The SAGE Glossary of the Social and Behavioral Sciences

Editorial Board

The SAGE Glossary of the Social and Behavioral Sciences

Edited by
Larry E. Sullivan

John Jay College of Criminal Justice,
City University of New York

Los Angeles | London | New Delhi
Singapore | Washington DC

A SAGE Reference Publication

For information:

SAGE Publications, Inc.
2455 Teller Road
Thousand Oaks, California 91320
E-mail: order@sagepub.com

SAGE Publications Ltd.
1 Oliver's Yard
55 City Road
London EC1Y 1SP
United Kingdom

SAGE Publications India Pvt. Ltd.
B 1/I 1 Mohan Cooperative Industrial Area
Mathura Road, New Delhi 110 044
India

SAGE Publications Asia-Pacific Pte. Ltd.
33 Pekin Street #02-01
Far East Square
Singapore 048763

Printed in the United States of America.

Library of Congress Cataloging-in-Publication Data

The SAGE glossary of the social and behavioral sciences/Larry E. Sullivan, editor-in-chief; associate editors, R. Burke Johnson, Cynthia Calkins Mercado, Karen J. Terry.
    p. cm.
Includes bibliographical references.
ISBN 978-1-4129-5143-2 (cloth)
  1. Social sciences—Dictionaries. 2. Psychology—Dictionaries. I. Sullivan, Larry E.

H41.S24 2009
300.3—dc22   2009007803

This book is printed on acid-free paper.

09 10 11 12 13 10 9 8 7 6 5 4 3 2 1

Publisher:	Rolf A. Janke
Acquisitions Editor:	Jim Brace-Thompson
Editorial Assistant:	Michele Thompson
Developmental Editor:	Sara Tauber
Reference Systems Manager:	Leticia M. Gutierrez
Reference Systems Coordinator:	Laura Notton
Production Editor:	Kate Schroeder
Copy Editor:	QuADS Prepress (P) Ltd.
Typesetter:	C&M Digitals (P) Ltd.
Proofreader:	Penelope Sippel
Cover Image:	Michelle Montone Flyte, M.F.A.
Cover Designer:	Janet Kiesel
Marketing Manager:	Amberlyn McKay

Contents

List of Entries

D

T

About the Editors

EDITOR-IN-CHIEF

Larry E. Sullivan is Associate Dean and Chief Librarian at the John Jay College of Criminal Justice and a professor of criminal justice in the doctoral program at the Graduate School and University Center of the City University of New York. Prior to his appointment at John Jay in 1995, he was the chief of the Rare Book and Special Collections Division at the U.S. Library of Congress, where he had responsibility for the nation's rare book collection. Previous appointments include Professor and Chief Librarian at Lehman College of the City University of New York, Librarian of the New-York Historical Society, and Head Librarian of the Maryland Historical Society. He became involved in the criminal justice system when he worked at the Maryland Penitentiary in Baltimore in the late 1970s. That experience prompted him to begin researching prison history and to write the book *The Prison Reform Movement: Forlorn Hope* (1990; revised edition, 2002). He also began collecting literature written by felons, and his private collection of convict literature has been on public exhibition at the Grolier Club in New York and at the John Jay College of Criminal Justice. He based his book *Bandits and Bibles: Convict Literature in Nineteenth Century America* (2003) on these prison writings. He is the author, coauthor, or editor of over 50 books and articles in the fields of American and European history, penology, criminal justice, art history, and other subjects, including the above books, *Pioneers, Passionate Ladies, and Private Eyes: Dime Novels, Series Books, and Paperbacks* (1996; with Lydia C. Schurman), and *The New-York Historical Society: A Bicentennial History* (2004). His three-volume *Encyclopedia of Law Enforcement* (Sage, 2005), of which he is editor-in-chief, is the first such work that covers both the theory and the practice of policing and has been called unique by reviewers in its comprehensive coverage of worldwide law enforcement. His most recent publication is "'Prison Is Dull Today': Prison Libraries and the Irony of Pious Reading," which appeared in *PMLA*, the journal of the Modern Language Association of America, in 2008. Besides his many publications in journals, he has written entries in numerous reference publications over the years, including the *Worldmark Encyclopedia of the States, Collier's Encyclopedia, Encyclopedia of New York State, Encyclopedia of the Prison, International Dictionary of Library Histories, Dictionary of Library Biography, Encyclopedia of Library History, Dictionary of Literary Biography*, and the *Dictionary of the Middle Ages*. Future articles will appear in the *International Dictionary of Creative Women*. He serves or has served on a number of editorial boards, including the *Encyclopedia of Crime and Punishment*, the *Handbook of Transnational Crime and Justice*, and the journal *Book History*. He has delivered papers at meeting of the American Historical Association, the Modern Language Association, the American Society of Criminology, the Academy of Criminal Justice Sciences, the Society for the History of Authorship, Reading and Publishing, and the American Library Association, among others. He has consulted on the development of criminal justice libraries and on rare book and manuscript collections. At John Jay, in addition to directing the largest and most comprehensive criminal justice library in the world, he teaches graduate and doctoral-level courses in advanced criminology and philosophy of punishment and conducts a seminar on philosophy of science for forensic science PhD and master's students. Works in progress include the books *Theories of Punishment* and *Crime, Criminals, and Criminal Law in the Middle Ages* for a series on medieval life and culture. He holds an MA and PhD in history from The Johns Hopkins University, an MS in library science from The Catholic University of America in Washington, D.C., and a BA from De Paul University in Chicago. He was also a Fulbright Scholar at the University of Poitiers in Poitiers, France, where he studied medieval history and literature.

ASSOCIATE EDITORS

R. Burke Johnson is a professor in the Department of Professional Studies at the University of South Alabama. He is first author of *Educational Research: Quantitative, Qualitative, and Mixed Approaches*, which is published in its 3rd edition (2008) by Sage. He is author or coauthor of numerous articles and chapters and has published in the *Educational Researcher, Journal of Educational Psychology, Evaluation Review, Journal of Mixed Methods Research*, and *Evaluation and Program Planning*. He is an associate editor with the *Journal of Mixed Methods Research*. He also was the guest editor of a special issue on mixed methods research in the journal *Research in the Schools* (the special issue is available online at www.msera.org/rits_131.htm). His current interests are in research methodology (especially mixed), the philosophy of social science, and social theory. He holds three master's degrees (psychology, sociology, and public administration). His PhD is from the REMS Program (Research Evaluation Measurement and Statistics) in the College of Education at the University of Georgia.

Cynthia Calkins Mercado, PhD, is an assistant professor of psychology at the John Jay College of Criminal Justice in New York. Her research broadly encompasses sex offenders, risk assessment, and sex-offender-specific legislation, including residence restrictions, community notification, and Sexually Violent Predator (SVP) statutes. She is also involved in a major study of the causes and context of sexual abuse of minors by Catholic clergy. Broadly speaking, her work seeks to examine the empirical assumptions underlying policy decisions in the area of sexual violence.

Karen Terry is a professor in the Department of Criminal Justice at John Jay College of Criminal Justice and the director of the doctoral program in criminal justice at the Graduate School and University Center of the City University of New York. Her primary area of research interest is in sexual victimization and sex offender supervision and management. Some recent publications include *Sexual Offenses and Offenders: Theory, Practice and Policy* (2005) and *Sex Offender Registration and Community Notification: A "Megan's Law" Sourcebook* (1998). She has been involved with numerous research projects regarding sexual offenses and offenders. She was the principal investigator for a national study on the nature and scope of child sexual abuse in the Catholic Church from 1950 through 2002 and is currently the principal investigator for the study of the causes and context of that crisis. She is also the editor of the bimonthly *Sex Offender Law Report*. In addition to her research on sexual abuse, she has published books and articles in the field of policing and has received grants from the Department of Homeland Security to support the education of students in terrorism-related fields. She holds a doctorate in criminology from Cambridge University.

Contributors

Valerie Allen
*John Jay College of Criminal Justice,
City University of New York*

Cemalettin Ayas
Ohio State University

Paige Baggett
University of South Alabama

Gahan Bailey
University of South Alabama

Virginia Barber-Rioja
*John Jay College of Criminal Justice,
City University of New York*

J. Jackson Barnette
Colorado School of Public Health

Elizabeth Bartels
*John Jay College of Criminal Justice,
City University of New York*

Abigail Baxter
University of South Alabama

Alexander Beaujean
Baylor University

Michael Bender
Tilburg University

Michael Blitz
*John Jay College of Criminal Justice,
City University of New York*

Hope Brasfield
University of South Alabama

Mary Michael Campbell
University of South Alabama

Kristin Chong
*John Jay College of Criminal Justice,
City University of New York*

Jean N. Clark
University of South Alabama

Effie Papatzikou Cochran
*John Jay College of Criminal Justice,
City University of New York*

Kimberly A. Collica
Westchester County Jail and Penitentiary

K. M. T. Collins
University of Arkansas, Fayetteville

Kathleen Collins
*John Jay College of Criminal Justice,
City University of New York*

Roddrick Colvin
*John Jay College of Criminal Justice,
City University of New York*

Julie P. Combs
Sam Houston State University

Chris L. S. Coryn
Western Michigan University

Maria Josephine D'Agostino
*John Jay College of Criminal Justice,
City University of New York*

Tarika Daftary
Graduate Center, City University of New York

Gayle V. Davidson-Shivers
University of South Alabama

Peggy M. Delmas
University of South Alabama

J.V. Dempsey
University of South Alabama

Ann C. Eckardt
Hofstra University

Patricia Eckardt
Adelphi University

Nancy Egan
*John Jay College of Criminal Justice,
City University of New York*

Matt J. Eliot
Univeristy of Washington

Diane Endall-Bruno
Graduate Center, City University of New York

Kristin Englander
*John Jay College of Criminal Justice,
City University of New York*

Marcia Esparza
*John Jay College of Criminal Justice,
City University of New York*

Yu Feng
Indiana Univeristy, Bloomington

Kathleen M. Fitzhenry
Independent Scholar

Laureen A Fregeau
University of South Alabama

Natasha A. Frost
Northeastern University

Gennifer A. Furst
William Paterson University

Sandy Gibson
Rutgers University School of Social Work

Lior Gideon
*John Jay College of Criminal Justice,
City University of New York*

Paula E. Gormley
*John Jay College of Criminal Justice,
City University of New York*

Robert M. Gray
University of South Alabama

Andre Green
University of South Alabama

Dana Greene
New Mexico State University

Maria (Maki) Haberfeld
*John Jay College of Criminal Justice,
City University of New York*

Richard L. Hayes
University of South Alabama

Dáñiellè D. Holt
Loyola University Chicago

Yi-Min Huang
University of Washington

Dawn Hurst
University of North Texas

Marjorie Icenogle
University of South Alabama

Burke Johnson
University of South Alabama

Ursula Johnson
University of North Texas

Brenda Gayle Juarez
University of South Alabama

Wendi M. Kappers
University of Central Florida

Barbara Bussell Kawulich
University of West Georgia

Lila Kazemian
*John Jay College of Criminal Justice,
City University of New York*

Mansureh Kebritchi
University of Central Florida

Ken Kelley
University of Notre Dame

Kimora
*John Jay College of Criminal Justice,
City University of New York*

Bianca Klettke
Deakin University

Kathryn Kloby
Monmouth University

Louise Krasniewicz
University of Pennsylvania

Jennifer Langhinrichsen-Rohling
University of South Alabama

Anne Elizabeth Lee
Pratt Institute

N. L. Leech
University of Colorado, Denver

Robert D. Leier
Auburn University

Miri Levin-Rozalis
Ben Gurion University of the Negev

Eric J. Loomis
University of South Alabama

Cristina Martinez
Independent Scholar

Wes Martz
Kadant Inc.

John Matteson
*John Jay College of Criminal Justice,
City University of New York*

Dabney Hunter McKenzie
Troy University

Dee McKinney
East Georgia College

Chuck McPherson
University of South Alabama

Venezia Michalsen
*John Jay College of Criminal Justice,
City University of New York*

Vaughn S. Millner
University of South Alabama

Dara Persis Murray
Rutgers University

Jennifer Nabors
University of Georgia

Susan Nordstrom
University of Georgia

Patrick O'Hara
*John Jay College of Criminal Justice,
City University of New York*

A. J. Onwuagbuzie
Sam Houston State University

Michael Quinn Patton
Organizational Development and Evaluation Consultant

Gianni Pirelli
*John Jay College of Criminal Justice,
City University of New York*

Ashley Powell
University of South Alabama

Carol Price
University of Tennessee, Knoxville

Geoffrey Rab
*John Jay College of Criminal Justice,
City University of New York*

Kelly Rawls
University of South Alabama

Rosemary C. Reilly
Concordia University

Thomas G. Reio
Florida International University

Jennifer Richards
University of Tennessee, Knoxville

Clark Robenstine
University of South Alabama

Elizabeth Romey
University of South Alabama

Flora Rothman
*John Jay College of Criminal Justice,
City University of New York*

Kenneth Royal
University of Kentucky

Marilyn Marks Rubin
*John Jay College of Criminal Justice,
City University of New York*

Andrew Rudyk
*John Jay College of Criminal Justice,
City University of New York*

Meghan Reilly Sacks
*John Jay College of Criminal Justice,
City University of New York*

Vincenzo Sainato
*John Jay College of Criminal Justice,
City University of New York*

Iris M Saltiel
Troy University

Susan Pitts Santoli
University of South Alabama

Carsten Schmidtke
Oklahoma State University-Okmulgee Arts & Sciences

Daniela C. Schroeter
Western Michigan University

Ellen Sexton
*John Jay College of Criminal Justice,
City University of New York*

Eddie Shaw
University of South Alabama

Zachary Shemtob
*John Jay College of Criminal Justice,
City University of New York*

Diane Sivasubramaniam
Barnard College, Columbia University

Gary J. Skolits
University of Tennessee

J. R. Slate
Sam Houston State University

Agnes Smith
University of South Alabama

Lloyd Soobrian
Berkeley College

Andy Stanfield
University of South Alabama

Tori Steber
University of South Alabama

Tres Stefurak
University of South Alabama

Alene Sullivan
Ernst & Young

Larry E. Sullivan
*John Jay College of Criminal Justice,
City University of New York*

Daniel W. Surry
University of South Alabama

Olga Teploukhova
*John Jay College of Criminal Justice,
City University of New York*

Shirley Timmons
Clemson University

Hasan Tinmaz
Baskent University

Ellen Tufano
St. John's University

Karyn W. Tunks
University of South Alabama

Lisa A. Turner
University of South Alabama

Jim van Haneghan
University of South Alabama

April Vannini
European Graduate School

W. Paul Vogt
Illinois State University

Jeannette Waegemakers Schiff
University of Calgary

Martin A. Wallenstein
*John Jay College of Criminal Justice,
City University of New York*

Christopher Ebun Warburton
*John Jay College of Criminal Justice,
City University of New York*

Lori Westmoreland
University of South Alabama

Tom Clark Wilson
Chapman University

Marilyn Kay Wilson-McGowan
University of South Alabama

Sue-Lin Wong
*John Jay College of Criminal Justice,
City University of New York*

Haci Bayram Yilmaz
Ohio State University

Hsiu-Ting Yu
Leiden University

Annmarie Zand Scholten
University of Amsterdam

Sarah E Zappe
Pennsylvania State University

Tina Zottoli
*John Jay College of Criminal Justice,
City University of New York*

Introduction

A *glossary* is a specialized dictionary that provides short, core definitions related to a specific discipline or language. New disciplines develop their own language, jargon, concepts, and terms that may not be familiar to any student or scholar coming to these various fields for the first time, and in fact the language of the social sciences may be unintelligible even to the intelligent layman. Many glossaries currently exist for discrete disciplines, but to compare how terminology is used in different fields of scholarly endeavor, the student must make an exhaustive search through many volumes to find even a simple comparison. The *Sage Glossary* is the first attempt to deal with this issue comprehensively and to combine and compare terminology in nine separate social and behavioral science disciplines: communication, economics, education, geography, media studies, political science, psychology, public administration, and sociology. We have also added terms used in the methodology for social science research because we feel that these methods are integral to an understanding of all the disciplines included here.

When the social sciences became fashionable in the late 19th century, scholars followed the methods of the physical or natural sciences in the belief that their theoretical decisions or findings were "objective." The social sciences closely follow the scientific method as far as they can, but they cannot verify, even falsify, in the same way as the physical sciences because they are dealing with human behavior in the past. Many of these methods and concepts were formulated in an attempt to first explain, and then predict, behavior. The entries on economics are prime examples of the use of statistical modeling to predict the behavior of financial markets. And anybody who reads the daily newspaper or watches the ubiquitous cable television news shows knows how predictable human behavior is. In the *Sage Glossary*, the student has one reference companion germane to all the disciplines, one that will place the development of concepts in their proper historical context and further the understanding of how these disciplines operate. Admittedly not all terms are included, but we wanted to keep the work to one volume as a convenient *vade mecum*, or a one-volume inclusive reference library. Therefore, we have made the entries short—from 50 to 425 words. The terms are organized in an A to Z fashion. In some cases, the terms have different definitions and applications according to which of the disciplines they represent. In these cases, we have listed multiple definitions and have indicated which disciplines correspond to each definition.

This is not an encyclopedia, nor is it intended to be so. Nor is it a dictionary with short, one-line entries. Our glossary falls in between the two, with enough content to lead the reader to understand the social sciences in comparative context and to stimulate further inquiry. The concepts in the social sciences have become so specialized over the years that we have attempted to follow Samuel Johnson's aim as stated in the preface to his great dictionary (published in 1755): "To interpret a language by itself is very difficult; many words cannot be explained by synonimes, because the idea signified by them has not more than one appellation; nor by paraphrase, because simple ideas cannot be described. . . . To explain, requires the use of terms less abstruse than that which is to be explained, and such terms cannot always be found; for as nothing can be proved but by supposing something intuitively known, and evident without proof, so nothing can be defined but by the use of words too plain to admit a definition" (p. 5). We have provided just such general explanations here, ones that can be understood by the intelligent reader, student, or academic coming to a discipline for the first time or who needs a refresher on the latest use of a term.

I had the vision for this *Glossary* when I reflected on the time I began my doctoral studies many years ago and turned to one of the great glossaries of the Latin language, the *Glossarium mediae et infimae latinitatis*, compiled by Charles du Fresne, sieur du Cange in 1678, to understand the medieval Latin of chronicles, charters, and other documents. Many of the Latin words used in the Middle Ages do not correspond with classical Latin or have variations of meaning from the Latin of Vergil and other writers from whom we learned our Latin in high school and college. Simply referred to as *Ducange*, this work in 10 volumes explains in good classical Latin how medieval Latin words differ considerably from their classical roots and how we could greatly misinterpret important primary source materials by relying on our knowledge of classical languages. Du Cange was one of the first glossators to study the historical development of languages, and his work is an indispensable guide to understanding the use of Latin in medieval documents and texts. When we had to turn to Old French, we had Jean Baptiste de La Curne de Sainte-Palaye, who in the

18th century produced the multivolume *Glossaire de la langue française*. We must also mention that most medieval manuscripts used a sort of shorthand to facilitate scribal copying of texts. In the university cities of the Middle Ages, there was a robust market for textbooks, and scribes had to reproduce numerous copies to keep up with the demand. The first printers also, such as Gutenberg in his great bible of 1455, followed manuscript tradition and used similar Latin abbreviations. How was one to interpret these? For paleographical research, our handy guide was Adriano Capelli's *Dizionario di abbreviature latine*, or the *Lexicon abbreviaturarum* (1912), which explains which symbols signify missing letters in a written or printed work. Such scholarly compilations were products of Enlightenment thinking that attempted to sum up all knowledge in ambitious multivolume works or, as in Capelli, to show how to actually read earlier works. Most important, scholars couldn't advance in their intellectual pursuits without the use of such reliable reference tools.

The Enlightenment compilers and textual scholars were following an old tradition, by applying critical tools to the interpretation of words and concepts. We can go back many centuries to works such as Isidore of Seville's famous *Etymologies* of the early 7th century, which claimed to summarize all known knowledge, sometimes in fascinating and naïve descriptions. Isidore's work in 20 volumes is a combination encyclopedia, glossary, and dictionary and inspired numerous medieval encyclopedias, such as the 9th-century *De rerum naturis* of Rabanus Maurus and the 13th-century *Speculum naturale* by Vincent of Beauvais. Most of these medieval works were compiled *ipsa verba* from classical and other sources and in many cases were compilations of excerpts from earlier works (sometimes even close to *florilegia* [anthologies or excerpts of other works on a theme]), with little substantiation of facts or sources and no critical analysis. These writers just built on the works of others. The early modern and Enlightenment scholars weighed sources, and editors and authors went at their work in the scientific manner then gaining ascendancy. In this sense, they checked historical usage and attempted to validate sources. We can just think of textual scholars such as the 15th-century Italian priest Lorenzo Valla, who exposed the Donation of Constantine, on which the medieval popes based their claims to temporal power, as a definitive forgery through linguistic proof of anachronistic Latin terms.

The coining of new terms in science and other disciplines follows the language usage model of early modern Europe, when scientists and academics such as Isaac Newton still wrote their books in Latin. Newton, in the *Philosophiae naturalis principia mathematica* (1687), and Jophannes Kepler, in his *Astronomia nova* (1609), had to describe phenomena with Latin words whose meanings were different from those in the Roman period or that didn't exist then. How was one to explain astronomical phenomena or the calculus in terms that weren't even thought of in the Roman era of good

Ciceronian Latin? Since Latin was only spoken and written in ecclesiastical or intellectual quarters, explanatory scientific terms had to be improvised or created. Cultural additions were subjected to the same process, as they are today in many languages.

Our *Glossary* is all the more necessary for the comprehension of concepts because the social and behavioral sciences are relatively new disciplines and much of the jargon used in research and academia has taken on a variety of different meanings. If we look a bit at the history of these disciplines, we realize how recently academics organized associations devoted to the furtherance of their study. The American Economic Association dates only to 1885; the American Psychological Association was founded in 1892 and the American Anthropological Association in 1902; the American Sociological Association first gathered officially in 1905; communication scholars organized the National Communication Association in 1914 (under a different name); the American Society of Criminology broke away from the sociological associations in 1941; and the National Association of Schools of Public Administration only goes back to 1970. Therefore, it is time to recognize and codify the concepts and technical language used in these new disciplines in a succinct, concise, and, especially, comparative manner in order to provide a reference resource for the research universe of the social and behavioral sciences.

In writing and editing this book, we acknowledge how the Islamic terrorist attacks on the World Trade Center on September 11, 2001, changed the way we look at the world, especially in social and behavioral science terms. Many of the authors of our entries thought no more than to state "9/11" without further explanation. This date is now an integral part of our culture, how we look at globalization, communication throughout cultures, sociological and criminological research, economics—in fact all the disciplines included in this book. Our assumptions of the world and its phenomena change along with the contextual change. The 20th-century philosopher Ludwig Wittgenstein explained it best when he insisted that all our attempts to understand what we call facts will always be relative to the framework of a particular form of life, especially in the historical and cultural sense.

It is the importance of understanding the different uses, receptions, and interpretations of concepts that led me to work on this present *Glossary*, and I feel that it follows in the Enlightenment tradition of summarizing known knowledge of specialized conceptual usage in each discipline. One of the first glossaries in the English language, Thomas Blount's *Glossographia* of 1656, defined specialist words introduced into the English language from other languages and disciplines. Blount mentioned that he had problems understanding these new words and his *Glossographia* would smooth the way for others reading works in sciences such as geometry, mathematics, architecture, and others. Blount also provided etymologies of words, being one of the first to do this in English. We have attempted to follow a 21st-century version of this model.

The most difficult process in putting this book together was the selection of entries. We could argue at length on what should or should not be included in such a glossary, but we planned to have enough entries to make the work fairly comprehensive and inclusive, but not overwhelming, in one volume. I was fortunate in having superior associate editors and colleagues who helped compile the lists. I trust that we have kept the lacunae to a minimum and have provided references to even more specialized terms for further study.

I would like to thank the associate editors—Burke Johnson (education and research methods), Karen Terry (sociology and criminology), and Cynthia Mercado (psychology) for their thoroughness in carrying out their editorial duties. Meghan Sacks, my managing editor, was a constant source of support during every phase of this project. My assistants at John Jay, Elizabeth Clark-Wilson, Kristin Chong, and Kimberly Teets helped me wade through the arcana of online publication systems. Their assistance was invaluable in bringing this project to fruition. As always, I want to thank the librarians of John Jay College's Sealy Library for their continuing support and dedication to the pursuit of knowledge.

Larry E. Sullivan

A

Abdication The act of removing oneself from political office. This term, usually associated with monarchies or the papacy, is derived from the Latin *abdicatio*, which means "disowning" or "renouncing." Under Roman law, the term was also used for family disownment. Common reasons for abdication include unfitness for the throne, a political coup, or simply old age. In Great Britain, approval of both houses of parliament is necessary before an abdication can be effectuated. One of the most famous abdications in recent British history is that of King Edward VIII of the United Kingdom in 1936. King Edward VIII abdicated his throne to wed twice-divorced American Wallis Simpson, who was not considered suitable as queen. As part of the His Majesty's Declaration of Abdication Act (1936), any descendants of King Edward VIII were also ineligible for the throne.

The functional equivalent of an abdication in a democracy would be a resignation.

Abduction Charles Sanders Peirce (1839–1914), the American philosopher and founder of the Pragmatic School of philosophy, maintained that the process of discovery in science is as important as that of proof and must, therefore, meet logical criteria. Peirce claimed that we must not leave scientific discovery to chance, because, in the end, it is the discovery process that creates and advances science and human knowledge. In scientific research, two logical inferences prevail: deductive research logic and inductive research logic. By formulating a third research logic (to be distinct from research methodology), which he called "abduction," that aimed to cover "the logic of discovery" (Rescher, 1978; Rosenthal, 1993), Peirce enables us to conduct rigorous research stemming from a single fact in the field.

According to Peirce, in a process of discovery, we confront a new or surprising fact (a problem), decide how to address it, create an initial explanation, and test this explanation against *all* our observations and facts to see if it works. Even one observation that does not fit this preliminary explanation tells us that the explanation is not good enough.

At this stage of drawing conclusions, Peirce demands that we take our explanations or conclusions, convert them into hypotheses "on probation," and explore farther into a wider scope of data. In each such cycle, our explanations become broader, more general, and more abstract (Levin-Rozalis, 2000; Peirce 1955a, 1955b; Yu, 1994).

A hypothesis on probation is said to meet the logical criteria not if it corresponds with a conception of external reality or theory but, rather, only if it resolves the dilemma, problem, or difficulty for which it was formulated (i.e., it explains the "'surprising fact"). With this logic, Peirce created an inseparable link between new facts that we face in the "real world" (as it is perceived in our minds) and their explanation (Josephson & Josephson, 1996; Levin-Rozalis, 2000, 2004). For more information, see Josephson and Josephson (1996), Levin-Rozalis (2000, 2004), Peirce (1955a, 1955b), Rescher (1978), Rosenthal (1993), and Yu (1994). ***See also*** Deduction Versus Induction

Ability Grouping The practice of placing students into instructional groups based on past academic performance or apparent academic potential. This practice can be used within a single classroom to group students for projects and classwork or used to determine assignment of students to teams or teachers. For more information, see Westchester Institute for Human Services Research (2002). ***See also*** Tracking

Aborigine A proper noun naming the indigenous people of Australia. The term is also used as a common noun meaning a human, plant, or animal that has resided in a geographical region before any colonists arrived. An aborigine is a native or the earliest inhabitant of an area.

Abscond The action of secretly running away to hide oneself. The most common usage refers to the behavior of someone who has escaped to evade detection or arrest. The term *absconder* is used to describe someone who has skipped out on bail.

Absolute Advantage A theory of international trade originally put forward by Adam Smith (1723–1790). This theory is largely based on resource endowment and acquisition of skills for efficient production. Although endowment is a gift of nature, special skills and techniques are required for production of goods. The theory postulates that efficient trade depends on specialization on the production of goods for which a nation is well-endowed and efficient. Production of those goods reflects a nation's absolute advantage. A nation must then produce and export the goods of its absolute advantage and import the goods of its absolute disadvantage. A corollary of the theory of absolute advantage is the labor theory of value, which assumes that the cost (not the opportunity cost), and therefore the price of a good, depends exclusively on the amount of homogeneous labor required to produce it. For more information, see Salvatore (2006). *See also* Comparative Advantage

Absolute Threshold   The smallest amount of a stimulus that can be identified by an organism. The term is most often used in audiometry when determining an individual's threshold of hearing with psychophysical methods that were first developed by Gustav Fechner (1801–1877). The absolute threshold is not considered a discrete point but is marked by the percentage that an individual recognizes the presented sound correctly at the minimum sound level and a given frequency. The threshold of human hearing has been reported as 20 µPa (micropascals) for the frequency of 1,000 Hz (hertz). The human auditory system is best adapted to perceive stimuli between 1,000 and 5,000 Hz. For more information, see Gelfand (2004). *See also* Perception; Subliminal Message; Threshold

Absolutism *(political science)*   The principle by which a leader possesses absolute power, with no restraints. An absolute government would be considered an *autocracy* (derived from the Greek word *autokrates,* which means ruling by one's self). An absolute or autocratic state is said to be the opposite of a democratic one. Popular opinion has minimal influence, while criticism of leadership is stifled. Once an autocratic leader reaches power, opposition groups are usually outlawed. Strict adherence to the leader's views is expected among citizens, pervading most areas of a citizen's life. King James I, the first Stuart King of England, who took the throne in 1603, used the medieval European doctrine of the divine right of kings to support his absolutism, claiming that the legitimacy of his office was directly ordained by God. He further declared that his subjects must obey the king as they would God. The king was also answerable only to God not to parliament or anyone else.

Proponents of an autocratic state claim that an absolute leader is "the best" to serve office. The 17th-century English philosopher Thomas Hobbes (1588–1679) supported absolutism, claiming that natural law supports the notion that a single ruler is necessary to keep the peace in society. In reality, autocratic leaders most often attain their positions through violence and retain their leadership through imposition of a police state. Historical examples of autocratic world leaders include Adolf Hitler, Mao Tse-tung, and Benito Mussolini. For more information, see Burgess (1996).

Absolutism *(public administration)*   A form of autocracy in which all political power is wielded by a single monarch. While the term *absolutism* may be used in a variety of different contexts, it primarily denotes a period of European governance from approximately the 17th to 19th centuries. Before the 17th century, power was largely shared between the monarchy and the nobility. Seeking to usurp the nobles' (and often the Church's) authority, monarchal rulers began to claim themselves uniquely ordained by God (in a tradition known as the "divine right of kings") and therefore the only earthly individuals qualified to rule in God's name. Although it remains unclear how powerful such monarchs truly were, the idea of absolutism spread across the European continent and resulted in some of the first standing armies in Western history. Although it was ultimately brief, the so-called Age of Absolutism thus had an undeniable influence on subsequent European history. For more information, see P. H. Wilson (2000).

Abuse   Although often easy to recognize, this term is surprisingly hard to define. This may be due to the many types of abuse, which all center around the cruel treatment of a person or animal. When a father hits his child or a husband his spouse, few objective observers will likely argue against the existence of abuse. Considerably more nebulous is the concept of emotional abuse. Using words to demean or humiliate another individual may be seen as personally cruel, but at what line this becomes abusive can be considerably difficult to determine. Other forms of abuse may be sexual, whether it is abuse at the hands of a family member or the unwanted advances of a partner or spouse. Autocratic managers also tend to verbally abuse their underlings. Increasingly common has been the extension of the concept of abuse toward the environment as well, for example, in regard to the destruction of particular fauna or the increasing ramifications of global warming on the external world.

Access   The ability to have an entry point for information, particularly in one's engagement with communications technologies. An individual or group's access to information is influenced by contextual social, political, and economic structures. In media studies, access to information is understood through the deconstruction of messages filtered through the media industry. *See also* Censorship; Exposure

Access, Open   The free and widely available information throughout the World Wide Web. Once an article's author or copyright holder gives express consent, an open-access journal or archive may post its content over the Internet. Open-access literature is particularly popular among authors, researchers, teachers, students, and libraries and includes a spectrum of academic disciplines (from criminology to physics). Journals are usually peer reviewed and often subsidized by certain universities or professional societies (although they may make extra money through advertising). While archives may also be university funded, the recent advent of open-source software now allows anyone with the appropriate money and knowledge to construct their own archive. Since mainstream scholarly journals do not generally pay academics for their articles, authors ultimately lose no money in choosing to publish through open-access. University tenure and promotion review boards, however, are still resistant to giving the same weight to open-access publications as to peer-reviewed journals.

Since open-access technology is predicated on the author's consent, unlike film or music downloading, it has not proven a source of particular controversy or debate. For more information, see Suber (2004).

Acclamation A term derived from the Latin verb *acclamare,* meaning "to shout." This word comprises the prefix *ad* (to) plus *clamare* (shout). In the Middle Ages, certain street vendors—those who walked through the streets hawking their wares in loud tones or shouting— were known as *clamators.* We see this type of person on cable television business shows where the commentator walks around the studio recommending (or not) stocks at annoyingly high decibel levels. The word eventually took on the meaning of overwhelming praise manifested through oral praise or applause. The term takes on a particular resonance in the political arena at presidential nominating conventions, where a candidate is said to be chosen "by acclamation." To give but two examples, George Washington was nominated and elected first president of the new United States by virtual acclamation (he had no opponents); the Democratic Convention in 1936 nominated Franklin Roosevelt by acclamation from the floor of the convention.

Accommodating A theoretical framework examining the ways in which individuals make adjustments while communicating in a variety of contexts. The communication accommodation theory aims to predict and explain these adjustments and how they create, maintain, or decrease social distance in interactions. It explores the various ways in which individuals adjust the way they communicate, the motivations for the adjustment, and its consequences. There are many social situations in which individuals accommodate or modify the way they speak. Examples include speaking to the elderly or children. Many adults accommodate their speech to the needs of a child, who may otherwise not be able to understand adult concepts. Almost every relationship in every individual's life involves some sort of accommodation of speech and communication, particularly those developed in a job setting. Speech styles, such as intonation, rate, dialect, and volume, can be adjusted for individuals to communicate their feelings, ideas, values, and attitudes.

Accommodating the way individuals communicate is not specific to speech but also to nonverbal behaviors. For example, when speaking to someone from another culture, one may increase the use of arm movements. Motivations for accommodation can include gaining approval and increasing communication effectiveness. In this way, accommodating can be a way to identify with the speaker/listener. Social distance can be maintained, however, by emphasizing differences

through communication, such as different speech styles between the speaker and the listener. For more information, see Giles et al. (2005).

Accountability *(education)* The principle that schools should provide data to show that students are learning the required material and take responsibility for improving student achievement, if necessary. Often, accountability is demonstrated through scores on standardized tests. Schools are then assigned grades or rankings based on results. *See also* No Child Left Behind (NCLB)

Accountability *(political science)* There are two contradicting views of the origin of this concept. Some scholars argue that accountability is a product of classical democracy dating back to the 8th century BCE. The contrasting view contends that classical democracy itself arose from a concept of accountability that has been traced back to the 5th-century BCE Athenian legal institution of *euthyna,* literally translated as "the action of setting straight" (von Dornum, 1997). *Euthyna* was a public procedural mechanism for all officials, which provided the citizens with a full public account of all actions taken by any official. If auditors suspected wrongfulness on the part of the official, sanctions would be imposed.

Modern discourse on accountability posits itself in democracy and, within it, presumes a legitimate relationship between two actors, be they individuals, institutions, or nation-states, in which an actor has the right to hold another to a set of standards and responsibilities. If the obligations are not met, a sanction, whether positive or negative, maybe imposed on the agent. It may be noted that the accountability mechanism always operates ex post facto. The sanction punishes the unauthorized or illegitimate use of power as deemed fit by the delegated institution. For more information, see von Dornum (1997) and Grant and Keohane (2005).

Accountability *(sociology)* The principle of holding people responsible for having participated in, contributed to, or effected an occurrence. To be accountable is to be liable for what has taken place. Accountability often implies obligation and a subsequent expectation to act to counter or explain the behavior for which one is accountable. Accountability is an important component of the criminal justice system, particularly as it relates to law enforcement. In a democratic society, the police are accountable to the community for their actions.

Accounting Keeping records of business transactions, including summaries of assets and liabilities. The first examples of writing, and hence the first historical accounts, were found in Sumer and other areas of Mesopotamia in the 4th millennium BCE. These consisted of cuneiform characters engraved on clay tablets used for bookkeeping purposes in business transactions. From that time until the 15th century, accounting techniques were rudimentary, using basic

A

listings, usually in chronological or geographical order, of business inputs and outputs, purchases, inventories, and other transactions all listed together. In 1494, the Franciscan Friar Luca Pacioli published the mathematics textbook *Summa de arithmetica, geometrica, proportioni et proportionalita* (Venice, 1494). Although this book contained mathematics as known in the 15th century, one chapter described the method used by Venetian merchants that we now call double-entry bookkeeping. Pacioli also wrote about the recording of receivables and inventories, income, expense accounts, the year-end closing of ledgers, balanced accounts, and other methods that we still use today. Indeed, some historians date the beginning of the modern age (and even the beginning of the Renaissance) from Pacioli's treatise on accounting. Accountants have basically followed his precepts, with some modifications, for more than 500 years.

Metaphorically, the term takes on ethical and religious significance, as when one is told to balance one's accounts of good and evil. In fact, this sentiment is depicted in Christian liturgical and popular art with St. Peter holding a key and a book, the latter with a record or account of good and evil deeds, the former, the key to heaven, which he will use based on the balancing of accounts (see the Bible, Matthew 16:13–21).

Accreditation   An external review of an institution's competency in meeting its standards for student performance. It is a process in which a peer review team measures, assesses, and evaluates a school's proficiency in maintaining high standards and then bestows certification on the institution if it meets the relevant standards. Since the early 20th century, a number of professions have taken on accreditation standards through oversight bodies. Among the most important are universities and the health care professions. Practitioners in each field adopt their own standards of accreditation, and some are required to do so by state and/or federal governments.

Accreditation in Postsecondary Education
Accrediting agencies are authorized by the U.S. Department of Education to evaluate postsecondary educational institutions against quality standards. If the institutions meet those standards, they are then granted accreditation. This accreditation serves as a type of quality assurance, ensuring that educational institutions provide students an acceptable level of education.

Acculturation *(communication)*   The process of culture change as the result of contact between two or more distinct cultural groups. It can be contrasted with "enculturation," which is learning a particular cultural tradition from members of a particular culture. The term *acculturation* was commonly used in the context of a dominant, Western, technologically advanced group encountering a less-technological, so-called primitive group, usually a group of aboriginal people. It was thought that these encounters always resulted in the smaller, indigenous group being adversely affected and their

cultural complex being overwhelmed or destroyed. Acculturation could result in changes in language, identity, expressive behavior, political affiliations, rituals, religious beliefs, value systems, marriage patterns, and technology.

More recent interest in ethnic identity, resistance to assimilation, pluralism, global culture, and multiculturalism has made the term somewhat unwelcome as a mode of viewing cultural contact. All cultural contacts go both ways, and even in examples of conquest or first encounters, the exchange of cultural information, people, and goods usually makes such contact a source of change in both parties. In addition, few groups have ever been in total isolation from other populations, and mechanisms for evaluating, incorporating, or rejecting outside elements exist in every culture. The process, then, is more dynamic than is simply that suggested by episodes of colonialism, imperialism, and conquest. Resistance to all aspects of acculturation does not necessarily preserve an "original" culture but can, instead, lead to the development of a new version of that culture that focuses on resisting change. Acculturation is studied by anthropologists, social psychologists, political scientists, economists, and other scholars interested in what happens when two cultures meet. For more information, see Said (1978). ***See also*** Culture (communication); Enculturation; Ethnocentrism (communication, education); Linguistic Differences

Acculturation *(psychology)*   A term introduced by American anthropologists, as early as the 1880s, to describe the process of culture change occurring when two different cultural groups come into contact with each other. Acculturation was then mainly seen as a group-level phenomenon, while in more recent times, interest has grown in the study of individual-level phenomena, referred to as "psychological acculturation."

Early research on acculturation focused on the pathological symptoms of so-called culture shock, while more recently, acculturation has been studied from a social-psychological perspective, from which researchers examine its cognitive, affective, and behavioral components. Major influences come from work in stress and coping. A seminal model of acculturation was developed by John Berry in 1980, which can best be understood in the context of migration, where it is most typically put to use in the investigation of first- and second-generation immigrants. The model comprises four different options or strategies that result from combining the dimensions of cultural maintenance and cultural exploration. (1) *Assimilation* refers to the process of turning away from the original culture (country of origin, familial cultural context) in favor of the host culture. (2) In contrast, a *separation* focuses on the mainte-nance of the original culture and the rejection of the host culture. (3) Individuals high in an *integration accul-turation orientation* strive to maintain their original cul-tural identity while exploring and adapting to the new cultural context at the same time. (4) Individuals with a *marginalization orientation* reject both their original cul-ture and the host culture.

Although the acculturation process has consequences for both the host culture and the minority immigrant group, the latter is usually more affected. While the original model has a categorical design, current approaches focus on the two underlying dimensions of maintenance and commitment. Most recent frameworks differentiate between acculturation conditions, orientations, and outcomes and between public and private domains of acculturation orientations. The public domain involves all activities aimed at participation in social life within the host country (e.g., education and job), while the private domain involves personal and value-related issues (e.g., marriage and child-rearing). Such frameworks allow for a better understanding of individual differences in acculturation, in particular in public and private domains of acculturation, and they also provide a better foundation for refinements in the assessment of acculturation. For more information, see Sam and Berry (2006). ***See also*** Acculturative Stress; Cross-Cultural Research; Ethnic Identity; Multicultural Research

Acculturation *(sociology)*   The process undergone by different cultural groups when they interact and adopt cultural patterns from one another. The process of acculturation is one of being changed through assimilation into an alternate culture. Frequently, the acculturated culture in reference is the dominant one in the society.

Acculturative Stress   Stress caused by psychological, somatic, and social difficulties when adapting to a new cultural context. The term *acculturative stress* has been used synonymously with *culture shock* and *psychic conflict* (the conflict people experience when coping with conflicting cultural norms). Acculturative stress is considered a crucial psychological variable affecting an individual's affective and cognitive well-being. Whether or not acculturation is experienced as stressful depends on affluence, social support, and the degree of dissimilarity of the cultural contexts, among other factors. Most often, acculturative stress has been investigated in first- and second-generation minority immigrants, who generally report lower levels of affective and cognitive well-being than nonimmigrants. For more information, see Sam (2006). ***See also*** Acculturation; Cross-Cultural Research; Ethnic Identity; Multicultural Research; Stress

Achievement Motivation   A form of motivation aimed at achieving a personal standard of excellence, related to experiences of "doing better." With power and affiliation, the achievement motive represents one of the three basic motives formulated by Henry Murray in 1938. Motivation is differentiated into implicit (or operant) motives and explicit (or respondent) motives. (Implicit achievement motivation is also known as *need for achievement,* or nAch; explicit achievement motivation is also known as *self-attributed need for achievement,* or sanAch.) Both are generally unrelated and are linked to different behavioral correlates. Explicit achievement

motivation is readily articulated and involves seeing oneself as a hard worker and wanting to take on challenging tasks. In contrast, implicit achievement motivation reflects a less conscious preoccupation with self-improvement and an intrinsic enjoyment of interesting and challenging tasks. For more information, see McClelland (1985).

Achievement Tests   Measures of students' attainment of specified learning outcomes. By comparison with aptitude tests, achievement tests measure acquired knowledge and skills following instruction or training. The format of achievement tests may vary, including multiple-choice, short-answer, essay, or other item types. ***See also*** Criterion- and Norm-Referenced Measurement

Acquit   To judge a defendant "not guilty" (which will set the individual free from the criminal charge for which he or she was tried). Once a person is acquitted, all criminal liability is removed. An acquittal is a verdict that stems from judicial proceedings and is but one possible resolution of a criminal trial.

Act *(political science)*   A bill that has been approved by at least one house of Congress. It is called an "act" because it indicates the action of one body of Congress. In popular usage, many acts are still commonly referred to as "bills." If the act is also approved by the other house of Congress and the president, it will become a law. If the president vetoes the act, a two-thirds majority of both houses is needed to override his veto for the bill to become law. State legislatures also produce acts, which follow their respective legislative processes to become law.

Act *(public administration)*   Legislation (a bill or joint resolution) that has passed both chambers of Congress (in the case of the federal government) or a state legislature and has been signed into law by the president or the state governor or has passed over his or her veto, thus becoming law.

A *bill* is the principal mechanism employed by lawmakers for introducing their proposals (e.g., enacting or repealing laws) in the appropriate chamber of the legislature. Bills introduced in the U.S. Senate, for example, are designated S. 1, S. 2, and so on depending on the order in which they are introduced. They address matters of either general interest ("public bills") or narrow interest ("private bills"), such as immigration cases and individual claims against the federal or state government. Once passed, public bills become public laws (i.e., they have general applicability nationwide), and private bills become private laws, which have restricted applicability to the individual(s) involved.

A *law* is a rule of conduct established and enforced by the authority, legislation, or custom of a given community, state, or nation, including federal or state constitutions or statutes, judicial decision, common law, rule of court, executive order, or rule or order of an agency. Consequently, not all laws are the products of legislation. For example, the Supreme Court decision *Perry v. Sindermann* concerned the failure of a Texas state community college to reemploy a professor who had criticized the college administration. Although the school employees' manual stated that the school did not grant tenure, the reality was that all teachers were routinely reemployed except the one who criticized the school, exercising his First Amendment freedom of speech right.

The term *act* may also be applied technically to a bill that one house has passed but that has not yet become a law. Subsequently, when both houses of Congress pass an act and it becomes a law, it is assembled with other laws (chronologically) in a bound volume titled *Statutes at Large* for the federal government or *Session Laws* in the case of, for example, the state of Illinois. For more information, see Illinois General Assembly (n.d.), *Perry v. Sindermann* (1972), U.S. House of Representatives (2003), and U.S. Senate (n.d.).

Action Potential   The abrupt electrochemical changes traveling down the axon of a cell that allow communication between neurons. Normally, the channels of the cell body are closed, which ensures that the cell membrane is polarized (i.e., the inside of the cell is slightly more negatively charged than the outside). On activation of the neuron, these channels open, allowing positively charged molecules to enter the cell, which depolarizes the cell interior and results in the action potential and "firing" of the neuron. The depolarization of the cell interior either surpasses the given balance or not, thereby allowing only for a binary (on/off) communication down the axon. For more information, see Kandel, Schwartz, and Jessell (2000). *See also* Axon; Dendrites; Neurons; Soma; Synapse

Action Research   A type of research that seeks to solve a specific problem within an organization, program, community, or unit by directly involving members of the unit studied who might actively participate in research design, data collection, analysis, and representation. It is not uncommon in an action research project for the researcher(s) to take on a facilitator role and lead the research efforts of the employees, volunteers, or community members involved. Action research is considered informal in terms of design, data collection, and data representation. Results are usually presented and used only within the organization studied rather than disseminated to a larger audience. Other names for action research are "action learning," "team learning," "reflective practice," and "internal evaluation" (Patton, 2002). For more information, see Patton (2002). *See also* Basic Versus Applied Research; Critical Theory; Qualitative Research

Activation-Synthesis Theory   A theory put forward by James Allan Hobson and Robert McCarley in 1977 that describes dreams as by-products of activity in the hindbrain (rhombencephalon) during phases of rapid eye movement (REM) as part of the natural sleep cycle. According to this theory, hindbrain activity creates random, meaningless messages that activate other brain areas, especially the cerebral cortex. Dreams then result from the effort of the cortex to make sense of, or synthesize, these messages by drawing on memories, feelings, and other information stored in the cortex. For more information, see Hobson and McCarley (1977). *See also* Brain (Encephalon); Psychoanalysis

Active Listening   An approach to interpersonal communication that requires sensitivity and open-mindedness on the part of the listener and a willingness to share information and opinions on the part of the speaker. Listening actively allows the one who is hearing to comprehend the underlying message beneath the content of the words voiced, to evaluate fairly the speaker, and to reconsider previously held attitudes. Being heard in a nonjudgmental manner gives the speaker the confidence for self-expression without fear of criticism or intimidation and a sense that what he or she has to say is of value. Active listening has been used successfully in the workplace and in other social settings, as well as in health and mental health practice, to bring about changes for the better in both the listener and the speaker. Learning the art of active listening takes practice. For more information, see Rogers and Farson (1987). *See also* Critical Listening; Empathetic Listening; Evaluative Listening; Passive Listening

Activism *(political science)*   Any type of individual or collective action performed with the purpose of creating political or social change. Activism can be organized at the local, national, or international level. Targets of change can be governments, in an effort to change policy, or private individuals, in an effort to alter personal behavior. Change-promoting activities can range from peaceful rallies and demonstrations to violent acts of terrorism or political assassination. Notable activism in the history of the United States has included the women's rights movements of the late 19th century and early 1970s, the civil rights demonstrations of the late 1950s and early 1960s, and the Vietnam War protests of the 1960s. Examples of contemporary activist causes are global warming, homosexual rights, voter registration, and immigration. Young adults, especially college students, are most popularly associated with activist participation. The Internet is increasingly being used as a tool for activists to increase public awareness and orchestrate collective organization and mobilization.

Activism *(public administration)*   An organized attempt to foster political or social change. This is usually in response to certain institutional policies that are viewed as morally or politically restrictive. Activism can take myriad different forms, including (but not exclusively) marches, letter-writing campaigns, civil disobedience, boycotts, or even physical attacks on perceived oppressors. Activists need not necessarily demand a direct change in law, but they can advocate more profound shifts in cultural behavior (such as animal rights vegetarians or gay acceptance movements). While the 1960s were undoubtedly considered the "hey-day" of Western activism, social protests remain prevalent throughout world affairs. Perhaps most interesting is activism's inherent subjectivity; people (even of the same culture) may bicker over whether someone is an activist or a criminal ("one man's terrorist is another man's freedom fighter") or if a particular movement seeks to spur change or merely engender chaos.

Actuality   The concrete and tangible ways of being for the individual in what is considered to be the "real" world. In media studies, the term is determined largely from the philosopher Pierre Levy's 1998 work "Becoming Virtual: Reality in the Digital Age," wherein actuality is viewed, along with reality, virtuality, and possibility, as a mode of existence. For Levy, actuality is defined by environmental context. The notion of actuality brings up questions of its relationship to agency, subjectivity, and representation. Furthermore, the term is used to explore the increasingly borderless experience between the "real" world and social networks, particularly communicating online and offline. ***See also*** Experienced Reality

Actuarial Judgment   A decision that is made by applying a particular set of rules, based on empirically based statistical relations between predictor variables and an outcome variable. The actuarial approach to behavioral judgment and decision making is often contrasted with the clinical judgment approach, in which decisions are based on the unsystematic and subjective mental processes of a human judge. Research shows that, across a multitude of decision-making domains (e.g., college grades, criminal recidivism, surgical outcomes), actuarial models are more accurate in making predictions about highly complex outcomes than are trained human judges. For more information, see Dawes, Faust, and Meehl (1989). ***See also*** Clinical Judgment

Actus Reus   A Latin term that means "guilty act." It is one of two necessary elements of a crime, the other being *mens rea* or "guilty mind" (the intent to commit the crime). The *actus reus* is the physical act of a crime. Each element must be independently proven beyond a reasonable doubt to convict someone of an illegal act. ***See also*** *Mens Rea*

Adaptation (*psychology*)   A learning process through which an organism's (sensory) responsiveness to a stable, unchanging stimulus decreases over time. In particular, habituation, as a special form of adaptation, occurs when sensitivity to sight, sound, smell, taste, or touch decreases over time after repeatedly encountering an unchanging stimulus. In contrast, sensitization is characterized by exaggerated responses to unexpected, potentially threatening stimuli. Adaptation occurs—to some degree—to all kinds of stimuli and in all kinds of animals. For more information, see Pinel (2005). ***See also***

Behaviorism; Habituation; Learning; Sensory Adaptation; Systematic Desensitization

Adaptation (*sociology*)   The manner in which social systems react to their environment. Any social system—a nation-state, a corporation, or a family—must adapt to its environment, or it will break down. Talcott Parsons popularized this sociological meaning of the term in the middle of the 20th century. Adaptation is a component of Parsons's theory of social system survival. Adaptation is one of four "functional prerequisites" (the others being goal attainment, integration, and pattern maintenance) that any social system must exercise in order to prevail.

Parsons asserts that specialized subsystems develop to fulfill these functional prerequisites. The subsystem that corresponds to adaptation is the economy.

Adaptive Expectations   A forecasting theory that is used to estimate the future direction of economic variables based on past occurrences or indicators and the margin of error associated with past predictions.

Adaptive expectations is an integral component of the Phillips curve, the curve that shows an inverse relationship between unemployment and inflation. *Inflation* is defined as a function of past inflation, cyclical unemployment, and supply shock (exogenous occurrences that have an impact on production—e.g., change in oil prices). If economic agents base their expectation of inflation on past inflation, inflation easily becomes inertial unless it is checked by something else. Consequently, if there is no supply shock and if unemployment is at the natural rate, that is, the nonaccelerating-inflation rate of unemployment (NAIRU), inflation becomes inertial as a result of expansionary monetary policy. The theory was first developed by Irving Fisher (1867–1947), but like all forecasting techniques, it has the potential of exaggerating or underestimating the future value of economic variables.

The concept of adaptive expectations was popular in the 1950s, but it fell into relative insignificance in the 1970s, partly as a result of high inflation and unemployment (stagflation). For more information, see Mankiw (2006). ***See also*** Monetary Policy; Recession; Stabilization

Ad Hoc   Originally a Latin phrase meaning "for this purpose." Ad hoc solutions are specifically tailored to address a unique problem or scenario. Something ad hoc by its very definition cannot be generalized and therefore cannot be used for more than one function. Examples could include a financial plan aimed at a specific company or a committee formed to examine and address a unique issue or scenario. In the social and natural sciences, adjustments in theories or postulates are also known as ad hoc. Such corollaries can prevent a central thesis from collapsing entirely and may thus add a necessary revision or reformulation to the initial hypotheses. Ad hoc adjustments can stretch from evolutionary conjectures to theories of relativity and are often proposed years after an initial theory's formulation. For more information, see Gould (1979).

A

Adjournment   A term generally used in reference to legislative activities, meaning, in that context, "termination of a legislative day on the completion of business, with the hour and day of the next meeting being set prior to adjournment." A related term, *adjournment sine die,* Latin for "without a day; an indefinite period," generally refers to "the final adjournment of a legislative session" (Illinois General Assembly, n.d.).

When used in reference to the U.S. Congress, *adjournment sine die* means "the final adjournment of an annual or the two-year session of a Congress." The Congress of the United States also uses other, constitutionally significant, related terms. *Adjourn for more than three days* is important because "under the Constitution, neither chamber may adjourn for more than three days without the approval of the other. Such approval is obtained in a concurrent resolution approved by both chambers." Additionally, *adjournment to a day and time certain* means "an adjournment of the Senate that fixes the day and time for its next session" (U.S. Senate, n.d.).

Adjournment is also used in judicial proceedings, where the term means "a temporary postponement of the proceedings of a case until a specified future time" (New York State Unified Court System, n.d.). For more information, see Illinois General Assembly (n.d.), New York State Unified Court System (n.d.), and U.S. Senate (n.d.).

Adjudication   The final step in the judicial process. To adjudicate a dispute is to examine and resolve the case through judicial procedure and due process of law. A legal argument that has been heard and settled has been adjudicated. In an adversarial system of justice, two sides argue their case before a neutral party, usually a jury or judge, who renders a decision. The way to officially challenge the judgment is to file an appeal. **See also** Adversary System of Justice (political science, sociology); Appeal; Due Process of Law

Adjustment   A modification that facilitates ease or comfort with the environment. An adjustment is an alteration of any size or shape that results in a different relationship with existing conditions. Adjusting is the act of changing to better fit the circumstances. **See also** Adaptation

Adlerian Counseling   An approach to counseling founded by Alfred Adler, a Viennese psychiatrist, during the early 20th century. Adler viewed humans as purposeful, creative, and social, often standing in stark contrast to Freud's more pessimistic take on humanity. The focus of counseling is on the future, maladaptive conscious and unconscious beliefs, and the capacity of the individual to make free choices, all while seeking to address the whole person through an equalitarian therapeutic relationship. Adler's approach is often viewed as the blending of cognitive-behavioral and humanistic counseling modalities.

Administered Prices   Set market values for specific goods and services established by a governmental, bureaucratic agency or a firm (or collection of firms) with a substantial amount of market power. There may a set or designated minimum or maximum price for the affected items. An example of a minimum price would be the national minimum wage or minimum-price standards for various agricultural products set by a farm price support system. Alternatively, an example of a maximum price would be maximum rent prices for various residential properties set by a local government. These price control measures are often maintained by public or private sanctions for individual buyers or sellers who may be inclined to engage in market transactions at prices different from the administered prices. For example, OPEC, the cartel that controls the prices of oil products among a number of oil-producing countries, may try to fine or otherwise punish member countries that contract to sell oil products at prices below administered levels.

Administration   Alexander Hamilton, early on in the new republic (1788), articulated well the use of this term:

> The administration of government, in its largest sense, comprehends all the operations of the body politic, whether legislative, executive, or judiciary; but in its most usual, and perhaps its most precise signification. it is limited to executive details, and falls peculiarly within the province of the executive department. The actual conduct of foreign negotiations, the preparatory plans of finance, the application and disbursement of the public moneys in conformity to the general appropriations of the legislature, the arrangement of the army and navy, the directions of the operations of war, these, and other matters of a like nature, constitute what seems to be most properly understood by the administration of government.

Woodrow Wilson (1877/1983) defined it as follows: "Administration is the most obvious part of government; it is government in action; it is the executive, the operative, the most visible side of government, and is of course as old as government itself." Wilson added,

> Public administration is detailed and systematic execution of public law. Every particular application of general law is an act of administration. The assessment and raising of taxes, for instance, the hanging of a criminal, the transportation and delivery of the mails, the equipment and recruiting of the army and navy, etc., are all obviously acts of administration; . . . The broad plans of governmental action are not administrative; the detailed execution of such plans is administrative.

Recognizing that the study of administration in Europe was more advanced than in the United States, he advocated adapting those studies to America.

One of the Europeans who had a great impact on American concepts of administration, although he recognized that European systems were different from American systems, was Max Weber (1922). Among other things, he identified the characteristics of modern governments as follows:

> In public and lawful government these three elements constitute "bureaucratic authority"; I. There is the principle of fixed and official jurisdictional areas, which are generally ordered by rules, that is, by laws or administrative regulations; 1. The regular activities required for the purposes of the bureaucratically governed structure are distributed in a fixed way as official duties; 2. The authority to give the commands required for the discharge of these duties is distributed in a stable way and is strictly delimited by rules concerning the coercive means, physical, sacerdotal, or otherwise, which may be placed at the disposal of officials; 3. Methodical provision is made for the regular and continuous fulfilment of these duties and for the execution of the corresponding rights; only persons who have the generally regulated qualifications to serve are employed.

For more information, see Hamilton (1788), Weber (1922), and Wilson (1877/1968).

Administrative Accountability   The means by which public agencies and their workers manage the diverse expectations generated within and outside of the organization. Romzek and Dubnick (1987) identify four key accountability systems: legal, bureaucratic, professional, and political. *Legal accountability* is imposed by a specific entity outside of the organization, taking the form of policy mandates, laws, or contracts. Public administrators are responsible for implementing these initiatives. *Bureaucratic accountability* systems are embedded within the hierarchical structure of the organization to ensure checks and balances. The central aspect of this system is the supervisory relationship between superior and subordinate. Objectives and expectations are clearly specified in agency policies, procedures, and manuals. *Professional accountability* has grown to meet the complex problems addressed by public organizations. Operating through professional norms, values, and codes of ethics, employees acknowledge that they will be rewarded and punished for their behavior in the organization. *Political accountability* works to ensure responsiveness of public administrators to external parties interested in agency action, such as elected officials, taxpayers, and independent auditors acting on behalf of one or more of these constituencies.

More than 60 years ago, scholars rigorously debated whether public administrators were accountable to elected officials or should be judged in accordance with professional standards. This argument is now known as the famous Freidrich-Finer debate of the early 1940s.

Carl Freidrich (1941/1978) argued that public administrators, with their training and technical competence, were capable critics of their performance. Herman Finer (1941/1972), on the other hand, countered that elected officials serve as representatives of the public interest in a democracy and therefore urged that administrations should be accountable to elected officials as they represent the interests of citizens. For more information, see Finer (1941/1972), Freidrich (1941/1978), and Romzek and Dubnick (1987).

Administrative Advocacy   Any attempt by interested parties, which may include individuals, organizations, and governments, to shape or influence the policies or regulations of administrative agencies when they implement responsibilities given to them by the legislature by means of enacted legislation. Agencies have discretion as to how programs are implemented, and the actual policies implemented may be more favorable to some parties than to others. Consequently, those interested will try to shape the policy and regulation to their benefit. Administrative procedures that are similar at all levels of government generally encourage public input into the regulatory process by means of all rulemaking processes—informal, negotiated, or formal. All are preceded by a notice of proposed rulemaking inviting comments and recommendations. The agency proposing the rules is required to evaluate the comments, though it does not have to accept any of them, and to explain its rationale for issuing any final regulations. Advocacy, however, can also take the form of petitions for rulemaking and the bringing of lawsuits against agencies for improperly deciding to issue or not issue appropriate regulations.

Administrative advocacy may also involve monitoring program operations, engaging others in the practice of monitoring regulations and guidelines that control implementation of legislation, directing public attention to proposed regulations, or challenging policies or regulations in court when they are inconsistent with the law.

In *Massachusetts v. Environmental Protection Agency* (2007),

> a group of private organizations petitioned the Environmental Protection Agency (EPA) to begin regulating the emissions of four [greenhouse] gases, including carbon dioxide, under the Clean Air Act, which requires that the EPA "shall by regulation prescribe . . . standards applicable to the emission of any air pollutant from any class . . . of new motor vehicles . . . which in [the EPA Administrator's] judgment cause[s], or contribute[s] to, air pollution . . . reasonably . . . anticipated to endanger public health or welfare." EPA denied the petition, reasoning that (1) the Act does not authorize it to issue mandatory regulations to address global climate change, and (2) even if it had the authority to set greenhouse gas emission

A

standards, it would have been unwise to do so at that time because a causal link between greenhouse gases and the increase in global surface air temperatures was not unequivocally established. The agency further characterized any EPA regulation of motor-vehicle emissions as a piecemeal approach to climate change that would conflict with the President's comprehensive approach involving additional support for technological innovation, the creation of nonregulatory programs to encourage voluntary private-sector reductions in greenhouse gas emissions, and further research on climate change, and might hamper the President's ability to persuade key developing nations to reduce emissions.

The petitioners, joined by various intervening states, including Massachusetts, and local governments, sued the EPA in the D.C. Circuit, maintaining that the EPA decision was "arbitrary, capricious, an abuse of discretion, or otherwise not in accordance with law." They lost in the D.C. Circuit and appealed to the Supreme Court, which reversed the lower court's decision. The Supreme Court stated, in pertinent part,

The sovereign prerogatives to force reductions in greenhouse gas emissions, to negotiate emissions treaties with developing countries, and (in some circumstances) to exercise the police power to reduce motor-vehicle emissions are now lodged in the Federal Government. Because congress has ordered EPA to protect Massachusetts (among others) by prescribing applicable standards . . . and has given Massachusetts a concomitant procedural right to challenge the rejection of its rulemaking petition as arbitrary and capricious, . . . petitioners' submissions as they pertain to Massachusetts have satisfied the most demanding standards of the adversarial process. EPA's steadfast refusal to regulate greenhouse gas emissions presents a risk of harm to Massachusetts that is both "actual" and "imminent," . . . and there is a "substantial likelihood that the judicial relief requested" will prompt EPA to take steps to reduce that risk.

Administrative advocacy also means appearing before the administrative body that is deciding on the application of a party for a license. For more information, see *Massachusetts v. Environmental Protection Agency* (2007).

Administrative Agency   An agency delegated power by Congress, or the appropriate state or local legislature, to act on behalf of the executive branch of a federal, state, or local government. Agencies are formed to further the protection of the public good. Members of an administrative agency consist of specialists in the relevant field. The power allowing the federal government to create agencies rests in the "necessary

and proper" clause of Article 1, Section 8 of the U.S. Constitution: "To make all laws which shall be necessary and proper for carrying into execution the foregoing powers, and all other powers vested by this Constitution in the government of the United States, or in any department or officer thereof." In the United States, the first administrative agencies were created in the late 1700s to provide pensions for wounded soldiers and to determine appropriate tariffs on imports. The first permanent administrative agency, the Interstate Commerce Commission (ICC), was formed in 1887. Agencies may also commonly be referred to as commissions, bureaus, departments, or divisions.

Administrative Discretion   The authority given by the legislature to an agency to make a choice or judgment about how to implement a program or statute. Among the details left to administrative discretion is the promulgation of regulations. The agency is free to issue regulations "in accordance with the sound exercise of discretion" (U.S. General Accounting Office, 2004). When the legislature leaves the details of implementation to the agency, "there is an express delegation of authority to the agency to elucidate a specific provision of the statute by regulation" (*Chevron U.S.A., Inc. v. Natural Resources Defense Council, Inc.,* 1984), and "any ensuing regulation is binding in the courts unless procedurally defective, arbitrary or capricious in substance, or manifestly contrary to the statute" (*Flynn John J. v. Cmsnr IRS,* 2001):

To say that an agency has freedom of choice in a given matter does not mean that there are no limits to that freedom. Discretion is not unbridled license. The decisions have frequently pointed out that discretion means legal discretion, not unlimited discretion. (www.gao.gov/atext/d04261sp.txt)

Where a particular action or decision is committed to agency discretion by law, the agency is under a legal duty to actually exercise that discretion. [In one line of cases,] the principle has evolved that the failure or refusal to exercise discretion committed by law to the agency is itself an abuse of discretion. (www.gao.gov/atext/d04261sp.txt)

Most exercises of administrative discretion are subject to judicial review under the Administrative Procedure Act (APA) or the state equivalent. Sometimes, however, an action that, according to the APA, is "committed to agency discretion by law" is not subject to judicial review: In "rare instances statutes are drawn in such broad terms that in a given case there is no law to apply" (Senate Report No. 752, 1945).

Under federalism, conflicts between the different levels and courts may arise when state administrative agencies are required to apply the provisions of federal law to particular issues. For more information, see *Chevron U.S.A., Inc. v. Natural Resources Defense Council,*

Inc. (1984), *Flynn John J. v. Cmsnr IRS* (2001), Senate Report No. 752 (1945), and U.S. General Accounting Office (2004).

Administrative Due Process   The premise that all individuals in the United States (including noncitizens) are entitled to (owed) a certain degree of procedure before their life, liberty, or freedom is taken from them. In other words, before an individual can be deprived of life, liberty, or freedom, certain procedures must take place. The due process clause is found in the Fifth and Fourteenth amendments of the U.S. Constitution.

Under administrative law, government agencies as well as regulatory agencies must follow certain administrative procedures when working with private parties. These administrative procedures are written guidelines that are intended to protect the private parties from the capricious or unjust use of governmental authority. In addition, these procedures help protect the individual rights of these private entities. These stipulations require that government agencies or commissions observe specified guidelines that are designed to be neutral and objective. It is felt that since the government has a greater amount of resources than these private parties, steps must be taken to protect these private parties from governmental abuses. Part of the protections and safeguards of administrative due process is that any decision adverse to a private party is subject to appeal.

Administrative due process as applied to the legal system indicates that individuals must exhaust all legal remedies in their respective state legal systems before they can use the federal court system. In other words, before individuals can take a case to a federal district court, they must first exercise all of the appropriate legal remedies available to them in their particular state legal system.

Administrative Law   The body of law that flows from and surrounds the actions of administrative agencies that make legislative or substantive regulations, the authority for which has been in essence delegated by the legislature to the executive. These laws have a future effect and adjudicate the compliance of covered entities with the regulations or claims to entitlement to statutorily bestowed benefits. The definition includes the requirement that agencies "keep the public currently informed of their organization, procedures and rules . . . provide for public participation in the rule making process . . . prescribe uniform standards for the conduct of formal rule making and adjudicatory proceedings, i.e., proceedings which are required by statute to be made on the record after opportunity for an agency hearing . . . [and] restate the law of judicial review" (U.S. Department of Justice, 1947). This includes proposed rules, final rules, decisions, and judicial interpretations as to whether the rules or decisions meet or failed to meet the standard of fairness, are not arbitrary, and are legal.

Although administrative law can be traced back to the first Congress, rulemaking and adjudication were irregular. In January, 1935, for example, not until a dispute about a Presidential Executive Order appeared before the Supreme Court was it determined that an issue in dispute concerned a provision that had been revoked. The Court stated, "Whatever the cause of the failure to give appropriate public notice of the change in the section, with the result that the persons affected, the prosecuting authorities, and the courts, were alike ignorant of the alteration, the fact is that the attack in this respect was upon a provision which did not exist" (*Panama Refining Co. v. Ryan,* 1935). To fix this situation, Congress, in 1935, passed the, Federal Register Act, which empowered the archivist of the United States to establish a division within the National Archives to be responsible, with the Government Printing Office, for the publication of a daily *Federal Register* under the authority of a newly established Administrative Committee of the Federal Register. It is the official gazette of the U.S. Government and is published every federal working day. It provides legal notice of administrative rules and notices and presidential documents in a comprehensive, uniform manner. The Federal Register contains Federal Agency Regulations; Proposed Rules and Public Notices; Executive Orders; Proclamations; and Other Presidential Documents. The final rules and presidential documents are compiled annually into the Code of Federal Regulations (CFR). It is an annual codification of the general and permanent rules published in the Federal Register by the executive departments and agencies of the federal government. (McKinney, 2006).

Publication of rules solved one problem, but another problem was the need for public knowledge of administrative procedure as well. This took the form of the enactment of the Administrative Procedures Act (APA) in 1946. Initial study of the problem began before World War II, but final action was delayed until after the war. When passed, the APA included the following sections: § 551 Definitions; § 552 Public information; agency rules, opinions, orders, records, and proceedings; § 552a Records maintained on individuals; § 552b Open meetings; § 553 Rule making; § 554 Adjudications; § 555 Ancillary matters; § 556 Hearings; presiding employees; powers and duties; burden of proof; evidence; record as basis of decision; § 557 Initial decisions; conclusiveness; review by agency; submissions by parties; contents of decisions; record; § 558 Imposition of sanctions; determination of applications for licenses; suspension, revocation, and expiration of licenses; and § 559 Effect on other laws; effect of subsequent statute.

Agency rules are often described as "quasi-legislative" pronouncements because they resemble statutes. Agency adjudication is often referred to as "quasi-judicial" because it involves individualized determinations of the legal rights of particular persons or entities. Thus, for example, an agency's determination that a particular person is disabled and meets the requirements for

A

receiving vocational services is an administrative adjudication because that decision assesses, the legal rights of that particular person. The criteria for qualifying as "disabled," however, might well come from an administrative rule, which is applicable to all persons claiming the right to such vocational services. (New York State Department of Civil Service, 2008)

For more information, see Administrative Procedures Act (1946), McKinney, R. J. (2006), New York State Department of Civil Service (2008), *Panama Refining Co. v. Ryan* (1935), U.S. Department of Justice (1947).

Administrative Order   In public administration, the term *administrative order* has been defined in at least four ways. The principal definition is within the context of administrative law and has evolved to mean "an agency adjudication of particular applicability that determines the legal rights, duties, privileges, or immunities, or other legal interests of one or more specific persons." In other words, "an order includes solely agency legal determinations that are addressed to particular, specific, identified individuals in particular circumstances. An order may be addressed to more than one person" (National Conference of Commissioners on Uniform State Laws, 2007a). Another version of this "administrative order" is a written decision issued by an administrative law judge or quasi-judicial entity (Arizona Revised Statues, ARS 36–301, Definitions).

The term, however, is also used in court administration. For example,

> an "administrative order" is an order issued by the Supreme Judicial Court, regarding one or all of the courts and offices of the Judicial Branch, which directs, changes, or clarifies a practice or procedure of any court which is intended to have an effect on its customers or the general public in its dealings with the court. (State of Maine Supreme Judicial Court Administrative Order JB-05–2)

In the Department of Defense, "administrative order" means "an order covering traffic, supplies, maintenance, evacuation, personnel, and other administrative details" (*Department of Defense Dictionary of Military and Associated Terms* JP 1–02).

And in at least one instance (Alaska) at the state level, the term is used as, among other things, a means by which the governor assigns functions in the executive branch that are not otherwise defined in law. For more information, see Arizona Revised Statutes, *The Department of Defense Dictionary of Military and Associated Terms*, National Conference of Commissioners on Uniform State Laws (2007a), and State of Maine Supreme Judicial Court Administrative Order JB-05–2.

Administrator   One appointed to provide leadership skills and management abilities to direct and supervise the operations of a business or agency such as a school or government office. Administrators make minimal changes in existing processes and organizational structures as they facilitate progress toward goals and objectives.

Adolescence *(education)*   The stage of human development that occurs between childhood and adulthood. It begins with the onset of puberty and ends when the individual reaches the age of 18 to 21. During adolescence, individuals experience changes in cognition, social-emotional relations, and physical and hormonal growth that result in sexual maturity. ***See also*** Cognitive Development; Human Development

Adolescence *(psychology)*   The period of transition in which a child matures into an adult. The beginning of human adolescence is marked by a growth spurt. This spurt usually happens at the age of 12 for girls and is accompanied by numerous physical changes (e.g., the development of breasts and growth of pubic hair, onset of menstruation). For boys, this growth spurt begins generally at the age of 14, also accompanied by a multitude of physical changes (e.g., enlarging testes, pubic hair, facial hair, first ejaculation, voice deepening). By the end of adolescence, females are menstruating and males are producing live sperm, signifying sexual maturity. Adolescence is also marked by various psychological changes and challenges. Young people develop abstract thinking abilities and a clearer sense of psychological (and ethnic) identity, and they advance in their moral reasoning. Independence from parents and peer groups become important concerns. Peer groups usually have a positive effect when providing emotional support and can at times be more important than parents. Several developmental stage models have addressed the importance of adolescence in human development. In Sigmund Freud's model, adolescence marks the "genital phase" of psychosexual development, while for Jean Piaget, who focused on cognitive development, it is the "formal-operative stage." Erik Erikson, in his theory of psychosocial development, identified the identity crisis as the central aspect of adolescence. For more information, see Lerner and Steinberg (2004). ***See also*** Developmental Psychology; Personality

Adoption Studies   Studies that investigate babies that are adopted very early in life to determine the influence of socialization and genetics on psychological variables. The first studies aimed at separating "nature" and "nurture" were conducted in 1924. The rationale for conducting adoption studies is that if adopted children's characteristics are more like those of their biological parents, it is more likely that genetics play a determining role for the development of these characteristics than nonshared environmental influences. For example, psychological traits of adopted children tend to be more similar to their biological parents than their adoptive parents: IQ scores of adopted children were more similar to their biological than their adoptive parents, and adopted children are ten times more likely to develop schizophrenia if their biological mother suffered from schizophrenia. If twins are investigated in adoption studies, the role of heredity can be identified relatively clearly. Advances in the Human Genome Project have allowed scientists to begin identifying DNA differences responsible for certain attributes and behaviors to better understand the interaction of heredity and environment. For more information, see Plomin, DeFries, McClearn, and McGuffin (2001). *See also* Developmental Psychology; Evolutionary Psychology; Heritability; Nature–Nurture Debate; Twin Studies

Adult Education A course of action for assisting adults in their lifelong learning, including adapting to innovations in rapidly changing modern societies through the improvement of their knowledge, skills, and abilities. *See also* Continuing Education; Lifelong Learning

Adult Learning Theory The body of knowledge that comprises what is known about how adults learn. In the 1970s, those involved in the education of adults sought to separate their field of work from that of learning in general, which had previously been researched mainly by psychologists and educational psychologists. Adult learning theory differentiates between itself and other areas of education as well as between how children learn and how adults learn.

Knowles's (1980) concept of andragogy (the art and science of helping adults learn) is among the better-known models in adult learning. The essence of Knowles's model lies in the following assumptions about adults: (a) they are more self-directed than dependent; (b) their accumulation of experiences is a rich resource for learning; (c) their readiness to learn is directly related to the tasks required in their social roles; (d) they are more subject centered than problem centered in learning; (e) they find internal motivations more powerful than external ones; and (f) they need to know why it is important to learn something. Knowles viewed these assumptions as critical to the design of educational programs for adults.

Other theories of adult learning include Illeris's (2002) three dimensions of learning model, Jarvis's (1987) model of the learning process, McCluskey's (1963) theory of margin, and Mezirow's (2000) theory of transformative learning. Illeris's three dimensions of learning are cognition, emotion, and social context, among which learning continually interacts. Jarvis holds that change occurs in a person as a result of the person having experienced dissonance, which led to learning. Adult development and the timing of learning are central to McCluskey's theory of margin, while Mezirow's transformative learning occurs as a change in the adult's consciousness through the process of learning. For more information, see Illeris (2002), Jarvis (1987), Knowles (1980), McClusky (1963), Merriam,

Caffarella, and Baumgartner (2007), and Mezirow (2000).

Advanced Placement (AP) A program designed by the College Board offering college-level courses in high school that span 22 subject areas. High school students can receive college credit by scoring 3 or above (on a scale of 1 to 5) on an AP exam in any subject area. *See also* International Baccalaureate Schools (IB)

Adversary System of Justice *(political science)* The manner in which criminal cases are prosecuted under a common-law system. Great Britain and her former colonies adopted the common-law approach. There are two adversarial sides to a criminal trial: the *defense,* a private or court-appointed attorney representing the *defendant,* and the *prosecution,* a public attorney prosecuting on behalf of the victim. The burden of proof is always on the *prosecutor,* and a defendant is presumed innocent until proven guilty. A jury of one's peers and/or a judge hears the evidence of the case and makes a final determination. In contrast to this is the inquisitorial system, which is present in civil law countries. There is no private defense, and it is not mandatory that a jury hear a trial nor is the presumption of innocence present. An investigating public officer collects evidence about the case on behalf of the victim *and* the defendant. The judge also takes an active role in the collection of evidence.

Adversary System of Justice *(sociology)* A tradition of jurisprudence in which parties are situated in opposition to one another. Typically, there are two sides. A series of rules and legal principles rooted in due process guide the procedure. The resolution of this adversarial process is a decision rendered by an impartial third party or an agreement reached by those involved. The United States uses an adversary system of justice. *See also* Due Process/Due Process Model

Adverse Impact Hidden discrimination toward a particular minority group. Such an occurrence is not necessarily intentional and is especially relevant in terms of hiring practices. According to the Equal Employment Opportunity Commission (EEOC), "a substantially different rate of selection in hiring, promotion or other employment decision which works to the disadvantage of members of a race, sex, or ethnic group" constitutes adverse impact. The EEOC currently provides an "80% rule" of thumb to determine the presence of adverse impact. In this framework, if the target (or minority) group selected is four fifths or greater than the reference (or majority) group selected of the applications received, then adverse impact is considered to have taken place. For example, let us say a particular place of employment has 50 applicants for positions, including 40 (declared) whites and 10 (declared) Hispanics. If 10 of the (declared) whites are then given a position and 2 (declared) Hispanics, the 80% rule has not been statistically violated because 20% of the hires were from

A

a minority group. For more information, see USLegal (n.d.). *See also* Discrimination

Adverse Selection   The result of asymmetric information. Information is asymmetric when all participants in a market do not have the same amount of material information. Adverse selection occurs when poor-quality participants or goods in a market are treated much more favorably because of skewed or unbalanced information. Adverse selection creates price distortions in the market.

Consumer perception of market products based on adequate information will drive prices down for goods that are likely to perform poorly (be a lemon) or create disutility. Poor-quality and high-quality goods will not be traded at proximate prices, and there will be little or negligible price discrimination because of information asymmetry.

Adverse selection is a risk-based theory in which consumers take risks because of lack of information. Sellers of low-quality products are well disposed to sell their products, but sellers of high-quality products are not necessarily so. The net effect is that both good- and poor-quality products are perceptibly misconstrued to reflect price expectation. *See also* Asymmetric Information

Advertising *(economics)*   Communication about a company's products or services for sale, through electronic media, television, newspapers, magazines, billboards, and any other forum that has visibility. Companies try to convince consumers to buy their products through advertising because of competition from other companies. In addition, companies use advertising to differentiate their products and to create consumer awareness of and familiarity with a company's products. Advertising is done by companies engaged in pure competition, monopolistic competition, and oligopolistic competition. When companies charge prices for their goods above marginal cost, these companies need to advertise to compete for more buyers by attracting them or convincing them through advertising of the superiority of their products and services. Advertising has been criticized for making people buy something that they do not want. Critics claim that most advertising is psychological rather than informational. It manipulates people to buy. On the other hand, companies claim that advertising is used to provide information about their products. For more information, see Mankiw (2007).

Advertising *(media studies)*   The paid promotion of goods, services, or ideas by an identified sponsor through any form of media. Because advertising is paid for, as distinct from publicity, the advertising message's content and placement can be controlled by the sponsor. Through the analysis of audience characteristics, or demographics, advertisers try to target their messages based on audience's particular needs or desires. Typically, advertising is the biggest source of income for American media outlets.

In America, the earliest advertisements were in the form of signboards at inns. The 18th century witnessed the publication of the first newspapers, and through them, sponsors sold goods or services. By the early 20th century, modern advertisers began applying psychological principles to their advertisements and moved away from a long description of their products' benefits, using instead images and minimal copy in newspapers and other print formats to appeal to the emotions and create a desire for their products. This shift, used to great effect in radio and later television advertising, coupled with the obvious profit motivation, has created skepticism among the public, who believe that advertisements are meant to persuade rather than inform. Although government legislation and oversight is the main deterrent against false or deceptive advertising, the media have established some codes, and the advertising industry itself has developed standards.

As media forms and technologies changed throughout the 20th century, so too did the types of advertising messages. Currently, in addition to traditional print, outdoor, and broadcast advertising formats, many Internet-advertising techniques have become increasingly popular and have resulted in ethical debates that tend to focus on format over content. These techniques include "in-line" text ads that highlight certain words that, when clicked, bring the individual to an advertisement. Also, "contextual advertising" displays advertisements along with other search results in response to entering search words in a search engine. Critics of these techniques argue that they blur the line between real news or information and advertisements. Others say that they are less intrusive than print or broadcast advertising genres, as the interactive nature of the internet allows the audience to choose the advertisements it wants to read. For more information, see Turow (1997). *See also* Public Relations

Affect   Emotive responses to stimuli, in contrast to actions or to cognitive responses. Deriving from the Latin *afficere*, the word means "to have had something done to one," implying a certain passivity. The complex interrelationship between cognition and affect is the subject of varied and extensive psychological studies on questions such as the following: What different areas of the brain control different emotions? Does affect occur independently of cognition, or is it strictly a postcognitive response? To what extent can affect be consciously controlled and alter behaviors? Advertising psychology invests heavily in studying the control of affect and its contribution to impulse buying.

Affect expresses itself through an array of physiological reactions (muscular contraction, secretions) and visible symptoms (voice changes, facial expressions), suggesting that conscious choice plays little part in emotional response. Yet affect is also socially constructed. Cultural anthropology studies differing taxonomies of affect across cultures and the differing social valence they give to emotions.

See also Affective Domain; Behavioral Effects; Emotional Communication

Affective Domain An element of a theory first presented by Bloom and Krathwohl (1956, 1965) that encompasses both a system of knowing or perceiving and a hierarchical taxonomy of objectives for instruction and assessment. The five levels in the taxonomy are presented as levels of maturity, wherein the subject's development could be described by a systematic hierarchy: *Receiving,* or awareness, is the lowest level. Then follow *responding,* or a reaction or behavior related to an experience; *valuing,* or involvement or commitment relative to the experience; *organization,* or making the event one's own by integrating it into one's priorities; and *characterization,* or acting consistently with the new value. As the descriptions suggest, higher levels involve deeper and more personal ownership of the material at stake. In writing learning goals or instructional objectives, teachers are able to specify their instructional targets and plan accordingly. Consequently, the verbs used as descriptors become the target objectives, and students' work can be assessed more accurately. For more information, see Bloom (1965) and Bloom, Englehart, Furst, Hill, and Krathwohl (1956). ***See also*** Motivation Theory

Affidavit A formal declaration of fact, in writing, that has been made under oath. An individual, often a witness in judicial proceedings, swears to the truthfulness of his or her statement before an authorized party. Affidavits carry significant legal weight.

Affiliative Behavior Any activity that builds or creates unity in a group. The term *affiliative behavior* is most commonly found in academic discourse in the fields of anthropology and psychology. It only refers to those actions that are likely to be understood as pleasing and appealing. Examples include smiling, head nodding, and waving. Affiliative behavior facilitates human connections.

Affirmation The idea that a point is factual or a proposition is true or valid, based on a previous decision or judgment that confirms that something is true. An affirmation can also be a solemn declaration that is made under oath in a court of law. The privilege of affirming was first granted to the Quakers during the reign of William III (king of England, Scotland, and Ireland, 1689–1702). Later, this privilege was granted to other people. An affirmation can be given in place of an oath when the person has no religious ties.

Affirmative Action *(political science)* The principle according to which laws may prohibit discrimination in the workplace, in terms of hiring and promotions, and in education, in terms of admissions, against minority groups, such as women, Latino/a, and other historically disadvantaged groups. The term first came into use in 1935 in the National Relations Act. Affirmative action provides a framework for governmental agencies to promote equality for African Americans. During the 1950s and 1960s, in legal cases such as *Brown v. Board of Education of Topeka* (1954), the Supreme Court ruled that, as African Americans have equal rights before the law (as established in the Fourteenth Amendment of the U.S. Constitution), practical measures must be taken to address violations of those rights.

As a tool to decrease social inequality for racial minorities in the United States, the concept was further developed during the presidency of Lyndon Johnson through the establishment of the Office of Federal Contract Compliance and the Equal Employment Opportunity Commission in 1965. Through these offices, affirmative action made it possible for all public institutions and organizations to consider the historical inequalities affecting minority groups, including women (as of 1971), in their hiring and admissions decisions.

Yet the policy came under criticism from African American civil rights leaders, who claimed that a policy could not overturn the legacy of slavery and racial discrimination and that more drastic measures were needed to correct historical inequalities.

As a result, during the 1970s and 1980s, civil rights organizations such as the National Association for the Advancement of Colored People (NAACP) and the National Organization of Women (NOW) advocated for programs intended to provide limited kinds of preferential treatment for victims of long-term racial or gender-based discrimination.

Spheres in which specially designed civil rights actions have been applied include education, voting, the housing market, university admissions, and employment (in federally funded agencies as well as in the public and private sectors). Affirmative action policies can frequently be found in the realm of education, and these govern (in many states) admission of students to institutions of higher education.

To this day, affirmative action continues to be at the center of intense debate. "Intensely controversial in the United States" (Mervin, 2003a), it has generated much legal and political debate. Some observers argue, for example, that affirmative action undermines the spirit of American society, that is, its ideal of equality of opportunity. Some critics have also noted that preferential treatment could lead to reverse discrimination, which would hurt white males in many contexts as well as (paradoxically) Asian Americans applying for university admission, for example. Both California (1996) and Michigan (2006) held successful referenda against reverse discrimination in admissions to public universities. For more information, see *Brown v. Board of Education of Topeka* (1954), Dallek and Boyer (2001), and Mervin (2003a).

Affirmative Action *(public administration)* Among the most controversial of contemporary public policies, affirmative action (often called "positive discrimination" in Europe) seeks to aid traditionally marginalized

A

(usually race-based) groups in gaining access to business or academic institutions. This can be achieved in a number of disparate ways; minorities may be given preferential treatment when applying to universities or certain occupations, or a certain quota can be set aside for their exclusive accommodation.

Proponents of affirmative action argue that such policies are necessary for a variety of different reasons. First, preferential treatment may seek to explicitly address and ameliorate past prejudices, granting opportunities to the current generation that were cruelly denied their ancestors. Second, and perhaps more persuasively, proponents argue that regardless of historical discrimination, minority members continue to enter life with a distinct disadvantage; African Americans, for example, are often born into greater poverty than their white counterparts, and therefore an extra boost may be necessary to level the social and economic playing field. Furthermore, the continued persistence of racism (whether conscious or structural) may inherently disadvantage people of color, and affirmative action can thus provide both a practical and adequate remedy.

Although affirmative action's proponents have largely been successful, such policies have come under increasing scrutiny (perhaps most recently from the U.S. Supreme Court). Relevant criticism usually comes in two primary forms; while some critics seek to abolish affirmative action altogether, others believe that it should be socioeconomically rather than racially based. The former opponents of affirmative action criticize such policies as nothing less than "reverse discrimination." According to these critics, discrimination is a negative phenomenon no matter what the particular context, and affirmative action thus wrongly advantages minority groups at the majority's expense. Other critics argue that affirmative action debases the very notion of a meritocracy, privileging unqualified minority candidates over harder-working and/or more intelligent competitors. Finally, some contend that affirmative action will ultimately harm those it seeks to help, positing minorities as "children" in need of greater government assistance and subsequently creating a cycle of state dependency.

More nuanced criticisms of affirmative action accept such policies in principle but ultimately object to their current administration. Seeking to go beyond racial or gender boundaries, the so-called socioeconomic critics argue that affirmative action should be entirely predicated not on racial but on financial needs. In this viewpoint, social advancement is primarily restricted through class inequality, and affirmative action (as practiced) thus largely benefits upper- and middle-class minority members only. A more socioeconomic "action" would conceivably benefit not only poor African Americans but also those Caucasian (and presumably Hispanic and Asian) Americans currently left behind. For more information, see Fullinwider (1980). *See also* Cultural Diversity; Discrimination

Affirmative Action in Education   A voluntary employment plan developed by a school district or other educational hiring authority to include persons of all backgrounds, especially minority group members who have experienced past discriminatory employment practices. To be viewed as lawful, affirmative action plans must be based on lingering effects of past discrimination that support a compelling governmental interest.

Afterimage   The term used for residual images perceived after staring at an image for about 30 seconds and then switching to a white space. The color black (in the original picture) will result in a white afterimage, while green will result in red and yellow will result in blue. Afterimages are explained by the structure of ganglion cells and their photoreceptors. The center-surround receptive fields of ganglion cells form the basis for opponent colors. Some ganglion cells have a center that responds best to green wavelengths and a surround whose photoreceptors respond best to red, while other ganglion cells pair blue and yellow, or black and white (as the main types). When either the center or the surround of a ganglion cell's receptive field is stimulated, the other area is inhibited, thus producing a short-term afterimage. For more information, see Shimojo, Kamitani, and Nishida (2001). *See also* Adaptation; Cones; Perception; Sensory Adaptation

Ageism   Discrimination or stereotyping of individuals based on their age. The term most frequently refers to discrimination against older individuals regarding issues of employment hiring, firing, and promotion. Ageism also can be used to describe differential treatment or views on children and teenagers. *See also* Discrimination (public administration, sociology); Stereotype (communication, psychology)

Agency   In the field of public administration, a permanent federal, state, or local government organization that provides administration of discrete functions. It is an administrative division of the government, usually established though legislation or executive orders at the federal, state, or local level. Some agencies are referred to as "independent agencies," as they operate outside of the direct control of the executive branch. Others operate directly under the supervision of a cabinet-level position or executive-branch department. Oversight and judicial review of agencies at the federal level is usually provided through congressional statutes. Examples include the National Institutes of Health (NIH) and the Federal Bureau of Investigation (FBI). *Agency* may also refer to nongovernmental organizations (NGOs). These organizations are privately run and funded and usually do not have government representatives. *See also* Agency Mission; Government

Agency Mission   Part of the broader agency strategic management process, that is, the formulation and implementation of a strategic plan. Since the 1993

Government Performance and Results Act (GPRA), governmental agencies have been required to develop a five-year strategic plan. An agency's mission statement is based on what the government by law has authorized the agency to do. This mission statement sets out what the agency does and how it does it. The strategic goals that are developed are linked to the agency mission and explain the goals of the agency programs and the results they are expected to bring about. ***See also*** Strategic Planning

Agenda *(communication)*   A word derived from the plural gerundive of the Latin verb *agere,* meaning "to do." Thus, in modern parlance it is a list of things to do or discuss in a set order at a meeting. The agenda begins with a call to order and ends with a call for adjournment. During the meeting, the agenda may also include approval of the minutes, old business, and new business. An agenda can also be called "orders of the day." In this case, the participants usually get the list of activities before the meeting takes place. Usually, the agenda serves as a guide for the leader of the meeting and, distributed beforehand, allows participants to prepare for the discussions. Usually, the person who sets the agenda, for example, a congressional leader, controls the meeting.

Agenda *(political science)*   The goals of an organization, in relation to the political issues that form the primary focus of its debate and subsequent action. Government bodies, nongovernmental agencies, and special-interest groups possess agendas that highly influence U.S. politics. What determines our nation's political agenda is debatable. Lobbyists and special interest groups compete for a politician's time and attention in an effort to "push" their agendas. In addition, lawmakers and party officials struggle to get their concerns addressed by federal, state, or local legislatures. The mass media also play a central role in furthering the issues that will be of concern to constituents.

Political agenda is also the term used when an individual or individuals manipulate a situation in an effort to enhance their political position. When one's political agenda is disguised in the form of another or is the ulterior motive for a completely separate agenda, it is referred to as a "hidden agenda."

Agenda Building   A concept proposed in 1983 by Lang and Lang, after their study of the Watergate scandal, according to which, in a collective process, the public, the government, and the media all reciprocally influence each other. (The Langs posit that this concept is a more accurate reflection of the effects of mass media than the concept of *agenda setting* in that the media do not determine the public agenda independently of the political landscape or the public.) The process occurs in several feedback loops, in which political actors see themselves in the media; the media pools information, thus creating repetitive coverage; and then public responses, through opinion polls, are relayed back to both the media and politicians. For more information,

see Lang and Lang (1983). ***See also*** Agenda Setting (media studies, political science, public administration)

Agenda Setting *(media studies)*   The idea that although the media can't tell people *what* to think, they do control what people think *about*. McCombs and Shaw were the first to propose an agenda-setting effect, in a study that focused on the 1968 presidential election in Chapel Hill, North Carolina. In it, they found an extremely high correlation between the coverage of an issue and the public's perception of the importance of that issue. Over 250 subsequent studies have since examined agenda setting. Although largely supportive of the concept, researchers have looked at other variables in conjunction with media coverage—such as environmental circumstances or interpersonal experience—that were also found to have effects on public opinion. For more information, see McCombs and Shaw (1972). ***See also*** Agenda Building

Agenda Setting *(political science)*   The process in which political issues are brought to the public's attention, primarily through mass media. The mass media are central to agenda-setting goals owing to their inherent task of deciding which issues deserve news coverage and, further, how much prominence such coverage merits. Agenda setting in the media was first brought to national attention with the work of Maxwell McCombs and Donald Shaw in their study of the impact of the media on the 1968 presidential election in North Carolina (*Public Opinion Quarterly,* 1972).

There is an ongoing political debate as to whether the government dictates media coverage or whether the reverse scenario holds true. For example, government agencies engage in agenda setting by controlling the availability of sensitive information and making rules concerning its access. On the other hand, the mass media industry determines which issues are valued by lawmakers, due to their desire to appease voter concerns.

Agenda Setting *(public administration)*   The first phase, and generally considered the key part, of the public policy-making process. It is through the agenda-setting process that decision makers identify which problems need action. There are several different actors involved in the process, including the president, elected officials, the media, interest groups, and the public. The agenda-setting process includes phases such as problem recognition (how problems are identified by decision makers); salience, or the relative importance one gives to an issue; gatekeeping, or the control of salience; and framing, which attributes importance to issues.

Decision makers are influenced by many actors, including the media, interest groups, and the public. *Policy generation* refers to producing solutions to the identified problem. Solutions are often generated by experts and think tanks. For action to occur on the proposed solutions to the identified problem, the political climate must be relevant. For more information, see Kingdon (1995). ***See also*** Public Policy

Aggravating Circumstances   Conditions relating to a criminal act that intensify the severity of the crime. The increased severity is generally understood as an imperative to enhance punishment. The term is commonly associated with death penalty statutes. In 1972, the Supreme Court called into question the constitutionality of capital punishment on the grounds that it was not administered fairly. In response to this objection, legislatures developed capital punishment laws with more structure. A common development was the mandate that a crime's aggravating circumstances be weighed against the mitigating circumstances to determine whether the death penalty is an equitable punishment. ***See also*** Mitigating Circumstances

Aggregate Demand Curve   A curve showing an inverse relationship between the general price level and real output or gross domestic product (GDP) when other variables are held constant (ceteris paribus).

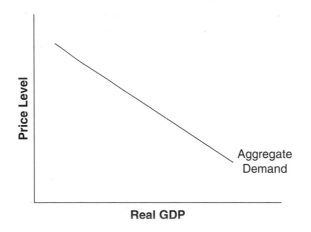

Aggregate Demand

Unlike a single market demand curve, the aggregate demand curve is a summation of demand in a macroeconomy (an economy as a whole) in relation to changes in the general price level (usually measured by the consumer price index, or CPI). The summation of demand reflects the reaction of consumers, investors, and foreigners to changes in price level.

A change in the general price level generates wealth, interest rate, and international trade effects, because when prices change, people may desire more or less money (wealth effect) and foreigners may buy more or less (international trade effect) goods depending on the direction of prices. If people are getting poorer because of a decline in purchasing power, they will try to sell assets to compensate for the decline in purchasing power. This will put upward pressure on interest rates (interest rate effect), which will result in less investment demand. As prices go up, ceteris paribus, total demand falls. For more information, see Boyes and Melvin (2002) and Mankiw (2006). ***See also*** Gross Domestic Product; Recession

Aggregate Expenditure   The sum of expenditures in a macroeconomy. To calculate the sum of expenditures in a macroeconomy, an accounting identity is used to account for the expenditures of the components of a macroeconomy. These components include household consumption (C); business investment expenditure (I); Government spending (G); and net spending in the global economy—net exports (NX). With the exception of autonomous government spending, the other variables are dependent on disposable income, the interest rate, and the exchange rate.

The aggregate expenditure model is a Keynesian model that makes the argument that the amount of goods and services produced, and therefore employment, is directly related to total spending in an economy (aggregate expenditure). When aggregate expenditure falls, total output and employment will fall because businesses will be ill disposed to produce goods and services for which markets are not available; conversely, when aggregate expenditure increases, businesses will be well-disposed to increase output and employment.

Well-targeted tax reductions increase household consumption; a reduction in interest rates stimulates investment demand; and a depreciation of the exchange rate relative to foreign currencies increases export capacity. (Of course, the ability to export is also a function of foreign absorption [elasticity], trade restrictions, product quality, and other economic variables.) ***See also*** Aggregate Demand Curve; Aggregate Supply Curve; Demand

Aggregate Supply Curve   The aggregate supply curve shows a positive relationship between the general price level and output when all other variables are considered to remain unchanged in the short run (see illustration). In the long run, when the economy is believed to be at full capacity, there is no noticeable relationship between the general price level and output. All attempts to stimulate aggregate consumption result in inflation. In the short run, when prices are sticky, there is no such upward pressure on the general price level as consumption increases.

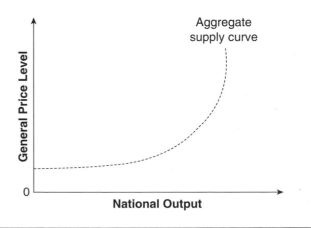

Aggregate Supply

Algorithm   19

The aggregate supply curve shows that when other economic variables are held constant (ceteris paribus), producers have an incentive to increase production in the intermediate period as prices increase. Other economic variables include input prices (resource cost), market power (the ability to set or control prices), productivity, and taxation or subsidy. These economic variables explain why the aggregate supply curve may shift to the right or left when the ceteris paribus restriction is relaxed. For more information, see Mankiw (2006) and McConnell and Brue (2008). *See also* Aggregate Demand Curve; Demand

Aggression   The character of an act that is intended to cause harm to another person. Evolutionary theory postulates that aggression is a basic survival mechanism that increases the chance of survival, both across (predator/prey) and within species. Additionally, aggression in males, evolutionarily speaking, may increase their chance of producing offspring. Biological influences moderating aggression include genetic, hormonal, and neurotransmitter influences, including the neurotransmitter serotonin, which curbs impulsive behavior. Indeed, lower levels of serotonin may predispose individuals to respond aggressively to social provocation. Similarly, testosterone is associated with higher levels of aggression. According to social-cognitive theorists (e.g., Albert Bandura), aggression is a learned behavior similar to many other forms of behavior, handed down by parents through role modeling and observational learning. Additionally, sociocultural influences such as poverty, prolonged unemployment, family breakdown, and exposure to violence in the community and family may facilitate aggressive behavior. In more general terms, sociocultural influences may shape what culturally accepted form aggression may take. For example, Americans resort more to physical aggression, while Japanese tend to exhibit aggression in verbal conflicts. Furthermore, a strong link between alcohol use and violent behavior (including domestic violence, homicide, and sexual violence) has been found, presumably due to loosening inhibitions under the influence of alcohol. Certain negative emotions, such as anger and frustration, are also linked to aggression. Additionally, environmental influences, such as rising temperature, can contribute to higher levels of aggression. At least two different types of aggression can be distinguished: hostile (affective/retaliatory) and instrumental (predatory/goal oriented). For more information, see Berkowitz (1993). *See also* Amygdala; Social Psychology; Social Skills Training

Agoraphobia   An anxiety disorder involving fear or discomfort in unfamiliar places, often combined with the fear of an unexpected panic attack occurring in these places. Often this includes a strong fear of being away from home, resulting in the individual being confined to his or her residence. Agoraphobia has a prevalence of about 5% in the U.S. population. Agoraphobia (and panic disorder) can be successfully treated with a gradual exposure therapy, often combined with cognitive therapy and antianxiety and antidepressant medication. For more information, see Barlow (2002). *See also* Antianxiety Drugs; Anxiety Disorders; Behavior Therapy; Panic Disorder; Phobia

Agricultural Policy   A set of laws and policies established to regulate domestic agriculture and imports of foreign agricultural products. Practices are commonly adopted to control price stability, supply level, product quality, and farm productivity and to deal with employment, land use, and food surplus. Such policies are also implemented to create a safety net in unexpectedly severe economic conditions and to slow the depopulation of rural areas.

While each country has its own ever-changing policies as it adapts to technological advances in the production of agriculture and to environmental challenges, generally speaking, there are two main methods of subsidizing agriculture. One method is to increase farmers' incomes should they fall below a level specified as acceptable. Often, farmers are required to set aside some of their land in exchange for this support. The second method is for the government to guarantee a minimum level of farm prices by buying up supply surplus and storing it or destroying it if prices otherwise fall below the guaranteed level. To minimize the direct cost of such a subsidy, governments may use trade barriers such as import levies to limit competition from cheaper world agricultural markets. Such domestic policies are often implemented as an insurance measure, in case it becomes difficult to buy agriculture products from abroad.

U.S. agricultural policies originated in the 1800s as the United States moved out of the colonial period and began to exploit the country's natural land and resources to produce tobacco and lumber for export. As land became overexploited and soils were depleted, it became necessary for Congress to intervene and diversify areas of settlement. Thus, the Homestead Act was born. Throughout the decades, the transition to industrial agriculture coupled with broader economic shifts has prompted the creation of multiple agricultural policies. One of the most recent U.S. agricultural policies, developed in 2002, emphasizes environmental concerns, organic and alternative agriculture, and energy production.

While agricultural policies largely address domestic concerns and are commonly a dominating factor in economic policies, they are also an important factor in foreign policies, affecting trade and the country's output. Agricultural policy is largely embedded in cross-border trade agreements such as the North American Trade Agreement (NAFTA), created to facilitate cross border movement of goods and services between Mexico, Canada, and the United States.

Algorithm   A systematic procedure or formula for solving a problem. Often applied in formal reasoning (or logical reasoning) situations, an algorithm involves a

A

formulaic, logical, statistical, or mathematical set of rules for problem solving. For many problems (e.g., Are all swans white?), strict formal algorithmic approaches, based on the full number of possible observations, are rarely practical by comparison with informal approaches (heuristics) that are based merely on a sample of observations, even though they may fail in some cases. For more information, see Jahnke and Nowaczyk (1998). **See also** Heuristic

Alibi   A statement made by a person accused of committing some act (usually a crime) that he or she was otherwise occupied or elsewhere during the time when that act was committed. This contention renders it impossible for that individual to have committed the act. An ideal or airtight alibi is one that can be supported by other people or by incontestable facts.

Allocation   In government budgeting, *allocation* refers to the division of appropriations among executive agencies using percentages that are based on legislative provisions. In strategic planning, *allocation* generally refers to resource allocations to achieve an organization's goals and objectives.

Allocational Effects   The outcome related to actions initiated by federal, state, and local government to alter the economy's pattern of output. If the private market were able to distribute all resources of the economy in a satisfactory way, there would be no allocative role for the government. Whether goods or services are produced by the government or produced privately, government's expenditures are allocative, and various patterns of taxation and subsidization influence the way in which goods and services are produced and consumed. Regulations also have allocational effects in that they encourage expenditures on some things and discourage or forbid expenditures on other things.

The U.S. government's issuance of transfer payments such as Social Security is a prime example of an allocational effect. Since recipients tend to spend their incomes in different patterns from other persons, any change in the amount allocated to this program would change the distributive pattern of goods and services produced and consumed by the nation's economy.

Alternative Assessments   Nontraditional forms of assessment (usually in an educational context) generally contrasted with standardized multiple-choice tests. Alternative assessments can sometimes take the form of performance assessments, in which the test taker is asked to construct a product or demonstrate a process. For example, in an entrepreneurship course, rather than having students complete a multiple-choice test on definitions, an alternative assessment might require students to develop, market, and sell a product or service, with scores derived using a rubric addressing the main objectives of the assessment. Other types of alternative assessments may include portfolios, oral presentations, journals, or exhibits. **See also** Performance Assessment

Altruism *(economics)*   Selfless consideration for the welfare of others without regard to reward or recognition. In theories of conduct, the term is an antonym of *egotism*. Altruism is a social behavior and value orientation that is central to many religious traditions and schools of thought.

The term *altruism* can first be traced to Auguste Comte, a French mathematician and philosopher who wrote during the early 1800s and who coined the French word "altruisme" to describe the ethical doctrine he supported. A few years later, it entered the English language as *altruism*. It is frequently used in a physiological sense, but many different perspectives exist; theories of altruism are no longer the province of philosophical and ethical thought but have become a focus of discussion among biologists, ethnologists, psychologists, and sociologists.

Biological altruism and the evolution of altruism in the animal kingdom have been the topic of much debate ever since Darwin. In the late 19th century, Darwin explored altruism's place with respect to genes and evolutionary theory. In evolutionary biology, an organism is said to behave altruistically when it acts in a manner that benefits others, at a cost to itself. By behaving altruistically, an organism reduces the number of offspring it is likely to produce itself but boosts the number that other organisms are likely to produce. Varying from the everyday concept, in biological altruism, cost and benefit are measured in terms of reproductive fitness; therefore, the conscious intention of helping another is not present.

In society, the concept of altruism often divides people into two groups: those who believe that altruism is a moral ideal that should be upheld by all humans and those who believe that it is a personal choice. While the promotion of altruistic behavior is central to most religions, including Christianity, Buddhism, Judaism, Islam, and Hinduism, altruism is also often regarded as the type of ethical principle that should guide the actions and duties of those in positions of power, such as political figures. To the contrary, philosophers such as Friedrich Nietzsche and David Kelley have voiced criticism of the doctrine and theory of altruism, indicating that treating others as more important than oneself is degrading and demeaning and that there is no rational ground for the notion. For more information, see Kelly (1998) and Nietzsche (1886/1955).

Altruism *(psychology)*   Unselfish concern for another's welfare. "Helping behavior" is formed by cultural norms and expectations instantiated by the family and the immediate social environment. Children increasingly help others to gain social approval until, in their late teens, helping behavior occurs even when no one is watching, out of a belief that it is morally good. Three major theories explain why people help without external reward. The first approach, the *cost-reward theory,* claims that people find the sight of a victim distressing and offer to help in order to reduce their own unpleasant (physiological) arousal. The evaluation of the costs associated with helping and not helping determines the occurrence of actual helping behavior. If the costs for the potential helper are low (i.e., not much effort is required to help) and the costs for the victim of not being helped are high (increased distress), helping behavior becomes more probable. Furthermore, the clarity of the need for help (e.g., the victim asks for help) increases the probability of helping behavior, while the presence of others inhibits helping behavior. This latter result has become known as the *bystander effect* and is explained by a diffusion of responsibility, with the bystanders assuming that others will help the victim. Other factors, such as personality, environment, and communication skills have been found to moderate the bystander effect. The second approach, the *empathy-altruism theory,* claims that helping occurs, even if the associated costs are high, when people feel empathy toward the person in need. However, it is still under debate whether people actually help out of an empathic concern or for more selfish reasons (e.g., reducing personal distress at the plight of others). The third perspective on altruism is rooted in *evolutionary theory.* Because natural selection focuses on inclusive fitness or, in other words, the survival of the genes and not necessarily the individual, helping kin (siblings, cousins, etc.) can promote fitness. Helping, even dying for, individuals whose genes one shares potentially increases the likelihood that at least some of our genetic characteristics are passed on to the next generation and will thus benefit future reproduction. For more information, see Madsen et al. (2007). ***See also*** Bystander Effect; Empathy-Altruism Hypothesis; Evolutionary Psychology; Kinship Selection Theory; Reciprocal Altruism

Alzheimer's Disease A major cause of dementia, characterized by a nearly complete loss of cholinergic neurons (that use acetylcholine as a neurotransmitter) in areas of the forebrain and limbic system that are particularly important for memory. The disease was named after the German neurologist Alois Alzheimer. Alzheimer's disease has a prevalence of 3% by age 75, with an average duration of 7 years from onset to death. Patients with Alzheimer's disease first become emotionally flat, then disoriented and mentally vacant. Severity of symptoms and duration depend on intelligence, gender, and education. Highly intelligent people show signs of Alzheimer later than the general populace, and women and well-educated individuals deteriorate more slowly. Drugs that enhance the availability and action of acetylcholine (among others), as well as cognitive therapies, are used in treating individuals suffering from Alzheimer's to slow down cognitive deterioration. For more information, see McFarlane, Welch, and Rodgers (2006). ***See also*** Cognitive Therapy (psychology); Memory (psychology); Neurotransmitters

Amnesia Loss of memory, which can occur in several forms. *Retrograde amnesia* describes the loss of memories of past events, while *anterograde amnesia* is the loss or impairment of the ability to encode or store new memories. *Childhood amnesia* (or *infantile amnesia*) describes the usual occurrence of amnesia during early infancy and childhood, typically before the age of three, and is currently explained by the advent of language, which renders previously stored information inaccessible to the language-based memory. Physical causes for amnesia include head trauma, degenerative brain diseases such as Alzheimer's disease, blockage of blood vessels to the brain, chronic infections, or alcoholism. Usually, performance on recall tasks is more affected by forms of amnesia than performance on recognition tasks, which in themselves provide a retrieval cue. Ordinary forgetting should not be confused with amnesia, as forgetting can be explained by several theoretic approaches. *Decay theory* postulates a gradual fading of unrehearsed memory traces as a function of time, while *interference theory* postulates that memory is disrupted by the interference of previously learned or newly learned material. *Retrieval theory* identifies the source of forgetting in the failure to access material stored in memory due to an encoding failure or a lack of retrieval cues. For more information, see Riccio, Millin, and Gisquet-Verrier (2003). ***See also*** Anterograde Amnesia; Forgetting Curve; Memory (psychology); Retrograde Amnesia

Amygdala A set of almond-shaped structures in the limbic system that play an important role in emotions (e.g., aggression, rage, fear) and the association of features from different sensory modalities. The amygdala helps regulate emotional states in response to unpleasant or aversive stimuli. Also, when the amygdala is electrically stimulated, the most frequent emotional reaction is fear or worry. Such an internal alarm system, signaling potentially threatening stimuli, has been linked repeatedly with evolutionary adaptation. More recently, the amygdala has been associated with grief, despair, positive emotions, and activity in response to erotic photographs. For more information, see LeDoux (2007). ***See also*** Brain (Encephalon); Classical Conditioning

Analysis of Covariance (ANCOVA) A general linear model (GLM) with one quantitative dependent variable and a mixture of categorical and quantitative independent variables. ANCOVA is often used as an extension of analysis of variance (ANOVA), where the means of different groups or treatment levels are compared for statistical significance after "adjusting" or "controlling for" the relationship between the dependent variable and the quantitative independent variable (called the "covariate"). ***See also*** Analysis of Variance (ANOVA); General Linear Model (GLM)

Analysis of Variance (ANOVA) *(education)* Comparison of variance among means of groups, with variance attributed to chance or error. ANOVA is used to compare means of different groups ("between") or means of the same group ("repeated observations") or combinations of these group types.

A

Analysis of Variance (ANOVA) *(psychology)* An inferential, statistical procedure to investigate differences in one dependent variable between two or more groups, often involving more than one independent variable. An analysis of variance evaluates the differences among means relative to the dispersion in the sampling distributions. Two estimates of variance are compared. One estimate comes from the differences among scores within each group and is considered error variance. The second estimate is derived from differences in group means and is therefore considered an expression of group differences or treatment effect (effect of experimental condition) plus error. If these do not differ significantly, it is concluded that all the group means (experimental and control) come from the same sampling distribution of means and variations are only due to random error. If the group means differ significantly, the null hypothesis (that the means are the same) is rejected in favor of the alternative hypothesis. Differences among variances are investigated as a ratio, with the differences of sample means as the numerator and the error variance as the denominator. This ratio forms an *F* distribution whose shape depends on the degrees of freedom in both numerator and denominator. The combination of degrees of freedom results in a list of critical *F* scores for testing the null hypothesis. Further statistical indicators in an analysis of variance include the sum of squares (i.e., the sum of squared differences between scores and their means) and the standard deviation (the square root of variance), a variability measure in the original format of the dependent variable. For more information, see Howell (2007). ***See also*** Statistics (psychology)

Anarchism An extreme political philosophy that rejects any form of government, or authority, in society. Anarchism as a social movement flourished between 1860 and 1939; the movement is associated with the era's European working class movements, including Russian Revolution (1917–1918) and Spanish Civil War (1936–1939).

There are many different types of anarchism, all sharing a belief in the dissolution of government but emphasizing different areas of interest and concern to its followers. Among them are *anarcho-syndicalism, anarcho-primitivism, green anarchism, anarcha-feminism, anarcho-communism, anarcho-collecivism, anarcho-individualism,* and *anarcho-capitalism. Anarcho-syndicalism* reflects the view that anarchy can only come about through organizational action and industrial unionization. *Anarcho-primitivism* proposes that all forms of civilization be destroyed, as it reflects domination in society, and that we should return to primal living. This is similar to *green anarchism,* which calls for a return to an agricultural, preindustrial society. *Anarcha-feminism* places emphasis on patriarchy as a central problem in society and a major reason for a call for anarchy. *Anarcho-communism* and *anarcho-collectivism* focus on the self-sufficient commune as the preferred lifestyle once anarchy is realized; each member would receive goods according to his needs and contribute according to his abilities. *Anarcho-individualism,* on the other hand, calls for no organization in society and for each individual to fend for himself or herself. *Anarcho-capitalism* calls for all property to be privatized. The word *anarchy* stems from the ancient Greek word *anarchia,* meaning "without rulers." For more information, see Wolff (1998).

Anchorage A term used in advertising to describe the use of text, in the form of a slogan or caption, to interpret an image. First introduced by the French theorist Roland Barthes along with the concept of relay, which is the relation of text within a sequence of images (as in a comic strip), anchorage leads the reader to a message that has been previously selected, instead of allowing the reader to put his or her own interpretation on the image. Therefore, the text becomes a form of control and has a repressive value with respect to the messages that can be drawn from the image. For more information, see Barthes (1977).

Anchoring Effect First investigated by Amos Tversky and Daniel Kahnemann in 1974, this effect describes the psychological heuristic of relying too heavily on one specific piece of information (i.e., an anchor) as a result of the way in which information is presented. In one of the first studies by Kahneman and Tversky, participants were asked to estimate the percentage of African countries in the United Nations. Before that, some were asked to first decide whether the percentage was more or less than 45%, while other participants were asked whether it was more or less than 65%. Participants who had seen the higher percentage consistently produced higher estimates than participants who were initially presented with the lower percentage. Since these first experiments, the anchoring effect has been shown to be a very stable cognitive bias, having many implications for behavioral decision making, including courtroom behavior about monetary awards. For more information, see Tversky and Kahneman (1974). ***See also*** Heuristic; Hindsight Bias

Animation The illusion of movement created by means of an inanimate object. This illusion is created by what Peter Mark Roget referred to as persistence of vision—after seeing an image, human beings retain it through the afterimage, which creates the appearance of continuity and movement. Traditional animation involves a frame-by-frame drawing—each one called a cel. These cels are then photographed onto adjacent pieces of motion picture film. Today, these processes have been replaced with computer animation.

Early technologies such as flipbooks in the 16th century were followed by the phenakistoscope, the kinematoscope, and the zoetrope, which were used throughout the 19th century. The basic principles of automation used in these devices, combined with the experiments and techniques of filmmakers in the emerging cinema, resulted in the development of cartoon films. In 1906, J. Stuart Blackton created a short film called *Humorous Phases of Funny Faces,* which was composed of a series of blackboard drawings of crude faces changing expressions. Only 30 years later, Walt Disney dazzled audiences with the beautifully animated *Snow White and the Seven Dwarfs.* By the turn of the 21st century, digital imaging techniques used in movies such as *The Matrix* were blurring the line between animation and live action.

Animation is now being used with tremendous effect in multimedia computer applications. Three-dimensional animation techniques and digitized graphics have produced incredibly realistic characters and scenes in video games. So much so that certain uses of animation have come under legal scrutiny. A 1993 joint hearing examined the perceived negative impact of games such as *Mortal Combat, Night Trap,* and *Lethal Enforcer* because of their use of digitized human beings engaging in violent activity. Other games that were being marketed at the time were not emphasized during the hearings because, although they contained equally or sometimes even more violent content, the animation used was not as realistic. As the result of the hearings, the industry adopted a video-game-rating system. More recently, animation techniques used to depict minors engaged in sexual activity were deemed as violating the Child Pornography Prevention Act of 1996 and became the subject of a U.S. Supreme Court Decision (*Ashcroft v. The Free Speech Coalition,* 2002). The Court upheld the lower court's decision finding the ban overbroad and therefore unconstitutional. For more information, see *Ashcroft v. The Free Speech Coalition* (2002) and Auzenne (1994). *See also* CD-ROM Games

Annexation The process by which a geographical area is declared part of a country's sovereignty. In most cases, the country that annexes is the stronger political entity, and the annexation is a unilateral act of coercion. A recent example of an annexation involving the United States is that of Hawaii in 1898. Hawaii was becoming a strategic commercial and military concern for the United States during the 1800s. There was additional concern of Hawaii being annexed by European powers, particularly since France and Great Britain forced Hawaii during the 1830s to sign economic privilege agreements. The U.S. sugar industry was fast becoming an integral part of the Hawaiian economy, and American planters feared the threat of high sugar tariffs. After Queen Liliuokalani expressed a desire to create a stronger monarchy in 1893, the United States deposed her that same year. Interest in U.S. annexation began in 1894, but it was not until the McKinley administration that annexation occurred.

Anomie A society's state of instability due to the breakdown or absence of norms. Émile Durkheim introduced the sociological concept of anomie in 1893 in *The Division of Labor in Society* and continued to expand on its meaning in *Suicide.* In "mechanical" or nonindustrialized societies, people are closer knit and simply behave like one another. In "complex" industrialized or modern societies, social bonds are weak, and therefore, socially created and reinforced values are what regulate and control human behavior. Social change, such as a shift in the economy or urban migration, unseats established norms, and a period of normlessness or anomie sets in. Durkheim equates anomie with lawlessness, and in such times, he posits, deviance increases. As society responds to increased deviance, norms are again established and come to restrain deviant behavior.

The concept of strain, that social structures encourage people to commit crime, derives from Durkheim's work on anomie. In criminology, strain theorists attribute crime and criminal activity to environmental pressures, in particular to blocked opportunities that prohibit the achievement of socially approved goals (e.g., economic success). For more information, see Bellah (1973) and Durkheim (1893/1977, 1897/1997). *See also* Criminology; Deviance; Functionalism

Anorexia Nervosa An eating disorder characterized by self-starvation, self-induced vomiting, laxative use, and dramatic weight loss. About 95% of people suffering from anorexia nervosa are young females, though prevalence of this disorder is increasing. Although obsessed with food and its preparation and experiencing hunger, individuals with anorexia typically refuse to eat, resulting in serious weight loss, which may cause irreversible physical damage (e.g., reduction in bone density). Although rarely, individuals with anorexia may die of starvation, biochemical changes, or suicide. Anorexia nervosa is most likely caused by a combination of genetic predisposition, biochemical imbalances, social factors, and psychological influences. Psychological factors include a self-punishing, perfectionistic personality and a culturally reinforced obsession with thinness, attractiveness, and weight loss. Individuals with anorexia are usually treated with a combination of drugs, hospitalization, and psychotherapy. For more information, see Bulik, Sullivan, Wade, and Kendler (2000). *See also* Bulimia Nervosa; Clinical Psychology

Anterograde Amnesia Loss of memory for any event that happens after damage to the brain. Physical causes for amnesia may include head trauma, degenerative brain diseases such as Alzheimer's disease, blockage of blood vessels to the brain, chronic infections, or alcoholism. In particular, damage to the hippocampus impairs the formation of new (especially episodic) memories and their transfer from short- to long-term memory. Implicit memory, procedural memory, and working memory are not necessarily affected by anterograde amnesia. For more information, see Corkin (2002). *See also* Amnesia; Dissociation; Forgetting Curve; Memory; Retrograde Amnesia

Anthropology The comparative, social-scientific study of humanity, focusing on the development, history, and manifestations of human life. A common method of anthropological research is ethnography. This diverse academic discipline embodies many dimensions of study.

A

Applied anthropology focuses on using the theories, methods, and knowledge associated with anthropology to address and resolve contemporary problems. Cultural anthropology focuses on the variations and parallels among human cultures both past and present. The aspects of human societies that cultural anthropologists may explore include languages, social structures, art, and religious practices. Physical or biological anthropology focuses on human evolution and the variations between humans. The origins and history of the human species are explored within this dimension of the field. Forensic anthropology focuses on the human skeleton. This branch of the discipline uses trace material such as bone fragments to investigate causes of death. Forensics is a division of both applied and physical anthropology and is used to investigate crime. *See also* Archaeology; Artifact; Culture (sociology); Ethnography (sociology)

Antianxiety Drugs   Tranquilizers (also known as anxiolytics) first developed in the 1950s to reduce the mental and physical tension associated with anxiety. Similar to barbiturates, these early anxiolytics could be lethal on overdose. Therefore, benzodiazepines (e.g., diazepam/Valium) grew in popularity in the treatment of anxiety, given the lower risk of lethal overdose. However, the side effects of benzodiazepines (including severe physical dependence) and their potentially fatal combination with alcohol, led to the development of buspirone (BuSpar), a slower-acting drug that eliminates some of the problems of benzodiazepines. Notably, antidepressants that increase serotonin have also been successfully used to treat anxiety. For more information, see Gorman (2003). *See also* Anxiety Disorders; Psychoactive Drug; Psychopharmacology; Sedatives

Antidepressants   Drugs prescribed to relieve the symptoms of depression or low mood. Several classes of antidepressants can be distinguished. Monoamine oxidase inhibitors (MAOIs) are effective in treating many cases of depression but can result in elevated blood pressure if food high in tyramine (found in aged cheeses, red wine, chicken livers) is consumed. Tricyclic antidepressants (TCAs) are prescribed more often than MAOIs and generally produce fewer side effects, though they are associated with side effects such as fatigue, dry mouth, dizziness, blurred vision, low blood pressure, and constipation, among others. Moreover, combining tricyclics with alcohol can be fatal. Today's most popular group of antidepressants includes those that affect the neurotransmitter serotonin. The most prominent drug in this class, fluoxetine (Prozac), was introduced in 1986 and is as effective as older antidepressants, though associated with fewer side effects. In 50% to 60% of patients, medication results in improved mood, greater physical activity, increased appetite, and improved sleep. For more information, see Olfson et al. (2002). *See also* Depression (psychology); Psychoactive Drug; Psychopharmacology

Anti-Federalist   A movement active in the 1780s in political opposition to the Federalist movement. The Federalists supported a stronger national government than the one put forth in the Articles of Confederation. On the other hand, the Anti-Federalists envisioned the United States as a small republic composed of self-reliant, politically active citizens. A fear existed among the Anti-Federalists that a powerful, centralized government would only lead to tyrannical oppression from the very type of establishment they had sought to escape from when leaving Great Britain. At the Convention of 1787, the Federalists and Anti-Federalists debated their respective causes and compromised with the ratification of the U.S. Constitution and accompanying Bill of Rights. Prominent Anti-Federalists were Patrick Henry and Richard Henry Lee of Virginia and Samuel Adams of Massachusetts.

Antipsychotic Drugs   A type of drugs (also known as neuroleptics) first introduced in the 1950s and aimed at reducing the intensity of psychotic symptoms such as hallucinations, delusions, paranoid suspiciousness, disordered thinking, and incoherence in many patients, including those with schizophrenia. Neuroleptics may produce mild side effects, such as dry mouth, blurred vision, urinary retention, dizziness, and skin pigmentation problems. They may also produce serious physical side effects, such as muscle rigidity, restlessness, tremors, and slowed movement. Development of tardive dyskinesia, an irreversible motor disorder resulting in uncontrollable tic-like movements, is the most serious side effect associated with antipsychotic medication and may affect up to 25% of patients taking neuroleptics. Newer antipsychotic medications such as clozapine (Clozaril) have effects similar to the phenothiazines (the most common class of neuroleptic antipsychotic drugs) but do not cause movement disorders. Several other neuroleptics have been developed recently, including risperidone/Risperdal and olanzapine/Zyprexa, which are also associated with fewer side effects than older classes of antipsychotic medication. For more information, see Lieberman et al. (2005). *See also* Psychoactive Drug; Psychopharmacology; Schizophrenia

Antisocial Personality Disorder   A personality disorder characterized by impulsive, selfish, unscrupulous, and even criminal behavior, often combined with a lack of remorse, anxiety, or guilt. From the perspective of public welfare and safety, it may represent the most serious, costly, and intensively studied personality disorder. Described as "moral insanity" in the 1800s, people with antisocial personality disorder have also been referred to as "psychopaths" or "sociopaths," though psychopathy is typically used today to refer to antisocial individuals who especially lack in affective or emotional response. About 3% of men and 1% of women in the United States can be diagnosed with antisocial personality disorder. Some studies suggest a genetic predisposition in the form of abnormal brain development or chronic underarousal of the central nervous system (resulting in sensation seeking), though the precise etiological causes of this characterological pattern remain unknown. Developmental factors (e.g., disrupted family environment or poverty) may also contribute to the development of this personality pattern. For more information, see Mealey (1995). ***See also*** Personality; Personality Disorders (psychology); Psychopathy

Antitrust   Trusts are otherwise known as combinations or mergers. Businesses combine to dominate a market, minimize competition, or maximize profit by controlling prices. In the United States, trusts became particularly repugnant in the 19th century, as various businesses incorporated and formed trusts to defraud consumers. The creation of the Standard Oil monopoly in the 19th century inspired many other industries to consolidate into similar trusts, including linseed oil, cotton seed oil, lead, sugar, distilling, matches, tobacco, and rubber. Wealth soon became concentrated in the hands of a few.

Monopolies had long been illegal in common law, but in the 1880s, more stringent laws were made, and some dissolved trusts. A trust dissolved in one state, however, could incorporate in another where the laws were much more amicable or lenient, with lax enforcement. The problem soon became a matter of federal rather than state regulation.

The railroad monopoly and price gouging hit farmers the hardest, as they were charged excessive rates and given poor service. The *Munn v. Illinois* case of 1877 cleared the way for the regulation of what had seemed to be private property (railroads).

The 1887 Interstate Commerce Act regulated the price wars and legislated that all prices should be just (fair); and then, in 1890, Congress passed the Sherman Antitrust Act.

The Sherman Act made every contract and combination in the form of trust illegal and a conspiracy in the restriction of trade or commerce. For some time the act was, however, used as an instrument to prohibit labor strikes, more so than combinations, until it was enhanced by the Clayton Act of 1914 to define its jurisdictional parameters. The Robinson-Patman Act of 1936 further improved on the authority of the Clayton Act to outlaw price discrimination (a mechanism of antitrust practices). Illicit combinations tend to reduce quantity, provide poor service, and charge exorbitant prices in the absence of competition. The Securities and Exchange Commission (SEC) and the U.S. Justice Department currently play a decisive role in the permission and punishment of trust activities. For more information, see *Munn v. Illinois* (1877) and Nevins and Commager (1992). ***See also*** Market Failure; Regulation (economics)

Anxiety Disorders   Disorders characterized by an enduring feeling of apprehension, fear, or unease that disrupts everyday life. Several types of anxiety disorders, which together represent the most common psychological disorders in the United States, can be identified. (1) *Phobia* is characterized by an intense, irrational fear of an object or situation that that is not proportional to the object's potential. Examples of specific phobias include fears or avoidance of heights, blood, animals, and air travel. *Social phobia* is characterized by anxiety or fear in social situations, often involving fear of being criticized or disliked by others. *Agoraphobia* is characterized by a fear of being away from a safe place (typically the home) and is often associated with the fear of having a panic attack in an unfamiliar place. (2) *Generalized anxiety disorder* is characterized by an excessive and long-lasting anxiety that is not restricted to particular objects or situations and often accompanies other psychological problems (such as depression or substance abuse). (3) *Panic attacks* are marked by intense heart palpitations, pressure or pain in the chest, dizziness, perspiration, and faintness. Anxiety also forms the basis for (4) *obsessive-compulsive disorder,* in which obsessive thoughts or acts (e.g., checking locks, washing, repeating words, etc.) are carried out to avoid some dreaded outcome. (5) *Posttraumatic stress disorder* follows a traumatic and threatening event and is characterized by anxiety, depression, sleep disturbance, and especially flashbacks (in which the person may reexperience the traumatizing event). Causes for anxiety disorders include biological factors (heredity for the disorder or a predisposition) as well as psychological factors (especially environmental stressors and learning experiences). Treatment options include behavioral and cognitive therapy and anxiolytics (antianxiety drugs). For more information, see Bouton, Mineka, and Barlow (2001). ***See also*** Antianxiety Drugs; Anxiety Disorders; Panic Disorder (psychology); Phobia; Posttraumatic Stress Disorder (PTSD)

Aphasia   Difficulty in understanding or producing speech resulting from an impairment of or damage to the association cortex, which has implications for all the functions of the cerebral cortex, including the auditory cortex (for spoken language), the visual cortex (for written language), and the motor cortex (production of speech). Two main forms of aphasia can be distinguished: When motor areas, known as Broca areas, are impaired, the mental production of speech suffers, resulting in "Broca's aphasia." Damage to the Wernicke's area (in the temporal lobe), which is involved in the interpretation of both speech and written words, can leave a person able to speak but unable to understand spoken or written words ("Wernicke's aphasia"). For more information, see Spreen and Risser (2003). ***See also*** Wernicke's Area

Appeal   The process by which a higher court is petitioned to examine a judgment made by a lower court. It is a legal challenge to a particular element in a trial court's process, not a claim against the court's

A

finding in the case. Appeals raise procedural and/or constitutional issues. The argument underlying an appeal is that the outcome is possibly tainted due to problematic procedure. Examples of the subject of complaints found in appeals include the inclusion or exclusion of evidence, a judicial ruling during the course of the trial, the prosecutor's behavior, or how the jury was instructed. **See also** Adjudication; Appellate Court

Appearance and Dress   The importance of paying attention to appropriate dress and external appearance when appearing in public forums as a speaker or participant. During most of the past century, public speakers adhered to formal dress-code policies. Audiences assumed that proper appearance made for a good self-concept and was highly correlated with organizational pride and appropriate behavior. Appropriate dress consisted of suits and ties for men and suits and blouses for women. Clean, shined shoes were also deemed necessary, and the wearing of large earrings and other ostentatious jewelry was discouraged. Exceptions to this appearance and dress policy were usually made for speakers who had certain religious objections and needed to wear clothes that fit the expectations of their religion.

These codes were somewhat upended during the rise of information technology in the last generation of the 20th century. Billionaire software executives and the like began appearing in large public forums wearing jeans and open-collared shirts. Clearly, not suits and ties, but money, made the man. For the most part, however, those who need society's approval follow the more formal dress code of former years. For an example of a dress code, see Moody Bible Institute, www.moody ministries.net/crp_MainPage.aspec?id=80 (accessed May 9, 2009).

Apellate Court (political science)   Any court that has the authority to hear appeals of a lower court's decision. In most cases, the appellate court reviews only for legal errors in a case and not the findings of fact of the lower court. If facts are reviewed, it is usually only for "clear error." A panel of judges hears a case in an appellate court, instead of the single judge present in a trial court. Furthermore, an appellate court has no witnesses or jury present. Appellate court judges are expected to write reasons for their decisions in published "opinions," whereas this practice is unusual at the lower court level. Specialized appellate courts exist in the federal and state systems; among them are the federal Court of Customs and Patent Appeals and the Court of Military Appeals.

Appellate Court (sociology)   A legal venue, a court of appeals that reviews decisions reached by the lower courts. Typically, appellate courts do not conduct criminal or civil trials. The primary role of the appellate court is to resolve legal questions and controversies that emerge from previous court cases. **See also** Adjudication; Appeal

Appellate Jurisdiction   A court's authority to review a lower court's opinion. Appellate jurisdiction is in contrast to "original jurisdiction," in which only cases of first instance are heard. The Appellate Court has very few cases of original jurisdiction. At the federal level, the Supreme Court has original jurisdiction over cases involving disputes between states. And at the state level, appellate courts have original jurisdiction over cases involving lawyer disbarment. The federal court and most state courts have a three-layer structure in hearing cases. The "trials court" is the court of first instance, at the intermediate level is the "court of appeals," and at the final level is the "supreme court." In some states with a smaller population, there are no intermediate appellate courts.

Applied Research   Research attempting to find a solution for a specific problem, in contrast to (pure) basic research, which is more concerned with the advancement of insight and knowledge itself. Usually, applied research involves an investigation of topics directly related to research issues that originate from practical experience (e.g., studying methods of enhancing the educational experience of children with mental retardation or performing an outcome evaluation to determine if a drug treatment program is effective). For more information, see Cozby (2004). **See also** Basic Research

Appointment   "Any personnel action that brings an individual onto the rolls (staff) of an agency." It is also referred to as "accession." An appointee is the person being hired. The appointing officer, also commonly known as the appointing authority or appointing power, is the person "having power by law, or by duly delegated authority, to make appointments" (U.S Office of Personnel Management, n.d.). "Appointing officer means a person having power by law, or by lawfully delegated authority, to make appointments to positions in the service of the Federal Government or the government of the District of Columbia" (5 CFR 210.102(b)(1)).

Marbury v. Madison (1803), the U.S. Supreme Court case enshrining the concept of judicial review, is in fact a case dealing with the basics of appointment. It established the principle that appointment is effective when the last thing that needs to be done is done, namely, documenting the decision to appoint the individual concerned. Neither mailing of the decision or commission or warrant nor possession of the appointing documents is required.

As *Marbury* makes clear, the appointment procedure is a decision-making process, performed by those with discretionary authority, that requires the appointing authority to evaluate the applicant in order to determine fitness:

The appointment to an official position in the government, even if it be simply a clerical position, is not a mere ministerial act, but one involving the exercise of judgment. The appointing power must determine the fitness of the applicant; whether or not he is the proper one to discharge the duties of the position. (*Keim v. United States,* 1900)

In responding to the question of whether the executive must appoint the person certified as the highest scorer on a competitive civil service examination, the Attorney General of the United States (13 Op.A.G. 516) said no, because

the power of appointment conferred by the Constitution is a substantial and not merely a nominal [ministerial] function, and the judgment and will of the constitutional depositary of that power should alone be exercised or have legal operation in filling offices created by law.

A public officer's duty is ministerial

only when it is absolute, certain and imperative, involving merely the performance of a specific task when the law imposes, prescribes and defines the time, mode and occasion for its performance with such certainty that nothing remains for judgment or discretion. (*Kierstyn, v. Racine Unified School District,* 1999)

Additionally, inherent to the appointing authority or the appointment power is the power to terminate the appointee without the authority to terminate having to be stated in the law: "In the absence of specific provision to the contrary, the power of removal from office is incident to the power of appointment" (*Keim, loc. cit.*). For more information, see 5 CFR 210.102(b)(1), 13 Op.A.G. 516 (1871), *Keim, loc. cit., Keim v. United States* (1900), *Kierstyn, v. Racine Unified School District* (1999), *Marbury v. Madison* (1803), and U.S. Office of Personnel Management (n.d.).

Apportionment   A plan, approved by the Office of Management and Budget, to spend allocated resources from a specific fund. The purpose of apportionment is to ensure that agencies spend their funds within imposed limits so as to avoid deficient or supplemental appropriations. Once the budget has been approved, since most likely an agency did not receive all requested funding, the apportionment process serves as a mechanism to manage spending. In the execution phase of the budget process, line agencies submit their budget plan to the Office of Management and Budget explaining how apportioned funds will be used. For more information, see Lee, Johnson, and Joyce (2008). *See also* Discretionary Spending

Appreciation   The incremental increase in the value of an asset over time. Increases in value relate to any type of asset, such as real estate, stocks, bonds, or currency. Increases in value can occur as a result of changes in inflation or interest rates or due to growth in demand or weakening supply. An increase in the value of financial assets such as stock is referred to as *capital appreciation* and can be a result of the improved financial performance of a company.

Appreciation is often used in accounting to refer to an upward adjustment of the value of an asset. More commonly, a downward adjustment is made to the value of an asset as the asset loses value due to use or age. Such an adjustment, *depreciation,* is the opposite of appreciation.

Appropriation   The process that local, state, or federal governments use to set aside funds for a specific purpose. At the federal level, the power of the government to appropriate funds is delineated in Article 1, Section 9, of the U.S. Constitution, which allows "appropriations made by law." The House and Senate Appropriations Committees draft legislation to allocate these funds. The legislation is then presented to Congress for its approval each fiscal year. The Committees are also empowered to draft supplemental spending bills, which are designed to address emergency situations that may arise during the fiscal year. The term *pork-barrel* is used to describe appropriations gained by representatives for their own districts to enhance their popularity among constituents.

Appropriation Bills   Legislative bills that allocate local, state, or federal government funds for a specific purpose. At the federal level, the power of the government to appropriate funds is delineated in Article 1, Section 9 of the U.S. Constitution, which allows "appropriations made by law." There are at least 11 appropriation bills each year, which together fund the federal government; these bills need to be enacted prior to October 1, the date of the new federal fiscal year.

The House and Senate Appropriations Committees draft legislation that allocates these funds; this is then presented to Congress for its approval each fiscal year. The Committees are also empowered to draft supplemental spending bills that are designed to address emergency situations that may arise during the fiscal year. The term *pork-barrel* is used to describe appropriations gained by representatives for their district to enhance their popularity among constituents.

Aptitude–Treatment Interaction   An interaction effect is a joint or multiplier effect of two variables. For example, in a drug interaction, two drugs that are harmless when taken singly can be harmful when taken together. Research designs investigating the possible interactions of participants' aptitudes and an experimental treatment are called "aptitude–treatment interaction designs." For example, a method of instruction (the treatment) might work differently for students with high and low IQs (the aptitude). Trait-treatment interaction is a more general version of the

A

same phenomenon and examines the effects of any kind of trait—for example, gender, age, or ethnicity, and not only research participants' aptitudes—on the effects of treatment. This is also called an "attribute–treatment interaction."

Arbitrage   Taking advantage of price differentials in two or more markets to earn a profit. For example, if a good is selling at a higher price in one market and at a lower price in another market, speculators and others can purchase the good selling in the lower-priced market and then sell it in the higher-priced market and earn a profit. This opportunity for profit will eventually be eliminated because increased demand for the cheaper goods will eventually raise the price of the good in the lower-priced market to equal the price of the good in the other market. Arbitrage opportunities exist in many markets, including the foreign exchange market, where currencies can be bought cheaply in one market and sold in the expensive market. Arbitrage opportunities are temporary and quickly disappear when price differentials no longer exist. For more information, see Mankiw (2007).

Arbitration   A form of alternative dispute resolution. Mediation and nonbinding resolution are types of arbitration. In theory, arbitration is a consensual process.

Toulmin's Layout of Argumentation (named after the British philosopher, Stephen Toulmin) is based on a model that identifies six aspects of argument that are common in any field. The substance of the argument may change from one field to another, but the parts remain the same. These parts of the argument include the following aspects: data, claim, warrant, backing, reservation, and qualifier. The Toulmin model is a key ingredient in learning aspects of argumentation. Effective debate incorporates all six aspects mentioned above. Although it was originally meant for legal argument, Toulmin (1979) adapted the method to general communications theory. For more information, see Toulmin (1958) and Toulmin, Riecke, and Janik (1979).

Archaeology   The scientific study of past human lives by means of researching physical objects. Archaeology is considered a division or subdiscipline of anthropology. Archaeologists examine, explain, and reconstruct past societies and cultures by scrutinizing the material evidence of their existence. Excavation, locating and removing articles from a concentrated geographic region is a common methodology. As science and technology become more sophisticated, so too do the abilities of archaeologists to date and detect artifacts. By piecing together evidence, from architecture to diet, archaeologists record and analyze the way humans lived in the past and the societies in which they lived. The work of archaeologists can be controversial as conflicts arise regarding ownership of found artifacts. The discipline of archaeology has also been subject to

challenges regarding its tradition of Eurocentric analyses. **See also** Anthropology; Artifact; Culture (sociology)

Archetype   A perfect or original example, or model, of a kind of entity. *Archetype* can also refer to an ideal. In the influential psychological theory of Carl Jung, an archetype is an image or idea that arises in the collective unconscious and is manifested in dreams and art. In literature, an archetype is a symbol that represents a universal. **See also** Collective Unconscious; Symbols/Symbolic Reality

Archival Research   Research that involves review of records or documents in archives, typically undertaken with the goal of describing the characteristics of individuals, groups, or organizations. Archival data are typically collected for purposes other than research and thus may not always be maintained in a form suitable for research. Advantages of the use of archival data include naturalistic quality, access to rare participants, the possibility of retrospective longitudinal designs, and low reactivity. Archival data may also be less expensive to collect than original data. Disadvantages include the fact that access to archival data may be difficult and, moreover, the validity of the investigated variables may depend on how systematically the data was originally collected. Finally, archival research does not easily allow for causal explanations, given that it does not employ a true experimental design. For more information, see Kellehear (1993). **See also** Case Study Research (education, psychology); Field Research; Laboratory Research

ARCS Instructional Motivation Model   The four-step model of instruction originated by John Keller in 1987. The steps are to generate the following: *attention,* or students' interest and curiosity captured through variety, visual aids, references to real and imaginary people, and problems or paradoxes; *relevance* to students' personal, educational, and career goals; *confidence,* by ensuring student success with clear assignments, explicit criteria, practice, and specific feedback; and *satisfaction,* by reinforcing accomplishments, applications to the real world, incorporating new skills, and acknowledging the risks taken. For more information, see Keller (1987). **See also** Instructional Design

Argumentativeness   An attitude characterized by the tendency to emphasize differences in an exchange of communication between two or more people. Situations in which argumentativeness can be provoked include miscommunications over intended meanings and confusion over relayed information between the parties involved, in formal or informal contexts.

Conflict management strategies can be employed to work through the divergence, either in work or personal situations. Interpersonal communication models of conflict resolution focus on exploring the influences of gender, race, and class on the argumentative individual as well as the situational components that have contributed to the argumentativeness mode. These tactics seek to achieve negotiation and positive decision making from the parties in conflict.

Argumentativeness is generally considered to be a negative mode of communication that is aggressive and generally verbal (rather than nonverbal behavior). *See also* Defensiveness

Aristocracy   A government ruled by a self-appointed social elite that believes in its own superiority. The word *aristocracy* is Greek in origin (*aristos* [the best], *kratia* [rule]). The concept of aristocracy was articulated by the Greek philosopher Plato (428–347 BCE), who developed in his *Republic* the ideal of a government composed of a council of the intellectually and morally superior members of a society governing for the common good. As the aristocratic concept developed in Medieval Europe, leadership came to belong instead to the wealthy elite, who believed that they were "the best" by means of privileged birthright alone. Plato had rejected this practice of hereditary leadership, believing instead that the aristocracy should be achieved through meritocracy or the recruitment of the intellectually gifted. *See also* Democracy (political science)

Arraignment   A pretrial stage of a criminal proceeding, when the suspect is first informed by the court of the charges against him or her. The suspect also enters his or her plea of guilty or not guilty. Further court dates are scheduled by the court, and the defendant has the opportunity to obtain counsel if he or she has not done so already. Some states hold arraignments in lower courts only and transfer cases to upper courts if felony charges are filed. At the federal level, arraignment proceedings are specified in Article 4, Rule 10 of the Federal Rules of Criminal Procedure. *See also* Adversary System of Justice (political science, sociology); Arrest

Arranged Marriage   A matrimonial union orchestrated by parties other than the bride and groom. Typically, the parents of those to be married negotiate the terms of the deal. Arranged marriages are a long-standing tradition in many cultures.

Arrest   The act of taking someone into governmental custody, thereby depriving that person of freedom, because he or she is suspected of having committed a crime. Sworn law enforcement officers have the authority to arrest someone once they have determined that a crime has taken place and that a particular individual is the likely responsible party. An arrest has taken place only if a person is not physically free to leave. The police are required to meet a constitutional standard of probable cause in order to arrest someone. An arrest warrant is an official judicial determination that there is sufficient probable cause to arrest someone.

Arrest rates can be calculated for a given area by dividing the number of arrests by the population of that area. Arrest rates are compiled annually by the FBI, with information from local jurisdictions, and published in the Uniform Crime Reports. *See also* Probable Cause

Arson   The intentional burning of an object. Criminal arson is understood as either setting fire to someone else's property or setting fire to one's own property with fraudulent intent. Any fire that has been deliberately set with malicious intent is arson. A person who purposely starts such fires is an arsonist. In 1979 arson was added to the list of Index I crimes and became one of the eight serious offenses tracked yearly in the FBI's Uniform Crime Report (UCR). *See also* Uniform Crime Report (UCR)

Art Education   Curricula involving the pursuit and construction of artistic and aesthetic knowledge and skills. Art education, in the visual and tangible arts, includes understanding, responding to, and producing drawings, paintings, sculpture, and variations of design. In addition to facilitating acquisition of art knowledge and skills, qualified art educators attempt to stimulate critical thinking, relate art to social issues, and build cultural identity.

Articles of Confederation   After the Revolutionary War, the 13 states constituting the new nation were organized under the Articles of Confederation. This "constitution" was in effect from 1781 until the present Constitution was ratified in 1789.

At the time, the states were concerned about a strong central government; they were afraid that their individual needs would be ignored with a national government that had too much power, with the resulting abuses that oftentimes went along with that power. The Articles sought to establish a constitution that provided individual states the largest share of power.

The Articles set up a national legislature that could raise an army and a navy, declare war, borrow and coin money, run a postal system, and handle relations with American Indians. Each state could send two delegates to Congress but had only one vote. Delegates from 7 of the 13 states had to be present to establish a quorum and conduct business. Delegates were elected for one-year terms and could not serve for more than three years in any six-year period.

Having neither an executive nor a judicial branch, but only a unicameral legislature, the government was largely ineffective in spite of its progressive stand, and the Articles of Confederation contained many flaws. For example, the government could not really enforce its mandate over individual states because it left it up to each of them to collect taxes and provide for security. Thus, the Articles' main mission was to enforce foreign policy and negotiate treaties. Each state had a veto power, and states' interests took precedence over the national or common good. After much deliberation, the states agreed to call a Constitutional Convention in 1787 in order to replace the Articles. For more information, see Articles of Confederation (2001), Jensen (1940), Kaminski (2001), and Rakove (1979).

A

Articulation   A clear manner of communication, particularly for the individual in the public sphere. Articulation is seen in the selection of appropriate words to suit the speaker's intended meaning and the ability to speak fluently in making words distinct from one another. Effective articulation is considered, particularly in interpersonal and organizational communication studies, to be marked by the ability of the speaker to disseminate information to audiences and for audiences to grasp the intended meaning of the speaker. This can create a cycle of giving and growing knowledge between individuals and groups. The articulation of ideas can result in a two-way communication (e.g., between the speaker and audience) that involves discussion of problems (topical to the context, or of a communicative nature) and problem solving. *See also* Oral Style

Artifact   An article made by humans; a product of human creation. Artifacts are objects that play a role in our way of life. In various disciplines, including history, anthropology, and sociology, artifacts are used as data that explain human cultures, time periods, and behavior.

Asperger's Syndrome   A disorder characterized by severe delays and deficits in social and motor skills as well as more general social difficulties similar to autistic deficits. In contrast to autism, Asperger's syndrome (also called Asperger disorder) is not accompanied by delays in the development of language and cognition. The syndrome is named after Hans Asperger, who, in 1944, described a group of young boys who showed severe deficits in social skills, despite otherwise normal intelligence. Individuals with Asperger's syndrome often exhibit a very narrow, restricted, and repetitive interest in particular subject areas, with an abundance of knowledge in these areas of interest. Due to their lack of empathic perspective taking, individuals with this disorder experience many difficulties in social interactions, from being awkward conversationalists to engaging in odd or repetitive patterns of behavior. Fine motor problems are common as are deficits in physical dexterity. Although the precise etiology of this disorder is unknown, there appears to be a significant genetic contribution. Interventions are typically behavioral in focus, emphasizing the enhancement of social skills and adaptive behaviors. For more information, see Baron-Cohen and Klin (2006). *See also* Developmental Psychology

Assault   A violent attack against another person. An assault is a verbal or physical confrontation with the intent to do injury or harm. The criminal law classifies assault into various categories. *Aggravated assault* is any attack that involves a weapon. The level of harm is not pertinent to this classification. A *simple assault* is an attack in which no weapon was used and the victim incurred minor injuries. *Assault and battery* is a legal term conveying that a person has been the victim of physical violence. *Attempted assault* recognizes the intent to harm regardless of what actually occurred. Statistics regarding assault differ greatly along gender, racial, and economic lines. *See also* Battered Woman Syndrome; Rape, Forcible; Sex Offense/Crime

Assertion   The declaration of one's views in an exchange of communication. The mode of assertion can be positive (showing confidence in one's beliefs) or negative (showing defensiveness in relation to another's views). An assertion can occur in the public sphere (such as a work setting) or a private conversation (such as an interpersonal exchange). Effective assertion is the ability to express one's beliefs and/or needs and receiving confirmation that one's audience has understood and respected the speaker's communication. This enables a process of problem solving and negotiation between parties, rather than negative modes of assertion such as submission or aggression. *See also* Debate

Assessment   An evaluation process in which knowledge, skills, attitudes, or beliefs are formally documented, often toward the goal of enriching what is known or understood about a particular individual. Assessment instruments can be objective, with only one correct "answer" (e.g., multiple-choice questions), or subjective, with multiple correct answers (e.g., essays, open-ended questions). Differences in the use and the definition of objective and subjective assessments exist between various disciplines, often having to do with the way the data are treated for analysis. Many assessments rank the test results according to a specific criterion (e.g., a driving test) or a population norm (e.g., IQ tests). Another broad distinction is whether the assessment is carried out in a formal (usually written) or an informal way. Objectivity, reliability, and validity are considered the fundamental criteria of an assessment. Objectivity is achieved when the result does not depend on a particular evaluator, while reliability is attained when the assessment can be repeated with the same results. Finally, validity refers to the degree to which test scores truly measure what they are intended to measure. For more information, see Keeves (1997). *See also* Reliability; Validity

Assessment in Postsecondary Education   The systematic and ongoing process of gathering, analyzing, and using data for improvement purposes. Typically, constructs such as knowledge, skills, attitudes, and beliefs are examined in measureable terms based on explicit and clearly predefined outcomes. Once the collected data are analyzed, the results may be used to determine the extent of change, growth, impact, or effectiveness occurring within a particular sample, organization, or class. The assessment process culminates when assessment results are used for improvement purposes. An example might include determining whether one's educational interventions increased students' learning and/or performance. Areas in which obtained scores are unsatisfactory often require reassessment of intervention techniques and adoption of new (or different) strategies intended to improve learning.

Asset   Something of economic value that can be exchanged or traded. Assets can be highly liquid (quickly convertible into cash) or illiquid. For accounting purposes, an asset that is highly liquid is normally referred to as a "current asset" and is normally given the foremost position on the balance sheet of a company. A current asset has a useful lifespan of less than a year—for example, accounts receivable, marketable securities, and cash balances. A long-lived asset, on the other hand, has a longer life span—for example, plant, equipment, and patents. Under generally accepted accounting principles, most assets are recorded at their historical cost (book value) except in exceptional cases. In corporate finance, cumulative asset is a combination of shareholders' equity and total liabilities (debts).

Assimilation   In linguistics, the process by which a sound becomes similar to an adjacent or nearby sound. In assimilation, one segment influences another to produce a specific sound. Vowels, for example, acquire a nasal quality when followed by the sound /n/. The phonological patterning of the language, discourse styles, and accents are some of the factors contributing to observable assimilation. Four configurations are found in assimilations: an increase in phonetic similarity (1) between adjacent segments or (2) between segments separated by one or more intervening segments and changes (3) to a preceding segment or (4) to a following one. An example of assimilation occurs in the word *cupboard,* where the sound /p/ in the word *cup* has undergone what we call complete assimilation to the sound /b/ of *board.* For more information, see Crowley (1997).

Association   A term used in the field of anthropology to refer to identification, contact, and connection among people, concepts, or things. Association also refers to grouping entities based on such connections. There are three primary means by which to associate. A *group* is a collection with fixed boundaries and whose members share belonging. Examples include families, corporations, and nations. A *network* is a web of connections with no set boundaries, and members may only be linked to a few other associates. Examples include customers or friends. A *category* is any grouping of people with one or more shared attributes or goals. Examples include African Americans, teenagers, or football fans. ***See also*** Anthropology; Categorization; Group; Network

Asymmetrical Federalism   *Federalism* is a principle of organization of a political system. It refers to the distribution of power across different levels of government.

In the United States, federalism refers to the division of governmental powers between the national and state governments. The founding fathers of the Constitution instituted a federal system to persuade the independent states to join the Union and acquiesce in the creation of a powerful central government. Up to that point, a federally organized country had been perceived as a club of member states. Under the U.S. Constitution, each citizen belongs to two governments, national and state.

Under federalism, both the central government and the state governments have direct control over their own separate areas of jurisdiction. These independent powers are sanctioned by the Constitution.

Countries around the world have attempted to institute a federal system. Examples of these countries include Australia, Canada, Brazil, the Federal Republic of Germany, India, Russia, and Switzerland.

Among political scientists, there are debates about the nature of federalism. One school stresses the amorphous nature of federalism and its operational complexity. A second school highlights the distinctive role of regional governments in federal systems, however designated—as states, provinces, republics, or cantons.

Asymmetric federalism or asymmetrical federalism is found in a federation in which different constituent states possess different powers; that is, some states have more powers independent of the national government than other states, although all states have the same constitional status.

The difference between an asymmetric federation and federacy is difficult to define. A federacy is essentially an extreme case of an asymmetric federation, either due to large differences in the level of autonomy or the rigidity of the constitutional arrangements. An asymmetric federation, nevertheless, must have a federal constitution, and all states in the federation have the same formal status ("state"), while in a federacy, an independent substate has a different status ("independent region"). For more information, see Beer (1993), Elazar (1991), Nathan (2001), and Rittberger and Bulpitt (2003).

Asymmetric Information   Information is asymmetric when material information is not generally shared with all participants in a market. This means that, in the credit market, for example, borrowers may have valuable information that lenders do not have but that might be critical to make informed decisions. Borrowers typically like to present themselves in the most favorable light to secure a loan and might therefore conceal or distort unfavorable information. By so doing, they put lenders at a disadvantage. Technological innovation has, however, made it possible to minimize disparities in access to quality information.

Asymmetric information can lead to adverse selection and moral hazard. Adverse selection occurs when poor-quality participants or goods in a market are treated much more favorably because of skewed or unbalanced information. The sale of "lemon" (poor quality) cars at market prices is an example of adverse selection that is the result of uneven distribution of information.

A moral hazard occurs when risks are undertaken with the foreknowledge that the costs associated with the risks will be paid by someone else and not the risk taker. This problem is evident in the relationship between depository institutions (banks) and insurance companies.

A

Banks that invest or give loans without prudence because they know that they will not be responsible for the cost of their losses engage in the furtherance of a moral hazard. Of course, information is imperfect in such situations because the insurance companies are unaware of the motivations for risk taking by the depository institutions. The east Asian financial crisis of the late 1990s has been partly attributed to moral hazard. Concern over moral hazard has also affected the financial crisis in the United States in 2008. *See also* Insurance; Market Failure; Risk

Atavism   A condition of savagery associated with regression to a "prehuman" state of evolution. An atavist or atavistic person is considered a primitive "throwback" supposedly representative of an earlier stage of human development. The term gained prominence with the work of Cesare Lombroso (1835–1909), an Italian medical doctor. He was a pioneer in that he applied the emerging empirical scientific method, positivism, to the study of crime. The work of Charles Darwin inspired evolutionary deterministic theories. Lombroso's work followed this tradition. He autopsied bodies, measured skull sizes, and compiled biological data on those convicted of crime in Italy. In his 1876 book, *Criminal Man,* he posited a criminal typology in which the "atavistic born criminal" was a distinct category. The atavist, he claimed, is devolved in that he has the innate physical traits of earlier man, which drive him to act criminally. Lombroso fathered the biological determinism school of criminology and the field of criminal anthropology. *See also* Anthropology; Criminology; Positivism (sociology)

Attachment Theory   A framework for the investigation of deep and enduring relationships that are formed in early infancy. The British psychologist John Bowlby drew attention to the importance of attachment after he observed orphaned children in World War II. He concluded that forming an attachment to a caregiver (usually the mother) is an important developmental task and separation from the caregiver or loss of the bond results in depression and emotional difficulties. Children as young as three months learn to recognize the mother and are able to differentiate her from a stranger. Virtually all children prefer their mother to a stranger by the age of six or seven months. After that, separation from the mother is experienced as stressful. Children vary in their attachment (amount of closeness and contact) to their mother, resulting in different attachment styles, which have been investigated with a test (called "Strange Situation") developed by Mary Ainsworth: In an unfamiliar playroom, the effects of separation from the mother, appearance of a stranger, and return of the mother are observed. Most infants exhibit a *secure* attachment, using their mother as a home base, exploring and periodically returning for contact and comfort. When the mother returns after the separation, infants are happy to see her. Some infants, however, display an *insecure* attachment. If the relationship is

avoidant, they avoid or ignore their mother on her return. If the relationship is *ambivalent,* they may greet their mother after the separation but immediately react angrily and reject the mother. If the relationship is *disorganized,* infants' behavior is inconsistent and disturbed (e.g., crying when the mother returns, reaching out to but not looking at the mother). The specific attachment style has long-term predictive validity for relationships with other people, including romantic relationships. Research has shown that the effectiveness of different attachment styles varies by culture, which has been explained by different socialization practices. For more information, see Bowlby (2005). *See also* Developmental Psychology; Insecure Attachment

Attendance/Truancy   Parents have the legal responsibility to comply with state statutes governing the school attendance of their children. State statutes typically specify age, admission, and exemption requirements. Truancy is the failure to attend school without a valid reason such as illness, death in the immediate family, or other excuse provided to a school official.

Attention Deficit Disorder (ADD)   A relatively common neurological disorder most often diagnosed in young children. ADD, or ADHD, consists of (a) inattention/distractibility and/or (b) impulsivity/hyperactivity symptoms. Diagnosis is based on an interview and objective testing, and symptoms must exist before age seven. Stimulant medications and behavioral therapy are effective in treating ADD. *See also* Executive Functions

Attention Deficit Hyperactivity Disorder (ADHD) A developmental disorder exhibited by 3% to 7% of children, most commonly boys. Symptoms include impulsivity, concentration difficulties, and excessive motor activity. Three subtypes exist: primarily inattentive, primarily impulsive, and combined inattention and impulsivity. Due to their impulsivity, children's learning is usually impaired, leading to poor performance on clinical tests of attention, memory, decision making, and other cognitive processing tasks. Although genetic predisposition appears to play an important role in the etiology of this disorder, postnatal brain damage, lead poisoning, and low birth weight have been ascribed a causal role. Evaluations of active or hyperactive children vary across cultural contexts due to differing norms, and this results in differing prevalence across cultures. ADHD can be treated successfully with medication and/or psychotherapy. Drugs such as metylphenidate (Ritalin) are have been shown to have success in suppressing the symptoms of ADHD. ADHD is also known as hyperkinetic disorder. For more information, see Daruna, Dalton, and Forman (2000). *See also* Psychopharmacology

Attitude   A manner of behavior (verbal and/or nonverbal) in an exchange of communication. An attitude can belong to an individual or a group. An attitude affects the modes of communication: In verbal cues, attitude can be reflected in tone of voice and word choice (being of an argumentative or peaceable nature), while in nonverbal cues, attitude can be seen in body language (such as defensive or confident posturing) and actions. An attitude has the potential to be altered through self-reflection and by learning communications techniques. Organizational communication is concerned with the attitudes of employees and with influencing their ability to effectively execute projects. Interpersonal communication is concerned with the attitudes of parties insofar as these affect their ability for positive communication and subsequent potentials for negotiation and problem solving. An individual's or group's attitude is shaped by subjective experience, which can derive from gender, race, or class factors, as well as social, political, and economic structures. **See also** Argumentativeness; Defensiveness; Oral Style

Attribution   A reference to the source one uses for a journalistic article, book, and the like. For instance, a journalist can "attribute" a piece of information to an "unknown source high in the government" or to a specific, named, person. Conversely, a source can tell a journalist a piece of information and specify "not for attribution," meaning that she or he cannot be named. One can also use the term to identify an unsigned work of art through style, brushwork, time period, paint, and other features, as in a determination that the painting may be "attributed to the workshop of Lorenzo Eduardo." In a theoretical sense, the term refers to the determination of a cause of behavior. Communications theory uses the term to explain actions. In this sense, "attribution" is based on understanding the cognitive processes that lend themselves to acting out in a certain way. Although attribution processes are very much a part of the use of language, this theory is more germane to social psychology. **See also** Attribution Theory

Attribution Theory   A framework for explaining the process with which people explain behavior. According to Harold Kelley and other researchers, understanding attributions requires the investigation of three key variables: consensus (the degree to which other people's behavior is similar to the actor's), consistency (the degree to which the behavior is the same across time and/or situations), and distinctiveness (the extent to which an actor's response to one situation stands out from responses to similar situations). Kelley's theory suggests that people are most likely to make internal attributions (i.e., stressing the disposition of the person) to the causality of an actor's behavior when there is low consensus (i.e., other people do not behave like this), high consistency (the actor always behaves like this in different situations), and low distinctiveness (the actor behaves like this in similar situations). Otherwise, external attributions (emphasizing situational constraints) prevail. The degree to which internal and external attributions

about the causality of behavior are made depend on the cultural background of the observer. Individuals from interdependent contexts more often attribute behavior to external causes, while individuals from independent cultural contexts more readily infer that the causality for the actor's behavior is rooted in internal disposition. Such cultural influences extend to the *fundamental attribution bias*, the tendency to overestimate the influence of internal factors while underestimating the impact of external factors in explaining behavior: Individuals from interdependent cultural contexts are less prone to this bias than individuals from independent cultures or societies. A further bias is the *actor-observer bias*, characterized by predominantly attributing the behavior of others to internal attributes, while attributing one's own behavior to external factors. This general tendency is moderated by the *self-serving bias*, the tendency to take personal credit for success but to blame external causes for failure. Again, both the actor-observer bias and the self-serving bias can be found in all cultural contexts, but to varying degrees. For more information, see Kelley (1973). **See also** Fundamental Attribution Error

Auction   A market transaction that is based on declaration of competing prices by a number of potential buyers (bidders) and the willingness and ability to pay for goods or assets at an openly determined price. Auction is an alternative pricing mechanism by which the value of goods or assets is determined by those with direct interest in them within a specified period of time. Sellers normally pay a fee to the auctioneer for facilitating the exchange.

Bidding may be done by buyers or sellers. In the English auction, buyers make progressively higher bids until the highest bidder is willing and able to pay for the good. Alternatively, in the Dutch variety, sellers may offer progressively reduced prices until a buyer is willing and able to pay for a good or asset.

In the sealed-bid auction, bidders are given a single chance to make offers without knowledge of each other's offers, and the highest bidder obtains the good in question. A variant of the sealed-bid auction is the Vickery auction, in which the highest bidder ends up paying the price of the second highest bidder.

An auction might make provision for contingencies. In the Swiss auction, contract bids are contingent on unanticipated occurrences. The results of such auctions are not immediately binding because economic circumstances or structural conditions can change. In situations where the best (prime) bidder cannot fulfill his or her obligation, the next best bidder is considered, but the prime bidder has obligations to compensate for adverse price disparities.

Auction is a very old system of economic transaction with enduring traditions. Modern financial markets such as the New York Stock Exchange continue the practice of auction by selling assets through public outcry and formal rules.

Technological innovation has also made it possible for articles of trade to be auctioned on the Internet by eBay and other auction houses. In addition, buyers are now exposed more than ever before to a variety of goods and assets. This exposure has been enhanced by innovation, diffusion of information, and linkage of auction markets.

Prices of auctioned goods or assets may, however, price the unfortunate and less wealthy out of auction markets. In this respect, auction markets, like other markets, are susceptible to failure by not providing goods to those who are willing to have them but lack the ability to pay. ***See also*** Market; Market Failure

Auction Politics A political campaign strategy in which the candidates compete to make the most financially attractive promises to voters. The candidates are the metaphorical "bidders," and the election win is the item "on the block." The term is commonly used in Irish politics, less so in the United States.

The historian T. Ryle Dwyer first introduced the notion of auction politics in describing the Irish politician Jack Lynch's 1977 successful campaign strategy. Lynch's Fianna Fail government party was facing a low chance of victory in the 1977 general election. Lynch turned the election into a landslide victory through his issuance of an economic "manifesto." The manifesto promised voters a series of economic incentives, including the abolishment of car tax and grants to first-time home buyers.

A less common usage of the term is the notion that state power can be bought by the electorate. For example, a legislator will follow the dictates of the campaign donor who will contribute the most.

Audience The intended receiver in an exchange of communication. An audience can be an individual or a group in face-to-face communication (a friend or group of colleagues) or an online setting (a user from a networking site). The audience may provide feedback to the sender, depending on the context of communication.

Audio Having to do with sound, its recording, and its transmission. In 1860, Edouard Léon Scott de Martinville was the first to record sound using a hog's hair bristle that made grooves on a cylinder coated with lamp black. This device could not play back the music, however. It was not until 1877 that Thomas Edison developed the first device that could do both. A few years later, Emile Berliner, working on Edison's ideas, began using flat disks instead of cylinders and invented the gramophone to play back the sound on the disks. The electric record player and vinyl disks eventually replaced these earlier technologies. In the meantime, the radio was gaining popularity. It and the recorded sound industry shared a symbiotic relationship that survives to the present day. By the 1940s, German engineers developed audiotapes and eventually, these tapes were put into a small, manageable-sized cassette. Later, Thomas Stockham invented digital recording, which could be played back

with a laser beam, and the compact disc (CD) made it to market in 1983. By the end of the 1990s, the MP3 file format emerged, enabling music to be compressed into small files and users to store large quantities of recordings. These smaller compressed files also allowed for the downloading and swapping of music on the Internet at very rapid rates. As audio technology evolved, it had a huge impact on the advertising industry and gave birth to the recording industry, simultaneously changing leisure time and popular culture. Audio technologies have been used with great effect in education, research, art, and in products for the disabled. These developments have also affected the legal system, through disputes over patents, copyrights, profanity, and censorship. ***See also*** Broadcasting; Radio; Recordings

Audio Tapes A form of communication technology prominent in the late 20th century. Audio tapes are a playback medium that allows for continual listening to voices and music recorded on a magnetic tape enclosed in a protective plastic shell. Audio tapes have largely been replaced by digital networking technologies. ***See also*** Communication Medium

Augustus, John A humanitarian of faith, considered the father of probation in the United States. Augustus (1785–1859), a shoemaker, was driven to help those he understood to be in need of reformation rather than punishment. He provided bail for a defendant, charged in the Boston Police Court, for the first time in 1841. Augustus went before the court and advocated that defendants be released into his custody. He assumed legal responsibility for them, provided their bail, and found them housing. His work paved the way for probation, the practice in which a convicted offender, instead of going to prison, remains in the community under some type of supervision. ***See also*** Bail; Parole; Probation

Authentic Learning Learning that centers on "real-world" tasks. Scaffolding from teachers, social interaction, and personal insight link the learning application to students' lives. Students are encouraged to explore, discuss, discover, and form meaningful constructs, through problem-solving or projects. Motivation is usually increased because students see the real-time application to their current lives.

Authoritarian A type of government in which strict adherence to the views of the government is required of its citizenry. Criticism of the government is not allowed, and censorship of speech and the press is the norm. An authoritarian government is usually associated with a totalitarian and nondemocratic regime.

The term *authoritarianism* was first used by the German philosopher Theodor W. Adorno (1950) in *The Authoritarian Personality*. Adorno's work was the product of a growing scholarly interest in understanding the German people's adherence to Nazism. Adorno's thesis, borrowing from Freudian psychoanalytic theory, was that people attracted to authoritarian regimes are those with an "authoritative personality." These individuals possess deeply repressed resentment against their parents' use of oppressive authority in their childhood, and as adults they take out such resentment on minority out-groups. Authoritarian personalities are marked not only by an ironic submission to authority but also by bigotry and intolerance of ideas other than their own. For more information, see Adorno (1950/1993).

Authoritarianism   A personality trait composed of three elements: (1) an acceptance of conventional or traditional values, (2) a willingness to unquestioningly follow the orders of authority figures, and (3) a tendency to act aggressively toward individuals or groups that have been identified as potentially threatening by authority figures. Authoritarianism is strongly linked with prejudicial behavior and a strong differentiation of in-group and out-group behavior. People with a strong authoritarian orientation perceive the world as a dangerous place and seek safety in their in-group. In-group favoritism is common to most people, and members of out-groups are usually perceived as less attractive and less socially acceptable than members of the in-group, thereby enhancing self-esteem. This common favoritism results in prejudice when an individual's motivation to enhance self-esteem causes him or her to disrespect other people. Authoritarianism also influences socialization; authoritarian parents tend to be firm, punitive, and unsympathetic and value obedience from the child. For more information, see Altemeyer (1996). *See also* Personality; Prejudice (psychology); Stereotype (psychology); Trait

Authority   The right or power to direct and demand performance and obedience, enforce laws, determine or judge. It also includes the right to specify the means and methods by which work will be executed. The term is derived from the Latin word *auctorius*.

A *public authority* is a type of public benefit corporation, or public corporation contracted by a state to perform a defined public service. A public authority typically takes on a more bureaucratic role and is granted broad powers to regulate or maintain public property. The organization is generally run by boards of directors who are appointed rather than elected. Such corporations are often found in common-law jurisdictions, such as the British Commonwealth countries, and often operate in heavily regulated industries, such as transportation. In a broader sense, a public authority could represent any corporation that exists for a charitable or nonprofit purpose. Most likely having roots in mercantile capitalism, the first public authority on record is the Port of London Authority, established in 1908.

While the terms *power* and *authority* are often used interchangeably, their meanings are distinct. When power is legitimized, it is called authority. The transformation of power into authority is seen in the relationship between supervisors and subordinates in organizations. For example, university faculty have authority over graduate assistants because they direct and supervise their work. Department chairs have authority over faculty for the same reasons. Those in authority are responsible for keeping activities aligned with goals. Authority is most effective when it is respected by subordinates and supported by superiors. Thus, for a department chair's authority to be effective, he or she should be respected by the faculty and supported by the dean.

Authority is often linked to legitimacy. People obey authority as long as they believe that it is legitimate. College students obey their instructors because they recognize their academic credentials and expertise in a particular area as legitimate. Faculty members obey their department chair because he or she has been vested with power by the college's dean. Although authority is distinct from leadership, authorities may be leaders. There are also examples of individuals having authority but not being leaders. The timekeeper at an academic competition might have authority, but he or she is not necessarily a leader.

The sociologist Max Weber made distinctions between three types of authority: rational-legal, traditional, and charismatic. *Rational-legal authority* depends on written rules and laws for its legitimacy. This type of authority is extended to individuals by virtue of the office that they hold. For example, a student government association president has rational-legal authority because he or she was elected to a position by the student body. When the student leaves his or her position as president of the Student Government Association, he or she no longer has the authority of his or her former office. *Traditional authority* derives from long-established customs and social structure. This type of authority may be seen in a family where a patriarch has power over other members of the family, or in a monarchy, where the king has power over the member of the kingdom. *Charismatic authority* derives from the charisma or personality of a leader. Charismatic authorities are obeyed because followers have a strong emotional attachment to them. Examples include Dr. Martin Luther King and Jim Jones, of Jonestown, Guyana. For more information, see Bolman and Deal (1997) and Pfeffer (1981).

Autobiographical Memory   The memory for information related to the self. This is mostly considered part of the episodic memory but can be distinguished from mere episodic memories by several features. First, autobiographical memories are more complex than other types of memories. According to Martin Conway, autobiographical memories are organized in different levels of specificity, from lifetime periods (e.g., when I lived in Berlin) to general events (e.g., the times I went to the theater) to event-specific knowledge that contains sensory or affective information. Recently, the life story was added to this model as a more comprehensive level.

Autobiographical memory is further set apart from other memory forms by unique features such as the "reminiscence bump" (an accumulation of memories recalled from the age of transition to adulthood), childhood amnesia (the inability to recall events before the age of three), and flashbulb memories (memories of high affective intensity that can be recalled seemingly to the last detail). For more information, see Bluck (2003) and Conway (1990). *See also* Flashbulb Memory; Long-Term Memory (LTM); Memory (psychology)

Autocracy   Although this word denotes a type of government in which all political power is wielded by a single individual, it also metaphorically encompasses an administration or organization that is run by one person who has effective control over decisions (etymogically, it derives from the Greek *autokaratia,* or "ruling by one's self). This leadership and management style is in contrast to an oligarchy (where power is wielded by a strict set of persons) or a democracy (where power is primarily wielded by the people). Some of the 19th- and 20th-century business conglomerates or trusts were effectively controlled by one person in the same way as an autocracy. For more information, see Fredrich and Brzezinski (1965). *See also* Authoritarianism; Democracy (political science, public administration); Totalitarian

Automaticity   The ability to do things without thinking about them. This ability requires learning, repetition, and practice. When the skill is mastered, the mind can simultaneously focus on other activities or thoughts. Examples include walking, riding a bike, reading, and writing. It is measured by processing speed or accuracy of responses of the secondary task (e.g., riding a bike) that is performed simultaneously with a primary task (e.g., thinking about a math problem).

Autonomic Nervous System   The subsystem of the peripheral nervous system that carries messages between the central nervous system and the heart, lungs, and other organs and glands, thereby decreasing or increasing the activity in these organs. Although the autonomic nervous system (ANS) is influenced by the brain, it controls activities that are normally outside of conscious control (e.g., digestion, perspiration) and is thus labeled autonomic. The ANS consist of two parts: (1) the *sympathetic system,* which mobilizes the body for action in the face of stress (with responses that are often labeled as the fight-flight-syndrome), and (2) the *parasympathetic system,* which regulates the body's energy conservation. These two systems can thus often create contrasting effects (increasing/slowing down the heart rate). For more information, see Berthoud and Neuhuber (2000). *See also* Central Nervous System (CNS); Parasympathetic Nervous System (PNS); Peripheral Nervous System (PNS); Sympathetic Nervous System

Autonomy   The state of being self-governed; a condition in which one is independent and self-determining, free from external controls. The term can be applied to an individual, a group, an institution, a state, or a people. It is an essential concept in the disciplines of philosophy, political science, and theology. *See also* Political Science

Availability Heuristic   A mental shortcut in behavioral decision making through which judgments are based on information that is most easily brought to mind. It can thus be considered a part of *informal reasoning.* Like most heuristics, this shortcut tends to work well in most cases. It can, however, lead to biased judgment, especially when mental availability does not reflect actual frequency. For example, news reports on airplane accidents are mentally more available than car accidents, though car accidents happen with considerably greater frequency. For more information, see Gigerenzer, Todd, and the ABC Research Group (1999). *See also* Heuristic

Aversion Therapy   A type of therapy based on aversion conditioning, in which nausea, painful electrical shocks, or other unpleasant stimuli are paired with a behavior or habit that one aims to extinguish. Aversion therapy relies on behavioral therapy approaches, with the central tenet of aversion therapy being that behaviors can be unlearned through conditioning techniques. Just as behaviors are learned through their pairing with pleasant consequences (or rewards), behaviors can be unlearned through their pairing with unpleasant consequences (or punishment). Behavioral therapy has been used most commonly to treat smoking, gambling, substance use disorders, and paraphilic behavior. For more information, see Flor, Birbaumer, Hermann, Ziegler, and Patrick (2002). *See also* Behavior Therapy (education, psychology); Operant Conditioning; Punishment (psychology, sociology)

Avoidance   The act of circumventing the expression of one's beliefs or feelings in an interaction with one or more parties. Avoidance can be nonverbal (e.g., withdrawal from social situations) or verbal (the artful manipulation or evading of information) and is generally viewed as a lack of contact. Anxiety, apprehension, and uncertainty are emotional processes considered to be associated with avoidance behavior. Avoidance can negatively influence one's ability to develop and maintain professional and personal relationships. Similarly, avoidance can function in a cyclical way, as seen in studies that draw on psychological notions of early attachment (especially parental attachment), wherein it affects the ability to form attachments later in life. Avoidance is considered to be a manifestation of conflict—intrapersonal, interpersonal, intragroup, and intergroup. Management of avoidance can be realized through use of communications tactics, which draw on notions from psychology. Avoidance is a form of destructive, rather than constructive, communication.

Axiology   The branch of formal philosophy concerned with moral concepts, standards of right conduct, and the nature of good and bad. Axiology pertains to moral judgments about what makes actions right or wrong and not with questions of which actions are right or wrong. ***See also*** Ethics (communication, education, public administration, sociology)

Axon   A neuron fiber that transmits signals from the cell body of the neuron to the area where communications with other neurons takes place. There is usually one axon per neuron, with many terminal branches. The axon is covered with myelin (glial cells), which supports the structure of the axon and provides nutrition. Axonal transport can take place both from the cell body (anterograde) and from the axon terminal (retrograde). Two terms can be distinguished in describing axons, which are always used in relation to a particular brain region or structure. Axons carrying information into the region are *afferents,* while axons carrying information away from the region are *efferents.* Accordingly, all axons can be described as both efferents and afferents. The axon terminals contain synaptic vesicles (filled with synaptic transmitters, also called neurotransmitters) that can be emptied into the synaptic cleft to chemically transmit a signal to the receptor molecules of the postsynaptic membrane, thus innervating the target cell. For more information, see Pinel (2005). ***See also*** Glial Cells; Myelin Sheath; Neurotransmitters; Soma; Synapse

B

Background Checking of Teachers The procedure meant to uncover any information in a teacher's background that would make unsupervised access to children inappropriate and unsafe. These checks vary from state to state; they may uncover information through fingerprinting or during an investigation based on personal data, such as the teacher's social security number.

Badlands Areas composed of irregular topography resulting from wind and water erosion. Badlands are commonly found in Nebraska and South Dakota. Vegetation is lacking in these barren lands, and the formation of canyons and ravines is typical. As the name suggests, agriculture and travel are both difficult due to the lack of rain and the atypical formation of the land. The soft sedimentary rock found in the badlands is composed of loosely anchored clay, leaving the land particularly susceptible to erosion. Scarce vegetation and erosion make the badlands a place where fossils are easily found. Peaks, valleys, and ridges are also common in the badlands, which can also be recognized by their unique range of colors. In popular culture, the Badlands of America frequently serve as outdoor sets for Western movies.

Bail The monetary amount or condition of pretrial release; a bond (guarantee) or other security provided to the court by a person who agrees to be responsible for a defendant to appear at each stage of the trial. The amount of bail is set by the judge at the initial appearance; the full amount or a percentage of the bond may be required, in cash or other type of security (e.g., property). A bail bondsman may post bail in exchange for a fee in all but four states—Illinois, Kentucky, Oregon, and Wisconsin. The bail bond system is widely criticized as discriminatory against poor and middle-class defendants. This commercial or profit-making aspect is unique to the United States.

Approximately two thirds of all defendants are granted and pay bail, with another third remaining in pretrial detention. Defendants accused of violent offenses or some drug offenses are generally ineligible for bail. About one third of those released have their bail revoked and are returned to jail for committing a new offense, failing to appear in court as scheduled, or committing some other violation. ***See also*** Pretrial Detention/Release

Balanced Budget (*economics*) A term used when the sum of money a government collects is equal to the amount it collectively spends on goods, services, and debt interest.

Within his popular theories, the 20th-century British economist John Maynard Keynes regarded a balanced budget in the public sector as being achieved when a government possesses enough fiscal discipline to be able to maintain equilibrium between revenues and expenses over various business cycles. The maintenance of such a delicate balance results in a deficit during low economic periods counterbalanced by the production of surplus in periods of high economic activity.

While it is common for most U.S. states to require the local government to pass a balanced budget, the U.S. Constitution does not require the Congress to do so. While the modern movement to pass a balanced-budget amendment to the U.S. Constitution dates back to the 1980s, initiatives for the government to pass this type of amendment began during the Depression. The balanced-budget amendment, historically favored by the Republicans, would amend the U.S. Constitution by requiring, through law, that Congress pass a federal budget that balances projected revenues and expenditures, with certain exceptions (most notably at times of war). The lack of such a law has led to deficit spending, consequentially creating national debt. The most recent time when either the U.S. House or the Senate has passed a balanced-budget amendment was in 1996, when it was passed by the House. To date, both the House and the Senate majority necessary to pass an amendment has not been achieved.

One of the common arguments in favor of a balanced budget is that Congress can simply not discipline itself. Moreover, such arguments are driven by concern for national debt; federal budget deficits rose to new highs during President Bush's term (in nominal dollars). Conversely, creating a balanced-budget amendment is criticized by individuals and groups such as the Ludwig von Mises Institute, which condemns the balancing of a "future estimated budget" rather than "the actual budget at the end of a given fiscal year." The Institute also asserts that "balancing the budget by increasing taxes is like curing influenza by shooting the patient; the cure is worse than the disease" (http://mises.org/econsense/listof articles.asp, http://mises.org/Econsense/ch65.asp). ***See also*** Debt; Deficit

Balanced Budget (*political science*) A term used when government expenditure equals government revenue. In the United States, public opinion polls consistently find that a balanced budget is of great concern to American voters, although a number of leading economists stress that an annual balanced budget is not necessary if long-term financial planning is employed. The Congressional Budget and Impoundment Control Act of 1974 was one of the first recent attempts by Congress to help balance the budget. The Act made the budget process more organized as congressional involvement in the budget process was increased, while the President's control was limited. Nearly two decades later, President Clinton's Balanced Budget Act of 1997 resulted in a $69 billion budget surplus a year later. A national debate ensued on how best to spend the budget. The result was the decision of the Bush administration in 2001 to enact a $1.3 trillion tax cut over a 10-year period. The 2008 federal deficit was the largest in U.S. history. ***See also*** Debt; Deficit

Balance of Payments (BOP) *(economics)* A summary statement of the economic transactions between the residents of one country and the rest of the world. Transactions that result in the receipt of payments from foreigners are recorded as credits, and transactions that cause payments to be made to foreigners are recorded as debits. A double-entry accounting (bookkeeping) procedure is used to record all transactions, once as a credit or debit and then as an offsetting debit or credit. Errors and omissions are characterized as statistical discrepancies.

In an ideal situation, credits must be equal to debits for BOP to be in equilibrium. When credits exceed debits, a nation is said to have a BOP surplus. Conversely, when debits exceed the surplus, a nation is said to have a BOP deficit. Deficits that are chronic or persistent are considered unsustainable and must be addressed by policy intervention, which may include devaluation in addition to fiscal and/or monetary constraints. Fiscal constraint means a reduction in government spending or an increase in taxes to reduce disposable income. Monetary restraint means an increase in interest rate to discourage borrowing or a reduction in the money supply.

The BOP has three main components: (1) the current account, (2) the capital account, and (3) the official reserve account. Transactions involving exchange in goods and services, income on investments (interests and dividends), and unilateral transfers (gifts or bequests) are recorded in the current account section. The capital account shows net changes in the asset holdings of a nation when official reserve assets are excluded. It includes direct investments, such as buildings and factories; securities, such as stocks, bonds, and treasury bills; and bank claims and liabilities. The official reserve account measures change in a nation's assets during one year. Official reserve assets include gold holdings, special drawing rights (SDRs), and official foreign currency holdings. For more information, see Carbaugh (2007), McConnell and Brue (2008), and Pugel (2007). ***See also*** Debt; International Monetary Fund (IMF)

Balance of Payments (BOP) *(political science)* A statement that reflects a country's international transactions and balances the amount of money flowing in and out of a given country. The BOP reflects activity in both the public and the private sectors of a state's economy. When money flows into a country, it is known as credit; when money flows out of a country, it is known as debit. Ideally, the credits and the debits should balance (equal zero), but this is rare. The BOP is divided into three major parts: (1) current account, (2) capital account, and (3) financial account. The current account refers to the funds related to goods and services flowing in and out of the country. The capital account records international capital transfers; this category includes nonfinancial and nonproduced assets. The financial account tracks international business and real estate investments, stocks, and bonds. The current account should ideally balance with the capital plus the financial accounts. ***See also*** Debt; International Monetary Fund (IMF)

Balance of Powers The achievement of an equal distribution of power between states or sublevels of government within a state. In international relations, a balance of powers prevents a country from becoming more powerful than the others, as a result of weaker countries banding together to form a united front against a powerful sovereign. This is especially marked during times of war when a dominant country has aggressed against a weaker nation; states often join the side of the weaker power in peril. The balance of power concept has been traced back to the classical Greek period. In Thucydides' *History of the Peloponnesian War* (431 BCE), he attributed the war to the escalation of power in Athens and the threat it posed to the Spartans.

The separation of powers also refers to the democratic principle of limiting the powers of any one branch of government. In the United States, it is also known as a system of "checks and balances" and was deliberately written into the U.S. Constitution. The framers developed the U.S. system in an effort to avoid tyrannical leadership emblematic of Great Britain. Powers are separated among the three branches of the federal government (executive, legislature, and judiciary) and between the federal and state governments. There is a list of enumerated powers—concurrent, those shared with the states, and exclusive, those exercised only by the federal government or the states—in the Constitution. For more information, see Sheehan (1996) and Thucydides (431 BCE). ***See also*** Separation of Powers

Ballistics The science or study of the motion, behavior, and effects of projectiles. In forensic science, ballistics is the science of analyzing firearm use in a crime. The flight path of a bullet includes travel down the barrel, path through the air, and path through a target.

Ballot A voting method where little balls of different colors are deposited secretly into a wooden "ballot box" to signify a voter's preference. It is commonly used to describe any type of secret, as opposed to an open, voting method. The earliest use of ballot voting can be traced back to ancient Greece.

Bandwagon Appeal A fallacy based on the technique prominent in advertising that if popular people use a particular product, the product itself is popular and of high quality. Many who buy the product do not take into consideration that the celebrity touting the merchandise is paid to do so. Also, the bandwagon appeal becomes operative when some product, entertainment, and other such thing becomes faddish because of word-of-mouth or other communicative techniques. An appeal to popularity is very strong and involves peer pressure to wear a certain type of clothing, drive a certain model automobile, or go to a popular school or college. Such "snob appeals" are prevalent among all classes. The use of the phrase "Everyone else is doing it" is a good example of explaining or defending one's behavior according to the bandwagon appeal. *See also* Bandwagon Effect

Bandwagon Effect The term used to describe the social phenomenon of individuals favoring a popular trend merely because it is popular. The phrase originated in 1848, during Zachary Taylor's successful run for the presidency. During Taylor's campaign, Dan Rice, a popular clown of the era, invited Taylor to join his circus bandwagon. This brought Taylor such recognition from the townspeople that other political contenders also wanted to "jump on the bandwagon." This phenomenon poses particular concern in contemporary politics; it is feared that surveys and voter exit polls sway voters toward favoring popular opinion and candidates instead of voting according to their true knowledge of the issues at hand. *See also* Bandwagon Appeal

Bank A depository institution and a financial intermediary. As a financial intermediary, it is a facilitator of finance. Although thrifts (savings banks) played a vital role in the past, contemporary banks may be classified into three broad categories: (1) credit unions, (2) commercial banks, and (3) central banks.

Credit unions are banks that perform banking functions for private members. Commercial banks are open to the public, and they specialize in providing banking services to individuals and institutions or businesses. Central banks provide banking services to national governments and perform regulatory, supervisory, and administrative functions. They are generally responsible for the overall performance and stability of a financial system.

Credit unions and commercial banks perform an important function of transferring and creating money. They transfer money by collecting savings from surplus spending units so that deficit spending units can have access to loans or credits. By doing so, these banks reduce transaction costs and the cost of borrowing money. Banks request interest (the cost of borrowing money) for loans that are issued and as such raise revenue from the issue of loans.

Other countries of the world have a central bank. In the United States, there is a Federal Reserve System, which consists of regional and district banks. The U.S. central banking system is therefore decentralized with presidents and vice presidents, regional and district officials, and the Board of Governors, consisting

of the chairman of the Federal Reserve Board and the vice chair.

Central banking in the United States is comparatively new (a 19th- and 20th-century undertaking), but unlike most countries, the U.S. central bank enjoys a reasonable amount of autonomy, which enables it to frame an independent monetary policy to stabilize the economy.

Monetary policy involves the increase or decrease of the money supply, which is usually done through open-market operations (the buying and selling of U.S. securities) to affect the liquidity of commercial banks and the performance of the economy.

To minimize the occurrence and persistence of a financial crisis, central banks impose reserve requirements on depository institutions. They also supervise and regulate their operations to ensure fairness, secured deposits, and equal access to credit. In the U.S. depository, institutions can only undertake measured risks because they are forbidden to engage in unlawful risk taking.

A central bank acts as a lender of last resort so that it can provide banks in peril with financial assistance. Central banks may also perform convenience functions such as clearing checks, transferring money domestically and internationally, and making money available to depository institutions. *See also* Deregulation (economics); Financial System; International Monetary Fund (IMF); Stabilization

Barriers to Intercultural Communication Owing to the inevitable changes between cultures, breakdowns in communication are bound to occur. Such occurrences are costly to the multinational enterprise because of the resulting workplace problems and their effect on returns, revenues, and customer relationships. In addition, a firm's competitive advantage can be compromised due to barriers in intercultural communication. Three main obstacles to intercultural communication can be highlighted: (1) language, (2) modern technology, and (3) mindset.

When we use language, slang and jargon hamper intercultural communication and can be insulting to people from other cultures. The presence of globally known brands, products, and services does not mean that the local people possess the same level of language sophistication as the producers of advertisements for these items. Some words mean very different things in different languages.

With the advent of modern technology, especially the Internet, it is likely that there will be some degree of miscommunication between people of different cultures. This is especially true with the use of short message service (SMS) and e-mail messages. For example, e-mail eliminates nuance, language tone, and body language that can result in misconstrued messages and miscommunication.

When we use language, it is also important to take into account the mindset of the person you are communicating with at any given time. It is important that one knows how to manage conflicts well, since one will be dealing with people from other cultures who are quiet, shy, individualistic, private, or independent; all these different mindsets lend themselves to possible breakdowns in communication. The Austrian philosopher Ludwig Wittgenstein stated that the "meaning" of a word could only be understood or elucidated in the context of how it is used. For more information, see Sluga and Stern (1996). ***See also*** Jargon; Language; Slang

Barter *(economics)*   A system that served the function of money before the development of money. In the absence of money, trade was conducted through the exchange of goods. For example, a farmer will barter his corn for some goods that he needs. If the farmer needs a pair of shoes, then he will barter his corn or exchange the corn for a pair of shoes. This system was very cumbersome. If you have a horse to trade, you must search for someone who has the need for the horse and at the same time has a good that you want. The swap rate also became a problem in this system. If a farmer with a cow needs four chickens and another farmer has only two chickens, the farmer with the cow cannot give up half of his cow. Because barter was cumbersome, it was eventually replaced by the development of money as a medium of exchange. For more information, see Case and Fair (2003) and McConnell and Brue (2008).

Barter *(sociology)*   The trade of goods or services without the use of money. Bartering was commonly used in precapitalist or premarket economies instead of market exchange based on a monetary system. Bartering is common inside a jail or prison, where money is considered contraband.

Basal Ganglia   A group of six subcortical nuclei, including the neostriatum, which includes the caudate and putamen; the paleostriatum, which includes the external globus pallidus (GPe) and the internal globus pallidus (GPi); the subthalamic nucleus (STN); the substantia nigra (SN); the thalamus; and the red nucleus. These nuclei innervate each other, thereby forming a neural system that is important for motor control, particularly automated or involuntary movements, and that has also been called the extrapyramidal system. Disordered movement due to impairment of the basal ganglia and its associated structures has been linked with Parkinson's disease. For more information, see Pinel (2005). ***See also*** Brain (Encephalon)

Basic Research   An attempt to expand our understanding of (psychological) phenomena, even if such knowledge does not necessarily lead directly to any practical benefits, thereby distinguishing itself from *applied research*. Scientists conducting basic research usually work for universities or government-funded agencies. Recently, distinctions between applied and basic research have become less clear-cut, in that many basic research findings often have practical utility and, likewise, applied research findings may have implications for our understanding of basic psychological processes. For more

information, see Nihei and Miura (2002). ***See also*** Applied Research

Basic Versus Applied Research   The difference between the two kinds of research lies in their respective aims. Basic research refers to research aimed at acquiring new, fundamental knowledge and theoretical understanding about basic human and other natural processes without any particular application in view. Applied research also is conducted as an original investigation to acquire new knowledge, but it is primarily directed toward practical objectives with the aim of providing relatively immediate solutions.

Battered Woman Syndrome   Also referred to as battered person or wife syndrome, this is a criminal defense used when a person (usually a woman) accused of assault or homicide acts in self-defense. The condition can result from persistent and severe domestic violence, which leads to the belief that she is unable to escape from and is responsible for the abuse.

Beccaria, Cesare   An Italian philosopher (1738–1794). His famous *An Essay on Crimes and Punishment* (1764) is considered the foundation of the classical school of criminological theory. His work led to criminal law reform in western Europe and influenced the developing American system. He was critical of the corporal and largely arbitrary and harsh punishments of the time and called for a rational system of punishment that fits the crime. He argued that punishment should be swift and certain and not be excessive for the crime. He called for a system of law created by government that should be specific and not capricious. For more information, see Beccaria (1764/1983). ***See also*** Classical Criminology

Beck Depression Inventory (BDI)   The BDI is a 21-item, brief, self-report instrument to assess symptoms of major depressive disorders. The BDI is now in its second edition and provides cutoff scores to classify the severity of symptoms in the mild, moderate, or severe range. The instrument has been shown to have excellent reliability and validity.

Behavioral Economics   The belief that economics, similar to behavioral psychology, is a science of highly organized behavior. In behavioral economics, scientific research is applied to human and social-cognitive and emotional biases to better understand and explain how they affect elements of the economy such as market prices, returns, and consumer choice. The study of behavioral finance and economics encompasses social psychology within large groups as well as individual psychology. Many of the theories are concerned with the rationality, or lack thereof, of economic agents.

As a discipline, behavioral economics is regarded as a sophisticated and well-developed component of behavior analysis that has existed since the late 1700s. In the early stages of development, concepts linking human behavioral theories and psychology to economic principles emerged in studies such as Adam Smith's *The Theory of Moral Sentiments* (1759), which described the psychological principles of individual behavior during the Classical period. Despite the early emergence and relative acceptance of such theories, by the 20th century, psychology had all but disappeared from economic discussions.

Gradually, as the use and development of behavioral economics began to incorporate various models such as those related to expected utility (e.g., game theory) and discounted utility (e.g., deterministic utility streams), which had already gained wide acceptance, the science began to be acknowledged. In the past couple of decades, the field has made a few significant strides with largely publicized conferences and journals, most notably the special 1997 edition of the *Quarterly Journal of Economics,* "In Memory of Amos Tversky," which was devoted to the topic of behavioral economics. More recently, the field received recognition and was highlighted when Daniel Kahneman was awarded the Nobel Prize in 2002 for his development of prospect theory and related studies that integrated insights from psychological research into economic science, most notably concerning human judgment and decision making under uncertainty.

Behavioral models often may be used to integrate psychological principles with the theories of neoclassical economics in order to explain economic behaviors and their outcomes. There now exist methods to test these models based on real-world data and the results of experiments simulating real-life economic activities, such as stock market trading and auctions. These new methods involve transactions based on monetary compensation. Originally, behavioral economic theories were developed mainly from the conclusions drawn from experimental observations and survey responses. Brain activity patterns, while an economic decision is being made, are also observed using functional magnetic resonance imaging (fMRI).

Behavioral economics is mainly concerned with the following:

- *Framing:* the presentation of a rational-choice problem
- *Heuristics:* the habit of making a decision based on the "rule of thumb," or the most common practice, rather than making a decision after performing a rational analysis of the situation
- *Market inefficiencies:* explaining market anomalies, such as mispricing, that do not reflect rational market expectations

For more information, see Herbert (1959) and Smith (1759/2000). ***See also*** Neoclassical Economics

Behavioral Effects   One of three types of media effects, along with cognitive and affective. Whereas cognitive and affective effects research tries to determine the impact of media on an individual's perceptions, beliefs, and attitudes, behavioral effects research seeks to detect whether behavior can actually be altered as a result of exposure to some form or forms of mass communication. There are, naturally, inherent problems in studying the latter because, ethically, research that will harm subjects or cause harm to others cannot be conducted. Researchers are more likely to study cognitive and affective effects, suggesting that the research on media effects may be understated. Nevertheless, numerous studies have tried to assess the mass media effect on social behavior—that is, whether excessive exposure to violent television content increases aggression—and health behavior—that is, whether advertising can lead to diet choices or changes in alcohol consumption. For more information, see Perse (2000). ***See also*** Media Effects

Behavioral Geography   A branch of human geography that focuses on an individual's relationship with the environment. The term can cause confusion and is sometimes assumed to be behavioral in nature. However, behavioral geography is actually a quantitative approach to environmental perception and is cognitive in nature. Pioneered in the 1970s, this type of geography challenged neoclassical economic determinism, which governed the study of human geography until the late 1960s. Behavioral geography is concerned with a human being's cognitive reasoning, focusing on spatial perceptions, decision making, and values. More specifically, behavioral geography involves an individual's perception of his or her environment, even though the perception may be drastically different from the objective reality. This discipline is praised for having acknowledged the individual's role in geography and for its utility in explaining human perception through a geographical approach. This type of geography relies on many other disciplines, including psychology, sociology, and anthropology. The study of behavioral geography is recognized for having integrated several disciplines to better understand human perception of the environment. ***See also*** Cultural Geography

Behavioral Observation   The structured and systematic assessment of behavior through observation. Observational measures, therefore, can be used to measure anything a person does that researchers can observe (e.g., eye contact between people in conversation and aggression in children on the playground). Behavioral observation requires carefully recording the observed behavior for later analysis. Participants' behavior is either directly observed or indirectly recorded through videotape or audiotape. Behavioral observation scales, designed to facilitate direct observation, are often used in performance appraisal in the industrial/organizational sector. Behavioral observation has a potential advantage over self-report measures because it does not involve direct questioning and is thus usually less reactive. This is especially the case if the research participant is not aware that measurement is occurring, does not realize what the purpose of the measurement is, and cannot change his or her responses even if he or she wishes to. For more information, see Furr and Funder (2007). *See also* Assessment

Behaviorism *(education)* The name for an early-20th-century movement in psychology claiming that scientific psychology must study objective observable behavior rather than subjective mental events. Behaviorism dominated learning theory in psychology for much of the 20th century and is still used today in areas such as applied behavior analysis, token economies, and behavior therapy.

Behavioral scientists study voluntary and involuntary behavior. The first to systematically record studies of behavior were Pavlov and his followers, who studied reflexive (autonomic, automatic, and involuntary) behavior. B. F. Skinner called this *classical conditioning* because it first proposed a relationship between a behavior and an external event. With classical conditioning, a neutral stimulus (which produces no response) is repeatedly paired with an unconditioned stimulus (which produces a natural response), and over repeated trials, the neutral stimulus becomes conditioned and produces (by itself) the natural response. For example, a hungry dog is presented with a neutral stimulus, such as the ringing of a bell, immediately followed by an unconditioned stimulus, such as the sight and smell of food, and the natural response of salivation occurs. After repeated pairings of these two stimuli, presentation of only the previously neutral stimulus (ringing of the bell) produces the natural response of salivation. The previously neutral stimulus has become a conditioned stimulus.

Also called operant conditioning (from the Latin word *opus,* meaning a work or action), the study of voluntary behavior patterns is a learning theory attributed to B. F. Skinner. In operant conditioning, a behavior (work, action, *opus*) may be followed by reinforcement or punishment. Positive reinforcement is anything that is pleasing, increasing the likelihood of the original behavior being repeated. This reinforcement may be inherently pleasing, such as food or praise. It may be a learned valuing, such as accumulating points, leading to prizes, or paychecks for work. Punishment following a behavior is something that is aversive, decreasing the likelihood of the behavior being repeated. Negative reinforcement following a behavior includes the threat of punishment with a way of escape. If there is noncompliance, there is punishment; if there is compliance, there is no punishment (escape), and the escape behavior is said to be negatively reinforced.

In classical (or Pavlovian) conditioning, the series of events is basically reversed from operant conditioning. Whereas the classical conditioning paradigm consists of an event (stimulus) followed by a behavior, the operant conditioning paradigm consists of a behavior followed by an event (reinforcer). Classical conditioning is also different from operant conditioning, in that Pavlov's work only involved autonomic, nonvolitional bodily response (such as salivation, pupil dilation, heart rate, and muscle tension associated with eating); Skinner's behaviorism, on the other hand, involved volitional control, or choice of behavior, which was learned as a result of the type of reinforcement given during prior and similar behaviors. For more information, see Pavlov (1902) and Skinner (1938). *See also* Classical Conditioning; Operant Conditioning; Reinforcement; Reinforcer

Behaviorism *(psychology)* A concept that emphasizes the role of learning (especially classical and operant conditioning) and behavioral observation in psychology and dominated psychological research between 1920 and 1960. John B. Watson, heavily influenced by Ivan Pavlov, believed that the observable behavior of animals and humans is the most important and parsimonious source of scientific information in psychology. Unlike earlier researchers (especially, the structuralists and functionists), he did not propose to use behavior as the basis for inferences about consciousness, but he advocated that psychologists should ignore mental events (because they cannot be observed) and base psychology only on overt behavior occurring in response to environmental stimuli. Behaviorists like Watson assumed that adaptation to the environment is achieved through learning and that this basic principle holds true for all kinds of animals, including humans. Following Watson, the American psychologist B. F. Skinner worked on mapping out the details of how reward (reinforcement) and punishment shape, maintain, and change behavior in operant conditioning, mainly by experimenting with rats and pigeons. For that, he developed the so-called Skinner box, an apparatus to train rats and pigeons to push a lever in order to obtain food rewards. He saw the organism as a "black box," solely shaped by learning experiences. Based on Skinner, Kenneth Spence and Clark Hull's stimulus-response psychology refined the basic approach of behaviorism, until the dominance of behaviorism ended with the paradigm shift during the cognitive revolution, which was put forward particularly by Donald Broadbent (1958) and Ulrich Neisser (1967), who, among others, criticized behaviorism (especially, on the basis of the linguistic approach) and emphasized cognitive processes. The basic principles and methods of behaviorism, classical and operant conditioning, reinforcement patterns, and stimulus-response theory, are influential milestones in psychology, especially, in clinical psychology (i.e., behavioral therapy). For more information, see Baum (2005), Broadbent (1958), Hull (1951), Malone (1990), Neisser (1967), Pavlov (1902), Skinner (1938), and Watson (1913). *See also* Behavioral Observation; Behavior Therapy; Classical Conditioning; Operant Conditioning; Skinner Box

Behavior Management All actions taken by a classroom teacher to promote the types of positive student behaviors that will create an environment conducive to learning. Many teachers institute concrete behavior management plans that include clearly identified expectations of student behavior and spell out the consequences for inappropriate behavior. ***See also*** Behavior Modification

Behavior Modification   An intervention method for behavioral change based on behaviorism, especially the principles developed by B. F. Skinner. A basic assumption underlying this approach is that though the link between stimulus and response exists (classical or Pavlovian conditioning), it is the outcome produced by the action that shapes behavior. Therefore, any attempt to change behavior must be done through an empirical analysis of the stimuli and reinforcements (rewards) surrounding the targeted behavior. This analysis is called the "ABC" approach, with observations examining antecedents, behaviors, and consequences. Once a behavioral baseline is recorded, it is analyzed, patterns are identified, and an intervention plan is created that is aimed at consistent antecedents (stimuli) and/or consequences in order to increase or decrease the targeted behavior.

Two main principles are used when implementing behavior modification programs. *Operant conditioning* is the modification of behavior through the management of the consequences. Behavior is strengthened when it is followed by a reward and weakened when followed by something aversive. Reinforcements are the rewards that support behavior, such as primary reinforcers (food or drink); secondary reinforcers (smiles or pointing toward a desired prize); and generalized reinforcers (money or attention). Positive reinforcement prompts an increase in a behavior through a system of rewards; negative reinforcement encourages behavior by removing an aversive consequence. Behavior modification interventions use reinforcements that follow a clear set of basic principles: (1) reinforcement follows the targeted behavior and follows it as soon as possible; (2) reinforcement fits the targeted behavior and must be meaningful to the individual; and (3) multiple reinforcers are more effective than a single reinforcer.

Behavior modification can also discourage unwanted behavior through punishment, the application of an aversive stimulus in response to a targeted behavior. However, punishment has been shown to not necessarily eliminate behavior but only suppress it.

Behavior modification reinforcement schedules define and identify the amount of behavior change required or the time that must elapse between reinforcers. Some schedules are continuous, providing reinforcement every time the target behavior occurs, while others use a fixed or variable interval that is either time or objective related. A token economy system is an example of a behavior modification reinforcement schedule. Awarding "tokens" for meeting positive behavioral goals strengthens the positive behavior. The tokens themselves are not reinforcers but are accumulated and are used to gain a more desired object or activity.

Behavior modification forms the foundation of many approaches to classroom management and is also termed *applied behavior analysis* (ABA). ABA has been used in the areas of health and exercise, parenting, and teaching students with autism spectrum disorders. For more information, see Miltenberger (2003) and Skinner (1938). ***See also*** Behaviorism (psychology); Classroom Management; Operant Conditioning; Reinforcer

Behavior Therapy *(education)*   An action-oriented therapy aimed at changing maladaptive behavior through application of behavioral learning theory principles and procedures. Behavior therapy focuses on modifying the factors that influence maladaptive behavior, and clients are expected to take an active role in solving their problems (i.e., in changing their behavior). There are several types of behavioral therapies based on the theories of classical and operant conditioning, including principles such as systematic desensitization, classical extinction, reinforcement, and punishment.

Classical conditioning, first demonstrated by Ivan Pavlov, shows that behaviors can be elicited in response to specific stimuli and new stimuli can be conditioned to produce the desired responses. For example, when a neutral stimulus is repeatedly paired with an unconditioned stimulus (which produces a natural response), the neutral stimulus slowly becomes conditioned and produces (by itself) the natural (and desired) response. Based on classical conditioning, *systematic desensitization* is a therapy usually used to treat phobias by teaching the client how to remain relaxed when presented with the feared object or situation. The therapist and client develop a hierarchy of the feared object or situation and work from the least feared to the most feared object or situation. Slowly, the client is able to remain relaxed, even in the presence of the highly feared situation (e.g., holding a previously feared snake in one's hands). The goal of *flooding and implosive therapy,* based on classical extinction, is to reduce the fear or anxiety response by exposing the client to an intensive level of the anxiety-provoking stimulus. As with all behavioral therapies, the goal is to change behavior. The difference between flooding and implosive therapy is that while flooding exposes the client to a live representation of the feared stimuli, implosive therapy uses the client's imagination to carry out the extinction of the fear and anxiety. The goal is to enable the client to extinguish his or her own anxiety responses. The goal of *aversive counterconditioning therapy* is to eliminate an undesired behavior by repeatedly pairing it with an aversive stimulus (i.e., a stimulus that elicits an unpleasant response). Here, the client learns to avoid the undesired or maladaptive behavior.

Several behavior therapies also are based on the theory of operant conditioning, which asserts that behaviors are likely to occur when they are reinforced and unlikely to occur when they are punished. In *reinforcement therapy,* response consequences are applied such that the person is rewarded for performing the desired or target behavior (positive reinforcement), punished for performing the undesired or maladaptive behavior, or negatively reinforced by allowing avoidance or escape from an aversive experience. One commonly used behavior therapy is *token economy,* in which operant conditioning principles are applied in a group environment. The limitation of behavior therapy is that behavior therapy may change behavior but it doesn't change feelings and thoughts. Another criticism is that insight is not encouraged because the symptoms, rather than their causes, are treated. For more information, see Pavlov (1902). *See also* Classical Conditioning; Cognitive Behavioral Therapy (CBT); Operant Conditioning; Punishment (psychology, sociology); Reinforcement; Social Learning Theory (education, sociology); Systematic Desensitization

Behavior Therapy *(psychology)*   Treatments that use classical conditioning principles to alter behavior. According to behavior therapy, most psychological problems are learned behaviors that can be changed by taking action to replace them with new behaviors, not by searching for underlying problems as in psychodynamic or humanistic approaches that focus on insight or self-awareness. For example, in case of a panic attack, behavior therapy suggests first to identify the signals, rewards, and punishments, as well as other learning-based factors, that led to the panic attack and then to develop new responses to the identified constellation of factors. The behavioral approach and the social-cognitive approach, inspired by Watson, Pavlov, Skinner, and others, proposes that classical conditioning, operant conditioning, and observational learning can be used to alter disordered human behavior. The features of such a behavioral treatment include the development of a productive therapist-client relationship, careful listing of the behaviors and thoughts that need to be changed, the therapist acting as a sort of teacher (providing learning-based treatments, homework assignments, etc.), and continuous monitoring and evaluation of treatment. Methods relying on classical conditioning are usually called behavior therapy, methods focusing on operant conditioning are called behavior modification, and approaches designed to change thinking patterns are called cognitive behavioral therapy. Techniques in behavior therapy involve (a) systematic desensitization (visualizing anxiety-provoking stimuli while remaining relaxed), (b) modeling (demonstration of desirable behaviors), (c) positive reinforcement (setting up contingencies to be strengthened through reinforcement), (d) extinction (removing reinforcers that usually follow a particular response), (e) aversion therapy (reducing the appeal of stimuli by pairing them simultaneously with aversive stimuli), and (f) punishment (presenting the aversive stimulus after the undesirable response). For more information, see Baum (1994), Miltenberger (2003), Pavlov (1902), and Skinner (1938). *See also* Aversion Therapy; Behavior Therapy (education); Classical Conditioning; Operant Conditioning; Systematic Desensitization

Belief   The act of deciding on or being convinced of the truthfulness or reality of a proposition. Belief involves accepting the proposition even when logic or rationality would suggest the opposite. Belief can be associated with faith when the belief under consideration is religious and requires acceptance of a system of related beliefs. *See also* Construction of Reality

Beltlining   A form of arguing in an unfair way, attacking the other person by "hitting below the belt." This metaphor comes from boxing, where the literally low blow (beneath the boxer's beltline) calls for a foul. Psychological hitting below the belt entails using intimate information against another and engenders hurt, anger, and resentment. Beltlining is a passive-aggressive form of communication, usually ineffective in conflict resolution, and it leads to ever-increasing retaliation.

Benchmarking   The systematic process of collecting performance data, identifying best practices, and implementing those practices. Benchmarking is primarily concerned with quantitative measures of efficiency, productivity, and outcomes. However, qualitative data from observations and interviews are useful when identifying best practices, particularly in service organizations. *See also* Performance Assessment

Bench Trial   A trial before a judge. This occurs when a defendant waives the right to a jury trial in a criminal trial or there is no right to a jury trial (e.g., the defendant is charged with a misdemeanor). The judge alone decides the defendant's guilt and the subsequent sentence type and length. Bench trials are generally faster than jury trials and less formal. A defendant might choose a bench trial over a jury trial if the evidence is technically complicated or if there has been negative publicity about the case that may influence the jurors. Bench trials tend to result in more acquittals in cases such as police in-the-line-of-duty shootings and those that have received media attention and speculation.

Bench Warrant   An order issued by a judge in a criminal or civil proceeding. A bench warrant is a court order that authorizes law enforcement officers to take an individual into custody on sight. Usually, a bench warrant is issued for a person who has failed to make a required court appearance or has violated some other order or requirement of the court (e.g., paying child support). If on bail, the bail is generally revoked and the person held until trial as the defendant is deemed a flight risk, having already demonstrated untrustworthy behavior.

Bentham, Jeremy   An advocate of utilitarianism, the philosophy that society should act so as to produce the greatest good for the greatest number of people. Bentham (1748–1832) is often regarded as Cesare Beccaria's British counterpart and also a member of the classical school of criminology. He formulated the algorithm for "felicific calculus," which could calculate a crime's punishment so as to be just enough to act as a deterrent and not as excessive vengeance. He is also the inventor of the panopticon, a circular prison design with an officer tower in the center so that all cells could be viewed at any time. **See also** Utilitarianism (political science)

Best Practices and Effective Schools Since the identification of "effective-school correlates" (clear school mission, high expectations for success, instructional leadership, frequent monitoring of student progress, opportunity to learn and student time on task, safe and orderly environment, and home-school relations) in 1979 by the Harvard researcher Ron Edmonds, much research has been conducted on what are the best practices that contribute to effective schools. Among these best practices are a positive school climate and strong leadership, which support teacher behaviors such as planning, classroom management, and instruction. These teacher behaviors, in turn, promote student success, involvement, and appropriate coverage of necessary content. The result of these best practices is improved student achievement.

Research indicates that a positive school climate can be created through an emphasis on academics, an orderly environment, and clearly stated expectations for success. The leadership processes that help build and maintain a positive school climate are consensus building, modeling, and feedback. Because leadership is so important to effective schools, research has shown that behaviors common to principals of effective schools include (a) being supportive of good teaching, (b) building healthy relationships with parents and with the community, (c) being both task oriented and goal oriented, (d) being assertive instructional leaders, (e) clearly defining and communicating school policies (f) delegating responsibilities to others, and (g) communicating expectations for everyone. In effective classrooms, achievement on standardized tests is linked to the amount of time a student is actively engaged in working on academic content, the amount of content the student covers that is actually on the standardized test, and the student's level of success on daily assignments and unit tests. For more information, see Edmonds, R. (1979), Harris (2006), and Squires, Huitt, and Segars (1983). **See also** Leadership (Definition and Types)

Beyond a Reasonable Doubt The standard of proof required for conviction in a criminal trial. This is a standard that generally requires a reasonable person to say with moral certainty that a person is guilty of a particular act. Lesser standards of proof include preponderance of the evidence or clear and convincing evidence, which is used in civil cases.

Bicameral Legislature An organized political body consisting of two distinct upper and lower legislative houses, which serve to check and balance each other. This type of governance became popular during the 18th and 19th centuries in Europe and in the European colonies. Bicameralism originated in Ancient Greece and Rome, but it did not come into modern usage until the 14th-century English parliament. Bicameralism originally allowed for an upper house to be chosen by the monarchy or nobility and the lower by the people, the conservative upper house serving as a check against the lower house's popular will. Other European powers and newly formed colonies also came to adopt the bicameral approach.

Article 1 of the U.S. Constitution requires bicameralism at the federal level, but it is not a requirement of the states. All states but Nebraska currently have a bicameral legislature. The Convention of 1787 established a bicameral Congress as the legislative arm of the federal government. Congress is made up of two Houses, the Senate (the upper house) and the House of Representatives (the lower house). The Senate provides equal representation (two Senators) for each state, while the House provides representation proportional to each state's population. Senators are elected to six-year terms and the House of Representatives to two-year terms. The Constitution originally established that Senators were elected, or appointed, only by state legislatures, but the passage of the Seventeenth Amendment (1913) changed this to a vote of the people instead. For more information, see Tsebelis and Money (1997). **See also** House of Representatives; Senate

Bifurcated Trial A two-stage trial, required in all capital cases, where the first stage determines a defendant's guilt or innocence and the second part decides whether the defendant should be sentenced to death. The bifurcated trial was developed as a remedy to what the U.S. Supreme Court found to be the arbitrary imposition of the death penalty in *Furman v. Georgia* (1972). In civil cases, bifurcation separates liability and damages decisions. Some states require a bifurcated trial when a defense of mental disease or defect is used. For more information, see *Furman v. Georgia* (1972).

Bifurcation The judge's power to divide and decide on legal issues presented in a single suit in separate trials. This is in contrast to severance, which creates separate suits out of the legal issues. Factors considered in the decision to bifurcate include the complexity of the issues for the jury.

Bilingual Education Refers to a wide range of program forms and services that use two languages to deliver instruction. Often controversial, bilingual education seeks to promote the scholastic success of minority language students in culturally plural societies as these students acquire proficiency in the majority language. In the United States, as in many destination countries around the world, bilingual education has become a civil and human rights matter, which both affirms the nation's multilingual past, present, and future and represents the deep historical patterns of domination and struggle over economic, political, and social control in society.

Bill The name given to most legislation drafted by either House of Congress. Bills may originate in either House of Congress, except for all bills raising revenue, which the Constitution requires to originate in the

B

House of Representatives. Bills can be public, relevant to the public at large, or private, concerning only individuals or private entities.

Bill of Attainder   An act that declares a person "attainted," or guilty of a crime, without the benefit of a trial. The U.S. Constitution under Article 1, Sections 9 and 10 prohibits Congress or state legislatures from passing bills of attainders. The drafters of the Constitution considered these bills to be an abuse of power of the British monarchy. Technically, bills of attainder under British law only refer to crimes for which the penalty is death. Anything less than death was handled by bills of "pains and penalties." It was decided by the Supreme Court in *Fletcher v. Peck* (1810) that bills of attainder should include bills of pains and penalties under the U.S. Constitution. For more information, see *Fletcher v. Peck* (1810).

Bill of Rights *(political science)*   A formal statement indicating the privileges, liberties, and rights citizens have by virtue of belonging to a community of human beings living in a society. Accordingly, these inalienable rights cannot be taken away by the state. The idea of fundamental, sacred human rights is deeply rooted in the history of Western civilization. Its significance was sharpened by the debate leading to revolution and independence in the United States and gained strength from the 18th-century Enlightenment with its stress on reason and the individual.

In the United States, the Bill of Rights consists of the first 10 amendments to the Constitution. Its origin stems from the Virginia Declaration of Rights, an influential document drafted in 1776 to proclaim the inalienable natural rights of men, including the right to rebel against an unjust government. The Declaration was adopted by the Virginia Convention of Delegates on June 12, 1776. It influenced a number of later documents: the U.S. Declaration of Independence (1776), the U.S. Bill of Rights (1789), and the French Revolution's Declaration of the Rights of Man and of the Citizen (1789). The Declaration of the Rights of Man and of the Citizen is a document defining a set of individual and collective rights of all the estates (clergy, aristocracy, and all the rest of male France) as universal, brought on by the French Revolution.

This statement of rights sets up the boundaries of the state's power to avoid denying rights to the citizenry. The French Declaration of 1789 together with the U.S. Constitution stand out as the most enlightened statements protecting the fundamental rights of humankind. Also of significance is the Charter or Fundamental Laws of West New Jersey (1677), which guaranteed the right of due process to the individual.

Through its Bill of Rights, the U.S. Constitution is often used as the best example for stating the rights of its population. For example, the Fifth Amendment guarantees due process before the law and, therefore, prohibits discrimination based on any social ground. The Bill of Rights cannot be changed by written law (statutory law) as it is considered to be a "higher law." For more information, see Mervin (2003b) and Patrick, Pious, and Ritchie (2001). *See also* Constitution (political science)

Bill of Rights *(sociology)*   The first 10 amendments of the U.S. Constitution, generally considered the most important and basic personal freedoms guaranteed to each person by the federal government. Added to the Constitution on December 15, 1791, they are also the main source of the standards for procedural law. Most notable to the criminal justice system are (a) the First Amendment right to freedom of speech, the press, and religion; (b) the Second Amendment right to bear arms; (c) the Fourth Amendment right against illegal searches and seizures; (d) the Fifth Amendment right against self-incrimination, protection from double jeopardy, or being tried for the same crime twice; (e) the Sixth Amendment right to a speedy and public trial, a trial by jury, and the right to counsel; and (f) the Eighth Amendment right against cruel and unusual punishment and excessive bail. The Fourteenth Amendment, or Due Process Clause or Incorporation Amendment, assures that these rights are guaranteed by the states as well. *See also* Constitution (sociology)

Biofeedback   The feedback provided to people about their internal bodily functions, which aims to give some degree of voluntary control over physiological processes. Individuals are attached to monitoring devices that provide them with constant information about their physiological functioning. Rising tones, for example, may signal an increase in heart rate. People can thus learn strategies to modify their physiological functions, including their heart rates, blood pressure, muscle tension, body temperature, and brain wave patterns through, for example, electromygraphic or thermal feedback. Research supports the effectiveness of biofeedback in the treatment of incontinence and chronic pain, among others. For example, thermal feedback has proven particularly useful in treating migraine headaches. For more information, see Sarafino and Goehring (2000). *See also* Biopsychology; Electroencephalograph (EEG)

Biological Diversity   The earth is composed of several different types of biological systems. Included in this category are plants, animals, and various microorganisms. Biological diversity refers to the wide range of species found in the various biological systems. In addition to species, the earth is composed of different ecosystems, such as the desert and the rain forest. Therefore, biological diversity actually includes both the various species and the ecosystems in which they can be found. The term, also referred to as biodiversity, considers the assortment of species resulting from thousands of years of evolution. The different species contribute to the maintenance of the ecosystem in which they are found, making the existence of various species a central component of the survival of ecosystems. Climate changes and actions of human beings are believed to have a negative impact on biological diversity, causing extinctions of different species and the destruction of ecosystems. However, efforts are being made by governments, scientists, and citizens to regulate human activities and preserve biological diversity. *See also* Ecosystem

Biopsychology The psychological specialty that investigates the physical and chemical processes that cause and occur as a response to behavior and mental processes (also called physiological psychology, neuroscience, or biological psychology). For example, biological psychologists have found that patients experiencing hallucinations, in the form of hearing voices or seeing things, exhibit brain activity in those regions that process auditory and visual information. Research methods include the enhancement of neural functions through electrical stimulation, psychopharmacological manipulation, or transcranial magnetic stimulation or the disablement of certain neural functions via electrolytic, chemical, or other forms of lesions. Neural activity is often measured by functional magnetic resonance imaging (fMRI); electroencephalography (EEG), or the measurement of single neurons; and functional neuroanatomy. In humans, research often focuses on patients with brain damage. Especially for clinical psychology and psychopharmacology, the investigation of the link between neural activity and pathological symptoms promotes the understanding and treatment of psychological diseases and has contributed important therapeutic data to a variety of conditions, including Parkinson's disease, Huntington's disease, Alzheimer's disease, depression, schizophrenia, autism, and anxiety. For more information, see Pinel (2005). *See also* Biofeedback; Electroencephalograph (EEG); Magnetic Resonance Imaging (MRI)

Biosphere The zone of the earth in which life occurs. All living organisms, including plants, animals, and man, are found in the biosphere, which comprises air, land, and water. This zone of the earth, about 10 kilometers in total, stretches from a thin layer of crust below the earth's surface into the atmosphere just above the earth's surface. The biosphere, which contains all the earth's ecosystems and different forms of life, evolved approximately 4 billion years ago. All living things found in this zone of the earth rely on each other and the surrounding environment for survival.

Human actions have resulted in a notable impact on the biosphere. In particular, the activities of the human race have contributed to environmental problems such as pollution and the extinction of species. It is integral to the future survival of the biosphere to alleviate some of the negative consequences of the increasing human population. Preservation of the earth's ecosystems is necessary for the survival of the earth's natural resources.

Bipartisanship A term used when two opposing parties in a political system support a legislative act. In the United States, bipartisanship support refers to having both Republican and Democratic sponsorship. Bipartisanship can be formed from the outset, having a house member of each party sponsor the legislation, or it can be achieved through eventual compromise. Bipartisanship is notorious for slowing down the legislative process, with eventual legislative gridlock the feared result. For this reason, congressional committees are oftentimes purposefully formed on a bipartisanship basis. At the federal level, bipartisan support for a measure is variable, depending on the political issue at hand and in which house of Congress the act is up for vote. For example, bipartisanship in Congress is often associated with foreign policy and national security issues.

Bipolar Disorders Formerly known as manic depression, the term is used to describe mood swings that alternate between periods of elevated or euphoric mood (manic episodes) and periods of depression. Between these poles, periods of normal moods can occur. During a manic episode, people become restless, excited, and talkative; spend lavishly; become involved in sexual escapades; and may appear, among other things, out of character with their usual personalities. Other symptoms are rapid speech, flight of ideas (changing topics repeatedly), and an inflated sense of self-worth to the point of delusion. During these periods, they may have boundless energy and little need for sleep. After the transition into the depressive episode, they feel hopeless and are in despair. During this transition, some people commit suicide to avoid falling into the depression that they anticipate. About 1% of the population of the United States suffers from bipolar disorders. Currently, no single cause for bipolar disorders can be identified, although it is assumed to have a very strong hereditary aspect. Medication usually aims at stabilizing the mood to prevent relapses into manic or depressive episodes. The most prominent drugs to stabilize mood are based on lithium. Treatment of the manic episode may require the use of antipsychotic drugs (e.g., quetiapine, olanzapine, or chlorpromazine). For more information, see Sachs, Koslow, and Ghaemi (2000). *See also* Antipsychotic Drugs; Depression (psychology); Lithium; Mood Disorder; Psychopharmacology

Black Economy Otherwise known as the underground, informal, illegal, or parallel economy, in which illegal and unreported economic activities take place. The precise size of an underground economy is usually not known because economic activities are surreptitious. Policymakers try to have an understanding of the underground economy by estimating illegal and unreported activities.

The economic activities in the underground economy are diverse and include trade in stolen goods, drug trafficking, prostitution, gambling, smuggling, tax evasion (avoidance), unreported income from work, and unreported illegal payments to workers. In some countries, the shadow economy has progressively

B

expanded over the years, and this growth is strongly reflected in the shadow labor economy.

There are various propitious conditions for a black economy. Countries with relatively low tax rates, fewer laws and regulations, and an evident respect for the rule of law tend to have a comparatively smaller shadow economy. On the other hand, higher tax rates and social security contributions tend to provide a disincentive to report income and taxes.

Taxation and government regulation may contribute to the creation of shell corporations and the offshoring of businesses. Regulations include license requirements, environmental laws, and laws regulating working conditions, which might impose severe start-up and variable costs.

It must be noted that the general motives for the black economy are debatable. Some economists have argued that discriminatory enforcement of regulation and poor governance have more explanatory power over the shadow economy than taxes. Notwithstanding the motives of the underground economy, its presence has significant effects on the official economy.

Transactions in the underground economy are conducted in cash, which increases the propensity to demand money, potentially causing a demand-pull inflation. Studies that have focused on the effect of the shadow economy and its growth have generally ended in inconclusive results. Some studies indicate that the shadow economy depresses growth, while others reach a contrary conclusion.

Studies that conclude that the shadow economy is adversarial draw attention to a shrinking revenue base of government, which constrains spending on social services and the infrastructure to depress the level of employment in the official sector. It is possible for the underground economy to generate procyclical tendencies that prolong cycles of economic performance.

Recipients of unemployment benefits who take jobs in the parallel sector cause distortions that make it difficult to stabilize the national economy. Lucrative multiple payments have the effect of enlarging the shadow economy rather than minimizing it.

Economists use direct and indirect approaches to measure the underground economy. Direct approaches include sample survey and tax audits, while indirect approaches include national income statistics, labor force statistics, and currency demand. For more information, see Schneider and Enste (2002). **See also** Corruption (economics); Gross Domestic Product; Growth; Macroeconomics

Blame   To hold someone or something accountable for one's deeds or misdeeds. Blame does not necessarily imply the truth but is the tendency to censure and lay responsibility on someone for a wrongful action. Blame can take the form of outright condemnation and frequently involves lying. Blame can also be applied to groups and is often seen in organizations and bureaucracies when managers do not take full responsibility for

their decisions and actions. Gerald Weinberg, a noted systems theorist, believed that the flow of blame in any organization was a clear indicator of the health of the organization. Weinberg further stated that a sign of a dysfunctional organization was blame flowing downward from management to staff. For more information, see Weinberg (1975).

Block Scheduling   The term used for scheduling of fewer but longer classes to increase in-class time length for students in middle or high school. Advocates point out that it allows more in-class time by avoiding period-switching delays, more electives to be taken over the year, and more class content to be covered in comparison with traditional daily schedules. It has been criticized for exceeding students' attention spans and producing long time periods in which students are not taught some subjects.

Blog/Blogging   The abbreviated but commonly used form of weblog, a type of Web site that delivers frequently updated information, usually in reverse chronological order. Both terms were first used in the late 1990s, when blogs were generally started by individuals posting personal information and opinions, in contrast to commercial or institutional Web sites. As free, user-friendly blogging software programs were developed, vastly increasing numbers of people started blogs, eventually creating a digital community known as the "blogosphere." Bloggers range from personal diarists, read by a few loyal followers, to staffers of mainstream news organizations, followed by millions. Blogs are characterized by regular and frequent updates, the inclusion of numerous hyperlinks, and, often, comments posted by readers. As the future of traditional journalism came into question with the popularity of online newspapers and with escalating criticism of media monopolies, blogs—perceived by many as an inherently democratic medium—have taken on a more prominent role in mass communication. **See also** Internet; Journalism; Networking; Twitter

Blue Laws   Laws designed to enforce moral standards, particularly that Sunday is a day of rest or worship. The laws prohibit specific activity, such as sale of alcohol or hunting on Sunday. Most blue laws are no longer enforced or have been repealed.

Body Language   The conveyance of emotions and attitudes through conscious and unconscious expressions, gestures, and movements. Body language is more formally known as kinesics and is considered to be a form of nonverbal communication.

Among the better-known "figures of speech" in body language are stare downs, which establish dominance; hunched or droopy shoulders, which indicate timidity or discouragement; raised eyebrows, which express surprise or fear; and arms crossed in front of the body, which shows defensiveness.

Body language—both in its expression and its interpretation—often is cultural. While looking someone straight in the eye may be interpreted as straightforward behavior in America, it might be interpreted as rude and intrusive in certain Asian cultures. In America, a salute normally indicates respect, while a raised clenched fist signals resistance. For more information, see Beattie (2003) and Fast (1971). ***See also*** Nonverbal Communication; Nonverbal Dominance

Booking   The process of making a record of a suspect's arrest. On being taken into custody, a suspect will be searched and his or her personal information, fingerprints, and photograph will be taken. Information about the alleged crime will be noted, and a criminal background check will be conducted. The suspect is then generally placed in a police holding cell or local jail.

Boot Camp   Modeled after military training camps, boot camps have been used in the U.S. penal system since the 1980s. Also referred to as shock incarceration, boot camps are an alternative to prison that may be offered to young, first-time, or low-level offenders. The time served, generally between 90 and 180 days, is significantly shorter than a prison sentence. The activities include military-style marching and exercising as well as mandatory education and counseling programs. While less expensive than traditional incarceration, research has failed to demonstrate that boot camps are a more effective correctional tool.

Borderline Personality Disorder (BPD)   A disorder that is characterized by a lack of stability in interpersonal relationships, in the self-image, as well as in emotion. People with BPD tend to be impulsive and prone to angry outbursts, have an intense fear of abandonment, and frequently display suicidal gestures or report suicidal ideation. The prevalence of BPD varies between 1% and 2% in the general population. A number of studies suggest a link between childhood abuse, trauma, and the development of BPD, as well as a strong influence of a genetic predisposition. BPD can be treated with several specific forms of psychotherapy (e.g., dialectical behavior therapy), with varying degrees of success. In general, treatment, especially hospitalization, is very difficult due to the demanding personality attributes of the patient, especially in a therapist-patient relationship. Medication with antidepressant and antipsychotic drugs has been shown to have some effect. For more information, see Gunderson (2001). ***See also*** Antidepressants; Antipsychotic Drugs; Personality; Personality Disorders; Psychoanalysis

Bossism   The name given to an American political system in which corrupt politicians, also known as "political bosses" or "political machines," engaged in rampant patronage and corruption. Bossism was common in the Northeastern cities from the early 20th century until the 1940s. Industrialization, coupled with large-scale immigration, created fertile grounds for political bosses who met immigrant job demands with civil service positions. Since the early 1950s, political reformers and the increased intervention of state and federal government into local politics have curbed—but not wholly eliminated—the workings of political machines. One of the most infamous bosses include William M. "Boss" Tweed, who held influential jobs in New York City from 1865 to 1871, including as public works commissioner, state senator, and Grand Sachem of the Tammany Hall Society (Democratic Party Club). He engaged in rampant patronage, vote-buying, and embezzlement schemes. It is estimated that the Tweed ring bilked the city of $75 million to $200 million, an enormous sum for the period.

Boundary   A type of border or limit. A boundary is the feature that separates two or more connected entities. Boundaries can be artificial or natural, with the former being constructed and the latter being more physically noticeable. A boundary is typically thought of as the border between states or between countries, and throughout history, disputes, battles, and wars have been fought over these sometimes artificial lines.

Bounded Rationality (*economics*)   In modeling complex human behavior to obtain utility maximization, economists normally assume that humans are rational. Being rational presupposes the ability to process substantive information. This assumption enables economists to achieve optimal results (the best outcomes given substantive limitations) in order to make inferences about human behavior and utility maximization.

The theory of bounded rationality maintains that humans do not entirely behave in a rational way to maximize utility because the information to make rational decisions is not always adequate or available. Apart from the claim to rationality, the theory holds that humans are equally emotional, and therefore, they make choices that are based on emotions rather than rules of logic.

Utility, or profit maximization, is further complicated by multiple objectives or alternatives with consequences for choice. As such, the limitation of information compels decision makers to follow a heuristic procedure rather than one based on formal rules of logic or rationality. In effect, rationality is bounded or restricted somehow.

The leading proponent of bounded rationality, Herbert Simon, a political scientist, argues that humans use common sense rather than complex rational theories to make decisions. He maintains that humans make complex decisions that do not lend themselves to the computation of expected alternative utilities, and as such, decision outcomes are contingent on the decision-making processes.

Rather than promoting utility or profit maximization, utility or profit satisficing (compromise choices) is strongly advocated by the theory of bounded rationality to suggest that in the absence of all pertinent

B

information, it will suffice to make use of the best available information in order to arrive at economic outcomes. The satisficing theory tends to do well in the study of corporate behavior, where complete information about costs and revenue tends to be ex post rather than ex ante.

Bounded rationality exhibits inherent weaknesses. Heuristic procedures do not apparently differentiate between complex and simple choices, and there is a considerable problem with isolating individual decisions or choices from institutionalized ones. Critics of bounded rationality argue that the social context in which people act and interact inures on institutional performance but that this context is not given adequate consideration by the theory.

Contemporary innovation imposes limitations on the applicability of the theory because bounded rationality applies to some situations that do not take adequate consideration of novelty and creativity. When innovation or creativity becomes substantive, it becomes impractical for rationality to be bounded. For more information, see Dequech (2001), and Simon (1947). *See also* Innovation (economics); Profit; Rational Expectations; Satisficing (public administration); Utility

Bounded Rationality *(education)*   A decision-making model developed by economist Herbert A. Simon that describes how individuals make decisions in the real world. The classical model of decision making assumes that decision makers have complete information upon which to make optimally rational decisions, whereas this descriptive theory recognizes the limitations of human information-processing capabilities. In reality, decision makers have limited time, resources, and information, all of which contribute to conditions of uncertainty. Uncertainty exists when all possible alternative courses of action cannot be identified, when the probable consequences of each alternative cannot be calculated, and when the consequences of every alternative cannot be compared. Under conditions of bounded rationality, individuals search for plausible alternative courses of action until an acceptable alternative is identified. Simon refers to this selection process as *satisficing*: selecting a satisfactory alternative rather than searching until the optimal solution is found. For more information, see Simon (1979).

Bounded Rationality *(public administration)*   The classical thinkers, such as Bentham and Beccaria, assumed that human beings were each "perfectly rational" entities. This presumed that each individual had all the information necessary to make perfectly rational decisions, based on perceived costs and benefits. This state of "hyperrationality" is subsumed into most economic models, along with the assumption that people would not behave in a way that violated their preferences.

Ostensibly, the process of rational choices and decisions involves selecting the best alternative among two or more options, given the preferences for the choices and the assumed benefits resulting from the consequences of those choices. The process can be simplified into three steps: (1) identification of the alternative choices, (2) assessing the likely outcomes resulting from each alternative, and (3) determining which choice will yield the greatest efficacy. In reality, there is a limited likelihood that all potential alternatives will be properly listed, weighted, and evaluated.

Herbert Simon, winner of the 1978 Nobel Prize in Economics, is believed to have first coined the term *bounded rationality* in his text *Models of My Life*. His argument was that people are not "hyper" rational but merely partly so. He argued that the world is a much larger and complex place than individuals can fully comprehend; moreover, their ability to rationalize is therefore bound by their experiences, time, and, cognitive capabilities; nonetheless, they desire to logically situate situations so as to make choices with a *rationale*.

Simon argued that the actors and entities would develop models and procedures for decision making whereby the best result could be approximated. According to Simon, agents and entities make decisions with imperfect information and therefore make errors of expected utility, and this leads to inferior decision making. Simply stated, Simon argued that the agent's ability to make purely rational decisions is bound by the limitations of the human mind and the specific structure and cognitive capacity of the individual's mind. For more information, see Simon (1991). *See also* Utility

Bow Street Runners   In 1749, Henry Fielding founded what is widely regarded as London's first professional, organized police force. It consisted of formally paid constables who served writs (written orders from a judicial body) and made arrests by traveling throughout the country on behalf of the Bow Street magistrate, or judge. The Bow Street Runners replaced "thief catchers," who were unorganized and prone to corruption by the offenders they were pursuing. In 1792, additional offices based on the Bow Street model were put in place, serving as the basis for the future Scotland Yard.

Brain (Encephalon)   Control center of the central (brain and spinal cord) and peripheral (somatic and autonomic) nervous system. It is anatomically dominated by the cerebral hemispheres (telencephalon), sitting atop the brainstem. The brain tissue is folded into gyri, which are separated by furrows (sulci), thereby increasing the cerebral surface area. The major sectors of the cerebral hemispheres are the frontal, parietal, temporal, and occipital regions (or lobes). The outer shell of the brain is called the cerebral cortex. The cortex is responsible for the more abstract "higher" functions, in contrast to the "lower" parts of the brain, which are involved in respiration and heart rate. The occipital cortex receives visual information, while most sound information reaches the temporal lobe, and information about touch is processed by the parietal lobe. The frontal lobe is crucial for motor control. A large bundle of axons (corpus callosum) connect the brain hemispheres. Anatomically, two distinct cell bodies can be identified: (1) white matter, referring to bundles of nerve fibers, and (2) gray matter, referring to areas rich in cell bodies. The brain can be divided on the basis of its ontogenetic development into the forebrain (prosencephalon), midbrain (mesencephalon), and hindbrain (rhomben-cephalon). After these general regions, the cerebral hemispheres develop (telencephalon) and then a further region of the forebrain (diencephalon), including structures such as the thalamus and the hypothalamus. Next, two divisions in the hindbrain develop, the beginnings of the cerebellum (metencephalon), and the bridge (pons) and the medulla (myelencephalon). The midbrain, pons, and medulla are usually called the brainstem. These five general areas can further be divided into nuclei, tracts, and other specific structures. Most structures can be found both in the left and in the right hemisphere. Apart from ontogenesis, the brain can also be divided into functional regions. For example, the basal ganglia are a group of six subcortical nuclei, which form a neural system important for motor control, particularly automated or involuntary movements, and have been associated with Parkinson's disease. The limbic system, a widespread group of brain nuclei, is involved in the mechanisms of emotion, learning, and memory. The brain and its functions are usually investigated with imaging techniques such as functional magnetic resonance imaging (fMRI), positron emission tomography (PET), and electroencephalography (EEG). Behavioral tests can help identify certain impairments in the brain, and anatomical (post mortem) analysis of brain tissue can further specify their location of origin. For more information, see Pinel (2005). ***See also*** Basal Ganglia; Brainstem; Central Nervous System (CNS); Electroencephalograph (EEG); Magnetic Resonance Imaging (MRI)

Brainstem The midbrain (mesencephalon), bridge (pons), and medulla together constitute the brainstem. It can be considered one of the phylogenetically oldest parts of the human brain. Several main functions of the brainstem can be distinguished. First, all peripheral information (ascending pathways) to the cerebrum or cerebellum has to pass through the brainstem. Likewise, all descending pathways (mostly from the upper motor neurons) either have to pass through the brainstem or originate in its nuclei to connect to the spinal cord. Furthermore, the brainstem has integrative functions involved in cardiovascular control, pain sensitivity, alertness, and consciousness. Due to this crucial integrative nature of the brainstem, damage to this organ is followed by symptoms such as visual distur-bance, changes in sensation, problems in coordinating movement, and hearing problems. For more infor-mation, see Pinel (2005). ***See also*** Brain (Encephalon); Cerebellum; Medulla; Pons

Brainstorming *(communication)* The process of stimulating ideas. This can occur in the context of inves-tigating conflict in communication, as a means of problem solving, or it can be used in an intrapersonal or group setting to produce ideas for a project. The goal of brainstorming is to produce understanding of a situation. ***See also*** Consensus (communication)

Brainstorming *(public administration)* A widely used technique to encourage creative thinking in public policy or organizational change. The aim is to generate new ideas and proposals in order to address a policy problem and foster policy action. Brainstorming is often conducted in informal meetings between people who have a shared interest in solving a problem. The brainstorming process entails generating a list of policy alternatives. Ideas are generated and listed without critique or evaluation. The second phase of brain-storming is to narrow down the list to several options that are worthy of more in-depth discussion and potential action. Brainstorming can also be refined to include written suggestions rather than an open meeting with discussion. ***See also*** Policy (public administration); Policy Analysis

Breaking and Entering The criminal act of going into a residence or other property with force and without authorization. This is also considered illegal trespassing in some jurisdictions. Breaking and entering a building with the intent to commit theft is burglary.

Broadcasting Generally, the transmission of radio, television, cable, and satellite signals to a wide audience. The term was borrowed from agriculture, where it was traditionally used to refer to the casting of seeds over a large area. Work on sound transmitting by inventors like Guglielmo Marconi in the late 19th century and, later, Lee De Forest and Edwin Armstrong eventually led to the detection and amplification of radio signals. Radio broadcasting began in the 1920s and hit its stride in the following two decades, only to be eclipsed shortly afterward by television broadcasting. Within a few decades, the majority of American families had tele-vision sets. The advent of cable broadcasting occurred in the 1950s, and satellite broadcasting followed a decade after that.

Each new phase of broadcasting caused astonishing changes in popular culture, leisure time, and information dissemination. These phenomena were accompanied by the understanding that some sort of responsibility and regulation was required. This responsibility is based on the premise that the airwaves belong to the public and that broadcasters must therefore act in the public interest. In fact, case law has demonstrated that the print media enjoy much more freedom under the First Amendment than broadcasters and that whenever the public interest is weighed against the latter, the courts hold that the public interest is overriding. The broadcast industry is subject to government regulation, specifically through the Federal Communications Commission (FCC). It is self-regulated, however, relying on many of the tenets first imposed by The National Association of Broadcasters' (NAB) 1929 Codes of Practices. The term is also used metaphorically to make something known to a wide audience. For more information, see Hilmes (2007). *See also* Cablecasting; Radio; Satellite Systems

Broken Windows   A concept derived from an article by James Q. Wilson and George L. Kelling published in March 1982 in *The Atlantic Monthly*. The authors argued that neighborhood disorder creates fear and gives out crime-promoting signals. According to the theory, targeting small problems, such as vandalism on walls, litter on sidewalks, or broken windows in abandoned buildings, will prevent more serious crime from occurring. Based on this concept, the New York City Police Department implemented a "zero tolerance" policy for policing petty crimes in 1990. The 1990s was a time of significant decrease in crime in New York City, which was largely attributed to the policing approach's focus on maintaining community order and safety. Critics of the theory argue that even those cities that did not adopt this approach saw their crime rates drop during this period. For more information, see Wilson and Kelling (1982). *See also* Zero Tolerance Policing

Brown v. Board of Education of Topeka   A 1954 legal challenge brought by parties in four states to address the legal question as to whether or not segregated educational facilities for white and black students satisfy the "separate but equal" doctrine standard. The U.S. Supreme Court ruled that "separate but equal facilities are inherently unequal" (*Brown v. Board of Education of Topeka*, 1954). The separate but equal doctrine had been set by the 1896 *Plessy v. Ferguson* Supreme Court case. For more information, see *Brown v. Board of Education of Topeka* (1954) and *Plessy v. Ferguson* (1896).

Bubble   An economic condition where excess buying occurs and a run-up in prices results (referred to as an economic bubble, speculative bubble, market bubble, or financial bubble). While the exact cause of a bubble is unknown, the stage is typically followed by a crash or "burst," when prices suddenly drop. In an economic bubble, it is not uncommon for prices to fluctuate significantly, blurring the equilibrium between supply and demand patterns. Often, bubbles are identified in retrospect due to these consequences.

In general, economic bubbles are considered to affect spending power, as assets are overvalued and people tend to spend more. Ultimately, this spending pattern results in a negative impact on the economy when the bubble "bursts," as assets have been misallocated and market participants react by retracting their spending. Historically, this succession of "boom" and "bust" was evident during the Great Depression in the 1930s and in Japan in the 1980s. In more recent times, the United States experienced a technology bubble in the early 2000s

and a housing and credit bubble that burst in 2008, resulting in the greatest fiscal crisis since the 1930s.

Budget   An estimate or summary statement of expected income and outlays (expenditures) in the distant or near future. Economic agents—individuals, households, businesses, and governments—typically have a plan for future revenues and expenditures. The sources of revenue for these agents are somewhat diversified. The income of the U.S. government is primarily dependent on tax revenue from individuals and corporations.

Not all expenditures and revenues are listed in the U.S. national budget. Items that are excluded by law are referred to as "off budget." For example, some federal agencies such as the postal service and social security trust funds (old-age and survivors insurance and disability insurance) have been excluded from the listed outlays. The Budget Enforcement Act of 1990 excludes these entities from the deficit targets and other enforcement calculations, except for the administrative expenses of social security.

A budget deficit occurs when outlays exceed revenues. Conversely, a surplus occurs when revenues exceed outlays. Economists use the standardized (full employment) budget to determine the deficit at full employment when tax revenue changes. For more information, see McConnell and Brue (2008) and Melicher and Norton (2005).

Budgeting   The act of making a statement of financial position and priorities, which takes the organization's funds and allocates them to support its goals, functions, programs, or projects. The most common form is the line-item budget, which allocates funds to broad categories of expenditure such as travel, salaries, and equipment. A criticism of line-item budgeting is that the categories do not clearly identify specific projects, programs, or functions. An alternative is a performance budget, which allocates funds to specific goals of the organization and enables clear identification of inputs and outputs. Another alternative is the program budget, which allocates funds to actions that achieve the organizational goals and can encompass multiple units of the organization. Zero-based budgeting is a technique in which each unit defends its entire budget by creating a series of budget packages of alternative fund requests. Perhaps, the most prevalent budgeting technique is incrementalism, where units request an incremental increase to the previous year's budget. *See also* Bureaucracy (education, political science, public administration)

Bulimia Nervosa   An eating disorder characterized by eating massive amounts of food and then expelling the food through self-induced vomiting and/or the use of strong laxatives. Such "binge-purge" episodes may occur as often as twice a day. Like individuals with anorexia nervosa, individuals with bulimia nervosa are focused on being slender and are, typically, female.

Although bulimia is generally not life threatening, the consequences can be extremely severe and result in long-term health problems, including dehydration, nutritional problems, dental problems (from the acids associated with vomiting), and intestinal damage. The preoccupation with eating and avoiding weight gain also makes it difficult to lead a productive life. The prevalence of bulimia ranges between 1% and 3% of adolescent and college-age women. Causes for bulimia include perfectionism, low self-esteem, stress, a culturally encouraged preoccupation with being thin, depression, and other emotional problems. The role of biological factors (e.g., defective satiety mechanisms) is still under debate. Bulimia nervosa is usually treated by individual or group therapy (and sometimes with antidepressants). For more information, see Herzog et al. (1999). ***See also*** Anorexia Nervosa; Antidepressants; Group Therapy

Bullet Theory   An early theoretical model of media effects that presumes that the mass media fire messages like bullets and all individuals are susceptible to these powerful messages in the same way (also called magic bullet theory). This is also sometimes called the hypodermic needle theory, where, metaphorically, messages are injected like drugs. Although it seemed strange to presume that all individuals would react the same way to a message, theorists argued that the creators of the messages wanted people to get particular messages. Therefore, despite the varying backgrounds and social influences of the individuals, there would still be some consensus on the interpretation of the message.

Although the roots of the bullet theory are often attributed to Lasswell, who looked at the effects of World War I military propaganda on individuals, his work followed earlier studies of the effects of movies on children's play habits, behavior, and attitudes toward social issues. This work was evolving at the same time when sociologists were positing that society, largely because of the Industrial Revolution, was fragmenting and people were becoming more isolated.

The direct effects theory eventually fell out of favor when more limited or indirect effects theories became popular. A study performed in response to the radio broadcast of the "War of the Worlds," which caused great panic among its listeners, found that certain characteristics of the listeners did, in fact, influence whether they checked other sources of information before succumbing to panic. Later, Lazarsfeld, Berelson, and Gaudet looked at the 1940 presidential election and determined that people were not as isolated as earlier presumed and that they interacted within groups. Therefore, it was presumed that people were more capable of resisting messages and choosing those that were more in accord with their own attitudes and interests.

Although there is very little support for direct effects theories such as the bullet theory (any direct effects research usually focuses on cases where there is a huge amount of exposure to a message and the audience is a

vulnerable population, such as children or adolescents), they represent a milestone in mass communications studies as they represent the first phase of media effects research. For more information, see Lasswell (1927), Lazarsfeld, Berelson, and Gaudet (1944), and Perse (2000). ***See also*** Hypodermic Needle Model; Indirect Effects Theory; Industrialism; Media Effects

Burden of Proof   The standard that must be met to prove legal allegations. In criminal trials, where a person's liberty is at stake, the burden of proof is "beyond a reasonable doubt." In civil cases, where money is at stake, the burden of proof is "preponderance of the evidence" or clear and convincing evidence, which requires a lower standard of certainty.

Bureaucracy *(communication)*   The structure and set of regulations in place to control activity, usually in large organizations and government. It is represented by rules and procedures that dictate the execution of most or all processes within the particular body. Included in the structure are formal divisions of power, along with a hierarchy and the relationships that form from that hierarchy within the organization. The practice of bureaucracy can lead to informal influence. When one says that something is "very bureaucratic," the person is stating that there are many delays on the road to the solution, which are inherent in any organization that follows rules set by the same group.

Bureaucracy is outlined in the fields of sociology and political science as the way in which the administrative execution and enforcement of rules takes place in a socially organized manner. There are four structural concepts that are key to any definition of bureaucracy: (1) a clear division of administrative labor within the organization; (2) a personnel system with patterns that are consistent in terms of how people are recruited and maintained for linear careers; (3) a hierarchy among offices, which allows for status and authority to flourish; and (4) formal and informal networks that connect the organization so that information flows between departments. In addition, cooperation is emphasized between the formal and informal networks.

The following are examples of bureaucratic organizations: schools; courts; ministries; the military; local, state, and federal governments; corporations; and hospitals.

The word *bureaucracy* comes from the word *bureau,* used from the early 18th century in western Europe to refer to a writing desk and the workplace (office) where officials worked. The term *bureaucracy* came into use shortly before the French Revolution in 1789 and from there rapidly spread to other countries.

Karl Marx and Friedrich Engel mention bureaucracy in their theory of historical materialism. They state that the historical origin of bureaucracy is to be found in four sources: (1) technology, (2) religion, (3) commerce, and (4) the state.

B

Max Weber studied bureaucracy. He described the ideal type of bureaucracy in positive terms, considering it to be a more rational and efficient form of organization than the alternatives that had come before it. For more information, see Gruber (1987). ***See also*** Division of Labor; Hierarchy

Bureaucracy *(education)*   A type of organization that concentrates authority in the hands of specific administrators or managers according to a defined hierarchy. Bureaucracies often are characterized by numerous levels of authority, fixed procedures, impersonal human interactions, and clear divisions of labor. The bureaucratic model of management features a top-down, centralized model of decision making. ***See also*** Division of Labor; Hierarchy

Bureaucracy *(political science)*   A widely used concept in the social sciences. Broadly speaking, it can be best defined as a body of administrative officials and the procedures and tasks involved in a particular system of administration developed by modern societies.

The sociologist Max Weber is generally recognized as having made the most original contribution to the study of how large organizations are driven by rational management. Weber believed that the bureaucratic organization, as found in modern societies, is technically superior to all other forms of organization. The features of a bureaucracy include elements such as rules, regulations, specific goals, and specific jurisdictional areas. Regular activities required for the purposes of a bureaucracy are distributed as official duties, authority to give commands required for discharge of these duties, and procedures to carry out the administrative duties. For Weber, a bureaucracy constitutes an "ideal type," a standard to use when comparing various societies. Wouldn't our lives be driven by chaos if it were not for the orderly routine of bureaucratic institutions, such as education or health? Weber believed that the more rational people became, the greater the need for institutions based on rules and procedures.

Some observers have noted that to fully realize its significance, bureaucracy should be understood in the context of democracy as well as domination. This is because the exercise of power requires the rational operation of the means of control and authority. Also within the context of domination and democratic rule, the development of a bureaucracy heavily depends on the degree of legitimacy assigned to those in power.

There have been numerous criticisms of bureaucracy since Weber's theory prompted intense interest in the subject. The most significant criticism is the notion that Weber's "ideal type" does not really exist. Scholars have noted, for example, that corruption and political conflict could jeopardize Weber's presumed balanced system of interaction.

The most important criticism came from the sociologist Robert Michels (1911), who wrote on the political behavior of the intellectual elite and contributed to elite theory. Michels, like Weber, was also concerned about the deeply rational nature, and therefore dehumanizing effects, of bureaucracy. Accordingly, Michels believed that bureaucracies developed in the iron law of oligarchy.

Michels was much more pessimistic than Weber because he came to the conclusion that the formal organization of bureaucracies inevitably leads to oligarchy and therefore is dominated by a small, self-serving group of people who achieve positions of power. The emergence of oligarchies can occur, according to Michels, in large organizations because it becomes physically impossible for everyone to get together every time a decision has to be made. Consequently, a small group is given the responsibility of making decisions, and therefore, bureaucracies are doomed to be dominated by a handful of elite bureaucrats. It follows that this elite would aim at securing their power rather than representing all the people working under their supervision. For more information, see McLean and McMillan (2003), Michels (1911/1999), and Weber (1904/1949). ***See also*** Division of Labor; Hierarchy; Oligarchy (political science)

Bureaucracy *(public administration)*   A concept in sociology and political science that refers to a form of organization that consists of an administrative structure based on hierarchical authority-based relations. A bureaucracy is usually established in large organizations and is typically characterized by a structural model consisting of divisions of responsibilities (authority delegated among individuals, offices, or departments) held together by a central administration, a hierarchy, established procedures (written laws and regulations), and impersonal relationships. Examples of bureaucracy include governments, schools, courts, hospitals, and corporations.

The term was coined in 18th-century France and first appeared in English in 1818. While the term was traditionally used with a pejorative implication, later in the century, Max Weber became the first writer to view bureaucracy more favorably. Weber, who systematically established the characteristics of a bureaucracy, described the bureaucratic concept as a more rational and efficient form of organization than the alternatives that preceded it. He believed that the most rational orchestration of an organization involved abiding by rules in a hierarchical office where promotions and appointments are based on merit as opposed to social customs or personal allegiance. He considered it technically superior to all other forms of organization and hence indispensable to large, complex enterprises.

Modern bureaucracies developed in most large states as government grew in size and the role of the bureaucracy to implement government's decisions became crucial. While it was deemed a necessary component of a state, in practice, however, bureaucracy came to be regarded as tending to lead to concentration of power at the top of an organization and plagued by inefficiency due to conformity to procedures. Due to the shortcomings that have in practice afflicted large administrative structures, bureaucracy usually invites disapproval and implies lack of initiative, a narrow outlook, excessive adherence to rules and routine, and red tape. For more information, see Weber (1922). *See also* Division of Labor; Hierarchy

Bureaucrat　An individual who works for a bureaucracy, a large hierarchical organization or government agency. The label *bureaucrat* holds a negative connotation, implying a worker who is routine in his tasks and lacks independent thought and creativity. According to Max Weber (1991), a bureaucrat

> in the great majority of cases is only a single cog in an ever-moving mechanism . . . entrusted with specialized tasks and normally the mechanism cannot be put into motion or arrested by him, but only from the very top. (p. 228)

The first known use of the term was attributed to the French civil servant and physiocrat Vincent de Gournay (1712–1759) by his contemporaries. It was first used in English in 1818. The term is western European in origin (*bureau* [office] in French and *kratos* [power] in Greek). For more information, see Weber (1991). *See also* Bureaucracy (political science)

Bureau of Justice Statistics (BJS)　The BJS is the United States' primary source for official criminal justice statistics and operates under the Department of Justice. The mission of the agency is to collect, analyze, and make public information on crime, offenders, victims, and the criminal justice system at the federal, state, and local levels.

Burglary　A crime that involves unlawful entry into a building with the intent to commit a crime, generally to steal. Burglary is a Part I Index crime in the Uniform Crime Reports compiled by the FBI annually. *See also* Uniform Crime Report (UCR) (Part I/Part II Offenses)

Business Cycle *(economics)*　Short-run fluctuations of output and employment around a natural (long-run) rate. The business cycle has four phases, which may be sequentially referred to as (1) peak, (2) downturn (slowdown, or recession), (3) trough, and (4) recovery. Recessions could be mild or severe. A recession is characterized by falling output and unemployment for approximately two consistent quarters or more. A severe recession, such as that of the 1930s, is known as a depression. Because prices are downwardly inflexible, they tend to drop when a recession is severe.

The trough of a recession or depression is the prelude to recovery. This prelude may be either brief or long. The recovery is the phase of expansion when output and employment are on the rise. The correlation between expansion and employment may be fuzzy because of technological innovations. Some economists might, therefore, talk about an *oxymoronic* "jobless recovery." This means that a high level of unemployment does not reflect a surge in real GDP (gross domestic product). Traditional economic theory maintains a positive correlation between increasing employment and economic recovery. Unemployment that is closely tied to the business cycle is known as "cyclical unemployment," because unemployment increases during a recession but tapers off during a recovery.

There has been no shortage of theories to explain the business cycle. Some of the major theories are irregular innovation, irregular productivity, and irregular spending. To avoid destabilizing recessions and inflation, policymakers now seek policies to stabilize an economy. Prior to the Great Depression of the 1930s, it was widely believed that the market is capable of correcting itself. The severity of the depression and the inability of the markets to clear made it worthwhile to explore alternative theories: One of the most significant alternative theories is that of John Maynard Keynes, which calls for deliberate policy intervention to stabilize an economy. For more information, see Case and Fair (2003), Keynes (1936), Mankiw (2006), McConnell and Brue (2008), and Schiller (2006). *See also* Fiscal Policy; Keynesian; Monetary Policy; Recession; Stabilization

Business Cycle *(public administration)*　The periodic but irregular up-and-down shifts in economic activity, measured by fluctuations in real GDP (gross domestic product) and other macroeconomic variables. The business cycle is unpredictable and irregular. The cycle involves fluctuations, over time, between periods of relatively rapid growth of output (recovery and prosperity) and periods of proportional stagnation or decline. During some years, most industries are booming and unemployment is low; during other years, most industries are operating well below capacity and unemployment is high. The cycle is defined by four sequential phases: (1) a contraction, a slowing of the pace of economic activity—if this is serious enough, it is called a recession; (2) a trough, the turning point when the contraction turns into an expansion—if this is serious enough, it is called a slump or a depression; (3) an expansion, when the pace of the economic activity speeds up; and (4) a peak, the turning point in the cycle.

The combination of expansions and recessions, the ebb and flow of economic activity, is called the business cycle. During an expansion, output rises, employment rises and unemployment falls, new constructions increase, and inflation may rise if the expansion is quick. On the contrary, during a recession, the output of goods and services declines, employment falls, and unemployment rises; new constructions also decline. Business cycles are dated according to when the direction of economic activity changes. The peak of the cycle turns to the last month before several key economic indicators, such as employment, output, and retail sales, begin to

B

fall. The trough of the cycle turns to the last month before the same economic indicators begin to rise.

Typology and length of business cycles are:

- The Kitchin inventory cycle (3–5 years)—named after Joseph Kitchin, with four periods: (1) expansion = increase in production and prices and low interest rates, (2) crisis = stock exchange crash and bankruptcies of several companies, (3) recession = decrease in price and output and high interest rates, and (4) recovery = stocks recovery thanks to the fall in prices and incomes
- The Juglar fixed investment cycle (7–11 years)—named after Clement Juglar
- The Kuznets infrastructural investment cycle (15–25 years)—named after the Nobel laureate Simon Kuznets
- The Kondratieff wave or cycle (45–60 years)—named after Nikolai Kondratieff
- The Forrester cycles (200 years)—named after Jay Wright Forrester
- The Toffler civilization cycles (1,000–2,000 years)—named after Alvin Toffler

See also Gross Domestic Product; Recession; Stabilization

Buyer's Market   Also called a soft market, it refers to a market where there are more sellers than buyers, resulting in purchasers holding much of the power in negotiations. The law of supply and demand typically causes the lowering of prices as a result of the excess supply and abundance of goods (such as stocks, housing, etc.) available for sale relative to demand. A buyer's market can occur as a consequence of negative news in the financial markets, a drop in stock prices, or the general recognition in the market that prices are too high. Additionally, overbuilding, population decrease, or an economic downturn often causes a buyer's market.

In contrast to a buyer's market is a seller's market, which is an economic environment where more demand than supply of a product exists. In a seller's market, the ability to set the terms and prices is in the seller's hands. *See also* Demand; Supply

Bystander Effect   A phenomenon in which the probability that a person will help another person decreases as more people are present. One of the most cited examples for the bystander effect is the Kitty Genovese incident, which took place in New York in 1964. During a 30-minute struggle, Genovese was stabbed repeatedly, but none of the witnessing neighbors intervened or called the police until it was too late to save her life. A prominent explanation for why the presence of others prevents a person from offering help is the diffusion of responsibility: People think that someone else will help the victim. The degree to which the presence of others reduces helping behavior depends on several factors. With strangers, poor communication may increase the diffusion of responsibility, while being surrounded by friends increases the probability of helping. Also, the personality of the helper plays a central role, especially the individual's capacity for empathy. Furthermore, environmental factors influence the likelihood of helping; individuals in urban areas are less likely to help than people in rural areas. Several theories, such as cost-reward theory, empathy-altruism theory, or evolutionary theory, provide a framework to better understand helping behavior and the bystander effect. For more information, see Dovidio and Penner (2001). *See also* Altruism (psychology); Empathy-Altruism Hypothesis

C

Cabinet A select group of appointed government advisers to aid a government leader. In the United States, the Cabinet is composed mainly of the secretaries of different departments in the executive branch of government (State, Treasury, etc.). The role of the Cabinet is implied in Article 2, Section 2 of the U.S. Constitution.

Cablecasting Television delivered by coaxial cable strung on telephone poles or buried underground. Although the technology existed by the late 1940s, its growth was hindered by conventional broadcasters, who lobbied to prevent cable's development. Community antennae television (CATV) service, however, was allowed to serve smaller towns that did not have their own television stations. In this way, cable technology could be used to distribute distant signals from traditional broadcast systems to rural areas that they could not otherwise reach. Then with the development of communication satellites in the 1970s, the future of cable was ensured. Whereas regular network television largely developed programming that appealed to a wide audience, the proliferation of cable channels led to more specialized programming, and many of these programs had a tremendous influence on popular culture. Now the most dominant entertainment medium, cable has been blamed for the "dumbing down" of America as more people watch television than use printed media. *See also* Broadcasting

Cache A French word meaning to hide. *Cache* refers to a hiding place or storage unit. It can also be the placement of short-term information or data that are quickly accessible from a computer's hard disk. Previously viewed Web pages are stored temporarily and updated continuously in Internet caches, allowing pages to upload more quickly and reducing the burden on individual Web servers.

Cameras in the Courtroom The use of any audio- or image-recording devices during courtroom proceedings has been an issue debated across the country for decades. Laws have varied across the states on the legality of allowing such recording, usually based on the notion that a fair trial cannot be conducted with excessive publicity. Many states now allow judges to permit recordings at their discretion, and some require all parties concerned to agree. Constitutional arguments in favor of court proceedings' coverage include the First Amendment rights of the press to access court proceedings. The Supreme Court does not allow its hearings to be televised. One famous example of cameras in the courtroom was the televised O. J. Simpson murder trial in 1995. ***See also*** Reality Programming

Camera Surveillance The use of a camera to scrutinize an individual or a group. Traditional surveillance involved any means of gathering information through observation, even interpersonal supervision. Camera surveillance, on the other hand, is part of what social scientists call the "new surveillance"—that is, the use of new and emerging technologies in extracting personal or group data. Closed-circuit television (CCTV) is used to a much greater extent in Britain than in the United States. First introduced in the mid-1970s in a few Underground stations, two decades later, more than three quarters of the country's budget for crime prevention was being used to install CCTV in parking lots, city centers, and crime "hot-spots." Even in the United States, where there is much more resistance to CCTV, several cities have introduced it as part of an overall crime deterrence scheme. The American Civil Liberties Union warned that we may be on our way to becoming a "surveillance society." Very little empirical research has so far been done on the effectiveness of CCTV. What has been done suggests that CCTV does not act so much as a deterrent but rather serves as a valuable investigatory tool once a crime has been committed. While CCTV cameras are used in public places where there typically is no expectation of privacy, there is some suggestion that the ready acceptance of this type of surveillance may result in a lowering of privacy expectations across the board, the result being a kind of surveillance creep. For more information, see Staples (1997).

Cannon-Bard Theory A theory of emotion developed in 1927 by Walter Cannon and Philip Bard. This theory defends the view that emotion-eliciting stimuli or events trigger physiological arousal and the experience of emotion simultaneously and independently. The Cannon-Bard theory suggests that emotions originate in the thalamus, which is the part of the brain that sends messages from the sensory organs to the autonomic nervous system, cerebral cortex, and skeletal muscles, thus affecting arousal, conscious thought, and motor behavior. For example, if you hear a sudden loud noise while at home alone, you may simultaneously feel afraid and experience heart palpitations. Cannon stated that bodily

C

sensations alone could not evoke emotions. In fact, individuals who are injected with hormones that energize the body report feeling aroused but do not report feeling any specific emotion. In addition, emotions are sometimes elicited by an external stimulus instantly, that is, before the physiological reactions have had enough time to be activated. Finally, physiological reactions have been observed to be too vague in isolation to allow one to differentiate among emotions. For example, both fear and anger may be associated with heart palpitations. The Cannon-Bard theory originates as an alternative to the James-Lange theory of emotion, which suggests that emotions follow the physiological reaction triggered by the emotion-eliciting stimulus. For more information, see Rolls (1999). *See also* James-Lange Theory; Two-Factor Theory of Emotion

Canon Law   The law of the Roman Catholic Church that delineates the regulations and processes of the Church, such as the obligations, rights, and moral duties of Catholic patrons; the structure and hierarchy of the Catholic Church; and the administration of the holy sacraments. The first great compilation was in the 12th century under the Benedictine monk Gratian, who produced the Decretum (or *Concordia discordantium canonum* of ca. 3,800 texts), which formed the Church's legal basis (with many revisions throughout the centuries) until the early 20th century. The Canons, revised again in 1983, are only amendable by the Pope. For more information, see Malone (2007).

Capital   Man-made facilitators of production are generally referred to as capital. Capital is one of three main factors of production. The others are widely considered to be land and labor, although entrepreneurial (managerial) skill may also be considered. Examples of physical capital are computers, machines, plants, and buildings, which can be used to produce output. Physical capital is subject to depreciation over time, and in the computation of national income, allowance is made for such depreciation. Other forms of capital include financial capital (stocks and bonds) and human capital (education). Capital goods may, alternatively, be referred to as investment goods because they contribute to growth (increased output) in the future. *See also* Fixed Cost

Capital Budgeting   A key factor in long-term strategic planning for state and local government. The capital budget is distinguished from an operating budget because of its focus on the infrastructure and not the day-to-day expenses. A capital budget is concerned with long-term investments such as bridges, roads, schools, and water treatment plants. State and local governments rarely have all the funds up front to finance capital projects from the regular revenue. Since the benefits of the project will be spread over many years, so is the cost. State and local governments usually finance capital projects through debt, that is, by borrowing from investors such as banks and capital markets or by issuing bonds. The debt does not count toward determining a balanced budget. Capital budgets emphasize how government funds are used as an investment in communities and often are a part of the wider comprehensive-planning process. For more information, see Lee, Johnson, and Joyce (2008). *See also* Balanced Budget (economics, political science)

Capital Controls   The government-imposed restrictions that prevent financial investors from freely transferring financial assets in and out of a country, also known as exchange controls. Capital controls may be used to protect a fixed exchange-rate regime from speculative attack. For example, a government may require foreign exchange earnings to be turned over to authorized dealers so that it can then reallocate foreign exchange to domestic traders in search of foreign goods at government-stipulated prices. Also, foreign savers may be prevented from buying a certain amount of government securities or holding a certain amount of domestic stock.

By controlling capital, governments normally try to put themselves in a unique position so that they can encourage or discourage certain types of financial transactions by setting the prices for the conduct of such transactions via discriminating foreign exchange prices. Such controls have the potential of limiting capital reversibility while facilitating balance-of-payments stabilization at the same time.

The evidence in favor of capital controls is not entirely satisfactory. Capital controls may be seen as a symptom of financial crisis and may, in fact, lead to a self-fulfilling prophecy of capital flight. Additionally, they may foster a robust and threatening underground economy in which bribery and corruption in black (parallel) markets can make currency valuation very problematic and stabilization very painful. In such situations, the cost of borrowing capital increases considerably.

Some economists favor capital controls for incoming, short-term capital to avoid sudden reversals, but others see it as an allocation hazard and a basis for the stagnant stock prices in Chile during the 1990s. The avoidance of sudden reversals is favorable for lengthening the maturity of debt so that policymakers can buy time to liberalize capital markets and develop their financial sector. For more information, see Carbaugh (2007), Daniels and Vanhoose (2005), and Pugel (2007). *See also* Exchange Rate; Free Trade; Liberalization; Market Failure; Stabilization

Capital Gain   An increase in the market value of an asset—that is, the positive difference between an asset's adjusted purchase price and selling price. For example, when a share is sold at a price that is greater than the cost of its acquisition, there is a gain in the value of capital. Various financial instruments are susceptible to capital gain and tax as long as they are held for more than 12 months (long term) or less (short term). Federal statute specifies the minimum holding period before capital gain can be taxed. Taxable financial instruments include stocks, bonds, and mutual funds. The gain is conventionally not actually realized until the asset is sold.

Capital gain is taxed because of the appreciation of capital or the realization of profit based on the income brackets of the recipients. To encourage investment or the ownership of capital (entrepreneurship), the tax rate on long-term capital gains is usually smaller relative to the marginal tax rates on income. For example, taxpayers in the range of 10% to 15% are taxed 5% on capital gain, while those in a higher income bracket—for example, in 2009, 25% ($33,951) and over—have been charged 15% on capital gain.

There has been a recurrent opposition to capital gain tax because some critics of the tax see it as a disincentive to investment or risk taking. Lower tax rates on capital gain in the United States were originally scheduled to end on December 31, 2008, but they were extended for an additional two years. Gains that are reinvested are taxed just as gains that are received in the form of cash. *See also* Capital

Capitalism *(economics)*   An economic and social system that encourages private ownership and means of production where personal profit can be acquired through investment of capital and employment of labor. Production is generally led, income distributed, and investments, distribution, and pricing of goods and services determined through the operation of markets. The term is said to have been first cited in 1854, while the term *capitalist* emerged in 1792 but was first used in its modern sense by Werner Sombart in the early 20th century in his book *Der Moderne Kapitalismus* (1916). Capitalism is considered synonymous with a laissez-faire economy, private enterprise system, and free-price system.

Along with the institution of private property, *capitalism,* as a term, is believed to have been brought into formal existence between the late 15th century and the 18th century in Europe. Various economic transformations, including agricultural change, urbanization, industrial development, and commercial expansion, led to the accumulation and productive investment of capital. Labor became more of a commodity and new forms of social organization, used to exploit economic opportunities, emerged. Changes in economic, social, and political form are regarded as fundamental to the transition from feudalism to capitalism. Although such changes led to the emergence of capitalism, noncapitalist forms existed alongside such economic trends and inevitably shaped its formation. During the rise of capitalism throughout this period, John Locke played an important part in the development of associated economic theories. Locke argued that the right to private property is a natural right. Karl Marx, Friedrich Engels, and Max Weber also largely influenced the development of capitalist theories.

Capitalism has evolved over the past 500 years, with various concepts involved in defining capitalism, such as investments, markets, and private ownership, evolving along with changes in theory, law, and practices. Since its inception, theories of capitalism as a coherent economic system have been highly contested and defended. Proponents of capitalism emphasize capitalism's ability to promote economic growth, as measured by gross domestic product (GDP). It is argued that an increase in GDP brings about improved standards of living. It is also asserted that capitalism offers more opportunities for individuals to raise their income than socialist or traditional feudal societies.

Critics of capitalism—primarily coming from the left but some from the right and some from religious elements—argue that market exchange and commodity production are threats to cultural and religious traditions. Other contentions involve a seemingly unfair and inefficient distribution of wealth and power, various other forms of economic exploitation, unemployment, and economic instability. For more information, see Schumpeter (1939) and Sombart (1916).

Capitalism *(political science)*   An economic system that came into existence following the demise of feudalism and subsequent shift of dynamics between the proletariat and the bourgeoisie in 18th–19th-century England. Since then, the discourse on capitalism has been grounded in the works of Karl Marx, specifically *Das Kapital* (1867). Capitalism does not possess a finite form; it should be discussed within the realms of characteristics because its form and development change and depend on the historical narrative of the particular nation-state. However, capitalism's premise of private ownership of the means of production is based on the multidimensional interactions between labor and personal profit and on private owners' ability to accumulate capital and reap profits. In this structure, labor, the means of production, is provided by nonowners who sell their labor power to owners. Owners, through the accumulation of capital, gain the power and authority to shape markets and thereby to regulate profits. Arguably, the hypocrisy inherent in this structure is that rather than closing the gap, it has solidified class division, though mobility is possible and little "classical capitalism" exists today in the West. Ironically, in times of economic crisis, labor unions take large stakes in companies for a certain measure of job security. Therefore, labor becomes the capitalist. This change happened, for example, in the airline industry in 1994, when the unions ended up with 55% of the stock of United Airlines through their stock ownership plan, and United became the largest employee-controlled company in the United States. Similarly, the United Auto Workers have agreed to a large ownership stake in the Chrysler bankruptcy of 2009 and the company's plan to merge with the Italian automaker Fiat. For more information, see Amin (2008) and Marx (1992).

Capital Market   The market in which the purchase and sale of stocks and bonds take place. The capital market allocates savings efficiently by bringing together buyers and sellers of financial assets. Companies can raise money from the capital markets by issuing stocks, which are then bought and sold on the stock exchange. Also, governments and corporations can borrow money in the capital markets by issuing bonds. In addition to the capital markets, there is another financial market called the money market. This market primarily refers to banks and other short-term lenders where companies can borrow and invest money on a short-term basis—less than a year—through certificates of deposit and marketable securities. The capital market is also called the securities market. This capital market consists of a primary market and a secondary market. The primary market is where the initial offering of a company's stock is issued for the first time. Companies that want to raise money for the first time will go through the primary market through a syndicate of investment bankers and securities dealers. The investment banks or securities dealers make a market or the stock by raising the money privately and giving the money directly to the company. The syndicate or investment bankers charge a commission for their service. After this process, the company's stock is then listed on the secondary market, which can be the New York Stock Exchange or NASDAQ (National Association of Securities Dealers Automated Quotation). The company's stock is now listed on the stock market at the price determined by the market. The secondary market is where investors can buy and sell the company's stock. The overall stock market performance is linked to the economy and vice versa. When the economy is booming, the stock market will also be rising, and when the economy is in recession, the stock market will be declining. For more information, see Ehrhardt and Brigham (2003), Emery, Finnerty, and Stowe (2004), and Smart, Megginson, and Gitman (2007).

Capital Punishment   The execution of a person by the state for a capital crime, typically first-degree murder accompanied by one or more aggravating circumstances. First codified during the 18th century BCE by King Hammurabi, the United States is one of the few industrialized nations that still use the death penalty. Globally, China, Iran, Saudi Arabia, and the United States are responsible for nearly all executions. Thirty-six states in the United States employ the death penalty for capital crimes. Lethal injection is the most common method, followed by electrocution and the gas chamber. California has the most inmates on death row, while Texas executes the most prisoners annually. Proponents claim that the death penalty serves as a deterrent to murder, although extant research does not support this claim. Recent exoneration of some death row inmates via DNA evidence has produced considerable controversy about the use of the death penalty. Opponents argue against its disproportionate application to people of color. The Supreme Court declared capital punishment to be unconstitutional in *Furman v. Georgia* (1972) but reinstated it in *Gregg v. Georgia* (1976). Recent cases have

provided exceptions for death sentences in capital cases if the defendant is under the age of 18 or is mentally ill or retarded. All capital cases must employ a bifurcated process, and only juries can impose a sentence of death. For more information, see *Furman v. Georgia* (1972) and *Gregg v. Georgia* (1976).

Capital Structure   The percentage composition of a company's debt and equity structure used to finance the acquisitions of the company's assets. The capital structure of a company comprises debt and equity. This combination is referred to as the debt-to-equity ratio. This ratio is meaningful in determining the riskiness of a company. Creditors can use this ratio in determining whether a loan should be given to the company. All companies need capital to fund their long-term expansion goals and short-term financing needs. The short-term needs may include investment in inventories, payment of taxes and salaries, advertising, and basic operating expenses. The long-term needs may include purchasing capital equipment, buildings, plants, and other assets that can be used to generate revenues. Companies usually have a target debt-to-equity ratio that they will maintain. This target ratio is also referred to as a target capital structure. Companies can issue long-term and short-term bonds and also can raise money in the capital markets or stock market by issuing shares. The mix of debt and equity is carefully analyzed to make sure that companies maximize shareholder value by maintaining the right debt to equity ratio. Generally, the price of debt is cheaper than the price of equity. Shareholders who provide equity financing will always demand a higher return for investing in a company. This return, on average in the past 80 years, was about 12%. On the other hand, bond holders will expect a lower return. When companies need financing, they have the option to go the debt route or the equity route or a combination of both. Taking on additional debt without any new equity issue will increase the debt ratio and increase the riskiness of the firm if this ratio exceeds 50%. This is especially true if a company experiences a drop in sales and it cannot meet its debt obligations. This will put the company at risk of bankruptcy. Companies can reduce the debt ratio by issuing more equity, which will bring down the debt ratio. For more information, see Emery, Finnerty, and Stowe (2004) and Smart, Megginson, and Gitman (2007).

Career Criminal   A person who commits multiple crimes across his or her life span and, unlike most offenders, does not "age out" of crime. Criminal offending often begins in adolescence and continues into adulthood past the age of 25. Offenders with the highest frequency of law-violating behavior tend to begin their criminal careers at an earlier age than those who commit less serious crime and commit such crime less often. The frequency, seriousness, and prevalence of criminal offending increases with age, and predicators of adult offending are often based on juvenile offense patterns.

Definitions vary among researchers, but the number of offenses committed over a length of time is often used as an integral part of the classification. This small group of offenders is responsible for the majority of crime committed. It is estimated that approximately 6% of offenders commit most of the serious crime. The age of onset, individual personality characteristics, family relations, peer groups, school experiences, and so forth are variables correlated with the persistent offender.

Career Development   The purposeful accumulation, progression, and management of multiple factors (e.g., educational, physical, sociological, psychological, political, economic, and chance factors) by individuals and organizations to positively influence individuals' attitudes, behaviors, and the significance of their "work-related self." Development continues throughout one's life span. Career development involves continual assessment of work patterns and change within both individuals and organizations. Individuals regularly re-examine how they are affected by various factors, and they change and reevaluate their roles as workers.

Career Planning   Actions, ongoing and purposive, that are initiated by individuals, groups, or organizations to continually prepare people for the assumption of and improvement in their occupations or vocations. Planning can be multidimensional, including cognitive and behavioral domains, and can be based on forecasted skills and attributes that are expected to have marketability for the future. Careers that are planned can be traditional or nontraditional, as well as currently defined or undefined. Planning can be enacted individually or collectively. The purpose of career planning is to produce successful, productive, and satisfying careers.

Cartel   An organization of producers with the explicit or implicit motive of fixing prices and regulating the share of output in a particular market by collusion. Collusion may be overt, such as that of the Organization of Petroleum Exporting Countries (OPEC), or covert, as was the case in the Borden, Pet, and Dean Food companies. The product of a cartel may be standardized (e.g., oil) or nonstandardized (e.g., steel).

Cartels are illegal in the United States, meaning that any collusion to determine prices and output in the United States will have to be surreptitious (covert) and will be in violation of antitrust laws. Since illegal cartels are difficult to detect, only verdicts in antitrust cases involving the rigging of prices and adjustments of output can actually determine their existence. In 1996, it was determined that business executives met secretly in Europe, Latin America, and the United States to distort the market prices and quantity of livestock feed. Subtler forms of collusion involve gentlemen's agreements that are struck during informal gatherings and events. These forms of collusion are much more difficult to detect and prosecute.

A cartel is a form of oligopoly that is difficult to maintain because of the potential to cheat, mainly due to cost differentials and economic conditions. Members of a cartel cannot realistically maintain a commitment to sell at a certain price when there is an enticing opportunity to maximize profit or when the cost of production makes it essential for them to offset the per unit cost of production because of excess capacity and recessionary conditions. Cheating, in turn, is a precondition for price warfare and the ultimate disintegration of cartels.

Collusion makes a market less efficient because the price of the product sold in such a market is persistently marked up above the marginal cost and minimum per unit cost of production. Cartels are, therefore, an example of imperfect markets in contradistinction to competitive markets with long-run, efficient outcomes. ***See also*** Market; Monopoly; Perfect Competition

Carter Doctrine   President Carter's foreign policy stance to protect U.S. interests in the Persian Gulf region. Formulated in 1980, the doctrine was a reaction to the Soviet Union's invasion of Afghanistan and the rise to power of Ayatollah Khomeini in Iran in 1979. Afghanistan was perceived to be a stepping stone to Soviet hegemony in the Gulf. The twin advantages of access to warm-water ports and control over a major portion of the world's oil supplies were seen as the historic aims of Soviet foreign policy, which the Soviets were determined to realize.

President Carter and Zbgniew Brzezinski, his national security adviser, believed that these two events were a serious threat to U.S. interests, mainly access to oil resources. In the words of Brzezinski, the doctrine was "to make it very clear that the Soviets should stay away from the Persian Gulf." Within this doctrine, the use of military operations was considered to be a justifiable means to contain the Soviet and the Ayatollah's threat. As a result, the Carter administration expanded military aid to countries such as Israel and Egypt.

For many observers, the Carter Doctrine was a variant of President Truman's policy of containment in force during the early stages of the Cold War era. The doctrine contradicted President Carter's projection of his administration's determination to restore a moral dimension to U.S. foreign policy (especially concerning human rights) because it left the overarching foreign, geopolitical goals of the United States unchanged—the expansion of U.S. control over natural resources.

The major policy initiative generated by the doctrine was the creation of a Rapid Deployment Joint Task Force equipped for instant dispatch to the area in case of an attack. It also involved renewed U.S. efforts at securing bases that could be used for the deployment of military operations. Carter's implementation of his doctrine lacked force and was woefully inadequate; it had to wait for the "Reagan Corollary" to the doctrine for any meaningful military assurances of enforcement. For more information, see Evans and Newnham (1992) and Smith (1986).

Case Law   Law based on judges' decisions in cases that set a precedent for future cases. Case law is a vital component of our legal system and a major element of the substantive and procedural criminal law. Case law helps define, clarify, or modify existing decisions or statutes.

Case Study Research *(education)*   The in-depth study of one or more bounded units or systems. A case can be a single person, such as a faculty member, or a group of people, such as a college department. A case could also be a policy, such as a university grade-forgiveness policy, or a program, such as a Women's Studies program. The case study approach is particularly appropriate for answering questions of how and why. Case study research typically relies on multiple sources of data (e.g., interviews, observations, audio or video recordings, documents). Case study researchers often investigate the case(s) over an extended period of time. A case study can focus on a single case study or on multiple cases in a comparative case study. When multiple cases are examined, data are analyzed first within each case and then comparisons are made across cases, where the researcher looks for similarities and differences. Although case study research can be weak for making generalizations, naturalistic generalizations (i.e., generalizations to similar cases or similar situations) are appropriate.

Case Study Research *(psychology)*   A type of descriptive research that involves in-depth observation of one or more individuals or cases. Instead of using large samples of individuals, case studies are based on the premise that in-depth examination of one individual can result in meaningful information about many individuals. Psychologists can use many tools to obtain information about one case, such as interviews, behavioral observations, biographical or historical material, or psychological tests. Case studies have played a very important role in psychology, and Sigmund Freud, for instance, based his psychoanalytic theories of personality on case studies done with individual patients. One of the main criticisms of the case study method is that it can have limited generalizability, especially when the cases are particularly atypical. ***See also*** Longitudinal Study; Quasi-Experimental Research

Castration, Chemical   A medical procedure that eliminates testosterone production. Surgical castration, which is viewed unfavorably in the United States, is the removal of the testes to stop the production of sex hormones. It was often used during the eugenics movement in the early 20th century to sterilize criminals or individuals thought to be feebleminded. Today, castration is a form of punishment or serves as a treatment alternative to incarceration for sexual offenders. In chemical castration, sexual offenders are given large doses of anti-androgens, such as medroxyprogesterone acetate (MPA), commonly known as Depo Provera. The administration of the weekly injectable hormone decreases sexual desire, urges, thoughts, and almost all ability to engage in sexual activity. Although participation is voluntary, refusal to submit to treatment can result in probation revocation or a lengthy prison term. Side effects can include weight gain, impotence, lowered sperm count, nausea, hypertension, labored breathing, and so forth.

Catch-Up Effect   A theory of convergence that postulates that poor countries or regions tend to grow faster over time because of low levels of capital per worker. Beta convergence occurs if poor countries grow faster than rich ones, and sigma convergence occurs if the cross-sectional standard deviation of real per capita income for a group of countries is declining.

In practical terms, evidence has not generally demonstrated that there is convergence. Rich countries continue to grow at a faster rate relative to poor countries so that the two sets of countries do not reach long-run equilibrium at the same time (when investment offsets depreciation, or the steady state), partly because there have been differences in the rate of savings. In other words, there has not been absolute convergence.

Alternatively, conditional convergence takes into consideration differences in the rate of saving that will enable rich and poor countries to get to long-run equilibrium (converge) at different rates. Convergence is growth theory that is contingent on saving, capital accumulation, and depreciation. For more information, see Mankiw (2006) and Gylfason (1999). ***See also*** Growth

Categorization   A cognitive process of organizing information about people, other living matter, inanimate objects, and natural phenomena into specific groups or classes according to various criteria. Categorization helps people store and retrieve information; by using categorization, people experience a simplification of their environments.

Categorization can be likened to putting data into mental storage bins. Using inference and inductive reasoning, people categorize information important to conducting their everyday and professional lives. Researchers, for instance, categorize the results of their studies, often creating new categories for storage and retrieval of that specific information. Categorization is not a static process; as information, professions, or fields of study change, so can the names and characters of categories.

Because of the potential of the human mind, there are no limits to the creation of categories. There is much debate, however, about the maturing processes of the human mind and at what point in the life cycle a person becomes capable of categorizing. For more information, see Lindlof and Taylor (2002) and Markman (1989).

Cathartic Effects/Hypothesis   Research prevalent in the 1960s suggested that crime and violence in the mass media may be a direct or at least a contributory cause of aggressive behavior. But one point of view suggested that exposure to this type of programming may, under appropriate conditions, have a desirable, cathartic effect. The notion of a medium having a cathartic effect on its subjects dates back to Aristotle. It surfaced in modern mass communications research in 1961, when Seymour Feshbach performed a study that found a reduction in aggressive acts by college students under certain conditions. When these students were first insulted and made angry and then exposed to a film about boxing, they exhibited less hostility than students who were not first insulted. Feshbach theorized that the exposure to aggressive material had a drive reduction effect—offering viewers a release from their own aggressive potential. He did not, however, rule out guilt or revulsion as the cause for the decrement in hostility. Although there has been a modest amount of support, most research has had conflicting results when studying the effects of media violence on behavior, and therefore, the hypothesis is treated with skepticism. For more information, see Feshbach (1961). *See also* Media Effects

Caucus A private meeting of members of a political group to plan activities or policy. In the United States, Republican and Democratic caucuses are instrumental in deciding their respective presidential and vice-presidential nominees. This nomination process has existed since the late 1700s but has evolved on a state-by-state basis.

Causal Models of Aggression Media effects research models that are used as tools in inquiring into any theory that suggests that there is causation between violence in the media and aggressive behavior. Since the mid-1950s, media theorists have tried to find a causal link, but as in all causal models, correlation does not denote causality. Social scientists generally agree that causation cannot be proved but can be inferred and that the better the model employed, the more comfortably the inference can be made. Early social science theories generally stayed away from causal terminology. It was not until the 1960s that these direct cause and effect models were replaced with multivariate causation. Researchers who doubt or deny the extent of the media's effects on aggression typically point out the flaws in the causal models and in inferring causality.

Most research that attempts to link media with aggression is based on social learning theory—that is, the idea that individuals' aggressive or criminal behavior is learned from exposure to their environment and the people around them. This exposure can be to people in the media. There are three dominant types of research methodologies: the field survey, the field experiment, and the laboratory experiment. Researchers generally seek to examine any of three assertions when performing these experiments: (1) that viewing violent media content will have a cathartic effect, (2) that viewing violent media content will have neither a stimulative nor a cathartic effect on aggression, and (3) that viewing violent content

will stimulate aggression. The last is supported by causal models such as *x* produces *y* or *x* leads to *y*. Most current research, however, has looked at media violence coupled with at least one other variable, such as the viewer's cultural background, sex, class, and age. Other studies have looked at the nature of the violence portrayed and its effects: Was the portrayed violence against people or objects? Was the violence real or fictional? These multivariate theories can be supported by more complicated models represented by equations and path diagrams. Research of this nature has been performed with respect to various mediums, such as television, print and Internet pornography, and video games. *See also* Behavioral Effects; Cathartic Effects/Hypothesis

Causation A cause is a phenomenon that brings about or determines a change, an effect, or a result. Demonstrating that one thing has caused another can be difficult. Hence, causation is a highly complicated and controversial concept. Some scholars deny that it is possible or appropriate to study cause in the social and behavioral sciences. Others claim that cause in the human disciplines is no different from cause in the natural sciences. Others point out that even in the natural sciences, causal determinism is seldom clear; uncertainty rules in the natural sciences, too.

Most researchers would agree that for a causal relation to exist, some conditions are *necessary* but not *sufficient*. (To win the lottery, it is necessary to buy a ticket, but it is not sufficient.) For A to cause B, it is necessary (not sufficient) that A precede B—what comes after cannot cause what comes before; it is necessary (not sufficient) for A and B to covary or to be correlated. A correlation between two variables does not prove cause, but if two variables are causally related, they will be correlated or covary (change together).

There are probabilistic, multiple theories of cause; these contrast with simple, deterministic definitions. In simple, deterministic causation, whenever A occurs, B always occurs. Such causal events are rare at best in the social and behavioral sciences. By using the strict, simple, deterministic definition of cause, scholars find it easy to reject the notion of cause as applicable to human thought and action. In disciplines studying people, multiple and probabilistic causation is the norm. For example, inflation in the economy can be caused by the Fed lowering interest rates, by declining productivity, by rising wages, by "irrational exuberance," or by deficit spending by the government—or by some combination of these. No one of them is sufficient to produce inflation, and no one if them is even necessary. However, any one of them or several of them in combination can make inflation more *probable*. Causal determinists say that this is to confuse *likelihood* with cause; they think that probabilism expands the concept of cause to the point where it loses all meaning.

One form this debate takes in the social and behavioral disciplines is whether it is legitimate to infer causation from nonexperimental evidence. Many believe that only evidence from an experiment allows one to make justifiable causal inferences. Those engaged in nonexperimental research make causal inferences using probabilistic methods of statistical control. Experimentation does not settle the debate. For example, in physics the issue pitted Einstein (deterministic) against Heisenberg (probabilistic) in the interpretation of experimental data. **See also** Correlation (education, psychology); Path Analysis; Statistical Control

Cause   During voir dire, questions are asked of potential jurors to determine their appropriateness for jury duty. Potential jurors can be disqualified based on their prejudices or bias. If such biases exist, the prosecutor or defense attorney can ask the judge to remove the juror for cause. If the judge concurs with the challenge, the juror is removed and replaced. There are typically no limits on the number of challenges for cause that can be effected by either side. **See also** Peremptory Challenge

CD-ROM Games   Although video arcade games have been around since the early 1970s, and home video game stations shortly after that, the introduction of home computers in the 1980s saw the introduction of the computer game. When CD-ROM technology emerged in the late 1980s, the computer game industry was transformed. With their capacity to hold very large amounts of information, CD-ROMs could be used to create more sophisticated, interactive types of computer games. Their storage capabilities allowed game producers to develop multimedia games that incorporated text, video, and audio capabilities. The most popular games include action adventure, fantasy, and sports and military simulation. Most games are for entertainment, but some have been developed for other purposes, such as education or advertising.

Because of the increasing sophistication of the quality of the games and the proliferation of home computers, the U.S. computer game industry is among the most profitable entertainment businesses. As a result, the use of games, particularly by younger consumers, has been the subject of a great amount of research. Studies on their impact have addressed topics such as the possible addictability of games, the impact of violent content on young users, and the reinforcement of gender stereotypes in some of their content. A rating system for games went into effect after a 1993 joint hearing looked into the impact of violence in video games on their users. Other research has suggested that there are several benefits to video game playing. For example, it has been suggested that the interactive nature of the games helps develop creativity and problem-solving skills. Also, games have been used with some effect in both physical and emotional therapeutic exercises. For more information, see Kent (2001). **See also** Animation; Interactive Media

Celerity   The word means swiftness. In criminology, the celerity of punishment, discussed by Cesare Beccaria

in his *An Essay on Crimes and Punishments* (1764), helps members of society and the individual offender form a connection between the criminal act and the appropriate punishment. For punishment to have a deterrent effect, it should occur shortly after the commission of criminal conduct. Delays in punishment will negate the efficacy of the deterrence model. For more information, see Beccaria (1764/1983).

Censorship *(communication)*   The practice of supervision over behavior and morality. Censorship is historically inculcated in the tension of power relations, both structurally (in the Foucauldian sense, wherein institutions function to censor their subjects) and in day-to-day communication (e.g., between a supervisor and an employee). Censorship is shaped by cultural ideologies surrounding truth and is generally concerned with the control, interpretation, content, and dissemination of information. Ideologies relating to censorship include who has access to and who needs protection from information. Furthermore, the ability of an individual to effectively articulate may be undermined by self-censorship and structural censorship. These types of censorship are largely determined by the subjectivity of the individual, which is shaped by factors such as age, race, gender, and class, as well as structural positioning. Late 20th- and early 21st-century debates about censorship often occur over questioning the information found in communications media, such as books or the Internet. The power of these texts to aid in intellectual freedom (supported through literacy and critical thinking) may be sites of concern for censors, who do not want the presence of competing ideologies in their communities, families, and other groups. Moreover, critics have identified communications technologies as potential threats to face-to-face communication because of the loss of a shared sense of space and temporality. Critics maintain that the online space is contributing to a sense of fragmentation in communication and a type of disconnected intimacy in human relationships. Hence, the use of communications technologies is often subject to the censorship of parents, schools, and spouses. Audiences who have access to the content of media are censored as well, as seen in parental control software. Censorship attempts to edit (and perhaps delete) access to and the exchange of ideas, the growth of personal opinion, and the relationship of audiences to media messages. **See also** Access; Frame of Reference; Gatekeepers; Industry (media studies); Opinion Leadership

Censorship *(media studies)*   The act of prohibiting, discouraging, or condemning cultural practices that are considered inappropriate, dangerous, or obscene by one element of a culture. Censorship can be performed by any religious, political, social, governmental, commercial, or moral group regardless of its affiliations or political agenda. Through censorship, particular images, ideas, words, materials, acts, or information are suppressed (or suppression is attempted) with the intention of protecting citizens from their purported influence. The goal of censorship is the control of the free expression of ideas by labeling some types of information as subversive, profane, vulgar, or necessarily secret. Censorship is a common component of most cultures because there are always competing ideas about what constitutes appropriate behavior in every society. Even democracies are not immune to censorship efforts. The past several decades in the United States have seen the banning of books by libraries and schools, attacks on political and sexual art, attempts to outlaw offensive movies, prohibitions against vulgar speech, and attacks on music lyrics and music artists. Scientific information has also been censored by some government agencies through rewriting research reports, focusing attention away from scientific data, and removing dissenting scientists from government panels. Censorship can be enforced by laws, community values, personal example, education, economic pressure, or force and violence. Censorship can be a violation of the First Amendment right of freedom of speech, and it is often the conflict between free speech and controlled behavior that becomes the focus of many censorship controversies. Self-censorship is the practice of quieting one's own expression of ideas because of the fear of reprisals or punishments. ***See also*** Culture (communication, media studies)

Censorship *(political science)* Attempts to suppress certain freedoms that are guaranteed in the First Amendment to the U.S. Constitution, which prohibits Congress from establishing laws against the freedom of religion, speech, press, assembly, and the right to petition grievances against the government. *Schenck v. United States* (1919) set a precedent for censorship. Ordinarily, the First Amendment is upheld; however, under conditions of clear and present danger, Congress has the right to suppress First Amendment rights to ensure national security. The extent to which a state implements censorship depends on the calculation of harm, which is directly connected to the historical, cultural, and political environment in a specific time period. For more information, see *Schenck v. United States* (1919).

Censure A formal statement by an authoritative entity denouncing an individual. There are no formal rules regarding the act of censure. An individual may be censured for various reasons. In 1834, President Andrew Jackson was the first president to be censured by a vote in the Senate, 26 to 20. The president had refused to turn over a controversial document to the Senate.

Center This political concept originated alongside the left–right political groupings in the Estates-General during the French revolution beginning in 1789. When asked to choose between the left or right political ideology, many remained uncertain, thus standing in the middle ground of both political ideologies.

Center polity seeks to find a balance between the extremes at a pace that enables progression without stagnation. Modern-day centrists are also known as moderates. For more information, see Lukes (1990).

Central Agency An office of government that holds power over an area of operations. Central agencies are common in countries with centralized systems of government. Although there is a tradition of decentralization in the United States, there are a number of central agencies at the federal level. A recent example of the establishment of a central agency is the Department of Homeland Security (DHS) created in law in the Homeland Security Act of 2002 and established in 2003. DHS was formed in direct response to the 9/11 terrorist attacks; it was believed by government officials that better information sharing and coordinated action between federal agencies would have been beneficial in helping to prevent the attacks. The DHS united 22 federal agencies and approximately 180,000 federal employees under a central command. Agencies in the DHS include the U.S. Secret Service, the U.S. Coast Guard, and the Immigration and Naturalization Service.

Centralization *(political science)* A system of government in which one central authority has direct control over an area of operations. The opposite of centralization is decentralization, a system of dispersing authority to the more local level. One example of centralization versus decentralization involves the question of who holds the proper authority over local police forces. In many European nations, police forces are under the command of a national force with headquarters in the nation's capital office and regional offices scattered throughout the country. For example, in Italy, nonmilitary police forces are under the auspices of the national Polizia di Stato, or State Police, with headquarters in Rome. This is in contrast to the American system, where there is a national, nonmilitary police force—the Federal Bureau of Investigation—with jurisdiction pertaining to only certain delineated crimes. The remainder of crime control is handled through an estimated 25,000 independent state, county, and local police forces.

Centralization *(sociology)* The concentration of power in one central or individualized location or group (a feature of bureaucracies). Orders, guidelines, rules, policies, procedures, and regulations are passed down through a hierarchical structure, from the top to the bottom. Although most probation and parole departments are decentralized, most prison systems continue to use a centralized system of management.

Central Limit Theorem Upon repeated sampling and regardless of the shape of the population we sample from, the sampling distribution of a sampled statistic (i.e., mean, proportion, mean difference, or proportion difference) becomes more like a normal distribution, and the variability of the sampled statistic decreases as sample size increases.

C

Central Nervous System (CNS)   The largest part of the nervous system, made up of the brain and the spinal cord. The brain is the centerpiece of the body's nervous system and is enclosed within the cranial cavity. The spinal cord is a long, thin, tubular column enclosed within the vertebral column, which runs from the lower back up to the base of the skull. The CNS is primarily devoted to the storage and transmission of information. Together with the peripheral nervous system, the CNS has an essential role in controlling behavior. *See also* Brain (Encephalon); Peripheral Nervous System (PNS)

Central Tendency   The general term for the middle point of any score distribution, where the scores of any measurement lie between the highest and lowest scores. Central tendency is typically described with three measures: the *mean, median,* and *mode.* The mean is the arithmetic average of the scores and is calculated by adding all the scores and dividing this sum by the number of scores. The median is the middle point of any ordered (from lowest to highest or highest to lowest) set of numbers; it is the 50th percentile. The mode is the most frequently occurring score(s) of any distribution of scores.

Centrist   A modern-day ideology denoting a moderate, middle-of-the road political position between the extremes of the left and the right. A centrist believes that, in this changing world, the Left and Right movements have become archaic and are no longer functional. The centrist's views are neither left nor right and hold an ideology between these positions. The term most likely originates from the time of the French revolution of 1789, when the moderates were seated in the center of the Convention, between the radicals on the left and the royalists and conservatives on the right.

Cerebellum   A primitive structure attached to the back of the brainstem. The term is derived from Latin and means "little brain." This structure is the oldest in the nervous system, and although it plays an important role in learning, memory, and the processing of certain aspects of music, its main function is to control the balance and coordination of complex, voluntary movements. The cerebellum receives and integrates sensory information and feedback on the position of the body and makes calculations as to what muscles must be activated. Lesions within the cerebellum cause feedback deficits that affect fine movement, equilibrium, and posture. *See also* Brainstem

Cerebral Cortex   The outermost covering structure of the brain and the most highly developed brain structure in humans. Its name originates from the Latin *cerebellum* and *cortex,* which mean "brain" and "bark," respectively. Because the cerebral cortex is the newest, evolutionarily speaking, part of the brain, complex animals have larger cerebral cortexes in relation to the rest of the brain than do lower forms of organisms. The cerebral cortex is responsible for higher-order mental processes, such as thought, attention, memory, and language. The cerebral cortex is classified on the basis of topographical conventions into four lobes serving different functions: occipital, temporal, parietal, and frontal. *See also* Brain (Encephalon)

Cerebral Lateralization   The localization of brain functions attributed to either the right or the left hemisphere. Using a number of methods, researchers have collected evidence for hemispheric lateralization of the human brain. In general, the left hemisphere is believed to largely control verbal activities, such as reading, writing, or speaking. The left hemisphere, on the other hand, plays an essential role in nonverbal activities, such as visuospatial abilities, recognition of faces and other people's emotional states, and the processing of music. One of the tools used to make determinations about hemispheric lateralization is comparing people with damage to either hemisphere. *See also* Corpus Callosum

Certiorari   A legal document or writ that asks for judicial review and seeks public relief. If the writ of certiorari is granted, the senior court will review the case of the lower court for legal errors. In the Supreme Court, four out of the nine Justices must vote to review the certiorari petition.

Chain Gang   Prisoners who are chained and shackled together to engage in work detail (e.g., cleaning trash from local roads, cleaning public parks, etc.) outside the secure prison structure. Chain gangs were abolished in the 1960s but reappeared in the mid-1990s. Opponents argue that chain gangs are abusive and pose serious physical risks to prisoners.

Change Management   The systematic methodology for planning, monitoring, adapting, controlling, and producing desired change. Proactive rather than reactive management is of key importance. Change management is especially important for individuals and organizations existing in rapidly changing environments. Change management focuses on desired end states or outcomes and requires constant monitoring of performance to provide ongoing feedback on performance measures. One famous "change theorist" is the social psychologist Kurt Lewin (1899–1947), whose change management model includes three stages: unfreezing, change, and refreezing/institutionalizing the change. He argued for dynamic (i.e., changing) homeostasis (i.e., equilibrium), in which the needs of change and stability are continually balanced as the person or organization moves forward in time. Change management is supported today by management and marketing information systems, but it is always designed to produce and support the desired change or outcome. Change management does not have to be a one-time process, and it can be incorporated into an organization's plan to efficiently and effectively support an organization's mission. For more information, see Marrow (1969).

Chain of Command (*education*) A top-down organizational approach popular in bureaucratic and, especially, military organizations, in which the hierarchy of task authority passes down an organizational structure, with each person being directly accountable to the person or position directly above him or her. The organization operates on the basis of superior and subordinate relationships, and authority is based on position in the organizational structure.

Chain of Command (*sociology*) A hierarchal structure of order and discipline used in militaristic and paramilitaristic agencies. Orders are disseminated from the top to the bottom. Traditionally, lower-ranking officers must report and can only receive orders from the next-higher-ranking officer. Going outside the chain of command is unorthodox and could result in disciplinary action.

Chain of Custody The rules that must be followed during the collection of evidence. The process includes chronologically documenting where the evidence was retrieved, the person or persons who had custody of the evidence, and where it was transferred, stored, and analyzed. In a criminal case, this log is especially important to preserve the integrity of the evidence and preclude allegations of evidence tampering. For more information, see Giannelli (1983).

Change of Venue A pretrial motion that requests the transfer of a case from one jurisdiction or court to another. Transfers can be made to differing towns, counties, or states. In high-profile cases, a change of venue may be necessary because an impartial jury will be difficult to select locally. The right to an impartial jury is inherent in the Sixth Amendment and the due process clauses of the Fifth and Fourteenth amendments. When cases are highly publicized or emotionally charged, moving the case allows for more juror objectivity and prevents specific bias (i.e., making preconceived decisions regarding the case based on prior knowledge).

Change Theory The theoretical model regarding the process of transformation from one state or phase to another on an individual or system level. Individual change models focus on different factors to explain and facilitate change. Of the many that exist, some current ones rely on the following factors:

Self-efficacy: This means self-assessment of one's ability to achieve change based on prior success, physiological states, and outside sources of information. Self-efficacy determines the amount of effort an individual will expend initiating and maintaining change. The health belief model, for example, contends that individuals take health-related actions if they believe that they can successfully enact those actions with confidence.

Behavioral learning theory: Behavior is persistent because it is rewarded. Therefore, to establish change, social reinforcement must be withdrawn from the unwanted behavior to extinguish it and applied instead to the desired behavior.

Social-cognitive theory: Change is determined by the reciprocal interactions between environmental determinants, personal characteristics (such as cognition or affect), and previous behavior. Since each factor affects and is affected by the others, change efforts must involve all these factors when designing, implementing, and evaluating change processes.

Kurt Lewin, an early change theorist, posited a three-stage model for system change that is still quite popular and forms the basis for other frameworks. An underlying assumption is that people and systems tend to seek equilibrium, safety, control, and stability. Change, therefore, entails a deep psychological process that involves unlearning and relearning—a restructuring of thoughts, perceptions, feelings, and attitudes. Thus, the first stage, *unfreezing*, requires effort to loosen the status quo and habitual ways of being and thinking, overcome inertia, and create a sense of willingness to embrace change. Motivation to change must be generated before change can occur. The second stage, *transition*, is the provisional space where the change begins to occur. Lewin emphasized that change takes time and resembles a journey more than a single step. This transitional space represents the series of adjustments individuals and systems must make in their psychological and behavioral patterns to achieve the change. The third stage, *freezing* (also called *refreezing*), involves establishing the desired change as a new habit so that it becomes the standard way of being or operating. Without the process of refreezing, individuals or systems may revert to old, established patterns. Current ideas about change are influenced by the evolving conceptualization of the nature of human beings from preferring homeostasis to seeking novelty. This twofold view explains the seemingly contradictory patterns of people seeking yet resisting change. One formulation of this twofold view is found in the systems concept of dynamic homeostasis. For more information, see Bridges (1991), Holman, Devane, and Cady (2007), and Marrow (1969). ***See also*** Change Management

Channel Any means of communicating information, including memos, reports, meetings, newsletters, telephone, Internet, and the like. In technology, the term is used for a part in a communication system that connects a data source to a data sink. In radio and television communication, for example, it is a specific radio frequency—denoted by a letter or a number—that is used by the receiver to tune in to the channel. In the Internet Relay Chat (IRC) network, a channel is a "room" in which people can communicate with each other. A channel also refers to television channels and is used frequently in terms such as *favorite channel* meaning the network one prefers.

Character Education   A focus on the development of children's skills and attitudes regarding moral values. Students engage in lessons by reflecting on various common traits that are essential for good character and becoming responsible citizens. Character traits might include responsibility, respect, honesty, fairness, integrity, human dignity, compassion, loyalty, and self-discipline. The goal of character education is to help reduce antisocial behaviors through learning problem-solving and conflict-resolution strategies.

Charge   Based on sufficient evidence and prosecutorial discretion, this is the legal process of obtaining an indictment to formally charge someone with a crime. Conducted after arrest but prior to arraignment, it is a vital step in proceeding with a criminal case. States may bring charges through two processes: a grand jury, which issues a true bill or an indictment, or a preliminary hearing, which results in an information.

Charter Schools   Alternative, public, nonsectarian schools that are operated independently of local school boards. They have open admission policies and are not required to adhere to certain state educational regulations. These tuition-free schools are held accountable by the state to demonstrate that student achievement does not fall below the state average.

Chief Justice   The presiding member of the Supreme Court, the court of highest appellate jurisdiction, or the presiding member of a state's supreme court. The U.S. Chief Justice is one of nine judges appointed for a lifetime position by the President and confirmed by Congress. The *United States Code* refers to him as Chief Justice of the United States, whereas the other eight justices are termed associate justices of the Supreme Court of the United States. A state chief justice is appointed for a limited term. He or she serves as chair of the court and can influence the state's political and social ideology. For more information, see Langer and Wilhelm (2005).

Child Abuse and Neglect   The physical, emotional, or sexual mistreatment of a person typically under 18 years of age. Cases of child abuse occur most frequently in the home and are most common in single-parent households or blended families. However, children can be abused outside the home, by acquaintances or, less commonly, by strangers. Victims of child abuse are at risk of developing low self-esteem; anxiety; eating, personality, or sleep disorders; other psychiatric problems (such as posttraumatic stress disorder, withdrawal, deviant behavior, aggression); and a plethora of other behavioral problems. Neglect and abuse can also lead to physical injury and, in severe cases, death. The exact cause of child abuse is not known, but many abusers have themselves been previously victimized. Sociological, psychological, or biological factors contribute to the abuser's behavior. Preventative efforts have focused on community education and interventions for families at high risk. Once abuse is formally recognized and reported, agencies such as child protective services and the police department will be involved.

Child Molester   A person who sexually abuses a minor, typically under 18 years of age. Some child molesters suffer from a disorder known as pedophilia, which is a sexual attraction to prepubescent children. The *Diagnostic and Statistical Manual of Mental Disorders* (fourth edition; *DSM-IV*) requires that such offenders be at least 16 years old and engage in sexual contact with a child 5 years younger. In cases of incest (sexual relations between family members), the offender is most often attracted to a child at the beginning of adolescence, during the start of physical maturation. Offenders are mostly male and can be heterosexual, which is more common, or homosexual. Most child molesters abuse children they know. They often gain the trust of their victims and then make threats to keep the victim from reporting such behavior. Results regarding the successful treatment of child molesters are mixed, and recidivism rates are affected by the individual characteristics of the offender, such as previous offenses, force used during such offenses, their plethysmography score (a measure of sexual arousal), personality disorders, and so forth. Official statistics show low levels of recidivism for child molesters, though many offenses are unreported. ***See also*** Pedophilia/Pedophile

Children's Programming   The notion of children as an audience sector germinated in the 1930s in the radio industry. Like adult programs, children's programs were used as vehicles for sponsors, but many addressed social issues and concerns. After World War II and throughout the 1950s, the "Golden Age of Television" witnessed the development of children's programs that would assuage the growing backlash against what the public and lawmakers saw as too much violence on television. Shows such as *Howdy Doody; Kukla, Fran and Ollie;* and *Super Circus* were shown in the evening and were watched by both children and adult audiences.

In the 1960s, sponsors reassessed their advertising techniques and as prime-time slots became more expensive to advertisers, children's programs were moved to Saturday mornings. Dominated by superhero cartoons, these were replaced by less violent programs in the 1970s. The civil rights movement, the launch of Public Broadcasting (PBS), and community antennae television (CATV) all had a pronounced impact on children's programming. In the 1980s, when the Federal Communications Commission (FCC) relaxed its rules on commercial airtime, networks dropped many shows that were geared toward children in favor of adult programming, as these could attract more advertising revenue. In response, the Children's Television Act was passed in 1990. It stipulated that broadcasters provide proof that they offer educational children's programs if they want to have their licenses renewed. Later, guidelines got stricter, and networks were required to offer three hours a day of children's programming. These strict guidelines, coupled with competition from cable broadcasters whose specialty niche channels included children's programming channels, caused network broadcasters to look for ways to get out of the children's market. Now, networks typically lease a block of time to outside production companies or repurpose programs that were not originally considered children's programming. Since the turn of the new millennium and the advent of digital television technology, much of the focus on children's programming has been on interactivity. Concern over advertising to children in an interactive environment has led to FCC restrictions. For more information, see Bryant (2007).

Chi-Square Technique A statistical analytic technique used to examine the relationship between two categorical variables. The chi-square (denoted χ^2) tests hypotheses about the distribution of observations into categories. The *null hypothesis* states that the observed frequencies are the same as the expected frequencies. When the observed frequencies are sufficiently different from the expected frequencies, the value of chi-square goes up and the null hypothesis is rejected. However, if the value of the observed frequencies is similar to the value of the expected frequencies, the value of chi-square is small and the null hypothesis is retained. *See also* Null Hypothesis (psychology, sociology)

Christopher Commission Formally labeled the Independent Commission on the Los Angeles Police Department (LAPD) and chaired by the attorney Warren Christopher before he was the U.S. Secretary of State, the Christopher Commission's purpose was to investigate the LAPD's use of excessive force in minority communities in the aftermath of the Rodney King beating. Rodney King, who was chased by the LAPD for speeding, was beaten severely by four LAPD officers. The Commission examined factors such as use of excessive force, the adequacy of training, recruitment practices, and disciplinary procedures within the LAPD. They found that the LAPD used excessive force without following departmental guidelines and that many of the disciplinary problems and problematic behavior exhibited by officers was attributed to poor management and supervision.

Chromosomal Abnormality Abnormalities exist when chromosomes exhibit atypical numerical properties (i.e., there is more than or less than one pair of chromosomes) or structural properties (i.e., there is extra chromosomal material, or a fraction of the chromosome is missing). Such abnormalities can lead to conditions such as Down syndrome, mental retardation, autism, or Turner's syndrome. Although some chromosomal abnormalities are believed to be inherited, most are purely accidental and occur during the conception or gestation process.

Chromosomes Cell structures found in all biological cells that contain deoxyribonucleic acid (DNA) and DNA-bound proteins. Chromosomes contain single pieces of DNA molecules in the form of genes. Each cell nucleus contains 46 chromosomes organized in 23 pairs. The mother donates one member of a chromosome pair, and the father donates the other member of the chromosome pair. Therefore, the two members of a chromosome pair are not identical. Geneticists have numbered these chromosomes from the largest to the smallest. *See also* Deoxyribonucleic Acid (DNA) (psychology, sociology); Genes; Genetics

Chronemics The examination of the perception of time in a particular culture and historical period. The study of chronemics focuses on nonverbal communication. In a low-context culture, if one calls for a meeting at 14:15, participants are expected to be punctual. In other cultures, the perception of the meeting time is approximate. Social status also plays a role: Someone at the top of the organizational or social hierarchy can be late to a meeting or event and be excused because of his or her status, whereas others will be criticized for tardiness. Those lower on a hierarchy are expected and willing to wait. Chronemics is especially important for cross- or intercultural communication. A time-oriented, capitalist culture—rooted in the Industrial Revolution, which gave rise to time and motion studies—has little understanding of the lack of punctuality and organizational work habits of other countries, and vice versa.

Chronology A sequence of events ordered or listed by time, traditionally from the earliest to the most recent. Chronologies can be placed into various categories to show progression in particular topical areas, such as a chronology of correctional history, a chronology of major medical developments, or a chronology of sociological theories.

Chunking The recoding of information into "chunks." This term is used in cognitive psychology and mnemonics. Chunking improves our short-term memory by making a more efficient use of our capacity. A variety of studies have provided evidence to support the notion that humans have a short-term memory capacity of "seven plus-or-minus chunks." However, studies have also shown that we can learn to increase the size of those chunks. Most of us make regular use of the phenomenon of chunking in the way we group phone numbers or other information. *See also* Memory (psychology); Mnemonics; Short-Term Memory (STM)

Cinema A term that is sometimes used interchangeably with *film* and *the movies* but also has a larger scope.

Cinema (or *the cinema*) generally refers collectively to the entire range of activities or products related to the motion picture industry and the academic or cultural practices encompassing all movies and not just an individual film. The cinema is thought to have the characteristics of a commodity, a form of communication, a spectacle, a special effect, a tool of ideology, or an apparatus that creates the modern subject. For more information, see Cubitt (2004). ***See also*** Film

Circuit Court   A court that has jurisdiction over multiple geographical areas. In the federal system, there are 13 circuit courts, which serve as part of the federal appellate division. Cases on appeal are typically reviewed by three judges and decided by the majority. Some states have circuit courts that preside over multiple counties or towns. Circuit courts are considered courts of general jurisdiction.

Circumstantial Evidence   A compilation of information or facts from which, when examined collectively, a strong and compelling inference can be made regarding the theory of a case. This differs from and may not be as strong as direct evidence, which would include physical evidence such as DNA or witness testimony. However, many cases are prosecuted successfully with circumstantial evidence. In criminal cases, it can be used to infer guilt and in civil cases, liability.

Citizen Participation   The involvement of citizens in the public decision-making process to make government more accountable, responsive, and transparent. The involvement of citizens in the decision-making process emphasizes the role of citizens as contributors to the policies and programs that affect their lives and simply as recipients of government services. There are several different mechanisms to involve citizens in the decision-making process, including more traditional forms such as public hearings, legal and administrative arbitration, and advisory boards. More innovative and interactive mechanisms have been developed, such as electronic town meetings. Regardless of the techniques, there exists a tension between administrators and citizens. Administrators often view citizen involvement as time-consuming and inefficient, whereas citizens often view their involvement as perfunctory. ***See also*** Decision-Making Theory

Civil Commitment   The legal process by which persons can be involuntarily committed to a mental or psychiatric institution. Commitment procedures vary from state to state, but in general, a person has to fit two criteria to be admitted against his or her will: (1) the person is mentally ill and (2) the person poses a danger to self or others. Such danger has to be imminent. Formal commitment is by direct order of the court and can be requested by doctors, family members, guardians, and so forth. A formal hearing, in which the patient has a right to legal representation, will be conducted. Informal commitment can be done at the discretion of

medical personnel. Patients can be detained if staff believe that they are too dangerous or unstable to be released. Any person behaving in an unruly manner can be taken to a hospital and committed for 24 hours to 20 days by the two-physician certificate (i.e., two doctors must sign the commitment order). Detainment after this time period requires a formal judicial hearing.

Civil Disobedience (*political science*)   The term refers to actions of opposition and defiance by citizens to protest against what they perceive as injustice on the part of their government. The discourse on civil disobedience began with Henry David Thoreau's "Resistance to Civil Government," later renamed "Civil Disobedience." It is based on the premise that a government, which represents the interest of the people, is also capable of perversion and abuse, for which it is equally accountable. The injustice may take the form of a specific law or public policy, though the real rationale for action lies in the underlying structure that the unjust policy represents. When injustice occurs in the underlying structure, this theory claims that each citizen has the right to oppose and defy the government. This action, violent or nonviolent, is a purposeful denial of governmental authority with the specific intent to overthrow and draw attention to the unjust, underlying structures. Americans often label nonviolent actions as civil disobedience, though according to Thoreau's theory, the action can be either violent or nonviolent.

Individuals who have led such acts include Mahatma Gandhi, Martin Luther King Jr., Leo Tolstoy, and Rosa Parks. For more information, see Rosenwald (2000).

Civil Disobedience (*sociology*)   The denunciation of governmental rules, the refusal to obey certain laws, or a protest against policies and/or governmental action. Civil disobedience is commonly nonviolent, and protestors can illegally occupy a building, form a cordon, or demonstrate peacefully. The likelihood of arrest is high. Leaders such as Martin Luther King Jr. and Mahatma Gandhi used civil disobedience to draw attention to their cause.

Civilian Review Boards   The first civilian review boards were in New York City (New York Civilian Complaint Review Board [CCRB], 1953) and Philadelphia (Philadelphia Advisory Board, 1958). In the 1970s, many other cities formed review boards, the most influential of which were in Detroit (Board of Police Commissioners), Chicago (Office of Professional Standards), Berkeley (Police Review Commission), and Kansas City (Office of Citizen Complaints). The CCRB is the largest civilian review board in the United States and presides over thousands of complaints annually. The CCRB comprises 13 civilian board members, appointed by the mayor, and is charged with examining and investigating complaints of misconduct lodged by community members against the New York City Police Department (NYPD). Anyone who has information on police misconduct, such as use of excessive force or abusive language, corruption, abuse of power, failure to perform one's duties, and so forth, can file a complaint.

Civilization The word originates from the Latin *civilis,* meaning "citizen" or "civilized." A civilization is a group of people that constitute a culture or a community. Civilizations tend to be advanced cultures with multifarious social structures, well-developed laws, and varied economic, educational, and cultural opportunities. Its citizens share similar values, norms, and belief systems and are deemed superior to people in less developed or primitive societies. They have a highly developed political system and a greater dichotomy between the social classes than primitive societies. A civilization often expands to other areas through the introduction of its normative structure and philosophies to less advanced cultures. Some primitive societies have readily incorporated the characteristics intrinsic to civilizations, while others were forced to adapt.

Civil Law *(political science)* A branch of law that defines relations between citizens, as opposed to criminal law, which concerns relations between citizens and the state. In English, the concept derives from the French *droit civil.*

As used in the American legal system, civil law is noncriminal law, such as the law of property, commercial law, administrative law, and the rules governing procedure in civil cases. But civil law also refers to a body of law distinct from the common-law systems of the English-speaking world.

Civil law legal systems were derived from Roman law. This particular legal tradition developed in Europe and spread throughout the world as a by-product of the European expansion that took place beginning in the 15th century. European countries such as France, Germany, Italy, and Spain follow the Roman law tradition as embodied in Justinian's Code from the 6th century, and until recently, so did all of Latin America.

Civil law systems depend heavily on written codes of private law, such as the French Civil Code (Code Napoléon) of 1804, as primary sources for authoritative statements of the law.

Civil law systems differ from common-law systems in the substantive content of the law, the operative procedures of the law, the legal terminology, the manner in which authoritative sources of law are identified, the institutional framework within which the law is applied, and the education and structure of the legal profession. They follow an inquisitorial model, which involves an investigation. To compare, in the United States, custom is the primary source of law—that is, the use of precedent, or stare decisis (earlier court decisions). In the United States and its territories, only three jurisdictions are considered civil law systems—Louisiana, Puerto Rico, and Guam—but because of the strong influence of common law in these jurisdictions, they are really mixed systems of civil and common law.

There are a number of significant differences between civil and criminal law in the United States. For example, in civil law, a private party (e.g., a corporation or an individual person) files the lawsuit and becomes the plaintiff. In criminal law, the government, which is called the prosecution, always files the litigation.

One of the most fundamental distinctions between civil and criminal law is in the notion of punishment. In criminal law, crimes are divided into two broad classes: (1) *felonies* have a maximum possible sentence of more than one year of incarceration and (2) *misdemeanors* have a maximum possible sentence of less than one year of incarceration. For more information, see "Civil Law" (2006) and Merryman (1969).

Civil Law *(sociology)* This branch of law involves a dispute between private parties. Civil cases examine tort violations (breech of a duty that was owed), contract violations (breech of a promise that was made), or any other private matter. Civil cases can be decided by a judge or by a jury. The standard of proof to find someone liable or guilty in a civil matter is *preponderance of the evidence;* this is a much lower burden to meet than what is required in criminal cases. If a defendant is found liable, punishment is in the form of compensatory or punitive monetary damages payable to the plaintiff.

Civil Liability A defendant being found guilty in a civil case or lawsuit by a preponderance of the evidence. The defendant is responsible for paying monetary damages. Damages can be compensatory (monetary relief for actual damages), punitive (monetary relief as a form of punishment), or a combination of both. Such damages are ordered by the court.

Civil Liberties A concept that has been much debated and is often discussed against the backdrop of civil rights. Though scholars have attempted to make a distinction between the two, the divisions are still quite vague and unclear. Therefore, civil liberties cannot be discussed as a finite definition but rather as a set of premises.

All contemporary discourse on civil liberties dates back to J. S. Mill's "On Liberty." Civil liberties cannot be thought of in terms of specific laws and statutes. Rather, civil liberties are ideologies that one believes ought to be valued and respected. Transience characterizes these ideologies. Civil liberties are individual or group conceptions restricted to the immediate historical atmosphere accounting for the social, political, economic, and cultural period. Civil liberties are a matter of what individuals or groups decide for themselves regardless of the reason for which they do so. The positions that these individuals and groups take are a matter of predilection, and the hierarchical structure of civil liberties is determined by a calculation of utility. When such a liberty becomes a legally recognized right, it then becomes a civil right, though it still retains its status as a civil liberty. For more information, see Cohen (1988–1989) and Mill (1859/1989).

Civil Rights   Unlike civil liberties, a civil right is enacted and protected through legislation, wherein any violation warrants and gives cause for action in both civil and criminal proceedings. Examples of civil rights include the freedom of speech, the freedom of assembly, the freedom from involuntary servitude, and many others.

In the United States, the Thirteenth Amendment (1865), the Civil Rights Act of 1866, and the Fourteenth Amendment (1868) marked the beginnings of enforceable civil rights law. The Thirteenth Amendment abolished slavery and gave the right of citizenship to exslaves and anyone born in the United States. This monumental step was betrayed by the "black codes" enacted in many states during the Reconstruction period after the Civil War. Congress then passed the Civil Rights Act of 1866, which was a prelude to the Fourteenth Amendment, passed to override the black codes. However, though civil rights suits were brought to court, civil rights jurisprudence failed to flourish until *Monroe v. Pape* (1961) in the Supreme Court under Chief Justice Earl Warren. *Monroe v. Pape* (1961) held police officers, but not municipalities (Chicago, in this case), accountable for an unreasonable search under the Civil Rights Act of 1871. The cause for action sought to show that individual rights, though safeguarding citizens from the nation, only gave actionable cause against states when the nation should also be held accountable. Arguably, *Monroe* grounded civil rights litigation in the Fourteenth Amendment's due process clause, paving the way for civil rights jurisprudence. It was not until *Monell v. Department of Social Services* (1978) that the Supreme Court made municipalities liable for the actions of their officers. For more information, see *Monell v. Department of Social Services* (1978), *Monroe v. Pape* (1961), and Weinberg (1991).

Civil Rights Act of 1964   A law, signed by President Lyndon B. Johnson, that outlawed segregation in businesses, public places, and public schools. The act also enforced voting rights and prohibited employment discrimination, which outlawed hiring, firing, and promotion based on gender or race. ***See also*** Desegregation

Civil Rights Acts   Civil rights are the liberties citizens are entitled to within a particular jurisdiction. Civil rights can be written, implied, or derived from common law. When citizens deem certain rights to be inadequate or inequitably applied, civil rights movements have materialized as a way to redress such social wrongs. The United States has passed several civil rights acts. The Civil Rights Act of 1866, initially vetoed by President Johnson and subsequently affirmed by Congress, entitled all citizens, with the exception of Native Americans, to own property, enter into contractual agreements, and sue and testify in a court of law. The Civil Rights Act of 1871, also referred to as the Ku Klux Clan (KKK) Act, was passed to provide African Americans legal redress against abuses inflicted by the KKK. The most vital stipulation, 42 US Section 1983,

allows individuals to sue state officials for constitutional torts. It is the most common type of suit brought by state inmates against state prison officials. The Civil Rights Act of 1875 gave everyone, regardless of race, equal treatment in public institutions. The Civil Rights Act of 1957 gave southern African Americans access to polling places. The Civil Rights Act of 1960 enhanced the 1957 Act by passing penalties for anyone who prevented someone from voting. Federal inspectors were deployed to ensure the integrity of the voting process. The Civil Rights Act of 1964, one of the most important pieces of legislation in U.S. history, prevented any type of discrimination based on race, religion, gender, or country of origin. As a result, the Equal Employment Opportunity Commission was formed to address issues of discrimination in the public and private sectors. The Civil Rights Act of 1968, known as the Fair Housing Act, prevented discrimination in the selling and renting of dwellings. The Civil Rights Act of 1991 provided a jury trial for discrimination claims and provided a monetary remedy for emotional distress in such claims.

Civil Society   The space between the market and state where actors come together based on shared purposes, values, and interests that are distinct from those of the market or the state, often referred to as the third sector. Civil society is considered important for creating a strong civic culture and strengthening democracy. Civil society includes not only the individuals who participate but also civil society organizations. Civil society is composed of diverse organizations, including voluntary and social organizations, charities, nongovernmental organizations, trade unions, faith-based organizations, social movements, community groups, women's organizations, self-help groups, business associations, coalitions, and advocacy groups. Civil society organizations serve a significant role in informing and educating the public about different issues and their rights as citizens. They provide the foundation for citizens to request service or information, make informed decisions, participate in politics, and hold government accountable. ***See also*** Nongovernmental Organization; Nonprofit Organization

Claim-Makers   Individuals or institutions that influence audiences to think, feel, or give meaning to a concept that matches the individuals or institutions' intention. Persuasive claims are considered to be of a verbal, visual, or behavioral nature. The media industry is considered to be a claim-maker as its presentation of information to audiences has the potential to affect audiences' meaning-making processes. Social constructionist theory has contributed to the body of research on how audiences construct individual meaning. Along the lines of that tradition of scholarship, the sociologist Donileen Loeske's 2003 work *Thinking About Social Problems* examined the relationship between media claims and audience interpretation. For more information, see Loeske (2003). ***See also*** Industry (media studies); Opinion Leadership

Clan   A group of individuals inextricably linked by a common ancestor. Such links can be biological or symbolic. These kinships can be matrilineal, patrilineal, or inclusive of both lines of female and male descendents. Clans are often smaller groups within a larger tribe. In other cultures, the word *clan* can also indicate informal political or economic contacts.

Class   A group with a specific classification that shares similar or comparable properties. Social class involves ranking groups according to their income and/or social status. Most societies are stratified and have social classes that are based on a hierarchical structure, such as lower class, middle class, and upper class.

Classical Conditioning   A type of learning in which organisms learn to associate stimuli. It is also known as Pavlovian conditioning, after Ivan Pavlov (1849–1936), a Russian physiologist who incidentally discovered classical conditioning while studying the digestive system in dogs. Pavlov leashed his dogs in a harness and placed food in their mouths, after which he measured the saliva flow through a tube inserted into their cheeks. After several repetitions, Pavlov observed that his dogs started to salivate before the food was placed in their mouths. They would salivate merely by seeing the assistant in charge of bringing the food or listening to his footsteps approaching the cage. Pavlov realized that the dogs had learned to anticipate the food and to associate the food with, for example, the sound of approaching footsteps. Pavlov called the saliva the *unconditioned response* (UR) because it is a reflex naturally triggered by food, which he called the *unconditioned stimulus* (US). He then introduced a bell ring as a *neutral stimulus* and repeatedly rang the bell before presenting the food to the dogs. After several repetitions, the dogs were conditioned to salivate to the sound of the ring alone. The bell then became a *conditioned stimulus* (CS) and the salivation a *conditioned response* (CR). After this simple experiment, researchers started to condition different types of animals as well as humans to react to a variety of neutral stimuli. Classical conditioning often takes place without awareness. ***See also*** Conditioned Response (CR); Conditioned Stimulus (CS); Operant Conditioning

Classical Criminology   A philosophy originally developed during the Enlightenment in the 18th century by Cesare Beccaria and Jeremy Bentham. Due to inconsistencies and the arbitrariness of the judicial process, in addition to the widespread use of torture as a practice for punishment and the extraction of confessions, both philosophers called for the humane treatment of prisoners. They spoke against the use of corporal and barbaric punishments, which were inherently incongruous with the underlying principles of a civilized society. Certain principles characterize the classical-criminology perspective. For punishment to deter future crime, it should be certain (the offender's chance of being apprehended and prosecuted is highly probable), swift (the time between the act and the punishment should be as brief as possible), and severe. Punishments should be based on gradations of seriousness according to the nature of the crime; in sum, the punishment should fit the crime. Punishments that are too lenient will not deter future criminal behavior, and punishments that are too severe could beget more crime. Crime can be controlled through the threat of formal punishment, and punishment serves two vital deterrent purposes: *specific deterrence* sends a message to the individual offender, while *general deterrence* sends a message to society. Sanctions should encompass the principle of utilitarianism—that is, providing the greatest good for the greatest number. Beccaria and Bentham believed that crime was a rational choice on the part of the offender: All people were rational beings and made decisions based on the concept of free will; prior to the commission of an act, an offender weighs the costs and benefits of crime; if the benefits exceed the costs, crime would be the logical decision. Crime is often viewed as more attractive because it involves less work with a greater payoff, and offenders will typically choose acts that are pleasurable for them. The classical school has developed into rational choice theory.

Classical Economics   An economic theory that emphasized free-market operations and the labor theory of value in the 18th and 19th centuries. Some of the foremost thinkers of this period include Adam Smith, who published his *The Wealth of Nations* in 1776; Jean Baptiste Say (1776–1832); David Hume; David Ricardo, renowned for his *Principles of Political Economy and Taxation* (1817); Thomas Malthus, author of *An Essay on the Principle of Population* (1798); John Stuart Mill, who published his *Principles of Political Economy* in 1848; and Karl Marx.

The forerunners of this economic tradition were the French Physiocrats, who were advocates of laissez-faire because of their concern about the mercantilist philosophy of trade regulation or interventionist policy to acquire bullion (precious metals). Hume's response was that trade regulation and balance-of-trade surpluses were inflationary and unnecessary because precious metals will flow to areas or nations with lower prices, thereby defeating the purpose of regulation.

Similar thoughts were shared by Adam Smith, who argued that nations can acquire wealth and derive mutual benefits from trade if they specialize in the production of goods for which they have absolute (natural) advantage and acquire skills to trade freely. As a popularizer of Smith's idea of free markets, Jean Baptiste Say argued that there could not be a general glut in the market because supply creates its own demand; that is, products are being paid for by products. According to Say, the demand to produce goods means that money and employment will be generated in other sectors of an economy. Recessions occur when the demand for production is not evenly distributed and some sectors are imperiled.

Although some manufacturing took place, value (price) was extensively measured in terms of the labor required to produce goods (the labor theory of value). The classical economists did not quite have a consensus on value creation but espoused extensive agreement on free markets. Ricardo made strong arguments for rewarding capital and the business class to stimulate growth. He was not a passionate advocate for the repeal of the Corn Law in Britain, but he pointed out that the tariff (tax) on grain benefited unproductive landowners.

The question of value was subsequently challenged by later classicalists, such as Jevons, Menger, and Walras, who argued that value is reflective of marginal cost and benefit rather than labor, which may not even be of value in the production of certain goods. This was the era of marginalism, which became prominent in the late 19th century.

Classical economics faded into oblivion in the 20th century, when it became increasingly apparent that the market cannot "go it alone." The Great Depression of the 1930s and other related issues of market failure created distrust in the pristine form of classical economics. For more information, see Fusfeld (1999), Malthus (1798), Mill (1848/2004), Ricardo (1817/1996), and Smith (1776/1994). ***See also*** Business Cycle (economics, public administration); Laissez-Faire (economics, political science); Market; Market Failure

Classical Measurement Theory The earliest measurement theory, which focuses on the reliability of the *observed score* on a test for estimating the *true score*. The true score is the theoretical, unobservable score for an individual regarding his or her level of a specified construct. The observed score is the actual score as measured by the test. More specifically, the observed score is based on a set of specific items given under a set of circumstances at a particular period of time. Items on a test are drawn from a universe of all possible items measuring the construct. Because the true score cannot be observed for an individual, the observed score must be used as an estimate. The observed score can be influenced by various factors, introducing error into the estimate of the true score. The relationship between the true score and the observed score is often expressed as the following:

$$x = t + e,$$

where x is the observed score, t is the theoretical true score, and e is random error. Over repeated administrations of an instrument, the expected value of the observed score is equal to the expected value of the true score. The expected value of error over repeated administrations is equal to 0.

According to classical measurement theory, the reliability of an instrument refers to the relationship between the true score and the observed score. Because the true score is unknown, reliability must be estimated by other means, typically through the correlations of parallel tests. These parallel tests can come in various forms, with estimates of reliability stemming from multiple test versions (equivalent forms reliability), halves of the same test (split-half reliability), or the average of all possible halves of the same test (internal consistency). Because reliability is considered to be inversely related to error, classical measurement theory focuses on increasing the reliability of scores and, subsequently, reducing random error.

Although still widely used in the development of both large- and small-scale tests, classical test theory faces several criticisms. Reliability and score estimates using classical test theory are said to be test dependent, or reliant on the particular set of items on the test. In addition, the estimates are sample dependent, or reliant on the specific sample that completes a given test. Error estimates are associated with a given group of test takers and do not differ from person to person. In addition, the ability estimates and the item difficulty levels are on a different scale, making it difficult to compare them. Other measurement theories that address some of these concerns include item response theory and generalizability theory. ***See also*** Item Response Theory

Classification (*education*) Although there is overlap in some content areas, classification schemes in education are generally structured along the lines of *taxonomies* and *typologies*. Taxonomies are rational, law-based, observed interrelationships. Often, but not always, taxonomies are hierarchical in nature, and the taxonomical units, referred to as *taxa* (singular *taxon*), are applied in a parent-child scheme. The most famous taxonomy is the Linnaean biological system, which is a binomial system based on formal taxonomic ranks: kingdom, phylum, class, and so forth.

Though less structured than the biological system, there are a number of taxonomies of learning outcomes, including those of Gagne and Bloom. These taxonomies classify learning outcomes based on their rational relationships. They serve as bases for analyses for purposes of assessment and the systematic design of learning materials.

Typologies are much more common than taxonomies. Often these interrelationships are arbitrary and frequently not lawlike. Typically, they are less logically based than taxonomies. Whereas taxonomies are the study of taxa, typologies are the study of types. Types arise to describe many content areas. In psychology, there are personality types; in architecture, there are historical types; in any language, there are types of accents. Typologies are emphasized in education to "chunk" content into working classifications in order to help learners organize conceptually. For more information, see Bloom (1956).

Classification (*sociology*) The process of formally and scientifically categorizing different groups for some precise purpose. Categories share distinct characteristics and are comparable in terms of structure, configuration, constitution, composition, or origin. Plato originally spoke about the process of classification, also known as categorization, of objects according to their similarities;

such categories should be mutually exclusive and mutually exhaustive.

Classroom Management When the teacher controls the classroom, learning is more effective. Classroom control includes managing student behavior through discipline and structure, making the classroom environment conducive to learning, the planning and delivery of content through appropriate activities, and controlling the physical aspects of the classroom to ensure safety and a positive learning environment. These actions eliminate barriers to learning.

Glasser (1984) taught that balance in the classroom is an important psychological component for students to witness and possess a sense of control in their world. Behaviorism predicts that the right set of rewards and punishments will modify student behaviors toward optimal learning conditions. Transactional analysis suggested that the adult ego state embodied by the teacher would help keep the student-child ego state in check. Ginott recommended that communication between teacher and student be considered foremost in classroom management; criticism and blame are seen as the greatest barriers to learning. Fredric Jones (2000) proposed that teacher presence translates into classroom management, through class administration, verbal interchange, body gestures, and circulation throughout the classroom.

More recent models of classroom management have emphasized the importance of sensitivity to cultural diversity among students. Because of the diversity of learners in any classroom, it is important that teachers know the needs, customs, and cultures of all students. Sensitivity and education about unique differences will help students feel safe and accepted, will decrease confusion, and will diminish moral or cultural conflicts. For more information, see Ginott (1995), Glasser (1984), and Jones (2000). *See also* Classroom Procedures

Classroom Procedures Structure and order make classroom experiences more predictable and learning more efficient, provide smooth transitions, and help students feel safe and relaxed. There are five primary areas in which teachers should communicate expectations and regulate student adherence: (1) the beginning of class (being on time, bringing materials, sharpening pencil); (2) behaviors required during lessons (procedures about talking, asking questions, doing one's own work); (3) transitions (getting or replacing classroom materials, turning in work, forming groups); (4) work production, such as use of correct materials (folders, notebooks, pen vs. pencil) and procedures (name on paper, putting in bin, turning in assignment when finished); and (5) preparation for exit (gathering materials, writing down homework, clarifying due dates or details). *See also* Classroom Management; Learning Outcomes

Clearance Rate A term used by police departments to denote the completion of an investigation. Once a case has been cleared, the case has been solved. Recent research shows a steady decline in crime clearance rates; this decrease may be related to factors such as changes in the relationship between the offender and the victim, changes in police resources, different types of crimes being committed (e.g., Internet-based offenses), and reduced help from the public (decreased community willingness to assist the police in their investigations, particularly in urban areas). The less time that passes between the crime and the police's subsequent investigation and the more detectives assigned to a case, the more likely clearance rates will increase.

Clear and Present Danger Test A test, in American law, that determines whether or not speech is protected under the constitutional First Amendment. The Supreme Court formulated the clear and present danger test in *Schenck v. United States* (1919) when it unanimously affirmed the lower court's decision to convict Charles Schenck on criminal charges under the Espionage Act of 1917. Mr. Schenck, secretary of the Socialist Party, had argued that he was protected under the First Amendment for his mailing of leaflets to 15,000 eligible servicemen, during World War I, urging draft dodging. Justice Oliver Wendell Holmes wrote in the Court's opinion that a

question in every case is whether the words used are used in such circumstances and are of such a nature as to create a clear and present danger that they will bring about the substantive evils that Congress has a right to prevent. It is a question of proximity and degree.

For more information, see *Schenck v. United States* (1919).

Clemency A procedure used by the executive branch of government to lessen a lengthy prison term and guard against disproportionate sentences enacted by the legislative or judicial branches. The President of the United States has the power to grant clemency to federal inmates, while state inmates seek reprieve from their state's respective governors. Some jurisdictions have strict requirements for submission, while others are less rigorous in application.

Client-Centered Therapy Also called person-centered therapy, this is a form of humanistic psychotherapy originating with Carl Rogers (1965) during the 1940s and 1950s. The therapist seeks to establish three conditions: (1) empathy, (2) unconditional positive regard, and (3) therapist congruence, which will allow the client's innate "actualizing tendency" to emerge and correct maladaptive behaviors. For more information, see Rogers (1965). *See also* Humanistic Counseling; Person-Centered Therapy (PCT)

Climate Average weather conditions over an extended period of time. The climate, determined mostly by quantitative analyses of temperature and precipitation, helps predict patterns and variations in weather conditions, usually over at least a 30-year period. Climate can be used to understand what types of agriculture and livestock will flourish in different parts of the world. The three major climate groups are the low-latitude climates, which are characterized by tropical conditions; the midlatitude climates, which are best understood as climates affected by both tropical and polar air masses; and the high-latitude climates, which are those climates affected mostly by polar air masses.

Clinical Judgment   The process of reasoning or making decisions that concern patient or client care. Clinicians may make decisions based on scientific evidence, prior clinical experience, personal experience, or some combination thereof. Mental health professionals often use their clinical judgment to make decisions about personality, diagnosis, prognosis, dangerousness, treatment options, or vocational selection. The degree of accuracy of clinicians' judgments about diagnoses has been found to be variable, though generally acceptable when diagnoses are made following the *Diagnostic and Statistical Manual of Mental Disorders* (*DSM*). Research in the area of clinical judgment has, however, found that clinicians tend to be overconfident about their clinical judgment and that use of actuarial or other formulaic decision-making tools may enhance decision-making accuracy. ***See also*** *Diagnostic and Statistical Manual* (*DSM*) (psychology)

Clinical Psychology   The largest and perhaps most typical branch of psychology, involving the scientific study and application of psychology with the purpose of evaluating, diagnosing, preventing, and treating psychological distress or dysfunctional behavior. In contrast to other branches of psychology, such as developmental or cognitive psychology, that attempt to understand "normal" behavior, clinical psychology attempts to understand and treat individuals with "abnormal" cognitions, perceptions, emotions, and behaviors. Clinical psychology is based on the premise that humans have the capacity for change; therefore, clinical psychologists seek to diagnose and treat psychological disorders such as depression, anxiety, and psychosis. In addition, clinical psychologists also routinely engage in teaching, research, development, program administration, consultation, and providing expert testimony for the courts. The historical roots of modern clinical psychology can be traced to the American psychologist Lightner Witmer (1867–1956), who in 1886 opened the first psychological clinic to treat children with learning disabilities. He subsequently developed the first journal and training program in a new profession, for which he coined the name clinical psychology. Although a research-based, laboratory psychology was already gaining momentum in the early 1800s, the field generally rejected the idea of an applied psychology. In Europe, Sigmund Freud (1856–1938) also contributed to the development of psychology as an applied science removed from the laboratory through clinical practice.

Two main areas of expertise for many clinical psychologists include psychological assessment and treatment. Psychological assessment involves the use of intelligence, achievement, personality, and neuropsychological tests as well as clinical observations, to attain a better understanding of the individual's psychological problems. Psychological treatment through psychotherapy involves a relationship between a clinical psychologist and a patient, couple, family, or group, where the psychologist employs a series of techniques to relieve psychological distress or otherwise improve coping strategies. There are different theoretical approaches to psychological treatment, which generally include psychoanalysis or psychodynamic therapies, behavioral therapies, cognitive behavioral therapy, and humanistic therapy. In the United States, clinical psychologists are required to have a doctor of psychology (PsyD) or a doctor of philosophy (PhD) degree. PhD programs integrate research, whereas PsyD programs are more focused on practice. For more information, see Ludy (2005). ***See also*** Developmental Psychology; Psychoanalysis (psychology)

Cloning   The process of replicating DNA, resulting in the creation of an identical structure or organism. Rife with ethical concerns, reproductive cloning, which involves the transfer of a nucleus from a donor egg to a nonnucleus cell, may result in certain DNA mutations. The first mammal to be successfully cloned was Dolly the sheep, in 1996; she died six years later.

Closed Economy   An economy in which there is very little or no international trade. A much more restrictive definition of a closed economy is an economy in which there is no international trade, an autarkic economy. This condition is not practical because countries are somewhat interdependent; that is, no country can be entirely independent to such an extent that it does not trade with others. A much more reasonable interpretation of the concept is, therefore, contingent on the degree of openness to international trade or the exchange of goods, services, and assets. The degree of openness is normally estimated by the amount of imports and exports in and out of a country. This measure is usually indicative of the extent of the restrictions that are imposed on the free flow of trade. Socialist and communist economies are examples of closed economies because of limitations on free-market operations and property rights. For more information, see Case and Fair (2003). ***See also*** Capitalism (economics, political science); Mixed Economy; Open Economy; Socialism (economics, political science)

Closed-Mindedness   An unwillingness to consider the value of the ideas, philosophies, or worldviews of others or to accept various people, cultures, or institutions. Closed-mindedness is the opposite of open-mindedness and is exhibited by people at all educational and economic levels.

Arie Kruglanski calls closed-mindedness, together with open-mindedness, a phenomenon of human behavior, arguing that people adhere to preconceived viewpoints as a means of closure toward information that could delay them from making judgments or decisions. He states that people have the potential to open their minds and reconsider opinions.

Sanford I. Berman states that unconscious assumptions affect how people think, speak, and behave, as well as how they view themselves, and that a human tendency toward misevaluation leads people to draw conclusions from inference rather than fact. Noting that the world is complex while a human's knowledge is limited, he argues that people can open their minds by learning to think beyond the more immediate acts of assumption and misevaluation. For more information, see Berman (2001–2002) and Kruglanski (2004). *See also* Cognitive Dissonance (communication, media studies); Intolerance; Semantics; Stereotyping

Closed Primary   In the early 20th century, the Progressive movement began a reform calling for primary elections, which intended to shift power from political parties to the people. In general, there are four types of primary elections: closed primaries, semiclosed primaries, open primaries, and semi-open primaries.

In closed primaries, voters must register prior to election time, must be affiliated with a specific political party, and can only vote within their respective party's primary election. Voters who are unaffiliated or independent cannot vote in closed primaries. Moreover, voters who are affiliated with a specific party cannot vote in a different party's primary. Candidates in closed primaries compete for votes within their party rather than among the general population; therefore, to oust an incumbent, a challenger must win a majority of the votes within the primary constituency. For more information, see Brunell (2004).

Cloture   The term refers to restriction of a debate in a legislative body, especially by putting the matter to vote. In the U.S. Senate, cloture is found within Senate Rule 22. The first cloture rules were adopted by the Senate in 1917. The primary purpose was to place a time limit on a debate of a pending matter. It is the only procedural rule that allows the Senate to overcome a filibuster. Cloture must be voted on, three fifths of the full Senate must agree, and once enacted it limits the consideration of a pending measure to 30 additional hours. Furthermore, cloture limits the time a senator may speak on the motion to one hour. However, senators can have the time limits extended through a written request following the guidelines found in Senate Rule 22. For more information, see Koger (2006).

Cluster   A small group with comparable properties, generally. It has different meanings depending on the

context in which it is used. A scientific cluster refers to a subset of molecules, a data cluster refers to a type of data analysis, a computing cluster refers to a small network of computers working collectively, and so forth.

Cluster Analysis   The process of formally and scientifically categorizing data with similar properties. Used during statistical data examination, it is a scientific tool to solve classification issues. A data set will be divided into smaller categories and separated equally by distance. The distance between the cluster subsets will influence the shape of the overall cluster.

Cluster Sampling (*education*)   A method for selecting a random sample from a population to participate in a research study. With this sampling method, the population is divided into collective groups (called clusters), and clusters (rather than individuals) are randomly selected. In one-stage cluster sampling, all individuals in the selected clusters are included in the final sample. In two-stage cluster sampling, clusters are randomly selected, and individuals are randomly selected from each cluster.

Cluster Sampling (*political science*)   A multistage research method that involves first dividing a study population into randomly selected "clusters," or groups, before randomly selecting subject participants from the clusters. In contrast is single-unit sampling, which involves randomly selecting survey subjects from an entire subject population group, without first breaking the population into clusters. An example of a cluster sample could be found in a survey of what political issues are of interest to American college students. The survey would first randomly select colleges (the clusters) from a list of all colleges in the United States and then randomly select students from only these colleges. A single-unit sample would, instead, randomly select college students from all the colleges in the United States. Cluster sampling is often less costly and more feasible than single-unit sampling. Cluster sampling is more accurate if the population to be sampled is relatively homogeneous in nature.

Coaching   Assistance provided to a learner that supports the development and strengthening of skills and abilities and helps the learner benefit from his or her experiences. Typically, the learner demonstrates some degree of knowledge about his or her pursuits. Coaching events range from daily, on-the-job training to periodic opportunities to share ideas in personal and professional arenas. Coaching can be provided by one's superior or a peer; the focus is on practical or technical areas of expertise.

Coalition   Individuals, groups, political parties, or states who join together at a particular time for a limited period to advocate a specific agenda. For example, in parliamentary democracies, coalitions are formed during elections and are a necessity. In many parliamentary democracies, no specific party usually attains a majority status and must, therefore, form partnerships to gain control of the government. Parties that are ideologically similar will come together and form what is known as a minimally winning coalition. It is considered a minimally winning coalition because if any one member leaves the government, the coalition will lose its power by falling into minority status, at which time a new coalition will be formed. Political parties with a majority status will have no need for partners and have no need to form a coalition. For more information, see Back (2008).

Coattail Effect   Lower candidates on a party ticket are elected into office because they are of the same political party as a popular candidate at the top of their ticket. The coattail effect in presidential elections has been irregular in the 20th century. This phenomenon has been attributed to the ability of incumbents to increasingly distance and insulate themselves from other party members in the eyes of their local constituency. A recent example of a likely coattail effect was in the 2004 presidential election of Republican George W. Bush, which also witnessed Republicans gaining control of both Houses of Congress. The term is also used when referring to political agenda setting, when an otherwise uninteresting issue receives public attention only because it is purportedly related to another issue of great interest to the public—for example, the call for stricter motor vehicle license requirements in light of the terrorist attacks of 9/11.

Code of Ethics   A set of principles that define certain model behaviors and practices for members of an organization or institution. In journalism, a profession that enjoys sweeping constitutional protections, a code of ethics establishes a benchmark for self-evaluation and promotes responsibility and cooperative relationships. Journalism ethics have coevolved along with journalism since the debut of printed news in the early 17th century. It was not for another three centuries, however, that American newsmakers would adopt a national code. The first, in 1923, was developed by the American Society of Newspaper Editors (ASNE). In 1926, the first professional journalist association, Sigma Delta Chi (later called the Society of Professional Journalists [SPJ]), borrowing from ASNE, wrote its first Code of Ethics. Both these codes stressed objectivity and truthfulness. The SPJ Code of Ethics, most recently revised in 1996, seeks to describe the role that journalism plays in society and provide normative standards for the profession and its practitioners through four tenets: (1) seek truth and report it, (2) minimize harm, (3) act independently, and (4) be accountable. Adherence to these principles is strictly voluntary.

In addition to the industry code, most individual news outlets have their own codes of ethics. According to a 1999 analysis by the ASNE of 33 current codes of ethics, public relations and education are the two most important functions of these codes. In enumerating concerns, the most prevalent is conflict of interest. The study also noted that many codes do not have any discussion of privacy, racial stereotyping, conflicts between the advertising and editorial departments, and enforcement. For more information, see Steele and Black (1999) and Ward (2004).

Code of Hammurabi   The codified rules of King Hammurabi (1792–1750 BCE), the king of Babylonia. Babylonia was the leading state of the 18th century BCE and was often credited with laying the foundation for civilization. The Code of Hammurabi—also known as Lex Talonis, the law of retaliation or the "eye for an eye" doctrine—consisted of 282 clauses, 50 of which pertained to crime and punishment.

Code of Law   A set of laws that dictate the behavior of a society. One of the oldest preserved written codes of law is the Code of Hammurabi, dating back to ancient Babylonian times—written sometime between 1700 and 1800 BCE. The sixth king of Babylon, Hammurabi, claimed to have received the words of the Code from Shamash, the god of justice. The laws in the Code are multifaceted, pertaining to criminal law and punishment, civil law matters, and commercial rules and regulations. Hammurabi had the codes inscribed onto a stone, which was discovered centuries later by the French archeologists De Morgan and Scheil in 1901 in Susa, Iran. The Code is currently on display in the Louvre, Paris. In modern society, virtually all nations have some type of legal code in place. In secular societies, such as the United States, federal, local, and state legislators are charged with drafting their respective legal codes.

Code Switching   When people with multiple-language proficiencies mix their languages during conversation, they are code switching. For example, if a person is bilingual, he or she tends to use parts of both languages to converse with another person. For example, a Spanish native speaker may say, "I bought a car *negre*," using the grammatical rules of Spanish, which place the adjective after the noun, rather than saying, according to English rules, "I bought a *negre* car." Code switching is frequently used in the United States, especially among some Spanish-speaking Americans who communicate using "Splanglish," a mixture of English and Spanish.

Coercion (*political science*)   A legal term in British and American law used when one is forced, physically or mentally, to do an act that one would not do otherwise. "A person is guilty of criminal coercion if, with purpose unlawfully to restrict another's freedom of action to his detriment, he threatens to: commit any criminal offense; accuse anyone of committing a criminal offense; expose any secret tending to subject any person to hatred, contempt, or ridicule, or to impair his credit or business repute; or take or withhold action as an official, or cause an official to take or withhold action" (Model Penal Code Section 212.5). *Coercion* also refers to physical or mental force used by officials to produce a confession. The question of the "voluntariness" of the accused is central in the court's determination of whether or not a confession was coerced by law enforcement officials.

Coercion *(sociology)*   The use of threats, violence, physical force, sexual force, intimidation tactics, and so forth to force another person to do something or to stop doing something against his or her will. Once someone is coerced, he or she will succumb to the pressure and cooperate with or remain submissive to the coercer. Although the person submits to the coercer, he or she is not acting voluntarily. Coercion limits the victim's freedom, as well as his or her responsibility for his or her own behavior. The three main types of coercion are physical, psychological, and economic. Physical coercion, the most common of the three, involves inflicting physical injury or violence on a person or a person's loved ones. There is also nonphysical coercion, which involves the *threat* of physical injury against the victim or the victim's loved ones. In psychological coercion, the victim's relationship with others becomes the source of the threat, such as in blackmail. This can also involve nonviolent verbal coercion, typically perpetrated by someone the victim knows. The coercer uses bullying, pleading, begging, or guilt to obtain his or her objective. Economic coercion typically involves the exploitation of someone with inadequate resources. The victim can be forced to pay an inflated price for a needed item. Economic coercion is common in correctional facilities, especially in the underground or sub rosa prison economy. This includes trading goods for sex, drugs, and other forms of contraband.

Coercion is not always viewed as ethically wrong. A state will often use coercive tactics against its enemies and its citizens to remain sovereign through its use of a formal system of law. Coercion can also be used in modern discourse to describe being placed under enormous social pressures.

Cognition   The way in which individuals process information. It is also defined as the mental processes that mediate between a stimulus and a response, including perception, memories, expectations, abstract reasoning, judgment, or intelligence. The concept of cognition did not gain popularity in the United States until the 1960s, although European psychologists like Wilhelm Max Wundt and William James had introduced the concept of cognition years earlier. The invention of the computer greatly contributed to the increased interest in mental processes, and the way in which humans process information has been compared with the computer processing strategies. The human brain and computers alike receive information from the outside, convert that information into meaningful components, store the information, and retrieve information from memory when necessary. *See also* Behaviorism (psychology); Cognitive Behavioral Therapy (CBT)

Cognitive Behavioral Therapy (CBT)   A group of treatment techniques that aims to change disordered behaviors, cognitions, and feelings through well-established principles of learning. CBT assumes that maladaptive behaviors are learned though reinforcement, and the goal of therapy is thus to unlearn those behaviors. As opposed to psychodynamic therapy, CBT is not concerned with the patient's past or the roots of the problem but rather with the present symptoms. The goal is to identify problematic behaviors, establish concrete behavioral goals, and change the dysfunctional behaviors through a focused and short-term period of therapy. An important aspect of CBT, which distinguishes it from the more purely behavioral therapies introduced by John Watson or B. F. Skinner, is the incorporation of cognitive processes. Indeed, CBT assumes that dysfunctional thoughts can cause disturbed emotions and behaviors, though like pure behavioral therapies, CBT applies both classical conditioning and operant conditioning techniques. *Flooding* is a behavioral technique in which the patient is exposed to the fear-provoking stimulus until the anxiety is extinguished. *Systematic desensitization* uses *counterconditioning* to treat anxiety by conditioning the patient to pair the feared object with relaxation (or a similar response that is incompatible with anxiety). Some operant conditioning techniques include using rewards and punishments, by establishing clear reinforcement programs, and social skills training for people who experience difficulty in social situations. CBT has proved to be especially effective for the treatment of anxiety disorders such as phobias, obsessive-compulsive disorder, or panic disorder, and some types of depression. ***See also*** Anxiety Disorders; Classical Conditioning; Cognitive Therapy (psychology); Operant Conditioning; Phobia

Cognitive Development   The development of the ability to think, including the construction of thought processes, learning structures, and systems in the brain, including remembering, symbolizing, problem solving, categorizing, reasoning, judging, creating, and decision making.

Jean Piaget developed the most influential and widely used theory of cognitive development. His genetic epistemological theory focused on the ability to more accurately represent the world. A process fundamental to this development is the construction of *schemata* (schemes), mental structures that are an organized way of making sense of experience and the world. Schemes change with age and cognitive expansion. Schemata are constructed through two processes. *Adaptation,* in which schemes are built through direct interaction with the environment, consists of the complementary activities of *assimilation* (the use of existing schemata to interpret the external world) and *accommodation* (the adjustment of old schemata or the creation of new ones after seeing that existing schemes do not accurately represent the world). *Organization* is the internal reorganization of schemes and linkage with other schemes to form a strongly interconnected cognitive system. Piaget posited that schemata become increasingly sophisticated as human beings move through four basic periods of developmental growth:

1. *Sensory-motor period (years 0–2):* Infants learn to "think" by interacting with the world through their five senses. They begin to develop essential spatial abilities and an understanding of the world by enacting goal-directed behavior, appreciating physical causality, anticipating events, internally representing absent objects and past events, imitating, and playing make-believe.

2. *Preoperational period (years 2–7):* This is a period of rapid development of representational or symbolic activity. Children learn to represent objects by using images and words, are able to classify objects according to simple criteria (all *blue* pegs), and are able to understand spatial symbols (e.g., simple maps). However, thought is generally not logical and includes animism and elements of egocentrism.

3. *Concrete operational period (years 7–11):* Children demonstrate the beginnings of thought that is logical, flexible, and organized when applied to concrete information and experience (e.g., hierarchical classification and seriation). However, there is a lack of capacity for abstract thinking.

4. *Formal operational period (years 11 and older):* This signals the development of abstract scientific thinking and the ability to reason logically and draw conclusions from the information available.

Challenges to Piagetian theory focus on (a) whether cognitive growth is a matter of domain-general changes or involves a variety of domain-specific changes, (b) the role of language in cognitive development, and (c) whether a constructivist approach provides a fully accurate account or whether human beings are born with an innate body of knowledge. For more information, see Gruber and Vonèche (1977). ***See also*** Cognitive Learning Theory

Cognitive Dissonance *(communication)*   A theory, advanced by the American psychologist Eric Festinger in the 1950s, that posits that individuals experience discomfort or unease when newly presented information contradicts their beliefs or assumptions or when other people make requests that conflict with their values. To find relief from the discomfort or unease such inconsistencies cause, people are likely to resort to various defense mechanisms, including dismissing or avoiding the information, convincing themselves that

conflicts do not exist, or settling the differences even if not to their satisfaction.

In the decades that followed, researchers studying cognitive dissonance in relation to communication theory have theorized that humans tend to seek information that supports their beliefs and preconceived notions as well as their decisions. For example, in the 1980s, John Cotton wrote that humans rarely absorb information in a passive manner; instead, they tend to be selective in choosing and screening data, not only to bypass material unnecessary to specific searches but also to find matter that justifies what they want to believe and how they want to behave.

Experiments tend to be empirical in nature, and the results of such experiments have not been consistent. Among the more recent is a series of three experiments begun in 2005 by the psychologists Laura Brannon, Michael Tagley, and Alice Eagly, faculty members at three midwestern universities. They conducted experiments to see whether the strength of people's attitudes moderates the effect of selective exposure. They concluded that it did but also raised the possibility that other variables moderate the effect. For more information, see Brannon, Tagley, and Eagly (2007), Cotton (1985), and Festinger (1957). ***See also*** Selective Exposure

Cognitive Dissonance *(media studies)*   The condition that emerges when one simultaneously holds two contradictory thoughts or beliefs or when one's beliefs are inconsistent with one's actions. It can also refer to the attempts one makes to reduce the emotional discomfort brought on by this condition.

The theory of cognitive dissonance was first articulated in 1957 by the social psychologist Leon Festinger. Festinger was led to announce his theory by research conducted while writing his book *When Prophecy Fails*. While studying a doomsday cult whose leader had predicted that the earth would be destroyed by aliens, Festinger observed that after the projected date of destruction passed without incident, the cult's followers not only refused to renounce their beliefs but actually intensified their attempts to win new converts. Festinger's theory stated that two contradictory cognitions—in this case, the believers' confidence in their leader and the failure of his vision to come to pass—serve as an impetus that drives the mind to invent new beliefs or modify existing ones so as to reduce the friction between the two ideas and, hence, the sense of inner division that the dissonant beliefs have generated.

Festinger asserted that two elements of knowledge are in dissonant relation if, considering these two alone, the obverse of one element would follow from the other. He argued that dissonance, being psychologically uncomfortable, will motivate the person to try to reduce dissonance and achieve consonance. Not only do people try to reduce existing dissonance, Festinger claimed, but they may also actively avoid situations and knowledge that are likely to increase dissonance. Studies have revealed that cognitive dissonance can be especially acute when a subject is required to behave publicly in a way that contradicts her or his inner beliefs. One way of resolving this dissonance is to change one's beliefs to correspond with the required behavior.

Cognitive dissonance is likely to persist even after the decision that prompted it has been made. For instance, studies indicate that purchasers of new cars are more likely to read advertisements about the model they have purchased than ads featuring different cars. These car owners evidently hope to allay their lingering uncertainties by seeking out information that reinforces their choices. Some research has shown that people tend to pay attention to only those parts of a given message that support their preexisting beliefs and to ignore those parts that contradict these views and might, therefore, produce dissonance. The Beatles' "Nowhere Man," "blind as he can be/Just sees what he wants to see," exemplifies a cognitively dissonant state of mind. For more information, see Festinger (1956, 1957) and Severin (1988).

Cognitive Dissonance (psychology)   A psychological state of tension that results when there is conflict between our beliefs and our behaviors. According to Leon Festinger (1957), we all hold numerous cognitions and beliefs about others, the world, and ourselves, and these beliefs sometimes collide. One way to cope with this state of tension is to change the attitude so that it is consistent with the behavior. For example, if you wait in line several hours to see a movie that ends up being terrible, you may unconsciously reduce cognitive dissonance by changing your mind about the quality of the movie. For more information, see Festinger (1957). **See also** Cognition

Cognitive Learning Theory   A theory that emphasizes the brain and its functioning in learning, through processing, memory, thinking, and mental executive functions such as planning, organizing, and categorizing. The cognitive-learning process begins with attention and recognition. As we process information, we categorize it and organize it based on prior experience, memory, and logic. Then when we want to retrieve the information, we use the same memory, categories, and plan of organization to "find" it and use it later.

Piaget (1928) presented four stages of cognitive development, asserting that we think differently in each stage, based on the *schemas* we develop. A schema is the mental process we use to understand and remember an object, idea, or event. In each of Piaget's stages, our understanding becomes more mature because we gain more information, more experiences, and more efficient ways to perceive or organize the experiences we have. Piaget further believed that errors are vital in this process, so that in each stage we improve our cognition by correcting errors or misinformation in previous stages.

Piaget, Bruner (1961), and others also suggest that an important part of cognitive learning is constructivism, or individual schema development, resulting in the unique

way each individual perceives (and, therefore, processes and remembers) an event or experience. Each person's perception is based on experience, both with the content at hand and with the process of learning and remembering.

Many cognitive researchers study and emphasize the role of language in cognition. A common language is the means by which any experience or construct can be translated to large numbers of people so that they understand the event similarly. Cognitive learning theory is devoted to exploring the different ways that people develop constructs. Studying both similarities and differences in the processing of individuals assists researchers and educators in understanding the complexity and depth of the learning process. This continued study leads to improved instruction because cognitive processing can also be taught along with the content or events to which it is attached. For more information, see Bruner (1961) and Piaget (1928). **See also** Cognitive Development; Constructivist Learning Theory; Intersubjectivity; Learning Theory

Cognitive Strategies   There are many ways to process or learn information. There is no universal "best" way to learn. Learning effectiveness is defined in relation to content, age or level of the learner, structure of the environment, and research-based approaches. There are many ways to get information into long-term memory storage, including methods of memorization (repeating, chunking, practice), making meaning (abstracting, elaborating, schematizing, organizing), mnemonic devices (acronyms, acrostics, peg word and loci methods), metacognitive cuing (advance organizers, signals, summaries, review questions), and mathemagenics (note taking, class work, homework, and other review methods). There are also metacognitive processing strategies, such as self-evaluation, self-monitoring, and self-regulation. Finally, there are academic-related behaviors that benefit learning, including simple things such as regular class attendance, paying attention, taking notes, reading assigned items, time management, asking for help, forming study groups, and developing or following a study plan. **See also** Cognitive Development; Constructivist Learning Theory; Learning Theory

Cognitive Therapy (education)   Aaron T. Beck developed this type of psychotherapy in the 1960s. Beck's cognitive therapy is an insight-focused therapy that emphasizes recognizing and changing negative thoughts and maladaptive beliefs. While working with clients, Beck (1985) found that their daily cognitions, such as their thoughts, expectations, perceptions, images, assumptions, beliefs, and schemata, influenced their emotions and behavior. Beck's theoretical assumption is that a person's emotions and behavior are determined by his or her perceptions, which structure his or her experience. The purpose of cognitive therapy is for clients to identify distorted and maladaptive cognitions and change them into more rational and positive thought patterns. Beck believes that clients can

C

be active participants in modifying their disruptive cognitions and then be relieved from a range of psychological conditions.

Most of the thoughts that a person has in any given situation are automatic thoughts. These automatic thoughts are based on beliefs a person has about himself or herself and the world, which leads to an emotional response. Automatic thoughts can lead to "logical errors," which do not allow for objective reality but usually go in the direction of self-deprecation. These habitual errors in reasoning are cognitive distortions, faulty assumptions, and misconceptions. Some cognitive distortions are *arbitrary inferences, selective abstraction, overgeneralization, magnification* and *minimization, personalization,* and *polarized thinking.* Arbitrary inference is thinking the absolute worst scenario and outcomes for most situations, without relevant supporting evidence. Selective abstraction occurs when conclusions are formed based on an isolated detail of an event. Overgeneralization is the process of forming a strong belief based on a single incident and applying that belief inappropriately to other events that may be similar or dissimilar. Magnification involves perceiving something negative to a greater extent than one should, and minimization involves perceiving something positive to a lesser extent than one should. Personalization occurs when individuals relate external events to themselves without a logical basis for doing so. Polarized thinking occurs when a person thinks or interprets in all-or-nothing terms.

According to Beck's cognitive therapy, these cognitive distortions need to be reconstructed. Clients first identify emotions and the positive and negative consequences of those emotions. Next, clients identify situations and stimuli that begin the sequence of events that lead to certain feelings and behavior. Unproductive behaviors need to be identified, then the automatic thoughts that precede the behavior. These thoughts are researched to find the underlying maladaptive beliefs or cognitive biases that produce the thoughts. With the therapist's help, the client begins to question the objectivity and rationality of the thoughts. Finally, the client develops new, constructive cognitions to be used in similar situations in the future. For more information, see Beck and Emery (1985). *See also* Cognition; Rational Emotive Behavior Therapy (REBT) (education, psychology)

Cognitive Therapy (psychology)   A psychotherapy approach that attempts to change disturbed behaviors or emotions through cognitive restructuring techniques that aim to change patterns of maladaptive thinking. It is assumed that cognitions, or the ways that people think and make sense of their environment, mediate between outside events and distressful emotions. According to this approach, individuals with symptoms of psychological disorders have a dysfunctional way of interpreting important life events, and therefore, the goal of therapy is to change these erroneous patterns of thinking. Albert Ellis and Aaron Beck are considered the most important pioneers of this approach to therapy.

According to Ellis's (1997) rational emotive behavioral therapy (REBT) approach, mental distress is not caused by negative environmental events but by rigid and maladaptive ways of construing these events. To change these ways of thinking, REBT therapists confront clients on their faulty ways of interpreting events through the use of challenging questions. Beck's (1985) cognitive behavioral therapy (CBT) assumes that people who are depressed or otherwise suffer distress view the world, the future, and themselves in a negative manner; thus, the focus of Beck's cognitive therapy is on challenging the underlying irrational or dysfunctional belief that supports this worldview. Although CBT and REBT share much in common, Beck's approach to therapy is more gentle and collaborative than that employed by Ellis. For more information, see Beck and Emery (1985) and Ellis and Dryden (1997). *See also* Cognition; Cognitive Behavioral Therapy (CBT)

Cohesiveness   The term implies "sticking together." The definition of cohesiveness comes from group dynamics and field theory. This theory looks at how one pursues goals and how one behaves in this pursuit. Cohesiveness results when people form groups and have a feeling of belonging. These groups have a feeling of loyalty, high morale, and shared goals.

Generally, cohesive groups are more productive than noncohesive groups, particularly where group size is relatively small. When groups are more cohesive because their members care about their task, they will usually be more productive than groups that are not cohesive because their members do not care about their task. Researchers have found that a person's commitment to the group and its goals is a determining factor in the success of the group.

Cohort   A group of people who share a common trait, such as the year they were born, or share a common experience, such as employment, disease, or educational level. A *cohort study* is a longitudinal examination that follows a particular group over a lengthy period of time. A *cohort analysis* compares two or more cohort groups and investigates changes between such groups over a certain period of time.

Cold War   The name given to the tension-filled, 45-year period from the end of World War II to the fall of the Soviet Union in 1991. The tension was due to the competitive relationship between the United States and the Soviet Union. Both nations emerged from the war as the world's leading superpowers, and archrivals, having ideologically opposite political and economic systems. Although already unmatched in military capabilities, the two nations engaged in an active nuclear arms race. The frightening standoff never escalated into any direct warfare—the threat of world destruction apparently keeping relative peace.

The term *cold war* to describe the U.S.-Soviet relationship was popularized by the 1947 publication of the journalist Walter Lippmann's book titled *The Cold War*. The term can be attributed to a comment made by the British author George Orwell two years earlier, who stated that a world living under a nuclear threat was not a world at peace but rather in "a cold war." For more information, see Lippmann (1947) and Orwell (1945).

Collaboration   Cooperation between two or more people, entities, or organizations to bring about results, such as solutions to problems or the creation of practices or technologies. Collaboration is in use across various disciplines of study and across various occupational and professional fields. Educators, librarians, scientists, medical personnel, business executives, community activists, and artists collaborate.

Technological advances from the printing press to the telegraph to the Internet have increased the possibilities for collaboration across distances. For example, the knowledge and procedures for early computer systems programming came about through a collaborative effort called Share, a voluntary group of IBM computer users in businesses across America in the late 1950s.

Collaboration can be used in a pejorative sense, particularly in reference to cooperation with oppressive regimes or totalitarian governments, and especially in reference to the Nazis in 1930s and 1940s Europe. For example, the name of the Nazi puppet head of Norway during World War II, Vidkun Quisling, is used as a negative term for collaborationist. For more information, see Akera (2001).

Collaborative Planning   An interactive process that promotes the sharing of expertise, experience, and resources among general-education and special-education professionals. Effective collaboration provides a framework for developing an inclusive classroom that addresses the needs of all students. It involves equal participation and cooperation as professionals work to provide comprehensive and appropriate responses to students' difficulties in the classroom. Collaborative planning provides an opportunity for general-education and special-education professionals to work together to design interventions and evaluate their effectiveness, thus ensuring that students are supported in achieving learning and behavioral goals.

Collateral   A term derived from the Latin *collateralis,* meaning parallel, secondary, or additional. In the military, *collateral damage* is accidental destruction incurred during military activity. In law, *collateral attack* means to file an appeal; it is asking for a reversal of the initial judgment or asking to challenge a ruling in another case.

Collective Bargaining   A form of negotiation between a group of unionized workers and an employer. Collective bargaining has existed since the 19th century. Although the phrase *collective bargaining* was coined by two British labor reformers Sidney and Beatrice Webb in the 1890s, such an approach to negotiation between

unionized workers and employers was already common in the United States. The right to collective bargaining in the United States was formalized by the establishment of the National Labor Relations Act of 1935, known as the Wagner Act. Collective bargaining has since become an accepted practice in most Western countries with a high level of industrialization.

While many different negotiation styles exist, there are two basic forms: *traditional bargaining* and *partnership bargaining*. In the traditional mode, each side presents its proposal and demands, and the other side responds with a counterproposal. This adversarial approach is considered by many to be negative as each side has little or no understanding of the issues at hand. The partnership style is considered positive and the more modern and commonly used style of negotiation; it is focused on understanding and education by both the labor union and the employer. With the partnership approach, both sides present a list, and discussions ensue around the related concerns.

The ultimate goal of the process is the formation of a collective bargaining agreement or contract, which most typically establishes hours, wages, benefits, promotions, and other employment terms. While negotiations can be conducted between more than one group of workers and more than one employer, single-plant, single-employer bargaining is the most common. A collective bargaining agreement is limited to a degree by federal and state laws as such an agreement cannot accomplish what the law prohibits.

If collective bargaining fails as a way to settle the differences between management and labor, a union often stages a walkout or strike to pressure management to accede to the union's demands. Union members are permitted by federal law to picket during a strike as long as the demonstration does not exhibit intimidation or violence. Boycotts are also often used as a union strategy to pressure management: members of the public, in addition to union members, are discouraged from conducting business with the firm in dispute. On the other hand, management may use tactics such as a lockout to pressure employers and close the business, keeping union members from working until the dispute is settled.

Collective Rights   The rights guaranteed to a group of people communally as distinguished from the rights of individual people. It includes the right to unionize with fellow workers and to engage in collective bargaining with employers, as well as the right to bring a class action suit in a court of law. In some cases, the rights of individuals and the rights of a group can overlap, or they can be in conflict with one another. In 1948, the UN's General Assembly approved the Universal Declaration of Human Rights. It included the protection of fundamental liberties, such as civil and political rights.

Collective Security   A political strategy in which governments enter into an agreement that an attack on any one member will bring about a collective, retaliatory attack by the others. There are a number of difficulties that arise from this seemingly logical deterrence strategy. The challenges facing the United Nations in its attempts to bring about collective security at the global level are outlined in Thomas G. Weiss, D. P. Forsythe, and R. A. Coate's (2004) *The United Nations and Changing World Politics*. The first challenge is the issue of military strength, especially concerning nuclear power. If the aggressor has such capabilities and the other countries do not, an attack against the aggressor would be unlikely. Secondly, critics claim that nations will inevitably become too self-interested to always abide by the pact; for example, it is improbable that a state would readily violate long-established alliances in an effort to help another unknown state. A third issue is economics: whether states' economies could really withstand the pressures of military engagement at all times. A fourth issue is whether all battles would be considered equal by participants. States have historically treated some nation's problems as more—or less—important than others.

According to Weiss et al., examples of successful UN collective security efforts include collective action against the Iraqi invasion of Kuwait in 1991 and the suppression of a military coup against President Jean Bertrand Aristide in Haiti in 1993. For more information, see Weiss, Forsythe, and Coate (2004).

Collective Unconscious   An analytical psychology concept, first identified by Carl Jung (1934/1981), that refers to inborn, unconscious material that is shared among all humans and is accumulated across generations. Jung broke with Freud's tradition and maintained that the unconscious consists not only of individual repressed experiences but also of memories or experiences from our ancestral past. He distinguished it from the personal unconscious particular to every individual. The existence of a collective unconscious would explain why so many humans are afraid of snakes or heights, given that these may be fears inherited from our ancestral past. Jung later changed this term to *objective psyche,* believing that it is common to everyone. For more information, see Jung (1934/1981). ***See also*** Psychoanalysis (education, psychology)

Collectivism   A cultural orientation that stresses cooperation and human interdependence. Collectivistic cultures focus on the community and give priority to group goals over individual goals. The collectivist individual is a loyal member of the community and acts in consideration of the best interest of the community rather than simply for himself or herself. In collectivist societies, the society as a whole is perceived as being more valuable than the discrete individuals who form that society. Hofstede (1980) conducted a worldwide study of 116,000 IBM employees and found that the most collectivist individuals were from Venezuela, Colombia, Pakistan, Peru, Taiwan, and China. For more information, see Hofstede (1980). ***See also*** Individualism (psychology, public administration)

Collectivist Culture   One in which people tend to view themselves as members of groups, such as families, work units, tribes, and nations. They usually consider the needs of the group to be more important than the needs of individuals. Most Asian cultures, for example, tend to be collectivist. China is a collectivist culture. The fundamental difference between individualist and collectivist cultures lies in the handling of the relationship between individuals and the community. An individualist culture highlights personal interests, which is not an issue in a collectivist culture.

In a collectivist culture, the community is more important than the individual. In Singapore, for example, the community takes precedence, and the government enforces strict rules to maintain a collectivist culture. The most well-known example is the law forbidding spitting on the street in Singapore. This rule exists to ensure that the health of the community is taken into account, as well as cleanliness.

Collectivists claim that an emphasis on individualism reflects egocentrism rather than the good of the community. In a collectivist culture, individual rights are not of great concern since the focus is on the needs of the community.

If individuals give up personal benefits for the sake of others, they are considered to be altruistic. That means that they put community first (since a community consists of many individuals). Their deeds embody the spirit of collectivism.

In collectivism, one gives priority to the goals of one's group and to defining one's identity in terms of group attributes. Collectivists tend to have fewer interpersonal relationships, but the ones they do have are typically very stable and long term. In social situations, collectivists avoid blunt honesty and sensitive issues and instead exhibit a self-effacing humor as a way of preserving social harmony. For more information, see Vadi, Allik, and Realo (2002). ***See also*** Barriers to Intercultural Communication

Colonialism   The practice of a strong nation extending its control territorially over a weaker society. Colonialism is not restricted to a time or place as it was practiced by the Greeks, the Romans, and the Ottoman Empire, but has become more widely identified with the practices of the Europeans in the later centuries as an extension of the civilization of European people to peoples considered inferior and coming from backward societies.

Colonialism is often used synonymously with *imperialism,* although the two may be mutually exclusive concepts. Colonialism occurs when the domination involves the transfer of a population from the dominant country to a new territory, where the new residents live as permanent settlers while maintaining their political allegiance to their country of origin. Imperialism, on the other hand, often describes cases in which a government administers a territory through indirect involvement, such as Britain, France, Spain, Belgium, and Portugal's rule over African nations in the late 19th century and the American administration of Puerto Rico, the Virgin Islands, and Guam.

Aspects of colonialism include racial and cultural inequality, including the imposition of language and norms on the subordinated group, the acquisition of resources by the dominant group, political and legal domination, and the exploitation of the ruled.

In recent decades, neocolonialism has emerged as the indirect control of a weaker society through its economic and cultural dependence on the more powerful society. Neocolonialism exists as the continued control of former colonies through the ruling native elites who are obedient to the former colonial powers, while local populations are exploited for their labor and resources. Some have likened neocolonialism to the worst form of imperialism, since, unlike in colonialism, there is no accountability to the dominant power's country. **See also** Globalization (economics, political science, sociology); Imperialism; Westernization

Cominform　The Communist Information Bureau was formed in 1947, with its headquarters in Belgrade. The organization was the successor of the Comintern, its mission also the overthrow of capitalism and the establishment of a global Communist state. The Cominterm was composed of nine European member Communist parties: the Soviet Union, Czechoslovakia, Poland, Hungary, Romania, Bulgaria, Yugoslavia, France, and Italy. In 1948, Yugoslavia was removed from the organization because Marshal Tito (1892–1980) refused to follow the dictates of the Russian leader Joseph Stalin. In 1956, the Cominform was dissolved by Nikita Khrushchev (1894–1971) as a sign of peace with the West and of making amends with Yugoslavia. **See also** Comintern

Comintern　The Communist International was the international organization of the Communist Party, founded by Vladimer Lenin (1870–1924) in 1919 and headquartered in Moscow. The Comintern sought the revolutionary overthrow of capitalism and the establishment of communism worldwide. One method advocated by Lenin was to help sponsor independence movements in the colonies of the European powers. The Second Comintern Congress in 1920 established the conditions for member parties, including the requirement of absolute obedience to the dictates of Moscow. Until Joseph Stalin (1879–1953) rose to leadership in 1929, Russia held two foreign relations strategies. The first was to enhance Russia's relations with foreign powers using standard diplomatic measures, while the second was to overthrow these same foreign powers through the activities of the Comintern. Stalin tended to prefer the former over the latter. The Comintern was dissolved by Stalin in 1943, reportedly due to the negative sentiments of the Allied powers toward the organization. **See also** Cominform

Commerce Clause　One of the many enumerated powers of Congress listed under Article 1, Section 8, Clause 3 of the U.S. Constitution. The wording specifies that Congress has the power to "regulate Commerce with foreign Nations, and among the several States, and with the Indian Tribes." The clause has been interpreted to mean that Congress has power over interstate and international commerce, while the states have authority over intrastate commerce. Its scope has been defined broadly by the courts and includes areas such as federal crimes, civil rights in employment practices, and environmental protection law. The clause additionally implies that intrastate commerce regulations should not unduly burden interstate commerce. The Supreme Court ultimately decides, on a case-by-case basis, if a disputed state legislation interferes with the relevant interstate commerce.

Commission Plan　A commission is created to investigate a topic of public concern; it is usually authorized to collect information on a topic and produce a report of its findings, which should include a recommended plan of action. In the United States, presidential commissions are appointed by Congress and approved by the President. For example, the National Commission on Terrorist Attacks Upon the United States, also known as the 9/11 Commission, was an independent, bipartisan commission created in late 2002. The commission was mandated to create a detailed account of the circumstances leading up to the 9/11 terrorist attacks and prepare recommendations to prevent future attacks. The 10 appointed members of the commission included 2 former state governors, 4 former congressmen, 1 former high-ranking military official, and 3 former government attorneys. Many of the commission members had also previously served on other presidential commissions.

Committee of the Whole　All members of a legislative body acting as one committee. Rules that govern committees would, therefore, apply, instead of the legislative body's usual procedures, resulting in expedited action. In the United States, a Committee of the Whole exists in the House of Representatives. The committee deliberates and debates legislation but cannot independently pass bills. Action is expedited because there is a smaller quorum requirement (100 members instead of a simple majority), a "five-minute rule" for debates (five minutes allowed to express support and five minutes allowed to express disapproval), and prohibition of the time-consuming motions "to adjourn, lay a measure on the table, recess, recommit, reconsider, or for the previous question." The recommendations of the committee are reported to the full House by the committee chair. The House votes whether to pass or fail the bill or recommit it.

Commodity　A tangible good that generates utility (satisfaction) and is exchangeable. Tangible goods include coffee, wheat, computers, and gold. Commodities are traded in markets, which is generally referred to as a *commodity exchange.* A much broader definition of commodity includes all products that are traded in a commodity exchange. These products will include international currencies and bonds.

The values of commodities are susceptible to changes because of price movements, perceived inflation, or changes in supply and demand. When commodities are in abundance, their prices tend to fall. Conversely, when they are scarce, their prices tend to rise. If the demand for commodities is greater than the available supply of commodities, the prices of commodities tend to rise in order to offset the increasing demand.

To hedge against unwanted losses, unexpected changes (shocks), and adverse price movements, the participants of a commodity exchange may enter into *futures contracts* that will guarantee the sale or purchase of commodities at contracted or prearranged prices. They agree to make margin payments (deposits) and subsequently maintain the margin on a daily basis to reflect price changes until the contracts mature.

Common Law *(political science)*   A legal system that follows the tradition of having current law derived from judges' decisions in past cases. This principle is known as stare decisis, Latin for stand by what is decided. It is unusual for a judge to depart from precedent, but if he does do so, the judge is required to detail the reasons for his departure in a written decision. If no available cases on the legal matter at issue exist in the court's jurisdiction, similar cases or ones from nearby jurisdictions are presented in their place. The written laws in a common-law system are usually written in a vague manner, and the details are determined as they arise. The United States is an example of a common-law nation, as are other former colonies of Great Britain. A common-law system is different from a civil law system, where the rule of law is based on written codes and not on judges' decisions.

Common Law *(sociology)*   Law that developed from custom rather than in a written or statutory format, also known as Anglo-American Law. Originally developed by the English courts during the 12th and 13th centuries, common law is also known as *case law* or *judge-made law.* If a statute does not exist, judges have the right to develop and formulate law. Laws are based on tradition and earlier judicial precedents. Once a court rules on a particular matter of law, that ruling sets a precedent (other judges will use that decision to guide future cases) for forthcoming cases in the same jurisdiction under the principle of stare decisis. Common law is the basis for many statutory laws, as well as the underlying foundation of vital historical documents such as the Constitution, the Bill of Rights, and the Declaration of Independence. All the states in the United States, with the exception of Louisiana, and all of Canada, with the exception of Quebec, follow common law.

Common Property   More than one person having a vested or legal interest in land or real estate. It can refer to one or more tenants who hold a property title to a piece of land that does not specify a certain percentage of ownership to any one individual. Common property can include a condominium or homeowner's association in which every tenant owns an equal share of the property. Lands that are owned by the government for use by everyone, such as national parks, are also common property.

Communication   The process of conveying information from one person to another. The sender is the one who sends the message. The receiver is the person who gets the message. If a message is communicated well, the sender and the receiver will understand it. People have to understand a common language in which messages are exchanged between each sender and receiver. There are many ways to communicate: listening, speaking, writing, touching, looking at one another, using paralanguage, using body language, and assigning sign language.

Communication is defined as a process by which we assign and convey meaning in an attempt to create shared understanding. A person needs a wide array of skills to communicate well. Those skills include speaking, analyzing, questioning, observing, and evaluating.

We learn to communicate by interacting with our families, attending school, going to church, and taking part in work. Collaboration and cooperation occur in communication.

Communication can occur through different forms of media, including radio, television, and newspapers. All these forms of communication are subjective.

Communication is usually described via a few major dimensions: content (what type of things are communicated); source, sender, or encoder (by whom); form (in which form); channel (through which medium); destination, receiver, target, or decoder (to whom); and purpose, or the pragmatic aspect. Between parties, communication includes acts that confer knowledge, experiences, advice, or commands and ask questions. Communication content and form make messages that are sent toward a destination. The target could even be the person who started the message, but it usually involves another person or persons, or a group of people.

Communication can be viewed as processes of information transmission governed by three levels of semiotic rules: (1) syntactic (the formal properties of symbols and signs), (2) pragmatic (concerned with the relations between the signs or expressions and their users), and (3) semantic (study of the relationships between signs and symbols and what they represent).

Communication is social interaction where at least two interacting agents share a common set of signs and a common set of semiotic rules. This rule sometimes ignores *auto communication.* Auto communication includes self-talk.

There are three types of communication: (1) body language, (2) voice tonality, and (3) words. A language is a syntactically organized system of signals—such as voice sounds, pitch, gestures, or written symbols—that communicate thoughts or feelings.

Nonverbal communication is the process of communicating through sending and receiving wordless messages. Such messages can be communicated through gesture, body language, facial expression, eye contact, object communication—such as hairstyle or clothing, or symbols. C. David Mortensen (1997) stated that we do most of our communicating in a nonverbal manner. For more information, see Mortensen (1997).

Communication Apprehension Trepidation about communicating. This may be the most common fear in America. In 1999, the National Communication Association found that less than 25% of all Americans are comfortable communicating. Communication apprehension ranges in severity from mild nervousness to disabling phobia. The stronger the communication apprehension, the less likely the person is to communicate. Communication apprehension may be restricted to specific contexts, such as asking for a date, interviewing for a job, talking to someone in authority, chatting at a party where one does not know anybody, meeting new people, speaking up in a group, or formal, public-speaking situations.

In the public context, communication apprehension manifests itself in the form of *stage fright*. Stage fright may be the most prevalent phobia in the United States. The Bruskin Report (1973) found that stage fright was the most common fear of Americans, suffered by more than 40% of those surveyed. People undergoing stage fright or other forms of communication apprehension can feel various physiological and psychological symptoms related to "fight or flight" instincts. Psychologically, time appears to slow down and the individual becomes acutely aware of self and of the reactions of others. Physiologically, the person's heart rate becomes faster, the breathing becomes quicker and shallower, and the individual may perspire and may suffer from butterflies in the stomach or trembling of the extremities. In extreme cases of communication anxiety, individuals may suffer panic, nausea, vomiting, and fainting.

The energy and awareness generated by mild communication apprehension may actually improve communication. Severe communication apprehension can usually be reduced to manageable levels by exposure to the anxiety-producing situation and communication training. For example, individuals who have undergone assertiveness training report lower levels of communication anxiety and higher levels of assertiveness. Individuals who have taken public-speaking classes learn how to manage their stage fright. For more information, see Barnlund (1968), Bruskin and Associates (1973), Lucas (2007), McCornack (2007), and National Communication Association (1999).

Communication Flow The flow of data from one device to another. Adjustments are made to the flow of data to ensure that the receiving device can handle all the incoming data. This can be of particular significance when the sending device transmits information faster than the receiving device can obtain it.

Communication flow has been applied to many contexts: technology, business, politics, media, psychology, journalism, and the law. The flow of communication can move in different directions. In a business setting, downward communication involves the flow of information passing from a higher authority to a lower authority; upward communication would involve the opposite direction of flow. Horizontal or lateral communication involves distributing information between individuals of the same level of authority, such as peers and coworkers. Communication can move between different departments and groups of an organization or can be informal and uncontrolled, such as rumors or gossip.

Several theories of communication flow exist. The *hypodermic needle* or *magic bullet theory* proposes that the mass media has a direct, powerful, and immediate effect on the public. The 1940 presidential election influenced the creation of the two-step flow of communication theory, which posits that mass media information is channeled to the masses through opinion leadership (an individual who is an active media user): (1) the opinion leader receives the information and then (2) interprets, explains, and diffuses the media content and its messages for individuals with less access to and understanding of the media. This model led to the formation of the multistep flow of communication theory. This theory (also known as the diffusion of innovations theory) is an approach to examining how, why, and how quickly new ideas, innovations, and technology can spread throughout a community. For more information, see Institute for Working Futures (2005) and Lazarsfeld, Berelson, and Gaudet (1944).

Communication Medium The channel through which information flows from sender to receiver. The communication medium generally refers to a communication technology, such as television or the Internet. However, language can also be considered a communication medium, such as in an exchange between human beings. The standard comprehension of the communication medium is based on information theory developed by Norbert Weiner and adapted by Claude Elwood Shannon and then Warren Weaver. The Shannon-Weaver model of communication outlines the process through which a message is transmitted through signals into a channel with noise and arrives at its destination to be decoded by the receiver. For more information, see Weaver and Shannon (1963). ***See also*** Audio Tapes

Communication Theory A collection of ideas, hypotheses, and models that seeks to explain the process by which information is exchanged between individuals and between other entities, such as machines or organizations. The most basic elements of communication are the sender, who creates and transmits the message; the message itself; and the receiver, who can be either an intended or an unintended recipient of the message. More advanced theories of communication include elements such as the *channel, feedback,* and *noise.* The channel is the medium by which the message is transmitted, such as voice, writing, gesture, data, telephone, or symbol. Feedback is the response to the original message that is generated by the receiver. The concept of feedback establishes that communication is not a linear process but a dynamic and interactive exchange, often described as a loop, between sender and receiver. Noise is anything that interferes with the transmission of the message, such as a loud sounds, language and cultural differences, and technical problems.

Communication theory also stresses the importance of shared experience to the communication process. According to the theory, communication is greatly facilitated if the sender and receiver have similar experiences and backgrounds. *Encoding* and *decoding* are also key elements of many communication theories. Encoding is the act by which the sender assigns an intended meaning to a message. Decoding is the act of assigning meaning to a message by the receiver. If the sender and the receiver have dissimilar experiences or if noise interferes with the transmission of a message, the encoded and decoded meanings of a message can be dramatically different. Major subcategories of communication theory include mass communication theory, organizational communication theory, and interpersonal communication theory.

Communism (*economics*) The theory of social organization that advocates the communal ownership of all property and that all basic economic resources be held in common. It first appeared in English in 1843 (from the French *commun),* preceded by the first use of the term *communist* in English in 1841 by Goodwyn Barmby in his London Communist Propaganda Society. Modern communism theory is grounded in the ideas of Karl Marx, who hoped to see a society where no socioeconomic differences exist between different types of labor or places of habitation, be it rural or urban. In practice, communist economic systems are composed of production facilities that are state owned, and production decisions are made by official policy as opposed to being directed by market action.

Communism first emerged as a theory of government with the ancient Greek idea of the Golden Age, a belief in a world of communal bliss and harmony without the existence of private property. During the English Civil War of the 1640s, a number of Christian communist groups arose, notably the Diggers, led by Gerrard Winstanley. During the Industrial Revolution in the 18th century, the reinforcement of capitalism triggered the conditions that led to the commencement of modern communism. The endurance of terrible factory conditions, wages, and hours by the industrial class led to protests and a revolt against economic inequality and private property. In 1848, *The Communist Manifesto* of Karl Marx and Friedrich Engels was published, and Marxian theories soon began to dominate left-wing thought. The Marxist movement, however, continued under the name of socialism.

Modern communism began to develop in 1903 with the split of the Russian Social Democratic Party into Bolshevism and Menshevism. Years of revolts and movements to bring about the downfall of capitalism and establish an international socialist state ensued. The Bolshevik victory, led by Vladimir Lenin, in the Russian Revolution of 1917 led to the establishment of the Russian Communist Party. In 1919, Lenin established the Comintern, or an association of communist parties of the world whose ultimate goal was to establish a harmonious, classless society. Under Joseph Stalin, however, the possibility of building a true communist system in one country alone was asserted. By 1943, the Comintern had been disbanded, and communism had been greatly strengthened by the many governments modeled on the Soviet communist plan. The Soviet Union's "satellite" nations of Albania, Poland, Czechoslovakia, Hungary, Bulgaria, Romania, East Germany, and Yugoslavia all employed communist governments, and by 1950, the Chinese Communists held all of China, with the exception of Taiwan, under communist rule. Furthermore, a communist administration was installed in North Korea as well as in some nations of the Middle East and Africa. Marx's utopian ideal society in reality was based on a systematic repression of human rights to gain the condition of harmony that he sought. The modern history of communist states bears this out well, and it brought about their demise.

The collapse of communism began in 1985, when Mikhail Gorbachev became the leader of the Soviet Union and relaxed communist statutes. By 1991, the Soviet-bloc nations of Poland, East Germany, Czechoslovakia, Bulgaria, Romania, and Hungary had all dissolved dictatorial communist rule, and the Soviet Union was disbanded. Communist parties, or their descendent parties, remain politically important in Russia and in many eastern European nations as well as many of the other nations that emerged from the former Soviet Union. Into the 21st century, communism still held power, to some degree, in China, Cuba, Laos, North Korea, and Vietnam. Many of these governments, however, have made concessions to nonsocialist economic activity. For more information, see Marx and Engels (1848/1969) and Ozinga (1991).

Communism (*political science*) A political and economic philosophy. As a political doctrine, it is based on the notion that societies are best organized around the common ownership of wealth, without discrimination based on people's capacities to generate income. As an economic philosophy, communism provides a method of analysis that looks at classes as the unit of analysis rather than individuals or firms. Karl Marx, a sociologist, is considered the founder of the systematic analysis of communism as a set of ideas that stresses the economic exploitation of the working class by the ruling class. Writing in the early 19th century, Marx believed that the main characteristic of human life in modern society is *alienation*. A communist regime was desirable because it secured economic provisions for everyone regardless of people's capacities to generate an income. Provided with economic security, people could then aspire to develop their potential as human beings; that is, communism contributed to the full realization of human freedom. This in turn would mean the end of workers' alienation from their own productive capacity.

Marx sponsored a dialectical and historical view of modern societies. For him, communism could emerge from the wealth produced through the development of the "mode of production," or the capitalist-economic system. Using a historical method of analysis, Marx examined the different modes of production over time and, specifically, the dynamic interrelation of productive forces and human relations. At each historical stage, the level of development of the material forces shapes specific ways in which those who own the means of production (the bourgeoisie) and the proletariat, or exploited class, struggle for ownership of the material forces. For Marx, the struggle between these two opposing political classes will ultimately result in victory for the working class, which in turn will lead to the establishment of a communist society, where private ownership (by the bourgeoisie) is abolished and the means of production and subsistence will belong to the broader community. This notion of how societies can be best organized relies on the idea that the development of capitalism and the struggle of the working class could evolve into a communist society.

Revisions to Marx's theory of class struggles came from Vladimir Lenin, who made more precise observations of the differences between communism and socialism in projecting a classless society. A standard text to understand the writings of Marx, written in collaboration with Friedrich Engels, is *The Communist Manifesto,* first published in 1848.

Communism exists in a much-changed form and in only a few countries today. In China, for example, while the Communist Party underwent a series of conflicts over ideology and practice, communism is synonymous with the political philosophy of Mao Zedong (1893–1976). Contrary to classic communism, which relies on the proletariat to achieve a classless society, Mao believed in the peasantry and that a peasant uprising could lead to a socialist society. Although the Marxist revolution in Russia was largely a peasant revolution, Russian Marxists still believed that a true communist revolution would originate from and concern workers rather than peasants. Mao, on the other hand, aggressively sought the recruitment of the peasantry and soldiers. For more information, see

"Communism" (2005), Marx and Engels (1848/1969), and Whitefield (2003).

Community A term derived from the Latin *communitas,* meaning the same. *Communitas* stems from *communis,* which means "shared by many." A community comprises individuals in a social group, within the larger society, who share the same regional area and possess mutual concerns. Individuals identify with their community; it enables them to achieve a sense of belonging. Defining communities only in terms of geographical location is limited; they are also based on mutually shared beliefs, culture, norms, values, history, experiences, language, class, or interests. A community can involve interconnectedness among members, who share strong bonds or ties. It is a network of relationships that can be supportive and exist at places of employment; houses of worship; professional, political, or leisure organizations; educational institutions; and so forth.

Community Colleges Organizations providing postsecondary education in the form of two-year programs. These programs lead to certificates and the potential to transfer to four-year institutions toward completion of bachelor's degrees, or technical training to be applied to a trade. Community colleges also serve the needs of their community through recreational and leisure course offerings.

Community-Based Corrections Programs that punish offenders outside a secure environment but still provide a measure of supervision, also known as extra-institutional punishments, alternative sanctions, or intermediate sanctions. This includes programs such as probation (community supervision, by the Department of Probation, in lieu of incarceration), parole (community supervision, by the Division of Parole, after release from jail or prison), halfway houses (programs that provide supervision and a place for an offender to live), house arrest (requiring the offender to remain in his or her premises during specified time periods), electronic monitoring (an enhanced form of house arrest that requires the offender to wear a monitoring bracelet), fines (money paid by the offender to the state), restitution (money paid by the offender to the victim), asset forfeiture (economic sanctions that allow for the confiscation of property and money that are linked to criminal activity), and community service. Courts can mandate other types of programs as part of community-based corrections, including parenting programs, drug and alcohol counseling, driving information courses, therapy, or anger management.

Community-based corrections offer a variety of benefits. These alternatives reduce jail and prison overcrowding, they are more cost effective than incarceration, the treatment programs are more varied, they are less stigmatizing for the offender, and they aid in the reintegrative process of offenders. Servicing offenders in the community limits disruption to the offender's personal life (i.e., job, family, schooling, etc.). Others have criticized community-based programs for their limited effectiveness, for net widening (bringing more people under the control of the criminal justice system), and for possibly putting public safety in jeopardy.

Community Development   The process by which various civic and governmental groups, as well as citizens, unite to remedy or address a particular or group of issues or concerns. Policymakers, public administrators, and other parties use the term to describe when members of a given neighborhood take action to solve a problem or lobby for a particular program or service.

Civic groups, police precinct community groups, school board groups, political clubs, senior centers, and children's programs all have events and meetings. Through these meetings, concerns and issues relating to the community are brought from the street level and are given an opportunity to be discussed and deliberated in a public forum. This is a critical first step in the development of eventual action or inaction. At this step, the members and leaders of a particular group could take action or advise the individual citizen regarding a unique concern. If other people share the same concern or want to see the same or a similar issue addressed, they can take action. This action could be in the form of a column in a community newsletter or newspaper, petitioning, posting of flyers, seeking input from local elected officials or relevant public administrators at the various executive levels, protesting, or any other form of civic engagement and involvement. It should also be noted that while the concept of community development usually implies a "top-down" approach, the roles could also be reversed; that is, elected officials or the management of an agency could take the lead. *See also* Civil Society

Community Identity   Residents who live in a particular neighborhood tend to link part of their self-identity with the community in which they reside. These individuals define themselves, at least in part, by where they live. They take pride in their communities and share a certain bond with other community members. Community identity enables members to have a sense of belonging.

Community Policing (COP)   An approach designed to bridge the gap and alleviate the conflict between the police and the communities they serve. It replaces reactive strategies with proactive policing tactics. The cornerstone of this model is problem solving, not crime fighting. The Broken Windows Theory by Kelling and Wilson has been credited with reinstating a community-based model of policing. The idea is that one broken window left unfixed will lead to other broken windows. Neighborhoods with broken windows appear disorderly and breed more crime and fear among current residents.

Police need the help of urban residents to solve and prevent criminal activity. To foster good relations between the police and the community, cops were encouraged to return to a traditional style of policing. It is a style that allows the police and residents to know one another. Increasing public confidence and preserving safety and order are its main goals. Foot patrol is the best way for cops to have a visible presence. COP programs have been implemented in many areas and enable the police to interact with residents on a more personal level. For more information, see Kelling and Wilson (1982).

Comorbidity   The presence of more than one psychiatric diagnosis occurring in a singe patient at the same time. Although the *Diagnostic and Statistical Manual of Mental Disorders* (*DSM*), which is used for the classification of mental disorders, presents disorders separately, many people diagnosed with one disorder have a tendency to present with symptoms of other mental disorders. For example, more than 50% of people diagnosed with anxiety are also diagnosed with another mental disorder, often major depression or substance use disorders. *Dual diagnosis* is the term used to indicate the diagnosis of both a mental disorder and a substance abuse disorder. For more information, see Kendall and Clarkin (1992). *See also* Diagnosis; *Diagnostic and Statistical Manual* (*DSM*) (psychology)

Compact Discs (CDs)   Thin, plastic disks (diameter 12 cm, or 4.8 in.) originally developed in the 1970s and 1980s at Philips Research Laboratories and SONY Corporation for the playback of 74 minutes of digital audio files. The first commercial compact discs (CDs) were sold in 1982. They soon replaced the play-only phonograph record and recordable cassette audio tapes as the popular consumer format and are still the most common physical medium for the sale, recording, and playback of consumer audio, even though much digital audio is now downloaded. CDs are played on devices that use a laser to read the information on the disk without touching the surface, resulting in less wear and damage to the medium. The CD became the preferred medium for the installation and backup of digital computer files with the development of the CD-ROM (compact disc read-only memory) format. *See also* Recordings

Comparative Advantage   A theory of international trade that was put forward by David Ricardo in his publication *Principles of Political Economy and Taxation* (1817). Comparative advantage was an improvement on two theories of international trade: (1) mercantilism and (2) absolute advantage.

Mercantilism, one of the earliest theories of international trade, presented international trade as a zero-sum game in which little or no consideration was given to mutual benefits from trade. Trade was to be highly regulated to acquire bullion (precious metals).

The French Physiocrats challenged the fundamental arguments of mercantilism by advocating the theory of laissez-faire (lit. "to let alone"—a term coined by the Physiocrat François Quesnay) in the 18th century, based on which Adam Smith promoted the theory of absolute advantage and free trade as the most important way for nations to generate wealth.

Smith's theory of absolute advantage was based on the labor theory of value and efficiency. Nations, he argued, can benefit from trade if they specialize in the production of the goods for which they are efficient because of endowment and acquired skills or advantage and export those goods while importing the goods and services for which they have an absolute disadvantage.

In the 19th century, Ricardo responded to Smith's theory by arguing that even if nations have an absolute advantage in the production of multiple goods, there is still a basis for mutually beneficial trade if nations specialize in the production of the goods for which they have comparative advantage (advantage based on opportunity cost). This theory is otherwise considered to be the theory of comparative cost.

Comparative advantage is more of a dynamic than a static theory because over time the comparative advantage changes as a result of productivity growth; thus, even if a nation has a comparative advantage in the production of electrical equipment today, that advantage can change if another nation becomes more adept and experiences growth in productivity.

In the 1920s and 1930s, Eli Heckscher and Bertil Ohlin improved on Ricardo's theory by defining the basis of comparative advantage in terms of factor or resource endowment in what became known as the Heckscher-Ohlin (HO) theory. The theory became associated with the equalization of factor prices due to international trade.

In the 1950s, Wassily Leontief conducted two studies to discover that although the United States is capital intensive, U.S. imports were more capital intensive than exports. This finding became known as the *Leontief paradox*, which challenged the general applicability of the HO theorem. Notwithstanding the Leontief finding, comparative advantage remains an important theory of international trade and is widely used to explain the basis of specialization in contemporary international trade. For more information, see Blaug (1992), Carbaugh (2007), "International Trade (Leontief Paradox)" (2009), Pugel (2007), Ricardo (1817/1996), and Salvatore (2006). *See also* Absolute Advantage; Labor Theory of Value; Laissez-Faire (economics, political science); Trade Theory, New

Comparative Education   A field in which researchers compare aspects of formal, nonformal, or informal education in two or more countries. Researchers seek to understand educational systems and policies in their sociocultural, political, economic, philosophical, theoretical, and historical aspects. Formal education refers to K–12 schooling in public and private school

settings. Nonformal education refers to education that is offered outside the formal sector to both children and adults by agencies and organizations such as CARE, 4-H, the YMCA, and so forth. Informal education refers to the transfer of information that occurs through interaction of family or community members when they participate in a pleasure or work-related activity.

Comparative education is a subfield of international education, in which researchers study and report on education in countries other than the United States. Areas of study and research include (a) the American role in international education, (b) national and international security and education, (c) international economic development, (d) development education and Women in Development (WID), (e) globalization and education, (f) international education policy, (g) colonialism and neocolonialism effects on education, (h) foreign policy studies, (i) regional and area studies (addressing world regions), (j) peace education, (k) international business and education, and (l) international environmental education.

Popular academic journals publishing research and other academic work in comparative and international education include *Comparative Education, Comparative Education Review* (CER), the *International Journal of Comparative Education, Research in Comparative and International Education* (RCIE), *International Education Journal: Comparative Perspectives* (IEJ), *Current Issues in Comparative Education* (CICE), *Compare: A Journal of Comparative Education,* and *International Journal of Educational Development.*

Professional organizations in comparative and international education include the Comparative and International Education Society (CIES), which sponsors an annual conference where professionals in the field meet and present their work; the World Council of Comparative Education Societies (WCCES), which promotes the study of comparative and international education throughout the world; and the Association of International Educators (NAFSA, formerly National Association for Foreign Student Advisers) which is an association for individuals in international education at the postsecondary level to promote educational opportunities across national boundaries. For more information, see Comparative and International Education Society: www.cies.us, *Current Issues in Comparative Education* (n.d.), Gutek (2006), Kubow and Fossum (2003), and World Council of Comparative Education Societies: www.wcces.net.

Comparative Politics   The subdivision of political science that uses the empirical *comparative method* in the study of politics. The aim of this inductive method is to find general rules and principles (e.g., common causes and consequences) through the study of events—usually historical—and discovering what is common between them. An example would be a study of the causes of European civil wars during the 20th century. The comparative method would compare all civil wars in

Europe in the 20th century (dependent variable: war) and examine what variables all the nations had in common (independent variables: economy, birth rates, religion). A danger of this method is that the correlation between the dependent and the independent variable might be due to an extraneous third variable.

John Stuart Mill's (1806–1873) "Joint Method of Agreement and Difference" is commonly used by social scientists as a comparative method. This method involves searching for cases where (1) the observed change in the independent variable is the only thing *in agreement* between subject groups and (2) the observed change in the independent variable is the only thing *different* between subject groups. The sociologist Neil J. Smelser in *Comparative Methods in the Social Sciences* (1976) argued that the comparative method should not be treated as a distinct method of investigation, since the majority of social science research involves the comparison of subject populations and looking for observed differences. For more information, see Smelser (1976).

Comparative Psychology   The branch of psychology concerned with the scientific study of the behavior of humans, animals, and living beings such as bacteria and plants. This discipline places special emphasis on comparative methods that examine the differences and similarities between humans and other animals that may provide information about developmental processes and evolutionary relationships. Comparative methods are also employed to compare modern animal species with ancient animal species. Comparative psychology was recognized as a differentiated discipline in 1994 under the name of "physiological psychology and comparative psychology" by Division 6 of the American Psychological Association (currently known as the division of behavioral neuroscience and comparative psychology). One of the main goals of comparative psychology is to attain a broader and deeper understanding of human behavior through research on animal behavior. Some instances in which research on animal behavior has shed light on human behavior include Ivan Pavlov's discovery of classical conditioning through the study of the digestive system of dogs and Harry Harlow's research on maternal deprivation in rhesus monkeys. Some topics frequently studied in comparative psychology include heredity, mating and parenting behavior in primates, and evolution. The work of Charles Darwin and George Romanes (frequently considered the father of comparative psychology) mark the beginning of modern research in animal behavior. Since the 1990s, comparative psychology has integrated the study of animal cognition by taking the principles of human cognition and testing them in animals. This new line of study has provided rich information about cognitive abilities in animals, such as learning and memory. For more information, see Tobach (2006). ***See also*** Classical Conditioning; Evolutionary Psychology

Compensatory Education   Programs or services for students who are considered "at risk" and those not performing at grade level. These programs and services are provided in the classroom or are provided in addition to regular classroom instruction. Examples include before- or after-school tutoring, summer and weekend programs, providing extra time to take tests, and having someone read test questions to a student. The idea behind compensatory education is that programs or services provide "compensation" for students not currently meeting performance standards or students who were not provided with appropriate services in the past.

Competence   The ability to perform a task successfully. To complete a job, one needs certain knowledge, skills, and abilities that are germane to the task at hand. Competence means that one is qualified for taking on a position. Competence implies that the person is able to interpret a situation in a given context and to have the ability to implement a solution that advances the goals or aims of the organization. David McClelland developed the occupational competence movement in the 1960s. This movement attempts to describe competence in terms of self-image, values, traits, and motive dispositions that are found to consistently distinguish outstanding from typical performance in any given role or job. McClelland noted that different competencies predict outstanding performance in different roles. Thus, McClelland concluded that "competence" for one job might not predict outstanding performance in a different role. For more information, see McClelland (1973).

Competencies   An integrated set of skills, wisdom, and actions necessary for successful teaching. Through experiences, the competencies of well-qualified practitioners constantly evolve as the situation and the context dictate. Individuals demonstrate their competencies over time through observable behaviors. ***See also*** Competence; Competency

Competency   The mental capacity or mental ability of an individual person. In law, competency pertains to the mental capacity of a defendant. One who cannot understand the legal proceedings or assist in his or her own defense is deemed incompetent. In other instances, legal guardians are appointed for adults who are found incompetent to make decisions regarding their finances, health care, and so forth.

Competency to Stand Trial   An individual's ability to understand the nature and purpose of court proceedings. In other words, a defendant not only needs to be physically present at trial, but he or she also needs to be mentally present—that is, to understand the purpose of the proceedings and be able to assist in his or her own defense. This concept is applicable at every stage of the court proceedings, from pretrial hearings to criminal trials or sentencing hearings. The national standard for competency to stand trial was formulated in *Dusky v. United States* (1960), which put forth that a defendant must have "sufficient present ability to consult with [one's] attorney with a reasonable degree of rational understanding, and a rational as well as factual understanding of the proceedings against him."

This concept is an important doctrine in the criminal justice system for several reasons. Defendants must be able to understand what they are being accused of so that they can meaningfully participate in the court proceedings. In addition, it is considered morally acceptable to punish a convicted defendant only when he or she fully understands the reasons why he or she is being punished. Finally, defendants need to have the capacity to defend themselves if the adversarial system is to be considered fair and just. When psychologists conduct competency evaluations, four abilities are generally examined: (1) the capacity to understand the legal proceedings, (2) the capacity to communicate with attorneys, (3) the capacity to appreciate one's role in the proceedings, and (4) the capacity to make legally relevant decisions. At least 25,000 criminal defendants are referred for a competency-to-stand-trial evaluation in the United States each year. For more information, see *Dusky v. United States* (1960). ***See also*** Forensic Psychology

Competition   A market structure in which there are many buyers and sellers and in which no individual or group can significantly influence market outcomes. Competition is usually used with some regularity in conditions or assumptions to model efficiency in economics. From a theoretical perspective, competition is alternatively defined as perfect competition.

To observe the outcome of efficiency in this market structure, it is also assumed that the participants in the market have freedom to enter and exit the market, that the products of this market are homogeneous or identical, that buyers and sellers are reasonably knowledgable of market conditions, and that sellers are price takers.

These assumptions provide a basis for intuitively understanding the operations of the competitive market. Because participation in the market is unrestricted, profits can be made in the short run but not indefinitely. The prospect of earning a profit will encourage other sellers to enter the market until superprofits are competed away. Competitive firms will stay in production for as long as they can cover their fixed cost. Inability to cover fixed cost will force firms to exit from a market.

In the long run, price in the competitive market will be the equivalent of the per unit cost of production, and it will be enough to attract just enough resources from alternative areas of production. As such, scarce resources will be efficiently allocated in production and consumption; that is, the incremental or marginal cost of production will be the equivalent of the change in total revenue as the result of additional units sold.

Although perfect competition might seem to have limited theoretical appeal because of its assumptions, it is a much more realistic approximation of markets with identical products, such as agricultural goods and differentiated products. It models efficient markets more than any other market structure and has provided a basis for policy making in support of competition.

Antitrust laws and laws prohibiting price gouging, price discrimination, and restraint of trade are intended to foster competition and improve consumer welfare by making more goods and better services available while maintaining prices at competitive levels.

In international trade, nations promote free trade to acquire advantages from competition and innovation. Some of these advantages come from the diversification of articles of trade and competitive prices.

Competition may, however, endanger infant industries and result in unfair trade practices, poor-quality products, and unemployment when it is promoted across international boundaries without equal commitment to enact or enforce equitable laws. For more information, see McConnell and Brue (2008). ***See also*** Antitrust; Economics; Free Trade; Mergers and Acquisitions; Monopoly; Perfect Competition

Competitive   An adjective that describes behavior characterized by the desire to succeed, either by performing better than another person or by exceeding a standard or record. The term is frequently seen in literature concerning athletics, business, economics, management, media, and politics.

Earlier studies regarding competitive behaviors tended to look for the negative consequences, but several done within organizational entities in the past two decades have concluded that competitiveness can foster cooperation and bring about higher levels of achieving goals. For example, in large news organizations, reporters compete with each other to identify and develop the stories most likely to be highlighted on broadcasts, on Internet sites, and in print.

A study conducted in mainland China, in which 64 managers and 28 subordinates participated, showed several instances of interpersonal competitiveness to be advantageous. In that study, two engineers cooperatively consulted with each other while competing to complete an assignment and to gain status. For more information, see Tjosvold, Johnson, Johnson, and Sun (2003). ***See also*** Achievement Motivation; Attitude; Empathy; Political Behavior

Complaint   A grievance against something that is displeasing or offensive. In common law, a complaint is a legal document filed by a plaintiff against another party because the plaintiff has been injured or wronged; such a complaint results in a civil suit. When a felony has been committed, a victim can file a formal complaint with the proper authorities; such a complaint can result in the arrest of the accused.

Compliance-Gaining Strategies   Methods of effecting cooperation or of inspiring others to follow prescribed courses of action or to fulfill expectations. Compliance-gaining strategies involve interdependence and can be gently persuasive or harshly insistent. Suggestions, advice, requests, directions, demands, orders, and threats are all strategies.

Anyone or any entity can develop or use compliance-gaining strategies. Their effectiveness continues to be studied in many fields, including business, medicine, and education, not only for their value in imparting knowledge about environments or professional relationships but for the insight they provide about persuasion.

Business studies show that managers seeking compliance use a variety of strategies, perceived to be either positive or negative in approach. They may give subordinates facts and arguments in support of a request; they may try friendliness as they attempt to win the cooperation of subordinates; they may use social pressure, making allies of other subordinates or managers; they may bargain or negotiate, offering favors and perks in reward for cooperation; they may become forceful, and behave in an angry or threatening manner; they may look for support from those who are in higher levels in their organizations. Results gained through any strategy or set of strategies depend on many factors, including attitudes toward gender and power.

Compliance-gaining strategies used by professional individuals, such as physicians, may differ somewhat from those used by managers in organizational structures. One study found that doctors who use humor in their approach to patient care are more likely to inspire their patients to follow prescribed health plans—including medication schedules, fitness courses, and dietary guidelines and restrictions—than those who behave in a more authoritarian manner.

Compliance-gaining strategies are not limited to those who have authority. For instance, a study on how college students perceive the role of graduate teaching assistants yielded a secondary set of results on how students use compliance-gaining strategies to influence instructors—for instance, blame, emotional displays, and flattery. For more information, see Golish (1999), Sullivan, Albrecht, and Taylor (1990), and Wrench and Butterfield (2003). ***See also*** Persuasion

Compromising   The practice of making concessions to settle conflicts or differences of opinions between parties in personal, business, or political relationships.

The appropriateness and occurrences of compromising have been studied by researchers in the fields of interpersonal communications and management, among them M. Afzalur Rahim, whose studies in organizational conflict management strategies have been recognized since the 1970s. According to Rahim, compromising is most appropriate when the goals of each party are mutually exclusive, when each party is equally powerful, when there is a lack of consensus between parties, when integrating or dominating styles do not succeed, and as temporary solutions to complex problems. Compromising, he added, is not appropriate when one party is dominant or when a

problem's complexity calls for more involved methods of problem solving.

Researchers studying interpersonal relationships, including marriage, have found higher levels of satisfaction between people who can compromise. For more information, see Rahim (2002) and Rahim, Kaufman, and Psenicka (2004). ***See also*** Consensus; Problem Solving (communication)

Computer-Based Instruction/Computer-Assisted Instruction/Computer-Adaptive   Instruction
Delivering instruction via computer-based technologies, such as multimedia and the Internet, is called computer-based instruction (CBI). In CBI, individuals are presented with materials, assessed for mastery, provided with corrective feedback, and then prescribed further instruction. Computer-assisted instruction (CAI) is CBI adopted by a teacher as a supplement to a lesson, as an aide or tutor. Computer-adaptive instruction (CADI) is used in the instructional context involving learners with special needs, such as those with mobility, visual, and hearing impairments. In CADI, these learners are assisted with specialized technologies, such as speech recognition software and screen readers.

Computer Crime   Crime in which the computer, used as the primary instrument, facilitates the commission of criminal activity. It is also known as cybercrime. Unauthorized use of a computer can result in theft of service, forgery, identity theft, embezzlement, interruption of service, establishment of fake accounts, cyberstalking, implementation of computer viruses, and so forth. Sexual predators are known to solicit potential victims via the Internet, which is a type of computer crime.

Computerized   Tomography   (CT)   Scan   A diagnostic imaging technique introduced in the 1970s in the medical field. In this procedure, a series of X rays are taken to obtain cross-sectional pictures of the brain. A computer transforms the X rays into an image that depicts horizontal images of the brain. While this procedure is being conducted, the patient must lie on a table without moving while the table slowly passes through a large X-ray machine. This procedure is often used to diagnose brain abnormalities, such as brain tumors or strokes. ***See also*** Electroencephalograph (EEG); Magnetic Resonance Imaging (MRI); Positron Emission Tomography (PET) Scan

Concentration (economics)   The extent to which a number of firms account for a proportion of sales in an industry. Concentration is said to be high when very few firms account for a high percentage of sales in an industry. This is a propensity toward monopolizing an industry.

The U.S. government has traditionally discouraged trusts or combinations in restraint of trade since the 19th century, when antitrust laws were passed to promote a much more favorable competitive market environment. Prominent statutes to check conspiracy and restraint of trade include the Sherman Anti-Trust Act of 1890, the Clayton Act of 1914, and the Robinson-Patman Act of 1936.

Preference for competition, unlike in the monopolistic structure, is based on the view that competition leads to efficiency, reasonable prices (hence, improved welfare), and the provision of better services. Natural monopolies may arise because of initial outlays and the per unit cost associated with production. Yet in today's market environment, the probability of having a complete monopoly is highly unlikely.

The U.S. government has established guidelines for mergers based on a concentration ratio that calculates the percentage of market shares of firms within an industry to determine allowable mergers. On rare occasions, horizontal (competitive) mergers may be permitted if one firm is endangered and suffering from major losses.

The Federal Trade Commission (FTC) and the Justice Department use the Clayton Act to prevent such mergers when they are inappropriate. For example, the U.S. government blocked the mergers between Staples and Office Depot (two major office supply retailers) and WorldCom and Sprint. Vertical (supply-producer-distribution) mergers escape antitrust regulation more often because they eliminate intermediation more than competition. For more information, see McConnell and Brue (2008). *See also* Market; Natural Monopoly; Perfect Competition

Concentration *(sociology)* Specialized attention given to particular stimuli. It is a particular focus in which one is completely engrossed in one's present activity. In sociology, concentration can mean a disproportionate representation of a population, object, or characteristic within a small area. For example, there is a concentration of poverty or crime in many urban neighborhoods. Sociologists may examine a concentration or accumulation of a particular ethnicity or religion in a small geographical area. Certain concentrations, such as ethnic ones, may inhibit assimilation and economic or geographical mobility.

In economics, concentration relates to funds and investments. When individuals have concentrated investments, they are investing in one type of stock; their portfolios are not diversified. Banks can concentrate their loan process by only lending money to one specific type of industry. This is risky because if the industry fails to thrive economically, the bank will also lose substantial money and profits.

Concrete Operational Stage The third stage in Piaget's four theoretical stages of child development. During this stage (between about 7 and 11 years of age), the child's reasoning becomes more logical, systematic, and rational. One major characteristic of preoperational (i.e., the stage prior to the concrete operational stage) children is *centration,* or focusing attention on one aspect of a situation while excluding others. This ability is demonstrated using "conservation tasks," which aim to examine a child's understanding of whether quantity, length, or number of items is related to the arrangement or appearance of the items. Another key element of the concrete operational stage is the elimination of egocentrism, or an enhanced ability to view things from the perspective of others. For more information, see Piaget (1962/1999). *See also* Conservation

Concurrent Two factors existing simultaneously or side by side. If two or more agencies or individuals form a cooperative agreement, they demonstrate concurrent efforts. In the law, two courts can have concurrent jurisdiction (both courts have legal authority over a case), witnesses can have concurrent or similar testimony, and defendants can receive concurrent sentences for two or more charges (multiple sentences are served at the same time, and the punishment is the length of the longest sentence).

Concurrent Powers The power to enact and oversee legislation in certain areas, granted in the U.S. Constitution to both Congress and the state legislatures. The powers are held in common between the federal and state governments but otherwise operate in a mutually exclusive manner. Examples of concurrent powers include the powers to collect taxes, borrow money, build public works, charter banks, establish courts, assist agriculture and industry, and protect public health. Concurrent powers stand in contrast to an "exclusive power," which is only assigned to the federal government. If a conflict arises regarding a concurrent power, according to the supremacy clause, Article 6 of the U.S. Constitution, the federal interest will prevail.

Concurrent Validity A measure's ability to correlate or vary directly with a measure of the same construct or indirectly with a measure of a different but related construct that has been previously validated. Therefore, concurrent validity is determined by comparing a new test with one that has already been demonstrated to be valid or acknowledged to be the "gold standard." Concurrent validity is often calculated by obtaining the correlation coefficient between the results of the two measures (the new and the already accepted measures) administered to the same population. For example, if you are developing a new test of intelligence, you may compare it with the Wechsler Adult Intelligence Scale (WAIS), a previously validated test of intelligence. *See also* Content Validity; Discriminant Validity

Conditional An adjective that describes release based on good behavior during incarceration. In most jurisdictions, an inmate earns his or her conditional release after serving two thirds of his or her maximum sentence. Inmates can lose good-time credits for disciplinary infractions, and those with a maximum sentence of life are not eligible. Conditions apply to the release and, if violated, can result in parole revocation.

C

Conditioned Response (CR)   A learned response evoked by a stimulus that has been classically conditioned. Ivan Pavlov (1849–1936), a Russian physiologist, first coined this term after incidentally discovering classical conditioning while studying the digestive system. He leashed his dogs to a harness and placed food in their mouths to measure the saliva flow. He soon realized that his dogs started salivating before the food was even placed in their mouths. They salivated merely by seeing the assistant in charge of bringing the food. He called that response a CR because it is learned and not instinctual or innate like the response of salivation to the food (which he called an unconditioned response). For more information, see Pavlov (1927/1960). ***See also*** Conditioned Stimulus (CS)

Conditioned Stimulus (CS)   An originally neutral stimulus that is classically conditioned to induce a response. Ivan Pavlov (1849–1936), a Russian physiologist, first coined this term after incidentally discovering classical conditioning while studying the digestive system. He trained his dogs to salivate to the sound of a bell. The bell was originally a neutral stimulus because it did not evoke any response. However, after pairing it with food several times, the dogs began to salivate to the sound of the bell. The bell is then called a CS because it evokes the conditioned response of salivation. A large number of neutral stimuli can, through association with unconditioned stimuli, eventually become a CS in both animals and humans. For more information, see Pavlov (1927/1960). ***See also*** Classical Conditioning

Cones   The cone-shaped, specialized type of nerve cells located in the layer of the retina closest to the back of the eyeball. Cones are photoreceptors that are sensitive to color under relatively high levels of illumination. Most cones are clustered in the center of the fovea and become sparser as they approach the periphery of the retina. Cones are less sensitive to light than the rod cells of the retina, which are highly sensitive to high levels of illumination and activate for black and white vision in soft light. Therefore, cones allow the perception of color. ***See also*** Cornea

Confederation   A formal association of states loosely bound by an agreement. In many cases, this treaty establishes a central governing mechanism with specified powers over member states but not directly over citizens of those states.

By definition, the difference between a confederation and a federation is that the membership of the member states in a confederation is voluntary, while the membership in a federation is not. A confederation is, thus, less binding than a federation.

The nature of the relationship between the bodies constituting a confederation varies considerably. Likewise, the relationship between the member states and the central government, and the distribution of powers among them, varies considerably. Some looser confederations are more comparable to international organizations, while tighter confederations may resemble federations.

In principle, the states in a confederation would not lose their separate identity through confederation and would retain the right of secession. In practice, this right might be difficult to execute, and the constituent units of a long-standing confederation might appear to be little different from those of any other federal state. For example, in the Swiss confederation, while cantons are designated as "sovereign" and enjoy considerable decision-making autonomy, the powers of the federal government have expanded over time and secession would not seem to be a practical possibility. Other nations that have been confederations at some point in their history are Ireland, the Netherlands, Canada, and Germany.

In the United States, a confederation form of government existed from 1781 to 1789. In the South, the secessionist Confederate States of America existed from 1861 to 1865.

In a nonpolitical context, confederation is used to describe a type of organization that consolidates authority from other semiautonomous bodies. Examples include sports confederations or confederations of pan-European trade unions. For more information, see "Confederation" (2006), Grant (2003), and Schmidt, Shelley, and Bardes (2006).

Conference Committee   An ad hoc, temporary committee appointed by Congress to resolve differences on House and Senate versions of the same—often complex—bill (e.g., appropriations bills). It is also known as the U.S. Congress Conference Committee. For the President to veto or approve any bill, the House and Senate versions need to be in identical form. Conference committees are formed only after both Houses have passed their version of the bill. The committees choose their own chairman and decide the rules of procedure, the only caveat being that members discuss only the disagreed-on provisions. The committee proceedings are public, unless the members vote to keep them closed. The alternative to forming a conference committee is to exchange amendments between Houses; either House may accept the other's amendments.

Once the committee has finished its work, conference papers are issued. The conference papers are a compilation of the conference report and the joint explanatory statement, also called the conference manager's statement. The conference report contains the negotiated legislative text, and the joint explanatory statement explains, oftentimes in further detail and simpler language, the negotiated legislation. Once the committee has created its version of the bill, it must be voted on by both Houses for approval. Sometimes the committee cannot make an agreement, or it issues a partial conference report with amendments still under disagreement. For more information, see Kura (2001).

Confession   The act of admitting one's guilt or the act of taking responsibility for one's actions. In the Christian faith, parishioners confess their sins to the church's spiritual leader or quietly through prayer; confession is necessary to obtain forgiveness from God. In the law, a confession is when one admits one's guilt or culpability for the commission of a criminal act.

Confidence Intervals   A range of numbers that is inferred from a random sample that has a known probability of including the population parameter. One's level of confidence is in the long-term process, not in a particular interval. For example, 95% confidence intervals include the true population parameter (e.g., a population mean, population percentage, or population correlation coefficient) 95% of the time, in the long run; and 99% confidence intervals include the true population parameter 99% of the time, in the long run. Confidence intervals can be made more precise (i.e., made narrower) by using larger sample sizes (e.g., 500 rather than 300) or by relying on a lower level of confidence (e.g., 90% rather than 95% confidence interval). Confidence intervals are contrasted with *point estimates,* in which a single number is used as the best estimate of the population parameter instead of a range of numbers. ***See also*** Estimation (Point and Interval); Inferential Statistics

Confidentiality/Anonymity   An element of the ethical concept of the right to privacy. Confidentiality refers to the researcher acquiring information from research participants but ensuring that the participants' identities cannot be known by anyone other than the researcher. Anonymity is a stronger condition, in which data are collected and stored in a way that participants' identities are never known, even to the researcher. ***See also*** Ethics in Research

Confirmation Bias   A type of cognitive bias in which one tends to look only for evidence that confirms one's beliefs and to ignore or pay less attention to evidence that contradicts one's beliefs. This tendency is thought to be pervasive and to negatively affect the way individuals approach problems or make decisions. This type of selective thinking can also affect hypothesis testing, because researchers may actively, though unintentionally, look for evidence that will confirm their hypothesis. For more information, see Nickerson (1998). ***See also*** Hypothesis Testing

Conflict   *(communication)*   Disagreement in goals, which causes discord, leading to physical, psychological, social, or other forms of attack. This discord may be real or imagined, but any conflict situation involves a real perception. Conflict can occur between individuals or within individuals. In politics, conflict can lead to violence, oppression, war, or revolution. Conflict can result in stress in organizations. A clash of interests and values can lead to conflict. Kenneth Thomas and Ralph

H. Kilmann identified five basic ways of addressing conflict. (1) *Avoidance* is to avoid or postpone conflict by ignoring it, changing the subject, and so forth. Avoidance can be useful as a temporary measure to buy time or as an expedient means of dealing with a very minor, nonrecurring conflict. (2) *Collaboration* is working together to find a mutually beneficial solution. (3) *Compromise* is finding a middle ground in which each party is partially satisfied. (4) *Competition* is asserting one's viewpoint at the potential expense of another. (5) *Accommodation* is surrendering one's own needs and wishes to accommodate the other party. Finally, the Thomas Kilmann Instrument can be used to assess one's dominant style of addressing conflict. For more information, see Kilmann and Thomas (1977).

Conflict   *(sociology)*   A battle between two opposing entities or a difference between two perspectives. Conflict can exist as an internal battle (intrapersonal conflict), in which a person is literally fighting against himself or herself, or as an external battle, in which one is fighting or struggling with something outside oneself. According to conflict theorists, societies, which are constantly undergoing change, are rife with conflict. This includes strain, antagonism, rivalry, and discord in relation to goals and values. In criminology, conflict means that the criminal law is determined by groups in society that hold economic, political, and social power and that everyone in society does not have equal input on the law. Conflict causes a divide between the social classes. Social order is not maintained by general consensus but rather by those who hold power. ***See also*** Conflict Criminology; Conflict Model

Conflict Criminology   A view popularized in the 1960s and based on the theoretical focus of the philosopher Karl Marx. The law, which is influenced by those who hold the political, social, and economic power in society, is used as a means to control the poor or society's marginalized citizens. This is in direct opposition to the consensus perspective, which states that the law serves the views of the citizen majority. Instead, the state is viewed as the tool of the capitalist. The social inequality inherent in capitalistic systems begets criminal activity. The poor will commit nonviolent crimes to obtain money, and they will commit violent crimes to vent their rage and frustration over oppressive social conditions. Society will rid itself of crime only if it rids itself of capitalism. As long as capitalism exists, power struggles will exist, and crime will be the result of that struggle.

Conflict Management   People have different approaches when it comes to resolving conflict or stress in relationships. It is important to keep in mind the aspects of *escalation* and *de-escalation.* If there is a move toward escalation, there is a strain in the way the person is "standing their ground." If there is a move away from escalation, one person takes the other person's feelings into account. In addition, the person involved is attempting to "save face" and move on. Sternberg and Soriano (1984) studied personal styles of conflict management (conflict resolution). They believed that a person's personal style of conflict stays rather consistent no matter what type of conflict he or she encounters. There is no one kind of strategy that works in conflict management, since we all have different ways of interpreting the same series of events. We also have our own style of dealing with conflict, depending on our upbringing, our belief system, and our knowledge about an issue. Conflict management differs, too, when we deal with people who are silent, refuse to get involved in the conflict, or are utterly abusive in the situation. For more information, see Sternberg and Soriano (1984).

Conflict Management/Resolution   Strategies that address conflict situations. One way to describe conflict management is along two behavioral dimensions, ranging from low to high: (1) *assertiveness,* in which individuals attempt to achieve personal goals, and (2) *cooperativeness,* in which individuals work to preserve relationships with others. These two dimensions are used to describe five styles of conflict management, whose appropriateness is contextually determined:

1. *Competing:* high concern for goals but low concern for relationships

2. *Accommodating:* high concern for relationships but low concern for goals

3. *Avoiding:* low concern for goals and relationships

4. *Compromising:* moderate concern for goals and relationships

5. *Collaborating:* high concern for goals and relationships

For more information, see Thomas and Kilmann (1983). ***See also*** Negotiation

Conflict Model   A model of criminal justice that proposes that the main agencies of the criminal justice system—that is, the police, the courts, and the prison system—are competing with one another rather than working in concert to achieve the same goal. For example, judges may impose long sentences without realizing the impact they will have on the prison system, and while the police may want offenders to serve long periods of confinement, prison officials must facilitate early release to ameliorate costs and prison overcrowding. As these agencies compete for prestige, public support, funding, political status, and so forth, they undermine the system as a whole. Many agencies in the criminal justice system do not readily share information. This is apparent in the lack of communication between the county and the state and between the state and the federal system, and insufficient interstate cooperation. ***See also*** Consensus Model

Conflict Resolution   An attempt to solve or resolve a dispute, argument, or conflict between opposing parties. Historically, this was a common practice among tribal societies, known as sentencing circles. Sentencing circles were less about deciding innocence and guilt; they were focused on conflict resolution and the restoration of social harmony. Today, this model is found in restorative justice strategies.

Conflict Styles   When people are involved in conflict, they engage with each other with their words, tone of voice, and actions. These behaviors are called conflict styles. Those conflict styles in large part determine the outcome of the conflict. The way we behave when in conflict can lead to the conflict escalating or being suppressed, ignored, or resolved, resulting in either positive or negative consequences. Conflict styles are often described as comprising five basic styles: (1) avoidance, (2) competition, (3) compromise, (4) accommodation, and (5) collaboration.

Avoidance is deciding not to engage in conflict. Competition involves a winner and a loser. Compromise involves a person giving up something for the benefit of the whole. Accommodation involves appeasement. Collaboration implies that people work as a team.

The Search for Common Ground, located in Washington, D.C., points out that these conflict styles are not often consciously chosen. However, they can emerge as actions that have been learned since childhood from everyday encounters, disagreements, debates, or arguments. We tend to use a style that fits the situation.

Baxter, Wilmot, Simmons, and Swartz (1993) used a representative study to illustrate how subtle and sensitive the tones of an open-ended verbal conflict can be. For example, exhibiting laughter during a tense moment in a conflict can disperse the energy, thus changing its focus. In addition, if a third party gets involved in the conflict, it can be neutral and get the parties to focus on the conflict. In essence, there are many different styles of conflict. For more information, see Baxter, Wilmot, Simmons, and Swartz (1993).

Confluence   A point of meeting or joining together. Typically used to denote the place where bodies of water converge, confluence can also be used to explain the points where latitudinal and longitudinal lines meet. The most notable areas of confluence include rivers, streams, and canals.

Conformity   A tendency to bring our beliefs and behaviors in line with group norms. Conformity can result in group solidarity and harmony insofar as it results in members of the group thinking or acting similarly. However, conformity may have harmful effects if individuals follow unhealthy group norms, such as when adolescents drink or engage in other risky behavior as a result of peer pressure. Private conformity refers to internalized change in behaviors or opinions, whereas public conformity refers to a superficial change in behavior and opinions to comply with the majority, though previously held beliefs are privately maintained. Solomon E. Asch (1955) was the first psychologist to demonstrate this phenomenon in the laboratory. For more information, see Asch (1955). *See also* Social Change

Conglomerate A single corporate entity that is composed of a variety of distinct corporate entities. A conglomerate is formed when firms in separate marketplaces merge with one another. The smaller firms' different markets rule out the possibility of competition between the newly acquired entities and also allow a profitable market in one entity to benefit a less profitable entity in the conglomerate's portfolio (e.g., revenue profits from one can be invested in upgrades in another). A disadvantage of a conglomerate is the inherent difficulty in managing effectively several unrelated business ventures. Conglomerates started to appear in the American market after World War II and experienced their heyday in the 1960s.

Congress The Convention of 1787 established a bicameral Congress as the legislative arm of the federal government. Congress first met on March 4, 1789, at New York City's Federal Hall. The Congress moved, in 1790, temporarily to Philadelphia and then moved to its permanent home in the nation's capital in 1800, to land donated by Maryland and Virginia for this purpose. Congress is made up of two houses, the Senate and the House of Representatives; the Senate provides equal representation (two senators) for each state, whereas the House provides representation proportional to each state's population. Senators are elected to six-year terms and Representatives to two-year terms. As decided by the Supreme Court in *U.S. Term Limits, Inc. v. Thornton* (1995), states cannot impose term limits on state representatives to Congress. A bill can be introduced in either branch, except for bills raising revenue, which can only be introduced in the House of Representatives and need majority approval of both houses before being sent for the President's approval. For more information, see *U.S. Term Limits, Inc. v. Thornton* (1995).

Conjugal Visit A program that allows inmates to visit with their families overnight for a few days in a private setting. It is also known in many states as the Family Reunification/Preservation Program. Most visits, which are limited to legally married spouses and immediate family, take place in trailers located on the prison's property. Conjugal visits are used as a tool to maintain family bonds during incarceration.

Connotation The secondary meaning or representation of a word or thing. The generally accepted view of connotation is that it is viewed in relationship to the dominant meaning (denotation), although some scholars dispute their distinct separation. The connotation is shaped by the cultural context in which language is constructed as a set of codes, rather than by individual subjectivity. Significantly, connotation has been elaborated on in the work of the linguist Ferdinand de Saussure, the semiotician Roland Barthes, and the media critic John Fiske. With Barthes, connotation is of the second order of signification. Ultimately, ideological meaning is determined by both connotation and denotation. For more information, see Barthes (1967). *See also* Denotation

Consecutive Sentence Two or more sentences that are served one after the other. The length of punishment equals the sum of all the sentences. On the day the offender completes the punishment for his or her first offense, he or she will begin serving the sentence for the next charge. This differs from concurrent sentencing, in which the offender serves all sentences at the same time; consecutive sentencing punishes the offender for a longer period of time.

Consensus *(communication)* The generally agreed-on opinion held by two or more parties, usually pertaining to a group. A consensus may involve feelings of anxiety over loss of autonomy by group members. Consensus processes may refer to problem solving, negotiation, and decision-making models of communication. In such contexts, roles are defined, and specific vocabulary is used to reach agreement on the course of action and the tasks to achieve the decided ends. Groups with high versus low levels of consensus may have different types of communication, particularly in decision-making tasks. A positive consensus group involves members seeking collaborative insight to achieve a common rather than a personal end. *See also* Brainstorming (communication)

Consensus *(political science)* A decision-making process in which, ideally, all group members are in agreement with the outcome. The most common type of consensus model of government is a democracy, which requires a numerical majority in governance. The word *consensus* is derived from the Latin *cum* (with) and *sentire* (to feel).

Consensus Model A model that proposes that the three main agencies of the criminal justice system—that is, the police, the courts, and the prisons—work or should work together and cooperatively to achieve the same goals. The criminal law embodies the values, norms, goals, and beliefs of the citizen majority. The law provides a vital social control function; it precludes offenders from taking advantage of others' vulnerabilities for their own personal gain. Behavior that is inherently destructive seeks to undermine the social harmony and the social fabric of society. Hence, the majority believe that the law serves the purpose of protecting all citizens, and all behavior prohibited under the law is agreed on by the citizen majority as being reprehensible. This differs from the conflict model, which views the system as a competition for resources and power. *See also* Conflict Model

Consent   The act of giving one's permission. One must give consent for medical procedures, warrantless searches, contractual partnerships, and so forth. The *age of consent* refers to the legal age when one can consent to marriage, sexual relations, reproductive health exams, treatments, or procedures. A *consent decree* is a judicial order that mediates a conflict between opposing parties. *Informed consent* is a legal paper that is signed before submitting to a medical procedure, a contractual agreement, and so forth; it provides all the knowledge necessary to make an informed decision. Consent is also a defense that can be used in a criminal or civil trial to negate responsibility. For example, in rape cases, the defendant may claim that the victim consented to sexual activity. In civil action, the defendant may claim that the plaintiff consented to the terms of the agreement.

Consent/Assent   The ethical and legal responsibilities of a researcher to notify individuals of their rights as research participants, to instruct individuals in the procedures involved with participation, and to obtain permission from individuals to use their data for research or other purposes. When conducting research with minors, parental consent is required, because minors cannot provide informed consent; minors can, however, provide assent, and ethical researchers are obliged to respect and act based on the minor's assent or dissent. ***See also*** Informed Consent (education, psychology)

Conservation   The notion that the physical characteristics of objects do not change even if there are superficial changes in appearance. According to Jean Piaget (1896–1980), children do not understand the concept of conservation until they reach the *concrete operational stage* of development, which occurs at about the age of seven. For example, children in the preoperational stage are not able to recognize that if you pour a long and thin glass of water into a shorter and wider cup, the quantity of liquid stays the same. The child in the preoperational stage, typically a preschooler, believes that the tall and thin glass contains more liquid than the shorter, wider cup. Piaget believed that conservation represents a significant advance in cognitive development, setting the stage for more cognitively advanced stages of development involving abstract reasoning and moral judgment. ***See also*** Concrete Operational Stage; Developmental Psychology; Preoperational Stage

Conservationism   A movement based on the idea of the preservation of natural resources for human consumption. Its development was based in part on the belief that nature's resources are limited and should be preserved. President Theodore Roosevelt and his chief forester, Gifford Pinchot, were not the first public figures to concern themselves with conservation, but they were the first to apply the word *conservation* to describe environmental policy. Conservation happens in places we can see and draw on a map. It includes policies based on boundaries and clearly identifiable resources.

In the earliest phase of American history, up to circa 1890, conservation was not a priority. Rather, the dominant theme was the advance of the frontier. The frontiersman maintained an attitude based on the assumption that the American West contained inexhaustible resources. The second phase of American history, however, began with the emergence of conservationism, which led to the alteration of the fundamental attitudes that were nurtured during the first phase.

Two factions have emerged in the United States in the second phase of the conservation movement. One advocated the careful use of finite resources without rejecting the basic assumption that the resources are there to be exploited. The other faction, described as advocating "aesthetic conservation," argued for the preservation of natural land for its own sake and for public enjoyment. This group's activities led to measuring environmental values in other than strictly economic terms and to the establishment of national and state parks, monuments, and wilderness areas. The national parks would include not only forests, seashores, lakeshores, and scenic trails but also monuments, historical sites, and battlefields—man's creations alongside nature's.

Conservationism thus includes a symbiosis between nature and man. The conservationist mission welcomes humankind as in integral and legitimate part of nature's landscape. The Roosevelt administration took the view that the purpose of conserving nature was to continue using it—forests for lumber, ranges for grazing, rivers for electrical power. However, the later years of the 20th century have manifested public controversies throughout society about the nature of man's activities (i.e., mining, logging, fishing, manufacturing, agriculture) that provide the fundamental materials and sustenance that humans either require or would like to have. For more information, see Huber (1998).

Conservatism   A political philosophy or ideology that favors tradition and slow social change, where allegiance to traditional values, religion, culture, or the fatherland is largely valued. The term, drawn from Latin, means to protect or to preserve social hierarchies. Thus, the term encompasses concerns about stability and historical continuity.

Conservatism as a political philosophy is difficult to define; it encompasses numerous movements, and conservatives sometimes disagree about which parts of a culture ought to be maintained. Moreover, since different cultures have different established values, conservatives in different cultures have differing goals. Some conservatives seek to preserve the status quo or to reform society slowly. Modern conservatism draws from the work of intellectuals such as Edmund Burke, an English thinker and politician, widely regarded as the father of conservatism. As a political philosophy, Burke elaborated a powerful critique of abstract social theories, the perfectibility of man, and radical social engineering in response to the French Revolution. Burke's conservatism extended to economic affairs; he preferred minimal state intervention, preferring to let the market determine its own rate of change.

Conservatives have sought to defend particular practices and institutions—a traditional conception of institutions such as the family, a traditional sense of patriotic obligation, and religious and moral standards. All these may be seen as vital to a decent society but are difficult to defend in a liberal framework that is sometimes seen as reducing all obligations to individual choice. Today, followers of conservatism would argue that self-interest is universal, but the dignity of individuals is bound up with the exercise of self-reliance and personal responsibility in pursuing one's interests, and therefore, ultimately, political responsibility lies on individuals. Margaret Thatcher, who served as the Prime Minister of the United Kingdom from 1970 to 1990 and was the leader of the Conservative Party from 1975 to 1990, is an example of a current conservative politician. For more information, see Kramnic (1999), and Rabkin (2001).

Consocialism A model form of democracy, developed by the Swedish political scientist Arend Lijphart (1936–), in which many nations can coexist peacefully under one state. It is also known as consociationalism. The concept of consocialism was developed by Lijphart in "Typologies of Democratic Systems" (1968), when studying the Netherlands to discover how deeply divergent religious communities coexisted without conflict. Lijphart divided Dutch society into three religious groups—Roman Catholic, Calvinist, and secular—and called these "pillars." The ordinary members of each religion of each pillar did not interact much, but the elite members regularly interacted and negotiated differences. The consociationalism system is based on vertical and horizontal trust: vertical—that is, among the ordinary members of the pillar and their leaders acting on their behalf, and horizontal—that is, between pillar elites to stand by their word to one another. Strategies of elite cooperation include defining conflicts as technical or legal rather than ideological or avoiding discussion of conflicts altogether. According to Lijphart, consociationalism requires the following four elements: (1) all nations are represented in all important decision-making bodies of the state, (2) representation in the decision-making body is proportional to the national representation that exists within the state, (3) the formalized rules of procedure in policy making require the approval of each of the nation's leaders, and (4) each nation holds exclusive decision-making authority over issues that are only of that nation's concern. For more information, see Lijphart (1968).

Conspiracy An agreement by two or more people to commit a crime. It has its roots in 14th-century English common law. It was first broadly applied in the United States in the 1800s. Today, it forms the basis for a variety of prosecutions dealing with a wide range of issues. They include drug violations, murder for hire, bank robbery,

and extortion. Indeed, it is one of the most commonly charged crimes. Consider, for example, that in the United States, more than one quarter of all federal criminal prosecutions and a significant number of state cases involve prosecutions for conspiracy.

In general, the offense of criminal conspiracy consists of the following elements: an agreement between parties to execute an illegal activity, the defendant's intent to enter into the agreement, the defendant's knowledge of the illegal conspiracy, and the commission of an overt act by any one defendant in furtherance of the conspiracy.

Criminal conspiracy involves many complex matters. For example, agreement among conspirators is central to the offense, yet rarely is there clear and direct evidence of an agreement, such as a written statement, a videotaped meeting, or a digitally recorded conversation. Another difficult issue concerns the type of evidence that will be admissible against specific defendants in proving their intentional membership in the agreement.

Conspiracy as a basis for criminal prosecution remains controversial in the 21st century. Critics contend that conspiracy trials are often too large, often containing as many as 10 to 15 individuals tried together. Perhaps the most serious criticism is whether the notion of conspiracy is needed at all, at least in many of the instances in which it is currently employed. *Conspiracy theory* has come to signify a series of hypotheses based on the idea that certain groups of people are actively conspiring together. A variety of conspiracy theories question the mainstream account of the September 11, 2001, attacks in the United States. Many critics allege that governmental officials knew of the impending attacks and intentionally failed to act on that knowledge. The common suspected motives were the use of the attacks as a pretext to justify overseas wars, to facilitate increased military spending, and to restrict domestic civil liberties. Other popular conspiracy theories are that the AIDS/HIV virus is man-made, the Apollo moon landing was a hoax, the John F. Kennedy assassination was the result of a government-led conspiracy, and Princess Diana of England was murdered by the royal family. For more information, see Johnson (1973), Marcus (2002), and Pierce (2005).

Conspiracy Theory The belief that an event, a situation, or a set of people is controlled by unknown or secret forces, which usually have unsavory intentions. The conspiracies are supposedly intended to seize or hold political power, keep shocking information from the public, protect parties guilty of a crime, or overthrow social institutions. Conspiracies may be controlled by unidentified figures or by known institutions such as the CIA, the FBI, or the U.S. government; they may refer to known religious groups, such as Jews or Catholics, or they may assume an unprecedented new cabal; they may be attributed to aliens, communists, racial or ethnic minorities, or to a stranger. What all conspiracy theories have in common is the idea that common people have gained secret knowledge that a powerful elite is trying to keep hidden and that uncovering the conspiracy will help explain things that were previously hard to understand.

Conspiracy theories develop for several reasons. They are a way of making sense of information that is difficult to organize or comprehend. When logic and rationality do not provide a good story to explain something, conspiracy, attached to a series of seeming coincidences, can do the job. Events that appear random and hard to reconcile with known causes can be brought under control if a conspiracy is used to explain them. The effects of actions by large institutions, such as governments or corporations, are difficult to explain because of their complexity; conspiracy can account for their actions in a comprehensive way. Conspiracies are hard to disprove because any opposition to a conspiracy theory can be seen as another part of the conspiracy and as an element of a cover-up.

Conspiracy theories are popular ways to talk about the unknowable. Big, disturbing events, such as the attacks of 9/11 or the John F. Kennedy assassination, spawn conspiracies because they seem too random or unexpected. The 9/11 conspiracy theorists were not satisfied with the explanation that Al Qaeda operatives were responsible and have developed a series of theories that blame the U.S. government. The Kennedy assassination has nurtured decades of conspiracy theories, in part because the government's official explanation (in the Warren Commission Report) contained inconsistencies and inaccuracies. Theories such as the crashing of an alien spaceship in Roswell, New Mexico, in 1947, and the subsequent transport of alien bodies to "Area 51" in the Nevada desert, have become acceptable ways of talking about encounters with the unknown. For more information, see Becker (1994) and Shermer (1997). *See also* Belief

Constituency (*political science*)   The voting base of a government representative. In the United States, a constituency refers to the voting base, or the residents of the congressional district, of a member of the House of Representatives. The U.S. Constitution, Article 1, Section 2, requires that each state have at least one congressional district and that each district not exceed 30,000 persons.

Constituency (*public administration*)   A group of individuals whose shared interests are represented or solicited by a specific person, corporation, or institution. In business, it can refer to a company's target population, whereas in politics, this group of individuals may support or be represented by a specific political candidate or party. It may also refer to a specific geographical area that is served by a political representative.

Constitution (*political science*)   A set of fundamental rules governing the politics of a nation. The term encompasses the institutions, practices, and principles that define an autonomous political organization or a system of government, and the written document that

defines such a system. A constitution marks the existence of a polity that claims its own sphere of authority. This authority may be defined in terms of a particular region, a particular people, or particular issues. Such authority need not be national. In federal systems, for example, each local government may have its own constitution. All in all, a constitution defines how a political system and its institutions will be governed. Because institutional design affects both the distribution of political power and the making of governmental policy, the structure of the state is often hotly contested in debates over making or amending a constitution. Constitutions are more difficult to amend than ordinary laws. Furthermore, constitutions with more specifically delineated rights are typically less forthcoming about how the citizen who feels deprived of these rights may seek redress.

Although some observers claim that constitutions inherently limit government—for example, by regularizing the governmental process and thus prohibiting capricious action—historically, constitutions have been made to empower states. The American and French Revolutions led to the first written constitutions. These constitutions organized institutions and established fundamental political principles. In both France and the United States, written constitutions aimed at establishing governments based on popular consent and respect for individual rights. Constitution making was a recurrent feature of both nationalist and bourgeois revolutions in the 19th century. After World War II, colonial and occupying powers sometimes refused to relinquish sovereignty to indigenous peoples until constitutions acceptable to them were adopted. Now, a written constitution has become almost a prerequisite to international acceptance for new nations.

The Constitution of the United States was signed in 1787 in Philadelphia, Pennsylvania. The members of the Constitutional Convention convened in response to discontent with the Articles of Confederation and the need for a strong, centralized government. The delegates to the Convention rejected the idea of revising the Articles of Confederation. They agreed to develop a new framework for the new national government.

The proposed Constitution was submitted to the states for approval. Although the vote was close in some states, the Constitution was eventually ratified, and the new federal government came into existence in 1789. The Constitution established the U.S. government as it exists today. It builds into the government a set of checks and balances, or safeguards. It does this by preventing any one of the three branches of government (executive, legislative, and judicial) from acquiring dominance over the others. The Bill of Rights is the first 10 amendments to the Constitution. For more information, see Elster and Slagstad (1993), Hart and Stimson (1993), and Sartori (1962).

Constitution (*sociology*)   Adopted on September 17, 1787, the U.S. Constitution is the supreme law of the land. All laws—statutory, administrative, case law, and so forth—must adhere to the principles inherent in the Constitution. The Constitution comprises a preamble, 27 amendments, and 7 original articles. It establishes three branches of government: the legislative, which enacts law (Article 1); the judiciary, which interprets the law (Article 2); and the executive branch, which enforces the law (Article 3). Article 4 describes the states' powers and limits. Article 5 explains the process of amending the constitution. Article 6 establishes the Constitution as the supreme law of the land, and Article 7 explains the process of ratifying the Constitution.

The first 10 amendments of the Constitution are known as the Bill of Rights. The First Amendment establishes rights to free speech; freedom of religious expression, to assemble, and to petition; and freedom of the press. There is also an implied right to privacy. The Second Amendment provides citizens with the right to bear arms. The Third Amendment precludes the government from using private homes for soldiers unless consent is received from the homeowner. The Fourth Amendment protects against unreasonable searches and seizures; there is also an implied right to privacy. The Fifth Amendment provides due process rights, protection from double jeopardy, and the right against self-incrimination. The Sixth Amendment grants rights to a speedy trial, trial by jury, and counsel. The Seventh Amendment provides a trial by jury in civil matters. The Eighth Amendment prohibits the government from imposing excessive bail, fines, or any punishment deemed to be cruel and unusual. The Ninth Amendment states that the rights listed in the Constitution and the Bill of Rights are not exhaustive. And the Tenth Amendment provides the states with powers not specifically issued to the federal government. The subsequent amendments provide for the abolition of slavery, due process rights incorporated by the states, presidential term limits, and so forth.

Constitutional Amendment An addition to the Constitution. All 27 amendments that have become the law in the United States have been proposed by two-thirds majorities in both houses of Congress and ratified by three fourths of the states. In some instances, the authors of these amendments aimed them directly at the Supreme Court. Taken together with the high court's interpretation of them, these amendments are a barometer of the social, economic, and political change within the constitutional system.

The framers of the U.S. Constitution realized that this document would have to be revised to meet new needs that would arise as times changed. George Washington, presiding at the Constitutional Convention of 1787, recognized the importance of Article 5 of the Constitution, which specifies how formal changes, or amendments, may be made. The Constitution was first amended in 1791. Amendments 1 through 10, known as the Bill of Rights, were ratified together by the end of 1791. This Bill of Rights limits the power of the federal government, thus protecting the civil liberties and rights of individuals. These rights include the freedom of speech, press, and religion; protection against unwarranted searches and seizures; and provision of due process and other rights for people accused of criminal behavior.

Amendments 13, 14, and 15 are known as the Civil War amendments. They were passed in the wake of the Union victory over the southern states of the Confederacy. These three amendments were passed to protect the rights of former slaves. The Thirteenth Amendment, approved in 1865, prohibits slavery. According to Amendment 14, all citizens (natural-born and naturalized) have the same legal rights and privileges. Amendment 15, adopted in 1870, barred the federal and state governments from denying any citizen the right to vote on the basis of race, color, or former enslavement.

Amendments 19, 23, 24, and 26 extended and protected the voting rights of certain groups of people. The Nineteenth Amendment, ratified in 1920, guaranteed the voting rights of women. In recent years, proposed amendments have been directed to modify or reverse court decisions concerning, for example, school prayer and Bible reading, abortion, flag burning, and congressional term limits. For more information, see Bernstein and Agel (1995), Kyvig (1998), McComas (1992), Ritchie (1989), and Patrick, Pious, and Ritchie (2001).

Construct A concept that is shaped by social, political, and economic structures, as well as being a product of their ideologies. A media construct can be formed by numerous constituents (culture, subjectivity, etc.). In media studies, constructs are used from interdisciplinary fields, such as sociology, psychology, history, and English. The media industry and its messages can be viewed in a cyclical fashion with culture, in the creation of institutional constructs for audience consumption through media technologies, as well as having members of a culture articulate constructs about the functioning of the media. Ultimately, constructs are formed on the individual, group, and institutional levels. *See also* Definition (communication, media studies)

Construction of Reality A stance taken in relationship to the question of what is real and how reality is determined. One concept of reality is based on the idea that reality is what actually exists in the perceivable world; it is external to humans and independent of their understanding or perception of it. This approach takes reality as a given, as something that humans cannot change just because they approach it with a different culture or perspective. The construction of reality, on the other hand, is concerned with how—under specific circumstances and in the context of a specific culture—we define what is real and how we claim to know this reality. In the first approach, reality is a constant; in the second approach, reality is continually shifting, and the study of it reveals the workings of a particular culture.

The nature of reality is important because it is the basis for defining truth, validity, value, and other judgments. The construction of reality is an issue in everyday life because the world of reality is already predefined for an individual by his or her culture. The language of that culture has terms and concepts for supporting that reality, and the behaviors of members of that culture make that reality tangible and believable. Without this shared vision of reality, meaning would be difficult to comprehend and could not be confirmed and reinforced through interactions with others. For more information, see Berger and Luckmann (1966). ***See also*** Cultural Context; Culture (communication, media studies, sociology); Ethnocentrism (communication); Realism

Constructive Speech   The writing and presentation of a public address that is composed, or constructed, in a manner that is logical, persuasive, and nonincendiary. While elements of critique and calls for change can be evident in constructive speech, the tone of argument is civil and designed to convince people about the necessity and wisdom of suggested courses of action.

Constructive speech is the province of public speakers, such as diplomats and elected officials, as well as members of academic forensic, or legal, debating (public speaking) teams. Those who debate, for instance, are trained to introduce their arguments point by point, to clearly define terms, and to provide substantial support for their platforms by quoting experts and authorities and by citing case histories, laws, statistics, and other examples. For more information, see New York University (2009) and Oregon School Activities Association (2009). ***See also*** Persuasion; Public Speaking

Constructivist Learning Theory   Learning is an individual experience, wherein each individual builds or constructs his or her own idea or meaning of concepts or events, based on current and past experience. The theory explains how a group of individuals could have the same experience or exposure to an event or concept, at the same time, in the same environment, and yet the individuals form varying conclusions, report differing facets and results, and remember the event quite differently when recalling it later.

Some educators use constructivism as their didactic methodology. In discovery learning, Bruner (1961) advocated hands-on, experiential involvement rather than traditional reading and lecturing to study content. The more a student explores, questions, and experiences an idea or experience, the more the information makes sense, is remembered, and is valued.

Constructivism includes social or communal dialogue in which individuals share findings, question or debate one another, and collaborate to accomplish a task. The teacher provides a structure or framework, which includes boundaries but encourages individual and group creative exploration.

Constructivism is studied extensively in language and communication applications. Since constructivism posits that meaning making is as unique as the individual making the meaning, those who explore verbal exchange are also concerned with ways to make ideas, concepts, and experiences result in a common understanding of a construct. For example, David Ausubel proposed, in his work on the receptive process, that a common understanding or agreement about meaning is primary. Then discovery learning could follow, in which unique or differing opinions or perceptions could be explored. In other words, only after we agree on a single meaning can we explore possible different meanings.

Piaget (1928) viewed cognitive constructivism as involving the processes of assimilation and accommodation. In the former, experiences are fit into existing schemes. In the latter, schemes are modified, or new schemes are created. Over time, each individual develops an upward spiral in his or her ability to understand more and more complex levels of information. For more information, see Bruner (1961) and Piaget (1928). ***See also*** Cognition; Cognitive Development; Cognitive Learning Theory

Construct Validity   The degree to which a construct under investigation is accurately measured and interpreted. Construct validity is viewed in contemporary psychometric theory as a general framework for all other forms of validity (content related, criterion related, etc.). Construct validity is a major concern of researchers who seek evidence to warrant their research findings because without adequate measurement, empirical research cannot be trusted.

Constructs are characteristics of the human and natural world. Researchers study constructs singularly and in relationship to other constructs. Some examples of constructs are motivation, self-esteem, self-efficacy, stress, dyslexia, and intelligence. Researchers have difficulty measuring many constructs because constructs can have multiple features and might lack agreed-on definitions. Because many constructs are complex and difficult to measure, researchers sometimes rely on *multiple operationalism,* which is the use of several measures to represent a construct more adequately.

When one needs to measure a construct, it is advisable to select an existing measure, if one is available. This is because the construction of an original measurement instrument is a complex, time-consuming, and expensive process and is best conducted by professional test developers or psychometricians (i.e., professionals trained in the theory and practice of measurement).

There are many strategies available for obtaining evidence of construct validity. A general strategy is to develop a theory about what the construct is and how it should relate to other measures of similar and different constructs. Then, one must collect data to test the theory. One has *convergent validity* evidence when the construct of interest correlates strongly with other measures of the construct; one has *discriminant validity* evidence when the construct of interest does not correlate with measures of

C

different constructs. *Content-related* validity evidence is obtained when a group of experts examines the instrument measuring the construct and concludes that the items, tasks, and questions adequately represent the construct. *Criterion-related* validity evidence is obtained when scores on the measurement instrument accurately predict or indicate performance on a known criterion. For example, if scores should predict some future phenomenon, then *predictive validity evidence* should be obtained. Evidence of construct validity also can be obtained using the *known-groups technique;* that is, groups that are known to differ on the construct are measured and the accuracy of the measuring instrument is assessed. Construct validation is a continuing process because perfection never is attained and time-sensitive items will need updating. *See also* Multitrait-Multimethod Analysis; Reliability; Validity/Validation

Consumption   The ultimate utilization of goods and services by consumers, excluding the products used in the production of other goods (i.e., the machinery used to make the goods). The term is derived from the Latin *consumere,* to use up, generally referring to food, which, in the Middle Ages and Early Modern period, constituted commodity consumption for most people. While the majority of one's income was spent on food in the 16th century, by the 18th century more of the population had become consumers in the modern sense of the word. Consumption has evolved to include the use of products or goods for one's satisfaction beyond immediate needs. This subjective view is associated foremost with the economist and political philosopher Jeremy Bentham (1748–1832).

Consumption, primarily determined by income and price, is closely linked to production and the wholesale and retail trades, thus creating the foundation of a modern capitalist society. While manufacturers seek to increase consumption through advertising and marketing, modern governments are ultimately able to control the levels of consumption through taxation. Although taxation, to an extent, limits the amount of disposable income, thus affecting what can be spent on service and goods, growth is supported by fiscal innovations, such as the stock exchange and consumer credit and related interest rates.

Consumption, central to most economies and globalization, is typically the main component, and one of the primary determinants, of the growth of a country's gross domestic product (GDP). However, growth in consumption is increasingly associated with issues such as environmental degradation, poverty, hunger, and even the rise in obesity.

Contact Hypothesis   The proposal that under certain conditions, the direct contact of member of different groups (e.g., members of two ethnic groups) will improve their relationship. However, for contact to have this effect, it is proposed that the two groups need to be of equal status at the time of contact and that there need to be

individual interactions among the members of the two groups. Furthermore, it is suggested that the two groups should have a common goal and, moreover, that cooperation is needed to reach that goal. The contact hypothesis predicted that school desegregation was going to result in a decrease in racism; although improved race relations did not immediately follow desegregation, it may be the result of the aforementioned conditions not being met. *See also* Racism (education, psychology)

Contagion   The overspill of an economic or financial condition from one country to other countries. Contagion is usually the result of cultural and economic (trade) links between the affected countries, and it involves access to credit, foreign exchange volatility, and capital withdrawals.

Nervous creditors tighten credit availability to other countries when there is a perception of information asymmetry in their dealings with one country that might have economic or cultural ties with the others. This was evident in East Asia in the 1990s and Latin America in the 1980s. International investors normally pull back from one country, as they did in Mexico or Thailand, to evaluate the situation in other countries; so that without a disturbance in one country, it is unlikely that the others might have been affected.

The credit crunch reduces export and investment capacities but also heightens the pace of destabilizing speculation, which rapidly degenerates to a widespread, financial crisis and, in much more serious cases, currency crashes (the speculative attack and devaluation of a currency). For more information, see Pugel (2007) and Carbaugh (2007). *See also* Asymmetric Information; Devaluation; Stabilization

Containment   The U.S. foreign policy developed during the early 1950s designed to discourage or prevent the territorial expansion or expansion of the influence of the Soviet Union and other communist states. It was the strategy of the United States during the Cold War. First articulated by President Truman in 1947, containment involved maintaining a U.S. military presence around the world, as well as supporting ally regimes economically and militarily.

George Kennan, a top official at the U.S. embassy in Moscow, defined the new approach in a long telegram he sent to the State Department in 1946. Pointing to Russia's traditional sense of insecurity, Kennan argued that the Soviet Union would not soften its grip over key areas of the world. Moscow's pressure to expand its power had to be stopped through "firm and vigilant containment of Russian expansive tendencies." This would entail "a vigilant application of counter-force at a series of constantly shifting geographical and political points corresponding to the shifts and maneuvers of Soviet policy." Kennan believed that the implementation of a containment strategy would remain pivotal until the time when the Soviet Union's totalitarian system led to significant, if not profound, internal changes and a consequent moderation in Soviet external behavior, if not its demise.

The Berlin blockade, the Soviet Union's detonation of an atomic bomb, and the Chinese communists' seizure of power in 1948–1949 reinforced the image of global confrontation and provided added impetus to the militarization of containment. A high-level policy review commissioned by the Truman administration in response to these events recommended the modernization and expansion of U.S. military capabilities.

The globalization of U.S. containment policy reached its highest point with the large-scale deployment of U.S. ground forces to Vietnam. The Johnson administration steadfastly contended that Vietnam was a symbol of U.S. resolve and that failure to meet the communist challenge there would undermine the credibility of American commitments elsewhere.

In the mid-1980s, Soviet President Mikhail Gorbachev, faced with intractable economic and social problems at home and a hostile external environment, initiated a sweeping internal reform program (i.e., perestroika). These profound domestic changes were accompanied by correspondingly dramatic changes in Soviet external behavior (e.g., the 1988 decision to withdraw from Afghanistan) and the recognition of the demise of communist regimes in eastern and central Europe in 1989).

In the post-Soviet era, the ascendance of China as a great power in East Asia revived the issue of containment. U.S. officials, however, have eschewed the term because of its Cold War connotation. For more information, see George (1947), Harbutt (2001), Ulam (1973), and "Containment, Strategy of" (2001).

Content Analysis *(education)*   A data analysis strategy used to study the content of texts and discourses. Qualitatively oriented researchers who use content analysis (CA) seek to understand the meanings, symbols, and communicative nature of texts, through either deductive or inductive measurements. They recommend focusing on what readers do with a text, how they relate to texts, and the social meanings. Quantitatively oriented researchers use CA to determine the amount and frequency of words and concepts found in textual data. Both qualitative and quantitative approaches can provide useful information. ***See also*** Discourse Analysis

Content Analysis *(media studies)*   A systematic means of understanding, categorizing, or describing a message's content. It differs from the interviews or questionnaires used in survey research in that a content analyst, rather than generating his or her own data, investigates the texts of existing documents, broadly defined, to reach conclusions about the thinking, methods, or objectives of the people or organizations that created those documents.

The work of a content analyst typically begins with identifying a question to be answered or a hypothesis to be tested. He or she then defines the characteristics of the data to be investigated, often including the time frame, geographic area, and type of document (e.g., action movies, newspaper editorials, political advertisements, rap lyrics) that will be analyzed. The analyst then typically creates categories for classifying the messages' contents and assesses the content of each datum according to predetermined, objective criteria. The content of a document may be assigned some coded value, which enables it to be compared with other documents. Content analysis aspires to be quantitative and objective rather than subjective and anecdotal. A sophisticated use of content analysis often requires the researcher to extend his or her investigation beyond the document itself and to observe it in light of other variables, such as audience demographics, prevailing social attitudes, or known information about the nationality, education, or bias of the persons who originated the message.

An example of content analysis would be a study of news articles written during a given time period about a particular overseas political movement, observing the frequency with which pejorative words, such as *terrorist,* are employed as opposed to more positively connotative phrases, such as *freedom fighter.* The results of such an analysis might reflect the tendency of news media either to affirm or contradict their government's attitude toward the movement. Content analysis is frequently employed to identify bias or persuasive agendas in media messages. For more information, see Severin (1988).

Content Validity   The extent to which a test includes or represents all the content or domain of the construct that is being measured. In clinical psychology, a test developed to measure a psychological disorder, such as depression, needs to contain items that correspond to the symptoms involved in the disorder. The opinion of experts about the construct being measured may be one manner by which to determine content validity. Content validity requires more elaborate statistical procedures than *face validity,* which refers to whether a measure *appears* to measure that which it is intended to measure. A common method for establishing content validity consists of asking different judges or raters about whether the item is essential to measure the construct. The higher the degree of agreement among judges, the greater the level of content validity. ***See also*** Criterion Validity; Face Validity

Context   The words around a statement or passage that help clarify the meaning of a word. Words, placed in a different context, can have entirely different meanings. Context also refers to a particular setting or area, or the circumstances that initiate an event. Theorists are often concerned with understanding the historical, cultural, social, or political context of an event; explanations of behavior change depending on the context.

Context Analysis   An instructional design component in which three types of context (i.e., facilitating, constraining, and missing environmental factors) are analyzed for the benefit of instruction and learning. The three context types are: (1) orienting context, (2) instructional context, and (3) transfer context. As part of the analysis of what learners bring to the learning environment, their goals, perceived utility of the instruction, and perceptions of accountability constitute the orienting context. Instructional context includes those factors related to the physical environment, such as equipment, seating, noise, transportation, lighting, temperature, and accommodation, as well as the scheduling of the course. To connect learning with the real world, opportunities need to be created for the transfer of learning. So the analysis should include the analysis of diverse situations for application, practice opportunities, and support from the transfer context. To conduct a context analysis, surveys, observations, and interviews can be used for collecting data.

Contexting A strategy of choosing the appropriate mix of verbal and extraverbal communication to get a message across. Certain cultures demand that great attention be paid to the context of a message. Situations within cultures also demand that we pay attention to the context of a message. There are high-context (HC) and low-context (LC) frameworks. Low context involves verbal skills and self expression. High context involves nonverbal skills and limited expression.

In his book titled *Beyond Culture* (1976), Edward T. Hall mentions that an LC communication is one in which the mass of the information used is vested in the explicit code. Direct, verbal skills and the ability to give detailed, exact information are most important. Such communication is frequently used in business, law, and the classroom. It is unstable, not necessarily linked to the past, quick to change, hectic, and carries a danger of information overload. Because the transmitted message does not depend on the contextuality of its information, it is slower, less efficient, and less personal. Low context communication can express distance or displeasure as when we address people by their full name because they upset us. An LC message needs all informational specificity to put a decision in context. An LC message needs all the information to put the decision in context.

An HC communication or message is one in which most of the information is either in the physical context or internalized in the person. Very little information is coded. It is indirect communication using nonverbal skills. It is rooted in the past, slow to change, and used through understanding the social context (including the social background) of a person. Raising the contexting indicates warmth in the relationship. This is seen in the use of informality in greeting people or the use of friendly nicknames. There is more concern about group consensus than individual decision making. For more information, see Hall (1976).

Context of Situation In communication, every act takes place in an environment with extralinguistic features. Textural environments can serve as contexts for

conversation. The Polish anthropologist Bronislaw Malinowski (1884–1942) coined the expression after linguistic theory was developed by John Rupert Firth (1890–1960). Malinowski posited that one could only extrapolate meaning from its use in a social situation. Historians derived meaning from placing an event in a temporal or historical context. Firth identified and described situation types according to their extralinguistic features. For more information, see Firth (1957) and Malinowski (1947).

Contextual Constructionism The assessment and evaluation of data that are put forth as "objective" but in fact, when examined in context, may present a biased or skewed picture of reality. For instance, in reporting the news, journalists may quote from sources a statistic that supports their story. While the statistic is genuine and received from a credible source, it may not offer an accurate portrayal of the truth. For example, a news story may claim that crime in New York City is down as the number of convictions has dropped by 10% from the previous year. Applying contextual constructionism to this factoid, the reader would have to know that the conviction rate is not an accurate portrayal of the number of criminal incidents. Victimization surveys are the most reflective of what is actually happening as many victims do not make complaints. Of those that do make complaints, only a fraction of them result in arrests. Then, only a portion of arrests result in prosecutions. Even further down the line are convictions, as not all prosecuted cases end in convictions. What a 10% decrease in convictions may, in fact, represent, is any number of alternative explanations, none having to do with a decrease in crime: that more victims are afraid to come forward, that the police or prosecutors' office are not staffed as well as the previous year, or that more cases are being pled out. It has been suggested in the field that some journalists may feel that a story is complete once they've found a credible source to back up their story; however, it is part of a journalist's responsibility not only to present accurate data but to gain an understanding of the story's perspective and present it in its proper context. For more information, see Paulos (1995).

Continent One of the earth's largest masses of land. Found above sea level, continents are made of connecting tectonic plates and are often surrounded by major bodies of water. There are seven landmasses currently recognized as continents: North America, South America, Europe, Asia, Africa, Australia, and Antarctica.

Continental Climate The climate most typically found in the center of a continent. These climates are usually characterized by extreme weather conditions as they are located far from the ocean, which tends to have a mitigating effect on weather. More specifically, the distance from the ocean leaves these regions with a lack of precipitation, dry air, and a wide range in yearly temperatures. The winters in a continental climate are generally very cold, while the summers are extremely hot. Both the midwestern United States and Russia are marked by continental climates, which are only found in the Northern Hemisphere.

Continental Divide   A natural boundary of terrain that divides a continent into separate bodies of water and controls into which ocean precipitation will flow. In the United States, the Continental Divide, also known as the Great Divide, separates the water that runs into the Atlantic and Pacific oceans. With the exception of Antarctica, all continents possess continental divides, and some continents, including North America, possess several.

Continental Plate   A type of tectonic plate, which is a thick, movable plate found in the earth's lithosphere. Continental plates are portions of the earth's crust that come together to form the landmasses known as continents. The other type of tectonic plate is an *oceanic plate,* which tends to be much thinner than a continental plate. When continental plates collide with oceanic plates, they produce volcanoes and earthquakes. Additionally, continental plates collide with each other to form mountain ranges.

Contingency Approach   A management strategy that argues that effective management involves a contextualized and tailored approach to planning, organizing, leading, and controlling. A key concept is that there is no single best way; rather, what is correct is highly situational, given the needs of the entity and the resources available. This form of management should be used flexibly and efficiently to ensure the well-being of the entity and of the people who participate in the development of the organization. The necessity for change depends on the operation of the entity and the circumstances faced. Some changes may even be environmental when directly dealing with equipment technology and the growth of employment. All these factors must be taken into consideration when delivering a successful contingency approach.

Contingency Contracting   A written and signed agreement—between teacher and student, with parents' involvement—containing a target behavior, performance expectations, consequences of compliance and noncompliance, and a timeframe. Being written, it eliminates confusion and problems of memory, and it allows renegotiation when necessary. *See also* Behavior Management; Behavior Modification; Token Economy (education)

Contingency Table   A matrix used to display information in cells formed by the intersection of two or more categorical variables. Contingency tables are used to show the number and percentage of cases falling into different cells of the table and the relationships between variables. To check for relationships, one calculates percentages for the cell counts in the table. *Column percentages* add up to 100% for each column; *row percentages* add up to 100% for each row. To determine if two variables are related, follow these rules: (a) if examining column percentages, then make cell or group comparisons across the rows, and (b) if examining row percentages, then make comparisons down the columns. Relationships observed in contingency tables can be checked for statistical significance using the chi-square statistic. Numerical measures of relationships also are available (e.g., contingency coefficient, Cramer's *V*). Contingency tables with more than two variables also can be constructed.

Continuance   The postponement of a hearing, trial, or other court proceeding. The request can be made by one or both parties or by the presiding judge. Judges have the authority to hear cases and render decisions; this authority also allows them to grant continuances. Continuances are denied if the sole purpose is to delay the trial; there must be a justifiable reason, or the continuance could violate the defendant's Sixth Amendment right to a speedy trial. If there are multiple defendants in the same case, a continuance granted for one of them automatically applies to all.

Continuing Education   A program offered by a college, university, professional training group, and so forth that consists of educational activities intended to develop, maintain, or increase the knowledge, skills, and professional competence of a person or staff in a particular area. The term *continuing education* often refers to instructional courses designed especially for part-time, adult students, which may or may not award academic credit hours.

Continuing Resolution   The U.S. federal government's budget (fiscal) year begins on the first day of October. All agencies and programs that require annual funding must have been appropriated funds by the start of the fiscal year to continue to operate. If an appropriations bill for a specific agency or program is not passed by the start of the fiscal year, Congress may pass a stopgap appropriations act known as a continuing resolution, which must be signed by the President to take effect. While continuing resolutions do prevent the shutdown of government operations and are generally short-term in nature, they may also be somewhat restrictive and may prevent affected agencies and programs from moving forward.

Contraband   Materials or objects that are illegal to possess. The term is derived from the Latin *contra,* meaning against. Such objects can be dangerous, such as guns, chemical warfare agents, and so forth, or illegal, such as stolen goods. In correctional facilities, contraband is used to connote objects that inmates are not allowed to possess.

Contract   A promise that is made between parties, based on written or oral agreements. The word *contract* is derived from the Latin phrase *pacta sunt servanda,* meaning a pact that must be kept. Contracts are legally binding, and a breach of contract can result in legal remedies or civil penalties.

Contributory Negligence   A tort claim, currently known as *comparative negligence* in most U.S. jurisdictions. It was used as a common-law defense in cases where the defendant was charged with negligence but stated that his or her negligence was in part based on or contributed to by the careless actions of the plaintiff. Remedies or damages are typically reduced, depending on the role the plaintiff played in contributing to the overall negligence.

Control Group   The group in an experiment that is not exposed to the independent variable (e.g., does not receive the treatment or intervention). The control group provides a basis for comparison. Optimally, the control group should be identical to the experimental group in every way except for the fact of not having received the intervention or experimental manipulation. To reach this goal, research participants are randomly assigned to the control and experimental groups. When all other factors or aspects of the experimental environment are kept constant, the difference observed in the dependent variable (between the control and experimental groups) may be attributed to the effect of the independent variable. *See also* Dependent Variable; Experimental Group; Independent Variable

Convenience Sampling   A sample of research participants that a researcher uses simply because it is easily accessible or readily available. While sometimes necessary to complete a research study, the disadvantage of convenience samples is the difficulty in supporting generalization of the findings to the larger population. *See also* Sampling

Convention   The Democratic and Republican Party conventions meet every four years to nominate their respective party's presidential candidates. Delegates from each state are sent to the convention to formally cast their votes for the presidential nominee. The reality is that the candidates have already been chosen by party members voting in each state's primary or caucus. This change in procedure came about after the 1968 Democratic National Convention in Chicago. Many Americans were unhappy with the Democrats' nomination of Hubert Humphrey, who subsequently lost the 1968 campaign to Richard Nixon. Political conventions are not mentioned in the U.S. Constitution.

Conversion Disorder   A type of mental disorder whereby an individual experiences neurological symptoms (e.g., numbness) that cannot be explained by physical causes. Instead, it is believed that the problems arise as a result of mental problems or, in other words, that the individual has converted or otherwise conceived his or her psychological problems to be medical problems, when in fact there is little or no medical basis for the problems. The *Diagnostic and Statistical Manual of Mental Disorders* (*DSM*) specifically defines a conversion disorder as a condition where the client presents with symptoms that suggest a neurological deficit or sensory condition but that cannot be explained fully by a medical condition and the clinician therefore judges the onset of the symptoms to be associated with a psychological stress.

Convict/Conviction   A slang word that means a person who was convicted of a crime and is sentenced to serve time in jail or prison; when a person charged with a particular crime is found guilty of that crime by a court of law. The guilty verdict, whether set forth by a judge or a jury, is the conviction.

Cooperative Federalism   The federal principle is based on the notion that unity can be found in diversity. In federal organizations, authority is divided between a center and the periphery. The two most influential manifestations of the federal principle emerged under the names of *dual federalism* and *cooperative federalism* in the history of the United States. While the two strands of federalism share the federal idea of dual administration, they differ in how the two levels of government relate to each other.

Cooperative federalism is a concept that was first used in the New Deal period (1933–1941) to refer to, among other things, federal aid programs that established national regulatory measures administered by the states and funded by Congress. The idea of cooperative federalism served as a euphemism for the centralization of policy making in the national government at the expense of states' rights and autonomous decision-making processes. Since the 1930s, the Supreme Court has given broad constitutional approval to grant-in-aid programs, the primary form of cooperative federalism.

In Europe, there is a current discussion on whether cooperative federalism is the federal model that best represents the law-making function in the European Union. Scholarship demonstrates the evolution of the European legal order from a dual federalism to a cooperative federalist philosophy. This transition from dual to cooperative federalism is viewed as a positive development that will benefit both levels of government—the European Union and the member states—since the ideal of structuring the law-making function according to the problem at hand is more flexible and efficient than the idea of mutually exclusive spheres of power. The mechanism of common federal standards supplemented by territorially differentiated national solutions best expresses the idea of unity in diversity. For more information, see Belz (2005) and Shutze (2009).

Cooperative Learning/Instruction   A teaching method where a small group of mixed-ability learners work together to solve a common problem. Each learner takes equal responsibility for solving the problem and learning; that is, learners must work together to ensure that everyone has acquired an understanding of the concepts and material in question. The most successful cooperative learning occurs when there is a combination of rewards for attaining group goals and individual accountability. Teaching students communication and helping skills increases the likelihood of success of instructional efforts employing cooperative-learning methods.

Cooperative learning is one of the cornerstones of constructivist approaches to teaching and learning. In general, constructivists (e.g., Piaget, Vygotsky) posit that engaging in cooperative learning is more akin to real-world learning environments where knowledge about the world is co-constructed through group interactions. Research suggests that cooperative-teaching methods are useful, particularly for minority students who are younger, urban, and of lower socioeconomic status. *See also* Constructivist Learning Theory

Copycat Effect/Crime   The incorporation of elements from a media-portrayed crime, either real or dramatized, into a subsequent crime. Gabriel Tarde, at the beginning of the 20th century, was the first to suggest that certain sensational criminal incidents prompted similar acts. It was not until the 1970s, however, with the emergence of widespread copycat crime, that his assertions received any attention.

Because of the inherent difficulties in empirically researching the copycat effect (i.e., identifying those subjects most likely to be susceptible, making a direct link between one crime and a subsequent crime) the information on copycat crime, though pervasive, is largely anecdotal. Most of the empirical research on the copycat effect has been performed in relation to suicide. What little has been performed with respect to crime has used offenders as subjects.

Anecdotal evidence has shown that the copycat effect of the media on crime has a twofold impact on society: (1) it creates crime where it previously would not have existed, resulting in an increase in crime, and (2) it informs the behavior of established criminals. The great preponderance of anecdotal case histories supports the latter. Also, there have been empirical studies that suggest that while a large number of the perpetrators who mimicked media crimes recall using techniques they learned from television viewing, for the most part, copycat offenders had already possessed the intent to perform a crime before they imitated a technique. Many were already part of the offender population. In turn, there is little empirical evidence to suggest that the media have a direct, criminalizing effect on noncriminals.

Society has witnessed scores of copycat crimes, from heinous crimes such as school shootings, terrorist acts, and over-the-counter drug tampering to other offenses, such as certain types of property theft. Their repeated incidence has led many advocacy groups to call for some restrictions on crime reporting (at least, sensationalized crime reporting) and programming. These efforts, however, have been largely curbed by the doctrines of freedom of the press and freedom of speech, coupled with the difficulties in collecting empirical data to support their arguments. For more information, see Coleman (2004), Surette (1990), and Tarde (1903/1962, 1912). *See also* Crime Programming on Television; Media Effects

Copyright   A legal protection provided to authors of works in music, writing, art, architecture, and other areas of production. A copyright protects a work from unauthorized reproduction and lets the author control its display, reproduction, performance, or sales and distribution. Copyright protects both published and unpublished works. International copyright regulations vary; in the United States, copyrights are registered with the U.S. Copyright Office. In "works for hire," the copyright resides with the employer and not the employee. Violation of copyright protections is illegal and subject to criminal penalties. One limitation of the rights of copyright owners is called "fair use"; it refers to the right of the public to duplicate parts of a copyrighted work for criticism, comment, news reporting, teaching, research, or parody. *See also* Plagiarism

Cornea   A transparent, curved membrane that covers the iris and the pupil. The cornea acts like a "window" because the outside light rays first pass through it. Together with the lens, the cornea merges the outside light, helping the eye to focus, though it also contributes significantly to refraction. While the curvature of the lens can be adjusted depending on the distance of the object, the curvature of the cornea is fixed. Lesions within the shape of the cornea cause *astigmatism*, an optical defect that causes selective blurring of the image. *See also* Cones

Coroner   A public official who must investigate the causes of death, especially in cases where the cause appears suspicious or the death occurs under unusual or unnatural circumstances. The coroner has the power to order an autopsy when the cause of death is questionable. The word is derived from the Latin *corona*, meaning "crown" or "official of the crown."

Corporal Punishment   *(education)*   The act of administering physical blows to the body of a student, typically to the buttocks using a paddle, to cause pain but not injury in order to influence the student's behavior. The U.S. Supreme Court in *Ingraham v. Wright* (1977) ruled that corporal punishment did not violate a student's constitutional right to be protected against cruel and unusual punishment. For more information, see *Ingraham v. Wright* (1977).

Corporal Punishment (*sociology*) The infliction of physical pain for the purpose of punishment. A common practice in most criminal justice systems, especially prior to the Enlightenment, barbaric corporal punishments, such as scourging, drawing and quartering, flogging, and stoning, were used to extract confessions and inflict pain on convicted criminals. In the United States, corporal punishment in the home, the school, or the prison system is viewed with disapproval.

Corporate Crime/Law Crimes that are committed by corporations or by people affiliated with corporations. It can include white-collar crime, organized crime, or a combination of both. White-collar criminals can often enlist the assistance of organized-crime members, and organized-crime members may use legitimate businesses to commit illegal activities. Such crimes can include embezzlement, stocks and securities fraud, and so forth. Corporate law pertains to statutes that establish the legality of corporations. Corporations are governed by state corporation laws, trade regulation laws, contract laws, consumer protection laws, labor laws, and so forth. Corporations are considered a legal entity and are separate from their stockholders.

Corporate Media A system of media that is owned, produced, and distributed by corporate interests. Many argue that because the U.S. system of media is dictated by the demands of a capitalist marketplace, journalism is restricted and biased, filtering out information that does not suit the corporate agenda, thereby leading to restrictions in public discourse. Criticism and wariness of corporate media ownership became more and more acute in the 1980s when the relaxation of ownership regulations led to the creation of vast mega corporations. This environment spawned groups such as Fairness & Accuracy in Reporting (FAIR), formed in 1986 to oversee the media, monitor accuracy and bias, and advocate the breaking up of these large media conglomerates.

Others, however, say that the claim that a handful of transnational media moguls control media outlets is hugely overstated. Instead, they point out that larger corporate-owned outlets have grown only in relation to the growth of developed economies. Also, they maintain that these outlets provide more diversity and editorial content than smaller nonprofits or privately owned outlets, which often display ideological biases. For more information, see Compaine (2002), McChesney (2004), and Soley (2004). ***See also*** Deregulation (media studies, political science)

Corporation A form of organization, often called a "C-Corporation," that exists as a legal entity and has centralized management, limited liability, transferable shares, and continuity of existence. A corporation is created as an artificial person, in accordance with law, and with the purpose of engaging in activities of a business nature. While a corporation exists separately from its owners, the shareholders, it has many of the same rights, abilities, and responsibilities as held by humans. A corporation can hire or discharge employees; enter into contracts; and have the right to own, sell, rent, or lease property. Furthermore, corporations are subject to risk, lawsuits, and income tax liabilities.

In comparison with other major forms of business ownership, such as sole proprietorship and partnerships, corporations are considered a more flexible model with which to conduct business on a larger scale, and a corporation is the predominant form of business entity in the United States. As most corporations are businesses for profit, capital for corporate activities is raised by selling shares of stock. Every share of stock represents a portion of ownership of the corporation and is typically transferable.

From a stock issuance standpoint, there are two types of corporations: public and private. With a public corporation, anyone has the ability to purchase shares of stock, and the stocks are often traded on a stock exchange. On the other hand, a private company only issues stocks to specific individuals, such as members of the principal stockholder's family. A corporation is governed by a board of directors, which is elected by its shareholders and makes the major decisions.

Since 1776, when the power to grant incorporation moved from the Crown to individual state legislators, corporations have evolved through the 20th century to provide a very broad purpose and to include multiple forms of corporations with distinct features, such as charitable, cooperative, municipal, and religious corporations. Additionally, a number of business entities exist that are similar to corporations. Such organizations include professional corporations, not-for-profit corporations, closed corporations, limited-liability companies, and S-Corporations.

Corpus Callosum A structure that connects the left and right cerebral hemispheres. It is a 4-inch-long, ¼-inch-thick structure that consists of millions of flat bundle axons. The corpus callosum is the largest white matter brain structure and is responsible for most of the interhemispheric brain communication. When the corpus callosum is severed, patients experience different degrees of "disconnection," known as a *split-brain condition*. A surgical operation conducted to separate the two hemispheres (corpus callosotomy) is rarely performed as a last resort in intractable epilepsy. ***See also*** Cerebral Cortex; Cerebral Lateralization; Split Brain

Corpus Delicti Translated from the Latin, the term means the body of the crime or corpse. It is a legal term that requires the presence of material evidence and elements of the crime for conviction. Before a defendant can be held criminally accountable, the court must prove that an actual crime transpired (*actus reus*) and that the defendant had a criminal mind (*mens rea*).

Corrections The component of the criminal justice system that punishes offenders after conviction. As indicated by its name, corrections is an attempt to correct or rehabilitate the offender. This philosophy fell into disfavor in the 1970s and was replaced with a more retributive model. Corrections can include sentences of jail or prison, in addition to community-based or extra-institutional punishments, such as halfway houses, electronic monitoring, house arrest, fines, restitution, asset forfeiture, drug programs, community service, boot camps, work release, shock incarceration, probation, parole, and so forth. Correctional facilities are a form of institutional punishment and can include jails to hold detainees, inmates sentenced for one year, or state inmates temporarily while awaiting court appearances or instate transfers. They are locally managed, and in most jurisdictions, they are supervised by the sheriff's department. Prisons are specifically reserved for convicted felons who are serving more than a year's sentence, and they are managed by the respective state's Department of Correctional Services or the Federal Bureau of Prisons.

Most state systems use a centralized system of management; there is one main administrative unit in charge of establishing the standards of procedure. Federal systems tend to be decentralized and focus on unit management. States facilities are classified according to security level and can consist of supermaximum, maximum, medium, and minimum security facilities. Federal facilities are classified as administrative segregation, high security, medium security, minimum security, and low security. Inmates are classified in a reception center according to their security level (i.e., instant offense, past record, etc.), and their treatment needs (i.e., programmatic, medical, or mental health requirements). Depending on behavior, an inmate's security classification can change several times during his or her incarceration. **See also** Community-Based Corrections; Jail; Prison/Prisoner; Probation

Correlation (*education*)   A measure of how closely two variables are associated. For example, education and income are correlated: When education is high, income tends to be high; when education is low, income tends to be low. This is an example of a *positive* correlation or a *direct* relation: The values of the two variables tend to move in the same direction. A *negative* correlation or an *inverse* relation is one in which the values of the two variables tend to go in opposite directions, such as nations' education levels and their birth rates: Nations with high education levels tend to have low birth rates; countries with low education levels tend to have high birth rates. Note that *positive* and *negative* do not mean *favorable* or *unfavorable*. The relation between weight and diabetes is "positive" but a health risk; the relation between class size and student learning is "negative" but a good outcome.

Correlation coefficients expressing these relations range from +1.0 for a perfectly positive relation, through 0 when there is no relation, to –1.0 when the relation is perfectly negative. The original and most common correlation is the Pearson *r*. There are several adaptations of the Pearson *r* for different types of data, such as ranks or categories rather than continua, but they are all expressed using coefficients that run from +1.0 to –1.0.

A *multiple correlation* is between one dependent variable and two or more independent variables. It is expressed with a capital letter *R*. An important measure for both the two-variable (or bivariate) and the multiple correlation is the *squared correlation*, expressed as either r^2 or R^2. The *squared coefficient* tells you the proportion of variance in the dependent variable that can be explained by the independent variable or, in the case of the multiple *R*, the proportion that can be explained by all the independent variables taken together. For example, say that in a sample of college graduates, the multiple correlation *R* between their college grade point averages (GPAs) and their high school GPAs and SAT scores is .50. Then R^2 is .25, or 25%. That means that knowing the independent variables enables you to predict the dependent variable 25% better. In other terms, 25% of the differences in the dependent variable are explained by the independent variables, and 75% are not.

A *partial correlation* describes the relation between two variables while controlling for (partialling out) the effects of one or more other variables. For example, in the same sample of graduates, if the simple correlation between high school GPAs and college GPAs is .40, a researcher could use a partial correlation to see what that correlation is after subtracting any effects of SAT scores. If the partial correlation was .30, that would mean that the correlation would have been .30 if all students had the same SAT score. **See also** Regression Analysis

Correlation (*psychology*)   A statistical tool used to measure the strength and the direction of a linear relationship between two variables. Correlations are expressed in numerical terms using *correlation coefficients* that range from –1.0 to +1.0. Two variables are positively correlated when they simultaneously increase or decrease in the same direction. On the other hand, two variables are negatively correlated when they simultaneously increase or decrease in different directions. The higher the correlation, the stronger the relationship is between the two variables, regardless of whether that relationship is positive or negative. The Pearson product moment correlation coefficient is the best-known correlation coefficient. **See also** Statistics (*psychology*)

Corruption (*economics*)   The abuse of power to satisfy individual or parochial group interest. The corrupt individual is, therefore, an official or fiduciary who uses his status unlawfully to procure benefits for himself or others to the detriment of society.

Corruption may be systemic and analogous to organized crime. Systemic corruption occurs when the segments of a government that are supposed to prevent corruption by way of inspection, evaluation, enforcement, budgeting, and auditing are in fact highly corrupted. In such situations, there is usually a conspiracy of principals and agents to be corrupt.

Corruption is a major concern for international businesses because of the harmful effects it has on investment and economic growth, and many countries have at least made the symbolic gesture of signing treaties to prevent corruption. In 1996, the Organization of American States adopted the Inter-American Convention Against Corruption. The Organization for Economic Cooperation and Development (OECD) adopted the Convention on Combating Bribery of Foreign Public Officials in International Business Transactions in 1997. The African Union adopted the convention on Preventing and Combating Corruption in 2003. And the United Nations ratified its Convention Against Corruption in 2005. Consequently, although some might argue in favor of a "grease hypothesis" (i.e., that corruption speeds up the wheels of commerce), corruption is unequivocally a crime in international law.

In 1977, the U.S. Congress passed the Foreign Corrupt Practices Act, which makes it illegal for U.S. companies to bribe foreign government officials. The act was amended in 1988, inter alia, to differentiate between lack of knowledge and willful bribery. It has become recurrently difficult to distinguish grease payments from bribery.

Some economists believe that corruption is a drag on growth and that it impedes foreign direct investment (FDI). Therefore, corruption hurts developing countries, in particular, where FDI and capital inflows have the potential to augment meager national savings.

Curing corruption will require better systems rather than laws or new codes of conduct. It is believed that reducing monopoly power (by promoting competition), limiting the exercise of discretion (by making rules transparent and less ambiguous), and demonstrating exemplary behavior, will minimize the propensity to have systemic corruption. The World Bank and Transparency International compile data on the intensity of corruption in various countries. For more information, see Folsom, Gordon, and Spanogle (2004), Perkins, Radlet, and Lindauer (2006), and Slomanson (2003).

Corruption *(sociology)* A word that describes an individual or an entire system not performing its duties as required or performing such duties unlawfully or improperly. In the criminal justice system, police corruption occurs when a police unit or police officers perform their job improperly by taking bribes, using their power to engage in criminal activity, engaging in brutality against suspects, planting evidence, and so forth. Corruption can exist in the court system if prosecutors fail to prosecute cases or engage in malicious prosecution or if jury members or judges are bribed or coerced. In corrections, corrupt correctional officers may physically or sexually abuse inmates, bring contraband into the prison for profit, and so forth. Corrupt

politicians may vote for or against a piece of legislation for financial or personal gain. Corruption is an extremely serious charge as it undermines the fabric of the government's system of social control.

Cost-Benefit A quantitative analysis and decision-making tool used by public and private entities to assess the efficacy of policy decisions or projects. Cost-benefit analysis measures both costs and benefits in the context of a single metric, typically currency units. For example, in the United States, costs and benefits are measured with respect to the U.S. dollar, whereas in England they would be assessed with respect to the British pound.

Under analysis, if the benefits exceed the costs (called a positive net benefit), then decision makers can use the analysis to justify moving forward with the policy under analysis; however, if the policy or project fails to meet expectations, then the initial analysis can be used as a way of assessing the quality and justification of the decision making. Cost-benefit analysis is useful for assessing the efficacy of a single project, or it can be used to compare the relative benefits and costs of many projects. Thus, decision makers can more precisely determine in which direction to apply their limited resources in order to achieve the greatest efficacy.

Cost-benefit analysis is applied to many areas of decision making (e.g., criminal justice, public health, critical infrastructure projects, etc.). Ostensibly, any policy or decision-making venue where the costs or benefits can be quantified in a single measurement can be analyzed using this approach; however, this approach is not without its problems. Estimates of costs depend on information that may be incomplete or invalid; moreover, this form of analysis frequently relies on past projects as predictors of future ones. That said, this approach can be incredibly useful and cost-effective when the assumptions and related cost-benefits are understood and measured accurately.

Cost-Benefit Analysis (CBA) *(economics)* An economic theory that maintains that rational individuals base their decisions on the comparison of costs and benefits. Beyond the realm of individual or private CBA, public decisions made by governments are classified as social CBA. Social CBA has implications for nonmarket participants and the use of scarce resources.

Externalities are generated when nonmarket participants incur part of the costs of market transactions and governments will have to decide whether to tax or subsidize a particular activity. Such a decision is normally evaluated on the basis of social cost versus social benefit. To encourage or discourage any activity, a planner must know the social value (shadow price) of the activity. If the market price is less than the social value, the scale of the activity should be expanded. CBA measures social value.

Since economic resources are scarce relative to societal wants, resources must be allocated in such a way that they are not overallocated or underallocated to an

C

economic activity. This means that the marginal social cost must be equal to the marginal social benefit (the additional benefit must be equal to the additional cost).

Advanced econometric techniques, such as constrained optimization and linear programming, can be used to estimate incremental costs and benefits. For more information, see Brent (1997).

Cost-Benefit Analysis (CBA) *(political science)*   A process of weighing the pros (benefits) and cons (costs) of a given project. A CBA can be economic or social in nature, the benefits either strictly financial in the former or for the betterment of society in the latter. One of the classic works exploring cost-benefit analysis is E. J. Mishan and E. Quah's (1976) *Cost Benefit Analysis,* where they assert that the CBA is based on the principle of a Pareto improvement. A Pareto improvement is the principle that at least one person would become better off and no one would become worse off from the idea. In most cases, to achieve a Pareto improvement, the aggregate winners must compensate the aggregate losers so that no one suffers. According to Diana Fuguitt and Sharon Wilcox in *Cost Benefit Analysis for Public Sector Decision Makers* (1999), public policy analysis using CBA should assess the following three questions: (1) Is this policy better than no policy at all? (2) Is public policy better than using resources in public or private investments?, and (3) Does the policy's future value offset current consumption?

When governments use CBA, there are a number of difficulties that may arise, including government costs being higher than anticipated, difficulty in assigning monetary value to social reforms, and the undue influence of professional economists. Some critics also contend that the breadth of politics may be beyond the scope of analysis. For more information, see Fuguitt and Wilcox (1999) and Mishan and Quah (2007).

Counsel   A person who can provide representation in a court of law or provide legal assistance (also called a lawyer or an attorney). The right to counsel during criminal legal proceedings is a fundamental right implied in the Fifth Amendment and expressly written in the Sixth Amendment. Miranda warnings, which include the right to remain silent and the right to counsel, are implied in the due process clause of the Fifth Amendment and incorporated to the states via the Fourteenth Amendment. This right to counsel applies prior to formal court proceedings (i.e., at pre-indictment lineups, interrogation, etc.), while the Sixth Amendment right to counsel applies at the start of formal court proceedings, such as arraignment.

Counseling   Interventions and strategies to help people develop more satisfying lives. Generally regarded as a process, *professional counseling* serves individuals, groups, couples, and families with a wide range of functions and addresses internal concerns, relationship difficulties, personal growth, educational concerns,

stress management, career development, substance abuse, adjustment difficulties, life transitions, wellness, and pathology. Professional counseling's hallmark is the helping relationship.

There are many specialties within the field of counseling, including mental health counselors, school counselors, rehabilitation counselors, and marriage and family counselors, to name a few. The profession's governing body is the American Counseling Association. ***See also*** Therapy

Counseling Psychology   A branch of applied psychology with its roots in the vocational guidance and veterans' services movements of the early and mid 20th century. Counseling psychology emphasizes the scientist-practitioner model of training and has contemporary emphases in the following areas: counseling and psychotherapy, positive psychology, life-span development, vocational development, health psychology, and cultural factors.

Counterconditioning   A technique often used in behavior therapy to treat the fear and anxiety associated with phobias. An individual is conditioned to display a behavior that is in opposition to the undesirable behavior by gradually being exposed to the anxiety-provoking stimulus. Initial exposure to the stimulus is at such a low intensity that the undesirable behavior is not displayed. Patients are taught coping mechanisms, such as relaxation techniques, which would run counter to their fear-induced behaviors. Gradually, exposure to the stimulus is increased such that the individual no longer experiences fear or anxiety. ***See also*** Behavior Therapy (education, psychology); Phobia

Counterculture   The values and norms of behavior of a cultural group or subculture. A counterculture does not follow the mainstream of society. It is a form of political opposition. A counterculture can reach critical mass and persist for many years. A counterculture movement expresses the ethos, aspirations, and dreams of a specific population during an era. It is a social manifestation of a worldview. A counterculture refers to a group rather than an individual.

In his book *The Making of a Counter Culture* (1995), Theodore Roszak questioned how the counterculture could change the established system. Roszak was opposed to a highly sophisticated industrialized society. He did not like the modern aspects of the industrialized world in which people planned, rationalized, and strived for order in their lives.

You can read texts that precede Roszak's thoughts about the counterculture world. Those books include Ginsberg's *Howl* as well as C. Wright Mills's *Causes of World War III. Mad* magazine was also a precursor to the counterculture world of the 1960s in the United States.

Roszak condemned consumerism. He stated that mass consumption of goods would lead people to a meaningless existence. He believed that the counterculture should get rid of the scientific worldview and replace it with a "non-intellective consciousness," which is a personal form of transcendence that does not condone materialism. Finally, Roszak believed that the counterculture needed to drop the ego.

There were two models of countercultures: Freud and Marx. Marx dealt with ideas, and Freud dealt with the mind. Roszak felt that Freud and Marx were integral to the counterculture because they were part of a social and psychic revolution.

The counterculture adopted *The Tibetan Book of the Dead* and applied it to the psychedelic experience. Roszak applied the writings of Herbert Marcuse to the discussion of Eastern religion and the counterculture.

Roszak set up an argument between science and mysticism. He related this discussion to the role of technology in modern society.

One of Roszak's most famous quotes about the counterculture was cited in his text *The Making of a Counter Culture* (1969/1995):

> At the bohemian fringe of our disaffected youth culture, all roads lead to psychedelia. The fascination with hallucinogenic drugs emerges persistently as the common denominator of the many protean forms the counter culture has assumed in the post-World War II period. (p. 155)

Roszak disliked psychedelic drugs because he felt that they distracted people so that they were not as politically conscious as they needed to be in society. In fact, Roszak felt that American society was becoming too dependent on drugs.

To Roszak, counterculture was counter to the Age of Reason and the Enlightenment. He warned us to avoid machines and not become robots in the modern world. For more information, see Ginsberg (1956/1995), Mills (1958), Roszak (1969/1995), and Sambhava (1993).

Counterfactual Thinking   The tendency to imagine alternative outcomes to an actual result that might have happened but did not. Although we do not engage in counterfactual thinking after every experience, we tend to engage in this type of "what if" thinking when we regret actions that resulted in negative outcomes, as opposed to thinking this way as the result of inaction. Counterfactual thinking can result in positive or negative emotions. If we imagine that the alternative outcome is better than the actual outcome, we might feel disappointment; however, if we imagine that the alternative outcome is worse than the actual outcome, we are perhaps more likely to feel relief. For more information, see Kahneman and Miller (1986). ***See also*** Cognition

Counterplan   Part of argumentation theory in communication, commonly exploited in the activity of policy debate. It allows the negative viewpoint to defend a separate plan. In that plan, the counterplan has to be nontopical and competitive, have advantages and disadvantages, and be effectively used along with a disadvantage. The affirmative viewpoint needs to expose the flaws in the counterplan and show why the ideas presented by the negative viewpoint are a bad idea. When someone argues in a debate with a counterplan, the object is to explain what the negative viewpoint is and why it should be done. In summary, a counterplan allows a nontopical, reasonable alternative to the affirmative plan. Such reasoning is often used in hypothesis testing in social science methodology.

Coup d'Etat   The illegal overthrow and replacement of a nation's leadership by an insurgent group, usually working from within the government. A coup differs from a revolution because it is not carried out by the "people," instead it is instigated by government insiders who have access and hence the ability to seize control of the police and military powers. The first notable coup d'etat was Napoleon's overthrow of the French Directory in 1799. Modern coups d'etat are limited to unstable global government regimes, never having occurred in either Great Britain or the United States The term is French for strike against the state (*coup* [blow or strike], *état* [state]).

Court   A legal forum for resolving disputes, reviewing matters of law, or adjudicating criminal matters. Both federal and state courts are based on a hierarchical system. The only court established by the U.S. Constitution (Article 3, Section 1) is the Supreme Court; all other courts are established by statute. Typically, federal courts are courts of general jurisdiction; they can handle both civil and criminal cases. The first level of the federal court system is the trial court, known as the U.S. District Court; all federal cases are tried in this court. Every state has at least one district court. The intermediate courts, known as the U.S. Court of Appeals or U.S. Circuit Courts, do not hear evidence; they serve as a medium for review and appeal of both state and federal cases. There are 13 federal circuit courts in the United States, and each has jurisdiction over a particular geographical area.

The highest appellate federal court is the U.S. Supreme Court. Their holdings constitute the supreme law of the land, and all other courts are bound by their decisions. Most cases come to the Supreme Court through writ of certiorari; four or more justices must agree to review to the case. Out of 6,000 petitions that are brought to the Supreme Court annually, approximately 200 cases are reviewed.

In the state system, the lower court is also the trial court. Depending on the state, they are known as circuit, district, superior, or municipal courts. These courts can be courts of general jurisdiction or courts of specialized jurisdiction. Specialized courts hear cases pertaining only to a particular area, such as family court, traffic court, or drug court. Most states have two appellate divisions, an intermediate appeals court and the highest state appellate division, known in most areas as the state supreme court.

Credibility   The subjective and objective levels of the truthfulness of a message. If the message is credible, it is trustworthy, and it shows expertise of some kind.

Credibility in communication is very important on the Internet. In the 1990s, the Internet emerged as a wonderful tool for sharing information. However, was the material credible? This was such an important question because so many people relied on the Internet. People used to rely on television, radio, movies, and newspapers for information. The Internet was soon becoming the main source of information for people in the United States.

Flanagin and Metzger (2007) explored the level of credibility posed by the Internet. The researchers discovered that most people did not verify the information that they found on the Internet. People generally believed what they read on the Internet. Flanagin and Metzger discovered that people generally found the news on the Internet to be credible. This was because people generally liked the depth of content, the design features, and the site complexity. On the other hand, people generally felt that personal sites had the least credibility. The researchers also discovered that college students generally felt that the Internet was very credible. College students relied on the Internet for academic as well as personal information.

Since the 1990s, many Americans have found the Internet to be a very credible source for medical information as well as retirement information. In addition, many people have no hesitation about booking their own airline flights on the Internet, thus bypassing travel agents. Students will often select their own courses online without going to a Registrar. Many people prefer to make purchases over the Internet instead of taking the time to go to a store to select items. At the core is the belief that digital media now allow for credibility that was not in existence before. That this belief is faulty, at best, has given rise to the very strong emphasis on information literacy in college curriculums. The problem, of course, is for those who navigate the Internet on their own. For more information, see Flanagin and Metzger (2007).

Crime   Behavior that violates the penal law. A crime is a deviant behavior, which violates the norms, values, and morals of society. Crimes must be understood in both a historical and a cultural context. The law is dynamic and constantly changes. Behaviors deemed deviant in one time period may not be viewed as such in the current time period. In the same respect, behavior considered criminal or deviant in one country may not be viewed so in another. Governments are responsible for controlling criminal behavior; such behavior undermines society's process of social control, reduces citizen confidence, and jeopardizes public safety.

The legislature is charged with developing the penal law, both the substantive and the procedural components. The substantive law defines the elements of the crime and the punishments or sanctions associated with the commission of such crimes. The procedural law outlines the rules for fair and equitable procedures in the justice system, such as the rules that must be followed for making an arrest; interrogating, charging, or arraigning a suspect; giving instructions to a jury; and so forth. In common law, crimes were divided into two categories, *mala in se* and *mala prohibitum*. *Mala in se* crimes were behaviors deemed inherently evil in and of themselves, such as murder, while *mala prohibitum* crimes were behaviors categorized as illegal under statute, such as drug use. Currently, crimes are divided into *misdemeanors* and *felonies*. Misdemeanors are less serious offenses, can only impose a mandatory imprisonment sentence of one year, and must be conducted in the presence of a law enforcement officer to result in an arrest. A felony is a serious offense, can result in imprisonment for more than one year, remains on an offender's record for life, and can bar individuals from certain employment, housing, educational opportunities, voting, and so forth. A suspect can be arrested for a felony with or without a warrant; law enforcement does not have to witness the act to effect the arrest.

Law enforcement agencies are responsible for executing the law and are essential in crime prevention. They use proactive and reactive responses to crime. The district attorney's office is responsible for formally charging a suspect with the crime, obtaining an indictment, and formally prosecuting the offender to the fullest extent of the law. The court system will hear evidence in criminal cases. If the case is not dropped or plea bargained, the court will render a verdict; once the offender is convicted, the court will impose a sentence within the confines of existing legislative statutes. Once sentenced, agencies that make up the corrections department will be responsible for executing the sentence.

Crime Control/Crime Control Model   A perspective, initially pioneered by James Q. Wilson in the 1980s, highlighting the need for harsher punishments. According to Wilson, crime was not caused by economic desperation, it was a consequence of greed. He argued that offenders had little stake in conventionality, were more likely to take risks than other people, and chose crime because it was exciting and required little work. Hence, addressing the causes of poverty would not reduce criminal activity; harsh punishments were the answer. The crime control model is concerned with protecting society by controlling dangerous offenders. Offenders will be deterred through the fear of harsh formal sanctions. Increased law enforcement, mandatory punishment, and incarceration will reduce criminal activity. The theorists want the focus of the system to be on the victim, not the offender. They advocate for the abolition of the *exclusionary rule*, by which technicalities allow key evidence to be excluded from trial and subsequently may allow the guilty to go free.

Crime News   Those legal trials that spill over into the entertainment media—because of the celebrity of the participants or the salacious nature of the crimes—have become the most dominant element in crime and justice coverage. The slogan "If it bleeds, it leads" developed in the late 1970s in response to the prevalence of newscasts that led with crime blocks—a unit of news stories that focused on the worst criminal incidents. A study by Graber (1980) found that the media overreported violent crime and underreported property crime, thus skewing the public perception of crime. By the late 1990s, stations in some parts of the country responded to viewer criticism that suggested that crime, which had been on the decline in most urban areas, was being overemphasized. Some even set standards that ensured that rather than simply recounting of all the crime committed in any given day, in cases where the crime did not pose a threat to the community, the story should provide a context for understanding the crime.

Often, the coverage of media trials, like in other crime news reporting, misleads the public about the nature of the justice system and its role in society because, in many instances, the most bizarre cases are selected. In arguing the appropriateness of media coverage, the First Amendment rights of freedom of speech and the press have always been juxtaposed with the rights afforded the accused under the Sixth Amendment. After the sensationalized trial of Bruno Hauptmann in 1935, most states banned TV, radio, and photographic equipment from courtrooms. Later, however, as equipment got less intrusive, and throughout the 1980s, most courts reevaluated their bans. By the turn of the century, all states allowed cameras in the courtroom and most left it to the discretion of the judge to allow television coverage.

In 1991, Court TV, which provided live coverage of media trials, was launched, and its coverage of the O. J. Simpson trial in 1994—the most publicized trial in history—has resulted in much subsequent analysis. Proponents of virtually unrestricted television coverage argue that the trial gave the American public a valuable civics lesson, educating people about the workings of the judicial system, its strengths, and its weaknesses. Others say that the trial was dragged out and its legal integrity compromised by lawyers who were performing for the cameras and that time spent by the media on the one trial was attention taken away from other issues. For more information, see Alexander (2004) and Graber (1980). *See also* Media and the Judicial System

Crime of Passion   A homicide or attempted homicide, typically committed with provocation and without premeditation or deliberation. In most jurisdictions, such murders are classified under the category of manslaughter or attempted manslaughter. It

is not considered a justification to homicide, but it does mitigate culpability and reduce the level of blameworthiness.

Crime Prevention   A policy or proposal enacted to reduce the incidence of crime, deter potential offenders, and reduce the prevalence of victimization. Crime prevention can be achieved through both informal and formal sanctions. Informal sanctions, or primary prevention, target individual factors and address one's stake in conventional bonds. The more one is attached, committed, and involved in family, school, work, church, and so forth, the less likely one will violate such bonds by engaging in criminal activity. Community programs, especially those targeted at at-risk youths, fall under the umbrella of secondary prevention. Formal sanctions, also known as tertiary prevention, focus on the initiatives, punishments, and sanctions set forth and implemented by the criminal justice system.

Crime Programming on Television   Programs that are centered on a crime theme, either reality based or fictional, which seemingly fill the networks' program schedules. While situation comedies, sports, and feature-length movies are the most popular types of programs with audiences, the most dominant type of drama genre is crime shows. These appeal to audiences because unlike other types of drama, which often tell stories in a serialized fashion, episodes of crime dramas are usually closed-ended—the audience is treated to a story with closure within the designated timeframe. Also, the networks have episodes that repeat well as they do not have to appear in any particular order—making them more lucrative to produce for syndication.

Since the 1960s, when congressional hearings met over the violent content of *The Untouchables*, social scientists, lawmakers, and industry regulators—arguing on one side or the other—have sought to address the depiction of violent crime on television. Behavioral effects studies have tried to explore whether exposure to this type of programming can lead to more aggressive or violent behavior, either immediately or as the result of prolonged exposure. These studies are limited, however, because of the inherent difficulties in performing this type of research. Explorations of cultivation theory have sought more to determine whether prolonged exposure may result in changes in perception or attitude. Some research has suggested that frequent viewers may overestimate the amount of violent crime in society and believe that the number of violent crimes surpasses the number of property crimes. This fear of crime, however, is often tempered by "just resolution" in which the police and the judicial system almost always prevail—another distortion of reality. For more information, see Sparks (1992). *See also* Behavioral Effects; Cultivation Theory; Syndicated Programs/Syndicates

Crime Rate   The measure of the incidence or prevalence of crime in a given time period or in a given geographical area. Crime statistics are reported in the Uniform Crime Report (UCR) (aggregate statistics complied by the FBI based on official police arrests); the National Crime Victimization Survey (NCVS) (statistics compiled by the Department of Justice and the U.S. Census Bureau based on reports from victims of crime); and self-report data (information collected by researchers based on reports from offenders about crimes they committed). The most common method for determining the crime rate in a given jurisdiction is to use the formula in the UCR, which is the total number of crimes divided by the population, multiplied by 100,000. Once a rate is derived, crime rates in jurisdictions of all sizes can be compared. Crime rates are used to evaluate neighborhood safety, to modify existing crime control policies, or to assess whether a particular law enforcement strategy is effective.

Criminal Homicide   The killing of one human being by another without justification. This is considered a *mala in se* crime, a crime that is evil in and of itself. The word *homicide* is derived from the Latin *homicidium; homo* means human being, and *caedere* means to cut or to kill. Criminal homicide can include many different categories of murder, such as first-degree murder (killing with premeditation, deliberation, and malice aforethought), second-degree murder (murder of depraved indifference), felony murder (someone getting killed during the commission of another felony crime), voluntary manslaughter (murder committed with provocation), involuntary manslaughter (murder committed through recklessness or negligence), and so forth.

Criminal Justice   A society's formal system of social control. It is a tool for implementing and executing the law, in addition to punishing those unable to follow the law. It begins with initial contact by the police and can end with the offender's re-entry into society; it involves a series of sequential steps, including investigating criminal activity, making arrests, gathering evidence, bringing formal charges, conducting trials, rendering sentences, and carrying out punishments. The criminal justice system consists of three main components: (1) the police, who are responsible for executing the law, investigate and deter crimes; (2) the court system comprises the prosecutor, the judge, and the jury, which is a legal forum for trying criminal cases; and (3) corrections is responsible for executing the sentence of a convicted defendant. For criminal justice to be most effective, each agency should work cooperatively with the others. ***See also*** Conflict Model; Consensus Model

Criminal Law *(political science)*   A body of law that defines criminal offenses and punishments for convicted persons. The general purposes of the criminal laws are to (a) define the acts or omissions that are proscribed and their consequent punishments, (b) define the mental states that constitute each offense, and (c) differentiate between serious and minor offenses.

In the United States, criminal law refers to *substantive criminal law*. Substantive criminal law stemmed from common law. Common law, which originated in England, is known as judge-made law since judges used previous case decisions as precedent for their own judicial decisions. Substantive criminal law is based on legislative action and is found in federal and state statutes defining crimes against the state, persons, habitation, property, public order, public morals, nature, the environment, and the administration of justice. On the other hand, *criminal procedure* describes the processes, such as arrest, charging, trial, and sentencing, through which the criminal laws are enforced.

In criminal law cases, the prosecution must prove two basic elements beyond a reasonable doubt. The first is the *actus reus*. This is the committed act. The second is the *mens rea*, or mental state, of the actor at the time of the offense. The prosecution must prove that the act was indeed an offense, rather than an accident, and that the actor had an unjustifiable or inexcusable intent to commit the offense.

In American jurisprudence, the punishment goals of the criminal law are *retribution, incapacitation, deterrence,* and *rehabilitation.* Under the principle of retribution, offenders ought to be punished for their acts, and the doctrine of just deserts asserts that the punishment ought to be proportional to the crime committed. Incapacitation is meant to keep offenders away from society, especially through imprisonment. Deterrence is intended to discourage either the offender, through specific deterrence, or society, through general deterrence, from committing future offenses. Rehabilitation is intended to prevent further offenses by transforming the offender into a productive member of society.

Under common law, crimes were classified as *mala in se* or *mala prohibita. Mala in se* crimes were acts that were considered wrong in themselves because they violated the natural and moral principles of a civilized society. These acts consisted of serious crimes, such as murder, rape, and robbery. *Mala prohibita* crimes were acts that were wrong because they were prohibited.

A modern way to classify crimes is by the punishment an individual will receive if convicted. One classification is from most to least punishment. *Felonies* constitute crimes receiving the most punishment, since they are punishable by more than one year of imprisonment. Felonies include serious crimes, such as murder, arson, weapon possession, or terrorism. Next are *misdemeanors,* which consist of less serious crimes, such as possession of narcotics, trespassing, or public intoxication. Misdemeanors are punishable by up to one year of imprisonment. The least serious are *violations,* which are punishable by suspension of a privilege or a fine. Violations typically include the breaking of local ordinances, such as traffic offenses, or the accumulation of trash on one's property. For more information, see Lippman (2006). ***See also*** Common Law

Criminal Law *(sociology)*   A set of statutes, also called penal law, enacted by the legislature to define crimes, to establish the punishment for such crimes, and to set forth the procedures for investigating and prosecuting such crimes. Each jurisdiction differs in its criminal law, and crime definitions vary according to state. The first written laws were established in early civilization by the Babylonian King Hammurabi, who was responsible for developing the Code of Hammurabi (1760 BCE).

Criminal law serves to publicize society's norms and values and serves several philosophical purposes: rehabilitation (to correct an offender's behavior), retribution (to punish offenders for the crime they have committed), deterrence (to prevent offenders from committing crime in the future), incapacitation (to incarcerate offenders so that they are unable to commit crimes in the community), and restitution (to repay society for social harm).

Criminally Insane   A defense that can result in a verdict of not guilty by reason of insanity. If a defendant is found criminally insane, he or she has been successful in the use of the *insanity defense* during a criminal trial to negate *mens rea*, or criminal intent. Insanity is a legal term, not a psychological diagnosis, and is very difficult to prove. Most people who suffer from mental illness will not be excused from their criminal behavior under an insanity defense unless the mental illness is such that it affects their ability to appreciate the difference between right and wrong or they do not have the capacity to understand their behavior, or both.

Criminology   The interdisciplinary and scientific approach to the study of criminal behavior. It includes disciplines such as psychology, sociology, economics, biology, and physiology. The word *criminologia* was coined by Raffaele Garofalo, an Italian law professor, in 1885. Criminologists focus their studies on criminal behavior, crime patterns, the consequences of punishment, the effectiveness of punishment, rehabilitation, and the etiology and prevalence of crime. Criminology includes multifaceted theories such as biological positivism (criminal behavior is inherited), sociobiological positivism (criminal behavior is a combination of biology and environmental factors), psychological determinism (criminal behavior is due to personality disorders, mental illness, etc.), or sociological determinism (criminal behavior is due to environmental factors).

Criterion- and Norm-Referenced Measurement
Two frames of reference that define how scores on tests are interpreted. Criterion-related measurement interprets scores by comparison with a predefined standard of performance. Scores on criterion-referenced tests usually provide feedback about strengths and weaknesses in defined areas of performance. Norm-referenced measurement interprets an individual's scores by comparison with the scores of others, usually displayed on a table of norms. Norm-referenced tests do not generally provide as much feedback on the specific strengths and weaknesses of an individual. Depending on the frame of reference used for interpretation of scores on a specific instrument, different psychometric problems are presented. ***See also*** Norm Group

Criterion Contamination   A criterion measure being influenced by something other than the performance related to the construct. Contamination is also often defined as the failure of an actual criterion measure to overlap with the ideal or the ultimate criterion measure. Contamination can occur for several reasons, such as low reliability, rater bias, cheating, or other construct-irrelevant influences. Contamination is contrasted with *criterion deficiency*, where the criterion fails to measure important aspects related to the construct. An example of criterion contamination might occur on a test intended to measure math aptitude that is highly influenced by respondents' verbal abilities. ***See also*** Validity/Validation

Criterion Validity   The degree to which the results of a test predict or agree with a criterion measure to which it, theoretically, should be similar. The results of the test are generally used to predict performance in a "real-life" situation. For example, a college admission test has good criterion validity if it directly correlates with college grades or some other measure of college performance. There are four types of criterion validity depending on the criteria used as the standard for judgment: predictive validity, concurrent validity, convergent validity, and discriminant validity. ***See also*** Concurrent Validity; Construct Validity; Content Validity; Discriminant Validity; Predictive Validity

Critical Listening   An essential element of the critical-thinking process. The critical listener is an active listener. He or she does more than hear; he or she senses, interprets, evaluates, and responds to claims being made, to arguments being offered, and to analogies and examples being used.

Though critical listening involves evaluation, it differs from what the psychologist Carl Rogers defines as *evaluative listening* in that critical listening opens the mind to effective interpretation and knowledge gathering, while evaluative listening closes the mind with a mental critique process that bars understanding.

Critical listening is important in all stages of life, and teaching school-age children to listen critically is considered to be particularly essential. As children learn language, they learn to think.

At higher educational levels and in professional fields, the need for critical listening remains constant. Researchers at Alverno College in Milwaukee, noting the lack of listening instruction at the college level, developed the integrative listening model, a four-stage process for developing effective listening skills, among them the ability to set goals for listening, for evaluating what is heard, and for recognizing filters such as culture, age, and physical well-being, which affect how well one listens. The researchers also referred to an earlier study at Alverno in which students were asked to evaluate why listening skills were critical to their majors. Music majors noted that not only did they need to be able to listen critically to their own and their classmates' performances, they needed to polish their critical listening skills so that they could effectively teach others to perform. For more information, see Hunsaker (1991), Jalongo (2008), Kirschenbaum and Henderson (1989), and Thompson, Leintz, Nevers, and Witkowski (2004).

Critical Theory   Theory associated with the Frankfurt School, particularly Max Horkheimer's 1937 essay "Traditional and Critical Theory." Traditional theory, Horkheimer argues, discounts the possibility that its truth value might itself be historically conditioned. Its apparent disinterestedness reflects the apparent freedom of the bourgeois economic subject. When society itself is irrationally organized and alienated from itself, so also is reason. The very division between theory and praxis arises as the effect of alienated thought. Traditional theory is powerless to transform its object of knowledge, for its job is strictly to understand by means of an unwavering eye on the "facts." It is, ultimately, under the rule of the empirical because, in the face of any discrepancy between fact and theory, theory is modified in light of fact.

In contrast, critical theory seeks to transcend alienated thinking by linking itself to praxis and by acknowledging the historically contingent nature of knowledge. To critique empirical reality, critical theory must both accept that reality as its object and run counter to common sense. It must find some way of articulating the discrepancy between theory and fact without capitulation to the latter, and it can only do this by speaking a language alien to the empirically self-evident. Committed to working for the reasonable organization of society, yet continuously taking for its object a society unreasonably organized, critical theory is necessarily at odds with everything about which it speaks.

Central to the Frankfurt School's "critical" project was a focus on the role of mass culture and the media. Early studies regarded the media as ideological, as disseminators of the false consciousness of capitalism. The culture "industry" cannot critique society for it serves society as a *divertissement* from the reality of labor and unemployment. However, the work of Jürgen Habermas on the public sphere and communicative action offers a more productive way to understand the mediatory role of culture. The public sphere refers to discursive spaces, such as coffee houses or newspapers, where social issues are identified and debated. These spaces can only operate in democratic societies where public policy arises through fair debate (the word *parliament* derives from the Old French *parlement,* meaning discussion). It is in the act of rationally ordered communication that freedom is formed and performed. By the exercise of communicative reason, social beings cohere, giving to the media a transformative role in public debate. In witness to these transformative

possibilities and to the indissoluble connection between literature and social reality, critical theory—broadly incorporating philosophical, sociological, psychoanalytical, and political methods—occupies a central place in literary studies. For more information, see Habermas (1962/1989) and Horkheimer (1937/1972). ***See also*** Empiricist Tradition; Hegemony (media studies); Ideology (media studies, sociology); Marxism; Popular Culture

Critical Thinking   A process of discerning information in a balanced manner that employs curiosity, logic, open-mindedness, and skepticism and, therefore, discards bias, prejudice, and preconceived notions. Critical thinking is essential to everyday life tasks and decisions, both commonplace and academic, and its use is encouraged by professionals in many fields, including educators and health and mental health practitioners. While it does not guarantee arriving at the truth, it is an effective means of searching for it.

Critical thinking requires the development of interdependent mental skills. Initially, a critical thinker needs to be able to make claims—declarative sentences that can be true or false but not both and do not depend on personal sentiment. A critical thinker also needs to be able to define words and terms.

A critical thinker learns to see through concealed claims, which are attempts to convince by rhetoric rather than argument; to evaluate the premises of his, her, or another's arguments; and to ascertain the validity of such arguments. A critical thinker learns to repair his or her arguments, to compound claims, and to make counter arguments, reasoning that some claims fit all, some, or no situations. In the critical-thinking process, a person can use analogies (comparisons) to illustrate arguments, and use examples of cause and effect, keeping in mind that there is a difference between "because" and "can cause." A critical thinker learns to explain his or her arguments, to avoid fallacies, to write effective arguments, and to make decisions. For more information, see Epstein (2003) and Ruggiero (1989). ***See also*** Active Listening; Critical Listening; Evaluative Listening

Crony Capitalism   A pejorative term used to describe a society, usually marked by an allegedly capitalist economy, where the close relationships between businessmen and government officials are used to succeed in business. Consequently, the success of a business is determined by favoritism by the ruling government rather than by a free market and the rule of law, thus corrupting public-serving and political ideals. Such favoritism is usually granted in the form of special permits, tax breaks, government grants, and other incentives. In crony capitalism, favoritism can also be shown based on race, religion, or ethnicity, which is especially so in developing countries. Countries noted for exhibiting or having exhibited crony capitalism include the People's Republic of China, India, Mexico, Brazil, Malaysia, Russia, and Indonesia, as well as most of the ex-Soviet countries.

The rise of crony capitalism has been blamed on both socialists and capitalists alike, with either party placing the blame on the other. Socialists have often declared crony capitalism to be the inevitable result of any capitalist system, asserting that people in power, whether business or government, intend to stay in power, and the only way to do this is to create networks between government and businesses that support each other. They believe that because businesses' main objectives are to make money and since money typically leads to political power, business entities will inevitably use their power to influence governments. On the other hand, while capitalists are also generally opposed to crony capitalism, they consider its occurrence to be the result of socialists' need to control the state, which requires close cooperation between businesses and governments.

At one end of the spectrum, crony capitalism exists in less extreme forms, such as collusion among market players. The market players, while still competing against each other to an extent, will combine efforts and present a united front to the government when requesting subsidies or aid. Such groups are referred to as trade associations or industry trade groups. Newcomers and other players in the market may find themselves alienated from these associations, finding it hard to gain market presence or find loans. To the other extreme, crony capitalism is usually associated with more powerful government interventions, such as ambiguous laws and regulations; these laws, when enforced, can greatly impede virtually all business, providing an incentive to stay in the good books of government officials.

In its worst and most extreme form, crony capitalism can devolve into corruption. Bribes to government officials and tax evasions are typical by-products of extreme crony capitalism.

As an example, crony capitalism has been evident in the process of privatization in Russia, notably with the transfer of major oil companies into private hands at extremely low prices. As crony capitalism implies that a tacit understanding exists between the country's government and oligarchs or business leaders, this method of privatization had an extreme, negative effect on the economy: The influence of the crony capitalists over the process led to a warped system of property rights.

Cross-Cultural Research (*psychology*)   Research that examines differences and similarities in people from different cultures and societies. Cross-cultural studies examine the relationship between human behavior and culture and typically use field data from different societies to test hypotheses about human behavior and culture. Cross-cultural research in psychology examines human behavior under different cultural conditions. Research in cross-cultural psychology can take two different approaches: the *etic* approach, which focuses on what things mean to individuals outside the culture, and the *emic* approach, which focuses on what things mean to members of the culture. Some examples of cross-cultural psychology research include differences in personality or manifestations of psychopathology across cultures. For more information, see Berry, Poortinga, and Pandey (1997). *See also* Comparative Psychology

Cross-Cultural Research (*sociology*)   A study or analysis that compares two or more different cultures. It can involve research conducted in a particular discipline that examines the effect of culture on behavior or behavior observed within and between communities, in addition to varying beliefs and institutions. Community members have similar practices, beliefs, values, social roles, expressions, and norms; these factors result in community cohesion. Such factors are interrelated with historical context and the physical and social environments in which people reside. Cross-cultural research allows social anthropologists to compare and contrast these various social elements and examine commonalities and contradictions across both different and similar cultures of varying time periods.

Cross-Examination   The questioning of a witness by opposing counsel. It comes after direct examination and may be followed by a redirect. Questions asked during cross-examination are limited to matters discussed during direct examination. Attorneys can often ask leading questions during cross-examination and attempt to discredit the witness's credibility and testimony.

Cross-Sectional Research (*psychology*)   A method frequently used in developmental research that involves examining individuals of different ages all at the same time. Individuals are tested at a single point in time, and groups are compared at different ages on independent variables, such as intelligence. Using this type of strategy, researchers can compare the IQs of different generations of individuals. Although cross-sectional studies are quick to implement, their results should be interpreted with caution because the observed differences might be due to a difference in generations and not by age. This phenomenon is called *cohort effect*. *See also* Longitudinal Research

Cross-Sectional Research (*sociology*)   A time dimension study that takes a cross section of some phenomenon or population at one time and studies that cross section meticulously. Cross-sectional studies are frequently descriptive or exploratory. Their aim is to appreciate changes over a period of time; however, their results are based on observations at one particular time. It is a scientific method that compares two different groups based on similar factors at one point in time. Such studies have to use representative sampling procedures in order to establish validity and reliability. Such studies can measure the rate of specific conditions or elements and establish correlations between them. Cross-sectional studies use surveys to gather data and are a good measure of knowledge, beliefs, perceptions, behavior, and attitudes among study participants.

Cross-Validation   Any process of checking a conclusion by testing it with a different sample, data, or method. Can field observations be confirmed in the laboratory? Will an experimental result be replicated with different participants? Will survey findings be consistent with different respondents? When developing a theory with one set of data, it is especially important to cross-validate it using different data. *See also* Validity/Validation

Crystallized Intelligence   A type of general intelligence that involves the ability to use verbal skills, factual knowledge, and experience; it can be distinguished from *fluid intelligence*, which can be understood as a type of intelligence that is independent of acquired knowledge. First identified by Raymond Cattell (1971), the two types are correlated with each other, and most tests of intelligence evaluate both modalities. However, they are believed to be based on distinct neural and mental systems, and when examined independently, separate developmental patterns are identified. Crystallized intelligence remains relatively stable over time, while fluid intelligence tends to decline with age.

Crystallized intelligence involves the accumulation of factual knowledge as indicated, for example, by the number of words in one's vocabulary or one's ability to add or subtract. This type of intelligence is observed to increase gradually, stay relatively stable through adulthood, and decline slowly after approximately age 65. Crystallized intelligence is also more susceptible to change, and we are able to enhance crystallized intelligence through continued engagement in cognitively demanding tasks, such as reading books or doing math. The verbal subscales of the Wechsler Intelligence Scales are believed to be good measures of crystallized intelligence. In general, crystallized intelligence correlates highly with measures that rely on general knowledge and experience, such as vocabulary, analogies, or general information. Since crystallized intelligence involves the ability to access information from long-term memory, it appears to be a function of the hippocampus, the part of the brain responsible for the storage and use of long-term memories. For more information, see Cattell (1971). *See also* Fluid Intelligence; Wechsler Adult Intelligence Scales (WAIS)

Culpability   An individual's level of responsibility or blameworthiness for a particular behavior or action. The word *culpability* is derived from the Latin *cupa,* meaning "fault." In the law, the level of culpability, or lack thereof, can aggravate or mitigate a criminal charge. Levels of culpability include a crime that is committed intentionally, knowingly, negligently, or recklessly.

Cultivation   To cultivate means to mature or grow. In science, cultivation or tillage is a method of preparing soil to enhance plant growth. In sociology, cultivation is the development of culture, behavior, attitudes, relationships, beliefs, intellect, values, norms, and so forth through training and exposure. The more education and training one receives, the more cultivated one becomes.

Cultivation Theory   The view that television is part of a complex social system that cultivates people's perceptions of the world. Before the development of cultivation theory, media research was largely devoted to determining any immediate impact that a single message can have on individuals' attitudes, beliefs, or behaviors. Cultivation theory, however, suggests that the effects are cumulative as the result of significant exposure to television.

Research on cultivation theory was first funded by the National Commission on the Causes and Prevention of Violence in 1968. Rather than look for measurable changes, George Gerbner and others posited that television, as the main entertainment medium, socializes people into society. Therefore, while no one television show can have an impact on an individual's behavior, watching a lot of television can cultivate a view of reality that affects our judgment of the world and real situations. Furthermore, people who spend much time watching television tend to exhibit many commonalities of perception. The research found that excessive exposure to television caused people to perceive the world as a much more dangerous place—what was called the *mean world syndrome*. Thus, heavier television viewers tend to favor more punitive crime measures, such as the death penalty.

The original study prompted what was to mark the beginning of the Cultural Indicator's Project—the longest-running research project in the world. The project has amassed a huge database of television programs and characters. Each item in the database is then subjected to analysis. Rather than a unidirectional, stimulus-response model, Gerbner and his researchers describe their strategy as three pronged: (1) institutional process analysis, which examines the conditions under which the messages that are distributed are selected; (2) message system analysis, which monitors the repetitiveness in television programming; and (3) cultivation analysis, which explores the impact television viewing has on the individual's worldview. Subsequent applications of the theoretical model have been applied to gender roles, concepts of aging, occupations, minority stereotyping, and other concepts. For more information, see Gerbner and Gross (1976) and Stossel (1997). *See also* Media Effects

Cultural Assimilation (*communication*)   A range of pathways taken by an outsider to integrate and resemble others in the predominant culture. The broader term *outsider* is often used, and most scholarship uses the term *immigrant* to denote that the study of and the discussion around cultural assimilation should not be viewed narrowly. The imposition is suggestive. Milton Gordon (1964) developed a dichotomy distinguishing cultural assimilation from *structural assimilation*. According to Gordon, cultural assimilation requires outsiders to become collectively alike. Structural assimilation occurs only when one becomes institutionally incorporated.

This terminology should not be confused with *acculturation*. Assimilation presumes full integration, while acculturation refers to partial amalgamation or, rather, an exchange of cultural parts wherein the individual picks and chooses what new aspects are incorporated into his or her identity. Acculturation is a partial exchange, and much of the native culture remains and is transformed, thus creating a new identity partially alien to both new and native cultures. Assimilation assumes a rewrite of the native culture; as such, cultural assimilation in its strictest form does not occur. Both processes transform the new and old cultural environment: The outsider both takes and leaves behind a cultural fingerprint influencing the social structure, thus making full assimilation an ideology rather than a practical matter. Assimilation is not unidirectional. To understand this, we must also examine the various conceptions of culture.

Culture is a medium used to conceptualize and experience the world. Essentialists view culture as fixed, while others argue that culture is transient and a vague conglomeration of forms differing in depth and attributed to a group. Such forms include beliefs, values, norms, behaviors, and social structures that have developed and evolved historically: in essence, passing the test of time. Certain aspects have become fixed, while others continue to evolve. Therefore, culture is both fixed and transient, allowing it to be studied. The underlying theoretical constructions used are recurrent forms of interactions.

The field of communications examines how various forms and patterns of communication influence the way an individual both constructs and receives confirmative signals indicative of integration into the predominant culture. Forms and patterns of communication and indicative cues include verbal and written language, various forms of media and telecommunications, communicative actions, and communicative expressions. Examples include books, magazines, various forms of mass media, music, humor, and slang. Forms of communication affect the way an individual assimilates into the culture and can be used to label the individual. For example, the use of specific words labels the user ideologically and can be used to identify the user's particular place of assimilation. More specifically, an English-speaking Chinese educated in Hong Kong will use "pardon" as a form of etiquette, as compared with an English-speaking Chinese educated in New York, who is more likely to use "excuse me." Language, the use of specific words or phrases, is a medium that creates a reality or an identity.

Moreover, the advent of modern communicative technology has changed the old conceptions of assimilation. In addition, political movements—beginning in the 1960s—that emphasized pride in racial and ethnic identities and created a hyphenised culture—mitigated against full cultural assimilation, as was the case in the United States in the 19th and 20th centuries with immigrants from southern and eastern Europe. It is becoming easier to both maintain the native identity and adopt a global identity. As technology expands its reach within the global economy, the discussion will shift, and key theories will need to be able to account for such developments. For more information, see Gordon (1964), Heller (2006), and Pedraza (1999).

Cultural Assimilation (*education*) The expectation that all other groups believe in and subscribe to the culture of the dominant group, which is in a position of social or economic power and control relative to other groups. This is based on strong ethnocentrism. ***See also*** Culture (communication, education); Ethnocentrism (psychology, sociology)

Cultural Context The aspects of the social and cultural situation that must be considered to interpret or understand a phenomenon. Any idea, text, information, object, person, place, or experience requires an examination of the cultural group that creates or uses it, the surroundings in which it occurs, its history and connection to traditions, its utility, and its symbolism. This approach is grounded in the idea that meaning is not inherent in any entity but is created through the interaction of that entity with its use. So, for example, a Beatles song played at a concert full of screaming girls in the 1960s has a different range of possible meanings than the same song played as elevator background music in the 21st century. The context limits the meanings that are possible and also makes it more likely that they can be articulated and understood.

If human behavior is seen as symbolic action that has meaning only when acted in public for others to see and evaluate, then cultural context provides the necessary conditions for that sharing to take place. Cultural context is thought to work because meanings have to be learned and used in particular ways for them to be shared. The context can clue participants into the acceptable way to act on or articulate an idea or action. Behavior that is acceptable or expected in one context (a baseball game, a wedding) would be considered inappropriate or offensive in another (a church, a funeral). Some contexts are broad and thus more flexible, while others require strict adherence to very structured rules, languages, and reactions. The anthropologist Clifford Geertz called the practice of describing cultural context a "thick description" because of all the details needed to make sense of even the simplest situation. For more information, see Geertz (1966b). ***See also*** Culture (communication, education, media studies); Ritual (communication, sociology)

Cultural Determinism The view that an individual's personality, behavior, economic level, social status, and so forth are created solely by cultural factors. A vast number of societies believe that their customs and rituals establish the identity of their political and economic structures. Individual identity and status are determined by cultural elements, not by biological factors.

Cultural Diffusion An anthropological term used to describe the dissemination of cultural elements, such as ideas, rituals, religion, customs, values, norms, beliefs, and language, between two varying cultures. *Direct diffusion* is when two cultures live in close proximity and share cultural elements. *Forced diffusion* is when one area is dominated by another area, usually during war, and the victor's culture is forced on the defeated. *Diffused culture* is when cultural traits are passed from one area to another by an intermediary.

Cultural Diversity   The variety of different cultures within a single society or geographical area. This may be represented by a number of distinct personal characteristics, including (but not limited to) a mix of disparate languages, races, religions, and ethnicities within a single social group. The amount of cultural diversity may vary depending on the area of focus; when speaking of cultural diversity, one can refer to anything from a seemingly diverse workplace to a relatively heterogeneous nation-state. On the structural level, cultural diversity may be enforced through policies of multiculturalism, or the attempt to preserve specific cultural heritages within one society or state. These policies can be aimed at incoming immigrant groups or long-standing but egregiously disenfranchised minorities.

While proponents of multiculturalism believe that such strategies promote greater tolerance and respect for marginalized populations, opponents argue that multicultural agendas may actually lead to greater ethnic strife and social division. Another major argument has centered on the importance of cultural diversity in educational environments. According to many scholars, a diverse cultural environment can be both intellectually and socially healthy; students not only gain a variety of different perspectives in the classroom, but they also learn how to properly function with people from all different walks of life. Although not the only argument for affirmative action (nor even the most prominent one), advocates of cultural diversity thus often emphasize this beneficial aspect of such policies.

Businesses have also begun to stress the value of fostering cultural diversity. This includes not only employing people of different races and ethnicities (although this is certainly the primary concern) but also allowing qualified minority candidates into management or high-level positions. Indeed, many businesses have begun to offer seminars or workshops specifically tailored to celebrate and encourage greater cultural diversity in the workplace. For more information, see United Nations Educational, Scientific and Cultural Organization (n.d.). ***See also*** Affirmative Action (political science, public administration); Discrimination

Cultural Ecology   The scientific study of human beings and their relationship to the environment and other living organisms. Cultural disparities are analyzed by social scientists through an ecological process. Individuals construct culture as they acclimate to the environment. Cultural rituals and practices are influenced by opportunities and strain in one's surrounding area.

Cultural Evolution   The processes of cultural and societal change over time. Cultural evolution comprises three vital components. The first component is the individual. As individuals change, they change their environment. The second component is the community. The community offers a supportive function and provides a cohesive unit, which reinforces belief and value systems. The third component is society. Society influences the former components, and all three influence cultural change.

Cultural Geography   A branch of human geography that studies the various characteristics of a human culture in a particular location. Human geography, a more modern development under the discipline of geography, examines the relationship between human beings and the environment in which they exist. With a strong focus on spatial relations, human geography combines disciplines, examining the impact of social, economic, political, and cultural forces on human behavior.

Some of the characteristics examined in this field include clothing, language, education, government, and religion. Cultural geographers also measure the variation of culture from location to location in the hope of better understanding the environmental factors affecting behavior.

Spatial divisions, which can be thought of as the division of habitable space, play a large role in cultural geography. Spatial divisions, such as the division between states or countries, are the main focus of cultural geography. While these divisions can be created by territory, they are also decided by cultural, language, or religious differences.

Carl Sauer (d. 1975), who taught at the University of California at Berkeley, is most notably associated with the study of cultural geography and is frequently referred to as the father of cultural geography. Sauer developed many of his writings in response to and as a criticism of environmental determinism. He is best known for his 1925 scholarly monograph "The Morphology of Landscape," which helped change the focus of geography from economic determinism to cultural landscapes. Newer theories of cultural geography tend to focus more on cultural identities than on landscapes and emphasize the importance of postmodernism and poststructuralism. For more information, see Sauer (1925).

Cultural Pluralism   A social process of accommodation in which cultural groups are modified by and through their presence in and experience with the dominant culture, while at the same time maintaining their intrinsic cultural characteristics. The dominant culture is modified as well by the groups' presence. ***See also*** Cultural Assimilation (education); Culture (communication, education, media studies)

Cultural Relativism   The idea that the beliefs, values, norms, and so forth of a particular individual must be understood, examined, and studied in their cultural context. Culture affects these elements, and differences in such factors among individuals are relative to cultural encounters. In discerning the differences between right and wrong, therefore, absolute truths do not exist; all truths are relative and are the result of cultural experiences, and one culture cannot be judged by the values or standards of another.

Cultural Revolution   A general disruption in people's everyday habits, feelings and desires, and way of life. The goal of a cultural revolution is to transform people into a new society. The Russian Revolution marked Vladimir Lenin's reference to a general cultural development of the country under socialism, with an emphasis on the instillment of literacy and hygiene and a gradual transformation from the backwardness that Lenin saw as the legacy of tsarism. The label *cultural revolution,* however, was coined in 1978 by Western historians to mean a class war and define the period in Russia from 1928 through 1931.

In Russia, the cultural revolution was one major avenue by which the governing party's respect for backward others, the proletariat, was absorbed into the Bolshevik's revolutionary ideology. Between 1905 and 1920, the Bolsheviks instituted cultural enlightenment into the mainstream. The Bolsheviks were members of a wing of the Russian Social-Democratic Workers' Party, which advocated seizure of power by the proletariat. After 1917, Vladimir Lenin, leader of the Bolshevik Party, launched the cultural revolution in earnest. In 1928, communist militants transformed the term. It no longer involved mere teaching to read and write but rather evolved to mean the militant restructuring of the entire ideological superstructure through class struggle, at the outcome of which the proletarian class would take power and govern.

The cultural revolution in China was initiated by Communist Party Chairman Mao Zedong in 1965 to revive the economy and usurp power from the existing government. Mao believed in an authoritarian party leadership and that industrialization and state ownership would transform society into the communist ideal. He also emphasized a need for personal transformation of thought away from capitalism and toward the Communist Party and the peasant ideals that emphasized socialist tendencies. The revolution, however, was characterized by political zealotry, purges of intellectuals, and social and economic chaos.

To fulfill his plan, Mao organized China's urban youths, called the Red Guards, who shut down China's schools and persecuted teachers and intellectuals, who were seen as carriers of bourgeois ideals. Torture was common. The Red Guards also destroyed cultural icons, such as art, architectural treasures, and cultural monuments, associated with precommunist China. The Red Guards, however, ultimately splintered into rival groups. They were disbanded in 1969 and sent into the rural hinterlands. The revolution ended after Mao's death in 1976. In the end, an estimated 1,000,000 people died from the purges.

Other cultural revolutions have existed throughout the world, although the Soviet and Chinese cultural revolutions were perhaps the most noted. To Westerners, cultural revolutions were introduced in colonized nations by the introduction of hospitals, medicines, Western goods, and education. And commodities and customs judged Western were deemed superior to those considered local. Colonial administrators often suppressed barbaric practices revered by indigenous groups, such as human sacrifice, slavery, and physical cruelty. Missionaries further contributed to changes by discrediting local gods and weakening the spiritual foundations of society before introducing Western spiritual ideals.

Another well-known cultural revolution occurred in Iran from 1980 through 1987, when Ayatollah Ruhollah Khomeini imposed a theocratic government based on the Islamic principles of the Qur'an, after denouncing the Western direction Iran was taking. Iran's cultural revolution began after the Islamic Revolution in 1979 with the forced exile of Mohammad Reza Shah Pahlavi, Iran's king, who was considered to be a Western sympathizer. As a result, an unknown number of academics from universities and schools were executed. For more information, see David-Fox (1999) and MacFarquhar and Schoenhals (2008). ***See also*** Communism (political science)

Cultural Values   The key ideas, ideals, and norms of a given culture that serve to regulate and guide a person's life. Values form the internal compass of an individual. They guide actions and shape decision making in both individuals and organizations. The collection of values is a value system.

The study of mass media and its effects on values is generally placed in two contexts: (1) the modern period, which begins in the 19th century with the arrival of the Industrial Revolution, and (2) the postmodern, post–World War II period. In the modern period, values were typified by the belief in concepts such as democracy, freedom, justice, individualism, rational order, and the scientific method and in a work ethic that leads to material success. Values were thought to be hierarchical, in both the individual and the culture. These hierarchies may differ. As values are held in common by members of a culture, they make social life possible, yet they can cause friction within a social group and make change difficult, usually when the individual's hierarchy differs from the culture's. The postmodern context suggests that the value system is not hierarchical but, rather, more like a complex map. The pronounced disillusionment that marks postmodern thought has manifested in a shift in values: opposing hierarchy, questioning scientific reasoning, recycling culture, and embracing paradox.

Research tends to indicate that values are acquired through the process of socialization and that the media, along with the family, schools, and so forth, are agents of socialization. It has been suggested, on the one hand,

C

that the media reinforce values. For example, most crime dramas are resolved with the forces of good prevailing over the evil forces—that is, an arrest, a conviction, or the death of the criminal—thus reinforcing the cultural values of rational order and justice. Also, some researchers have suggested that the media can be consciously used to acquire norms and values and that many individuals, particularly adolescents, use it for that purpose. However, cultivation theorists suggest that being exposed to too much media can result in a cumulative effect that degrades cultural values and skews the viewer's concept of reality. For example, if somebody watches too much violent television, he or she will believe that the world is a far more dangerous place than it is. This *mean world syndrome* represents an unconscious erosion of cultural values such as freedom and justice. For more information, see Campbell, Martin, and Fabos (2007). ***See also*** Cultivation Theory; Industrialism; Postmodernism

Culture *(communication)* A term developed by anthropologists but widely used across academic disciplines and in vernacular speech to refer either to a group of people sharing a way of life and worldview (a culture) or to the system of meanings shared by this group (culture). In the 19th century, anthropology defined its goal as one of identifying and describing the discrete cultures of the world and understanding the different ways they lived and understood their lives. The widely used definition of culture (promoted by E. B. Tylor) that underpinned this mission was that culture was a "complex whole" that included everything a person acquired as a member of a particular society, including beliefs, customs, habits, and knowledge. Anthropologists studied the cultures of the world by living with them and describing their religions, economic systems, environment, languages, rituals, and other cultural activities.

The two aspects of the term *culture* were equated, and "a culture" had a "culture" that could be described and delimited. Cultures were thought to be basically static entities, which could evolve as whole units into other forms (e.g., from tribal to civilization). Culture became thought of as the characteristic, which humans possessed and used, that set them apart from nonhumans.

The definition of culture was reoriented by the anthropologist Clifford Geertz, who emphasized its symbolic, world-making aspects and the continual process of reformulation in response to changes. Geertz, drawing on the work of Max Weber, called culture a semiotic activity, based on the idea that humans spin "webs of significance." Culture referred to the shared and learned patterns of meanings that were necessary for comprehending and acting in a particular world. Culture was studied by doing a careful and detailed description of how meanings were made and used. Critiques of

Geertz suggest that *culture* is an outdated term that does not deal well with mass media, global exchange, and mobile populations.

A less academic use of culture relies more on Tylor than on Geertz. Culture is seen as something people possess by being a member of a local, regional, or national group and something that can be seen in the entities created—music, food, rituals, costume, language—as well as a way of looking at the world. Culture (or being cultured) has also been used to refer to aspects of educated and elite activities, such as the arts and classical music, but this usage is less common today in a multicultural world that recognizes that different people have different approaches and beliefs. But the terms *mass culture* and *popular culture* are still used to distinguish everyday life from the more refined world of the arts. For more information, see Geertz (1966b) and Tylor (1871/1974). ***See also*** Enculturation; Socialization (media studies, sociology); Symbols/Symbolic Reality

Culture *(education)* The shared beliefs, values, customs, language, and so forth of a group of people. These contribute to the group's sense of peoplehood and are transmitted from generation to generation. They are often modified by experience or through contact with other cultural groups. All human beings have culture. When applied to individuals, culture refers to the broad set of beliefs, values, customs, traditions, worldviews, and so forth that influence how a person thinks about things, perceives events, and acts.

Culture *(media studies)* A term derived from the Latin *cultura,* the basic sense of which refers to the growth and tending of plants and land. Cultivation suggests refinement, giving us the current usage: the ideas, customs, and artistic expressions of a society, its material practices and symbolic meanings. The history of social communication and the preservation of culture is usually charted as a linear evolution from oral to print to electronic culture, despite the fact that all three can and do coexist.

In oral traditions, the archive is memory, and this changes the nature of verbal interaction. Information is embedded in long, episodic, digressive stories that teach as much as they entertain. Complex patterns of repetition, variation, epithets, and ring composition mark the delivery of stories continuously retold. Knowledge, under these conditions, is socially produced, learned in the context of personal relationships. Oral culture reinforces shared values and traditional beliefs, creating a tendency toward consensus rather than individualism.

Print complicates face-to-face relations by introducing the text as a third element, even when books are read aloud to groups. The change in social formation that print culture is said to have brought about presupposes a model of solitary reading. Because the reader encounters knowledge in the form of a book rather than a social encounter, there is a greater detachment from "facts," which are separable from and independent of the reader. Print culture thus objectifies knowledge as empirical fact. Mass access to print widens education and brings about the democratization of power and the belief in liberal values.

In *Orality and Literacy,* Walter Ong argued that electronic communication had led to a *secondary orality,* whereby information is processed through convergent media rather than exclusively through the printed word. The *digital revolution* has dramatically altered the nature of communication and information. By converting a physical sound or image into information, recorded in binary digits of 1 and 0 in varying sequences, digital technology can remaster and misleadingly alter the original "event." Computer-generated technology can create virtual worlds that blur the distinction between real and imagined experience.

Instantaneous transmission of data through cyberspace and interactive media have globalized communication by collapsing physical distance into virtual space and have altered the nature of the information transmitted. *Hypertext* or *hypermedia* (terms coined by the information technology theorist Ted Nelson) denotes the reading of online texts in multiple dimensions. In hypertext fiction, the form of the story and of the process of reading becomes labyrinthine. The single direction of linear reading breaks down into a rhizome of branching possibilities, and the one world of words set in fixed order fragments into many. For more information, see Nelson (1965) and Ong (1988). *See also* Face-to-Face Communication; Oral Tradition; Printing; Virtual Reality

Culture *(sociology)*   A term derived from the Latin *cultura,* which originated from the Latin *colere,* meaning to cultivate. Culture is the conduct, traditions, language, mores, customs, beliefs, institutions, art, literature, laws, religion, dress, and so forth that are passed down to community members from generation to generation. The examination of behavior requires an understanding of culture and of a community's philosophical ethos. It is inclusive of everything a community shares and can comprise both material and nonmaterial elements. Material culture incorporates artifacts and their symbolic meaning. Nonmaterial culture contains conceptual designs such as language, myths, and beliefs. Society is the result of individuals who share a culture. Culture is vital for the survival of individuals and society, and cultures cannot survive without support from individuals within such a society. Sharing cultural practices allows each generation to progress and grow more than the generation before. Over time, societies become more technical and advanced. Each society possesses its own unique culture.

Culture-Bound Syndrome   A combination of psychiatric symptoms that are unique or specific to certain societies and cultures. Culture-bound syndromes are present throughout the world. They are not objective, structural dysfunctions or biochemical abnormalities in the organisms that can be objectively identified, and they are not recognized in other cultures. However, the abnormalities are readily identified within the culture and tend to involve dramatic symptoms of short duration. These conditions are commonly treated by the folk or indigenous medicine of the culture.

The existence of culture-bound syndromes is controversial and is not accepted by all mental health practitioners or anthropologists. Recognizing the need to consider symptoms that are not common in European or American societies when evaluating individuals from other cultures, the fourth edition of the *Diagnostic and Statistical Manual of Mental Disorders* (*DSM-IV*) included a list of the most common culture-bound syndromes. Some of the culture-bound syndromes listed in the *DSM* include *amok,* a syndrome usually found in males from Southeast Asia and the Caribbean. This syndrome involves sudden outbursts of aggressive behavior and rage, sometimes followed by ideas of persecution and, finally, by fatigue or withdrawal. *Nervios* is also a culture-bound syndrome, usually found in Latin societies, that involves periods of intense distress characterized by headaches, stomachaches, dizziness, and nervousness. *Koro* is a syndrome usually found in South and East Asia and involves intense fear that the external sex organs will retract into the body, causing death. *See also Diagnostic and Statistical Manual (DSM)* (psychology)

Culture of Poverty   Views about poverty that are passed down from generation to generation in impoverished neighborhoods. Residents possess feelings of indifference, skepticism, and disempowerment, in addition to a grave mistrust of social institutions that offer assistance to the poor. These feelings preclude community members from taking advantage of the availability of such social service programs and prevent individual and familial socioeconomic advancement.

Currency Board   The commitment by one country to allow its currency to be converted to, or exchanged for, another country's currency at a fixed exchange rate. The monetary or central bank in a country that chooses a currency board monetary system must ensure that it has an adequate amount of the foreign currency that will be exchangeable for the country's domestic currency. Since the domestic currency is exchangeable for the foreign currency at a fixed exchange rate, the country selecting a currency board system must have sufficient foreign reserves to cover the money supply of the country. This means that the country cannot expand or introduce any additional currency unless that amount is backed by an equal amount of the foreign currency.

C

Therefore, the country must have 100% of the foreign currency or *anchor currency* selected. The currency selected is generally a widely traded, acceptable, and stable currency. The U.S. dollar is a popular currency selected by countries that choose to implement a currency board monetary system.

A currency board can be an independent body working alongside the central bank. Or a currency board can replicate the role of the central bank in managing the currency of the domestic economy. A board does not engage in monetary or fiscal policy. Its sole role is to ensure that the domestic currency in circulation is matched by the foreign currency or anchor currency. Once a currency board is established, the central bank is neutralized, and the currency board will match or issue the inflows and outflows of foreign currency with the domestic currency. Thus, the central bank does not influence the value of a domestic currency in relation to a foreign currency. A currency board is more independent and freer from political influence than the central bank. A currency board brings more stability to domestic prices and inflation. It gives foreign and domestic investors more confidence in the stability of the currency. For more information, see Carbaugh (2007) and Krugman and Obstfeld (2006).

Curriculum   The courses or programs of learning offered by an institution of education. A curriculum provides the model for learning, and it includes the goals and objectives of learning. A curriculum also includes criteria for referencing and measuring whether learning goals and objectives have been achieved.

Curriculum Development   The process used for developing the curriculum of an institution of learning. The curriculum development process is used to define institutional goals and objectives for learning. This process is also used for aligning institutional goals and objectives for learning with external governing standards, such as state and accreditation associations.

Curriculum Evaluation   The assessment and judging of the merit and worth of the broad processes, elements, and resultant outcomes encompassed within an educational curriculum. Curriculum evaluation may include curriculum planning and design processes (needs assessment evaluation), curriculum implementation (process evaluation), and assessing the effectiveness of the implemented curriculum in creating desired student change (outcomes evaluation). ***See also*** School Evaluation

Curriculum Guide   An instructional guide for developing curriculum content. A curriculum guide is used to assist educators in developing curriculum content for a specific subject area. This guide identifies associations between learning objectives for a specific subject area and learning objectives within curriculum content areas.

Curriculum Integration   A curricular approach in which the various disciplines—usually the core subjects of language arts, math, science, and social studies—are organized around a theme, topic, or project and taught in combination rather than as traditional, single-content disciplines. The disciplines are brought together to help students understand how various concepts are related in a meaningful way in the real world. The basic tenets of this methodology focus on holistic teaching, constructivism, interactive scholarship, and exploratory and experiential learning. Teachers of the various disciplines (at the same grade level or across grade levels) engage in team planning to determine the lesson objectives, content standards, learning activities, teaching strategies, and forms of assessment.

Curriculum Mapping   The documentation and description of real-time classroom events showing what occurs in classrooms over time. It includes fewer details than lesson plans and syllabi and more details than a list of course and unit descriptions. Curriculum mapping was developed after World War II as traditional scope and sequence charts and promoted later by Jacobs (1997) as an effective tool that engaged teachers and staff in a collaborative effort to increase managerial control. The curriculum mapping can be used to communicate with various persons interested in the school curriculum. A typical curriculum mapping includes essential questions, content pieces, activities, and assessments. For more information, see Jacobs (1997).

Custody   A term derived from the Latin *custodire*, "to guard." In the criminal justice system, a person is taken into custody or seized after law enforcement effects an arrest or after a reasonable person does not feel free to leave during questioning or subsequent detainment by law enforcement. The suspect's information, such as name, age, race, criminal charge, and so forth, and his or her photograph and fingerprints are entered into the computer system. The suspect may also be interrogated or asked to stand in a lineup. In the United States, custody procedures are dictated under the Constitution's Fourth Amendment, which guards against unreasonable searches and seizures.

Customs   The traditions, behaviors, and mores that are passed down from generation to generation. They are long-established practices and serve a symbolic purpose. Customs give cultures their unique characteristics. In the criminal justice system, Customs is the law enforcement agency responsible for monitoring goods, services, and noncitizens passing in and out of a country's borders.

Cutback Management   The systematic process employed by political and managerial leaders to guide their organizations through periods of resource scarcity. The term emerged in the 1970s and 1980s, when public administrators, particularly at the state and local levels, were challenged by economic stresses attributed to stagflation, a combination of inflation and high unemployment. In subsequent years, attention to cutbacks has also been associated with increased political support for "smaller government."

Experts reject the reliance on incremental, across-the-board cuts as an inadequate strategy for dealing with such challenges and recommend that the process begin with a more careful analysis of the organizational, programmatic, economic, and political environment. Cutback management requires leaders to look at the agency's mission and priorities, legal mandates, and the potential impact of cuts on performance, morale, and employee retention. Opportunities for innovation are considered, including options such as fees, contracting out, layoffs, and hiring freezes. Identification of and communication with stakeholders is urged to gain their support for change.

Organizations slated for cutbacks may adopt various strategies to resist them, including targeting popular programs for reduction or elimination. Sometimes conflicts are fought internally as units of an organization seek to protect their own programs and resources. Skilled leadership and widespread participation in planning have been regarded as keys to successful navigation of the cutback experience.

C

D

Damages A legal term for an award paid by a defendant or sought by the plaintiff that compensates for harm, injury, or loss. It is a remedy found in the civil court system. The size of the payment is said to reflect the wrong done by the defendant and is that necessary to relieve the plaintiff's suffering.

Dance/Movement Therapy Therapy that uses movement for exercise, rehabilitation, and cognitive-physical intervention. Instructors are trained, often at the masters' level. Sessions are provided in public and private schools, hospitals, rehabilitation facilities, and fitness clubs. The intervention improves self-esteem, reduces stress, and teaches muscle control and mind-body communication. **See also** Health and Physical Education; Rehabilitation

DARE An acronym for the Drug Abuse Resistance Education program. DARE is a national nonprofit organization founded in 1983 in Los Angeles, California, by the city's police department. DARE incorporates a curriculum designed to teach young people skills that will help them avoid gang involvement, refrain from drug use, and steer clear of violence. Specially trained police officers conduct DARE classes in schools and classrooms around the country, and the curriculum has been adopted in other nations. DARE instructs students from kindergarten through the 12th grade. Studies regarding the effectiveness of DARE have been inconclusive.

Data, Extant/Existing Preexisting evidence that researchers can consult, rather than generating their own data. Extant data and documents are often available in archives. They are widely used in fields such as sociology, political science, and economics. Examples include census data, vital statistics, and survey archives such as the General Social Survey.

Databases for Literature Searches Numerous electronically accessible databases for literature searches exist. Among the most important in the social and behavioral sciences are *PsycINFO, Sociological Abstracts (Sociofile), Dissertation Abstracts,* and ERIC (Educational Resources Information Center). There are many others. Because no database is exhaustive, researchers should generally research their topic in several. The chief advantages of electronic searches are speed and specificity. First, speed: Searches that took days in print versions of sources, such as *Dissertation Abstracts,* take only minutes when conducted electronically. Specificity is more important: One can combine multiple criteria for defining the topic of a search and thus efficiently zero in on the subject of interest. **See also** Meta-Analysis

Deadly Weapon A term used in legal statutes to refer to instruments capable of or likely to inflict serious harm, bodily injury, or death. The presence of a deadly weapon during the commission of a crime, regardless of its use, usually increases the severity of the act, and the punishment is enhanced accordingly.

Dealignment A term used when voters no longer align themselves with any particular political party. Dealignment stands in contrast to "realignment," which is when voters shift from one party to another. The United States has been experiencing dealignment since the 1970s, when voters began identifying themselves less with their parties and more as "independents." This shift has been attributed to shifts in regional, ethnic, and racial demographics in the United States. Great Britain has also experienced voter dealignment, although British dealignment has more to do with traditional social class loyalties rather than partisan ones. A replacement of partisan voting is "retrospective voting," when voters punish or reward candidates based on a prior administration's performance.

Death Row The area of a prison where those awaiting capital punishment are housed. Death row was historically a hallway or hallways of cell blocks. The term death *house* typically refers to the area in the prison where executions take place.

Debate The act of considering a point of discussion. A debate generally occurs between two or more parties who deliberate on their competing viewpoints. Most debates seek the goal of conflict resolution and negotiation. An adjudicator may become involved to decide the outcome of a debate in which claims are the focus. Argumentation is a key element in a debate, as well as other modes of rhetoric (such as metaphor and narrative). Furthermore, important aspects of argumentation include evidence, reasoning, reservations, and claims. Stephen Toulmin's (1958) model of argumentation has been important to the field of rhetoric in the study of argumentation. For more information, see Toulmin (1958). **See also** Assertion

Debt An obligation to pay money or something of value at a future date in accordance with an expressed or implicit agreement. A debt may or may not be secured. A secured debt is a collateralized debt for which the debtor uses assets to ensure that the debt will be paid, failing which the assets can then be converted into cash to fulfill the debt obligation.

Debts may be issued by businesses or governments through bonds (IOUs), such as Treasury bonds, or they may be in the form of personal or sovereign (national) loans to be repaid by current or subsequent governments. The cost of a debt is the interest rate that must be paid in addition to the principal. This interest rate is normally based on expected inflation over the life span of the debt, and it is alternatively referred to as the inflation premium.

Credit acquisition is another form of debt. The annual percentage rate (APR) is the contracted annual rate of interest that must be paid when incremental payments are made on time. This rate is normally higher than stipulated in situations of late payments or default.

Debt Forgiveness In the 1970s and 1980s, numerous developing countries contracted a huge amount of debt to such an extent that it became burdensome to pay the principal and the interest. The poor countries were particularly endangered as it became evident that the provision of social programs was being compromised by debt obligations. Between the late 1980s and 1990s, poignant calls were made for national debt forgiveness based on what some perceived to be the odiousness (illegal and hateful nature) of the debts, largely attributable to creditor overindulgence of profligate illegitimate regimes.

In 1999, Congress put together an International Financial Institution Advisory Commission (Meltzer Commission) and gave it a wide mandate to inquire into the organization and functions of the World Bank, the International Monetary Fund (IMF), and the regional development banks and make recommendations for improvement.

One of the recommendations of the commission was that the debt situation of the poor countries merits attention and debt reduction, contingent on financial reforms, must be considered. In 1999, the IMF and World Bank's Highly Indebted and Poor Countries (HIPCs) Initiative, which was first launched in 1996, was enhanced to provide economic relief (debt forgiveness) to countries with a track record of good economic policies in order to bring their debt to sustainable levels, that is, to meet debt repayment obligations without recourse to further rescheduling or accumulation of arrears that will compromise growth. In 2005, the G8 countries and multilateral institutions agreed to forgive debts to the tune of $55 billion. The gesture was seen as noble but inadequate. At the end of 2007, HIPCs reaching completion point obtained $32.5 billion, and non-HIPCs obtained $182 million in debt relief (evaluated at the value of Special Drawing Rights, SDR). For more information, see Vines and Gilbert (2004) and Warburton (2005). **See also** Debt; International Monetary Fund (IMF)

Decatur Studies In 1955, Katz and Lagerfeld published their findings of a two-part study performed on a cross-section of 800 women in Decatur, Illinois—chosen from a group of Midwestern towns as representative of a "typical" town. This study explored the role of the individual in the flow of mass communications. Previous research had largely focused on various media as the vehicles of communication. Respondents were interviewed twice about marketing, fashion, public affairs, and moviegoing. Changes in opinions in any of the four categories were noted. Respondents were then asked who or what media had influenced their opinion. The study found that respondents were more influenced by other individuals than by the media and that communication had traveled in a two-step flow—from the media to the opinion leader and then to less active members of the population. It also found that the opinion leaders who influenced the subjects in certain areas shared certain characteristics. This study spawned a huge amount of subsequent research in the 1960s and 1970s. For more information, see Katz and Lazarsfeld (1955). **See also** Indirect Effects Theory

Decentralization The transfer of part of the powers of a central or national government to the local authorities. It involves planning, decision making, and management of public functions from the central government to field organizations. Decentralization policies are a part of initiatives to support rural development and development in developing nations.

There are several benefits of decentralization. First, it allows for local levels to tailor development plans and programs to the needs of heterogeneous populations. Second, it is less structured and, therefore, less bureaucratized. Third, it allows for a greater knowledge of, and sensitivity to, local needs, which provides for an increase of more realistic plans for programs and projects. Fourth, it facilitates the spread of national government policies into remote areas. Fifth, it allows for a greater representation of political, religious, ethnic, and tribal groups in decision making. Sixth, local governments can take over functions not usually performed well by the central government, such as maintenance of the infrastructure. And seventh, officials in the national government will be relieved of routine tasks so that they can plan and supervise the implementation of national policies.

There are several degrees of decentralization that are based on factors such as the degree of transfer of authority, local citizen participation, and the benefits for the political system. As such, decentralization can be viewed as a continuum. On one end is deconcentration, which includes shifting of the workload from the central government to offices outside the capital. These offices generally do not have local discretion in decision making. Since decision making remains at the center, these offices may be limited to transmitting orders and implementing decisions.

Next, delegation involves decision making and management by organizations under indirect control of the central government. In such arrangements, the responsibility and resources for implementing specific tasks are usually assigned under a contract. The organization with which the central government has contracted has some autonomy in interpreting the tasks assigned. Delegation represents extensive decentralization.

At the other end of the continuum is devolution, which involves independent levels of government operating outside the control of the central government. Devolution allows local residents to participate in administrative affairs through representatives elected to local government. For more information, see Rondinelli (1980). *See also* Centralization (political science); Delegation; Devolution

Deception An intentional act of misleading or providing information that is not true or that is partially true. Deception can also involve concealment or withholding of information. In psychological experimentation, deception refers to a research procedure that involves misleading participants about the real purpose of the study. This procedure is legal in psychological research and in some cases is necessary to avoid jeopardizing the results of the study. For example, deception is frequently used in experiments that involve a placebo group where participants are not told whether they are in the placebo or experimental groups. When deception is used, participants need to be explained the real purposes of the experiment afterward; this procedure is referred to as "debriefing." The American Psychological Association also recommends that to mitigate the breach of trust between the experimenter and the participants, investigators can choose to withhold information instead of providing untruthful information. *See also* Experimental Research

Decision Analysis An analytical process for making decisions under conditions of uncertainty and complexity. Uncertainty can be caused by lack of information, lack of time, and other general factors that can "bound" the decision-making process. Complexity is usually a function of the intricate and intractable nature of the problem or issue. The analysis process involves breaking down complex decisions into smaller—more manageable—components. The smaller components allow decision makers to make simple and familiar choices.

Since complexity and uncertainty bound the decision-making process, decision analysis uses existing literature and/or experts to develop estimates of the likelihood of particular events or outcomes occurring based on each small decision made. The aggregation of each small decision, via mathematical models, helps the decision makers arrive at a more comprehensive decision with respect to a complex problem or issue.

There are several analytical models that involve mapping strategies to address a complex problem or issue. The most common model is the decision tree (or the closely related influence diagram). Decision trees can be used to graphically represent multiple strategies for a desired outcome.

In recent years, decision analysis has become a practical tool in many sectors. For example, the banking industry bases some of its investment strategies on the results of decision analysis. Decision analysis has also been used for analysis of mergers and acquisitions, capital investment, and new product development. Finally, governments are using decision analysis for policy-making decisions. For example, the U.S. federal government used decision analysis to decide whether strategic oil reserves should be based on the potential disturbance of the world's oil supply or some other factors.

Decision-Making Theory A theory that seeks greater understanding of how ideal or real decision makers make or should make decisions. The traditional aspects of this theory are concerned with how optimal decisions can be reached, known as normative or rational decision theories. In this type of decision-making theory, it is critical to understand the ways in which humans strategize and generate multiple alternatives when making the optimal choice or decision. A criticism of this perspective is that psychologists theorize that people do not typically make perfectly optimized choices. Another area of decision-making theory attempts to understand how humans actually make decisions without optimizing, known as descriptive or naturalistic decision theory. Here, the focus is on the ways humans use prior experiences to make decisions in certain contexts. Naturalistic decision makers are more concerned about situation awareness rather than generating multiple alternatives. Decision-making theory is an area of study examining the human psychological phenomenon in all cognitive, behavioral, and social activities. For more information, see Janis and Mann (1977) and Zambok and Klein (1997). *See also* Satisficing (public administration)

Declarative Memory A type of long-term memory that stores facts or explicit memories. Declarative memory consists of both *semantic* memories for facts about the world (e.g., who the president is, what a dollar is worth) and *episodic* memories for facts about ourselves (e.g., where we were born, what our favorite color is). Declarative memory is distinguished from *procedural memory*, which refers to our stored knowledge of well-learned habits or skills. Declarative memories are often lost in people with amnesia, whereas they are still able to retain procedural memories. ***See also*** Amnesia; Long-Term Memory (LTM); Procedural Memory

Decoder   A device that is used to retrieve information that has been encoded, that is, scrambled in an electronic signal. In this manner, the information can then be interpreted. In communication, a synonym for *decoder* is *receiver*. The receiver accepts the information. For example, a person can receive (decode) the news. The person accepts the information as valid and acceptable.

Deconstruct   A term coined by the philosopher Jacques Derrida, who himself is playing on a term used by Martin Heidegger, *Destruktion* (destruction), and *Abbau*. *Abbau*—"dismantling" or "unbuilding," from *bauen* (to build)—better captures, than does *Destruktion*, the careful disassembling and reassembling of the Western philosophical tradition that Heidegger's and Derrida's work represent. Derrida himself refused to constrain deconstruction to any kind of critical method because any method or critique instantiates precisely the metaphysics of presence that deconstruction seeks to avoid. Yet in popular parlance, the term is used loosely: in a positive sense, to think critically and in a negative sense, to render meaning empty, obscurantist, and relative. ***See also*** Construct; Postmodernism; Structuralism (media studies, sociology); Text

Decoy   An object or a person used to lure or lead someone in a particular direction. A decoy can be used to distract attention toward or away from another entity. Decoys are tactical tools frequently employed by law enforcement. For example, a female police officer may go undercover as a prostitute to act as a decoy to arrest a John.

Deduction Versus Induction   These terms refer to two distinct patterns of inference. In general, an inference is deductive if the truth of the premises purports to guarantee the truth of the conclusion and inductive if the truth of the premises purports to make the truth of the conclusion more probable but does not guarantee it. The use of the word *purports* in these definitions allows for the existence of arguments that fail to possess the associated properties. Thus, there may be deductive arguments that purport to guarantee their conclusions but do not (and are thus invalid) or inductive arguments that fail to make their conclusions more probable (and are thus inductively weak).

Many inductive arguments involve inferences from specific cases to general ones, as with arguments by enumeration (which infer from the presence of a property in a sample to its presence in a larger population) and arguments by analogy (which infer the presence of a property in a subject from its presence in analogous instances). But not all inductive arguments exhibit this structure. For example, causal arguments, which infer the presence of a cause from certain conditions, are inductive and yet may infer from one particular case to another.

Deductive arguments are either valid or invalid. An argument is valid if and only if it is logically impossible for the premises to be true and the conclusion false. In such a case, the truth of the premises guarantees the truth of the conclusion. Inductive arguments are either strong or weak. An inductively strong argument is one in which the truth of the premises makes the truth of the conclusion more probable but does not guarantee it. By these definitions, no valid argument is strong, and no strong argument is valid.

Deductive inferences exhibit other properties not possessed by inductive inferences. Among them is monotonicity. Assume that P is a set of premise statements and C a conclusion statement that is inferable from P. Let A be any set of additional statements. The inference is monotonic if C is still inferable from the union of P with A. All deductively valid inferences are monotonic, because if C validly follows from P, then it validly follows from the union of P and A. (Note that even if A contains the denial of C, the argument is still valid since the premises cannot possibly be true.) In contrast, no inductively strong argument is monotonic. Given any inductively strong argument, there exists some statement such that its addition to the premises would render that argument weak.

Defense   One of the opposing sides in an adversarial justice system. A defendant is brought up on charges by the prosecution. Typically, a defense attorney represents the defendant in court and defends the accused against the charges. The counsel's role is to ensure that the defendant's due process rights are upheld and that he or she receives a fair trial. The Sixth Amendment states that those accused by the government have a right to counsel. In 1963, the Supreme Court ruled that one's right to an attorney has no value unless the state provides defense attorneys to those unable to afford one themselves. ***See also*** Adversary System of Justice (political science, sociology); Due Process/Due Process Model; Prosecutor

Defense Mechanisms   *(education)*   A concept that originates from the psychodynamic theories of Freud and involves the unconscious psychological strategy of tension reduction, which allows us to cope with anxiety, an aversive psychological state that individuals attempt to avoid. Defense mechanisms are developed by the ego to deal with the demands created by the id, the superego, and reality. According to Freud's topographical model of personality, the ego deals with reality. Therefore, the ego has to deal with the demands frequently conflicting with the id and the superego. The defense allows the unconscious feeling that we cannot consciously tolerate to be expressed only indirectly in a disguised manner. When the anxiety becomes too overwhelming, the ego activates defense mechanisms to protect the individual. Feelings of anxiety are often accompanied by embarrassment, shame, or guilt. The id is the primitive, pleasure-oriented part of the personality. Therefore, defense mechanisms work either by blocking the unacceptable impulses or by distorting or transforming them into more acceptable ones. This distortion of perceived reality decreases the anxiety and the psychological tension felt by the individual. There are several defense mechanisms that have been described by researchers. Anna Freud, Sigmund Freud's daughter, described 10 defense mechanisms used by the ego. While defense mechanisms can be unhealthy when overused, they also can be adaptive as they allow us to function normally. For more information, see Freud (1937). *See also* Denial; Displacement; Projection (communication, psychology); Rationalization; Regression

Defense Mechanisms *(psychology)*   Mechanisms used to distance oneself from awareness of anxiety-producing thoughts, feelings, and desires. According to Freudian psychoanalytic theory, defense mechanisms are used to protect the self or the ego from unpleasantness. Unconsciously, the id impulses are in conflict with the ego and superego's needs, values, and beliefs. Although defense mechanisms distort a person's awareness, which makes the thought, feeling, or desire tolerable, they often can lead to harmful problems. There are many defense mechanisms that have been hypothesized, but denial, repression, projection, regression, rationalization, and displacement are commonly cited. Denial is when a person does not accept reality and acts as if the thoughts, feelings, and behaviors that are producing anxiety do not exist. Repression means that an individual unconsciously suppresses the ideas, impulses, and memories that cause anxiety from coming into awareness. Projection is the process by which a person attributes his or her own traits, attitudes, and emotions onto another person. Regression causes a person to escape from reality and go back to an earlier stage of development. Rationalization means to take a situation that is confusing or irrational and make it clear and rational while concealing a person's motivations and how she or he truly feels, thinks, and acts. Displacement is the process of transferring emotions or desires from the original object or person onto a safer object or person. *See also* Psychoanalysis (education, psychology)

Defensiveness   An attitude that is characterized by difference in an exchange of communication between two or more people. Situations in which defensiveness can occur are from miscommunication over intended meaning or confusion over relayed information between the parties involved in formal or informal contexts. Conflict management strategies can be employed to work through the divergence, either in work or in personal situations. Interpersonal communication models focus on exploring the influences of gender, race, and class on the defensive individual, as well as the situational components that have contributed to the

defensiveness mode. These tactics seek to achieve negotiation and positive decision making among the parties in conflict. Defensiveness is generally considered to be a negative mode of communication that is marked by hostility and self-protectiveness that arise in reaction to perceived attacks by one or more parties in an exchange of communication. This attitude can be reflected in verbal messaging and nonverbal behavior. *See also* Argumentativeness

Deferral   A term that has several meanings in both public and private administration. In accounting, it refers to any account where an asset or liability is realized at a future date or a tax shelter tool that accelerates deductions and postpones taxable income. In an executive branch, deferral refers to a delay in the spending of appropriated funds or an action or inaction that delays the availability of a budget obligation.

Deferred Sentencing   The legal practice of affording an offender a term on probation in lieu of a conviction and subsequent punishment. Typically, if the offender completes probation without violating its terms, the charge is dismissed, and in effect, the person was never convicted. If someone violates the probation, a conviction is handed down, and the offender is sentenced accordingly.

Deficit   A situation that arises when a government spends more money than it is collecting in revenue within a given time frame. A deficit is different from a debt, which is the accumulated amount of negative funds of the government. A deficit is not necessarily a negative force to a nation's economy and can be stabilizing in times of high unemployment. On the other hand, deficits in times of high employment can lead to inflation and a decrease in private investments that can affect a nation's long-term capital formation and economic growth. The opposite of a national deficit is a budget surplus, when the amount of revenues of a government surpasses its expenditures. *See also* Inflation

Definition *(communication)*   The meaning of a word or phrase. Stipulative definitions give a new meaning either to a term already in use or to a new term. A descriptive definition can be shown to be right or wrong depending on the usage of the term.

Definition *(media studies)*   An agreed-on statement that expresses the meaning of a word, term, or thing. The meaning of a definition is formed by its cultural usage; thus, the meaning of a definition can shift over time. In addition, a definition is shaped by social, political, and economic structures and their ideologies. *See also* Construct

Deflation *(economics)*   The decrease in general price levels, characterized by the rise in the value of money. This economic situation, often caused by the reduction in the supply of money or credit, leads to the fall in prices, wages, and credit. In addition to the decrease in the supply of money, deflation can be caused by a decrease in the demand for goods, an increase in the supply of goods, or an increase in the demand for money.

Deflation can be induced by contractions in overall spending and a decrease in consumer demand in a country as a result of a decrease in government spending, personal spending, or investment spending. Consequently, unemployment rises or salaries are cut, corporate profits fall or factories close. Often defaults on individual and company loans increase, and ultimately, the country enters into an economic recession or depression. To remedy an economy characterized by deflation, or to mitigate deflation, the Federal Reserve has the power to use a monetary policy to increase the money supply and induce rising prices, causing the opposite effect, or inflation.

Some economists believe that deflation is a purely monetary effect of government-enforced slimming of credit or increases in interest rates, which in effect increases unemployment. In some instances, the government induces deflation by imposing interest rate increases and tightening the money supply to suppress inflation and slow the economy.

Deflation should not be confused with disinflation, which refers to the slowing rate of inflation or general levels of prices. ***See also*** Depression (economics); Inflation; Recession

Deflation *(political science)*   A general decrease in the prices of goods in a nation's economy. Deflation often goes hand in hand with economic recession or depression. The United States and Great Britain experienced a period of deflation during the Great Depression. Until this point, most Americans believed in a laissez-faire approach to the economy, that a capitalist system cures itself. Influential economists, particularly John Maynard Keynes (1883–1946) from Britain, endorsed government intervention in the marketplace. These developments in economic policy have contributed to the fact that the United States and Britain have not experienced a severe financial recession or depression until the credit bubble and stock market crash of 2008. The U.S. government began deregulation of certain financial instruments and services under the James Earl Carter presidential administration (1977–1981). This movement picked up steam under the following Ronald Reagan administration. Under the presidency of William F. Clinton (1993–2001), the government repealed the Glass Seagall Act of 1933, which prohibited banks from being active players in the securities business (The Gramm-Leach–Billey Act). Stemming from this and other deregulation activities, large securities firms and banks made enormous profits with unregulated hedge funds and with very complicated mortgage "securitization" instruments, credit default swaps, and the like. Easy credit, little control, much risk, and other plays for easy money, all

came together in 2008 to cause a meltdown of the economy. The George W. Bush administration and its doctrine of free markets did little to bring back any form of strict regulation. The state of the economy in 2009, with the bailouts of big banks, insurance companies, auto companies, and the like, makes it almost mandatory for the government to put back in place strong regulatory measures in order to bring back confidence in the American and world economic systems. In the United States, deflation is generally measured through the U.S. Department of Labor Consumer Price Index (CPI) and Producer Price Indexes (PPI). Deflation is the opposite of inflation, which is the rise in the price of goods. Sometimes a period of stagflation exists, when there are alternate periods of both inflation and deflation during an economic recession. ***See also*** Depression (economics); Inflation; Recession

Degree   A legal term used to value and rank the seriousness of a criminal act. An illegal act in the first degree is more serious than one in the second degree. This unit of measure is used to calculate and classify punishments so that the justice system can honor the principle of proportionality.

Deindustrialization   The transformation caused by technological and economic factors when industrial activities are removed or reduced in a country, particularly those dependent on heavy industrial or manufacturing industries. Typically, a series of economic and social changes ensue as industrial activity lessens. Since manufacturing jobs typically pay well, a consequence of deindustrialization can be the decline in wages and average standard of living.

Not necessarily a result of globalization in all instances, a prominent example is the substantial deindustrialization that the United States has experienced as foreign competition has threatened the U.S. steel, automotive, and electronic industries.

While deindustrialization refers to the decline in manufactured goods or employment in the manufacturing sector, it can also refer to the shift from manufacturing to the services sector, marked by an increase in the share of jobs. Deindustrialization can also be interpreted as the declining share of external trade represented by manufacturing, leading to the failure to maintain a surplus of exports over imports and eventual economic decline.

Many theories exist to explain deindustrialization, some dating back to the 1800s. Some economists see the process as both a cause and an effect of economic performance—on the one hand, a result of poor economic performance and, on the other, representing a positive, mature economy—not as a symptom of failure but as a natural outcome of successful economic development associated with rising living standards. ***See also*** Globalization (economics)

Delayed Reaction   The postponed feedback to the communication of another party; generally pertains to a verbal reply. This interval might provide the necessary time for an individual to cognitively process the information relayed to him or her and to construct a response. The pause in an exchange of communication can also correlate to an individual's emotional processing (particularly relating to overwhelming feeling) that inhibits the ability to provide an answer. A delayed reaction can also be a function of a second thought about an idea. An individual's subjectivity shapes his or her style of communication, thus holding the potential to shape the nature of his or her reactions. ***See also*** Feedback (communication)

Delegates   In the United States, those members of the Republican and Democratic parties sent to their respective national conventions to vote for a presidential candidate. A delegate is also the name given to a member of the House of Representatives who represents a U.S. territory instead of a state. ***See also*** House of Representatives

Delegation   (1) The practice of assigning tasks and responsibilities to subordinates by a supervisor or manager. A potential problem that can occur with delegation is suggested by the "principal-agent problem." That is, can the supervisor who has delegated authority to the subordinate be confident that the subordinate will carry out the agenda and wishes of the supervisor rather than his or her own agenda/wishes? (2) Select members of an organization who are assigned to represent that association's interest to another party.

Deliberation   The legal decision-making process a jury engages in when deciding a case. Deliberation begins after each side has presented its argument and the judge has instructed the jury. While deliberating, the jury is expected to consider and weigh all they've heard so as to reach a decision. ***See also*** Jury

Delinquency   Illegal behavior conducted by someone who is not yet an adult. In response to a growing social perception that juvenile offenders are distinct from adult offenders, the first juvenile court was established in Illinois in 1899. A separate justice system, in which young people are to be treated differently, was quickly instituted around the country. This created a new class of offender—the juvenile delinquent. Jurisdictions routinely enact legislation that deems certain behaviors, such as truancy or running away, illegal only if committed by a juvenile. Therefore, delinquency encompasses a wide range of behaviors. ***See also*** Juvenile Justice System; Status Offense

Delivery   The enunciation of words. It also involves the vocal and bodily behavior during the presentation of a speech. This involves tone, pitch, volume, rate, and vocal quality.

Tone involves the sound of a definite pitch and vibration. Tone can also mean the pitch of a word that

one uses to express differences in meaning when one is speaking. Finally, tone implies a particular pitch or change of pitch that constitutes an element in the intonation of a phrase or sentence.

Pitch involves the difference in the vibration frequency of one's voice that adds to the total meaning of speech. A definite relative pitch is a significant part of any speech.

Volume is the degree of loudness (intensity of a sound) when a person speaks. It is important to speak loud enough for the audience to hear you. Microphones can be used to enhance the volume. It is also important to develop a pleasing volume level. No one wants to be shouted at. On the other hand, no one wants to strain to hear someone's voice.

Rate involves the speed at which a language is spoken. Word reference forums claim that German is spoken at a leisurely pace, while French and Spanish are spoken at a much faster rate.

Vocal quality is perceived within the harmonics of a voice. Harmonics are dependent on the levels of estrogen and progesterone.

In speech delivery, it is important to be aware of your tone, pitch, volume, rate, and vocal quality. For more information, see Kleiven (1973). ***See also*** Speech; Verbal Communication

Delivery Systems   Systematic and multiple-method processes for delivering services or products. Delivery systems are groups of interrelated individual systems. These systems include the means, the technology, and the devices for delivery.

Delusions   Firmly held beliefs that are not based in reality. Even in the face of contradictory evidence, individuals who experience delusions will typically not abandon these fixed beliefs. In addition, individuals who experience delusions may struggle to understand why others find their beliefs implausible. Delusions may be present in a variety of psychological conditions, including delusional disorders, depression, mania, organic disorders, or drug overdose; they are very common in schizophrenia. Delusions observed in schizophrenia are frequently called "bizarre" delusions, in reference to their unrealistic and strange content. Some common types of delusions are delusions of persecution (the belief that one is being persecuted, plotted against, or mistreated), delusions of control (the belief that other people or forces are controlling one's mind), delusions of reference (the belief that one is being referred to by gestures, comments, or things), and delusions of grandeur (the belief that one is extremely powerful). ***See also*** Schizophrenia

Demand   The willingness and the ability of consumers to purchase goods and services. The allusion to willingness and ability gives the concept a particular meaning in economics. When economists talk about demand, they allude to effective demand, which is a combination of willingness and ability. A consumer might be willing to purchase a good, but that is all there is to it. The consumer does not have the ability or wherewithal to purchase the good and therefore cannot obtain the good from a market.

Given certain regularity conditions or assumptions, economists have tried to model consumer behavior to derive the law of demand, which states that if other factors that can affect demand don't change, consumers will buy more of a good as the price falls and less of a good as the price increases.

Practical theories such as revealed preference and marginal utility are used to indicate the choices that rational consumers will make when price, income, and marginal utility change. These theories have been used to determine the law of demand. The theory of revealed preference postulates that if consumers are rational, prices and income are sufficient to justify the law of demand by observing consumer spending in the marketplace when changes in price and income occur. This theory may be contrasted to that of demand based on satisfaction or utility derived from the consumption of a good.

The theories of revealed preference and utility are practically inseparable when a comprehensive approach is used to understand consumer behavior. Price is a common denominator in both theories. Demand is theoretically contingent on several factors, including taste or preference, income, price, the number of buyers, marginal utility, the prices of related goods (substitutes and complements), expectations of future prices, time horizon, and whether or not a good or service is essential. For more information, see Case and Fair (2003), McConnell and Brue (2008), Salvatore (2002), and Schiller (2006). ***See also*** Aggregate Demand Curve; Elasticity; Income; Price; Utility

Democracy (*political science*)   A form of government in which power is vested in the people and exercised directly by them or through their elected representatives under a free electoral system. Democracy means rule by the people. It is based on consent of the governed whereby power flows from the people to their leaders. Democratic governments rely on constitutions and their adherence for survival.

The theory of modern democracy was not formulated until the Age of Enlightenment in the 17th and 18th centuries, when philosophers defined the essential elements of democracy as follows: (a) separation of powers among the executive, judicial, and legislative branches of government; (b) protection of basic civil and human rights; (c) religious liberty; (d) freedom of opinion; (e) an equal right to vote; (f) good governance, which requires a focus on public interest and absence of corruption; (g) the choosing of government through elections; (h) active participation of the people in civic life; (i) the application of the rule of law to all; and (j) the separation of religion and State.

One of the most important contributions to democratic practice is the system of checks and balances

to ensure that political power is dispersed and decentralized. The idea of checks and balances stems from the belief that government is best when its potential for abuse is curbed. There are two meanings of checks and balances: federalism and separation of powers. Federalism exists where there is a strong central government and constituent smaller units, such as states, which allows states to check the power of the federal government. Separation of powers ensures that political power will not be concentrated within a single branch of the national government but rather be divided among the branches so that none could accumulate too much power.

There are many types of democracies. Two that are found in the United States are representative and liberal. In representative democracies, citizens elect officials to make political decisions, formulate laws, and administer programs for the public good. Liberal democracy is a form of representative democracy in which the elected representatives discharge their functions under the purview of a constitution, which limits their powers. This ensures that the rights of individuals are safeguarded. A liberal democracy has elections, more than one political party, an independent legislature, and an independent judiciary.

There are a number of ways to elect officials in a democracy: plurality elections, proportional representation, and majority elections. The plurality system is the simplest means of determining the outcome of an election. In plurality elections, a winning candidate gains more votes than any other single opponent. Proportional representation means that each political party is represented in the legislature according to its percentage of the total vote nationwide. It is carried out when voters cast ballots for political parties rather than individual candidates. In the majority system, the candidate or party receiving more than 50% of the vote in a constituency is awarded the position. For more information, see Dahl (2000). ***See also*** Election; Federalism; Rule of Law; Separation of Powers

Democracy (*public administration*)   Originating back to ancient Greece, when Athens (ca. 500–330 BCE) called itself a *democracy*, the term refers to a government in which supreme power is vested in the people, exercised either directly or indirectly through elected representatives. Elections are typically held with freedom of speech, freedom of the press, and some degree of rule of law. The term is a literal translation of the Greek *dēmokratia*, and when used as a descriptive term, democracy is synonymous with "majority rule."

Although it originated in ancient Greece, modern conceptions are largely different, and no universally accepted definition of democracy exists. The formal mechanisms of democracy vary, with direct democracy at one end of the spectrum and representative democracy at the other. Direct democracy means that people participate directly in the activities of State with voting techniques such as referendums (Switzerland), while in contrast, in a representative democracy, sovereignty is exercised by representatives of the people, elected on a geographical and population basis (United States). Most democracies are representative democracies.

In the United States, separation of powers, or the division of political power among several bodies as a precaution against tyranny, is often regarded as a necessary element, while in other countries, such as the United Kingdom, the underlying philosophy of democracy is parliamentary sovereignty, where the parliament is supreme to all other government institutions. Although most political systems have considered themselves democracies since the mid 20th century, many have not stressed individual rights or emphasized other elements typical of Western democracy such as the encouragement of competing political parties.

With the collapse of authoritative dictatorships in Latin America and the end of one-party Communist rule in Eastern Europe and sub-Saharan Africa, the number of countries holding multiparty elections has recently increased. Despite the increase in countries holding multiparty elections, the rights and freedoms of citizens in many nations in the world are limited, and many countries in Africa, for example, have reverted to authoritarian governments with sham, and sometimes violent, elections (e.g., Zimbabwe in 2008). *See also* Election; Federalism; Rule of Law; Separation of Powers

Democracy and Education   John Dewey's most important book on education, *Democracy and Education* (1916), discusses what Dewey saw as the inherent connection between education and democratic ideals. Since education as a social process has no meaning until we define the kind of society desired, democratic societies should seek to cultivate democratic dispositions in children. A democratic education is continuous with the student's experiences, provides opportunities for testing ideas, and is founded on the continuity of experience. For more information, see Dewey (1916/1997). *See also* Experience

Democratic Leadership   A style of leadership that assigns individual rights and privileges to all parties in a group or organization as the followers are engaged by a leader to achieve goals. Democratic leadership encourages participation by all parties engaged in similar pursuits and requires equitable distribution of both power and responsibility.

Democratic Socialism   Promotion of socialism and democracy in the governance of people. Democratic socialists, those who accept democratic socialist principles, believe that the economy and society should be run democratically to meet the needs of the whole population rather than make profits for a few, as in a capitalist system. Democratic socialists see the political empowerment of society's disenfranchised—that is, workers—as a necessary step in the transformation of capitalism into a more humane social order. Their base of support is trade unions. The key element of democratic socialism is workers' meaningful participation and control of daily life at work and in the community, with managers elected by and responsible to workers and community members. The focus is on the abolishment of the capitalist system.

Democratic socialism took root in Europe after World War I. Democratic socialist parties actively participated in government in Great Britain, Germany, Sweden, Belgium, the Netherlands, and other nations where democratic socialism is more accepted than in the United States. Since the 1930s, the United States has been the only industrially advanced capitalist democracy without a large established social democratic or socialist political party.

Democratic socialism is not the same as social democracy. The division between social democrats and democratic socialists stems from the former party's peace with capitalism while concentrating on humanizing the effects of capitalism. Social democrats supported and tried to strengthen the basic institutions of the welfare state, such as pensions for all, public health care, public education, and unemployment insurance. Democratic socialists, on the other hand, have argued that capitalism could never be sufficiently humanized. Their dual task has been to secure socialism against capitalist opposition and secure socialism in a way that develops socialism's democratic potential. They estimate their success in terms of advances in a democracy before, during, and after a socialist transformation. In short, democratic socialists want socialism to help lay the basis for making major advances in a democracy. For more information, see Marković (1982). *See also* Capitalism (political science); Democracy (political science, public administration); Socialism (economics, political science)

Demographics (*economics*)   Statistical data for a defined human population with relation to their size, structure, and distribution and the relative change over time. Demographic information is very often culturally based and typically includes variables such as age, gender, race, income, occupation, and educational attainment. Detailed demographic information is often recorded in a region or country census and is periodically updated. In addition, records of events such as birth, deaths, migrations, marriages, divorces, and so on complement population censuses.

Demographic data are often used by governments to measure trends ranging from immigration patterns to wealth distribution. Data are also largely used during election periods to predict voting outcomes and to focus campaign efforts. Demographics are used by governments to measure the overall characteristics of a population on a macroscale, such as average age and generational characteristics. Demographic data relating to employment rates are one of the key indications of an economy's health. Governments study trends in areas such as population to predict and prepare for economic impacts. For example, demographic studies have shown that sharp population increases, such as during postwar periods, may contribute to heavy increases in unemployment when this segment of population enters the workforce. Furthermore, when this same population becomes elderly and retires, health care spending and retirement pensions are likely to consume a growing share of the gross domestic product. Given that these are provided by the state, this could mean increasing public spending and higher taxes.

Demographics are also often used in government, economic, or marketing research to identify consumer markets. Data used by businesses to identify markets for their goods and services have historically been the foundation of target marketing. In addition to enabling businesses to identify their customers and determine how likely they are to purchase their goods, studying demographics aids businesses in identifying changes in the needs of the marketplace.

Demographic data are used to create customer profiles for target audiences, which are then used to define marketing strategy. Demographic data are commonly accessed through government census bureaus or "cluster systems," which take large numbers of demographic variables and combine them to create profiles of individuals and households.

Demographics can often lead to demographic profiling, which results in generalizations about a group of people. Demographic profiling is often criticized as demographic data refer to aggregates of data and the overall conclusions may not apply to each person within that group.

Demographics *(media studies)* A segment of the human population, that is identified by its objective information for the purposes of market research. Statistical information about these subgroups is commonly concerned with age, gender, race, income, employment status, location, ownership (home, car), and educational background, as these factors are considered as contributing to an individual's purchasing decisions. Market researchers use this information to construct demographic profiles, which identify subgroups of the population and the representative characteristics of a member of a subgroup in relation to being a consumer. David Foot and Daniel Stoffman's (1999) work *Boom, Bust and Echo* addresses the powerful relationship between demographics and media trends. Advertising and marketing strategies are highly influenced by demographics to match their products with an attractive demographic group for consumption. For more information, see Foot and Stoffman (1999). ***See also*** Psychographics

Demographic Transition The changing patterns, in both mortality and fertility, associated with a society's shift to an industrialized state. The pattern of a preindustrial social structure is one in which high birthrates are balanced by high death rates. In an industrialized society, lower death rates are balanced by falling birthrates.

Demography *(geology)* The systematic study of population attributes, including age and gender distribution, birth and death rates, marriage and divorce statistics, disease, and other data pertaining to population demographics. Demography is a science that requires the application of rigorous quantitative analysis and draws from disciplines such as sociology, anthropology, and economics. Demography is used for many purposes, the most common known being to collect census information. Demographers collect information about the population for certain industries as well. The advertising, marketing, and real estate industries rely on demographics to appeal to certain target groups. In addition, government uses demography to help identify social and political priorities and assist in the development of governmental policies. While demography can be used to provide basic descriptive statistics such as age and sex, it can also be employed to make larger social, economic, and political connections.

Demography *(sociology)* The scientific study of human populations. Demography is a social science sometimes referred to as *population studies*. The field of demography encompasses inquiry into a wide variety of population characteristics including but not limited to composition, mortality, growth, and changes over time. Demographic studies often explore relationships between significant population statistics and other forces such as economics and politics.

Dendrites Branched extensions from the cell body of a neuron, or soma, that participate in the transmission of neural impulses by receiving incoming impulses. Dendrites (derived from the Greek word *dendron*, "tree") receive and process most of the excitatory electrical stimulation from sensory organs or other neurons and conduct the electrical impulses to the cell body. Dendrites receive electrical impulses by other neurons via synapses. The higher the number of neurons, the more is the information that can be received. For more information, see Stuart, Spruston, and Hausser (2007). ***See also*** Axon; Neurons; Soma; Synapse

Denial A defense mechanism that is based in the psychodynamic theories of Freud. According to these theories, defense mechanisms are unconscious methods to minimize anxiety. Denial is the refusal to acknowledge a fact or an external source of anxiety. The individual rejects or minimizes a fact that is too uncomfortable or anxiety provoking, even despite clear evidence of its existence. The anxiety-provoking external event is forgotten and eliminated from awareness. For example, the husband of a woman who is terminally ill may refuse to recognize that she is dying and may plan to take her on a long trip when she recovers from her illness. ***See also*** Defense Mechanisms (psychology)

Denotation The dominant meaning, or representation, of a word or a thing. The generally accepted view of denotation is in relationship to the secondary meaning (connotation), although some scholars dispute their distinct separation. Denotation is shaped by the cultural context in which language is constructed as a set of codes rather than by individual subjectivity. Significantly, denotation has been elaborated on in the work of the linguist Ferdinand de Saussure, the semiotician Roland Barthes, and the media critic John Fiske. Barthes sees denotation as the first order of signification. Ultimately, ideological meaning is determined by both connotation and denotation. *See also* Connotation

Deoxyribonucleic Acid (DNA) *(psychology)*   A nucleic acid that is mostly located in the cell nucleus, though a small amount of DNA can also be found in the mitochondria. Almost every cell in a person's body contains the same DNA, which is hereditary in all humans, almost all organisms, and some viruses. DNA is organized into structures called chromosomes in the form of firmly coined strands of large molecules. The main function of DNA molecules is the long-term storage of information. DNA is often referred to as a set of blueprints as it contains all the instructions needed to synthesize proteins, which supply the biochemical basis for heredity. Within each DNA molecule are segments called genes, which carry this genetic information. *See also* Chromosomes; Genes; Genetics

Deoxyribonucleic Acid (DNA) *(sociology)*   Stores and copies genetic material in living organisms. DNA, as it is commonly known, consists of two spiraling and repeating units of nucleotides joined together by chemical bonds. DNA's physical construction, a double-helix, is an image that has become widely familiar. Francis Crick and James Watson are credited with discovering DNA in 1953. In 1962, they were awarded the Nobel Prize for what is consistently identified as one of the most important scientific discoveries of the 20th century. DNA accounts for how organisms are constructed and explains heredity. *See also* Chromosomes; Genes; Genetics

Dependency Theory   The name given to a theory promulgated by S. J. Ball-Rokeach and M. L. DeFleur in 1976. It suggests that people have various dependencies on the media and that these dependencies vary from person to person, group to group, and culture to culture. It asserts that audiences in modern urban-industrial societies have a particularly high dependence on reliable, up-to-date mass information.

Dependency theory stresses the existence of a strong triangular relationship that unites society, the media, and the audience. When, for example, society experiences a great deal of conflict, uncertainty, and change, popular dependency on the media increases. As societies and media technologies become more complex and as the amount of information to be synthesized increases, the functions of the media become more specialized, more diverse, and more apparently essential, satisfying the needs of the audience by reducing its sense of ambivalence regarding a given issue, making sense of a complicated issue, or supplying audience members with a means of orienting themselves toward a body of information. In a modernized society, the media typically serve not only as the principal provider of entertainment but also as a key source of political, economic, and emergency information. The more functions served by the media in society, the deeper the dependency of society on them. Of course, the media supply not only factual data but also interpretive gloss; and the more media-dependent an audience is, the more likely it is to accept the media's definition or explanation of a particular event or situation.

While it has been postulated that dependency on mass media generally increases as a function of the individual's wealth and education, there are reasons for questioning the universal truth of this supposition, which is sometimes referred to as the "knowledge gap." While it may be true that wealthier, better-educated people may have more access to and familiarity with the media, it is also arguable that they are less passive, more skeptical consumers of information and therefore somewhat less likely to accept at face value the conclusions offered by media presentations.

Not all people become dependent on the same kind of information medium, and it has been suggested that people who become dependent on different media tend to have different overall concepts of the world. Moreover, it seems likely that the more a person depends on one particular medium, the more likely he or she is to accept the ideas expressed through that medium. For more information, see Ball-Rokeach and DeFleur (1976), Becker and Whitney (1980), Miller and Reese (1982), and Severin (1988). *See also* Knowledge Gap; Mass Media

Dependent Variable   The factor in a research study that is being measured. The dependent variable is often hypothesized to be affected by the researcher's manipulation of the independent variable. The dependent variable is never controlled by the experimenter but "depends" on the experimental situation. For example, if a researcher were to investigate the effect of viewing violence on television on children's aggression, children's displays of aggression would be the dependent variable. To prove causal relationships between two variables, the dependent variable has to change only as a direct response to the manipulation of the independent variable. *See also* Experiment; Independent Variable

Deportation   The legally forced removal of people from a geographical place. Typically, those being deported are foreigners—people who are not native to the location from which they are being driven. Deportees are often sent back to the place considered to be their native land. Many courts now require deportation of illegal immigrants, and sometime legal immigrants, if found guilty in a criminal case.

Deposition   A judicial process in which a witness is formally questioned prior to a criminal or civil trial.

This inquiry takes place outside the courtroom. The statements and evidence given in a deposition are under oath and carry significant weight. This official testimony will be used during the course of the legal proceedings. Deposition is also a legal term and when used as such refers specifically to the document created when a witness is deposed. In political science, when someone has been removed from a position of power, he or she is said to have been deposed.

Depression *(economics)* An economic situation characterized by decreasing business activity, falling price levels, high unemployment, excess supply, deflation, and public fear. An economic crisis that is less severe and considered a more normal part of a business cycle is usually known as a recession. A recession is defined as two consecutive quarterly declines in gross national product. If a recession continues long enough, it could develop into a depression. While recessions are typically limited to a single nation, depressions, such as the Great Depression, can encompass many countries. Although the transition point from a recession into a depression is not clearly defined, it has been noted that a decline in gross domestic product of more than 10% constitutes a depression.

Throughout the 18th century, depressions primarily had noneconomic causes, such as weather-induced crop failures or wars. Since the early 1800s, depressions have been increasingly industrial, although the Japanese recession in the 1990s was partly caused by a reduction in consumer demand. In modern times, the common causes of a severe economic downturn may include overexpansion of commerce, industry, or agriculture; underconsumption and overinvestment; a regional discourse or a war; or a stock market crash. The most notable depressions in history included the Great Depression in the 1930s, which affected most of the world; the Long Depression, which lasted from the 1870s to the 1890s; and the severe economic downturn in Japan in the 1990s.

A depression develops when demand decreases and overproduction forces a decrease in production, discharging of employees, and wage cuts. Consequently, unemployment and decreases in wages affect purchasing power, and the crisis escalates.

Governments typically apply methods to both prevent and alleviate recessions and depressions. Some economists are advocates of deficit spending by the government to encourage economic recovery, while others support a more "hands-off" method where the government does not interfere with the natural market forces. Tax rate cuts, increased public welfare, job reeducation programs, and interest rate adjustments are among the measures taken by governments to alleviate economic downturns. *See also* Deflation; Demand; Recession; Supply

Depression *(education)* A psychiatric condition differentiated from normal sadness or bereavement by its duration and intensity. Referred to in the *Diagnostic and Statistical Manual of Mental Disorders* (fourth edition, text revision; *DSM-IV-TR*) as major depressive disorder (MDD), depression is characterized primarily by either chronically depressed mood quality or anhedonia and accompanied by various combinations of the following symptoms: lethargy or agitation, concentration difficulties, hopelessness, sleep/appetite disturbances, decreased self-worth, shame/guilt, and suicidality. MDD is most often recurrent but is highly treatable with a combination of psychotherapy and medication. Early treatment yields a more positive long-term prognosis. Significant evidence exists that MDD has a genetic component that interacts with environmental stresses and idiosyncratic personality and cognitive factors. *See also* Dysthymia

Depression *(psychology)* An emotional state typically characterized by low mood, despondency, and feelings of hopelessness. Individuals who are depressed tend to feel pessimistic about the future, unhappy, or "down in the dumps." While feelings of sadness or depression are common, a clinical diagnosis of major depressive disorder (according to the *Diagnostic and Statistical Manual of Mental Disorders* [fourth edition, text revision; *DSM-IV-TR*]) is characterized by more severe symptoms that last for at least two weeks. Symptoms of a diagnosable major depressive disorder include depressed mood or intense sadness, loss of pleasure, disturbance of appetite and sleep patterns, psychomotor retardation or agitation, loss of energy, feelings of worthlessness and guilt, difficulties concentrating, and recurrent thoughts of suicide or death. Depression is a risk factor for suicide. Major depressive disorder is one of the most common disorders encountered by mental health professionals. Women experience depression at higher rates than men, with nearly twice as many women suffering from depression than men. Single people experience depression at higher rates than separated and divorced people. Different causal factors have been linked to depression, and much remains to be known about its etiology. Psychological models of depression link stressful events to depression. Biological models of depression have linked depression to genetic factors, altered neurotransmitter activity, hormonal changes, and low levels of activity in the left anterior or prefrontal cortex. Seasonal changes have also been connected to depression. The "diathesis-stress model" of depression proposes that some people have vulnerability factors that, when paired with stressful life events, increase the risk for depression. Depression is usually treated with antidepressant medication and/or psychotherapy. Electroconvulsive therapy is also used with severely depressed patients. *See also* Diathesis-Stress Model; Dysthymia

Deregulation *(economics)* The elimination of laws that can conceivably prevent the efficient performance of markets. It is usually carried out by lawmakers to correct wrong judgment in the past or to address changing economic and social circumstances. It is possible for deregulation to be followed by reregulation. The Financial Institutions Reform, Recovery and Enforcement Act of 1989 was enacted to reregulate thrifts after a period of deregulation and failure of the savings and loan (S&L) institutions.

The ultimate aim of deregulation is to reduce the amount of restrictions that are imposed on economic activity so that the markets can function under less restrictive or regulatory conditions to produce much more efficient outcomes. Some critics of deregulation are normally apprehensive about the impact of deregulation on consumer welfare and the environment.

Deregulation has affected markets, financial institutions, savers, and investors in the United States and Europe. Many of the regulations in the United States that were enacted in the 1930s (as a result of the Great Depression) were phased out in the 1980s. For example, the Depository Institutions Deregulation and the Monetary Control Act (DIDMCA) of 1980 phased out Regulation Q, which imposed interest rate ceilings and set the interest rate ceiling on demand deposit at 0% under the Glass-Steagall Act of 1933. The removal of interest rate ceiling was partly intended to make thrift institutions more competitive, but the overambitious drive to be competitive without adequate safeguards contributed to the failure of the thrifts in the 1980s. The DIDMCA also expanded the asset and liability powers of banks and thrifts to enable them to give loans to businesses and offer more services to customers.

In the spirit of deregulation and competition, the Garn-St. Germaine Depository Institutions Act of 1982 made it possible for depository institutions to compete with money market mutual funds by creating money market deposit accounts and the Super Negotiable Order of Withdrawal (NOW), that is, special interest-bearing checking accounts.

Deregulation also hit the energy market in the late 1990s as a result of the increasing demand for energy supply. By the 1990s, the Clean Air Act (1963) restricted the ability to supply an increasing amount of energy to meet U.S. consumer demand in the absence of a significant substitute and sufficient power-generating facilities. On a state-by-state basis, there was a movement to deregulate the energy industry to meet the escalating demand.

In the airline industry, the Airline Deregulation Act (ADA) of 1978 removed government control from commercial aviation to make the passenger airline industry much more responsive to market forces. Economic integration, such as that of the European Union, and globalization have increased the desire to deregulate markets, but deregulation has not always been without dire consequences—bankruptcies, downsizing, unemployment, financial crisis, and environmental pollution. For more information, see Burton and Lombra (2003), Schiller (2006), and Stiglitz (2003). *See also* Efficient Market Hypothesis; Laissez-Faire (economics, political science); Monopoly; World Trade Organization (WTO)

Deregulation *(media studies)*   A climate of relaxed business regulations aimed at promoting competition and more efficient markets, which began in the 1970s. In the communications industry, it eventually culminated in the Telecommunications Act of 1996. This act removed the restrictions that had previously limited the number of television and radio stations that any corporation could own. It also allowed for cross-ownership so that a company could own television and radio stations or cable and broadcast networks in the same market. Proponents say that deregulation leads to competition and better financial support for outlets, while critics suggest that the resultant market consolidation has led to less variety in programming and less diversity in opinions and promotes content that only supports sponsors and other commercial interests. For more information, see Wilson (2000). *See also* Corporate Media

Deregulation *(political science)*   The reduction or elimination of government power in a particular industry, usually to create more competition within the industry and stimulate the economy. Some industries subjected to deregulation have been the airline, telecommunications, electric utility, trucking, cable television, banking, and natural gas industries. Deregulation aims to increase the efficiency of markets in certain industries by encouraging competition.

Deregulation expanded in the mid-1970s as a result of increased dissatisfaction with governmental regulatory policies. The costs imposed on consumers were high when the markets were monopolistic, and regulated industries often controlled government regulatory agencies to serve the industries' interests rather than those of consumers. Deregulated markets were expected to encourage expanded services and better technology while offering increased choices, lower costs, and lower rates for consumers.

Although initially valued, deregulation has received mixed results. On the one hand, social regulation to protect consumers has increased with the expansion or creation of regulatory agencies such as the Occupational Safety and Health Administration, the Federal Drug Administration, the Equal Employment Opportunity Commission, and the Environmental Protection Agency. The goals of these agencies have been to provide safer working conditions, better health products, more impartial employment practices, and a cleaner environment. In addition, deregulation for some industries, such as natural gas, has created spot markets. A spot market occurs when buyers and sellers agree on price and delivery terms "on the spot," with delivery to occur in the very near future. These markets embody competition since they allow buyers to directly determine prices with sellers. Also, in the telecommunications industry, deregulation has brought vast improvements in technology and innovations with lower prices for basic services.

On the other hand, in an industry such as the electric utility industry, consumers in deregulated states have not always paid significantly less for their electricity than customers in still regulated states. Furthermore, since deregulation, airlines have dramatically increased airfares. Some airlines also have virtual monopolies in particular city hubs. In other industries, deregulation has contributed to large scandals, such as in the California electricity crisis of 2000 and 2001, the savings and loan crisis of the 1980s and 1990s, and the subprime mortgage crisis of 2007–2008. Some experts suggest that a mixture of regulation with some deregulation provides the best environment for competitive markets. For more information, see Winston (1993). *See also* Competition; Efficient Market Hypothesis; Laissez-Faire; Monopoly

Descriptive Statistics (*education*)   The numeric characteristics of observed data from a sample or population that describe or summarize the data. They include descriptions of the central tendency (mean, median, mode), variability (variance/standard deviation, interquartile range, range), and shape (modality, skewness, and kurtosis) of the distribution of data. *See also* Inferential Statistics

Descriptive Statistics (*sociology*)   The mathematical means of organizing data that focuses on describing and summarizing characteristics of the data. Descriptive statistics are different from inferential statistics, which focus on reaching conclusions and deducing suppositions about data. Statistical computations that are descriptive help order and condense large amounts of information into manageable and meaningful arrangements. Examples of descriptive statistics are mean, median, mode, frequency distributions, and measures of variability. *See also* Inferential Statistics

Desegregation   The landmark court case *Brown v. Board of Education* in 1954 made it illegal for students to be segregated in public schools based on race. The U.S. Supreme Court ruled that segregation was illegal and all children be granted the right to an equal education, which reversed the *Plessy v. Ferguson* ruling that stated separate but equal facilities was legal. After the *Brown* ruling, state educators had to desegregate their schools, meaning redrawing school boundary lines and/or bussing mainly black students to other schools or districts. There was great resistance in the South to desegregation in their public schools. For more information, see *Brown v. Board of Education of Topeka* (1954) and *Plessy v. Ferguson* (1896). *See also* Brown v. Board of Education of Topeka; Civil Rights Act of 1964

Despotism   When a ruler holds unlimited authority. The drafters of the U.S. Constitution considered Great Britain to be a despotic government and sought to prevent the United States from following this model. This fear became a leading reason put forth by the Anti-Federalists for less national powers at the 1787 Constitutional Convention. George Washington additionally warned of the potential of despotism in his 1796 Farewell Address to the American people:

It is important, likewise, that the habits of thinking in a free country should inspire caution, in those intrusted with its administration, to confine themselves within their respective constitutional spheres, avoiding in the exercise of the powers of one department to encroach upon another. The spirit of encroachment tends to consolidate the powers of all the departments in one, and thus to create, whatever the form of government, a real despotism.

See also Authoritarian; Dictatorship; Totalitarian; Tyranny

Detain   A legal term that means keeping someone in official custody. The person who is being held is known as the detainee. The writ allowing someone to be detained is known as a detainer. People held for a relatively short period of time are held in detention, either in a police station or in a jail. *See also* Custody

Detention Center   A facility used to house those who have been temporarily detained by an order of the court. Typically, detention centers house people awaiting adjudication or those being held for a relatively short period of time. The term also refers to certain institutions that house juveniles.

Determinate Sentence   A prison or a jail term for a fixed amount of time. An offender with a determinate sentence must serve the complete sentence before being eligible for release. With the emergence of prisons, sentences were determinate. Indeterminate sentencing became the fashion toward the end of the 19th century, with a resurgence of determinate sentencing at the end of the 20th century. There has been a move back toward determinate sentencing with a recognized need for "truth in sentencing." *See also* Indeterminate Sentence; Parole; Prison/Prisoner

Deterrence (*political science*)   A military strategy in which one actor (A) tries to prevent an action by another actor (B) by threatening punishment or retaliation if B initiates the action that A seeks to avoid. Deterrence is aimed at preserving the status quo. The use of deterrence became more intricate with the invention of atomic and nuclear weapons and the onset of the Cold War. After World War II, deterrence became the defining feature of military strategy in the United States. From 1946 through 1995, the United States had engaged in 395 uses of physical force to influence other nations through either direct military coercion or indirect political posturing.

For deterrence to be effective, a nation must meet three criteria. First, the deterring actor (A) must be capable of carrying out the threat. The doctrine of mutually assured destruction (MAD) requires that A possess a guaranteed second retaliatory strike capability, which will survive its opponent's first strike. Second, A must communicate to the deterred actor (B) what actions B is not supposed to take and what will happen if action is taken. Third, the threatened response must seem credible to B. Credibility requires that A has, in addition to the capability, the will to carry out the threat. Thus, for deterrence to work, there is usually a cost-benefit analysis conducted by B. The cost is that of the perceived risk of punishment after A makes good its threats. This is counterbalanced against the gains of engaging in the proscribed action.

A problem with deterrence has been the idea of self-deterrence, which occurs when retaliatory threats lack credibility because the risks to domestic survival are too great, as in nuclear war. The image of war, especially nuclear war, is too horrible and the risks of nuclear escalation too great to chance a confrontation. For example, in 1979, in response to the Soviet invasion of Afghanistan, the United States declined to participate in the Moscow Olympics. This response gave the USSR the ability to act with impunity under the protection of MAD. For more information, see Fordham (2004). *See also* Cold War; Containment; Sanction (political science, sociology); Superpower

Deterrence *(sociology)* A goal of punishment, deterrence supposes people can be discouraged from acting if the cost of doing an act outweighs the benefits derived from that act. Deterrence is rooted in the premise that people are rational and make decisions about their behavior by conducting a straightforward cost-benefit analysis. Deterrence theory emerged in the second half of the 18th century as ideas associated with the Enlightenment came to be applied to matters of crime and punishment. Cesare Beccaria popularized the concept of deterrence with his seminal book *Essays on Crimes and Punishments*, published in 1764. According to Beccaria, the utility of punishment in a society is to prevent crime by deterring criminal acts. He asserted that if the pains of a punishment outweigh the gains and advantages of a crime, people will be deterred from committing that act. His theoretical argument is considered the first criminological theory and gave rise to the classical school of criminology. Deterrence, as Becarria understood it, relies on the swiftness and sureness of the cost rather than its severity. The cost must be absolutely associated with the act, only then will people have to calculate it into their reasoning. There are two kinds of deterrence, general and specific. General deterrence is in operation when the populace is dissuaded from acting as an undesirable cost has come to be associated with a particular act. Specific deterrence occurs when someone has endured the cost of an act and because of that experience is dissuaded from ever acting in that way again. *See also* Beccaria, Cesare; Classical Criminology

Detoxification The reduction or elimination of toxic substances from the body through metabolic change and excretion. Detoxification can be facilitated through simple supervision of the elimination of substances, through chemical and mechanical assists such as neutralizing drugs and gastric lavage (pumping out the stomach), or by fasting, special diet, and saunas. *See also* Drug; Substance Abuse

Devaluation The deliberate reduction of the par (pegged) value exchange rate of a currency by a nation's monetary authorities. In the fixed exchange rate regime, the monetary authorities strive to keep the exchange rate virtually fixed or pegged even if the preferred pegged rate differs from the market rate.

During the interregnum of the world wars, nations devalued their currencies to have a competitive edge in the global economy. This practice became known as "competitive devaluation." International trade and finance was characterized by volatile and chaotic conditions, for which more formal rules, payment arrangements, and relative foreign exchange stability became more desirable. The International Monetary Fund (IMF) was created to foster exchange rate stability, increased flow of trade, and balance-of-payments equilibrium.

In the contemporary international financial system, devaluation occurs when it becomes very costly to sustain a fixed-exchange-rate regime as a result of a severe balance-of-payments deficit. When a significant and persistent misalignment of exchange rate occurs, nations with chronic balance-of-payments problems must give up precious reserves or assets to sustain a fixed-exchange-rate regime. At some point, the loss of reserves or assets becomes unsustainable or impractical. With the failure of interest rate hikes or fiscal and monetary policies to completely remedy severe balance-of-payments problems, a nation's monetary authorities, in compliance with Article IV of the IMF's Articles of Agreement or the principles of international economic law, may then decide to devalue its currency.

The essence of devaluation is to make exports cheaper in order to promote export earnings while making imports expensive to discourage spending. The results of devaluation, as a mechanism for correcting balance-of-payments problems, are inconclusive and largely depend on refractory political and economic conditions.

Generally, devaluation has not worked very well for African and Latin American countries because of the rigid structure of their economies, the lack of diversity in their articles of trade, corruption, and the lack of adequate absorption of their export products in the relatively richer countries. As a result, inflation, unemployment, and riots are sometimes the ocular results of devaluation in these countries. One of the major problems with devaluation is that the burden of its implementation is not equitably distributed. The indigent tend to suffer the most, although current stabilization programs require a Poverty Reduction Strategy Paper (PRSP). For more information, see Carbaugh (2005), (2007), Lowenfeld (2003), Pugel (2007), and Salvatore (2006). *See also* Balance of Payments (BOP) (economics); Corruption (economics); Elasticity; Exchange Rate; Fiscal Policy; International Monetary Fund (IMF); Monetary Policy

Developing Countries The bases for characterizing countries as "developing" are very fluid and controversial.

D

The expression is considered to be analogous to the classification of countries as "Third World" in the 1950s and 1960s, which suggested the amount of poverty and lack of industrial progress that were inherent in the nonaligned countries. Much more contemporaneously, the fluidity of classification has much to do with the less than clear lines of demarcation on the basis of national income, economic liberalization, and individual government opinions.

Countries that are classified as developing by the World Bank include countries with low or middle levels of gross national product (GNP) per capita as well as the relatively high-income countries such as China, Israel, Kuwait, Singapore, and the United Arab Emirates. Similarly, countries in transition (undergoing liberalization of markets) are sometimes classified as developing because of their national income but also as developed because of their relatively high level of industrialization.

The World Trade Organization (WTO) provides no yardstick of measurement to demarcate "developing" from "developed" countries, and member nations are left with the option of self-categorization that is subject to impeachment when potential benefits to be derived (because of status) are seemingly at variance with status declaration.

Notwithstanding the nuances and lack of homogeneity, developing countries share common traits that distinguish them from high-income developed countries. These include low living standards, low levels of productivity (hourly output per worker), high population growth and dependency burdens, dependence on agriculture and primary exports, and dependence and vulnerability in international relations.

The structure of the economies of developing countries makes it imperative for them to push for fair and liberal conditions of trade to sell their agrarian products and raw materials in international markets. They are consequently, and understandably, oftentimes at loggerheads with much more developed nations on matters of sovereign debt repayment and international trade agreements—arguing for some amount of restriction to foreign imports and extensions for the implementation of the provisions of inconvenient trade treaties that are declaratory of intent.

The common features of underdevelopment are usually attributable to (a) inadequate capital (physical, human, and financial), (b) insufficient capital accumulation (because of high dependency and poor saving), (c) political corruption, (d) relatively high mortality rates, (e) information asymmetries, (f) underdeveloped financial markets for credit expansion, and (g) excessive sovereign debt.

For comparative analysis, economic indicators such as the GNP and the human development index (HDI) are commonly used to determine *intra-* and *inter*group development levels. But the HDI and GNP are less than perfect measures of development.

Since 1990, the United Nations Development Programme (UNDP) has calculated the HDI for several developing countries to include life expectancy, school enrollment rates, and literacy rates. Additional indices are now used to consider poverty rates and gender-related development. The GNP, like the HDI, is also fraught with problems. Not all transactions can be realistically computed, and a substantial and inestimable amount of economic transactions are conducted in the shadow, parallel, or underground economy, which holds a very robust status in most of the developing countries. The attempt to perfect the economic measurements of development levels attests to the ongoing problem of accurately classifying the levels of economic development to which countries belong. For more information, Perkins, Radlet, and Lindauer (2006) and Todaro and Smith (2008). *See also* Corruption (economics); Debt; Growth; Trade Theory, New; World Trade Organization (WTO)

Developmental Disability   Any physical and/or mental impairment that significantly limits an individual's daily functioning (e.g., independent living, learning, mobility, economic self-sufficiency, expressive and receptive language, self-care, self-direction). Onset is before 22 years of age. Growth, development, and/or learning are influenced. The impairments are chronic and severe. *See also* Disabled Persons; Mental Retardation (education, psychology)

Developmental Education   A field of research and practice in higher education rooted in developmental psychology. Often using various learning theories to promote the intellectual, social, and emotional growth of students, developmental education typically focuses on individual differences and needs by providing students personal, academic, and career counseling; academic advising; tutoring; mentoring; and course work. *See also* Developmental Psychology

Developmental Evaluation   Uses evaluation methods and processes to facilitate innovation by adapting to emergent, uncertain, and complex nonlinear dynamics.

Emphasis is on rapid, real-time feedback, adjusting an intervention model to changed conditions, using systems thinking and complexity science as frameworks for innovation, and learning lessons. It goes beyond improving a model (formative evaluation) to dynamically developing the model. For more information, see Patton (2008).

Developmentally Appropriate Instruction   A term whose use reflects different views on the relationship between development and instruction/learning. With development viewed as preceding learning, instruction is provided only when the learner is developmentally ready. In contrast, the view that instruction leads development allows instruction to be appropriately challenging and yet supportive of individual needs.

Developmental Psychology   The discipline that examines the changes that occur throughout the life span in humans' behavior and reasoning as a result of environmental, biological, and psychological factors. This branch of psychology attempts to answer the question of how individuals change as they age. Developmental psychology examines changes occurring throughout all stages of life, from conception, infancy, childhood, adolescence, and adulthood to old age. Since the focus of this discipline is on different areas of development and different influences on development, it is important to approach developmental psychology from different theoretical perspectives. An important concept in developmental psychology is that of "maturation." *Maturation* refers to "those aspects of development that are primarily under genetic control and which are relatively uninfluenced by the environment" (Slater & Bremner, 2003, p. 5). When thinking about what contributes to development, age by itself has no impact on development, but maturation and the different experiences that intervene between the life stages are what influence development. Therefore, developmental psychologists study *age-related changes* and the different factors that underlie these changes. Developmental psychologists use a variety of research strategies to answer questions related to development. To study behavioral changes related to age, both *cross-sectional* and *longitudinal* studies are employed. These types of research designs are combined with research methods to study development. The research methods most frequently employed include observational, experimental, and correlational technique, as well as psychological assessment. Observational studies involve repeated observations of the same individual at different points of time. Experimental studies are aimed at finding the *causes* of development, whereas correlational studies investigate the associations between variables. Finally, developmental psychologists employ a varied number of tests that are frequently used for clinical and educational assessment purposes. For more information, see Slater and Bremner (2003). ***See also*** Cross-Sectional Research; Longitudinal Study

Development Economics   The application of economic development theories to improve the general social and economic welfare of society. Economic development is concerned with improving the standard of living of a country's citizens and increasing the national income of the country. Economic development is achieved by increasing the rate of economic growth; the improvement in education, health care, and industrialization; the building of stable political and legal systems; and the availability of basic services, such as electricity, water, transportation, and others. One of the key theories in development economics is that economic development cannot take place without investment. This investment can come from within the country or from foreign sources. The theory further suggests that investment is a function of the savings in a country and therefore countries with a high savings rate tend to have greater economic development.

Development economics also try to explain why some countries are more developed than others. Development economists study a country's economic, political, and legal systems and try to explain the reasons why some countries are poor and others are rich. Development economists then can recommend policies that alleviate poverty and improve the economic welfare of a nation. The study of economic development is one of the newest branches of economics. Development economics became popular after the 1950s, when the world witnessed the rising poverty of developing countries in Asia, Africa, and South America despite some of these countries achieving high economic growth rates. A group of economists studied the problems and called for a better approach in dealing with absolute poverty, inequitable income distribution, and rising unemployment. From the 1950s to the 1980s, many studies were conducted in the area of economic development, and the consensus was that governments in developing countries must thrive to achieve three broad goals: (1) the improvement and availability of basic human needs to include food, housing, shelter, and adequate health care; (2) raising the material living standards of its people by creating more sustainable jobs, increasing national incomes, and increasing the availability of institutions that enhance cultural and recreational activities; and (3) making more economic and social choices available to the people and making them less dependent on economic aid. With these goals in mind, economic development or development seeks to transform poor countries by reducing poverty and improving the economic and social welfare of its citizens. The economic development of a country is measured not only by material gains but also by the United Nations Human Development Index, which measures longevity—measured by life expectancy at birth; adult literacy; and real per capita income—as measured by the purchasing power of each country, which reflects the differences in cost of living. For more information, see Todaro and Smith (2006). ***See also*** Economic Growth; Economics; Investment

Deviance   Refers to any behavior outside the socially dictated boundaries of normal, correct, or proper activity. Deviance encompasses a variety of behaviors. Criminal behavior is commonly defined as deviant, but behavior need not be against the law to be deemed deviant (e.g., tattoos and piercings). Deviant behavior is a socially constructed category. It is relative to what is considered ordinary or typical. Deviance is informed by culture, time, and place; therefore, the dictates are always changing in accordance with social norms. That which is deviant in one society or group may be customary and acceptable in another. Deviance is used to describe both behavior and individuals. A question related to deviance is whether it refers to behavior beyond the socially prescribed norms or acts that are committed by a small percentage of the population. The term is used in both contexts. The study and analyses of

D

deviance have inspired multiple schools of thought. Functionalists view deviance as a critical sociological component. These theorists view a society's processes of naming, identifying, and responding to deviance as serving to create and sustain social cohesion. The rituals and practices associated with deviance specify and affirm social values. Labeling theorists question whether there is a single collective sense of what is normative behavior. They view the labeling of deviance as a social process that alienates and marginalizes those judged deviant. It is a practice focused not on behavior or actions but on people. Critical theorists assert that the classification of deviance serves to reinforce the distribution of power within a society. Feminists challenge that which has historically been identified as deviant by highlighting the biased nature of such cataloging. Postmodernists challenge the dualistic, binary, and static construction of deviance studies. They recognize a fluidity and nonessentialist nature in both people and behavior. *See also* Crime; Criminology

Devolution   When a local or regional form of government is statutorily granted independent powers from a central government. In the United States, only state and federal powers are granted under the Constitution. Local governments need to be devolved from state authorities as stated in Section 10 of the U.S. Constitution: "The powers not delegated to the United States by the Constitution, nor prohibited by it to the States, are reserved to the States respectively, or to the people." The U.S. territories (American Samoa, Federated States of Micronesia, Guam, Midway Islands, Puerto Rico, U.S. Virgin Islands) and Native American governments are also devolved from federal authorities. England has devolved some forms of government powers in Scotland, Wales, and Northern Ireland. The word *devolution* is derived from Medieval Latin (*devolvere* [to roll down]).

Diagnosis *(education)*   The critical analysis of a situation, condition, or problem or the conclusion(s) reached by this process of critical examination. A diagnosis can also refer to the label applied to a specific condition. Although commonly associated with medical procedures, it is widely used in other professions to descriptively identify a problem. In the behavioral sciences, the process of diagnosis usually consists of a history of the situation, the current status, assessment tests, and interviews with clients and collaterals. The resulting diagnostic statement is a concise summary of the results of this investigation. *See also* Dual Diagnosis

Diagnosis *(psychology)*   The classification and labeling of an individual's problems within one or a set of categories of abnormal behavior. The classification of mental disorders is guided by patterns of behavior, thought, and emotion. The *Diagnostic and Statistical Manual of Mental Disorders* (*DSM*), developed by the American Psychiatric Association (APA), is the most widely used tool for diagnosing mental disorders. For more information, see APA, *DSM-IV-TR* (fourth edition, text revision, 2000), the last revision of the *DSM*. *See also Diagnostic and Statistical Manual* (*DSM*) (education, psychology); Differential Diagnosis

Diagnostic and Statistical Manual (DSM) *(education)*   The most widely used system for the classification of mental disorders in the United States. The *DSM* was first published by the American Psychiatric Association in 1952. The last edition (text revision) was published in 2000 (*DSM-IV-TR*). This manual contains a comprehensive list of 410 mental health disorders organized in 17 broad categories. It provides a list of symptoms in concrete behavioral terms for each disorder as well as an explanation of the number of symptoms that are required to be present to meet the diagnosis. In addition, preceding each diagnostic criterion is a description of the prevalence for men and women, the approximate age of onset, predisposing factors, and the expected prognosis. One of the innovations of the third edition of the *DSM* was the inclusion of a multiaxial classification system. After the *DSM-III*, diagnoses include a rating in five different categories: Axis I includes all diagnostic categories except personality disorders and mental retardation, which are classified under Axis II; Axis III includes general medical conditions; Axis IV includes psychosocial and environmental factors; and Axis V includes the individual's general level of functioning. The *DSM* has been criticized for promoting the stigmatization of individuals with mental illnesses, for lacking reliability (low levels of agreement between two mental health professionals who diagnose the same patient), and for being biased against some gender, racial, cultural, or socioeconomic groups. Despite the criticisms, the *DSM* facilitates a common nomenclature and provides the operational definitions required for research. *See also* Diagnosis (education, psychology); Differential Diagnosis

Diagnostic and Statistical Manual (DSM) *(psychology)*   Currently in its fourth edition, the *DSM* is the most widely used classification system for mental disorders. The *DSM* consists of broad categories of disorders and specific symptoms required to meet the criteria for each specific disorder. The classification system is based on scientific consensus. The fifth edition is scheduled for release in 2012. *See also* Diagnosis (psychology); Differential Diagnosis; Psychological Disorder

Dialectic   In the ancient world, the term is most associated, as recorded by Plato, with the Socratic method of refutation of his interlocutors by means of questions that uncover the others' error (*elenchus*). Exposing the absurd consequences of their assertions frees them from ignorance and helps them "deliver themselves" (as in pregnancy) of the truth within them. Socrates thus acts as a midwife (his own metaphor), or in another famous metaphor (in the *Apology*), he likens his needling questions to a gadfly stinging the Athenians out of their intellectual torpor. Although Plato emphasizes the centrality of reason in dialectic, Socrates' dialectic is also a process embedded in personal encounters, where it retains its nontechnical sense of conversing (hence Plato's "dialogues"). In the course of classical to Western scholastic philosophy, dialectic became a synonym for formal logic, as in the medieval trivium, which consisted of grammar, dialectic (i.e., logic), and rhetoric. In German idealist philosophy, especially Hegel, dialectical logic replaces formal logic. Formal logic disallows contradiction: It is impossible that *x* can simultaneously be *x* and not *x*. But in dialectical logic, it is only through contradiction that truth emerges as a reconciliation of opposites. For Hegel, contradiction is an objective condition of reality. Hegelian dialectic became the departure point for the Marxist philosophy of dialectical materialism, in which Marx famously stood Hegel on his head by materializing the idealism of dialectic and, at the same time, rendering matter as a dynamic process rather than a fixed object. Only when reality is regarded as a totality and not in discrete parcels can the dialectical contradictions that objectively exist emerge. Reality is not a fixed phenomenon but the outcome of the interpenetration of opposites. Class struggle and conflict are the means by which reality emerges. Apart from these precise senses, dialectic loosely refers to the productive encounter of opposite forces. ***See also*** Critical Theory; Marxism (political science, sociology)

Dialectical Organization

This idea emanates from the concept of the process that the social world is in a continual state of becoming. This view evolved as the antithesis to the bureaucracy. In a dialectical organization, communication is more horizontal and upward than in a bureaucracy, where communication is vertical and downward. Dialectical organizations are goal oriented and use available means to reach goals. These organizations are flexible and charismatic. Clients are seen as equal to or superior to the organization, and the organization seeks to make the system responsive to the needs of its clients. The major features of a dialectical organization—goals, hierarchies, technology, informal relations, and so on—are functions of social construction.

Dialectical organizations are oriented to change. Rather than being a fixed entity, which characterizes bureaucratic organizations, the dialectical organization is seen to be in a continual state of becoming, a process. Whatever occurs in the organization is the result of goal pursuit. The organization is committed to the concept of progress.

Components of the organization are intertwined rather than isolated. This interconnectedness can be seen when considering the contradictions, that is, ruptures, breaks, or inconsistencies, within an organization. Dialectical organizations are fundamentally based in contradiction growing from distinct, semiautonomous spheres of social action both within and without the organization. They are typically scenes of multiple contradictions, which may permit reorganization or fragmentation.

Contradiction feeds into the social fabric of dialectical organizations. Contradiction constructs the production of process by providing a continuing source of tensions and conflicts, which may shape consciousness and action to change the present order, set limits on and establish the possibility of reconstruction, produce crises that enhance the possibility of reconstruction, and define the limits of a system.

Contradictions may be generated by special interests in the larger society and imposed on an organization. A dialectical organization, such as a prison, often has the dual purpose of rehabilitation and incapacitation. Some contradictions within dialectical organizations directly reflect features of the larger economic-political system. Management-labor conflict, for example, is a product of contradictory arrangements inside dialectical organizations and sets limits on innovations, on morale levels, and in other areas. The mobility of participants in pursuing their interests and reaching out for alternative structural arrangements is a significant feature of power in dialectical organizations. For more information, see Benson (1977). ***See also*** Bureaucracy (communication, education, political science, public administration); Horizontal Communication; Process Evaluation

Dialogue

A spoken or written exchange of words between two or more people. At its best, dialogue is more than conversation; it serves as an open forum that allows all parties involved to become more aware of the beliefs, opinions, and knowledge of others—hence, to become more informed and to develop broader viewpoints.

In the second half of the 20th century, the American physicist David Bohm began to develop fundamentals for effective dialoguing as a means of sociotherapy for a troubled world and formed collaborations with the Indian philosopher Jiddu Krishnamurti and the English psychiatrist Dr. Patrick de Mare. For more information, see Bohm (1996).

Diathesis–Stress Model

A psychological model used to explain abnormal behavior, with the central tenet being that disorders result from a combination of genetic factors and environmental stress. The *diathesis* is a genetic vulnerability or predisposition toward developing a disorder. Abnormal behaviors or psychological disorders are triggered when this genetic predisposition is combined with environmental factors or life events that are perceived as stressful (*stress*). According to this model, both the diathesis and the stress are required to trigger psychological disorders. Although the diathesis, or vulnerability, is generally considered to be the result of certain gene combinations, it can also be the result of psychological and/or sociocultural causal factors. The diathesis is considered to be a distal necessary contributory factor that is not sufficient by itself to cause or explain the disorder. Though stressful life events are considered to be the more proximal contributory factors, they are also not sufficient in isolation to cause the disorder. For example, although schizophrenia is believed to include a strong genetic component, environmental stressors must trigger this genetic predisposition for the disorder to develop. In recent years, the concept of *protective factors* has frequently been incorporated into the diathesis–stress model. Protective factors (e.g., having at least one parental figure who is supportive and warm) modify how people respond to environmental factors and may make them less likely to experience the undesirable effects of the stressors. For more information, see Zubin and Spring (1977). ***See also*** Genes; Schizophrenia; Stress

Dictatorship   A government in which a single leader or party, such as the military, exercises absolute control over all citizens. Power in a dictatorship is maintained through intimidation, terror, suppression of civil liberties, and control of the mass media. The ruler in a dictatorship is called a dictator. A dictator's rule is absolute, that is, not constrained by a constitution or laws. Most current dictatorships are found in Africa and Asia. Some other terms for dictatorship are despotism, tyranny, totalitarianism, absolutism, authoritarianism, and autocracy.

The term *dictatorship* originated in the ancient Roman Republic from *dictatura*, a military office that exercised power during national emergencies, such as foreign attacks, for temporary and limited purposes. A *dictatura* was authorized by the Roman Senate, usually for no more than six months. A dictatorship thus was known as an extralegal institution for the defense of the constitution. During the 1880s, dictatorship came to be contrasted with democracy and to be referred to as a form of government. It is this meaning that is in current use.

Dictatorships can be differentiated according to how the ruling leader or party comes to lead the nation. A dictatorship may come into power through democratic elections. Once elected, however, the dictator will then ban all opposing parties and cancel future elections, except to rig them in order to present the illusion of democratic legitimacy. A dictatorship may also begin or continue through appointment by the ruling party, where the dictator inherits power from a deceased relative. Third, a dictatorship may come into existence through a coup d'etat, whereby an existing part of the government, usually the military, suddenly overthrows and replaces the existing state leadership.

In the United States, support for right-wing dictatorships, that is, authoritarian, antidemocratic regimes that are neither socialist nor communist, came after World War I in response to the belief that right-wing dictatorships could ensure stability while simultaneously opposing communism. In 1920, the United States refused to recognize the communist government in Moscow since the administration of Woodrow Wilson believed that the rulers of Russia did not rule by consent of the people. The American government believed that the new government of Russia, itself a dictatorship, threatened American values and interests. This belief was used to demonstrate opposition to left-wing dictatorships, such as those in China in 1949, Cuba in 1961, and Vietnam in 1975, which supported communist values. In response, the United States denied trade and aid to those governments to force change. These ideological justifications for U.S. support of right-wing dictatorships have influenced American policy up to today. For more information, see Schmitz (2006). ***See also*** Absolutism (political science, public administration); Authoritarian; Autocracy; Coup d'Etat; Democracy (political science, public administration); Despotism; Totalitarian; Tyranny

Differential Association   A criminological theory that supposes criminal activity is a learned behavior. Edwin Sutherland, a sociologist associated with the Chicago School, developed the theory of differential association. The term first appeared in his 1939 publication *Principles of Criminology*. Through his work with delinquent subcultures, Sutherland came to believe that criminality was no different from any other behavior. Deviance, he posited, is learned much in the same way that all other behaviors are learned. Differential association claims that the environment and peers help individuals determine if a behavior is acceptable or objectionable, and those individuals learn to act accordingly. Associations and interactions teach people how to behave. This general theory of crime accounts for how someone comes to break the law and explains which laws are broken. Differential association claims that criminality derives from a combination of contact with forces that value criminality and isolation from forces that scorn such behavior. For more information, see Sutherland (1939). ***See also*** Criminology

Differential Diagnosis   The process of differentiating between two or more psychiatric disorders that have similar or overlapping signs or symptoms. This practice involves a process of elimination used by qualified clinicians to correctly diagnose a specific disorder. The first step is to create an initial list of possible diagnoses. Then, after further evidence has been collected, the process involves attempting to eliminate diagnoses from the list until preferably only one diagnosis remains. This method allows the clinician to make a reasonable prognosis and devise a treatment plan or intervention. If the patient's condition does not improve after the selected treatment or therapy for the disorder or disorders finally selected has been implemented, then the diagnosis or diagnoses need to be reassessed. ***See also*** Diagnosis (psychology)

Differential Item Analysis   A statistical analysis procedure that scrutinizes the degree of difference in the fairness of a test item (a single question on a test). Differential item analysis references the fairness of a test item in relation to the racial, ethnic, and gendered profile of the persons taking the test. The level of knowledge and ability is assumed to be similar throughout the sample but not a factor in this particular analysis. The question this analysis answers is as follows: To what degree was the test item structured so that persons with different racial, ethnic, and gendered profiles would submit the same or a similar response?

Differentiated Instruction An instructional approach in which the instruction addresses the needs of academically diverse learners and is intended to engage and support all learners. It adapts instructional content, process, and product in response to learners' different cognitive resources, such as goals, needs, interests, and prior knowledge and abilities.

Diffusion An anthropological and sociological term that refers to the dispersal of social practices and cultural traits from one group to another. This conceptualization of diffusion first appeared in *Primitive Culture* in 1871. Diffusion accounts for the presence of traditions and customs beyond their society of origin. Such practices include language, technologies, beliefs, and rituals. For more information, see Tylor (1871/1974). *See also* Anthropology; Culture (sociology)

Diffusion of Innovations The process by which an innovation is communicated to the members of a social system. This occurs through certain channels over time. The French sociologist Gabriel Tarde was one of the first to study the concept, or what he referred to as the laws of imitation. His examination sought to explain why some innovations are widely accepted while most are ignored. In 1962, Everett Rogers, in his book *Diffusion of Innovations*, examined an enormous body of research on the theory from six different disciplines. He described the process as being broken down into four elements: (1) the innovation, (2) the channels of communication, (3) time, and (4) the social system. There are five stages from innovation to adoption: (1) awareness or first knowledge of an innovation, (2) developing an attitude or interest, (3) evaluating and deciding whether or not to accept the innovation, (4) implementing the idea, and, finally, (5) adoption. Prior conditions, such as perceived need, previous practice, level of innovativeness and societal norms, and characteristics of the decision-making unit and of the innovation, all influence the process and adoption. Having synthesized the available research, Rogers determined that the great preponderance of the literature on the theory shared three basic concerns: (1) the factors that affect an innovation's rate of diffusion, (2) the characteristics that determine early and late adopters, and (3) how the network structures of the adopters affect the order of adoptions. Because mass media is the most efficient way to spread awareness of an innovation, advertising and public relations professionals, considered change agents in the theory, can use an understanding of the process and prior conditions to

great advantage for their clients. For more information, see Rogers (1962) and Tarde (1903). *See also* Advertising (media studies)

Diffusion of Responsibility The notion that the presence of others inhibits helping behaviors because of the belief that others in the group will intervene. This phenomenon has been used to explain the "Kitty Genovese incident." Genovese was a young woman who was stabbed to death in Queens, New York, while many people witnessed the crime but failed to intervene because they assumed that someone else was already helping. Laboratory research has also provided support for this phenomenon, given that individuals who work in groups tend to diffuse responsibility and contribute less than they would if working individually. Indeed, the larger the group, the less responsibility each member assumes. For more information, see Latane and Nilda (1981). *See also* Bystander Effect

Diplomacy The art of conducting relationships for gain without conflict. Diplomacy seeks maximum national advantage without using force or causing resentment while furthering a state's geographic or economic interests. One maxim in furthering that goal is by quid pro quo; that is, the best way to get information is to exchange an idea for equal or more valuable information possessed by the other party. Methods of diplomacy previously included secret negotiations, information gathering, treaties, and conferences. Current methods also include conflict resolution, peacemaking, scholarships, information dissemination, and the creation of Web sites.

Diplomacy may involve bilateralism, which includes negotiations between two states. Diplomacy may also involve multilateralism, which involves either international negotiations among multiple countries or negotiations over more complex issues with more actors, such as experts, citizen groups, and nongovernment organizations. There are two stages in multilateralism: negotiation and treaty making. The United Nations is an example of a multilateral organization.

Public diplomacy is one type of diplomacy that builds on information exchanges between a government and peoples of other nations. The goals of public diplomacy in the United States are to engage, inform, and influence overseas audiences. To accomplish these goals, the State Department's Under Secretary for Public Diplomacy and Public Affairs has an annual budget of about $800 million with 700 diplomatic offices in 260 domestic and global posts. Diplomacy efforts include academic and professional exchanges, English language teaching, and information programs. The other diplomatic arm, the Broadcasting Board of Governors, has an annual budget of about $650 million that funds broadcast entities in 59 languages to 125 media markets around the world.

After the September 11, 2001, Islamist terrorist attacks, there has been a notable decline in favorable opinion toward the United States, especially in Arab

Muslim societies, which have felt resentment even before the 9/11 events. Such anti-Americanism has harmed U.S. businesses through boycotts of American products, increased security costs for U.S. companies abroad, higher foreign opposition to U.S. trade policies, and a decline in the ability of the United States to attract the world's best talent to join the American workforce. The U.S. Government Accountability Office recommends that the United States engage in greater public diplomacy efforts in Muslim countries. For more information, see Al-Orabi (2002). *See also* Conflict Resolution; Negotiation

Direct Broadcast Satellite Systems (DBS) Systems that downlink hundreds of channels for a fee. These systems are the biggest competitor to the television and cable industries. In the mid-1970s, the first satellite dishes—with diameters of up to 40 feet—were developed. They received cable channels, and in the following two decades, they sprang up in rural areas, where it would have been too expensive for the cable companies to wire. Many of these rural customers faced legal challenges by satellite broadcasters, and the cable companies started scrambling their channels, forcing consumers to purchase their services. As technology improved and restrictions were relaxed, the systems became a more widespread alternative to standard cable or broadcast signals. Now, dishes can be purchased—some no bigger than a dinner platter—that offer 300 to 500 channels with digital-quality pictures. *See also* Broadcasting; Cablecasting

Direct Democracy A pure democracy where all decisions are made directly by a majority vote of the people of a nation. The framers of the U.S. Constitution were fearful of tyranny through majority rule under a direct, or "pure," democracy. The framers instead preferred a representative government—also called a republic—where legislators elected by the people make laws and appoint officials. During the Progressive Era (1890–1913), social reformers lobbied for the introduction of direct democratic measures in an effort to curb abuses by the local party bosses. The most significant of these measures was the introduction of the initiative, referendum, and recall at the state level. The first state to have these measures was South Dakota in 1898; at present, 24 states have the initiative and referendum process and 18 the recall. *See also* Republic

Direct Examination The judicial process by which an attorney initially questions a witness he or she has called to the stand. It is sometimes referred to as the "examination-in-chief." The purpose of these opening questions and their responses is to make one's case. *See also* Cross-Examination

Direct Instruction An instructional method that emphasizes explicit teaching of essential skills and knowledge. Instructional objectives include clearly defined learning outcomes that directly result from instruction. Lessons are planned to highlight the active role of a teacher (sometimes assisted by technology) in the following: (a) articulating well-defined objectives, (b) reviewing prerequisite skills and knowledge, (c) presenting at an appropriate pace new materials that are organized into steps, and (d) having students practice each step and providing feedback. To help students build knowledge and transfer their learning, the teacher uses among many others, advance organizers, questioning, demonstrations, prompts, rule-example-rule, and worked examples.

Direct Speech A phrase used to describe the practice of using the exact words spoken by another speaker. The words are indicated by the use of quotation marks (" ") in the writing—for example, "'Here is the book,' she stated." There are no modifications in direct speech, as the original words spoken by the speaker are used verbatim. Direct speech is a kind of construction that is an ordered arrangement of grammatical units that form a larger unit. Different usages of the term *construction* include or exclude stems and words.

Disabled Persons Individuals with a physical, mental, or cognitive impairment, which restricts their ability to function in major life activities such as communication, mobility, performing manual tasks, and self-care. The nature and severity of the impairment are to such an extent that these individuals are unable to perform or are substantially limited in their ability to perform an activity compared with an average person in the general population. Their disability could be related to mobility, cognition, sensory, or speech impairments and may result in the need for supportive services.

Discharge Petition A process in which a bill is forced out of committee without the go-ahead from committee leadership. Discharge petitions are only associated with the House of Representatives and state legislatures. A discharge petition can be filed after a pending bill has not been acted on for 30 legislative days. A discharge petition requires 218 votes, a majority of the House, to be passed. The process allows greater power to individual representatives than traditional House leadership. *See also* Bill

Discipline In the educational setting, the establishment of a set of norms by which students abide for the school to be a safe environment where learning takes place without student disruption and misbehavior. Creating a healthy discipline environment is a process that generally includes rules and consequences for behavior that is inconsistent with the mission of the school and may also include rewards for exhibiting positive behavior. A principle of school discipline is that schools should help students develop into law-abiding citizens demonstrating self-discipline to live in a civil society. While some educational institutions establish a schoolwide discipline model, teachers may also have individual classroom discipline models they implement in their classrooms. A classroom discipline model often used by first-year teachers is assertive discipline. Other commonly used models include reality therapy, discipline with dignity, and judicious discipline.

Discourse   From the Latin meaning "running to and fro," the term basically means conversation, although it more precisely refers to the institutionalized body of opinions and conversations that inform all disciplines or specialisms. It is out of and through a discourse consisting of many voices that meaning is constructed and that power operates. Statements that appear self-evidently true (or false, funny, authoritative, or blasphemous) are only so within a local context of assumptions about appropriateness and meaningfulness. Discourse analysis studies the assumptions and implied rules by which meaning is constructed. Truth can thus be considered less the intrinsic property of some statements than the effect of successfully operating discourse. Grammatical correctness does not guarantee, and is not necessarily essential to, meaningful communication and successful discourse. Discursive formations shift over time and across cultures; and therefore, the study of discourse requires that attention be paid to the historical and social conditions by which utterances become meaningful. *See also* Discourse Analysis; Semiotics (education, media studies); Structuralism (media studies, sociology); Text

Discourse Analysis   The analysis of written text, spoken language, or signed language to reveal the discourses within it or the linguistic and rhetorical devices involved in its construction. This is a broad term for an analysis technique that is used by social scientists in a variety of disciplines such as linguistics, anthropology, social psychology, cognitive psychology, sociology, international relations, communication studies, and translation studies. Given this variety, it is not uncommon to find a diversity of interests among discourse analysts, such as gestures, sounds, turn taking, and relations between discourse and power. Definitions of what is a discourse also abound. A simple definition is that a discourse can be a verbal exchange between people, or it can be the system set of images and metaphors used to construct an object or idea. Thus, there is a wide variety of opinions among scholars as to what a "discourse" is and what "discourse analysis" entails. Some notable discourse analysts include Harvey Sachs, Emmanuel Schegloff, Gail Jefferson, and Michel Foucault.

One of the most common uses of discourse analysis is by postmodernist and poststructuralist theorists. The postmodern and poststructuralist view of a discourse largely rests on a connection to power and knowledge. These theorists question how the discourse is produced, how it functions, who controls the discourse, what its social effects are, and what is allowed or not allowed in the discourse. Some key authors who wrote methodological texts about using discourse analysis include Malcolm Coulthard, Norm Fairclough, and James Paul Gee. For more information, see Bove (1990), Burr (2003), Butler (1992), Childs and Williams (1997), Crotty (1998), Foucault (1978), and St. Pierre (2000). *See also* Discourse; Postmodernism; Poststructuralism; Qualitative Data Analysis; Qualitative Research

Discovery Learning   A popular instructional philosophy that originated with Jerome Bruner (1961), in which inquiry-based learning required that students "experience" their content by active involvement. Under this perspective, students are encouraged to experiment, elaborate, discover, and explore in learning, or "learn by doing." In constructivist instruction, the process of discovery is as important as the content, if not more so. Questions are used more than lectures, and activity and inquiry are valued more than collecting information. For more information, see Bruner (1961). *See also* Constructivist Learning Theory

Discretion *(political science)*   The power given to an individual or an agency from a principal agent (e.g., legislature) to make a decision according to their best judgment. In criminal law, the analogy is often found within discretionary sentencing rules where judges are given more flexibility to decide on an appropriate punishment. In general, the flexibility of discretion increases as the vagueness in the legislature increases and decreases when there is heavy and appropriate oversight. For more information, see Brehm and Gates (1993).

Discretion *(sociology)*   The opportunity to exercise choice in decision making. Discretion is the ability, power, or authority to choose whether or not to act and to decide which action to take. Discretion implies the use of personal judgment. Discretion may be guided by rules and regulations, moral principles, or desired outcomes.

Discretion is a crucial element in the criminal justice system. The police use discretion when deciding who to stop and who to arrest. The prosecutor chooses whether or not to charge a defendant as well as with what to charge the defendant. The judge and jury are specifically mandated to use discretion and to make choices based on their determinations. Discretion is necessary in the criminal justice system, particularly in policing, for many reasons. Legally, police officers are supposed to enforce all laws and enforce laws equally among all people in every society. However, they often use discretion not to stop or arrest because to enforce every law would strain limited resources. Additionally, there is no way to define all the circumstances that an officer may encounter. Some officers, however, may abuse their powers of discretion and overenforce the law by arresting individuals in minor situations, where they usually would not arrest, based on their personal prejudices against a particular group. *See also* Criminal Justice

Discretionary Spending   There are two types of spending authorized by the U.S. Congress. These are discretionary spending and mandatory spending. The level of discretionary spending is controlled by appropriation bills that are passed by Congress on an annual basis. Mandatory spending is authorized by permanent law and does not require an annual appropriation. Discretionary spending now accounts for close to 40% of the federal budget each year. Of this, about half goes to the Department of Defense, Homeland Security, and other security-related spending. The other half of discretionary spending funds domestic spending by several departments, including the Department of Health and Human Services and the Department of Education. *See also* Appropriation Bills

Discriminant Validity   The degree to which a measure of a construct is observed not to be similar to (diverges from) the measure of another construct to which it theoretically should not be related. In other words, discriminant validity is a measure of the degree to which the measures of two constructs that theoretically should not be related are in fact not related. A correlation coefficient is typically used to estimate the degree to which any two measures are related or unrelated to each other. For example, a successful demonstration of discriminant validity would show that a measure or test of depression is not highly correlated with a measure or test of intelligence (which it theoretically should not be related to). *See also* Concurrent Validity; Content Validity

Discrimination *(public administration)*   The targeting of particular persons or groups based solely on their possession of a distinct characteristic. Such prejudice may be predicated on race, religion, gender, age, disabilities, or a number of other individual features. Title VI of the Civil Rights Act of 1964 prohibits workplace discrimination predicated on "race, religion, sex, color, or national origin." Federally funded programs are explicitly barred from discrimination based on these individual faculties, perhaps most prominently in the realm of housing or other assistance programs. In the domain of criminal justice, racial profiling has especially proven a point of contention, and the police have been subsequently sued or reprimanded for encouraging supposedly discriminatory policies. More recently, the Age Discrimination in Employment Act has been passed to prevent employees from victimizing those 40 years and older and the elderly (usually considered as those 65 years or above). Although equally pernicious, gender discrimination has proven somewhat more complicated to identify and ameliorate than that involving race or age. Although Title VII of the Civil Rights Act specifically demands equal pay for males and females in the same profession, this has often failed to practically occur. Women thus often complain of a "glass ceiling," or an invisible barrier preventing occupational progress or significant raises in wages. Perhaps the most recent form of discrimination to enter the popular conscience has been based on disability (usually physical rather than mental). Passed in 1990, the Americans with Disabilities Act thus attempts to address disparities in employment, public transportation, accommodation, and telecommunications regarding the disabled.

Although few persons are going to openly and publicly support discrimination, some nevertheless contend that such policies consequently lead to "reverse discrimination." In this scenario, minority groups benefit at the expense of the majority and are thus given "special rights" rather than "equal rights" (e.g., see the debate surrounding Affirmative Action). For more information, see Cornell University School of Law (2009). *See also* Affirmative Action (political science, public administration)

Discrimination *(sociology)*   The practice of distinguishing between individuals or groups based on prejudicial determinations. Discrimination also refers to exclusion, rejection, and negative treatment related to bigotry. To discriminate is to treat people unfairly or differently by reason of characteristics, stereotypes, and biases. Discrimination is to participate in, or be subjected to, selective treatment. Laws vary by jurisdiction. But it is commonly illegal to discriminate or treat people differently based on certain attributes, including race, disability, ethnicity, gender, age, and sexual orientation. *See also* Civil Rights; Stereotype (psychology)

Discussion Methods of Teaching   A strategy that focuses on students meeting educational objectives through meaningful, purposeful, and productive communication. Through discussions, students engage in critical thinking, analyze multiple viewpoints and perspectives, investigate alternative solutions to problems, and evaluate resolutions. The teacher serves as a moderator, ensuring that all students participate and stay on the topic. Discussions typically end with a summary or group consensus and help students develop the principles of living in a democratic society.

Disinformation   Deliberate dissemination of false information. Disinformation differs from other propaganda in that it seeks to manipulate its audience on a purely rational level. Whereas other kinds of propaganda speak to the willingness of the audience to think unreasonably, disinformation supplies the listener with false data with the expectation that the listener will apply his or her reason to the information and reach an unwittingly erroneous conclusion. For instance, the alleged counterfactual assertions of the George W. Bush administration regarding weapons of mass destruction in Iraq may be regarded as disinformation. Also, totalitarian regimes are notorious for disseminating false information to create solidarity and retain a hold on power.

Disinformation may also involve the presentation of a fact in a way that obscures or withholds other facts that are essential to understanding the information correctly.

An example is the reporting of the German navy's sinking of the British passenger liner *Lusitania* in 1915. Whereas the British and American governments decried the attack as a senseless slaughter of the ship's 1,200 passengers, they did not report that the ship was also an armed auxiliary cruiser, freighted with tons of military material.

Disinformation is also different from misinformation, which is the transmission of false information by someone who is unaware of its falsity. For more information, see Severin (1988).

Dismissal A judicial decision that ends all actions against the defendant. A defendant petitions the court to have the charges against him or her dropped by making a motion to dismiss. A judge may decide to dismiss a case based on procedural errors or based on the weak merits of the case.

Disorder A term used in the medical field to describe mental or physical illness. The term can be used generically, meaning that there is an ailment present, or can be used to name a particular sickness, such as attention deficit disorder. There are a vast number of specific disorders. In the fields of psychology and psychiatry, disorders are listed and explained in the *Diagnostic and Statistical Manual of Mental Disorders*.

Displacement In criminal justice discourse, this term refers to the shifts in crime patterns that can occur in response to policing initiatives. Displacement is typically associated with changes in street-level policing tactics such as community policing and hot-spot policing. As the police engage in these new strategies to reduce crime, criminal activity moves to another geographic location or shifts to another time of day, or new targets and criminal activities arise. This is important because even as crime appears to be dropping, it may be that criminal activity has not diminished but rather has been displaced. In anthropology and human rights law, displacement refers to the forced movement of people from their original residence to other areas. Internally displaced persons (IDPs) have been defined by the United Nations as people who have not crossed an international border but have been forced to leave their homes because of violence or man-made disasters. Displaced persons (DPs), including refugees, are those who have fled across an international border. In the field of psychology, Sigmund Freud first introduced the term *displacement*. He presents displacement as the process by which individuals shift their emotions, positive or negative, onto another object or person that is somehow connected to the original object of feeling. This is understood to be an unconscious process and is often revealed in dreams. Freud identified displacement as a defense mechanism. The term *displacement* is also used to describe a particular function of verbal communication. Language is a means to convey ideas and things that are not spatially or temporally occurring at the moment of the communication. This is considered displacement. *See also* Community Policing (COP); Human Rights; Language

Dissent The feeling or action of opposition and disagreement. The term commonly refers to those who contest established, dominant, or authoritative forces. To dissent is to refuse to comply or conform. The refusal to agree is a form of dissent. Differing opinions are dissenting opinions. If all the justices do not agree on the outcome in appellate court cases, some of the judges may write a dissenting opinion that explains why they disagree with the majority.

Dissident An individual who adopts and promotes an ideology that differs from an already established set of principles accepted by a majority within a state. The label of a dissident varies within the particular historical period and depends on the policies of the state. The dissident seeks to actively promote an ideology or change an existing policy using both nonviolent and violent acts.

Dissociation A phenomenon in which one's experience is detached or separated from one's awareness or conscious memory. In other words, dissociation is thought to occur when two parts of the mind are operating independently. Some common examples of dissociation include walking somewhere and realizing that you do not remember how you got there or why you wanted to go there in the first place. *Déjà vu*—the feeling that you had lived a situation before even if you had not—has also been considered by some to be a dissociative experience. However, individuals who are formally diagnosed with dissociative identity disorder (DID), as categorized in the *Diagnostic and Statistical Manual of Mental Disorders* (*DSM*), experience more severe dissociative experiences that have serious consequences for memory. These disorders include amnesia and fugue states and dissociative identity disorder, formerly known as multiple personality disorder. *See also Diagnostic and Statistical Manual* (*DSM*) (education, psychology)

Dissolution The act of examining the underpinnings in the disintegration of a relationship between two or more parties. Dissolution is considered to be a permanent severing of a relationship. Relationship dissolution generally refers to the act of one individual initiating the dissolution rather than both people. Dissolution can also occur in business contexts. Dissolutions can be managed through dissolution communication strategies, or exit strategies, as per Hirschman's 1970 model in *Exit, Voice and Loyalty*. The dissolution communication strategies can use either direct or indirect communication. The dissolution process may be complicated by individuals' conflict management style, shaped by their subjectivity. For more information, see Hirschman (1970). *See also* Strategy

D

Distance Education   A mode of education where learner(s) and teacher(s) are physically separated from each other and the instructional processes are fulfilled via information and communication technologies. Distance education alters the conventional patterns of education and provides opportunities of learning whenever and wherever you need. ***See also*** Distance Education/Online Learning/E-Learning

Distance Education/Online Learning/E-Learning
Sometimes all these terms are believed to be the same thing. However, *distance education* (or learning) is the broader term. Distance education is any instruction in which the instructors and learners are separated by time and/or location and are brought together through one of various delivery methods, not just electronic or telecommunication systems. Other forms of delivery for distance education include correspondence courses, broadcast systems, communication networks, electronic or telecommunications systems, and the Internet and World Wide Web (also known as the Web). However, as technologies advance and become more accessible across the globe, the definition of distance learning could narrow through emphasis on the use of interactive telecommunication to connect a learning group (instructors and students) with the instructional resources.

In contrast, *e-learning* (electronic learning) is a narrower term and is often used in U.S. business and industry training and in international settings. E-learning refers "to the use of any electronic applications and processes for instruction [or training], including CBT (computer-based training), WBI [Web-based instruction], CDs (compact discs), and so on, whereas WBI is defined as instruction via the Internet, Intranet, and Web only" (Davidson-Shivers & Rasmussen, 2006, p. 10).

Online learning is readily interchanged with *Web-based instruction* (or learning). Both terms refer to learners and instructors being at a distance from each other in time and place and connected together through Internet- and Web-based technologies. Additionally, Davidson-Shivers and Rasmussen (2006) suggest that there are three forms of online instruction (or learning). (1) Web-based instruction is a virtual classroom in which all instruction takes place only through the Internet and the Web. (2) Web-enhanced learning, sometimes called Web-blended learning, occurs when the instruction is split between face-to-face meetings involving the instructor and students in a classroom and online meetings by the group, which take place entirely on the Internet. (3) Web-supported instruction refers to the instructor and students meeting face-to-face in classroom settings, but students are given "Web assignments and activities to support classroom activities" (p. 24).

Another term, *distributed education* (or learning), is sometimes interchanged with distance education (or learning) because both concepts suggest that participants interact with each other at differing times and places. Additionally, including the use of technology, such as computers and communication technologies, adds to the confusion to blur the definitional lines. Some suggest that distance learning emphasizes that students and instructors are distanced by time and place, whereas distributed learning emphasizes that instructors and students may interact or connect in the traditional classroom, in some virtual classroom, or in some combination of both venues through the use of computer and communication technologies. For more information, see Davidson-Shivers and Rasmussen (2006). ***See also*** Distance Education; Internet

Distributive Justice *(education)*   A political-ethical theory that focuses on issues of what is just in society, not in terms of procedural laws but in terms of allocations of goods. Distributive justice is concerned with how society distributes the burdens and benefits of the economy to the individual. One of the major proponents of distributive justice theory is the political theorist John Rawls. A key principle in Rawls's version is the Difference Principle, which states that all services, liberty, knowledge, and equality are to be allocated equally unless an unequal allocation will result in an advantage to those least favored in society.

Distributive Justice *(political science)*   A theory governing the provision of benefits (be it economic activity, political rights, or social benefits) within a society, arising out of the concern for maintaining a productive and just society. It is not possible to constrict the ideas of distributive justice into a formal definitive definition; rather, it needs to be discussed in terms of a set of principles varying on the item of allocation, the pattern of allocation, and the justification of allocation. The justness of the distribution is seen as either a product of the process of allocation or a product of the outcome and in some schools, both. Principles of distributive justice include egalitarianism, the difference principle, resource-based principles, welfare-based principles, and libertarian principles. All these together constitute "social justice." For more information, see Zucker (2001).

Distributive Policy   Government policies can serve several functions: redistributive, distributive, or regulatory. Redistributive policies can provide goods and services in the form of subsidies, grants, tax breaks, or regulatory provisions. Such policies benefit few or many as they allocate resources or services for issue areas such as highway infrastructure, public education, the military, or national parks. Many people label these kinds of programs "pork barrel." *Bringing home the bacon* is a phrase used to describe the success of some elected officials, such as members of Congress, in providing agricultural subsidies or public works programs to their constituents. (The first recorded modern use of this term was in reference to the great lightweight boxer Joe Gans, who telegrammed his mother that he was "Bringing home the bacon" after he beat Oscar "Battling" Nelson in a championship fight in 1906.) Elected officials often determine who gets what as they work to please their constituents. Most often referred to as *pork*, these types of programs are often used as a bargaining tool by legislative leaders for mobilizing constituent support and votes for key pieces of legislation or for reelection. In return for votes, special projects or programs that are meaningful to legislators are inserted into legislation, thus securing a benefit to distribute to constituents in the lawmakers' home districts or state. The programs are inserted into the budget even in times of lean budgets and scarce resources. Alaska's "bridge to nowhere" is a well-known example of pork barreling. The Gravina Island Bridge was proposed to replace the ferry that connects Ketchikan, Alaska, to the Ketchikan International Airport on Gravina Island. The bridge was projected to cost $398 million. Members of the Alaskan congressional delegation were the bridge's biggest advocates in Congress, who helped push for federal funding. Support for the project waned when the Alaska delegation was unable to prevent changes to federal funding levels that more than doubled Alaska's portion of the bill for construction. In addition, it was not all that clear that the bridge would in fact meet the need to shuttle airport patrons. For more information, see Anderson (1997) and Davidson and Oleszek (2006). *See also* Redistributive Policy; Regulatory Policy

District Attorney A court officer responsible for prosecuting people accused of crimes. A district attorney conducts criminal proceedings on behalf of the people and represents the state, one side in an adversarial justice system. In some jurisdictions, district attorneys are elected to their posts, and in others they are appointed. They operate at every level of government: city, county, district, state, and federal. *See also* Due Process of Law; Prosecutor

District Court A level of judicial court. In the United States, the term *district court* is applied in several ways. Some states use it to describe their appellate courts, others use it to name courts of limited jurisdiction, and yet others have no district courts at all. There are 94 federal judicial districts with trial courts, district courts that hear criminal and civil cases at the federal level.

Divergence Difference or disagreement. In communication, a divergence of opinion indicates that the writers or speakers are expressing different viewpoints about the topic. Divergence of opinion is important in scholarship since one must know different, opposing arguments to refute them. No person can win an argument without knowing the divergent opinions that exist for any topic. Divergence can also imply that there is a departure from a particular viewpoint or that one's mental world has a different cultural construction. Also, when one learns to be a critical thinker, one learns to think "outside the box," or not in the usual way.

Diversification The application of techniques used to manage or reduce the risks of a broad range of investments exposed to uncertainties from the external and internal environments. The external environment includes, but is not limited to, the stock market, the economy, government policies, interest rates, and currency fluctuations. The internal environment is specifically related to individual firms.

An application of diversification is in stock portfolio management. An investor can reduce his or her portfolio risks by holding a portfolio of stocks above 25. This means that holding more stocks in a portfolio can spread the risk among a larger diversified base. However, these stocks in the portfolio must be diversified across many industries to ensure that if one industry is in recession, other industries are in boom. For example, an investor should not have all his or her stocks in, say, the automobile industry or any single industry. *See also* Investment

Diversity Involves acknowledging, respecting, and appreciating the differences that people have in terms of their appearance, beliefs, and lifestyle. There are primary and secondary dimensions. Primary dimensions are core elements that cannot be changed: race, age, gender, sexual orientation, and physical and mental abilities. These characteristics form the heart of people's identities and shape the filters through which they view the world. The greater the number of primary differences, the greater is the challenge to establish trust. Secondary dimensions are those that can be modified or changed, including spiritual practices, education, relationship status, and income. Though diversity can be challenging, the benefits outweigh the difficulties since it fosters (1) the reduction of prejudice, (2) the vitality of groups by providing new perspectives, (3) productivity by providing a wider range of resources, (4) creative problem solving, and (5) perspective taking. Diversity also means the inclusion of traditionally marginalized groups in the composition of institutions, communities, corporations, and government. *See also* Prejudice (psychology); Prejudice and Discrimination

Divided Government A stalemate, or policy gridlock, is more likely to occur during periods of divided government. It exists when one political party controls the presidency and the other political party controls at least one house of Congress. Some of the reasons for a policy impasse as a result of a divided government are evident. Members of the same political party, for example, are likely to share similar points of view regarding the appropriate size of government, the scope of government actions, and the level of government intervention required to effect positive change through public policies. Although divided government can present a number of challenges for generating cooperation or consensus around a policy issue, policymaking can proceed even under these circumstances. One such illustration is the Clean Air Act

Amendments (1990), which is an expansive piece of legislation. It was passed in spite of split party control of the White House and Congress. On the other hand, the Carter administration operated with democratic control of the White House and Congress, yet President Carter's priority legislation was not passed by Congress. More often than not, the American legislative process is slow moving, as policy changes may be incremental or gradual. In many instances, presidents can play a vital role in pushing policies onto the agenda and through the legislative process. President Johnson, for example, spearheaded health care reform with the passage of the federal Medicare Program (1965), as well as pushing for broad-sweeping social and systemic change with civil rights policies and the War on Poverty.

Divine Right   A concept that originated from the practices of the Eastern monarchies and Hellenistic philosophy. In its earlier embodiments, found in Egypt, Syria, and Mesopotamia, the king was considered a direct kin of God. It has been argued that this concept later developed in Western ideology to deal with the political problems posed after the Reformation, though it was fully accepted that the king was a direct kin of God rather than God's lieutenant on earth. In Western political theory, divine right vested sovereignty on the king, whose power and authority came from God alone, not his subjects. However, others argue that from an ideological point of view, divine right condemned disobedience and did not exclude the king from obeying his own laws. It instead created a hierarchy that required the king to obey the norms and laws of God.

Early divine right theorists included John Aylmer, Thomas Bilson, and John Bridges. For more information, see Burgess (1992).

Division of Labor   A term going back to Plato and summarized and modified by Adam Smith in his 1776 *An Inquiry Into the Nature and Causes of the Wealth of Nations* to refer to the partitioning of the capitalist economy into specialized occupations and production types. This specialization was criticized by Karl Marx. In organizational theory, it refers to the differentiation of jobs into specialized positions and tasks, including the proper allocation of people and machines. For more information, see Smith (1776/1977). ***See also*** Scientific Management (public administration)

Docket   The formal schedule of upcoming judicial cases and an official record of judicial proceedings. The docket is both the calendar of forthcoming events in a particular court and the name of the book in which that record is kept.

Doctrine   A political philosophy specific to a particular moment in history reflecting the historical and social ideologies of a nation-state or a particular group.

For example, in the 1990s, prior to the bombing of the World Trade Center on September 11, 2001, the American political philosophy regarding war reflected a post-Vietnam perspective. Under the philosophy, or doctrine, of General Colin Powell, the United States fought "short" wars, decisively, infrequently, and with paramount force. The events of 9/11 arguably produced a shift in both historical and social ideologies, altering the political doctrine of war. Political conflict and instability abroad became clear threats to homeland security, thereby shifting the political objective from one of dissolving conflicts quickly and forcefully to establishing governance abroad aligned with American interests. Under President George W. Bush and his leading general, David Petraeus, wars are prolonged, ambiguous, and require coercion, not necessarily by means of brute force. The Petraeus doctrine has overturned the Powell doctrine. The main problem with this doctrine is that an existential enemy became difficult to define, and the United States began fighting a war with a doctrine itself (e.g., Islamist terrorism). President Barack Obama (2009–) is still shaping his war doctrine, but so far it differs little in substance from that of the Bush administration. For more information, see Bacevich (2008). ***See also*** Political Philosophy

Doe, John/Jane   The generic name used in the place of an actual name. These universal names are used in a court of law when a party's actual identity is either unknown or must be kept private and off the record. It is also an idiom used to connote everywoman or everyman.

Domestication   The process by which humans appropriate animals or plants so that they are better suited to human use. Domestication involves the control and manipulation of characteristics so as to discipline plants and animals for their utility toward human endeavors.

Domestic Violence   Physical, sexual, or emotional abuse of people in intimate relationships. The U.S. feminist movement of the 1970s brought attention to the nature and prevalence of domestic violence, and the term gained prominence. Domestic violence refers to violence, intimidation, and harm perpetrated by one person against another or others with whom the person is in a relationship. Typically, the term refers to incidents and patterns of terrorization in the home, within a family unit, and between those with personal connections. Domestic violence often involves a cycle of recurring acts that escalate so that the perpetrator cultivates and maintains power and control over the victim/s.

Dominance   A term used by Marxist theorists to describe the hierarchy and interaction of elements involved in social formation. Louis Althusser (1968) first used the term in the 1960s to explain a process of dominance and subordination that results in social structures. Dominance is control over a particular person or peoples. In psychology, dominance refers to the disposition of individuals who exert control over others. It can also refer to a part of the brain being more active than another part. ***See also*** Marxism (sociology)

Dominant Construction A semiotic term referring to the preferred or hegemonic reading of a particular message. It takes place when the message's recipient fully shares and accepts the seemingly natural or transparent meaning of the message. Dominant construction may be contrasted either with "negotiated construction," in which the recipient partly agrees with the natural meaning but somehow modifies it to reflect his or her own position, or with "oppositional construction," in which the recipient understands the dominant meaning but rejects it in favor of some other position or frame of reference. For instance, a feminist may view a Disney film from the 1950s and interpret it oppositionally as an encoding of gender stereotypes, whereas a dominant construction might fail even to perceive the presence of gender politics.

The terms *dominant construction* and *preferred reading* are open to philosophical challenge, since one may ask precisely how one knows such a construction when one has found it. In the context of advertising analysis, for instance, it is not necessarily justifiable to assume that it is in the interests of advertisers to create one "preferred" reading of the advertisement's message. Intentionality suggests that the author of the message has consciously manipulated the text and images, and it implies that the visual, technical, and linguistic strategies work together to secure one preferred reading of an advertisement to the exclusion of others. On the contrary, it seems likely that not all the messages one may read in an advertisement are present by design. Some theorists suggest that the concept of dominant construction may be applied more easily to news and current affairs than to other mass media genres. For more information, see Chandler (2001) and Myers (1983). ***See also*** Semiotics (media studies)

Dominion Either the act of exercising control over something or the condition of being controlled. In the individual sense, dominion concerns that an individual be free from constraints imposed by the actions of others and also that citizens subjectively know that they are entitled to this freedom. An individual will have dominion when he is exempt from constraints imposed by the actions of others.

More specifically, *dominion* also refers to the overseas possessions of the British Empire in the late 19th century. These nations were semiautonomous and were distinguished from the less autonomous dependencies controlled by the British Empire. The dominion nations included Canada, Newfoundland, India, Pakistan, Australia, New Zealand, and South Africa. Their decline occurred around the time of World War II, when these nations gained independence subsequent to the decline of British colonialism.

Dopamine A substance that functions as a neurotransmitter in the brain and activates five types of dopamine receptors (D1, D2, D3, D4, and D5). Dopamine acts as an inhibitor and is mainly involved in the regulation of motor movement and in reward-related activities. Dopamine also functions to regulate sleep, mood, and attention. Parkinson's disease, which involves loss of control over voluntary movements, is thought to be caused by the loss of neurons that produce dopamine. The dopamine hypothesis theorizes that schizophrenia is associated with excess dopamine receptors in the brain. ***See also*** Neurotransmitters

Double Jeopardy (*political science*) The concept can be traced back to *The Digest of Justinian* (529–534 AD). The origins of the modern-day *double jeopardy* found in the United States paralleled the development of the modern criminal procedure, both in the late 15th century. Conceptually, it was developed in 1642, on completion of Sir Thomas Cook's *First Institutes*, which set forth the framework for double jeopardy to protect citizens against the state for even relatively minor offenses. A century later, Sir William Blackstone would coin the term *jeopardy* and give it importance.

The double jeopardy clause is found in the Fifth Amendment in the Bill of Rights, which states that no person shall "be subject for the same offense to be twice put in jeopardy of life or limb." For more information, see Thomas (1998) and A. Watson (1998).

Double Jeopardy (*sociology*) A legal term that means to be tried more than once for the same criminal violation. The Fifth Amendment to the U.S. Constitution has a double jeopardy clause to protect citizens from being tried again for the same offense after having been acquitted or convicted. It also disallows multiple punishments for the same conviction.

Downward Communication A traditional management practice for the dissemination of information through a formal chain of command. Organizations using downward communication pass down verbal and written information from the upper rungs of the administrative ladder to the lower rungs. The information, handed down through chains of managers to subordinates, may include messages about organization policies and work practices to be instituted, as well as employee evaluations.

Studies and evaluations of downward communication have pointed to positives and negatives in the practice. Downward communication does delineate the hierarchy within an organization, giving employees at various levels direction about job performance expectations. On the other hand, as a message gets passed down, it gets larger, and sometimes distorted, with additions made in the process of manager-to-subordinate clarifications; information passed down from the top usually needs several changes before it can be applied to the set of employees at whom it is directed. For more information, see Goris, Vaught, and Pettit (2000) and Huang and Kleiner (2005). ***See also*** Horizontal Communication; Lateral Communication; Upward Communication

Drama A word derived from the Greek for acting. Drama from its earliest times to today retains this essential sense of performance in which actors assume roles, act, and speak. In theory, one could have a wordless drama, as in a mime or a dumb show, but the usual form employs characters and dialogue as well as action, and often music, song, and dance. Drama occurs across the media, on TV, radio, stage, film; combines with different genres, as in docudrama, which dramatizes real events; and can feature in the classroom as pedagogic strategy. Western tragic drama was traditionally preoccupied with great men and women (comedy more often representing the lower classes), but contemporary drama—for example, the "kitchen sink drama" of the mid 20th century—often represents the concerns of the marginalized person, the squalor and boredom of daily existence, and the realities of poverty and discrimination. In common parlance, drama is often synonymous with melodrama, denoting sensational events and heightened emotion—hence the epithet *drama queen*. Less pejoratively, drama refers to any vivid representation or event. Drama in many cultures is embedded in religious and political life, although in contemporary Western culture, it is largely regarded as entertainment for its own sake.

Sticking to the core meaning of drama as doing, Aristotle (in the *Poetics*) defines tragic drama as the imitation of an action that is serious, complete, and of a certain size. The action represented cannot be trivial but must test free choice to its limits. In having magnitude, the action cannot consist of simply one event but must represent a unified chain of consequences ensuing from the protagonist's deeds. By "imitation" (mimesis), Aristotle refers to the dramatist's ability to show things as they should be rather than as they are in ordinary life. Although contemporary drama has long since challenged these conventions, they remain a part of the development of the theory of dramatic representation. For more information, see Aristotle (1996). ***See also*** Representation (media studies); Theater

Dress Codes   Policies, rules, or regulations that govern the appearance, such as facial hair for men, or types of dress that students or employees may wear. To withstand legal challenges, dress codes must further the aims of the organization or agency and not violate an individual's constitutional rights.

Drift   A criminological theory of delinquency developed by David Matza and Gresham Sykes in the late 1950s. These American sociologists posited that young people drift, or coast, into illegal behavior through a process of rationalizing delinquent behavior. This occurs alongside weak or weakening social connections. Delinquent drift takes place when young people neutralize the illegality or wrongness of criminal behavior by justifying their actions or disassociating from the harms they cause. ***See also*** Criminology

Drug   Any substance, chemical or organic, that affects the body or mind of a living organism. The field of medicine roots its distinct drug classification system based on the treatment and prevention of disease and the toxicity and power of the drug. The legal system classifies drugs as controlled substances. Certain drugs are illegal; it is against the law to possess, use, and distribute these substances. Though the illegality of controlled substances varies across place, time, and amount, common examples include heroin, cocaine, and marijuana. The law also regulates and controls the use and distribution of legal drugs, such as pills prescribed by a physician. Compulsive use of a drug, often driven by chemical and emotional dependency, is known as drug addiction. Addiction, sometimes referred to as substance abuse, is the deliberate continuous use of a drug for nonmedical purposes. Drug court is a collaborative judicial process focused on steering a defendant away from drug dependency. This is done through mandatory substance abuse treatment and monitoring. Drug courts are often part of diversion practices aimed at keeping people out of the criminal justice system. ***See also*** Substance Abuse

Drug Enforcement Administration (DEA)   A division of the U.S. Department of Justice. The DEA's role is to enforce all laws relating to controlled substances. President Richard Nixon created the agency in 1973 to establish a centralized force to fight "a war on drugs."

Drug Testing   The practice of administering urinalysis, breathalyzer, hair analysis, or other means of medical testing to determine the use of illegal substances or drugs by a student or employee. Policies that address drug testing of students or employees must be thoughtfully developed to avoid impairing Fourth Amendment rights to privacy. ***See also*** Drug

Dual Diagnosis   In the strictest terms, the term refers to any two co-occurring medical, psychiatric, developmental, or substance abuse disorders. Common alternative terms are comorbid disorders, co-occurring illnesses, concurrent disorders, and dual disorders. The term *dual diagnosis* is most commonly used to refer to the combined presence of any psychiatric disorder (identified on Axis I or II of the *Diagnostic and Statistical Manual of Mental Disorders* [fourth edition; *DSM–IV*]) and a substance abuse disorder. Recently, the term *concurrent disorders* has become widely preferred. For more information, see Lehman, Myers, and Corty (2000) and Mueser, Drake, and Wallach (1998). ***See also*** Comorbidity; Psychological Disorder; Substance Abuse

Dual Federalism   The earliest period in the intergovernmental system of the United States is characterized by what is referred to as dual federalism. Disputes often arose about how much power the federal government should have and what should be addressed by the states. This stage and governmental arrangement lasted well into the 20th century. Dual federalism refers to how federal and state governments both sought to establish their own separate spheres of power and influence. Some describe the relationship between federal, state, and local governments as a layer cake. That is to say, the three levels worked parallel to each other and rarely together. There was very little cooperation or coordination between federal and state levels of government. In many instances, the relationship between the two was rife with tension and conflict. As urban centers grew and society increased in its complexity, the federal government worked to address broad policy issues. New grant programs, for example, increased federal involvement in the construction of highways and in vocational and higher education. While states were appreciative of federal money and investments, they were generally cautious of the infringement of federal government on state responsibilities. In many circumstances, federal and state functions remained very distinct. The federal government, for example, generally limited itself to the larger issues and concerns around national defense and international trade. The federal government, however, began to assert itself on issues such as establishing a national bank and the parameters for interstate commerce. This was met with resistance and challenges. Under the leadership of Chief Justice John Marshall, the Supreme Court supported the expansion of federal government and its ability to influence public policies. Yet major conflicts persisted. Some of the more significant conflicts include the disagreement over the spread of slavery and the subsequent Civil War. ***See also*** Federalism

Dualism   The term (derived from the Latin word *duo*) refers to a philosophical position that assumes that there is a nonmaterial or spiritual reality over and beyond the physical reality. Therefore, our beings are not only composed of a body. There are different types of dualism. The mind-body dualism assumes that the body and mind are separate although interacting entities. This concept originated with Rene Descartes (1596–1650), a French mathematician and philosopher. He popularized the concept of reality as dichotomized into matter, or spatial substance, and spirit, or thinking substance, that includes God. The material substance is physical, and it is assumed to be the basis of the empirical world (i.e., what we see, hear, or sense). The spiritual substance is the nonmaterial world that forms the basis of the nonempirical world (psychological or mental world). Dualism assumes immortality because the other reality besides the body can survive death. ***See also*** Reality Principle

Due Process/Due Process Model   A legal and judicial framework, forwarded by the U.S. Constitution, that prioritizes and guarantees the protection of individual rights. The Fifth, Sixth, and Fourteenth amendments' due process clauses guide procedure and practice at all stages of the criminal justice system so that individual rights are safeguarded against injustices and abuses of governmental power. Due process ensures procedural fairness and impartiality as a person faces a threat to his or her liberty. A due process model of justice emphasizes and honors citizens' rights by controlling governmental authority and buttressing individual autonomy. This is realized through processes, due to the individual, that restrain and structure criminal procedure. The primary value of such a system is protecting civil liberty, as opposed to the crime control model in which the primary value is cutting down on the amount of crime. Due process maintains that it is better for a guilty person to go free than for an innocent one to be falsely punished. ***See also*** Crime Control/Crime Control Model

Due Process of Law   The exercise of governmental power with regard for the fundamental fairness of the rights of individuals. Due process of law distinguishes between procedural due process, which concerns how the law ought to be justly applied, and substantive due process, which examines the sources of fairness beyond the text of the Constitution. In American jurisprudence, the central premise of due process is that all levels of government must operate within the law and provide fair procedures. Due process for individuals is required when the state acts against their rights to life, liberty, and property.

Procedural due process includes rights that dictate how the government can lawfully take a person's rights when the law gives it the power to do so. The law must be clear and fair and must apply a presumption of innocence to comply with procedural due process. Some of the rights that procedural due process includes are (a) the right to a fair trial, (b) the right for the accused to be present at trial, (c) the right to be heard by an impartial jury, (d) the right to appeal decisions, (e) the right to counsel, and (f) the right cross-examine witnesses.

The due process clause not only requires due process, or procedural rights, but also protects substantive rights. The question of substantive due process is whether the government's deprivation of a person's life, liberty, or property is justified by a sufficient purpose. Substantive due process looks to whether there is a good enough reason for such a deprivation. In its decisions, the Supreme Court has determined that substantive due process protects abstract liberty interests, including the right to personal privacy, bodily integrity, and self-determination.

The due process clause is found in both the Fifth and the Fourteenth amendments. These guarantees initially had no application against the states. According to the Fifth Amendment, "no person shall . . . be deprived of life, liberty, or property, without due process of law." The Fifth Amendment's due process clause stated that the Bill of Rights would protect citizens against the federal government.

The Fourteenth Amendment, however, applied the due process clause of the Bill of Rights to the states. The Fourteenth Amendment's language also states, "Nor shall any State deprive any person of life, liberty, or property without due process of law." Although the Fourteenth Amendment was ratified in 1868, it was not until the 20th century that the Supreme Court, through its case decisions, incorporated the most important elements of the Bill of Rights and applied them to the states. For more information, see Hyman (2005). ***See also***

Bill of Rights (political science, sociology); Constitutional Amendment; Substantive Due Process

DUI/DWI   Acronyms that stand for "driving under the influence" and "driving while intoxicated." These terms are used within the criminal justice system to describe the illegal behavior of operating a vehicle while drunk or under the influence of another substance. One must meet a legal standard of intoxication, usually determined by blood-alcohol or dexterity tests, to be deemed DUI or DWI.

Duress   One of several justifications used in defenses to mitigate or absolve criminal culpability. A duress defense asserts that the defendant was coerced, pressured, or threatened into committing the crime and would not have done it otherwise. Duress is an affirmative defense, which means that the burden of proof lies with the defendant.

Duty to Warn   The responsibility of a therapist or a counselor to breach confidentiality when a patient or client identifies someone who is in clear or imminent danger. In these situations, the therapist or counselor must determine the seriousness of the situation and, in some situations or jurisdictions, notify the potential victim and/or others who might be able to protect the person. This concept has its legal precedent in the case of *Tarasoff v. Regents of the University of California* (1976). In this case, Prosenjit Poddar, who was seeing a therapist at the University of California's student health center, informed the therapist that he intended to harm Tatiana Tarasoff, who had rejected Poddar. The therapist notified the campus police after finding out that Poddar intended to purchase a gun. However, the police questioned Poddar and did not find him to be dangerous. Two months later, Poddar killed Tarasoff. Although not all jurisdictions have a statutorily defined duty to warn or duty to protect provision, some courts have ruled similar to California, thus requiring therapists to breach confidentiality in order to protect identified victims. For more information, see *Tarasoff v. Regents of the University of California* (1976). ***See also*** Therapy

Dyadic Communication   Communication between two people. A husband and wife, a parent and child, a job interviewer and the interviewee, a police interrogator and a suspect, two people on a date, a beggar and a passerby, two partners in a business are all examples of dyads. Dyadic communication has special characteristics. In face-to-face communication, dyads allow for more accurate and immediate feedback than would a large audience or even a small group. Communication apprehension often lessens in established dyads when compared with larger groups. Within dyads, power roles may influence the ability to decode messages. Within groups and organizations, different dyads may have different levels of cohesiveness and importance to the participants. For example, the relationship between a boss and an employee differs from that between two coworkers. Dyads are important basic units for communication. In addition, Dyads are the building blocks for larger groups and organizations. For more information, see Barry and Crant (2000) and Wilmot (1987).

Dysfunction   A breakdown or disturbance in normal or expected function. Dysfunction conveys an abnormality or difficulty that results in something not working properly. It is used in the disciplines of medicine, psychology, and sociology. In medicine, the term is used to describe the impairment of an organ or a body part. In psychology, the term is used to describe a malfunctioning social group or a mental disorder.

Dysthymia   A type of mood disorder that involves a mild, but persistent and chronic, depression. Individuals with a diagnosable dysthymic disorder experience chronic depression for at least two years, though they may experience intermittent normal moods. Symptoms of dysthymia are not severe enough to merit a diagnosis of major depressive disorder, though typically, individuals who suffer from dysthymia are depressed most of the day, almost everyday, over a period of years. A feeling of pessimism and an inability to experience pleasure are common, as are appetitive and sleep disturbances. Low energy levels, concentration difficulties, indecision, low self-esteem, and suicidal ideation are also associated with this syndrome. This set of symptoms may impair the individual's social, occupational, or other areas of functioning. ***See also*** Depression (education, psychology); Diagnosis (psychology)

E

Early Childhood A period or a stage of human development from two to six years of age, preceded by infancy and followed by middle childhood. During this period, children known as preschoolers grow more slowly in overall body size than they did in infancy. Their brain development, particularly in the left hemisphere, supports fast language skill development. Their attention span continues to improve, and their recognition memory becomes very accurate. Their motor skills are refined in terms of body balance and control of hands and fingers. In the meantime, they begin to show a sense of morality and establish peer relationships.

Early-Intervention Programs Systems of supports offered to infants or young children (birth to age three) and their families when delays in development in physical, cognitive, social, communicative, or adaptive areas are present. Designed to assist the family and to promote typical growth and development of the child, these intervention programs are used to reduce the need for future special education services. In the United States, Part C of the Individuals with Disabilities Act (IDEA), a federal law reauthorized in 2004, requires states to publicize these programs, specify eligibility criteria, and provide services to infants and preschool children with special needs. Services, partly funded by the federal government through grants to the states, include assessment, evaluation, and appropriate interventions and therapies (e.g., speech and language therapy, vision services, family training, physical therapy, occupational therapy, and special instruction). Ideally, professionals collaborate with the family to create an individualized family service plan (IFSP) and to provide integrated services for the child in natural settings, including the home, child care centers, and community centers. *See also* Developmental Disability; Individualized Family Service Plan (IFSP); Individuals with Disabilities Education Act (IDEA); Head Start

Eating Disorders A syndrome of maladaptive behaviors surrounding an individual's eating habits and/or an individual's attempts to maintain a low body weight. There are three eating disorders defined in the *Diagnostic and Statistical Manual of Mental Disorders* (text revision; *DSM-IV-TR*): anorexia nervosa, bulimia nervosa, and eating disorder, not otherwise specified, which includes binge-eating disorder. Anorexia is characterized by chronic and intense fears of gaining weight accompanied by ongoing attempts to limit caloric intake, resulting in a body weight consistently below what is typical for the individual's age and height. The disorder is typically accompanied by an absence of menstruation in women. Bulimia is characterized by discrete periods of eating in excess accompanied by a subjective sense of lacking control over eating behavior during these periods. Also, bulimia involves recurrent attempts to compensate for this caloric ingestion through compensatory behaviors, for example, self-induced vomiting, use of laxatives, fasting or intense exercise, and so on. Both disorders are thought to be linked to an underlying distorted self-perception of one's physical body, and many theorists link these disorders to exposure to unrealistic cultural ideals for male and female physical appearance. Both disorders are much more prevalent in women, and theories of these disorders often include a gender-specific component to account for this divergence. There are also several lines of research that suggest both genetic/biological as well as family dynamics components that may be present in the etiology of eating disorders.

Eclecticism An approach to psychotherapy, which is differentiated from an "integrative" approach, that espouses utilization of conceptualizations and interventions from across a broad range of existing therapeutic modalities. Eclecticism is pragmatic in that interventions are matched to the client, rather than derived from a single theory. This approach is among the most frequently endorsed by mental health practitioners, next to cognitive behavioral therapy. *See also* Psychotherapy

Ecological Determinism A theoretical paradigm that stipulates that changes in human settings are governed by changes in the environment. From this perspective, changes in the physical environment (e.g., climate) result in changes in human behavior, attitudes, and culture. *See also* Ecology; Social Ecology

Ecological Psychology A branch of psychology that focuses on the environment to facilitate the study of human behavior and adaptation, and development. According to ecological psychology, human behavior and development can be understood best in terms of its links to environmental contexts and situations in which the individual is immersed. Bronfenbrenner, for instance, stresses viewing human adaptation and development in terms of a sociocultural context. In a somewhat different vein, James and Eleanor Gibson suggest that the environment is the source of perceptual learning and development; by proactively exploring one's environment in the service of seeking new information about the properties of objects and events (affordances or opportunities for action), one's learning and likelihood of adaptation are said to increase. For more information, see Bronfenbrenner and Morris (1998), Gibson (1979), Gibson and Gibson (1955), and Gibson and Pick (2000). *See also* Perception (communication, psychology); Situated Cognition

Ecology   The scientific study of interactions and relationships among organisms, as well as their interactions with the environment. The most basic assumption of ecology is that all organisms (vegetation, animals, humans, etc.) are interdependent and that they interact with nonliving things. Social ecology is a philosophical paradigm that stipulates that environmental problems result from the hierarchical structure of society. According to this perspective, the hierarchy in social classes and the increased power of specific social groups justifies the domination and exploitation of the environment. Social ecologists argue that the exploitative attitudes observed in society (such as racism, differential treatment of different social classes, etc.) share similar underlying processes with destructive behavior toward the environment (pollution, waste of resources, etc.). Social ecologists also argue that environmental challenges can only be undertaken once these social issues of hierarchy and power have been addressed. *See also* Ecological Determinism; Ecosystem; Social Ecology

Econometrics   A scientific method to measure or estimate economic variables or models (formal representation of a theory, usually in mathematical form). Variables are generally observable phenomenon with changing quantitative values. When they are categorical (qualitative), for example, male or female, they can be transformed into quantitative variables if they are given numerical values or codes. Econometrics is an abridged combination of two words: economics and metrics (measurement).

Econometric analyses may involve one or more theoretic model specifications, but the basic principle is to obtain unbiased and credible results in order to ascertain economic laws and make sensible economic predictions or policies. One of the most popular techniques of econometric analysis is regression analysis. Regression analysis examines the dependence of one variable (dependent variable) on one or more independent variables by minimizing errors in estimation. The results of estimation by regression analysis indicate correlation rather than causation. For more information, see Gujarati (2006) and Warburton (2006). *See also* Economics; Regression Analysis

Economic Determinism   A philosophical school of thought used to explain historical development. Economic determinists posit that economic conditions, more specifically, the "mode of production" or "commodity form," determine the intellectual, social, and political reality of the era. The truth of social existence is thereby legitimized by economic conditions and the means by which the substances are produced rather than the noneconomic, humanistic factors. From a strict view of economic determinism, humanistic variables, such as race, gender, and culture, have no influence over the ideologies of that period.

The discourse on economic determinism began in the mid-19th century with the works of Karl Marx and Friedrich Engels. Modern-day discourse surrounding economic determinism continues to be centered on Marxism, though many supporters of Marxism deny Marx's emphasis on the strict impact of economic influences on social reality, while others argue from the opposite position. For more information, see Blanshard (1966). *See also* Marxism (political science)

Economic Growth   An increase in national output, if and when it occurs. This concept must not be confused with development, which is a broader indicator of economic performance and policies affecting education, health, and income distribution. Gross domestic product (GDP) is the main economic variable that is used to measure economic growth or performance.

The pace of economic growth across the world is not even. Some nations continue to grow faster than others because of differences in the availability of economic resources and deliberate policy measures that are adopted by policymakers. Growth may be stalled or retarded because of population pressures and gyrations in economic performance attributable to the business cycle or contingent shocks, such as natural disasters or unforeseen impediments.

The main determinants of the level of economic growth are education, saving (for capital formation), innovation, level of inflation, fiscal and monetary policies, the quality of the financial system, the efficiency of labor, the rate of capital deepening (a process that ensures sufficient capital per worker) or widening (increase in capital stock that barely keeps pace with the labor force and depreciation of capital), and returns from international trade.

The growth rate of GDP is calculated by the annual percentage increase, and the average rate of growth calculates the average of the annual percentage increase. The annual percentage increase may be revised downward to accommodate the rate of inflation.

Economists have used several theories to model growth, one of the earliest being that of Harrod-Domar in the 1940s, which focused attention on capital accumulation and fixed proportions of capital and labor for growth. In 1956, the Solow neoclassical model improved on the Harrod-Domar model by allowing for variability and substitution between capital and labor but taking technological change as residual (exogenous).

Much more recent models make technological change endogenous and argue for increasing returns to scale (doubling input can more than double output). These recent models have been used to explain growth without a steady state in industrialized countries. For more information, see Mankiw (2006), McConnell and Brue (2008), and Perkins, Radlet, and Lindauer (2006). *See also* Business Cycle; Capital; Fiscal Policy; Gross Domestic Product; Inflation; Monetary Policy

Economics   The study of how individuals, households, and societies choose to use their scarce resources efficiently in order to satisfy their diverse wants. By definition, economics is a social or behavioral science because it studies human behavior just like other social sciences, but it emphasizes the need to make wise choices in order to use scarce resources in an efficient way to satisfy diverse wants.

Resources are the factors of production, the inputs, and managerial skills that are required to produce goods and services. These are land, labor, capital, and entrepreneurial skill. The factors of production are scarce because of the limitless wants of economic agents and the competing uses to which the resources can be committed. Scarcity is therefore a relative concept, meaning that economic resources are scarce relative to limitless wants and the competing demands for available resources.

Scarcity necessitates choices and costs. Individuals, firms, and societies must then choose the way and manner in which they want to use scarce resources in order to avoid waste and inefficiency. Whenever a choice is made, there is a corresponding cost—the sacrificed alternative, otherwise known as the opportunity cost.

Economists have determined that incremental (additional or marginal) cost-benefit analysis is the underlying principle that rational humans will use to make choices. Humans will evaluate the marginal cost against the marginal benefit when making choices, and they will act on the weights of benefit and cost.

Intuitively, humans will prefer the benefits to costs, but by acting on such a preference, the use of aggregate societal resources will not be equitably distributed. There will be overallocation and underallocation of resources, which is an inefficient outcome. Therefore, societal resources must be allocated to attain equilibrium of marginal social cost and marginal social benefit, the precondition for efficient allocation. By doing so, a society will be producing what it wants at the least possible cost.

Economics has diverse fields but two broad categories. The field of economics includes industrial organization (the structure and performance of industries and firms); economic development (the study of, inter alia, poverty, education, health, and income distribution); international economics (economics in trade, finance, and development); labor economics (the factors affecting wage rate and employment); econometrics; public economics (government in the economy); welfare (normative) economics; and law and economics.

The two broad categories of economics are microeconomics and macroeconomics. Microeconomics is the study of individuals, households, and firms, while macroeconomics studies the aggregate economy and aggregate variables, such as national income, national saving, the general price level, and the national employment rate.

Economics seeks to deal with normative and positive issues. Normative issues are based on value judgment (good or bad), with little or no empirical justification for the conclusions reached. Positive economics is probative and uses theory to justify conclusions. Econometrics incorporates the methodology of economics. The major goals of economics are to attain efficiency, equity, growth, and price stability. For more information, see Boyes and Melvin (2002), Case and Fair (2003), Mankiw (2006), McConnell and Brue (2008), Perkins, Radlet, and Lindauer (2006), Pugel (2007), Salvatore (2002, 2006), and Schiller (2006). *See also* Cost-Benefit Analysis (CBA) (economics); Econometrics; Growth; International Economics; Stabilization

Economic Sanctions   Domestic restrictions or penalties imposed on international trade from one country to another primarily for political reasons. Generally, such sanctions are placed for purposes of foreign policy or national security. Economic sanctions have historically included trade barriers, import duties, tariffs, and export duties.

Economic sanctions have been in use for two millennia, tracing back to 432 BCE, when officials in Athens denied traders from the state of Megara access to Athens's harbor and its marketplace. Thousands of years later, the imposition of sanctions has become one of the major tools of international governance. Between the years 1945 and 1990, the United Nations (UN) Security Council, authorized under Article 16 of the UN Charter to use economic restrictions to address "threats of aggression" and "breaches of peace," approved such sanctions on only two occasions. Since 1990, the number of sanctions approved by the UN Security Council has increased significantly to 11. Sanctions have been imposed on nations including Yugoslavia, Libya, Somalia, Liberia, and Haiti.

Despite increases in UN-approved sanctions, the United States ranks as a nation that has imposed sanctions, alone or in conjunction with other nations, far more frequently than any other nation in the world, including the UN; since the 1990s, almost 200 sanctions have been imposed by the United States, both unilaterally and multilaterally.

Not always imposed because of economic circumstances, economic sanctions are also used in an effort to discourage nations from taking actions considered undesirable or harmful on a global basis, such as supporting terrorism, proliferating weapons of mass destruction, violating human rights, trafficking in drugs, or despoiling the environment. Economic sanctions are regulatory in nature, and despite the seemly beneficial nature and purpose of the sanctions, they are highly controversial and contested.

While proponents view sanctions as a means of international governance and peacekeeping, critics believe that using economic sanctions against a nation undermines the economy of the society in question by preventing the importation and production of necessities. Sanctions such as those against Robert Mugabe's brutal dictatorship in Zimbabwe, Africa, combined with the country's own disastrous economic policies, have brought the country to complete collapse, with poverty, disease, and an inflation rate reaching a quintillion percent. Consequently, the most vulnerable and least political members of a society are denied the means to basic human survival, such as potable water, food, and medical care. *See also* World Trade Organization (WTO)

Economic System   A system combining processes relating to the production, distribution, and consumption of goods or services in any given society. Economic systems are made up of individuals and institutions, and the state of relationships between these two components results in changes in the dynamics of the system. The processes underlying economic systems vary according to differences in geographic, cultural, political, and environmental characteristics. The main types of economic systems consist of capitalism, socialism, and communism. *See also* Economics; Economy

Economy   A multidimensional concept that refers to a system of capital accumulation through the production, exchange, distribution, and consumption of goods and services involving economic structures, organizations, and actors competing for power and hegemony. The production of specific goods and services depends on the ability of the actor, the availability of social and structural resources, and the availability of natural resources. In the modern economy, goods take the form of commodities. Class relations, power, and hegemony are determined by the relationship of production between economic actors.

The development of an economy is intertwined in the political and social history of the particular nation-state. It cannot be separated, nor should its development be discussed without a proper discussion of the nation-state's polity. The political structure of the nation-state governs the laws of accumulation, distribution, and competition. The modern economy is not autonomous from the nation-state; if either failed, it would cause a domino effect, collapsing or disabling other systems.

In the modern economy, there exists a dichotomy between both the formal and the informal economy. For more information, see Fuchs and Collier (2007). *See also* Capital; Competition

Economy, New   A concept that is, generally, less precisely defined than "economy" but alluding to effects of technological innovation and globalization that inure on the mode of production, cost of production, unemployment, national income, and prices of goods and services in the 1990s and thereafter.

In terms of the mode of production, it celebrates the extension of capitalism and liberalization to other areas of the world, particularly in Africa, Latin America, and Asia, which were once slow to embrace market capitalism. As such, the new economy marked an era of economic integration in which regional organizations are formed and trade barriers broken down to foster trade and investment. The World Trade Organization (WTO) played a crucial role in this transition.

The explosion of new technological products is an integral part of the new economy. These products—the Internet, personal computers, notebooks, cellular phones, fax machines, and digitized equipments—make communication and economic transactions a lot faster and cheaper. Opportunities for efficient management increased (reduction in bureaucratic red tape), outsourcing and offshoring boomed, and e-commerce became an important mechanism of exchange. The new technology transformed economies and diversified the sources of income. Traditional sources of income, such as the automobile industry, housing, farming, and mining, faced fierce competition from the high-paying information technology sector.

The old economy espoused strong indications of inflationary growth. In the new economy, the prices of the new products tend to fall on the dynamic time path because of rapid diversification and less supply constraints. Additionally, new innovation brings with it multisectoral implications for noninflationary growth or low unemployment and inflation.

The transforming effect of technological innovation is consistent with Schumpeter's "creative destruction"—the destruction of monopoly power and the old ways of doing business as a result of innovation and new products. The effects of innovation were envisaged in the old economy, but the forces that propel change in the new economy are predominantly unanticipated but stimulating. Prior innovation triggers a cascading effect, with consequences for new output and performance, hence the oxymoronic expression *the new old economy*.

Intensive debates continue over the measurement of technological change and the contribution of innovation to output in the new economy, partly as a result of stagnant wages, the quizzical contribution of the Internet to national income, miscalculation of contributions of the service industry to growth, and valuation of new products relative to the old. For more information, see Rauch (2001), Schumpeter (1950), and Shepard (1997). *See also* Globalization (economics, political science); Liberalization; Weightless Economy; World Trade Organization (WTO)

Ecosphere   *See* Biosphere

Ecosystem   A system consisting of the entire group of organisms (or living things, such as animals, vegetation, etc.) and the nonliving environment (such as minerals, rocks, etc.) located in any given area. Ecology, on the other hand, is the scientific study of interactions and relationships among organisms, and their interactions with the environment. The living and nonliving components of the ecosystem are said to be interdependent; that is, they exert reciprocal effects one on another. Ecosystems greatly vary in size and can range from a small pond to an entire ocean. *See also* Ecological Determinism; Ecology; Social Ecology

Editing The process of modifying media texts (composed of words, film, sound, and/or images) to create a final work for audience consumption. This may involve organizing images, correcting language, and altering sound. The methods of editing pertain to the type of text. Digital technologies are used as tools in editing.

Educational Law The study of constitutional provisions, state and local laws, state school board regulations, and local school district policies that govern matters related to the operation of public and private schools. Educational law is a field of study that encompasses a wide range of legal subject matter, which includes the structure of education law, school attendance, special education regulations, student discipline, employment law, separation of Church and State, tort liability, and constitutional protections.

Educational Policy A policy that designs and regulates education at three levels: federal, state, and local. In the United States, the Tenth Amendment to the Constitution limits the federal role in public education. Most education policy is determined at the state and local levels. Prior to the mid 20th century, the design and regulation of public school education were typically left to local school districts. During and since the 1980s, control moved from local to federal and state and then to state and building levels (with site-based management). Accountability measures and earmarking of federal money keep federal control over the implementation of policy significant.

Prior to the 1980s, educators, educational administrators, and others directly involved in schooling were considered to be the experts on education policy and were primary players in policy making. Beginning in the 1980s, federal and state governments have played an increasing role in educational policy making. Today politicians, business, and "think tanks" rather than educators are making education policy.

State-level policy since the 1980s has focused on control of K–12 curricula (through state standards) and on teacher preparation through both state standards and testing. Federal education policy has focused primarily on tying education success to U.S. economic competitiveness and the success of the United States as a world power. Historically significant federal policy includes the National Education Defense Act (1958),

L. B. Johnson's War on Poverty (compensatory education programs, including Head Start), A Nation at Risk, Goals 2000, No Child Left Behind, and numerous U.S. Supreme Court decisions.

Research on education policy includes a wide variety of approaches at local, state, national, and international levels. These include classroom-based action research, research employing local, state, and federal statistical data, and qualitative school and community-based studies. The George W. Bush administration stipulated that "scientific" research be the foundation for federal education policy. Scientific research, in this case, was narrowly defined as specific types of quantitative approaches embedded in an essentialist philosophical perspective.

Federal and state educational policy has historically targeted special populations and has been influenced by each of the three branches of government—for example, Native Americans (Indian Education Act—legislative), African Americans (*Brown v. Board of Education of Topeka* [1954]—judicial), women (Title IX—legislative and judicial), children below the poverty level (NCLB and Head Start—executive), and language minorities (Bilingual Education Act—legislative, *Lau v. Nichols* [1974]—legislative, NCLB—executive).

Popular academic journals publishing research and other academic work on educational policy include *Educational Policy, Journal for Critical Education Policy Studies (JCEPS), Journal of Education Policy (JEP), International Journal of Education Policy and Leadership (IJEPL),* and *Education Policy Analysis Archives (EPAA).*

Educational policy centers and institutes (think tanks) representing various political perspectives and agendas conduct research on public school policy issues, such as school accountability, school vouchers, school choice, academic standards, after-school programs, technology, and teacher quality. Professional organizations, centers, and institutes in educational policy include Center on Educational Policy, Educational Policy Institute, The Center for Research in Educational Policy, Brookings Institution, Education Policy Studies Laboratory (EPSL), Program on Education Policy and Governance (PEPG), Center for the Study of Education Policy, Commonwealth Educational Policy Institute (CEPI), Peabody Center for Education Policy (PCEP), The Center for Educational Policy Analysis (CEPA), Center for Education Policy, Applied Research, & Evaluation (CEPARE), and Institute for Research on Education Policy & Practice (IREPP). For more information, see *Brown v. the Board of Education of Topeka* (1954), Christensen and Karp (2003), Fowler (2004), Larson and Ovando (2000), *Lau v. Nichols* (1974), National Clearinghouse for English Language Acquisition and Language Instruction Educational Programs (2008), and U.S. Department of Education: www.ed.gov. *See also* U.S. Constitution and Education

Educational Psychology A broad term that encompasses both the study of how people learn in educational settings as well as the provision of

E

psychological services by practitioners in a school setting. Educational psychology, as a modern scientific discipline, traces its roots to the late 19th century with the application of the scientific method to educational problems. William James's book, *Talks to Teachers on Psychology,* published in 1899, is considered the first book on educational psychology, while Edward Thorndike, whose work on instrumental conditioning in the early 1900s influenced later theories of learning, is widely considered the father of educational psychology. Today, the title "educational psychologist" usually refers to psychologists who focus on learning outcomes (as influenced by both student attributes and instructional processes), the effectiveness of educational interventions, the psychology of teaching, and the organizational and social psychology of schools. Educational psychologists are concerned with how students learn and develop, and their research often informs a number of areas within education, such as curriculum development, special education, and classroom management. Educational psychologists who provide psychological services in school settings are usually called *school psychologists,* to distinguish them from educational psychologists (who are primarily involved with research). School psychologists collaborate with teachers, parents, and administrators to remediate students' learning and behavior problems by assessing for learning disabilities or other psychological impairment, often recommending psychological interventions that help students deal with academic and emotional difficulties. In the United States, enrolling in a two-year master's in educational psychology (MEd) program is the typical route to becoming an educational psychologist. Individuals with an MEd can conduct basic and applied research, as well as evaluate the program needs of schools. To provide psychological services to students in a school setting, however, earning an education specialist (EdS) degree in school psychology is typically required. For more information, see James (1899/2008) and Thorndike (1898). *See also* School Psychology

Educational Technology   A discipline of theory and practice for utilization of technologies in instructional contexts. Both the theory and the practice serve the purpose of integrating media into instructional processes and materials so that the effectiveness of the teaching-learning process can be maximized.

Effectiveness *(communication)*   The ability to bring about intended results and/or ensure that performance expectations are met. From a communications standpoint, effectiveness is indicated not by how well a message is crafted but by how well the intended audience receives and acts on the message. Communications can fail when target audiences filter out messages because they do not trust them or they perceive that the sender lacks conviction, according to the business consultant David Lapin.

Experts in the fields of public relations and communications management maintain that effectiveness in communications is not theoretical but organizational. James E. Grunig, for instance, advises that the "communications subsystem" of an organization be integrated into organizational goals.

According to a 2007/2008 return-on-investment (ROI) communication study by Watson Wyatt Worldwide, the most financially successful organizations keep their customers in mind while making employees feel it necessary to do business operations and monitoring and updating the effectiveness of communication programs. For more information, see Grunig (1992), Lapin (2004), and Watson Wyatt Worldwide (2009). *See also* Downward Communication; Horizontal Communication; Upward Communication

Effectiveness   *(public administration)*   Effective administration is necessary for a successful public policy. Effectiveness depends on an organization's personnel, experience and language, and administrative norms. These factors determine the ability of an organization to change and its ability to address public problems successfully. Effectiveness is defined as the impact programs have on solving identified problems. To advance toward goals, agencies create and operate programs. Program evaluation is used to access how programs have contributed to ameliorating a problem as well as the capacity of employees to achieve tasks and goals. Effectiveness is a key variable used to decide future funding. For more information, see Makielski (1967). *See also* Budgeting; Evaluation (public administration)

Effect Size Indicator   A measure of size of effect or strength of relationship between treatment and outcome variables. It is often used to help a researcher make a judgment of practical significance. It can be in the form of an odds ratio, a difference between or among group parameter estimates in units of standard deviation, or a variance-accounted-for statistic (eta-squared and Cramer's V). The most common metric effect size indicator, attributed to Cohen (1988), is the standardized effect size (d), which is the difference in parameter estimates divided by the pooled standard deviation. For more information, see Cohen (1988). *See also* Statistical Versus Practical Significance

Efficiency   The overall productivity of an agency in terms of budgetary allocations. Given the limited resources and unlimited demands by citizens for services, managers seek to maximize allocated resources in order to achieve the agency mission. Managers examine how different units and departments perform, to assess efficiency, on the basis of a performance measurement system. Efficiency assessment is necessary to ensure that public funds are spent properly and specific goals and objectives are being achieved. Performance measurement systems are tools that provide a mechanism to reduce the operational costs and prevent waste and fraud. The information collected is public information made available to citizens through the Freedom of Information Act (FOIA). Therefore, efficiency is key to maintaining accountability and transparency in government. ***See also*** Accountability; Performance Auditing; Sunshine Law

Efficiency Analysis   The quantitative and qualitative study of the expenses related to achieving specific goals. It is a critical part of any program planning, and it also is important in retrospective program evaluations. Efficiency analyses are critical in securing and maintaining funding for any program of intervention. A key idea in efficiency analysis is that evidence of program effect is insufficient; evidence of efficiency also is required.

The importance of efficiency analysis is obvious when one considers that resources are finite and the needs of systems almost always outstrip resources. As a result, planning and decisions regarding the expenditure of resources are typically guided by the rank ordering of needs and wants, an understanding of the available resources, and the expected and observed outcomes of programs that are designed to achieve the set goals. When resources are limited, it is desirable to choose those alternatives that are the least costly for reaching a particular objective or that have the largest impact per unit of cost. This is intuitively obvious because the most cost-effective solution will free up resources for other uses or allow a greater impact for any given investment in comparison with a less cost-effective solution.

Major types of efficiency analysis include cost-benefit analysis, return on investment (ROI), and cost-effectiveness analysis. All three of these assume that evidence of program effect is available and attempt to relate effect to benefits and costs in different ways. In cost-benefit analysis, the benefits and costs resulting from the program are identified and converted to monetary (e.g., dollar) units. Once this information is obtained, total costs are subtracted from total benefits to determine whether the program has a positive net benefit. Another way to compare costs and benefits is with a benefit-cost ratio (i.e., total dollar benefits divided by total dollar costs); a value of 1 is the break-even point, and values greater than 1 indicate positive program impact. ROI is a financial ratio of total benefits minus total costs divided by total costs. Values greater than 0 on the ROI index indicate a positive ROI. In cost-effectiveness analysis, costs are determined as in cost-benefit analysis (i.e., total dollar cost is determined), but benefits are not converted to monetary units. Cost-effectiveness ratios (total costs divided by total effects in natural units) are calculated to indicate the cost per unit of program output/effect. An effect-to-cost ratio also is informative and indicates how much program output/effect is obtained per dollar spent. If cost-benefit, cost-effectiveness, or ROI data are available for competing programs, then relative comparisons can be made, and the most efficient program across the set of programs can be selected for funding. ***See also*** Accountability (political science, sociology); School Audit

Efficient Market Hypothesis   A theory initially developed in the 1960s by E. F. Fama, M. C. Jensen, and R. Roll. Fama formalized the theory by publishing one of a series of papers on this theory that states that it is impossible to beat the stock market because all prices and information on the market are already incorporated in the price of a stock. Because a market is efficient, it incorporates all the relevant information instantaneously before an investor or speculator can beat the market. The efficient market hypothesis theory is a well-studied and documented theory in economics. There is widespread disagreement and controversy on this theory because some economists and investors believe that one can beat the market by mathematical trading and by building mathematical models. Some investors believe that by using charting—a form of technical analysis—one can predict the stock price. The efficient market theory, however, has an exception; that is, one can beat the market if one has insider information on the company stock. For example, if one knows before the market opens the next day that the company will announce a loss in earnings and that person buys the stock the day before, then that investor has beaten the market and the efficient market hypothesis does not hold. However, insider trading is illegal and is subject to heavy fines and a prison sentence. In addition to technical analysis and mathematical trading, there is a group of investors who believe that they can beat the market by applying value-based investment strategy. They reason that the value or price of an asset is the present value of its future stream of earnings or cash flow. Investors can search for stocks that are underpriced based on the present value of their future cash flows. Accordingly, these investors can beat the market, and the efficient market hypothesis does not hold. An efficient market exists when security prices reflect all available public information about the economy, the financial markets, and the targeted company. All new information is instantaneously captured, and therefore, this causes the prices of stocks to move randomly and makes it impossible to predict the randomness. This movement in prices is sometimes called a *random walk* because changes in the prices will not follow any defined pattern. Here is where technical analysts using charts claim that they can beat the market by "predicting the random walk" by charting the patterns. The efficient market hypothesis describes three forms of market efficiency: (1) weak-form efficiency, (2) semistrong efficiency, and (3) strong-form efficiency. The weak form states that the price of an asset incorporates all past or historical financial information about that stock. The semistrong states that all publicly available information is incorporated in the price of the stock, and the strong form states that the price of an asset incorporates all information—both public and private. For more information, see Fama, Fisher, Jensen, and Roll (1969), Ehrhardt and Brigham (2003), Emery, Finnerty, and Stowe (2004), and Smart, Megginson, and Gitman (2007). ***See also*** Insider Trading; Market

Egalitarian Society   A society that aims to minimize discrepancies between different social classes and to distribute wealth and power uniformly across these different classes. Egalitarian societies emphasize the importance of an equitable distribution of resources, as well as equality of rights and benefits among different social groups (according to gender, ethnicity, age, socioeconomic status, etc.). In egalitarian societies, all individuals are born equal, and all members of society are said to have a right to equal opportunities. These types of societies are often referred to as *classless societies*. *See also* Equal Educational Opportunity; Equality (political science); Equal Protection

Ego *(education)*   A Latin word meaning "I," which entered the psychology lexicon most pervasively through the work of Sigmund Freud. In his original formulation, ego referred to the conscious, rational mind, which managed the unconscious impulses originating from the biological drives of the id and socially based unconscious mandates of the superego. *See also* Id; Superego

Ego *(psychology)*   In psychoanalytic and psychodynamic theories, the *ego* is conceptualized as the conscious part of a tripartite personality (including the *id, ego,* and *superego*). The ego, which is not thought to be present at birth, develops over time and enables an individual to gratify the impulses of the id, or pleasure principle, through assistance of the superego, or conscience. The ego operates on the reality principle, as opposed to the pleasure principle, which governs the id, and allows the individual to express desires and drives in realistic and socially appropriate ways. In modern parlance, the word *ego* is also used to mean one's self-esteem or an inflated sense of self-worth. For more information, see Freud (1923). *See also* Id; Superego

Elaborative Rehearsal   A type of cognitive processing proposed by Craik and Lockhart's (1972) "Levels of Processing" model of memory. In contrast to maintenance rehearsal, which involves rote repetition of information in working memory, elaborative rehearsal involves the deep processing of material through the formation of associations, the grouping of material into categories, and the use of memory strategies to retain the information. Such deep semantic processing results in the production of durable memories. For more information, see Craik and Lockhart (1972). *See also* Memory Strategies

Elastic Clause   Also known as the *necessary and proper clause,* this clause refers to Article 1, Section 8, Clause 1.18 of the U.S. Constitution, which grants Congress the power "to make all laws which shall be necessary and proper for carrying into execution the foregoing powers, and all other powers vested by this Constitution in the government of the United States, or in any department or officer thereof." Legal scholars debate the extent of the authority granted to Congress under the elastic clause. One of the earliest cases in which the Supreme Court considered the extent of the elastic clause was in its decision in *McCulloch v. Maryland* (1819) to allow Congress the authority to establish a national bank. The Court held a broad interpretation of the clause, deeming it necessary and proper for Congress to establish the bank in order to carry out its powers of taxation and coining and borrowing money. For more information, see *McCulloch v. Maryland* (1819). *See also* Congress

Elasticity   A measure of responsiveness to changes in economic variables. It measures the effect of a percentage change in an economic variable on the percentage change of another economic variable. When the percentage change is measured over an arc, the elasticity coefficient is denoted as *arc elasticity*. If it is measured at a specific point, the elasticity coefficient is referred to as *point elasticity*.

There are four main types of elasticity coefficients in economics: (1) elasticity of demand, (2) elasticity of supply, (3) income elasticity, and (4) cross-price elasticity. Elasticity of demand measures the responsiveness of consumers to a price change, using the formula $\%\Delta Q_d/\%\Delta P$, where $\%\Delta Q_d$ is percentage change in quantity demanded and $\%\Delta P$ is percentage change in price. If the calculated elasticity coefficient is less than 1, demand is said to be price inelastic, meaning that the responsiveness of consumers to a price change is not that significant. Goods with inelastic demand have the potential of increasing the total revenue of sellers when their prices increase. This is normally the case for essential goods such as drugs.

If the calculated elasticity is greater than 1, demand is price elastic, and the response of consumers to a price change is substantial. The total revenue of sellers can easily decline if there is a price increase on goods with elastic demand. Demand tends to be price elastic when goods are inessential, require a substantial amount of income to be spent on them, and are easily substitutable. An infinitely elastic demand and a perfectly inelastic demand show an independent relationship between price and quantity.

The elasticity of supply can similarly be calculated, but with different implications. Elasticity of supply is more useful to determine time periods in the market; for example, the market period is a time when supply is perfectly inelastic and cannot be adjusted. In the short run, supply is relatively elastic and can be adjusted. The long run is a time period when supply is very elastic and inputs can be highly variable.

The income elasticity coefficient (the percentage change in the quantity of a good purchased in relation to a percentage change in income) is used to determine whether goods are normal (positive coefficient) or inferior (negative coefficient), and cross-price elasticity (the percentage change in the quantity of one good in relation to the percentage change in price of another good) is used to determine the substitutability or relationship of goods (positive coefficient for substitutes and negative coefficient for complements). For more information, see Boyes and Melvin (2002), Case and Fair (2003), McConnell and Brue (2008), and Salvatore (2002). *See also* Demand; Income; Perfect Competition; Price; Supply

Election A selection process whereby individuals compete for a specific role and to act in a designated capacity and wherein power and responsibility are bestowed, not necessarily for the greatest good. Elections consist of formalized rules governing participation of all actors involved. There are numerous electoral systems, though the prevailing view is categorized by voter representation. Such systems include plurality majority systems and proportional representation systems. For more information, see Endersby and Krieckhaus (2008). *See also* Representative Democracy

Electoral College The system in the United States under which the president and the vice president are elected. The people of each state do not vote directly for the president, instead they vote for electors, who then vote for president. Electors are generally chosen by their state political party; the number of electors per state is proportional to the state's representation in Congress. Electors are not bound to vote according to popular vote under constitutional or federal law, but a majority of the states require them to do so. The legal basis of the electoral system is in the U.S. Constitution; a constitutional amendment would be required to change the process. Over the past 200 years, 700 such proposed amendments have been submitted to Congress. It is rare that the electoral and the popular votes do not match, but it has occurred in the 1800, 1824, 1876, and 2000 presidential elections. *See also* Election

Electroconvulsive Therapy (ECT) A controversial psychiatric treatment in which seizures are induced for therapeutic purposes. Although widely used in the 1940s and 1950s to treat psychiatric disorders, today ECT is used most often to treat severe, treatment-refractory major depression. It is less frequently, though also successfully, used in the treatment of mania and schizophrenia. ECT is rarely, if ever, the first line of treatment; its use is more typical in severe cases where symptoms do not remit with other therapeutic interventions. ECT is usually administered in a course of 6 to 12 treatments, up to several times a week. The exact mechanism of action of ECT remains unknown, but it appears that ECT increases brain-derived neurotrophic factor (BDNF) in drug-resistant depressed patients. BDNF is a protein that stimulates the growth and differentiation of new neurons and synapses. ECT has been shown to be an effective treatment for many patients, and many report both short- and long-term improvements in their quality of life. Side effects include confusion and memory loss for events around the time period of treatment. ECT is not thought, however, to cause long-term brain damage. Nonetheless, certain types of ECT have been associated with persistent memory loss. Informed consent is a standard of modern ECT, and involuntary ECT treatment is uncommon in countries that adhere to contemporary standards of medical care. *See also* Depression (psychology)

Electroencephalograph (EEG) The most widely used brain-imaging technology in neurology and neuroscience research. EEG is the recording of the brain's electrical activity through electrodes attached to the scalp. In clinical use, the EEG is thought to provide gross anatomical correlates of brain activity and is the primary tool for the diagnosis of epilepsy. EEG technology is also used to record event-related potentials, which are electrical activity in the brain that follows the presentation of an external sensory stimulus.

Electronic Media Forms of communication and transmission of information that use electronics to deliver the content to a user. Electronic form of transmission means that electrical energy can be used to move the content simultaneously and consistently to many users at the same time. It also means that information can be conveyed and retrieved in nonmaterial forms. Some common forms of electronic media include the telegraph, telephone, television, radio, and computers. Some forms of electronic media rely on information recorded on materials such as videotape, audio CDs, or film and are translated for use or viewing on electronic media devices. These material forms of storage are referred to as analog media because they use wave signals to capture and store information or, as with film, they use light and chemical reactions to transform a physical medium for later translation by an electronic device. Digital media, on the other hand, are stored in the form of digital codes, arrangements of ones and zeroes to represent information. However, the term *digital media* is now also used to refer to various forms of information recording on magnetic tape, such as those used in digital video cameras. Analog photography refers to cameras that use light-sensitive emulsions on a plastic film, while digital photography refers to the capture of image information on memory devices such as flash drives or cards. Analog-to-digital transfers make information more easily transmitted by electronic media and also create questions about copyright. Digital or electronic publishing of text, images, and music are widely practiced. For more information, see Kroker and Kroker (1997) and Negroponte (1995). *See also* Copyright; Hypermedia; Media; Media, New; Television and Social Behavior

Electronic Monitoring A sanction designed to incapacitate criminal offenders while permitting them to remain in communities through the use of surveillance technologies. Active electronic monitors, such as the bracelet and global positioning satellite (GPS) transmitters, send continuous signals reporting offender location back to a central command center. Electronic monitoring is sometimes used in conjunction with house arrest. *See also* Community-Based Corrections; House Arrest

Electroshock Therapy   A method of treating depression that involves medically induced seizures. It is now reserved for treating recurrent, severe, and drug/psychotherapy-resistant forms of depression. Electroshock therapy has been shown to reduce depressive symptoms, though the effect is often short-lived. Modern methods minimize risks, though concerns persist regarding its effect on memory. *See also* Depression (education)

Elementary Education   The first phase of compulsory schooling, which provides a foundation in central academic disciplines such as reading, mathematics, and science. While starting age and duration of elementary education vary among countries, in general, it starts at age five or six and continues for six or seven years.

Elite Theory   A theory that posits that irrespective of the form of government, a privileged few (elites) will always control the state. Classic elite theory is based in part on the works of Robert Michels, Gaetano Mosca, and Vilfredo Pareto.

Modern elite theorists have expanded the application of elite theory distinguishing political elites and providing an analysis to understanding the ways in which elite groups differentiate and proliferate to maintain power. Political elites radically affect national political outcomes by their status of authority in influential organizations, movements, or social groups. The authoritative status may be given based on merit or be taken by right or might. Some argue that for proliferation to occur, elite groups must compete for mass support and, in doing so, give each citizen greater political participation or the perception of participating.

Modern elite theorists (other than the above) include C. Wright Mills, Floyd Hunter, James Burnham, Robert D. Putnam, John Higley, and Michael Burton. For more information, see Svanikier (2007). *See also* Pluralism (political science)

Emancipation   A concept that is an extension of the discussion relating to citizenship. Political emancipation refers to having the full and absolute rights inherently possessed by a citizen of a nation-state during a particular period in history, regardless of the individual's characteristics (i.e., physical) or status (i.e., social). Simply stated, who you are as a private individual is completely separate from who you are as a political individual (citizen).

One of the most influential works in the theory of emancipation was written by Karl Marx. His work "On the Jewish Question" argues that it is foolish, though an important first step, to ground emancipation and seek it in the political structures because it offers only an illusion of freedom, wherein freedom is a mechanism of bourgeois control. Marx states that individuals are not truly emancipated until the individual can recognize that there is only an abstract separation of private and political individual and that to be truly emancipated, one cannot separate the two identities abstractly. One must be recognized as a whole, and only then can the

individual reach true emancipation, which he terms *human emancipation*. In historical and practical terms, in U.S. history, the term refers to the emancipation of humans from slavery as embodied in the Thirteenth Amendment to the Constitution. This amendment was ratified in 1865 and was preceded by President Abraham Lincoln's Emancipation Proclamations in 1862 and 1863. Emancipation is also a legal instrument by which minors are emancipated from the control of their parents when they reach the age of majority or through marriage or other means. For more information, see Kouvelaskis (2005). *See also* Equality (political science); Marxism (political science)

Embargo   An economic sanction used by one nation against another in an act to denounce a specific policy or deed enacted by the other, theoretically providing an impetus for change. It is generally considered a containment strategy, and as such, the embargo can continue for as long as it takes to bring about the change. In both academic and political arenas, its efficacy is often debated.

Historically, in the United States, the use of the sanction began with President Thomas Jefferson in the Embargo Act of 1807. Jefferson saw it as an alternative to war and argued that it provided both social and military benefits to the initiator. Although he may have seen the embargo as a moral necessity to condemn the actions of belligerent nations, it was an economic disaster for the fledging economy and was one of the more spectacular failures of Jefferson's presidency.

Perhaps the longest-standing embargo to date, enacted by the United States, is the embargo against Cuba, which began in 1962. The embargo continues to punish Cuba for the expropriation of property owned by U.S. nationals in Cuba, without compensation, and arguably was used to contain the spread of communism throughout Latin America. It remains in effect mainly because of the political pressure by anticommunists and the Cuban community in the United States. For more information, see Foley (1900) and Smith (1998). *See also* Economic Sanctions

Emic and Etic Perspectives   Two perspectives of reality used when investigating a social system—commonly used in ethnography. "Emic" is an insider's view of a behavior, system, or culture and presents a native, local, culture-bound position. An emic account is one that is idiographic, one that accurately represents the multiple realities of the members of a specific community. "Etic," on the other hand, is an outsider's viewpoint and generally presents a nomothetic perspective, one that is abstract, culturally neutral, and scientific. An etic account represents the view of the trained observer or researcher. For more information, see Fetterman (1997). *See also* Ethnography (education)

Eminent Domain   A government's right to claim private property if intended for public use (e.g., schools, parks, highways, etc.). The government can only exert this right if the owner of the property is given fair compensation, based on market value.

Emotional Communication   A theory that focuses primarily on how the emotions affect communication between people and organizations. Research in this area includes examining how communicative partners convey or transmit content or the substance of messages through emotions. For example, facial expressions have been studied as a way of communication since the 19th century with the work of Bell (1844) and Duchenne (1867/1990). Charles Darwin (1872/1965) took previous work further and analyzed how facial muscles lent to emotional expression or communication. More recent studies have focused on how we perceive fear, happiness, excitement, anxiety, and other emotional states through body language, expressions, and the patterns of response to certain external or internal stimuli. Many studies treat emotions as an independent variable that influences the communication process (e.g., Burleson & Planalp, 2000). Specific emotions can affect different behaviors. For example, anxiety can affect a job interview or a public speech. All researchers, however, agree that understanding various human emotions is critical in appreciating the dynamics of the mutual interaction between people in both singular and multiple settings, as well as in and between different cultures. For more information, see Bell (1844), Burleson and Planalp (2000), Darwin (1872/1965), and Duchenne (1867/1990). *See also* Communication

Emotional Development   The aspect of human development that refers to the progression of one's capability to express, regulate, and control one's emotions. Emotions are feelings brought into consciousness by a thought or event. They can be positive, such as happiness and excitement, or negative, such as sadness or fear. Emotional development begins during infancy and extends through adulthood. It is usually conceptualized as part of social development and is related to cognition and psychological well-being. Achieving successful emotional development is identified in terms of demonstrating prosocial behaviors. *See also* Attachment Theory; Language Development

Emotional Intelligence   The ability to perceive and manage one's emotions and to get along with others. The term first appeared in the work of Payne (1985), was further researched by Salovey and Mayer (1990), and was popularized by Goleman (1995). Although it originates within one's self, emotional intelligence (EI) is expressed when interacting with others. EI has four facets: (1) sensing (internal, physiological, and cognitive) and naming one's own feelings (external, learned from social cues); (2) recognizing behaviors associated with emotions; (3) managing or manipulating one's own emotional behavior; and (4) manipulating, influencing, or controlling the emotions of others. These facets are not in stages and are not inherently positive or negative. They occur concurrently and require constant cognitive processing. For more information, see Goleman (1995),

Mayer and Salovey (1993), Payne (1985), and Salovey and Mayer (1990).

Empathetic Listening   A kind of listening similar to active listening in that it requires sensitivity on the part of the listener. Beyond that, empathetic listening calls for the listener to express a perception of what the speaker is saying. An empathetic listener makes a habit of understanding someone else before expecting that he or she will be understood in return.

Empathetic listening does not involve pity or sympathy; it calls for the ability to comprehend another person's spoken and unspoken thoughts and attitudes and to relay them back. An empathetic listener asks questions to demonstrate his or her involvement and to reinforce the speaker's perspective.

In the 1950s, the psychotherapist Carl Rogers defined empathetic listening as the accurate perception of another person's internal frame of reference, and he hailed the empathetic listener as the catalyst for furthering understanding between people. He deemed empathetic listening to be the most potent approach that a psychotherapist could take to help someone in therapy improve his or her personality, relationships, and ability to communicate with others. Writing for a more general audience in the *Harvard Business Review* in 1951, he suggested that his readers try listening with understanding when they find themselves arguing with a spouse, a friend, or a small group of people, by encouraging each person involved to restate the ideas and feelings of another—accurately and to each speaker's satisfaction.

In addition to the field of psychotherapy, empathetic listening has been recommended as an effective communications tool in fields such as education, nursing, sales, and marketing. For more information, see Rogers (1959) and Rogers and Roethlisberger (1951/1991). *See also* Active Listening; Empathy; Evaluative Listening; Passive Listening

Empathy   The ability to understand and sympathize with another's experiences without actually being subjected to these experiences. Individuals with highly developed empathy are extremely sensitive to the feelings and experiences of others. Empathy is often referred to as the ability to put oneself in another person's situation.

Empathy–Altruism Hypothesis   A hypothesis put forth by Batson in the late 1990s, which maintains that people will be more likely to help those for whom they feel empathy without receiving something in return. Such help is proportionate to the empathy experienced and can be provided even at great cost to the helper. Without empathy, we are motivated by external reward. Nonetheless, this hypothesis does not necessarily presuppose that empathy results in altruism, as the reward for helping can be many and can include relief of distress from watching another person suffer. For more information, see Batson (1998). *See also* Empathy

E

Empirical   A type of research that is based on information collected through observation or experiment rather than theory. Empirical studies aim to objectively test and investigate specific research questions or hypotheses through verifiable methods. Empirical research implies that it is possible to measure the outcome variable and, by the same token, to test and prove (or disprove) any given hypothesis. Empirical research can be quantitative or qualitative in nature. Studies of a quantitative nature tend to involve numbers, data, and statistical methods. Studies of a qualitative nature generally offer more in-depth information. It is often argued that the depth of information obtained through empirical studies of a qualitative nature compensates for their limited ability to generalize results. ***See also*** Empiricism; Qualitative Research; Quantitative Research

Empiricism   The epistemological view that knowledge must originate in sensory experience. Empiricists deny that knowledge may originate through nonsensory channels such as intuition or innateness. The scope of empiricism can vary. For instance, concept empiricism maintains that sense experience is our only source of our knowledge of concepts. Belief empiricism maintains that all propositional knowledge, that is, knowledge expressible in sentences that can be true or false, must originate in experience. ***See also*** Essentialism; Idealism; Ontology

Empiricist   Tradition   Although elements of empiricist thinking can be traced to philosophers from the earliest times, empiricism proper is said to have emerged as a formal philosophical position from the 17th to 19th centuries with the work of John Locke, George Berkeley, David Hume, and John Stuart Mill. In the 20th century, empiricism influenced the work of George Russell and G. E. Moore and led to the development of analytic philosophy. Empiricism stands in opposition to the rationalism of continental European philosophy, most notably the philosophy of René Descartes, which asserts the innateness of ideas and their independence from physical experience. Deriving from the Greek word for experience, empiricism asserts that all theories must be justified by observation and experiment. Some propositions, however, seem self-evident and in need of no empirical verification—such as "All bachelors are unmarried." Empiricism allows for these exceptions in the deductive sciences of mathematics and logic. Thus, without any experiment, one can assert that the square of the length of the hypotenuse equals the sum of the squares of the lengths of the other two sides. Such propositions are, however, fundamentally tautological, for their conclusions are embedded within their initial terms, and therefore, they do not offer new knowledge. The deductive sciences cannot then tell us about how the world actually works. The empiricist tradition maintains that any knowledge worth having must be verified by observation and experiment and that all knowledge ultimately derives from sensation. The requirement of experiment renders knowledge probable rather than certain and always subject to revision in light of new knowledge. Even though the same experiment performed countless times yields the same result, there is no reason why one more iteration of the test should not produce a different result and modify the hypothesis. The empiricist tradition remains skeptical of dogmatic assertion and is open-minded to the possibility of new theories. ***See also*** Critical Theory; Empiricism; Logical Positivism; Materiality; Positivism

Empowerment   Any act, policy, or process that enhances fairness and equity toward or reverses discrimination against marginalized individuals or groups, such as those defined by economic status, race, ethnicity, language, religion, or gender. Empowerment processes increase the self-determination of individuals and groups. ***See also*** Empowerment Evaluation

Empowerment   Evaluation   A type of program evaluation in which program participants evaluate their own programs, often with the advice of an outside evaluator. The purpose of this kind of evaluation is not to judge whether the program's funding should be continued; rather, it is to help program participants better accomplish their own goals. ***See also*** Process Evaluation

Encoder   A mechanism or person who converts a message or information into a code. It is also a device that is used to change a signal (message) into a code. The code can compress information for storage or transmission to another site. An encoder can be used to translate codes. ***See also*** Decoder

Encoding   The process of transforming information from one format to another. Decoding is the opposite of encoding. In cognition, encoding is a basic perceptual process of interpreting incoming stimuli. Technically speaking, it is a complex, multistage process of converting relatively objective sensory input, such as light and sound, into a subjectively meaningful experience.

Character encoding is a code that pairs a set of natural language characters. This includes the use of an alphabet with a set of something else, such as numbers. This can also include electrical impulses.

Text encoding uses a markup language to tag the structure and other features of a text in order to facilitate processing by computers. Semantics encoding of formal language is a method of representing all terms used in the language. For example, this is done in programs or descriptions of language. Encryption transforms information for use in secret missions. A person can compress a video file using a codec to transmit the file in a very short period of time. For more information, see Dyson (1999). ***See also*** Encoder

Encoding   Specificity   A principle, proposed by Thompsen and Tulving in 1973, that specifies that there is a relationship between the contextual setting at the time one encodes a memory and the contextual cues available at the time one later recalls that memory. Specifically, recall memory is better if the setting or cues available at encoding are available when recall is required. For example, students might do better on an exam taken in the same room where they learned the material. Tulving suggested that the probability of successful retrieval of a memory increases as a function of the overlap between the information present at retrieval and the information stored in memory. For more information, see Tulving and Thomson (1973). *See also* Memory (psychology)

Enculturation *(communication)*   The process of becoming a member of a particular culture by learning the rules, values, and expectations of that culture. Every cultural group has a process for passing on its cultural practices and beliefs to those born into it or those who join it through marriage, adoption, or other means. Humans depend on this sharing of their learned traditions since culture is not passed on genetically. The job of culture is to make explicit the categories that are important to know, show how these categories create the desired order, define the elements of disorder that could threaten the culture, and communicate this to members of the culture through symbols, rituals, language, and behavior. Humans learn the limits of acceptable and expected behavior in their group as well as the consequences of stepping outside the boundaries of what is acceptable. The enculturation of children takes place from birth through child-rearing practices, educational systems, play, rituals, language, and the behavior of other members of the culture. It is a system of taken-for-granted practices that are considered acceptable ways to bind children to their cultural system, habituating them to these practices. An enculturated human will have culturally appropriate behavior that he or she generally accepts as correct and desirable. The enculturation of adults is usually more direct and requires the additional step of transforming the adult from being the member of one culture to being the member of the new one. For more information, see Barrett (1984). *See also* Construction of Reality; Culture (education, sociology); Ethnocentrism (education); Linguistic Differences

Enculturation *(sociology)*   Occurs when the values, norms, and practices advocated by a given culture are adopted by an individual or group. Enculturation is a form of socialization or assimilation into a culture. This cultural transmission of customs and values is particularly relevant among groups who are in the process of being initiated to a given culture, such as children or individuals who immigrate to a foreign country. For instance, various studies have investigated processes by which young children learn the values of the culture that they are exposed to. Other research has explored how immigrants assimilate into the culture of their host country, as well as the effect of the socialization process on economic, educational, and social conditions. *See also* Cultural Assimilation; Cultural Values; Socialization

Endocrine System   A system of ductless glands, integrated within the central nervous system, which regulate the secretion of hormones. The major glands that form the endocrine system are the hypothalamus, pituitary, thyroid, parathyroid, adrenal, pineal, and sex glands (ovaries in females and testes in males). The pancreas can also be considered part of the endocrine system given that they produce digestive enzymes. In general, the endocrine system regulates processes that occur slowly, such as growth and development. The endocrine system is integral in regulating mood, tissue function, metabolism, and reproductive processes. Hormones travel from the endocrine glands to target cells via the bloodstream. In addition to target cells, specialized proteins in the blood bind to some secreted hormones, to aid in controlling hormone levels. In a healthy endocrine system, secretion is regulated to maintain the necessary level. Disorders of the endocrine system result in too much or too little production of necessary hormones. *See also* Hormones; Hypothalamus

Endorphin   Naturally occurring peptides with opioid properties, produced by the pituitary gland and the hypothalamus during strenuous exercise or other extreme physical or emotional excitation. Endorphins bind to opiate receptor sites in the brain and can produce pain relief and a sense of mild euphoria.

Energy   A system's capacity to do work. While energy is not visible, it is essential to all daily activities and takes on several different forms. The two main forms are known as kinetic and potential energy. Kinetic energy, sometimes referred to as movable energy, refers to the energy a moving object has from its motion. Some of the common known forms of kinetic energy include electrical and thermal energy and sound. Potential energy is energy that is stored in an object. Its name is derived from its ability to change into other forms of energy. Common types of potential energy include chemical and nuclear energy. The two primary sources of energy are renewable and nonrenewable sources. Renewable sources, such as solar energy, are easily replenished, whereas nonrenewable sources, such as petroleum, are limited. These two sources of energy are converted to provide essential secondary sources of energy. The supply and use of both chemical energy and nuclear energy are politically contentious in national and global political and economic relations, and such supplies have been subject to manipulation by energy companies (e.g., the Enron scandal of 2001).

English and Language Arts   The study and manipulation of the interdependent components and procedures of the human communication system, including the active processes of listening, reading, speaking, writing, and thinking. The study of English involves the mechanics and conventions of the language arts and may include the study of literature. Thinking underlies all the processes because the learner is either adding to content knowledge or expressing knowledge.

English as a Second Language (ESL)   English learned or used in English-speaking countries, such as the United States and Britain, by immigrants and ethnic minorities, whose first language is not English. In this context, English is the dominant language for administration, commerce, and education, and therefore, learners need English for social and/or academic survival. In the case of ESL, students need English language skills to master core academic subjects. This concept also is used in former British colonies in Asia and Africa, where English is not the first language of any group. *See also* Foreign-Language Education

Entertainment Media   Both the forms of media whose general purpose is to engage viewers' attention and serve as a means of diversion, escape, gratification, or relaxation as well as the vehicle of those forms. In the first usage, examples include television programs, film, consumer magazines, novels, Web sites, computer games, music, "soft" feature news, political talk radio, and, in some circumstances, advertisements. In the second usage, the term may refer to the physical magazine, book, CD, or DVD that contains the entertainment content. Streaming video and computer games are virtual vehicles of this usage of the term. The line between the two usages can be quite fine given that, for example, television is a medium of entertainment and television itself delivers entertainment media.

Though *entertainment media* as a whole describes those outlets that are commonly differentiated from news or information media, news about celebrities and other types of "soft" feature stories, for instance, would likely fall under the category of entertainment. Entertainment media are outlets for the expression of popular culture and as such are subject to stigmatization, possibly criticized for pandering to the masses. The blurring of the line between news and entertainment can have an impact on factual information. The cable channel Comedy Central's program *The Daily Show* offers an example of entertainment that parodies a news program and has been touted as a common source—especially for young adults—of actual news information. Advertising, too, is often enjoyed for its entertainment value alone and is increasingly produced with such consumption in mind. *See also* Infotainment; Mass Media

Entitlement   A legislation that establishes the legal obligation of the U.S. federal government to provide benefits to all persons, units of government, or other entities that meet the eligibility criteria set forth in the authorizing legislation. Social Security, Medicare, and Food Stamps are examples of some of the better-known entitlement programs. Congress generally controls entitlement programs by establishing eligibility criteria and benefit or payment rules in the authorizing legislation—not by providing budget authority in an appropriation act such as that which funds discretionary spending. The only way to limit who gets entitlement funding is for Congress to change the eligibility rules.

Entitlement Programs   In the budgetary process, the term refers to those programs that provide financial benefits to the public. Eventually, the public feels "entitled" to receiving these moneys under these programs, and legislators may attempt to drastically revise them only at the expense of their own political careers. Once passed into law, the programs become mandatory, do not need reauthorization, and give those who meet the qualifications a legal right to receive the benefits. The most important entitlement programs in the United States are Social Security, Medicare, Medicaid, federal retirement plans, and support to agriculture. The past several presidential administrations have proposed curbing the latter, but interest groups usually ensure that such legislative proposals are defeated. In the political economy, such programs cause problems because they eat up one half to two thirds of the yearly budget and make it difficult for the government to plan and fund new programs. *See also* Entitlement

Entrapment   A situation wherein a law enforcement officer persuades or encourages an individual to engage in a criminal offense that he or she would otherwise not engage in. Entrapment may be used as a defense against criminal charges. The defendant must prove that his or her involvement in the offense would not have occurred in the absence of the law enforcement officer's influence. *See also* Defense

Enumerated Powers   A set of rules found in Article 1, Section 8 of the U.S. Constitution, which limits the authority of Congress to those powers enumerated in the Constitution. The power of Congress is not to exceed these.

According to the enumerated powers, Congress has the right to (1) impose taxes; (2) pay debts; (3) borrow money; (4) regulate foreign and domestic commerce; (5) regulate currency and therefore institute punishments for defrauding the U.S. government; (6) promote development of the arts and sciences, therefore securing patented rights; (7) establish a court system; (8) set up roads and post offices; (9) establish rules and punishments for international offenses; (10) declare war; (11) maintain both structural (rules, recruitment, etc.) and financial support of the armed forces; and (12) make laws that are "necessary and proper." For more information, see The Constitution of the United States of America (2008). *See also* Constitution (political science)

Environment *(geography)*   Also known in science as the natural environment, it encompasses all conditions that affect living organisms. Essentially, a combination of all the surroundings of an organism, the environment comprises physical, biological, and chemical factors. These include all things that are living and nonliving. Living components include plants, animals, and human beings, and nonliving components include air, land, and water. All these surroundings interact to influence organisms, and it is the totality of the interactions that form the environment and contribute to the survival, development, and depletion of living organisms. It is essential to protect the environment, as it is the life support system for all living things. Environmental movements ("Green Parties" and the like) have garnered political and some legal strength since President Richard Nixon created the Environmental Protection Agency in 1970.

Environment *(sociology)* The circumstances, objects, individuals, beings, or other influences surrounding an individual. In the field of sociology, the environment surrounding an individual consists of the social and cultural characteristics that are likely to exert an impact on an individual's (or a group of individuals') behaviors and thoughts and to shape the dynamics between the members of the group or between the individual and his or her surroundings. An environment implies the presence of conditions or influences that are in close proximity and directly related to the individual. Family, school, and work are examples of environments that are in close proximity to the individual and that are likely to affect cognitive patterns and behaviors.

Environmental Determinism The idea that the physical environment decides culture (also known as *geographical determinism*). Popular in the early 20th century, the tenets of environmental determinism stand in stark contrast to the idea that social forces determine culture. Environmental determinism found momentum with the introduction of Darwin's theory of evolution, and while it enjoyed a period of popularity, it was heavily criticized for having racist and supremacist implications. After environmental determinism fell out of favor, it was replaced with a more subtle implication of environmental influence, one that acknowledged environmental possibilism. Now seen as a theory ridden with flawed overtones, environmental determinism has been replaced in the field mainly with the idea that social forces shape culture.

Environmental Economics The study of the use and management of scarce environmental resources. These resources are usually endangered and nonrenewable or irreplaceable. Environmental resources constitute land, air, and water.

Environmental issues include endangered elephants and tigers; pollution and increased levels of carbon monoxide (which leads to asphyxiation problems); global warming and increasing sea levels; logging, which results in flooding and erosion of land; and the dumping of toxic materials into the ocean (which endangers and destroys oceanic life).

Environmental economics deals extensively with three major economic decisions confronting economic agents: (1) what to produce given the limited environmental resources so that the environment can be preserved, (2) how to produce for current optimal consumption without compromising future growth and development (sustainable development), and (3) for whom to produce.

The third question usually involves equity issues relating to humans, particularly those with limited income who are priced out of markets. From a broader environmental perspective, the third question takes a global dimension to include consideration of the welfare of fauna, which is also contingent on the flora, and the welfare of those nations that are poor and trying belatedly to increase national income (to converge) without the technology that is crucial to forestalling environmental degradation.

Environmental economics therefore involves an understanding of the process of environmental degradation and designing environmental policies to mitigate or halt the damage to the environment. Effective policy making depends on finding out the causes of environmental degradation and how to target these causes to reduce their effects.

The motives for environmental degradation can be classified under three broad categories: (1) accessibility to environmental resources or lack of restraint (the tragedy of global commons), (2) poverty, and (3) disequilibrium between profit maximization and social responsibility.

Domestic and international policies currently lay emphasis on preservation through reservations and the outlaw of trade in animal parts of endangered species. For example, in 1972, the United States passed the Endangered Species Act to protect animals that are in danger of extinction. The Convention on International Trade in Endangered Species (CITES) has been instrumental in regulating the international trade of animal parts from Africa and Asia.

In poor areas of the world with corrupt officials and lax law enforcement situations, the indigent turn to the environment as an immediate source of income by cutting down trees for fuel and engaging in the poaching of animals for income. The slashing and burning of trees intensifies air pollution.

In the United States and across the globe, laws have been enacted and treaties ratified to minimize environmental degradation in the process of maximizing corporate profit. U.S. federal statutes classify hazardous materials; stipulate transportation storage, emission, and disposal requirements; and call for prompt disclosure of exposure to hazardous materials. These statutes could be found under Titles 15, 33, and 42 of the U.S. Code (USC). Examples include The Clean Air Act of 1970; Ocean Dumping Act, 1972; Toxic Substances Act, 1976; and The Oil Pollution Act of 1990.

International treaties such as the Kyoto Protocol (2005) are policy measures to reduce the emission of pollutants believed to be causing global warming. Other treaties pointedly inveigh against dumping into the seas. For more information, see Field and Field (2006). ***See also*** Economics; Equity (economics, political science); Externality; Regulation (economics, public administration)

Environmentalism A movement based on preserving the natural environment. Unlike conservationism, which occurs in observable places and conceives of clear boundaries, environmentalism protects things not easily seen, such as the air. The environmental movement has existed in the United States since the 19th century. The movement has since turned from a desire to protect the earth's resources to a cause based on influencing the moral choices of American consumers and pushing for ethical practices in both government and business.

The environmental movement began in earnest during the Industrial Revolution in the United States, when fears of overindustrialization prompted a drive to undo the harms of modern civilization. This movement, however, did not gain in strength until the 1960s, when the concern for the environment turned into an organized effort.

In the 1960s and 1970s, Congress passed legislation to preserve natural resources such as air, water, land, and animals. In 1970, President Richard Nixon established the Environmental Protection Agency to consolidate tasks related to the environment that were currently executed by other agencies. In 1972, the first international Earth Summit was held in Stockholm, Sweden. This meeting addressed the environmental effects of industrialization, such as acid rain and oil tanker spills. Subsequent meetings focused on issues such as global warming, depletion of the ozone layer, landfills, ecotourism, renewable energy sources, and the unequal distribution of wealth caused by the exploitation of natural resources across the planet. ***See also*** Conservationism

Environmental Perception   An individual's perceptions about his or her surrounding environment (also known as *environmental geography*). This view is concerned with subjective rather than objective reality, as it is the perception that serves as the focal point. Environmental geographers are concerned with how perceptions are formed and how they influence an individual's decision-making process. Environmental activism gained momentum in the late 1960s and provided an impetus for the close study of environmental geography. Using human attitudes and responses to natural hazards has become a popular method for developing environmental impact assessments. Studies involving environmental perception have become an important and well-recognized method for developing environmental policies. ***See also*** Environment (geography)

Epidemiology   The study of how a disease originates and spreads in any given population and/or time period. Epidemiologists seek to establish factors that are associated with disease (risk factors) as well as factors that may protect from disease (protective factors). Epidemiological studies do not always establish causation but can identify correlations between a given factor and a higher or lower incidence of disease in a population. Such research is important in informing public health policy for the prevention and treatment of disease.

Epistemology   The study of knowledge, justification, and rationality. There are several areas of epistemological investigation. One is what kinds of knowledge there may be, such as propositional knowledge or knowledge *that* such and such is the case, and knowledge by acquaintance. Another area studies the structure of justification, such as whether justification must rest on foundations or whether it may include coherence considerations. Epistemologists also investigate the nature of knowledge itself, whether, for instance, it is more than justified true belief, and the thesis of skepticism, which claims that there is no knowledge at all. ***See also*** Knowledge

Epoch   A given period in history or in an individual's life characterized by significant or memorable developments or events. An epoch highlights an important turning point in time. For instance, one may make reference to an epoch of recession, epoch of imperialism, epoch of warfare, and so on. An epoch is a subdivision of a period.

Equal Educational Opportunity   The egalitarian ideal that all students should receive full access to the same high-standard academic curriculum to enable them to achieve social and economic success. Although it is not a guarantee of individual success in a meritocratic society, equal educational opportunity is nonetheless considered a fundamental requirement for democratic schooling.

Equality *(political science)*   Thomas Jefferson wrote, "All men are created equal" and stated that "an equal application of law to every condition of man is fundamental." Since then, the discourse on equality has remained fixed on these concepts. Equality amounted to equal treatment under the law. However, the terms *equality* and *law* have come under increased scrutiny. The idea of legal impartiality compounded what was understood as equality. The debate centered on an individual's opportunity to participate effectively in any aspect of society. Equality, therefore, was defined as the availability of given opportunities to all members of society regardless of the individual's choice to act on the given opportunity. One cannot assume legal impartiality, and it alone is not sufficient. The law, static in many regards, limits the range of opportunities and choices an individual with different beliefs, cultural background, gender, and sexual orientation can make.

The current debates conceptualizing equality center on what it means to have an opportunity, examining if the opportunity given allows for equal choices to act or if it is a reflection of a set of multifaceted justifications for unequal treatment. Issues around this area range from genetic cloning rights to same-sex marriage. Some of the more perspicuous philosophers think that providing a set of political conditions and liberties in which one can pursue social and economic goals is sufficient for a democratic, rights-oriented, society. For more information, see Allen (2007) and Foley (1900). ***See also*** Equal Protection; Natural Rights

Equality *(public administration)*   Although a seemingly simple idea, this concept has garnered a considerable amount of philosophical and practical debate. In theory, equality demands that all responsible agents be treated similarly. Of course, what such similarity entails and in what manner it should be allocated have long divided social scientists. While some advocate an equality of opportunity (that everyone should start from the same basic playing field), others have demanded an equality of outcome (that true equality is only reached when everyone has the same social and economic placement). Furthermore, although (at least in the Western world) the idea of racial, religious, and sexual equality is nearly universally accepted, debates continue on whether this equality should be privately or publicly (i.e., governmentally) enforced. Thus, while state advocates often argue the necessity of government intervention in maintaining equal rights, their opponents stress that forcefully promoting equality may inherently undermine individual freedom. For more information, see Honderich (2005). **See also** Equal Educational Opportunity; Morality

Equal Protection   A clause, included in the Fourteenth Amendment of the U.S. Constitution, stipulating that the law must be applied uniformly across all members of society, irrespective of gender, ethnicity, class, age, health, or any other trait. For instance, the clause maintains that all individuals should have access to the same legal services (which includes access to the law, to lawyers, to courts, etc.) and that there should be fair and equitable treatment of all individuals who come into contact with the legal system. In sum, equal protection of the law advocates objective, unbiased, equal, and fair treatment of all members of society by the law. **See also** Constitution; Equality (political science)

Equal Rights Amendment (ERA)   A proposed amendment to the Constitution of the United States that aims at securing equality for women before the law. The Equal Rights Amendment was introduced in 1923 by Alice Paul, a lifelong women's political activist of the National Woman's Party. It was preceded by the Nineteenth Amendment, which secured equal suffrage for women in 1920.

To this date, the ERA has not been ratified by the U.S. Congress, although every year since 1982 the amendment has been reintroduced in Congress. Attempts to pass the ERA have been failing since 1920 (the year women won the right to vote), partly due to the conservative backlash against women, although at times, it has gained support. In 1940, for example, the ERA was backed by the Republican Party. In 1970, the National Organization for Women (NOW) became responsible for promoting ERA, and only two years later, the House of Representatives and the Senate passed ERA as the proposed Twenty-Seventh Amendment to the Constitution. That same year, in 1972, 22 states ratified it, of the

38 needed to make the amendment law. In 1973, only 8 states signed on, and by 1976, support halted. Right-wing leaders such as Phyllis Schlafly argued that the amendment would take away rights such as spousal support and that women would be sent into combat, among other objections. In addition, many states' rights advocates feared that the ERA would strengthen federal power over local jurisdictions. Fundamentalist religious groups also opposed the ERA. On June 30, 1982, the final, extended deadline for ratifying the ERA passed, with only 35 of the required 38 states having ratified it. In 2007, in the 110th Congress, the amendment was reintroduced as S. J. Res. 10 (Senator Edward Kennedy, Massachusetts), and H. J. Res. 40 (Rep. Carolyn Maloney, New York). The sponsors did not include any deadline in the ratification process, but so far, little attention has been paid to the legislation.

Despite its defeat, the movement for the ERA contributed to important revisions in American law. During the 1970s, feminist legislators helped write new laws addressing discrimination in the Social Security system, in banking and credit, and in educational funding. Women's groups have mounted court and legislative challenges to the ratification deadline. The most recent is based on the "Madison Amendment," which is now the Twenty-Seventh Amendment and was passed after a 203-year period. Under this argument, the ratification process is ongoing, with no deadline, and when the needed three states approve the amendment, the ERA would become the Twenty-Eighth Amendment to the Constitution. Not all agree, however, and the legal argument continues.

The ERA has also had a lasting impact on women's lives in the United States as it provided a focal point for the feminist movement. The ERA struggle helped build the feminist movement in the United States to the point where, in 1989, one out of three women in the United States was reporting to poll takers that she considered herself a "feminist"—about the same percentage as considered themselves Democrats or Republicans. For more information, see DuBois (2001) and Mansbridge (2001). **See also** Equality (political science, public administration); Suffrage

Equilibrium   A state of equality or balance in which economic variables and/or constants are equal or reflective of market expectations. The concept of equilibrium is central to economic analysis on three levels—individual decision making, market performance, and the macroeconomy (national economy). Individuals make decisions about how to spend limited income to balance the consumption of desired goods in order to maximize utility. Consumers are in equilibrium when the marginal utility of the last unit of money spent on one good is the same for all goods consumed.

Markets are in equilibrium when the expected quantity of goods, services, assets, and inputs demanded (d) is equal to the expected supply (s). The estimated price and quantity at which supply is equal to demand are known as the equilibrium price (*pe*) and quantity (*qe*), respectively (see below).

Consumers and private investors demand finished products and assets, while businesses demand both inputs and assets in the factor (input) and financial markets. Private and institutional investors can also sell assets in financial markets at mutually agreeable (equilibrium or market) prices.

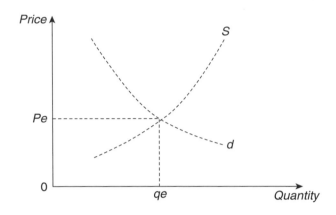

Equilibrium

The macroeconomy is in equilibrium when aggregate demand is equal to aggregate supply. Although equilibrium suggests a balance, not all equilibrium is desirable or stable. For example, a national economy might attain equilibrium, a point at which policy implementation can lead to an improved outcome of increased output and lower prices. It is also possible that shocks can destabilize a prevailing equilibrium. For more information, see McConnell and Brue (2008) and Schiller (2006). ***See also*** Demand; Market; Price

Equitable Funding and Expenditures This concept can be looked at from both the student and the taxpayer's perspectives and at local, state, and federal levels. Public education is generally financed through a combination of federal, state, and local taxes. Federal education funding is 7% to 9% of state education budgets. Local funding made up the bulk of funds prior to the 1990s; however, since the 1990s, state taxes have made up 70% to 80% of local education budgets. The percentage varies by district and state. An "upbeat economy" is historically tied to the launching of major new federal education programs and increased federal funding for education. Since public schools are ultimately funded and administered at the local level, local school administrators who reflect the interests of their constituents generally address school finance and equity issues.

Equity defined in school finance is equal spending per pupil and is complicated by a variety of factors. For example, equal per pupil expenditures do not guarantee equal educational outcomes. Some groups (special-education students, English-language learners, migrants, rural students, low-income students) require a larger per pupil expenditure than others to approach opportunity for equal outcomes. The *Serrano v. Priest* (1971) ruling established the principle of "fiscal neutrality," meaning that students' education may not be affected by their financial status or that of the community, only by the financial status of the state in which they live.

The Education Trust found that although the funding gap between high- and low-poverty school districts has somewhat diminished, in most states, high-poverty and high-minority districts receive substantially less funding than low-poverty districts. One solution to inequitable funding has been equalization, or the allocation of federal dollars to states on a "needs" basis. In his popular 1991 book Savage *Inequalities,* Jonathon Kozol made the general public more aware of the vast inequalities in education quality and funding between low- and high-poverty school districts.

Equity for taxpayers funding education continues to be debated and researched. Equitable taxation would be based on ability to pay (wealth and income). Traditional property tax is regressive (poor people pay a larger percentage of their income/wealth for the same education tax funding) and does not provide a base for equitable funding. Property values vary geographically and over time and do not reflect an individual's ability to pay taxes.

Equity in financing and expenditures issues for consideration in research include the "weighted"-pupil approach, equity at the school level, funding equity versus equal learning, assessed valuation per pupil, equity in taxation for school funding, equalization, alternative funding sources to property taxes, effects of federal earmarking, comparative state, local, and federal funding, and so on. For more information, see *Serrano v. Priest* (1971).

Equity *(economics)*   The fairness, part ownership, and value of a business. Fairness is a normative and subjective concept with hardly any form of widespread agreement. Because it is based on human perception, there is no empirically acceptable algorithm for it in economics.

Equity as fairness is a highly regarded theory in welfare economics as a way to redistribute income much more fairly in order to alleviate the plight of the poor or less fortunate in society. This means that taxes should be much more equitable, proportionate, and progressive. Those who make more income in society should be mandated to pay proportionately more taxes than those who make less for income to be less concentrated and for social services to be optimally provided. Critics argue that such a notion punishes innovation, hard work, and self-accomplishment.

In the market place, equity alludes to the fair price—the price that is generated by competition—which reflects efficiency and economic profit. In an imperfect market structure, it is the price for which average revenue is equal to per unit cost of production. It is believed that sellers will break even by selling at such a price when a market is imperfect. The problem is that such price regulation inhibits the potential to make profit or further investment and violates property rights.

Equity may also refer to part ownership of a firm, such as possession of common stock, which carries the risk of losses as well as speculative rewards. Capital from stock issues is regarded as capital equity, unlike debt equity (bonds). The net value of a business is also known as equity. *See also* Economics; Market; Perfect Competition

Equity *(political science)*   A legal concept of fairness, found within common law jurisprudence and involving the use of equitable principles to remedy unjust results in common law.

King James VI of Scotland, later James I of England, founded the principle of equity in England and based it on his own written works, most notably *The True Law of Free Monarchies,* written in 1597. *The True Law of Free Monarchies* was both a justification of the monarch's absolute authority and a mandate of the king's duties to God to reign justly, maintaining just laws. However, he asserted that righteous laws may also contribute to the greatest wrongs, wherein lies the necessity for royal discretion undoing an injustice created by the strictest letters of the law but limited in extent so as not to give what is not justly deserved. For more information, see Fortier (1998). *See also* Common Law (political science)

Equity Theory   The process by which an individual (Person A) is motivated to reduce cognitive dissonance when Person A perceives that his or her efforts, compared with those of another (Person B), are rewarded unfairly. In this process, Person A compares his or her ratio of rewards (outcomes) received relative to efforts (inputs) expended against the perception of the ratio of rewards and efforts of Person B. For example, if you perceive that your rewards-to-efforts ratio is *less* than the ratio of another person, then, according to equity theory, you will be motivated to equalize the ratio by reducing your efforts (decreasing the denominator) or by attempting to increase your rewards (increasing the numerator). If you perceive that your rewards-to-efforts ratio is *greater* than the ratio of another, you will be motivated to equalize your ratio by increasing your efforts to justify the larger reward or by attempting to reduce your rewards. According to the theory, when you cannot change inputs or outcomes, you may (1) psychologically distort your perceptions of your own inputs or outcomes or the inputs and outcomes of the comparison person, (2) choose another person or group for comparison, or (3) leave the inequitable situation by quitting the job or by increasing absenteeism. For more information, see Adams (1963). *See also* Cognitive Dissonance (psychology)

Eras of Policing   Different means, methods, or approaches used by law enforcement agencies to tackle issues of crime. There are three commonly acknowledged eras of policing: the political era, the professional/reform era, and the community policing era. The political era, which is generally associated with a time prior to the 20th century, refers to a period when the police was under the control of politicians. The professional/reform era makes references to a period in which the police addressed the issue of crime using technological tools, such as sophisticated emergency response systems. Other community problems were not perceived to be a part of the police's responsibilities during this period. The third era, the era of community policing, aimed to address crime as well as other community problems that may exert an impact on crime rates. The era of community policing adopts a problem-solving approach and seeks to strengthen ties between the police and the community. *See also* Community Policing (COP)

ERIC   An Internet-based bibliographic and full-text database of education research and information, sponsored by the Institute of Education Sciences of the U.S. Department of Education. The ERIC (Education Resources Information Center) collection indexes more than 600 journals, books, conference papers, technical reports, policy papers, and other education-related materials. For more information, see ERIC: www.eric.ed.gov. *See also* Databases for Literature Searches

Error in Fact/Error in Law   The first error occurs when wrongful conclusions are drawn about a given case based on information presented during the trial. An error in law refers to a misunderstanding of the law, its applicability, and the rules dictating standard legal procedure relevant to a given case.

Escapism   The avoidance of reality by diverting the mind with some form of entertainment. Escapism is identified as one of the motives for media content selection in uses-and-gratification research—an investigation into the psychological origins that predict media gratification. In a study performed by Conway and Rubin, the psychological variables most linked to escapism were sensation seeking and anxiety. Entire entertainment businesses—radio, television, films, video games, and so on—have flourished on the premise that their programs or products help people escape. Excessive escapism has been examined with respect to some forms of media—that is, Internet or video game addiction. For more information, see Conway and Rubin (1991). *See also* Entertainment Media

Essentialism   The metaphysical view that at least some entities have essences that consist of essential or necessary properties. For example, an essentialist might maintain that a cow must necessarily possess the property of being a ruminant and that such a property constitutes part of the cow's essence. Essentialists generally take essential predications, such as this one, to be *de re,* or "of things." That is, essentialists will deny that essential predications are simply *de dicto*—products of definition, stipulation, or ways of speaking. Anti-essentialists will deny that there are genuine *de re* essential properties of things. ***See also*** Metaphysics

Essential Question   An interrogatory statement focusing on the key idea of instructional content. The ideal essential question (EQ) stimulates critical thinking and inquiry; it provides a frame of reference related to specific learning objectives. Teachers use the EQ to guide student decision making throughout the lesson or specific curriculum. ***See also*** Taxonomies

Estimation (Point and Interval)   In inferential statistics, estimation is the process of approximating some unknown parameter of interest. Point estimation uses the single value of an estimator (e.g., such as the mean, variance, or correlation) as the estimate of the value of the unknown population parameter of interest. Interval estimation uses a lower and an upper limit, a band, to bracket the estimated value of the unknown parameter of interest with a specified degree of probabilistic assurance. For example, 95% confidence intervals, which include the true population value 95% of the time, are common. ***See also*** Inferential Statistics

Ethical Relativism   The idea that morality is entirely dependent on a specific time and place. Ethical relativism is perhaps the most controversial (and forcefully repudiated) position in all philosophy. Whereas philosophers like Immanuel Kant and Plato offered an absolute and binding moral code, ethical relativists deny the very possibility that morality can be universally grounded. Although ethical relativists may argue from a number of different positions, many of their claims are often anthropologically based; in discrete societies, moral codes have diverged dramatically, differing from time to time and place to place. Whereas some societies find female genital mutilation deplorable, for example, others imbue this action with deep religious and cultural connotations. Critics have countered that some common human values are indeed universal; prohibitions against "unjustified" (although this term itself is much open to dispute) murder can be found in nearly every society, and people therefore supposedly possess moral intuitions concerning what is right and what is wrong. Others posit some "basic forms of good" that lend themselves to rule making. Moral relativism also runs counter to nearly all religious beliefs, which stress the notion of a pure and solid "good" (as demanded by God, Allah, etc.) that humans must unwaveringly follow. Of course, the entire notion of moral relativism contains a seemingly irresolvable contradiction; if its premises were universally accepted, this would contradict the very definition of relativism! Due to such obvious criticisms, few philosophers have advocated a purely relativist stance (although it remains a common critique to use against one's intellectual opponents). Indeed, it is difficult to determine how a "true" relativist would actually behave. Would such an individual live by his or her own made-up moral code (and from where would this code spring)? Or would such an agent be rendered morally immobile, regarding all ethical actions as inherently empty and intellectually pointless? For more information, see Honderich (2005). ***See also*** Morality

Ethics *(communication)*   An area of philosophy that studies good conduct in life. Ethics involves "the right action" and "the greater good." Morals encompass the practice of ethics. Personal ethics involves the study of individual morality. Socrates, Aristotle, Epictetus, and G. E. Moore are considered seminal ethical thinkers. In communications and media, as in business, ethics takes the form of normative and applied ethics, as in a "code of ethics," which specifies right action in performing duties and reporting news. For example, to engender trust in the readership, journalistic standards of news accounts should be balanced and fair, with sources verified and reliable. This is summed up in the slogan "Neither fear nor favor" in reporting. It is unfortunate that in the 21st century, because of the proliferation of unbalanced and biased news accounts, the mixing of fact and fiction, the use of composite portraits in the writing of stories, and other irregularities, public opinion on the media's ethical codes has dropped to an all-time low. ***See also*** Code of Ethics; Morality

Ethics *(education)*   The philosophical analysis of moral judgments and the systematic inquiry into human conduct with the goal of discovering both the rules that ought to govern action and the goods that we should seek in life. These two different questions provide two traditions in ethics: one concerned with the rightness or wrongness of action, the other with the ends or goals of action and their goodness or badness. The first of these traditions is the deontological and the second, the teleological. Teleological theories hold that the morality of an action is determined by its consequences or benefits. Right conduct is that which maximizes the good. One variation, ethical egoism, states that if any person performs an action that increases his or her own good, then that action is right. The most obvious criticism is that this reduces ethical behavior to that which benefits the self alone. The more substantial variation of teleology is utilitarianism. Developed in its most influential form by the English philosophers Jeremy Bentham (1748–1832) and John Stuart Mill (1806–1873), its central doctrine is that right action is that which produces the greatest good for the greatest number. Though utilitarianism is said to account for the obvious problem of egoism by considering an action's consequences for everyone, it is not immune from criticism. Teleological theories in general require that we know all the possible consequences of an action, but utilitarianism in particular can justify results that seem morally objectionable, at least to many. For example, an action that causes pain for you individually can be justified if it results in good or pleasure for more others. The best-known form of deontology is the German philosopher Immanuel Kant's (1724–1804) categorical imperative: "So act that the maxim of your will could always hold at the same time as a principle establishing universal law." The idea of universality means, first, that there are no exceptions to universal moral rules: If an action is wrong, it is always wrong. Second, impartiality is required: The universal moral rule applies to each of us, with no individual exceptions. Third, universal moral rules must be applied consistently: We must not accept or reject a moral rule depending on circumstances. One other core belief is that we are to treat persons as ends, not as means. Thus, utilitarianism would be rejected since it ends up treating some individuals as though they are means to the ends of others. One significant criticism of deontology is the question of how to decide whether to have some action become a universal moral rule without considering the consequences of the action. *See also* Axiology

Ethics *(public administration)*   The moral values, principles, and customs of an individual or group. The word is derived from the Greek word *ethos*, which means "character," and from the Latin word *mores*, which means "customs." In philosophy, ethics is the study of human conduct in light of moral principles and the standards by which actions can be considered right or wrong.

Among the major ethical theories in the 20th century was instrumentalism, studied by John Dewey, which dictated that morality lies within the individual and is relative to a person's experience, and emotivism, developed by Sir Alfred J. Ayer, who determined that ethical considerations were merely expressions of the subjective desires of the individual. Intuitionism, studied by G. E. Moore, postulated an immediate awareness of the morally good. Similarly, deontological ethics, with intuitionists like H. A. Prichard and W. D. Ross, proposes a distinction between good and right, arguing that moral obligations are intrinsically compelling, despite whether or not their fulfillment results in some greater good.

Since the mid 20th century, other theories have been developed, such as prescriptivism, supported by R. M. Hare, which compares moral precepts to commands, the distinguishing factor being that moral precepts can be universally applied. *See also* Axiology

Ethics *(sociology)*   The study of morality and its impact on behavior. Ethics also refers to the set of moral principles adopted by any given individual or the distinction made between "right" and "wrong." Various ethical theories have been developed, such as principle ethics theory, ethical realism theory, utilitarianism, cognitive moral development theory, and many more. Principle ethics theory stipulates that unlike conflicting laws and rules, conflicting principles promote moral reasoning. Ethical realism theory states that when confronted with conflicting norms, the individual faces a moral dilemma and is compelled to choose the least harmful option. Utilitarianism argues for moral standards that promote the best interests of and

minimize the harm caused to all parties concerned. Cognitive moral development theory stipulates that ethics and moral reasoning are not innate but can be developed and learned; this ethical theory was developed by Lawrence Kohlberg. *See also* Morality

Ethics in Counseling and Therapy   A set of behaviors based on socially accepted standards of what is considered right or wrong. Ethics guides the actions of individuals and groups of people. When applied to a specific profession or discipline, ethics consists of those rules of conduct that are considered morally, and in many instances also legally, acceptable. They include relationships with clients, confidentiality, and attitudes toward clients such as dignity, respect, and recognition of diversity. Each medical and human behavior profession has a code of ethics that details the values and practices to which all members must adhere. For more information, see Burke and Miranti (1992) and Pope and Vasquez (2007). *See also* Ethics in Research

Ethics in Research   The principles that guide research with the aim of protecting the rights of participants. Since research delves into the physical, mental, and social lives of human beings, researchers have an ethical obligation to ensure the rights, privacy, and welfare of individuals and communities that form the focus of their investigations. Research ethics defines what is and what is not legitimate *to do a*nd what "moral" research involves. Research ethics focuses on principles rather than fixed rules, and has been developed to balance two competing values: the pursuit of scientific knowledge and the rights of those being studied. This is an evolving process as society, in general, and the research community, in particular, become more aware of the ramifications of their actions.

Generally, there are four ethical issues that must be resolved before the research process can proceed. The first involves the degree of potential *harm to participants,* which ranges from physical harm (untested drugs or live viruses) to psychological harm (stress or loss of self-esteem) to legal jeopardy. Current practices include anticipating risk before beginning the research process, screening out individuals who may be at greater risk, and doing no harm. If some stress is required, follow-up counseling or treatment is made available. The second issue is *informed voluntary consent* to participate. This involves full disclosure to participants on what participation entails and explicit consent to participate, in the form of a signed or verbal consent. If deception is necessary, researchers do not misrepresent the risks and debrief participants truthfully afterward. If research is conducted with vulnerable groups (children, captive populations such as inmates, or individuals with decreased mental competency), additional steps are taken (e.g., consent by a legal guardian and assent by the participant) to ensure informed consent. An additional dimension is the freedom to withdraw from the research at any time without penalty. The third issue, the *right to privacy,* guarantees the participants'

E

confidentiality or anonymity. According to the condition of confidentiality, the researcher knows the identity of the participant but does not reveal it to anyone; according to the condition of anonymity, which is preferred, participant identity is also unknown to the researcher (i.e., the research cannot connect the data to particular research participants). Ethical researchers violate privacy only to the minimum degree necessary and only for legitimate research purposes. This includes invasions of privacy through observation in quasi-private spaces, spying, or eavesdropping. In addition, researchers protect the information on research participants from public disclosure by using pseudonyms or numerical coding or altering identifiable characteristics. The fourth issue is the *confidentiality of data*. The source of information is kept secret from the public, and the researcher holds the source in confidence.

Though there are institutional review boards that hold researchers accountable, ethical responsibility rests with the researcher to avoid exploitation; to honor guarantees of privacy, anonymity, or confidentiality; and to not coerce participants. For more information, see Gregory (2003). ***See also*** Ethics; Institutional Review Board (IRB) (education, psychology)

Ethnic Identity One's sense of identification with the ethnic group(s) to which one believes one belongs. Ethnic identity describes the relationship between the individual and the group or the extent to which an individual's perceptions, feelings, and behaviors are related to or influenced by membership in an ethnic group. The ethnic group is often, but not always, the individual's group of biological heritage. The four generally accepted components of ethnic identity are (1) ethnic awareness (recognition and understanding by in- and out-ethnic groups), (2) ethnic self-identification (the name or label of one's ethnic group), (3) ethnic attitudes (beliefs and feelings about in- and out-ethnic groups), and (4) ethnic behaviors (behavioral patterns or activities and actions that are thought to be specific to one's ethnic group).

Ethnicity Affiliation to a social group composed of members who tend to share common cultural, historical, geographical, and religious characteristics. Ethnicity is a social construct; one's ethnic group may change as a result of changes in the way society defines ethnicity.

Ethnocentric The idea that one's own ethnic or cultural group is superior to other groups from a different cultural and ethnic background. An ethnocentric view reflects a refusal or an inability to understand the values, practices, and cultures of other ethnic groups. ***See also*** Ethnicity

Ethnocentrism (*communication*) A perspective on the relationship between one's own culture and that of others. An ethnocentric perspective evaluates anything from another culture using one's own values and beliefs, filtering everything seen in that culture with a bias that promotes the superiority of one's own culture. Under ethnocentrism, any cultural entity of another culture—its religion, dress, language, behavior, religion, political system—is automatically inferior or suspect. Ethnocentrism can be considered an example of how culture operates to make its own workings seem natural and normal. If culture has the job of convincing its people that the world they are creating is distinctive and worthwhile, then some degree of ethnocentrism may develop as a result.

Anthropology is an academic discipline founded on the effort to combat ethnocentrism and to consider all cultures as equally relevant and valuable. Using an insider's point of view, anthropological studies have shown that each culture has its own perspective and systems of value, truth, and reality and that all these are equally valid ways for people to organize their lives. This approach has earned anthropology the reputation for cultural relativism, the concept that each culture must be understood in its own terms rather than evaluated in relation to a set, external standard.

Ethnocentrism is often thought to be the result of not having exposure to people who are different. Under an ethnocentric perspective, difference is viewed as problematic and something that should be ignored, eliminated, or assimilated. Ethnocentrism is one way to describe the strife between different religions or ethnic groups, but the disagreements between these groups are not necessarily based on ignorance of the other. For more information, see Drummond (1981). ***See also*** Belief; Cultural Context; Culture (communication, education, media studies, sociology); Stereotyping

Ethnocentrism (*education*) The belief that one's culture is the best, superior to all others. Based on this belief, the individual sees it as logical and appropriate that other groups abandon their inferior cultures and subscribe to the individual's. This is often reinforced through power relationships between groups. ***See also*** Culture (communication, education, media studies, sociology)

Ethnography (*education*) A qualitative research method concerned with discovering and describing the culture of a group of people. A culture includes the group's shared beliefs, values, practices, norms, rituals, language, and material objects and artifacts. Ethnography focuses on the group rather than the individual. The goal of ethnographic research is to uncover and describe the cultural characteristics of the group being studied. Fieldwork for ethnography typically consists of observations, interviews, and document gathering. The researcher (i.e., the ethnographer) spends an extended period of time in the setting conducting fieldwork to understand the group's culture. It is important to document both the emic perspective (i.e., the view of the culture from the inside, from the insider's perspective) and the etic perspective (i.e., the view of the "objective" outsider).

Educational ethnography was born out of the field of cultural anthropology. In the 19th and early 20th centuries, anthropologists examined what they called "primitive" cultures by immersing themselves in the societies of other countries for lengthy periods of time. They wrote extensive accounts of their experiences of these ways of life. Anthropological interviews and observations became standard tools for collecting data in the field, which educational ethnographers would later use.

Beginning in the 1950s and continuing through the 1980s, educational researchers turned their interests to the American school system, conducting fieldwork in classrooms and schools. Since the 1980s, educational researchers have been fine-tuning the way they conduct ethnography. There has been much discussion on the ways ethnographers interpret the groups of people they are studying, as well as the perspective that ethnographers take to present their findings. The complete objectivity of ethnographers has been called into question, along with the assumption that there is one correct perspective from which to report ethnographic findings.

There are many types of ethnographies, including critical ethnography, confessional ethnography, authoethnography, and microethnography. Critical ethnography is the study of the shared patterns of a marginalized group, such as special-needs children. This type of ethnography aims to advocate for the group it presents in its study. Confessional ethnography is a report of the researcher's experiences in the field. Autoethnography is a highly reflective, self-examination by the researcher set within his or her own cultural context. Microethnographies focus on a specific aspect of a cultural group and its setting. For more information, see Creswell (2002). ***See also*** Qualitative Research

Ethnography *(sociology)* A branch of anthropology and sociology that is dedicated to the study of human cultures. Ethnography is concerned with acquiring a better understanding of processes within a cultural group or community. Ethnographic research requires that the researcher be present in the field and observe and interview various members belonging to the culture of interest. The ethnographic approach, just like any other method used in qualitative research, provides more in-depth information about a given community than quantitative methods (surveys, etc.) and provides better insight into the processes underlying the cultural group of interest. ***See also*** Qualitative Research

Ethos The general ambience, attitude, organization, or "style" of a culture. It was a term used by the culture-and-personality or psychological anthropology school because it was helpful in discussing the relationship between individuals and their society. If a culture has a particular ethos, its members would tend to have certain related personalities. The term is not widely used today, but the concept is one that appears in stereotypes. ***See also*** Stereotyping

Eugenics A practice that was concerned with improving the future of the human race by controlling human reproduction. Based on the principles of genetics, eugenics emphasizes the importance of increasing reproduction among individuals who are defined as superior and restricting reproduction among (or sterilizing) individuals who have physical or mental deficiencies. In the early part of the 20th century, eugenics was used to sterilize those who were habitual criminals or thought to be feebleminded. ***See also*** Castration, Chemical

Eurocentric Curriculum An educational system in the United States focusing on European Americans, their cultures, their history, and their institutions. Textbooks, discussions, and activities promote only European American standpoints and accomplishments; faculty, guests, and community business partners are mostly European Americans. The history, cultures, and future prospects of minority students are limited or ignored. ***See also*** Cultural Diversity; Race Discrimination

Euthanasia Medically assisted death (often referred to as assisted suicide). Euthanasia is among the most controversial of practices and is currently illegal in most countries. Often described as intentional killing for the benefit of the patient, euthanasia can be achieved by an act (providing lethal drugs) or omission (failing to provide life-sustaining treatment).

Evaluation *(education)* The systematic process of determining the merit (quality), worth (value), and/or significance (importance) of evaluands (e.g., programs, policies, and products) or evaluees (e.g., personnel), or the product thereof. While every person to some degree engages in evaluation on a daily basis, professional evaluation involves the use of systematic investigation to collect and synthesize factual information (what so?) in order to render evaluative conclusions (so what?) about an evaluand's goodness, value, and importance. ***See also*** Evaluation, Logic of; Formative Evaluation; Goal-Free Evaluation; Goals-Based Evaluation; Summative Evaluation

Evaluation *(public administration)* The final stage of the policy-making process. In this stage of the policy process, a program or policy is examined to determine whether it is meeting its intended goals and objectives, how well it is working, what is not working, and what modifications should be made to improve performance on overall impact. The evaluation process is conducted by various actors, which can include interest groups, the media, the recipients, legislative oversight committees, the General Accountability Office (GAO; www.gao.gov), presidential commissions, or staff within administrative agencies. Evaluations present a number of challenges. Policy goals, objectives, targets, and performance indicators are not always clearly articulated during the policy formulation stage. In many instances, policies are designed with little regard for measuring performance and showing results. More often than not, policy evaluation is not accounted for in program budgets, and in practice, it is overlooked. The GAO conducts policy evaluation of federal policies and programs as well as state-level initiatives and can serve as a useful resource when designing a program evaluation. For more information, see Anderson (1997) and Peters (2007). *See also* Policy (public administration); Policy Analysis

Evaluation, Logic of   A concept that pertains to the definition of evaluation, definitions of its major concepts, its nature and relationship to other disciplines, and the rules of inference that govern it. The *definition* of evaluation is based on three evaluative predicates: (1) merit (goodness without consideration of cost), (2) worth (goodness under specific consideration of cost), and (3) significance (importance or relevance). Although many definitions of evaluation exist, they are often too narrow (e.g., limiting evaluation to general social/behavioral science research) or too broad (e.g., taking anything that generates useful information as professional evaluation).

There are three *purposes* of evaluation: (1) improvement (formative evaluation), (2) accountability (summative evaluation), and (3) knowledge generation (ascriptive evaluation). Evaluation objects are referred to as *evaluands;* evaluation subjects are called *evaluees.* Evaluation is practiced in varying disciplines and fields of study in the arts, humanities, social and behavioral sciences, engineering, and business. *Branches* of evaluation include policy, program, personnel, performance, product, portfolio, proposal, intradisciplinary, and meta-evaluation.

The distinguishing feature between evaluation and research is the centrality of *valuing* in evaluation. In contrast to the value-free doctrine commonly practiced in the social sciences, evaluators purposefully ascribe value. The working logic of evaluation consists of four major steps: (1) establishing the criteria of merit (i.e., On what components or dimensions must the evaluand do well?), (2) constructing standards (i.e., How well should the evaluand perform?), (3) observing/measuring performance and comparing it with the standards (i.e., How well did the evaluand perform?), and (4) synthesizing and integrating information into an evaluative conclusion (i.e., What is the relative or absolute merit or worth of the evaluand?).

Fundamental operations for determining the absolute or relative merit, worth, or significance of an evaluand can be subdivided into two categories: (1) *primary operations* (grading, ranking, scoring, apportioning, and synthesis) and (2) *secondary operations* (weighting—assigning importance levels; barring—setting minimum performance levels, which cannot be compensated for by better performance on any other dimension or component; and profiling—the graphical illustration of performance).

Professional evaluators strive for *essential claims* that are based on scientific evidence and require the establishment of factual and value premises. *Factual premises* comprise descriptive information, while *value premises* provide relevant and indisputable standards that are applied to the facts to establish conclusions about the absolute or relative merit, worth, and significance of an evaluand. These describe the key function of evaluative inference, namely, to move validly from factual and definitional premises to evaluative conclusions. Other value claims are open to dispute in evaluation, including personal preference (subjective claims that are not definitionally true and cannot be validated), market claims (which can be verified by common sense and law), and contextual claims (prima facie factual claims that hold true in a given context). For more information, see Fournier (1995), Mathison (2005), and Scriven (1991). *See also* Evaluation (education); Formative Evaluation; Summative Evaluation

Evaluation Dissemination and Utilization   The process of sharing information regarding evaluation procedures and products with stakeholders, policymakers, and researchers in a timely and impartial manner and using the evaluation results to make decisions about programs. There are three major types of utilization. First, *instrumental use* occurs when evaluation results are used to modify, stop, or extend the scope of a program. Second, *conceptual use* occurs when an evaluation affects the decision maker's thinking about a present or future program. Third, *process use* occurs when persons participating in the conduct of an evaluation change as a result of their participation. A highly controversial type of utilization is *symbolic use*, which occurs when an individual uses evaluation information for political self-interest. For more information, see Quinn (1997) and Weiss (1988). *See also* Evaluation (education)

Evaluative Listening   Critical assessment, during the process of hearing, of the statements made by another person.

As defined by the psychologist Carl Rogers in the 1950s, evaluative listening is an immediate reaction, highly influenced by emotion and preconceived notions, underscoring the human tendency to judge, approve, or disapprove. In Rogerian psychology, evaluative listening has a negative connotation in that it implies that the listener is not receiving the statements made by the speaker in an open-minded manner. Rogers argued that evaluative listening is a barrier to interpersonal communication and most likely to cause the two or more parties engaged in discourse to miss the viewpoint of the other(s). He suggested empathetic, active listening as the preferred gateway to effective communication.

In a keynote address given at the inaugural convention of the International Listening Association in 1980, Professor Ralph G. Nichols, University of Minnesota, echoed Rogers's sentiments on the negative impact of evaluative listening, stating that the "wise listener is attentive, and non-evaluative; he asks only unslanted questions, and praises those statements made by an adversary which he can honestly praise."

More recently, however, the term *evaluative listening* has come to be used interchangeably with critical listening, especially in educational circles. In that sense, evaluative listening is seen as a positive process in which the person doing the hearing logically considers the information and sentiments being presented by a speaker. Evaluative listeners are likely to effectively discern information—for example, from candidates for political office or from advertisers—before making decisions. For more information, see Nichols (1980), Rogers and Roethlisberger (1951/1991), and Thompson, Leintz, Nevers, and Witkowski (2004). *See also* Active Listening; Critical Listening; Empathetic Listening; Passive Listening

Evidence   Anything used to determine the truth of an assertion. In a criminal case, evidence is material used to determine guilt or innocence. Although various types of direct, physical, testimonial, and circumstantial evidence are usually admissible in criminal cases, there are notable exceptions. Hearsay evidence is generally inadmissible, and physical evidence can be suppressed (i.e., excluded from consideration) if it is gathered in violation of a defendant's constitutional rights. A defense attorney seeking to have evidence suppressed will request a Mapp hearing, asking the judge to apply the exclusionary rule. *See also* Circumstantial Evidence; Exclusionary Rule (political science, sociology); Testimony

Evolutionary   An attribute that refers to an ongoing and gradual progression from one stage or phase to another. *Evolutionary* denotes some degree of development and is applicable to a wide range of areas, such as disciplines (biology, ecology, psychology, etc.), research, and so on. For instance, evolutionary biology refers to the gradual changes in traits and characteristics observed between different generations. *See also* Evolutionary Ecology

Evolutionary Ecology   The study of the development and evolution of various living things or species. Evolutionary ecology shares some common traits with evolutionary biology, which aims to study the gradual changes in traits and characteristics observed from one generation to another. Evolutionary ecology is concerned with the histories and changes occurring within species over time, as well as the changes in dynamics between different species. *See also* Evolutionary

Evolutionary Psychology   A discipline that seeks to identify evolved emotional and cognitive adaptations of human psychology. Evolutionary psychology proposes psychological adaptations or evolved cognitive mechanisms that emerged over the course of evolution through the process of natural selection to solve recurrent problems in human ancestral environments. Evolutionary psychologists propose that universal behaviors and emotions, such as fear of spiders and snakes, reflect these adaptations. Evolutionary psychology adheres to the main tenets of evolutionary theory, which maintain that traits appear through natural and sexual selection within an environment of evolutionary adaptiveness, via inclusive fitness (e.g., mate selection). Essentially, this means that variation in genetics allows the selection of some organisms over others in a particular environment; those traits that make an organism best suited to the environment will be promulgated. Evolutionary psychologists argue that understanding the psychological functions of the human brain requires understanding of the problems that had to be overcome in the environment at the time in which humans evolved, generally accepted to be during the Pleistocene era. Evolutionary psychology proposes that in Pleistocene environments, problems such as growth and development, survival, mating, and social relationships were resolved via the processes of natural and sexual selection.

Modern evolutionary psychology maintains that human psychology consists of a large number of functionally specialized mechanisms that produce manifest behavior and that this manifest behavior depends on underlying psychological mechanisms triggered by external and internal stimuli. Moreover, modern evolutionary psychology suggests that natural selection is the only identified causal process capable of creating these mechanisms and that psychological mechanisms are specialized to solve problems that recurred for humans over evolutionary time. Researchers in the field rely on comparative methods (e.g., human with nonhuman species, human with human in different contexts) as well as traditional experimentation to test evolutionary hypotheses. Methods of study include archaeological research, observation, and self-report. *See also* Natural Selection

Exchange Rate   The rate at which the currency of one nation can be exchanged for the currencies of other nations. In mathematical form, it is the ratio of the value of the domestic currency to the value of a foreign currency or currencies. This ratio is normally representative of the nominal exchange rate. It is nominal because the values of the currencies are not calculated to reflect their respective purchasing power. The real exchange rate takes into consideration the purchasing power of the respective currencies, that is, the amount of goods that can be purchased in physical or real units.

The real exchange rate is the product of the nominal rate and price indices of a foreign country in relation to the domestic country. Exchange rate can be set to determine potential price movements in the foreign exchange market. The rate for immediate delivery is known as the "spot rate," and the rate for future delivery is known as the "forward rate." Exchange rate can also be classified as fixed or flexible (market based). For more information, see Carbaugh (2007), Mankiw (2006), McConnell and Brue (2008), and Pugel (2007).

Exclusionary Rule *(political science)*   A legal principle that evidence collected in violation of the due process clause of the U.S. Constitution against unreasonable searches and seizures may not be used against a person in court. The purpose of the exclusionary rule is to deter the police and prosecutors from illegally collecting evidence. The origins of the exclusionary rule may be traced to 1886, when the Supreme Court in *Boyd v. United States* held unconstitutional the compulsory production of business papers.

In 1914, the Supreme Court's decision in *Weeks v. U.S.* established that evidence obtained in violation of the Fourth Amendment's protection against unreasonable searches and seizures could not be used against a person in federal court. In 1961, the exclusionary rule was applied to state courts through the Fourteenth Amendment in the decision of *Mapp v. Ohio*. The exclusionary rule was extended to violations of the Fifth Amendment in 1966 in *Miranda v. Arizona,* which provided protections against self-incrimination for suspects in police custody who were subjected to questioning. For more information, see *Boyd v. United States* (1886), *Mapp v. Ohio* (1961), *Miranda v. Arizona* (1966), and *Weeks v. U.S.* (1914). *See also* Due Process/Due Process Model; Due Process of Law

Exclusionary Rule *(sociology)*   A judicially created remedy for the violation of a defendant's constitutional rights. Constitutions provide citizens with rights protecting them against undue government intrusion but offer few remedies for violations of those rights. The exclusionary rule, which makes evidence seized illegally by government agents inadmissible in criminal courts, was first announced in the case *Weeks v. United States* (1914). In *Mapp v. Ohio* (1961), the U.S. Supreme Court extended the exclusionary rule to the states. Defense attorneys seeking to have evidence suppressed will request a suppression hearing (also known as a *Mapp* hearing) asking the judge to apply the exclusionary rule to physical or testimonial evidence that has allegedly been obtained illegally. The judge makes a determination as to the legality of the evidence and uses that determination to rule on the admissibility of the evidence. For more information, see *Mapp v. Ohio* (1961) and *Weeks v. U.S.* (1914). *See also* Circumstantial Evidence; Evidence

Exculpate   To release from blame, accusation, or guilt. When an individual is exculpated, he or she is found to be innocent of the accusations brought against him or her. Exculpation extends beyond the realm of the criminal justice system and does not necessarily entail an act that is criminal in nature. *See also* Acquit; Exonerate

Execution   The legally authorized killing of a person following conviction for a capital offense. Although most Western nations have outlawed executions, the United States retains the death penalty and executes persons convicted of capital murder. Since the 1980s, the most common method of execution has been lethal injection. *See also* Capital Punishment; Death Row

Executive Branch   Under the federal political system, the branch of government responsible for implementing, or executing, the law. To compare, the legislature does not implement but makes the law, which the executive branch enforces. The president cannot be part of the legislature, a dimension that confirms the separation of powers doctrine.

Under the separation of powers doctrine, the term *executive branch* refers to the president of the United States and his or her cabinet. The president appoints the cabinet staff.

The role of the executive involves enforcing the law and conducting the foreign relations of the state along with commanding the armed forces. The executive branch of government also issues executive orders. The Senate and the House of Representatives act as a check on the president with their right of impeachment (House) and conviction (Senate). The president, in turn, can veto congressional legislation, which the latter can override with a two-thirds vote. In the United States, a person can become president if he or she is a minimum of 35 years of age and is a natural-born citizen who has lived in the country for at least 14 years.

The executive branch model of government can be traced back to the French thinkers of the 18th century, who devised a political system based on the legislature, the judiciary, and the executive. For more information, see Robertson (1985), Scruton (1982), and The White House (2009). *See also* Separation of Powers

Executive Federalism   A concept used in European constitutional law to describe the system in which executive members of national governments meet in an intergovernmental federal body to negotiate and create federal law. While there are many variations of executive federalism, Katy LeRoy and Cheryl Saunders, in *Dialogues on Legislative, Executive, and Judicial Governance in Federal Countries* (2006), assert that "the common denominator is a high level of policy making by governments acting collectively, relying on executive dominance of their respective legislatures to ensure that their decisions are given effect" (p. 42). According to Philipp Dann, in *Principles of European Constitutional Law* (2006), three basic components of executive federalism exist. The first is what Dann calls "a vertical structure of interwoven competencies," meaning that the federal level creates laws, and it is the responsibility of the executives of the member states to uphold the law in their respective states. This requires cooperation from member state executives to participate in the creation, the adaptation, and the review of federal law. A second characteristic is that a council of executives from member states exists to organize state cooperation. A third characteristic is a decision-making model of consensus instead of a simple majority rule.

A major advantage of the executive system is that it enhances cooperation and coordination between national governments. Disadvantages include the limitation it places on democratic citizen involvement in decision making, complaints of undue secrecy of legislative bodies, and a lack of accountability. The European Union is said to use executive federalism, with the Executive of Ministers representing member states. Germany has a similar system of executive federalism, the Bundesrat representing the Lander governments. In Canada, executive federalism refers to the meetings of the First Ministers. For more information, see Dann (2006) and LeRoy and Saunders (2006). *See also* Executive Branch

Executive Functions A constellation of higher-order regulatory and supervisory functions that allow individuals to exert control over and coordinate their behavior. In a sense, they are the functions that orchestrate the lower-order cognitive processing of the brain. Therefore, *executive function* is really an umbrella term used to describe a set of global functions, such as planning, mental flexibility, attentional allocation, working memory, and inhibitory control, that guide purposeful behavior and effective performance. These functions allow one to plan for and anticipate outcomes, adapt strategies according to feedback, and direct attentional resources to meet the demands of novel events and situations. Although the integrity of the entire brain is necessary for intact executive functioning, research has consistently associated executive functioning with frontal-lobe activity, particularly that of the prefrontal cortex. Likewise, because executive functions are not domain specific, executive disruption may manifest itself as diffuse impairment across several cognitive domains. As long as executive functions remain intact, a person can withstand considerable cognitive loss and still continue to be independent, social, and productive. On the other hand, no matter how well preserved the underlying cognitive capacities are, impairment of executive function may disrupt a person's ability for self-care, independence, or social relationships. There is no single test or even battery of tests that identifies all the different features of executive function. For a review of neuropsychological measures that are commonly used to assess executive functioning, see Lezak, Howieson, Loring, Hannay, and Fischer (2004). *See also* Brain (Encephalon)

Executive Privilege A privilege of the U.S. president, and other executive branch members, to be exempt from judiciary or legislative disclosure requests. It is ordinarily understood as extending only to national security or foreign policy matters. The privilege is based on the constitutional doctrine of separation of powers but is not mentioned in the Constitution. Precedent can be found in *U.S. v. Reynolds* (1953), when the Supreme Court overruled a lower-court decision ordering the disclosure of an Air Force accident report; Chief Justice Vinson opined that "the Court should not jeopardize the security which the privilege is meant to protect." In *U.S. v. Nixon* (1974), the privilege was not extended to President Richard Nixon's criminal proceedings. The earliest known use of the term was in the U.S. Court of Appeals case *Glass v. Ickes* (1940), which upheld Harold Ickes's (President Franklin D. Roosevelt's Secretary of the Interior) immunity in a defamation suit. For more information, see *Glass v. Ickes* (1940), *U.S. v. Nixon* (1974), and *U.S. v. Reynolds* (1953). *See also* Separation of Powers

Existential Counseling An approach to psychotherapy that has roots in existential and phenomenological philosophy and in the psychotherapies of Viktor Frankl and Ludwig Binswager. Emphasis is placed on the inherent isolation in which humans exist and their consequential need for personal meaning. Counseling involves helping clients take responsibility for the freedom available to them to create meaning and make adaptive choices. *See also* Phenomenology

Existentialism A position within philosophical thought that rejects the Cartesian project and aims for a philosophy that erases the subjective/objective dichotomy. Existentialists, such as Sartre, Merleau-Ponty, Kierkegaard, Levinas, and Nietzsche, insist that there can be no being-in-itself and that instead the essence of being emerges in acts and experiences that are constantly in flux and becoming. The existentialist notion of becoming dissolves the mind-body dualism and the related idea that essence precedes existence. Existentialist thought highly regards the value of being "true to oneself" since there is no self other than that created in experience. While existentialists have often been misunderstood and accused of fostering rampant individualism, in actuality, they assert that to live authentically one must acknowledge the choice of being responsible for one's own and others' lives and the freedom and moral duty to make such choices. To live inauthentically would be to disregard such responsibilities and consequences by relinquishing them onto external forces. For more information, see Cooper (1999). *See also* Dualism; Phenomenology

Exonerate To pronounce a person previously convicted of a crime factually innocent. Despite safeguards to help ensure that only the guilty are convicted of criminal offenses, wrongful convictions do occur, and innocent people are sentenced for crimes that they did not commit. Exonerations, or legal pronouncements of actual innocence, serve to remedy miscarriages of justice. Organizations such as the Innocence Projects, state innocence commissions, and the 2004 Justice for All Act provide convicted offenders who proclaim their innocence avenues for seeking exoneration. Since 1976, more than 125 death row inmates have been exonerated, and since 1992, 200 convicted offenders have secured exonerations through DNA evidence. *See also* Convict/Conviction

E

Expectancy Theory   The process by which individuals are motivated by their expectancies of the probability of receiving a valued reward. The theory includes three components, all of which must be present for motivation to occur. First is the valence (value) an individual attaches to the expected reward. If the reward offered is not valued, the individual will not be motivated to put forth effort to achieve the reward. Second is the expectancy that one's effort will lead to successful performance. Again, if an individual has low expectancy that effort will lead to successful performance, motivation will be lacking. Third is the individual's belief that successful performance will be instrumental in obtaining the reward. If the individual does not believe that successful performance will result in the valued reward or if the individual believes that the reward will be granted despite unsuccessful performance, motivation will be lacking. For more information, see Vroom (1994).

Experience   The sum of knowledge or skills gained from participating in any activity. In John Dewey's view, education must be conceived as a continuing reconstruction of experience. This continuity of experience means that every experience both takes up something from those that have gone before and modifies those that come after. Since learning and doing develop together, students must be given authentic opportunities to test learning in real, direct experience. Only then will learning have use, value, and meaning for the student. *See also* Democracy and Education

Experienced Reality   The individual's subjective experience of and knowledge obtained from the world. The Husserlian phenomenological perspective of experienced reality is concerned with knowledge that is instantly introduced to the consciousness. The media industry and its messages are viewed as constructing reality for audiences through the ubiquitous presentation of highly subjective information. Critics assert that the media influence the subjectivity of individuals and the individual's knowledge about reality, particularly relating to other cultures and countries to which the individual does not have firsthand access. Furthermore, digital media technologies have been identified as having the potential to complicate a user's experience of his or her own reality through the negotiation of the real versus virtual worlds, wherein a user may have difficulty assessing the information obtained in those spaces. *See also* Actuality

Experiment   A set of observations made after the controlled manipulation of one or more independent variables that represent the presumed causes of some behavioral or physical phenomenon (called, generally, the *dependent variable*). The goal of an experiment is to find support for or attempt to falsify a hypothesis concerning a presumed causal relationship between two or more variables. Experimentation is the cornerstone of the empirical approach to acquiring deeper knowledge about the physical or social world. For more information, see Martin (2004). *See also* Control Group; Experimental Group

Experimental Group   A group that receives an experimental manipulation (treatment) that is hypothesized to cause a particular change in state or behavior. Experimental studies designed to identify causal relationships between variables must include at least one experimental group that receives a treatment and a comparison group, usually called the *control group,* that is similar in every way except that it does not receive the treatment. *See also* Control Group; Experiment

Experimental Research   A type of research in which experimental conditions are manipulated or created (in the laboratory or field) for one or more groups of research participants to determine whether participants' thoughts and/or behaviors change as a result of their participation in the experiment. The key ingredients under the researcher's control in experimental design are (a) the use of one or more pretests (i.e., measurement on the outcome variable before the experimental manipulation starts), (b) the use of one or more posttests (i.e., measurement on the outcome variable after the experimental manipulation ends), (c) comparison groups (e.g., a control group that receives no treatment, an experimental group that receives the treatment, and any additional comparison groups that receive different types or amounts of the treatment), and (d) the assignment mechanism used to place participants into groups (with random assignment being the superior assignment mechanism). *See also* Nonexperimental Research in Quantitative Research

Experimental Research Designs   The defining characteristic of such research designs is control (i.e., purposeful manipulation) of the independent variable(s). The strongest experimental designs also have random assignment of participants to treatment and control groups. In experiments, researchers do something to the research participants (they intervene, administer a treatment, or modify an environment), and they examine the results of this activity. They do not simply observe or ask questions.

In a simple design, participants are randomly assigned to an experimental group or a control group. Random assignment is crucial because it makes the groups equivalent (within the limits of probability) at the beginning of the experiment. It is also important that experimenters control the treatment so that they know its nature, size, and timing. The experimental group receives the treatment, and the control group does not; the researcher then determines if the groups differ on the dependent (outcome) variable.

The varieties of experimental design are numerous. Here, only a brief overview is provided. See the work by Shadish, Cook, and Campbell (2002) for a classic treatment of the subject. Using standard notation,

O stands for observation and X stands for treatment. Here is a simple before-and-after experiment without a control group:

O   X   O

Simple Pre-Post Design

For example, an anxiety scale is administered to the patients; this is the pretest (the first O). Then, an experimental therapy is tried (the X). Next, follows a second administration of the anxiety scale, which is the posttest (the second O). A *simple pre-/postdesign* is a weak design because without a control group, the experimenter cannot be sure that any reduction in anxiety is due to the therapy. There are many rival explanations for the outcome.

A strong experiment, with random assignment (symbolized R) to control and experimental groups, is notated as follows:

R   O   X   O (experimental group)

R   O   O (control group)

Basic Randomized Experiment

In a *basic randomized experiment,* by comparing two equivalent groups (one that receives and one that does not receive the treatment) and by giving both groups the pretest and posttest, the researcher can be *much* more confident about the effect of the therapy (X).

The number of possible combinations of groups, observations, and treatments is very large. Each combination produces a different experimental design; each has specific strengths or helps avoid specific kinds of weaknesses. For example, if the experimenter worried that the pretest might influence participants' posttest scores, a *Solomon four-group design* could be used. It is depicted as follows:

R   O   X   O

R   O   O

R   X   O

R   O

Solomon Four-Group Design

Groups 1 and 2 are the same as in the second figure, but Groups 3 and 4 omit the pretest. Adding Groups 3 and 4 to the design controls for any effects the pretest has on the posttest. For more information, see Shadish, Cook, and Campbell (2002). *See also* Experimental Research; External Validity; Internal Validity; Rival Hypotheses; Variable (education, sociology)

Expert Testimony   Statements made in court by a qualified individual (or expert) based on his or her knowledge, education, training, or previous experience.

Expert testimonies are very different from lay-witness testimonies, which are not based on expertise but rather on observation or recollection of events. Some examples of qualified individuals who may provide expert testimonies are forensic psychologists, psychiatrists, medical doctors, and so on. Expert testimonies are used to address the legitimacy of evidence presented in court. *See also* Expert Witness (psychology)

Expert Witness *(education)*   A specialist in an area of knowledge (by education and/or experience) who can provide pertinent information to the court in criminal and/or civil cases. Unlike other types of witnesses, who may only provide facts, experts may also offer personal opinions relevant to each specific case. *See also* Expert Testimony

Expert Witness *(psychology)*   An individual who by virtue of knowledge, skill, experience, training, or education can provide scientific, technical, or other specialized knowledge to the court when such information is deemed necessary to assist the trier of fact in understanding the evidence or determining an issue in a legal proceeding (adapted from the Federal Rules of Evidence, Article 7, Rule 702). Whereas lay witnesses are restricted to testimony of direct observations, expert witnesses provide opinions to the court on the basis of scientific evidence or specialized knowledge. In the United States, potential expert witnesses must be qualified by the court as experts. Prior to 1993, the dominant vehicle by which federal and most state judges assessed the admissibility of expert testimony in court was the Frye rule, based on the decision of the Supreme Court in *Frye v. US* (1923), which stated that the scientific evidence on which testimony was based had to be "sufficiently established or generally accepted by the field to which it belongs." In 1993, the Supreme Court's decision in *Daubert v. Merrell Dow Pharmaceutical* ruled that expert opinion be based on inference derived by the scientific method and gave the Court the responsibility of determining whether the reasoning or methodology underlying the evidence is scientifically sound. About half of U.S. states adhere to the *Frye* rule. For more information, see *Daubert v. Merrell Dow Pharmaceutical* (1993), *Frye v. US* (1923), and Poythress and Slobogin (2007). *See also* Expert Testimony

Explanation   A description that clarifies the context, meaning, and consequences of a certain situation or object. It can establish rules and laws and clarify them. Certain disciplines, such as history, art, literature, and social science, use different methods of explanation, ranging from descriptive to inductive. Explanations uncover new knowledge, forming the basis of research.

Explicit Memory   Conscious and intentional memory of previous experiences and learned information. Explicit memory for autobiographical events is generally referred to as *episodic explicit memory,* whereas memory for nonautobiographical information is referred to as *semantic explicit memory*. Semantic explicit memory includes memory for things such as historical events, facts and figures, vocabulary, and mathematics. It also includes memory for faces and names that allows us to recognize others. Coding of explicit memory depends on conceptually driven, top-down processing, during which a person makes associations to previously learned information or experience. Recall of explicit memory is largely influenced by the way in which the information was originally processed. The neural structures that have been associated with explicit memory include many of the limbic structures (e.g., amygdala, the hippocampus) and the prefrontal cortex. *See also* Implicit Memory

Exploratory Data Analysis   A term attributed to Tukey (1977), who proposed the use of existing and innovative graphic (box-and-whisker and stem-and-leaf plots) and numeric methods to simplify data description and stimulate generation of new hypotheses for testing.

Exploratory Evaluation   An activity designed to measure and judge the merits of a government policy or program. An exploratory evaluation refers to the method and approach by which the evaluation is conducted with no original basis of study or model used. Exploratory evaluation usually occurs after the fact. Other methods are used to either formulate or evaluate policy, such as systems analysis, simulation, and benefit-cost analysis. At the onset of the evaluation, hardly anything is known about the policy, and the approach is initially about abstracting and generalizing the policy and related information at hand. It is imperative to approach the subject matter from several different viewpoints, either from the angles of various established policies or just from miscellaneous practical points of view. *See also* Evaluation (public administration)

Ex Post Facto   A Latin expression for "after the fact." Ex post facto occurs when laws prohibiting a given behavior are enacted after the commission of the act. Such laws are inadmissible in the United States, since the individual's behavior was not considered to be an offense at the time of the act.

Exposure   The presentation of information through the media to audiences. Exposure is not limited to human beings based on gender, race, or age; instead, the relationship between exposure and audiences is focused toward the question of access. The exposure to media messages can occur through communications media, such as television and the Internet. Exposure can be direct (as seen in interactive media, such as online or telephone usage) or passive (such as television or radio). There can also be different levels of exposure and consumption based on frequency of engagement with media texts by audiences. In addition, market researchers strategize the placement of their products in media texts for the goal of maximum exposure to

attractive demographics. Censorship may be practiced by those who wish to limit the exposure of certain media messages to others. There is a contemporary debate about young people's exposure to, and subsequent influence by, the media. *See also* Access; Salience

Expressiveness   The degree to which someone uses language to communicate a thought. The degree of expressiveness will vary depending on the cultural influences. There is less agreement among social scientists on why these differences exist. While some researchers propose that innate differences in how infants in different ethnic groups react to distress underlie the subsequent differences in emotional expressivity, other theories support the view that cultural and family environments influence a child's expressiveness.

Culture and family environment influence children's facial expressivity and create differences among children of the same ethnicity, as suggested by results from a study of four groups of young Chinese and American girls. In general, adopted Chinese girls were more expressive than Chinese American and mainland Chinese girls.

The nonverbal channel of communication includes visual information (such as the face), the vocal channel involves the tone of voice, the verbal channel relies on the spoken word, and the audiovisual channel combines visual and verbal cues. A great deal of expression can be shown in one's face, and when it is combined with expressive voice quality, a person can communicate in a very animated manner. For more information, see Ambady and Rosenthal (1992). *See also* Communication

External Costs   Costs that are not directly controlled or incurred by a "demander" in a market but are the consequences of an exchange. Frequently, these costs cannot easily be quantified, and the burden of these costs can be on individuals or society. An example of an external cost would be the loss of civil liberties and freedoms as a consequence of increased police surveillance; however, external costs can be positive. For example, the pollen, an allergen, is transformed into honey by bees; likewise, carbon is transformed into air by trees.

Externality   A spillover cost or benefit to a society, and sometimes to the rest of the world. Externality may be linked to the overallocation and underallocation of resources. A spillover cost or benefit affects a third or *external* (nonmarket) party. Private costs are borne by producers and consumers of a good because producers incur costs in the process of producing a good, which can be transferred to consumers who will derive satisfaction from the consumption of such a good.

The social cost is the combination of the private cost and external or environmental cost. This identity makes it feasible to see that the external cost is the social-private cost differential. External benefits can analogously be understood as the social-private benefit differential.

The market supply curve of a firm or a firm's marginal cost (damage) curve (when it is not a monopolist) does not capture all the costs associated with production. The costs are much higher. As such, spillover costs are associated with overallocation of resources, a situation in which society is using up more resources than are necessary to produce the optimal outcome. Environmental pollution is a good example of external cost.

Conversely, external benefits indicate that the allocation of societal resources is suboptimal because the market is only responding to private wants, not social wants. For example, those who can afford the high cost of acquired immune deficiency syndrome (AIDS) drugs will purchase them, but not those who cannot afford them. Society is endangered because of the potential spread of the epidemic. If, however, a social planner can intervene with inoculations and preventive mechanisms, even those who are not immediate beneficiaries ultimately become beneficiaries because of the external effects of reducing infections. Those who are not active participants in the AIDS drug market become beneficiaries. Alternatively, policymakers can subsidize production of AIDS drugs.

Externality is therefore the result of market failure. The market cannot always achieve the best or optimal outcome, and therefore, some amount of intervention by policymakers may be warranted to minimize the external effects of market failure. Tools at the disposal of policymakers include regulation, taxes (to minimize external cost), and subsidy (to increase external benefit). For more information, see Field and Field (2006), McConnell and Brue (2008), and Schiller (2006). *See also* Cost-Benefit Analysis (CBA) (economics); Deregulation (economics, political science); Fiscal Policy; Market; Market Failure

External Validity   The degree to which research findings can be generalized. External validity includes the extent to which research findings can be applied to the population of interest. External validity also includes the extent to which research findings can be extended to different people, places, settings, times, outcomes, and treatment variations. *See also* Internal Validity

Extinction *(psychology)*   The eradication of a behavior. Behaviors will become extinct naturally if they are not rewarded in some manner. However, the schedule of reinforcement of a given behavior will determine how easily the behavior will become extinct. For example, if a conditioned response has been created with a regular and predictable reward or punishment, then the absence of that reward or punishment will quickly lead to extinction. If, however, the reward or punishment has

been applied intermittently (or irregularly), then experiencing the conditioned stimulus sets up an expectancy for reward or punishment, which maintains the behavior and makes it more resistant to extinction. Another way of extinguishing a behavior is by making a person accustomed to the stimulus that produces the behavior, without responding. Many psychological interventions for anxiety use such techniques. *See also* Operant Conditioning

Extinction *(sociology)*   An extinct entity or behavior is one that no longer lives or exists or that has ceased being used. The state of extinction alludes to a particular being, species, and so on that is in the process of becoming extinct.

Extradition   The delivery of an accused person suspected or convicted of a crime or a fugitive from the state where he or she has taken refuge to the state that asserts jurisdiction over that person. The purpose of extradition is to allow the demanding state to prosecute the accused. Extradition is an act of international legal cooperation in that almost all extraditions take place under the authority of bilateral treaties. Such treaties often require evidence that the accused violated the laws of both jurisdictions. Within the United States, the Constitution imposed a duty on governors, under Article IV, Section 2, to deliver fugitives from justice found in their respective state. This is commonly referred as *interstate rendition*. *See also* Jurisdiction (political science)

Extraneous Variable/Evidence   In research, a third variable, which may contribute to the explanation of the dependent variable through its effect on the independent variable; in an investigation, additional information obtained from external sources that may affect the outcome of a situation or case. *See also* Variable (sociology)

Extrinsic Motivation   Motivation that comes from outside an individual, such as the drive to obtain money or rewards, which provides pleasure that the task that one does to obtain the reward does not provide in itself. Extrinsic motivation might cause a person to work on a task even when he or she has no interest in it because the anticipated reward for doing the task provides satisfaction (e.g., the paycheck). Companies use extrinsic motivation to obtain customer loyalty by mechanisms such as reward cards or airline miles programs. The main problem with using extrinsic motivation to obtain desired behaviors is that the focus is on the reward and not on the behavior; once the reward is removed, the behavior is usually extinguished. *See also* Intrinsic Motivation

F

Face-Saving In certain high-context cultures, conflicts present dilemmas to the parties involved because of the social weight placed on maintaining a positive self-image. To these cultures, it is more important not to "look bad," or to "save face," than to admit a mistake. As a result, conflicts can continue and spiral out of control because neither side will admit any wrongdoing. Skillful negotiators stress on minor concessions so that both parties can claim a way out of what can be a dangerous bind and, thus, emerge with a positive self-image, with nobody claiming total victory. Negotiators William Ury and Martin Linsky discourage gloating when somebody wins, since such behavior tends to encourage resentment and perhaps future, and more serious, conflicts. On a global scale, we can see that agreements such as the Treaty of Versailles in 1919, which ended World War I, only bred resentment on the part of Germany and was a key component in the events that led up to World War II. Ury and Linsky refer to the Cuban Missile Crisis of the early 1960s and the delicate negotiations that kept the United States and the Soviet Union from nuclear disaster, as well as four other disasters that involved such face-saving. For more information, see Ury and Linsky (1985). *See also* High-Context Culture

Face-to-Face Communication The exchange of information between human beings who share the same time and space. This type of communication is defined by verbal interactions, although nonverbal behavior can also be evident (such as facial expressions and body language). Face-to-face communication can occur in formal and informal contexts. It can be marred by conflict; however, interpersonal communication strategies can be learned to overcome these obstacles. Listening is a critical factor in face-to-face communication, as a feedback loop is a part of this interaction. Topics discussed in face-to-face communication can range from the offering of personal advice to a job performance appraisal. In the late 20th and early 21st centuries, face-to-face communication has often become replaced by computer-mediated communication due to social networking technologies. Critics argue that face-to-face communication plays a significant role in developing connections between individuals in ways that digital technologies cannot replicate. Face-to-face communication is commonly referred to as FTF.

Face Validity The subjective assessment of whether the measured variable appears to be an adequate measure of the conceptual variable. Therefore, face validity (also called a priori validity) can serve as a preliminary indication of the construct validity of a measured variable. Usually, face validity is high if the content (and the associated responses) of an item is intuitively appealing, as in the Rosenberg Self-Esteem Scale ("I feel that I have a number of good qualities"). However, face validity may not always be a desirable characteristic of items. Items explicitly revolving around controversial themes such as racism may not be suited to assess the conceptual variable because participants might feel offended or do not want to indicate their true response, particularly when anonymity is not guaranteed. In such cases of high reactivity, low face validity might be a more desirable feature. For more information, see Shaughnessy, Zeichmeister, and Zechmeister (2000). *See also* Validity

Facial-Feedback Hypothesis According to this hypothesis, facial movements associated with an emotion will induce the corresponding emotional state. Consistent with this hypothesis, several studies demonstrate that smiling can induce positive feelings, in part perhaps because it also prompts you to recall positive experiences. The facial-feedback hypothesis is associated with the James-Lange theory of emotion, which postulates that physiological states induce emotional states, in contrast to the Cannon-Bard theory, which postulates that sensory information triggers the experience of fear. Cognitive theories (e.g., the Schacter-Singer theory) argue that physiological feedback may not vary enough to create the many different emotions people experience and propose that cognitive interpretation, or attribution (e.g., the cognitive appraisal theory by Lazarus), is needed to account for this variation. For more information, see Zajonc, Murphy, and Inglehart (1989). *See also* Cannon-Bard Theory; James-Lange Theory

Fact A piece of information that can be verified to exist by observation or that is generally agreed on as true. A fact is distinguished from hypotheses or theories, which are tools used to explain or interpret known facts. *See also* Theory (communication, psychology, sociology)

Faction A subset of individuals within a larger political organization who share a common objective and band together in efforts to achieve it. In the United States, there are informal issue-oriented factions within the Republican and Democratic political parties. According to a *New York Times* piece by Bill Marsh (2006,

October 1), the following factions exist within both parties. Among the Republicans are the (1) leave-us-alone—opponents of government intervention, especially fiscal; (2) cultural—concerned with religious and moral values and their apparent decline; (3) security—supportive of military intervention to support democracy efforts abroad; and (4) old-guard—in favor of abortion rights, an environmental policy, and tax cuts—factions. Among the Democrats are the (1) social justice—the younger set, ideological and issue driven; (2) old-line—the older set, committed to New Deal agenda; (3) centrist—most closely following the Republican ideology; and (4) new left—anti-establishment, anticorporate, and antibureaucratic—factions. For more information, see Marsh (2006).

Factor Analysis *(education)*   A factor is a set of related variables. Factor analysis is used to find factors or clusters of intercorrelated variables, such as a group of items on a survey instrument that refer to the same concept. Exploratory factor analysis is used to discover factors. Confirmatory factor analysis is part of structural equation modeling. ***See also*** Structural Equation Modeling

Factor Analysis *(psychology)*   A multivariate statistical technique used to investigate the underlying pattern of correlations among a set of measured variables and to provide a simplified structure of the relationships among these variables. Factor analysis is employed to reduce the number of variables by creating or extracting a smaller number of (higher order) factors, each of which is a linear combination of the scores in the original measured variables. The number of factors is quantified that adequately expresses the variation in the variables (indicated by the factor-loading matrix), and then (depending on the research question) the factors are mapped (rotated) onto the variance to achieve an independent factorial structure. Then, scores of individuals can be expressed as factor scores instead of item scores. Exploratory factor analysis is used when the researcher has not yet formed clear expectations on how these variables relate to factors, while confirmatory factor analysis allows testing specified relationships between items that are assumed to form factors. This can also be achieved by applying structural equation modeling (SEM) and other techniques. ***See also*** Statistics (psychology)

Factor Analysis *(sociology)*   A multivariate statistical method used to explain patterns of relationship among a large number of variables. Factor analysis identifies the underlying independent variables ("factors," or latent variables) that were not measured but nonetheless significantly affect variation in the dependent variables. Factor analysis allows for the reduction in the number of variables to a smaller number of factors with a minimum loss of information. Factor analysis is also useful in the identification of groups of interrelated variables. Originated by the British psychologist Charles Spearman, factor analysis is used widely in the social sciences and marketing. ***See also*** Statistics (sociology)

Factorial Design   An experimental design in which two or more independent variables, at least one of which is manipulated, are studied to determine their separate and joint effects (called main effects and interaction effects). The treatment conditions are determined by "crossing" the independent variables. For example, if one independent variable has two levels (e.g., pill and placebo) and the other has three levels (high, medium, and low amounts of sleep), there would be 6 (3 × 2) experimental conditions to which participants would be randomly assigned. They would experience their "condition" and be measured on the dependent (i.e., outcome) variable that the researcher hopes to influence. The advantage of factorial designs over one-factor-at-a-time experiments is that they are more efficient and they allow interaction effects to be detected. ***See also*** Experimental Research; Variable (education)

Fair Trade   Equitable and humane conditions for production, compensation, and access to goods and services at fair prices. There are three significant components of the theory: (1) fair protection, (2) buying commodities at competitive prices, and (3) avoidance of labor abuse.

A corollary aspect of fair trade is free trade, which means the removal of unfair restrictions from the free flow of goods across national boundaries. In actual fact, nations are engaged in managed trade, since no nation will permit the unfettered flow of all sorts and conditions of goods across its boundaries. The hallmarks of fairness are the lack of discriminatory trading practices, that is, the extension of "the most favored nation" (MFN) provision to all trading partners and the removal of illegal subsidies to producers to promote competition.

Fair trade also means that products must be sold at competitive prices and that producers must be rewarded accordingly. Pointedly, businesses must avoid dumping (selling at cheaper prices abroad to eliminate competition), and producers must get a fair price for their products by eliminating expensive intermediation and barriers to their products.

The evasion of environmental laws, payment of starvation wages, and abuse of labor laws (unfair trade practices) enable some businesses to produce at very cheap cost to outperform their competitors. Poverty and income inequality in developing nations are normally associated with unfair trade—adverse prices for agricultural products and subsidy of farming in some developed countries. The World Trade Organization (WTO) is responsible for the promotion of free and fair trade, and it is the international institution within which unfair trade practices and trade disputes can be resolved. For more information, see Carbaugh (2007) and Dunkley (2004). ***See also*** Free Trade; Globalization (economics, political science); World Trade Organization (WTO)

Fallacy   A part of the argument that is flawed and so makes the entire argument invalid. There are various types of fallacies. A formal fallacy is a deductive argument that has an invalid form. An informal fallacy is a mode of reasoning whose flaw is not in the form of an argument.

False Negative In inferential statistics, this term is also known as the "Type II error," "β error," or "error of the second kind" and describes the error of failing to reject a null hypothesis (groups do not differ significantly in the variable x) when the alternative hypothesis would be more adequate (groups differ significantly in the variable x). The probability of committing this error is formulated as "β," and the power of the statistical test is "$1 - β$." False negatives may occur due to random error in measurement. They may also occur due to low effect sizes of the investigated relationship between variables, which determines the power of the statistical test. The β cannot be set like α, the significance level of a test, which influences false positives (Type I error). In any research, there is a trade-off between making false negatives and false positives: Lowering α (i.e., decreasing the chance of rejecting a correct null hypothesis) increases β (increasing the probability of rejecting a correct alternative hypothesis). For more information, see Cohen (1977). ***See also*** False Positive; Hypothesis (psychology); Null Hypothesis (education, psychology, sociology); Statistics (psychology, sociology)

False Positive In inferential statistics, this term is also known as the "Type I error," "α error," or "error of the first kind" and describes the error of rejecting a null hypothesis (groups do not differ significantly in the variable x) when it is actually true. The probability of committing this error is formulated as "α" and can be set by the experimenter (conventionally, it is set to .05 or .01). For α = .05, the chance of erroneously rejecting the null hypothesis is 5 out of 100. However, false positives may still occur due to random error in measurement. The probability for false positives is closely linked to false negatives (the error of failing to reject a null hypothesis when the alternative hypothesis would be more adequate): Lowering α (i.e., decreasing the chance of rejecting a correct null hypothesis) increases β (increasing the probability of rejecting a correct alternative hypothesis). For more information, see Cohen (1977). ***See also*** False Negative; Hypothesis (education); Null Hypothesis (education, psychology, sociology); Statistics (psychology, sociology)

Family An institutionalized social group of adults and children united by ties of affinity (marriage), consanguinity (blood), or adoption, usually residing in a single household. While other family forms (e.g., polygynous) have existed throughout history, the basic family unit in Western cultures is a nuclear family, which consists of a married couple living with their immediate children. Families including more than these basic individuals are considered an extended family—a kinship group of a married couple, their children, and other close relatives, such as aunts, uncles, and cousins. The functions of the family are the care, socialization, and enculturation of children; provision of basic physical, economic, and affective security for its members; and serving as a legitimated site for procreation.

Family Counseling Therapy or interventions that treat the family as a unit or a system. Counseling involves the unit because the entire family is affected by the behaviors, needs, or characteristics of one or more members. Counseling is solution based and may include interventions that are behavioral, cognitive, physical, or emotional. The focus is on relationships and communication so that the whole family benefits and target problems can be managed, solved, or eliminated. ***See also*** Systems Theory in Counseling; Therapy

Family Court A court that is convened to handle and decide civil and criminal matters concerning parents, spouses, and juveniles according to family law. Family courts may decide matters such as custody of children, the dissolution of marriage, visitation, child support, paternity, juvenile delinquency, and the issuance of orders of protection in domestic violence cases. Family court hearings are heard and decided by judges or magistrates; there are no juries in family court. In family court proceedings, children may be appointed a representative, such as a law guardian, to serve in the child's interests. ***See also*** Delinquency; Juvenile; Juvenile Justice System

Family Education Rights and Privacy Act (FERPA) A federal law established in 1974 to protect the rights of students by controlling the release of their personal information (also known as the Buckley Amendment). FERPA ensures that students may access their academic records, while unauthorized individuals are denied such access.

Family Therapy The treatment of two or more individuals from the same family system, often with one individual as the initial client and the family ultimately becoming an additional client or clients. This form of treatment originated from the idea that the problems and disorders displayed by one family member usually reflect problems in the functioning of the entire family unit. The goals of family therapy are not only to alleviate the problems of the initial client but also to create harmony and balance in the family system. Like group therapy, family therapy focuses strongly on the interaction within the family, and observation of this behavior often serves as a starting point for treatment. There are several different forms of family therapy. Structural family therapy concentrates on dysfunctional family communication patterns and on breaking up rigid patterns of alliances that are associated with the emergence of problems. Behavioral therapists use the group format to increase acceptance of so-called behavioral contracts that can help establish rules and reinforcement contingencies to encourage desirable behavior. Couples therapy, in which communication between partners is typically the focus, can be considered another form of family therapy. For more information, see Beels (2002). *See also* Psychotherapy

Fascism   An ideology that includes historical, cultural, and political facets or secondary references. As a political ideology, it represents an extreme right-wing ideology that stresses the subordination of individuals' interests to the interests of the state and the nation. It includes ideologies troubled with fears of cultural decline and social disorder. From this perspective, a fascist regime often stresses notions of racial superiority (often white supremacy), and it seeks to exorcise society's "internal enemies" menacing the unity of the nation. One of the prime examples of a fascist regime has been in Italy under Benito Mussolini (1883–1945).

Contemporary theorists find fascism difficult to define, partly because fascist ideology has varied widely. Among fascist states of the 1920s and 1930s, there were, however, certain common features, organizational strategies, and similar enemies. A common feature of fascism is that they hold simplistic ideologies because they subordinate complex societal problems to single causes and single remedies. They are also fundamentalist because they rely on notions of the world as being "good" or "bad" and therefore there is no such thing as neutrality. In their political regimes, they created police states, one-party systems led by a charismatic dictator. On the other hand, their economic systems are aimed to develop some form of national socialism. Unlike Marxian socialism, the state was not to take over the means of production. Fascist socialism was directed at the interests of the nation, not a particular class. In foreign policy, fascist regimes are, for the most part, expansionist: Mussolini revived Italy's vision of an African colonial empire, Adolf Hitler's Third Reich aspired to a great empire in Europe, and the Spanish Falangists longed for African territories and natural resources.

So complex has the term become that these days fascism applies to anything from right-wing terrorist groups in Italy to military dictatorships, from the police to criminal gangs. Following the events of 1989 and the end of Soviet influence in Eastern Europe and the Balkans, fascist-inspired movements and popular uprisings have surfaced in a number of these regions. Scholars have noted that there is a strong likelihood that additional fascist-style regimes might arise in this region of the world. They would feed on the conflicting nationalisms in the area, and they might be spearheaded by the military. Even if such regimes were to emerge, however, it appears unlikely that they would pose a threat to the international order in the way Nazi Germany precipitated the crisis of World War II. Nevertheless, the rise of fascist regimes might be an expression of fascism's appeal to the masses.

Federal Bureau of Investigation (FBI)   A law enforcement agency that serves as the investigative branch within the U.S. Department of Justice. The FBI was established in 1908 and maintains headquarters in Washington, D.C. In addition to investigating federal offenses, the FBI is charged with collecting and distributing crime data through the Uniform Crime Reporting Program. *See also* Index Crimes/Offenses; Uniform Crime Report (UCR) (Part I/Part II Offenses)

Federalism   A system of government whereby sovereignty is divided among a strong central authority and constituent subunits. Authority is divided between at least two levels, such as national and state governments, whereby each level retains sovereignty over matters in some areas. The authority each maintains is constitutionally authorized.

Federalism gained momentum in the United States in the past two decades of the 19th century, especially after the Civil War. The earliest Federalists believed that a strong central government would facilitate the economic and political strength needed to maintain independence, especially from England. The Anti-Federalists, however, argued that federalism would replace one tyranny with another. The system that was created was a dual federalism in which both the federal and the state governments were considered coequals. Although dual federalism existed theoretically, in practice, the federal government had the greater power over states' interests.

After the Depression of the 1930s and two world wars, the federal government became even more centralized. The provisions of the New Deal recognized that a strong federal government was needed for a national economic crisis. The national government assumed authority over areas of economic regulation and development that had previously been the domain of the states. Since then, there has been a gradual shift to cooperative federalism, which asserts that the national government is supreme over the states. *See also* Cooperative Federalism; Executive Federalism

Federalist   A proponent of both a strong union and adoption of the U.S. Constitution, as well as a member of the Federalist Party. The Federalists, who took their name from the Federalist Papers, were conservatives who encouraged the growth of industries and favored the needs of merchants and landowners. Federalists themselves were mostly wealthy merchants, large land owners in the North, and small farmers and businessmen. They were geographically concentrated in New England and the middle-Atlantic states.

In the 1790s, the Federalist Party was formed. It was led by Alexander Hamilton and John Adams. It dominated the U.S. government until 1801, when Thomas Jefferson took office as president. The Federalists believed that the national government was obligated to preserve the public peace against both internal and external attacks, regulate commerce with other nations and interstate trade, and supervise political or commercial discussions with foreign countries. Furthermore, the Federalists believed that the national government should be in charge of the states and that it had a duty to protect the states. The essays that Hamilton wrote for the collection that came to be known as The Federalist Papers analyzed the weaknesses of the Articles of Confederation, considered the first constitution of the United States. According to the Federalists, the Articles of Confederation had established a central government too weak for law enforcement, interstate commerce, and defense.

After the U.S. Constitution was adopted, a division grew in the government, and the War of 1812 began the demise of the Federalist Party. The other dominant political party, the Democratic-Republican party, founded by Thomas Jefferson and James Madison, opposed the policies of the Federalists. Contributing factors that helped end the Federalists' reign were their foreign policies, internal conflicts, and the death of Hamilton in a duel with Aaron Burr in 1804. For more information, see Elkins and McKitrick (1995) and Madison, Hamilton, and Jay (1788/1987). *See also* Articles of Confederation

Federalist Papers   A collection of 85 essays intended to promote the ratification of the U.S. Constitution by countering the arguments of the Anti-Federalists who were against the ratification of the Constitution. The Federalist Papers were written and published between late 1787 and early 1788. The majority of the papers were written by the Federalist Alexander Hamilton (51), while the rest were written by James Madison, a Democratic-Republican (29), and John Jay (5). The Federalist Papers illustrated the tension between Madison, who wanted a weaker central government, and Hamilton, who wanted a strong central government over the states.

The Federalist Papers were originally signed "Citizen of New York," but the signature was changed to "Publius," the defender of the ancient Roman republic, since one of the writers was not a citizen of New York. The papers were later published in states other than New York. New York was first chosen as the site to publish the Federalist Papers as it was one of the remaining pivotal states where ratification of the new Constitution was most in doubt. Alexander Hamilton decided that a massive propaganda campaign was needed in New York to convince New Yorkers to ratify the Constitution. As a result, a barrage of publications was sustained four times a week in New York newspapers. The three writers did not agree on all ideas, but they did agree on republicanism, federalism, separation of powers, and free government, each of which was dealt with in the Federalist Papers. The Federalist Papers possibly provided the greatest insight into interpreting the source of the Constitution.

Federal System   The Constitution of the United States implemented the federal system, also known as federalism. Under this political system, the governments' powers are constitutionally divided between the national or federal government and the local or state governments. This system allows independence to local governments to exercise sovereignty in specific areas, such as taxation.

Federal system should be seen as a political organization (polity) uniting various local governments into one overarching political system, allowing each political unit to maintain levels of autonomy. In theory, a federal system allows for local sovereignty, where each authority is responsible and has authority over local issues. Ultimately, however, the federal government, or executive branch, has sovereignty over the regions of the country.

In the United States, all local governments and the federal government base their power to govern in the written Constitution. A sophisticated judiciary system is in place deciding on conflicts, where the federal government, ultimately, and when necessary, reasserts its decisions.

To compare, European countries such as Switzerland have a federation of different autonomous areas with different languages and religions. For more information, see Robertson (1985) and Scruton (1982).

Feedback *(communication)*   A process of sharing ideas, concerns, and suggestions between people in an organization or organizations with the intention of improving organizational performance. Negative feedback implies criticism within the organization. It helps maintain stability in a system in spite of changes outside the organization. Positive feedback implies constructive, praiseworthy behavior within the organization. It amplifies divergent possibilities (e.g., change of plans) and allows growth and evolution within the organization. Positive feedback allows equilibrium to foster in the organization. Examples of feedback in government are elections and the mass media. Examples of feedback in organizations include marketing research and performance appraisals.

Feedback *(education)*   Information provided to a learner to compare his or her actual understanding and performance with expected understanding and performance. This information can be cognitive (e.g., correctness of an answer, supply of specific knowledge, and learning strategies), metacognitive (e.g., reflective knowledge about the learning process), and/or affective (e.g., verbal or material rewards for motivating a learner). Feedback can be provided in an immediate or delayed manner. The sources of feedback can be multiple and sometimes mediated by technology: teacher, self, peers, materials developers, and new learning experiences. Therefore, feedback has an important role but different functions in different learning theories.

Feedforward   A system that reacts to and anticipates changes in the environment. Derived mainly from physical and applied sciences such as engineering, the object of this system is to calculate any disturbances or deviations upstream or in the way of one's path. With feedforward, one uses an algorithm with certain corrective tools to anticipate problems in the system and

F

maintain a desired state. In communications and other social science systems, the concept is useful in focusing on solutions and positive outcomes rather than any failures in the past.

Felon/Felony   The term *felon* refers to a person convicted of a felony offense. Felony offenses are the most serious criminal offenses and are best understood when contrasted with misdemeanors. The distinction between felony and misdemeanor offenses is typically made by reference to the amount of punishment a person could receive if convicted. Felonies are offenses for which a person can be sentenced to more than one year in prison. Murder, robbery, rape, and burglary are all felony offenses. Some offenses, such as assault, drug possession, and larceny-theft can be charged as felony or misdemeanor offenses. *See also* Index Crimes/Offenses; Misdemeanor; Offender/Offense

Felony Murder   If a person dies during the commission of a serious felony offense, the person committing the felony can be charged with felony murder, even if she or he did not intend the death. The felony murder doctrine, which has been abandoned in many countries, applies in all U.S. jurisdictions. *See also* Felon/Felony; *Mens Rea;* Murder; Offender/Offense

Feminine/Masculine Culture   One of the five cultural dimensions developed by the Dutch organizational anthropologist Geert Hofstede and used in intercultural training. According to Hofstede, nations can be categorized (and assigned a score) as either predominantly masculine or feminine based on a variety of national sociocultural characteristics. Masculine characteristics include a preference for achievement, competitiveness, heroism, and assertiveness. Feminine characteristics include modesty, equality, unity, empathy, and the use of negotiation and compromise in conflict resolution. The strongest indicator of a masculine country, however, is the size of the gender gap: The gap is significantly larger in masculine countries than in feminine ones. A feminine culture exhibits less differentiation between the genders, and equality is more prevalent.

With regard to interpersonal communication, in a masculine culture, where sex roles are more rigid and males are more dominant, there is generally less—or at best merely superficial—interpersonal interaction between the sexes than in a feminine culture. In a feminine culture, interpersonal communication is more intimate.

On a group level, practical application of Hofstede's dimensions is found mostly in intercultural communication, especially business, where professionals and companies can potentially engage in more effective working relationships on understanding these cultural underpinnings.

In terms of media and mass communication, the concept can also be played out in advertisements produced by a country. For instance, research has supported the idea that ads generated in feminine countries tend to depict relationships. For more information, see Hofstede (1980, 1998). *See also* Gender Differences; Sexism

Feminism   A critical theoretical framework based on the assumption that women are oppressed and exploited by virtue of gender. Many forms of feminism exist, such as Marxist, liberal, radical, psychoanalytic, socialist, existentialist, and postmodern (Crotty, 2003). Feminism is often divided into "waves" or time periods, with the "First Wave" referring to the suffrage movement in the 19th and early 20th centuries. The "Second Wave" refers to work during the 1960s to late 1980s. The "Third Wave" began in the 1990s and continues through the present. Major authors include Judith Butler, Patricia Collins, Betty Friedan, Sandra Harding, bell hooks, and Simone de Beauvoir. For more information, see Crotty (2003). *See also* Critical Theory; Essentialism; Standpoint Epistemology

Feminist Counseling   Counseling that promotes a framework of both personal and professional development through a nonsexist belief system and encourages egalitarian relationships. Feminist counseling emerged as a reaction to traditionally established counseling approaches that embraced societal beliefs associated with male-dominated power structures. *See also* Counseling

Fetal Alcohol Syndrome (FAS)   A pattern of physical and mental defects that affects up to half the babies born to women who regularly abuse alcohol during pregnancy. Unlike many other substances, alcohol can cross the placental barrier and affect the nervous system of the embryo. FAS is characterized by mental retardation and facial deformities (e.g., underdeveloped upper jaw, widely spaced eyes, and flattened nose), as well as many secondary impairments (e.g., mental health problems) arising from prenatal damage to the central nervous system. FAS is considered the leading preventable cause of mental retardation. Heavy use of alcohol during pregnancy can lead to miscarriage, premature delivery, and stillbirth. For more information, see Stratton, Howe, and Battaglia (1996). *See also* Developmental Psychology

Field Experience   A critical part of teacher preparation programs that involves teaching practice in the school setting. The practice provides preservice teachers an opportunity to apply what they learned in their school of education and to connect theory with practice. Also known as "classroom observations," "practice teaching," or "student teaching."

Field Interview   A brief contact between a police officer and a citizen, on foot or in a vehicle, based on reasonable suspicion. Individuals may be stopped and questioned in field interviews to prevent and investigate crimes or to promote community relations. ***See also*** Reasonable Suspicion

Field Notes A written account of a qualitative researcher's observations. Field notes might include a diagram of the physical setting of the observation, observer commentary, descriptions, and direct participant quotes. Depending on the researcher's preference and the circumstances of the study, field notes may be written up on-site or off-site.

Field Research Research that involves participant observation and data collection (e.g., through surveys) in a less controlled setting than that used in laboratory research. Laboratory research strives to reduce the influence of variables that may affect the study of the desired relationship between variables. Because field research does not necessarily allow for controlling confounding variables, statistical criteria (objectivity, reliability, and validity) are often at stake. The advantage of field research lies in its (potentially) ecologically valid character, as it takes place in the natural environment rather than in artificial laboratory settings. Furthermore, some groups of participants may be difficult to reach with laboratory methods. Field research can often provide initial observations that may stimulate further and more controlled research and, therefore, could be regarded as important in hypothesis generation. The combination of the ecological validity of natural settings with an experimental approach has resulted in the so-called field experiment. For more information, see Stangor (2007). ***See also*** Archival Research; Case Study Research (psychology); Laboratory Research

Fieldwork The collection of data in the field, as opposed to in the laboratory or in other controlled environments. Fieldwork involves observation of natural behavior and events in physical or social settings and interaction with respondents in their natural environment (e.g., through surveys, interviews) to supplement observations. In that their presence may affect subjects' natural behavior, fieldworkers may or may not identify themselves as researchers during observation and data collection. Fieldwork may produce both qualitative and quantitative data for analysis and can be integrated with data from other sources. ***See also*** Ethnography (sociology); Interview (sociology); Participant Observation (sociology); Qualitative Research

Film A term often used interchangeably with "cinema" and "movies," although each term can take on different meanings depending on the theoretical perspective of the user. *Film* refers alternately to a technology (filming), a physical analog medium (film), a category of media (film/cinema/movies), an industry (the film industry), and a product (a film), all related to recording or projecting sound and/or images generally recorded with a camera. All the practices, creations, and industries that circulate around film are related by their goal of using moving images (with or without sound) to convey information or create a narrative. The creation of motion pictures was dependent on several technologies, including the invention of photography (recording images on light-sensitive materials) in 1827; the marketing of photographic film on rolls in 1889 by The Eastman Company; the invention of motion picture cameras, including one by Thomas Edison in 1891; and the first commercial projection of motion pictures by the Lumière Brothers in 1895.

Motion picture film records 24 frames per second and projects these images back at the same rate. The ability of the human perceptual system to perceive this succession of still images as uninterrupted motion has often been attributed to a concept called "persistence of vision," in which each frame supposedly burns itself into the retinal, only to be replaced by the next image that blends with it. But persistence of vision does not explain the sense of motion humans perceive, and it is more likely that we see movie motion the same way we see real-world motion, with neural motion detectors that help us comprehend changes in visual material.

The film industry developed in many places around the world at the turn of the century, including the United States, India, Scandinavia, Japan, Australia, and Europe. Early films showed everyday life as well as historical and fantasy subjects. Later, newsreels were an early form of factual reporting, which were replaced in the 1950s by television news. Hollywood began developing a film industry around 1908 and simultaneously developed a star system, promoting the actors in the motion pictures as desirable cultural icons whose personal lives were as important as their movie roles. As significant features of the cultural landscape, movies have been subjected to various forms of regulation, censorship, and voluntary rating systems that still guide the industry today. For more information, see Anderson and Anderson (1993), Corrigan and White (2004), Cousins (2004), and Prince (2004). ***See also*** Censorship (communication, media studies); Cinema; Narrative

Financial System A system in which there is interaction among financial institutions, policymakers, savers, and borrowers. Financial institutions are intermediaries that facilitate the interaction of surplus spending units (savers or investors) and deficit spending units (borrowers) in financial markets. In an effective financial system, policymakers ensure the smooth operation of financial institutions by promulgating rules and laws and ensuring adherence to regulations to prevent the collapse of the financial system. The major policymakers of a financial system are the lawmakers and the central monetary authorities of a nation.

Financial institutions consist of depository institutions (banks), contractual organizations (insurance companies), securities firms (investment companies, investment banks, and brokerage firms), and finance firms (finance companies, including mortgage banking firms). Apart from the regulatory, supervisory, and administrative role of monetary authorities, they ensure the creation and transfer of money. Financial institutions accumulate and lend or invest savings, while the financial markets facilitate the transfer of financial assets. For more information, see Burton and Lombra (2003), McConnell and Brue (2008), and Melicher and Norton (2005). *See also* Asset; Bank; Equity (economics)

Financing of Schools   The federal, state, and local income streams help in the financing of schools. Generally with some strings attached and in a marginal way, the federal government contributes to the funding of local school systems. Local education agencies also rely on the state to shoulder part of the education finance burden, a burden that differs dramatically depending on what state you reside in and how steady the income stream is that funds the educational initiatives of that state. On the local level, funding for schools is obtained through the assessment of property taxes, and bonds are typically issued to cover additional expenses not usually covered by property tax revenues, such as the building of a new school. These funding sources for education are not permanent and are subject to fluctuation when the economy dictates.

The economy drives the amount of revenue available to state and local education systems to disburse for education. A strong economy implies that more money is available to more fully fund educational initiatives statewide. With many states lacking what amounts to a "rainy-day fund," weak economies demand that state funding for education get cut or "prorated." This trickle-down system of funding passes these deficits down to the local education agencies, making budgeting for education difficult and unpredictable for administrators on all levels. When funds are cut statewide, difficult financial decisions must be made, often leading to diminishing returns for student learning outcomes.

Economics plays a role at the local level as well, affecting the quality of the education that is provided for the community. Gross inequities in education still exist between school districts due to differences in property tax income at the local level. There remains a serious educational disparity between "the haves and the have-nots": those students who live in heavily populated, wealthier school districts versus those who live in more rural, less populated, and poorer areas. Higher property taxes means that there is more money to spend per student in wealthier systems, so the education these students receive is generally superior to the one that students receive in poorer areas. Many smaller systems have been forced to close their school doors when the money wasn't there to pay the bills.

School reform and school finance reform are inextricable connected. True school reform will not be possible without an equitable funding system for all schools, but it is a complicated task that cannot be fixed by the stroke of a lawmaker's pen. In many cases, it involves the revision of the state constitution altogether. *See also* School Reform

Finding   The formal decision of a court (i.e., judge or jury) on issues of fact or law in a trial. In the process of a lawsuit, a judge may ask a jury to decide on "specific findings" as a part of their deliberation. Finding also refers to the result of a research project based on the data.

Fingerprint   The impression of the ridges on the undersides of fingers and thumbs. Fingerprints may be deposited on surfaces by natural secretions or other solutions (e.g., ink). Fingerprint patterns are unique, often used for identification in criminal investigation, the military, and employment. *See also* Evidence; Forensic

Firearm   A device (e.g., rifle, pistol) that can be used as a weapon by discharging either single or multiple shells, shots, or bullets propelled at high velocity using an explosive substance such as gunpowder. In the United States, firearm ownership restrictions are highly controversial because the Second Amendment of the Constitution protects the right to arms. *See also* Constitution (political science); Weapon

Fiscal Policy   Political decisions by government about taxes and spending to influence conditions in the larger economy such as employment and housing.

There are essentially two sides to fiscal policy: taxation and public expenditure. Policies may change tax rates or the rules about liability to tax or change spending on real goods and services.

Public expenditure may be categorized into two components: (1) expenditure on goods or services and (2) transfer payments. Because aggregate demand is an increasing function of government spending and a decreasing function of taxation, these instruments can affect economic activity. In times of recession, when aggregate demand is too low in relation to the productive capacity of an economy, a combination of tax cuts and public expenditure may be used to stimulate demand. In times of inflation with excessive aggregate demand, a reversal of these instruments will help diminish excess demand and stabilize prices.

"Easy" fiscal policy refers to policies such as cutting taxes and increasing government spending while overlooking the resulting budget deficits and increases in governmental debt. "Tight" fiscal policy includes policies that tend to limit effective demand. This may include high taxes or little public spending.

Fiscal policy was shaped by Maynard Keynes's theory of employment. Keynesianism believed that the government should manipulate the net levels of taxes and spending to decrease the likelihood of economic crises. Besides the particular programmatic goals of a budget, the net amount of money it added or subtracted from the economy came to be seen as the government's primary mechanism to combat inflation and unemployment.

Since the 1980s, fiscal policy has remained generally "tight" in most countries in the Western world. The severe fiscal and economic crises of 2008 have prompted calls for a return to Keynesianism to shore up the badly weakened global economic infrastructure and bring back some fiscal stability. The United States and other governments' plans to inject billions of dollars in the economy and even buy stakes in financial institutions point in this direction. For more information, see Heyne, Boettke, and Prychitko (2002).

Fiscal Stress There is no generally accepted definition for this term. In its broadest terms, fiscal stress can mean the inability of a government to meet the demand for public goods and services. Another measure assesses a government's ability to maintain structural balance, that is, to be able to pay for recurring expenditures with recurring revenues. A government that is unable to maintain structural balance would be defined as fiscally stressed. Another alternative is to define a fiscally stressed government as one that exhibits a consistently negative financial position, a low current ratio, declining per capita general fund balances, and increasing current and long-term liabilities compared with operating revenues.

Fiscal Year An accounting period of 12 months established by an organization to mark the commencement and conclusion of annual financial records. A fiscal year does not always begin in January and end in December and is used to differentiate a budget or financial year from a calendar year. For example, in 1976, the U.S. government changed the beginning of its fiscal year from July 1 to October 1. This change resulted from a law passed in 1974 that allowed the government to have more time to get its budget in shape and incidentally allowed a change in government bookkeeping for that year.

Five-Factor Model of Personality A trait approach in identifying the core structure of personality. Its roots can be traced to Gordon Allport and William Cattell. Cattell asked people to rate themselves and others on items describing a particular trait that Allport had invented. Cattell then used factor analytical techniques to investigate which of these items form clusters (i.e., are closely interrelated and distinct from other items) in order to identify the core structure of personality. Through these analyses, he identified 16 factors (e.g., shy vs. bold, trusty vs. suspicious) that he believed reflected the basic personality found in everyone and developed the "Sixteen Personality Factor Questionnaire" (or 16PF). More recently, factor analyses by Robert Costa and William McCrae suggest only five distinct factors, resulting in the so-called "big-five model," or "five-factor model" of personality. These components are (1) openness to experience, (2) conscientiousness, (3) extraversion, (4) agreeableness, and (5) neuroticism. Different investigators consistently find these factors in data from numerous sources (personality inventories, peer ratings, adjective checklists). Some of these factors appear in many countries and cultures. The "big five" have since been

employed to investigate the impact of personality on a multitude of psychological topics ranging from personality disorders to well-being. For more information, see McCrae and Costa (2004). **See also** Factor Analysis (psychology); Personality

Fixations Constellations of personality traits that are characteristic of a particular stage (oral, anal, phallic, latency, genital) in the psychosexual being, according to Sigmund Freud's psychoanalytic theory. According to Freud, fixations may result from either excessive or inadequate gratification in any of the stages of development. For example, too much gratification in the oral stage (12–18 months) may lead to oral fixation in adulthood, such as smoking, alcohol abuse, and overeating. Too little gratification, in contrast, may result in passivity, dependence, and pessimism; suggesting that one's needs for nurturance were not met during infancy. For more information, see Freud (1966). **See also** Psychoanalysis (psychology)

Fixed Cost An expenditure that does not vary with output. As a result, fixed cost does not intrinsically depend on output. It is cost incurred even when a firm does not produce anything, as for example, rental payments. Fixed cost is part of the total cost of a firm, and it could be estimated as the difference between total cost and variable cost (a cost that varies with output). Fixed cost may also be referred to as sunk cost because it is not an optional expense in the short run, when a firm cannot vary all its costs. For more information, see Boyes and Melvin (2002) and Case and Fair (2003).

Flashbulb Memory Particular experiences that are subjectively thought to be preserved in great detail and vividness. They are considered a special form of autobiographical memories, and their most intense version can be found in individuals who are unable to forget a traumatic experience and who may feel stressed by this intrusive memory. Common examples of flashbulb memory are memories of extremely stressful personal events (such as a victimization experience) as well as historic events, such as the events of September 11, 2001, or the assassination of John F. Kennedy. Despite their vividness and detail, flashbulb memories are as inaccurate and prone to distortion as other forms of long-term memory. For more information, see Conway (1995). **See also** Autobiographical Memory; Long-Term Memory (LTM); Memory (psychology)

Flooding A procedure for reducing anxiety that involves keeping a person in a feared, but harmless, situation. By preventing the person from using the usual rewarding pattern of escape, the person learns that the situation can be managed. Flooding is based on extinction, or the process of removing the reinforcers that typically follow a particular response. Flooding, which breaks up the association between a conditioned (anxiety provoking) stimulus and the fear, is an example of an exposure technique and is considered a part of behavioral therapy. Although it is effective, flooding includes presenting the patient with distressing stimuli (e.g., a client with arachnophobia touches a spider) to desensitize the individual to this fear. A gradual exposure technique is typically used, with exposure to the feared stimulus occurring gradually along a hierarchy of fears. For more information, see Barlow (1988). *See also* Extinction (psychology); Operant Conditioning; Systematic Desensitization

Fluid Intelligence   The basic power of reasoning and problem solving according to Raymond B. Cattell. Fluid intelligence can also be described as mental flexibility and involves the type of intelligence needed to solve problems quickly, perceive relationships among patterns, remember newly acquired information, form and recognize concepts, and reason abstractly and rapidly. Crystallized intelligence, in contrast, is a specific and often fact-based knowledge gained as a result of applying fluid intelligence. Fluid intelligence declines with age, while crystallized intelligence shows less decline and may even improve in certain areas (e.g., increased vocabulary). For more information, see Cattell (1987). *See also* Crystallized Intelligence; General Intelligence

Fluid Versus Crystallized Intelligence   These concepts were developed by Raymond Cattell and John Horn. Fluid intelligence refers to one's natural ability to detect patterns and relationships, particularly in novel tasks. Fluid intelligence typically peaks in adolescence or the early 20s and slowly declines throughout adulthood. In contrast, crystallized intelligence consists of learned and/or acquired knowledge and has the potential to increase throughout adulthood. Currently, these concepts are included in the Cattell-Horn-Carroll hierarchical model of intelligence. *See also* Intelligence Quotient (IQ)

Focus Group (*communication*)   A method of research in which an interviewer or team of interviewers seeks information or opinions from a small gathering of individuals, typically 7 to 10 people. To facilitate open discussion among members, focus group organizers are more likely to select people with shared rather than diverse characteristics. Focus groups are used in the marketing and advertising fields to determine product development or the likelihood of success of a product and in the education, political science, and public policy fields to determine traits and trends among populations. Responses gleaned from focus groups can be valuable for developing survey questions. *See also* Research Methodology

Focus Group (*education*)   A type of group interview used to collect qualitative data on topics of interest to a researcher. The group moderator serves as a facilitator in a focus group, managing group dynamics and interactions and keeping the group focused on the topics of interest. A focus group typically includes 6 to 12 participants and one or more group moderators. A group moderator might provide little structure or direction, or

a high amount of structure and direction. The discussion is usually recorded so that the data can be analyzed in depth at a later time.

Focus Group (*sociology*)   A qualitative research tool that collects and analyzes data from group interviews. A trained moderator guides the interview in an interactive setting to explore a particular topic by gathering the experiences, attitudes, and perceptions of a selected group of people.

Forcible Compulsion   The physical force or express or implied threat or intimidation used to compel a person, using fear of immediate death or physical injury to himself, herself, or another person or fear that he, she, or another person will immediately be kidnapped. Forcible compulsion of a child below 16 years of age may involve expressed or implied intimidation by another person 4 years older than the victim. The legal definition of consent often employed in sexual assault cases may require proof of forcible compulsion sufficient to overcome the resistance of the victim. *See also* Consent; Rape, Forcible; Sex Offense/Crime

Forcible Entry   The unlawful entry into a residence or other dwelling with the intention of taking possessions from that dwelling. Entry may be by breaking in or by forcing occupants out by violence or threat of violence after a peaceful entrance. *See also* Breaking and Entering; Burglary

Foreign Direct Investment   A long-term capital flow or investment in which a nonresident entity has significant management control of voting stock (10% or more) over an enterprise in a foreign or host country. Unlike short-term capital flows, foreign direct investment (FDI) is not immediately susceptible to reversibility. The bulk of FDI activities in developing countries are undertaken by multinational or transnational corporations. A transnational corporation is a firm that is headquartered in a home country but controls assets of enterprises that are central to its profitability in foreign or host countries.

Supporters and critics of FDI have made passionate arguments to show the benefits and drawbacks of FDI. In the 1960s and 1970s, many developing countries adopted steps to discourage FDI because of its extractive or exploitative tendencies. The era of the 1960s and 1970s coincided with the dawn of colonialism for most countries, and the bitter effects of colonialism had not subsided.

Political and legal institutions were mostly weak and susceptible to corruption in the developing countries. As such, foreign investors were closely associated with corruption and a new form of imperialism closely entwined with the extraction of raw materials and mining. In the mid-1980s, however, developing countries adopted measures to increase the flow of long-term capital in order to augment the paucity of national saving, finance investment, create jobs, import innovation, and position themselves favorably in the global economy. FDI also flows North (to rich countries), but in relative terms, the bulk of FDI tends to flow South (to poor countries).

Although FDI is sought to improve the economic prospects and performance of countries, it continues to generate issues involving the repatriation of profits, taxes, and control over natural resources (sovereignty). Some economists classify FDI activities under three broad areas—(1) natural resources, such as petroleum, minerals, and agricultural production; (2) manufacturing and services, such as apparel and processed food; and (3) labor-intensive manufacturing, such as apparel, electronics, textiles, and toys. The efficacy of FDI ultimately depends on the purpose and nature of long-term investment, as much as the policies and institutions in the host and parent countries. For more information, see Perkins, Radlet, and Lindauer (2006) and Stiglitz (2003). ***See also*** Corruption (economics); Globalization (economics); Investment

Foreign-Language Education   Language-learning experience, primarily as a school subject, provided to individuals who learn a language or languages with no recognized institutional or social role in their own community. That is, learners learn a language or languages not spoken within their own communities for purposes such as communication, cultural exchange, and interdisciplinary studies. ***See also*** English as a Second Language (ESL)

Forensic   Application of scientific information to legal and criminal settings. "Forensics" involves a wide range of specialties from natural and social science disciplines that apply information, research, and methods to criminal and legal evidence. Such disciplines include psychology, science, anthropology, computing, and pathology. *Forensic* is derived from the Latin *forensis*, which refers to a forum. A forum was used in ancient Rome as a place of business, public, governmental, and legal affairs. It gradually became a commonly used word in the English language with the growth of forensic medicine (later becoming forensic pathology). In modern society, the word *forensic* is restricted to disciplines that are applied to the collection, examination, and analysis of evidence pertaining to criminal and legal settings. New forensic techniques for examining crime scenes are important and have revolutionized the study of evidence for trials, resulting in more definitive or less ambiguous guilty and innocent court decisions. But many of these techniques are time-consuming tasks that technicians undertake in laboratories or painstaking examinations of crime scenes. Although forensics is a more recent phenomenon, there is currently an influx of forensic-related programs on television that have become widely popular with the viewing audience. With the increase of both fictional and nonfictional stories of crimes and legal cases reported in the media, there is now a concern that these programs confuse audiences, presenting a glamour that is lacking in the real work of technicians and scientists, misleading techniques, and incorrect information regarding forensics.

Forensic Psychology   A specialty area of psychology that deals with issues at the intersection of psychology and the law. Forensic psychologists may, for example, be employed to provide expert testimony to the courts, assess a defendant's competence to stand trial, assist in the selection of jurors, or evaluate whether someone is malingering (i.e., faking) mental illness. Forensic psychologists may also be appointed by the court to evaluate the defendant's state of mind at the time of the offense or a defendant's risk of committing future dangerous behavior. Forensic psychologists may carry out research or provide testimony on issues related to eyewitness testimony, jury decision making, false confessions, or the detection of deception. Furthermore, some forensic psychologists assist the courts in child custody cases. For more information, see Adler (2004). ***See also*** Competency to Stand Trial; Expert Witness (psychology); Insanity; Profiling

Forfeiture   The loss of property or assets to the state due to a violation of law; used as a tool in the prevention of crimes (e.g., drug trafficking). Assets are usually confiscated in civil proceedings, either as proceeds from or as instruments used to facilitate crime.

Forgery   The creation or alteration of an object or written document with intent to deceive or defraud. Most forgeries occur in connection with money (e.g., checks) but may also involve deeds, public documents, wills, and contracts. Counterfeiting is usually regarded as a type of forgery. ***See also*** Fraud

Forgetting Curve   The rate of forgetting over time. The forgetting curve was first investigated by the German psychologist Hermann Ebbinghaus in the late 1800s. He conducted research on his own memory performance by learning "nonsense syllables" (e.g., "pof," "xem"). To compute retention, he used the *method of savings*, which involves computing the difference between the number of trials needed to learn the list of items and the number of trials to relearn the list. Ebbinghaus found a decline in savings as time passes, with the most dramatic drop in the first nine hours. The shape he discovered (especially the initial drop) was confirmed in numerous studies with different methods and materials. Ebbinghaus also found that forgetting is not necessarily complete, with savings persisting over time. For more information, see Baddeley (1999). ***See also*** Learning; Long-Term Memory (LTM); Memory (education, psychology); Short-Term Memory (STM)

Form   Often contrasted with content, the relationship between the two and the priority of the one over the other being vexed. At its simplest level, content refers to substance, while form refers to shape or structure. The form of a verbal composition represents *how* something is said, content represents *what* is said. Form extends to all phenomena, whether the structure of a society, work of art, body of law, and so on. The question is in which—form or content—consists the reality of the phenomenon, whether form is simply an empty shell that contains content or substance, or whether content is itself determined by the form in which it is expressed. ***See also*** Content Analysis (media studies); Genre; Structuralism (media studies)

Formal Communication System　The network of communication activities, personnel, documents, and other artifacts within an organization. These may include (but are not limited to) organizational newsletters, in-house journals, training films, bulletins, plans for meetings, training sessions, video archives, communication officer(s), memos, calendars, schedules, motivational posters, telecommunication protocols, financial documents, instruction manuals, as well as various forms of communication hardware—telephones, VCRs, computers, and fax machines.

Formal communication systems within organizations typically follow two trajectories: vertical and horizontal. The latter entails much of the above but may also include oral transmission of organizational information. For example, an employee may have the duty to inform fellow employees of a new directive or policy; an employee may be responsible for updating the organization's Web site to keep all members abreast of meetings, events, and policies. These transmissions are considered both formal and horizontal. In general, as part of an organization's communication system, these transmissions must be approved with regard to form and content by someone in authority. Typically, someone will be responsible for maintaining a record of these communications, the record itself becoming part of the formal communication system.

The formal *vertical* communication system would include all forms in which directives, direct orders, requests for information, and performance are transmitted "down" from those in authority to those required to answer to that authority. These may include reports of all kinds, memos, e-mail, letters, and oral communication. As with horizontal communication, when the formal communication is vertical, it may be public or private.

It should be noted that formal communication systems are only sometimes "one way." Much of the time, there are means by which recipients of such communications may—or perhaps are required to—respond, such as through memos, e-mail, reports, and oral communication.

Any organization's formal communication system will also include the ways in which it transmits information to outside individuals and/or groups (including other organizations). Common examples range from pamphlets and fliers to more elaborate reports and prospectuses, but organizations may also use broadcast media, the Internet, print advertisement, and/or personal representation. It may also be argued that an organization's product or output is part of the formal communication system.

In addition, the term *formal communication system* as it is regularly used with regard to learning-disabled individuals within and without educational settings, refers to a system that is documented, used consistently among various people and locations, and follows the individual wherever he or she goes. In most such cases, the system is unique to one person only and designed to address that individual's specific expressive and receptive communication needs. For more information, see Chance and Edward (2002), Olmstead (2002), and Yates (1993).

Formal Group　An organization that follows structured rules or customs to appear or be orderly and manageable. This structured group follows an ordered sequence of steps for decision making within the organization. McBurney and Hance (1939) wrote about the value of group discussions organized around formal, reflective thinking. Implied in this development is an *input-process-output* (I-P-O) model of group discussion. I-P-O models assume that the manipulation of factors conceptually prior to group discussion will affect the discussion process, which, in turn, will affect factors conceptually subsequent to discussion. Educators presumed that a group's use of a formal procedure, such as reflective thinking, would lead to improvements in the structure and content of the group's discussion, which, in turn, would improve the quality of the group's decision. For more information, see McBurney and Hance (1939).

Formal Operational Stage　According to Jean Piaget's theory, this stage follows the concrete operational stage and is thus the fourth stage in cognitive development. It is theorized to begin around age 11, when children exhibit the first signs of abstract thinking, and it marks the point of full cognitive maturity. Not all children enter this stage at the same age, and about two thirds of all people may not fully develop abstract thinking abilities, thereby remaining in the concrete operational stage even as adults. Formal operations are characterized by the ability to think logically about abstract ideas, generate hypotheses, and engage in deductive thinking. For more information, see Piaget (1983). ***See also*** Concrete Operational Stage; Preoperational Stage; Sensorimotor Stage

Formal Theories of Organization　Theories that focus on structural and managerial arrangements that are designed to achieve maximum efficiency and productivity. The typical elements include organizational centralization to strengthen control and coordination, division of labor to encourage specialization, and scientific approaches to determine the "one best way" to accomplish the organization's work.

While many formal organization concepts emerged in the work of pioneers such as Frederick Taylor, Max Weber, and Luther Gulick in the 20th century, their ancestry is also recognizable in much earlier ecclesiastical and military hierarchical structures and emphasis on rules. In both early and later models, the elements serve the purposes of control and predictability.

Formal models dominated the organizational theory literature during the 1920s and 1930s but soon faced challenges from two quarters. The earlier critics pointed to the lack of attention to employees' needs. This weakness, identified by the Hawthorne studies, "discovery" of the informal organization, and by the works of Chester Barnard and Mary Follett, pointed to the importance of employees' roles in ensuring organizational success. The ability to retain absolute control was being threatened.

A later challenge came from those who regarded the "closed organization" envisioned in formal theories as inadequate to the pressures of an increasingly complex environment. The need to accommodate change played havoc with the predictability and stability that managers preferred. ***See also*** Human Relations Theories of Organization

Formative Evaluation   Improvement-oriented determination of merit, worth, and/or significance with the intent to inform decision making about the state of an evaluand's/evaluee's (e.g., program, policy, personnel) components or dimensions. This type of evaluation supports decision making about which program components or staff member competencies require improvement. ***See also*** Evaluation; Summative Evaluation

For-Profit Schools   Companies that provide alternative educational experiences, often for academically or economically challenged children. The two most common versions are (a) educational management organizations (EMO), which co-operate schools within districts or establish charter schools, and (b) for-profit schools, which receive money or vouchers for children attending schools and are operated like a business.

Forum   A public space or assembly place (from the Latin *forum*). In ancient Rome, political discussions took place in such an area. The word also implies having the opportunity for open discussions. One of the most popular modern forms of the forum is the Internet forum. This is the discussion board on the Internet, where participants can voice their written opinions about current topics.

Fragment Theory   An interpretation of the ideological development of colonial societies based on what fragment of evolving European society the founders identified (also known as the Hartzian model). The theory was conceived by the Harvard political scientist Louis Hartz (1919–1986) in *The Liberal Tradition of America* (1955), a study tracing America's ideological foundation. Fragment theory claims that the ideology underpinning a nation can be traced back to the mother country *at the time* when the founders of the nation departed from it; therefore, developments that occurred in the mother country after the founders left would not be reflected. Hartz went so far as to argue that the Old World experiences of the founders were even more formative for the new nation than those gained in the New World.

According to Hartz, 17th-century Europe was composed of the feudal, radical, and liberal ideological fragments. The liberalism of the United States can be traced back to the founding fathers—religious dissenters and members of England's rising middle class. In contrast, Hertz asserted that Latin America was founded by feudalists and Australia by proletariat radicals, explaining the differences these nations share in political traditions. Critics of the fragment theory assert that it is overly simplistic and offers insufficient historical evidence to back its sweeping claims. For more information, see Hartz (1955, 1964).

Frame of Reference   A specific perspective suggesting beliefs or assumptions about an issue or thing that is put forth for audience consumption. Media studies focuses on the frames constructed by media sources (such as news organizations) that characterize, relay, and construct meaning about events and individuals in the public sphere. Media frames are viewed as influencing the perception of individuals in the direction of the viewpoint presented in the frames. The selection of rhetoric and visual communication are of particular attention in the construction of media frames; these elements of study can be specialized to examine the representation of gender, race, and other constructs. Framing theory is used particularly in political communication and is frequently applied to analyze television programs, candidate speeches and Web sites, and the coverage of social movements. ***See also*** Censorship (communication, media studies); Gatekeepers; Industry (media studies)

Framing Effect   People's thinking and their decisions are influenced by the way situations and possible outcomes are described. The framing effect is best illustrated by a now famous example from Kahneman and Tversky. In Scenario 1, participants are told about a disease and two programs to treat 600 people. If nothing is done, all the people will die. Selecting Program A means that 200 people will be saved, while choosing Program B means that there is a one-third chance that all people will be saved and a two-thirds chance that no one will be saved. Most participants choose Program A. In Scenario 2, participants are told of a ship that hit a mine and that all passengers will die if action is not taken immediately. If Option A is adopted, 400 passengers will die. If Option B is adopted, there is a one-third chance that no passengers will die and a two-thirds chance that no passengers will be saved. In this scenario, most participants choose Option B. Logically, they should have chosen the same option in both scenarios. The only difference is whether the problem is phrased in terms of potential gains or losses. People tend to be more conservative when choosing between two gains and more willing to take risks when choosing between two losses. For more information, see Kahneman and Tversky (2000). ***See also*** Heuristic

Franchise   A form of business, also referred to as the "turnkey business" model, where a license is granted by a company (franchisor) to an individual or company (franchisee) to be able to operate a specific outlet using the franchisor's name for an agreed-on franchise fee. In exchange, the franchisee consents to use the franchisor's products and is provided with specified ongoing business and operational services such as marketing, selling, and distribution. Fees are typically structured as an initial fee and then as an ongoing percentage of gross sales of the business. Dating back as far as the 1850s, with products such as the sewing machine and telegraph systems, current franchising is particularly prevalent in the food service and hotel industry.

Frankpledge System   A system of policing and law enforcement, originating in England, which divided a community into tithings (units) of around 10 adult males, representing their households. Groups of tithings were associated together in wards, or leets. Within a tithing, members were bound and held responsible for one another's behavior. The leader of each tithing was known as the capital pledge, chief pledge, or tithing man. If a member of the tithing committed a crime, the tithing was responsible for producing him for trial in court and vouching for his guilt or innocence. **See also** Law Enforcement

Fraud   The willful and deliberate misrepresentation of fact made for the personal profit of the money, property, services, advantage, or legal right of another person. Also called "theft by deception," fraud may be actual (direct) or constructive (abuse of a trusting relationship). Prosecution of fraud occurs in both civil and criminal courts and usually results in the awarding of damages for the loss or cancellation of a fraudulent contract. Fraud may involve the use of forged checks, fictitious identities, the postal service (mail fraud), or electronic devices (Internet or wire fraud) with the intent to deceive. **See also** Theft; White-Collar Crime

Free Association   A technique used in psychoanalysis, whereby the client is encouraged to say anything that comes to mind, no matter how trivial or irrelevant it seems. Sigmund Freud believed that these free associations would eventually lead to the expression of deep-seated wishes and desires that reflect underlying conflicts. In classical psychoanalysis, the client lies on a couch while the therapist sits off to the side, thus creating an atmosphere that encourages the client to focus on his or her own thoughts. For more information, see Freud (1949). **See also** Psychoanalysis (psychology)

Freedom of Information Act   Many countries have freedom of information legislation, which clarifies the procedures by which the public is given the right to access government records. The legislation is passed to enable rather than to restrict access, and in it the public usually enjoys the presumption of disclosure, meaning that no reason for requesting the information needs to be given and, in the event of records being withheld, that the burden of proof lies with the relevant government body to explain their reasons. In the United States, the Freedom of Information Act (FOIA) refers to federal legislation passed in July 4, 1966, by President Lyndon B. Johnson to ensure public access to federal records (whether print, tapes, maps, photographs, or any other medium) in an agency's possession. The FOIA is complemented by the Privacy Act, passed in 1974, which protects the release of personal records by means of the "no disclosure without consent" rule. The Privacy Act was signed by President Gerald R. Ford as a response to Watergate and its abuse of the privacy of individuals. Access to records is gained by a written request to the relevant agency, which is required to provide information about how to apply. Checking the relevant Web site of the agency is the most efficient way to get information about filing a request. Representatives of news media organizations and educational institutions are generally excused from fees beyond the reproduction costs.

The presumption of disclosure gives the public automatic right of access except under special circumstances, and the FOIA provides for this in a number of specific exemptions, such as National Security Information, Confidential Business Information, Personal Privacy, and so on. Government agencies have also been known to invoke the "Glomar" response (named after a case on appeal won by the CIA), in which they neither confirm nor deny the existence of requested records. Although it is a fixed piece of legislation, the FOIA can be understood as a document under continuous modification, whether through extension or restriction. Multiple amendments have been made to it in light of events such as Watergate, the advent of electronic information, and the Islamic terrorist events of September 11, 2001, directly after which President George W. Bush imposed restrictions on access to presidential records in an executive order signed on November 1, 2001. On March 25, 2003 (following the declaration of war on Iraq), President George W. Bush further restricted the scope of the FOIA with the Executive Order on Safeguarding Classified Information. The Homeland Security Act, signed into law on November 25, 2002, has raised concerns about the invasion of the privacy of U.S. citizens, who can be legally investigated and surveilled if targeted as potential terrorist threats. **See also** Censorship (media studies); Democracy (political science); Freedom of Press

Freedom of Press   A legislation passed in many countries that guarantees the press the right to publish information and opinions freely. This guarantee is restricted by whatever legislation exists to protect publication of information classified in the interests of national security (e.g., the Official Secrets Act of the United Kingdom). The right of free speech published in any medium is enshrined in the Universal Declaration of Human Rights (1948), and freedom of the press is commonly held to be essential to any healthy democracy. Nongovernmental organizations such as

Reporters Without Borders (RSF—Reporters Sans Frontières) work worldwide to protect the rights and interests of journalists in the course of news coverage. RSF publishes annually an index of countries ranked in order of press freedom. Out of a range of five categories (good, satisfactory, noticeable problems, difficult situation, very serious situation), the United States in 2008 ranked "satisfactory."

Censorship and freedom of speech have always been at the center of the political process, the trial of Socrates being one of the best-known cases of the conflict between the two. Prior to the 18th century, censorship of free speech was usually couched in terms of heresy or treason. The papal *Index Librorum Prohibitorum* (an instrument of the Counter-Reformation) and the English Licensing Order of 1643, which disallowed the publication of any book without government license, were indications of the direct control by the Church and the State of the dissemination of ideas. In "Areopagitica: A Speech of Mr. John Milton for the Liberty of Unlicensed Printing to the Parliament of England" (1644), Milton spoke in favor of press freedom. His "speech" was also published as a pamphlet in direct contravention of the Order. Later legislation in England, such as the Bill of Rights (1689), gave the protection of civil rights necessary to bring about the wide circulation of newspapers in the 18th century, which published everything from political opinion to the "tattle" of the London coffeehouses (as in the *Tatler*, founded 1709). In North America, the earliest independent newspapers were published in the 1720s, in particular the *Pennsylvania Gazette*, owned by Benjamin Franklin, who also wrote for it. Freedom of the press from the passing of any prohibitory law by Congress is explicitly granted by the First Amendment to the U.S. Constitution (1791). That freedom, however, remains vulnerable to criminal sanction or damage suits. In a landmark case, *New York Times Co. v. United States* (1971), the Supreme Court upheld the continued publication of the Vietnam War report, the *Pentagon Papers*, which President Nixon had sought to suspend. For more information, see Herring (1993) and *New York Times Co. v. United States* (1971). *See also* Censorship; Freedom of Information Act; Printing

Free-Market Environmentalism   A type of environmentalism that advocates the elimination of governmental control over the environment. Instead of governmental legislation regulating the environment, private property rights, contract law, and tort law are believed to be more effective. Some free-market environmentalists liken government regulation to medieval feudalism and market socialism. The movement traces back to the logic of the Coase theorem developed by the Chicago School economist Ronald Coase in his article "The Problem of Social Cost" (1960). According to the Coase theorem, government intervention is unnecessary when there can be bargaining among economically self-interested private individuals. For the theorem to apply, the following conditions are

necessary: (1) clear property ownership rights, (2) a limited number of affected parties, and (3) bargaining costs kept to a minimum. For example, a builder buys 100 acres of farmland to build a shopping mall. The neighbors of the farmland object to the builder's plans. Under the theorem, the neighbors can offer the builder money not to build the mall or to limit the mall's size. If the builder finds it more profitable to accept the neighbor's financial incentives than to build a shopping mall, he will do so.

There is the assumption in free-market environmentalism that higher incomes, produced by a free-market economy, will produce a higher demand for environmental quality. This is supported by a 1991 study by the University of Chicago economist Don Coursey, which estimated that for every 10% increase in income, there is a 30% to 50% increase in demand for environmental quality. Free-market environmentalists still do take the chance that citizens might prefer to destroy nature—for example, demolish a farmland to build a shopping mall—but assert that it is their right to do so. For more information, see Anderson and Leal (2001) and Coase (1960).

Free Recall   Tasks such as essays or fill-in-the-blank questions in which people are asked to recall information they have previously learned while having minimal retrieval cues to help their memory. In free recall, individuals are asked to recall as much as they can in any order they wish. In a serial recall, individuals are asked to recall items in a particular order, and in paired-associates recall, individuals are asked to recall previously memorized pairs of items. Free recall tasks generally produce less accurate results than recognition tasks in which individuals are presented with more retrieval cues (e.g., seeing the correct answer among the choice of alternative answers in a multiple choice task). For more information, see Anderson (2000). *See also* Learning; Memory (psychology)

Free Trade   Exchange of goods, services, and assets across national boundaries with very little or no interruption. In politics, as well as economics, there is nothing like absolute freedom. This means that to obtain the maximum or optimal benefit from trade, only the necessary safeguards or restrictions should be considered in economic relations. Excessive restrictions inhibit improvement on general welfare because they sustain prices above the market clearing rate, limit consumption, promote inefficiency, discourage innovation, and prevent fair competition or movement of economic resources across national boundaries.

Free trade is analogous to *openness* to trade, and for comparative and analytical reasons, some economists measure the degree of *openness* of an economy in terms of its volume of trade (exports and imports) in relation to its national income. Trade may be restricted to protect infant industry, safeguard health, foster employment, ensure desirable product quality, attain fair labor standards, and prevent environmental degradation. Restrictions are normally in the form of tariffs (taxes) or nontariff barriers, including quotas. Some of the reasons outlined above for restricting trade may ostensibly be used by some nations to prevent freer trade and competition.

In contemporary trading relations, disputes arise over the right to protect articles of trade or engage in discriminatory trade practices. The World Trade Organization (WTO) guarantees the formation of a dispute panel once a trade dispute is initiated for resolution within its jurisdiction. It then sets time limits for each stage of the resolution process.

The policy to remove perceived restrictions on trade is generally referred to as liberalization. Liberalization is integral to economic integration of nations into the international economy. Some nations are increasingly moving toward integration by creating a free-trade area and optimum currency area, although some express reservations about the intensity and consequences of liberalization as promoted by some policymakers and international institutions such as the International Monetary Fund (IMF).

In a free-trade area, members remove trade barriers among themselves but keep separate barriers against trade with nonmembers. The North American Free Trade Agreement (NAFTA) and the Economic Community of West African States (ECOWAS) are examples of a free-trade area. The European Union (EU) is a much more advanced example of economic integration, which is otherwise known as an "economic union" (common tariff and monetary policy) or "optimum currency area" (single-currency area). For more information, see Bhagwati (2004), Carbaugh (2007), Lowenfeld (2003), and Stiglitz (2003). ***See also*** Closed Economy; Globalization (economics); International Economics; International Monetary Fund (IMF); World Trade Organization (WTO)

Free Vote   A type of vote, also known as a conscience vote, in a legislative body where legislators are expected to vote according to their personal conscience rather than the official line indicated by their political party. Free votes are typically left for moral, religious, or ethical issues. They are typically found in liberal democracies, such as the United States.

Frequency Histogram   A graphic presentation of data that consists of a set of bars, each representing how frequently different values or scores occur in a specified data set. It is mostly used to illustrate (statistical) differences between categories or to illustrate relationships by comparing several histograms when tables would be less clear in conveying the intended information. A frequency histogram is slightly different from a bar chart, in which the bars are usually not touching each another. For more information, see Stangor (2007). ***See also*** Statistics (psychology)

Frisk   A police action of searching a possible criminal suspect for concealed weapons by patting down the

person's outer clothing. Also called a "pat down," a stop and frisk without a search warrant was made legal in the U.S. Supreme Court case of *Terry v. Ohio* (1968). A "Terry stop" is considered legal if a police officer has a reasonable and articulable suspicion that an individual is armed and dangerous to himself or others and had been, is, or is about to engage in criminal activity. In practice, it is generally preferred that women are frisked by female officers and men are frisked by male officers to avoid accusations of impropriety. For more information, see *Terry v. Ohio* (1968). ***See also*** Reasonable Suspicion; Search and Seizure

Fruit of the Poisonous Tree   A legal doctrine that describes evidence discovered and collected by the police as the result of an illegal search or other unconstitutional means (such as a forced confession). Such evidence is considered tainted by its source and is not admissible in court. The metaphor is that the original evidence (the "tree") was illegal, and therefore tainted, so that anything that "grows" from it is likewise tainted. The doctrine, stemming from the exclusionary rule, was created to deter the police from using illegal methods to obtain evidence. ***See also*** Confession; Evidence; Exclusionary Rule (political science); Search and Seizure

Fugitive   A person who has been convicted or accused of a crime and is fleeing from custody or prosecution to avoid being arrested or punished. Fugitives who cross state lines may be tracked down and extradited to the state where the crime was originally committed.

Fugue   A sudden loss of personal memory and the adoption of a new identity in a new place, often accompanied by significant stress. The fugue is, like dissociative amnesia, not due to direct physiological effects that can typically be found in other types of amnesia. According to psychoanalysis, repression is one of the key processes in the genesis of dissociative disorders, assuming that individuals experiencing a fugue act out otherwise unacceptable impulses. It was furthermore suggested that dissociative disorders such as dissociative identity disorder (DID) may be linked to repeated abuse in childhood, though this suggestion has not been empirically confirmed. For more information, see Ross (1997). ***See also*** Amnesia; Anterograde Amnesia; Dissociation; Multiple Personality Disorder (MPD); Retrograde Amnesia

Full-Service Schools   Public schools used by school districts for educational purposes and by communities to provide additional education, family support services, and partnerships with local agencies. These have become the "center of the community" and are designed to reduce obstacles that prohibit success in many financially challenged communities.

Functionalism   A theory of mind according to which mental states are defined by their functional roles. A functional role may itself be characterized as a set of cause-effect relationships, a set of input-output relationships, or simply the role a state plays in a system. For instance, a functionalist would maintain that the mental state of desiring is defined by a functional role, such as a certain set of stimuli (inputs) and responses (outputs). Functionalists acknowledge the "multiple realizablity" of functional roles, which is the idea that a given functional role can be realized in a variety of organic or even inorganic systems.

Functional Theory A theory that suggests that the mass media are part of a complex social system and each medium serves a necessary function within that system. A functional analysis examines each component or subsystem of the system to determine whether it contributes to the stability of the system. If it has a negative influence on the system, it is said to be dysfunctional. In performing a functional analysis on the mass media, there are four approaches. The first is to analyze the functions of the mass media as a system. The second is to analyze each type of mass media—that is, newspapers, movies, and television—as a system. The third approach looks at each organization as a system—that is, a large urban newspaper, a movie studio, and a television network. Finally, the fourth approach looks at each communication activity as a system—that is, surveillance, correlation, transmission, and entertainment.

As an example, using the first approach, a functional analysis can determine that even parts of the system that are looked on negatively—that is, media content that is considered in low taste—serve a function and are necessary for the operation of the mass media. Low-taste media content is widely distributed and appeals to the masses despite the negative reaction from critics. To ascertain its function, one must look at all components of the system of mass media; the first being the audience. This component is linked to market research organizations that seek to explain the complicated mechanisms that determine audience response. Also linked to the audience is the distributor. The audience provides its attention, and the distributor provides content and advertising. The distributor of the content links to other subsystems in the various media—that is, the broadcasting network, the movie chain, and the newspaper syndicate. These, in turn, sell content to local outlets for money. The distributor is linked to the producer of the content, who in turn is linked to the sponsor. To this complex mix of research organization, producer, distributor, and sponsor is linked the advertising agencies that provide their messages to the distributor and are paid by the sponsor. Other subsystems such as regulatory bodies exert control over the entire system. These regulatory subsystems are affected by external conditions such as the societal norms and beliefs that surround the entire system. Because the predominant internal condition of the system is financial, all are dependent on the first component, the audience. Therefore, content—in this case, low-taste content—that appeals to the mass audience is a key element in the complex social system of mass media as any great change in audience behavior would seriously disrupt the entire system. In this way, functional theorists explain the survival of some extremely bad, even repugnant, content, as its removal would upset the system's financial equilibrium. Changes in content would depend on changes in other components, such as the education level of the audience. For more information, see DeFleur (1970) and Wright (1960).

Fundamental Attribution Error The tendency to overemphasize dispositional, or personality-based, explanations for behaviors observed in others while underemphasizing the role and power of situational influences. In the classic demonstration by Edward E. Jones and Keith Davis (1967), participants were presented with pro- and anti-Fidel Castro speeches under one of two conditions: (1) the speaker chose the position freely or (2) the position was randomly selected (by tossing a coin). Subjects were to rate the pro-Castro attitude of the speakers in the condition they were assigned to.

Participants still rated the people who gave the pro-Castro speeches as having a more positive attitude toward Castro than those giving anti-Castro speeches. The fundamental attribution error represents, like other cognitive biases, a concept that was derived from Western, particularly North American, psychology. Researchers have found that in other cultural contexts, the strength of this error varies. In many interdependent cultural contexts, individuals are less likely to attribute people's behavior to internal, dispositional causes than individuals from Western, independent contexts. Instead, individuals, predominantly from Asian cultures, focus their attribution of behavior on the contextual, situational demands in which a person is immersed. For more information, see Jones and Harris (1967). *See also* Attribution Theory; Heuristic

Fundamentalism In American politics, the term refers to a conservative right-wing political special-interest group that allies itself with the Republican Party. The term originally referred to the conservative Protestant movement in the United States, which rose in reaction to liberal Protestantism of the late 19th and early 20th centuries. Fundamentalist Protestants remained arguably uninvolved in mainstream politics until the late 1970s. Grassroots political organizations grew in response to the threat of gay rights legislation, legalized abortion, and the proposed Equal Rights Amendment. The fundamentalists also pushed for school prayer, increased military spending, and religious school vouchers. One of the most politically formidable of these organizations was the Moral Majority, started by Reverend Jerry Falwell in 1979; it dissolved in 1989 but was reestablished in 2004. The group was succeeded by the Christian Coalition, founded by Reverend Pat Robertson in 1989. The Christian Coalition enjoys an impressive membership base and remains a powerful influence in American politics into the 21st century.

F

Fundamental Principle of Mixed-Methods Research
A guiding principle or logic in mixed-methods research stating that the researcher should strategically mix or combine qualitative and quantitative research approaches to produce an overall mixed-methods research design with complementary strengths and nonoverlapping weaknesses.

Furlough   A temporary release from incarceration. Furloughs are designed to ease the transition from prison to the community through allowing approved temporary leaves of absence as inmates approach release. Furlough programs, which were introduced in the 1960s, were designed to further the goals of rehabilitation and reintegration. ***See also*** Community-Based Corrections; Incarcerate; Parole

G

Gambling Wagering money or something of value on the outcome of a future event or game of chance with the goal of winning additional money or goods. In many places, gambling is illegal; its legal status depends on factors such as the type of gambling, where it occurs, and the age of the gambler. To pay off gambling debts, other crimes may be committed, such as check forgery and theft. *See also* Forgery; Theft

Game Theory A concept that is used to explain decision-making processes involving political alliances, individuals, and businesses with the goal of conflict resolution and utility and profit maximization. In economics, game theory is being used to analyze market structure with few producers (oligopoly). In this context, the theory suggests that strategic action and reaction have consequences. Every action is assumed to create a reaction, and action can only be undertaken after a careful calculation of its consequences or payoff.

Game theory therefore implies that strategic decisions must be made to maximize utility or profit based on the reaction functions of others and the payoffs of individual decisions. Although the incentives for making choices may be known, the actual choices that will be made are presumed to be unknown in certain situations. The theory is normally simplified in terms of the prisoner's dilemma to rat or not to rat in order to get minimal punishment. As far as businesses are concerned, the choice of strategy in this simplified form is limited to a dominant and nondominant strategy.

The dominant strategy produces the better result regardless of what the competitor does, whereas the nondominant strategy produces the desirable result based on what a competitor does. In practical terms, however, firms actually make ex post decisions once they have knowledge of what their competitors are doing or have done. This real-life situation is alternatively modeled by sequential game theory—a situation in which a firm actually reacts to a strategy that has been adopted by another.

Game theory is used to rationalize collusion, incentives for cartel members to cheat, interdependence, and relative price stability within certain industries. The earliest form of game theory analysis was a duopolistic example put forward by Antoine Cournot in 1838.

Game theory can be cooperative or noncooperative. Cooperative game theory results in coalitional outcomes (alliances in politics) or mergers (in economics). In noncooperative game theory, the actors base their strategies on rationality (knowledge of ordering and timing) to make choices and achieve selfish outcomes that are much more desirable than the cooperative ones.

In 1950, John Nash expanded game theory and demonstrated that finite games always tend toward an equilibrium point at which all players choose actions that are best, given the positions or choices of their opponents. This concept of noncooperative (Cournot-Nash) equilibrium in game theory has made a strong showing in economic analysis since 1994, when the game theorists Nash, John Harsanyi, and Reinhard Selten received the Nobel Prize in economics. For more information, see Boyes and Melvin (2002) and McConnell and Brue (2008). *See also* Equilibrium; Market

Gang An organized group of people with its own culture that includes unique symbols, signs, codes, and languages. Gangs are often thought of as composed of urban youth whose affiliation provides identity, replaces family, and is involved in illegal activity. In the United States, gangs have a history that dates back to before the Civil War, where the first criminal gangs were formed in poor, urban areas, such as in New York City. Today gangs are diverse in their goals and belief systems and can include street gangs such as the MS-13, Bloods, Crips, and Latin Kings, as well as extremist groups such as the Ku Klux Klan. The organization of gangs varies from loosely disorganized groups that engage in occasional and unplanned criminality such as vandalism to hierarchical, tightly knit territorial gangs that rule regional drug markets. Prisons are increasingly riddled with gang problems, and today, inmates are often segregated based on gang affiliation as enemies housed together will inevitably lead to violence and murder.

Gatekeepers Individuals at institutions who make the decisions to present or deny information from audiences. Gatekeepers decide how and what information is covered. These actions relate to the construction of media frames. Critics assert that this mode of authority is a type of censorship. This term particularly applies to individuals working in news organizations, ranging from journalists to reporters. The psychologist Kurt Lewin initiated the term in his 1947 work "Frontiers in Group Dynamics," applying it to the function of the news media. McCombs and Shaw connected gatekeeping to agenda setting, a powerful theory introduced in their 1976 work "Structuring the Unseen Environment."

G

See also Censorship (political science); Frame of Reference; Industry (sociology)

Gender Differences Distinctions in attitude, behavior, conversational habits, perception, and physical and intellectual skills between men and women, whether innate or socially constructed. Studies and literature concerning the validity and veracity of gender differences came into prominence during the Women's Movement of the late 1960s. Prior to that, the social philosophers Mary Wollstonecraft and John Stuart Mill had challenged assumptions about gender prevalent in late-18th-century and early-19th-century England, when the Industrial Revolution brought about distinct places in the workplace and home for men and women, respectively.

Writing in the late 1980s, Cynthia Fuchs Epstein reviewed literature concerning gender differentiation and noted that while sociological studies prior to the Women's Movement had been biased against women and based on unchallenged assumptions, studies conducted during the new wave of feminism also fell prey to both personal and "institutionalized" biases. She maintained that gender differences, except for those distinctions of a sexual/physical nature, can be traced to hierarchy not biology—thus concurring with the feminist "minimalist" model for sexual difference. She also explained a "maximalist" feminist model, which maintained that gender differences were innate and should be celebrated and configured into a distinct woman's culture.

In 1989, Christine Williams published a study juxtaposing the behaviors and adjustment processes of two professional minorities: males who trained to be nurses and women who trained for the Marine Corps. Her findings showed that the male nurses were more concerned with projecting masculine identities than the women recruits, who were concerned with projecting feminine identities. *See also* Feminine Culture; Feminism; Self-Perception

General Adaptation Syndrome A term, originally described by Hans Selye (1907–1982), used to describe the body's short-term and long-term reactions to stress. Stressors in humans are events or situations that impinge on us physically or psychologically. They can be external, such as work pressures, surviving natural disasters, chronic health problems, or the loss of a loved one, or internal, such as recurring fears, worries, prolonged grieving, conflicts, or the inability to solve a problem.

Selye described three distinctive phases in the syndrome's progression: alarm, resistance, and exhaustion. Phase 1, alarm, is the immediate reaction to stress that occurs when we suddenly encounter a major stressor or a flood of minor ones. The body mobilizes its flight or flight response, whereby the sympathetic nervous system is activated, increasing the heart rate, shutting down digestion, and releasing epinephrine. The initial response can decrease the effectiveness of the immune system, making a person more susceptible to illness

during this phase. If the stressor remains salient, the individual might move to Phase 2, resistance. Resistance is the body's adaptation to stressors that continue to attack. The parasympathetic nervous system gets activated to keep functioning within reasonable limits, but the sympathetic nervous system remains active, gradually draining the individual's physical resources. If the stressor is chronic, the individual will eventually reach the third phase, exhaustion. At that point, the individual may experience tissue damage, reduced immunity to illness, ulcers, and in some severe cases cardiovascular symptoms or even death.

The general adaptation syndrome is not inevitable; it is influenced by a number of individual characteristics such as overall health and nutritional status, sex, age, socioeconomic status, and genetic makeup, among others. Selye observed that people vary in their perceptions of stressors and that health problems result from maladaptive responses to them.

General Intelligence A theoretical concept denoted as *g* and developed by the British psychologist Charles Spearman in 1904. Using his previously developed method of factor analysis, Spearman found that one general factor (*g*) could account for the relationship among a number of cognitive abilities. His analyses suggested that if a student performs well in one cognitive domain, he is likely to perform well in other domains too. Similarly, if he performs poorly in one area, he is less likely to succeed in others. Spearman theorized that in addition to the discrete abilities a test may measure, it also measures "*g*" to varying degrees. Likewise, *g* cannot be inferred from a single test. Although the concept of general intelligence has become the foundation of psychometric models of intelligence testing, there is much controversy around the methods for measuring *g*. Opponents of current methods of intelligence assessment suggest that tests are culturally biased and assessments of intelligence better reflect one's social class and educational opportunities as opposed to an innate ability. In contrast to this criticism, different social groups demonstrate similar distributions of general intelligence. Furthermore, genetic and biological correlates of *g* weaken the social construct theory of intelligence. *See also* Cognition

Generalizability The degree to which results of a research study on a sample from a given population can be applied to the population at large. Due to the inherent need for control in scientific research as well as the difficulty in obtaining truly representative samples, it is sometimes difficult to generalize findings to a natural setting. The more control a researcher exerts over the study, the less the results will generally be generalizable to the larger population. For more information, see Sirkin (2005).

Generalizability Theory (G Theory) A more comprehensive model of measurement consistency than the classical reliability theory, which examines how various contributors to measurement error contribute to score variability. Generalizability analyses look at how factors such as test form, rater, items, occasions, and other factors (called facets) operate to introduce measurement error within a universe of assessment scores. The goal of such analyses is to determine how robust measurement is in the face of these sources of variability.

General Linear Model (GLM)   A general framework that incorporates a wide variety of statistical techniques. Different variable types, for example, continuous or discrete, can be incorporated into the GLM framework. The GLM includes (a) a bivariate form, (b) a simple multivariate form, and (c) a full multivariate form. The simplest form of GLM is the bivariate model, $Y = \beta X + e$, which includes one dependent variable (Y) and one quantitative or one two-group categorical independent variable (X). In the equation just shown, Y is the dependent variable, X is the independent variable, β is the coefficient expressing the relationship between X and Y, and e is the error or probabilistic component. The bivariate GLM includes techniques such as simple regression and two-group analysis of variance (ANOVA). The simple multivariate form of the GLM, $Y = \beta_0 + \beta_1 X_1 + \beta_2 X_2 + e$, includes one dependent variable and two or more independent variables (or a single categorical independent variable with three or more levels). This GLM model includes techniques such as multiple regression, ANOVA (with a single categorical independent variable with three or more levels or ANOVAs with two or more independent variables), analysis of covariance (ANCOVA), and repeated measures ANOVA. The full multivariate form of the GLM incorporates multiple dependent variables and multiple independent variables and includes statistical techniques such as MANOVA and MANCOVA. *See also* Analysis of Covariance (ANCOVA); Analysis of Variance (ANOVA) (education, psychology); Regression Analysis

General Semantics (GS)   A popular movement (or cult) in the 1940s and 1950s that was largely responsible for making the term *semantics* widely known among the general public. (The linguistic term *semantics* comes from the Greek and refers to the study of meaning [*seemasia* (n) = meaning, sense, importance, gravity, significance; *seemeno* (v) = to mean or to signify].) Although not an academic discipline then, it was often confused with "linguistic semantics."

GS is based on the philosophy of the Polish engineer Alfred Korzybski (1879–1950), whose main ideas were drawn from the work of Bertrand Russell and Albert Einstein. Korzybski wanted to use the scientific method to understand how language shapes thought. His basic idea, which was presented in his 1933 book *Science and Sanity: An Introduction to Non-Aristotelian Systems and General Semantics,* was that language, especially the structure of vocabulary, because it is so deeply

imprinted on the speaker's mind, plays a major role in unconsciously determining the way human beings think and behave.

The GS movement's early, leading popularizers were Stuart Chase and S. I. Hayakawa and, more recently, Harry Maynard, who used the tenets of GS successfully in public relations and advertising. Stuart Chase, along with his book *The Power of Words,* faded away, although at the time, his work had the salutary effect of alerting readers to the dangers of propaganda. Hayakawa's book *Language in Thought and Action* is still recommended reading. Another popular book on GS is the 1980 *Metaphors We Live By,* by George Lakoff and Mark Johnson.

Modern GS followers and teachers claim that GS goes beyond the study of meaning and encompasses a way of thinking about language and its relationship to the word, thought, and behavior; hence, it gives its practitioners a way of thinking outside the box, which is an advantage, especially in the field of communication. GS is taught in interdisciplinary college courses dealing with education and communication, speech, and language arts. *See also* Semantics

Genes   The basic functional units of heredity. Genes are nucleotides within the DNA that transfer biological information from cell to cell. These pieces of DNA occupy a unique location on a specific chromosome, and most genes control the production of proteins. The information encoded on genes determines how different cells in the body will function and, to some degree, the physical and functional characteristics that develop throughout an organism's life span. Humans are thought to have approximately 35,000 genes. *See also* Deoxyribonucleic Acid (DNA) (psychology, sociology)

Genetics   The science of heredity in living organisms. The modern science of genetics began with Gregor Mendels's work in the 1800s with pea plants and was greatly advanced in the 1950s with the discovery of DNA, which is made up of sequences of amino acids and proteins that create a genetic code. Today, the study of genetics has advanced so that scientists can identify how specific genes affect particular traits. While the nature versus nurture debate has long existed in the social sciences, today it is widely recognized that nature (biology and heredity) interacts with nurture (environmental factors) to determine the final organism. *See also* Deoxyribonucleic Acid (DNA) (psychology, sociology); Genes

Genotype   The genetic makeup of an organism (often referred to as our "genetic blueprint"), specifically the allelic composition of an organism or cell. For organisms that reproduce sexually, the DNA structure is inherited from both the organism's parents. For asexual organisms, it is a direct copy of the DNA of the parent. The genotype regulates the organism's formation from production of protein molecules to metabolic synthesis and determines the expression of a trait (phenotype). *See also* Deoxyribonucleic Acid (DNA) (psychology, sociology); Phenotype

Genre   A kind, type, or class of artistic or cultural composition, and ultimately descends from Latin *genus* (as in genus and species). The analogy between genre and genus is not exact, however, as the classifications determined by genus describe naturally occurring phenomena, whereas the classifications determined by genre are socially constructed. Although genre is often associated with literary composition (poetry, fiction, drama), it includes any cultural composition, whether painting (portrait, still life), music (classical, rock), or TV program (soap, sitcom). Earlier, classical genres were generally prescriptive and identified by form. Modern genres are more descriptive than prescriptive but can create a circular logic of identifying generic characteristics from examples, which themselves are classified according to the generic characteristics. All genres operate within given conventions—and presuppose a tacit agreement between author and audience, which exerts a normativizing influence over cultural expectations and performance—and are thus connected to ideology and hegemony. *See also* Form; Hegemony; Ideology

Geochronology   The science of dating and determining the time sequence of events in the history of the planet. Geochronologic units of analysis include the eon, era, period, epoch, and age. Geologic research is the determination of the ages and composition of rocks.

Geographical Isolation   Also known as allopatry, the term is used in the study of evolution. When part of a population of the same species becomes geographically separated from the others, it may evolve characteristics that are different from the original species due to natural selection.

Geographical Race   A biological term referring to any population that differs genetically from any other population of the species. Developed as a way to retain the use of "race" as based on continental location, the term is a misnomer since every population of every species differs somewhat from other populations. Today, race is generally recognized as a socially constructed, not a biological, concept.

Geography *(education)*   Study of the physical and human features and characteristics of the earth, including their evolution or history, their location, and their distribution.

Geography *(geography)*   A very broad discipline, basically understood as the study of the world or physical environment in which humans, animals, plants, and other living beings live. Geographers are interested in the earth's features and the manner in which life is apportioned. Considered a science, geography has also facilitated the integration of social sciences such as anthropology, sociology, and economics.

There are two main divisions of geography. The first, known as physical geography, is traditionally recognized as a science of the earth that focuses on the study of the physical features found in the earth's spheres. Physical features found in the earth's spheres include land, water, climate, and plants. Physical geographers contribute to our knowledge of the earth's processes and identify strategies for preserving the earth's natural resources.

The study of human geography, a more modern development in the field of geography, focuses on human interaction with the natural environment. Although once including environmental determinism, the field of human geography shifted toward cultural geography. Cultural geography, the most notable subfield of human geography, best illustrates the focus of human geography. Cultural geographers examine man's relationship with the environment and how spatial relations shape culture, including religion, customs, politics, language, and more. Human geography has become well accepted in the field of science and has found significant value in identifying the relationship between geography and human behavior. *See also* Cultural Geography; Geography

Geomorphology   Geomorphologists examine the processes that produce the earth's various land formations. Some of the land formations examined in geomorphology include mountains, volcanoes, and valleys. Known as the Father of Geomorphology, William Morris Davis pioneered the study and classification of the earth's land masses in the 19th century. By the 20th century, geomorphology had progressed to include not only the description of processes that shape land formations but also the ongoing processes that shape the earth's structures. The progression marked a more quantitative approach to this science, as geomorphology can be used for predictive as well as descriptive purposes. For instance, geomorphologists can predict the effects of climate change and other extreme conditions on the earth's surface. Although physical processes such as weathering and erosion help shape the earth's land, the actions of human beings are also responsible for shaping land formations.

Geopolitics   A view of global politics that emphasizes the international competition for valuable land and natural resources. The origins of the philosophical underpinnings of geopolitics trace back to the German geographer Friedrich Ratzel's (1844–1904) "organic state theory," which viewed nations as organisms biologically programmed to compete for resources and living space. The term was coined in an 1899 article by Rudolf Kjellen (1864–1922), a Swedish political scientist who wrote of Sweden's geographical boundaries and the importance a state's natural resources play in determining its power.

Kjellen, a former member of the Swedish Conservative Party, became a supporter of the German empire after Sweden's failure to prevent Norway's independence. Kjellen's writings were adopted by the German geographer Karl Haushofer (1869–1946) and transformed into the Nazi concept of *geopolitik,* which viewed German imperialism as biologically justified. The field fell out of favor due to its association with Nazism but regained eminence during the Cold War years and beyond.

Gerrymander   The intentional rearrangement of electoral boundaries to give a particular political party an advantage in the outcome of elections by minimizing the electoral impact of an opponent's supporters. This is accomplished by either concentrating the opponent's supporters in a small number of districts or spreading them across many electoral districts so that they will be the minority. Gerrymandering is also known as reapportionment and redistricting. The term *gerrymandering* originated from Elbridge Gerry, a signer of the Declaration of Independence and the fifth vice president of the United States, in 1813. In 1811, he became the governor of Massachusetts. His administration was known for dividing electoral districts for political advantage.

Gestalt Theory   A psychological theory that focuses on the brain's perceptive processes and proposes a holistic approach to cognitive processing. Gestalt theorists follow the assumption that the whole is greater than the sum of its parts. Therefore, a behavioral, psychological, or physiological experience cannot be reduced to separate events without the risk of losing the meaning of the whole percept. The parts may represent a different relationship when considered outside the whole, but when combined, the parts form a greater meaning. Gestalt theory was a response to the theory of atomism that proposed that parts of an element were as significant as its entirety. Atomistic theorists believed that experiences were absolute, regardless of their context. According to the Gestaltists, it is a dynamic interaction of individuals and their surroundings that determines their behavior and relationships. Max Wertheimer is often credited as the founder of Gestalt psychology; however, Christian von Ehrenfels was the first to propose the idea of gestalt theory in the late 19th century. Wertheimer applied the theory to visual perception. He, along with Wolfgang Kohler and Kurt Kafka, was driven by the fact that organisms are often presented with incomplete parts in our visual fields, yet our minds are capable of perceiving the whole out of distinct elements. According to Gestalt theory, we are able to perceive wholes because our brain demonstrates self-organizing tendencies that construct entire forms from incomplete parts, especially with regard to visual recognition of figures. Out of gestalt theory came the law of Pragnanz, which states that individuals prefer to organize elements in a manner that is easy and simple to understand. Following from this law, several other principles describe the ways in which humans perceive stimuli in its entirety. For example, the law of similarity states that humans group items that are similar together, thereby making them easier to perceive. The main criticism of Gestalt theory is that it is merely a descriptor and does not explain how these perceptions occur.

Gestalt Therapy   Treatment based on the principles of Gestalt psychology. Gestalt therapy includes a variety of therapeutic counseling techniques aimed at encouraging clients to develop wholeness and integration of self. Clients are urged to resolve unfinished business and integrate their past and present experiences. With emphasis on the here and now, the focus is on action rather than on thinking or talking. ***See also*** Counseling

Gifted   An adjective describing a person endowed with some quality or talent. A gifted child displays asynchronous development, in which advanced cognitive abilities and heightened intensities across any of several domains produce a lived experience that is qualitatively different from that of chronological age-peers, whether or not the child is presently achieving at a high level in the academic arena.

Glass Ceiling   A metaphor for the invisible barrier holding women and members of minority groups from attaining the top jobs in their chosen fields of employment. Glass ceilings allow them to see to the top of the corporate ladder but keep them from climbing the rungs.

The term *glass ceiling* is believed to have been popularized after appearing in the 1986 *Wall Street Journal* cover story report on women in management. The reporters made the point that although in the 1980s women were filling almost a third of all management positions, most had little authority and were not well paid. "The executive suite seemed within their grasp, but they just couldn't break through the glass ceiling," they stated.

In 1991, the U.S. Department of Labor established a federal Glass Ceiling Commission to study the barrier as it applied to women and minorities. In its final report in 1995, the commission stated that breaking the glass ceiling must be an economic priority in America. ***See also*** Gender Differences; Minority Group

Glial Cells   Cells that provide physical support for neurons and, therefore, structure for the brain. They are important in the manufacture of myelin sheathing, provision of nutrition, and destruction of pathogens and removal of dead neurons. In the human brain, glia are estimated to outnumber neurons by about 10 to 1. The most abundant type of glial cells are astrocytes, which are thought to be involved in the blood-brain barrier. Myelin sheaths are formed by another important glial cell, called the oligodendrocyte.

G

Global Education   Basically defined as a global perspective (Hanvey, 1976). In today's increasingly globalized, multicultural, and interconnected world, it refers to a concerted, holistic effort to create a tolerant, just, and peaceful society for the future by empowering citizens through learning about the perspectives of "the other." ***See also*** Globalization (economics, political science, sociology); Global Village

Globalization *(economics)*   Economic integration of national economies into the international economy through trade. Globalization is mainly the result of technological innovation that reduces the cost of production and facilitates the rapid movement of economic and financial resources as well as finished products across national boundaries.

By definition, globalization is not a novel phenomenon. The first wave of globalization occurred roughly between 1870 and 1914, as a result of the removal of trade barriers and new technologies that reduced transportation costs as a result of the introduction of railways and the shift from sail ships to steamships. The second wave of globalization occurred after World War II until about 1980. It was largely propelled by manufacturing and *agglomeration economies* (clusters and vertical linkages) to exploit location and minimize costs associated with transportation, coordination, and monitoring.

The latest wave is characterized by the breakthrough of some developing countries into the world markets for manufactures by taking advantage of labor-intensive skills. These countries include China, Bangladesh, Mexico, and Thailand. The latest wave has been expedited by the advent of the Windows operating system, uploading, outsourcing, insourcing, off-shoring, and supply-chaining (the immediate replacement of goods sold as a result of electronic communication with the supplier). Technological innovation also eliminates the reliance on intermediaries. For example, rural farmers can now bypass the dominant classes and castes to participate directly in markets because of information diffusion.

Contemporary globalization is not without aversion. Critics point to unemployment (as a result of job displacement and changing structure), increasing poverty, child labor, wage depression, inconvenient cultural transformation; and environmental problems caused by the agents of globalization (including transnationals, the World Trade Organization, and the International Monetary Fund) in some areas of the world. Those in favor of globalization see the problems in terms of the lack of efficient management of irreversible globalization. For more information, see Bhagwati (2004), Carbaugh (2007), Friedman (2006), Lowenfeld (2003), and Stiglitz (2003). ***See also*** Closed Economy; Foreign Direct Investment; Free Trade; International Monetary Fund; Poverty; World Trade Organization (WTO)

Globalization *(Political science)*   Processes of change that lead to greater interdependence of human affairs by linking together and expanding human activities across physical locations. This process includes the establishment and maintenance of cross-border economic, political, and sociocultural relations, also known as *deterritorialization*. Deterritorialization activities include commerce, war, academic seminars, and e-mail correspondence. They take place irrespective of the geographical location of participants.

Although the term was first used around 1960 in its current sense, economists have made it commonplace in the past 20 years, although there has been disagreement about the causal forces behind it as well as the point at which it started. Its growth is tied to the economy.

It has been argued that globalization began in the Portuguese movement to colonize territories in the 15th century; the end of World War II marked an increase in multinational companies with the creation of the International Monetary Fund and International Bank for Reconstruction and Development (later known as the World Bank). These institutions were created by the General Agreement on Tariffs and Trade, first signed in 1948 and later amended, which, among other interests, promoted the reduction of tariffs and the construction of free-trade zones.

For many years, economists, social scientists, political scientists, journalists, environmentalists, and many others have been debating the merits and harms of globalization. Part of the controversy surrounding globalization concerns its effects on poverty. Some have suggested that there has been a growing material inequality spawned by economic globalization, in which a gap has widened between wealthy and poor countries. Multinational corporations invest in poor countries, make profits from low wages and access to natural resources, and per capita incomes in poor countries have fallen to the point where half of the world's 3 billion population lives on less than $2 per day. On the other hand, those favoring globalization point to the above average drop in poverty rates in countries where globalization has taken a strong foothold, while countries that do not embrace globalization have poverty rates that have remained stagnant. ***See also*** Capitalism (economics)

Globalization *(sociology)*   International integration of the sociocultural, technological, economic, and political aspects of several societies into a single society. The term is often used in the context of economic globalization where nations become connected through trade, investment, migration, and technology. There is also social and political globalization, where people freely travel between nations and countries and are regulated by a global government. Globalization has influenced crime as well, as people, weapons, drugs, and other commodities are internationally traded illegally. While there is an international criminal court located in The Hague, Netherlands, countries such as the United States and China have refused to participate. The court investigates large-scale crime such as genocide. As knowledge of these crimes is disseminated, there are increasingly calls for international justice movements, such as aiding the people of Darfur, Africa.

Global Village The concept of the entire world being one community linked by telecommunication technologies. The term also is used metaphorically to describe both the Internet and the World Wide Web.

Coinage of the term has been attributed to the Canadian media scholar Marshall McLuhan, who first used it in 1962. Preceding McLuhan in the concept of a world connected by technology, however, was the Belgian Paul Otlet. Before his death in 1944, Otlet predicted that the technologies of cinema, telephone, radio, and television would bring the world together, that seated in an armchair, everyone would be able not only to see and hear but also to participate by applauding, giving an ovation, adding a voice to the cries of appreciation, or singing with the chorus.

The global village is historical in scope and has political ramifications. Some economists and media specialists applaud the global village as a means of promoting commerce, democracy, and the exchange of ideas; others criticize it as cultural or media imperialism. **See also** Internet

Global Warming A term frequently used to describe the future warming of the earth's surface. It is the increase of the earth's mean temperature that has occurred in the recent past. This recent warming of the earth's atmosphere is said to be caused by the rising emission and trapping of greenhouse gases, otherwise known as the "greenhouse effect." The increase in greenhouse gases is thought to be the result of human activities, including the burning of fossil fuels and deforestation. The notable increases in the earth's temperature have caused sea levels to rise and will likely lead to extreme weather conditions and adverse impacts on the environment. The anticipated consequences of global warming, which include physical, economic, and social impacts, have brought the issue to the forefront of world policy. Major suggestions to reduce the effects of global warming include recycling, using less energy and water, burning less gasoline, and planting more trees. The very fact of global warming is a hotly debated political topic and has arguments on both sides. What is not in question is that the earth is getting warmer. **See also** Greenhouse Effect

Goal Analysis An instructional design approach for identifying an instructional problem and defining an intervention. Such an analysis is typically based on accurate input from experts who know the instructional problem and learners. It can also use the data from a needs assessment to prioritize a need for determining instructional goals. Six steps are usually followed to conduct a goal analysis: (1) identify an aim, (2) set goals, (3) refine goals, (4) rank goals, (5) refine goals again, and (6) make a final ranking. **See also** Task Analysis

Goal Articulation The process of clearly defining and expressing group goals in an organization or group. This process is usually the function and responsibility of the organization or group leaders. The proper documentation and thoroughness by which this process is executed is regarded as a key step in developing support for official goals.

Goal Congruence The conformity by which fundamental goals are created and the process by which they are decided in an organization or group. Goal congruence refers to the agreement among both leaders and followers on the central objectives of the organization. Often, if this objective is not accomplished, internal tension and ultimate difficulty in defining and achieving goals occur.

Goal-Free Evaluation The determination of merit, worth, or significance without explicit consideration of a program's stated goals or objectives, sometimes referred to as needs-based or values-based evaluation. Goal-free evaluation considers what an evaluand is doing instead of what it intended to do. Needs assessments are central elements in goal-free evaluation. **See also** Evaluation (public administration); Goals-Based Evaluation; Needs Assessment

Goals-Based Evaluation Determination of the extent to which the evaluand (e.g., intervention, program, organization) achieved its goals or objectives. The criteria used in a goals-based evaluation are limited to the goals of the evaluand; process, comparisons, and side effects are generally not considered in this type of evaluation. A goals-based evaluation is most appropriate when goals are clearly defined, measurable, meaningful, and time based; direct human behavior; and are linked to the values of the program or organization. **See also** Goal-Free Evaluation

Good Time Time taken off a sentence of incarceration for good behavior. Standard good time in some places equates from 10 to 15 days each month, while in some jurisdictions, earned good time can be accrued for participating in treatment programs such as education and vocational training. Good time can be revoked for violating prison rules.

Government A political system through which a body of people is administered and regulated. The fundamental purpose of government is to maintain basic security and public order. Governments serve several functions. Most exercise executive, judicial, and legislative powers, as well as provide internal and external security. Many also provide welfare services, regulate the economy, and establish educational systems. Some governments control the religious affairs of their people.

The form of government instituted in a state differs according to the power holders of that state. Power may be held by one individual as in a monarchy, dictatorship, or autocracy. Plutocracy and theocracy are examples of rule by a few individuals. Democracies exemplify rule by the majority.

Although governments may operate only on a national level, others consist of more than one level of government. Their systems contain local governments, which are smaller and have lesser powers than the national government. Their administration may also be partially or wholly subsidized by the national government.

Governments also differ according to the distribution of power at the local level. This distribution may be unitary, federated, or confederated. In unitary governments, smaller organizational units within a country are governed constitutionally as one single unit, and the national government has the right to recall delegated power. Federations comprise separate smaller units that have a separate constitutional existence and are both partially self-governing and united by a central government. Confederations consist of governments of several political divisions, or states, in which each division retains considerable independence. **See also** Autocracy; Confederation; Democracy (political science, public administration); Dictatorship; Monarchy; Theocracy

Government Corporations (GCs)   Bodies formed by the government to serve a public-interest need, also called "government owned corporations" or "public corporations." There is less bureaucracy in the GC's activities than in a regular government agency, which is believed to improve efficiency and output. GCs may be wholly owned by the government or a "mixed enterprise," where corporate control is private but the government has investment and/or broad representation. There is an international trend of privatization of government services—for example, ZIM shipping carriers in Israel (2004), British Rail in Great Britain (2002). GCs can be an in-between option for officials.

In the United States, the first GC was established in 1791, with the creation of the First National Bank of the United States. The authority for establishing a GC at the federal level is derived from the U.S. Constitution's "necessary and proper" clause. GCs receive capital from congressional appropriations for their activities, can sue and be sued, sign contracts, and borrow money. GCs are traditionally formed in response to crisis; for example, during the Great Depression and both World Wars, more than 100 government corporations were formed to meet specific public needs. The largest government corporation in the United States today is the Tennessee Valley Authority (TVA). The TVA was chartered during the New Deal to control flooding in the Tennessee Valley and is at present one of the major electricity providers to the country. **See also** Privatization (political science)

Government Failure   Government actions may work to tax, control, and regulate, but in some instances, action or inaction can lead to a government failure or the deepening of a market failure that requires some form of corrective action. Determining the proper level of government intervention has its challenges, and there are several reasons for government failures. The pursuit of self-interest among politicians and civil servants, for example, can often lead to a misallocation of scarce resources. For example, logistical decisions about road construction, schools, and hospitals may be decided with at least one eye to the political consequences. The pressures of a looming election or the influence exerted by special interest groups can create an environment in which inappropriate government spending and tax decisions are made. This can result in increasing the level of welfare spending leading to an election or bringing forward major items of capital spending on infrastructural projects without the projects being subjected to a full and proper cost-benefit analysis to determine the likely social costs and benefits. Critics of government intervention in the economy argue that politicians have a tendency to look for short-term solutions or "quick fixes" to difficult economic problems rather than conducting an analysis of long-term considerations. The risk is that myopic decision making will likely yield short-term relief for particular problems, but it does little to address structural economic difficulties. Regulatory capture can also occur whenindustries under the control of a regulatory body (a government agency) appear to operate in favor of the "vested interests" of producers rather than consumers. Some economists argue that regulators can prevent the ability of the market to operate freely, while the economic collapse in 2008 suggests that too little government involvement can lead to major market failures. **See also** Market Failure

Government Propaganda Effects   The term *propaganda* comes from the *Congregatio de propaganda fide,* or Congregation for the Propagation of Faith, established by the Catholic Church in 1622. The concept, however, is much older than the name. The dissemination of wartime propaganda dates back at least to Sun Tzu's *The Art of War,* written before the Common Era. It was not until World War I, however, that propaganda was used in a massive, highly organized fashion. Writing in the 1920s, Harold Lasswell defined propaganda as the control of opinion by significant symbols or, to speak more concretely and less accurately, by stories, rumors, reports, pictures, and other forms of social communication. A message may be considered to be propaganda only if it serves to benefit the generator of the message instead of its recipient.

Prior to World War II, the United States began to take a major interest in educating its citizens about the potential effects of propaganda. This concern led to the establishment of the Institute for Propaganda Analysis and the publication of *The Fine Art of Propaganda,* a book directed toward a large popular audience that identified seven common devices of propaganda. The devices were assigned simple, catchy names: "Name Calling," which associates an idea or its proponents with a repellent label; "Glittering Generality," the association of something with a positive term so that the audience will approve it without considering its actual merits; "Transfer," the association of something prestigious or authoritative with something else to make the latter more acceptable; "Testimonial," having some respected or reviled person pronounce something good or bad; "Plain Folks," representing the speaker and his ideas as good because they are "of the people"; "Card Stacking," the selection and use of facts or falsehoods, illustrations or distractions, and logical or illogical statements to present the best or worst possible case for something; and "Band Wagon," presenting something as overwhelmingly popular or unpopular and implying that joining the crowd that supports or rejects it will give one a sense of inclusion and belonging.

The effectiveness of government propaganda is contingent on a number of factors, including the education level of the recipient, his or her predisposition to believe the message, and, in the case of bandwagon propaganda, the degree of perceived unanimity in support of the message. Regimes in which propaganda has proved most influential, like Nazi Germany, have been those in which the state enjoyed a virtual monopoly on public communication and could reinforce its messages through organized terror. Joseph Goebbels, Hitler's infamous propaganda minister, is said to have observed, "A sharp sword must stand behind propaganda, if it is to be really effective." For more information, see Lasswell (1927) and Severin (1988). ***See also*** Bandwagon Effect

Grade Equivalent Score Score derived by comparing raw test scores with the average score obtained by grade-level norm groups. For example, if the average test score for fifth graders is 65, a student who scores 65 would have a grade equivalent of 5. ***See also*** Criterion- and Norm-Referenced Measurement

Grandfather Clause An exception that allows an old rule to apply to a current situation, while a new rule applies to all other current and future cases. It is often used to indicate that an exception has been granted. The original grandfather clause was in the Jim Crow laws to prevent certain groups, particularly people of color, from voting. Exemptions from poll taxes and literacy tests were made for those who had descendants who were able to vote before the American Civil War.

Grand Jury A jury that examines evidence presented against a person accused of committing a crime and, if the evidence warrants, makes formal charges on which the accused person is later tried. The grand jury was created to prevent arbitrary prosecution by the state. Grand juries were incorporated into the U.S. criminal justice system with the Fifth Amendment of the Constitution. Today, approximately half of all states use them, generally depending on the type of crime. A grand jury has the power to act as an independent investigatory body that can compel witnesses to testify, and it can serve as a check on the prosecution (the state) to determine if there is probable cause for prosecution (the charging decision). If the grand jury finds probable cause, it issues a true bill or indictment; if it fails to find probable cause, no bill is issued. All proceedings of the grand jury are secret, and the defendant is not able to participate. ***See also*** Indictment; True Bill

Grand Larceny Larceny is theft or permanent removal of another person's possession without violence. Grand larceny is usually defined as the theft of a significant amount of property. Generally, in the United States it is an amount of $200 or more, whereas in New York it is $1,000. The crime is generally regarded as a felony.

Grants Financial packages given to fund research interests. These can be given to either social or natural scientists and can come from a variety of sources, including federal (i.e., tax-based) programs, nongovernmental organizations, and private research institutions. Researchers must usually apply for grants in advance and present a convincing argument to explain for what purpose and in what amount the capital is needed. Often, various researchers will compete for a single grant, and the process can therefore be quite competitive. Arguments have pivoted around whether government funding is appropriate for noninstrumental projects and if private funding is more efficiently allocated.

Grants of Power Delegations of power from the national to the state level. Grants of power are conveyed through constitutions, statutes, and charters. Under a federation, such as the United States, certain powers are reserved for constituent states that have some level of sovereignty. Federations consist of a union comprising partially self-governing states united by a central government.

One idea of federalism, expressed through the Tenth Amendment of the Bill of Rights, reserves to the states those powers not granted to the federal government. According to the Tenth Amendment, which was ratified in 1791, "The Powers not delegated to the United States by the Constitution, nor prohibited by it to the States, are reserved to the States respectively or to the People."

States may further grant powers to local or municipal governments through home rule powers. Home rule powers are different from federation powers in that home rule powers may be temporary and ultimately reside in the state government. Territorial governments, Native tribunal governments, and the District of Columbia are further examples of jurisdictions practicing home rule powers. ***See also*** Bill of Rights

Graphic An illustration representing an arrangement of visual elements, which can be either functional or artistic in nature. A graphic can stand alone but usually accompanies text to make a message visually appealing or to bring greater clarity to a message. A graphic can be found in any medium, including printed material, television, or the World Wide Web. More and more, regardless of the medium used for display, the graphic is being generated via a computer. The enhanced capabilities of computers have made it possible not only to produce graphics for all mediums but also to create extraordinary graphic images that can be manipulated in applications such as electronic games, scientific visualization, or computer-aided engineering and design. *See also* Animation; CD-ROM Games

Graphic Organizers   Vsual teaching and learning tools with many purposes. They allow students to generate ideas, organize information, construct knowledge, and synthesize the relationships among various concepts and topics in a pictorial way. Teachers may use them to introduce and summarize content and to assess students' thought processes.

Graphic Violence   As with many qualitative judgments affecting media, a clear definition of graphic violence is elusive. It is perhaps safe to say that what constitutes violence on the screen is measurable against real life. One is, in effect, recognized by the other. For instance, children do not typically regard cartoons or video games as disturbingly violent, in part because these are seen as standing at a tangible remove from real life. On the other end of the spectrum, children appear more likely to be disturbed by media representations of real-life violence, as in news reports, than by violent drama.

Typically, concerns about graphic violence in media tend to be manifested with regard to a group younger than the people expressing the concern. Whereas adults worry about how viewing graphic violence will affect children and teenagers, teenagers worry about its influence on children, whereas older children regard younger children as the at-risk group. This phenomenon, called displacement, arises frequently in media studies; people tend to worry most about the effects of the media on someone else.

Graphic violence in media receives criticism on three grounds: (1) that viewers will be inclined to incorporate what they have seen into their own conduct (behavioral effects), (2) that they will incur emotional harm from the disturbing stimuli (emotional effects), or (3) that media representations of violence may, over time, influence societal attitudes, making violence more acceptable within the culture or, perhaps, making certain groups more acceptable targets of violent behavior (ideological effects). Because the ideological effects of graphic violence are assumed to take place over long periods, these supposed effects are almost impossible to quantify. Much of the psychological research has focused on harmful behavioral effects. Here, too, however, researchers face substantial challenges in reproducing normal viewing conditions, both because experiments tend to feature an artificially controlled media diet and because the experimental subject may consciously shape his or her responses in the hope of pleasing the experimenter.

Despite—or perhaps because of—the difficulty in compiling reliable data regarding the effects of graphic violence in media, concern over graphic violence remains powerful. One study reflects that by the age of 12, the average child will have seen more than 100,000 violent acts on television, including some 13,400 violent deaths. One significant study has found that violent behavior among 19-year-olds is more closely correlated to the amount of violent television watched in third grade than to factors such as domestic disharmony, frequency of punishment by one's parents, or the regularity with which one's parents have attended church. In 1982, the National Institute for Mental Health stated a consensus belief among researchers that violence in media does lead to aggressive behavior in children and teenagers who watch the programs. For more information, see Severin (1988). *See also* Visual Images

Grassroots Lobbying   A tactic used by political interest groups to organize local collective action in an effort to influence larger-scale policy making. Grassroots lobbying occurs when the public is called on by an interest group to contact legislators individually regarding an issue. Contact is usually in the form of phone calls, petition drives, requests for meetings, and letter-writing campaigns. This practice is in contrast to "direct lobbying," which occurs when individuals, or groups, contact a legislator on behalf of an interest group.

The political organization of massive numbers of ordinary Americans has had a profound effect on the history of American politics. Some of the most notable grassroots lobbying efforts have included the industrial workers' movement of the 1930s, the Southern Civil Rights movement of the early 1960s, and the women's liberation movement of the 1970s. More contemporary efforts include antiwar movements, faith-based campaigns, and environmentalist concerns. Grassroots lobbying gains its success, in part, from the general political apathy of the American public. Since the vast majority of American citizens rarely communicate with their legislators, it is quite noticeable when they do.

Despite grassroots lobbyists' prior achievements in the United States, critics claim that their effectiveness is inevitably limited. They maintain that resistance from powerful political and financial establishments overpowers any grassroots efforts that might alter an embattled status quo. Furthermore, the more global the political stage, the more difficult it is for grassroots campaigns to extend their sphere of influence. Nonetheless, grassroots efforts only show signs of gaining in popularity.

Politically, the term *grass roots* was first used by Republican Senator Albert Jeremiah Beveridge of Indiana to describe the Progressive Party in 1912: "This party comes from the grass roots. It has grown from the soil of the people's hard necessities." *See also* Interest Group (political science, public administration)

Greenhouse Effect   The ability of atmospheric gases to trap heat expelled from the earth's surface, commonly thought to be responsible for global warming. The greenhouse effect is also responsible for providing the earth with insulation, without which the planet would be too cold for most forms of life to exist. The greenhouse effect is a natural process that allows gases in the atmosphere to trap heat, thereby warming the earth. The current level of gases found in the atmosphere, however, is at historically high levels and is responsible for increasingly warmer temperatures. The burning of fossil fuels such as coal and oil, along with other human activities, is thought to seriously contribute to increasing the gases in the atmosphere. The result, according to many scientists, is the rise in the earth's average temperature, commonly referred to as global warming. The warming of the earth's surface is predicted to have devastating consequences and has led to efforts to reduce emission of greenhouse gases. Tension exists between proponents of curbing the emissions of greenhouse gases and those who advocate economic growth without investing in more environmentally sound technology. *See also* Global Warming

Grievance A complaint filed in the criminal justice system by an inmate or group of inmates against a specific employee or the correctional institution itself. The build-up of grievances over time is often cited as the cause of prison riots. Inmates at Attica were grieving their deplorable living conditions, which included being issued one roll of toilet paper per month.

Grooming Behaviors A social activity that allows animals living near each other to bond and build relationships by influencing and caring for each other. Sexual grooming refers to the social behavior of a potential child sex offender, who attempts to make a child more accepting of sexual advances. This can occur in person or over the Internet, such as in a chat room or through e-mail correspondence. The child is befriended, and a relationship is cultivated so as to build trust between the offender and the child. *See also* Sex Offense/Crime

Gross Domestic Product The total value of all the goods and services produced within a nation for a given period of time. Gross domestic product (GDP) is an economic indicator of the overall performance and income of an economy. GDP per capita (per head) is normally used for comparative analysis. The GDP of the United States is computed on a quarterly basis by the Bureau of Economic Analysis.

The income and expenditure approaches are the two main methods used to calculate GDP. The income approach calculates the total income of everyone in the economy, and the expenditure approach computes the total expenditure on an economy's output of goods and services. The income approach computes compensation of employees, proprietors' income, rental income corporate profits, capital consumption allowance, indirect business taxes, and net foreign factor income.

The expenditure approach computes household expenditure (C), government expenditure (G), expenditure on investment by businesses (I), and expenditure by foreigners on domestic goods and services minus domestic expenditures on foreign goods and services (net exports, NX). It turns out that these approaches can be used interchangeably, because for the economy as a whole, income must be equal to expenditure (every transaction has a buyer and a seller).

The nominal value of GDP—that is, GDP calculated by current price level (consumer price index) and output—does not necessarily reflect the economic well-being of a nation over time because the value of GDP can be inflated as a result of an increase in the price level rather than output. To deal with this problem, the real GDP is used as an alternative. Real GDP uses anchor, base, or constant prices instead of current prices, and it is the ratio of nominal GDP to GDP deflator.

Not all transactions are included in the computation of GDP—for example, used products, intermediate goods (goods used for further processing), stock market transactions, domestic services, and activities in the underground economy are not accounted for. The underground economy is a robust economy with surreptitious economic activities beyond the reach of policymakers. For more information, see Mankiw (2006), McConnell and Brue (2008), and Schiller (2006). *See also* Aggregate Demand Curve; Business Cycle; Economic Growth

Gross National Product (GNP) A quantitative measure of a country's production of goods and services by its citizens. In addition to economic activity created by companies located in the specified nation, the GNP also includes income earned by residents from overseas investments and excludes income earned within the domestic economy by foreign investors. The GNP is a significant measure of economic health and is measured annually or quarterly. *See also* Gross Domestic Product

Grounded Theory A method of qualitative research that builds theory from the inductive analysis of data. Rather than starting with a theoretical framework or perspective, the grounded theorist builds the theory directly from the data. The focus is on building, generating, or constructing a theory rather than testing an existing theory. According to the founders of grounded theory, Barney Glaser and Anselm Strauss (1967), the characteristics of a good grounded theory are *fit* (Does the theory fully fit the data?), *understanding* (Is the theory readily understandable to researchers and practitioners?), *generality* (Does the scope of the theory apply to more than one group or people or one setting?), and *control* (Does use of the theory allow users to affect the world?). Analytic techniques and concepts include constant comparison, theoretical sensitivity, theoretical sampling, and theoretical saturation.

The goal for the grounded theorist is to become immersed in the data in order to see embedded meanings and relationships. A noted difference between using the grounded theory method and other methods is that the line between data collection and data analysis is blurred,

G

meaning that the two activities are conducted iteratively (collect data, analyze data, collect data, analyze data, etc.) as well as simultaneously (i.e., the researcher continually considers the theoretical meaning of the data while the data are being collected). During data analysis, the grounded theorist analyzes the data constantly by sifting, rearranging, and examining different categories, themes, and patterns throughout the collection and analysis periods. Another aspect of grounded theory is that the data collection and analysis drives the sampling. To test the boundaries of or refine an emerging category or pattern, the grounded theorist will seek new cases. Grounded theory development is said to be complete when theoretical saturation occurs (i.e., when no new concepts are emerging from the data and the theory has been thoroughly validated). In addition to the founders Glaser and Strauss, Juliet Corbin and Kathy Charmaz are two currently noted grounded theorists. **See also** Qualitative Data Analysis; Qualitative Research

Group   A collection of people who share characteristics, interact with each other, work well together, and share to a degree some common ideas and identity. Society is an example of a group. A group usually has some cohesion and some form of ties, whether strong or loose. The German sociologist Ferdinand Tönnies (1855–1936) made one of the earliest contributions to the study of groups with his concepts of *Gemeinschaft* (small, closely knit communities based on family ties, friendship, and a strongly shared value system) and *Gesellschaft* (large, formal communities with weak ties and little consensus). There are various types of groups. Primary groups consist of small groups with kin-based relationships, such as a family. Secondary groups are large groups whose relationships are more formal. An example of a secondary group would be a school. Reference groups are groups to which an individual conceptually relates himself or herself. For example, in a reference group, an individual can adopt a goal based on the principles learned from the reference group. Success of a group is based on each member playing an active, productive part in the organization. Groups need not have face-to-face communication as the proliferating number of Internet groups illustrate.

Group Counseling   A modality of counseling/psychotherapy that provides counseling simultaneously to a small group of clients who typically have similar problems. This approach allows clients to hear each others' stories and receive feedback from other clients and is cost-effective. Group counseling/therapy is widely used across a wide range of settings and client populations.

Group Dynamics   A field in social psychology focusing on the study of groups and group process, especially the study of small groups. The famous social psychologist Kurt Lewin is usually credited with coining the term *group dynamics*. Lewin used the phrase to designate the scientific discipline that studies group dynamics.

Scholars and teachers use terms such as perceptions, motivation, goals, organization, interdependency, and interaction to define important qualities of groups. Group dynamics research has examined topics such as individual versus group performance, brainstorming, the risky shift phenomenon, groupthink, diffusion of responsibility, pressures to uniformity, power in groups, and motivational and structural properties of groups. Small-group research also has examined many characteristics of groups, including the physical environment (e.g., interaction distance, seating arrangements, leadership emergence, communication networks), personal environment (e.g., group size, biographical characteristics, personality characteristics of groups members), social environment (structure, status and roles, norms, leadership styles), and task environment (goals, task typologies, task complexity).

An example of small-group research is stages of group development. Bruce Tuckman (1965) conceptualized a popular four-stage model of forming, storming, norming, and performing. First, during *forming,* the group members come together and meet one another, statuses and roles are unclear, anxiety and uncertainty are common, and discussion addresses the purpose and tasks of the group. Second, during *storming,* competition, arguing, defensiveness, formation of factions, and power struggles are said to occur. Third, during *norming,* agreements are made, responsibilities become clear, members accept and identify with their statuses and roles, and norms regulating behavior emerge. Fourth, during *performing,* the group follows its norms and works toward goal fulfillment. Tuckman (1975) later added a fifth stage, called *adjourning.* In this stage, the group has completed its task and breaks up. This stage is the opposite of the first stage in that it involves "unforming." The final meeting group meeting is held. Members experience a sense of accomplishment but simultaneously experience difficulty in "breaking up."

Although group dynamics is a relatively old discipline in social psychology, group dynamics research remains robust, and its research is published in many journals. Examples of these journals include the following: *Group Dynamics: Theory, Research, and Practice; Group Processes & Intergroup Relations; Small Group Research; Journal of Personality and Social Psychology; Journal of Experimental Social Psychology; Human Relations;* and *Journal of Social Psychology.* **See also** Group; Group Norms; Small Group

Group Norms   Members of a team develop particular ways of interacting with each other. For group norms to develop, effective interpersonal communication is vital. Therefore, it is important for the group to pay attention to how work is assigned, who holds people accountable for actions, and how the group makes decisions.

Group norms develop when members of the group commit to using the adopted guidelines. Those rules govern the conduct of the group. There is no recommended number of group norms for each group, but it is important to recognize that conformity to rules is vital. It is important for the group to periodically evaluate the adopted rules to see if they are still viable.

If someone does not follow the group rules, the person can be punished. Punishment in a civilized society means that one will be excluded from the group—a terrifying prospect to many. These group norms coordinate the way in which we behave in groups. There are group norms that set the standards for dress, speech, and appearance within the group. ***See also*** Interpersonal Communication

Groups   The term refers to three or more individuals who form a collective distinguished by seven properties:

1. Groups have a reason to exist, and individuals join groups to achieve *common goals* they are unable to achieve alone. Clarity and commitment to collective goals are factors that separate successful from unsuccessful groups.

2. Group members are significantly *interdependent,* in that what affects one member is likely to affect all members.

3. Group members *interact and communicate,* verbally and nonverbally, with each other in meaningful ways over time.

4. *Relationships within the group are structured* by norms (cultural rules regulating interaction and behavior) and social roles (differentiated sets of behaviors, expectations, and obligations defining suitable actions in social situations).

5. Group members perceive themselves as having an identity associated with *belonging* to the group.

6. Groups are composed of members who *mutually influence* each other through their interpersonal relationships and interactions.

7. Membership in the group *satisfies a personal need* or confers some reward, motivating members to be part of the group.

Since a fundamental characteristic is a common purpose, various types of groups exist. A *primary group* provides the basic human needs of support, affection, and a sense of belonging. Its main task is to perpetuate itself in order to continue maintaining interpersonal ties. Families are an example of a primary group. *Secondary groups* exist to fulfill a necessity, accomplish a task, or achieve a goal. They form the majority of groups individuals belong to at work or school. The following are some types of secondary groups:

- *Problem-solving or task groups:* groups convened to solve a problem or accomplish a task, who then disband

- *Social groups:* groups providing a context to pursue common social or recreational interests in a friendly setting
- *Decision-making groups:* groups charged with the task of making a choice from among several options
- *Self-help groups:* groups whose members give each other support, encouragement, and mutual aid with personal problems
- *Therapy groups:* groups led by a professional that assist members to manage or overcome difficulties using therapeutic methods
- *Study or learning groups:* groups that assist their members in the acquisition of new knowledge and skills
- *Committees:* elected or appointed groups whose function is to carry out an assignment
- *Work groups or teams:* groups in the workplace responsible for achieving tasks or performing duties on behalf of the organization (teams generally are self-organized and self-managing)
- *Service groups:* groups whose activities are dedicated to worthy causes for individuals within and outside the group
- *Public groups:* groups convened to work though issues on behalf of the public

See also Group Dynamics

Group Therapy   A form of psychotherapy where a small group, typically no more than 12 people, meets regularly to discuss their problems with one or more therapists in the same room. The voluntary disclosure of personal information by patients is believed to be therapeutic both to the patient and to other group members. A social network is formed, allowing clients to feel less isolated with regard to their problems, which is thereby thought to enhance coping. A psychologist forms the group based on a variety of factors, including gender, age, diagnosis, and amenability to therapy. Some group therapies, however, may be formed by groups of lay individuals, such as Alcoholics Anonymous, centered on the idea of providing a supportive, therapeutic network among peers who suffer from like difficulties. ***See also*** Psychotherapy

Groupthink (communication)   A thinking process in which the members of an in-group (organization) hold a set of beliefs to maintain cohesiveness against appraising opposing, rational information and bad outcomes. As a result, the group may make a very quick decision that is irrational. Individual decisions are not recognized. The goal is to minimize conflict. William H. Whyte coined the term *groupthink* in 1952 in *Fortune:*

Groupthink being a coinage, and, admittedly, a loaded one, a working definition is in order. We are not talking about mere instinctive conformity. It is, after all, a perennial failing of mankind. What we are talking about is a rationalized conformity, an open, articulate philosophy which holds that group values are not only expedient by right and good as well. (p. 89)

Irving Janis (1972) originated the scholarly study of groupthink with his case studies of flawed decision making by the government, including the Bay of Pigs Invasion under the John F. Kennedy administration and the Watergate Scandal under President Richard M. Nixon. Groupthink is particularly prevalent in organizations with strong in-group cohesive decision makers who place importance on conformity and unanimity.

Groupthink *(psychology)*   A thought process that occurs when there is a breakdown in independent thinking within a group. Groupthink may result in flawed decisions if, in an effort to reach group consensus, members do not critically analyze ideas and fail to consider alternative opinions. Famous examples of negative results of groupthink include the *Challenger* explosion in 1986 and the Bay of Pigs Invasion in 1961. Irving Janis, who coined the term *groupthink,* proposed that groupthink happens when the group is highly cohesive and feels an "illusion of invulnerability." High levels of confidence, reluctance to consult an outside opinion, and lack of objective leadership may increase the likelihood of the occurrence of this phenomenon. Similarly, this may be more likely to occur when group members fear rejection, strive to fit in, and feel pressure to reach a unanimous decision. The more insulated the group is, the less likely that an opinion will be challenged or that alternative ideas will be put forth. If members of the group do have a dissenting opinion, they often do not speak up, thereby implicitly accepting the group decision. For more information, see McCauley (1989). *See also* Risky Shift

Growth   An increase in national output, if and when it occurs. This concept must not be confused with development, which is a broader indicator of economic performance and policies affecting education, health, and income distribution. Gross domestic product (GDP) is the main economic variable that is used to measure economic growth or performance.

The pace of economic growth across the world is not even. Some nations continue to grow faster than others because of differences in the availability of economic resources and deliberate policy measures that are adopted by policymakers. Growth may be stalled or retarded because of population pressures and gyrations in economic performance attributable to the business cycle or contingent shocks, such as natural disasters or unforeseen impediments.

The main determinants of the level of economic growth are education, saving (for capital formation), innovation, level of inflation, fiscal and monetary policies, the quality of the financial system, the efficiency of labor, the rate of capital deepening (a process that ensures sufficient capital per worker) or widening (increase in capital stock that barely keeps pace with the labor force and depreciation of capital), and returns from international trade.

The growth rate of GDP is calculated by the annual percentage increase, and the average rate of growth calculates the average of the annual percentage increase. The annual percentage increase may be revised downward to accommodate the rate of inflation.

Economists have used several theories to model growth, one of the earliest being that of Harrod-Domar in the 1940s, which focused attention on capital accumulation and fixed proportions of capital and labor for growth. In 1956, the Solow neoclassical model improved on the Harrod-Domar model by allowing for variability and substitution between capital and labor but taking technological change as residual (exogenous).

Much more recent models make technological change endogenous and argue for increasing returns to scale (doubling inputs can more than double output). These recent models have been used to explain growth without a steady state in industrialized countries. For more information, see Mankiw (2006), McConnell and Brue (2008), and Perkins, Radlet, and Lindauer (2006). *See also* Business Cycle; Capital; Fiscal Policy; Gross Domestic Product; Inflation; Monetary Policy

Guilty *(psychology)*   The state of feeling guilt or the state of being found justly chargeable with or responsible for crime or breach of social conduct. People often feel guilty when they believe they are responsible for an act deemed morally or legally wrong. When an individual feels responsible for a situation but cannot improve on it, guilty feelings can also occur. People may also feel guilty when their actions do not coincide with their values.

Guilty *(sociology)*   The state of being responsible for an act, generally an offense, crime, or violation of moral or legal standards. A person can be deemed guilty by others, as in the case of a judge or jury. Guilt can also be an individual affective state that results from acting (or not acting) in a manner in which one regrets. Once a defendant is found guilty or pleads guilty in court, he or she will be sentenced accordingly. *See also* Not Guilty; Plea

Gun Control   A political issue surrounding the ownership, use, and regulation of firearms by individual people. Guns are blamed for the United State's high rate of violent crime, and there is a movement to restrict ownership of firearms, whether specific types or in general. The largest group against gun control, the National Rifle Association (NRA), points to the Second Amendment as granting individuals the right to own firearms. Those in favor of stricter gun control point to violent crimes and accidental deaths that occur because of access to guns, whereas those who oppose argue that crimes are generally committed with illegally acquired guns and point to the Second Amendment as establishing their right. *See also* Firearm

H

Habeas Corpus A Latin expression meaning "you have the body." A writ of habeas corpus is an order from the court requiring that the custodian produce the prisoner so that the court can determine the legality of the prisoner's detention. Habeas corpus protects individual citizens against unlawful government detention.

Habitat *(geography)* The physical environment in which living organisms reside. A habitat is occupied by a particular species, as each environment accommodates different forms of life. Habitats provide the appropriate conditions for survival, which include food, shelter, climatic conditions, and protection for the species that occupy them. The preservation of habitats is a significant environmental concern. Both physical and human factors have contributed to the destruction of certain habitats, leading to refuge areas for endangered species. Habitats are also used to describe the environments in which human beings exist, including the physical environments in which individuals work and reside. ***See also*** Environment (geography)

Habitat *(sociology)* The natural environment that supports the life and growth of an organism or a community of organisms, including all living and nonliving factors of the area. Human habitats are the total (e.g., physical, social, urban) environments in which people live, work, and recreate. ***See also*** Environment (sociology)

Habitual Offender Offenders who re-offend at exceptionally high rates relative to the average offender (sometimes referred to as persistent or chronic offenders). Marvin Wolfgang, a world-renowned American criminologist, is most famous for his work advancing our understanding of habitual offenders. Wolfgang, Figlio, and Sellin studied juvenile offenders in Philadelphia and demonstrated that a small number of chronic offenders were responsible for more than half of all criminal offenses and for almost three quarters of all serious criminal offenses. Habitual offenders have since been increasingly targeted by legislation aimed at their incapacitation. For more information, see Wolfgang, Figlio, and Sellin (1972). ***See also*** Career Criminal; Offender/Offense

Habituation A physiological process whereby the brain ignores or becomes accustomed to environmental stimuli that remain constant. The human brain appears to be prewired to pay more attention to changes in the environment than to things that remain constant. This reduced responsiveness to a repeated stimulus has been identified as the simplest form of learning. According to Solomon's *opponent process theory,* habituation is a conditioned response that counteracts an initial involuntary response to a stimulus. After a stimulus is repeated over and over (i.e., remains constant), the opposing conditioned response occurs faster and with greater intensity. For more information, see Solomon (1980). ***See also*** Learning

Halfway House Residential facilities designed to facilitate the transition from prison back to the community (sometimes referred to as transitional houses). Halfway houses are staffed facilities that allow for limited and graduated freedom while maintaining strict rules for their residents. Offenders nearing the end of their prison terms are often moved from prisons to halfway houses. ***See also*** Community-Based Corrections; Offender/ Offense; Parole; Prison/Prisoner

Hallucinations Sensory perceptions that occur in the absence of any causal external stimulus. Hallucinations are a hallmark symptom of schizophrenia. Hallucinations can occur in all five sensory modalities, but auditory hallucinations are by far the most commonly reported. Auditory hallucinations occur in approximately 70% of patients with schizophrenia and can take several forms. Command hallucinations involve voices that tell the individual what he or she should think, feel, or do. Patients with schizophrenia often report voices that keep up a running commentary of the patient's behaviors or events the patients come across in their environment, or they report that voices are arguing. Visual hallucinations are less common but involve patients seeing imaginary people or creatures. Hallucinations can occur in healthy individuals who are under intense physiological stress, such as sleep deprivation, and they can also occur as a result of using drugs with hallucinogenic properties. For more information, see Ohayon (2000).

Halo Effect A form of observation that is potentially inaccurate because it relies on bias toward a particular personality trait that leads to a false generalization, whether positive or negative. It was first empirically supported by Edward L. Thorndike (1920) in a study that asked army officers to rate their soldiers. The halo effect is also caused by the influence of preconceived notions, assumptions, or traits. This effect also encompasses the perception of positive qualities in one thing or one part that later gives rise to the perception of similar qualities in related things. Solomon Asch, for example, found that attractiveness gave the impression, false or true, of competence in other personal traits. The reliance on such wrong impressions contributes greatly to cognitive errors and bias and can lead to poor leadership, faulty decision making, and failure in an organization.

Harold Kelley in his implicit personality theory also found that first impressions influence our view of others and can lead to unfounded expectations. When we seek out the endorsements of products by certain celebrities or their views on subjects on which they are especially ignorant, we have egregious examples of the halo effect. For more information, see Asch (1946), Kelley (1973), and Thorndike (1920). *See also* Attribution Theory; Implicit Personality Theory

Hamiltonianism   A political ideology that resembles the views of Alexander Hamilton (1757–1804), first Secretary of the Treasury and leader of the Federalist Party. Hamilton was an ardent supporter of a strong central government and distrustful of the popular will. Hamiltonianism is often contrasted with Jeffersonianism, named after Thomas Jefferson (1743–1826), the third President of the United States and leader of the rival Democratic-Republican party. Hamilton's politics was publicized in *The Federalist Papers* (1787–1788), a compilation of essays, written with John Jay and James Madison, debating the framing of the Constitution. Hamilton is said to have written 51 of the 85 essays. Hamilton was one of three New York delegates at the Convention; his constitutional proposal was closely modeled on the British parliamentary system. He advocated that senators and a "national governor" be chosen by special electors to hold lifetime terms. Additionally, assembly members should be chosen by the people and should serve three-year terms; the national governor would choose the state governors.

On the other hand, Jeffersonianism supported a weak federal government and strong state- and local-level governments, believing that this arrangement better represented the will of the people. This view extended into the operations of the different spheres of government. For example in the economic arena, Jeffersonians preferred an agricultural economy rather than an industrial one and were wary of big business. Hamiltonians, on the other hand, promoted government involvement in the protection of business and the mercantile class. For more information, see Frisch and Ashbrook (1992) and Madison, Hamilton, and Jay (1788). *See also* Federalism; Federalist Papers

Hands-On Learning   A strategy by which a student learns a concept through the use of manipulatives rather than the classroom lecture alone. It is a kinesthetic approach to learning. The physical manipulation of a concept aids the cognitive process by adding a physical experience through the student's senses. This strategy can be used in the teaching of all subjects.

Haptics   The study of touching behavior. Touching is a part of human communication in interpersonal relationships and can be important in conveying physical intimacy. Touching, however, can be interpreted both positively and negatively. Some people like to be touched, while others find it abusive and harassing. Acceptable levels of touching vary from culture to culture and are interpreted differently. For example, it is natural in the United States to shake hands when meeting for the first time, but a kiss or hug may not be acceptable until one is on more intimate terms with the other. *See also* Human Communication

Hate Crime   A crime committed against a person or property based on a perceived association with a particular social group. Sometimes referred to as bias crimes or bias motivated crimes, hate crimes may be either personal or property crimes and are, typically, committed based on the victim's race, ethnicity, religion, gender, disability, or sexual orientation. Hate crimes are considered more harmful than traditional crimes, because they target not just the individual victims but also the entire community or group with which the victim is associated. Most states have passed laws criminalizing hate crimes and providing for additional punishment for crimes motivated, in whole or in part, by hatred. *See also* Criminal Law (political science, sociology); Prejudice (psychology)

Hawthorne Effect   *(psychology)*   Similar to the placebo effect in medicine, this effect occurs when people change their behavior simply as a result of being a participant in a research study or because they know that they are being observed. The behavioral change is usually in a socially acceptable direction. The Hawthorne effect was originally discovered in the 1920s by a group of Harvard psychologists who were conducting a study at the Hawthorne Works of the Western Electric Company, with the study designed to assess whether varying levels of lighting had an effect on worker productivity. Investigators found that productivity increased for all groups, including the control group, regardless of the level of lighting. Several subsequent studies were conducted examining the Hawthorne effect in various other work settings. The major contribution of these studies was in determining that workers' behavior was influenced not only by the physical environment but also by social factors in the workplace. However, some researchers have questioned the validity of the effect because of problems with the experimental designs. They cite practice, experimenter feedback, and pay-for-performance as additional factors that could have caused the increase in performance across groups. In summary, these criticisms do not nullify the argument that in some cases there will be a behavioral effect that results from participants' reactions to the experiments themselves; however, they suggest that such effects are not always present and that when they are, direct causal factors can include several distinct possibilities. For more information, see Jones (1992). **See also** Experiment

Hawthorne Effect *(sociology)*   An effect observed at a Chicago General Electric plant in the early 20th century that describes a temporary improvement in the behavior or productivity of a group of people being observed, probably due to teamwork and communication resulting from the perception of increased attention.

Head of Government   The chief executive officer of a state, who is responsible for leading a team of ministers or cabinet members who control the central institutions of that government. In democratic presidential systems, the head of state is also the head of government. In parliamentary systems, the head of government may be a premier or prime minister.

Head of State   A person or a collective that represents a political state and may also be known as the chief of state. The head of state personifies the legitimacy of the state and exercises political powers in accordance with the constitution of the country. The three main categories of heads of state are (1) monarch, (2) president, and (3) dictator.

Head Start   A federally funded program that provides various services to eligible children and their families for the purpose of promoting school readiness. Project Head Start was first developed as a preschool program designed to meet the needs of economically disadvantaged families in 1965, as part of President Johnson's War on Poverty. Head Start was initially sponsored by the Office of Economic Opportunity, transferred to the Office of Child Development in 1969, and is currently a part of the Administration for Children and Families. In 1995, Early Head Start was established to serve children from birth to three years of age, which focuses on healthy development of newborns, infants, and toddlers. Head Start also provides services targeted for specific populations, including the Migrant and Seasonal Program and the American Indian-Alaska Native Program. The Head Start Reauthorization Bill of 2007 included services for the unique needs of homeless children in America. **See also** Compensatory Education; Early Childhood; Poverty

Health and Physical Education   An education course of study in health and physical activity or fitness. Health and physical education courses explore the promotion, development, and maintenance of a healthy lifestyle through cognitive, affective, and psychomotor activities.

Health Care System   A system made up of a group of independent but interrelated elements that constitute a unified whole and designed to look after the health care needs of a population. The modern health care system comprises three components: (1) personal medical care services, which are involved in prevention, diagnosis,

treatment, and rehabilitation; (2) the institutions and personnel that provide these services; and (3) government, public, and private organizations, which finance service delivery. These arrangements rely on the interrelationships of the people needing the health care services; the professionals and practitioners providing the health care; and the public and private agencies organizing, planning, regulating, financing, and coordinating the services.

The health care system's concern for the delivery of services is related to access. Access is influenced by the characteristics of health care consumers, such as age, education level, economic status, race, ethnicity, cultural heritage, and geographical location. These determine when and where consumers seek health care services, their expectations of care and treatment, and the extent to which they wish to participate in decisions about their own medical care.

The evolution of the modern medical industrial complex is built on the acceptance of germ theory as a cause of disease. Prior to the 1800s, women took care of illnesses. Doctors, who had little formal training, were summoned to the home in cases of life-threatening illnesses. In the early 1800s, health care, in terms of the creation of public departments of health, emerged in the face of epidemics, such as cholera, yellow fever, and diphtheria and poor sanitation. Doctors began treating patients under one roof.

By the end of the 1920s, the first large medical insurance company, Blue Cross, was established. In the 1930s, doctors were being paid through a fee-for-service system, in which patients paid a fee for each service that they received. World War II marked the beginning of health maintenance organizations (HMOs), which would become pervasive in the 1980s.

The post–World War II era marked the beginning of an expanding workforce, advancements in medical care and medical science, an increase in health care costs, and technological advancements in drugs and equipment, which precipitated the professionalization of nonphysician therapists and technicians. In the 1960s, the U.S. government established the Centers for Disease Control, the U.S. Food and Drug Administration, and the cabinet-level Department of Health and Human Services.

By the 1980s, HMO's dominated the organization of health care and reimbursement to physicians. The fee-for-service system faded as doctors found themselves less in control of the health care services and instead working for corporations that made profits in prepaid health care by reducing costs, restricting services, and focusing on prevention. The fee-for-service was replaced by capitation, also known as managed care, a system that set a fee per patient for a given period of time. Patients, therefore, have been forced to become more directly involved in their own health care. As a result, the use of the Internet and alternative medicine have proliferated, as patients rely more on their own resources to get the care that they need. For more information, see Starr (1982). **See also** Public Programs

Health Psychology   A relatively new branch of psychology that is concerned with how biology, behavior, and the environment interact to influence health and illness. Health and illness were once assumed to be strictly biologically determined; however, as medical science improved, it became evident that despite the advances in medicine, chronic illnesses such as heart disease, cancer, and substance abuse continued to rise. Over the past quarter-century, it has become clear that many chronic illnesses could be prevented or treated through behavior and lifestyle changes. These realizations fueled the advancement of health psychology, which employs the bio-psycho-social approach to understanding illness. Health psychology is closely related to clinical psychology; however, the emphasis of health psychology is on the effect of mental illness and environmental stressors on the individual's physical well-being. Health psychology is concerned both with treating physical and mental illness and with applying psychological science to promote healthy lifestyles, prevent illness, and advance social issues relating to psychological health. There are four different approaches to health psychology: (1) clinical, (2) public health, (3) critical health, and (4) community. Clinical health psychology is very similar to clinical psychology and is also considered to be a major contributor to the field of behavioral medicine. Clinical health psychologists educate patients in behavioral change and conduct psychotherapy. Public health psychology is primarily concerned with epidemiological research aimed at determining the causal relationships between psychological and environmental factors and physical health at the population level. Interventions are usually on a large scale and aimed at institutional and environmental change. The community health psychology approach is similar to the public health approach, but it is concerned with causal effects at the local level. Interventions are often organized with the help of local businesses and hospitals to facilitate the improvement of the physical and mental health of the local community. Finally, critical health psychology can be considered an advocacy branch that is concerned with the universal right to health care and the equitable distribution of health care in societies. For more information see Taylor (1990). ***See also*** Clinical Psychology; Psychology

Hearing, Legal   Preliminary legal proceeding before a judge or any other decision-making body or officer, without a jury, in which charges, evidence, testimony, and arguments are presented to determine issues of fact and law. Hearings are usually brief and informal and may be held before or during a trial to decide specific questions or motions, such as the admissibility of evidence, that will determine how and whether a trial may proceed. The support of the defendant's due process has meant that hearings are now used for administrative decisions that were once made informally. ***See also*** Trial

Hearth Areas   A term used to describe the origin of an idea or innovation and the following diffusion from the hearth to other areas. While diffusion from the hearth to other regions facilitates the spread of different cultures, values, and traditions, cultural obstacles can also impede the process of diffusion. Hearth areas are not just an important factor in acculturation, but they also play a key role in the larger concept of globalization, where the spread of ideas and innovations occurs globally. Globalization, while praised and critiqued on different fronts, is responsible for the interconnectivity of markets, politics, and cultures worldwide. ***See also*** Globalization (political science)

Heartland Theory   A theory formulated by the British geographer Sir Halford Mackinder, in 1904, to describe a nation that extends its power and influence over other nations, based on the logic that the dominant nation controls the "heartland." The theory asserts that the dominant nation is self-reliant and has superior militaristic and economic policies and, therefore, cannot be defeated by other empires. Although the heartland nations have changed throughout history, Eastern Europe was conceived of as the original heartland nation. This theory brought to light the importance of geopolitics, a discipline pioneered by the Swedish political scientist Rudolph Kjellen in the early 1900s. Geopolitics examines the geographic, economic, political, and social influences over the state and the state's relationship with other world powers.

Hegemony *(media studies)*   A term (from the Greek for "leadership") mostly associated with the political theorist Antonio Gramsci, who used it to describe how capitalist power maintains itself in the modern state—namely, less through repressive force than through a correlation of political coercion and civil consent. Hegemony explains how the masses can voluntarily cooperate in their own domination by a ruling class. Gramsci describes the structure of civil society in terms of trench warfare. His choice of a military metaphor is pointed, implying that political and military science are identical and that a capitalist government *is* a form of war. As in trench warfare, it is impossible to engage the enemy head-on because its military strength is dispersed through a wide system of trenchlike structures, such as the judiciary, government, compulsory education, the church, and mass media. Because democracies refuse to vest absolute authority in any single person or executive body, and because the democratic state machine is always bigger than any individual or group of individuals, power is exercised through a totality of discrete institutions that on the face of it are often in conflict with each other. Modern versions of hegemony turn from the metaphor of the trench to the web, conceiving of power as a potentially endless network of relations that continually shift to incorporate every position of dissent encountered. This model of power is dynamic and mobile, in which the media become the site of competing ideologies rather than the instrument of a single class interest; some are independently funded, and some are owned by large corporations. They have the appearance of autonomy; they "perform" power by continuous representation, coverage, and management of information; by "covering" apparently everything of note or interest, they assimilate positions of dissent; by claims to balanced reportage (in terms of both quantitative and qualitative coverage), they elicit the consenting agreement of the masses. *See also* Capitalism (political science); Critical Theory; Ideology (media studies, political science); Marxism (political science); Power

Hegemony *(sociology)*   A concept used by Gramsci that refers to the domination or authority of one over another, especially of one nation or social group over others. The influence becomes so pervasive that it appears abstract and inevitable so as to avoid scrutiny and maintain power. *See also* Society

Heliocentric   The modern theory of planetary motion, which replaced the geocentric Ptolemaic system in the early 16th century and places the sun motionless at the center of the solar system. Using ancient astronomical records, Copernicus determined that the planets, including the earth, revolve around the sun. This shift of worldviews of the universe generated much political and religious controversy and culminated in Galileo's heresy trial, conviction, and abjuration in 1633 in Rome.

Hemisphere   One half of the earth, dividing the earth into either Northern and Southern or Eastern and Western Hemispheres. The Northern Hemisphere, comprising mainly North America, Europe, and Asia, contains most of the world's population, whereas the Southern Hemisphere hosts significantly less of the world's population but contains the remaining four of the seven continents. The earth is also divided into Eastern and Western halves, usually demarcated by the Prime Meridian and consisting of Africa, Asia, Australia, and Europe in the Eastern Hemisphere and North and South America in the Western Hemisphere.

Heritability   The proportion of the variation in phenotype that can be explained by genetic variation among individuals. In other words, heritability is the extent to which genetic differences contribute to individual differences in observed behaviors or traits. The error in heritability estimates is generally high unless the sample size is very large. For human behavior, almost all estimates of heritability are in the moderate range of .30 to .60. It is important to note that heritability is a population concept. A heritability of .30 for a particular trait means that, on average, about 30% of the individual differences observed on that trait in the population may be attributable to genetic variation. It does not mean that for a given individual 30% of the observed trait is due to his or her genes. For more information, see the Stanford Encyclopedia of Philosophy entry "Heredity and Heritability" (http://plato.stanford.edu/entries/heredity/). *See also* Genes

Hermeneutics *(education)*   The theory and technique of interpretation. The word is derived from the Greek god Hermes, whose task it was to communicate messages from the gods to ordinary mortals. The development of hermeneutics is owed to the work of Friedrich Schleiermacher through the practice of scriptural interpretation. Other philosophers such as Heidegger, Gadamer, and Dilthey contributed significantly to hermeneutical studies. Dilthey, especially, can be associated with broadening the scope of hermeneutics beyond texts to encompass the study of human behavior and everyday experiences. Dilthey thus inspired generations of interpretivist ideographic researchers, who believe that meaning can only be recovered and understood in context. For more information, see Bleicher (1980) and Ricoeur (1981). *See also* Ontology; Phenomenology

Hermeneutics *(sociology)*   The study of the understanding and interpretation of texts (especially religious) and meaning systems. Hermeneutics requires empathy for the creator of the text and appreciation of the cultural and social forces that create context. Understanding is considered a circular process of transmission and interpretation.

Heterogeneous   A system consisting of elements or constituents that are different in kind or in nature. For example, heterogeneous societies may consist of people of varying racial, ethnic, age, and socioeconomic groups. *Heterogeneous* is the antonym of *homogeneous,* which indicates uniformity in structure or composition throughout. *See also* Homogeneous

Heuristic   An informal, usually experientially based, mechanism used to solve a problem or make a decision without analytic reasoning. Heuristics can be thought of as intuitive judgments that are made readily accessible by environmental stimuli. Heuristics were originally described by Tversky and Kahneman as simple and efficient rules, either genetically imprinted or learned, that humans use to make decisions when faced with information that is either too complex or incomplete. For more information, see Kahneman, Tversky, and Slovic (1982). *See also* Problem Solving (education)

Hidden Agenda   A particular action's veiled, nonexplicit purpose. For example, an individual may call his parents with the principal intention of asking for money. Embarrassed by the concept of openly begging for finances, the person may (seemingly casually) talk about hardships in paying rent and affording groceries, hoping that his folks will "unexpectedly" offer monetary support. Hidden agendas need not be restricted to conversations alone and can often be a necessary tool in social scientific research. One may wish to study the presence of narcotics in the local community and therefore need to override individuals' natural reluctance to openly share such private information. The researcher may thus ingratiate himself or herself with the local population and only reveal his or her true intentions after gaining the necessary trust and confidence. In such a scenario, however, ethical issues will also inherently rise to the surface, especially concerning the researcher's lack of full disclosure to his or her subject pool.

Hierarchy   A system wherein people or things are ranked according to a particular or series of factors. The Catholic Church, for example, is highly hierarchical in nature, with the rank of Pope at the top and priest at the bottom. The military is similarly structured, as each soldier must follow the commands of the officer directly above him or her. Social philosophers have long incorporated hierarchical notions into their ideas. Whereas Aristotle famously proclaimed humankind to be divided into a natural hierarchy (with men at its height and slaves at its base), thinkers such as Jeremy Bentham and William James sought to rank different human desires by their supposed importance. Feminist or postmodernist thinkers have also identified hierarchies, although from a considerably more negative perspective. Such scholars have detailed how gender or race hierarchies directly and indirectly repress "deviant" social groups, whether through drawing rules of inclusion or restricting their access to particular social or economic goods. The term is used in a more positive sense in management theory with influential ideas such as Abraham Maslow's "hierarchy of needs" in human organizations. For more information, see Maslow (1943) and Honderich (2005). *See also* Feminism; Human Relations Theories of Organization; Postmodernism

Hierarchy of Needs   A concept originally conceived of by Maslow in 1943 in the context of his theory of human motivation. The theory assumes that human motivation is arranged in a hierarchy, such that needs that have the greatest urgency will dominate behavior. Needs, which range in order of importance, include essentials for life (physiological needs), economic and physical safety and well-being, belonging and intimacy, esteem and approval, and finally self actualization. Self-actualization is the instinctual need to fulfill one's creative, moral, and intellectual potential. Lower-order needs must be met before motivation can be dominated by the higher-order needs. As an individual moves upward in the hierarchy of needs, needs in the lower levels will no longer be prioritized. However, if and when a lower set of needs is no longer being met, the individual will reprioritize those needs while not losing motivation to maintain the higher-order needs. Research has supported the position that lower-order needs do take precedence over higher-order needs, but critics have suggested that Maslow's hierarchy is too simplistic and too rigid to explain the motivation of those who cannot meet the lower-order needs but still strive for the higher-order needs. For more information, see Maslow (1943) and Neher (1991). *See also* Humanistic Theory

High-Context Culture   First made popular by Edward T. Hall in his book *Beyond Culture* (1976), this concept refers to a culture where communication is more implicit than explicit. The culture underlying the communication or surface act makes things understood indirectly, inferring the meaning and intention of words within the situational context without explicit, unwieldy, and excessive verbal constructs. Hall uses the American legal system as a prime example of both high- and low-context culture. While the court system eschews contextual interpretations with its overly explicit attempt to determine "facts," with highly codified rules of evidence and testimony, lawyers see themselves as a group apart and tend to understand implicitly what other attorneys are saying without wordy explanations. He quotes Richard Nixon, as vice president, who used to say, "Yes, I can deal with him—he's a lawyer, too." In other words, lawyers as a group have had similar connections and ways of communicating over a long period of time. Through this dichotomy, they see themselves unrealistically on a higher level than others and act accordingly. Hall terms this character defect as "extension transference."

Members of a certain social class or of private clubs who elect members because of their contextual similarity, whether of birth or merit, implicitly understand certain rules of behavior. Explicit codification is not necessary for understanding communications or verbal messages. The family, religious congregations, street gangs, and the like are also examples of this type of environment. Understanding is internalized because the group accepts the members and, therefore, needs less verbal and formal communication. Long-term friendships and relationships place knowledge in situational contexts, with less need for verbal explanation. Knowledge is more implicit. One understands without excessive detail and specific details are determined unnecessary. Therefore, high-context societies are more difficult for outsiders to enter because their communication structures and contexts are shared by the "in-group"—those who internalize and accept a certain code and have a feeling of belonging. Hall calls this "internal contexting," which allows for automatic, quick exchange of information and communication between persons of the same group, as well as relational decision making. Each person or interlocutor implicitly understands the meaning of the exchange. In such cultures, patterns of communication are difficult to articulate. As Hall puts it, "The more that lies behind [a person's] actions (the higher the context), the less he can tell you." For more information, see Hall (1976). *See also* Contexting; Low-Context Culture

High School   A secondary education institution providing generalized instruction in the humanities, social sciences, natural sciences, technology, fine arts, and vocational training to prepare students (of ages 14 to 19) for work or postsecondary education. Traditionally, a high school houses Grades 9 through 12, although some house Grades 10 through 12. *See also* Accreditation

High-Stakes Test   Achievement tests used to make important decisions about individuals based on scores. Examples include certification examinations, college admission tests, and high school graduation examinations. Failing to pass or to obtain an adequate score on these instruments has detrimental consequences for test takers. **See also** Achievement Tests

High-Stakes Testing   A state-mandated accountability test that measures students' yearly academic progress in math and reading from Grades 3 through 8 and once in high school as part of the No Child Left Behind Act (2001). In many states, student promotion, teacher retention, and teachers' salary are tied to these test results. **See also** Accountability; Achievement Tests

Hijack   The illegal and forcible stopping and seizure of a vehicle in transit, such as an airplane or ship, to rob it or to divert it to an alternate destination. Individuals or groups use hijacking for personal gain or political objectives; hijacking is a type of terrorist activity. **See also** Terrorism (political science)

Hindsight Bias   The inclination to see events that have already occurred as more predictable than they were before they occurred. The phenomenon has been demonstrated experimentally, in that subjects tend to remember their predictions of future events as having been stronger than they actually were, but only in those cases where those predictions turn out correct. Hindsight bias might cause people who know the result of an event to vastly overestimate its *predictability* or *obviousness* compared with the estimates made by people who must guess without advance knowledge. Thus, this bias can affect the outcome of legal cases where a judge or jury must determine whether a defendant was legally negligent in failing to foresee a hazard. For more information, see Fischhoff and Beyth (1975).

Hippocampus   A horseshoe-shaped complex of neurons located in the medial temporal lobe, posterior and adjacent to the amygdala. Humans and other mammals have two hippocampi, which join together via the fornix at the hippocampal commissure. The hippocampus is part of the limbic system and is involved in the consolidation of new memories, emotional processing, spatial orientation, and spatial navigation. It is not exactly clear what the role of the hippocampus is once memories have been consolidated and stored in the long-term memory; hippocampal damage can result in anterograde amnesia (loss of ability to form new memories) while sparing older memories. However, degeneration of the hippocampus results in eventual eroding of long-term memory and disorientation, the hallmark features of Alzheimer's dementia. Damage to the hippocampus does not appear to affect procedural memory, such as the ability to learn a new skill. **See also** Neurons

Histogram   A two-dimensional graphic that displays the frequency or relative frequency (percentage) distribution of scores or score categories. Scores or score categories are plotted on the horizontal (X) axis in increasing order from left to right and frequency or percent plotted on the vertical (Y) axis. **See also** Descriptive Statistics (education)

Historic Period   A well-known era or important period in the history of a human culture, with a distinctive place in space and time. Historians give such periods of time names for organization and classification purposes. Centuries or decades are commonly used for historic periods.

Holism   The belief that groups, organizations, or other collectivities exist independently of their individual parts. The opposite of holism is reductionism, the belief that a collective entity is nothing but the sum of its parts or can only be understood by analyzing the individual parts. A holist would argue, for example, that since a university (or a society or a nation) existed before its current members were born and would likely exist after they all die, a university is a real entity and not merely a convenient label for the people in it. Another example is the medieval term *manus mortua*, which is related to the corporative nature of the Christian Church. This legal concept stated that land or property is given over to a corporation that "never dies" and is hence perpetual. **See also** Reductionism

Holistic Approach   A philosophy of health care based on a concept of the "whole" person, whose mental and physical aspects are treated with conventional and nonconventional therapies, such as chiropractic medicine, naturopathy, and acupuncture, without the use of surgery and prescription drugs.

Home Schooling   The educating of school-aged children outside the public or private school environment, typically by parents or guardians. Home schooling is a legal option in all the 50 U.S. states and is often chosen for religious reasons or because of dissatisfaction with institutionalized educational settings. **See also** Educational Law; Educational Policy

Homework   A plan for students to complete assignments at home or outside class. The teacher must take into account each student's current level of proficiency, and the assignments should be directly related to the in-class learning objectives for the purpose of improving students' skills and abilities.

Homicide   The killing of a human being. It may be intentional or unintentional and is not always criminal. A judicially authorized execution is an intentional homicide that is not criminal, as is the killing of an enemy soldier during war. Homicides can be broadly grouped into two categories: (1) nonnegligent homicides and (2) negligent homicides. Nonnegligent homicide involves the purposeful, knowing, or willful, killing of another human being. Negligent homicide occurs when a person kills another human being in his or her care through inaction. Generally a pattern of negligence is required for a criminal charge of negligent homicide. *See also* Felony Murder; Index Crimes/Offenses; Manslaughter; Murder

Homogeneous   An object or system consisting of the same elements throughout. Societies, communities, and populations may be described as ethnically, culturally, demographically, or politically homogeneous, reflecting absence of diversity. *Homogeneous* is the antonym of *heterogeneous,* which indicates a composition of elements of different kinds or natures. *See also* Heterogeneous

Homogeneous Appeal   Although our society has begun to give broader acceptance to the idea that the media best serve the public interest by portraying a diversity of images, experiences, and viewpoints, the media remain responsive to the economic advantages of communication products with a uniform appeal. Communications may be said to have a homogeneous appeal when they are attractive to a broad mainstream audience and they contain features that give pleasure and comfort to almost everyone. This broad acceptance may arise from the item's familiarity or predictability, but it may also result from its ability to resonate with fundamental impulses that are present in most audience members, for instance, sexual attraction, a desire to nurture, or a need to identify with a stereotypical hero.

Market forces tend to promote media products with homogeneous appeal because media companies hope to reach and please large audiences, hence the formulaic premises of many Broadway shows and Hollywood movies. The predictable formats of local news broadcasts, the familiar plot trajectories of sitcoms, and the standardized attire and features of TV personalities may all be traced to the desire for homogeneous appeal.

Critics complain that the quest for homogeneous appeal leads to a fundamental conservatism in media presentations, tending to drive the diverse and idiosyncratic out of the marketplace while confirming audiences in their preconceived preferences and assumptions about the world. In debates involving the concept of homogeneous appeal, the public interest in innovation and diversity often comes into conflict with the media's interest in producing reliably profitable publications and programs. For more information, see Croteau and Hoynes (2005). *See also* Audience; Media

Hoover, J. Edgar   The director of the U.S. Federal Bureau of Investigation (FBI) from 1924 until his death in 1972. As director, Hoover was highly regarded as the man responsible for the growth and reform of the organization, due in no small part to his publicizing of the FBI's success in the capture of several well-known fugitives. After World War II, Hoover received authorization to investigate Communist activities, particularly foreign espionage in the United States. Hoover was also criticized for his surveillance and information-gathering methods, often considered an abuse of his authority, which involved illegal wiretaps and burglaries and which were alleged to inform threats to politicians. In particular, Hoover was criticized for his focus on surveillance of those he considered political radicals, including left-wing dissenters, such as Martin Luther King Jr., in the 1960s. Since Hoover's tenure as FBI director, subsequent directors have been limited to 10-year terms. *See also* Federal Bureau of Investigation (FBI)

Horizon   The meeting or dividing point between the earth and the sky. The true horizon line is not always visible, as it may be shielded by forestry, mountain ranges, buildings, and other types of obstructions. However, even if blocked from full view, a visible horizon line exists at any position. The term is often used metaphorically. For example, the philosopher Hans-Georg Gadamer used the term as a common, general framework for the situation of any particular interpretation. *See also* Hermeneutics (education)

Horizontal Communication   The sharing of knowledge or information between people within the same level of an organization or between departments or divisions within an organization. The term often is used interchangeably with lateral communication.

Horizontal or lateral communication is considered to be more effective than the more traditional downward communication, which is hierarchal in nature and relies on a top-to-bottom chain of command from high-level management to lower-level personnel. Having become the norm in business and other organizations such as not-for-profit and governmental agencies, horizontal communication has been shown to significantly increase cooperation and bring about efficient project completion as people work on related tasks.

The results of a 2007 online survey on the effectiveness of horizontal communication between television newscast directors and producers, however, disputed the value of horizontal communication, showing that the directors and producers who responded tend to be dissatisfied with, and even intolerant of, each other's expertise and work ethics.

Horizontal communication can be conducted in a face-to-face manner or by various electronic methods, such as Internet or intranet e-mailing, conference calls, and webinars. A 2006 study done at a medical center in Florida, for instance, showed that a system of posting patient nursing assignments online and making them accessible to all staff considerably enhanced horizontal communication. The staff considered the online posting system to be superior to the portable telephone system that preceded it.

Horizontal communication also refers to the software that commands the hardware in electronic devices such as satellites, televisions, radios, video cassette recorders, digital videodisc players, or VCR/DVD combinations. For more information, see Adams (2007). *See also* Collaboration; Downward Communication; Lateral Communication

Hormones Biochemical messengers that affect body states or growth by carrying signals from one group of cells to another, usually via the bloodstream. Hormone secretion is governed by the hypothalamus, generally via feedback loops with the pituitary gland. When hormone molecules bind to the receptors on their "target" cells, they initiate a sequence of intracellular signals that may alter the behavior of the target cells or stimulate (or repress) gene expression in the nuclei. For example, in times of emergency and stress, the pituitary gland secretes adrenocorticotrophic hormone (ACTH), which stimulates the adrenal glands to produce epinephrine, a hormone that serves to increase the heart rate and prepare the body for response. Because most hormones travel through the bloodstream to reach their destinations, their effects begin slowly and take time to wear off.

Hostage A person given or held by a captor as security to ensure the fulfillment of certain specified terms or conditions by another. The hostage taker may threaten harm to the hostage to further guarantee fulfillment of the obligation. The Geneva Convention forbids hostage taking. *See also* Abduction; Terrorism (sociology)

Hot Pursuit An exception to the rule that law enforcement needs a warrant before entering a private home or chasing a suspect into another jurisdiction. The exception applies when suspects are fleeing and evidence may be hidden or destroyed if officers stop for a warrant. *See also* Arrest; Warrant

House Arrest A sanction designed to incapacitate criminal offenders while permitting them to remain in communities. People under house arrest cannot leave their homes except as specified by the court or unless given explicit permission to do so. House arrest might be imposed pretrial or postconviction and is sometimes used in conjunction with electronic monitoring. *See also* Community-Based Corrections; Electronic Monitoring

House of Representatives One of the two legislative chambers created through Article I of the U.S. Constitution. The House of Representatives, which comprises Congress, was created to set checks on the Senate. The House is granted the power to initiate bills to impose taxes, impeach officials, elect the President in electoral college deadlocks, and authorize the expenditure of federal funds.

In 1911, Congress fixed the size of the House of Representatives at 435 seats. House members are elected every two years from the 50 states. Under Article I, Section 2 of the Constitution, seats in the House of Representatives are determined in each state based on the size of the population in the state, which is determined by the census every 10 years. The number of members is not to exceed 1 for every 30,000 of population. Each state has at least one representative. California has the most representatives at 53.

Representatives must be at least 25 years of age, a resident of the United States for 7 years, and a resident of the state from which he or she is elected.

The House of Representatives has eight leadership positions; the most prestigious is the Speaker of the House. The Speaker is the leader of the House and presides over debates and also appoints committee members. *See also* Congress; Electoral College; Senate

Hue and Cry A public clamor, protest, or alarm raised by bystanders to summon help in the pursuit of a criminal who was witnessed committing a felony act. Common law provided that those who failed to raise or respond might be criminally liable themselves.

Human Capital The knowledge and skills that make a worker more productive. Empirical evidence suggests that investment in human capital is a necessary precondition for the improvement of an efficient labor force. Human capital can be improved through formal education and on-the-job training. This requires investment in teachers, libraries, and quality instructional time.

Although early development models did not incorporate human capital, recent models show that human capital is as important as physical capital. Human capital explains to a greater degree the component of the Solow growth model (i.e., with improved technology, new capital is more effective than old capital—after Robert Solow, who received the Nobel Prize in Economics in 1987 for his work) that was once categorized as a residual, and it has been used contemporaneously to explain the international differences in standards of living.

To make human capital much more functional in terms of economic growth, some economists suggest that policymakers should direct resources to capital that generate the highest marginal products by relying on the market to efficiently allocate resources for capital improvement. Others encourage policymakers to be proactive in order to foster technological innovation that can lead to learning by doing and technological externality or knowledge spillover—a situation in which society benefits from a pool of knowledge that is the product of innovation. Yet some economists are skeptical about industrial policies because of the improbable measure of externality and the political biases that might inform the rewards of tax breaks or subsidies.

The promotion and sustenance of human capital is highly contingent on perception of rewards for innovation and quality education. Inadequate compensation and disincentives stifle the prospects of increasing human capital and, therefore, productivity and growth.

Countries that have benefited tremendously from the investment in human capital include the East Asian Tigers of Taiwan, Hong Kong, Singapore, and Korea. These countries modified their trading strategy in the

1980s to emphasize a skilled workforce in technological innovation, export-oriented growth, and competition in the global economy. For more information, see Mankiw (2007), Solow (1956), and World Bank (1993). ***See also*** Ecomonic Growth; Productivity

Human Communication   Transmission of information from one person to another person. A common system of signs, symbols, and/or behavior is used to deliver the message between individuals.

Face-to-face communication remains elusive and fascinating because so many things occur all at once. Each person participates in the definition and direction of the shared situation, and yet the totality of what is shared goes well beyond the grasp of any given person involved.

During periods of mundane human communication, virtually all that happens counts one way or the other, but this does not mean that everything counts equally.

Human communication is what two or more individuals feel, think, say, and do (together and alone) without any one member being in a privileged position to figure out what makes it possible and necessary for collective things to work out just the way they do. According to the communications arts professor C. David Mortensen, at the center of human action is an unfolding, incomplete, and unfinished communal struggle over the selective and strategic aspects of discourse and dialogue. Participation in the process may or may not reveal the source of what Mortensen describes as two major ecological secrets. This involves understanding what makes individual discourse possible in the first place (potentialities) and what mutual dialogue makes possible subsequently (unforeseen consequences). It turns out that very little may be revealed in the process.

Mortensen goes on to explain that what counts as the communicative value of face-to-face interaction turns out to be at least as complex as the magnitude of changes set into motion. The participants may know fully well, in point of fact, that they *do* make a real and decisive difference in the personal conduct of one another without any one source ever being able to pinpoint exactly what the consequences may be. Any direct personal encounter is apt to produce a rich mix of implicit urges, desires, intentions, expressions, coordinated lines of action, structures, functions, effects, and consequences. Distinctive features add up in a holistic and synthetic manner, which does not reduce itself to simple verdicts over whether the message sent equals the message received. In effect, B's response is amplified in response to A's response.

Finally, Mortensen concludes that what matters most in effective human communication is how vital and fully animated systems of human communication simultaneously and sequentially conceal what transpires. The main task is to locate a range of sensibilities in which an acute sense of miscommunication or problematic conversation occurs within some larger sphere, scope, or domain of what is presumed to qualify as communicative. For more information, see Mortensen (1994). ***See also*** Face-to-Face Communication; Group Dynamics; Interpersonal Communication

Human Development   The scientific study of emotional, physical, mental, and behavioral changes over a human's life span. The field of human development comprises various approaches and theories that attempt to explain universal truths of human development, as well as factors that can adversely affect normal human development from conception to death. The major human development theorists include Freud, Erikson, Pavlov, Skinner, Bandura, Piaget, and Vygotsky. Considered as an interaction of both physical and cognitive growth as well as personality and social development, human development is addressed from the biological, cognitive, personality, and social perspectives.

The biological, or physical, perspective recognizes the influence of genes and physical conditions that affect development. This approach addresses the brain, nervous system, and other biological functions that affect behavior.

The cognitive perspective recognizes the importance of mental processes, such as memory, learning, and problem solving, as well as changes in intellect. Cognitive development considers both the growth and decline of verbal, spatial, and reasoning abilities as well as the structure of thought over the life span.

Personality development involves enduring individual characteristics that evolve over a human's life span and differentiate people from one another. The study of personality generally includes the acknowledgment of the Big Five personality traits—neuroticism, extroversion, openness, agreeableness, and conscientiousness. Although these traits are considered stable over the life span, they can be influenced by life circumstances and other factors.

Social development refers to the influence of social relationships on human growth and change. The social domain includes the recognition that individuals change as a result of their interactions with others. Increasingly, developmentalists recognize that people live and behave in distinct contexts—that is, unique physical and social environments. Some developmentalists view context as an important agent for individual change and human development and as unique to each person depending on one's culturally specific context. Cultural contexts can include meanings and values associated with one's home, family, school, and community settings as well as one's own background and historical time period.

Patterns of growth and broad human changes are typically associated with stages or developmental periods that are age related. This view of development is embraced by developmentalists who believe in *continuity*. Continuity is the persistence of characteristics over a lifetime. Change is seen as gradual and the culmination of a process. Conversely, those who see human development as *discontinuous* are more likely to believe that human experiences cause characteristic changes over a lifetime even though human change is biologically based with distinct characteristics. The discontinuous view sees human development as less likely to occur in continuous stages. *See also* Cognitive Development; Context; Developmental Psychology; Personality; Social Psychology

Human Factors The dynamics affecting human performance, often in service of the reduction of human error and better systems design. Researchers in this field study the physical, cognitive, psychological, and social contributors to effective task performance, efficient systems use, and user satisfaction.

The terms *human factors* and *ergonomics* are often used synonymously. Ergonomic studies began in the workplace as researchers and designers conducted detailed studies of physiology and biomechanics to improve task performance through the improved design of related equipment. *Human factors,* a term first used in the U.S. aviation industry, distinguished itself initially through the inclusion of the cognitive, psychological, and social factors affecting task performance and user adoption of technology. Currently, both terms are being used to describe the research and development of optimal human performance through optimal systems design. For more information, see Wickens, Lee, Liu, and Gordon-Becker (2004).

Human Genome The whole set of hereditary information encoded in DNA, including the genes and the noncoding sequences of DNA. The human genome has 46 chromosomes (22 distinct autosomal pairs and the sex chromosomes), which hold approximately 3 billion DNA base pairs and contain an estimated 20,000 to 25,000 genes. The human genome has fewer genes than expected—less than two times that of many lower-order species, such as the fruit fly. However, some human genes are capable of coding for more than one protein, through a process known as alternative splicing. For more information, see The Human Genome Project Web site. *See also* Deoxyribonucleic Acid (DNA) (psychology, sociology)

Human Geography   *See* Cultural Geography

Humanism A philosophy that centers on the importance of human potential and creativity for self-actualization. It promotes the development of the whole person through a focus on affective domains instead of just cognitive ones. Humanism advocates experiential learning that is self-directed and self-evaluated and eschews external rewards.

Humanistic Counseling An approach to counseling/psychotherapy that is supportive and insight oriented rather than directive or interpretive. It has roots in European romantic and phenomenological philosophy. Emphasis is placed on an egalitarian therapeutic relationship, as well as the client's subjectivity, strengths, and capacity for free will. Therapy leverages the client's innate self-actualizing drive. *See also* Client-Centered Therapy; Self-Actualization (psychology)

Humanistic Theory The humanistic approach in psychology, often associated with Carl Rogers and Abraham Maslow, emphasizes subjective experience, conscious free-will, and human aspiration. In direct opposition to the more deterministic psychoanalytic and behaviorist theories that preceded it, humanistic theory presented an optimistic view of human nature, in which humans are active, creative, and concerned with growth. Humanistic theory holds that humans think consciously and rationally, can exert control over their biological urges, and can change their attitudes and behavior. Problems are believed to result from incompatibility between one's actions and one's beliefs about oneself. While the humanistic theory is often criticized as the least testable theory of personality, most psychologists agree that subjective experience guides personality development more strongly than objective reality. Humanistic psychology's emphasis on healthy personality development has influenced numerous popular self-help therapies. *See also* Hierarchy of Needs; Person-Centered Therapy (PCT)

Human Relations Theories of Organization The interpersonal interactions between human beings in a work situation that affect the productivity and profit of an organization, as well as the economic, psychological, and social satisfaction of the people within the organization. Technical ability is, typically, only one factor in achieving career success, whereas interpersonal skills represent a vital category of transferable skills. An interdisciplinary field that studies human behavior in organizational settings, drawing on the fields of communications, management, psychology, and sociology, human relations incorporates a variety of interactions between people, including their cooperative efforts, group relationships, and conflicts. This field of study is the essence, as all workers engage in some form of human relations activities. Good communication is cited as the foundation and most important component of effective human relations.

It is believed that the human relations movement, which first emerged in the mid 1800s, focused primarily on improving productivity, efficiency, and motivation. Originating in the 1920s with the Hawthorne Studies (at a factory plant outside Chicago), the movement refers to the study of and the researchers of organizational development, who study the behavior of people in groups. The Hawthorne studies explored the effects of social relations, employee satisfaction, and motivation on factory productivity. The Hawthorne Effect refers to the changing, short-term improvement in workers when they knew that they were under observation.

Douglas McGregor's theories of human motivation have been prominent in human resource management, organizational behavior, and organizational development since the 1960s. McGregor began with Abraham Maslow's hierarchy of needs (a theory in psychology that consists of a pyramid of five categories of needs, the most primitive at the bottom—physiological and safety, proceeding through love and belonging, esteem, and self-actualization).

McGregor's Theory X and Theory Y, although often regarded as unrealistic extremes, especially by rigid bureaucrats, remain the guiding principles and normative standards of positive approaches to human relations management and for improving. In Theory X, management assumes that employees are inherently lazy and dislike work. Consequently, workers need to be closely supervised and managed through a system of controls. In this theory, without an attractive incentive and reward program, employees will avoid responsibility and exhibit limited ambition. Theory Y asserts that employees may be self-motivated, have self-control, and are likely to accept greater responsibility and empowerment. Under this theory, it is believed that employees generally enjoy their work and have the desire to be proactive, creative, and forward thinking in their place of work. They will excel with fewer restrictions, and the rules required in Theory X will only stifle motivation and the satisfaction that comes with doing a good job. Theory Y cultures tend to be more entrepreneurial and successful, while Theory X cultures tend to be bureaucratic, stiff, and less productive. Government bureaucracy tends to regress to the lowest forms of Theory X, with its sometimes endless codes and regulations (one federal agency has 32 layers of approval control!). Rensis Likert also built a measurement tool for successful organizations that promotes this human relations theory. These theories, although not followed literally today, have been incorporated in most of the successful managerial leadership styles. For more information, see Likert (1967), Maslow (1943), and McGregor (1960). **See also** Hawthorne Effect (psychology); Organization (public administration); Organizational Culture (public administration); Organization Development (OD) (public administration)

Human Resource Management (HRM)   In education and business, the process of managing the organization's human resources (intellectual capital and skill) to achieve the organization's strategic objectives. An organization's human resources provide a distinctive competence when employees' knowledge, skills, abilities, and other characteristics (KSAOs) are superior to the KSAOs of competitors' employees. HRM activities can be grouped into nine categories: (1) organizational design, (2) recruiting and staffing, (3) training and development, (4) performance management and appraisal, (5) compensation and benefits, (6) safety and health, (7) organizational development, (8) employee relations and labor relations, and (9) management of employees across national boundaries. Activities in each of the nine areas must be aligned and focused on building human capital to support the organization's strategy.

Human resource (HR) departments are staff functions that provide HR services to support line managers, including recruiting, selection, training, compensation, benefits, and employee relations. HR specialists reduce organizational disruptions by listening to employee concerns and advocating on behalf of employees with managers. In addition, HR specialists serve as in-house consultants by providing advice and counsel to executives and managers on HR issues and assist with the creation of organizational policies, procedures, and rules. Fulfilling the consultant role requires HR specialists to have an in-depth understanding of employment and labor law and to keep abreast of legislation and regulatory changes and court decisions.

HR specialists help organizations adapt to changing competitive environments. Recent issues affecting competitive strategies and HR activities are globalization, the rapid rate of technological change, increasing customer expectations, controlling labor costs, labor shortages, use of contingency employees, offshoring, balancing work and family life, and the aging population.

In recent years, organizations' top HR executives (chief HR officers) are likely to report directly to the chief executive officer and are likely to participate in the formulation and implementation of the organization's strategic plans. Participation in formulation helps line managers understand the HR requirements of strategic options, and participation in implementation helps ensure that HR activities and processes are aligned with the strategy to develop human capital. When shifts in strategic direction require major organizational changes, HR specialists often take the role of change agents to lead and facilitate change efforts.

The Society for Human Resource Management (SHRM) is a global, professional organization representing over 250,000 HR professionals. SHRM provides information, educational resources, credentialing services, a code of conduct, and a job-placement network for its members. SHRM also supports research to expand the HR body of knowledge and provides up-to-date information regarding HR issues, pending legislation, and regulatory changes. **See also** Human Capital; Organization (education)

Human Rights   The inalienable moral entitlements individuals have in society. This means that regardless of people's race, nationality, political membership, religion, gender, or sexual orientation, all people possess, by virtue of their humanity, human rights.

The language of rights can be traced back to the revolutionary texts of the 18th century. Both the American Declaration of Independence of 1776 and the 1789 French Declaration on the Rights of Man and the Citizen made claims to a catalog of rights that emphasized the rights of citizens to participate in the formation of law.

In the 20th century, catalyzed by the horrors of World War II, world leaders came together to form the United Nations (UN) and to draft the Universal Declaration of Human Rights. On December 5, 1948, the UN's General

Assembly passed a Declaration of Human Rights, safeguarding fundamental freedoms, recognizing that the protection of human rights is universal (for everyone) and should be under international scrutiny and a matter of international concern. This declaration establishes a broad range of civil and political rights, including freedom of assembly, freedom of thought and expression, and the right to adequate housing and education. The Declaration also proclaims that social and economic rights are "indispensable," including the right to education, the right to work, and the right to participate in the cultural life of the broader community.

Translated into more than 200 languages, the Universal Declaration has had a huge influence; all around the globe, people and individuals appeal to the Declaration's provisions to win respect for their rights. At the same time, national and international courts have begun to invoke the Declaration in their judgments. Unfortunately, because of the unwieldy bureaucratic nature of the UN and the diverse political views of its members, the organization has had little success in enforcing the Declaration.

The international movement for human rights is differentiated by generation. The first generation concerns civil and political rights (such as freedom from arbitrary arrest), while the second generation of social and economic rights requires an active provision, for example, by imposing an obligation on government (such as affordable housing). A third generation concerns rights such as peace, development, and humanitarian assistance. While many of the provisions apply to individuals, some belong to collectivities, such as the right to national self-determination. Critics reject the idea of universality and argue that notions of human rights are driven by dominant Western ideas of individual rights. For example, only recently have the rights of indigenous peoples, as subjects of collectives, been recognized after long years of organized advocacy for their rights at the UN. For more information, see Buergenthal, Shelton, and Stewart (2002) and Clapham (2001). *See also* Civil Rights; Right

Human Variation The natural variation in gene expression between humans or groups of humans. It may be distributed geographically, due to natural selection (e.g., ethnic groups), or individually. The study of human variation promotes the understanding of population migrations and relations and the origins of disease.

Hung Jury A trial jury that is hopelessly deadlocked with irreconcilable differences of opinion and unable to come to the (usually) required unanimous verdict. The judge in a hung jury case declares a mistrial, leading to a new trial with a new jury. *See also* Jury; Trial

Hunter-Gatherers The earliest form of human society, in which people subsisted primarily by hunting, fishing, or foraging for edible plants and animals in the wild. Hunter-gatherer societies do not raise or herd animals or practice agriculture, though they have recently been argued to have been socially complex. A small number of such societies sill persist in remote areas of the world, on land generally not considered arable. Archeologists believe that humans subsisted exclusively by hunting and gathering until the end of the Mesolithic period, when agricultural practices are believed to have emerged. *See also* Society

Hydrography The scientific measurement and description of the waterways on the earth's surface, including oceans, rivers, lakes, and other bodies of water. Hydrographers use the skill of charting to convey and interpret hydrographic information. Hydrographers chart the conditions of the earth's waterways, including the depth of the water, the motion of the tides and currents, the features of the coastline, and the condition of the sea floor. Hydrography was traditionally used for navigating ships and boats through waterways; however, its utility has expanded to assist with the governance of water spaces, the protection of ports and harbors, coastal engineering, and offshore development.

Hyperinflation The excessively rapid inflation that causes money to lose its value to such an extent that dollarization and barter become much more desirable. One of the disastrous effects of hyperinflation is that inflation paranoia forces consumers to anticipate much more rapid inflation, which leads to economic disruptions.

Creditors are usually much more reluctant to lend money, and businesses hoard products to take advantage of much higher prices in the future. Hyperinflation discourages saving, and those with money invest in precious assets to hedge against galloping prices.

Hyperinflation is usually the result of excessive money supply created by unrestrained seigniorage. Governments tend to print money as a source of income when they cannot raise taxes or borrow money, especially during periods of war and flagrant mismanagement of national economies because of populism, corruption, and fraud.

Apart from the wartime experience in Germany, hyperinflation has been noticeable in some countries of Africa and Latin America, such as Zimbabwe (estimated at 66,000% in 2007), Argentina, Chile, and Bolivia. Argentina experienced hyperinflation in the early 1980s for nonpopulist reasons, but in Bolivia, the lack of access to the credit market because of excessive multilateral debts and commitment to populism resulted in hyperinflation in the vicinity of 300% annually in the 1980s. Hyperinflation in Bolivia was particularly instrumental in the rush to de facto dollarization. Countries with hyperinflation are almost always invariably susceptible to "original sin"—the inability to borrow in their local currency in financial markets. *See also* Inflation

Hypermedia A variation of the term *hypertext*, which refers to written text that is linked nonsequentially to other texts as well as to sound, images, moving images, and databases. Both terms are attributed to Ted Nelson, who in the 1960s was developing ideas for linking text on interactive computer screens to other forms of information. Hypermedia and hypertexts are considered open systems of information, which provide easy access to related information and open up the reading of a text to various interpretations because no reader will interact with all the hypertext options in the same way. Most hypermedia works via links to material that can be ignored, brought to the original text screen simultaneously, or substitute for the initial text screen. In all cases, a simple sequential, linear reading of the text is not expected. The challenge of hypermedia in research or academics is that it subverts the expectations of a traditional text and can leave the user uncertain as to the completeness, logic, or validity of a work that is against the linear tradition of argument. While hypermedia and hypertext are now common ways of interacting with information via Internet search engines, encyclopedias, such as Wikipedia, and most Web sites, when Nelson first proposed them, the technology was not available, and it took decades for computers to be powerful enough to process the information. Now projects such as Google Book Search, Project Gutenberg, and other e-books, as well as technologies such as Amazon's Kindle and Sony's Reader Digital Book provide the digital versions of texts. For more information, see Landow (1992), Rosenzweig (1999), and Ted Nelson's Web site. *See also* Electronic Media; Intertextuality

Hypnosis   A trancelike state induced by a hypnotist, which can be used for medical purposes to relieve anxiety or alter behavior. Not all people are susceptible to hypnosis; new research suggests that susceptibility to hypnosis is related to fear and sensory gating ability (the ability to block sensory stimuli from awareness). The neurosurgeon James Braid (1795–1860), called the "Father of Modern Hypnotism," ascribed the trancelike state to a physiological process resulting from prolonged attention to an object of fixation. Braid used hypnotism to treat various disorders and had little success, although other physicians at the time claimed better results. The neurologist Jean-Martin Charcot (1825–1893) endorsed hypnotism for the treatment of hysteria, and the reports of his success led to systematic experimental examinations of hypnosis across Europe. Charcot's pupil Pierre Janet (1859–1947) conceived of hypnosis as dissociation and was one of the first to draw a connection between events in the subject's past life and their present-day trauma, laying the groundwork for psychoanalysis. Effects of hypnosis include temporary improvements in sensory acuity and memory as well as posthypnotic suggestion. Modern applications of hypnosis, most typically, include postsurgery pain reduction, smoking cessation, and weight loss. *See also* Dissociation; Obsessive-Compulsive Disorder; Psychology

Hypochondriasis   A somatoform disorder characterized by chronic preoccupation and concern with one's physical health, often resulting in imagined illness or disease. The preoccupation is based on the misinterpretation of one or more bodily signs or symptoms and is more cognitively based than a conversion disorder. The preoccupation does not reach delusional intensity but generally persists despite medical evaluation and reassurance. Hypochondriasis is often viewed as an "obsessive-compulsive spectrum disorder" because individuals are preoccupied or "obsessed" with an imagined illness, which creates high levels of anxiety, leading to a compulsive need for medical reassurance. Techniques used for treating obsessive-compulsive disorders are also effective for treating hypochondriasis. The prevalence of hypochondriasis is estimated to range between 4% and 9% in those seeking outpatient medical treatment, and it typically begins in adulthood, affecting males and females at approximately equal rates. Hypochondriasis is not an attention-seeking behavior; persons with the disorder truly believe that they are sick and feel misunderstood. For more information, see American Psychiatric Association, *Diagnostic and Statistical Manual of Mental Disorders* (fourth edition, text revision, 2000). *See also* Obsessive-Compulsive Disorder

Hypodermic Needle Model   Also referred to as the direct effects model or magic bullet theory, this model uses a medical term to describe a mass communication theory describing mass media effects on an audience. The theory holds that the mass media wield a direct, immediate, and highly influential effect by injecting or shooting information into an audience, as a hypodermic needle does into a patient. The metaphor also reinforces the idea that many people will receive the same message at the same time. The term was frequently used during World War I in support of the idea that people were thought to be brainwashed, in effect, by mass media messages. It is related to the mass society theory held by a number of early sociologists who argued that in an increasingly large but isolated population, the conditions were favorable for people to be manipulated by certain messages. The hypodermic theory is today generally perceived as outdated and oversimplified, as it was coined before substantial research was done on mass media effects. It has since been criticized for promoting a pessimistic view of society and portraying audiences as impressionable, passive, defenseless, and having uniform reactions. The idea that each member of an audience receives and processes information in the same way has been discredited. In the 1950s and 1960s, the sociologists Elihu Katz and Paul Lazarsfeld put forth a limited-effects theory of personal influence, wherein people have control over media effects instead of the reverse. The original model did not take into account the intervening factors. Depending on one's personal orientation—intelligence level, previous experience, personality—the media will affect each person differently. For more information, see Bineham (1988). *See also* Bullet Theory; Mass Media Appeals; Mass Persuasion; Mass Society

Hypothalamus   A small area of the brain that forms the floor and part of the lateral wall of the third ventricle.

The hypothalamus is known as the "brain within the brain" because of its importance, via complex feedback loops with the pituitary gland, in the activation, control, and integration of the peripheral autonomic nervous system, the endocrine system, and somatic regulation. A properly functioning hypothalamus is required for physiological functions such as maintenance of body temperature, circulation, food intake and digestion, reproductive activity, and the development of secondary sexual characteristics. For more information, see Neff and Goldberg (1960). **See also** Brain

Hypothesis *(education)*   A researcher's prediction regarding the outcome of an experiment or other study, focusing on the relationship between two or more variables. The researcher collects data to test the adequacy of the hypothesis. **See also** Hypothesis Testing; Quantitative Research; Rival Hypotheses

Hypothesis *(psychology)*   A possible explanation for an observed behavior or event, which may or may not be correct. It is generally posed as a specific statement about the relationship between two or more variables, expressed as a prediction of cause and effect that can be tested scientifically. Hypotheses are based on data from previous research studies or the personal experiences and observations of the researcher. The variables in the hypothesis must be specified in a way that indicates how they will be measured. **See also** Hypothesis Testing; Variable (sociology)

Hypothesis *(sociology)*   A testable statement set forth to explain the observation of the relationship between or among variables. A researcher designs an experiment to test the hypothesis, and the research results are used to evaluate the hypothesis for confirmation or disproof. The "null hypothesis" states that any observed relationship between or among variables is due only to chance. Researchers test the null hypothesis by engagisng in "hypothesis testing," by which they make a prediction and accept or reject the null hypothesis according to the statistical significance of the research results. **See also** Hypothesis Testing; Null Hypothesis (sociology); Variable (sociology)

Hypothesis Testing   The method followed for inferring the difference between a population parameter and an external standard for the parameter, using a statistic from a random sample, or when we want to infer population parameter differences based on the comparison of sample statistic differences from random samples. There are two complementary hypotheses: (1) the null hypothesis, which represents no difference, and (2) the research hypothesis, which represents a difference. Hypothesis testing is the method used to decide which of the two hypotheses believed to be true. Statistical tests assess the viability of the null hypothesis. If the null is rejected, that is indirect support for the viability of the research hypothesis. Rejection of the null is based on the value of the probability that the observed or higher difference could have happened by chance, referred to as the p value. The p value is compared with the level of significance set by the researcher, referred to as the alpha (α) level. The α level is also known as the level of significance and the risk of a Type I error. If the p value is less than α, we reject the null hypothesis and have indirect support for the viability of the research hypothesis, and we symbolize this result as $p < \alpha$. The steps in hypothesis testing are as follows: (1) State the null and research hypotheses. (2) Determine the test statistic and the accompanying probability model. (3) Set the level of significance, α (often at .05 or .01). (4) Collect and analyze the data, determining the test statistic and the accompanying observed p value. (5) Compare the p value with α. (6) If $p < \alpha$, reject the null hypothesis as support for the viability of the research hypothesis; if the p value is greater than or equal to α (symbolized as $p \geq \alpha$), do not reject the null. There are four possible reality and decision outcomes. Two of these are errors. If we reject the null when it is true, we commit a Type I error, with a probability symbolized as α. If we fail to reject the null hypothesis when it is false, we commit a Type II error, with a probability symbolized as β. Two of these decisions are correct. If the null is true and we do not reject it, this is a correct decision with a probability of $1-\alpha$. If the null is false and we reject it, this is a correct decision, symbolized as $1-\beta$, which is also known as the statistical power. **See also** Hypothesis (education); Null Hypothesis (education, psychology)

I

Ice Age A long period of time during which the earth's temperature is drastically decreased, leading to the formation of wide-spreading glaciers and ice sheets. Scientific research shows that ice ages are the product of several natural forces, including continental shifting, plate movement, and changes in the earth's orbit, all of which contribute to dramatic changes in the earth's climate.

There have been several ice ages in history; however, the Pleistocene, commonly referred to as the Great Ice Age, is usually used to describe a period of time beginning approximately 1.6 million years ago and lasting until about 15,000 years ago, during which time the climate was so cold that ice sheets covered a large portion of the Northern Hemisphere.

Evidence of the Great Ice Age exists today and can be found in Greenland and Antarctica, where glaciers can be found in mountain ranges. In addition, glacial erosion and deposition demonstrates that the earth has a long history of ice ages, beginning before the Great Ice Age occurred. The evidence shows that ice sheets moved across considerable distances, changing the earth's landscape as they progressed. Glacial activity has also contributed to land formations, including valleys and mountains, and altered sea levels significantly. In addition, although many animals suffered extinction due to harsh climates, scientific research shows that human beings evolved during the time of the Great Ice Age.

There is current speculation that increased melting glaciers caused by global warming will trigger the next ice age; however, this is a topic of debate and uncertainty at this time.

Iconic Memory Also referred to as visual sensory memory, it is part of the sensory memory system. Iconic memory is a temporary visual buffer that holds information for a brief time (in contrast to information stored in long-term memory). Iconic memory was discovered by Sperling (1960), using a partial instead of a whole report technique. Sperling (1960) discovered that after approximately a one-second delay, the accuracy of the partial report technique neared that of the whole report technique and concluded that information in iconic memory is available for less than one second. For more information, see Sperling (1960). **See also** Memory (psychology); Short-Term Memory (STM)

Iconoclasm The word is derived from the Greek word for "image breaking" and is mostly associated with the debate within the Byzantine Empire during the 8th and 9th centuries, but it also refers to any overt violation or desecration of political or religious images.

To distinguish the Hebrew faith from pagan idol worship, the Second Commandment forbade making any physical likeness of God, but supporters of image veneration in the Christian church argued that the incarnation had superseded the Old Testament prohibition. By the end of the 6th century, image veneration of Christ and the saints was well established, but reaction against it was strong, particularly in the East, the reasons being both theological and political—namely, the power struggles between Church and State. There were two main periods of persecution of image venerators, AD 730 to 787 and AD 814 to 843, the date of the restoration of icon veneration. The monastic clergy largely supported image veneration and the emperors, iconoclasm, division of opinion between the two inevitably had some grounding in the struggle between Church and State.

There have been many periods in which religious and political symbols were systematically destroyed in acts of vandalism and censorship: (a) medieval reformist groups, such as the Wycliffites, strongly opposed image veneration; (b) Protestant reformists systematically defaced statues of saints throughout Europe; (c) French revolutionaries decapitated sculptures of monarchs; (d) flag desecration remains illegal in many states in the United States; and (e) in 2005, the Taliban demolished the 6th-century Buddhas of Bamyan. Much modern art can be thought of as essentially iconoclastic in that it takes "sacred" images and subjects them to defacement, distortion, and ridicule, in an effort to construct new images out of dead ones—for example, the surrealist painter Max Ernst's *The Virgin Spanking the Christ Child* (1926). Iconoclasm today raises questions about censorship, the place of art, and the relationship between the material object and its symbolic meaning. **See also** Censorship (communication, media studies); Vandalism

Iconography The study of figures, pictures, or images. This area of study looks beyond superficial images and is concerned with the symbolic and deeper meanings expressed through any form of visual display. Iconography aims to interpret the undertones in a given image.

Id One of the three core parts of Sigmund Freud's theory of the psyche in conjunction with the ego and superego. Originally derived from the German word *Es*, the id resides in the unconscious and is the driving force behind instinctual urges, such as food, sex, or aggressive impulses. The base of the libido, the id, is governed by the pleasure principle, which seeks to maximize pleasure by immediate gratification of its urges. For more information, see Freud (2000a). ***See also*** Ego (psychology); Psychoanalysis (psychology); Superego

Idealism   The philosophical view according to which mind or consciousness alone are ultimately real. Idealists deny that space, time, physical objects, or abstracta, such as numbers, have any existence apart from the mind or consciousness that perceives them. A related view is phenomenalism, which posits that all physical objects are constructions out of the data of sensation. ***See also*** Positivism (education, sociology)

Ideographic Versus Nomothetic   The two terms, developed by the German philosopher Wilhelm Windelband describe ways of interpreting and relating to empirical knowledge. Ideographic research takes a subjective stance and seeks to understand phenomena through a descriptive, case-specific lens and a focus on depth. Generalizations within ideographic research take place through the formation and application of interpretive concepts and processes and a focus on breadth. On the other hand, nomothetic research seeks an objective stance and seeks to create causal explanations, and especially predictions. Generalization is generally statistical. Ideographic research is associated with humanistic disciplines, such as anthropology, and is generally associated with qualitative or inductive research and methods, such as ethnography, oral histories, and the analysis of texts and material culture. Nomothetic research is associated with the natural sciences and with quantitative and deductive research and methods, such as macrosociological research (e.g., survey data collection and analysis) or socio-psychological experiments. ***See also*** Deduction Versus Induction; Qualitative Data Analysis; Qualitative Research; Quantitative Research

Ideology *(media studies)*   A system of ideas that underlies and regulates the behavior of groups and entire societies. Ideology connects into a totality of individual actions and beliefs that seem on the surface to lack any systematic connection or political significance. More often than not, it exists within individual thought as unconscious and implied belief. Because ideology functions at the collective and structural levels, it cannot be changed by individual action. In a general sense, ideological formations can be identified in every society. However, Marxist critics, who gave the word its currency, locate ideology specifically in a capitalist society, defining it as "false consciousness," by which is meant the imaginary relationship of individuals with their real conditions of existence. Because the relations of power are structurally unequal, capitalist ideology works to sustain that inequality. The Western media, apparently a free site of contested and conflicting ideologies, can be seen as complicit in exercising hegemonic control in society. ***See also*** Capitalism (economics, political science); Critical Theory; Hegemony (media studies); Marxism (political science, sociology); Power

Ideology *(political science)*   A system of ideas that aspires to explain and change the world. Ideology functions as the conventions that make up the dominant ideas in a society. The term was first coined in the late 18th century by Antoine Destutt de Tracy, who used *idéologie* to mean the "science of ideas." Ideology is a concept that is central to politics and is articulated by a dominant political group through culturally accepted symbols. These symbols are expressed through social institutions, such as the church, school, and family, and cultural forms, such as music, literature, dress, and television. Ideology is not necessarily meant to oppress or be forced but rather to legitimize the current order.

The concept of ideology was later developed by Marx. According to Marx, ideology is an illusionary representation of the relation of people to real conditions. To the Marxists, ideology was sometimes considered a pejorative term meaning "false consciousness." Ideologies were considered false because they hid the real world. People's beliefs resulted from what they are led to think rather than that which is true. Since the goal of the dominant group was to legitimize its power, it tended to disguise the exploitation of the disempowered. Ideology could, therefore, be revealed by uncovering the means of production and the people's relations to production. The ideology of capitalism creates a false consciousness, which can be seen as the expression of bourgeois interests.

Among the many ideologies throughout history are socialism, communism, fascism, liberalism, conservatism, Marxism, Nazism, and feminism. For more information, see Eagleton (1991). ***See also*** Communism (political science); Fascism; Liberalism (political science); Marxism (political science); Socialism (political science)

Ideology *(sociology)*   A system of ideas, beliefs, values, and doctrines expressed by any given individual, social group, or culture. Ideologies are often considered to be the foundation of any social, economic, or political system. Ideologies shape views, opinions, and behavior. Ideologies exert an influence on actions, as well as the general sense of identity, at both individual and group levels. Ideologies vary according to different types of systems. Ideology has been argued to be a concept that was developed by the Marxist paradigm. Marxists defined ideology as a set of values, beliefs, and ideas adopted by the dominant groups in society to maintain the hierarchical structure in any given community. ***See also*** Marxism (sociology)

Idiot Savant   A term coined by J. Langdon Down in 1887 for an individual who has savant syndrome. Savant syndrome is the coexistence of both a mental disorder (e.g., autism) and a superior skill, such as a mathematical ability, photographic memory, or musical talent or, less frequently, language abilities. Individuals with savant syndrome tend to be exceptional at their superior skills. Though individuals with savant syndrome tend to score below average on a standard intelligence measure, savant syndrome has also been observed in people with above average intelligence. The etiological origins of this syndrome are often congenital, with brain damage typically localized in the left hemisphere of the brain. As the right hemisphere tries to compensate for the damage, consequentially, this is often where the savant's specialty resides. Overall, more males than females are savants, with an estimated ratio of four to six males to one female. The 1988 movie *Rainman* is a popular depiction of an autistic savant. For more information, see Treffert and Wallace (2003). ***See also*** Intelligence Quotient (IQ); Mental Retardation (education, psychology)

Illusion of Control A phenomenon by which individuals believe themselves to have influence (or control) over a primarily chance-driven process. This theory was developed by Ellen Langer (1975), who observed that people overattribute the degree of personal influence they have over chance events. She found that when skill-related cues (e.g., choice, familiarity) were introduced into chance situations (e.g., card games, lottery), individuals overestimated their likelihood of success probability. For example, participants who got to choose their lottery ticket instead of receiving a random one were willing to resell their tickets for more than four times the price a participant with no choice was willing to sell the ticket for. By introducing a choice option, individuals erroneously overestimated the likelihood of winning. For more information, see Langer (1975). ***See also*** Decision-Making Theory

Immigration The entrance of people into a new country for the purpose of establishing permanent residence. While the term *immigration* has existed throughout history, modern immigration describes, specifically, long-term, legal, and permanent residence. Immigration is a significant historical as well as present and continual influence on society and an essential part of how nations continue to grow and diversify. However, immigration is often highly politicized and, in most countries, a major controversial political issue.

The motives for immigration are often economic or educational, although persecution, religious or political, may be a significant reason. Additionally, immigration can occur for personal reasons, based on a relationship, such as a family reunification or a transnational marriage.

Immigration can have positive and negative impacts on both the recipient country and the original country. For the host country, immigration offers benefits, such as the assumption of jobs that people in the host country will not or cannot do; immigrants are, typically, willing to work for longer hours for lower salaries; and when welcomed into the recipient country, immigrants can be of value to cultural diversity.

The negative aspects apply separately to immigrants and the host country. For the host country, some of the issues are the costs of migrants (who may potentially take advantage of the existing welfare systems); labor competition; environmental issues (the impact of population growth and pollution); national security (concerns of narrow-minded immigrant groups and terrorism); and crime, from trafficking of drugs and people to other types of crime and corruption. A drawback for immigrants is that they can be exploited for their cheap labor; and many die trying to flee the country of their origin.

Immigration is currently a prevalent topic in the news. As the world globalizes in terms of nations' economies, trade, and investment, borders are opened up more easily to facilitate the flow of goods and products. The International Integration and Refugee Association estimated that the past 50 years have seen almost the doubling of immigration. According to a similar study, developed countries' populations contain approximately 60% of immigrants, with 40% in developing countries. Twenty-eight countries make up 75% of the total immigrant volume.

With immigration comes illegal immigration, which refers to undocumented/unauthorized entrants: individuals who enter a country without authorization or who are inspected on entry into another state but gain admission by using fraudulent documents and are violators of the terms and conditions of a visa. Such violations of immigration laws occur frequently and have caused much discussion among local and national officials on the extent to which such crimes should be prosecuted. So far, the President, the Congress, law enforcement, or the business community, which uses and to a degree exploits illegal immigrants, has not been able to agree on a workable solution to the wholesale illegal immigration that the United States has experienced. ***See also*** Migration

Immunity Exemption from legal sanctions or penalties in the criminal justice system. For instance, informants may be granted immunity (i.e., an assurance that they will not be prosecuted for their involvement in an offense) in exchange for information about a criminal act or another criminal. ***See also*** Informant

Impeach The process of bringing charges against a public official for conduct that is deemed to be improper. When an individual is impeached, charges are brought before a tribunal. If proven guilty, the public official is removed from office.

Impeachment A formal criminal proceeding against a public official. The authority for a federal impeachment in the United States lies in the U.S. Constitution. The House has the authority to bring impeachment charges against the accused, and the Senate hears the trial. A three-quarters majority vote of those senators present is needed for conviction. If it is the trial of the President, the Chief Justice presides. Punishment in impeachment proceedings should not go beyond removal from office, but the accused is still liable to a regular trial "according to law." Furthermore, the President may not pardon impeachment offenses. In its history, the House of Representatives has brought impeachment charges against only 18 officials, 7 of whom were convicted. Two presidents had charges brought against them, but neither was removed from office. Presidents Andrew Johnson (1868) and William J. Clinton (1998–99) were both impeached by the House but not convicted by the Senate, and President Richard Nixon (1974) resigned before the House voted to bring charges. ***See also*** Impeach

Imperialism   A policy whereby the dominant interests of one nation expropriate for their own enrichment the land, labor, raw materials, and markets of another people. This is done either through territorial acquisition or by the establishment of economic and political hegemony over other nations. Although imperialism can exist without the creation of formal colonies, some political writers have likened imperialism to neocolonialism. Early imperialist empires include Egypt, Mesopotamia, and the Persian and Roman empires.

Two types of imperialism exist. The first, formal, or direct, imperialism occurs when a foreign state manages the day-to-day political, social, and economic interactions of another land. America's domination over the Philippines exemplifies formal imperialism. The second type, informal, or indirect, imperialism exists when a foreign state works through local political parties to manage a distant society. Informal imperialism is demonstrated by Britain's, France's, and Belgium's continued management of their respective former African colonies subsequent to their independence from colonial rule.

The objective of imperialism is to open up peripheral, or Third World, economies to the investments of dominant capitalist countries, thus ensuring a continual supply of raw materials, including cheap labor, at low prices. The economies of the periphery provide the setting to meet the needs of the dominant capitalist countries rather than their own needs, thereby producing an unending dependency in the poorer regions of the world.

Imperialism may not be a necessary condition for capitalism, but it seems to be a natural outgrowth of advanced capitalism, since imperialism allows for peripheral countries to provide a continual supply of raw materials at low prices. Marxists, who strongly oppose imperialism, argue that imperialism exists when a powerful nation protects its foreign markets through business. Marxists see imperialism as the ultimate state of capitalism.

Although Americans have believed themselves to be anti-imperial, some have argued that America was imperialist since Thomas Jefferson's purchase of the Louisiana Territory in 1803. In addition to investments overseas, the United States historically has been interested in expanding its capitalistic interests through collaboration with and training of foreign business leaders, diplomacy, financial grants, Hollywood depictions of affluence, and military dominance. In addition, much of the world has adopted American forms of culture, fashion, language, and other facets of daily living, or what might be called "cultural imperialism." For more information, see Foster (2006) and Parenti (1995). ***See also*** Capitalism; Globalization (economics, political science)

Implicit Association Test (IAT)   An implicit social cognition measure developed by Greenwald, McGhee, and Schwartz (1998). In IAT, a person has to rapidly categorize various stimulus items. According to IAT, a faster categorization indicates a stronger association, while a slower categorization indicates a weaker association. IAT is based on the assumption that some cognitive processes are unconscious yet influence the way people perceive stimuli and behave in the world. IAT has been used to measure age, race, and gender bias. For more information, see Greenwald, McGhee, and Schwartz (1998). ***See also*** Experimental Research

Implicit Memory   A type of memory that does not require conscious awareness during recall and stands in contrast to explicit memory. Most prominently, priming is a form of implicit memory, whereby a person's judgment is unconsciously influenced by presented stimuli prior to recall. Another common form of implicit memory is procedural memory, which is referred to as memory for "knowing how" (e.g., to play a guitar). Evidence for implicit memory as a different memory process stems from cognitive psychology experiments and patients with brain trauma. While explicit memory may be affected in amnesic patients, implicit memory can be found to be intact, providing evidence for this memory distinction. For more information, see Schacter (1987). ***See also*** Explicit Memory; Memory (psychology)

Implicit Personality Theory   A theory (sometimes referred to as IPA) about the general expectations people construct about another after learning something about that individual or noticing a particular trait in that individual. Often, these expectations reflect stereotypical attitudes, such as expecting fat people to be jolly or bespectacled people to be smart. However, not all such expectations are necessarily stereotypical or false.

The renowned Gestalt psychologist Solomon Asch (1952) is credited with having discovered that the presence of a particular trait often implies the existence of particular other traits. According to Asch, traits are *central;* they not only imply the presence of a potentially predictable array of other traits, they also are the ones that most powerfully influence people's impressions of, and responses to, the object or individual. For example, individuals may believe that a generally unhappy person must also be unfriendly or unsuccessful.

Gordon Allport (1954), a pioneer in the study of traits—which he sometimes referred to as dispositions, argued that central traits are basic to an individual's personality. He also identified secondary traits that may be recognizable within a culture but do not necessarily reveal consistent information about personality. In contrast, central traits, according to Allport, are those that are strongly identified with an individual's personality. Central traits are, in this context, a powerful form of nonverbal communication.

One implication of this theory is that people will form prejudices toward others on the basis of perceived traits, regardless of whether such traits are truly indicative of the underlying personality. For more information, see Allport (1954/1979) and Asch (1952/1987). *See also* Personality; Trait

Imprinting   Originally discovered by Douglas Spalding during the 19th century, it refers to a phase-sensitive learning period, during which an individual learns the characteristics of a stimulus object. Imprinting is often used in the context of filial imprinting, which refers to the process by which the young learn about the characteristics of their parents. Konrad Lorenz experimented with filial imprinting, infamously resulting in geese imprinting on his gumboots. For more information, see Spalding (1872). *See also* Evolutionary Psychology

Imprisonment   A type of incarceration reserved for those convicted of the most serious offenses (felonies). A person sentenced to serve more than one year of incarceration is sentenced to a term of imprisonment and will typically serve that term in a state or federal prison (as opposed to a local or county jail). *See also* Felon/Felony; Jail; Prison/Prisoner; Punishment (psychology, sociology)

Inadmissible   An adjective that describes evidence that is deemed too unreliable to be considered. Evidence or testimony is considered to be inadmissible if it was obtained by violating basic legal principles. For instance, a confession that was coerced is inadmissible in a trial. In this situation, the information is considered to be unreliable and is precluded from the case. Decision makers (judge and/or jury) disregard inadmissible evidence in their final decision regarding a verdict. *See also* Evidence; Exclusionary Rule (political science); Fruit of the Poisonous Tree

Inalienable   Rights   Freedoms that cannot be transferred to the government. In democracies, inalienable rights are also those not given by the government to citizens. Rather, these rights are endowed in every individual by virtue of birth and cannot be surrendered. They are natural rights given by God. The government cannot make laws that interfere with these rights. Inalienable rights include freedom of speech, freedom of religion, freedom of assembly, equal protection under the law, and the right to a fair trial.

Inalienable rights are found in the American Declaration of Independence, which was adopted on July 4, 1776. In it, Thomas Jefferson stated that inalienable rights, which he called "unalienable rights," are fundamental principles on which a democratic government is created. "We hold these truths to be self-evident, that all men are created equal, that they are endowed by their Creator with certain unalienable rights, that among these are life, liberty and the pursuit of happiness."

In return for these rights, citizens in a democracy are expected to cooperate with the government under the principle of the social contract. They are to give the state their loyalty, as well as participate in the mutual protection of the inalienable rights of all individuals. Those who infringe on others' inalienable rights are subject to punishment by the state. *See also* Democracy (political science); Social Contract

Incapacitate   One of the primary goals of punishment is to physically prevent a person from committing a criminal offense. The most well-known form of incapacitation is incarceration or imprisonment. People who have been confined to correctional facilities have been incapacitated by virtue of their confinement. Incarceration is not the only way to incapacitate criminal offenders. Electronic monitoring, where offenders are subject to active or passive monitoring of their whereabouts; house arrest, where offenders are forbidden from leaving their homes except as specified by the court; and day reporting, where offenders must report each day to a community corrections center, are all alternative forms of incapacitation. Civil commitment is also a form of incapacitation used for those who are a danger to themselves or to others. Historically and in other cultures, castration and amputation have also been used to incapacitate offenders. *See also* Civil Commitment; Community-Based Corrections; Incarcerate; Jail; Prison/Prisoner

Incarcerate   To physically confine a person who has been charged with or convicted of a criminal offense. Incarceration is a broad term that encompasses all types of penal confinement. Facilities designed to incarcerate include jails, prisons, juvenile facilities, and various types of detention centers. *See also* Incapacitate; Jail; Prison/Prisoner; Punishment (psychology, sociology)

Incest   Sexual acts between individuals of the same family, often within the immediate family. Incest involves individuals who are so closely related that the law would prohibit marriage between them. When incest involves a child, it is considered to be a form of child sexual abuse; such incidents have been shown to exert deep and lasting psychological effects on the child. The law aims to prevent incest in order to avoid the disruption of the peaceful domestic environment and the negative repercussions for the vulnerable victims, as well as the undesirable genetic effects that arise from inbreeding. Incest has been defined differently according to distinct cultures and historical periods. For example, in the 6th century under Pope Gregory the Great, the Catholic Church defined incest as extending to the fourth degree of consanguinity (first cousins), and this was finalized under Pope Innocent III in the Fourth Lateran Council of 1215. On the other hand, in Roman civil law, the Code of Justinian allowed first cousins to marry, and the Greek or Eastern Orthodox Church restricted marriage to the seventh degree (second cousins). In the United States, most states prohibit marriage to the fourth degree inclusive. *See also* Pedophilia/Pedophile; Sex Offense/Crime

Inchoate Offense   The planning and preparation for a criminal act or the attempt, but not completion, of the act. An inchoate offense requires intent on behalf of the offender to engage in the offense. Inchoate offense charges may be brought against an individual only in the absence of occurrence of the offense (as a result of arrest, accident, or any other reason). Conspiracy or attempts to commit a crime are the most common forms of inchoate offenses.

Incidence   The frequency of an event over a certain time period (usually a year), often expressed as a raw number. Incidence, typically, refers to the number of new instances or experiences in a given year. For example, if the incidence of HIV infection in prisons has been increasing, it means that more new infections are being reported in recent years than had been reported in previous years. Incidence is best understood when contrasted with prevalence. Prevalence refers to the commonality of a condition or event. HIV infection might be prevalent among prison populations even if the incidence in any given year was low. Incidence refers to the risk of contracting a particular disease (or experiencing a particular event), while prevalence indicates how widespread it is. *See also* Prevalence

Inclusion   The practice of educating special-education students within the regular classroom as opposed to separate special-education classrooms. Students continue to receive support services; however, those services are delivered in the regular classroom setting, often by a special-education teacher spending time in the regular classroom to address the students' needs. *See also* Mainstreaming (media studies)

Income   The flow of money or rewards to the factors of production for their use in producing output. Factors of production are normally inputs used in production— land, labor, capital, entrepreneurial skill. For example, land (including valuable resources embedded in land) can generate rent periodically, labor generates wages/income, capital acquires interest, and the reward for innovation and risk taking is profit. Income can therefore be defined as a flow of rent, wages/income, interest, and profit. Income as a flow is distinguishable from a stock of asset, such as a bequest or gift. Wealth cumulatively constitutes the flow and stock of assets. *See also* Capital; Interest; Labor; Profit; Wages

Income Tax   The tax paid on income and a source of government revenue to provide social and essential services. Individuals and businesses pay taxes on income

when they are not exempted from making such payments. A tax is progressive or equitable when those who earn more income pay proportionately more than those who earn less. In the United States, the marginal tax rate is the tax paid on the last amount of dollar earned. An income tax reduction has the potential of increasing disposable income, and therefore the amount of money that can be used to purchase goods and services in a national economy. *See also* Fiscal Policy; Income; Stabilization; Taxation

Incompetent to Stand Trial   The description refers to those who lack the mental capacity to understand the nature of the criminal proceedings against them or who are unable to assist in their own defense. Such persons cannot be prosecuted unless and until those competencies are restored. Evaluations will be ordered by the court if there are any concerns about the defendant's competency. Competency to stand trial is unrelated to the defendant's mental state or abilities at the time of the crime; it is determined on the basis of his or her competencies at the time of the trial itself. *See also* Competency

Incrementalism   A form of belief that change is best enacted gradually. This is in stark contrast to the notion that only sudden shifts or progressions can correct a particular problem. In terms of research, incrementalism seeks to build slowly on previous accomplishments and discoveries; such change, thus, addresses the problems at hand instead of attempting to overturn previous precedents or methodologies. In many ways, incrementalism is psychologically intuitive; human beings are generally risk-averse creatures and may thus seek to minimize their losses, even if this involves failing to maximize their possible gains.

Naturally, there has been much debate concerning the contributory effect of incrementalist policies. While proponents of incrementalism paint sudden progress as destabilizing and open to adverse consequences, critics argue that incrementalism is often too piecemeal and timely to serve any adequate purpose. Global warming lobbyists, for example, often argue that small change will come too late to actively save humanity from this increasingly dire threat. Only a revolutionary shift in daily practices and technological production can (in this viewpoint) reverse the current trend, and incrementalists are therefore both foolish and naïve to think in merely gradualist terms.

Similar debates can be found throughout much contemporary political philosophy. The British scholar Edmund Burke famously favored small legislative enactments over grand shifts in government, eschewing the possible adverse effects of revolutionary ideologies. This stands in sharp contrast to political movements such as those founded by Karl Marx and Friedrich Engels, who argued that only a profoundly structural change could properly alleviate human suffering. According to their position, gradual legislation could only (at best) provide a band-aid over social wounds, which might temporarily stop the bleeding but would ultimately fail to save the patient. *See also* Marxism (political science, sociology) Revolution

Incriminate   To make an admission of guilt regarding one's criminal behavior. An incriminating statement may take a written or an oral form and provides information about one's involvement in criminal acts. *See also* Guilty (psychology, sociology); Inculpate

Inculpate   To accuse, blame, or incriminate; to suggest guilt or culpability. *See also* Guilty (psychology, sociology); Incriminate

Independent Agencies   Bodies created by Congress to serve a specified public purpose and to operate with more independence from the executive branch, as do executive agencies. Executive agencies are the other type of federal agencies and are administered within one of the following 14 executive departments: Agriculture, Commerce, Defense, Education, Energy, Health & Human Services, Housing & Urban Development, Interior, Justice, Labor, State, Transportation, Treasury, and Veteran's Affairs. The first independent agency created in the United States was the Interstate Commerce Commission (ICC), created in 1886. There was a surge of independent agency creation during the New Deal era.

Independent agencies' independence is strengthened through the commissioner's staggered and fixed appointment terms, which usually overlap the President's, and the bipartisan requirement of a set maximum number of commissioners allowed from any one political party. The President still holds the same authority to choose the chairman of the commissioners of independent agencies, as he does for the executive agencies. A major difference between the two types of agencies is the power of the President to remove the commissioner. If it is an executive agency, the President may remove its commissioner at will. In contrast, a President may only remove an independent agency's commissioner for reasons delineated in the enabling legislation, resulting in less presidential control. This removal-for-cause requirement was established by the Supreme Court in *Humphrey's Executor v. United States* (1934). The Court ruled for the plaintiff, the estate of William E. Humphrey, who sued for back pay from the time Humphrey was removed as the commissioner of the Federal Trade Commission. President Franklin D. Roosevelt had removed Humphrey for political reasons alone; Humphrey had been appointed by the previous President and was not considered a New Deal supporter. For more information, see *Humphrey's Executor v. United States* (1934) and Zwart and Verhey (2003). *See also* Agency

Independent Variable   In social science, research refers to the variable that is being manipulated by the researcher. The independent variable stands in relationship to and may affect the dependent, or outcome, variable. The basis of experimental research is to discover whether specific independent variables have an effect on dependent variables, for example, whether watching violent video games (independent variable) has an effect on aggression (dependent variable) in children. *See also* Dependent Variable; Experimental Research

Indeterminate Sentence   A sentence that does not specify the precise amount of time to be served but instead offers a lower limit and an upper limit. Indeterminate sentencing, which is closely associated with a rehabilitative punishment orientation, was used across the United States until the 1970s. A theoretically perfect indeterminate sentence is a sentence of 1 day to 100 years. The lower and upper limits allow for variation in the amount of time inmates would serve based on their rehabilitative needs. On demonstration of rehabilitation, inmates would earn parole release. *See also* Parole; Rehabilitation; Sentencing

Index Crimes/Offenses   The FBI distinguishes eight index offenses from all other offenses and uses these eight offenses to measure crime rates nationally. The eight index offenses are reported in Part I of the Uniform Crime Reports issued annually by the FBI and include four violent offenses (murder, rape, robbery, and aggravated assault) and four property offenses (burglary, motor vehicle theft, larceny theft, and arson). Introduced in 1960, the use of the overall index crime rates was suspended in 2004 as a result of complaints that these rates are misleading because of the far more substantial contribution the property offenses made to the overall rate (larceny thefts accounted for approximately 60% of all index offenses reported). The FBI now reports violent crime rates and property crime rates separately. *See also* Federal Bureau of Investigation (FBI); Offender/Offense; Uniform Crime Report (UCR) (Part I/Part II Offenses)

Indictment   A "true bill" or formal charging document issued by a grand jury following a finding of probable cause. The indictment includes a statement of the facts relating to the nature, time, place, and manner in which the defendant is alleged to have committed the offense. Once indicted, or formally charged, the defendant will be arraigned and can make a plea. *See also* Grand Jury; Information; Preliminary Hearing; True Bill

Indigent   A person who lives in extreme poverty and who is unable to afford the most basic essentials, such as shelter, food, and clothing. In the legal system, an indigent individual is one who cannot afford the costs of legal representation required to face the charges brought against him or her. In such circumstances, a legal representative is appointed by the state to represent the defendant in court. Landmark cases that established the need for appointed representation include *Powell v.*

Alabama (1932) in capital cases and *Gideon v. Wainwright* (1961) for all felony cases. For more information, see *Gideon v. Wainwright* (1961) and *Powell v. Alabama* (1932). **See also** Public Defender

Indirect Effects Theory   A theory of media effects that suggests that the media causes responses in individuals but only as one variable among a variety of intervening influencing variables. Much of the early communications research supported the idea that there was a direct link between a message and a response. These so-called magic bullet or hypodermic needle theories gave way, instead, to more complex models, which suggest that responses can result from media messages indirectly and that environmental circumstances intervene between the message and the response. Katz and Lazarsfeld first introduced the concept of indirect effects with their two-step flow model, which suggested that messages were first relayed to opinion leaders, who, in turn, influenced other individuals. Building on this work, multistep models were developed. Indirect effects became a more recognized concept in mass communications research when Klapper, in his book *The Effects of Mass Communication* (1960), confirmed their significance. Despite this, however, indirect effect models are not examined as much as the direct effect models, as they are far more difficult to identify or link to a media event. The importance of further research in this area is frequently pointed out in the literature examining media effects. For more information, see Holbert and Stephenson (2003), Katz and Lazarsfeld (1955), and Klapper (1960). **See also** Decatur Studies; Media Effects

Indirect Speech   A kind of speech that is used to communicate what someone else said—in a third-person narrative—without quoting the person directly. The tenses of the verbs are often changed, and the exact words are not used. For example, in indirect speech, one would say, "She stated that she liked the school she was attending," when the person's exact words were "I like the school that I am attending." Indirect speech is often referred to as "reported speech," since someone else is reporting the information. It is almost always used in spoken English. If the reporting verb is in the past tense, the reported clause will also be in the past form. If reporting a general truth, the present tense will be used. **See also** Direct Speech

Individual Differences   How individuals differ in traits such as skills, aptitudes, and abilities to learn and perform. Learners may vary in their personalities, motivations, and attributions for their successes and failures when learning—all of which may affect how and why they learn. Additionally, they differ in their preferences for learning and their willingness to learn. Some traits may be more adaptive, whereas others are stable and less malleable, or resistant to change, especially as an individual matures to adulthood.

Examples of stable traits are gender, culture, and race. Even education and age are considered as stable traits. Traits that may be more malleable, or adaptive, could include effort and attributions of success and failure, among others. Individual differences may be considered in making the learning environment educationally appropriate, interesting, and relevant. **See also** Trait

Individualism (*political science*)   The political, moral, or social outlook that holds the individual as the primary unit of interest in a society. It views the individual as over and above the collectivity. Society is thus viewed as a collection of individuals. Individualism promotes a movement away from the mass, with the smaller circle of family and friends taking priority, ultimately leaving society at large on its own. As such, individuals are responsible for making their own choices consciously and accepting accountability for their decisions and behaviors. Individualism promotes the goals and desires of individuals.

The term *individualism* first appeared after the French Revolution in 1789. The French writer Joseph de Maistre used this term to describe his dissatisfaction with the revolution's dissolution of traditional social bonds, caused by political liberalism, in favor of promoting individual rights that allowed individuals to be their own moral referees.

Individualism is often compared with communitarianism. However, this dichotomy does not fully explain individualism's nuances. Rather, individualism stresses the priority of individual goals over external interferences with an individual's choices. Thus, individualism is at odds with any beliefs that stress societal, state, religious, or any other collective influences on the individual. It is important to note that individualism does not equate with isolationism. Individualism does not deny that living in society and cooperating with other people can offer tremendous benefits to the individual. **See also** Collectivism

Individualism   (*psychology*)   An ideology that emphasizes a person's personal needs, goals, and desires over those of the community or group. In individualism, a person's identity is determined by personal goals instead of group goals. Individualism stands in contrast to collectivism, which emphasizes group goals over personal goals. In a culture that emphasizes individualism, children are reared to be independent and self-reliant. Roughly, North American and European cultures tend to emphasize individualism, while Asian, African, and Middle and South American cultures tend to emphasize collectivism (Triandis, 1989). Whether a culture emphasizes individualism or collectivism has direct consequences on behavior. For example, individualistic cultures may be more prone to the fundamental attribution error, as well as the self-serving bias. That is, in individualistic cultures, people often attribute their own success to personal achievements and their failures to situational factors, while failures in others are attributed to personal factors. In contrast, people in collectivist countries may be more prone to the self-effacing bias, explaining their success as due to help from others, while failure is explained as a lack of effort on their part. Whether a culture emphasizes individualism or collectivism also affects the perception of romantic relationships. While individualistic countries emphasize marriages based on romantic love, collectivistic cultures may have marriages arranged by the elders. For more information, see Triandis (1989). ***See also*** Collectivism; Collectivist Culture

Individualism *(public administration)* Considered the very cornerstone of modern identity, this concept grants primacy to the individual actor. Interestingly, the celebration of a person's unique identity denotes a relatively recent phenomenon; people have long been historically defined more by their role within the collective (whether this be tribal or otherwise) than by any distinct or singular sense of self. Modern philosophers have deeply contemplated what being an individual therefore entails; is the notion of a sole identity granted at birth or only through one's membership within a larger collective? Furthermore, do individuals possess inherent rights, and if so, under what scenarios or circumstances may these rights be rescinded or restricted? While Kantians see individual agents as "ends in themselves," utilitarians consider the individual's interests only in relation to others. Modern psychology especially pivots itself around notions of individualism, with the most rigorous debates revolving around whether individuals are shaped through nature or nurture (or both). The natural sciences have also come to play an increasingly larger role in this debate, especially as more and more becomes known about the workings of neural processes on self-identification (and the ramifications thereof). Large bureaucratic organizations (e.g., the federal government) usually tend to stifle individualistic tendencies, which are drawn toward creativity and entrepreneurship. For more information, see Honderich (2005). ***See also*** Collectivism; Utilitarianism (public administration)

Individualist Culture A culture based on the notion of individualism. Although many philosophers and thinkers, particularly in Western society, have provided various definitions of individualism, individualistic culture focuses on important aspects of the individual instead of the collective structure. The individual is to be treated with dignity and be allowed to practice autonomy. It emphasizes the importance of a person's freedom and independence from society. The individual should also have privacy from other people, institutions, the state, and society as a whole. Individualism has been applied to many areas of life, such as politics, religion, economy, and ethics.

This moral philosophy has been applied to various cultures and societies. Countries such as the United States, Canada, Britain, and many European nations have individualist cultures. The values, desires, norms, and practices are rooted in an individualistic moral stance. The freedom to be autonomous is highly stressed. Thus, the actions of the individual are emphasized and greatly praised. For example, in the business industry, people are typically encouraged and often rewarded for their entrepreneurial efforts. In addition, they are given the opportunity to develop their own ideas. Pursuing individual goals and making decisions based on individual needs and desires are encouraged. This may create a competitive mentality in many areas of society, such as education, business, sports, politics, and so on.

In opposition to the individualist culture is the collectivist culture. Collectivism places emphasis on the needs of the collective whole, such as families, institutions, religions, the state, and society. The actions of the individual are driven by the goals of the collective unit. Thus, the collective unit benefits from the efforts of every individual. Japan is an example of a collectivist culture. Families, businesses, and ethics are primarily based on fulfilling the goals and needs of the whole unit, not individual desires. For more information, see Stevens (1973). ***See also*** Collectivist Culture; Individualism (political science, psychology)

Individualized Education Program (IEP) A written plan for a student who receives special education and related services in a public school. A requirement of the 2004 Individuals with Disabilities Education Act (IDEA), IEPs are created through the collaboration of a combination of parents, teachers, other school staff, transition services agency staff, and the student. IEPs must contain certain elements, including current performance; annual goals; special education and related services; participation with nondisabled children; participation in statewide and districtwide tests, dates, and places; transition service needs; needed transition services; age of majority; and measurement of progress. For more information, see U.S. Department of Education, Office of Special Education and Rehabilitative Services (2000). ***See also*** Special Education

Individualized Family Service Plan (IFSP) Federally sponsored under the Individuals with Disabilities Education Act (IDEA), this is a plan for children from birth through 3 years with developmental delays or disabilities and their families. Written like an individualized education plan (IEP) for older children with special needs, the plan includes current developmental level, available resources, and goals for intervention and development. ***See also*** Individualized Education Program (IEP); Special Education

Individualized Instruction An instructional approach in which each learner has a unique set of goals and objectives and is not evaluated in comparison with other learners. Individualized instruction is not one-to-one tutoring. It addresses the individual needs of learners, through the collaboration of teachers, students, parents, and other professionals in formal programs.

Individuals with Disabilities Education Act (IDEA)
A federal program, created in 1997 and updated in 2004, to authorize funding of education for children with disabilities. To qualify under IDEA, a child must meet the following three criteria: (1) the child must meet one or more of the categories of impairment included in IDEA, (2) the child's impairment(s) must be severe enough to adversely affect his or her educational performance, and (3) the child's impairment(s) must require special education and related services. For more information, see Library of Congress, Congressional Research Service (2005). *See also* Disabled Persons

Industrialism   The social conditions prompted by the rise of industrialization. From the mid-18th century to the mid-19th century, tremendous changes in manufacturing occurred first in Britain and then throughout Europe and North America. This revolution not only changed the way goods were produced, it forever altered the accumulation of wealth for both nations and individuals. Manufacturing innovations and machinery were adapted to agricultural use as well. While cities became more populated, causing a rise in poverty, unemployment, disease, and crime, they also spawned a growing middle class.

This revolution in industry also witnessed a revolution in print. The growth of the middle class meant a growth in literacy, which was no longer considered a privilege of the very wealthy. Inventions that made it possible to print reading matter much quicker than in the past led to the mass publication of pamphlets, magazines, and books, democratizing information and fostering individualism, a fundamental value in America. With so many ideas about, people became less reliant on their communities and their political and commercial leaders. Also, they were cut off from their cultural traditions. Sociologists theorize that as society became more fragmented and individuals more isolated, relationships once formed through bonds of a personal nature became more like contractual obligations. This made people more susceptible to persuasive influences, such as from the mass media. This susceptibility was used to an advantage by advertisers when industrialism led to a rise in consumerism. The industrial revolution made it possible to mass produce goods at the same time when workers felt the need to buy consumer items as a diversion from their repetitive work routines. The increase in printed materials allowed manufacturers to advertise their products to wider audiences.

Certain theories of mass media developed based on the perception of society as a group of isolated individuals and their subsequent susceptibility to propaganda. Direct-effects theories, such as the so-called hypodermic needle or magic bullet varieties, caused a consistent reaction among their viewers. This reaction could be uniform despite the differences in background among the viewers, because the creators of the messages were engaging in intentional manipulation. These

theories eventually fell out of favor and were replaced with new theories that suggested that the media's effects were not quite so direct. *See also* Advertising (economics, media studies); Bullet Theory; Hypodermic Needle Model; Media Effects; Printing

Industrial-Organizational Psychology   A specialty of psychology in which psychologists work to improve the domain of work and industry and the conditions for the people within them. Industrial-organizational psychologists employ psychological principles as well as research methods, including the use of psychometric tests, to improve the relationship between workplaces and employees. However, industrial-organizational psychologists do not solely work for employees' benefits. Often, industrial psychologists have to ensure that possible adjustments to improve workers' physical and psychological conditions also produce increased profitability in the workplace.

Industrial-organizational psychologists may work as scientists, by conducting research in the workplace that leads to the development of new findings and theories to advance knowledge in the field. Industrial-organizational psychologists may also work as work psychologists or consultants, by applying their knowledge to the solution of difficulties in the workplace. Finally, industrial-organizational psychologists may work as educators or consultants, by training staff or management in new methods or practices as derived by research.

Areas in which industrial-organizational psychologists work include human resources departments—for example, conducting personnel selection, training, and advancement. Furthermore, the tasks include improving employees' morale and work attitudes—for example, by examining work- and family-related aspects. Industrial-organizational psychologists are also asked to improve job satisfaction and efficiency of employees, by examining and enhancing organizational structures and processes. Finally, industrial-organizational psychologists may consult with companies regarding potential improvements and training in organizational behavior.

Problems that industrial-organizational psychologists may be asked to give advice on include how to hire more productive or better-suited employees, how to decrease absenteeism, how to strengthen communication skills between the workplace and employees, and how to increase job satisfaction. One of the methods an industrial-organizational psychologist may use in tackling these problems is to conduct a job analysis. During a job analysis, the psychologist methodically identifies the tasks, duties, and critical needs associated with a job, followed by the employment behaviors (knowledge, skills, abilities, and competencies) that are required. Based on the job analysis, the industrial-organizational psychologist may design a new system for applicant selection, improve staff performance assessment, outline training needs, and examine whether employees' payments are fair. Although a job analysis may consume time and money, it has been found that the rewards tend to outweigh the expenses. ***See also*** Job Analysis; Job Enrichment; Job Satisfaction

Industry *(media studies)* An economic branch of society that is concerned with the production of goods and their consumption by consumers. Production refers to the manufacturing of goods and their corresponding ideologies. Labor is involved in production; theories drawing on Marxism (particularly from the Frankfurt School) are thus important in the study of the media industry. The term *culture industries*, coined by Theodor Adorno and Max Horkheimer in their work, "The Culture Industry: Enlightenment as Mass Deception," addressed the manipulation of audiences while they consume goods produced by the media industry. Furthermore, Dallas Smythe argued that audiences are commodities that work while viewing media texts produced by industry in his 1981 work, "On the Audience Commodity and Its Work." Other important theorists referred to in media studies to examine the relationship between audiences, culture, and industry are Susan Willis, Herbert Schiller, Nicholas Garnham, and Edward Herman and Noam Chomsky. For more information, see Adorno and Horkheimer (1972) and Smythe (1981). ***See also*** Censorship (media studies); Frame of Reference; Mainstreaming (media studies); Media Outlet; Publication

Industry *(sociology)* Any business activity produced by an enterprise, commercial or noncommercial. Industry can also refer to a group of several enterprises that share a similar goal—that is, making profits within the same domain. For instance, different types of industries include the textile industry, the automobile industry, and the oil industry. In a narrower sense, *industry* refers to the act of manufacturing a given product within a certain field.

Inequality The disparity in the distribution of national income and economic welfare. The causes for inequality are diverse but include market failure, lack of opportunity for upward mobility, and adverse redistributive national and global economic policies. The lack of opportunity, which is usually the result of poor-quality education or lack thereof, poor health provisions, and the presence of racial and gender discrimination, creates an inequality trap that stifles upward mobility or perpetuates poverty in the poorest segment of society.

Some economists measure inequality in terms of income distribution, but development economists tend to focus on household consumption, measured in terms of expenditures in cash or kind. Wealth may alternatively be used as a broader indicator of available opportunity.

Traditionally, the Gini coefficient, a ratio, is used to measure income concentration or inequality by using a Lorenz curve (a curve that shows the total income received by any cumulative percentage of recipients) and a 450 line. The area above the Lorenz curve but below the 450 line is divided by the sum of the areas above and below the Lorenz curve to define a Gini coefficient

ranging from 0 to 1. The closer the coefficient is to 1, the greater the degree of inequality. For more information, see Perkins, Radlet, and Lindauer (2006). ***See also*** Income; Market Failure; Poverty; Welfare Economics

Inferential Statistics The use of randomly selected samples to draw conclusions about populations. It includes *estimation* (point and interval) and *hypothesis testing*. In estimation, numerical characteristics of samples (called statistics) are used to estimate the characteristics of populations (called parameters). In point estimation, the single value of a sample statistic is used as the best point estimate of the population parameter. In interval estimation, sampling theory is used to determine confidence intervals and indicate the general accuracy of the interval estimates. Rather than using a single number, as in point estimation, an interval estimate is a range of values that captures the true value of the population parameter a known percentage of the time (e.g., "95% confidence intervals" include the parameter 95% of the time in the long run). In hypothesis testing, researchers use sample data to test hypotheses about population parameters. ***See also*** Confidence Intervals; Estimation (Point and Interval); Hypothesis Testing

Inflation A sustained increase in the general price level. Because inflation is an indicator of the general upward movement of prices, it is normally measured by an index of prices, the most popular and influential being the consumer price index (CPI)—a normal rather than luxurious basket of goods and services consumed by typical urban consumers.

There is no consensus on the reasons for inflation, but some economists argue that it is a monetary phenomenon; meaning that it is the result of a rapid increase in the money supply (growth) relative to the production of output. In a simplistic monetary expression, inflation may be defined as "too much money chasing too few goods."

Economists, more often than not, distinguish between two types of inflation: (1) demand pull and (2) cost push. Demand-pull inflation occurs when the general price level increases because total spending exceeds an economy's capacity to produce. Cost-push inflation occurs not because total spending exceeds an economy's capacity to produce but because the cost of production is so high that it puts an upward pressure on the general price level. This form of inflation is largely attributable to resource or input cost. Resource cost may generate supply shocks in the form of escalating oil prices, as was the case in the 1970s, or prices of other raw materials.

Inflation bids up the cost of borrowing money. Monetary authorities raise the interest rate to check perceived excessive spending in order to stabilize prices, but creditors also revise their expectations of inflation upward and therefore increase interest rates to offset the inflation premium. Additionally, as real income (purchasing power) falls, owners of assets convert their assets into cash to neutralize price increases. Bond prices fall, and interest rates increases.

Fixed-income receivers, savers, and creditors are normally hurt by inflation when adjustments are not made to compensate for escalating prices. ***See also*** Hyperinflation; Interest; Money Supply

Informal Communication Systems Ways of communicating, especially in organizations, that do not involve formal meetings, written reports, memos, and other similar modes. These methods can involve "hallway communications," impromptu discussions, and spontaneous conversations. The groundbreaking theory of Leon Festinger (1950) illustrated how informal communication systems influenced group decision making. Whenever a group works together, the characteristics of individual members will affect the way they form opinions and conclusions. Festinger thought that the pressure toward conformity is the mediating variable. He took into consideration the group's cohesion, homogeneity, and factors such as standing against outside pressure. All these variables contributed to the group's accepting a uniform opinion. Such group pressure is endemic to most organizations, and many social psychologists and communication theorists have built on this theory. In another sense, informal communication systems can include technical methods such as video- or Internet-mediated ways of communicating instead of face-to-face communication. For more information, see Festinger (1950). ***See also*** Blog/Blogging; Group; Groupthink

Informal Group A term referring to a gathering of people—in person or online—that generates discussion about political and social issues. In their 2006 study, a group of researchers at the University of Tokyo looked at discussion patterns in Western and Asian nations and concluded that informal groups meeting in person are more likely to be homogeneous—of similar age, background, and interests—while groups that "gather" on the Internet have a greater chance of being heterogeneous—of diverse ages, backgrounds, and interests.

In her 2004 book, Katherine Walsh notes that informal, face-to-face groups range from senior citizens frequenting a morning coffee shop in Ann Arbor to people who, in the aftermath of September 11, 2001, conversed while stranded at airports, in their workplaces, or at their dinner tables. She points to the merits of informal interaction as a means by which "people collectively gather fundamental tools of political understanding." For more information, see Kobayashi, Ikeda, and Miyata (2006) and Walsh (2004). ***See also*** Democracy; Heterogeneous; Homogeneous; Reciprocity; Social Capital

Informal Institutions A society's code of conduct or values that affect individual behavior. Informal institutions differ from formal ones, which are official rules of society, for example, constitutions and legal codes. The terms *informal* and *formal institutions* were coined by the institutional theorist economist Douglass

C. North in his book *Institutions, Institutional Change, and Economic Performance* (1990), where he defined institutions as "the rules of the game in society" (p. 3). North's work analyzes the impact of political, economic, and social forces on institutions. North argued that informal institutions are as important as formal ones in determining the costs of doing business in an economy and the likelihood for economic partnerships to develop. For example, the laws affecting commerce would be a mechanism of the formal institutions, but people's attitudes and adherence to the law would be the informal institutions at work. In understanding the social norms embedded in an informal institution, the traditional scholarly method is to look for the social benefit it provides; other methods include discovering a norm's historical causes and engaging in a comparison of failed social norms to better understand successful ones. For example, in China, the informal institution of the communal values of Confucianism is adhered to as a method of countering state power. For more information, see Miller, Benjamin, and North (2007) and Li (2007). ***See also*** Social Norm

Informant An individual who provides information about certain individuals or events. In legal cases, the informant offers information in exchange for immunity and protection. The informant is generally an insider; that is, he or she has some degree of involvement in the milieu or the individuals being investigated. ***See also*** Immunity

Information In the criminal justice system, the term refers to a formal charging document filed by the prosecution. The information includes a statement of the facts relating to the nature, time, place, and manner in which the defendant is alleged to have committed the offense. After an information is filed, a preliminary hearing is often scheduled to determine probable cause. ***See also*** Grand Jury; Indictment; Preliminary Hearing

Information-Processing Model (*education*) A model that explains how information is received, stored in memory, and accessed or retrieved, as described in the stage model of Craig and Lockhart (1972). In the information-processing model (IPT), the *sensory register* attends to some incoming information while missing or disregarding other information. Because of continuous incoming sensory information, attention is focused on distinguishing which information is important. In *working memory,* the brain interacts with the newly attended information. Within 40 to 60 seconds, the brain must perceive, label, and sort information in preparation for permanent storage; thus, information can be lost, confused with similar information, or poorly processed. Once it is stored in *long-term memory,* the information is prepared for future access and retrieval. This is made more efficient by using cognitive networking and organizing. For more information, see Craig and Lockhart (1972). ***See also*** Learning Theory; Memory Strategies

Information-Processing Model *(psychology)* A theory of human cognition and memory, using the metaphor of a computer. The information-processing model assumes that people actively process information based on three stages: (1) encoding, (2) storage, and (3) retrieval. During the encoding stage, stimuli are taken in via sensory registers. This process is similar to input into the computer. During the storage phase, information retained in working memory may be transferred into long-term memory. This stage is similar to storing files on a hard drive. Finally, if the stored information is required, it is retrieved from long-term memory back into working memory. This process can be likened to retrieving stored files in order to create an output. Initially, the stages of the model were conceptualized as linear and sequential, reflecting either top-down or bottom-up processing. As computer systems became more complex, cognitive psychologists extended the model to include parallel processing. One such model is the parallel distributed processing model (Rumelhart & McClelland, 1986), which suggests that humans can engage in bottom-up and top-down processing simultaneously. The parallel distributed processing model has been supported by neuropsychological research and the finding that it can account for speed of processing. The information-processing model is currently the dominant model of human cognition. For more information, see Rumelhart, McClelland, and the PDP Research Group (1986). *See also* Memory (psychology)

Information Technology Although the term did not evolve until the 1970s, it has been used to describe any technology engaged in the inputting, processing, storage, transmission, and retrieval of information, such as the codex, printing systems, facsimile machines, satellites, and others. The modern idea of information technology (IT), however, involves the use of computers and computer-based management information systems. This modern idea of IT advanced along with computers, which evolved from vacuum tubes to transistors to integrated circuits to the computer chip. Changes in IT have affected individuals, industries, and society in profound ways.

IT professionals are responsible for computer and computer network systems within their organizations. Careers in IT include database administration, systems analysis, system development and programming, and end-user computing. IT departments are considered a supporting activity within an organization. They can be either centralized, in which case an enterprise has a central IT department, or decentralized, in which case the various departments or divisions have their own IT departments or personnel. The latter structure offers greater flexibility and specialization. A centralized IT department, however, is generally more cost-effective. *See also* Technology (media studies)

Informed Consent *(education)* An overt indication of one's willingness to participate in research and understanding of such participation. Assent is an overt indication by a member of a vulnerable population of his or her willingness to participate in research and understanding of such participation. For vulnerable research participants, the legally responsible party provides informed consent. *See also* Ethics in Research

Informed Consent *(psychology)* A legal term by which a person voluntarily agrees to an action or procedure based on the understanding of the presented facts and background underlying that action or procedure. In social science research, it is a legal and ethical requirement to obtain informed consent from a participant before he or she can participate in experimental research. The purpose of informed consent is to protect participants from harm. *See also* Experiment

Infotainment A media text that combines standard news information and feature stories. News pertains to public issues and the political sphere. Feature stories focus on celebrity culture and human interest. Infotainment generally is more popular in television programming than in other communication mediums. The term marks a tension in contemporary journalism, wherein critics charge that infotainment is not in accord with the traditional ethics of journalism. Infotainers include news anchors/personalities (like Barbara Walters and Katie Couric), who interview celebrities and also report on news. Furthermore, an extension of infotainment is the infomercial, advertisements under the guise of a typical television format. *See also* Media

Infraction Violation of laws, agreements, or other sets of rules and regulations. In the criminal justice system, an infraction refers to a misdemeanor offense, as opposed to a felony offense. The resulting punishment is generally a fine or some other form of similar penalty. *See also* Misdemeanor; Offender/Offense

Infrastructure The physical and organizational networks facilitating capital, which is usually provided by public agencies or governments. Contemporaneously, there has been a movement to privatize the provision of economic infrastructure in various countries in order to reduce public outlays. Infrastructure, also known as *social overhead capital*, includes roads, bridges, telecommunications, railways, and the sewage system—the bulk of which is referred to as public utilities. Infrastructure is a crucial basis for economic growth and development, especially because it can attract foreign capital to enhance productivity and create linkages (positive productive externalities for other industries).

Apart from physical infrastructure (capital), three areas of the service sector may also be considered infrastructural: (1) education in science and technology (human capital), (2) technological innovation, and (3) extensive health care delivery systems.

Infrastructural development or decay can be measured in terms of changes per worker, per household, and per square kilometer of land area. Typical changes can be measured in units of cubic meters of water and kilowatt-hours of power. For more information, see Perkins, Radelet, and Lindauer (2006). **See also** Capital

In-Group Favoritism   A term used in social identity theory to explain intergroup differentiation. According to in-group favoritism, people prefer the group that they belong to and identify themselves with. Evolutionary psychologists have suggested that humans developed the distinction between in-group and out-group to quickly discern whether someone is a friend or a foe (Krebs & Denton, 1997). A person who is classified as belonging to the in-group is seen as favorable. A person who is classified as not belonging to the in-group is often negatively stereotyped, potentially resulting in a biased perception of that person. For more information, see Krebs and Denton (1997). **See also** Out-Group Homogeneity Bias

Initial Appearance   A criminal defendant's first appearance before a judge following an arrest. Usually within hours of an arrest, a defendant will make an initial appearance before a judge. During this initial appearance, the charges are read, the defendant is informed of his or her rights, and a determination is made about pretrial detention (e.g., whether the suspect will be detained, receive bail, or be released on his or her own recognizance). Although they are sometimes separate proceedings, depending on the jurisdiction and the nature of the charges, the initial appearance might be combined with the arraignment. The defendant enters his or her formal plea during arraignment. **See also** Arraignment; Bail; Preliminary Hearing

Initiative   A process, rising in the late 19th to early 20th centuries in the United States, whereby either a petition signed by registered voters forces a public vote on a proposed change of legislation or executive or legislative bodies are forced to consider a particular issue. An initiative may be direct, whereby a measure is put directly to a vote after being submitted by a petition. Or it may be indirect, whereby a measure is first referred to a legislature and put to a popular vote only if not enacted by the legislature. In the United States, indirect initiatives put to the vote are called referendums, ballot measures, or propositions. **See also** Ballot; Referendum

Injunction   A court order that forbids an individual or an organization from engaging in specific acts. An injunction aims to prevent further harm by disallowing acts that led to the harmful consequences in the first place. Injunctions can be permanent or temporary. Restraining orders constitute one form of injunction. **See also** Restraining Order

Innovation (*economics*)   The first successful use of a new product or method or the introduction of a new enterprise on a commercial or extensive scale. New products or services (product innovation) and new methods of production or distribution (process innovation) are usually the offshoot of invention.

By introducing new products and processes, innovation becomes an engine of competition and productivity, which allows consumers to vary their choices and what they consume at a relatively cheaper cost.

Innovation has the potential of endangering smaller firms with diseconomies of scale and less capital to compete, because larger firms, which can increase output at low per-unit cost, can sell their products at much lower prices that cannot be matched by less efficient firms.

Firms that are adequately capitalized and with excess capacity are forced to become more efficient as a result of innovation, by investing in research and development (R&D) to reduce cost and produce competing new products. Executives, scientists, and skilled, salaried employees (collectively known as *intrapreneurs,* for providing a spirit of entrepreneurship) are actively undertaking R&D for their firms to be competitive and profitable.

The cost of R&D may be reduced by diffusion. Diffusion is the dissemination of innovation through imitation or emulation. Since innovation, unlike invention, is not patentable, savvy firms may copy or emulate the successful innovation of their competitors to minimize short-term losses and stay competitive over a longer time horizon.

Although earlier economists like Robert Solow were less successful in modeling technological progress (considered a residual) in their explanation of economic growth, innovation or technological progress accounts for a considerable amount of economic growth in contemporary growth theories. Empirical results indicate that technology or innovation makes labor much more efficient. For more information, see McConnell and Brue (2008). **See also** Competition; Growth; Weightless Economy

Innovation (*education*)   The term refers not only to the creation of a novel and useful idea, product, service, or process but also to the intentional implementation, dissemination, adoption, and reshaping of the idea within an organization or system. The aim of innovation is to improve effectiveness, efficiency, value, or competitive advantage. Though overlapping with the notion of creativity, innovation represents the application and marketability of creative outputs, generally within a work context, and is fueled by extrinsic incentives. Though the creative output need not be entirely unfamiliar to the system, it must entail some distinct change or challenge to the status quo. For more information, see West and Farr (1991). **See also** Organization Design; Organization Development (OD) (education)

Inquest   An official investigation about a given matter. The inquest may be held before a jury, and the verdict of the inquest is determined by the jury or the judicial officer (in the absence of a jury). For instance, an inquest may be requested in the case of a suspicious death to gather further information about the circumstances of the death. **See also** Investigate

Inquiry Teaching A problem-based teaching strategy that engages students in solving complex real-world problems by using the nature of scientific inquiry. Students become the investigators by using higher-order cognitive processes and focusing on "how" we come to learn rather than "what" we have learned.

Insanity A defense based on the idea that a person allegedly accused of a crime cannot be held responsible for it if unaware of the implications of his or her actions. For example, the U.S. legal system requires that both the *actus reus*, that is the "guilty act," proven beyond a reasonable doubt, and the *mens rea*, the "guilty mind," (i.e., criminal intent) have to be established to prove criminal liability. Thus, if a person is unaware of what he or she is doing, the *mens rea* cannot be established. A defendant who is found not criminally responsible is judged NGRI, "not guilty by reason of insanity," and may consequently be committed to a psychiatric hospital (Wrightsman & Fulero, 2005). Such defendants remain in psychiatric care for the duration they are evaluated; moreover, contrary to popular belief, they often end up confined in secure psychiatric hospitals for a longer period of time than they would have served in prison if convicted.

There is no uniform definition for insanity, and states vary with regard to their definitions of insanity; some states do not permit an insanity defense at all. Approximately half of the U.S. states continue to use the M'Naghten Rule, also known as the McNaughton standard. According to the M'Naghten Rule, a defendant can be found insane if he or she suffers from a "defect of reason or mind" and therefore did not understand the "nature and quality of the act he was doing" or did not understand the wrongfulness of the act (Wrightsman & Fulero, 2005). Due to criticism, the M'Naghten Rule was in some states replaced by the Durham test, only to be replaced by the ALI (American Legal Institute) standard (except for New Hampshire). The ALI standard was, at least initially, thought to be an improvement over M'Naghten, as it includes both a cognitive and a volitional prong. While the cognitive prong focuses on the defendant not being able to "appreciate the wrongfulness" of the act, the volitional prong focuses on the defendant not being able to "conform his or her conduct" (Wrightsman & Fulero, 2005) or, in other words, maintain control over his or her behavior. The ALI standard is now used in 21 U.S. states. For more information, see Wrightsman and Fulero (2005). **See also** *Actus Reus; Mens Rea*

Insanity Defense A criminal defense strategy that stipulates that the defendant cannot be found guilty in a given trial if he or she is deemed to be insane. The premise underlying the insanity defense is that individuals who are considered to be insane do not have adequate moral reasoning to understand right from wrong or they do not have any control over their actions. As such, individuals who do not understand the distinction between right and wrong cannot have criminal intent, or *mens rea*. In this regard, individuals who are deemed to be insane cannot be found guilty of a criminal offense. The first legal attempt at taking into account defendants' cognitive abilities occurred in England in 1843. Daniel M'Naghten attempted to assassinate British Prime Minister Robert Peel. Instead, he killed Edward Drummond, the Prime Minister's secretary. M'Naghten was under the impression that Peel was trying to kill him. At the trial, experts testified that M'Naghten had serious mental health issues, claiming that he was a paranoid schizophrenic with psychotic tendencies. As a result, M'Naghten was deemed insane, and he was found not guilty on the premise that he was not sane at the time of the offense. The defense of insanity was subsequently referred to as the M'Naghten Rule, which stipulates,

> Every man is presumed to be sane, and to possess a sufficient degree of reason to be responsible for his crimes, until the contrary be proved to their satisfaction: and that to establish a defence on the ground of insanity, it must be clearly proved that at the time of commiting the act the party accused was labouring under such a defect of reason, from disease of the mind, as not to know the nature and quality of the act he was doing, or as not to know that what he was doing was wrong. (United Kingdom House of Lords Decisions, 1843)

Various limitations of the insanity defense have been pointed out. One of the difficulties in establishing insanity is that there is little consensus regarding its definition, which may lead to a large degree of discrepancy in the characteristics and circumstances of cases pleading the insanity defense. Others have suggested that some individuals do understand the difference between right and wrong but have very little control over their actions, which makes it difficult to reduce the definition of insanity to simply knowing the distinction between right and wrong. Various tests have been developed to assess insanity, such as the M'Naghten Rule, the irresistible impulse test, and the Durham Rule. To address some of the limitations of these tests, the American Law Institute (ALI) developed the Model Penal Code test in 1962. This test had more breadth when compared with previous tests. When compared with the M'Naghten test, the ALI test shifted the emphasis from an absolute and complete understanding of right and wrong to a significant inability to grasp the difference between right and wrong. This test also included a component measuring whether individuals had the ability to control their actions. For more information, see United Kingdom House of Lords Decisions (1843). **See also** Defense; *Mens Rea*

Insecure Attachment The term refers to the types of nonsecure attachment between children and caregivers:

avoidant and anxious-ambivalent. Attachment plays a critical role in child development as well as in adult romantic relationships. Individuals whose primary attachment was insecure tend to have inferior social skills, poorer peer relations, and fewer close friends than individuals whose primary attachment was secure. Cultural differences have been noted in attachment development. While many children in the United States tend to be securely attached, the majority of German children show avoidant attachments, and many Japanese children show anxious-ambivalent attachments. These cultural differences can be explained by the different emphases in child-rearing practices; for example, Northern German parents emphasize independence from an early age. ***See also*** Attachment Theory

Insider Trading   The trading (buying and selling) of securities on material information not available to the general public. This information is obtained from within the company or from others before it is made publicly available. Those who are in possession of insider information can profit from it. Trading with insider information is illegal and is subject to penalties and even a jail sentence. Examples of insider trading of information include leaking earnings results before they are publicly available, leaking the results of FDA drug approvals, and tipping off others as to possible mergers and acquisitions in advance of announcements to the public. Other examples of insider trading or schemes include unlawful trading ahead of upgrades and downgrades of securities by institutional research companies. Also newspaper information gathered from interviews by company officials and others before it is published can be considered insider information. Under federal law of the Securities Exchange Commission (SEC), violating insider trading law depends on what information should not be disclosed to the person receiving the information, who disclosed it to the person, and whether that person knew that the information should not be disclosed to him or her. The issue of what constitutes material information is open to interpretation. Persons who knowingly use material inside information to buy and sell securities and recommend securities related to this information are generally considered to be trading in inside information. Insider trading is not only illegal, it is unethical and a cost to society. It is unethical to profit from inside information at the expense of others who are not privileged to such information. The victims of insider trading include corporate investors, shareholders, the company itself, the market, and market makers. If all information is completely transparent, then the price of the stock should be priced correctly, where everyone has the same access to the information. The strong-form version of the efficient market hypothesis, which measures how quickly and accurately the market incorporates new information in the price of a stock, suggests that security prices reflect all public and private information and therefore those with inside information

cannot profit from this information. However, the evidence available today does not support this theory. People still make abnormal profits from inside information. The efficient market hypothesis theory is a well-studied and well-documented theory in economics. However, there is widespread disagreement and controversy over this theory because some economists and investors believe that one can beat the market by mathematical trading with the help of mathematical models. There is clear evidence, however, that a person with information can beat the market. For more information, see Ehrhardt and Brigham (2003) and Smart, Megginson, and Gitman (2007). ***See also*** Efficient Market Hypothesis

Insight   In the context of problem solving, the term refers to the moment when suddenly a solution for a problem is discovered. The term *insight* is based on Karl Bühler's notion of the German *Aha-Erlebnis* (aha experience). An aha experience takes place when two previously unrelated thoughts are spontaneously connected and lead to the solving of a problem. Insight is similar to the notion of an epiphany or eureka moment. For more information, see Bolgar (1964). ***See also*** Problem Solving (communication)

Instinct   A form of intuitive response to an external stimulus. Decisions based on instinct do not reflect rational calculus and conscious thought but rather a natural reaction to a given situation. Instinct is said to reflect an innate predisposition to react in a given manner.

Institutional Review Board (IRB) *(education)*   A group of individuals responsible for approving and overseeing all research activities involving human participants within an institution. The goal of an IRB is the protection of human participants' well-being. IRBs exist to enforce federal regulations created in reaction to historical events that violated human rights. ***See also*** Ethics in Research

Institutional Review Board (IRB) *(psychology)*   A body that regulates, governs, and approves research to be conducted on human beings. An IRB has the power and authority to approve research, including research involving human beings, as well as to disapprove research. An IRB may require that an informed consent form be given to participants and specific information be added to the informed consent form. An IRB may conduct an ongoing review of the research projects, in accordance with the risk category the research was initially classified in, and it has the power to have a third party observe the consent procedures and research administration.

An IRB must encompass at least five members, according to the U.S. Department of Health and Human Services. These members must be of diverse backgrounds to ensure that issues such as race, gender, and community position will be addressed. For example, an IRB may not be entirely composed of men. Members must ensure that the rights and welfare of human participants are protected. An IRB must consist of people who have the professional competence to review the proposed research and who can ascertain that professional regulations, conduct, and practice as well as legal requirements are adhered to. *See also* Ethics; Ethics in Research

Institutional Subsystem The third prong of the structural functionalist social system model promoted by Talcott Parsons in the 1940s. Parsons recognized the three major levels of organizational structure. At the bottom is the technical subsystem. Above the technical subsystem is the managerial subsystem. At the top is the institutional subsystem, whose function is to relate the organization to the larger society. The institutional subsystem consists of intangibles, such as standards, norms, rumors, myths, knowledge, and ceremonies.

In an organization, the institutional subsystem, which may have a fiduciary function, may be a board of directors, who, although superordinate to the managerial subsystem, also have responsibilities to the organization. It may give legitimacy and support to an organization, as well as define the limits of what those in the managerial subsystem may do, while simultaneously defining the organization's function in the larger community. In a business organization, the board may decide the issue of dividend policies, profits, or whether to invest in an economic program. In education or health organizations, the board will likely be tasked with where to build a school or hospital. For more information, see Parsons (1959). *See also* Organizational Structure

Instruction The process by which specific content and skills are delivered to learners. There are many theories and methods for effective instruction. For example, depending on the educational philosophy of the teacher, instructional methods may be teacher centered (passive or transmission learning) or student centered (active learning).

Instructional Analysis A term typically associated with the instructional design process or approach. According to some instructional designers, it is considered as the front-end analysis, which involves identifying an instructional problem within an organization (school, university, or business) and justifying an appropriate resolution to that problem. Based on this definition, instructional analysis consists of the procedures used for analyzing the instructional goal, context, task, and learners. More typically, instructional analysis is considered to be another instructional design phase included within the analysis stage and would thus be known as instructional content analysis, instructional task analysis, or learning task analysis. The purpose of such content or task analysis is for the instructional designer to identify the subordinate skills or knowledge

steps that a learner must attain to meet the desired instructional goal. This analysis also determines the best or most appropriate sequence for learning those skills or knowledge steps to achieve the goal. For more information, see Davidson-Shivers and Rasmussen (2006). *See also* Instruction; Instructional Design

Instructional Design The systematic process used to develop education and training programs. There are a number of systematic models for designing instruction, all of which include the major components of the analysis of a performance problem and the design, development, implementation, and evaluation of an instructional solution to the problem. For more information, see Dick, Carey, and Carey (2005) and Gustafson and Branch (2002).

Instructional Objectives A description of what the learner should be able to accomplish after instruction. Instructional objectives help the teacher or instructional designer develop appropriate instructional strategies, materials, media, and assessment. They also help the learner identify knowledge and skills to master and keep learning on the right track. Objectives are based on the results of task analysis and curricular requirements. They are typically grouped into cognitive, affective, and psychomotor categories, and within each category, there are varying levels of knowledge and skills. They must be specified in clear terms of learning outcomes corresponding to particular categories and levels. To develop a complete set of instructional objectives, it must be kept in mind that the objectives should describe (a) specific performance, behavioral and/or cognitive; (b) output (e.g., essay), indicating specified learning outcomes; (c) conditions for performance (e.g., time and resources); and (d) criteria for determining whether the expected learning outcomes have been achieved. *See also* Instructional Strategies; Task Analysis

Instructional Strategies The design of sequences and methods of instruction for facilitating learning, especially concerning how to teach. The design of instructional strategies is informed by developments in psychological and educational research in learning, instructional design, curriculum development, and philosophy. The convergence and divergence of educational research findings indicate, on the one hand, that educational communities view learning as active meaning construction in general and, on the other hand, that learning is multidimensional with different foci on acquiring facts and skills, developing mental structures and cognitive abilities, or participating in resource-rich learning environments. While insights from this research help generate major instructional models and supporting strategies, instructional strategies serve instructional purposes defined contextually and thus can be used strategically in the face of different learning problems. In other words, effective instructional strategies have both theoretical and pragmatic grounding.

Instructional strategies are prescribed in direct response to instructional objectives, shaped by content and performance. Different categorizations of objectives result in different groupings of instructional strategies. At the same time, local instructional objectives should be embedded in a larger coherent instructional unit that emphasizes active learning. In this case, the grouping of instructional strategies can benefit from recent research on expertise, which indicates that adaptive experts are high on both processes that lead to innovation and processes that lead to efficiency through well-practiced routines.

Instructional strategies are also prescribed with the consideration of (a) desired instructional outcomes and (b) instructional conditions. Desired instructional outcomes include effectiveness (attainment of instructional objectives), efficiency (effectiveness as against time and costs), and appeal (learner enjoyment). Given that instruction has complex relationships with learning, learners, and resources, the design of instructional strategies should address the issue of when and when not to use certain strategies by looking into the nature of the learner, the learning environment, and the resources, as well as the learning. It should be noted that instructional strategies can be reconfigured due to dynamic learning processes, whereby instructional decisions are constantly made. As such, instructional strategies are a set of heuristics, or flexible problem-solving strategies.

Depending on the stages and needs of learning, instructional strategies fall along a continuum from direct to indirect instruction, from teacher fronted to experiential, from structured to ill structured, from interactive to independent, and from teacher (or peer) facilitated to technology mediated. Each instructional strategy features a variety of more specific instructional tactics, such as presentation, demonstration, role playing, discussion, brainstorming, and reflection. For more information, see Reigeluth (1999). **See also** Instructional Objectives

Instrument　A tool used in empirical research to measure any given concept. Instruments may take on many forms, such as questionnaires, surveys, interviews, and so on. When a researcher wishes to investigate any given concept, he or she may choose to administer instruments to a select sample in order to obtain information about the concept of interest. Instruments are made up of many items, which are then combined to measure the behavior or attitude of interest. For instance, in the field of psychology, the Jesness instrument is used to identify asocial personalities and personality types, and the Beck Inventory is an instrument used to assess depression. **See also** Empirical; Interview (education, sociology); Research; Research Methodology; Survey

Insurance　The transfer of risk to an entity that pools resources to compensate for losses associated with accidents, natural disasters, injuries, economic losses, and death. Individuals and businesses face uncertainty, which may result in the loss of value (risk). Risk may take various forms, including premature death, damage to property, and economic losses.

Besides risk transfer, some risks could be retained or controlled. Risk is retained when individuals and businesses assume responsibility for all or part of an unforeseen adverse occurrence. Drivers assume responsibility for part of the cost of an accident by their deductibles. Loss may be controlled by reducing the frequency of hazardous events or adopting safeguards to minimize the cost of eventual loss.

Insurance involves a contractual arrangement in which the insured promises to pay periodic premiums and the insurer takes an objective risk (the difference between actual losses and expected losses). Actuaries (skilled mathematicians and statisticians) determine the insurance premiums to cover compensation and profits.

Insurance companies take different organizational forms—stock companies (owned by shareholders), mutual companies (owned by policy owners), reciprocal exchange (self-owned unincorporated mutuals), and Lloyd's associations (associations that facilitate markets and services).

There are macroeconomic benefits from insurance. For example, the Federal Deposit Insurance Corporation (FDIC) insured deposits to develop confidence in the banking system and achieve financial stability in the aftermath of the Great Depression of the 1930s. It took on an even greater role of insuring deposits during the financial crisis of 2008. Insurance companies facilitate the transfer of articles of trade and promote capital formation by pooling resources and investing them in money and capital markets. For more information, see Kidwell, Blackwell, Whidbee, and Peterson (2008). **See also** Risk Management (economics)

Intake　In research or social work, the term refers to the first time a professional (social worker, researcher, etc.) meets with an individual to obtain more in-depth information about the individual's situation. In the legal system, intake is a practice that occurs when various individuals (offender, the police, probation officer, etc.) engage in a discussion to decide whether a given case should be handled formally (in court) or informally. Intake occurs before a preliminary hearing. **See also** Preliminary Hearing

Intelligence Quotient (IQ)　A measure, or score, of a person's mental ability or general cognitive functioning. IQ scores were initially developed for measuring children's intelligence and were computed via an actual quotient. That is, IQ was calculated by dividing the mental age of the child by the chronological age of the child and multiplying this figure by 100. Consequently, if a child's mental age corresponds to his or her chronological age, when the ratio is multiplied by 100, the child would have a measured IQ of 100. Though this manner of calculating IQ proved problematic and, as such, is no longer used, it provided a foundation for the development of the IQ measure.

The most widely used tests of intelligence are the Stanford-Binet and Wechsler measures. David Wechsler developed the first IQ test for adults, the Wechsler-Bellevue Intelligence Scale in 1939, which was later succeeded by the Wechsler Adult Intelligence Scale, the WAIS, in 1955 (and has been modified in several versions since). To differentiate between verbal and nonverbal abilities, the Wechsler scales introduced the computation of three types of scores: (1) the verbal IQ; (2) the nonverbal, or performance, IQ; and (3) the total (full-scale) IQ (made up of the verbal and nonverbal IQ). The Wechsler scales use a scoring system based on the normal distribution (i.e., a bell-shaped distribution, where the majority of cases fall toward the middle of the curve, with a mean of 100 and a standard deviation of 15. That is, the average intelligence score is 100, and nearly 100% of the scores fall within three standard deviations of the mean (i.e., between 55 and 145). For more information, see Wechsler (1939). *See also* Stanford-Binet Intelligence Test; Wechsler Adult Intelligence Scales (WAIS)

Intent In the criminal justice system, the term refers to an individual's aims, purpose, and intentions when engaging in an illegal act. Intent is a mental state in which an individual sets out to commit an act that is forbidden by the law. Intent implies that the individual engaged in a given act with the intention of stealing, defrauding, harming, killing, and so on. The principle of intent implies that punishment should only be incurred if it has been established that the individuals were morally culpable for their actions. When an individual is accused of an offense, the prosecution and defense teams attempt to determine the intent of the defendant at the time of the offense. For instance, if an individual is accused of murder, it must be demonstrated that the defendant had intent to kill. *See also* Mens Rea

Interactive Media Any two-way or multiple-way flow of communication that allows for active participation. Technically, there are varying degrees of interactivity. For example, if a film is shown on television, a viewer can watch it from beginning to end but is generally powerless to alter it. Except for turning the television on and off, there is no interactivity. If the television has a digital recording device, where the user can pause, rewind, and forward through commercials, then the activity becomes moderately interactive. Some television producers have experimented with audience participation segments, where viewers can not only vote on contestants but, in some instances, also text message plot suggestions that are incorporated into the plot—this is highly interactive.

Major improvements in speed and capacity in digital storage devices have led to a proliferation of digital interactive technologies. In only a few decades, technologies such as the mobile phone, the Internet, video games, and virtual reality have been introduced

and greatly improved. While the World Wide Web service of the Internet is probably the most widely accessed interactive technology, interactive video games and virtual reality software represent those with the most sophisticated upgrades in software. These allow users to interact by participating in the action and taking on a role in the fantasy scenario.

The rise of interactive media has had a profound effect on aspects of popular culture, interpersonal communication, learning, and leisure time. It has also led to a large body of research regarding the effects of the technologies on users. For instance, research on the use of video games has looked at the detrimental effects, such as repetitive strain injury, social isolation, game addiction, and the possible stimulation of aggressive behavior. On the other hand, proponents of their use have looked into whether video games can improve eye-hand coordination, visual attention capacity, and spatial intelligence. *See also* CD-ROM Games; Internet; Technology (media studies); Virtual Reality

Intercultural Communication/Cross-Cultural Communication The study of how members from different cultural groups interact with each other. "Culture" can be viewed as the shared norms, values, beliefs, experiences, attitudes, and practices that characterize a particular racial, religious, or social group. Due to the ever-increasing integration of individuals from different cultural groups in modern-day society, there has been an emphasis on creating ways to accommodate the communication process between individuals from these cultural groups.

Intercultural/cross-cultural communication involves assessing the factors that influence how individuals from different cultural groups interact with each other. Within each culture, there are established values and behavioral patterns. Learning to understand these values and patterns and accepting that one's own cultural group may be quite different from another cultural group is important in creating an unbiased and nonjudgmental way of interacting. For example, in some Asian cultures, it is usually unacceptable to maintain eye contact with someone who holds a superior position in a work setting. In Western society, eye contact is considered a sign of honesty and respect and should be maintained when meeting with a boss at work. Many individuals from different cultures have accents so pronounced that it is important to try and understand the pronunciation if the person is having difficulty in properly speaking the language.

There are several reasons for the importance placed on intercultural/cross-cultural communication. Currently, as businesses become more global and international, being able to effectively communicate with individuals from other cultures becomes crucial when establishing a business in the foreign market. This would also apply to how products are marketed to the public, particularly different cultural groups. Intercultural/cross-cultural communication is also important in an academic environment, as individuals travel to places around the world to obtain an education. The significance of intercultural/cross-cultural communication can be seen in many other areas, such as politics, economics, entertainment, and technology.

A critical aspect of intercultural/cross-cultural communication is to understand and accept the notion that there may be barriers or breakdowns in communication because of cultural differences. More specifically, keeping an open mind about these differences can prevent the development and use of stereotypes and prejudiced attitudes. Such stereotypes and prejudiced attitudes can lead to misunderstanding and conflict. Being aware of potential differences may not make the communication process between cultural groups easy, but it can reduce the possibility of conflict and may lead to education on the norms, attitudes, and behavioral patterns of the other group. For more information, see Breslin (1981) and Dahl (2004). *See also* Cultural Diversity; Culture (communication)

Interest   The payment to the lender for the use of borrowed money or financial capital. Interest is paid because the value of money depreciates over time as prices rise. Compensation is required for that loss and the postponement of consumption. Interest is also paid to minimize the cost of default.

The nominal-interest rate is a combination of expected inflation and the real-interest rate, whereas the real-interest rate is the difference between the nominal rate and expected inflation. The interest rate is normally one of the most telling indicators of whether people will be willing to hold more or less money. When the interest rate is high, people tend to hold less money and more money when it is low. *See also* Capital; Keynesian

Interest Group (*political science*)   An association of individuals or organizations that seek to advance a particular cause, usually through influencing public policy. An interest group tries to influence government without trying to form a government itself. An interest group may also be known as a political advocacy group, special-interest group, pressure group, or lobbyist group. Interest groups first appeared in the United States around 1830 through 1860 as social groups in the antislavery movement and business groups supporting railroad and oil company interests.

Interest groups rely on a variety of methods to influence governmental policy. Their activities include lobbying, direct action such as protests, and financial contributions to campaigns through political action committee (PAC) money. In the United States, interest groups pay particular attention to influencing Congress, sometimes by producing iron triangles comprising the interest group, congressional subcommittees, and governmental agencies. Interest groups further use the Supreme Court through *amicus curiae* briefs, white papers, or direct legal action.

Interest groups may be divided into categories based on their cause and membership. Some groups represent a single issue, such as children, animal welfare, consumer advocacy, or immigration. Other groups represent trade associations, such as the National Education Association, or trade unions, such as the AFL-CIO. Others, representing corporations, are hired specifically to advance issues to increase profits, such as taxation, environmental protection, and trade policy. Corporate interest groups have no outside membership. *See also* Iron Triangles (political science)

Interest Group (*public administration*)   A group of individuals concerned with a specific issue or agenda. Interest groups seek to influence legislators to either adopt or favor their particular cause. Interest groups may go by a number of different names, including lobby group (perhaps the second most common term for them), advocacy group, pressure group, or special-interest group. Interest group members may share a variety of disparate political outlooks or personal concerns but are ultimately united by a single issue.

It is difficult to draw specific boundaries regarding the diversity of pressure groups, but most of these organizations can generally be broken into a number of distinct categories. This includes business groups, which can range from large corporations and industries to smaller businesses with enough capital to invest in local or national politics; professional organizations, such as medical or dental associations; and trade unions (although the role of the traditional union has undoubtedly decreased in contemporary American society). Perhaps equally influential are promotional groups, which consist of people united by an explicitly political cause. The National Firearms Association embodies this particular category, as do more liberal organizations such as Greenpeace or the American Association of Retired People. Such organizations may also have an ethnic or international basis, as embodied by the Jewish-Israeli or Armenian-American lobbies. Finally, there are interest groups known as "Fire Brigades," which only unite around a specific cause during a particular time period. During the war in Iraq, for example, a variety of these organizations arose to protest against U.S. involvement in the Middle East and, subsequently, often pushed for American troops to return home.

Besides explicitly meeting with politicians and contributing to local and national congressmen, interest groups may attempt to hold large-scale demonstrations or invest in public awareness campaigns. Such organizations can also issue what are known as *amici curiae*, or legal briefs intended to influence and inform judicial opinion during active litigation. Although interest groups continue to wield a major influence in American politics, they have weathered increasing criticism from both ends of the political spectrum. Many opponents claim that lobbyists do not represent the "will of the constituents" at all but instead only benefit a particularly well-connected elite. Furthermore, critics contend that interest groups literally "buy off" their political targets, breeding a larger culture of corruption, and engage in clandestine and insidious quid pro quos (literally "something for something"). Their advocates continue to maintain, however, that interest groups are necessary for a true democracy to function, representing a plurality of public voices to relevant political actors. For more information, see Wright (2002). *See also* Diversity

Interest Party A political organization that combines the characteristics of both political parties and interest groups and runs candidates for legislative elections. An interest party is not quite a matured political party but is also no longer a mere interest group. One of the first interest parties was the French Union de Fraternité-Française, formed in the mid 1950s.

Interest parties differ from political parties in several ways. First, interest parties' scope of interest is narrower than that of political parties. The scope of interest usually surrounds only a single issue, even though the issue may address a broader public concern. Second, the form of the interest party is less structured than that of a political party. Third, interest groups have political histories whereby they often began as voluntary associations rather than making their first electoral appearance as interest parties competing for votes.

Unlike the political model in the United States, which distinguishes between political parties and interest groups, interest parties are found in other parts of the world. For example, ecological interest parties exist in places such as Denmark, Belgium, Ireland, Italy, and Switzerland.

Intergovernmental Relations The complex relationships between different levels of government, within the framework of political, fiscal, programmatic, and administrative processes. Intergovernmental relations are often simply referred to as federalism in action. A federal system of government shares power between the central government and regional governments (including states, provinces, cantons, and lands). Within its own area of jurisdiction, each government is legally supreme. In the United States, based on the Constitution, certain powers are reserved for the federal government, others are reserved for the states, and some power is shared. Intergovernmental relations extend beyond national-state relations and encompass national-local, state-local, national-state-local, and interlocal relations.

The U.S. Constitution, by defining federalism, sets forth features of intergovernmental relations through three constitutional provisions. The first is the creation of a federal system of government with a national government and state governments. The second is the allocation of specific powers or functions to the national government. The third is the power of the Supreme Court to interpret the Constitution, thereby having the authority to alter the powers and functions of national and state governments.

Since intergovernmental relations encompass numerous actors, including nonprofit organizations, there can often be confusion as to accountability; it is not always clear which level of government is responsible for specific actions. Furthermore, there is often duplication and issues of unfairness. Nonetheless, a federal system of government provides for policy making and debate in a large diverse society. For more information, see Starling (2008). *See also* Federalism

Internal Validity A concern with whether the variation in the independent variable(s) caused or influenced observed variation in the dependent variable(s). Threats to internal validity (e.g., selection effects, history, mortality, etc.) should be identified before making any conclusions. Furthermore, a research study can only be internally valid if it measures what it is intended to measure. *See also* Validity

Internal Validity, Types of The researcher's ability to control extraneous variables in an experiment so that he or she can legitimately conclude that an observed effect is due to the treatment. Internal validity is required if the researcher desires to make the claim that variations in the independent variable *caused* variations in the dependent variable. Careful design of the experiment helps reduce the threat to internal validity. Campbell and Stanley (1963) identified several potential threats to the internal validity of a study. *History* refers to the impact of other events occurring during the period of the experimental manipulation. To avoid threats relating to history, researchers try to control the experiences of the treatment and the control groups to the extent possible. *Maturation* refers to natural physical or psychological growth that participants in a study may experience, independent of the treatment in the study. The use of a control group helps reduce this threat. If the treatment group has a greater gain from pretest measurement to posttest measurement than does a carefully selected control group, the difference between the two groups' gains can be attributed to the treatment intervention rather than to the natural growth or maturation of participants.

Testing refers to potential changes or learning that participants may experience simply by completing a pretest measure. The participants may demonstrate greater scores on the posttest because they have been primed or have learned from the simple experience of taking the pretest. Observed gains from pretest to posttest are thus not legitimately attributable to the treatment.

Instrumentation refers to the learning gains (or losses) observed from the pretest to the posttest that are due to changes in the measures used. Instrumentation threats may be due to differential difficulty between the pretest and the posttest or observer drift on the rating scales.

This threat can be reduced by using the same measure at the pretest and the posttest and by periodic checking and training of raters for consistency.

Regression artifacts refers to the statistical tendency of very high pretest scores to become lower and very low pretest scores to become higher on the posttest measurement. This phenomenon is also called regression to the mean because some individuals who score at the extremes on the pretest measurement have scores that are closer to the mean on subsequent test administrations. When regression artifacts are present, pretest to posttest changes cannot be attributed to the treatment.

Selection refers to the systematic differences between the treatment and control groups because the groups are composed of different kinds of people. When the groups are systematically different on variables other than the independent variable, the difference between the groups cannot be attributed to the treatment. For example, the treatment group may have greater abilities on the construct of interest than the control group, which could taint the conclusions. Randomly assigning individuals to the groups is the best way to reduce this threat because it probabilistically "equates" the groups on all variables other than the independent variable. For more information, see Campbell and Stanley (1963). ***See also*** Experimental Research; Experimental Research Designs

International Aid The support rendered by the wealthier nations to the poor nations to finance their development. As such, it is a crucial component and the largest source of development assistance to the poor countries. The World Bank's International Development Association (IDA), which was established in 1960, provides interest-free (concessional) loans and grants to poorer nations to alleviate the level of poverty by enhancing economic growth, reducing inequalities, and improving living conditions. It also provides relief to countries that are in severe debt and in financial trouble. Repayments are stretched over 35 to 40 years, including a 10-year grace period.

The United Nations (UN) encourages relatively wealthier countries to provide a percentage of their gross national income (approximately less than 1%) in the form of international assistance or official development assistance (ODA). ODA flows comprise contributions of the donor government and government agencies at the bilateral and multilateral levels. Multilateral institutions such as the International Monetary Fund and the World Bank play a crucial role in the dissemination of multilateral aid.

To the extent that international aid is fungible, it may not always achieve its targeted purpose, particularly in situations where public officials are corrupt. Also, it is not unusual for international aid to be tied to a quid pro quo. For example, the purchase of exports from donor countries may be tied to aid.

International aid imposes a questionable debt burden on poor countries when sovereign debts are contracted under illegal circumstances and generate no national benefit. The theory of odious debts captures the illegality of debts, including concessional ones.

By the 1990s, the preconditions for international aid were adjusted to attain better results. The rules, institutional framework, and institutions promoting private and official flows (financial architecture) were designed to consider the national impact, in particular the reduction of poverty and improvement in efficacy.

Changes include (a) intensified debt relief (poverty reduction strategy requirements) for a larger number of poor countries (including bilateral and multilateral debt reduction); (b) "institutional" readjustments incorporating programmatic lending rather than project lending; (c) concerted, coordinated, or alignment lending, which emphasizes greater harmonization of lending terms and policies; and (d) national ownership of debt obligation by the recipient countries. For more information, see Claessens, Cassimon, and Campenhout (2007) and Warburton (2005). ***See also*** Bank; Debt; International Monetary Fund (IMF)

International Baccalaureate Schools (IB) An educational organization that offers three programs from elementary to high school: Primary-Years Programme (ages 3 to 12), Middle-Years Programme (ages 11 to 16), and Diploma Programme (ages 16 to 19). With over 2,000 schools in 126 countries, IB diplomas are internationally recognized.

International Date Line An imaginary line on the earth that separates two consecutive calendar days. The date in the Western Hemisphere, to the right of the line, is always one day behind the date in the Eastern Hemisphere. While the line has no force in international law, it is, however, recognized as a convenience.

Without the international date line, travelers headed west would discover on their return that an additional day had passed, even if they kept an accurate record of the number of days traveled. A historic example of this occurred during Magellan's cruise to circumnavigate the globe. Conversely, traveling eastward would result in one day less traveled.

In theory, the international date line can be anywhere on the globe; however, it has been conveniently drawn at 180° from the meridian, which goes through Greenwich, England. This is especially convenient due to the fact that the majority of the area is covered by oceans, with a few zigs and zags for islands or island chains that would be otherwise divided into two separate dates; that said, the whales swimming across the line do not seem to mind.

Through history, the precise position of the line has changed several times. For example, until the mid 1800s, the Philippines were on the Eastern side; however, as a colony it was more convenient for colonizers to change the date to make political and business relations with other colonies more convenient. Another example concerns Alaska; on its purchase by the United States in 1867, the line was adjusted to permit the land mass to have its date included with the lower 48 states. There is no international body that decides on which side of the line a nation lies; rather, it is a local choice.

International Economics A branch of economics that deals with the economic interdependence among nations, which involves international trade, international finance, and the effect of trade and finance on a nation's well being (development).

International trade theory deals with the reasons for trade and the consequences of trade. International trade theory has evolved over the years from mercantilism to globalization. Mercantilists generally believed that trade should be restricted for nations to acquire bullion (precious metals) in order to become wealthy and finance large armies and expansionary wars. By the 18th century, however, David Hume's price-specie-flow doctrine strongly discredited the mercantilist way of thinking. Hume showed that the mercantilist theory is self-defeating and futile because of the inflationary consequences of stock-piled bullion.

Subsequent theories of trade have focused on resource endowment and skill acquisition, absolute and comparative costs, and globalization (integration due to technological breakthroughs). Absolute advantage is based on resource availability and skill acquisition, while comparative cost is closely associated with the opportunity cost of production.

Nations trade for a variety of reasons, including differences in taste, climatic conditions, endowment, technological advancement, cost of production, and preferences; but nations also have a tendency to impose restrictions on trade in order to derive a competitive advantage or secure rational self-interest. They, therefore, frame an international trade policy.

As a result of international trade, nations must pay for the goods and services they consume. The items of the goods and services they consume are recorded in their balance of payments. Payments for goods and services consumed require foreign reserves or foreign currencies; as such, international economics deal with the mechanisms of acquiring, managing, and spending financial resources (international finance). International finance includes the role of the International Monetary Fund (IMF) and depository institutions (banks) in the settlement of payments.

Not all nations benefit equally from trade, but all nations obtain incremental benefits from trade. Consequently, trade is not a zero-sum game. Nations that benefit disproportionately from trade may encounter balance-of-payments or adjustment problems as they correct their deficits or salvage the value of their currencies. The IMF was instituted in the 1940s to deal with these kinds of problems in the short run. However, the policies of the IMF have not always been very successful in correcting the balance-of-payments problems.

Stabilization policies have wider repercussions because they affect the economic interaction of nations, as a result of adjustments, and the movement of economic resources. International economics also deal with the adjustment mechanisms. Adjustments may take several forms, such as (a) international migration of labor to areas of higher-paying jobs, (b) tariffs, (c) movement of capital to areas of high return, (d) demand for political changes or a more equitable distribution of national income, (e) demand to reduce poverty, (f) solicitation of loans from depository institutions, and (g) reform of the exchange-rate regime. For more information, see Bhagwati (2004), Lowenfeld (2003), Perkins, Radlet, and Lindauer (2006), Stiglitz (2003), and Warburton (2005). *See also* Absolute Advantage; Balance of Payments (BOP) (economics); Comparative Advantage; Devaluation; Exchange Rate; Free Trade; Globalization; International Monetary Fund (IMF); Mercantilism; Stabilization; World Trade Organization (WTO)

International Law A set of rules recognized by nations as governing their conduct toward each other and toward each other's citizens. In addition, certain international organizations (such as the United Nations), corporations, and sometimes individuals may have rights or duties under international law. International law is sometimes viewed as a by-product of the rise of the nation-state in the 17th century.

Broadly speaking, international law deals with the formation and recognition of states, the acquisition of territory, war, the law of the sea and of space, treaties, the treatment of human rights, transnational and international crimes, and international judicial settlement of disputes. Early concepts of international law focused only on the relationships between and among sovereign states. However, the 20th century has gradually brought the individual to the fore. A large body of international law exists in the form of treaties, conventions, and principles. Their enforcement depends on the states themselves, although one of the parties may appeal to the International Court of Justice or seek some other form of arbitration. Broad conventions cover a diverse range of topics from efforts to protect women and children from discrimination to the control of cyber crime. International law is not devoid of criticism. First, observers have noted that the private interests of states prevail. Commentators highlight the fact that states' private interests often override the wider public concern for compliance with international law and that international tribunals seem to play only a minor role in the enforcement of international law. Second, strong states ignore international law. Because international law is not enforced by a sovereign power (in contrast to national law), its significance is often disputed.

A more recent dimension of international law concerns the development of a universal jurisdiction capable of imposing respect for international law. For example, the 1990s saw the United Nations Security Council authorize the use of force in response to violations of international law and to provide humanitarian assistance. The Council also established two international criminal tribunals: for the former

Yugoslavia and for Rwanda. The international criminal court has attempted to bring to justice the leaders or former leaders of states such as Liberia and the Sudan, which have witnessed atrocities and genocidal actions. Such coercive measures suggest that the concept of global enforcement of international law is now more real than theoretical, although it is limited to the realm of threats to international peace and security, and even in this realm, it proves to be selective. For more information, see Jones (2003), Picker (2001), and Ratner and Abrams (2001). ***See also*** Law (political science)

International Monetary Fund (IMF) The International Monetary Fund (IMF) was founded in 1944 at the Bretton Woods conference in New Hampshire. The conference was an urgent attempt to deal with the interregnum problems associated with international trade and exchange-rate instability. John Maynard Keynes of Britain and Harry Dexter White of the United States came up with plans to allow deficit nations to recover from temporary balance-of-payments problems. Regulations of the IMF dealing with the purposes, membership, quotas, subscriptions, and exchange-rate arrangements are outlined in Articles I through III of the IMF's Articles of Agreement.

A major objective of the IMF was to create a pool of resources based on mandatory contributions from its members, which could be drawn by member states to settle balance-of-payments problems. Each member of the IMF is assigned a quota, which is indicative of its importance in the global economy. The greater the importance of a nation to the global economy, the larger its quota (contribution) is expected to be. Contributions to the IMF have been payable in hard assets: one quarter in gold, or Special Drawing Rights (SDRs) (after amendment of the articles), and three quarters in members' currencies.

Deficit nations purchase foreign currency using their own currencies to settle balance-of-payments deficit, and as their balance-of-payments position improves, they are expected to repurchase their currencies from the IMF. A nation can borrow a quarter of its gold tranche without restriction or conditions. The IMF charges interest rates and imposes conditions for borrowing its resources.

The resulting compromise out of the Bretton Woods system to deal with exchange-rate volatility was the *adjustable peg,* otherwise known as the gold exchange standard. The *adjustable peg* system allowed countries to peg their currencies and also to finance out of international reserves.

In the 1950s, a system of *standby arrangements* guaranteed members lines of credit with the IMF. The IMF introduced a new reserve asset, SDRs or paper gold, in the 1970s as a result of high inflation and illiquidity problems. The Bretton Woods system ultimately collapsed in the 1970s, partly because gold cannot keep up with the volume of trade and also because America could no longer defend the convertibility of dollars to gold. For more information, see Carbaugh (2007), Lowenfeld (2003), and Perkins, Radlet, and Lindauer (2006). ***See also*** Balance of Payments (BOP) (economics); Exchange Rate; Free Trade; Globalization; Stabilization

Internet A system of computer networks that interconnects worldwide and uses a set of telecommunication protocols called Transmission Control Protocol/Internet Protocol (TCP/IP). Together, these protocols provide for a virtual connection that allows for the transferring and forwarding of information, via packets of data, to intended locations. Social and behavioral scientists rely heavily on the Internet as a tool for gathering both primary and secondary data. Potential uses include obtaining raw data for analysis, finding information about a particular theory or methodology to be used in a research project, or reviewing literature to put new research in context. The study of the impact of the Internet itself is a prevalent research topic in all reaches of these disciplines.

The predecessor to the Internet was conceived in the late 1960s by the Advanced Research Projects Agency (ARPA), a unit of the U.S. Defense Department. The original network, Advanced Research Projects Agency Network (ARPANET), was designed to support communication among military computers, defense department laboratories, and selected university departments. Over the next two decades, the system proved to be useful to computer science departments, major industrial laboratories, and a growing number of departments in academia.

Colloquially, the terms *World Wide Web* and *Internet* are often mistakenly interchanged. Though the Web is the most widely used part and largest generator of traffic on the Internet, it is but one service of the Internet. The most salient characteristic of the Web is the use of hypertext, a virtual-network-based information system that allows users to browse a variety of linked Internet resources organized by graphics-oriented pages.

The Web is not the equivalent of the Internet but rather uses the Internet as its transport mechanism. Many people use the term *Internet* as a medium—for example, "I found the article on the Internet." In essence, they did find the article via the Internet but, more accurately and specifically, on the World Wide Web. Other services of the Internet include e-mail, remote access, file sharing, streaming media, and voice telephony.

In general, *Internet,* used with an initial capital letter, refers to the worldwide, publicly available IP Internet, while *internet,* with a lowercase initial letter, can refer to any interconnected set of distinct networks that can exist between any two remote locations. The term *intranet* is generally used for private networks.

In the early years of its existence, the Internet was supported by the U.S. Government but now depends largely on support from commercial interests. The overall responsibility for managing IP addresses and domain names (the unique name that identifies an Internet network system or Web site) rests with the

Internet Assigned Numbers Authority (IANA). For more information, see Hafner and Lyon (1998). ***See also*** Technology (media studies)

Interorganizational Networks The patterns and structure of relationships within various groups and organizations. An interorganizational network is often considered a strategic means by which to improve an entity's competitive advantage, manage uncertain environments, and satisfy their resource needs. Consequently, organizations enter into ties with other organizations that have resources and capabilities that can help them manage such constraints and environmental forces, which are beyond their direct control. Such coalitions are formed between task- or skill-specialized economic entities, independent firms, or autonomous organizational units and are characterized by trust and exchange of information with specific partners. Alliances are also formed in response to the need to share the costs and risks of technology development or large-scale projects, as well as to develop existing markets or penetrate new ones.

Growth in interorganizational networks began following the Industrial Revolution in the late 18th century with the functional-specialization organizations of the early steel markets, followed by the automobile companies of the early 20th century, which catered to limited markets, and continued through to the multidivisional organizations of the cement, steel, textile, and automobile companies, which aimed at providing a variety of products to more demanding markets. Growth was not accelerated until the 1980s. Over the past 15 years, partly as a response to the growing uncertainty that characterizes the international business arena, the number of interorganizational alliances has grown at an unprecedented rate across a wide array of industries and both within and across geographical boundaries.

Interorganizational networks are associated with a variety of risks and consequences, resulting in uncertainty about the decision to form such alliances. Most notably, organizations are challenged with obtaining information about the competencies, needs, and reliability of potential partners. Thus, there must be proper and extensive due diligence prior to the formation of a network. ***See also*** Network

Interorganizational Relationships Relationships between two or more organizations that share or exchange information or resources. Oftentimes, the goal of establishing interorganizational relationships is to increase the amount of available resources in an organization by drawing from the resources of a different organization. ***See also*** Organization (education)

Interpersonal Communication A variety of discursive methods used by individuals to achieve certain goals that include persuading, informing, comforting, challenging, and other modes of dealing with people. Many sensory channels are used, but increasingly, the term refers not only to face-to-face encounters but also to mediated interaction through technological devices such as computers (e-mail) and telephones (also with text-messaging capabilities).

All forms of interpersonal communication involve gaining knowledge of others. Varieties of interpersonal communication theories, strategies, and aims coexist. These include social penetration theory, or how we gain information about others; norm of reciprocity, or how individuals reveal themselves to others (dyadic effect or level of revealed intimacy); and compensation (one's behavior is countered by another, as in facial expressions; variations on this theory are expectancy violation, arousal labeling theory, discrepancy arousal theory, and cognitive valence theory), among many others. Depending on the knowledge gained, we interact with people more efficiently. We can better predict how they will think, feel, and act if we know them. We gain this information passively, by observing them actively, by having others engage them, or, interactively, by engaging them ourselves. Self-disclosure, as in revealed intimacy, is often used to get information from another person.

Interpersonal communication helps us understand the context in which someone is speaking or writing. Context and expression frequently determine the meaning of words. Content messages refer to the surface-level meaning of a message. Relationship messages refer to how a message is said. Content messages and relationship messages are sent simultaneously, but each affects the meaning assigned to the communication. Interpersonal communication helps us understand each other better.

Interpersonal communication also establishes or constructs identity and public image through the interaction of the roles and faces presented in our relationships with others. William Schutz (1958) has identified three needs involved in interpersonal communication: (1) inclusion, (2) control, and (3) affection. Inclusion is the need to establish identity with others. Control is the need to exercise leadership and prove one's abilities. Groups provide an outlet for this need. Some individuals shun leadership roles and look to groups to establish relationships and friendships. For them, groups provide the necessary control and support for certain facets of their lives and fulfill the basic human need for affection. For more information, see Berger (1997) and Schultz (1958). ***See also*** Communication Theory

INTERPOL An acronym for the International Criminal Police Organization. This is a consortium of international police forces based in Paris, France. The organization promotes collaboration among law enforcement and intelligence agencies across the world and aims to bring to justice international criminals, as well as those who escape abroad to avoid prosecution in another country. INTERPOL also promotes research on comparative and international criminal justice issues. ***See also*** International Law

Interrogation   A formal method of inquiry used by the police or other law enforcement officials that involves asking individuals (generally held in custody) questions about specific events or circumstances. With the exception of providing basic information, such as name and address, the individual being interrogated has the right to remain silent (under the Fifth Amendment) and is not under any obligation to answer questions raised during the interrogation. Furthermore, the individual being interrogated also has the right to request the presence of his or her lawyer, at which point the interrogation must stop. If the suspect's legal rights are violated, the information gathered during the interrogation cannot be used as evidence in court under the exclusionary rule. *See also* Exclusionary Rule; Fruit of the Poisonous Tree

Interscorer/Interrater Reliability   Consistency among raters, for example, similarity among the scores awarded by Olympic judges. When scores or ratings are continuously measured, reliability is usually measured by correlation coefficients. When ratings are categorical, Cohen's kappa is a common measure. Interscorer/interrater reliability matters for the same reason that other kinds of measurement reliability matter: Only if the scores are reliable (consistent), can they be added together to form a valid measure. *See also* Test-Retest Reliability; Validity

Intersubjectivity   The shared meaning and understanding created by two or more individuals through dialogical conversation. The concept was introduced by Husserl and is central to the research tradition of phenomenology. If one accepts the existence of multiple subjective realities within social contexts, intersubjective discourse creates subjective mutual awareness, coconstructs an intersubjective reality, and shapes a shared worldview. For more information, see van Manen (1997). *See also* Phenomenology

Intertextuality   The idea that understanding or interpreting a text or any media form can only take place by understanding the system of signs and symbols that are already in circulation because of other texts. Intertextuality is a direct challenge to the notion that a text holds its meaning within itself and that the reader or viewer merely needs to uncover an already determined meaning. Intertextuality instead proposes that a text must be read in relation to other texts, to already existing systems of meanings, and to the larger sociocultural practices that surround the text. For intertextual readings, the meaning of the text is never stable but necessarily changes in relation to other texts or cultural practices that are brought into play. A popularization of the term can be demonstrated by the cross-media references in many movies and television programs, which comment on or quote each other and make connections between seemingly unrelated texts. For more information, see Allen (2000). *See also* Text

Interventionist   A term generally used to refer to an actor who (with or without permission) involves himself or herself in the affairs of another. In politics, interventionism is generally viewed in a negative sense and usually refers to the forced manipulation of one nation-state by a more powerful one. This can be through either economic or military means and may be motivated by a number of different objectives (to seize resources, preempt a supposedly imminent attack, resolve a human rights crisis, etc.). In economics, interventionism is usually characterized by state involvement in market activities. Although economists often deride interventionism as socially ineffective and financially regressive, state enforcement is almost always considered mandatory in terms of contract enforcement and monetary circulation. Taxes and minimum-wage laws also constitute popular forms of economic interventionism, although their proper restrictions and scope are consistently under debate (whereas American liberals favor a more interventionist approach, traditional conservatives value a generally unregulated free market). For more information, see Boaz (1998). *See also* Free Trade; Regulation (economics)

Interview *(education)*   A method of data collection, in which the interviewer asks questions of the interviewee(s). Interviews require that the interviewer be skilled at asking questions, fully listening and probing when necessary for clarity, detail, and shared understanding. Interviews may be structured, semistructured, or unstructured. In structured and semistructured interviews, the questions are predetermined, while unstructured interviews are more informal, with more opportunity for variations in answers. Data collected during interviews may be captured through audio or video recording or in handwritten notes. *See also* Data, Extant/Existing; Qualitative Research

Interview *(sociology)*   A formal discussion in which an individual is asked to provide information about a specific topic. The interviewer is the person leading the meeting, and the interviewee is the individual answering the questions. There are two main types of interviews: (1) structured and (2) unstructured. Structured interviews follow very specific guidelines, with detailed questions, a predetermined ordering of issues to be addressed, and a standard format that is applied uniformly to all interviewees. In contrast, unstructured interviews do not have a predetermined format or detailed questions but rather focus on more general issues. While unstructured interviews are not as precise as structured interviews, the unstructured format often provides more in-depth information about the topic at hand. *See also* Qualitative Research; Research

Intolerance   The human inability or refusal to accept differences in behaviors, cultural identities, economic status, or religious and political beliefs. Intolerance reflects narrow-mindedness and bigotry and, throughout human history, has led to social injustices, ranging from discrimination and repression to civil strife, persecution, and genocide.

Among the notable studies on intolerance is the one conducted with Jewish American and African American veterans of World War II by Bruno Bettelheim and Morris Janowitz, in which interviewees of two historically repressed groups showed tendencies to reiterate stereotypes about each other.

The subject of intolerance has been addressed by world leaders, including the slain civil rights leader Dr. Martin Luther King Jr., the Dalai Lama, and the late Pope John Paul II. A 2002 United Nations report, issued for the 25th anniversary of The Declaration on the Elimination of All Forms of Intolerance and of Discrimination Based on Religion or Belief, noted no decrease in the incidence of intolerance. For more information, see Bettelheim and Janowitz (1964) and United Nations (2002). ***See also*** Intercultural Communication/Cross-Cultural Communication; Propaganda (political science); Racism (education, psychology); Stereotyping

Intrapersonal Communication   The internal processes that human beings use to communicate within themselves. Most individuals are familiar with interpersonal communication, which refers to communication between individuals. Intrapersonal communication refers to the internal factors that contribute to how individuals process information and how these processes lead to the development of attitudes, self-concepts, meanings of symbols, and memories.

A way to understand this concept is by comparing it with interpersonal communication. In interpersonal communication, an individual gives information (the sender) to another individual (the receiver). There is a constant interaction, both verbally and nonverbally, between the sender and the receiver. For intrapersonal communication, the individual both sends and receives the information within himself or herself. Thus, the individual is involved in what is considered as "self-talk." There is a symbolic interaction within the individual, as expressed through a type of mental speech. Many theorists, including Sigmund Freud and George Herbert Mead, have discussed the notion of internal processes and how individuals take the information they receive from the external world, internalize it, and have some sort of symbolic interaction within themselves when processing this information.

Intrapersonal communication is a complex area of research and study. The study of intrapersonal communication involves discussing the physiological aspects of human beings, particularly the structure and processing models of the brain. Cognitive theories, such as the role of memory and language, have been applied to the study and discussion of intrapersonal communication due to its importance in how people receive and store information. The processes involved with developing attitudes, self-concepts, symbols, and

beliefs and how speaking and listening to other people greatly contributes to these developments are also aspects of intrapersonal communication that have been emphasized. Other elements, such as culture, gender, and religion, can also influence the type of intrapersonal processes individuals can experience.

Although intrapersonal communication can involve the research of numerous theorists, knowledge of physiology, and awareness of concepts related to cognition and affect, it is a lifelong process that human beings may not be fully aware of. A variety of examples of intrapersonal processes occur in everyday life. For example, praying or reciting a poem is a conscious way by which individuals communicate with themselves. Daydreaming and nocturnal dreaming can be considered subconscious internal processes. Reading, writing, and using other bodily movements, such as counting on one's fingers, are examples of internal communication to understand ideas. Intrapersonal communication is a constant, complex process that helps individuals develop ideas, concentration skills, memory, and problem-solving skills. For more information, see Goss (1982) and Vocate (1994). ***See also*** Interpersonal Communication

Intrinsic Motivation   The drive that leads an individual to engage in an activity without being externally rewarded for that action. In the context of learning, a student is intrinsically motivated if the process of learning is considered important and brings him or her joy. In contrast, a student who is extrinsically motivated is driven by external rewards, such as good grades. Intrinsic motivation has been found to be related to high achievement and how much students enjoy the learning process. There is currently no unified theory of intrinsic motivation. ***See also*** Extrinsic Motivation

Introspection   A method of experimental research in which a participant self-observes inner, conscious sensations and perceptions (Wundt, 1888) (the term is derived from the German word *Selbstbeobachtung*). While the method can be dated as far back as Socrates, it was Wilhelm Wundt who employed the method in an experimental setting in 1879. As a result, Wundt was credited with establishing the first experimental psychology laboratory. In recent times, a similar method has been popularized by cognitive psychology experiments, coined "thinking-aloud" protocols, in which the participant has to think aloud while participating in experimental research. This method allows experimenters to observe the introspective act and is closely related to the concept of metacognition. For more information, see Wundt (1888). ***See also*** Experiment; Experimental Research

Investigate   To conduct an in-depth examination about a given topic, situation, or individual or to engage in a systematic examination of causes and facts related to any given query. In research, investigation entails the gathering of relevant information, analysis, and conclusions drawn from the inquiry. In the criminal justice system, an investigation is the gathering of evidence by the police about an illegal act or the person who is suspected of committing that act. *See also* Evidence

Investment An asset or item that is purchased with the hope that it will generate income or appreciate in the future. The word originated from the Latin word *vestis,* which means "garment." The term is used differently in economics and in finance. In economics, investment refers to the production per unit time of goods that are not consumed but are used for future production. The building of a factory used to produce goods and the investment one makes by going to college or university are both examples, tangible and intangible, respectively, of investments in the economic sense.

In finance, an investment is where an investor puts money into a vehicle or a monetary asset is purchased with the intent that the asset will provide income in the future or appreciate and be sold at a higher price. Investments can include the purchase of shares, bonds, or stocks. Such financial assets are then expected to provide income or positive future cash flows and may increase or decrease in value, giving the investor capital gains or losses. *See also* Capital Gain; Income

Ionosphere The uppermost portion of the earth's atmosphere, situated above the stratosphere. Located approximately 80 kilometers from the surface of the earth, the ionosphere earns its name because it is ionized by solar radiation, sometimes referred to as solar wind. Comprising three distinct layers, the ionosphere facilitates the transmission of AM (amplitude modulated) radio frequency waves back to earth, as radio signals are actually reflected off of this layer of the atmosphere. It is important to note that FM (frequency modulated) radio and television wavelengths are too short to be reflected back to earth by the ionosphere and are instead transmitted via satellite.

Iron Triangles *(political science)* Closed, mutually supportive groups having jurisdiction over a particular area of government policy. The cohesion of iron triangles allows them to dominate policy making in their areas of interest. Iron triangles, typically, comprise three elements, each located on one tip of the triangle model. On the lower left tip are interest groups, also known as constituencies, comprising members who share a common interest and can influence congressional votes by guaranteeing reelection of congressional members in return for supporting their programs. On the lower right corner are bureaucrats, who are often pressurized by the interest groups their agencies are designated to regulate. At the top are usually Congress, but sometimes House, committee or subcommittee members, who are responsible for oversight and regulation of policy. Congressional members may align themselves with a constituency for political support

while simultaneously supporting legislation that advances an interest group's agenda.

The term *iron triangle* was coined in 1964 by Douglass Cater, who theorized that public policy results from interested sets of actors. The central assumption of iron triangles is that bureaucratic agencies seek to consolidate their power base. They need constituencies to do this. Constituencies are well organized, have resources, are easily mobilized, and are active in political affairs, such as voting, lobbying, and granting campaign contributions. In addition, constituencies can provide useful information to the committees and agencies. If supported, congressional committee members can continue the pet programs or pork barrel projects important to the constituencies or do special favors for them.

In 1978, Hugh Heclo postulated an alternative theory to iron triangles. Contrary to Cater's characterization of iron triangles as closed and impenetrable, Heclo stated that issue networks, otherwise known as shared-knowledge groups, are more pluralistic and penetrable than iron triangles. *See also* Congress; Constituency (political science); Interest Group (political science)

Iron Triangles *(public administration)* Public policy is influenced, in many cases, by relationships between members of the federal bureaucracy, congressional subcommittees, and interest groups. These are often cozy relationships that are mutually beneficial and are referred to as iron triangles or subgovernments. Examining an iron triangle aligned with the issue of tobacco, a federal agency such as the Department of Agriculture, especially its division on tobacco, is likely to interact regularly with the subcommittees of the House and Senate agricultural committees. Such interactions are likely to involve budget requests and approval, hearings on division performance, and other implementation-related concerns. Interest groups, such as the tobacco lobby of both farmers and manufacturers, are likely to interact with both congressional committees and members of the bureaucracy. The bureaucracy, for example, will issue rulings on tobacco production and pricing. Interest groups may share information about the industry or may show support for agency budget requests. With congressional committees, interest groups can provide campaign contributions and support as a way of generating interest in their concerns. They may share industry information with members of Congress. Congress is responsible for drafting legislation that affects the tobacco industry. When an iron triangle exists, it is presumed that legislative decisions are influenced by the campaign contributions and information exchanged by members of interest groups. In the case of tobacco, farmers have enjoyed crop subsidies regardless of the health risks and impact of smoking on the public. This relationship has come under fire from others in the area of health care who are not generally involved in the tobacco policy process. *See also* Bureaucracy (public administration); Interest Group (public administration)

Irresistible Impulse   A form of defense that argues that the defendant was driven by uncontrollable urges at the time of the offense (also defined as a form of insanity), which led him or her to engage in the act. Irresistible impulse implies that the individual was aware of the fact that the act constituted an infraction but that he or she was driven by impulses beyond his or her control. *See also* Insanity Defense

ISLLC Standards (Interstate School Leaders Licensure Consortium)   Standards adopted in 1996 to guide the work of current and future school leaders. The underlying concepts of the six standards call for leaders to develop a vision of learning and, with integrity, manage resources to establish a culture of student success.

Isolationism   The refusal of a country to intervene in the affairs of other nations, by declining to enter into alliances, foreign economic commitments, and wars, in order to remain in a state of neutrality. The first articulation of an isolationist posture in the United States is found in George Washington's Farewell Address in 1796. In it, he states, "It is our true policy to steer clear of permanent alliances with any portion of the foreign world; . . . in my opinion, it is unnecessary and would be unwise to extend them." Thomas Jefferson further articulated isolationism in his first inaugural address in 1801: "peace, commerce, and honest friendship with all nations, entangling alliances with none." The Monroe Doctrine in 1823 later emphasized nonintervention in European politics.

The central tenet of isolationism, from the era of the founders until the end of World War II, was that the United States should take advantage of its geographic distance from Europe and refrain from intervention in its affairs. The reasons for this refusal for participation stemmed in part from Americans' views that America could advance the cause of freedom and democracy by means other than war. To Americans, the avoidance of involvement abroad was a less important consideration than preserving the nation's freedom to carry out the decisions that best defended its democratic values and economic interests. This sentiment would continue until the 1930s, with the belief that European affairs are full of insincerity, devious methods, secrets, treachery, weakness, and immorality, all of which would corrupt America's democratic idealism.

The first major departure from isolationism occurred when the United States agreed to enter World War I after German submarines sank American merchant ships. Isolationist sentiment, however, resurged as a response to Woodrow Wilson's unsatisfactory settlement of World War I. Legislators imposed tariffs on foreign goods to shield manufacturers and restricted immigration.

Neutrality in military and political conflicts overseas remained until the 1930s. Involvement in world economic, cultural, and humanitarian affairs became accepted, or at least not denounced. In 1939, the America First Committee was formed by a group of wealthy men, including the aviator Charles Lindbergh, which essentially promoted an anti–New Deal crusade against President Franklin D. Roosevelt. It was disbanded after Japan's attack on Pearl Harbor in 1941, which brought the United States into World War II. The end of World War II marked the end of the major isolationist policies. In 1945, the United States became a charter member of the United Nations. Today, neo-isolationists recognize that there is a connection between global events and American security. As such, these groups favor scaling back rather than renunciation of overseas commitments. For more information, see Kennedy (2002) and *Washington's Farewell Address to the People of the United States* (2000). *See also* Monroe Doctrine

Isotope   A type of chemical element containing a different number of neutrons than electrons and protons in its nucleus. All elements contain an atom, which consists of particles of positive and negative charges— protons and electrons. The protons and electrons are found inside the nucleus, with the proton determining what element the atom is. In addition, atoms contain neutrons, which surround the nucleus and have no electrical charge. Some isotopes are unstable, and in the process of stabilizing, isotopes can lose particles, a process usually referred to as radiation. Unstable isotopes are known as radioisotopes and can release three types of radiation, otherwise known as alpha, beta, and gamma rays. All these rays are capable of causing harm to human beings, as exposure to radiation can result in the formation of abnormal cells. However, the potential for harm depends on the frequency and duration of exposure to radiation.

Issue Networks   An arrangement that can have a significant influence on the policy-making process. Sometimes referred to as "subgovernments," issue networks are informal arrangements between policy actors with a particular interest and area of specialization in a policy issue. These issue areas, for example, may be national defense, the environment, energy, communications, or agriculture. In many instances, decision making about these policy issues tends to be highly specialized due to their complexity. Decisions are often made as a result of interactions between three key components: (1) congressional subcommittees, (2) an executive agency, and (3) an outside economic-interest group, such as farmers, the telecommunications industry, or the oil industry. Members of these components develop channels of communication and even specialized language or terminology to discuss the policy issue. When determining how much to spend on weapons systems and which arms to procure, for example, congressional armed services committees, the Department of Defense, and private defense contractors that build and provide weapons will interact to determine a course of action. In many instances, many within this issue network are likely to favor defense spending and will work together to increase national defense system capacities. Public input is often limited, with few inlets to determine public support or to foster public oversight. Many policy decisions are made in this way, keeping much of the discussion limited to issue insiders in the backstage of the policy arena. ***See also*** Iron Triangles (political science, public administration); Lobbying

Item Discrimination Index An index that examines whether a test item is able to distinguish between individuals with high-ability levels and those with low-ability levels. A popular calculation of the index is the corrected point-biserial correlation between the item score and the total test score. ***See also*** Classical Measurement Theory

Item Response Theory A set of methods that addresses the difficulty, reliability, validity, and fairness of test items. It is an improvement on classical test theory, which has the same goals but uses less advanced statistical techniques. The basic tool of item response theory (IRT) is logistic regression, which is a kind of regression designed to study dichotomous outcome variables, such as right or wrong. Logistic regression is used to calculate the odds that test takers will answer a question correctly. The odds for a particular item add up to its item characteristic curve (ICC). Easy and hard items have different curves.

IRT is most commonly applied to educational testing. A good test will be composed of items that differentiate (discriminate) among students. Items that all students get right, or wrong, will tell the tester nothing about the comparative knowledge of the students. National standardized tests often aim for questions that 30% to 70% of students answer correctly. Can a question answered correctly by only 30% of students be a good one? It can if the most knowledgeable students answer it correctly and few of the least knowledgeable students do.

If that is the case, then the question differentiates among students who know the subject more and less well, which is the purpose of most tests.

An important use of IRT is creating different versions of a test at equivalent levels of difficulty. An example of the use of IRT that may be familiar is computer-adaptive testing (CAT). If you have taken a test (such a medical or law school admission tests) on a computer rather than with pencil and paper, chances are the testers used IRT to supply you with questions and calculate your score. The program starts with a question of middling difficulty. If you answer it correctly, you get increasingly more difficult questions until you begin giving wrong answers. If you answer a question incorrectly, you get progressively easier questions until you start answering correctly. In this way your level of knowledge is assessed. Two people taking the same CAT on the same day are unlikely to get the same questions or even the same number of questions. Despite this, testing experts believe CAT to be fairer than the traditional methods because a CAT exam can more accurately determine your level of knowledge.

Another area of fairness in IRT is called differential item functioning (DIF). DIF occurs when an item's difficulty (its ICC) is different for different social groups. This is evidence that the item is unfair. A testing goal is to use only items that differentiate among individuals on the basis of their knowledge, not among groups on the basis of their social experience. ***See also*** Regression Analysis; Reliability; Validity

Item Veto A special power that allows a chief executive to prevent specific provisions of a bill enacted by a legislature from becoming law (also known as a line-item veto). For the federal government, the Line Item Veto Act of 1996 was signed into law by President Bill Clinton but was declared unconstitutional by the U.S. Supreme Court in 1998. ***See also*** Veto

J

Jail   Different from state and federal prisons, jails are generally operated at the local city or county level. Jails hold a variety of people, including those being detained before trial who were not granted bail or are unable to afford bail. Jails house offenders convicted of felony criminal charges who are awaiting sentencing of more than one year in a prison, as well as offenders found guilty of misdemeanors sentenced to serve less than one year. Jails also hold offenders convicted of felonies awaiting transfer to a state prison. Given the variety of people housed in jails, they are generally considered more violent than prisons where the populations are relatively stable over time. ***See also*** Prison/Prisoner

James-Lange Theory   William James and Carl Lange developed this theory independently in 1884. It proposes that emotions are a result of physiological changes. The emphasis of the theory lies in the proposal that physiological changes in the autonomic nervous system result in emotions, not that emotions cause physiological changes. There is limited empirical evidence for the theory. The James-Lange theory has been challenged by other accounts of emotions, particularly the Cannon-Bard theory of emotion and the two-factor theory of emotion. For more information, see James (1884). ***See also*** Cannon-Bard Theory; Two-Factor Theory of Emotion

Jargon   Words, terms, or idiomatic expressions commonly used among members of a profession, occupation, or social class but not easily comprehended or recognized by persons outside those groups. Jargon often has a pejorative connotation, and its use is discouraged in publications. ***See also*** Slang

Jeffersonianism   A social philosophy expounding the beliefs of President Thomas Jefferson. Jefferson preferred a weak central government with simultaneous strong local governments. Jefferson believed that such an arrangement would be more responsive to the popular will than a strong central government. This sentiment stemmed from Jefferson's strong faith in the ability of the citizenry to govern itself.

As a yeoman farmer, Jefferson believed that the American economy should rely more on agriculture than on industry and big business. Jefferson did not trust big business. He believed that Americans could remain virtuous by minding their own agricultural affairs and that the government should not shape its economy on behalf of commerce and industrialization.

Jefferson also believed that all individuals have inalienable rights, or liberties, which could not be infringed by government or laws. He accepted the principle that government is everywhere and always at war with natural freedom. From this principle, Jefferson deduced that the lover of freedom will be jealous of delegated power and will seek to hold the political state to strict account. As a result, Jefferson strongly opposed the existence of a perpetual constitution or law. Rather, he believed that such instruments should constantly be subjected to and evolve from the will of the people, and inalienable rights should always come first. Jeffersonianism thus promoted constant vigilance to safeguard the freedoms of the people from encroachment by the state. ***See also*** Natural Rights

Jeopardy   In the general sense, a risk of danger, peril, or loss. In the legal system, jeopardy is defined as the risk faced by defendants when charged with an offense and faced with possible conviction and punishment. The Fifth Amendment protects individuals against double jeopardy, which means that no person can be tried twice, in the same court, for the same crime. ***See also*** Double Jeopardy (political science, sociology)

Jim Crow Laws   Laws that were enacted after the American Civil War, mainly in the Southern states, which legalized the segregation between African American and Caucasian groups. In 1896, the U.S. Supreme Court ruled in favor of the separation of facilities for African Americans and Caucasians in *Plessy v. Ferguson*. As a result, a series of laws that restricted the African American population's rights were enacted. These laws were based on the belief that Caucasians were superior to African Americans in many ways. Jim Crow laws restricted the African American population's access to public services and facilities, such as schools, restaurants, hotels, and public transportation. The laws are said to be named after a popular minstrel song that portrayed African Americans. Violence and practices such as lynching were often used as a means of social control, to punish those who violated the laws. It was only after World War II that the Jim Crow laws began to disintegrate; legal initiatives such as the Civil Rights Act of 1964, the Voting Rights Act of 1965, and the Fair Housing Act of 1968 finally offered some legal remedy to the discriminatory practices of the Jim Crow laws. For more information, see *Plessy v. Ferguson* (1896). ***See also*** Civil Liberties; Civil Rights; Civil Rights Acts

Job Analysis   A method by which a job—one of several positions that share similar responsibilities—is decomposed into behavioral components such as the duties, tasks, and activities required for a particular job or class of jobs. It is also used to identify observable knowledge and skills, as well as verifiable abilities and other characteristics (KSAOs) needed to perform a job. KSAOs identified through a job analysis are independent from the personal characteristics of an incumbent. That is, job analysis focuses on the job rather than on those who do or will perform a job. In addition to KSAOs, job analyses produce information on task difficulty, task criticality, time spent on job tasks, task essentiality, importance of tasks, and essential functions of a job. The results of job analyses are used to improve (a) organizations' personnel recruiting and selection procedures by ensuring that such procedures are practical, efficient, and ethical; (b) job effectiveness by optimizing individual and team organizational placements and structures; (c) performance appraisal and promotion systems by offering information about specific performance criteria on which equitable reward systems can be based; and (d) safety and health by identifying job contexts or tasks that are less likely to lead to accident or injury. Job analyses are simultaneously descriptive, in that they provide information about how a job is done; prescriptive, in that they provide information about how a job should be done; and predictive, in that they provide information about how a job will be done. Occasionally, the results of job analyses are used to identify educational, training, or professional development needs for a particular job or job class within an organization. Job analysis typically uses subject matter experts, including incumbents and supervisors of the job being analyzed—who should have considerable knowledge and expertise about the job—as the primary sources of job information. The U.S. Department of Labor's Occupational Information Network (O*NET) is often used to accentuate, supplement, or validate the results of job analyses conducted within an organization, or as a source of information for identifying demonstrable KSAOs. Organizations are required by law to base their recruiting, hiring, and promotion procedures on the essential tasks and requirements of the job. Therefore, a credible job analysis can help define the essential tasks and requirements of a job to ensure that staffing procedures are legally defensible. However, a job analysis alone does not provide protection against legal challenges, but it is an essential component in designing personnel systems that can withstand legal disputes. No statute mandates job analysis in the United States, but several laws such as Uniform Guidelines on Employee Selection Procedures and the Americans with Disabilities Act require information derived from systematic job studies. **See also** Performance Appraisal (education, public administration)

Job Enrichment   An approach to job design meant to make jobs more interesting and challenging. Jobs are enriched when employees are given increased responsibility, accountability, and autonomy, which offers opportunities for personal growth and development. Job enrichment should not be confused with job enlargement, which increases the number of tasks performed. The job characteristics model of work motivation shows how increasing the core job dimensions of skill variety, task identity, task significance, autonomy, and feedback increases the meaningfulness of the job, feelings of responsibility, and intrinsic knowledge of job performance. Job enrichment is more motivating when employees have a high need for personal growth. Job enrichment may not increase motivation when employees have lower needs for growth and development. For more information, see Hackman (1977). **See also** Accountability (education, political science, sociology); Autonomy; Feedback (education)

Job Satisfaction   An employee's attitudes about various dimensions of his or her job. Attitudes are predispositions that are learned through direct and vicarious experiences and are composed of beliefs and thoughts, feelings and emotions, and intentions to act in a certain way toward an object, person, or situation. Researchers have identified over 20 dimensions of job satisfaction, including the work itself, the quality of supervision, relationships with coworkers, pay, status, and opportunities for promotion. Job satisfaction may be measured with a single question that assesses one's general satisfaction with the job, such as "Overall how satisfied are you with your job?" A second method summarizes responses to questionnaire items, measuring two or more dimensions of job satisfaction to calculate a global rating. A third approach assesses satisfaction with specific dimensions, using items or scales that measure each dimension separately.

The relationship between job satisfaction and employee performance has been debated for many years. It was hypothesized that satisfied employees would be more motivated to achieve higher performance and to increase productivity; however, early studies found inconsistent relationships between employee satisfaction and performance. These contradictory results inspired researchers to examine the causes, consequences, and situational variables that correlate with job satisfaction.

Frederick Herzberg conducted several studies from the 1950s through the 1970s investigating the causes of employee satisfaction and motivation. He argued that job satisfaction and job dissatisfaction are not opposite ends of a one-dimensional scale but are separate attitudes with different causes and different consequences. According to Herzberg, job satisfaction ranges from high satisfaction to no satisfaction, and dissatisfaction ranges from high dissatisfaction to no dissatisfaction. Herzberg argues that job dissatisfaction is caused by extrinsic job characteristics (job context or work environment factors), such as poor working conditions, low pay, low security, and low status, while job satisfaction is caused by intrinsic job characteristics (job content) that stimulate and fulfill an employee's need for growth and self-actualization, such as achievement, recognition, responsibility, opportunities for advancement, and interesting and fulfilling work.

Herzberg labeled factors that are related to job dissatisfaction hygiene factors; these factors are less likely to motivate employees to work harder or produce more. Factors related to job satisfaction are called motivating factors because these factors may increase employee motivation to be more productive. Hackman and Oldham (1976) suggested that the degree to which motivating factors will motivate an employee depends on the strength of the employee's growth needs. If the employee's need for growth and self-actualization is low, the motivating potential of the motivating factors will be low; however, if an employee's need for growth and self-actualization is high, increasing the motivating factors will motivate the employee to greater performance.

The relationship between job satisfaction and performance is complex. Some argue that job satisfaction leads to higher performance; others argue that successful performance leads to higher job satisfaction. But research does not consistently support either view. Research does show that employees with higher job satisfaction are usually more involved in their jobs and more frequently display organizational citizenship behaviors (going above and beyond requirements to help and support others in the organization). Studies have demonstrated that more satisfied employees generally have lower rates of absenteeism and lower turnover than less satisfied employees. Studies have also shown positive relationships between employee satisfaction and organizational performance, as well as positive relationships between employee satisfaction and customer satisfaction.

Possible causes of job satisfaction include (a) the extent to which the job fulfills the employee's needs, (b) the degree to which the job meets the employee's expectations about the job, (c) the extent to which the job helps the employee fulfill his or her instrumental values and achieve terminal values, (d) the extent to which the employee feels that he or she is treated equitably in comparison with others, and (e) the predisposition toward positive or negative affect. Individuals who have a tendency to view situations, themselves, and others in a positive way are found to have higher job satisfaction, while individuals who accentuate negative aspects are more likely to have lower job satisfaction.

Two questionnaires used to measure job satisfaction are the Job Descriptive Index and the Minnesota Satisfaction Questionnaire. For more information, see Hackman and Oldham (1976) and Herzberg, Mausner, and Snyderman (1959). *See also* Performance Assessment

Johari Window Named after its originators Joe Luft and Harry Ingram, this model is depicted as a window with four panes:

1. *Public area:* known to self and others

2. *Blind spot:* unknown to self, known to others

3. *Hidden area:* known to self, unknown to others

4. *Unknown:* unknown to self and others

Communication involves information: We know about ourselves; we do not know about ourselves; others know about us; and others do not know about us. Information is not static but moves from one quadrant to another by means of awareness, insight, self-disclosure, and feedback. For more information, see Luft (1984). *See also* Interpersonal Communication

Joinder A legal term that indicates the merger of several lawsuits or legal cases, or several parties within the same cases. Joinders occur when there is a common ground that joins all legal cases or parties together. A formal hearing must occur before a judge to proceed with a merger, at which point it must be proven that this merger of cases or parties will not cause harm to any of the parties involved in the existing cases.

Journalism A profession whose purpose is to communicate information, analysis, commentary, and entertainment to the public. The work carried out by reporters, editors, photographers, videographers, publishers, and producers involves collecting, preparing, and distributing news or current events of public interest via a variety of media. The products of journalism are generally frequently published periodicals including newspapers, consumer and trade magazines, television, radio, pamphlets, newsletters, film, books, and the World Wide Web. While the industry was closely associated with newspapers for centuries, it is now just as commonly associated with the electronic media.

Journalistic censorship involves the restriction, suppression, or altering of writing, speech, ideas, or opinions and can occur either before publication or broadcast (preemptive) or afterward (punitive). Those who seek to censor may do so because they find the words or speech to be morally, politically, or otherwise objectionable or because the revelation of facts would be harmful to a person, company, or other entity. Despite the fact that journalists' rights are protected by the First Amendment, indirect pressure or direct censorship can come from media owners, government agents, and special-interest or lobby groups. Journalists may also engage in self-censorship—either by omission or by evasion—out of fear of external censorship, libel claims, or other negative repercussions.

Journalists gather information from direct observation as well as from sources—people connected to a story, with whom they conduct interviews. Sources can include witnesses of an event, though the term generally implies an authority on a particular subject. To retrieve information from sources, reporters frequently need to promise that their identity will remain confidential, though an overabundance of anonymous sources can lessen a story's credibility. The first known case of a journalist seeking the right to silence occurred in the mid-19th century, when a *New York Herald* reporter refused to reveal a source and was subsequently jailed for contempt of Congress. Reporter's privilege refers to the invocation of the First Amendment on the part of journalists in keeping sources confidential in a court of law. In the 1972 landmark *Branzburg v. Hayes* case, the Supreme Court ruled against the conferral of such special privileges to journalists. The ensuing controversy over the ruling provoked some states to implement shield laws that would protect journalists against being forced to reveal sources. For more information, see Bates (2001), *Branzburg v. Hayes* (1972), and Kovach and Rosenstiel (2001). ***See also*** Censorship; Print Media; Privileged Conversations; Reporter

Judge   An elected or appointed representative whose job it is to ensure that principles of law are adequately implemented in a court of justice. The judge oversees proceedings in a courtroom and is responsible for making decisions about the outcome of legal cases based on current laws. Judges have power over the courtroom and the trial, are influential in advising the jury (in jury trial cases), and determine the appropriate sentence for the defendant when found guilty. Private deliberations between the judge and other individuals involved in the case (i.e., prosecutor, defense attorney, and experts) occur in the judge's chambers. It is also where the judge gets acquainted with the facts surrounding the cases. While the courtroom is public, the judge's chambers remain private. ***See also*** Court; Judicial; Jury; Supreme Court (U.S.)

Judicial   An adjective describing anything related to the administration of justice. The judicial system refers to the entire structure of courts that is responsible for enforcing laws and ensuring that justice is served. A judicial officer is an elected representative who has been appointed to ensure that principles of law are adequately implemented in a court of justice. The judicial officer oversees proceedings in a courtroom, and is responsible for making decisions about the outcome of legal cases. Judicial power refers to the power given to judges and courts to apply laws. Judicial review is a power given to the courts, enabling an assessment of the constitutionality of decisions rendered by other courts. ***See also*** Court; Judge; Jury

Judicial Activism   There has been little agreement surrounding the definition of this term in American jurisprudence. Broadly speaking, judicial activism occurs when a court invalidates enacted legislation. More specifically, judicial activism is the practice by judges of disallowing policy choices by other governmental officials or institutions that a constitution does not clearly prohibit. In other words, judges are engaging in judicial activism when they go beyond their roles authorized by a constitution to restrict the work of other government branches. Such behavior has prompted many legal scholars to question what the role of the judiciary should be in a democracy. At the heart of the concern over judicial activism is the fear that judges will impose their own personal preferences in their decisions.

The concept of judicial activism has existed in the United States before the term was created. Scholars had long debated the virtues of judicial legislation. It was in 1947 that Arthur Schlesinger, Jr. coined the term *judicial activism* in a *Fortune Magazine* article. Schlesinger's assessment of the current Supreme Court concluded that there existed differing views over what role the justices ought to take in a free society. One side appeared more concerned with settling particular cases in accordance with their own social preconceptions and the other side with preserving the judiciary in its established but limited place in the American system. The former came to be known as judicial activists, whereas the latter came to be known as strict constructionists.

Critics of judicial activism assert that it undermines the power of the legislature, thereby diminishing the rule of law and democracy. They argue that a judiciary, which often comprises appointed rather than elected members, has no legitimate grounds to overrule the policy choices of duly elected legislative representatives when there is no real conflict with the constitution.

For more information, see Kmiec (2004) and Schlesinger (1947) and the following landmark Supreme Court cases that exemplified judicial activism: *Lochner v. New York* (1905), *Mapp v. Ohio* (1961), *Marbury v. Madison* (1803), *Roe v. Wade* (1973), and more recently *Bush v. Gore* (2000). ***See also*** Democracy; Exclusionary Rule (political science, sociology); Judicial Review; Jurisprudence (political science, sociology); Rule of Law; Substantive Due Process

Judicial Review   The power of a court to review, overturn, or limit the enforcement of federal laws, state laws, regulations, or treaties that are determined to have violated or are in conflict with the U.S. Constitution. Judicial review also empowers the Supreme Court to declare acts of Congress and the President unconstitutional. This power, however, does not derive from the Constitution, since there is no explicit reference to this authority, but rather comes from legal precedent. Prior to the ratification of the Constitution, some colonial judges invalidated laws under colonial charters on the ground that they violated a constitutional provision.

Judicial review was formally declared by the Supreme Court in Chief Justice John Marshall's opinion in *Marbury v. Madison* (1803), which established judicial review as the foundation of American constitutional order. In his decision, the Court ruled that Section 13 of the Judiciary Act was unconstitutional, in violation of Article 30 of the Constitution. As such, the Constitution implicitly grants the Supreme Court the power to invalidate congressional acts that violate it. In 1810, the Supreme Court extended this authority to the states in *Fletcher v. Peck* (1810), in which it declared the Georgia legislature's repeal of a 1795 law authorizing the sale of land to private speculators unconstitutional. These decisions secured the Supreme Court as the chief interpreter and authority of the Constitution.

There has been ardent disagreement over whether judicial review is legitimate. Thomas Jefferson opposed judicial review as violating the principle of the separation of powers. He believed that each branch should decide constitutional questions for itself and only be responsible to the voters for its decisions. Others have argued that judicial review should only be relegated to the state judiciary since, under the Tenth Amendment, powers not specifically enumerated by the Constitution are reserved for the states. More recently, debate has centered on whether judicial review can exist in a democracy. According to some, judicial review limits the legitimate choices open to legislative bodies. Also, it imposes limits enforced by unelected, unaccountable judges and thwarts the aspirations of the people as expressed through their elected officials. Despite these ongoing debates, judicial review is America's most distinctive contribution to modern constitutionalism. For more information, see *Marbury v. Madison* (1803), *Fletcher v. Peck* (1810), and Waluchow (2007). ***See also*** Judicial Activism

Judicial Uses of Media Technology   The use of a range of devices that allow for the facilitation, broadcasting, recording, and preserving of trial proceedings as well as the use of cameras in the courtroom.

In the 1970s, devices such as slide and overhead projectors and video players were increasingly used to present testimony, exhibit evidence, or provide illustrative aids. An evidence or document camera can focus and zoom in on evidentiary exhibits and project the image onto a monitor. By the 1990s, as newer technology was developed, courtrooms employed videoconferencing, animations, simulations, and virtual reality environments. Laptop computers are now used for multitasking. Internet connections allow media and appropriate legal sites to broadcast real-time transcripts while simultaneously creating a public record and providing easy access to information.

Television camera coverage is allowed at some level in most states in both trial and appellate courts. Technological advances have made cameras less intrusive, and cable television has made media coverage more common. Their presence is controversial, however, and poses a dilemma. Critics maintain that cameras distort the trial process, thereby setting in opposition a defendant's right to due process with the First Amendment right to press freedom. Widespread use of such technology can provide a service to increase public access to court information and educate citizens about the judicial process. Media coverage can cause bias among jurors but can also bring forth witnesses. Judges are obligated to consider the privacy implications of witnesses and parties when providing such access. For more information, see Cohn and Dow (1998) and Federal Judicial Center (2001). ***See also*** Cameras in the Courtroom; Due Process of Law; Media and the Judicial System

Junior High School   In 1918, these schools were approved by the National Education Association Commission on the Reorganization of Secondary Education. Serving students between elementary and high school, junior high schools typically include the seventh and eighth grades. They began to decline in popularity with the advent of the middle school movement in the 1960s. ***See also*** Middle School

Jurisdiction *(political science)*   The territory within which a public entity may exercise its authority. Jurisdiction also refers to the power of a court to adjudicate a particular case or issue an order. State courts have general jurisdiction since they can hear any controversy, whereas federal courts have limited jurisdiction according to Article 3, Section 2 of the U.S. Constitution. They can only hear cases defined by the Constitution and congressional statutes.

Jurisdiction *(sociology)*   Authority executed by a court to obtain the facts about any given case and render a decision. There are two main types of jurisdiction: subject matter jurisdiction and personal jurisdiction. Subject matter jurisdiction is established if the court has the power to hear or make an assessment about the nature of the case at hand. For instance, some types of cases, such as violations of immigration laws, do not fall under the state courts' subject matter jurisdiction and must be presented in federal courts. Personal jurisdiction refers to the court's authority to make decisions regarding a given case. Jurisdiction also refers to the physical area over which an agency or leader has control. For instance, local law enforcement agents only have control over a set geographical area, typically a city, county, or township, and are unable to use their powers of authority in other areas. There may be overlapping jurisdiction between local, state, and federal agencies. ***See also*** Judicial; Police Power

Jurisprudence *(political science)*   The study of law. In the United States, jurisprudence commonly refers to the philosophy of law. Modern jurisprudence has been largely dominated by Western academics, even though jurisprudence is or has been studied by others, such as Islamic scholars. The study of jurisprudence dates back to Roman scholarship, which focused on the relationship between law and morals.

Among the purposes of the study of jurisprudence are to (a) explain and criticize bodies of law, (b) compare and contrast law with other fields of knowledge, (c) uncover the historical and cultural basis of a particular legal concept, (d) ask what the law ought to be, and (e) understand how the law applies to legal decisions.

Some of the schools of legal thought that consider jurisprudence are medical jurisprudence, therapeutic jurisprudence, feminist jurisprudence, and critical legal studies. ***See also*** Law (political science)

Jurisprudence *(sociology)*   Traditionally viewed as the study of the principles underlying laws and the legal system. In the current legal system, jurisprudence more commonly refers to the practice of basing judgments of current cases on judgments rendered by the courts in the past for cases characterized by similar circumstances. In this regard, current judgments also become precedents

J

for future cases. This practice ensures the uniformity of the application of the law and of principles of justice and minimizes the discrepancies in judgments delivered by the courts for cases involving comparable circumstances. *See also* Judge; Judicial; Justice (education, sociology); Precedent (political science, sociology)

Jury   A body of persons constituted to hear the proceedings of a trial and arrive at a verdict. A grand jury, which consists of up to 24 people, is seated to determine whether there is probable cause to hold accused defendants over for trial. Grand juries hear the prosecution's evidence and issue indictments against suspects if probable cause exists to establish that a crime has been committed and that the person accused likely committed it. Grand jury proceedings are closed to all parties other than the prosecution. Defendants and their attorneys are not present during grand jury proceedings. Petit juries, or trial juries, consist of 6 to 12 jurors convened to hear the facts of a case and issue an impartial verdict. Grand jurors are drawn from the same jury pools as trial (or petit) jurors. *See also* Indictment; Trial

Just Deserts   A legal principle that means getting what is deserved. In the philosophy of punishment, retributivists argue that punishment is a moral imperative—it must be imposed because it is deserved. Just deserts is a specification of this philosophy and requires that the punishment should fit the crime and offenders should get neither more nor less than they deserve. *See also* Punishment; Retribution

Justice *(education)*   The ideal of fair and equitable dealing or right action. Justice is presupposed when we ask questions about how we should act toward others. Although often used as a synonym for law, justice in the broader sense means fairness. In Aristotle's terms, justice as fairness consists in treating equals equally and nonequals unequally, in proportion to their relative differences. *See also* Equity (political science); Judge; Law (political science, sociology)

Justice *(sociology)*   A standard or principle of fairness and equity. The legal system is founded on principles of justice, which implies that the law is administered adequately, that all individuals are entitled to fair and equitable treatment from the law, including the right to a fair trial and sentence. Judicial officers are appointed to ensure that the principles of justice are respected.

Punishment based on the principles of justice aims to punish on the basis of blameworthiness and culpability rather than variables that are beyond the control of individuals. *See also* Equity (political science); Judge; Just Deserts

Just Noticeable Difference   The minimum amount by which a stimulus has to be altered, or varied, in order to result in an individual noticing a change in sensory experience. The just noticeable difference (JND; also referred to as difference threshold) is determined by the midpoint of trials during which an individual notices a sensory change from the previous sensation. It is used as a statistical measure and in Weber's law. *See also* Perception; Sensory Adaptation

Juvenile   An individual who is younger than the established legal age of adulthood. In the United States, this age varies from 16 to 18 years, but in most states it is 18. By law, juveniles cannot be charged for an adult crime unless the prosecutor requests a change of venue to a criminal court, and they generally benefit from more leniency in the juvenile justice system on the premise that they have not yet fully developed the level of moral reasoning that is expected from adults. Juveniles can also be convicted for status crimes, which are crimes only because of the age of the delinquent (i.e., truancy, possession of alcohol). *See also* Juvenile Justice System; Status Offense

Juvenile Justice System   The system used to process, adjudicate, and sentence juvenile offenders. This system consists of various establishments, including the police, the prosecuting agency, detention facilities, courts, and the probation department. It is the equivalent of the adult criminal justice system, but for minors. With the exception of more serious forms of offending, minors generally do not get the same treatment as adults and tend to benefit from more leniency from the legal system. Juveniles may be tried as adults if they are deemed to pose a threat to society. Differential treatment of juvenile versus adult offenders relies on the premise that youths are not as committed to criminality as adults and that it is more possible to deter younger and less experienced individuals from engaging in criminal activities in the future. Furthermore, juveniles are considered to be a vulnerable population that is more in need of supervision, education, and rehabilitation than punishment. *See also* Criminal Justice; Juvenile; Status Offense

K

Kansas City Patrol Experiment An experiment was conducted by the Kansas City Police Department in Missouri that changed perceptions about increased police presence and reduced crime rates. This study, which was assessed by a private research organization known as the Police Foundation, was criticized for methodological flaws. It was hypothesized that increased police presence, in marked cars, would decrease criminal activity. Three types of police practices were compared: (1) neighborhoods with one police car that conducted routine patrols, (2) neighborhoods with two or three police cars that conducted routine patrols, and (3) neighborhoods without police patrol cars. After one year (1972–1973), no discernable differences were noticed in crime rates, prevalence of crime reporting, residents' views of the police, and residents' fear of crime. Increased patrol did not decrease crime or increase citizen satisfaction; researchers advocated for funds to be used in other areas. *See also* Patrol

Keynesian Economic theory associated with the thinking of John Maynard Keynes is broadly referred to as *Keynesian*. The foundation of Keynesian economic theory is based on: (a) aggregate demand, (b) savings and investment, (c) labor market failure, and (d) expansionary fiscal policy.

A fundamental argument of Keynesian economics is that aggregate demand plays a critical role in determining the level of real output. There is a tendency for actual expenditure to fall short of planned expenditure. Actual expenditure is the amount that economic agents (households, firms, and governments) spend on goods and services, and this amount is what in effect determines national income. Planned expenditure is the amount that economic agents will like to spend on goods and services.

Aggregate spending induces more production and therefore more employment through a multiplier process once autonomous spending is initiated. Consequently, Keynesian theory holds that a recession is the result of a lack of spending in the economy.

Earlier on, classical economists made strong arguments for the self-adjusting market (the theory that the market is capable of achieving equilibrium in the long run). For example, one of the prominent classical economists, Jean-Baptiste Say, in his *Treatise on Political Economy, or the Production, Distribution and Consumption of Wealth* (1803), argued that supply creates its own demand, suggesting that whatever is produced will be consumed as soon as the price and wage rates are stabilized.

The Great Depression of the 1930s exposed the major weakness of the fundamental thinking of classical economists. The labor market failed to clear, financial markets collapsed, and an expansionary policy in the form of increased government spending (deficit financing) was used to get out of the depression. Keynes further argued that prices are sticky in the short run and that for a given (constant) interest rate or wage rate, an increase in government spending is capable of increasing investment and saving without causing inflation. Keynesian critics have questioned the wisdom of intervention in markets to stabilize the economy in the presence of lags and inflationary pressures.

A new school of Keynesians (neoclassical synthesis) emerged in the post-1940s to accept the practical conclusions of Keynes while conceding the theory that the market has a natural tendency to gravitate toward full employment. Other schools have since arrived; some questioning the insistence on market equilibrium, which might be unattainable even with a reasonable measure of price flexibility when sectors in a macroeconomy are intricately connected. For more information, see Boyes and Melvin (2002), Case and Fair (2003), Mankiw (2006), McConnell and Brue (2008), and Schiller (2006). *See also* Aggregate Demand Curve; Business Cycle (economics, public administration); Depression (economics); Gross Domestic Product; Laissez-Faire (economics, politics); Market; Recession; Stabilization

Kidnapping The abduction of any human being, regardless of age. Initially used as a term in Colonial America to describe the abduction of children for use as servants, kidnapping is a felonious charge. To kidnap someone means to hold the person against his or her will. It can include false imprisonment, detainment of the person without legal authority, which is punishable as a crime and/or tort, depending on individual circumstances. Kidnapping is a serious crime and will become a federal matter if the victim is taken out of the state. Some victims may experience Stockholm syndrome, a psychological disorder in which victims empathize with their capture. In response to child abductions, most states in the United States participate in the Amber Alert System (media notifications to the public that a child has been kidnapped). For more information, see Soothill, Francis, and Ackerley (2007). *See also* Abduction; Stockholm Syndrome

Kinesics The study of bodily movements, facial expressions, and other such movements as a way of communication, as accompaniments to speech. Kinesics is the study of nonverbal communication. Such nonverbal communication has been studied by the noted anthropologists Ray Birdwhistell, Gregory Bateson, and Margaret Mead. Birdwhistell coined the term after another word of his devising, *kineme,* his analogy to the linguistic term *phoneme.* **See also** Nonverbal Communication

Kinetic Energy   *See* Energy

Kinship Selection Theory   An explanation for altruism toward relatives, derived from evolutionary theory and the mechanism of natural selection. Kinship selection theory views helping, along with other human social behaviors, as an action that contributed to the survival of early humans. While helping others at one's own risk appears, at first glance, to be maladaptive, this approach is argued by modern evolutionary theorists to be too narrowly focused on the survival of the fittest individuals, whereas the important evolutionary mechanism is the survival of the individual's genes, even in others. Kinship selection theory predicts that animals are more likely to help and share resources with their relatives than with other members of their species. Furthermore, it predicts that the degree of altruism will increase with proximity of the relationship; animals will behave more altruistically toward closer relatives than toward more distant relatives. Because we share genes with relatives, helping a family member potentially increases the likelihood that our genes will survive via the beneficiary's future reproduction. Thus, kin selection produces indirect genetic benefits for the helper. For more information, see Burnstein, Crandell, and Kitayama (1994). **See also** Altruism (economics, psychology); Evolutionary Psychology; Natural Selection

Knapp Commission   New York City Mayor John Lindsay convened this five-member commission, named after its chairman, Whitman Knapp, in 1970 to investigate charges of corruption in the New York City Police Department (NYPD). An undercover officer, Frank Serpico, testified before the commission about corrupt practices in the NYPD, and in his testimony, he distinguished between two types of corrupt officers: the grass eaters and the meat eaters. The grass eaters accounted for most of the corruption in the NYPD, which included small infractions, such as minor forms of bribery. The meat eaters indulged in a more serious form of corruption, involving an active role by NYPD cops in making money illegally, such as bribes obtained through coercion and intimidation. The commission found that widespread corruption existed throughout the NYPD and recommended several changes, including better supervision by police managers, or "command accountability," and upgrading of selection procedures and standards for recruits. For more information, see Skolnick (2005). **See also** Corruption (sociology)

Knowledge   Justified true belief, according to the most widely accepted definition. Knowledge is related to objectivity, truth, and rationality. To say "I know the Earth is spherical" means "I believe this, I have good reason for believing this, and the Earth is in fact spherical." Schooling is concerned with three types of knowledge: (1) *knowledge that . . . ,* or fact knowledge; (2) *knowledge how to . . . ,* or skill knowledge; and (3) *knowledge to . . . ,* or dispositional knowledge.

Knowledge Gap   A hypothesis proposed in the early 1970s by the journalism professor Philip Tichenor and his colleagues at the University of Minnesota. Their research suggested that the mass media had the potential to widen the information differences between social classes. Because access to and control over the use of various media can vary significantly depending on socioeconomic class, people may acquire information differently. Members of higher socioeconomic classes tend to acquire information more readily, while members of lower classes may be less informed about the news and public affairs. The more the information becomes available in society, the wider the gap is believed to grow. In the Internet age, this concept is analogous to the digital divide. For more information, see Tichenor, Donohue, and Olien (1970). **See also** Mass Media

L

Labeling Theory This theory, also referred to as *social reaction theory*, is attributed to Howard Becker (1963), who argued that deviance is constructed by the social control groups that create the rules and define their violation. Deviance, then, is a label or status attributed by society. The manner in which these social control groups react to a person's behavior defines it as deviant. According to this perspective, there is no behavior, status, or characteristic that is inherently deviant; society chooses what to define as deviant. Edwin Lemert (1967) further recognized primary and secondary deviance. A person can engage in deviance without being caught or labeled, which is referred to as primary deviance. Secondary deviance occurs when the behavior is recognized by society and the person is labeled as deviant and adopts the label and acts accordingly. *See also* Classical Criminology; Conflict Criminology; Criminology; Qualitative Criminology; Radical Criminology

Labor A resource of mental and physical capabilities that is used up in the production process. The contribution of labor to production depends on its availability and efficiency. Societies with highly efficient labor tend to be much more productive than societies with less efficient labor. By and large, the availability of capital is fundamentally important to providing efficient labor.

Labor, like other factors of production, is a tradable resource in a market; its price is influenced significantly by the forces of supply and demand, but distortions might not always guarantee a market price for its use. For example, in contemporary societies, trade unions, wage regulation, inflation, and immigration influence the price and availability of labor considerably. *See also* Inflation; Market; Price

Laboratory Research Research conducted in a controlled setting, in which the experimenters attempt to exclude any extraneous factors that could influence their results. For example, laboratory research in psychology often requires that the experimenter control features such as the noise, temperature, or light level in a room, or the information given to a research participant. Laboratory research is generally employed in experimental studies, where an experimenter attempts to change a small number of situational features while holding all other features of the environment constant. In doing so, the experimenter can observe how the changed factors (independent variables) affect some measure of interest (dependent variables). However, in creating this controlled environment, some degree of verisimilitude is often lost. Laboratory research is often criticized on this basis: Many argue that the findings obtained in laboratory research are not generalizable to real-world settings. *See also* Dependent Variable; Generalizability; Independent Variable

Labor Market The term can be conceptualized using two basic constructs. What might be referred to as the macroeconomics of labor markets relates to concepts such as employment, unemployment rates, and labor force participation rates. The microeconomics of labor markets focuses on the role of individuals and individual firms. In the labor market thus defined, employers find willing workers, workers find paying jobs, and wages are established to the extent that they are not predetermined by, for example, union contracts. Labor markets defined in either construct may cover different geographic areas: local, regional, national, and international *See also* Macroeconomic Policy; Microeconomics

Labor Theory of Value An 18th- and 19th-century theory that states that the ultimate value of a good depends on the amount of labor required to produce it. The theory was first put forward by Adam Smith, but it was subsequently popularized by David Ricardo as he tried to explain the basis of trade and value (wealth). These economists were writing in an era in which capital did not have an imposing presence.

In the 19th century, Alfred Marshall introduced a competing theory of value based on marginalism, market demand and supply, and price. Price theory has since been intertwined with value. Influential writers of Karl Marx's variety separate price from (surplus) value and use the labor theory of value to explain the exploitation of workers in the capitalist system. Today, capital is considered to be equally important as labor in producing value, especially when value can be created with minimal or no labor-intensive effort.

Laissez-Faire *(economics)* An 18th-century political-economy theory developed by the French physiocrats to limit the intervention by government in market transactions. Its literal interpretation could take any of the following forms: *let them do, allow them to do,* or *let alone.*

The theory of laissez-faire was a response to mercantilism, which advocated intense regulation of trade by a government to amass bullion (precious metals)

in order to fight wars of aggression (expansionary wars) during the Middle Ages. The advocates of laissez-faire argued that the role of government should be limited to the protection of property rights, the enforcement of private contracts, and the provision of public goods (those goods that markets are unable to adequately provide)—for example, a national army and roads. It was hoped that consumers and firms can pursue their rational self-interest in the market place without the intrusion of a central authority. A major weakness of the theory is that the limits of legitimate intervention cannot be clearly defined. *See also* Capitalism (economics, political science); Classical Economics; Market; Market Failure; Market Forces

Laissez-Faire *(political science)* A free-market economic policy, which spread through Europe and the United States in the mid-1800s, whereby private contracts were freely negotiated without government intervention. States relaxed their protective measures, such as tariffs and subsidies, which had curtailed trade, especially beyond national borders. It was believed that such arrangements would encourage competition. As a result of laissez-faire policies, nations became neutral in competitions among businesses and interest groups vying for market and political power.

Competition, however, seemed to encourage monopolies rather than market regulation. Laissez-faire policies were thus modified, and today, most industrialized nations usually maintain strong government intervention in the economy through minimum wages, antitrust regulation, and trade tariffs.

Landslide Effect A snowballing reaction from audiences desired by the media industry that pertains to the active consumption of goods in two significant ways: financially and ideologically. Preconditional factors (social, economic, political) contribute to the climate for a landslide effect. It can be perpetuated by media campaigns that are focused toward elements such as brand recognition to drive revenues and profit. To achieve this consumer reaction, the brand has achieved a phenomenon of high visibility but not oversaturation. Another view of a landslide effect focuses on the issue of bias in the production and presentation of news. Similar to a frame of reference or censorship, the landslide effect can refer to an increasingly singular perspective on a public issue or figure that is constructed by the media industry (particularly by news organizations). This one-dimensional ideology can then be perpetuated among audiences, beginning with a small fraction and spreading to wider segments of the population. *See also* Industry (media studies, sociology)

Language Human communication by means of spoken words or sounds, written words or illustrations, and gestures. Language can refer broadly to the linguistic tongues of cultures and nations throughout the world and to the terms or patterns of speech used by specific professions or social groups.

Though animals manage to communicate, language is considered to be uniquely human. Early in the 20th century, the Swiss linguist Ferdinand de Saussure differentiated between language and speaking, calling language a product assimilated by an individual and speaking an act of choice; neither is an abstraction but a concrete reality seated in the human brain. The communications theorist Neil Postman defined language as "pure ideology," which, among other tasks, influences human concepts "about how we stand in relation to nature and to each other." According to Postman, an individual's native language is so embedded that it affects the very way in which he or she reasons, influencing his or her worldview and interpretation of information. *See also* Linguistic Differences; Worldview

Language Development A process concerned with the determinants, processes, and mechanisms of acquiring language. For decades, researchers from different disciplines and theoretical perspectives have investigated this issue along the continuum of nature (biology) and nurture (environment). Among many others, three theories have been influential: behaviorist, nativist, and interactionist.

From the behaviorist perspective, language development is due to environmental influences. Behaviorists believe that children learn language through recognizing and forming associations between experience and language. Therefore, they claim that young children's language development is the result of imitation as well as parents' and other caretakers' behavioral reinforcement.

The nativist view of language development was initially backed by Noam Chomsky's theory that humans are biologically programmed to acquire language. Specifically, Chomsky argues that the biological determinant is the inborn language acquisition device (LAD). The LAD includes a set of abstract rules that enable children to understand and use language. These rules constitute Universal Grammar and are invariant across languages and cultures. The biological account provides some theoretical and empirical evidence as to why children acquire ultimate language competency even with insufficient and defective linguistic input and without corrective feedback.

Research on brain injuries, confirmed with the help of modern brain-imaging technology, has established that the left hemisphere (side) of the brain is more responsible for language than the right hemisphere. The specialization of the hemispheres begins at birth, but during the critical period, the brain still has more cells that are plastic, that is, adaptable and not yet specialized, than at any later time in life. Brain plasticity is the nativist explanation for why language tends to be acquired more completely during childhood than later in life.

Studies of genes in the area of reading have contributed new discoveries to the understanding of language development. Particular genes have been identified as responsible for reading disabilities in some families. Twin studies as well as research involving biologically related families versus adoptive families also suggest the critical role of genes in the biological determination of language ability and individual differences in this regard.

The third, and most notably sociocultural, perspective on language development claims that innate abilities and environmental influences interact to enable language acquisition. The emphasis on social context of this perspective puts the human mind firmly in the socioculturally formed environments it inhabits. Therefore, language development entails environments where children use their cognitive and linguistic abilities to communicate socially with more capable members of their communities. It is through children's active participation in communicative activities, in this view, that they acquire competencies associated with language use in addition to the structural components of language.

Larceny   The unlawful taking and carrying away of another person's tangible property without permission to permanently deprive the rightful owner of it. Some states differentiate between petty larceny (usually classed as a misdemeanor) and grand larceny (considered a felony) by the property's monetary value. The word derives from the Latin word *latrocinium* (robbery). *See also* Theft

Latent Content   The content of an event, as measured by the appearance of themes as interpreted by the researcher. Latent content analysis is one way in which the content of an event or communication can be investigated, when it has been recorded in some permanent form (e.g., a written essay, a magazine article, a photograph, an audio-recorded or transcribed conversation). The researcher examines the recorded material and interprets the presence of a particular theme. The advantage of latent content analysis over its alternative, manifest content analysis, is that the researcher can be flexible in discerning the underlying meaning of an event. However, its disadvantage is that it is inherently more prone to subjectivity than manifest content. For more information, see Auerbach and Silverstein (2003). *See also* Manifest Content; Qualitative Data Analysis

Lateral Communication   The practice of disseminating information from person to person within the same level of an organization or between departments or divisions within an organization. The term *lateral communication* is often used interchangeably with horizontal communication, and both terms can be used in reference to communication between or among different organizations.

Lateral/horizontal communication differs from downward communication because it is not hierarchical, meaning it does not call for top management to pass information down through various layers of supervisors to workers on the lowest rungs of an organization. Lateral communication is collaborative, linking personnel as they accomplish the tasks of their jobs.

Lateral communication has replaced downward communication as the norm in organizations as varied as small companies, not-for-profit entities, corporations, and global consortia. Integral to that replacement is the growth of electronic communication and globalization, as well as the transformation of America's businesses from manufacturing to service-oriented enterprises.

Among the first management specialists to suggest the effectiveness of lateral/horizontal communication was the Frenchman Henri Fayol, who in 1949 proposed constructing a bridge between employees at similar levels. In contemporary times, lateral communication is accomplished in a number of oral or written ways. Face-to-face contact, though very effective, is not always possible. Telephone conference calls and webinars, as well as e-mailing and instant messaging, have allowed the establishment of virtual communities of colleagues who are able to communicate laterally across great distances. *See also* Collaboration; Downward Communication; Horizontal Communication

Law *(political science)*   A set of rules that proscribe or permit interrelationships among people and organizations, provide procedures for ensuring the fair treatment of people, and prescribe punishments for those who do not follow these established rules. A law is also the document that sets forth the rules governing conduct.

Law is determined by the state and can be classified in a number of ways. It can be classified according to its origin: common or statutory. Common law derives from earlier judicial decisions. Statutory laws are written rules established by an act of legislature, which are either signed by the executive or passed over the executive's veto by the legislature.

Law can also be classified according to class: civil (or private) or criminal (or public). Civil law is a body of rules that delineates private rights and remedies and governs disputes between individuals or organizations in areas such as contract, property, and family conflicts. Criminal laws define crimes and establish punishments by the state. Criminal law may be common or statutory.

Law can also be divided into natural or positive law. Natural law is normative and is based on a common understanding of what is right and proper. It generally originates from moral and religious precepts as well as a common understanding of fairness and justice. Positive law is determined by the institutional facts internal to a legal system. The facts may or may not meet moral standards. Positive law must be obeyed however much it falls short of moral ideals. What is law is a factual question and should be kept distinct from what the law ought to be. *See also* Civil Law (political science, sociology); Common Law (political science, sociology); Criminal Law (political science, sociology)

Law *(sociology)* bodies of principles and rules of conduct of an organized society or nation, established by a government or other legislated authority and enforced by threat of punishment from an authorized body. The principle source of American law is the English Common Law, though it is distinguished by the coexistence of federal and state systems. Important types of law include antitrust law, business law, constitutional law, contract law, criminal law, environmental law, family law, health law, immigration law, intellectual property law, labor law, maritime law, procedural law, public interest law, tax law, and torts.

Law Enforcement   The enforcement of the laws of a local, state, tribal, or federal justice agency to prevent or investigate crime and apprehend and detain individuals suspected or convicted of criminal offenses. Law enforcement agents, such as police officers, are empowered to use force in order to enforce the law and assist the governance of a society. Police functions may include the protection of citizens' life and property, the enforcement of criminal law, and criminal investigation, though specialized police units exist specifically for functions such as traffic regulation, homicide, explosive disposal, and crowd control. *See also* Police Misconduct; Police Personality; Police Power; Police Subculture

Leadership (Definition and Types)   Generally, the ability to motivate or persuade others to act in a certain way in order to achieve a goal. Leadership creates a relationship between the leader and those following. Because of this, leaders both shape their followers and are shaped by their followers. A leader's actions result in some sort of response from his or her followers, which in turn also affects his or her ability to take future actions. Thus, leadership is a mutual process of influence between the leader and the followers.

Frequently mentioned characteristics of good leaders include vision, the ability to communicate a vision, commitment to the cause of the organization, and the ability to inspire trust. Other positive leadership characteristics cited include everything from self-confidence, to courage, to flexibility.

There are many theories of leadership. One of these is the idea that leadership style is not fixed but should be adapted to different situations. This is explored in contingency theory and situational theory. For example, the job of a public school superintendent is different from that of a college department chair. How a leader will lead depends on many factors, including how willing and how able the followers are to do a good job. Thus, the leader's style may change depending on the situation. Trait theory suggests that leaders possess innate personal qualities that distinguish them from others. Most often, traits are considered to be inherent from birth, and on this basis, trait theory supports the belief that good leaders are born, not made. Behaviorist theories of leadership, on the other hand, suggest that leadership is defined by action and behavior rather than by personality. As such, leaders need not be born great but can learn to be great leaders through observation and practice. Higher-education programs in leadership support the notion that individuals can be trained to be good leaders. A further branch of research that examines the relationships between leaders and followers is found in the transformational theory of leadership. A transformational leader is focused on achieving a goal while at the same time concerned with the welfare of the individuals he or she is leading. The transformational leader wants his or her followers to believe in and help achieve the mutual goal, but he or she also wants the followers to reach their potential. For more information, see Bolman and Deal (1997).

Leader Versus Management   A leader is one who possesses attractive characteristics that engender others to willingly follow him or her toward the attainment of some goal. The leader's followers are inspired by respect for the role of the leader as well as for the leader himself (herself). The leader possesses other characteristics that inspire others to follow, including having good communication skills (both oral and written) and being knowledgeable, trustworthy, and charismatic.

Management is only one of several leadership skills, and it facilitates the impact of a leader. Management is directing the actions of another based on power assigned to the management or leader role. It may or may not be required of the leader to maintain followers or to attain outcomes; however, stronger leaders also apply management of others in attaining and/or working toward goals.

Learned Helplessness   The belief that one has no control over a particular situation, resulting in failure to try to exert control over the environment. The concept of learned helplessness originated as a result of a seminal study conducted in two phases by Seligman and Maier (1967). In Phase 1, dogs were exposed to either escapable or inescapable shocks. In Phase 2, all dogs were exposed to escapable shocks. The dogs that had been exposed to escapable shocks in Phase 1 learned to escape the shocks in Phase 2, but the dogs that had been exposed to inescapable shocks in Phase 1 did not attempt to escape the shocks in Phase 2, even though they now had the agency to do so. A number of subsequent experiments have demonstrated, across species, that when behavior has no effect on events, the result is learned helplessness, a tendency to give up any effort to control the environment. The learned helplessness model is a social-cognitive theory of depression, which suggests that depression results from the perception that one lacks control over the negative events in one's life, leading to a failure to attempt to avoid these negative events. This model posits that humans become depressed when they feel incapable of controlling the stressors in their lives, and they develop a depressive attributional style (judging the causes of negative events to be internal to themselves, stable over time, and pervasive across many aspects of their lives).

See also Depression (education, psychology); Locus of Control (education, psychology)

Learner Analysis The identification of pertinent characteristics of a targeted population of learners; this step is found in most instructional design models. The instructional designer may examine both general (age, gender, culture, education, etc.) and specific (prior knowledge and skills, attitudes, motivations, etc.) characteristics, but only those relevant to the design and development of effective instruction are taken into consideration. Identifying the relevant learner characteristics and the similarities and differences among a particular group of learners assists in creating instruction that is educationally sound, interesting, and relevant to its intended audience.

Learner-Centered Instruction An approach in which learners take control of their own learning and the teacher plays the role of a facilitator and resource provider. It has empirical support crystallized in the American Psychological Association's Learner-Centered Psychological Principles five global statements of which are as follows:

1. Learning progresses through common stages of development influenced by both inherited and experiential/environmental factors.

2. One's existing knowledge serves as the foundation of all future learning.

3. The ability to reflect on and regulate one's thoughts and behaviors is essential to learning and development.

4. Motivational or affective factors, attributions for learning, and personal goals, along with the motivational characteristics of learning tasks, play a significant role in the learning process.

5. Learning is both an individually constructed enterprise and a socially shared understanding.

Learning The modification of preexisting behavior and understanding, through experience. The behavioral and cognitive-behavioral approaches to psychology argue that human behavior, thoughts, attitudes, and beliefs are largely determined by that which an individual has learned, often via rewards and punishments he or she has experienced. Learning can be categorized as nonassociative and associative. Nonassociative forms of learning are those that result from the impact of one particular stimulus and include habituation (the decrease in responses to repeated administrations of an unchanging stimulus over time) and sensitization (the amplification of a response in response to repeated administrations of an unchanging stimulus). Associative forms of learning are those that result from the relationships or associations between events, and they include classical conditioning (the repeated pairing of a neutral stimulus with a stimulus that already triggers a reflexive response, until the neutral stimulus alone comes to evoke a similar response) and operant conditioning (the manipulation of the consequences of a behavior to influence the likelihood of the behavior occurring). A number of factors can influence the effectiveness of associative learning. For example, the degree of classical conditioning that occurs when two stimuli are paired depends on biopreparedness (the tendency for particular events to become linked in the natural environment so that certain signals or events are particularly suited to form associations with other events). Similarly, operant conditioning can be influenced by the timing and size of reinforcers (e.g., operant conditioning more effectively shapes behavior when the size of the reinforcer is large than when it is small and when the reinforcer occurs soon after the behavior of interest). *See also* Classical Conditioning; Conditioned Stimulus (CS); Habituation; Operant Conditioning; Reinforcement

Learning Centers A physical location where learning occurs. Learning centers are designed to facilitate learning. They offer courses and activities that contribute to a subject of learning. A reading center is an example of a learning center. It is a center where courses and activities are focused on learning how to read.

Learning Disabilities A disorder in which a person's ability to acquire basic skills such as reading, writing, speaking, listening, or computing results in achievement that is not commensurate with same-age peers. Typically, the disability is identified when a discrepancy (of specified magnitude) is found between a standardized ability measure and a standardized achievement measure, with the score on the ability measure being higher than the score on the achievement measure. A learning disability cannot be the result of a person's family background, economic conditions, or home language. *See also* Individuals with Disabilities Education Act (IDEA); Special Education

Learning Organization An organization that continuously engages in the acquisition of new knowledge, skills, abilities, or attitudes to grow, respond to changes in the environment, and improve product or service quality. Learning organizations expand their capacity to create their desired future by means of *generative learning*, the organizing principle of the system's life and culture. Popularized by Peter Senge (1990), learning organizations are characterized by five "disciplines," or bodies of theory and practice:

1. *Personal mastery:* the ongoing expansion of individual vision, capacity, proficiency, and competency to realize the results that matter the most

2. *Mental models:* scrutinizing and challenging deeply ingrained assumptions, generalizations, and beliefs that influence how individuals

understand the world, shape their thoughts, and enact interaction

3. *Shared vision:* the creation of a genuine, shared image of the future to be constructed together

4. *Team learning:* engagement in group dialogue as the means to transform individual thinking into collective knowledge in order to mobilize energy, achieve common goals, and draw forth synergetic wisdom and talent

5. *Systems thinking:* the ability to understand and optimize the forces, dynamics, and inter-relationships that shape the behavior of the system

Learning organizations attempt to generate three kinds of knowledge: (1) knowing-why (why individuals perform the work they do); (2) knowing-how (with what skills and expertise individuals go about their work, covering both formal and tacit knowledge); and (3) knowing-whom (the range of relationships individuals hold within and beyond the workplace). When generating organizational knowledge, learning organizations engage people's intrinsic motivation (knowing-why) to support a shared vision and purpose. They incorporate people's skills and ways of interacting at work (knowing-how) into a shared repertoire of practice. They draw on people's social investments (knowing-whom) in each other to create patterns of mutual engagement. Senge contends that the only sustainable source of competitive advantage is an organization's ability to learn faster than its competitors.

Despite disputes in the literature concerning a system's capacity to learn, learning organizations display the properties of distributed cognition. Individuals in relationship actively mold and influence each other's knowledge and reasoning processes, building work epistemology on the basis of what they tell and are told by others. Therefore, individuals in learning organizations are not bound by the limitations of any one person's cognitive capacity or experience. Distributed cognition within learning organizations gives shared meaning to the tasks individuals are enacting and allows them to make collective sense of the processes with which they are engaged. ***See also*** Organization Design; Organization Development (OD) (education, public administration)

Learning Outcomes Specific student-focused expectations following a unit of instruction, usually stated in observable and measurable terms. Learning outcomes are often tied to a taxonomy, or hierarchy of learning levels. Learning can be assessed at any level, and the progression can be followed by using continuously more complex verbs (repeat, paraphrase, describe, explain, analyze, create). Outcomes drive both the lesson plans and the assessment; sources include text resource materials and state education Web sites. ***See also*** Learner-Centered Instruction; Taxonomies

Learning Society A term used to describe a society in which all members have equal opportunities to learn, and all members are actively involved in lifelong learning. Learning societies aspire to better the lives of each of their members by striving to promote equality among economic, social, political, and cultural forces.

Learning Strategies A term that has been used very broadly to identify a number of strategic methods and actions used by a learner to process information in order to alter retrieval or perform a task. Individuals use learning strategies in particular settings to aid in the acquisition of skills and knowledge. They are individuals' own cognitive processes that help them attend, learn, think, and remember. They are also considered as cognitive tools that individuals intentionally use to accomplish a specific learning task. One or more of these cognitive tools may be used in the process. Examples of learning strategies include rehearsal strategies and elaborations. Rehearsal strategies allow individuals to repeat verbal information (names, symbols, facts, etc.) for maintaining information in working memory. However, elaborative rehearsal may facilitate information to be stored in long-term memory for later retrieval. Elaboration strategies allow individuals to understand and expand on new information by adding their interpretation or meaning to the information based on their own prior knowledge. In other words, they are adding more meaning to what is actually being presented within the instructional or learning environment by drawing inferences or making assumptions about what is being presented. Elaborating on new learning helps the learner make distinctions from other preexisting knowledge and provide other ways to retrieve the information.

According to some scholars, an individual acquires and refines learning strategies over time. Through acquisition and refinement of learning strategies, an individual may become an independent learner and thinker. Individuals may also be trained in the acquisition and use of learning strategies. However, some individuals may not acquire and use learning strategies effectively.

Learning Styles A subset of cognitive styles that refer to the cognitive structure and processes within individuals in order to make sense of and acquire knowledge and skills within a learning situation. In addition, learning styles also relate to learner preferences for and perceptions of processing information but do not necessarily relate to processing ability. These preferences assume that each individual knows how he or she learns best. Learning styles are said to relate to heredity, prior experiences, and the current demands of the learning environment. Several of the theories related to learning styles are based on Jungian psychology. Most learning-style instruments are self-report measures.

Learning Theory There are three traditional theoretical schools that explain how we learn. First, the cognitive model focuses on thought processes. Piaget proposed four stages of cognitive development, Vygotsky focused on the social context of cognitive learning, Bruner added discovery learning, and the information process theory discusses methods and levels of processing. Second, behaviorism posits learning as a change in behavior due to experience, with reinforcement as the vehicle of learning.

Third, Bandura's social learning theory posits that learning is enhanced by other people, through modeling, vicarious learning, verbal persuasion, or guided participation. For more information, see Bandura (1977) and Bruner (1961). *See also* Behaviorism (education, psychology); Cognitive Learning Theory; Discovery Learning; Information-Processing Model (education, psychology); Social Learning Theory (education, sociology)

Leftist   A political term that originated in the left-right political groupings in the French Estates General in 1789. Left-right political ideologies should be discussed on a continuum, even though both are positioned on opposite ends of the spectrum. The ideologies are constantly shifting abstract values that are dependent on the historical, cultural, and social developments of the particular nation-state.

Western political discourse on left or liberal ideologies is indebted to John Locke's *Two Treatises of Governments*. According to Locke, the governing body must respect the natural rights of its citizens and limit its powers. In doing so, the governing body forms a pact, and if it is broken, its citizens maintain the right and duty to revolt. Arguably, what differentiates left-right ideology is the idea of equal citizenship, allowing free and equal participation in political processes, and the "rectification principle," which seeks to remedy inequalities. Leftists claim to favor equalitarianism achieved through policies such as welfare, social security, and affirmative action. Equalitarianism is rarely achieved and is usually subject to the political realities of a political entity subjected to the pressures of interest groups. For more information, see Lukes (1990).

Legal Aid   Free legal services, from assessment of financial need to counseling and representation, provided to persons who have limited or no financial means to pay a lawyer (those who are indigent). U.S. law has required provision of legal services to indigents since 1964, so as to ensure that the constitutional right to counsel does not unfairly discriminate against those who cannot pay for legal services. *See also* Constitution (political science, sociology); Due Process/Due Process Model; Indigent

Legal Hearing   A preliminary legal proceeding before a judge or other decision-making body or officer without a jury in which charges, evidence, testimony, and arguments are presented to determine issues of fact and law. Hearings are usually brief and informal and may be held before or during a trial to decide specific questions or motions, such as the admissibility of evidence, that will determine how and whether a trial may proceed. The support of defendants' due process means that hearings are now used for administrative decisions that were once made informally. *See also* Trial

Legislation   Law or a group of laws that have been prepared and enacted by a legislature or other governing body through its lawmaking process. Legislation is usually proposed (as a "bill") by a member of the legislature (a "sponsor") to committees, which consider it for recommendation. During review, and before enactment as written law, legislation may be amended to eliminate technical problems or to accommodate interested and affected parties. After deliberation and debate, the legislature votes on the proposed laws. After the legislation becomes written law, the judicial branch is charged with its interpretation. *See also* Bill; Law (political science, sociology)

Legislative Branch   A representative lawmaking body of government. It may be unicameral or bicameral. It may represent entire populations, particular groups, or regions. And its members may be appointed or elected. The primary duties of the legislative branch are to write, debate, and pass bills into law. Other duties may include monitoring other branches of government, investigating national issues, raising taxes, proposing and adopting budgets, assisting constituents, and serving on committees to handle specific governmental matters, such as budgeting, national security, agriculture, and crime.

Two common types of legislatures are presidential and parliamentary. In a presidential legislature, the executive and legislature are clearly separate. The executive is neither part of nor appointed by the legislature. In a parliamentary system, such as Britain's, the executive is constitutionally answerable to the parliament. Members of a parliament may elect an executive. Members may also force the resignation of an executive after a motion of no confidence in that leader.

In the United States, the legislative branch follows the presidential model and is called the U.S. Congress. It is a bicameral legislature made up of the Senate and the House of Representatives. Both houses comprise elected members from all 50 states. Congress was established by Article 1 of the U.S. Constitution, which was intended to provide checks and balances within the legislative branch. The first Congress met in 1789. Today, Congress also includes agencies that provide support services, such as the Government Accountability Office, the Library of Congress, the Government Printing Office, and the Congressional Budget Office. A law must be passed by both houses by a simple majority before it can go before the President for approval. If the President vetoes a bill, then Congress can make it a law if two thirds of the members of each house vote to override the veto.

In state governments in the United States, the legislative branches are often called *assemblies*. *See also* Bicameral Legislature (political science); Bill; Congress; Executive Branch; Parliament; Unicameral Legislature

Legislature   A governing body that has the power to create and ratify laws. In the United States, the legislature exists as a distinct branch of government at the federal level. This is a separate entity from the executive and judiciary branches. The legislature is composed of Congress, which comprises the House of Representatives and the Senate, as outlined in the U.S. Constitution, Article 1.

Legitimacy   An important, yet problematic, concept since it is difficult to define. It may be stated as the popular acceptance of a governing regime or law as an authority. It arises from the conviction that a state action proceeds within the confines of law in two ways: (1) the action issues from a rightful authority and (2) the action doesn't violate a legal or moral norm.

The idea of legitimacy originated from Weberian sociology. According to Max Weber, there are three pure types of legitimate authority. The first, called *rational* or *legal authority*, is based on the belief in the legality of normative rules and the right of those elevated to authority under these rules to issue commands. Next, *traditional authority*'s claim to legitimacy rests on the sanctity of traditions and the legitimacy of those exercising authority under these traditions. The third, *charismatic authority*, rests on devotion to the pure, heroic, or exemplary characteristics of an individual.

Legitimacy has been recognized on both normative and positive grounds. In the normative sense, an entity has political legitimacy if it is morally justified in wielding political power. Legitimacy thus concerns itself with why citizens ought to obey a political authority. The empirical sense explains why or when people obey a particular government or policy, and, on the contrary, why they do not revolt or disobey. Ultimately then, legitimacy is rooted in public opinion and is more concerned about whether the normative standards that people embrace are met than in debating what those standards should be.

The right to choose leaders is not enough to establish political legitimacy. It also depends on the quality of a government. Weber himself viewed political legitimacy as not only whether citizens democratically chose their leaders or decided on policy but also how policy is implemented. In furtherance of this, one idea about what makes a government legitimate is the services and benefits a government can bring to the populace. It is the equity and moderation of such services, rather than the mere selection of leaders, that determines whether the citizenry sees a government as legitimate. For more information, see Rothstein (2007) and Weber (1947).

Lesson Planning   The process of determining instructional content and strategies to meet the goal of a lesson. Lesson planning links curriculum and instruction. A lesson must be planned thoughtfully, systematically, and coherently to be effective and efficient. First, set instructional objectives, and decide what to teach within a time frame, what instructional materials and media to use, as well as what students' prerequisite skills and knowledge are. Second, develop and structure instructional strategies, procedures, and activities. Third, design assessment in alignment with instructional objectives. Lesson plans are teaching guides and can be adapted to what actually goes on in the classroom.

Level/Unit of Analysis   The level of social reality to which theoretical explanations refer, ranging from the micro (an interaction or an individual) to the macro (school community), and the element that will be studied. Units are also the components that serve as the basis for coding data. ***See also*** Research Methodology

Lex Talionis   The principle of direct and equal retaliation, or punishment in kind (often referred to as "eye for an eye" justice). The principle of *lex talionis* is most explicitly incorporated in the Code of Hammurabi (a written code of law dating to 1800 BCE). ***See also*** Code of Hammurabi; Retribution

Libel   The defamation of a person in untrue written, printed, or broadcast words or pictures with the aim of harming that person and his or her reputation. Libel is distinguished from slander (i.e., oral defamation). A civil wrong, libel is usually remedied with monetary damages. ***See also*** Slander

Liberal Democracy   A form of government in which the decision-making powers of elected representatives is subject to the rule of law and a constitution that protects the rights and freedoms of the constituency. Liberal democracy is the dominant form of modern democracies, including the United States.

The concept of a liberal democracy originated in the Age of Enlightenment in Europe in the 18th century. At that time, many governments were led by monarchies. Several political philosophers, however, likened the monarchy to a tyranny in which rule was often arbitrary and despotic. They offered a different ideal of a government whereby individuals' rights were paramount and superseded the impositions of government. This ideal, known as liberalism, inspired the American and French Revolutions in the late 18th century.

A liberal democracy contains constitutional protections of individual rights against government power, consistent with the liberal ideal. In addition, the natural condition of the individual in a liberal democracy is independence and solitude, and individuals are separate, autonomous, and free agents. Thus, the chief concern of liberal democracies is conflict. Autonomous individuals living in private and separate spaces are the stakeholders, and conflict is their characteristic mode of interaction, whether the conflict be over scarce resources or hunger for power and glory.

Freedom is one of the hallmarks of liberal democracies. Specifically, liberal democracies are interested in the removal of interferences by government or other individuals to allow individuals to choose their own ends. Freedom further entails the absence of political constraints on individual action. The language of freedom can be found throughout the U. S. Constitution. These freedoms include the freedom of speech, of assembly, to bear arms, of the press, to vote, and of education. Other freedoms found in liberal democracies include due process, privacy, civil liberties, and property ownership. ***See also*** Constitution (political science); Democracy (political science, public administration); Liberalism (education, political science); Monarchy; Natural Rights; Rule of Law

Liberalism *(education)* A set of related beliefs emphasizing individual rights and equality of opportunity. The term is derived from the Latin *liber,* which is broadly associated with liberty and the concept of freedom. The modern ideology of liberalism traces its origins to the Enlightenment and the set of movements intended to promote individual religious, economic, political, and intellectual freedom. The "liberal arts" of classical antiquity were made accessible to everyone to provide the proper education necessary for the cultivation of the intellect as a tool for promoting individual freedom. In this way, liberalism has become synonymous with education as the vehicle for freeing the individual from the "constraints of ignorance, sectarianism, and myopia" (Association of American Colleges and Universities [AACU], 1998). The American philosopher, statesman, and president, Thomas Jefferson wrote in a letter to William Jarvis in 1820,

> I know no safe depositary of the ultimate powers of the society but the people themselves; and if we think them not enlightened enough to exercise their control with a wholesome discretion, the remedy is not to take it from them, but to inform their discretion by education. This is the true corrective of abuses of constitutional power.

Nonetheless, differences in the form or extent of these liberties have led to two generally competing forms of liberalism—classical and social liberalism. Classical liberalism takes the more traditional position that individual freedom should be maximized while minimizing coercion or state intervention. Accepting the right of individuals to be educated, classical liberalism discourages state intervention in favor of local rule; a plurality of educational institutions, approaches, and circumstances; and the right to bring up one's children according to one's own values and/or religious principles. Social liberalism advocates that the state take an active role in preserving and promoting the freedom of its citizens. Chief among these freedoms is the right to an education as a foundation for full access to and participation in the larger society. Members of the society are free to consider and to choose from among competing alternatives, and they are responsible for the consequences of their choices. The relationship between education and responsible civic participation is embodied most fully in the writings of the educational philosopher John Dewey.

The challenge for liberalism today is to create a society that is as free as possible to defend itself from groups within it that may seek to constrain the rights of the individual, while also tolerating the greatest range of viewpoints to ensure that everyone can live together across the generations.

Liberalism *(political science)* An idea that considers individual liberty to be the fundamental political goal of government. Liberalism has had many different meanings under different circumstances.

At different times, it has sought, for example, to protect the right to acquire property, to shield the individual against tyranny, to establish the doctrine of the inherent rights of men, to organize a world market, or to create individualism. In most instances, however, the needs of the time determine the role of liberalism. Fundamentally, liberalism defends and protects the rights of individuals.

The central idea of liberalism is that government should be neutral toward the moral and religious views that its citizens espouse. Government should provide a framework of rights that respects persons as free and independent, capable of choosing their own values and ends. Liberalism asserts a priority of fair procedures over ends. This is the ideology that has predominated later in American history. It emphasizes a freedom that consists of the capacity of a person to choose his or her own values and ends. American liberal political theory insists on toleration, fair procedures, and respect for individual rights.

Liberalism has experienced ideological transformations throughout history. Classical liberalism, espoused during the Age of Enlightenment by 17th- and 18th-century thinkers such as John Locke, David Hume, Adam Smith, and Immanuel Kant, had a broader meaning than its current form. Classical liberalism was concerned with improving the lives of the working classes. Classical liberals connected liberty to property. They believed in the distribution of power emanating from a free-market economy based on private property and in protection of the liberty of citizens against the encroachments of the state. They further believed that all rights, including liberty, were forms of property.

Modern forms of liberalism are found in the works of John Stuart Mill and Jeremy Bentham in the 19th century and John Rawls in the 20th century. This form is often known as *social liberalism,* which comes from the idea that emphasizes toleration and respect for individual rights. This liberalism favors a generous welfare state and a greater measure of social and economic equality. Liberty thus exists when all citizens have access to basic necessities such as education, health care, and economic opportunities. It is considered as the opposite of conservatism. ***See also*** Conservatism; Liberal Democracy; Republicanism

Liberalization   the removal of restriction from the goods, financial, and service markets. Liberalization is supposed to facilitate the efficient allocation of resources and, as a result, create opportunities for an increase in income. But efficiency is contingent on innovation and capital availability. Liberalization is normally accompanied by transparency of trade policies and a push to have simplified rules and nondiscriminatory practices in trade arrangements and market operations.

Liberalization of the goods market refers to the removal or minimization of impediments to the flow of goods across national boundaries. These impediments include tariffs and nontariff barriers.

Tariffs take the form of taxes—specific tariff (per unit tax); added-value tax, assessed on the value of a good (ad valorem tax); and compound tariff (a combination of the specific and ad valorem). Other forms of restrictions include quantitative restrictions (quotas) through import licenses, voluntary export restraints (VERs) via export licenses or restraints, product quality, government procurement policies for government-funded purchases, and domestic content requirements.

Financial and capital market liberalization alludes to the free movement of capital and access to capital across international boundaries. This means the removal of exchange controls so that nonresidents (foreigners) are able to purchase financial assets or equities from financial institutions in another country or borrow directly from international markets.

Financial liberalization, such as trade in goods, has to be managed carefully in order to prevent the sudden outflow of capital to avoid losses (capital reversibility) and spillover effect to other countries (contagion). The East Asian crisis of the 1990s espoused both reversibility and contagion.

Liberalization of the service and information technology sectors is a relatively recent phenomenon, which was contemplated in the 1960s and 1970s during the General Agreement on Tariffs and Trade (GATT) negotiations, although GATT came into existence in the 1940s. During the Uruguay Round of talks, which resulted in the reorganization of GATT into the World Trade Organization (WTO) in the 1990s, liberalization of trade in agriculture, service, and information technology as well as the protection of property rights became the dominant issues.

Debates on liberalization have been polarizing; some maintaining that it stifles economic progress of the poor and developing countries because of adverse competitive demands on the poor countries and the skewed implementation of liberalization (unfair trade practices). Liberalization of North American trade through the North American Free Trade Agreement (NAFTA) is also raising cause for concern about environmental and labor standards as well as unemployment in the United States. For more information, see Bhagwati (2004), Carbaugh (2007), and Stiglitz (2003). ***See also*** Free Trade; Globalization (economics, political science, sociology); Market Failure; World Trade Organization (WTO)

Liberation Pedagogy   More commonly known as *critical pedagogy*, it is based on the theory of Paulo Freire. He rejects the principle of neutrality in education by advocating teaching and learning processes focused on the formation of nonoppressive democratic culture (see Darder, Baltodano, & Torres, 2003). Essential to this task is the explicit development of critical conscience (conscientization), whereby individuals come to understand and overcome both personal and societal oppression (see Wilson, 2007). ***See also*** Action Research; Critical Theory; Critical Thinking; Literacy/-Illiteracy

Liberty   The freedom to act according to one's own free will and the freedom from coercion to act according to another's. The founding of the United States is based on the principal of liberty; the U.S. Declaration of Independence declared one's inalienable rights of "Life, Liberty and the pursuit of Happiness." One of the most historical symbols of American history is the Liberty Bell. Located in Philadelphia, the Bell was chartered to be built in 1751 by the Pennsylvania Legislature to commemorate the 50-year anniversary of William Penn's 1701 Charter of Privileges, the founding constitution of the state. Penn's Charter contained values considered universal to mankind, including religious freedom and citizen participation in lawmaking. The Bell contains the inscription "Proclaim Liberty throughout all the land unto all the inhabitants thereof," from Leviticus 25:10.

Licensed Professional Counselor (LPC)   A legal credential provided by a state licensing board and intended to verify practitioner's training and competency in order to protect the public. The credential typically requires a master's degree in counseling, a passing score on a test of counseling knowledge, and a period of postdegree-supervised counseling practice.

Licensure   The granting of a license to teach by a state or territorial government. Individuals are eligible for licensure after they have completed the requirements for an education degree and have passed the requisite exams. This process protects students by ensuring that teachers are proficient. ***See also*** Teacher Licensing

Lie Detector   An instrument, also called a *polygraph*, used to record physiological reactions during questioning. Involuntary physical reactions (e.g., blood pressure increases, pulse, perspiration, and respiration) are measured to indicate whether the answers are truthful. Most legal jurisdictions do not allow the use of polygraph results in court testimony because their accuracy is questionable. However, it is a useful tool in law enforcement investigations and in some treatment settings. ***See also*** Testimony

Lifelong Learning A broad term that encompasses the full spectrum of an individual's educational experiences from traditional school to other forms of learning, which may include nonformal, informal, and self-directed learning. The term is often used in connection with adult education in the higher-education setting. It also is used in the occupational and professional development setting. Lifelong learning refers to a lifelong commitment to continual learning and personal development and improvement.

Life Span The human growth and characteristics over a lifetime. According to the developmental psychologist Urie Bronfenbrenner's ecological systems model, five systems, from family to workplace to general society, affect an individual and his or her development simultaneously throughout the life span.

Likert Scale *(education)* A rating scale introduced in 1932 by the social psychologist Rensis Likert (pronounced LICK-ert). A Likert scale invites individuals to rate their level of agreement or disagreement with items measuring their attitudes or perceptions. While traditional Likert-type items have 5-point rating scales, the number of points may vary. Items in a Likert scale measure the same construct and are summed to produce an overall scale score. Likert scaling, or the use of multiple items, is important because single-item measures of constructs are notoriously unreliable. *See also* Rating Scale

Likert Scale *(psychology)* A rating scale that respondents use to answer a question asking the extent to which they agree or disagree with a particular statement. Likert scales are a popular response type, because they indicate the magnitude or strength of an opinion, as well as its direction. Attitudes elicited by these questionnaire items are often measured on a 7-point or a 9-point scale, where one end-point anchor indicates that the respondent agrees (or sometimes that the respondent strongly agrees) with the statement in question and the other end-point anchor indicates that the respondent disagrees (or sometimes strongly disagrees) with the statement. *See also* Rating Scale

Likert Scale *(sociology)* A rating measure used widely in survey questionnaires to assess respondents' attitudes, preferences, and subjective responses to statements. Developed by Rensis Likert, a set of items presents users with statements and standardized response categories on a continuum, such as *strongly agree, agree, neither agree nor disagree, disagree,* and *strongly disagree.* Likert items are usually presented along a horizontal line on which the subject circles or checks his or her response. The Likert scale is a composite measure constructed from the sum of responses to several Likert items. *See also* Instrument; Quantitative Research; Questionnaire; Survey

Linguistic Differences The concept that differences in the way a language is grammatically structured affect the way a culture based on that language will organize itself. The concept, which has both strong and weak versions, states that the very thoughts that are possible within the culture are constrained or made likely by the language. Differences in behavior in each culture are the result of these language and thought differences. The basis of this concept is the work of Edward Sapir and his student Benjamin Whorf early in the 20th century. Synthesized as the Sapir-Whorf hypothesis by other linguists, the idea that language helps organize reality rather than merely being a tool for communicating a reality that already exists was an important break from previous models of language. Before Sapir-Whorf, language was seen as expressing thoughts that reflected an already extant world. With Sapir-Whorf, a language's use of grammar—its metaphors, categories, concepts of difference, orientations to time and space—affect or perhaps even determine what ideas can be thought. Reality is constructed through language as well as being expressed through it. Research to prove or disprove the hypothesis has had mixed results depending on how strict a version of the hypothesis is used. Recent studies based in cognitive linguistics suggest that language structures and systems are far from internally consistent and their realization in the world is also varied. Alternative ways of conceptualizing the world are common in all languages, but there may be limits to the variability possible. This last idea has led some linguists to suggest that there are language universals that are more important than the differences that the Sapir-Whorf hypothesis claims are so important. *See also* Culture (communication, education, media studies, sociology); Language

Linguistic-Relativity Hypothesis Posits that language use influences thought and perception. The earlier, more rigid version of this hypothesis, also known as *linguistic determinism,* or the *Whorfian hypothesis* (after Benjamin Whorf, the amateur linguist who developed the theory), claimed that language actually determined the structure of thought and the perception of reality. Whorf (1956) argued, for example, that the number of words that Inuit Eskimos used for the English word *snow* caused them to develop a greater perceptual ability to discriminate among varieties of snow. However, studies by Rosch (1975) and others showed that perceptual ability is not determined by specificity of language use. Recently, some psychologists have recognized the merits of weaker versions of the Whorfian hypothesis. They recognize that while language does not determine what we think about, it may still influence how we think, since having more specific words for particular concepts can facilitate memory for the concepts themselves because of the availability of verbal labels for those concepts. Separate words may exist to express distinctions or nuances in a concept that are considered important in one culture, whereas the same word may not be so finely distinguished in another culture in which the concept is less important. Alternately, the conciseness with which concepts are expressed in a given language may also be a reflection of the prevalence of the concept or idea in that culture; concepts that are more foreign to the culture are difficult to express in its language. Thus, while language does not determine thought and perception, language and culture are important influences on thought and perception. *See also* Language

Linguistics   The scientific study of the nature and structure of language. Linguists who study grammar cover morphology (the formation of sounds and words), and syntax (the ordering of words into sentences and phrases). Linguistics also includes the study of phonology (the sound system of language), phonetics (the production, transmission, and reception of speech and nonspeech sounds), pragmatics (how language is used in different environments), and semantics (the study of meaning in language). Historical (diachronic) linguists study the history of languages' relations to each other and to human behavior. Comparative linguistics compares languages with each other.

Linkage   A connection, relation, or association between two or more entities. In the social sciences, linkages refer to the connection between political organizations (e.g., political parties, social movements, special-interest groups), citizens, and society or the state. Linkages may be formal or informal ties between individuals or groups or may reflect a more conceptual, subjective connection between an individual and organizations or the political system. For criminal justice agencies to work together, there should be communication or links between them and their investigations. Lack of communication results in linkage blindness. *See also* Linkage Blindness

Linkage Blindness   The inability of law enforcement to communicate or share information in a way that connects similar unsolved crimes. Linkage blindness is often attributed to the lack of cooperation between decentralized police departments or the lack of information-sharing technology. It is often blamed in reference to serial murderers (e.g., the Zodiac Killer). Aside from hindering arrest, linkage blindness may also delay the mobilization of police resources to investigate serious crimes because patterns go unidentified. New technology, such as the FBI's (Federal Bureau of Investigation) Violent Criminal Apprehension Program (ViCAP), alerts law enforcement to similar crimes across jurisdictions.

Liquidity   The degree of promptness with which assets can be converted into cash without excessive loss of value. By definition, money is highly liquid. Similarly, money in a checking account is considered liquid because it could be used to make immediate payments just as cash. The preference for liquidity is normally contingent on interest rate. *See also* Interest

Listening   Hearing with an intent to comprehend. Listening also can refer to nonauditory perception. For instance, a person is listening to his or her body by interpreting fatigue as a sign of knowing it is time to rest.

In terms of interpersonal communication, listening is considered both an art and a skill. In its most effective manifestations, listening requires sensitivity and open-mindedness on the part of the listener. Active listening and empathetic listening—terms defined by the psychologist Carl Rogers in the 1950s—are examples of highly effective listening. Active listening calls for the one who is hearing to comprehend the underlying message beneath the content of the words voiced, to evaluate fairly the speaker, and to reconsider previously held attitudes. Empathetic listening is active listening with the additional component of the listener making the effort to relay back the speaker's perspective. Rogers considered empathetic listening to be the most potent approach that a psychotherapist could take with someone in therapy.

Passive listening, on the other hand, involves conscious or unconscious choices to refrain from comprehending the underlying messages beneath the content of the words voiced, from evaluating the speaker fairly, and from reconsidering previously held attitudes.

Two other forms of listening are critical and evaluative listening. Both involve evaluative thinking, but critical listening is defined as opening the mind to effective interpretation and knowledge gathering, and evaluative listening is seen as a process of closing the mind with a mental critique process that bars full understanding of what the speaker is trying to impart. *See also* Active Listening (communication); Critical Listening; Empathetic Listening; Evaluative Listening; Passive Listening

Literacy/Illiteracy   The basic skills of being able to read and write in one's language of everyday conversation, and the lack of these basic skills. Literacy also means to be familiar with and knowledgeable about the language specific to a discipline. More broadly, literacy refers to an active understanding and appreciation of the world in which one functions and operates, including the ability to converse comfortably in the language spoken in that world and to incorporate the concepts discussed in that language into *other* conversations. For more information, see National Institute for Literacy: www.nifl.gov/nifl/webcasts/NAAL findings/ Transcript_081506.doc

Literature   A collection of textual or spoken works that share a common subject matter. Though the term traditionally refers to a humanities context and includes belles-lettres, prose, verse, fiction, or nonfiction with a recognized artistic value, the concept is appropriately applied to the social sciences realm as well. In the broadest sense, literature is a means of communication. An author or editor intends to communicate a message to be broadcast to a community of readers. The medium—be it a book, a magazine article, or a speech—is a vehicle of mass communication.

In general, literature is considered to be something worthy of and important to record and preserve as a cultural marker. However, the term can refer to material such as campaign literature or propaganda addressing a particular political candidate or social issue. That which might be considered ephemera at one given moment can be preserved for posterity and become part of the literature on a particular subject. Though the artistic or aesthetic notion of literature does not include journalism, for example, such writing is commonly referred to as "the first draft of history."

Regardless of the discipline, whether social or behavioral sciences, hard sciences or humanities, there is a body (or bodies) of scholarly work that is considered to be fundamental to the study of the field or subject. This body of work is analogous to the traditional literary canon. Researchers in a field habitually engage in a literature review at the start of a research project. Monographs, gray literature (reports, conference papers, newsletters, and other texts usually not published commercially), and journal articles comprise the types of literature that might be included in a literature review in any given social science field. In some disciplines, such as psychology and anthropology, journal literature might constitute more of the review, whereas in history, monographs might figure more prominently. ***See also*** Databases for Literature Searches; Discipline

Lithium A drug often used to stabilize mood in people with bipolar disorder. Administered as lithium carbonate, lithium has been found to be effective in 30% to 50% of patients with bipolar disorder. The effects of lithium (and mood stabilizers) may take up to two weeks to appear, suggesting that lithium affects the biology of depression via some long-term compensatory adjustment of the nervous system. Lithium use needs to be closely monitored because of possible toxic effects and mild impairments in memory. Severe overdoses can lead to coma or death. While newer anticonvulsant drugs have been used as an alternative to lithium, their long-term benefits in reducing mania and the risk of suicide have not been established, so lithium remains the standard drug for the treatment of bipolar disorder. ***See also*** Antidepressants; Bipolar Disorders; Depression (economics, education, psychology)

Litigation An adversarial, civil, legal proceeding in a public court meant to determine a legal question or to enforce legal rights and defenses. According to statutory law, litigation may result in damages being awarded or the imposition of an injunction to prevent or compel acts. ***See also*** Statute/Statutory Law

Lobbying The process of petitioning government to influence policy. It is considered one of the most treasured rights in a democracy and is even protected under the First Amendment of the U.S. Constitution. A lobbyist is an individual who engages in lobbying activities, which can occur in any branch of government and at the federal or state level. The ultimate aim of lobbying is to institutionalize change through the legislative process.

The terms *lobbyists* and *lobbying* were used first in the 17th century in the English House of Commons floor, a public room known as the lobby, where individuals, known as lobby agents, approached and sought favors from members of Parliament. In the early 19th century in the United States, government petitioners were called lobbiers, then lobbyists. They solicited members of Congress in the rotunda in the U.S. Capitol.

In the United States today, the functions of lobbyists include researching and analyzing legislative or regulatory proposals, monitoring and reporting on political developments, attending or testifying at congressional or regulatory hearings, working with coalitions, educating employees and corporate officials in an industry, supporting political campaigns in the form of political action committee (PAC) contributions, and communicating with governmental representatives. This last activity actually constitutes the smallest proportion of a lobbyist's time, although it receives the most public attention.

Since the 1976 Lobby Law in the United States, two types of lobbying have been officially recognized, especially for nonprofit organizations: direct and grassroots. Direct lobbying involves stating one's position on specific legislation to a legislator. Grassroots lobbying comprises stating one's position on specific legislation to the general public and asking the general public to contact legislators and members of government who participate in formulating a specific piece of legislation. The distinction was instituted by the Internal Revenue Service, which supported the 1976 law, to formulate guidelines for lobbying expenditures and define activities that do or do not constitute lobbying.

Over the years in the United States, lobbying had become a derogatory term due to the questionable tactics special interests used to win legislation. For example, in the 19th century, railroad lobbyists openly distributed checks to legislators on the floor of Congress. In the 1990s, legislators increasingly relied on lobby contributions for campaign financing. For critics, the problem with these activities is that they threaten to corrupt the fundamental notion of democracy.

To curb and account for lobbying expenditures, in 1946, the Federal Regulation of Lobbying Act was passed, which required registration and regulation of the financial reports of lobbyists. It was later challenged by lobbyists as being unconstitutionally vague. In 1954, in *United States v. Harriss,* the Supreme Court upheld the Act's constitutionality but narrowed its scope. Congress later passed the Lobby Disclosure Act of 1995, which was intended to increase lobbyists' accountability, not covered in the 1946 law. ***See also*** Congress; Grassroots Lobbying; Interest Group (political science, public administration); Legislative Branch; Regulatory Agency

Local Network Programming Programs created by local broadcast stations as opposed to networks. Since there were only local stations when television first began broadcasting to the public in the late 1940s, each station produced its own programming. Even after technology allowed stations to link to one another and to national broadcasting networks, local stations still produced a substantial amount of original material. The content of such programs reflected the culture, tastes, and particular events of the local region, and viewers developed a somewhat intimate relationship with the performers. Unlike stars from nationally broadcast programs, local personalities seemed more accessible and real.

Due to financial constraints on local stations, programmers were compelled to produce more creative and arguably risky content and formats than what might be seen on a national scale, where larger budgets allowed for more spectacle. Such independent-minded development was a breeding ground for some innovative styles, such as the "Chicago School" style, which included figures who went on to attain national fame, such as Studs Terkel and Dave Garroway.

Similar patterns appeared, however, among local stations. Common formats in the 1940s and 1950s included children's homemaking and quiz shows during the day and sports and movies on nights and weekends. The increased capability for national syndication in the 1950s was inversely proportional to the opportunities for generating local programming. In 1970, the Federal Communications Commission established the Prime Time Access Rule, limiting the amount of network programming that could be shown on local stations, but it was eliminated in the mid-1990s. Local programming is nearly a relic in the 21st century. The introduction of cable television has reduced local programming even further, since network programming is far cheaper for local stations to deliver. *See also* Broadcasting; Network

Location Theory   A theory that draws from the disciplines of geography and economics and is used to examine the geography of economic activities. Location theory places a heavy focus on spatial dynamics, looking at why certain economics occur in different locations, including cities, towns, counties, neighborhoods, and even certain blocks. Similar to various economic theories, location theory is grounded in the notion that individuals will pursue their self-interests, weighing the costs and benefits of their actions. Under this utilitarian approach, geographical locations are selected for their maximum utility—termed in location theory as maximum profit capability.

Locus of Control (*education*)   The beliefs that people hold about the causes of outcomes. People with an internal locus of control believe that their own behaviors or attributes are influential in controlling outcomes. In contrast, people with an external locus of control attribute outcomes to unpredictable and/or uncontrollable external factors. *See also* Attribution Theory

Locus of Control (*psychology*)   An individual's beliefs about the source of responsibility for life events and, consequently, the individual's general expectancies about whether his or her efforts can bring about desired outcomes and reinforcements. Locus of control can be internal or external. People with an internal locus of control attribute responsibility for life events internally to themselves and believe that they can obtain reinforcements through work and effort. People with an external locus of control attribute responsibility for life events externally to themselves and believe that reinforcements are controlled by external forces beyond their control. Rotter's (1966) Internal-External Scale is a psychological inventory used to measure an individual's general locus of control. Locus of control has generated much psychological research and has important applications to clinical psychology, the health sciences, and education. For example, people with an internal locus of control tend to work harder at staying physically healthy, are less likely to drive while intoxicated, and tend to achieve better grades in college courses. However, more recent approaches have conceptualized locus of control as a multidimensional construct, and studies find that locus of control is context specific, so that people can differ in their locus of control across different domains (e.g., academic, health). *See also* Attribution Theory; Learned Helplessness

Logical Positivism   Occurring in various yet standard forms from the first days of the Vienna Circle in the early 1920s to the beginning of World War II, this concept was characterized by a number of then radical and interrelated principles. Among these doctrines were the verifiability theory of meaning, the rejection of metaphysics, the emotive theory of moral judgments, and the assertion that legitimate philosophy consists solely of logical analysis. The fundamental doctrine was the theory of meaning, which maintained that the cognitive meaning of a sentence is its method of verification. Consequently, if a sentence is not verifiable or is not true by definition, it is cognitively meaningless. This doctrine ruled out much of traditional philosophy, leaving only logic, mathematics, and the sciences as capable of meeting the verifiability criterion. Philosophy thus became identified with analysis whose only task was expounding and clarifying the logical syntax of science. According to the emotive theory, since moral judgments do not state any facts, they are descriptively meaningless. Their purpose is not cognitive but instead the expression of emotion.

Logistic Regression   The prediction of a dichotomous criterion variable, that is, a probability or proportion from a set of continuous or categorical (in dummy-variable form) predictor variables. Since the relationship between predictors and criterion is nonlinear, a natural logistic conversion is used to predict the criterion variable.

Logistics   The planning, implementation, and management of the efficient and cost-effective movement of goods, information, or people. Movement may be by road, pipeline, air, rail, or water from point of origin to point of consumption to conform to customer requirements (frequently, military organizations).

Logos   The source, order, or accountable principle—the "telling"—in a discourse. It involves reasoning. For example, reason and intelligence are implied if one is capable of speech. Heraclitus established the term in Western philosophy as meaning the source and the fundamental order of the cosmos. Aristotle (in *Nichomachean Ethics*) used the term to differentiate between the reasoning part of the soul and the emotional. A similar meaning—logos as a generative intelligence—exists in Christianity. The New Testament Gospel of John begins with the sentence "In the beginning was the Word [Logos], and the Word was with God, and the Word was God."

Lombroso, Cesare   Trained in Italy as a physician, Lombroso (1835–1909) is generally regarded as the most influential figure in biological positivism and is nicknamed the father of modern criminology. He was greatly influenced by Charles Darwin's (1809–1882) work on evolution. Lombroso's best-known work, *The Criminal Man* (1876), is a comparative study of Italian soldiers and Italian prison inmates. In the inmates, he identified atavistic human beings, or those he characterized as less evolved, or evolutionary "throwbacks" and more primitive. These natural-born criminals could be identified by physical stigmata, outer characteristics including high foreheads, large ears, and elongated eye teeth. Lombroso was one of the first to distinguish between male and female offenders in *The Female Offender* (1895), where he described women as generally less evolved than men and more likely to be atavistic. Criminal women were considered more masculine than noncriminal women.

Longitudinal Study   Studies where the same group of participants is tested repeatedly over time. This design is often used in developmental research to examine the way personality and behavior change across the life span. The advantage of longitudinal designs over their alternative, cross-sectional designs (see definition), is that longitudinal designs do not suffer from cohort effects, in which people of particular age groups, or cohorts, share particular sets of life circumstances (e.g., being teenagers in the late 1950s versus being teenagers in the new millennium) so that development stage at comparison (e.g., comparing older adults with adolescents in 2008) is confounded with other life circumstances. The disadvantage of longitudinal research is in the high rate of attrition that occurs over time. Also, in the same way that cross-sectional designs are vulnerable to cohort effects,

longitudinal designs are vulnerable to secular trends (general trends that occur in society and that may affect the results of the longitudinal study by confounding age with time of testing). For example, finding that participants improve at programming software as they age may be the result of developmental changes, or it may be the result of general growth in societal proficiency with technology. *See also* Cross-Sectional Research; Developmental Psychology

Longitudinal Versus Cross-Sectional Data   The former are collected at two or more points in time. Cross-sectional data are collected at one time. For example, in a cross-sectional study concerning the effects of age, three different groups of individuals could be surveyed in the year 2010: 20-, 25-, and 30-year-olds. In a longitudinal study, individuals would be surveyed first when they were 20 years old (in 2010); the same individuals would again be surveyed when they were 25 (in 2015) and 30 (in 2020) years old.

Long-Term Memory (LTM)   The third stage in an information-processing model of memory that proposes three distinct stages of memory, which differ in the length of time that information is stored. The first two stages are sensory memory and short-term (or working) memory. Long-term memory allows the information to be retained for periods of time beyond the capacity of short-term memory; some information is stored in long-term memory for days or weeks, but other information may remain across a lifetime, and the capacity of long-term memory is believed to be limitless. During REM (rapid eye movement) sleep and deep, slow-wave sleep, information from short-term memory is converted, through a process called *consolidation,* into long-term memories. Information can also be transferred from short-term to long-term memory through rehearsal, particularly elaborative rehearsal, since long-term memory depends largely on semantic coding (coding by meaning). Conceptual models of long-term memory posit that this memory system holds declarative and procedural memory and is organized according to semantic networks. *See also* Declarative Memory; Memory (education, psychology); Procedural Memory; Semantic Network; Short-Term Memory (STM)

Low-Context Culture   First introduced by the anthropologist Edward T. Hall in his book *Beyond Culture* (1976), this concept refers to a culture where communication is more explicit than implicit as in a high-context culture. This culture of communication stems from a context of short-term relationships where proper actions or behaviors have to be spelled out for new members. Understanding comes directly from consciously codified external verbal communication. In this culture, the specific task is more important than continuing, long-term relationships with implied meaning in communications. Verbal communication is direct and elaborate, with little room for conjecture on the part of the interlocutor. Edward T. Hall uses the American court system as a prime example of low-context culture. He discusses the inadmissibility of contexting testimony in courts of law. This leads to the "opinion rule," where only established facts, without context, are admitted as evidence.

As Hall (1976) says, "Low-context systems do not afford equal treatment but favor those who can enlist the most articulate and skillful lawyers on their side." Therefore, these attorneys are adept at manipulating the system in admitting or excluding testimony favorable to their clients. They are even more successful if they come before judges who are not intelligent enough to discriminate the context of "facts" the attorneys present.

Low-context cultures also do not differentiate much between in-groups (high culture) and out-groups. Communication becomes explicit information exchange only to the extent necessary to accomplish tasks. Low-context cultures are marked by short-term compartmentalized relationships with consciously organized knowledge. Individuals require explicit explanations when they need clarity in a situation. In other words, meaning is not internalized as in high-context cultures. Low-context organizational situations, such as taking on a job in a chain store, are relatively easy to deal with because they are not usually marked by long-term relationships between like-minded social or professional groups. Low-context relationships usually have clear-cut rules and codifications of behavior, such as those found in sports teams, large community or school organizations, and the like. North America is usually characterized as a low-context culture, in which the communication style is more direct with elaborate verbal messages. For more information, see Hall (1976). ***See also*** High-Context Culture

Lynching The unlawful, premeditated killing (especially by hanging) of a presumed offender by a mob action, under the pretense of administering justice, without legal authority. Lynching was widely used against blacks during and after the Reconstruction in the American South, often to intimidate other blacks. ***See also*** Civil Rights; Jim Crow Laws

L

Macroeconomic Policy   A combination of monetary and fiscal policies designed to stabilize a macroeconomy. Fiscal policy involves government spending and taxing, while monetary policy is designed to target the money supply and interest rate.

Fiscal and monetary policies can be expansionary or contractionary. Expansionary policies are intended to stimulate employment and output, while contractionary policies are implemented to prevent or curb inflationary pressures.

Fiscal policy is expansionary when a government gives a tax cut to increase disposable income or spends money (deficit financing) to increase employment and output. John Maynard Keynes used a multiplier theory to show how an increase in initial (autonomous) spending can generate a multiplier effect to stimulate aggregate consumption. Some people are apprehensive about the effects of the multiplier theory because of leakages and inflation.

Monetary policy is expansionary when a nation's monetary authorities expand credit availability to increase investment consumption and output. In the United States, the Federal Reserve does so through open-market operations by buying government securities to make depository institutions more liquid. Contractionary policies are the direct opposite of expansionary policies. Because macroeconomic policies are prone to time lags (recognition, implementation, and outside lags) that force the performance of a macroeconomy to deviate from its long-run growth path, advocates of market solution advance the argument that the economy is capable of stabilizing itself.

Advocates of automatic stabilizers maintain that during periods of recession, government tax receipts fall, but a government makes transfer payments to dampen the effects of unemployment. Conversely, during periods of expansion, government increases its revenue base and makes less transfer payments because of increased employment.

Apart from the prospects of self-correction, the effects of macroeconomic policies can be elusive because people form expectations about policies. The expectations or reactions of people to policy choices may not necessarily affirm the policy objectives. Consequently, for policymakers to assess the impact of policy choices, they must be able to ascertain with reasonable foresight how people will respond to policy changes. This criticism of policy evaluation is popularly known as the *Lucas critique.*

The Lucas critique (from the work of the economist Robert Lucas) is applicable to the cost of disinflation (the amount of gross domestic product [GDP] that must be sacrificed to reduce inflation by a percentage point—the sacrifice ratio) when people have rational expectations, such as when they can incorporate all available information, including from the recent past (adaptive expectations), in their decision-making process to determine what might happen in the future. Workers and firms, by setting wages and prices that incorporate all information, can also have an impact on inflation and employment. For further reading, see Keynes (1936), Mankiw (2006), McConnell and Brue (2008), and Schiller (2006). *See also* Business Cycle (economics); Fiscal Policy; Inflation; Macroeconomics; Monetary Policy; Stabilization

Macroeconomics   The study of an economy as a whole. Unlike microeconomics, it studies aggregate economic variables, such as the general price level (using an index of consumer or producer prices), the national (un)employment rate, national saving, and national output income (gross domestic product).

Although microeconomic issues might affect a particular segment or group of individuals in a national economy, macroeconomic issues affect everyone in a national economy and the overall well-being of a nation. The government and the monetary authorities are the principal macroeconomic policymakers of a nation.

In the United States, there is emphasis on the independence of these entities so that monetary policy is not infected by parochial political ambitions or interests. The degree of independent monetary policy making in the United States is sometimes questioned because the chairman of the Federal Reserve is appointed by the president subject to the approval of lawmakers. The position is also a political creation that can be expunged, although that is very unlikely or improbable. In some other nations, there is a consolidation of macroeconomic policy making, with very little emphasis on independence. This makes it very difficult to make meaningful and rewarding macroeconomic policies.

Macroeconomic policies are generally designed to attain efficiency, equity, stability, and growth. Efficiency involves the production of what society wants at the least possible cost. By definition, there are allocative (distributive) and productive (cost sensitive) dimensions to efficiency.

Equity involves fairness in the distribution of national income. Fairness is arguably an elusive macroeconomic concept because of its subjective and normative connotations, but there are normally efforts to evaluate tax structure based on notions of tax burden and societal wants and needs.

Progressive taxes are taxes that are paid based on the amount of income earned (the higher the income, the greater the taxes). Regressive taxes (such as sales taxes) are taxes for which the greater burden falls on those who make less income relative to the wealthy. Issues of merit and rewards for hard work or future growth (via investment) characterize macroeconomic debates on fairness.

Stability and growth require macroeconomic policies that aim at stabilizing prices in the hope of increasing output or employment. Policies to stabilize a macroeconomy may be expansionary or contractionary. Expansionary policies are intended to deal with recessions or downturns, while contractionary policies are designed to deal with inflation or the propensity of an economy to overheat. Policy choices fall into two broad categories: (1) fiscal and (2) monetary.

Expansionary fiscal policy is the deliberate effort by a government to reduce taxes or increase spending. Expansionary monetary policy is the deliberate effort by a nation's monetary authorities to reduce the interest rate or increase the money supply. Contractionary policies are the opposite of expansionary policies. Some critics are skeptical about the use of policies to stabilize a macroeconomy, partly because of lags or wrong intervention. For further reading, see Case and Fair (2003), Mankiw (2006), and McConnell and Brue (2008). ***See also*** Economics; Fiscal Policy; Gross Domestic Product; Growth; Keynesian; Monetary Policy; Stabilization

Macrofamily   A classification term in linguistics referring to a proposed language family that unites a group of recognized language families. Such language families are grouped because they show sufficient similarities to suggest genetic relationships. When linguists accept a macrofamily proposal, it becomes a "language family." ***See also*** Linguistics

Madisonianism   An ideology based on the writings of James Madison, the fourth president of the United States. Madison's ideology is shown in his work as a founding member of the Democratic-Republican party, coauthor of the *Federalist Papers,* and framer of the U.S. Constitution and Bill of Rights. Madison's legacy was to limit the power of the federal government. He did not want an active national government.

The central proposition of Madisonianism was that groups or individuals will tyrannize—that is, deprive others of their natural rights—if unrestrained by external checks. These external checks are rewards and penalties applied by outside sources. Madison believed that if the tyranny is to be avoided, external checks are required and these checks must be constitutionally arranged. The accumulation of all power in the hands of a central government implies the elimination of external checks. Thus, in *Federalist* No. 47, Madison supported a separation of powers among the three branches of government with a system of checks and balances.

Checks and balances were further needed to limit the powers of special interests, which Madison called *factions*. Madison addresses the likely danger of factions in *Federalist* No. 51, in which he states that the only way to counteract the potential tyranny of factions is to have numerous factions. According to Madison, to the extent that the electorate is numerous, extended, and diverse in interests, a majority faction is less likely to exist. If it does, it is less likely to act as a unity. For further reading, see Dahl (2003) and Madison, Hamilton, and Jay (1788/1987). ***See also*** Anti-Federalist; Bill of Rights (political science); Constitution (political science); Federalist; Federalist Papers; Republicanism

Magazine   A periodical publication that is issued weekly, monthly, bimonthly, or quarterly. Content can range from the popular and general interest to the scholarly and technical. The concept of print magazines dates back to 17th-century Europe, though *Gentleman's Magazine,* established by Edward Cave in London in 1731, is generally considered the first periodical to be designated a magazine. Andrew Bradford's *American Magazine* and Benjamin Franklin's *General Magazine and Historical Chronicle* were both established in Philadelphia in 1741.

Magazines are generally financed by advertising fees and subscription or newsstand prices, through either paid or controlled circulation (e.g., in-flight magazines). For most of the 20th century, a magazine fit into one of four categories: (1) consumer magazines are generally supported by advertising and aimed at the general public; (2) trade and technical magazines are aimed at smaller specific audiences in businesses and industries and contain information about the occupations practiced by their audience; (3) public relations periodicals promote the interests of corporations, universities, government agencies, or nonprofit organizations among their employees, clients, or alumni; (4) literary or scholarly journals generally do not have a commercial interest other than remaining in publication and defraying the costs of production. Over the course of the 20th century, however, the scope of categories grew. Magazines—as compared with other media—became more specialized as publishers were increasingly interested in targeting audiences with specific interests.

With the advent of the Internet, a distinction was made between print and online magazines; some are published online only, while some are available via both formats.

The term *magazine format* applies to radio and television broadcasts that include distinct segments. The program time is sold to two or more advertisers, as opposed to a single sponsorship, which was the convention in the 1940s and 1950s. For further reading, see Tebbel and Zuckerman (1991). ***See also*** Newspaper; Print Media

Magistrate   A judge who is a federal public official and who presides over a range of routine judicial proceedings, such as preliminary hearings in criminal cases and issuing of arrest and search warrants. Magistrate judges serve to expedite the disposition of U.S. district courts' criminal and civil caseloads. ***See also*** Judge

Magnetic Resonance Imaging (MRI)   A technique that uses a magnetic field to create a computerized image of internal bodily structures. It is used in psychological research to measure brain structure, by exposing the brain to a magnetic field and measuring the resulting radio frequency waves to produce clear pictures of the brain. Its advantage over positron emission tomography (PET) scans is that it requires no exposure to radioactivity and produces a higher spatial resolution of anatomical details. A newer MRI technique, called functional MRI (fMRI), can detect changes in blood flow that reflect changes in neuron activity. By observing activity in an individual's brain while the individual performs certain tasks, researchers can link the individual's behavior with activity in specific brain structures. Thus, fMRI not only maps the brain structure but also can be used to study the function of particular brain structures. For further reading, see Westbrook, Roth, and Talbot (2005). ***See also*** Brain (Encephalon); Positron Emission Tomography (PET) Scan

Magnet Schools   A system of school education developed in the 1960s to attract students from across numerous school districts or zones. Magnet schools tend to offer a specialized curriculum, such as International Baccalaureate (IB), fine arts, mathematics, technology, and science and attract students who are interested in those areas of specialization. Magnet schools exist at the elementary, middle, and high school levels. Competitive admission processes often exist along with lotteries or applications for admission and parents signing contracts addressing acceptable student grades and behavior. In the 1970s, magnet schools became important in desegregating innercity schools by offering sought-after curriculum to students.

Mainstreaming *(education)*   The practice of placing special-education students in regular classrooms for specified portions of the school day. This practice is based on the Individuals with Disabilities Education Act (IDEA) requirement that students be educated in the least restrictive environment possible. Benefits include a stronger sense of belonging to the school community and a more authentic school setting. ***See also*** Inclusion

Mainstreaming *(media studies)*   The process of creating mass audience awareness about previously underrepresented groups through media messages. Individuals and groups seek mainstreaming to voice messages about their representation in the mainstream media as well as to heighten public awareness about their cause. Mainstreaming is thus a means for improving visibility in mass media messages, which historically perpetuates the dominant social, political, and economic ideologies. Moreover, media messages reinforce notions of

acceptability for members of the majority culture and either slight or construct demeaning representations of minority groups. A difficulty with mainstreaming, as critics charge, is that media messages may be constructed that reinforce the problematic stereotypes of the individuals and groups while they are attempting to mainstream, rather than offering new meanings; this corresponds to the notion of media frames. ***See also*** Frame of Reference; Industry (media studies)

Majority Government   When the party wielding executive power in a government controls the majority of seats in the legislature, it is known as government by the majority. This type of government is practiced in the Westminster system, the parliamentary system used in the United Kingdom and many formerly colonized nations. For example, in Canada, the party that wins more than half the seats in the House of Commons forms a majority government. Many voters prefer a majority government because legislation is passed more easily, and the leadership is able to win the confidence vote of the legislature. The opposite of a majority government is a minority government, where the party with the executive power does not control the majority of seats in the legislature. ***See also*** Minority Government

Majority Leader   The leader who is chosen from the party in the majority in each house of Congress. The leader's responsibilities include planning legislative agendas, meeting with the president on behalf of the party, and lobbying efforts. In the House, the majority leader is elected every two years. In the Senate, the leader is elected at the start of each new Congress. ***See also*** Congress

Mala in se   In Latin, this phrase translates as "wrong in itself." *Mala in se* offenses are those offenses that are considered evil in and of themselves and are best understood when contrasted with *mala prohibita* (prohibited because of legal statutes) offenses. Murder, robbery, rape, and burglary are all examples of *mala in se* offenses. ***See also*** *Mala Prohibita;* Offender/Offense

Mala prohibita   In Latin, this phrase translates as "wrong because prohibited." *Mala prohibita* offenses are those offenses that are only wrong because they are prohibited by statute. *Mala prohibita* offenses are not universally considered evil or wrong. Drug possession and gambling are examples of *mala prohibita* offenses. This is in contrast to *mala in se* offenses, which are wrong in and of themselves (such as murder). ***See also*** *Mala in se;* Offender/Offense

Malice   The intention to cause harm. Generally relating to the intent element (or *mens rea* requirement) in a crime, evidence that the person thought about the consequences of his or her actions demonstrates malice. In some jurisdictions, a demonstration of malice aforethought is necessary for a conviction of murder. ***See also*** Culpability; *Mens Rea*

M

Management   Broadly, the term refers to the directing and controlling of a group of people or entities, and the process used for the purpose of accomplishing a goal. During the early 20th century, Mary Parker Follett (1868–1933), who wrote on the topic, defined management as "the art of getting things done through people."

In an organization, management combines both policy and administration and the people who provide the decisions and supervision necessary to implement the organization's objectives. An organization can be a business, school, city, or governmental entity.

Key functions of management often regarded as necessary to achieve the organization's goals include planning, organizing, budgeting, staffing, reporting, directing, and coordinating. These functions are applied throughout an organization regardless of type or orientation. Management size can range from an individual to multilayered management hierarchies in large, complex organizations. The people to whom the management task is assigned are referred to as managers. For further reading, see Graham (1995). *See also* Organization (public administration)

Management by Objectives (MBO)   An appraisal tool that was popularized by Peter Drucker in 1954 in his book *The Practice of Management*. It generally refers to the systematic and organized management technique of setting attainable goals and objectives. Initially, MBO was a human resource management tool for improving communication about expected work between supervisors and employees and encouraging workers to focus on outcomes. Rather than the supervisor assigning objectives and tasks to the employee in a top-down manner, MBO requires negotiation between the supervisor and the employee and encourages discussion of the nature of the task, the quality of the work, and the resources needed to accomplish the tasks. When MBO is fully operationalized in an organization, each employee's objectives are related to unit goals and organization goals in a cascading manner.

Drucker was very specific about the importance of objectives, with the guiding principle of MBO being that all members within the organization have a clear understanding of its objectives as well as an understanding of their own roles and responsibilities in achieving the objectives. In addition, the use of MBO needs to be carefully aligned with the culture of the organization. For instance, in an organization that emphasizes employee empowerment, employees will discuss the resources they need to achieve their objectives. Typically, MBO requires periodic review of congruence among tasks and the resources required to perform those tasks. These MBO practices contribute directly to higher organizational performance.

MBO and its subsequent refinements are widely used in management today. More often than not, MBO is integrated into an organization-wide performance management system. The key difference between the earlier application of MBO and its more recent use relates to the setting of objectives. In the early years of its application,
targets were established for meeting objectives. Now, when MBO is used, rather than setting objectives from a cascade process, objectives are generally discussed and agreed on based on a more strategic picture being available to employees. For further reading, see Drucker (1954). *See also* Management

Management Information System (MIS)   The collective term used to describe the use of information technology (IT) to improve the effectiveness and efficiency of organizations. Most often, this means using computer resources to record and analyze an organization's data so that they can be used to assist managers in decision making.

Managerial Subsystem   Management is the process of integrating human and material resources into a total system for objective accomplishment. Prior to the 1970s, managers were seen as prey to environmental determinations. They were considered only as an element that responded to the determinations imposed on the organization by other variables. Since then, managers have been understood as possessing the capacity to choose or influence some of the environmental factors that influence their organizations, such as employees, customers, and sales.

A managerial subsystem is the means of linking other primary subsystems of organizations into a coherent framework. A managerial subsystem's primary role is to integrate activities toward the achievement of explicit and implicit goals. As such, the managerial subsystem has a functional imperative since at least some management is needed to balance the tugs exerted by other subsystems, as well as to fit the organization to its environment.

In the managerial subsystem, managers are responsible for making decisions, relating the organization to its environment, setting goals, developing strategic and operational plans, and establishing control processes. This subsystem spans the entire organization by directing technology, organizing people, and relating—that is, identifying a niche that must be filled—the organization to its environment.

The managerial subsystem comprises all the managers in an organization or industry. In a school, for example, the managerial subsystem includes the superintendent, principals, and school board. In a larger context, apart from a single organization, such as the culture industry, the managerial subsystem may include organizations that produce cultural products, such as publishing houses, film studios, and record companies. *See also* Management

Mandate   Authority to take action given to an official by virtue of his or her winning an election by a large margin. In such a situation, a public mandate is said to be granted by voters for the official's proposed policy or agenda. It is debatable how much of a margin of victory is necessary for a mandate to be granted, especially when it concerns a presidential candidate.

Mandatory Sentence A sentence that must be imposed on conviction irrespective of an individual offender's aggravating or mitigating circumstances. Mandatory sentences, which reduce the discretion that judges have historically enjoyed in sentencing criminal offenders, often come in the form of mandatory minimums. *See also* Discretion (sociology); Truth-in-Sentencing Laws

Manhattan Bail Project A project conducted by the Vera Institute of Justice in 1961. As the first pretrial screening program in the United States, this project was proposed to address long-standing injustices in the nation's bail system by assisting judges in making more consistent, informed release decisions. Instead of basing release on financial means, which left more indigent defendants in pretrial detention than their wealthier counterparts, the project assessed defendants' ties to the community. Specifically, the staff of the project interviewed defendants and verified the information about relationships, employment, education, and prior criminal record with third parties. The strength of the ties informed release recommendations and significantly positively affected the rate of return of released defendants. As a result, defendants with strong ties to the community are released on recognizance (ROR) rather than detained or released on bail. *See also* Bail; Released on Recognizance (ROR)

Manifest Content The alternative to latent content. It is another way in which content can be investigated when an event or communication is recorded. Manifest content is the content of an event, as measured by the frequency of some objective word, phrase, or action. The researcher observes the number of times the target material or behavior occurs. The advantage of manifest-content analysis over latent-content analysis is that manifest-content assessment is less subjective. However, its disadvantage is that the researcher is limited to observing the frequency of an event without considering the context of its occurrence (e.g., counting how many times the word *love* appears in a passage of text, without considering whether the word represents brotherly or sexual love). Coding events in this way, without consideration of their context, may lead to inaccurate conclusions. For further reading, see Auerbach and Silverstein (2003). *See also* Latent Content; Qualitative Data Analysis

Manipulation The practice of twisting information in a clever and unscrupulous manner for the purpose of influencing people and misleading them into action.

Examples of—as well as accusations about—manipulation have been noted in advertising content for products and services, in campaign messages by candidates seeking political office, in the reporting of news, in organizational communication, in recruiting posters for the armed forces, and in government information dissemination. Regarding the latter, the American presidential candidate Adlai Stevenson made a statement in 1957 about "distortion and manipulation of the news—not *by* the press, but *to* the press."

People often do not perceive deviations from the truth because the deviations are either minor or because they come from sources people deem reliable. Therefore, the deceivers succeed in misleading their targets, as noted by researchers such as Herbert P. Grice in 1989 and Steven McCornack, who wrote about information manipulation theory in 1992. For further reading, see Grice (1989), "Manipulation" (2008), McCornack (1992), McCornack and Levine (1990), and McCornack, Levine, Morrison, and Lapinski (1996). *See also* Media; Perception (communication, psychology)

Manipulative An object that can be manipulated or moved to develop motor skills and facilitate learning of abstract concepts. These objects are often used in arithmetic. Counting pennies is an example of using a manipulative to illustrate a principle of arithmetic.

Manslaughter A criminal homicide (or killing of a human being) where the level of culpability (or blameworthiness) is less than it would be in a murder. Voluntary manslaughter is an intentional killing that lacks the malice aforethought traditionally associated with murder. Those who kill in the heat of passion or following provocation are often charged with voluntary manslaughter instead of murder. Involuntary manslaughter is sometimes referred to as criminally negligent homicide and results when a person dies as a result of a defendant's reckless conduct. A person who is convicted of involuntary manslaughter has, typically, willfully disregarded a known risk. *See also* Culpability; Homicide; Murder

Manufacturing The process by which materials are transformed into intermediate and finished products. Two inputs, labor and capital, are instrumental to the transformation process. As such, manufacturing encompasses labor- and capital-intensive goods (handicrafts and high-tech goods) when the expression is used generically.

Disparities in endowment and colonialism have made manufacturing an integral aspect of international exchange. Labor-intensive countries export their raw materials or cash crops to much more industrialized countries for further processing or industrial production.

Fabrication (a process through which chips or electronic devices are created by photographic and chemical processes) and the transformation of raw materials into intermediate or finished products are closely representative of the modern usage of the concept.

In advanced economies, manufacturing is associated with engineering and industrial design, which produces cars, airplanes, tires, and steel and steel-related products. Some Southeast Asian countries, such as Taiwan and Singapore, unlike some former colonial countries of Africa and Latin America, were able to successfully use

M

manufacturing as an export-oriented growth strategy to foster growth and development. ***See also*** Capital; Labor

Manuscript   A handwritten or typewritten text that is the original or revised material written by an author prior to publication. The term *typescript* specifically refers to a typed draft, though *manuscript* is often used to describe any unpublished draft material. In magazine, newspaper, academic journal, and book publishing, a manuscript is submitted to an editor for consideration, and in the scholarly journal publication process, it may be reviewed by a small group of anonymous peers. Most publications stipulate that potential authors follow a specific set of style guidelines when preparing their manuscripts, such as for line spacing, margin width, and citations. While the term literally and historically refers to a text that is handwritten, in most cases only typewritten manuscripts are accepted for consideration.

In general, original manuscripts are discarded or simply filed away as the text moves along in the publication process. With the ubiquity of computers, editors may make notes on a hard-copy printout of the manuscript or using a word-processing editing tool. Therefore, the original manuscript may cease to exist, as changes can be made directly to the digital text, which in turn evolves into the finished product. Quite often, an unpublished manuscript will survive the process and, if considered valuable for research purposes due to the author's renown, become part of a body of work that is collected by a library, museum, or other historical archive. The manuscript may be the original version of a famous novel, letter, or diary penned by the author. In this context, the meaning broadens to include almost any historical document relating to the author's life.

A related use of the term, *manuscript method of speaking*, refers to the direct reading of a speech that has been written out word for word. ***See also*** Publication; Text

Mapping   The charting of locations on a plane surface. In the social sciences, data mapping has been used to chart and analyze patterns in social phenomena, such as illness, poverty, or crime. Specifically, crime mapping has been used extensively by both criminologists and law enforcement to allow visualization of patterns of criminal incidents and the location of other variables, such as public housing, schools, or ethnicity. Crime mapping has been facilitated by the use of geographic information systems (GIS) software, which uses spatial data analysis to display and analyze patterns in mapped data.

Marginal   An incremental or additional change, which may be in the form of cost or benefit. Marginal analysis is a principle that is used to evaluate the efficiency of economic decisions or resource allocation.

In economics, it is generally assumed that consumers will maximize utility from the consumption of a variety of goods when the marginal utility per dollar is the same for the consumption of the last unit of all goods consumed. This is also a precondition for consumer equilibrium when income is exhausted.

In a perfectly competitive market, producers will produce until the marginal cost is the equivalent of the marginal revenue. As such, scarce resources will only be used or allocated as necessary.

Marginal analysis is also used to understand rates of resource substitution—for example, how many tractors must be given up to get more computers or the opportunity cost of using more labor relative to capital.

Mathematically, rates of change denote the marginal concept when other variables are held constant. In other words, the slope of a line indicates the amount by which one variable (dependent variable) is going to change when an independent variable is increased or reduced incrementally (marginally).

The marginal concept also serves the useful social function of evaluating a shadow price. The shadow price has no real existence, but it provides a rationale for explaining whether a policy should be encouraged or discouraged, by assessing its incremental cost or benefit to society. An activity is deemed necessary if the social benefit outweighs the cost, although it is produced insufficiently. A social planner can subsidize its production until the marginal social cost becomes the equivalent of the marginal social benefit.

The marginal concept can therefore be usefully applied to production, consumption, and the evaluation of social policy. ***See also*** Econometrics

Maritime Effect   Large bodies of water, such as oceans, have an effect on the climate of certain locations and regions within a given proximity. The effect of an ocean's airflow on the climate of the surrounding areas, also known as the maritime effect, is generally milder temperatures and a decreased variation in temperatures. Although the ocean is generally slow to warm, it retains its warmth for a long period of time, which has a tempering effect on the climate. Precipitation is more common in areas with a maritime climate, as moisture levels are higher near the ocean. Maritime climates are common on the British Isles.

Continental climates, on the other hand, can generally be found in areas surrounded by significant land masses. The continental effect stands in contrast to the maritime effect and is characterized by more extreme weather conditions, widely varying temperatures, and a dry climate. Continental climates can be found in Russia and in many regions of the United States.

Market   A market is an institution in which buyers and sellers meet to exchange services, goods, and assets. Today, markets may be physical structures or electronic media. Improvement in technology has made it possible for market transactions to be executed electronically and not just in the exclusive domain of bricks and walls.

Economists classify markets under three broad categories: (1) the resource or factor market, (2) financial markets, and (3) the output or goods market. Markets allocate resources because market participants determine what will be bought and sold in markets by responding to the cost of production and the prices of goods, services, and assets.

These costs are reflective of what consumers are willing to pay in the markets (given the information they have) and what sellers are willing to accept in order to offset the cost of production and investment for growth.

By responding to costs, scarce resources are allocated for the provision of certain goods and services to the exclusion of others. Consequently, there is a social opportunity cost—the cost that society is willing to forego in order to sustain the production of certain goods and services.

In capitalist societies, markets are expected to reflect efficiency in two categories: (1) production and (2) allocation. Of course, the two categories are not mutually exclusive but interdependent. The first is alternatively defined as productive efficiency (producing at the least possible cost) and the second as allocative efficiency (producing what society wants). A wholesome definition of efficiency is therefore the production of what society wants at the least possible cost.

The definition of efficiency presupposes the lack of distortions. There is an implicit assumption that consumers are knowledgeable about competing prices and that goods and services are offered for sale at a fair rate of return (market price). The attainment of a fair price is normally considered to be contingent on the degree of competition because competitive markets allocate resources to such an extent that the prices (value) of goods are indicative of their per unit costs.

Allocation of resources depends on consumption and income because producers will respond to consumption. This means that those with inadequate income can be priced out of the market. Consequently, the market will fail to provide their wants. For further reading, see McConnell and Brue (2008) and Schiller (2006). *See also* Demand; Market Failure; Price; Supply

Market Failure   The result of the failure of markets to achieve efficiency. Failure is normally the result of too much confidence in the free operation of the market (market fundamentalism), an exceptional reliance on the theory that the market is capable of correcting itself. This view was predominant during the 18th century and part of the 20th century, until the Great Depression of the 1930s challenged the presumption of the classical view of the free market.

Markets may be inefficient for a variety of distortionary reasons—a conspiracy or collusion to restrain trade, corruption, deception, adverse income distribution, ill-defined property rights, and externalities (which are the result of overallocation and underallocation of resources). When a market cannot function on its own accord, policy intervention may be required to aid its optimal performance. This is usually done by regulation, and fiscal and monetary policies.

To address the issue of market failure, governments have regulated wages, rental rates for housing, interest rates (by usury laws), environmental pollution, unemployment benefits, product quality, and business performance.

Unfortunately, there is no guarantee that policy intervention will have the desired effects when time-sensitive adjustments are required, as in the case of the business cycle. Lags associated with untimely implementation (inside lags) and the unintended effects of timely implementation (outside lags) produce unwanted results.

When a reasonable determination is made that an activity must be expanded—inoculation or education, for example—but is not adequately provided by the market, it might be desirable for government to subsidize the activity in order to compensate for failure of the market or underallocation of resources. Conversely, when an activity creates harmful effects and there is overallocation of societal resources—pollution, let's say—it might make sense for regulation to discourage its expansion or proliferation. Policy may therefore have a useful social function that the market is not capable of providing. *See also* Business Cycle (economics, public administration); Corruption (economics); Externality; Free Trade; Keynesian; Laissez-Faire (economics); Market

Market Forces   The uninterrupted operation of supply and demand to determine market outcomes. Ideally, the freedom to buy and sell is supposed to determine market prices and desired output or efficient allocation of scarce resources.

Market forces may produce expected outcomes when certain conditions prevail. For example, consumers must be fully aware of competing prices, the market must be competitive, there must be diverse producers and substitutable products, and no producer must exercise a considerable sway over prices and the quantity that will be made available in the market. These are some of the necessary conditions for a perfectly competitive market structure, which is usually used as a model of an efficient market in economics.

The assumptions make it feasible to analyze consumer reaction to prices and producer reaction to consumption and costs. If prices are too high, consumers will generally indicate their unwillingness to buy at a higher price relative to a lower price. Of course, this also presupposes that the products in question are not necessities and that substitutes are available. At prices that are higher than what the market will permit, there will be an excess of supply of products. If all things remain unchanged, excess supply will force prices to fall in order to induce increased consumption or demand.

Conversely, if prices are too low, there will be an excess of demand. If all things remain unchanged, excess demand will bid prices up. Consumer and producer perception of unacceptable higher and lower prices will force the market participants to buy and sell goods, assets, and services at the efficient price—the price at which producers will be willing to produce the quantities that are wanted by buyers, thereby using society's resources efficiently.

M

In reality, the assumptions or conditions for free-market forces to operate are not always evident, partly because of shocks, corruption, collusion, asymmetric information, and deception in the marketplace. ***See also*** Asymmetric Information; Laissez-Faire (economics); Market; Perfect Competition

Marketing/Market Model   A model that pertains to the way information flows from producers to consumers. The model—which can apply to any type of media—assumes that media products are commodities like any other good or service and rests on the idea that consumers' needs in this area are similarly met by the economic model of supply and demand. Proponents of the market model argue that private profit-seeking media ownership—as opposed to government regulation—creates a favorable and efficient environment for meeting consumer demand and ultimately serving the public. The individual's interests are central, implying a definition of the term *public interest* that refers to information that interests the public. The market model is also analogous to the liberal-pluralist model discussed in media theory. Such a model is based on the idea that press freedom includes the freedom to own and operate the means of publication without government censorship. The media market will ostensibly self-regulate and address societal and individual accountability without official interference. A market model implies that media producers should provide what the public demands as opposed to professional journalists or political parties deciding what is best for them.

With regard to television, for instance, the market model refers to a network's function of bringing audiences to its advertisers. The advertising-driven model of television necessarily treats the audience not as citizens but as consumers and commodities. Viewers are in effect customers, and news or entertainment programs are products. Though the term *market* can apply to the actual area of signal-receiving, television-viewing audiences, the connotation of *market* in this realm is more likely to refer to *market* in the macroeconomic sense.

With regard to news production, the market model can be best understood in contrast to the public sphere model, which emphasizes the public interest role of the mass media. The goal of the latter is to provide information and education about issues and events that will help people act as responsible citizens. At various points in any news production, investors, advertisers, information sources, and consumers can propel the process. In addition to the public interest, investors' and sponsors' interests are also at stake. Market forces compel owners and clients of media organizations to minimize costs and maximize public consumption while protecting the interests of investors and sponsors. For further reading, see Croteau and Hoynes (2005) and McManus (1994). ***See also*** Hypodermic Needle Model; Propaganda Model; Prosocial Model; Public Interest (political science)

Marriage Counseling   Also called couples therapy, it brings both partners of a relationship together to strengthen or rebuild their relationship. Typically, there is a target problem, and couples see a licensed marriage therapist or counselor for a relatively short time. At times, the couple may be doing well but may desire to improve the relationship. Counseling includes learning effective communication patterns, talking about sensitive issues in a psychologically safe environment, and acquiring tools to communicate, solve problems, and negotiate issues. The couple explores values, personal history, opinions, differences, and habits. ***See also*** Family Counseling; Systems Theory; Therapy

Marshal   A judicial court official in charge of federal law enforcement, who may have duties similar to those of a sheriff, such as maintaining court order and security, transporting prisoners, serving official documents, protecting federal officials, making arrests, or participating in police activities. ***See also*** Law Enforcement

Martial Law   A system of law temporarily imposed on an area in wartime or during internal dissension when the domestic military forces take control of the administration of justice. The army may impose rules (e.g., curfew), take over administrative and judicial functions, and suspend safeguards (e.g., habeas corpus).

Marxism (*political science*)   The political and economic philosophy of Karl Marx and his sometime coauthor Friedrich Engels, who saw the economic system as forming the basis of all social and political relationships, including that of the state to each class. Marx, who was born in 1818, was trained as a philosopher in the mid-19th century but turned his focus toward economics and politics. His work has perhaps singularly inspired communist movements around the world.

Although Marx wrote more than 100 texts, several have been noted as defining his ideological viewpoints. Marx brought his own brand of socialism, known as scientific socialism, to the fore, which he distinguished from the socialism expounded by other socialists, whom he considered utopian idealists. Marx believed that the economic system in which profit is the ultimate aim of capitalism exploits the proletariat, who sell their labor. This profit relies on surplus labor, the value of work beyond that which is required to produce the value of wages paid, which results in exploitation.

Marx's philosophy can be considered the antithesis to capitalism. Marx believed that class struggle played a determining role in society's inevitable efforts to progress from bourgeois oppression under capitalism to a socialist and ultimately classless society. Marx defined class as a group of persons whose lives are determined by their possession of a common economic status in a society. Their status further determines their social relations to others, within their respective class and without. To Marx, the two main classes, the bourgeoisie, or capitalists, who owned the means of production, and the proletariat, who provided the labor for the bourgeoisie, were at odds with each other.

Marx never embraced capitalist ideals. He did not accept that the interests of the worker and the capitalist were in accordance in a capitalist arrangement, but instead he based his class analysis on the workers' struggle for better wages and work conditions against the capitalists' drive for greater profits. Marx believed that capitalism, which created a situation where industrial workers sell their labor as a marketable commodity, kept the proletariat classes impoverished until they would rebel to emancipate themselves from the oppression of their material environment. The rebellion would then end all class distinctions and forms of exploitation. The sense of powerlessness felt by the working class will cease as the means of production become common property.

Marx wrote about historical materialism and stated that history provided the chronology of class struggles. The historical evolution of mankind is the outcome of the modes of production, which determine the nature of each historical epoch. The relationships in a society are determined by its material conditions. Throughout history, society has been divided into classes depending on what is produced, how it is produced, and how products are exchanged.

Marx even likened literature, art, and other aspects of culture as a reflection of the ideology of the class to which the artist belongs. And religion for Marx was a response to the pain of being alive and suffering. Since the proletariat was accustomed to suffering, religion was needed. Religion existed for humans to assert their communal essence. It further provided a response to alienation in material life. Today in the West, Marxism is alive and well almost solely in the universities, where it is used as a hermeneutic device for looking at texts, culture, and the like, in a variety of disciplines. For further reading, see Berlin (1959). *See also* Capitalism (political science); Communism (political science); Socialism (political science)

Marxism *(sociology)*   The political and socioeconomic philosophy derived from the work of Karl Marx and Friedrich Engels. The fundamental ideology of communism, Marxism suggests that class struggle (the conflict between classes with opposing interests) and economics have been the main determinants of historical change in society, in which the bourgeoisie (the owning, nonworking class) has exploited the proletariat (the non-owning, working class) for profit. According to Marxism, the proletariat will revolt to overthrow the capitalist economic system of production and create a socialist society without class divisions. Recent adaptations of Marxism include Leninism and Maoism. *See also* Communism (economics, political science); Criminology

Mass Communication   The transfer of ideas, information, and symbolic content to a large number of people in dispersed locations, usually at the same time. It is contrasted with face-to-face or individual communication acts. The term usually refers to widespread communication

that requires a technological interface, a means of preparing and presenting messages to a large audience. The media that can deliver mass communication to dispersed audiences include newspapers, television, radio, books, magazines, movies, and the Internet. Devices such as telephones or e-mail, originally used by individuals for personal communication, have been transformed into mass communication devices via listservs, mass e-mailings, spam, telemarketing, text marketing on cell phones, and political robo-calling. This indicates that any form of technological communication is inherently a form of mass communication.

The process of mass communicating has traditionally been traced back through time to the development of the printing press in the 15th century and to the rise of newspapers, broadsides, magazines, and various forms of print and, later, electronic media. But it can also be argued that whenever humans congregate in groups, from the smallest band in prehistoric times to the large civilizations of the ancient Egyptians or the Maya, there is a need for mass communication, for dispersing a message to everyone associated with the community. It is simultaneously a way of establishing and testing the coherence of a group.

The term is not as common today as it was when electronic media were first becoming widespread and scholars were trying to explain the effects of everyone seemingly getting the same message across large distances and in different racial, ethnic, and religious communities. Early research in mass communication emphasized its negative effects, and its mere existence was considered proof of the negative consequences of populations moving out of small-scale rural communities and into large-scale urban regions. Today, "new media" and new communication devices have rapidly integrated into the flow of everyday life, being devices for both mass communication, directed at the users, and sending out individual messages.

Mass communication is a concern to some because it seems to indicate an institutionalized power that develops homogenized and singular messages coming from one source, with media producers distinct from message recipients. When it appears across national boundaries, it is said to indicate a globalization of that power and indicates the negative influence of having one cultural tradition dominate social life and the production of meaning. For further reading, see Thompson (1995). *See also* Communication; Mass Culture; Mass Media; Mass Society; Media

Mass Consumption   The consumption of consumer products on a large scale. Mass consumption implies that a large percentage of the population purchases or consumes the same products or services because large manufacturers produce and distribute their products widely. Examples of such mass commodities might include McDonald's, the Gap, Apple computer products, *The New York Times,* the sitcom *Friends,* feature films, and video games. Mass distribution relies on mass media,

M

which in turn have an impact on mass consumption. It is the media that disseminate information about consumable products and thus fuel consumption.

Media and information are themselves commodities for mass consumption. Information providers, such as newspapers, television broadcasters, Web sites, and the like, rely on mass media outlets for the eventual mass consumption of their product. Some theorists in the area of political economy suggest that the media, in addition to creating media content, ultimately produce audiences that are in turn a commodity whose attention can be sold to advertisers. Audiences are seen as consumers whose attitudes, behaviors, and knowledge can be shaped and manipulated by media products.

President Franklin D. Roosevelt's fireside chat in 1933 was the first time the public consumed political communication in real time and on a mass scale. Opportunities for media consumption have expanded dramatically since then with the advent of new technologies—first television and then the Internet. Some claim that society suffers from media saturation and that the media dominate our experience of the world. Indeed, consumption does not always imply the exchange of money, especially with regard to media consumption. Even when we read a billboard on a highway, we are in a sense consuming information, with the billboard itself a vehicle of mass media.

On the positive side, mass media consumption is a part of the cultural learning process and provides shared experience. This is beneficial both to those born into a particular culture as well as to those who are newcomers. A pessimistic view holds that the media portrayals of a nation, for instance, can distort reality. This is often discussed in relation to how immigrants or foreigners perceive a country and also how children perceive the world. Reliable studies have shown that violence displayed in mass media can lead to aggressiveness in children. Educators and psychologists also express concern about addiction to various types of media— television, video games, the Internet—because of overconsumption. Children's nutrition and weight issues have been of particular concern, with many implicating the mass media. The belief is that consumption of media leads to overconsumption of many of the unhealthy foods advertised on television. ***See also*** Acculturation (communication); Advertising (media studies); Commodity; Mass Culture; Mass Media; Mass Society

Mass Culture   The culture of the masses, encompassing a range of information, ideas, images, and entertainment that appeal to the tastes of the majority of people. The concept arose in the early 20th century with the advent of mass media technologies. *Mass culture* traditionally had a negative connotation because it was associated with lower-class audiences (as distinct from high or elite culture). However, most people participate in mass culture on some level as part of their normal experience. The term is dated and objectionable as class lines have blurred since the mid-20th century. Though *popular culture* is devalued

in some cultural arenas, it is frequently the more favorable term to use in place of *mass culture* when discussing mainstream culture as it does not carry the same pejorative and divisive implications.

Between the end of the 19th and the early 20th centuries, manifestations of mass culture included newspapers and magazines. This was followed later in the 20th century by the modern outlets of radio, television, film, and advertising. Mass culture is often compared with folk or traditional culture, which was produced before the existence of mass media, though critics of the modern notion of mass culture portray it as produced self-consciously as a commodity for consumption; as the result of industrialization, mass culture has been distanced from its origins of authentic cultural expression.

Fundamental to the discourse is the idea that mass media produce a homogenizing effect among audiences, which in turn creates a mass society of people who have unwittingly relinquished their individuality, personal preferences, and local culture and traditions. Corresponding to the negative connotation, such popular or mass culture is viewed as debased and is understood as a measure by which a citizenry is controlled. The mass culture itself is thought to be a result of the alienation of individuals, whose opinions and behaviors are susceptible to being managed by external forces such as advertising, television shows, movies, music, and video games.

Popular culture has become an area of study among scholars in recent decades and is increasingly perceived as a serious entity, appreciated on its own terms. Though many of the same characteristics historically described mass culture—nontraditional, mass produced, broad, mainstream, commercial, and undifferentiated—when applied to popular culture, the belief is that these aspects are worthy of study in the broad scope of cultural understanding. For further reading, see Baughman (1992) and Wilson (1995). ***See also*** Mass Media; Mass Society; Popular Culture

Mass Media   The "vehicles" that distribute information or entertainment content simultaneously to a wide or multiple audiences, such as television, radio, newspapers, magazines, advertisements, movies, books, CDs, Web sites, and video games. Mass media messages are characterized by the fact that they are created by a few for the consumption of a large, heterogeneous, and potentially widely dispersed audience. They are distinct from the more specialized media targeting a smaller audience, such as newsletters.

Mass media also refer to the organizations that produce and disseminate the content, such as television networks (ABC, CBS, NBC, CNN), media companies (Time Warner, Viacom, News Corporation), and print publications (*Wall Street Journal, The New York Times, Entertainment Weekly*).

The term is often referenced in a larger cultural context relating to the societal effects of mass media content. Mass media can have profound cultural effects and can shape the way people perceive certain issues and ultimately behave. Debates surrounding such effects are perennial, and both defenders and critics of mass media bring forth fervent arguments. From an optimistic perspective, mass media are seen as a socializing force promoting shared experiences and common values. They can provide educational opportunities and possibilities for positive social change. A pessimistic view sees mass media as leading the creation of a mindless, dumbeddown culture.

Mass media—unlike a communication tool like the telephone—have generally been considered a one-way communication technology; that is, information flows to consumers, who cannot provide producers with immediate feedback. In recent years, however, some media providers—most notably Internet sites and some television programs—have created the means to allow consumers to provide instant comments on media messages. For further reading, see McLuhan and Powers (1989) and Postman (1985). *See also* Entertainment Media; Mass Communication; Mass Consumption; Mass Culture; Mass Society; Media Effects; Television and Social Behavior

Mass Media Appeals Persuasive communication techniques employed as potentially effective and efficient measures to influence audiences of print or broadcast mass media. The goal of the appeal is to sway viewers or readers to either purchase a commodity or adopt a particular opinion. Examples include bandwagon appeals, which rely on the human instinct to go along with the crowd; testimonial appeals, which involve an influential person's positive personal experience with the product; and glittering-generalization appeals, which involve the use of provocative but usually nonfactual language that masks the real issue.

While conventional wisdom holds that one-on-one, face-to-face persuasion is most effective in changing attitudes and affecting opinion, research has shown that attitude changes can also result from group discussions. Political speeches provide an ideal example. While a candidate can meet thousands of voters over the course of a campaign, it is likely that his or her televised speech will be more efficient in disseminating a message and will have a more substantial impact. In addition, because the same message will be received by a large number of people, the resulting media coverage and ensuing social discourse will continue to emphasize the content of the speech. This model could be applied to any form of propaganda or message that a company, group, or individual producer or creator wishes to transmit. For further reading, see Petty and Cacioppo (1996) and Walton (1999). *See also* Bandwagon Appeal; Mass Media; Mass Persuasion; Propaganda (media studies); Propaganda Model

Mass Murder The act of deliberately and directly killing four or more people. Mass murder may be committed by individuals (e.g., spree killers or serial killers) or by organizations and may be considered as genocide. Mass murder typically occurs at a single time and location. *See also* Homicide; Serial Murder/Serial Killer

Mass Persuasion The term is sometimes used interchangeably with propaganda, which has a more negative connotation and is more directly manipulative and often deceitful, largely due to its association with the rise of Nazism. The term is also associated with notions of mind control and large-scale brainwashing. From early in the 20th century, democracies of the world have expressed concern about the social and political power of mass communication. Topics that touch on human emotions, self-image, and self-esteem make audiences more susceptible to their message and are therefore most influential. The complex process of mass persuasion does not assume a passive public, as does the discredited hypodermic model. Individual responses vary depending on exposure to the message and selective attention and retention.

Historically, mass persuasion has been used to persuade groups to adopt ideologies that generally benefit some of the population and potentially harm others, the most infamous example being Adolph Hitler's propaganda techniques during World War II. Also during World War II, in a classic case study, the singer Kate Smith persuaded radio listeners to buy millions of dollars' worth of government war bonds during an 18-hour radio marathon. The endeavor was found to be effective due to the show format, the public's image of the singer as a sincere and patriotic person, and the social climate during wartime.

In modern society, the collective power of mass media—newspapers, film, radio television, advertising, the Internet—provides ample opportunity for mass persuasion on a more subtle but still socially significant scale. For further reading, see Merton, Fisk, and Curtis (1946) and Sproule (1997). *See also* Hypodermic Needle Model; Mass Media Appeals; Propaganda; Propaganda Model

Mass Society A sociological concept referring to a fragmented society composed of isolated, lonely, and powerless individuals. Proponents of the theory view modern society as characterized by the breakdown of community and by the presence of increasingly heterogeneous and individualistic trends resulting from industrialization, modernization, and urbanization. Mass-society theorists of the 19th and 20th centuries included, among others, Louis de Bonald, Joseph de Maistre, Karl Marx, Friedrich Engels, Émile Durkheim, Gustave Le Bon, Georg Simmel, Ferdinand Tönnies, Herbert Marcuse, William Kornhauser, Karl Mannheim, and Hannah Arendt.

Mass-society theorists hypothesized that a large yet isolated population was vulnerable to manipulation by powerful institutions. The major institutions in a mass society are centralized and therefore designed and organized to address "the masses." In the 1920s and

M

1930s, as broadcast communication became available to many, the concept of mass society was intertwined with that of mass media, the latter being a prime example of such a powerful institution. Messages delivered via mass media can be presented to a large undifferentiated population simultaneously and in a context of alienation and anonymity are more likely to be perceived as authoritative than they might be in smaller, localized communities. Marx and Engels, for instance, speculated that in a mass society, those who controlled the media were easily able to control the opinions, behaviors, and culture of the masses, who then become "narcotized." In addition, because individuals abandon personal values in favor of those of the group in a mass society, behaviors become contagious. Consequently, a conformist consumer society would result and, many argued, could even be dangerous, notably in the case of political propaganda. For further reading, see Kornhauser (1959) and Mills (1963). **See also** Centralization (sociology); Community Identity; Marxism (sociology); Urbanization

Materiality   Often associated with Marxist thought, the term refers to the economic factors that affect human behaviors, attitudes, and achievements. Theorists who adhere to the ideology of materiality posit that a person's economic situation—income, property, earning power, relationship to the means of production, and the like—is more important than ideas in guiding his or her behavior. This notion is contrasted with idealism or "liberal idealism," which holds that ideas are the most important factors. In the context of media and communication scholarship, the general connotation of the word—concrete as opposed to ethereal—is also at play. The notion of *material* as concrete aligns with those economic elements that are considered static or irreducible.

The term is also used in a related context to describe the characteristics of the media. The communications theorist Marshall McLuhan described the media as one of the many "extensions of man," which also included other nonphysical or unfixed material. In his view—and many other scholars adhere to it—the media are a paradigm defined by the relationship between form and content. McLuhan's belief that "the medium is the message" implied that the ethereal component of the media has important content that has the ability to affect human behavior and society. Therefore, the materiality, the physical nature and dimension of the medium, is as important as or even more important than the content being delivered by the medium. Both the immateriality and the materiality of media objects and systems can be addressed. For further reading, see Gumbrecht and Pfeiffer (1994), McLuhan (1964), and Williams (1977). **See also** Marxism (political science); Media Ecology; Semiotics (media studies)

Material Witness   A person alleged to have information relevant to the subject matter of a criminal proceeding that is significant enough to affect the outcome

of the trial. Material witnesses may be held and trials may be delayed to ensure that they testify. **See also** Trial

Mathematics Education   The term refers to the methods of teaching and learning mathematics. It also refers to the research discipline that investigates how mathematics is taught and learned. This research discipline and its organization, the National Council of Teachers of Mathematics, have proposed several influential curricular reforms. As is common with educational reform proposals, these have been hotly debated in political as well as educational circles. The controversies have usually involved one form or another of two basic positions: (1) a traditional, standards-based curriculum that focuses on established routines to solve problems and (2) a reform-based curriculum that emphasizes student-centered learning and conceptual understanding.

Matriarchy   A form of social organization in which familial and political power and authority are possessed by women (especially the mother) and property and descent are traced through the female line. There are no known examples of strictly matriarchal human societies in the past or the present. Matriarchal societies are distinct from matrifocal societies, where women form the core of the household, and matrilineal societies, a relatively common system, where descent is traced through female bloodlines but power is held primarily by men. Matriarchies are distinguished from patriarchies, in which men are the source of community power. **See also** Patriarchy (sociology)

Meaning   A term that is almost impossible to define without referring back to itself: Meaning is the quality of some thing or idea that is intended or implied, what is meant or what that thing stands for. This suggests, as many philosophers have argued for centuries, that meaning may be the most important concept in the relationship between language, thought, and reality. Much research in the social sciences and humanities is directed at finding the meaning of some text, action, event, or thing. But the anthropologist Clifford Geertz has warned that since meanings are created through interactions between cultural actors, ideas, and things, we should be looking instead at how meanings are made, at the process of making meaning rather than the product that is supposed to be a singular meaning. For further reading, see Geertz (1966a) and Langer (1957). **See also** Culture (communication); Symbols/Symbolic Reality

Mean Worldview   A phenomenon wherein media consumers adopt the belief that the world is a more threatening, dangerous, and violent place than it really is, full of disease, natural disaster, corrupt authority figures, and violent crime (also called mean world syndrome). Theorists and media analysts—George Gerbner being a prime example—argue that television viewing has a positive correlation with the belief that the world is a mean place. Local television news is often implicated, as such newscasts tend to lead with and focus on crime and other negative news. The impact on the individual viewer of such a distorted view of reality may include feelings of fear and isolation, which in turn leads to a societal impact, where citizens are suspicious of one another and withdraw or disengage from social and political life. Research has shown that television violence is far more prevalent than its occurrence in actuality, causing viewers to overestimate the possibility of its occurrence in their own lives.

There is some debate surrounding the theory, and some researchers hypothesize that mass exposure to violence can actually help reduce the rates of violence and crime because the representations serve as a victimless outlet for one's feelings of rage and hatred. For further reading, see Fowles (1999), Gerbner, Gross, Morgan, and Signorelli (1980), and Surette (1992). *See also* Graphic Violence; Mass Media; Media Effects

Measurement   The detection of relations between objects on a property and the representation of these relations through symbols. The symbols used are usually numerical. The types of relations (equality, order, etc.) that can be detected correspond to different levels of measurement (nominal, ordinal, interval, ratio, absolute). The set of symbols or numbers used to represent the relations between objects is called a measurement scale. In the social sciences, unlike in physics, it is seldom evident how properties, such as anxiety, can be measured. These properties are measured indirectly, through tests, questionnaires, physiological registration (e.g., eye movements), and observations of behavior or the results thereof (e.g., the number of cigarette butts on the pavement). How these observed measurements relate to the unobserved property (anxiety) can be described, and in some cases tested, with a psychometric measurement model. For further reading, see Michell (1990). *See also* Measurement, Levels of; Reliability; Validity

Measurement, Levels of   The rules determining the types of mathematical operations or statistical formulas that can be performed on a variable with a set of characteristics. *Nominal* variables are those in which differences are defined in terms of categories, such as gender, major, or political affiliation. Nominal variables are often coded numerically, although there is no inherent order in the scores. Central tendency for nominal variables can only be measured through the mode. *Ordinal* variables are categorical variables that can be ranked. Examples include year in college and order of finishers in a race. Central tendency for ordinal variables can be defined as the median or mode. Scores can be added and subtracted. *Interval* variables have the additional characteristic of having defined units of measurement but no true zero point. For example, Fahrenheit and Celsius temperature are interval variables with defined units; however, neither zero Fahrenheit nor zero Celsius indicates an absence of temperature. Central

tendency of interval variables can be represented by the mean. Quantities of interval variables can be added, subtracted, multiplied, and divided; ratios cannot be computed as there is no true zero point. *Ratio* variables have the additional characteristic of having a true zero point. Examples of ratio variables include height, weight, grade point average, and Kelvin temperature (where zero is the absolute zero of temperature). Ratio variables have greater flexibility in terms of available computational and statistical analyses. All computational operations can be performed on ratio variables, including computation of ratios. *See also* Central Tendency; Inferential Statistics; Nonparametric Statistics

Mechanization   The use of machines, either wholly or in part, to assist human operators, historically replacing animals' role in physical labor. Mechanization does not replace human participation (automation) but requires human instruction. Mechanization is considered effective in increasing productivity and most recently involves the use of computers.

Media   The channels of mass communication for transmission of information. Such channels include newspapers, magazines and books, photography, film and videotape, radio and television broadcasting, Internet postings, and satellite transmissions. The term also is used in reference to the people who report or broadcast the information, also known as news, from various media outlets or who make the decisions on what information is considered newsworthy. Media, plural of medium, is considered to be a collective or group noun; therefore, single or plural verbs and pronouns are used interchangeably with the term.

The growth of the media has been fueled by a series of inventions and technology, such as the printing press, the telegraph, photography, moving pictures, radio, television, and the Internet. Each of these innovations made it possible to deliver information in greater quantities, to larger audiences, and at faster speeds. Although some of these inventions date back to 100 years or more, the American historian Daniel J. Boorstin places the burgeoning of mass media at the start of the 19th century, a time in which "man's ability to make, preserve, transmit, and disseminate precise images . . . grew at a fantastic pace."

The term *media* is sometimes used as a pejorative or spoken with a negative bias. Critics blame the media for being either too liberal or too conservative, for ignoring or putting too much emphasis on certain news items, and for promoting political and social agendas that are advantageous to corporations or other influential entities. For further reading, see Boorstin (1987). *See also* Broadcasting; Mass Media; Mediation (communication)

Media, New   A term used in the 1970s to describe the development of mass communication media that used digital rather than analog technologies. The term tends to be used now for interactive digital technology,

M

particularly that involving the Internet and cell phones. Typical new-media activities include blogging, cell phone texting, social networking sites, streaming video, and mapping software combined with advertisements or other local information.

New media are created by the convergence of older-media technologies and concepts with the flexibility and interactivity of computers. New media recombine in hybrid fashion elements of different technologies, creating a network affecting all members of society, with interactive abilities enabling users to generate and disseminate their own content.

Enzensberger (1974) believed new media to be egalitarian and inherently subversive, with substantial potential mobilizing power. He believed a new-media use in his time, television news broadcasting, to be a key factor in the growth of public opposition against the Vietnam War. More recently, cell phone texting has augmented the organizing capabilities of grassroots activists, notably during the "Battle of Seattle," demonstrations by anticapitalist activists during a World Bank meeting. Zapatistas were early adopters of the Internet, using it to disseminate far beyond the Mexican borders the words of their charismatic leader Marcos, bringing international attention to their cause. Skeptics of the ability of new media to politically empower ordinary people point to the collusion of government and corporations in effectively censoring Web search engines in China.

New media enable new art forms to be explored. A new novel genre has emerged in Japan, using cell phones rather than word processors for composition, with the resulting text typically characterized by short sentences and fast-moving melodramatic plots. The rights to some of these cell phone novels have been bought by publishing houses to be sold in a more traditional printed-book format.

Two opposing theories attempt to explain how and why new-media formats come about—technological determinism and cultural determinism. These theories can help explain how and why some technologies are widely adopted but not others. Forms of new media initially adopted by a community vary—for example, Internet use spread widely in Trinidad before cell phone adoption, with the reverse pattern occurring in neighboring Jamaica. For further reading, see Curran and Gurevitch (2005), Enzensberger (2000), and Lievrouw and Livingstone (2002). *See also* Cultural Determinism; Internet; Technological Determinism; Technology (media studies)

Media Agency   Beginning in the early 1990s, media-buying executives started forming their own agencies to buy media. Although traditionally a department in the full-service advertising agencies, these "unbundled" media agencies have evolved and added to their media-buying role other functions such as research and media planning. Once considered to take a back seat to the creative functions in advertising agencies, the specialized tasks of the newly created media agencies now attract more highly qualified, media-savvy business executives, offering clients better plans at competitive prices. These professionals not only determine what type of media advertisements are placed in but also where they are placed in the medium and how much space or airtime they should get. These decisions are based on the client's target market, the quality and nature of the creative work, and the client's budget for media allocation.

Although these businesses are relatively new, many of them have already had to adapt their business models as a result of the tremendous changes in the media landscape in just the past couple of decades; that is, the number of network and cable television channels have increased, national circulation magazines have risen in number, and new digital formats now dominate the market. As a result, part of a media agency's job is to keep its clients educated on new-media options. For further reading, see Horsky (2006). *See also* Advertising

Media and Pornography   Pornography is a form of sexually explicit media intended for audience consumption. The content might be delivered via magazine, video or DVD, film, or the Internet, all of which provide producers and distributors with huge profits.

Magazines depicting sexually explicit material existed in the 19th century but were not produced or sold on a mass scale. In the early and mid-20th century, the advent of radio and television opened the market for more efficient distribution of such material, though standards were generally stricter for broadcast than for print venues since access to print materials is easier to control. As cable television and new video technology became widespread in the 1980s, the standards were relaxed to a large extent, creating a controversial double standard; that is, there was a greater acceptance of pornography on cable and video than on network television. As with print media, there is assumed to be more control over access, and the effort to keep minors away from sexually explicit material constitutes a large portion of any debate about pornography. There has been significant debate and some research on the negative effects that viewing pornography has on individuals and society. With advanced technology and increased possibilities of access, those potential effects have expanded. With the dawn of the Internet in the mid-1990s, the availability of pornography increased exponentially and with it the concern about control and regulation, both of which have proven to be elusive and contentious.

In addition to technology, federal and corporate bodies have also affected the amount of and access to sexually explicit material available to the public. In the 1980s, the Federal Communications Commission decided not to regulate cable TV, and network TV chose to do away with the existing national code of broadcast standards. Both events gave more power and profit to creators and distributors of pornographic material.

Over the course of the 20th century, debates over the First Amendment and pornography ensued. The central question was whether pornography should be considered under the rubric of freedom of expression and therefore legally protected. Those seeking to severely restrict or ban pornography were concerned about the damaging effect such material might have on people's behavior, especially young, impressionable people who glean much of their understanding of sex and sexual behavior from the media. There was concern among many that pornography also perpetuates gender stereotypes and instigates violence against women. For further reading, see Eysenck and Nias (1978) and McNair (1996). *See also* Media Effects; Pornography

Media and the Judicial System   The two systems intersect throughout the judicial process, often challenging the basic tenets of the Constitution, pitting defenders of the First Amendment's rights to a free press and free speech against staunch supporters of the Sixth Amendment—the right to a fair trial. The impact of the media on the judicial system is especially underscored during media trials—those trials that because of their content are subject to intense, often sensationalized, media coverage. However, aspects of media coverage in pretrial procedures, even before a case goes to trial, often prove contentious.

For instance, once the grand jury has issued its report, witnesses in those proceedings are allowed to discuss their own testimony. Sensationalist journalism has sometimes been accused of deliberately thwarting the efforts of the justice system—so-called checkbook journalism, where witnesses are paid for a description of their forthcoming testimony. This has led to their appearances in court being cancelled. In addition, the media often have access to pretrial hearings and records, such as arrest warrants, police blotters, and court dockets. While it is the media's contention that the public has the right to know, potential jurors are members of the public, and prior knowledge of aspects of the case may adversely affect the objectivity of the jury pool—causing problems in jury selection or, later, in jury decision making. Sometimes, once the jury has been selected and the trial commenced, the judge may choose to sequester the jury in order to shield them from the media.

On the other hand, many aspects of the judicial process are closed to the media. Plea bargaining sessions are closed to the public, although many critics feel that the public has the right to know why a case did not go to trial. If a case goes to trial, at any point in the proceedings, the judge may issue a gag order on any of the participants, forbidding them to speak about the case. Judges and lawyers are bound by their professional ethics when dealing with the media. Judges, however, have been admonished for entertaining press relations during a trial, and lawyers have used the press to create a positive "spin" for their clients. Journalists, however, in endeavoring to protect the rights afforded them under the First Amendment, must also take into account their professional ethics and their role in a judicial process that guarantees a fair trial. For further reading, see Alexander (2004) and Westfeldt and Wicker (1998).

Media as a Cause of Crime   The search for a connection between depictions of violence in the media (especially in comic books, television, music, video games, and movies) and actual violent, criminal, or aggressive behavior has been the goal of a wide variety of psychological, social science, and criminology research projects. Concern with the connection often increases after specific events, such as the Columbine High School shooting incident (the student shooters used to play violent video games), or copycat crimes, which perpetrators often attribute to media depictions of similar incidents.

Attempts at finding either cause-effect relationships (violence in the media causes violent behavior) or correlations (increased television watching takes place in conjunction with increase in violent crimes) have provided contradictory data and inconclusive results. Nevertheless, many medical and governmental agencies have accepted the results and have promoted the control of media content through labeling, banning, or filtering technologies, such as the television V-chip.

A chief proponent of the connection, the psychologist L. Rowell Huesmann (2007) states that observing aggressive behavior, whether real or simulated, stimulates real aggressive behavior in both children and adults. Most major medical, governmental, and psychological organizations state conclusively that children will be affected by violence depicted in the media, will become "desensitized" to it, will imitate it, and will desire more of it.

In his review of the history of these studies, Richard Rhodes has pointed out that most of the methodologies and results are flawed because of poor statistical methods, small sample sizes, untrained observers of behavior, vague definitions of violence and aggression, and varying definitions of media violence and because they take place in laboratories rather than in real-life situations. Rhodes concluded that much of the concern with the supposed effects of media violence were really concerns about the shift of influence out of the hands of religious and governmental institutions and into the hands of those who control the media. For further reading, see American Academy of Pediatrics (2000), Huesmann (2007), and Rhodes (2000). *See also* Censorship (media studies); Electronic Media; Propaganda (media studies)

Media as a Tool for Disintegrative Shaming   The use of media outlets for the purpose of shaming an offender in a retributive and isolating fashion. Disintegrative shaming is distinct from reintegrative shaming, which does not seek to isolate the offender. Disintegrative shaming has a long history—punishments such as the stockade or public whippings were used to shame offenders into not repeating their behavior. The use of the media for disintegrative shaming reaches a potentially large audience and, therefore, may ensure that the offender is isolated from a much larger community. These methods are sometimes used by overtaxed criminal justice systems as an alternative to criminal sanctions.

M

In some cases, offenders have been forced to take out full-page newspaper advertisements in which they describe their crimes. Newspapers have also published the names and pictures of parents who don't make their child support payments or people who have been charged with driving while under the influence of alcohol. In the case of sexual offenders, while the primary purpose of media use is to protect the public, Internet sex offender lists have also been used for disintegrative shaming. In an extreme case in 2000, England's *The News of the World* began printing the names and offenses of sex offenders in a "name and shame" campaign. The campaign caused some hysteria, leading to the suicide of two of the offenders and the disappearance of another. Most research on the subject suggests that disintegrative shaming devices only further stigmatize the offenders, isolating them from society and sometimes even forcing them to only socialize with other offenders. This type of shaming impedes any chance of reintegrating the offender into society and may in fact have the negative outcome of causing a repetition or escalation of the initial behavior. For further reading, see McAlinden (2005). ***See also*** Punishment (sociology)

Media as Business Organizations   There are eight different media industries: (1) book publishing, (2) newspapers, (3) magazines, (4) recordings, (5) radio, (6) movies, (7) television, and (8) the Internet. Book publishing is the oldest business, with the first American book having been published in 1640. The Internet is the newest media industry. These industries are almost entirely privately owned (National Public Radio and the Public Broadcasting Service are two exceptions) and are motivated by profit. Except in the cases of book publishing, recordings, and movies, in which the bulk of the profits are made from sales to consumers, the greatest profits are derived from sponsors. As the purpose of mass media is to inform as well as entertain, this can sometimes result in conflicts of interest.

Although the majority of the profits are made from advertisers, consumers provide enough profit to lend power to their interests. Recently, the variety and advances in technology have given consumers far more power over media businesses than they had in the past: Improvements in memory and storage devices has provided more portability of products, and interactivity has given the consumer more control over media choices. Many organizations have had to modify or completely change their business models in order to remain competitive.

As deregulation has led to very few ownership restrictions, most media companies expand by acquiring other existing companies. Stock in these companies is usually publicly traded, so one company need only buy the stock of another when it comes available in order to make an acquisition. The number of companies is decreasing as large companies take over small companies. This concentration of ownership, where fewer companies own more types of media, has taken various forms—chains, cross-media ownership,

conglomerates, broadcast networks, and vertical integration. ***See also*** Corporate Media; Deregulation (media studies)

Media Bias   The lack of an impartial view of reported events on the part of newspapers, broadcasters, and other media outlets. Balanced reporting would require that both sides of an argument are equally represented, but such precise equality is impractical, if not impossible, to put into practice and to measure. Despite common claims of presenting fair and balanced news coverage, objectivity and neutrality are elusive in most media organizations.

According to the tenets of upholding democracy and a free press, a media outlet should not let its preferences be known unless it explicitly identifies itself as a particular type of advocacy organization. A well-known conservative radio show host would not likely be accused of bias since his audience knows what to expect from him. A major network or cable news operation, however, is bound by journalistic ethics to provide as fair and balanced a presentation as possible. Quite often, various media companies are accused of bias because the parent company or segments of its leadership do have political and cultural biases that may leak—intentionally or unintentionally—into reporting. The practice of newspapers endorsing candidates gives some indication of the political leanings of a newspaper, though ideally that preference should not interfere with the news reporting. Editorials and op-eds express opinions, but in those cases, the presence of bias is explicit.

Given that language is inherently value-laden, the choice of vocabulary can lead to commission of media bias. Sources and interview subjects whom a news outlet chooses to consult can indicate a particular bias. Omission of selected information is also a form of bias. ***See also*** Objectiveness in Media Coverage

Media Campaigns   Organized activities that use mass media to persuade targeted populations to undertake or desist from some course of action. Campaigns usually involve raising awareness of the issue at stake by providing information before asking the audience to respond in some way. The action goals desired are as varied as signing a petition requesting a change in official policy; donating money, time, or goods; voting; and changing personal behavior or beliefs. Government health departments use media campaigns to persuade people to stop smoking, exercise more, drink less alcohol, and eat better. Political parties campaign to get their candidates elected. Campaigns, typically, use many of the same marketing and advertising channels used by corporations to sell products. Advertising slots may be purchased on traditional media channels, including radio, television, newspapers, magazines, and the Internet. Personal endorsements may be provided by politicians, celebrities, and other public figures—often, though not always, unpaid. Public relations techniques may be used, with press releases provided and press conferences held to promote coverage of the campaign as a news story. Empirical studies have shown that media campaigns can be effective in changing behavior. Public health anti-tobacco campaigns in the United States achieved considerable success in reducing cigarette smoking. For further reading, see Howard (2006), Ibrahim and Glants (2007), and Rose (2005). *See also* Public Campaign

Media Ecology   An interdisciplinary study of media theory that cuts across a number of social and behavioral science fields, including communications, linguistics, sociology, anthropology, psychology, and rhetoric. Media ecology is best understood as an approach, rather than a strict ideology, to understanding the media as environments. Central to media ecology is the idea that media environments, such as books, radio, film, television, and the like, involve subtle, implicit, and informal dynamics and complex message systems; because people do not often think of these media forms as environments, as they would a courtroom, classroom, or workplace, they are usually not aware of their effects. Media ecology attempts to illuminate the impact these media have on people at numerous levels.

Definitions of the term are not hard and fast and can depend on both the cultural and the academic context in which it is used. Generally, the term refers to the interplay between media communication and human perception, understanding, values, and behavior. Media ecology is concerned with the contents and uses of various media as well as with the relationships between people, places, technology, and events. It borrows the word *ecology* from the physical sciences to imply the study of environments with regard to their structure, content, and impact on people.

The term was formally introduced by the educator and cultural critic Neil Postman, who established a program for media ecology at New York University in 1971. Marshall McLuhan, often associated with his statement "The medium is the message," is widely regarded as the spiritual father of media ecology. The field of inquiry also draws on the work of a wide range of scholars, including Walter Benjamin, James Carey, Harold Innis, Lewis Mumford, and Walter Ong. Some scholars define media ecology as a field of inquiry, whereas others place greater emphasis on its practical applications. There exist somewhat diverging academic threads, such as the New York School and the Toronto School, as well as those who use the term in a more generic way. For further reading, see Lum (2006), McLuhan (1964), and Postman (1979). *See also* Ecology; Media

Media Effects   The impact that mass communications have on individuals and society. While not all media effects are considered negative—convincing large numbers of people to vote or donate to a cause are potentially useful results—the term connotes those effects that garner criticism and concern for the well-being of the public. The results from exposure to mass media may be either intended or inadvertent. Intended effects are the result of efforts such as political or public information campaigns, whereas crime and violence are often unintended effects and cause the greatest concern.

Media effects can be manifested in a change of opinion, belief, or behavior or in the reinforcement, or intensifying, of an already held belief or pattern of behavior. The impact will vary depending on the consistency, frequency, and intensity of the messages being delivered. The content of the media messages and the characteristics of the audience are taken into account when studying the effects. Media effects rely on the social, political, and culture environment in which the messages were created.

The hypodermic needle and magic bullet models, wherein audiences are characterized as uniform and passive, were early models of media effects that were subsequently rejected. A theory of media dependency has become the more commonly accepted model, which, among its many facets, holds that the extent of media effects is closely tied to the degree of dependence that individuals and societies have on mass media; the impact can be cognitive, affective, or behavioral. The more power the mass media wields in a particular culture or the more unstable an individual or society is, the more likely the person or group is to be dependent on mass media. Under such circumstances, it is also more likely that a copycat or contagion effect will result.

The rise of television in the 1950s first brought such concerns to the fore, and researchers and public officials began to collect data and reports on the connection between violence portrayed on television and violent behavior in society. Research has shown that media portrayals—with their retelling of specific details—can trigger individuals to imitate negative or destructive behavior. Suicides and school shootings are two examples. The media has the power to provoke an epidemic of such behaviors. For further reading, see Ball-Rokeach and DeFleur (1976) and Cumberbatch and Howitt (1989). *See also* Bullet Theory; Copycat Effect/Crime; Dependency Theory; Graphic Violence; Hypodermic Needle Model; Reiterative Model; Television and Social Behavior

Media Imperialism   Commonly regarded as a subset of cultural imperialism, it encompasses the notion that industrialized, wealthy, and, therefore, powerful nations have the potential to exert economic, cultural, and social control over less powerful countries through mass media. When a culture consumes media products that are mostly created in another country—film, television, or news, for example—ideas and assumptions about that culture are propagated that could be inaccurate or in some cases manipulative. The relationship among economic, cultural, and informational factors is central to the concept. Media imperialism also refers to the practice of compelling less powerful nations to adopt or consume the media models of more powerful nations with the goal of wielding control or influence.

M

Those with economic power tend to have power with the media as well, and so the values of media owners are often reflected in the resulting communications. Media imperialism can thrive where structural wealth and information gaps exist. The flow of communication is imbalanced, and citizens have varied levels of access to receiving or managing the information. As a result, affected countries are at a political and economic disadvantage compared with other countries with more wealth, power, and, therefore, control.

The concept generally refers to the hegemonic influence of Western media over the media of developing countries. Communications and economics researchers in Latin America in the 1950s and 1960s first brought the idea of media imperialism to the fore when they analyzed the relationship between Latin American countries, Europe, and the United States and revealed a situation of dependency. Herbert Schiller, a proponent of the idea of imperialism, was writing about the subject in the United States in the1960s. Schiller argued that by collaborating with Western—industrialized, political, and military—interests, the U.S. media industries were promoting capitalist values in non-Western nations. For further reading, see Gerbner, Mowlana, and Nordenstreng (1993), Herman and McChesney (1997), and Schiller (1969). *See also* Hegemony (media studies); Imperialism; Media Bias; Propaganda Model

Media Languages   Language in this context refers to more than merely verbal language and words; it can also refer to other modes of communication, such as images.

Each medium uses a distinct mode of representation as a way of communicating, employing various cues that inform the audience as to the meaning of a particular message. Such cues include a variety of conventions, formats, symbols, narrative structures, and codes. Codes—which can be written, visual, or audio—are rules by which signs are assembled to create meaning. Media languages may generally fall into a few broad categories: (a) still graphic images, (b) written language, (c) sound, and (d) moving images.

The language used in a newspaper article is qualitatively different, for example, from the language used in a newspaper advertisement. Articles make use of direct representational conventions, whereas advertisements incorporate rhetorical—metaphorical or symbolic—strategies. Likewise, television programs, film, photographs, radio shows, video games, Web sites, and other mass media forms use particular conventions in delivering their messages. Audiences develop expectations of certain media languages as they become familiar with the elements of different media texts (the product of communication in any media). Certain conventions or stylistic traits are recognized, identified, and associated with certain media forms. We recognize the difference immediately because we have learned to distinguish media languages in much the same way as we have learned to understand our native spoken and written language.

Some of the same concepts used in studying a written language can be applied to analyzing media texts. For instance, the "grammar" of a film can be discussed, taking into account motion, sound, color, and camera angles, all of which operate on the meaning of the film, just as the grammar of a sentence can affect its meaning. For further reading, see Nicholas and Price (1998) and Ryan (2004). *See also* Language; Semiotics (media studies); Text; Visual Images

Media Liability   The legal claims emerging from the gathering and communication of information. Media organizations may become liable to legal action for a variety of causes, including defamation, product defamation, or copyright infringement. The law of torts has long made a technical distinction between slander, or spoken defamation, and libel, or written defamation. Under the landmark Supreme Court case of *New York Times v. Sullivan,* the media are protected from liability for libel and slander unless the plaintiff proves actual malice—that is that the publisher knew the controversial statements were false or acted in reckless disregard of their truth or falsity.

Although news media and other publishers have long had to be wary of claims such as libel and copyright infringement, attorneys and insurers have seen a noticeable rise in the past few years in the number and severity of media liability claims for errors and omissions. Unlike traditional claims involving allegations of libel, copyright infringement, invasion of privacy, piracy, and plagiarism, errors and omissions claims seek to impose liability on the publisher for physical injuries or economic loss allegedly caused by some error or negligence in the ideas or expressions contained in the published material.

Often, a claim or lawsuit may not involve a clear error or omission. For example, a client is not happy with the result and brings a claim to obtain a different result or avoid paying a fee. To shield themselves from damage by media liability lawsuits, media entities have recently taken to purchasing media liability insurance policies. For further reading, see *New York Times v. Sullivan* (1964). *See also* Libel; Slander

Media Monitoring   The practice of reviewing the contents of various mass media. Carried out in a systematic, formalized way, through content analysis, the content of media messages can be compared with external data as a measure of auditing or "truth checking." Monitoring can also be practiced in a less formal (and less time intensive) manner by watchdog groups and media critics. Whereas content analysis is presumed to be an objective and scientific practice, other types of descriptive monitoring may be carried out by media activists or politically motivated interest groups. Media critics and watchdog groups function under the assumption that with press freedom comes the responsibility to act legally and ethically. Often such groups are concerned about the breaches in democracy or ethics, on behalf of media organizations.

Approaches can range from a focus on media ownership, to consumption, to assessing media performance, or may include a combination thereof. The goal of monitoring is to ensure a balanced and realistic view of the world. The undertaking of media monitoring presumes that mass media are powerful and influential and, therefore, capable of shaping individual opinions and behaviors and influencing society. With the ever-increasing power of the media, via conglomeration and saturation, advocates are concerned about the potential for manipulation of a mediated reality. Media monitoring is an effort to provide a balanced view of what is actually occurring while being vigilant about not overrepresenting certain factors.

Content analyses may be found in scholarly communications journals, and other types of media monitoring may be published as articles in outlets such as *Columbia Journalism Review* and *American Journalism Review* and in publications of the watchdog groups, such as Fairness and Accuracy in Reporting. For further reading, see McQuail (1992), Nordenstreng and Griffin (1999), and Parenti (1993). *See also* Censorship (media studies); Content Analysis (media studies); Manipulation; Mass Media; Mean Worldview; Media Effects

Media Outlet   The utilization of a communication medium to connect media messages to targeted audiences for consumption. Examples of media outlets are radio stations, television stations, and newspapers. Media outlets provide direct exposure of products to key audiences, such as advertising lipstick in women's magazines. They also provide news or entertainment programming to audiences. In today's media landscape, most media outlets are owned by a few corporations or conglomerates; media ownership is generally considered to be highly concentrated. One example of media consolidation is the CBS Corporation, which owns the CBS television network, CBS radio, and the Simon & Schuster publishing house. *See also* Communication Medium; Industry (media studies); Publication

Media Relations   The processes by which persons and institutions interact with news media. In theory and practice, the study of media relations proceeds from the understanding that the media stand as gatekeepers between factual events and the public, deciding what stories will be told and how they will be framed and interpreted. Given the inescapable fact that information that passes through the media to the public is always transformed by the process, media relations are of keen interest to the sources that initially provide information to the media. Indeed, media relations can be understood as the tactics and policies by which sources of information influence the way in which the media communicate that information to the public.

As Daniel Boorstin observed in 1961, news media, in the process of representing reality, transform it into a "synthetic novelty." Whereas some may naively assume that news reporting supplies a window on the world, it

is more accurate to say that the news transforms images and data into a "constructed reality." Yet the first opportunity to shape this reality lies not with the media but with the media's sources, the so-called authorized knowers or possessors of expert knowledge, or other forms of authority that supply the raw material for their reportage. A crude notion of media relations might suggest that an authorized knower can effectively control the media's reporting of an event, both by choosing what details to dispense and by placing a particular spin on the information. A more refined view, however, recognizes that this control is seldom absolute, both because other sources may exist and because a source that selectively presents or spins its information will lose credibility over time. A more enlightened approach to media relations acknowledges that media relations consist of much more than the management of information. Properly understood, it also involves managing an ongoing, productive relationship with the media, informed by a mutual need for trust and reliability, as well as the recognition that the appropriate domain of public relations is, in fact, relationships. For further reading, see Boorstin (1961), Ericson, Baranek, and Chan (1987), Johnston (2007), and Ledingham (2003). *See also* Gatekeepers; Media; Public Relations

Media Technology and Police Interrogations
Video and audio are used to provide reliable recordings for the courts of interrogations and confessions occurring in police custody. Currently in the United States, recordings of confessions are more common than recordings of full interrogations.

Recording police interrogations reduces the risks of false confessions, protects the police against charges of using coercive tactics, improves the quality of interrogations, aids in monitoring by supervisors, and reduces court time. Recordings may be video or audio. Video recordings provide a more complete record of events, including body language. It is a law enforcement tool widely endorsed by law enforcement officers who have used it. Diverse local and international organizations, such as the New York County Lawyers' Association, the United Nations Human Rights Committee, and the European Committee for the Prevention of Torture, have called for the technique to be widely adopted and regulated.

Illinois became the first state in the United States to require electronic recording of all custodial interrogations in homicide investigations in 2005, followed by Maine and the District of Columbia. Hundreds of individual police departments across the country currently record interrogations, many doing so without the aid of written regulations or guidelines. However, most police departments in the United States still do not routinely record interrogations in serious felony investigations. Since 1984, recording of interviews in serious felony investigations has been mandatory in the United Kingdom, and in Northern Ireland since 1999. Canada, Australia, New Zealand, and the Republic of Ireland also require that such interviews be recorded. For further reading, see Linkins (2007), New York County Lawyers' Association (n.d.), and Sullivan (2004). **See also** Camera Surveillance; Videotaping in the Criminal Justice System

Mediation (communication)   A complement to the study of mass communication and how the media affect societies. Unlike the more commonly known legal meaning of the word—an intervention to bring about an agreement between two parties—mediation in the realm of communications and social science refers to an investigational approach to understanding the influence of the mass media on social, cultural, and political institutions and behaviors.

Mediation focuses on the messages found in print, broadcast, and Internet media, both implicit and explicit. The concept of mediation developed during the latter half of the 20th century, as the presence of broadcast journalism increased. Promoters of the need for mediation, including the Latin American writer Jesus Martin-Barbero, point to the media's power to create cultural, political, and social agendas; to inform in honest or deceptive manners; and to influence government affairs.

As more and more people become communicators because of access to the Internet, the scope of mediation continues to grow. For further reading, see Ruben and Lievrouw (1990) and Silverstone (2005). **See also** Mass Media

Mediation (sociology)   A nonbinding intervention between two or more parties facilitated through the active participation of a neutral third party (mediator) to promote agreement, reconciliation, settlement, compromise, or resolution of a dispute. Mediation is often used as an alternative to litigation in labor disputes, contracts, civil damages, domestic relations (e.g., divorce, custody, visitation), and workplace and international conflicts and may be ordered by a judge. The mediator must be viewed as impartial and is trained to facilitate dialogue and resolution between the disputants. Participants, likewise, must understand mediation to be voluntary, collaborative, and confidential for it to be effective. **See also** Litigation

Medical Model (education)   A theoretical stance that views mental health through a lens similar to that of physical disorders. Clients are diagnosed on the basis of observable signs and symptoms and use of classification systems such as the *Diagnostic and Statistical Manual of Mental Disorders* (fourth edition; *DSM-IV*). The emphasis is on bringing the client back to health by remediating his or her psychological deficits and abnormalities. **See also** Wellness

Medical Model (psychology)   A model of psychopathology that frames psychological disorders as disorders of underlying physical mechanisms (such as biochemical and physiological processes). Since this model views the etiology of any psychological disorder to be physiological, the implications of this approach are that research and treatment should focus on understanding and altering biological malfunctioning. This model has been criticized for failing to consider social and cognitive causes of psychological disorders. The biopsychosocial model, an alternative to the medical model, retains the disease model as the basic assumption but views psychological disorders as multilayered phenomena in which social, cognitive, and physiological factors play an important role. A primary assumption of the medical model is that mental illnesses have a physical cause and that diagnosis will assist in determining etiology, treatment, and prognosis. For further reading, see Monti, Rohsenow, and Hutchison (2000). **See also** Wellness

Medical Model (sociology)   A sociological model that has two meanings. First, it is an approach to illness common in Western medicine that focuses on providing heath care to treat diagnosed physical symptoms or causes of disease or illness. Doctors who subscribe to the medical model use symptoms to diagnose diseases, discover their causes, and implement treatments that minimize symptoms or eliminate those causes. The medical model is criticized for its omission of social, psychological, and behavioral aspects of illnesses, particularly in reference to mental illness and substance abuse. The medical model is distinguished from the holistic model of the alternative health movement. The medical model also refers to the use of medical terminology and actions in a legal case, also linked to the concept of therapeutic jurisprudence. Offenders may blame their offending behavior on medical or psychological issues and may, in turn, be required to participate in treatment for their offenses. This is common in cases of sexual offending, for instance, when offenders blame impulses beyond their control for their offense and, in turn, receive chemical castration as a component of their sentence. **See also** Wellness

Meditation   A practice in which the individual focuses his or her attention inward to achieve a greater sense of clarity and stillness. Involving both mind and body, meditation has been linked to increases in wellness and life adjustment. It is practiced in secular and religious contexts.

Medium   A system or device used to communicate and deliver messages, ideas, or information to audiences. A medium can be classified as print (such as a newspaper, magazine, or billboard) or electronic (such as a television, radio, or computer). A medium may also refer to the material on which data can be recorded or stored, such as a CD-ROM. **See also** Message

Medulla   The medulla oblongata is a structure in the hindbrain, which is the oldest (in evolutionary terms) and lowest part of the brain. The medulla contains neurons that transmit information from the spinal cord to the forebrain and is the section of the hindbrain that lies closest to the spinal cord, just below the pons and reticular formation. The medulla controls very basic autonomic functions, such as blood pressure, heart rate, and breathing, and reflexes such as coughing, sneezing, and swallowing. For further reading, see Carlson (2007). *See also* Brain (Encephalon); Brainstem

Megan's Law   A set of laws that require registration of those convicted of sexual offenses in statewide registries. Megan's Law is officially the name of New Jersey's version of this type of law and was named after Megan Kanka, a 7-year-old child who was abducted, sexually assaulted, and killed by a neighbor who had multiple convictions for prior sexual offenses. Megan's Law is intended to increase public awareness of sex offenders living in communities and requires that information about the offender (name, address, and photograph) and the offense (nature of the crime) be included in statewide repositories. Information in the sex offender registries is made public via the Internet, and some states require some form of community notification in addition to the registration. *See also* Sex Offense/Crime; Sexual Offender

Memory *(education)*   A complex system in an organism's mind that actively selects, transforms, stores, retains, retrieves, and uses information.

Memory research, which started more than 120 years ago, has evolved from experimental investigations of rote learning to studies on the processing of complex chunks of information and constructing of meaning in real-life settings.

Different models have been proposed to account for the nature of memory, but the multistage (or multistore) model is the currently dominant one. Based on a computer metaphor, this model is functional instead of corresponding to the neurophysiological locations in the brain. The assumption of the model is that information is processed in stages that are linked to the memory systems, each of which has a specific function. Generally, this model is composed of sensory registers (or sensory memory) and short-term and long-term memory. Incoming visual and auditory information is selectively and briefly processed in sensory registers and then passed on to short-term memory for processing of meaning. To prevent the loss of information from short-term memory, two processes occur to transfer the information to long-term memory: (1) rehearsal (repetition) and (2) encoding (relating information to what is already in memory). Information thus stored in long-term memory is there permanently for later retrieval.

With further research on activities that occur in short-term memory, the term *working memory* started to be adopted in order to better capture the complexity of mental operations attributed to short-term memory. One well-known model of working memory includes an executive system that selects incoming information and controls two subsystems responsible for visual-spatial and verbal information.

Unlike sensory registers and short-term memory, long-term memory is assumed to have unlimited capacity. Three different types of knowledge are organized in long-term memory: (1) declarative knowledge, (2) procedural knowledge, and (3) conditional knowledge. Declarative knowledge refers to factual knowledge, or knowing that/what. Procedural knowledge, in contrast, refers to knowing how to perform certain activities. Conditional knowledge is knowledge about when and why to use either declarative or procedural knowledge.

Within the category of declarative knowledge, further distinctions have been made between two types of memory: (1) semantic memory and (2) episodic memory. The former refers to memory for general concepts and principles and the associations among them. It can be recalled independently of how it was learned. Examples of knowledge stored in semantic memory are concepts, historical facts, word definitions, and chemical formulae. Episodic memory refers to storage and retrieval of vivid and specific personal experiences. It is recalled through association with a particular time or place. Examples of episodic memory experiences are the first date, a trip to the Grand Canyon, and dorm life at college. *See also* Explicit Memory; Implicit Memory; Long-Term Memory (LTM); Schemas; Short-Term Memory (STM)

Memory *(psychology)*   A mental storage system into which information is encoded and retained over varying periods of time and from which information may be retrieved, with or without conscious effort. Information may be encoded in acoustic (conversion of information into a string of recognizable sounds), visual (conversion of information into a visual image), or semantic (conversion of information into meaningful material or association of information with meaningful material) forms. Once encoded, material may be stored in memory indefinitely until it is retrieved. Although implicit memory describes the effortless retrieval and influence of past experiences, explicit memory describes the retrieval of a memory with conscious effort and may require the assistance of retrieval cues (cues associated with the original encoding that facilitate the retrieval of memory). A common distinction drawn at the retrieval stage is the distinction between more effortful recall (retrieval of information with minimal retrieval cues present) and less effortful recognition (retrieval of information in the presence of retrieval cues).

These three primary processes (encoding, storage, and retrieval), which lead to the formation of memories, operate in a sequence of stages: (1) sensory memory, (2) short-term (or working) memory, and (3) long-term memory. Impressions registered very briefly in sensory memory are transferred into short-term memory for further processing. Short-term memory allows the retention and processing of sensory information for a maximum of about 30 seconds and relies predominantly on acoustic coding. Through a process called consolidation,

M

information is transferred from short-term memory to long-term memory and may remain in long-term memory for the life span. Long-term memory is thought to have limitless capacity. Information in long-term memory is classified into procedural memory and declarative memory. Declarative memory is further sub-classified into episodic versus semantic memory, and retrospective versus prospective memory.

Information in long-term memory is organized according to semantic networks and schemas, and constructionist theory holds that memory is not a replica of past events but a reconstruction of past events based on information from many sources. However, this reconstructive process can lead to distorted memories of events and experiences, or even false memories. Decay (the gradual disappearance of the mental representation of a stimulus over time), retroactive interference, and proactive interference are processes by which forgetting can occur, as are retrograde and anterograde amnesia.

While the hippocampus appears to be important in forming new memories and in consolidating short-term memories into long-term declarative memories, memory is not stored in a particular structure or part of the brain. Rather, memories are encoded, stored, and retrieved by complex neuronal networks, or circuits of neurons in the brain. Long-term potentiation is the biochemical process by which repeated stimulation strengthens the synaptic connections between nerve cells, and it is thought that this process leads to the conversion of short-term memories into long-term memories. The precise physiological processes involved in the transfer and storage of memory are unclear, but research generally indicates that memories are probably stored in and around the cortex. However, different aspects of memories may be stored in different sensory regions of the cortex (e.g., the auditory features of a memory may be stored in the auditory cortex, whereas the visual features are stored in the visual cortex). For further reading, see Purdy, Markham, Schwartz, and Gordon (2001). *See also* Explicit Memory; Implicit Memory; Long-Term Memory (LTM); Schemas; Short-Term Memory (STM)

Memory Strategies   Memory aids that individuals use to remember information. One common memory strategy, especially for young children, is using something tangible or concrete to remember. An example is leaving an item in a physical location so as to not forget it, such as leaving homework by the front door to remember to take it to school. Other forms are cognitive approaches or mental tricks that usually involve some sort of repetition or associations, such as a mnemonic device. Mnemonic devices often use verbal mediation, the association of two words by another word or phrase that connects them together; visual imagery, which are mental pictures; or both, to facilitate the storage and retention of information in long-term memory. One example is the method of loci dates, which dates back to the ancient Greek and Roman empires. This type of mnemonic device superimposes structure by using

geographical locations to remember lists of items; each item is associated with a particular location along a particular journey, and these associations facilitate memory of each entry, in the correct order, as each landmark is reached. Another example is the keyword method, which uses both verbal mediation and visual imagery. This method is an especially effective mnemonic device for learning foreign languages. It uses verbal mediation, such as connecting a foreign word with a native-spoken word (the keyword), and then forms a visual image of that word with its native-language meaning. The keyword method is not only effective for learning foreign-language vocabulary, it can also be used in paired associates (i.e., states or provinces and their capitals, world leaders and their names). Using the initial letter is a trick to store and retrieve a list of facts. The individual uses the first letter of each word of each item in the list as a trigger for remembering all the items in the correct sequence. *See also* Memory (education)

Mens Rea   A Latin term that translates as "guilty mind." *Mens rea* is one of the necessary elements of proving an intentional criminal act. In criminal law, it is generally not enough to establish that a person has committed a bad act (the *actus reus* or crime); the prosecution must also demonstrate that the defendant had the requisite intent (or *mens rea*). *See also Actus Reus;* Corpus Delicti; Intent

Mental Maps   Cognitive functions in which the brain records and stores the spatial relations of a location. Cognitive maps should not be confused with cartographic maps, as cognitive maps are not always synonymous with the actual geographic features of a space. Cognitive maps represent a human's interpretation of his or her everyday physical environment and, therefore, rely primarily on an individual's perception and memory. In this way, cognitive mapping is subjective rather than objective in nature and is used to help an individual determine spatial relationships.

Mental Measurement Yearbook   Expert reviews of commercially available tests developed by the Buros Institute of Mental Measurements in 1938. The Yearbook's purposes are to provide adequate information for selecting appropriate instruments and to encourage rigorous standards for test development and measurement research. *See also* Achievement Test; Personality Test

Mental Retardation (*education*)   A developmental disability that is identified when one's intellectual ability and adaptive behavior are significantly below what is expected in the social community. It is defined by the current culture, and, therefore, the definition varies across time and place.

In the United States, the American Association on Intellectual and Developmental Disabilities (formerly the American Association on Mental Retardation) leads the way in defining mental retardation. In 2002, they proposed their 10th definition in 94 years. This definition states, "Mental retardation [intellectual disability] is a disability characterized by significant limitations both in intellectual functioning and in adaptive behavior as expressed in conceptual, social, and practical adaptive skills. This disability originates before age 18."

Both the American Psychological Association and the American Psychiatric Association provide similar definitions. The American Psychological Association differs in that the age of onset must be before 22 years. The American Psychiatric Association differs in that it includes specific areas of adaptive functioning in the definition.

In a more global sense, the World Health Organization defines mental retardation as follows:

A condition of arrested or incomplete development of the mind, which is especially characterized by impairment of skills manifested during the developmental period, skills which contribute to the overall level of intelligence, (i.e., cognitive, language, motor, and social abilities). Retardation can occur with or without any other mental or physical condition.

As can be seen from the current definitions, there is a consensus that mental retardation is indicated by significant co-occurring limitations in intellectual and adaptive functioning originating during the developmental period. A significant intellectual limitation is indicated by scoring approximately 2 standard deviations or more below the mean on an accepted IQ test. Similarly, scores of approximately 2 standard deviations or more below the mean on an accepted measure of adaptive behavior indicate a significant limitation in adaptive behavior. There is greater consensus on accepted measures of IQ than of adaptive behavior. ***See also*** Developmental Disability

Mental Retardation *(psychology)* A generalized impairment in intellectual and social skills. As an Axis II classification in the *Diagnostic and Statistical Manual of Mental Disorders* (fourth edition; *DSM-IV*), the label of mental retardation is applied to individuals whose measured IQ is less than about 70 *and* who fail to display the skills of daily living, communication, and other tasks expected of people their age. Today, the terms *developmentally disabled* or *mentally challenged* are often used instead of mental retardation. Level of retardation can be categorized as mild, moderate, severe, or profound, depending on the individual's cognitive abilities as well as his or her ability to function independently in daily life. For example, mildly retarded school-age children are able to acquire reading and arithmetic skills to about the sixth-grade level and can later function relatively independently and engage in productive work, whereas severely retarded school-age children are capable of basic speech and may be able to learn repetitive tasks in supervised settings. Profoundly retarded children show severe delays in all areas of development, but some may learn simple tasks in supervised settings.

Down syndrome is one type of mental retardation occurring when an abnormality during conception results in an additional 21st chromosome. There are many other forms of mental retardation with a genetic etiology, such as Fragile X syndrome (caused by a defect on Chromosome 23) or Williams syndrome (caused by a defect on Chromosome 7). Mental retardation can also have environmental causes, such as exposure to rubella, alcohol, or other toxins before birth; oxygen deprivation during birth; infectious diseases during childhood; or head injuries. In approximately 30% to 40% of cases of mental retardation, referred to as familial retardation, there is no obvious genetic or environmental cause. In these cases, retardation appears to be the result of a complex interaction of genetic and environmental causes that are not fully understood. In these cases, mental retardation tends to be mild.

Mental retardation is more accurately thought of as a disability than a disease and so does not parallel other psychological disorders included in *DSM-IV*. Appropriate support and teaching can allow many mentally retarded individuals to improve their level of functioning to some degree. In mildly mentally retarded people, recognition of simple stimuli and the rate of forgetting in short-term memory are normal. However, mildly retarded individuals show general deficiencies in metacognition (the knowledge of cognitive strategies, when to apply them and how to use them in new situations), and it is these deficiencies that most limit their intellectual performance. It is therefore important to assist children with mental retardation to develop appropriate cognitive strategies and to teach them to monitor the success of their strategies. For further reading, see Handen and Gilchrist (2006). ***See also*** *Diagnostic and Statistical Manual (DSM)* (psychology); Metacognition

Mental Set The tendency to rely on cognitive strategies that have worked well in similar situations in the past. Mental sets can aid problem solving when a new problem is similar to an old one, enabling the individual to reach the appropriate solution more quickly. However, the solutions to previously encountered problems are not always the best or most efficient solution to the current problem. Thus, mental sets are an impediment to problem solving if a new problem requires a different strategy for solution. For further reading, see Greeno and Simon (1988). ***See also*** Cognitive Strategies; Problem Solving (education)

Mentoring An ongoing process of support provided by a successful peer that engages a novice protégé in a variety of experiences related to a specific endeavor. Components of mentoring include coaching, providing feedback, modeling, and guiding to help others grow into effective contributors to their field or profession.

Mentor Teacher An accomplished teacher who is given the responsibility through administrative arrangement for inducting novice teachers into the profession.

M

Mentor teachers are expected to assist new teachers in getting to know teaching assignments and context, reflecting on teaching practices and planning on improvements, and being innovative in transforming teaching practices.

Mercantilism   A theory of national wealth acquisition, which was popular from the 16th century to part of the 18th century in some European countries, including Britain, Spain, and France.

Mercantilism is predicated on the idea that aggressive promotion of exports, more than imports, will lead to the acquisition of bullion (precious metals of gold and silver) or wealth. The thought of export as a basis of wealth led to the systematic colonization of territories to obtain raw materials and markets for finished products. The mercantilist era witnessed the colonization of countries in Africa, Latin America, the West Indies, America, and Asia by the French, the British, and the Spaniards.

The control of major routes of commerce was a crucial aspect of mercantilism, and powerful European nations tried to preserve an efficient fleet of ships in order to maintain sea power and economic dominance. The necessity to maintain a trade surplus, or a positive net exports position, became an urgent precondition for extensive government involvement in trade to limit the amount of imports and create monopolies. The mercantilists, such as Munn of England and Colbert of France, therefore proposed stringent restrictions on trade in the form of tariffs (taxes) and nontariff barriers.

Mercantilism was based on a much narrower perception of international trade. The reciprocity of trade was not given adequate thought, and wealth was largely measured in terms of bullion. Mercantilists viewed trade as a zero-sum game because wealth was considered to be fixed and it was also believed that one nation can only gain at the expense of others.

The mercantilist theory of international trade began to collapse during the 18th century. The physiocrats presented the view that natural laws direct economic activity and that wealth includes goods as well (not just bullion). Laissez-faire was a direct extension of the views of the physiocrats.

David Hume's price-specie-flow mechanism further exposed a major shortcoming in the mercantilist theory of persistent balance-of-payments surplus. The price-specie-flow mechanism indicates that excessive acquisition of bullion is inflationary and unnecessary. When money supply is excessive, there is an upward pressure on prices, which will then cause consumers to look elsewhere for cheaper products. As such, surplus gold or precious metals will move to countries with lower prices and less bullion.

In his *The Wealth of Nations* (1776/2007), Adam Smith subsequently showed that, contrary to the mercantilist thinking, trade can be mutually beneficial if nations specialize in the production of the goods for which they have abundant resources and acquired advantages (skills) to minimize the absolute costs that are associated

with trade. Specialization, or division of labor, increases output and global welfare. For further reading, see Carbaugh (2007), Salvatore (2006), and Smith (1776/2007). *See also* Absolute Advantage; Free Trade; Laissez-Faire (economics)

Mergers and Acquisitions   An interchangeable term used to describe the combination of two companies or corporations into one company. Only one of the firms survives, and the other is combined with the surviving firm. This is called a merger. An acquired firm can also be combined with the acquiring firm to form one company. Also, a corporation can acquire another corporation for strategic reasons without combining that corporation with the acquiring corporation. A merger can be distinguished by what happens to the company acquired. A merger will result in the combination of all the assets of the acquired company with those of the acquiring company, and then an entirely new corporation is formed. The acquired company ceases to exist, and the common stock of the acquired company is exchanged for shares in the new company. Thus, the terms *merger* and *acquisitions* are used interchangeably. Sometimes the press refers to mergers and acquisitions as takeovers or buyouts. However, a distinction must be made with the term *acquisition*. Acquisitions must be seen in light of the type of acquisition being made by the acquiring company. Companies acquire assets for investments purposes. Some companies can acquire the assets or buy a division of another company. For example, IBM sold its computer division to another company. This transaction is an acquisition of IBM's computer division and not a merger. However, if the company had acquired all of IBM's assets and then merged them with its assets, then this would be an example of how the term *merger and acquisitions* is used. When companies merge, the board of directors of each company generally agrees to the merger. A price is set for the shares of the company being acquired. Then, payment is made by exchanging the shares of the company being acquired for the shares of the acquiring company. Sometimes companies being targeted for acquisition will resist the offer and demand a higher price, or another company may try to acquire another corporation through a hostile takeover by openly buying the shares of the targeted company listed on the stock exchange. For further reading, see Ehrhardt and Brigham (2003), Emery, Finnerty, and Stowe (2004), and Gitman, Smart, and Megginson (2007). *See also* Corporation

Merit System   The process of hiring or promoting candidates for employment positions based on credentials and/or quality of work performance. The merit of a potential candidate can be determined by examining the prior job experience, educational qualifications, employment testing, and/or job performance. It can also be used to describe the screening process used by educational institutions to admit students into their program. This process is viewed as being more efficient and ethical than the alternatives, in which individuals are hired or promoted based on loyalty, political affiliation, or nepotism. The rationale behind this system is to offer the greatest incentive for current employees seeking promotion and other potential employees to improve their productivity.

Mesosphere One of the core layers of the earth's atmosphere, which lies just above the stratosphere and below the thermosphere. Extending approximately 30 to 50 miles above the surface of the earth, the mesosphere is characterized by cooler temperatures, which become lower with increasing altitudes. The mesosphere, often referred to with the stratosphere as the middle atmosphere, is the layer in which the atmosphere reaches its coldest temperatures. In addition, due to the extreme heat produced by friction between gases, the mesosphere is the layer in which most meteors burn before reaching the earth's surface.

Message The information relayed in an exchange of communication from a sender to a receiver. A message can be expressed through language, verbal or written. It can also be conveyed through nonverbal communication. The meaning of the information in the message is influenced by the context in which the message was constructed. *See also* Communication

Meta-Analysis *(education)* A research technique where one systematically analyzes individual studies using a common standard to examine each study's characteristics, findings, and results. The resulting analysis presents a synthesis of all the studies. Meta-analysis is used statistically in quantitative data analysis or as a comprehensive literature review in qualitative research. *See also* Statistics (psychology)

Meta-Analysis *(psychology)* A statistical technique for combining results across a large number of individual studies on a particular topic, with a variety of characteristics, to reach a unified conclusion. The literature on a particular topic often comprises a number of individual studies that produce differing, even contradictory, results. Each individual study is vulnerable, to some degree, to error variance (variance due to factors unidentified in the study) and only provides a rough estimate of the true relationship between variables.

In a meta-analysis, the researcher endeavors to consider all studies (published or unpublished) that have been conducted on a particular topic, with respect to specific inclusion criteria that the researcher explicitly outlines. Meta-analysis is based on the effect sizes (the strength of the relationship between the variables of interest) found in each individual study. These data are then statistically integrated to obtain a general estimate of the strength of the true relationship between the variables. By combining effect size information from many individual studies, encompassing a variety of participants, measures, and procedures, researchers assume that the accuracy of the resulting estimate will be higher than the estimate provided by any one particular study. For further reading, see Sutton, Abrams, Jones, Sheldon, and Song (2000). *See also* Inferential Statistics; Statistics

Metacognition The self-awareness one's own cognitive processes (knowledge and skills) for attending, encoding, and retrieving information out of memory. This means that an individual is aware of his or her own learning and cognitive processes in addition to the actual learning task at hand. It is often termed *thinking about thinking*. Additionally, this self-awareness and knowledge is used by the individual in relation to self-regulation in terms of setting learning goals and forming a learning plan, identifying and using effective strategies, and monitoring his or her own present knowledge state throughout the learning process. *See also* Memory (education)

Metacommunication The act of commenting on, analyzing, or reflecting on another communicative act. The metacommunication may contradict the other communication, reaffirm it, or cause its meanings to be more complicated and ambiguous. Metacommunications can take place before, during, or after the communication, and their position in time can have an effect on the reception of the communication. For example, warning someone that a story about to be told may be scary can set up the listener differently than when not issuing this warning. The exact effects of a metacommunicative act cannot be any more precisely predicted than the act of communication itself, which is always prone to multiple interpretations, unexpected effects, and misunderstandings. Metacommunications may try to predispose a listener or reader to a particular interpretation or attitude toward the text or communication; a metacommunication that attempts to express the idea "I am only joking" may or may not actually do so. Body language is an easy way to identify an example of a metacommunication: While the words being exchanged may have one implication, the body language—squirming, acting nervous, looking away—may communicate the opposite. Level of voice, tone, and asides have the same function. Metacommunication affirms the idea that language itself does not convey meanings directly but rather meaning is constructed between the participants in a communication. Meanings are as much teased out of the peripheral metacommunications, the situation, and the context of the act as they are out of the communication itself. For further reading, see Bateson (1972). *See also* Body Language; Communication; Cultural Context; Meaning; Reflexivity

Meta-Evaluation The formative or summative evaluation of evaluation processes and products. Standards against which evaluations can be assessed include, for example, the Joint Committee Standards for Program Evaluation, the American Evaluation Associations Guiding Principles for Program Evaluators, and the U.S. Government Accountability Office's

M

Government Auditing Standards (Yellow Book). ***See also*** Evaluation; Evaluation, Logic of; Formative Evaluation; Summative Evaluation

Metaphysics   The study of what is ultimately real— that is, of the structure and constitution of reality. Since it investigates the possible existence and nature of entities, such as God, causation, natural laws, and abstracta (e.g., numbers or propositions), metaphysics is broader in scope than empirical science, theology, or cosmology. In some applications, metaphysics is synonymous with ontology. ***See also*** Essentialism; Idealism; Ontology

Metaskills   Abilities that transcend or exceed expectations of talent and knowledge. *Meta* is a Greek and Latin prefix denoting higher order, and people who use metaskills make conscious efforts to regulate their behavior, to integrate their aptitudes, and to set and attain goals.

The psychologist Paul Karoly, writing in 1993, used the term *metaskills* for what he also called human "computational superstructures," such as memory, forethought, volition, self-regulation, the capacity to learn vicariously, and competency with spoken and written language. Karoly (1993) pointed to a metaskill identified (though not termed as such) by the philosopher William James: the setting and achieving of goals that evidences a remarkable human ability to bridge the present with the future.

Metaskills are perceived to be valuable in effecting societal changes. Cindy Gallois, writing in 2003 in the wake of the September 11 terrorist attacks on the United States, urged the development of metaskill training for the improvement of intercultural and interpersonal communication among various political, social, and ethnic entities. For further reading, see Gallois (2003) and Karoly (1993). ***See also*** Emotional Intelligence; Intercultural Communication/Cross-Cultural Communication; Self-Actualization (education, psychology); Self-Efficacy; Self-Regulation

Methodology   A set or system of methods, rules, and principles employed by a given discipline that govern how research is conducted. The social sciences employ diverse methodologies, including quantitative, qualitative, and mixed-methods approaches to research. ***See also*** Interview (education, sociology); Qualitative Research; Quantitative Research; Research; Survey (psychology, sociology)

Metropolitan Police Act   An act passed by the British Parliament in 1829 and championed by Home Secretary Robert Peel, who was concerned about the state of the police and crime in London. The act radically reformed the London police by creating a central police office (the Metropolitan Police Service of London) under two magistrates, replacing local constables and officials (except for the City of London). The Metropolitan Police Service, which started with a force of more than 1,000

uniformed men, is considered the first modern police force and served as a model for police services around the world. ***See also*** Law Enforcement

Microeconomics   A branch of economics that studies how individuals, households, and firms choose to use scarce resources efficiently in order to satisfy diverse wants or minimize losses. Individuals, households, and firms are considered to be economic units. By focusing on individual units rather than aggregate units or variables, the methodology of microeconomics is distinct from that of macroeconomics.

The economic variables of interest are usually prices, income or wages, employment, saving, and cost of production. Of course, these variables are important to the study of both microeconomics and macroeconomics and there might be a sense of overlap, but there are occasions when economists are interested in how individuals make a decision to work or to prefer leisure and on how hiring or production decisions are made. These micro decisions ultimately have an impact on the aggregate economy, and to that extent, they form an integral component of aggregate analysis, or the measurement of national economic performance.

Normative issues arise in microeconomics just as they emerge in macroeconomics. In microeconomics, they normally involve the ability of firms or industry to pay workers an efficient or decent wage, provide health coverage and old age benefits, and show restraint (social responsibility) in the use of environmental resources or provide compensation to society for the degradation caused. Firms may also be expected to show interest in fulfilling societal goals by their largesse; in effect, there is a welfare component to microeconomics. At the macrolevel, a government might be expected to promote these welfare-enhancing policies through legislation, in order to influence the aggregate outcome.

Economics has evolved as an empirical social science, and several theories in microeconomics and macroeconomics are drawn from scientific analyses to inform decision making at all levels. As such, microeconomics is also dependent on actual occurrences that are closely linked to cause-effect relationships, collectively known as positive economics.

Virtually settled empirical findings in microeconomics, which are the result of data collection and various hypotheses tests, are considered to be *laws*. These laws form proven guidelines to understand or rationalize economic decisions, even when there might be limited exception or aberrant variances to empirical observances.

Fundamental *laws* in microeconomics involve the basis of demand and supply in relation to price, scarcity and choice, and the opportunity costs that are the corresponding results of choices made. For example, the law of demand presupposes that under rational conditions, an increase in the price of a good will result in a reduction in the consumption of that good when real income falls, if other variables or factors do not instantaneously change (ceteris paribus). Similarly, an increase in wage rate will induce more workers to work, and an increase in the price of borrowing money (interest rate) will discourage investors or consumers from borrowing money.

Some economists argue that most decisions in microeconomics should be influenced by market conditions to obtain efficient outcomes. When expectations are realized, there is equilibrium in microeconomic markets, and when competition is promoted, microeconomic markets tend to be more efficient. Equilibriums do not last forever because markets are susceptible to shocks. Policy intervention can therefore ultimately influence the performance of microeconomic markets. For further reading, see Boyes and Melvin (2002), Case and Fair (2003), McConnell and Brue (2008), Salvatore (2002), and Schiller (2006). *See also* Demand; Economics; Market; Monopoly; Perfect Competition; Supply

Micropolitics   Formal and informal power used by administrators, teachers, parents, or students to execute their plans within a school. Conflict among stakeholders may occur across organizational systems when individuals interact with one another. Micropolitics are affected by outside influences, termed *macropolitics*. Micropolitics and macropolitics commonly influence each other.

Middle School   A school providing developmentally responsive education to students between elementary and high school. Various grade configurations exist, yet middle schools usually consist of at least three grades, including Grades 6 and 7. The middle school movement began strongly in the 1960s to meet the unique and diverse needs of young adolescents.

Migration   The process or act of movement by an individual or group from one country, region, or place to another, sometimes over long distances. Evidence of human migration has been found throughout history and prehistory. In the United States, for example, former slaves freed by the Emancipation Proclamation took part in the "Great Migration" from the south to the north. Migrations may be voluntary (e.g., in search of better living conditions, often from rural to urban areas) or involuntary (e.g., transportation of slaves or human trafficking). Migration is one of the driving forces of human evolution.

Minnesota Domestic Violence Study   A study of police response to domestic violence calls conducted by Lawrence W. Sherman in the early 1980s. The study consisted of a series of experiments in which police responding to misdemeanor domestic violence calls in Minneapolis (a) asked one party to leave the premises; (b) acted as mediators, counseling both parties; or (c) made an arrest. Arrests were found to be more effective than either of the other responses in reducing the frequency of reoffending. Findings from the study

led to the widespread adoption of mandatory arrest policies for domestic violence incidents, though the findings have not been replicated in all studies. *See also* Domestic Violence

Minnesota Multiphasic Personality Inventory (MMPI) *(education)*   The most widely used and researched self-report measure of abnormal psychiatric symptoms and personality. Constructed using criterion-keying methods and consisting of 567 true-false items, the test yields both validity scales and clinical scales that measure the degree to which the responses are similar to those of various clinical populations.

Minnesota Multiphasic Personality Inventory (MMPI) *(psychology)*   An objective personality test, in true-false format, comprising 567 items. It is the most commonly employed objective personality test when the goal is a diagnosis of psychological disorder. The MMPI was originally developed in the 1930s at the University of Minnesota and was revised and updated in 1992 to become the MMPI-2. The MMPI-2 is organized into 10 clinical scales, or groups of items, and additional scales measuring other personality dimensions and response tendencies. The items making up these scales have been shown in previous research to draw a particular pattern of responses from people with particular psychological disorders or personality characteristics. The more items a person endorses in the same direction as the diagnostic group, the higher the score the person receives on the scale. (For example, if a person displays the same response patterns as those of clinically depressed people, he or she will score high on the depression scale of the MMPI.)

Interpretation of the MMPI involves comparing a respondent's profile with the profiles of people already known to display certain personality characteristics. The MMPI produces scores for individuals on each scale, but interpretation of the MMPI usually focuses on the individual's overall pattern of responses across all the scales, particularly if a respondent displays unusually high scores across multiple scales.

While the reliability and validity of the MMPI have been generally well established, the validity of the MMPI has been criticized when used with minority respondents. Because of cultural factors, the perceptions and values of a respondent may be significantly different from those of the comparison sample, and abnormal profiles may be the result of culture-specific interpretations or responses, not psychological disorders. While the MMPI-2 has been developed with a more culturally diverse comparison population than the original MMPI, care must always be taken when interpreting MMPI profiles for members of minority groups. For further reading, see Butcher (2006). *See also* Personality (psychology); Personality Disorders

Minor   A person under full legal age, usually 18 (state laws vary in the U.S.). Minors (also called juveniles) do not have the same rights as adults and may be prohibited from driving, buying alcohol and cigarettes, and voting; they are usually tried in separate (juvenile) courts. They also are considered under the age of consent and, therefore, cannot consent to sexual acts or other such behaviors. *See also* Juvenile

Minority Government   Government by a party that does not control the majority of seats in the legislature. This type of government is practiced in the Westminster system, the parliamentary system used in the United Kingdom and many formerly colonized nations. It is more difficult under this arrangement for legislation to be passed, as there is the threat of a "no confidence vote" by the legislature. When the party wielding executive power does control the majority of seats in the legislature, then a majority government exists. Surveys find that voters prefer this type of government because it increases accountability and the likelihood of legislation getting passed. *See also* Majority Government; Parliament

Minority Group   A collective entity or cohort that when compared to another group (or groups) is assigned a lower status on some scale or standard. The assignment is made by a group outside the minority-defined group and in relation to a different group that is thought to represent or possess a more valued status. The standard on which the minority group designation is made may be based on diverse, even nebulous factors, including those that are biologically, psychologically, and/or sociologically based.

Minority Leader   The leader who is chosen from the minority party in each house of Congress. The leader is the spokesperson for the party, mobilizes support for the minority-party's agenda, and acts as the party's top strategist. It is helpful if the presidential administration is of the same party as the minority leader.

Miranda Rights   The rights that must be read to suspects prior to their interrogation, usually at the time of their arrest. This fulfills the requirement, set by the U.S. Supreme Court in *Miranda v. Arizona* (1966), that suspects must be informed of their Fifth and Sixth amendment rights. According to the Miranda decision, arrested persons must be told that (a) they have the right to remain silent, (b) anything they say may be used against them in a court of law, and (c) they have the right to legal counsel, which may be assigned if they are indigent. Confessions may not be introduced as evidence at trial unless the suspect was informed of his or her rights and made a knowing, intelligent, and voluntary waiver of those rights. For further reading, see *Miranda v. Arizona* (1996). *See also* Arrest; Constitution (political science)

Misdemeanor   A category of criminal offense less serious than a felony. Misdemeanors are generally punishable by a monetary fine or a jail term of less than one year. The U.S. federal government and many states divide misdemeanors into several classes according to their seriousness and consequences. *See also* Felon/Felony

Mistake of Fact/Law   A legal principle referring to either an unintentional error in comprehending facts, words, or the law, which may reduce or eliminate liability or culpability, or an erroneous conclusion about how the law applies to behavior (may not be used as a defense). *See also* Culpability

Mitigating Circumstances   Sometimes referred to as extenuating circumstances, they are those circumstances that reduce either the gravity of the offense or the blameworthiness of the offender. The age of the defendant; the absence of a prior record; the role of the offender in the commission of the offense (instigator or accomplice); a history of abuse, provocation, emotional disturbance; or evidence of mental illness might serve as mitigating circumstances. Mitigating circumstances are most often introduced by the defense, are generally considered at sentencing, and become particularly prominent in death penalty cases. A sentence of death typically follows a finding that the aggravating circumstances outweigh the mitigating circumstances. *See also* Aggravating Circumstances; Punishment (psychology, sociology); Sentencing

Mixed Economy   A market-oriented economy in which a government plays an active role in fine-tuning the economy, rather than allowing the invisible hand of the market to correct the market. A mixed economy therefore shows traces of market capitalism (market freedom and free ownership of the means of production, inputs) and socialism (public ownership of economic resources and regulation of markets). The mixed economy is a testimony to the imperfection of markets, which results in market failure.

By definition, socialist economies, which have started to embrace privatization and market outcomes, can also be classified as mixed economy. The fundamental difference is the intensity of privatization and reliance on the market, which is much more inherent and prevalent in capitalist societies. The use of the expression is therefore traditionally more akin to the capitalist orientation, in which private enterprises play a dominant role in the market relative to publicly owned enterprises.

Over the years, the underallocation or overallocation of resources to the provision of public and private goods has made the role of the public sector increasingly important. For example, in the United States, there has been a tendency to subsidize farming and tax cigarettes or regulate polluting industries. Planning and economic growth are not merely left to the market.

Policymakers respond to downturns just as central planners target economic output and prices. In capitalist societies, governments employ a significant amount of the labor force, redistribute income by taxation, and provide social services.

Therefore, in mixed economies, the major economic decisions of what to produce, how to produce, and for whom to produce are made by public and private agents. Private and public sectors compete for available inputs and respond to consumption propensities and deficiencies. ***See also*** Capitalism (economics); Laissez-Faire (economics); Market; Market Failure

Mixed-Methods Research   The type of research in which a researcher or team of researchers mixes or combines qualitative and quantitative research philosophies, techniques, methods, approaches, concepts, or language into a single research study or a set of related studies (also called mixed research and mixed methodology). The three types of mixed-methods research are (1) qualitative-dominant, (2) equal-status, and (3) quantitative-dominant mixed-methods research. Mixing usually is undertaken to obtain breadth and depth of understanding and corroboration. Mixed-methods research is one of the three major research paradigms, including qualitative research, quantitative research, and mixed research. ***See also*** Qualitative Research (education); Quantitative Research (education)

Mixed-Methods Research Validity Types   The production of defensible research is important in all types of research, including mixed-methods research. Another label for "validity" in mixed-methods research is "legitimation." In mixed-methods research, the researcher attempts to make inferences, called *meta-inferences,* from the qualitative and quantitative findings. We focus here on the nine validity or legitimation types provided by the mixed-methods researchers Anthony Onwuegbuzie and Burke Johnson (2006). First, *inside-outside legitimation* refers to the extent to which the mixed-methods researcher accurately understands, uses, and presents the participants' subjective-insider viewpoints and the researchers' "objective"-outsider viewpoints. Second, *paradigmatic validity* refers to the degree to which mixed-methods researchers document and justify their philosophical or paradigmatic beliefs and practices in the research study. Third, *commensurability legitimation* refers to the degree to which the researcher is able to make "Gestalt switches" between qualitative and quantitative viewpoints and integrate these viewpoints into a meaningful meta-inference. Fourth, *weakness minimization legitimation* is the degree to which the researcher combines qualitative and quantitative approaches to have nonoverlapping weaknesses. Fifth, *sequential legitimation* is the degree to which the researcher correctly addresses any effects resulting from the order of the qualitative and quantitative phases in a mixed-research study. Sixth, *conversion legitimation* is the degree to which any qualitizing of quantitative data (e.g., putting quantitative data into categories or themes) and quantitizing of qualitative data (e.g., putting qualitative data into numbers) produces accurate and useful meta-inferences. Seventh, *sample integration legitimation* is the degree to which appropriate generalizations are made from mixed (i.e., qualitative and quantitative) samples used in the research study. Eighth, *political legitimation* is the degree to which the interests, values, and standpoints of multiple stakeholders are accurately and fairly represented in the research study. Ninth, *multiple validities legitimation* is the extent to which the mixed-methods researcher appropriately addresses and resolves the relevant issues raised in the different types of qualitative and quantitative validity in the mixed-methods research study. This last type of legitimation indicates that to conduct high-quality mixed-methods research, the researcher must, at the same time, conduct high-quality qualitative and quantitative research. For further reading, see Onwuegbuzie and Johnson (2006). ***See also*** Emic and Etic Perspectives; External Validity; Internal Validity; Qualitative Research Validity Types; Validity in Quantitative Research

Mnemonics   Techniques that are developed and used specifically to aid or improve memory. They rely on strategies for placing information in an organized context so as to remember it. Types of mnemonics include acronyms (where the first letters of each of a list of words to be remembered are organized into a single word), acrostics (a verse or saying in which the first letter of each word represents an item to be remembered), visual imagery (where items to be remembered are imagined as being associated in a visual image), and the method of loci (where items to be remembered are imagined in particular physical locations, which the individual then mentally passes in a preplanned order). For further reading, see Cook (1989). ***See also*** Memory (education); Short-Term Memory (STM)

Modeling   A form of observational learning in which individuals learn by observing and imitating others performing certain behaviors. Modeling is often used in psychotherapy to help people acquire adaptive behaviors. In modeling treatments, the client watches the therapist or other people perform the adaptive behaviors, thus learning skills vicariously. Modeling is used most commonly in social skills and assertiveness training. Albert Bandura (1997) pioneered the use of modeling as a therapeutic technique to help people overcome phobias. In treatment for this type of anxiety problem, modeling can teach the client how to respond fearlessly while vicariously extinguishing conditioned fear responses. The combination of modeling and gradual practice is called participant modeling and is one of the most powerful treatments for specific phobias. For further reading, see Bandura (1997) and Faust, Olson, and Rodriguez (1991). ***See also*** Phobia; Psychotherapy; Social Learning Theory (sociology)

Modern Portfolio Theory   A statistical technique used to show how a diversified portfolio of assets, such as stocks, can reduce risk and improve the portfolio performance. The theory suggests that the risk of an

M

individual asset or stock should not be considered on the basis of its volatility or variation from its expected return. Instead, it should be considered in relation to its incremental or marginal contribution to the total risk of a portfolio of assets or stocks. The addition of an asset to a portfolio will affect the portfolio's risk depending on whether the individual asset has a negative or positive correlation to the price movements of the individual assets in the portfolio. Modern portfolio theory was first developed in 1952 by Harry Markowitz by applying mathematics to stock analysis. The theory was later refined and further researched by Sharpe, Miller, Fama, and others. The main idea behind this theory is that an investor can reduce the risk of and improve the expected return of a portfolio of stocks if the stocks in the portfolio are not correlated in their variability of returns to each other. For example, a portfolio should consist of stocks from different industries and in sufficient quantities to take advantage of diversification. The idea is to pick stocks in different industries that move in opposite directions. For example, if there is a recession in the automobile industry and there is a boom in the telecommunications industry, then stocks in a portfolio that fall in prices in the automobile industry will be negated by the stocks in the telecommunications industry. For further reading, see Ehrhardt and Brigham (2003), Emery, Finnerty, and Stowe (2004), and Markowitz (1952). ***See also*** Risk

Modus Operandi (MO)   The mode of operation. In criminology and forensics, the term is used to describe a characteristic pattern or signature. In the social sciences and program evaluation, the modus operandi method (MOM) is a technique popularized by Michael Scriven (1991) for investigating cause-effect relationships. Causal agents known to precede an effect are identified, and those not present or operating are eliminated by checking for the presence of the MO pattern. For further reading, see Scriven (1991).

Monarchy   A type of government in which the rule of law is vested permanently in a single individual. The term *monarch* is popularly reserved for nations where there is a hereditary line of succession for leadership. There are different types of monarchies; among them are elective monarchies, in which monarchs are elected into power rather than being born into it, and constitutional monarchies, in which according to the nation's constitution, power is shared by the monarch with a legislative and/or executive body. The notion of monarchy is derived through theocracy, the earliest form of statehood, where a high priest would rule or a king under the auspices of God. This concept developed into the 17th-century doctrine of the divine right of kings, meaning a king's rule was ordained by God. Most monarchies were abolished in the 19th century. Countries that retain monarchies (with governing authority) at present include Brunei, Oman, Qatar, Saudi Arabia, Swaziland, Jordan, and Morocco. ***See also*** Divine Right; Republic; Theocracy

Monetarism   A theory that advances the view that sustained money growth in excess of the growth of output produces inflation. The relationship between money growth and output has not, however, always been precise. For example, in the late 1980s, the rate of inflation fell below the rate of money growth, and this exception suggests that money growth may not necessarily be a sufficient condition for inflation.

Notwithstanding, monetarists argue that the solution to stable prices is the control of money growth, such that expected inflation must be checked by increases in the rate of interest. Rising price level in turn portends a depreciating currency, which can arguably be salvaged by increases in the rate of interest.

One of the empirical observations of monetarism is that escalating prices tend to first have an impact on output, which rises above its long-run growth path, albeit on a temporary basis, before the impact shows up on the price level. Contemporary policymakers now use the monetarist proposition of monetarism to deal with inflation, interest rate, and currency valuation. ***See also*** Capital Controls; Exchange Rate; Monetary Policy; Stabilization

Monetary Policy   The control or regulation of a nation's money supply by its monetary authorities. This function is normally delegated to the central bank of a nation. In some countries, monetary policy is not made independently by experts or professionals: There is pervasive interference by central governments to influence monetary policy through the printing of money to raise revenue (seigniorage) when collecting taxes and borrowing money become less viable. The result is usually an increase in the general price level (inflation), which causes economic instability as a result of inflation tax, flight capital, and the "original sin" (the inability of nations to borrow in their own currencies in financial markets).

In the United States, the Federal Reserve (Fed) makes monetary policy with a considerable amount of independence, so that monetary policy cannot be infected by political decisions. Inasmuch as the independence of the Fed is widely touted, it must be pointed out that the Fed was created by congressional statute and that since it is a creature of statute it can be abolished by statute. Additionally, the president of the United States appoints the chairman of the Federal Reserve Board as and when appropriate, subject to the approval of the senate, and the chairman of the Fed is obligated to give congressional testimonies.

Decisions to increase or decrease the money supply are normally made by the Federal Open Market Committee (FOMC), which consists of the seven members of the Board of Governors and five presidents (New York being a permanent member). The committee meets about every six weeks to discuss and make monetary policy. To increase the supply of money, the Fed buys bonds, through the New York desk, so that depository institutions can become liquid enough to extend credit to deserving investors and consumers. The opposite occurs when the Fed wishes to decrease the money supply. Other, less appealing measures to control the money supply include the reserve requirements for depository institutions, federal funds and discount rates, and margin requirements (the amount of money that can be borrowed to buy securities). The ultimate goal of monetary policy is to stabilize an economy, although time lags might make the goal a challenging proposition. For further reading, see Greenspan (2007) and Mankiw (2006). *See also* Business Cycle (economics); Hyperinflation; Inflation; Money Supply; Stabilization

Money Supply The stock of money (money measured at a particular period of time) rather than a flow, which can be estimated as a medium of exchange or a medium of exchange and store of value.

The narrower definition of the supply of money is generally referred to as *M1* because it is highly liquid and generally excludes the form of money that is characterized as a store of value. When the supply of money is aggregated as *M1,* it is computed to include currency (coins and paper money) in the hands of the public and all checkable deposits in depository institutions—including negotiable order of withdrawal (NOW) and automatic transfer services (ATS). Money held as vault cash is discounted to avoid double counting.

A larger measure of the money supply is *M2,* which includes *M1* (medium of exchange) and forms of money held for future use that are less liquid (near-monies). The broader measure consists of savings account, money market deposit accounts (interest-bearing money market securities or checking accounts), small (less than $100,000) time deposit accounts, and noninstitutional money market mutual funds. *M2* is a much more reliable measure because it captures the checking-saving interaccount transactions. Beyond *M2,* one of the broadest measures is money zero maturity (MZM), which focuses on monetary balances that are immediately available at zero cost for households and businesses.

The money supply can be increased or decreased through monetary policy. As a policy measure, an increase in the money supply is associated with an expansion of credit through interest rate reduction to stimulate further spending and investment, and it must not be confused with printing money. When an increase in the money supply outpaces the production of goods and services, the result is inflationary. For further reading, see Mankiw (2006) and McConnell and Brue (2008). *See also* Inflation

Monochronic Behavior The cultural habit of accomplishing tasks one at a time and of dividing time into linear compartments. According to the anthropologist and social researcher Edward T. Hall, monochronic behavior is most likely to be exhibited by Western folk, including Americans and northern Europeans—in particular, the Germans, the Swiss, and the Scandinavians.

Hall argues that dividing time into compartments is not in keeping with the rhythms of nature, and that monochronic time is a result of the Industrial Revolution. Since its inception in England, factory work has required people to be in place at set times, and since then, the sounds of bells and whistles have added to the belief that the constraints of time are a necessary order for living.

People who are monochronic gear their energies toward one project or toward one person or entity, Hall writes. They are less likely to be flexible in their business and personal dealings and tend to view parcels of time as commodities that can be saved, bought, or wasted. They are likely to concentrate on their job responsibilities, to take commitments seriously, to adhere to plans and schedules, to value privacy and promptness, and to respect private property. They are less likely to borrow or lend and are accustomed to expecting personal and business relationships to be short-term.

Because monochronic folk are what Hall terms *low context* in terms of prior knowledge, they need to seek information to complete chores, and they are also inclined to restrict the flow of information. For further reading, see Hall and Hall (1990). *See also* Low-Context Culture; Polychronic Behavior

Monologue A lengthy, undisrupted speech communicated by an individual. It is directed at one or more parties and pertains to formal and informal settings. A monologue might present the feelings of the speaker to the conversation partner(s). People can also have internal monologues, wherein one speaks to oneself consciously or semiconsciously.

Monopoly Theoretically, a monopoly exists when a single firm produces a product for which there are no close substitutes. From a much more practical perspective, innovation in electronics and communication and laws that have been made to facilitate competition or limit mergers have now made it very unlikely to have a pervasive monopolistic market structure. A monopolist is a price maker because he or she generally has control over the quantity to be produced and the price that will be charged for the quantities produced.

A monopolistic market can be created through patents and licensing (legislation), ownership of essential resources, and economies of scale. A patent gives an inventor the exclusive right to use his or her invention or allow others to benefit from it for a given period of time, thereby giving the inventor a monopoly power for the duration of the life of the patent. A substantial number of businesses, such as General Electric, Pfizer, and Xerox, have made tremendous growth because of patent rights.

As a result of the HIV epidemic, much more recent debates on human rights try to balance patent right (a form of human right) against the right to life (also a form of human right, with peremptory consideration in international law).

Licenses limit competition and entry into an industry or occupation—for example, commercial licenses for taxicabs or cable television. Similarly, a firm that owns or controls a resource that is essential to produce certain types of goods may limit or prevent others from using it—for example, the International Nickel Company of Canada, which controls 90% of the world's known reserves, and at one point in time, the diamond monopoly held by the DeBeers mining company of South Africa.

Although a monopolistic market that is generated by falling per unit cost (economies of scale) might be beneficial to consumers, the monopolistic firm is not generally perceived as efficient because of the tendency of the prices charged to exceed the marginal cost and per unit cost when a monopolist is in business. For further reading, see McConnell and Brue (2008). *See also* Antitrust; Innovation (economics); Market; Perfect Competition

Monotheism   The belief in the existence of one God, applied particularly to Christianity, Islam, and Judaism, though early Zoroastrianism and later Greek religion were also monotheistic. Monotheism may include concepts of the plurality of a single deity, such as the Holy Trinity concept in Christianity. *See also* Polytheism

Monroe Doctrine   A principle articulated by President James Monroe in his seventh annual message to Congress on December 2, 1823. The purpose of this message was to institute a policy against Europe's threat to support Spain's restoration of the colonies in the Americas, even though these governments had already declared independence from Spain.

The resulting address, which became known as the Monroe Doctrine, specified three main areas of U.S. policy: (1) recognition of the separate political systems between the Americas and Europe, (2) noncolonization of the Americas, and (3) nonintervention of the United States in European politics unless territory in the Americas was threatened. The Monroe Doctrine was intended to be a policy rule for the United States. It did not institute any protocols with Europe, and Europe was not asked to agree to it.

Although the intent of the doctrine was to narrowly apply only to those governments recognized as independent by the United States, it was later expanded to include American states that became independent after 1823, such as Brazil in 1824. And it later included Canada in 1936, when President Franklin D. Roosevelt gave his acceptance speech for an honorary degree of Doctor of Laws from Queen's University in Ontario, Canada. Roosevelt tried to turn the Monroe Doctrine from a unilateral declaration into mutual arrangements with other American governments.

The Monroe Doctrine was explicitly invoked on several occasions in U.S. history. In 1865, the United States summoned diplomatic and military policy pressure in support of the Mexican president, which enabled Mexico to successfully revolt against the French government. In 1904, when European creditors came to collect debts and threatened intervention in several Latin American countries, the United States sent its military to these countries to keep the Europeans out. And in 1962, when the Soviet Union tried to build missile-launching sites in Cuba, the United States put its naval and air guard around the island, forcing the Soviet Union to withdraw its missiles and dismantle its sites.

As a consequence of the Monroe Doctrine, the United States became the protector of the Central and South American states. Although the doctrine successfully kept France, Spain, and other powers out of the region, it also caused resentment among Latin American states, which did not agree with the United States throwing its weight about in Latin American affairs. For further reading, see Fenwick (1938). *See also* Doctrine

Montessori Programs   A teaching program that relies on student self-directed learning, where the teacher acts as a facilitator of knowledge. This method allows student learning to progress based on the student's cognitive development rather than at a predetermined pace. Montessori programs draw on the learning theories proposed by Maria Montessori and generally focus on early childhood through adolescence. For further reading, see Montessori (1912). *See also* Cognitive Development

Mood Disorders   A class of psychological disorders on Axis I of *Diagnostic and Statistical Manual of Mental Disorders* (fourth edition; *DSM-IV*), involving disturbances in mood states, such as mania or depression. Mood disorders may be divided into two general types: (1) depressive disorders and (2) bipolar disorders.

1. Depressive disorders are often called unipolar disorders, as they involve only the depressive pole of a spectrum of moods. The most common depressive disorder is major depressive disorder, which is characterized by feelings of worthlessness, changes in sleep or appetite, lethargy, and loss of interest in pleasurable activities. Seasonal affective disorder (SAD) is a type of depressive disorder characterized by a repeated pattern of severe depression in the fall and winter, followed by elevated mood during spring and summer. Dysthymic disorder (or dysthymia) is characterized by relatively mild but chronic depression, with clients typically experiencing depressive episodes for five years or longer.

2. Bipolar disorders are characterized by alternating moods that swing between euphoria and depression. The two major types of bipolar disorders are (1) bipolar disorder (see definition) and (2) cyclothymic disorder. In cyclothymic disorder, mood swings are milder than those seen in bipolar disorder.

Generally, a comprehensive consideration of the etiology of mood disorders is thought to require inclusion of biological, environmental, and psychological factors. Psychological models vary in their posited etiology of depression. Behavioral models hold that the primary psychological cause of depression is a shortfall in environmental reinforcement levels. More recently, cognitive psychologists have argued that depression is caused by maladaptive thought patterns and negative interpretations of events, called cognitive distortions. Seligman and his colleagues emphasize the importance of attributional style (the way in which individuals explain events in their lives) and learned helplessness as determinants of depression.

Mood disorders can be facilitated by environmental factors, particularly stress. Stressful factors that are most closely linked to vulnerability to depression include loss of a loved one, prolonged unemployment, financial hardship, serious physical illness, or marital problems.

Finally, biological factors that are thought to play a role in depression include irregularities in neurotransmitter functioning (particularly serotonin), abnormalities in neural pathways, and genetics. Twin studies demonstrate a strong role of heredity in mood disorders, particularly bipolar disorder. Antidepressant drugs increase the availability of serotonin and other neurotransmitters in the brain. For further reading, see Houghtalen and Privitera (2007). ***See also*** Bipolar Disorder; Depression (psychology); *Diagnostic and Statistical Manual* (*DSM*) (psychology); Dysthymia; Twin Studies (psychology)

Moral Education   The development of individuals' moral reasoning—for example, Lawrence Kohlberg's moral stages of development. Often distinguished from character education or indoctrination, moral education uses moral dilemmas and discussion to bring about changes in the way individuals think about moral issues. For further reading, see Kohlberg (1973). ***See also*** Character Education

Moral Imperative   A categorical imperative that commands that individuals follow basic ethical obligations to themselves and to others. The moral imperative was described by the philosopher Immanuel Kant, whose work dates back to the late 18th century. The moral imperative is categorical in that an action carries with it an absolute necessity; it is concerned with the morality of a duty to obey innate moral laws, and an innate moral duty is experienced by all through the existence of the conscience and feelings of guilt and shame, which tell us when we violate this moral duty. Furthermore, the moral imperative declares an action to be objectively necessary in itself, without reference to any purpose. The authority of a moral imperative comes from reason rather than experience. Reason exists when the individual acts from some a priori guiding principle.

A good will is the ultimate goal of morality. The good will is one that chooses to act because it recognizes that a particular action is the right thing to do. Kant also believes that individuals' obligations to perform good acts are irrespective of their feelings in the matter. Thus, motive should not be a consideration when deciding to act with good will.

Morality   The attempt to construct principles for governing right and wrong behavior. The most famous codes of morality can be found in religion; the Christian Bible instructs its readers how to avoid eternal damnation, for example, while Judaism offers the Ten Commandments, which must not be violated under any conditions. Morality forms a central element of much of the standard philosophy as well and is grouped under the category of ethics. The Greek philosopher Plato famously argued that people should act according to ideal principles (influencing many early versions of Judeo-Christian philosophy), whereas his successor, Aristotle, believed that life should pivot around notions of temperance. Perhaps, the most extensive system of morals was proposed in the 18th century by the philosopher Immanuel Kant, whose so-called categorical imperative offered supposedly universal principles of behavior. While Kant's system has engendered much admiration, it has also been heavily criticized; the controversial intellectual Friedrich Nietzsche believed that morality is not composed of universal laws but is a way for Christianity to perniciously maintain control over human action. For further reading, see Honderich (2005). ***See also*** Ethics

Moral Panic   A term that has been applied to events as disparate as medieval witch trials and 20th-century public outcries over child abuse, pedophilia, violent movies, and youth subcultures. It is a concept now found more in subdisciplines of criminology and deviance literature than in general sociology, the discipline where it originated.

Stanley Cohen studied the public and political reactions to gatherings of young adults at English resort towns in the mid-1960s. Britain was recovering from the economic austerities following World War II, and ordinary people had a little more money to spend. Young people were developing the Mods and Rockers subcultures, with distinctive clothing and music. Groups of strangely dressed Mods and Rockers converged at resort towns on holiday weekends, alarming the locals. Newspaper reports sensationalized the gatherings, with headlines such as "Day of Terror by Scooter Gangs" and "Youngsters Beat Up Town." Arrests were made, with heavy punishments meted out for relatively minor infractions. Police numbers were increased, and legislators were persuaded to pass laws counteracting the perceived threat. Cohen analyzed these events in developing his moral panic thesis, labeling the part played by the Mods and Rockers as "folk devils."

Cohen described moral panic as occurring periodically. Something or someone or a group is defined as a threat to societal values and interests. The threat is often something quite ordinary, which comes to be seen as extraordinary. The mass media report the threat (the folk devil) in a stereotypical and stylized manner, authorities denounce the threat, and experts promote their solutions. The perceived danger of the threat grows, in a "deviancy amplification process," with social disintegration seen as imminent.

Moral panic occurs during periods of rapid social change and may be an expression of wider concerns about risk. Moral panic may help define the moral boundaries of society and establish consensus. In demonizing and simplifying the perceived threat as deviant and "other," society reassures itself of its own essential righteousness. Draconian punishments may be legislated, with little regard for complexities. For further reading, see Cohen (1972/2002), Critcher (2003), and Goode and Ben-Yehuda (1994). **See also** Deviance; Labeling Theory

Moral Reasoning   The manner in which people think about and justify their behavior. People make decisions about what is or is not the right behavior in a particular situation based on several factors, such as cognitions, social learning, and emotions.

There are various theories that attempt to explain people's behavior based on how they reason morally. Three prominent theories are (1) Piaget's (1932/1965) theory of moral development; (2) Kohlberg's (1973) moral reasoning theory, based on a justice-related theme; and (3) Gilligan's (1977) moral care reasoning.

Piaget approached moral reasoning from a cognitive perspective. After observing children making decisions about moral dilemmas and then justifying their behavior, Piaget determined that children reasoned differently depending on their level of cognitive development.

Kohlberg's theory supports and extends Piaget's focus on cognitive development as it relates to moral reasoning. Kohlberg, too, provided children with examples of moral dilemmas and asked them to solve them. Based on their responses, Kohlberg classified moral reasoning into six hierarchical stages that people move through, one stage at a time. Each stage is contingent on successful completion of the previous stage, and progression through the stages reflects movement from an egocentric point of view to the eventual potential acquisition of a social conscience. Kohlberg did not believe that all individuals reached higher levels of moral development.

Carol Gilligan's theory is different from those of Piaget and Kohlberg. Gilligan proposed that compassion and caring be considered as motivators for moral reasoning, especially among females. She also suggested that a morality of care can progress from an initial egocentric perspective to concern for those unable to provide self-care and finally to the realization that all individuals deserve care and compassion.

Overall, moral reasoning as it relates to moral behavior is complicated and deserves further study. Behaviorists argue that moral actions are learned behavior resulting from reinforcement and/or observation of others. In addition, many believe that peer interaction, culture, and social conventions shape one's differentiation of right from wrong. Some researchers focus on emotions in their study of moral development. Others, such as Eisenberg (1989), investigate the roles of both cognition and emotion in understanding moral reasoning, particularly as it results in prosocial behavior—that is, behavior intended to help another. For further reading, see Eisenberg (1989), Gilligan (1977), Kohlberg (1973, 1984), and Piaget (1932/1965). **See also** Moral Education

Motivation Theory   Theoretical models of motivation attempt to explain why individuals choose to engage in a particular activity. Motivation theories often include four stages or levels of involvement: (1) *initiation*—reasons for engaging in an activity, how to instigate or encourage entry; (2) *direction*—why one engages, refuses, avoids, or exerts effort toward engagement; (3) *intensity*—effort and concentration during engagement; and (4) *persistence*—how long one continues the activity, especially in the face of challenge, hardship, or temporary failure.

The role of intrinsic or extrinsic motivation is also a common factor of interest. Intrinsic motivation involves having a personal stake, or personally valuing some facet(s) of the activity. When the impetus, reward, or encouragement is external, both endurance and persistence fade if the external forces diminish or disappear.

Behaviorism explains motivation in terms of rewards and punishments.

Control theory and drive reduction theory state that a deficiency or need motivates people. If the need is met, motivation levels decrease, unless the needs are persistent or recurring. For example, the power of hunger may drive us toward certain behaviors; since we know that it will occur again, we might continue the behavior pattern so that hunger will not recur.

Cognitive dissonance theory is also a drive reduction theory, explaining motivation in terms of problem solving. Usually, two contradictory cognitive concepts are encountered, so we are moved to action to eliminate discomfort and restore cognitive equilibrium. Holland (1997) and other career theorists suggest that people are motivated toward goals related to vocational preferences; the stronger our interest or commitment toward a vocational area, the more motivated we are to work and sacrifice in order to meet the vocation-related goals. Need achievement theory posits three needs that we have, in differing degrees: (1) the need for affiliation (a sense of belonging, closeness, or acceptance by others), (2) the need for achievement (the feeling that our value is inherently tied to what we produce or accomplish), and (3) the need for power (being in control of our own destiny or a sense of personal helplessness, which lead us to control or manipulate others). Our actions and investment of our resources are more strongly applied to our areas of greatest need. The most widely accepted needs-based theory of motivation is Maslow's hierarchy of needs. There are five levels, and upper-level satisfaction (self-esteem, self-actualization) is not sought until the "deficiency needs" of the lower levels are met (food, clothing, shelter; safety, belonging). For further reading, see Holland (1997) and Maslow (1943). *See also* Behaviorism (psychology); Career Development; Cognitive Dissonance (psychology); Cognitive Learning Theory; Extrinsic Motivation; Hierarchy of Needs; Intrinsic Motivation

Motive   The reason a person committed an action or refused to act. Motive is distinguished from intent, which refers to an individual's state of mind (intention) during a criminal act. A motive is admissible at trial, but proof of motive is not required for conviction. *See also* Intent

Motor Vehicle Theft   The unlawful taking, or attempted taking, of a motor vehicle (e.g., automobile, motorcycle), intending to temporarily or permanently deprive the owner of it. The category excludes vehicles that run on rails (e.g., trains) or do not run on land (e.g., aircraft, boats). *See also* Index Crimes/Offense; Theft; Uniform Crime Report (UCR)

Muckraking   The name given to the American investigative journalists who exposed the social injustices and political scandals of the early 20th century. Some of the most notable muckrakers included Upton Sinclair, author of *The Jungle* (1906), which uncovered abuses in the meatpacking industry, and Lincoln Steffens, who authored *The Shame of the Cities* (1904), which was composed of a series of articles printed in *McClure's* magazine between 1902 and 1903 detailing fraud and corruption in America's largest cities. The term *muckrakers* was first used by President Theodore Roosevelt in a 1906 speech to describe sensationalist-seeking journalists who were tarnishing the reputation of "honest men." The name is based on a character, the Man with Muckrake, in John Bunyan's *Pilgrim Progress* (1678). For further reading, see Bunyan (1678), Sinclair (1906), and Steffens (1904/1957).

Muller-Lyer Illusion   A visual image in which two identical lines appear to be of different lengths, because of depth cues provided by their surrounding features. In the Muller-Lyer illusion, two identical lines are presented, parallel to one another. One line is bordered at each end by an arrowhead, and the other line is bordered at each end by an inverted arrowhead. The line bordered by the arrowhead on each end appears to be shorter than the line bordered by the inverted arrowhead on each end, even though their lengths do not actually differ.

Although the complete explanation for this illusion is still under debate, a partial explanation involves the brain's interpretation of size and distance cues. When two objects, projecting the same-sized image onto the retina, appear to be at different distances from the observer, the one perceived to be farther away is judged to be larger. In the Muller-Lyer illusion, the line bordered by arrowheads resembles the outside corner of a room

that is close to the observer, and the line bordered by inverted arrowheads resembles the inside corner of a room that is farther away from the observer. Since both lines actually project the same-sized image onto the retina, the brain interprets the one that appears to be further away (the line bordered by inverted arrowheads) to be larger. For further reading, see Morikawa (2003). *See also* Ponzo Illusion; Visual Images

Multicultural Counseling   Sometimes referred to as cross-cultural counseling, it involves an awareness of attitudes and beliefs about specific cultures and incorporates that knowledge in counseling relationships with clients from diverse ethnic, racial, and cultural backgrounds. Multicultural counseling acknowledges power and privilege as related to various client populations and challenges—historically, the heavy reliance on white cultural values. As such, therapists are encouraged to acknowledge and confront their generalizations and stereotypes about individuals from diverse groups. Multicultural competencies have been developed by both the American Psychological Association and the American Counseling Association for the training and practice of psychologists and counselors, respectively. *See also* Counseling; Cultural Diversity

Multicultural Education   An educational reform movement that creates a learning environment that is both equitable and relevant for students from a variety of racial, ethnic, and socioeconomic backgrounds. Triggered by the rapidly changing demographics of the classroom and inspired by the civil rights movement of the 1960s, multicultural-education scholars and advocates have sought to increase the presence of women and underrepresented groups in the curriculum while developing instructional methods to meet the learning needs of our increasingly diverse student population.

Multicultural education is a developmental and progressive project that seeks systemwide change to create an educational environment founded in ethnic and cultural pluralism: an environment free from the biases embedded within mainstream culture that also values cultural difference as a source of knowledge, creativity, and dignity. Related efforts can range from the development of a single course to the design of an entire curriculum.

A number of approaches can be categorized under the general rubric of multicultural education, including the following:

Single-group studies: These content-oriented programs seek to raise awareness of the social oppression and the empowerment efforts of specific groups, such as women, sexual minorities, and people of color. Such coursework can build scholarly integrity by highlighting the cultural, scientific, and political contributions of those who have been historically marginalized within the curriculum.

M

Transition to mainstream education: These student–oriented programs seek to optimize the academic performance of those who have been underserved by traditional education, through the inclusion of culturally relevant content and teaching practices. Such programs have academic parity for diverse students as their underlying goal.

Social reconstruction: These socially oriented programs explore processes of social change through the study of oppression and activism and can engender personal empowerment through participation in social reform.

Many multicultural-education approaches are founded on a strong social justice perspective, illuminating the power relationships that underlie social oppression, ranging from the classroom, to the workplace, to the political process. In doing so, leaders within the domain of multicultural education suggest that the democratic ideals of equality and equity for all can only be achieved through a rigorous examination of topics such as racism, ageism, religious intolerance, and institutionalized privilege. ***See also*** Diversity; Social Justice

Multicultural Research   The study of behaviors and cognitions that occur when individuals from different cultures come into contact with one another. Traditionally, culture has been defined as the accumulation of values, rules of behavior, forms of expression, religious beliefs, occupational choices, and so on, by a group of people who share a common language and environment. However, while cultures are sometimes delineated (less than perfectly and to varying degrees) by national boundaries, most countries are now multicultural, hosting various subcultures within their borders. Multiculturalism has been rapidly increasing over the past decades, as people in an era of globalization routinely move from their cultures of origin to new, host cultures for varying lengths of time, for work-related or personal reasons. Thus, multicultural psychology generally investigates the impact of culture and cross-cultural interaction on behavior and mental processes and encompasses many fields and approaches within the discipline of psychology. As such, multicultural psychology has particularly important implications for immigrants, and prominent topics in multicultural psychology include the study of acculturation, counseling for members of minority cultural groups, and workplace interactions in multicultural organizations.

Often, multicultural psychologists apply theory and findings from the larger and older domain of cross-cultural psychology to direct research and theory in multicultural psychology. For example, cross-cultural psychology has demonstrated the difference between interdependent and independent self-construals, with people from Asian cultures tending to construe themselves as more interdependent, whereas those from Western cultures tend to construe themselves as more independent. This knowledge is applied by multicultural psychologists to formulate hypotheses and direct inquiry regarding the interaction of Asian and Western people in a multicultural setting. For further reading, see Mio, Barker-Hackett, and Tumambing (2005). ***See also*** Acculturation; Culture (sociology); Multicultural Counseling

Multilevel Modeling   A form of linear regression (also known as hierarchical linear modeling [HLM]). The defining feature of multilevel modeling is the allowance for the variance of the outcome variable to be analyzed at multiple levels, whereas simple and multiple linear regression models all have variance at a single level. The data that bests suit multilevel modeling are data that are naturally nested (e.g., students nested within schools). There is some variance that is accounted for between schools, in addition to the variance accounted for between the students nested within those schools. Hierarchical modeling allows examination of those naturally occurring levels of variance and the calculation of the proportion of variance that is within each level of the data (intraclass correlation).

Let us look at an example of multilevel modeling. You are interested in how well fifth-grade student scores in one school district on a particular math achievement test are predicted by the utilization of a tutoring program. There are 10 schools (with 20 students in each school) in School District A. If you were to use a simple linear regression model (Model 1), you would look at the average math score among the 200 students predicted by the tutoring program and the error term associated with the predicted average math score.

Model 1

Predicted student math score = Average student math score for 200 students (overall intercept) + Unit change in predicted math score with tutoring (overall slope) + Overall error term associated with the predicted math score measurement (for 200 students).

However, you know that there are distinct differences within each school that can affect math achievement scores, which we want to capture and examine, in addition to the variance examined overall in the original model between the 200 students. To accomplish this, you could develop a model such as the following:

Model 2

Predicted student math score = Average student score across schools for 200 students (overall intercept) + Unit change in predicted math score with tutoring (overall slope) + Estimation of how much each school's average predicted score (school intercept) and unit change in score for tutoring (school slope) differ from the overall districtwide average predicted scores and slopes + the error associated with the predicted individual students score within the individual school.

The goal of multilevel modeling is to interpret the within-group residual variance and the variability of intercepts and slopes across groups (information obtained from the multilevel model), in addition to the average intercept and average slope (information obtained with the general linear model). HLM is an appropriate model where units are nested within a distinct functional group or unit, such as patients nested within hospitals and repeated measures nested within a subject. For further reading, see Bliese (2003), Bliese, Chan, and Ployhart (2007), Bryk and Raudenbush (1992), Efron and Morris (1977), Gelman (2006), Gelman and Hill (2006), Hox (1994), Livert, Rindskopf, Saxe, and Stirratt (2001), Rindskopf (2006), and Schonfeld and Rindskopf (2007). *See also* General Linear Model (GLM); Regression Analysis; Variability

Multilineal Evolutionism A 20th-century anthropological theory that focuses on the evolution of societies, populations, or cultures without value judgments about the concept of cultural "progress" from primitive to modern. Multilineal evolutionism, contrasted with unilineal evolutionism, contextualizes societal development within its own history and environment. *See also* Society

Multimedia The term was originally used to describe works of art, particularly modern art, that include different media, for example, installation art works that use video or a sculpture that uses metal, paper, textiles, and paint. The term is now used to describe works that combine more than one digitized medium, usually two or more of video, still image, sound, and text.

A multimedia work may be as simple as a series of slide images advancing at specified intervals and accompanied by a sound track. More complex works can include graphics, animation, and interactive components—for example, Internet-based multiple-user virtual-reality games. Image, video, and sound files tend to be large, even when compressed, and require greater bandwidth for network delivery and more storage space than text-containing files.

Multimedia works can be produced quickly by anyone with some inexpensive software and hardware, as the thousands of video pieces on YouTube attest. But most user-generated content demonstrates that great multimedia works require significant artistic, aesthetic, and technical abilities. But relatively simple digital devices can be used to capture images and sound of newsworthy events by journalists and others and can be downloaded through the Internet or a satellite/cable connection to the newsroom or Web site or blog within an hour. The public now expects access to unfolding news stories almost instantaneously. Professional journalists have been joined in reporting by countless amateurs. Newsblogs and independent media (indymedia) sites are using multimedia as they create alternative news sources to the established press.

Retrieval is a major challenge facing multimedia works on the Internet. Search engines have become astonishingly efficient at locating text documents, but retrieval of image, video, and sound files based on their semantic content is still highly problematic. Tagging files with metadata in text form describing the content is useful but time consuming and subjective and requires human intervention. Automated indexing of multimedia files now relies on reading text associated with the files, for example, text on the Web page surrounding the link to the file or the "alt" text embedded with the file. For further reading, see Anderson (2006) and Pagani (2005). *See also* Media, New

Multinational Corporation A corporation that has offices, buildings, property, and/or resources in at least one country other than its originating country. Multinational corporations that have several facilities in several countries will usually have budgets that are much higher than those of many small countries. Some people view multinational corporations negatively because they believe that they have political influence in some governments and take advantage of developing nations, along with increasing the rate of job losses in their home countries. These corporations are often the result of deregulation and globalization. *See also* Corporation; Deregulation (political science); Globalization (political science)

Multiparty System Unlike the two-party approach practiced in the United States and Great Britain, a multiparty system exists when a government's legislature consists of three or more political parties. The multiparty system currently exists in some Asian, European, and Latin American nations. Shifting coalitions and alliances are commonly formed in an effort to have political objectives met. Advocates of the multiparty system stress how coalition building encourages compromise in policy making and representation of minority voters. Critics point out that multiparty systems can be unstable and legislation in such systems more difficult to get passed, especially in a timely manner. Double and multiparty systems are often associated with democracies and single-party systems with dictatorships. *See also* Democracy (political science); Single-Party System

Multiple Intelligences *(education)* A theory, developed by Howard Gardner, that involves reframing of the concept of intelligence from the "psychometrically conservative" view of the single *g* score to multiple disparate factors or intelligences (hence the term *multiple intelligences,* or MI). Intelligence is defined as the particular degree of mental power an individual possesses in a certain area. This is distinct from learning style, which Gardner defines as the way individuals approach problems and situations, and also from domain, which he defines as a field of human endeavor. One's degree of a given intelligence or intelligences can be inferred from the work one produces in relevant domains.

The eight currently identified intelligences are (1) linguistic intelligence, (2) logical-mathematical intelligence,

(3) spatial intelligence, (4) bodily kinesthetic intelligence, (5) musical intelligence, (6) interpersonal intelligence, (7) intrapersonal intelligence, and (8) naturalist intelligence. *Linguistic intelligence* refers to written or oral verbal ability, *logical-mathematical intelligence* refers to reasoning and numerical ability, *spatial intelligence* refers to facility with pictures or objects (two- and three-dimensional), *bodily-kinesthetic intelligence* refers to physical and movement ability, *musical intelligence* refers to musical ability, *interpersonal intelligence* refers to a facility with social situations and dealing with other people, *intrapersonal intelligence* refers to self-knowledge and self-awareness, *naturalist intelligence* refers to a facility with the natural world. According to Gardner, most academic settings focus primarily on linguistic and logical-mathematic intelligence, to the detriment of the other intelligences and those individuals in whom those intelligences are dominant. He has considered and presently rejected the inclusion of spiritual intelligence and existential intelligence.

Other models that treat mental ability as composed of multiple, not necessarily covarying, domains include Taylor and Schlichter's talents model, Dabrowski and Piechowski's overexcitability theory, and Jackson's integral practice model.

Some problems with MI theory from a statistical viewpoint have been put forth by researchers including Pyryt (2000) and Plucker, Callahan, and Tomchin (1996), who found that when tests for MI were evaluated using factor analysis, the MI in fact loaded on only the two intelligences measured by traditional or conservative intelligence tests, verbal and performance or nonverbal intelligence. The response of adherents to MI theory is that the paper-and-pencil tests inevitably load on only verbal and performance intelligence.

From a theoretical viewpoint, the primary critique of the theory comes when it is used to assert that "everyone is gifted at something." Theorists like Delisle have attacked what they see as the seductive egalitarianism of the approach, which reduces the concept of high ability to a series of discrete subsets, none of which is seen as any more relevant, far-reaching, or significant than any other. However, it should be noted that if the theory is applied correctly, there is no reason to assume that everyone will in fact be highly able in any of the MIs. For further reading see Delisle (1996), Gardner (1983), Pyryt (2000), and Plucker, Callahan, and Tomchin (1996). ***See also*** General Intelligence; Intelligence Quotient (IQ)

Multiple Intelligences *(psychology)* Eight independent types of intelligence postulated by Howard Gardner to underlie different forms of intelligent behavior. Early theories of intelligence posited a single underlying dimension, labeled general intelligence, or *g*, which governed all behavior. These theories were derived from evidence that people who scored highly on one cognitive test tended to score highly on other tests. However, these theories allowed for some domain specificity, arguing that all mental tests also measure specific abilities that are unique to each mental test; thus, a person's performance on any given test was a function of *g*, their general intelligence, and *s*, a specific factor. Intelligence tests, such as the Weschler Scales, were developed as a measure of *g*, the underlying general intelligence factor.

Subsequent theories of intelligence retained the notion of a single underlying *g* but argued that assessment of a single intelligence quotient (IQ) score was of little value without further consideration of specific primary mental abilities. Thus, Thurstone and Thurstone (1941) argued for further domain specificity in the study of intelligence and pointed to a set of seven primary mental abilities: (1) verbal comprehension, (2) numerical ability, (3) memory, (4) inductive reasoning, (5) perceptual speed, (6) verbal fluency, and (7) spatial relations.

More recently, however, Gardner (1999) rejected the idea of a single underlying dimension called "intelligence" and argued instead for the existence of several different types of intelligence, called multiple intelligences, which are independent from one another and vary from one person to another. While biology provides raw capacities on any intelligence type, cultures provide symbolic systems (such as language) to mobilize those raw capacities, and individuals may develop some capacities further than others. Thus, any given person could score high on a test of one type of intelligence and low on another type of intelligence. The eight separate types of intelligence identified by Gardner were (1) linguistic (vocabulary and reading comprehension), (2) logical-mathematical (skill at arithmetic and certain kinds of reasoning), (3) musical (abilities involving rhythm, tempo, pitch, and sound identification), (4) spatial (understanding the relationships between objects), (5) bodily-kinesthetic (skill at dancing, athletics, and hand-eye coordination), (6) interpersonal (ability to understand and interact with others), (7) intrapersonal (self-understanding), and (8) naturalist (ability to see patterns in nature).

Some critics of Gardner's theory argue that definitive proof is still required for the existence of distinct, orthogonal intelligences. Others note that Gardner's model fails to address tasks that require more than one type of intelligence; for example, the ability to maintain a conversation requires both linguistic and interpersonal intelligences, and Gardner does not indicate how these intelligences interact to affect performance on the task. A fundamental criticism is the seemingly arbitrary designation of eight types of intelligence. The theory is unclear on the limit to the number of types of intelligence that exist and on what constitutes an intelligence type; critics argue that there are no theoretical barriers to the creation of infinite additional and increasingly specific intelligence types.

The multiple intelligence model has, however, experienced notable success, particularly in educational settings. Schools have been prompted to enrich the educational experience by cultivating a broad spectrum of intelligence types in children rather than simply targeting their traditional foci of linguistic and logical-mathematical intelligences. For further reading, see Gardner (1999) and Thurstone and Thurstone (1941). *See also* General Intelligence; Intelligence Quotient (IQ)

Multiple Personality Disorder (MPD)   Also known as dissociative identity disorder (DID). Dissociative disorders affect the ability of an individual to maintain a cohesive unity of consciousness, resulting in unusual behavior. MPD (or DID) is a type of dissociative disorder that is characterized by the appearance of multiple personalities in the same individual. Each personality has its own distinctive traits, manner, and memories. In some cases, there is a core personality that is generally known to other people and hidden alternate personalities that only reveal themselves at certain times. The alternate personalities may display genders, ages, and sexual orientations different from the core personality, and the core personality may be unaware of the existence of the alternate personalities or of events experienced by them. Men with the disorder tend to have fewer distinct identities than women.

Psychodynamic theories posit that MPD is caused by the massive repression of unwanted impulses or memories, whereas social-cognitive theories argue that MPD is an extreme case of the normal variation in behavior that healthy individuals display across different social situations. Evaluating hypotheses regarding the etiology of MPD has been difficult, since it is so rare. However, the prevalence of MPD has increased, and this has been a controversial topic among psychologists. Some have argued that the prevalence of MPD has not increased but the frequency of diagnosis has increased because of the influence of media stories or because of clinician bias toward the diagnosis and the subsequent expectations placed on the client and rewarded by the clinician.

The controversy has led some to question the very existence of multiple personalities or to suggest that the increased prevalence of MPD may reflect its status as a socioculturally approved means of expressing distress. For these reasons, the authors of *Diagnostic and Statistical Manual of Mental Disorders* (fourth edition; *DSM-IV*) changed the name of the disorder from MPD to DID, to avoid perpetuating the myth that people can easily harbor multiple personalities that can be contacted through hypnosis or other related means. The term *DID* was intended to suggest that the dissociation between memories and other aspects of identity can be so severe that sufferers of the disorder may come to believe that they possess two or more distinct personalities. For further reading, see Gleaves, May, and Cardena (2001). *See also* *Diagnostic and Statistical Manual* (*DSM*) (psychology); Personality Disorders (psychology)

Multistep Flow of Information   During the early decades of the 20th century, the transfer of information from mass media to an audience was seen as similar to injection with a hypodermic syringe. This changed when researchers analyzing opinion formation among voters during the 1940 presidential election unexpectedly observed that personal contacts appeared to have been more effective in opinion formation than the mass media. They developed the concept of a two-step flow of information, where opinion leaders filtered and passed on information from mass media to their social contacts. With time and further research, this model was seen to be overly simplistic. Opinion leaders were not omnipotent but were each respected for specific areas of expertise. Young women, for example, influenced opinion on fashion and moviegoing.

The simple two-step information flow was expanded to a multistep model and used to examine how innovations, new ideas, or technologies are adopted by members of a community. Information exchange among peers is seen as more significant than a top-down unidirectional information flow. Someone deciding whether or not to adopt an innovation passes through five stages, according to the researcher Everett Rogers: (1) knowledge (of the innovation), (2) persuasion, (3) decision (to adopt or reject), (4) implementation, and (5) confirmation (that the decision was correct or not). Rogers classified people according to the relative speed with which they adopted an innovation, labeling them as innovators, early adopters, early majority, late majority, and laggards. Change agents can speed the rate of adoption.

The use of interpersonal communication and change agents along with mass media is widely seen as the most successful way to get people to adopt a new technology. Advertisers using viral marketing techniques are attempting to make use of interpersonal communication in order to persuade people to buy products.

Diffusion of news stories tends not to follow the two-step or multistep models, as most people get exposed to news stories directly from a medium—television, radio, Internet. But news of great interest to large numbers of people travels farther and faster; that is it has a high "news value." For further reading, see Rogers (1962) and Severin and Tankard (1997). *See also* Two-Step Flow of Communication

Multisystemic Therapy (MST)   A strategy for dealing with children with severe mental illnesses, offering home-based care (rather than hospitalization) and involving the wider community (families, schools, and neighborhoods) in the health care process. This strategy was originally developed in the late 1970s to address issues with existing mental health services for serious juvenile offenders. MST posits that antisocial behavior in young people can be attributed to factors in various life domains, such as their family, their community, their peers, and their school. As such, treatment strategies that target particular aspects of the youth's behavior in an artificial setting (such as in a treatment facility or under supervised release) neglect the fundamental causes of antisocial behavior. MST targets aspects of a youth's social network that are contributing to antisocial behavior, such as improving caregiver discipline practices and increasing association with prosocial peers. Developers of MST argue that it has grown because, while it demands a different structure for caregiver services than is currently offered in many parts of the United States, the reorganized support for the community-based service results in improved outcomes for children with marked emotional difficulties. In addition, the cost of care delivery is reduced, relative to the alternatives, and therapists, families, and clients generally view MST positively. Various national agencies have identified MST as promising in the treatment of juvenile criminal behavior, substance abuse, and emotional disturbance. However, critics argue that insufficient independent research has been conducted to establish the effectiveness of MST. For further reading, see Schoenwald, Ward, Henggeler, and Rowland (2000). *See also* Juvenile; Therapist/Therapy

Multitrait-Multimethod Analysis (MTMM) An approach to construct validation that examines the degree to which methods and constructs are distinguishable. The approach was first formalized by Campbell and Fiske (1959). In particular, an MTMM study provides evidence of the convergent and discriminant validity of a test that is designed to measure a particular construct of interest to a researcher. An MTMM study examines at least two different traits measured by at least two different methods. Measures of the same trait should converge (have strong positive correlations with one another). Measures of different traits should be "discriminant" (have low or zero correlations with one another or an inverse relation to one another if it is theoretically meaningful). Examining different methods provides evidence of the robustness of a construct to different ways of measuring it. If correlations between measures of the same construct are moderate or highly positive, even though they are based on different measurement methods (e.g., a Likert scale and an interview), then the validity of the construct is supported. However, if there are stronger correlations between different constructs measured by the same measurement methods (two different constructs measured by Likert scales) than between measures of the same construct based on different methods, then there are problems with the validity of the construct because of measurement artifacts. More recent versions of MTMM studies have used structural equation models to test the fit of theoretical models designed to examine the relationships that would be expected under the conditions of convergent and discriminant validity. For further reading, see Campbell and Fiske (1959). *See also* Construct Validity; Correlation (education)

Multivariate Explanation In anthropology, a method of explaining the evolution of a culture or society. Mutivariate explanations emphasize the interaction and aggregate of the interaction of several aspects of that society operating simultaneously or sequentially. Multivariate explanations are distinguished from monocausal explanations, which attribute the existence of a phenomenon to a single cause. Multivariate explanations have recently been used in studies of election behavior, household composition, crime trends, and health status. Multivariate explanations can be more generally applied to empirical research. Multivariate analyses are conducted to explain the causality of a behavior or issue from multiple perspectives. Multivariate explanations are considered valuable because they allow for complexity and richness not available in "single-factor" analyses, though neither approach can address causality. *See also* Quantitative Research; Society

Municipality An organized administrative district (e.g., city, town, village, borough) that has a corporate status and usually has powers of local self-government. A municipality usually has a clearly defined geographic space and population and has administrative leadership consisting of the mayor and the city council.

Murder The criminal, unjustified killing of one person by another sane person with expressed or implied intent and malice aforethought, without legal justification, excuse, or authority. Murder may be categorized as capital (meriting the death penalty); first, second, or third degree; or, in some jurisdictions, felony murder. Evidence of torture, kidnapping, relation to another crime (e.g., rape), or special victim categories (e.g., police officer) may be required for a first-degree murder conviction. Murder is distinguished from voluntary and involuntary manslaughter (lacking malice aforethought), justified or unintentional killings, suicide, capital punishment, and the wartime killing of enemy combatants by lawful combatants. *See also* Capital Punishment; Felony Murder; Homicide; Index Crimes/Offenses; Manslaughter

Music Education The teaching and learning of artistic auditory communication. Qualified teachers facilitate various areas of instruction, including music history, music theory, instrumental proficiency, singing skills, and general music skills. Participation promotes attentiveness, self-discipline, cooperation, and creativity and supports the understanding of language and math.

Mutation A sudden, permanent change in the nucleotide sequence of the genetic material of an organism that is transmitted to future generations. Mutations are usually harmless or deleterious but can be important to evolution by establishing potentially beneficial variations in an organism's gene pool. *See also* Genetics

Myelin Sheath A fatty substance formed from glial cells that surrounds neuron axons, increasing the speed of action potentials and allowing muscles to move more efficiently and smoothly. Myelin is found surrounding neurons in parts of the nervous system that require the most urgently delivered information, such as neurons responding to intense sensory information (e.g., a burning surface), which requires reflexive responses. Because myelin sheaths are white, the parts of the nervous system that contain myelinated axons are often called "white matter." In multiple sclerosis (MS), myelin breakdown slows the transmission of nerve impulses and leads to the disruption of vision, speech, balance, and other important functions. For further reading, see Lazzarini (2003). *See also* Action Potential; Axon; Central Nervous System (CNS); Neurons; Peripheral Nervous System (PNS)

Myers-Briggs Type Indicator (MBTI)   A self-report personality test, developed by Katherine Briggs and Isabel Briggs Myers, based on the work of Carl Jung. This assessment tool addresses one's preferred orientation toward the world either outside oneself or inside oneself (extraversion/introversion), one's preference for using one's senses or using facts to take in information (sensing/intuition), one's preference for making decisions based on principles or on human values (thinking/feeling), and one's preference for orienting oneself to the world in a structured manner or with flexibility (judging/perception). *See also* Personality Test

Myth   A traditional sacred story shared by a group explaining a historical or natural event, rite, or belief and linked to cultural identity and religious beliefs. Myths often occur in a timeless or prehistorical past (e.g., creation) and involve supernatural elements (e.g., gods, ancestors). In the social sciences, myths are commonly held beliefs that are not true (e.g., that sex offenders have high recidivism rates).

M

N

Narcolepsy A sleep disorder in which a person slips abruptly from an active, often emotional, waking state into several minutes of rapid eye movement (REM) sleep. Narcolepsy is associated with cataplexy, in which a sudden loss of muscle control results in an individual suddenly collapsing. Narcolepsy can be very dangerous, leading to a variety of accidents, as sufferers can fall asleep in the middle of everyday activities, such as driving. Narcolepsy may be caused by a deficiency or absence of the neurotransmitter orexin, otherwise known as hypocretin. Stimulant drugs (amphetamines) and daytime naps are used to help maintain wakefulness in narcoleptics. For more information, see Silber (2001). *See also* Psychological Disorder; REM Sleep; Stimulants

Narrative A derivative of the Latin word *narrare*, which means to tell or to relate. Broadly construed, it means the telling of any story or event—as in legal or medical case narrative, journalistic or historical narrative—and therefore applies well beyond any literary context. All narrative is told from a certain viewpoint, which in the case of a first-person narrator, is easily identifiable and often biased or limited. More usually, the narrator is in the third person, but third-person rather than first-person narrative is not necessarily more impartial, and it is important to study the implied assumptions of events narrated in an apparently "objective" manner. Narrative also distinguishes between the "what happened" and the specific sequence in which events are related, which, when analyzed, reveals the narrator's implied relation of cause and effect between events. Narrative never naively re-creates its original story but always interprets and reconstructs it through careful selection and manipulated juxtaposition of events. *See also* Discourse

Narrative Analysis A technique for interpreting the meaning of stories. In narrative analysis, the idea of a "story" is extended to include texts, such as interview transcripts, journals, life histories, memoirs, personal accounts, family stories, notes, graffiti, and nonfiction works. The narrative allows the analyst to view cultural and social patterns through the individual experience. *See also* Qualitative Data Analysis; Qualitative Research

Narrative Therapy A social constructionist method of counseling, which refers to assigning value to clients' perceptions as they are expressed in the clients' own words, phrases, and stories. Narrative therapists recognize that the stories individuals and families choose to tell are constructions of culture and a way of interpreting the world rather than stories based on universal truths. Counseling interventions, typically, include questions to help empower clients to examine their problems, discover their resources, and reconstruct their behaviors, thoughts, feelings, and relationships in ways they find satisfying and self-fulfilling. With encouragement and collaboration from the narrative therapist, old patterns of destructive thinking and perception are avoided and new stories, and thus a new reality, are constructed. *See also* Constructivist Learning Theory; Counseling

Narrowcasting A specific process in broadcasting wherein programmers explicitly target niche audiences who may share demographic characteristics, values, or special interests. Where broadcasting distributes media to a wide segment of the viewing public, narrowcasting fragments that audience. In the early days of television broadcasting, the three major networks—ABC, NBC, and CBS—each hoped to reach the largest audience they could. With the proliferation of cable television in the 1980s, cable companies increased competition, causing programmers to vie for different segments of the viewing public. Single-information-category cable networks emerged, such as the Food Network, Entertainment Sports Network (ESPN), Cable News Network (CNN), or Travel Channel.

Narrowcasting is both triggered and fostered by competition and the economics of broadcasting. It benefits advertisers, who can more efficiently market their advertisement campaigns to particular specific demographic groups that have been targeted by media companies. *See also* Broadcasting; Target Audience

Nation A sizable group of individuals who unite, due to shared perceptions of social reality and historical origin, to occupy a specific territory, declaring loyalty and duty to the same government. A nation is fully developed through the national consciousness of its people, whose historical calling is inherent in the ethical ideals found within their historical legacy.

The political power of the nation has been traditionally argued to be legitimatized only through the will of the people. However, due to the complexities of globalization and international politics, a group of people may come to recognize themselves as a nation and give power to a specific government whose political entity may not be recognized as a legitimate nation in the eyes of the global community. The word *nation* originates in the Latin word *natus*—to be born; hence, "nationality" refers to a place of birth. For more information, see Wandycz (2006).

National Board Certification   A procedure designed to improve the quality of teachers and their instruction. Teachers complete a portfolio documenting their mastery of critical, pedagogical, and instructional skills and a content knowledge assessment. The benefits of certification may include a reciprocal teaching license in most states, salary increases, and recognition as a "highly qualified" teacher.

National Crime Victimization Survey (NCVS)   A yearly national survey, federally funded and conducted by the Justice Department and the U.S. Census Bureau, that uses a large, carefully drawn sample of citizens who are asked about their victimization in the past year. The survey reports higher crime rates than the Uniform Crime Reports (UCR) from the Federal Bureau of Investigation, as crimes that went unreported to the police are more likely to be included in the NCVS. Twice each year, data regarding the frequency and characteristics of offenses including rape, robbery, assault, and theft are collected by telephone from about 75,000 people in 42,000 households. While generally considered more accurate than the UCR, the NCVS suffers from threats to its validity. Limitations include overreporting and underreporting of criminal victimization and underrepresentation of certain groups, such as people of lower-socioeconomic status. Perhaps most significantly, because respondents are asked about victimization, homicide goes unreported. *See also* Uniform Crime Report (UCR)

National Incident-Based Reporting System (NIBRS)   An improvement on the Uniform Crime Reports (UCR), this system was developed in 1982 by the Federal Bureau of Investigation (FBI) and the Bureau of Justice Statistics. NIBRS counts the crimes reported to the police. NIBRS differs from the UCR in several ways. While the UCR calculates the crime rate based on only 8 index crimes, NIBRS collects data on 22 categories of crime, including kidnapping/abduction, gambling, and extortion/blackmail, and distinguishes between attempted and completed crimes, as well as crimes committed against people, businesses, and households. The UCR also includes only the most serious charge in a criminal offense, while NIBRS collects data on the entire criminal incident, including all charges and the relationship, if any, between the victim and offender. Additional characteristics of both the victim and the offender, the type and value of property stolen, and the characteristics of anyone arrested in connection with the incident are also recorded. *See also* Uniform Crime Report (UCR) (Part I/Part II Offenses)

National Institute of Justice (NIJ)   A subdepartment of the U.S. Department of Justice, it is mainly concerned with issues relating to crime control and justice and is dedicated to research and evaluation that will inform effective policymaking in the areas of criminal justice and crime prevention practices. *See also* Crime Prevention; Justice; Sociology

National Interest   A necessary, selfish, and subjective set of political manifestos based on the self-preservation of a particular nation-state. It is a moral duty of the state to ensure the survival of its citizens; therefore, a minimum prerequisite of survival is required proceeding hierarchically from that base. In addition, it must be logically necessary. A national interest is determined by the specific historical period and is arguably derived from the nation's identity, which constantly shifts on a basic continuum. A vital national interest is one that a nation-state is willing to defend by whatever means necessary.

For example, the Commission on America's National Interest identified five vital national interests:

1. Preventing the threat of nuclear, biological, and chemical weapons attacks on American military forces at home and abroad
2. Preventing both nuclear and biological weapons attacks against American cities, civilians, or military forces
3. Maintaining the security, safety, and accountability of all global stockpiles of nuclear weapons and related material
4. Reducing American vulnerability to all forms of international and domestic terrorism and, additionally, persuading states that support such endeavors to desist
5. Preventing terrorist groups from acquiring weapons of mass destruction against Americans everywhere

For more information, see Belfer Center (n.d.) and Huntington (1997). *See also* Nation

Nationalism   A conscious self-awareness of one's ethnic, territorial, historical, and cultural identity, generally positive and usually associated with governmental or political boundaries. Nationalism is frequently the sentiment used to distinguish one nation from another. Nationalism has been suggested by some scholars as an early modern European phenomenon, though most claim that it gained force only in the late 18th and early 19th centuries, after the Napoleonic Wars.

A nationalistic awareness develops in individuals when they recognize a common identity and are integrated in the community regardless of differences in social class, religion, and education. This awareness constitutes one of the individual's highest values, instilling pride and loyalty to the collective entity. The emotional components of nationalism, however, are also a cause for disruption and violence, as illustrated by the clashes and warfare that have occurred between different ethnic groups and tribes in Africa since the late 20th century. *See also* Nation

Nationalization The process of extending public ownership of enterprises in a national economy (also known as "deprivatization"). Nationalization frequently occurs in the public utility sector of a macroeconomy. Public utilities, such as transportation, telecommunications, water supply, health, and natural gas, are normally taken over by the government when they are endangered by improper or inefficient management that imperils the provision of services or the stability of a government. These services are critical, and the demand for them is highly inelastic.

Private companies may also be appropriated by governments, although international law inveighs against such a practice, especially without adequate compensation. In some developing countries, foreign investments have been expropriated because of a perception of exploitation, evasion of tax laws, or corruption. For example, nationalization, or seizure of private property, occurred extensively in Zimbabwe after the apartheid regime (Rhodesia) collapsed. Nationalization is supposed to prevent profit repatriation, but corruption in most developing countries has made it difficult to rationalize or justify the basis of expropriation. Zimbabwe, for example, is in total economic collapse in 2009, with illegal appropriations, a scandalously inefficient and corrupt government, and a quintillion percent inflation rate. *See also* Privatization (political science); Public Interest (political science)

Naturalistic Observation A type of observational research that involves recording ongoing behavior in an organism or individual without attempting to change it. In naturalistic observation, the observation is conducted in the actor's natural setting in such a way that the actor's behavior is disturbed as little as possible by the observation process; often, the actor is unaware that he or she is being observed. For this reason, naturalistic observation is also referred to as unobtrusive or nonreactive research (to emphasize that the actors do not react to the presence of the observer). Naturalistic observation has begun to play a more prominent role as more social scientists are becoming influenced by the methods and theories of animal behaviorists, and it is often used in psychology as a method of generating fruitful hypotheses for further research. Typically, research progresses from naturalistic observation to laboratory observation, where psychologists aim to rule out sources of confounding that may occur in the original naturalistic setting. Objective measures of behavior are an important component of naturalistic observation, ensuring that extraneous factors do not contaminate the collection and interpretation of data in naturalistic settings. For more information, see McBurney and White (2007). *See also* Extraneous Variable/Evidence; Laboratory Research

Natural Law The set of rules that hold value in a wide variety of contexts. These laws are defined by nature and are influential in diverse environments. For instance, the belief in the existence of God may be considered to be a natural law, as it is valid in various cultural settings across the world.

Natural Monopoly A theoretical market structure in which productive efficiency is guaranteed by a single producer rather than by many because of technical factors. Technical factors may impinge on resource availability, outlays, and technological advancement. As output increases, the single producer enjoys extensive economies of scale (low per-unit cost), from which consumers might obtain lower prices.

The marginal cost of producing incremental (additional) units is negligible to such an extent that no other market structure can supply the good more cheaply. A competitive market structure, for example, would generate comparatively higher per-unit cost.

The amount of fixed cost necessary for production is a very important precondition for natural monopoly because it constitutes a significant proportion of total cost, which in turn affects per unit cost. The utility, mass transit, and cable television markets require substantial sunk costs to deliver services to consumers.

An efficiency-generated monopoly (natural monopoly) is different from other forms of monopoly. Monopoly may alternatively be generated because of licenses, patents, copyright laws, control over resources, and regulations that prevent others from entering into a particular market.

Although a single-utility company can deliver a product much more efficiently than other firms, the profit-maximizing potential of a monopolistic structure can make it less desirable to charge the fair rate of return or a price that is reasonably above the fair rate (per-unit cost) in order to guarantee retained earnings for investment or growth and compensation to investors. In such situations, cost advantage does not automatically translate into consumer gain. To prevent the exploitation of consumers, some amount of regulation may be desirable, but the idea of regulation poses a dilemma.

If natural monopolies are to be regulated, the regulated price must be sufficient for them to stay in business, which means that they should be able to cover per unit cost and retain enough earnings for future growth. Since the marginal cost is extremely low, the efficient price will be below per-unit cost. The efficient price is unfavorable except when sufficient subsidy is provided. Governments will have to raise money to subsidize production, which might mean an increase in taxes. Regulation must also take into consideration the right to enjoy ownership of property. In *Smyth v. Ames* (1898), the U.S. Supreme Court recognized the need to maintain a balance of societal interest and property right (including the reward). For more information, see Schiller (2006) and *Smyth v. Ames* (1898). *See also* Economics; Fixed Cost; Market; Market Forces; Oligopoly; Perfect Competition; Profit; Regulation

Natural Rights A political theory that maintains that an individual enters into a political or organized society

N

with certain basic rights that no government can deny. These rights are inalienable. They cannot be taken or given away. The idea of natural rights grew out of the social doctrines of the stoics of the first century CE. The most famous formulation of natural rights was pronounced by John Locke, in the 17th century, who believed that humans were inherently rational and carried into political society the same rights that they enjoyed in the natural state.

Natural law incorporates the belief that people should live their lives and organize their society on the basis of rules and principles handed down by nature or God. According to Locke, the most basic law of nature is the preservation of mankind. In his view, natural law proposes that no harm should come to another's life, health, liberty, or property. These rules and principles evolved from the state of nature. In the state of nature, every man is presumed to be born equal and possess the power both to punish transgressors and be punished for transgressions. However, Locke states that the punishment ought not to be arbitrary or excessive but rather rational and proportionate to the transgression. Punishment was Locke's justification for harm.

Natural rights, according to Locke, provided the legal and moral basis for many revolutions, including the American Revolution in the late 18th century. In addition to punishment, Locke justified forcible and violent removal of illegitimate rulers as a way for societies to assert their rights against arbitrary rule.

Natural rights were later articulated by Thomas Jefferson in writing the Declaration of Independence. Jefferson borrowed the language for this document from the English Declaration of Rights of 1689. The language he incorporated includes the ideas of inalienable rights, the equal creation of men, and the right to life, liberty, and the pursuit of happiness. Jefferson substituted *pursuit of happiness*, which Locke intended as the freedom of opportunity. Another example of natural rights is found in the United States Bill of Rights. These rights include the freedom of worship, the right to a voice in government, and the right to property. For more information see, Locke (1690/1988). ***See also*** Bill of Rights (political science); Inalienable Rights; Jeffersonianism; Utilitarianism (political science)

Natural Selection   A process based on Charles Darwin's theory of evolution, in particular the concept of "survival of the fittest." Organisms or entities that are the most effective and efficient at adapting to their environment earn the most prolonged existence. The level of success an organism has in adapting to the environment can be measured by the number of offspring an organism procreates and whether the offspring continue, in a similar manner, to successfully adapt to the environment. The theory of natural selection has been applied to a successful organization in that those entities that produce the best outputs outlast the outputs of similar or competing entities and thus have the most longevity.

Nature–Nurture Debate   An ongoing debate in psychology about the etiology of traits and behavior. It inquires as to the influence of genetic inheritance (biological nature) and environmental conditions (nurture) on personality and human behavior. This debate was much more clearly demarcated in the early 20th century, when behaviorism was prominent. Behaviorists argued strongly for the "nurture" side of the debate, asserting that all behavior is determined by learning and experience. Those on the "nature" side of the debate emphasized the role of biological processes in human development, arguing that human development proceeds through a series of genetically determined changes that unfold according to a biologically determined path.

Although the debate continues today, it is now a debate about emphasis; modern psychologists recognize that human behavior is influenced by a combination of genetics and environment and argue over the relative contributions of these factors to particular behaviors. Behavioral genetics is the study of how genes and environments work together to shape behavior; the research methods commonly employed to investigate these questions include twin studies and adoption studies. Evidence shows that genes account for about half of the variation observed in personality characteristics, but whether genetics influences the development of personality and behavior patterns depends largely on the environment in which a child is raised. Behavioral genetics also aims to identify the particular genes that contribute to hereditary behavior. However, this can be a difficult task; while some physical traits are determined by a single gene, many behavioral patterns and personality characteristics are driven by a complex combination of multiple genes interacting with environmental factors. For more information, see Rose (2001). ***See also*** Adoption Studies; Environment (sociology); Genes; Personality; Twin Studies

Needs Assessment   An analysis to identify the gap between the current and ideal situations and depicting the ways of reducing those discrepancies. If there is a problem in any instructional or program context, the initial step is the establishment of a needs assessment (aka analysis). It is a process of collecting problem-related information from all possible sources so that clear descriptions of the desired and existing states can be formed. By scrutinizing these states, the gaps are identified in terms of needs. Critical needs are selected from previously defined needs, and possible solutions to overcome the problem are described.

Negative Externalities   A negative cost that is external to a transaction and where the bearer of the cost has no direct control over the transaction. The classic example of negative externality is the acid rain that results from the pollution caused by a factory. All the related long-term effects associated with the pollution are exogenous to the economic activities that resulted in the pollution in the first place.

Negative Feedback   A process in which some aspect of the output signal of a system is passed (fed back) to the input. This often controls the dynamic behavior of the system. Negative feedback in an organization conveys poor or unsatisfactory performance. Arturo Rosenblueth proposed that that negative feedback could control behavior in a determinative, directive way, whether the feedback be in response to the behavior of people, animals, or machines. In organizations, feedback is a process that involves sharing observations and concerns between people or parts of an organization with the intention of improving the performances of the individuals and the group. Negative feedback is critical and corrective. In animals, the disruption of negative feedback can lead to undesirable results, such as a dramatic rise in glucose levels in the blood, which may result in a major illness, such as diabetes. *See also* Feedback (communication)

Negligence   The failure to take the necessary precautions that would be taken under regular circumstances in any given situation. Criminal negligence refers to a failure to exercise the degree of caution that is required by law for the protection of others.

Negotiation   A process of discussing or conferring with others to reach an agreement for the purposes of influencing others, settling disputes, setting the terms of an exchange, or deciding the terms of a contract.

Neoclassical Economics   A branch of economics that emphasizes the marginal cost-benefit theory of value. It is believed that the expression was originally used by the American economist Thorstein Veblen. Neoclassical economics is an algorithm (metatheory) for constructing economic theories. Its fundamental assumptions give it a generic theoretical appeal: (a) economic agents have preferences, (b) economic agents are maximizers of benefits and minimizers of costs, and (c) decisions are driven by the information available.

Classical economists, in the tradition of Adam Smith, David Ricardo, Jean-Baptiste Say, and to some extent Karl Marx, advanced the theory that the ultimate value of a good is the price or the value of labor required to produce it. The free market represented the reward to factor input (distributional aspect).

A major problem confronting the classical theory was the consumer's willingness to pay higher or lower prices for a good because of the utility or disutility associated with it, which has nothing to do with the value of labor expended to produce it. In actual fact, the production, extraction, or acquisition of very valuable goods— diamonds, for example—might require a fortune but very minimal effort.

By the third quarter of the 19th century, economists like Stanley Jevons, Carl Menger, and Leon Walras developed quantitative theories to reflect the relevance and importance of incremental (marginal) changes to the concept of valuation. Marginalism was consequentially linked with the concept of utilitarianism, already developed by Jeremy Bentham. Value was then related to individuals as maximizers of rational self-interest, be it

for production or consumption, because consumers and producers base their decisions on incremental costs and benefits.

Neoclassical economics also holds that investment is a function of saving and that changes in factor (input) payments generate equilibrium at full employment. Not all economists share the neoclassical view. Some reject optimization (neo-Austrians) and the market as a distributing mechanism of income (post-Keynesian). But dissenting neoclassical theories are largely perceived as unscientific because of their relative lack of application of scientific methodology

Neoclassical economics is largely credited with the theories of rational behavior, efficiency or optimality (proposed by Vilfredo Pareto), and equilibrium analysis. Its methodological framework fosters analysis of social systems designed to minimize distributive conflicts. The scientific contribution of neoclassical economics has far-reaching implications for the analysis of interdependent market behavior, utility maximization, loss minimization, environmental cost-benefit analysis, intertemporal consumption, and much more. For more information, see Fusfeld (1999), McConnell and Brue (2008), and Salvatore (2002). *See also* Classical Economics; Marginal; Price; Utility

Neoclassicism   A movement initiated in France in the 17th century characterized by an aspiration to go back to the arts that were prominent in previous centuries. In particular, there was, during this period, a desire to once again adopt the arts, literature, and music that were developed in Ancient Greece and Rome. For instance, neoclassical architecture, which was developed in the middle of the 18th century, was heavily influenced by the architectural designs popular in Ancient Greece.

Neoconservatism   A political philosophy, which emerged in the 1960s and 1970s, that rejected the ideals of leftists and liberals. Since the 1980s, under the auspices of Ronald Reagan's presidency (1981–1989), it has developed into the belief of the use of an aggressive approach in promoting the United States' unrivaled power to advance its values around the world. This belief originated from a small group of liberal and leftist intellectuals who grew disenchanted with the liberal excesses of capitalism and the reluctance to spend adequately on military defense. The neoconservative label was originally applied to liberals and leftists, who became anticommunist after World War II, and Democrats, who embraced republicanism in the post–Vietnam War era.

Neoconservatism emerged out of the critiques of both capitalism and communism. Neoconservatists viewed capitalism as deficient in the Puritan virtues, such as thrift, industry, temperance, patience, and persistence. Although the neoconservatists did not believe in a proletarian revolution, they supported a bourgeois life. They did not view the bourgeoisie as weak or evil but rather as a living testament to the values that enabled the capitalist system to continue. In

N

the 1980s, the neoconservatives abandoned their original critique of capitalism because inflation declined after the recession in the early 1980s and economic growth increased.

Neoconservatists took issue with communism since it represented antidemocratic ideals. The defining characteristic of neoconservative anticommunism was its moralism with two components. First was the conviction that the type of democracy practiced in the United States was worth defending on the grounds of its moral superiority to competing models. Second, American power had been a force for good in the world and ought to be increased to confront outside threats to democracy. For example, the belief in the democratic transformation in the Middle East started with Iraq. And support for Israel, as a key outpost of democracy, has been seen as crucial to the United States' military sufficiency in the Middle East.

The neoconservatists' ideological foundation was a tough-minded pragmatism in the face of liberal naïveté. Unlike liberalism, which focused primarily on principles such as liberty and equality and human rights, neoconservatism leaned toward the question of whether other countries were friends or foes of the United States. Unlike the conservatists, who opted for containment policies, especially toward the Soviet Union during the Cold War, neoconservatists supported direct confrontation, even if this meant taking preemptive military action. Under Reagan's presidency, in the 1980s, the neoconservatists were able to influence foreign policy. Most of the younger neoconservatists began as Republicans in the Reagan government. For more information, see Lindberg (2004). *See also* Capitalism (economics, political science); Cold War; Communism (economics, political science); Containment; Leftist; Liberal Democracy; Reagan Doctrine

Network In the United States, the term refers to the three commercial television systems CBS, NBC, and ABC. These networks, with local broadcast stations throughout the country, dominated television broadcasting from the 1950s through the 1980s. At their peak, at the end of the 1970s, they captured 90% of the television audience. Even in 2000, they had 50% of the television audience, despite competition from cable and satellite channels. Network stations broadcast their transmissions over the airwaves and so are theoretically accessible to any television receiver within their range, without the necessity of subscribing to a service.

From the start, the networks were financed by advertising. At first, this took the form of sponsorship of entire programs, with the advertisers controlling the content. This changed by the late 1950s in response to rising costs, with broadcasters taking over content control and selling advertising spots. Ratings dictated program content, with networks providing content that would appeal to, and not alienate, the mass audiences their advertisers sought. As market research showed that the most profitable demographic for advertisers was the young, affluent urban dwellers, shows were dropped that had higher audience ratings but whose viewers had a less appealing demographic makeup.

In the 1970s, the Federal Communications Commission (FCC), which regulates broadcasting, required local stations to broadcast no more than 3 hours of network-provided content per day. This "prime-time" period led to increased competition for advertising slots and thus increased revenue for the stations.

During the 1980s, commercial pressure increased. All three networks were taken over by conglomerates interested in maximizing profits. A fourth network, Rupert Murdoch's Fox, appeared, to compete for viewers. Video recorders and remote control devices passed control to viewers over whether or not they viewed the advertisements. The FCC loosened its regulations. Advertising increased, and the boundaries between programs and advertisements blurred.

Networks have been praised for the high quality of television dramas made in the early 1950s and news programs during the 1970s. But many criticisms have been made about network-generated content. By concentrating on providing mass-appeal, U.S.-centric entertainment, they have failed to allow television to develop its potential for improving education and elevating public experiences and discourse. Shallow superficial coverage of news, current affairs, and international affairs by the primary medium through which most U.S. residents still get their news has been a subject of continuing concern for media critics. For more information, see Gorman and McLean (2003). *See also* Public Service Broadcasting; Satellite Systems

Network Effect A marketing terminology that (a) defines the effect of diffusion of information about product quality or service on value and (b) makes a product or service more valuable as the number of owners of the product or service increases. A product or service becomes more valuable as people disseminate positive information about its quality. Conversely, they are prone to become relatively worthless as negative information is disseminated about their quality, which results in smaller adoptions. Networking (information dispersion) or word of mouth, therefore, has an effect on product sales or value.

Performance capacity tends to reinforce the network effect. Businesses with negative appraisals, whose products are neglected and do not show indications of growth, tend to reinforce notions of bad publicity (negative-network effect) and may end up perpetuating mediocre business performance. The value of ownership of such products declines progressively when the lack of ownership of such products does not create added value for those who own them.

Networking generates utility and value when ownership of a product or service becomes more valuable as others adopt a similar product or service—for example, a telephone. Additional ownership is normally measured in terms of a positive marginal benefit-cost ratio.

A key business decision is how to accelerate the adoption of value-enhancing goods. The adoption and benefit of goods may not be infinite. It can only continue until a critical mass (tipping point or saturation) is attained beyond which value diminishes and disutility sets in. Indicators of negative returns are congestion and poor-quality service as a result of increased consumption. *See also* Externality

Networking An interconnected system of numerous forms of organization and person-to-person and computer-to-computer communication. A computer network consists of interconnected computer relationships according to (a) scale (e.g., local area networks), (b) function (network architecture), (c) communication method (optical fiber, ethernet, wireless), and (d) topology (logical relationships as opposed to physical ones). Most scholars in the social and behavioral sciences, however, define network as the links between social acquaintances, friends, and relatives. Most important, theorists in these disciplines have emphasized the primary importance of the relational facets of social networks that link people's actions to the group, which take precedence over individual agency. We can describe networks as having nodes and relational links. A graph illustrating such links was first formulated by Leopold Euler in 1737. Jacob Moreno (1892–1974) described psychological networks in the sociogram in the 1930s as he attempted to explain school ties and friendships. The anthropologist Alfred Radcliffe-Brown (1881–1955) formulated a theory of the network as a web of relationships with interlocking and interweaving actions; he was one of the first to use the term as the metaphor we use today. Significantly, most of these theorists, such as the sociologist Pierre Bourdieu (1930–2002), emphasized the social capital the individual gains through belonging to informal networks that provide information, friendship, and personal attachments. These scholars showed how the numerous weak ties of wide-ranging acquaintances were more important in professional life ("getting ahead") than having only a network of close friends and family. On the other hand, in emergencies, the strong, or close, network was more beneficial and supportive. Theorists developed many of these ideas using set theory, mathematical models of graphs, multidimensional scaling, and other similar methods. Today, "social networking," through ever-expanding Internet sites such as MySpace, has become more important for facilitating communications among youth. These sites also pose the problem of individuals losing, and even retarding, interpersonal social skills that are gained only through face-to-face communications. We can compare this deficiency with the creation of the avatar in the computer games of the 1980s, which hid the real identity of a player. Also, the use of such pseudonymous identities can lead to tragedy and crime.

In late 2008, an adult woman went on trial for posing as a teenage boy whose comments allegedly led a 13-year-old girl to commit suicide. Pedophiles posing as teenagers also use the Internet to commit crimes. These sites encourage more and more intercourse between faceless people, and it is still to be seen whether the good consequences will outweigh the deleterious effects of anonymous communications that these artificial social networks make possible and encourage. For more information, see Scott (2002). *See also* Social Capital

Neural Networks The neurons that operate together to perform complex functions. Researchers have established that memories are not based in particular localized brain cells. Instead, memories are coded, stored, and retrieved by complex circuits of neurons in the brain, or neural networks. Based on research investigating the laws of learning and the ways in which neurons communicate and adjust their synaptic connections, psychologists have been attempting to develop models detailing how these networks are established. Cognitive psychologists posit that knowledge is distributed throughout the network of associations that connect elements of a concept and its various representations. Neural network models of learning focus on how the connections in these networks are developed through experience. Research shows that interacting with a concept in some way (e.g., reading the word *dog*) will strengthen the connections between that concept and the other elements of the interaction (e.g., the concept "dog" and the letters *D*, *O*, and *G*). For more information, see Houghton (2005). *See also* Learning; Neurons; Semantic Network; Synapse

Neurons Nerve cells that are specialized to quickly respond to signals and send signals of their own. They are the fundamental components of the nervous system. Like other cells, they have an outer membrane (a fine screen that blocks some substances and allows others to pass) and a cell body containing a nucleus (which carries the genetic information that determines how the neuron will function), and they contain mitochondria (structures that turn oxygen and glucose into energy). However, neurons are distinguished from other types of cells by certain features of their structure: (a) axons are long, thin structures that extend from the cell body, carrying signals from the neuron to other neurons; (b) dendrites are similar to axons except that they receive signals from other neurons and convey that information to the cell body; and (c) the synapse is a tiny gap between neurons, across which neurotransmitters must travel to carry information from one neuron to another. For more information, see Carlson (2007). *See also* Central Nervous System (CNS); Neurotransmitters; Peripheral Nervous System (PNS)

Neurotransmitters Chemicals that assist in the transfer of signals from one neuron to another.

N

Neurotransmitters are stored in vesicles at the tips of axons (long, thin structures that extend from the cell body of neurons). When action potentials (see entry) reach the end of an axon, a neurotransmitter is released into the synapse (the tiny gap between neurons), where it spreads to the next cell. When they reach the membrane of the next (or postsynaptic) cell, the neurotransmitters bind to proteins called receptors. Neurotransmitters bind to their own receptors, but they do not bind to the receptors of other neurotransmitters. Each neurotransmitter can bind to several different types of receptors, and the neurotransmitter can have different effects depending on the type of receptor to which it binds. Dopamine, serotonin, and norepinephrine are examples of neurotransmitters. For more information, see Carlson (2007). ***See also*** Action Potential; Axon; Dopamine; Neurons; Synapse

Neutral Competence *(political science)*   A description of government bureaucracies that serve to advise government officials in a nonpartisan manner. In the United States, the ideology of neutral competence traces back to the Progressive Era (1890–1913), one of many anticorruption reforms enacted during this period. The American political scientist Herbert Kaufman coined the term in his 1956 study "Emerging Conflicts in the Doctrines of Public Administration" and defined it as "the ability to do the work of the government expertly, and to do it according to explicit, objective standards rather than to personal or party or other obligations and loyalties" (p. 1060). Under the neutral competence ideal, federal civil servants can wield a great deal of influence on national policy concerns. The courts have persistently upheld this influence by highlighting bureaucratic expertise.

The trend also emphasized policy privatization, as the President and members of Congress hire staff members with expertise in various fields and/or contract with private consultants instead of relying on bureaucrats, especially in the fields of economics and foreign affairs. Francis E. Rourke in "Responsiveness and Neutral Competence in American Bureaucracy" (1992) comments that former civil servants who join universities, think tanks, or private consulting firms can have greater influence on policy than they had as government employees. Rourke further attributes this phenomenon to officials' questioning the neutrality of bureaucrats and doubting their impartiality due to agency bias (a bureaucrat's commitment to what's best for his or her agency). Another explanation for the privatization of policy experts might be the complete reverse. Officials may *not want neutral experts* and prefer committed party loyalists. Rourke hypothesized that this tendency is most likely true for presidents in times of transition who are seeking great change rather than those satisfied with the status quo. For more information, see Kaufman (1956). ***See also*** Bureaucracy (political science)

Neutral Competence *(public administration)*   A concept that has long been regarded as an essential value in the field of public administration. During the early years of the republic, the Federalist and Jeffersonian traditions held that federal employees should be qualified for their jobs and minimally involved in partisan political activity. With the Jackson administration's embrace of a more politicized system, patronage flourished and efficiency and integrity diminished in many agencies.

By the end of the Civil War, a reform movement emerged, which proposed a system of competitive examinations to promote efficiency in government operations and to reduce, if not eliminate, political corruption. After the Civil Service Act of 1883, or Pendleton Act, was passed, Woodrow Wilson, a supporter of the new system, portrayed the ideal new civil servant as an objective expert, trained for his job and immune to the temptations and pressures of political partisanship.

In addition to its roots in American public administration history, neutral competence was also an important aspect of Max Weber's concepts of *bureaucracy*, in which public servants, or bureaucrats, were to be selected for their competence and granted tenure to ensure their neutrality in that role.

As tenure was a featured element of civil service systems, neutrality assumed particular importance. Courts have protected most civil servants from loss of employment when a new administration takes office while also using tenure as a quid pro quo for limiting those employees' political activities outside the workplace.

By the latter half of the 20th century, some academics and practitioners began to question the emphasis on neutrality—and efficiency—and urged that public administration be guided by a broader range of values, including responsiveness, representativeness, and equity. ***See also*** Bureaucracy (public administration); Public Administration

News Coverage   Whether and how the reporting of news affects real-world events is a topic of debate. The CNN effect describes the hypothesis that U.S. foreign policy during the 1990s was driven by topics chosen to be shown on the 24-hour television news channel.

Margaret Thatcher, British Prime Minister during the period of IRA terrorism, described publicity as the oxygen on which terrorists depend. However, there is disagreement among scholars as to whether there is an actual causative link between media coverage and terrorist acts. Some argue that there is no hard evidence for such a contagion effect. At least one study has found that person-to-person communication is more important than media coverage in spreading terrorism. Those who believe that media attention encourages terrorist acts advocate restraint in media coverage, either as voluntary industry guidelines or as government-imposed censorship.

Definitions of terrorism vary but generally refer to the committing of violent acts to change policy. State terrorism gets far less coverage in the media than terrorist acts committed by nonstate actors. The majority of terrorist acts get little or no coverage, with a small number of terrorist acts attracting a great deal of media attention. The vocabulary and tone chosen by media organizations in reporting violent acts affect the audiences' perceptions of the act, for example, media choices between the terms *criminal, terrorist,* and *freedom fighter.*

The Internet is used by terrorist groups to communicate their views directly to the public. Mainstream media pick up and report information gathered from these sites, including broadcasting, in part or whole, terrorist-produced videos.

The media play an important role in counterterrorism efforts. Media can inform and reassure the public during and following terrorist events. Government Web sites may become overwhelmed by the great numbers of people attempting to access them, but media outlets, particularly television and radio, have the capacity to quickly convey official announcements to great numbers of people, for example, regarding health and safety. For more information, see Alali and Eke (1991), Kavoori and Fraley (2006), Nacos (2002), and Robinson (2005). *See also* Media; Media Outlet; News/News Production; Terrorism (sociology)

News Management The Pulitzer Prize–winning national correspondent James Reston used the phrase "manage the news" while testifying before a Congressional Committee on Government Operations in 1955. He was describing attempts by the U.S. government to control media coverage. The aim of news management, or spin, is to detract attention away from some events and toward topics more favorable to the spinners. It is practiced by presidents, politicians, corporations, and public relations professionals.

News management techniques include denying news reporters access to a location or allowing access only under strictly controlled conditions. Press releases and carefully staged "pseudo events," such as controlled interviews, are used. Friendly journalists can be simply asked not to report what they know: In 1961, Reston was aware of plans to invade Cuba but acquiesced to President Kennedy's request not to publish what he knew about what was to become the Bay of Pigs fiasco.

During the late 1960s and early 1970s, journalists covering the Vietnam War, Watergate, and the civil rights movements evaded efforts at news management. By aggressively researching stories, they found and reported evidence to the public of lying and media manipulation coming from the highest levels of government. This government control of news and construction of news events was resented by reporters and encouraged the rise of adversarial journalism. Reporters, no longer content with reporting the facts as told to them by the authorities, engaged in aggressively researching stories.

One form of news management carried out in the name of national security is the redacting of official documents requested through the Freedom of Information Act. For more information, see Schudson (1978) and Thomas (2007). *See also* Freedom of Information Act; Journalism; News/News Production

News/News Production New information about a topic of interest disseminated to a reasonable number of people. The size of the interested audience varies: The mass media may have a potential audience of millions, in contrast to a local newsblog or local paper, with a niche audience of thousands.

News reporting by the mass media includes newspapers, news programs on radio and television, and news Web sites on the Internet. Newspapers and news programs have limited capacity; therefore, journalists and editors act as gatekeepers when deciding what news to report and what not to report. Under totalitarian regimes, the state decides what news may be released to the public. In the United States, direct state censorship is much less of a concern, but critics argue that news coverage is adversely affected by corporate power, as advertising dollars finance much of the traditional media and much of the industry has become consolidated in the hands of relatively few corporate owners.

The market model of news production sees news as a commodity that responds to the economic laws of supply and demand. Consumers, acting in the marketplace, inform news producers by their actions as to which news products they are willing to support, by purchasing or subscribing to one newspaper in preference to another or one cable channel rather than another. Ratings of radio and television programs and other market research convey information about the audience to news providers and the companies that purchase advertising slots. Critics of the market model complain that the mass media responding to a mass market leads to a dumbing down of news reporting, with coverage concentrating on sensational stories and celebrity gossip.

The major mass-media news-reporting organizations have Web sites, including CNN, network television, and national newspapers. Blogs covering niche news categories, such as political and local news, are increasing their audiences and becoming increasingly professional, particularly with regard to their financial models, with many financing themselves and making profits by selling advertising on their Web sites. For more information, see Machin and Niblock (2006) and Stephens (2007). *See also* Marketing/Market Model; News Management; Newspaper; Propaganda Model

Newspaper A paper-and-print product published at frequent regular intervals, usually every day or every week, with the purpose of conveying the news of the day to readers, for profit. Most are sold to the reader singly or by subscription. Advertisers provide the bulk of the revenue to the publisher. Newspapers traditionally consist of sheets of newsprint folded together, in either tabloid or broadsheet format. Broadsheet papers have tended to be more "serious" and are aimed at a wealthier, better-educated audience, while tabloids excel at shorter, sensational coverage aimed at a mass market. This is changing, with some higher-end newspapers adopting the smaller, more reader-friendly tabloid format but keeping their high-end content characteristics.

N

Newspapers have a long history. The first newspaper in North America was printed in Boston in 1690 by Benjamin Harris, titled *Publick Occurrences Both Foreign and Domestick*, but was closed by the Massachusetts authorities after just one issue. As censorship concerns eased, the *Boston Newsletter*, in 1702, had more success and was followed more famously, in 1721, by James Franklin's *New England Courant*. During the 18th century, many newspapers flourished, often produced by printers and postmasters as sidelines to their regular trades. Stories were often copied from one paper to another, and extreme editorial bias was the norm.

The penny press emerged in the 1830s with a business model based on cheap, mass-circulation, mass-appeal papers. The previously dominant model had been high-priced, market-niche newspapers, with low circulation focused on wealthy readers defined mainly by occupation or politics.

Yellow journalism described the newspaper styles of the late 19th and early 20th centuries when competition for mass audiences pitted newspaper publishers, including Hearst and Pulitzer, against one another. Tactics included enticing popular reporters and cartoonists to rival publications and using sensational, exaggerated headlines and stories to attract readers. The word *yellow* in the term *yellow journalism* referred to a popular cartoon series about a remarkably ugly child, "the yellow kid."

The number of newspaper titles in the United States peaked around 1915, with subsequent consolidation in the industry leading to fewer titles.

Newspapers have historically ensured their continued existence and profitability by adopting innovative technology and business practices. Such radical changes have not always been popular: Computerization during the 1980s dictated the end of typesetting and other printing-related occupations, with bitter union-management fights.

Newspapers compete with other news providers, including radio, television, and, most seriously and recently, the Internet. Newspaper sales are declining, particularly among younger readers. Classified small advertisements have migrated to the Internet. Competition for readers from non-newspaper-affiliated, independent newsblogs is growing. Ironically, newsblogs have been accused of being parasites, gathering stories from the work of reporters employed by other media rather than generating their own.

Most U.S. newspapers now release their content on their Internet sites, in addition to publishing in the print format. Some papers experimented with requiring readers to pay for online access, but this business model has changed in most cases to free access for readers, with revenue coming from onscreen advertising. In response to competition from blogs, newspapers are adding reader response and discussion areas to their Internet sites. For more information, see Alterman (2008), Barlow (2007), Schudson (1978), and Stephens (2007). *See also* Objectiveness in Media Coverage; Print Media

Niche   A situation that is convenient or appropriate to an individual, given the individual's interests and needs. A niche refers to an area of comfort. A niche is a situation or set of circumstances in which an individual feels a sense of belonging.

No Child Left Behind (NCLB)   Public Law 107-110, signed on June 8, 2002, with the stated purpose of providing every child with equal access to a high-quality education. The NCLB Act is built on four principles: (1) accountability for results, (2) more choices for parents, (3) greater local control and flexibility, and (4) an emphasis on doing what works based on scientific research. For more information, see U.S. Department of Education. *See also* Educational Policy; Elementary Education; Literacy/Illiteracy

Noise   Unwanted sound, even though it is still considered a form of communication. Noise has the ability to change or distort the meaning of a message that is being communicated in human and electronic communication. Communication noise refers to influences on effective communication that affect how we interpret conversations. There are various types of communication noise. They include physical noise (such as a loud bang or cacophony) and psychological noise (such as racist jokes being told on a subway when one is reading). Noise can inhibit our communication, not allowing us to hear what needs to be heard or causing us to misinterpret what we are hearing. Noise affects the way the sender is able to effectively communicate, as well as the way the receiver is able to decode the message. *See also* Communication

No-Knock Law   A law that prohibits door-to-door solicitation from individuals who request exemption from such solicitation (similar to a "no-call" list in telemarketing). Individuals may request to be added to such a list, which would generally protect them from unwanted solicitors. Some exceptions to this law include scouting groups, trick-or-treaters, or even religious groups. In criminal justice, a no-knock warrant allows police officers to enter a premises without a warning knock if there is cause to believe that alerting the residents will lead to the destruction of evidence or give them time to leave the premises.

Nolo Contendere   A Latin word for "no contest." It is a legal term used when a defendant chooses not to plead either guilty or not guilty. In such a case, the defendant would plead *nolo contendere*. A no-contest plea occurs when an individual does not rebut the charges brought up against him or her but does not admit guilt either. This is essentially the same as a guilty plea in the criminal court, and an offender can be criminally sentenced. However, the *nolo contendere* plea cannot later be used against the defendant in a civil trial. *See also* Plea

Nomination   The selection of an individual by a political party to run for a particular public office. In the

United States, nominations are determined by the outcome of political caucuses and conventions of the Republicans and Democrats at the local, state, and federal levels. Independents can also become nominated by filling out a nomination petition and acquiring the requisite signatures.

Nonexperimental Research in Quantitative Research Quantitative research for which the researcher does not manipulate an independent variable or randomly assign participants to treatment groups. Terms such as *survey, correlational, descriptive, causal-comparative, ex post facto, predictive and explanatory, passive observation, natural experiments, meta-analysis*, and *cross-sectional and longitudinal* describe the members of this family of research in the social sciences. A useful new 3×3 classification system classifies nonexperimental quantitative research along two dimensions: (1) primary research objective and (2) time. On the dimension of primary research objective, studies can be descriptive, predictive, or explanatory; on the dimension of time, research can be cross-sectional, longitudinal, or retrospective. Thus, it is possible to have nine different types of nonexperimental quantitative research, each mutually exclusive.

A major limitation of nonexperimental research in quantitative research is that it is very difficult to provide evidence of causality. Indeed, some researchers claim that it is not possible to establish causality from this type of research, but this view is problematic. It is important to understand that experimental research is the most powerful means of establishing causality. However, under the proper conditions, one can provide tentative, preliminary evidence of causality with nonexperimental research. Certain procedures, such as matching or statistically holding the extraneous variable constant (e.g., partial correlations, analysis of covariance), can be used to control for the threat of potentially confounding extraneous variables identified by the researcher, thereby supporting a possible causality argument. In addition, causal modeling or structural equation modeling, another statistical technique, tests data against theoretical models for evidence of causality. Overall, with a substantial, consistent body of nonexperimental evidence as well as strong theoretical support, one at least can suggest plausible cause and effect. For an example of such research, one has only to think back to the decades of nonexperimental research suggesting the link between smoking and cancer before smoking was declared a causal agent of lung cancer.

Remember that while experimental research may be the gold standard in scientific research, it is not always feasible or ethical to conduct such research. Even as we might prefer experiments for establishing cause and effect, in educational research, we must often use nonexperimental research to address our important research questions. Researchers must be certain that the research questions guide the study and then employ the most powerful research methods available to answer

these questions. For more information, see Johnson (2001) and Johnson and Christenson (2008). ***See also*** Basic Versus Applied Research; Research; Research Methodology; Survey (sociology)

Nongovernmental Organization (NGO) A nonprofit organized on a local, national, or international level. Nonprofit organizations are set up for charitable purposes and comprise two categories: (1) member-serving organizations and (2) public-serving organizations. Nongovernmental organizations are a common type of public-serving nonprofit. Nongovernmental organizations are driven by people with a common interest in providing service to citizens and acting as advocates to bring citizens' concerns to government. Nongovernmental organizations provide services to their members including providing health and education services, sponsoring cultural and religious activities, and advocating for causes.

Nonetheless, nongovernmental organizations are structured quite diversely. Nongovernmental organizations are not simply member serving but also conduct operational and campaigning activities. The operational nongovernmental organizations achieve change through projects, whereas the campaigning nongovernmental organizations promote change through the political system. Despite the differences, all types of nongovernmental organizations are involved in fundraising, have a mostly volunteer workforce, and organize special events.

The main reason for the greater involvement of nongovernmental organizations is privatization. Privatization is the use of nongovernmental organizations to provide goods or services previously provided by government. Privatization removes government from the design and provision of a service. The reasons for removing government from a service delivery include the possibility for clients to receive more attention and the enhancement of competition among service providers.

In an effort to be efficient, contracting, a common tool used by government to privatize public services, is used with nongovernmental organizations. ***See also*** Nonprofit Organization; Privatization (public administration)

Nonlethal Force The use of force resulting in injuries or impairment of any type but not death. Police officers or other law enforcement officials are generally authorized to use nonlethal force in certain circumstances in which other means have failed, such as to prevent injury to a third party, when an individual resists arrest, and so on. Nonlethal force may be administered through physical force or through the use of various instruments, electronic (tasers, etc.) and nonelectronic (pepper spray, stick, etc.). While it is not used with the intent to kill, deaths do occasionally occur as the result of nonlethal force.

Nonparametric Statistics A set of data analysis methods not based on the assumption of normality of the data. They are sometimes referred to as being "distribution free," but that is misleading. They are not distribution free, but nor are they based on the normal distribution sampling; thus they are "normal distribution free." These tests are often used to compare medians, proportions, or frequencies or as an alternative to parametric methods to compare centrality when assumptions are not met. Generally, they have slightly lower statistical power than their parametric counterparts. ***See also*** Statistical Power; Statistics (sociology)

Nonprofit Organization   There are 27 types of nonprofits defined in the Internal Revenue Code (IRC). Nonprofits include churches, public schools, professional associations, research institutes, labor unions, cemetery associations, and veteran organizations. These organizations, although disparate, are all tax exempt. Therefore, if these organizations make a profit, they do not have to pay income taxes. However, most often when we speak or think of nonprofits, we are referring to 501(c)(3)s. These nonprofits are also tax deductible; thus, donations are considered as federal tax deductions.

Nonprofits are permitted to educate the public on the issues; however, most nonprofits categorized as 501(c)(3) cannot advocate for a specific bill or conduct activities that influence elections to public office and are limited in the amount of time and money they can put into lobbying. In contrast, 501(c)(4)s are not limited to lobbying but will not be able to receive federal grants. They can also engage in political campaign activity, and unlike a 501(c)(3), donations are not tax deductible. Nonprofits are also considered the administrative arm of government; they provide a venue for government to efficiently deliver services and aid in keeping government small. They are perceived as efficient, low-cost deliverers of services in local communities and contract with government to provide services. Their links to the local community make it possible to more effectively tailor programs and service delivery structures to local needs. Nonprofits deliver a large array of services, including job training, residential care, and health services. For more information, see Berry (2005). ***See also*** Citizen Participation; Civil Society; Effectiveness (public administration); Efficiency

Nonverbal Communication   The manner in which people communicate attitude, emotion, and intent through body stance and movement, facial expression, and vocal sound. The term also refers to the scientific analysis of body movement and sound.

There are several components within the study of nonverbal communication: (a) kinesics, (b) proxemics, (c) haptics, (d) oculesics, (e) vocalics, and (f) chronemics.

Kinesics, also known as body language, may be the most recognizable term for nonverbal communication. Included are facial and hand gestures, such as smiles and frowns, open palms and clenched fists, the way people relax and tense their bodies, and how they walk or position their heads.

Proxemics refer to interpersonal space factors, such as the physical distances people put between themselves and others, how they orient their bodies, and the physical planes they choose to inhabit. For instance, standing close to or leaning toward another person may indicate an attempt at intimacy, while standing tall when conversing with a shorter person may indicate a lesser willingness toward intimacy.

Haptics refer to tactile communications. A firm handshake may signal cordiality, and a gentle stroke across an arm or face may signal loving feelings.

Oculesics refer to eye contact and gaze. Meeting someone's eyes while listening may indicate interest; meeting someone's eyes while speaking may indicate sincerity.

Vocalics, also known as paralinguistics, are sounds without words, such as grunts, groans, cries of agony or exclamation, and laughter.

Chronemics refer to time spent on interactions, to their synchrony or congruence. A short peck on the lips between a married couple, for instance, may indicate a lack of time or disinterest. For more information, see Anderson (1985) and Burgee (1980). ***See also*** Body Language; Chronemics; Haptics; Kinesics; Oculesics; Proxemics; Vocalics

Nonverbal Dominance   The manner in which people use their bodies, consciously or unconsciously, to indicate their intent to supervise or lead others or to manage or control social encounters.

Nonverbal dominant behavior does not necessarily indicate evil or unhealthy intent. Often, it is perceived by the other person or persons within the social setting.

The person who holds a gaze longer or who can stare down another person is thought to be dominant. The person who reaches out first to firmly grip another's hand in greeting or who leans toward or towers over the individual he or she is addressing shows signs of dominant behavior. The person who frowns or whose eye movements and gestures show displeasure or anger is more likely to control a social encounter than the person whose countenance is pleasant. The person who strides ahead, who gets to the front of the line first, or who occupies the most favorable spot exhibits dominance. For more information, see Carney, Hall, and LeBeau (2005). ***See also*** Body Language; Nonverbal Communication.

Norm *(communication)*   A rule that is enforced by society. Norms affect human behavior. For example, norms function as a way to teach people to conform to a set of rules. Norms vary from culture to culture. They regulate human behavior and act as social controls. Christine Horn (2001) in *Social Norms*, edited by Michael Hechter and Karl-Dieter Opp, stated that "new norms are thought to emerge when costs of compliance with existing norms become too high relative to the rewards." Many people conform to norms because they do not want to become "outsiders." Violations of norms are punished with sanctions, possibly enforced by the law. Violators of norms are considered deviant by society. The existence of social norms is related to the enforcement of such norms. ***See also*** Deviance

Norm *(sociology)* A principle of conduct that is encouraged to be followed by members of any given group. Norms are somewhat more informal than rules, regulations, or laws. Norms offer a prototype of behavior that is deemed to be "normal" by society. While the violation of norms may result in disapproval from the group, it does not generally result in formal punishment (unlike the violation of laws or regulations). When a given practice or behavior becomes very common, it is said to *become the norm*. ***See also*** Deviance

Normal Curve *(education)* Represents a distribution of scores, observations, or statistics that has a specific, bell-shaped curve. Many human characteristics are distributed close to the normal. It was discovered in the early 1700s and recognized as a model for errors in the late 1700s. Relative to statistical methods, the demonstration that errors of sampling are normally distributed is of greatest utility to the data analyst. ***See also*** Central Tendency; Inferential Statistics

Normal Curve *(psychology)* A commonly observed phenomenon in psychological data. In a normal curve, or normal distribution, the majority of scores tend to fall in the middle of the distribution, with fewer and fewer scores occurring toward the extremes. In a truly normal distribution, scores are dispersed in such a way that the mean, median, and mode all have the same value. When a distribution has this property (or, as is more often the case with psychological data, when the shape of a particular score distribution closely aligns with a normal distribution), the standard deviation of the distribution can be used to describe how any particular score stands in relation to the rest of the distribution. In a normal curve, half of the scores fall above and half below the mean. Approximately 68% of cases fall within one standard deviation on either side of the mean, and approximately 95% of cases fall within two standard deviations on either side of the mean. Crucially for inferential statistics, the properties of a normal distribution can be used to describe the distance between a score on some dimension (raw score) and the mean of the scores on that dimension. A standard score (or z score) is an expression of the raw score, in terms of standard deviations, above or below the mean. For more information, see Howell (2002). ***See also*** Central Tendency; Inferential Statistics; Standard Deviation; Standard Score; Statistics (psychology)

Normative A term in political science given to the scientific analysis of what *ought to be* or *what is right* in a given political situation. In contrast is positive political science, which focuses on what actually *is* and seeks to *explain why*. An example would be an examination of why a nation went to war; a normative analysis would most likely identify a humanitarian motive instead of a self-interested one.

Normative Media Researchers have frequently considered the role performed by communications media in the maintenance and, at times, revision of societal norms. To the extent that the media either dictate or influence social consensus in behavior, opinion, or speech, they may be regarded as normative. However, the actual influence of normative media is far from certain.

Psychological research has illustrated that individual persons in situations of uncertainty tend to be swayed by group opinion. Studies have even demonstrated that some people will go along with a group even when doing so contradicts the clear evidence of their senses (Asch 1955, 1956). It has therefore been theorized that the mass media, with their power to communicate focused messages to huge audiences, possess the ability to influence individual behavior by stimulating public opinion for or against a given behavior. This assumption has inspired advertising campaigns with slogans such as "I bet a lot of your friends are using it and you don't even know it" (Severin 1988). It has also been the basis for public awareness campaigns in relation to public health issues, which have sought to inhibit hazardous behaviors by causing them to appear unpopular. Overall, however, there is little and inconclusive evidence of the association between individual exposure to public health communication campaigns and health behavior change. Whereas many public health communication campaigns have been found to increase public awareness to related health risks, only a few demonstrated behavioral change in response to campaign messages. There is also the possibility that the intended normative message may be misunderstood by the audience. For instance, television programs such as *All in the Family*, whose creators hoped that it might function normatively to diminish racial bigotry, actually tended to reinforce prejudices among those viewers who were already disposed to harbor racial bias. Research has also shown that the power of mass media to influence the outcomes of elections is less considerable than we are likely to assume; indeed, the influence of mass media on voters may be weak compared with the influence of people with whom the voter is personally acquainted. One reason for this diminished effect may be that consumers of mass media do not tend to actively regard themselves as part of the "group" defined by the audience of mass media messages, since they do not receive these messages with the rest of the group physically present.

Rather, mass media attempts to alter social norms are often more effective when they are combined with interpersonal communication. This has been shown to be true both with regard to well-organized charitable drives and with respect to many elections. For more information, see Asch (1955, 1956), Berelson, Lazarsfeld, and McPhee (1954), Severin (1988), and Yanovitzky and Stryker (2001). ***See also*** Mass Media; Public Opinion (media studies); Social Norm

Norm Group   A large and ideally representative sample drawn from a defined population. The test scores obtained from this sample are used to develop a set of standards for comparisons of subsequent scores of individual test takers from the same population. ***See also*** Criterion- and Norm-Referenced Measurement

Not Guilty   When charged with a criminal offense, the accused is given an opportunity to enter one of three pleas. The defendant can plead guilty, not guilty, or *nolo contendere* (no contest) at arraignment. When defendants plead not guilty, they assert their innocence at arraignment. Not guilty verdicts are issued when the prosecution fails to meet the burden of proof necessary to secure conviction. ***See also*** Arraignment; Guilty (sociology); *Nolo Contendere*; Plea

Null Hypothesis *(education)*   A statement about a population parameter that is used in hypothesis testing. It states that some condition concerning the population is true, such as the population correlation coefficient is zero or the difference between male and female population income means is zero. The null hypothesis is directly tested in hypothesis testing (not the alternative hypothesis). Usually, the null hypothesis states that there is no relationship or no difference between means in the population; this type of null hypothesis is known as the nil null (Cohen, 1994). However, the null hypothesis does not always state that there is no relationship (i.e., nil null). For example, researchers can test the null hypothesis that a correlation coefficient has a particular nonzero value. In practice, the nil null

hypothesis is usually tested, and it is the default used in statistical programs such as SPSS and SAS. ***See also*** Hypothesis Testing; Inferential Statistics

Null Hypothesis *(psychology)*   The prediction of no difference between groups, or no relationship between variables. It is the first step in inferential statistics, and the main purpose of inferential statistics is to test the null hypothesis. When a study is conducted with a sample of individuals, inferential statistics are applied to determine whether a result obtained in the experiment is likely to generalize to the entire population. Inferential statistical tests estimate the probability that the result of the experiment was obtained by chance. The null hypothesis is that there is no difference between groups or no relationship between variables; in other words, the null hypothesis is that the result of the experiment was obtained by chance and will not generalize to the population. An arbitrary criterion (typically .05) is used to test the null hypothesis; if statistical tests show that the likelihood that the outcome was obtained purely by chance is less than .05, or 5%, then the null hypothesis is rejected. When the null hypothesis is rejected, experimenters conclude that there is a difference between groups, or a relationship among variables, in the relevant population. For more information, see McBurney and White (2007). ***See also*** Inferential Statistics; Statistics (psychology)

Null Hypothesis *(sociology)*   A type of hypothesis used in statistics that stipulates that there is no statistically significant relationship between given variables. The null hypothesis relies on the assumption that there is an absence of variation (or zero variation) between a particular set of variables. ***See also*** Hypothesis (sociology); Research

O

Oath A formally affirmed promise to fulfill a pledge, often to God or an other form of deity. An oath is an attestation of the truthfulness of statements made by an individual and often has religious significance. In legal cases, individuals who address the court are asked to take an oath before their testimony. Failure to respect the oath constitutes a criminal offense (perjury). *See also* Perjury; Testimony

Objectiveness in Media Coverage Objectivity in reporting, the opposite of subjectivity, refers to an ideal situation where a journalist is a neutral, unbiased observer rather than a participant in a news story. Sociologists consider this impossible to attain. The closest a reporter can get is with a "just the facts" approach. Critics of "just the facts" news reporting say that there are always biases present due to the unquestioned assumptions of the reporter, the form of the news story, and the normal process of news gathering, which serve to reinforce official viewpoints and established power structures. The critic Marshall McLuhan in his "the medium is the message" statements pointed to the inherent inseparability of bias from the media.

In consciously subjective, interpretive accounts, the author deliberately includes context and opinion, as in editorials and political columns. The literary journalism seen in magazines is deliberately nonobjective. Another example is investigative or "muck-raking" journalism, where an aggressive approach is used to cover stories that those in positions of authority do not wish uncovered—as exampled infamously in the Watergate reports, leading to the attempted impeachment of President Nixon. Perhaps the most brilliant satirical critic of sloppy journalism and plagiaristic journalists was the early-20th-century Viennese journalist Karl Kraus, who almost singlehandedly wrote the articles in his paper *Die Fackel* (1899–1936). Kraus was a pioneer in comparing inconsistent quotes made by politicians and others, a style very popular on television news today.

Before the rise of news agencies, 19th-century newspapers in the United States proudly displayed their biases, particularly when it came to politics. To adequately serve a diverse array of customers, news wire organizations composed news stories as neutrally as possible. These stories would often then be published verbatim in local newspapers. Another factor leading to greater objectivity and professionalism in the 20th century was the growing tendency of newspapers to rely on advertising revenue. Newspaper editors became more reluctant to voice strong opinions if that would lead to advertisers withdrawing their ads. For more information, see Schudson (1978). *See also* News Management; Propaganda Model; Transparency

Objective Responsibility An individual or group's liability for a certain deed even if the party at fault had no intention of actually performing the guilty act. Objective responsibility is also known as "no-fault," strict, or absolute responsibility. Legally speaking, no criminal intent (or *mens rea*) is necessary to try someone seen as objectively responsible. There are only a small number of crimes punishable within this framework. These may include crimes such as felony murder (where an individual can be charged for homicide even if this was unintentional) or certain drug crimes (often when an individual is caught with someone he did not know was in possession of an illegal substance). Strict liability is also relevant to numerous tort crimes and is usually based on principles of recklessness; for example, an employer can sometimes be found guilty of hiring illicit immigrants even if he or she believed that these employees had legally emigrated. For more information, see Schulhofer (2001). *See also* Civil Liability; Subjective Responsibility

Objectives (Definition and Types) The intended result of an educational program. Objectives are used to guide evaluation processes. They refer to the goals of a successful educational program or intervention. They are statements that describe what a student should know or be able to do on successful completion of a program. There is debate over whether objectives should be written at a specific or a general level; the latter position is taken in this definition.

Educational objectives can consist of different types and measure different general skills and abilities. In the late 1960s, evaluators were encouraged to write objectives using behavioral terms that would be easily measurable. These objectives focused primarily on the skills and abilities that could be directly observed. One of the primary disadvantages of behavioral objectives is the tendency for writers to focus on trivial, yet observable and measurable, skills that do not necessarily correspond to the broader goals of an educational program. Evaluators are now encouraged to write fewer, but still measurable, goals that could encompass the broader, more general goals of the program.

O

Objectives can be written to correspond to existing taxonomies of skills, such as those measuring the cognitive, affective, and psychomotor domains. The cognitive domain includes skills related to memory, thinking, and reasoning. Bloom's taxonomy, a commonly used method of classifying cognitive skills, can be used to help guide written objectives into one of six levels of varying cognitive complexity. An example of an objective written for the comprehension level of Bloom's taxonomy would be the following: "Given a short fiction story, students should be able to identify the main ideas and themes in their own words." Objectives may also be focused on the affective domain, focusing on learners' attitudes, interests, and beliefs, or the psychomotor domain, focusing on learners' abilities to physically manipulate objects or tools.

Other researchers have introduced other methods of classifying educational objectives. For instance, Gagné (1977) describes six types of objectives: (1) reinstating refers to objectives focused on the lower-level cognitive skills of memorization and recitation; (2) discriminating focuses on the ability to distinguish between two objects; (3) identifying focuses on the ability to identify and distinguish between concrete concepts, such as color, by appearance; (4) classifying focuses on more sophisticated concepts that cannot be distinguished simply by appearance; (5) demonstrating focuses on the demonstration of rules, in which the learner must show that he or she understands what a rule means; and (6) generating refers to higher-order rule learning, in which the learner must demonstrate that he or she can solve a novel problem by developing a new rule.

Regardless of the taxonomy or classification structure used when developing objectives, evaluators should use these only as guidelines not as a rigid tool. For more information, see Gagné (1977) and Popham (1993). **See also** Taxonomies

Objective Tests   Tests formulated on the principle of maximization of objectivity and minimization of human subjectivity or bias in judgments by test takers and test performance scorers. An example would be multiple-choice questions measuring students' factual knowledge graded by a computerized process.

Objectivity/Objectivism   A philosophical approach that has multiple definitions, which are difficult to pin down. In general, objectivism refers to the assumption that truth exists independent of the human mind and is discovered through systematic observation of the environment. In science, the term implies that the investigator must be separate from the object of investigation and without bias. **See also** Positivism; Postmodernism; Social Constructivism

Object Language   In semantics and logic, the ordinary language used to talk about people, places, and things in the world. In contrast, metalanguage is an artificial language used by linguists and others to analyze or describe the sentences or elements of object language itself. In other words, object language is the language being referred to in a metalanguage. For example, in the sentence "When we talk about the 'computer,' we are simply referring to a kind of 'tool,'" the words *computer* and *tool* are the object language; the overall sentence is a metalinguistic observation about the object-linguistic terms. The concept was developed by 20th-century logical positivists such as the Polish American Alfred Tarski and the German American Rudolf Carnap.

Sometimes referred to as the target language, object language may also be understood as the language into which a text, or data, written in another language is to be translated. For more information, see Steinmetz (2008).

Object Permanence   A child learns that an object continues to exist even after the object can no longer be seen. This developmental milestone was identified by Piaget, who suggested that object permanence in not fully mastered by children until they are 18 months old and occurs during the sensorimotor stage. More recent research by Baillargeon indicated that object permanence may be learned by children as young as three and a half months. For more information, see Piaget (1936) and Baillargeon and DeVos (1991). **See also** Sensorimotor Stage

Obscene   Offensive to the general standards of morality in a given society. In the legal context, obscene acts refer to behaviors of a sexual nature that are often perceived as vulgar. Such acts violate the common sexual norms in a given society or culture. For instance, indecent exposure is often perceived to be an obscene act. It should be noted that definitions of obscenity vary from one culture to another.

Observation (education)   A method of data collection that can take place in a laboratory or in naturalistic settings. In the former, the researcher creates the standardized setting for observation; in the latter, observation is done in real-world, natural settings. In participant observation, researchers record their direct experiences in their field notes. Observation requires intense concentration and attention to detail. Data collected through observation may be captured through audio or video recording, handwritten field notes, or more standardized approaches such as recording the time and frequency of occurrence of predetermined categories. Things a researcher may focus on in observation include the context and physical environment, the kinds of participants present, the activities engaged in, the kinds of interactions, conversations, nonverbal communications, and the researcher's own behavior.

Observation (sociology)   The act of taking notice and documenting given event or behavior. In social science research, researchers may sometimes choose to observe a given group or social phenomenon in order to better understand the dynamics of the phenomenon at hand. Observation can be participant or nonparticipant.

See also Ethnography (sociology); Participant Observation (sociology); Participant-Observer; Qualitative Research

Obsessive-Compulsive Disorder   A psychological anxiety disorder characterized by an individual's uncontrollable urge or drive to engage in irrational rituals. For example, a person may have an unreasonable fear of germs and therefore feels the urge to constantly wash hands in an attempt to alleviate the anxiety. Classified as an Axis I category disorder by the *Diagnostic and Statistical Manual of Mental Disorders* (fourth edition, text revision; *DSM-IV-TR*), an individual must have either obsessions or compulsions, or both, to be diagnosed with obsessive-compulsive disorder. The onset of obsessive-compulsive disorder is often around early adulthood. Obsessive-compulsive disorder is estimated to occur in approximately 2.5% of the population. A mild genetic predisposition for the disorder has been identified. For more information, see American Psychiatric Association, *DSM-IV-TR* (2000). *See also* Anxiety Disorders

Obsessive-Compulsive Personality Disorder   A personality disorder, specified in the *Diagnostic and Statistical Manual of Mental Disorders* (*DSM*), that is characterized by maladaptive levels of scrupulosity, rigidity, perfectionism, preoccupation with work, inability to delegate tasks, attention to detail, miserliness, and hoarding of unimportant objects. It is differentiated from obsessive-compulsive disorder in that anxiety is not the primary drive behind the symptoms of obsessive-compulsive personality disorder. *See also* Personality Disorders (education)

Obstruction of Justice   The act of creating a hindrance or impediment in the justice process. Obstruction of justice is a criminal offense that includes any interference with the work of criminal justice officials in a given legal case and any attempt to hinder efforts carried out by government and legal authorities.

Occupational Therapy   Assistance given by trained (usually master's level) occupational therapists to improve quality of life through development of skills and abilities for home and work environments. Clients may have physical, mental, emotional, or developmental conditions such as injuries, illness, limited physical or mental capacity, substance abuse problems, sensory challenges, or other limiting conditions. The range of assistance includes grooming or self-feeding, computer skills, physical exercise, use of adaptive equipment, decision making, memory and abstract reasoning, problem solving, planning and using of work space, medical resources, and job search or training. Assistance is given at home, in a medical setting, at the job site, or in a professional facility. *See also* Rehabilitation

Oculesics   The study of eye contact in nonverbal communication or use of the eyes in communication. Oculesics includes direct eye contact, indirect eye contact, and duration of the eye contact. It is expected in American culture that a person will look directly at another when communicating with that person. However, it is considered rude in American culture to stare into the eyes of another person. If one avoids eye contact when communicating with another person, it is believed that that person is insecure and untrusting. Direct eye contact can be misinterpreted as being aggressive. Minimal eye contact can be misinterpreted as having a lack of interest in what a person is saying. The situation also affects the use and interpretation of eye contact. For instance, making direct eye contact with or staring at a stranger in a New York subway can be dangerous to one's physical well-being.

Oedipus Complex   Theorized to occur during the phallic stage of psychosexual development, it is characterized by a child developing sexual desires toward the parent of the opposite sex. Proposed by Sigmund Freud (1900–1953) and used as a rationalization of the formation of the superego, the Oedipus complex is based on Greek mythology. According to the legend, Oedipus, albeit unknowingly, killed his father, Laius, and married his mother, Jocasta. A child with Oedipus complex feels rivalry toward the same-sex parent while trying to attract the parent of the opposite sex. The child has to successfully resolve the Oedipus complex in order to advance in psychosexual development. That is, the child has to learn to resolve the feelings of hostility and competition with the same-sex parent in order to later be able to view that parent as a role model and to be able to identify with him or her. Freud proposed that not resolving the feelings of hostility and not being able to identify with the same-sex parent will ultimately hinder the child's developmental progress. The female equivalent to the Oedipus complex is the Electra complex. For more information, see Freud (2000b). *See also* Psychosexual Stages; Superego

Offender/Offense   One who commits an infraction of the law. An offender is a person charged with or convicted of a criminal offense. An offense is a violation of criminal law. Felony offenses are serious criminal offenses punishable by more than one year in prison; misdemeanor offenses are punishable by up to one year in jail; and infractions are the least serious offenses, for which offenders can receive no more than a few days in jail (and typically receive just a fine). *See also* Crime; Felon/Felony; Index Crimes/Offenses; Misdemeanor

Oligarchy (*political science*)   A type of government where rule is by a small elite power group. The degree of oligarchy can be determined by the percentage of the population holding leadership positions, the most extreme form being a monarchy. Members of an oligarchy commonly achieve their position through election, heredity, or property ownership.

According to Aristotle in *The Politics* (350 BCE), an oligarchy depends on the "customs and training" of a nation rather than its constitution. The German sociologist Robert Michels in *Political Parties* (1911) coined the term the *iron law of oligarchy*. Michels's theory posited that any organization or government, no matter how democratic at its inception, will eventually turn into an oligarchy. This is due to the increasing complexity of the organization and its transformation into a bureaucracy that is controlled by a small, isolated elite.

Oligarchy *(public administration)*   A small group of elite people having control, as a form of government, over a country, organization, or institution. This form of government usually exists in the order of family hierarchy, where children are born into royalty and/or wealth and raised as heirs to positions of power. Throughout history, oligarchies have exercised power for economic benefits and purposes and have relied highly on public servitude. Examples include Japan, during the Meiji Restoration; modern-day Russia; and, to some, the two-party political system in the United States and its procedural methods to exclude third parties from electoral politics.

Oligopoly   A few firms dominating an industry and competing against each other for the market share. *Oligopoly* is a Greek word meaning, in approximate translation, "few sellers." Oligopoly is generally described as competition among a few firms in the same industry. In the United States, three or four firms dominate some industries. For example, for more than a century the automobile industry was dominated by three American car companies. In addition, many other industries, such as oil, gas, steel, food, and beverages, are oligopolistic in nature. Firms operating in an oligopolistic market react when one firm cuts its prices for an identical good. In addition, they react to changes in quality and other technological improvements and improvement in the safety of products. An oligopolist strategy is based on how a firm thinks its competitor will react to any changes in pricing, advertising, marketing, and distribution. In oligopolistic competition, price and output are not totally determined by supply and demand. There is one key factor that influences the determination of prices and output—the reaction of one oligopoly to another. Models have been developed to measure how firms react to each other. A very popular model is game theory, which is widely used in explaining and predicting oligopolistic behavior. Some oligopolies produce and sell identical goods. For example, Exxon and Mobil produce and sell oil, and their products are undifferentiated from each other. Some oligopolies produce and sell similar products but differentiate these products from each other by product features, style, technology, and quality. For example, Ford sells the Mercury Sable and competes against Nissan on price, features, and functionality. However, Nissan competes on quality and reliability. The prices of similar products are more sensitive to any changes in a competitor's price. If an oligopoly raises its price for an identical good, customers will switch to another competitor's product because the products are identical. For more information, see McEachern (2006).

Ombudsman   An official, usually affiliated with the government, who is responsible for responding to individual grievances and complaints. The ombudsman also monitors government activity to ensure that the interests of the general public are respected.

One-Party-Dominant System   A political system in which one political party dominates the powers of government, although other political parties are allowed to exist (also known as a "dominant-party system"). Minority parties can still wield influence in a one-party-dominant system as they still represent the interests of a segment of the population. This makes democracy possible in a one-party-dominant system, unlike in a "one-party system," which is usually associated with authoritarian dictatorships. Nations where the dominant-party system exists or has existed are numerous, including the Institutional Revolutionary Party in pre-1994 Mexico and the Liberal Democratic Party in pre-1993 Japan. One-party-dominant systems can be caused by a number of factors: on the negative side, election fraud or suspect constitutional amendments, and on the positive side, great popularity among the people. For example, the predominance of the Progressive Conservatives in the Canadian province of Alberta (1971 to the present) was attributed, by R. K. Carty and David Stewart in *Provinces: Canadian Provincial Politics* (1996), to "extended periods of office-holding, few changes in government, one sided legislatures, and majority support for the governing party" (p. 78). Proponents of a one-party-dominant system point to how leaders can afford to take risks and plan for the long-term. Opponents note that a dominant party most likely shies away from controversial stands in an effort to sustain majority support. For more information, see Bogaards (2004) and Carty and Stewart (1996).

Ontology   The study of what ultimately exists or, alternatively, what a given theory or belief system must be committed to as existing. In the first sense, *ontology* is synonymous with *metaphysics*. In the second sense, ontology investigates what a set of beliefs or statements must assume exists for them to be true, but without committing to the truth of those beliefs or statements. Thus, in this second sense, one might investigate the ontology of the caloric theory, asking, for instance, whether the theory is committed to the existence of negative masses. ***See also*** Metaphysics

Open Economy   An economy in which goods, services, and resources are permitted to flow freely with very little rather than no restriction. The flow of capital (physical, human, and financial), labor, and entrepreneurial skill normally constitute a significant proportion of international exchange or trade. For this reason, the expression is also used to describe countries for which international trade constitutes a substantially significant proportion of national income or gross domestic product (exports and imports as a percentage of gross domestic product).

The degree to which an economy is open depends on a number of political and economic considerations. For example, dictatorial regimes tend to have a tight control over the money supply, imports, investment (including capital flows), and the use of international currencies. Inflation, output, and currency availability are normally indicators of trouble in such countries.

Some developing countries complain that they have inadequate access to foreign markets and are disposed to impose restrictions of their own to ensure fair trade and equitable returns. Weak and unstable economic systems are normally mindful of interest rate movements and the effects of such movements on capital flows, capital reversibility, and currency valuation or crisis. International organizations such as the World Trade Organization (WTO) and the International Monetary Fund (IMF) promote freer world trade and openness in economic relations. ***See also*** Capital Controls; Free Trade; International Monetary Fund (IMF); Laissez-Faire (economics); Trade Theory, New; World Trade Organization (WTO)

Open-Ended Versus Closed-Ended Questions Researchers use such questions in questionnaires and interviews to provide data for their study. An open-ended question allows the research participant to respond fully in his or her own words—for example, "Tell me about your study habits." This type of question is designed to elicit a detailed answer using the participant's own knowledge, experience, or feelings. Closed-ended questions include a set of response categories constructed by the researcher, and the participant must select from the predetermined response choices. An example of a closed-ended question is "How useful do you think your research methods course will be in your career?" (1) Not at all useful, (2) Not very useful, (3) Somewhat useful, (4) Very useful. To answer this question, the participant has to select one of the four predetermined responses.

Opening Statement A statement delivered by counsel in a trial, summarizing the arguments that will be emphasized in the legal case. In an opening statement, the counsel provides an overview of the nature of the case, as well as all the evidence and facts that will be used to disprove the opposing counsel's arguments. ***See also*** Counsel

Openness The term when used in communications means maintaining open communication channels through which information can be transmitted and shared by other people or systems. Thus, one definition of openness could be the degree to which individuals are able to use a communication system to organize themselves in any way they find adequate. However, openness

also implies the facilitation of both production and distribution of information, as in true dialogue, where all participating parties are given equal opportunity to share and disseminate information. Nevertheless, we cannot assume that total openness exists, and we can also not assume the lack of it. Openness in communication relates also to job satisfaction, where positive communication between employees and their immediate supervisors is an essential factor for successful *outward communication.* Openness in communication is also essential in alleviating stressors in an organizational environment, as it has an ameliorating effect on personnel, giving them a feeling of responsibility and a sense of participation in the organizational decision-making process. For more information, see Hoem (2006).

Open Party Caucuses In the United States, a Republican or Democratic caucus where voters can participate without having to be a registered member of the party. A registered voter of one party may even vote in the caucus of the opposing party, although no voter can vote in both. The alternative to the open party caucus is the closed party caucus, where primaries are restricted to those with party membership. States that allow open party caucuses or primaries are Alabama, Arkansas, California (Democrats only), Georgia, Idaho, Indiana, Michigan, Minnesota, Mississippi, Missouri, Montana (Democrats only), North Dakota, South Carolina, Tennessee, Texas, Vermont, Virginia, Washington, and Wisconsin.

Open-Seat Election An election where there is no incumbent candidate in the race. Open-seat elections occur due to term limits on certain positions or an incumbent's decision not to run again. According to the political scientists Robert S. Erickson and Gerald C. Wright (2001) in *Congress Reconsidered,* incumbents in congressional elections are reelected 95% of the time. Since the incumbent holds the clear advantage, open-seat elections are considered difficult to predict and are hotly contested. Factors such as candidate experience and candidate spending become crucial determinants of election success. National party performance also plays a dominant role for voters. For more information, see Erikson and Wright (2001).

Open Systems Theory For organizations to function well, they must achieve "negative entropy." Negative entropy means that new energy and external resources must be constantly infused into the organization to achieve external equilibrium. Open systems is a method that calls for organizations to take a holistic approach to problem solving by understanding how the internal structure and external environment interact. First, the central assumption of open systems theory is that every organization is social, in that all organizations are made up of individuals and groups that interact with their environment. There is no "one best way" to achieve success for organization because of the diverse and unpredictable nature of a social organization's interactions with its environment.

The development of open systems theory has its roots in natural systems theory, which focused on the microlevel study of an organization by approaching the analysis as a biologist might approach the study of the human body—as a living organism with a system of interdependent parts. Open systems theory takes the human organism concept a step further in the macrolevel study to understand how organizations make exchanges with the environment and maintain an external equilibrium.

The Dutch biologist Ludwig von Bertalanffy discovered open systems theory; however, it has been shown to be relevant across a range of natural and social sciences. Ostensibly, an open system is one that is characterized by an orchestration of components that are interdependent on each other; moreover, an open system is one that continuously interacts with its environment. Mechanical, organic, and social systems each have particular types of relations between the parts. Mechanical systems tend to be highly constrained, whereas social systems tend to have more loosely related parts with greater variability.

The definition of what constitutes a "system" varies. With respect to public management, an open system is one that takes in raw materials (such as capital, labor, and technology) and converts them into goods and services (vis-à-vis machinery, skilled labor, etc.) that are then returned back into the environment. In contrast, a closed system is self-contained and does not interact with its external environment. For more information, see Bertalanffy (1976).

Operant Conditioning A theory of learning developed by B. F. Skinner, proposing that voluntary behavior is shaped by whether the consequences of a behavior are rewarding or punishing. A behavior is positively reinforced when the response to it is followed by a rewarding or favorable consequence. For example, if a person tells a joke and consequently makes friends laugh, the laughter is a rewarding consequence and will result in the person telling jokes in the future. A behavior is weakened, or negatively reinforced, when the response to a stimulus is followed by a punishing or unfavorable consequence. For example, if a person tells a joke and no one laughs, the lack of laughter is an unfavorable consequence and will lead to the person telling fewer jokes or potentially stopping the behavior altogether. Different schedules of reinforcement have been identified (Skinner, 1938): fixed ratio, variable ratio, fixed interval, and variable interval. Generally, ratio schedules result in faster responses than interval schedules, and variable schedules result in increased resistance to extinction of the behavior than do fixed schedules. Operant conditioning is named after one of its core assumptions; that is, a person "operates" in the surrounding environment rather than merely reacting to it. For more information, see Skinner (1938). *See also* Classical Conditioning; Skinner Box

Operating Grants Grants used primarily for funding the general, ongoing operating expenses of nonprofit organizations and other institutions. However, occasionally, operating grants are awarded for short-term projects such as feasibility studies or pilot projects. These grants may be more difficult to obtain than normal grants, which tend to fund new projects rather then ongoing activities. Often the use of operating grants is unrestricted and not contingent on specific projects or activities. Typical uses of operating grants include the payment of rent or mortgage, salaries of employees, and office supplies; utilities; and other overhead expenses. Applications for operating grants typically require budget justification, a rationale for future expenses, and information about the future direction of research or projects. Occasionally, they are awarded to individuals instead of organizations. *See also* Grants

Operational Definition The description of the way a variable is being manipulated in experimental research. The operational definition conceptualizes the specific steps that are taken to manipulate a variable in order to measure what the variable is intended to measure. To fully understand a variable, the operational definition, as part of the definition of the variable, is critical in enabling research to be replicable for future research. *See also* Dependent Variable; Independent Variable

Opinion A personal view or the individual expression of a subjective judgment. Opinions refer to personal ideas that cannot be proved or disproved, as they vary according to individual perceptions. In legal terms, the opinion is the written finding of a case that explains the outcome of the case. When all the justices do not agree on the outcome of a case, there may be a majority and a dissenting opinion.

Opinion Leadership The act of an individual explaining the content of media messages to others who are accepting of this opinion. The opinion leader has access to the media and is thus more knowledgeable about its contents than those who do not. Opinion leadership emphasizes agency and personal influence in the filtering and interpreting of information relayed in media messages. This notion was proposed in the 1948 work of the sociologists Paul Lazarsfeld and Elihu Katz, *The People's Choice,* as a part of their two-step flow-of-communication model. They offered that an opinion leader is knowledgeable and highly regarded for his information on particular topics but not necessarily in other areas. Moreover, opinion leaders exist on many structural levels (social, economic, and political) and hold positions of authority in their communities. Critics maintain that the opinion leader, then, acts like a censor in the management and dissemination of media information for his or her audience. For more information, see Lazarsfeld and Katz (1948). *See also* Censorship (media studies); Claim-Makers; Salience

Oppositional Defiant Disorder (ODD) A disorder of childhood specified in the *Diagnostic and Statistical Manual* (*DSM*) that is characterized by defiance of authority, temper tantrums, argumentativeness, annoying others, being touchy or easily annoyed, holding grudges, blaming others for mistakes or misbehavior, anger/resentment, and spitefulness/vindictiveness. ODD is often comorbid with attention-deficit hyperactivity disorder, and half of the children diagnosed progress to conduct disorder.

Oral Interpretation Expressing literature in dramatic or interpretive readings out loud to an audience. The physical, emotional, and social dimensions of characters in literature are explored by the reader/speaker. In the process, the speaker attempts to develop effective speaking skills to convey a story through proper voice quality, volume, pitch, inflection, and rate. Gestures, body language, and voice quality all express the attitudes, thoughts, and emotions of the characters portrayed in the literature and make them understood and believable. It is very common for high school drama and speech departments to have oral interpretation competitions. The art of storytelling is conveyed in these dramatic presentations. Students learn to master decoding skills for fluency and comprehension in oral readings. The goal is to bring meaning to the text through oral interpretation.

Oral Style The manner of speech presented by an individual to one or more parties. It is marked by the use of spoken (rather than written) words that are employed in a shared language between the speaker and his or her audience. An effective oral style in an exchange of communication offers information with clarity, and the style of relating (informal or formal) is germane to the context of the conversation. Important elements in oral style are thus the appropriate use of language and the tone of voice of the speaker. An oral style can be entertaining, convincing, or educational, depending on the audience and the content of the information. Oral style is important in many settings, both personally (with friends and family) and professionally (in presentations to clients and colleagues). *See also* Articulation

Oral Tradition In *Orality and Literacy*, Walter Ong identifies certain features of oral performance which rely on rhythm, balance, repetitions, contrasts, standard "riffs" (descriptions of meals, arming scenes, etc.), formulaic epithets, proverbs, and other commonplaces. These motifs are learned narrative "habits," recalled without effort. Syntax itself is affected, resulting in a paratactic aggregation of clauses (and . . . and . . . then . . . then) as opposed to the hierarchy of clauses characteristic of written communication. In its "purest" form, oral tradition is entirely dependent on memory for preserving and communicating knowledge. Oral tradition encourages "copiousness"; while the speaker is thinking of the next idea, he or she will mark time with a formulaic filler rather than fall silent. Oral tradition is repetitive, for saying something once in a community is not enough. Shared values and beliefs are formed through the reiteration of the same thing many times in many ways. Laws come to be indistinguishable from formulaic wisdom, sayings, and proverbs. Oral tradition keeps its vocabulary close to the material world, avoiding abstraction and neutrality, for the speaker is rarely impartial. Verbal violence is part of the discourse; hence, bards routinely engage in flyting or poetic battles.

A purely oral tradition technically cannot be studied since the minute something is recorded, it is no longer purely oral. In reality, oral traditions coexist alongside literate traditions—witness the persistence of folkloric stories and ballads to the present. One of the most vibrant and popular oral traditions in currency is rap, the half-sung, half-spoken rhythms of a contemporary music genre. Emerging out of African American urban neighborhoods (the "Ghetto Toast") in the 1970s and 1980s, rap is an essential element of hip-hop culture. It exhibits many if not all of the classic characteristics of oral tradition: violent, graphic imagery and language; competitive "flyting" contests; contempt for overly or pre-scripted rhymes; ingenious extemporizing or "freestyling"; mannered bodily gestures in delivery; and emphasis on performance. For more information, see Ong (1988). *See also* Culture (communication, sociology); Oral Style; Popular Culture

Order The expression *law and order* is used to convey a candidate's platform that is hard on crime and tough on punishment. Law and order became fashionable after the civil disobedience and prison activism of the 1960s and 1970s and the rapidly rising crime rates of the 1980s. Before that, Americans preferred treatment and rehabilitation of offenders. Voters usually are punitive in their attitudes toward crime, especially the violent variety, so that politicians vie with each other to prove that they are tougher on crime. In addition to the adaptation of the death penalty by the majority of states, crime legislation reflective of this stance includes "three strikes" sentencing laws and the federal mandatory minimum sentencing law.

Organism In its most basic representation, usually described as any living thing. An organism is composed of a system of organs that operate independent of one another but ultimately must work together for the survival of the living thing. Organisms, which can be unicellular or complex, are capable of reproduction, evolution, and subsistence. Examples of single-celled organisms include bacteria, protists, and yeast. Examples of complex organisms, which at a minimum contain more than one cell and at a maximum billions of cells, include plants, animals, and human beings. Some sociological theories use the term metaphorically to describe their systems.

O

Organization *(education)* A system arranged in a hierarchical structure that apportions and facilitates work toward goal accomplishment. It is characterized by rules and defined systems of communication and control. It includes human, physical, work, and coordination elements.

Organization *(public administration)* An arrangement of people, technologies, and processes designed to achieve one or more goals. IBM, MTV, Microsoft, the U.S. Army, and the Catholic Church are all formal organizations; so is the local police department, large or small. A formal organization's existence and essential purposes has been determined by some authorized individual, group, or institution. The U.S. Army was established by the Continental Congress in 1775, the Catholic Church grew in service to that religion's adherents, and Microsoft was founded by Bill Gates and Paul Allen in 1975.

An organization also arises spontaneously and informally. Schoolchildren at recess may arrange themselves in hierarchies and self-organize for games, and not always in ways their teachers/monitors want. Employees affiliate at work due to proximity or shared tasks and interests, eventually engaging in concerted action—work slowdowns or formation of a bowling team—that may be at odds with their formal organizational roles. The interplay between formal organization and informal organization in a business enterprise or government agency creates an overall social system that is an important focus of management studies.

Organizational Change *(education)* Variations in the structure of an organization brought about by responses to problems or the need to increase efficiency, effectiveness, and worker satisfaction. The process of organizational change requires identification of areas in need of change and removal of obstacles that block change. Successful change occurs in organizational cultures that include a commitment to common goals, conflict resolution, human resource development, organizational learning, and proactive adaptation to changing environmental conditions.

Organizational Change *(public administration)* Major adjustments in how an agency or company goes about its business. Examples of organizational change would be a traditional college moving to offer its courses and programs online or an Internet provider keeping up with competitors by eliminating or drastically lowering monthly fees.

Organizations need to regularly adapt their structures, policies, and personnel to new situations in order to effectively pursue established and emergent goals. Organizations are also social systems whose members build up a substantial investment in the familiar values, stable relationships, steady benefits, and overall predictability that arise from day-to-day organizational

functioning. Any organization's need to adapt will always clash to some degree with entrenched and influential forces that strongly desire to keep things the same. Organizational change thus engages both executives and employees in critical analysis that frequently engenders conflict as the path to organizational renewal is decided on and then traversed.

Organizational Communication The broad spectrum of human interaction that occurs at, and between, every level or unit within complex organizations. Simply put, organizational communication entails listening, speaking, questioning, and sharing feedback. The forms in which these acts occur serve to define the nature and effectiveness of a particular organization's communication system. The architecture of organizational communication consists of three general axes: downward, upward, and lateral (or horizontal) communication. Downward communication within an organization may refer to employer-to-employee, supervisor-to-supervisee, or even mentor-to-mentee communication and management of individuals' behaviors within the organization. Those in charge may communicate to subordinates through meetings, memos, work orders, instructional manuals, bulletins, performance reviews, and so on. Upward communication in these contexts may entail product reports—both written and oral, various performance metrics, log books, data analysis, and more. Horizontal or lateral communication within an organization is likely to take forms such as informal conversation, e-mail and instant messaging, project collaboration, conflict management (this may also be part of downward communication), and more. Organizational communication is often referred to as the "grapevine"—that network of communication acts that serves to transmit information, ideas, feedback, and evaluation both within the organization and outward, from the organization to those outside. For more information, see Miller (2006).

Organizational Culture *(communication)* Sometimes called "corporate culture," the term refers to the assumptions, values, norms, behaviors, interactions, and artifacts of organization members. Clues about the organizational culture may be found in anything from the arrangement of furniture to what members typically talk about, what they wear, and how they decorate their work spaces.

Corporate culture comprises a system of interactions between and among members as well as between members and the physical environment of the organization. This concept of culture is particularly important when attempting to manage organization-wide processes.

There has been a great deal of literature generated over the past decade about the concept of organizational culture—particularly with regard to learning how to *change* that culture. When such changes are unsuccessful, the failure is often credited to lack of understanding about the strong role culture plays in organizations. That is one of the reasons why many strategic planners now place as much emphasis on identifying strategic values as they do on mission and vision.

There are different types of organizational culture, just like there are different types of personality. Various studies of organizational culture have distinguished a long list of these types. Some examples are given below:

Academy culture is one where members are highly skilled and tend to remain in the organization for long enough periods to be promoted through the ranks. Universities, large corporations, and hospitals are examples of this type of organizational culture.

Baseball team culture is one where members have highly desirable skills that are in demand in the open market. The organization must provide significant incentives for such members to remain loyal to the organization and can expect that other organizations will try to lure these members away with more attractive incentives.

The tough-guy macho culture is one where members are part of a fast-paced, highly competitive corporate environment, such as brokerage houses, car dealerships, and real estate companies.

Organizational culture may also entail specific problems or weaknesses within the organization. These may include a culture of mistrust among members, a culture of blame, where any and all mistakes must be attributed to a particular member or group, which then must pay some sort of price; this may include financial penalty, loss of vacation time, or even termination of membership. For more information, see Cummings and Worley (2005), Deal and Kennedy (1982), and Schein (2004).

Organizational Culture *(public administration)* The shared values, assumptions, expectations, attitudes, and beliefs that exist within an organization. These shared attributes affect the behavior of individuals within an organizational context, which in turn affects the behavior of the organization as a whole. A strong organizational culture occurs when there is agreement between the values and goals of individuals and the larger organization. A weak organizational culture occurs when there is a lack of alignment between individuals and the organization and may result in poor performance of employees or other problems in the functioning of the organization. Organizational values (beliefs about what an organization's goals should be and how they should be achieved) affect organizational norms, which influence the behavior of individuals within an organization. This in turn affects the overall performance of the organization. There may be other internal cultures in an organization, usually within specific groups or ranks of employees. *See also* Organization (public administration); Organizational Structure

Organizational Humanism A belief, based on a set of theories, that work holds intrinsic interest for the worker. Also known as the human relations approach, organizational humanism evolved as a reaction to the dehumanized view of organizations resulting from Weber's view of people in bureaucratic organizations, the principles of scientific management, and the Hawthorne experiments. Organizational humanism was based on the Western Electric Company experiments of Elton Mayo in the early 20th century and later popularized by Douglas McGregor's XY theory in 1960.

Organizational humanists believe that the rational design of organizations leads to highly specialized and routine jobs. According to this view, workers seek satisfaction in their work, want to work rather than avoid it, and can be motivated through positive incentives such as participation in decision making. The major goal of organizational humanism has been the elimination of unnecessary rules, rigidly confining jobs, and inflexible supervisory applications.

When workers are allowed to reach their ultimate potential through their use of skills and talents, they will have attained self-actualization. The responsibility of managers is to challenge employees and allow them to develop their decision-making skills and take on responsibility. This in turn will motivate employees to reach self-actualization. When employees are self-actualized, they will integrate their goals with the goals of the organization.

Organizational humanism thus postulates a link between participation and production. In other words, it is believed that participation increases satisfaction, which in turn increases the work effort. Unfortunately, research did not support this hypothesis.

Research has found that there is only a small relationship between participation and work satisfaction. An increase in work satisfaction does not predict an increase in work effort, having a voice in the work process does not increase work satisfaction, and workers do not necessarily prefer larger or more interesting jobs. Another major criticism of the human relations approach has been its nongeneralizability. The human relations perspective fails to understand that not all workers are motivated in the same way under a single motivational scheme based on an ideology regardless of occupational level, socioeconomic status, or job function. This approach is not a panacea for lack of employee motivation.

Although the term has fallen into disuse, aspects of organizational humanism still exist in attempts to "humanize" organizations. Examples of this perspective can still be seen. They include sensitivity training and encounter groups. For more information, see Kaplan and Tausky (1977) and McGregor (2006).

Organizational Structure The arrangement of an organization with respect to task allocation, centralization of power, and the mechanisms of coordination and control. Common forms of organizational structure include functional, matrix, and divisional structures. The determinants of organizational structure include the organization's size, the extent of routinization of processes, and the life-cycle stage of the organization, among other factors. A complex organizational structure implies a high degree of specialization or division of labor, numerous levels of hierarchy (i.e., vertical differentiation), geographic dispersion, and a tendency toward decentralization (i.e., decision making and authority are dispersed downward in the hierarchy). *See also* Organizational Theory

Organizational Theory   There is no single theory of organizations. Rather, there are many theories that have examined organizations, their structures, designs, and environments and the behavior of individuals who work in them. This collection of theories is referred to as organizational theory.

Classical organizational theory was popular through the 1930s. Its foundations lay in the Industrial Revolution of the 1700s and the areas of mechanical and industrial engineering and economics. The basic principles of the theory are (1) organizations exist to accomplish production-related and economic goals; (2) there is one best way to organize for production, which can be found through systematic, scientific inquiry; (3) production is maximized through specialization and division of labor; and (4) people and organizations behave according to rational economic principles.

From World War II through the 1950s, neoclassical organizational theory modified and extended the classical theory. A major theme of neoclassical organizational theory was that organizations did not exist as self-contained units in isolation from their environments. Neoclassical theorists began to take into account the role of individuals and conflict within an organization.

In the 1950s, the organizational behavior perspective gained in popularity. It emphasized humans as individuals and promoted organizations as open and honest environments. The basic principles of this perspective are (1) organizations exist to serve human needs rather than vice versa; (2) organizations and people need each other—organizations need ideas, energy, and talent, while individuals need careers, salaries, and work opportunities; (3) a poor fit between the individual and the organization will result in one or both suffering—either the individual being exploited or the individual exploiting the organization, or both; and (4) a good fit between the individual and the organization benefits both—individuals find meaningful, satisfying work, and the organization gets the talent and energy it needs.

Modern structural organization theory arose in the second half of the 20th century as a somewhat separate field of study from organizational behavior. It concerns the various levels of hierarchy within an organization, the relationship between an organization and its environment, and interorganizational relationships. The basic tenets of this more structural perspective are (1) organizations are rational institutions whose chief purpose is to accomplish established objectives; (2) there is an appropriate structure for any organization; (3) specialization and division of labor increase the quality and quantity of production, especially in highly skilled professions; and (4) changing the structure of an organization can solve most problems in the organization. One additional subfield of organizational theory is organizational development (OD), which focuses on applying social science knowledge to the planning and improvement of organizational functioning and effectiveness. For more information, see Shafritz and Ott (2001).

Organizational Theory, Modern   A subset of public administration theory. There is no single organizational theory. Rather, organizational theory comprises theories from diverse fields that contribute questions or perspectives, such as anthropology, sociology, social psychology, economics, and political science.

To define organizational theory, it is prudent to first define an organization. An organization is a dynamic system in which activities, relationships, and interactions are woven into a whole. Theorists have used modeling to show the processes and activities that identify an organization and give it purpose and direction. Although organizational theory came to the forefront in public administration research since the 1950s, it is still a developing field. Part of the reason why organizational theory is not fully developed is the wide variety of theorists and practitioners in public administration, the continued controversies within the field of public administration, and ongoing unresolved issues.

Since its early days, organizational theory has included aspects of bureaucracy; scientific management; human relations; leadership and organizations; individual, group, and organizational behavior; motivation; conflict; and resources. The four main categories of organizational theory are (1) theories of individual and group behavior, (2) theories of organizational structure, (3) theories of organizational processes, and (4) global or overall theories of organization.

In the United States, questions of organizational theory centered on whether it ought to be a subfield of management, sociology, or economics. It began to take shape as a subfield of management as it began to focus on questions of administration, specifically concerning how businesses and public sector organizations could be run more effectively. The emphasis was on morale, motivation, supervision, and leadership. The field drew from psychology and social psychology.

In the 1970s, the focus of organizations shifted to fields and populations beyond the organization, called neoinstitutional analyses. These analyses prioritized the social, cultural, and coercive influences on organizations rather than efficiency or interest-based explanations. These influences represented the entities that the organization regularly interacted with. The management of outside influences involved compliance with demands and collective arrangements such as joint ventures, interorganizational associations, and mergers. Theories such as the interactional approach viewed organizations as total systems in which group and individual interactions, activities, and sentiments were viewed as mutually dependent on each other and modified by forces both inside and outside the organization's environment.

At the same time, organization theorists used quantitative approaches to solve organizational problems. The result has been a conglomeration of approaches such as queuing theory, game theory, and contingency theory. Attention now was focused on the problem of resources, such as their acquisition and interorganizational interdependencies. For more information, see Gortner, Mahler, and Nicholson (1989) and Hilgert (1964).

Organization Design The decision-making process that aligns an organization's structure with its strategic goals and helps ensure that the organization successfully adapts to its external environment. The purpose is to divide the major organizational tasks among parts of the organization (*differentiation*) and to coordinate the efforts of each part across the organization (*integration*) in order to accomplish the organization's strategic goals. Design involves dividing requisite tasks into subtasks and assigning subtasks among work units and employees, configuring the flow of work processes, creating coordinating mechanisms among the units for the completion of tasks, establishing lines of authority, determining spans of control (the number of employees reporting to one supervisor), and determining decision-making responsibility. Organization design is influenced by the organization's technology (Joan Woodward) and the rate of environmental change the organization experiences (Tom Burns and G. M. Stalker). Organizations in stable environments tend to have mechanistic characteristics, including narrow spans of control, centralized decision making, and formalized rules and procedures, while organizations in turbulent environments have organic characteristics, such as wider spans of control and decentralized decision making. For more information, see Burns and Stalker (1961) and Woodward (1965).

Organization Development (OD) *(education)* The process of enhancing organizational effectiveness in accomplishing the organization's goals and improving the well-being of the organization's members by applying behavioral science concepts through intervention strategies. Planned interventions may focus on macro organizational changes, which improve the effectiveness of the whole organization, or micro changes, which focus on improving the effectiveness of selected groups and individuals within the organization. Four types of OD interventions commonly used are (1) techno-structural interventions, (2) socio-technical system designs, (3) organizational transformation interventions, and (4) human process interventions.

Techno-structural interventions are concerned with redesigning jobs to improve work methods, work or process flows, and relationships among workers. One approach to job redesign is the Job Characteristics Model, which enriches jobs to increase the motivating potential of the job. Another approach is process reengineering, which revolutionizes work processes for more effective and efficient production. A third consideration in techno-structural interventions is employee participation in the redesign of jobs and work flow.

Socio-technical systems design focuses on improving the fit between the organization's technology and social considerations among employees. The focus of these interventions is to improve the quality of work-life. Interventions may include participative management, self-directed work teams, quality circles, and flexible work options.

Organizational transformation interventions focus on changing the organization's culture, mission, business methods, and structure to transform the organization into a *new* entity. Often such a transformation requires the direction of a new leader at the top of the organization.

Human process interventions focus on changing employees' attitudes, values, skills, and interpersonal styles. These interventions should focus on changing behaviors at the group level. Employees who participate in human process interventions should be informed of the purpose of the intervention and should have freedom to choose whether or not to participate and free choice to implement the activity. Common interventions include team building and survey feedback.

The process of planning OD interventions includes (a) diagnosing the need for organizational change, (b) setting goals for the OD effort, (c) developing a plan of action, (d) conducting the intervention, and (e) evaluating the results of the intervention. Diagnosis is commonly performed using survey feedback. Anonymous questionnaires are completed by employees at all levels. The responses are analyzed and interpreted by a change agent. The change agent meets with managers and employees to discuss and explain the survey results, develop goals, and develop an action plan. The change agent is responsible for facilitating the design and implementation of all interventions. Change agents, who may be external consultants or internal members, should be experts in OD theories and practices. **See also** Job Enrichment

Organization Development (OD) *(public administration)* A planned intervention to align work culture, employee attitudes, and interpersonal/intergroup relations with the mission of the organization. Formal organizations are very susceptible to dysfunction. The leadership may cling to policies with diminishing effectiveness. Employees may see only their narrow tasks and unit identities, becoming alienated from and alienating other units with which cooperation is critical. Bosses may look on workers with disdain, and workers may disrespect their bosses, with these animosities built on stereotypes as much as reality.

These dysfunctions depress morale, reduce effort, spark conflict, and damage organizational performance. In the 1940s, 1950s, and 1960s, management theorists responded with programs of training, role plays, and self-analysis that made employees high and low more sensitive to such issues. "Sensitivity training" asked employees to recognize the impact of their attitudes, to test the reality of their stereotypes, and to arrive at new and more productive ways of thinking and behaving at work. Extensive training was provided, often at outside facilities, so that employees could develop new workplace attitudes and behaviors. In most cases, the basic work structures and production pressures remained unchanged, so trainees reverted to the old routines once back on the job.

Organized Crime   A network of individuals who aim to build profits through organized, illegal activities. Organized crime groups also aim to infiltrate the legitimate markets (a practice referred to as racketeering). The problem of racketeering has led to the adoption of new laws in the United States, such as the Racketeering Influenced and Corrupt Organization (RICO) Act of 1970, which was aimed at one of the most notable organized crime families in the United States, the Italian Cosa Nostra. Some have argued that organized crime groups are not as organized as we tend to assume and that these groups are mainly driven by market dynamics, which can be quite volatile. For more information, see Reuter (1983).

Other-Orientation   A characteristic of interpersonal effectiveness in which one partner of a communication dyad or group conveys empathy, attentiveness, concern, and interest via verbal and nonverbal cues (also referred to as altercentrism). Such signals include acknowledging and confirming the other's viewpoint.

Other-orientation is contrasted with self-orientation, or egocentrism, in which one interactant or participant is largely self-referential, assumes a shared frame of reference, lacks empathy, and tends to give direct advice.

Other-orientation carries a positive connotation as an indicator of communication competence and skill. While it can be perceived as overly accommodating, it generally indicates an ability to adapt to other people and effectively perceive others' viewpoints.

It is an example of phatic communication, that is, for social purposes and relationship building, as differentiated from the communication of information.

Self-other orientation, which relates to a social-psychological theory of interpersonal communication, is frequently discussed in terms of intimate or other significant relationships. There exists substantial research in the context of organizational psychology, especially relating to managerial skill, job performance, and job satisfaction. *See also* Emotional Communication; Empathetic Listening; Interpersonal Communication

Outcomes-Based Education and Evaluation   A recent accountability trend in educational evaluation focusing on whether students have met intended outcomes, including those knowledge, skills, and attitudes the students should demonstrate after completion of an educational program. Data are systematically collected in the form of carefully selected indicators to show the impact that a program has had on student attainment of the outcomes. Experimental designs allowing firm conclusions of cause and effect, however, are rarely used. Interpretations of the standardized test data are usually made summatively, to claim whether or not the program has met the intended outcomes. Formative evaluation, focusing on how to improve programs in need of improvement, is often deemphasized in this movement. *See also* Goals-Based Evaluation

Out-Group Homogeneity Bias   People perceive the characteristics of members of their own (in)group as more heterogeneous than the characteristics of members of other (out)groups. An intuitive explanation for this bias may be that people are more familiar with and know a larger number of in-group members. However, out-group homogeneity bias has been demonstrated irrespective of the number of members in the in-group and the out-group (Jones, Wood, & Quattrone, 1981). Most notably, out-group homogeneity bias was demonstrated in in-groups and out-groups based on males and females. Out-group homogeneity bias can lead to negative stereotyping of out-group members. For more information, see Jones, Wood, and Quattrone (1981). *See also* In-Group Favoritism

Outward Communication   Information that flows from individuals/employees in an organization to clients of that organization and other players that are interested in the organizational goals and activities. Different from downward or upward communication, outward communication is the spokesperson's chief role in an organization as he or she represents the organization before the public. Consequently, it is extremely important that the employees, and in particular the spokesperson, have a strong grasp and understanding of the philosophy, vision, mission, and objectives of the organization, and it is important how these are communicated to clients of the organization and to the public, depending on the nature of the organization. Clear explanation of policies, rules, and regulations promotes good public relations, and the image of the organization depends on it.

However, there is another important aspect to *outward communication*, which has to do with employees' self-esteem and the way in which they value their work. Such feelings may be transmitted, directly or indirectly, to significant others, who will receive such communication and will interpret it and disseminate it to others. This process will present the organization's goals and activities to other individuals outside the organization and, as a result, may help in shaping the perception of the organization in their eyes. Such outward communication can result in support or lack of support for the organization's goals and activities.

Consequently, when dealing with *outward communication* where employees have the ability to determine what information on the organization is available to individuals outside the organization, clients and the public in general through informal communication, job satisfaction becomes a crucial factor. Job satisfaction is related to open communication lines, positive communication between employees and their immediate supervisors, and personal feedback on job performance. Therefore, all personnel should have access to information when they need it most, such as availability of supervisors, the procedure manual, job descriptions, and work schedules. Such open access will enable them to do their jobs in the most effective and efficient manner. Communication should be clear and understandable. As a result, organizational goals and activities will be perceived clearly by outsiders.

Oversight Function (*political science*)   Under the U.S. Constitution, Congress is charged with the responsibility of government oversight—the review, monitoring, and supervision of operations and activities. Committees and offices are formed by an act of Congress to perform this function, which is a part of the "separation of powers" principle of the Constitution. In oversight, the legislative branch is checking the executive. The oversight function is an implied power of Congress granted under the broad "necessary and proper" clause of Article 1 (Section 8, Clause 18), allowing Congress the authority "to make all laws which shall be necessary and proper for carrying into execution the foregoing powers, and all other powers vested by this Constitution." The Supreme Court in *McGrain v. Daughtery* (1927) upheld this power when deciding on a case involving congressional investigation of the Justice Department. For more information, see *McGrain v. Daughtery* (1927).

Oversight Function (*public administration*)   The crucial governance function related to ensuring accountability and proper operation of an organization. In various types of organizations, this function is typically provided by top management and exists to initiate, scrutinize, and amend legislation; oversee the executive; and approve the budget and scrutinize its implementations relative to the operation of the organization. This authority exists to ensure that proper duties are put in place to protect the integrity of information and related operations associated with the entity. Within the public realm, this authority extends to all aspects of government, including the military, the police, and international relations. The function ensures that the legislature minimizes conflict of interest among its own members and holds the executive accountable for corrupt practices.

Overt Act   An explicit act that is committed in preparation for another crime. The act may be legal in itself but is a step in a series of acts that ultimately leads to a criminal behavior. For instance, purchasing tools that will be used to commit burglary is an example of an overt act.

O

P

Pacifism   The moral ideology that seeks to avoid warfare and embrace peace. There are four major types of pacifist ideologies: (1) pragmatic, (2) vocational, (3) humanistic, and (4) structural. Pragmatic pacifists reject acts of war because such acts will only hurt global peace in the long run, no matter what the short-term goals may be. For example, nuclear pacifists, those against the development of nuclear weapons, are considered pragmatic pacifists. Vocational pacifists oppose war based on the teachings of Christianity; this sentiment can also be derived from other faiths. Humanistic pacifists instead believe that on secular, moral grounds the protection of life is of paramount value, and no goal of war should compromise this value. Finally, structural pacifists are focused on transforming global relations in an effort to eradicate the desire for warfare.

Paleontology   An area of study that aims to investigate all forms of life that existed in previous periods in time. Paleontology is concerned with the study of plant and animal fossils and provides further insight into the social and biological development of human and living beings, and it can inform the study of evolutionary biology.

Panic Disorder *(education)*   An anxiety disorder specified in the *Diagnostic and Statistical Manual of Mental Disorders (DSM)* that is characterized by recurrent panic attacks—severe anxiety with a rapid and unpredictable onset and accompanied by a sense of impending doom, depersonalization, and physical symptoms often confused with a heart attack. In some, this leads to agoraphobia—the avoidance of public places. ***See also*** Anxiety Disorders

Panic Disorder *(psychology)*   A psychiatric condition defined in the *Diagnostic and Statistical Manual of Mental Disorders* (fourth edition; *DSM-IV*) and characterized by chronic, recurrent, and unexpected panic attacks, which are accompanied by either significant behavioral changes, such as rapid heartbeat, dizziness, dyspnea (shortness of breath), and trembling, or at least one month of continuous worry about having other attacks. Attacks on average last a short period, typically 10 minutes or less. For more information, see Reiter, Rifkin, Garssen, and Van Schawk (1989). ***See also*** Psychological Disorder

Papyrus   One of the earliest writing media, widely used in Ancient Egypt and exported to the Mediterranean.

Papyrus (from which *paper* is derived) refers to both the product used for writing and the grassy, marsh plant growing in the Nile delta from which it comes, *Cyperus papyrus*. The wetness of continental Europe rendered papyrus highly vulnerable to decay, although it was a highly stable medium in the dry Egyptian heat. Highly versatile, papyrus was used for making cloth, sails, and rope, as well as paper. The inner pith of the thick papyrus stem was cut lengthwise into long strips and laid side by side in overlapping sheets. Overlapping sheets of equal thickness were laid on top at right angles, and the two layers were press-dried and polished. The result was a thin, fairly flexible length of white material that was not initially bound into a codex, as parchment and paper subsequently were, but rolled into scrolls, using up to 20 sheets of papyrus per roll. Only later, in the Graeco-Roman era, was papyrus sewn into quires and bound. Doing so addressed the problem of the brittleness of papyrus, which was not flexible enough to be unrolled and rolled with much frequency. The script, made with a reed brush on one side of the papyrus, followed the lie of the fibers across the length of the scroll. If the papyrus was reused, it would be written on the back, and the script ran horizontally, against the fiber. Although less expensive than parchment, papyrus was still costly and was recycled (palimpsest). Another cheap alternative for everyday texts was unglazed pottery. The softness of papyrus allowed the development of a quicker, cursive hieratic script. Although it was soon replaced by parchment, papyrus use continued surprisingly for quite some time, until the 11th century in Europe and the 12th century in the Byzantine Empire. ***See also*** Oral Tradition; Parchment; Pictograph (media studies); Printing

Paradigm *(education)*   A set of presuppositions, beliefs, and practices shared by a community of researchers. It is a way of thinking held in common by the group, and it has many of the features of a social culture. A research paradigm includes beliefs about philosophical issues (ontology, epistemology), conceptual systems, research findings, and appropriate methodologies. Thomas Kuhn brought the idea of research paradigms to the attention of social and natural scientists with his famous book *The Structure of Scientific Revolutions* (1962). He argued that science usually operates in a period of conformity called normal science. During normal science, researchers work on what he called *puzzle solving,* meaning specific research problems that are legitimated by the paradigm and that do not challenge the core beliefs of the paradigm. Researchers are socialized into the paradigm by their textbooks, their professors, and professional journals. Books and certain published research studies serve as *exemplars,* which are examples of appropriate research sanctioned by the paradigm. Researchers study these exemplars and emulate them as they learn to become good researchers in the paradigm. Kuhn also famously pointed out that over time, paradigms are challenged by *anomalies,* and at some point, during what he called *revolutionary science,* paradigms are replaced by new paradigms that are radically different. For example, Newton's classical physics was replaced by Einstein's general relativity and quantum physics during the first 30 years of the 20th century. Paradigms are said to be *incommensurable,* which means that different paradigms have radically different languages and definitions and views of the world; this results in difficulty in communication across paradigms. People in different paradigms define concepts in different ways, and they "see" and experience different worlds because of the influence of the paradigm. One paradigm change in psychology was the shift in the adherence of many researchers from behaviorism to cognitivism. Because behaviorism still is used along with cognitivism in psychology, psychology would appear to fit into what Kuhn called a *preparadigmatic* discipline, which he thought was common in the young sciences. The concept of the paradigm is commonly used in education and literature to refer to different "epistemologies," and each is said to have its own set of appropriate or legitimate methods. At the broad level, the methodological paradigms are divided into quantitative research, qualitative research, and mixed-methods research. At the more epistemological level, paradigms include constructivism, critical theory, poststructuralism, postmodernism, feminism, and several other "standpoint epistemologies." Paradigm debates in education and the social sciences often concern what knowledge is, what kinds of research issues researchers should focus on, what methodologies are appropriate, the role of values in research, and appropriate standards for judging the quality of research. For more information, see Kuhn (1962). *See also* Theory (psychology)

Paradigm *(sociology)*   A model used by a scientific discipline to support given theories or laws. A paradigm determines the subject matter to be observed, why it needs to be observed, and how the results should be interpreted. Paradigms give legitimacy to theories and may be useful in uniting different theories under one broad category. *See also* Theory (sociology)

Paralanguage   Verbal elements of speech that communicate variations of meaning and emotion. The pitch, volume, and intonation of speech can affect how one understands a message. That is why the reading of a transcript of a speech, trial, radio program, and the like

is no substitute for hearing the speech patterns that convey nuances of meaning. Paralanguage plays a very important role in human speech. Paralanguage comprises sounds that sometimes do not have a written form. Examples of paralanguage include whistling, shushing, and hissing, as well as speech changes, such as the quality of the voice or the speed with which we speak. Other examples of paralanguage include sighing, crying, and sneezing. The tone of voice plays a big role in how we communicate. *See also* Speech

Paranoia   A symptom of mental illness comprising intense delusional fears or suspicions about other people, with anxiety that someone else intends to do harm to the self. Patients with psychological disorders, such as schizophrenia, or under the influence of certain drugs may manifest paranoia. *See also* Psychological Disorder

Paraprofessional   An individual trained to assist a certificated or licensed teacher in the K–12 setting. Paraprofessionals, also referred to as teaching assistants, teachers' aides, or instructional-support personnel, have grown in number since the 1960s, in response to the demand for more individualized student attention in the classroom.

Parapsychology   The study of paranormal psychological phenomena. Paranormal refers to unusual experiences that are not easily explained by known scientific principles. Some of the phenomena studied include psychokinesis, extrasensory perception, telepathy, hypnotism, apparitions, materialization, and survival of consciousness after death. Most paranormal phenomena can be categorized into either mental (obtaining information in paranormal ways) or physical (paranormal influences on physical objects) events. The Society for Psychical Research was the first formal gathering of parapsychologists and was founded in 1882 in London. This was the first systematic effort to organize scholars investigating paranormal phenomena. Parapsychology is considered a fringe science by some as it does not fit into the standard theoretical models accepted by mainstream science. For more information, see Irwin and Watt (2007).

Parasympathetic Nervous System (PNS)   A division of the autonomic nervous system. The PNS causes slowing down of the heartbeat, lowering of blood pressure, constriction of the pupils, increased blood flow to and from the skin, and peristalsis of the gastrointestinal (GI) tract. The PNS's major function is to return the body functions to normal after they have been alerted by sympathetic simulation. The PNS works in complement with the sympathetic nervous system. When the body senses danger, the sympathetic system prepares it to deal with this danger, and the PNS reverses this system when the danger has passed. The PNS is a portion of the visceral branch of the peripheral nervous system. The main nerves of the PNS are the 10th cranial nerves, also known as the vagus nerves. For more information, see Robertson, Low, and Polinsky (1996). **See also** Central Nervous System CNS

Parchment Animal skin (usually of sheep, goats, or calves) used as a writing surface. The term is often used interchangeably with *vellum,* which strictly speaking denotes only calfskin (Latin *vitellus,* "little calf"), which is top-grade parchment. Modern parchment can also refer to a high-grade paper made from wood pulp and rags and given a polished finish. The word derives from the Latin *pergamenum,* named after the Greek city of Pergamum, in Asia Minor. The story goes that its extensive library so rivaled that of Alexandria that the Egyptians placed an embargo on the export of papyrus, provoking Pergamum to improvise—hence the use of parchment. The material and lengthy preparation of parchment makes it a highly expensive medium. There is the sacrifice of an animal that if kept alive could provide wool or milk indefinitely. The flayed skin was soaked for days in a softening and detergent agent, such as lime. Scraping removed hair and flesh from the outer dermal layer. The skin had to be stretched tight on a wooden frame to achieve the necessary tension for scraping with sharp knives. Proper scraping was essential to ensure that the parchment could be used on both sides. Any adhering flesh would leave an intolerable stink. The scraped skin, once dry, was powdered to minimize grease spots, which resisted ink. Another scraping, and the material was ready to be cut, folded, and sewn into quires or gatherings and then bound into a codex. The copyist would buff the pages to give them grain and texture and to ensure absorption of the ink without bleeding. Before any writing began, the page itself had to be pricked, ruled, and planned out into guidelines in order to align the letters. The strength of parchment enabled the use of goose quills for writing, which offered a wider range of effects than reed brushes. **See also** Oral Tradition; Papyrus; Pictograph (media studies); Printing

Pardon The act of forgiving an individual for having committed a crime, usually granted by the government or some other sovereign power. An individual is eligible for a pardon when he or she is deemed to have repaid his debt to society. The pardon implies that the individual is no longer under the obligation to reveal (e.g., to potential employers) that he or she has been convicted of a crime in the past.

Parens Patriae A form of power granted to the state whereby the state aims to defend the best interests of individuals who are legally unable to do so themselves. Examples include cases involving children, individuals with mental disabilities, and other vulnerable individuals. In these instances, the state is the designated guardian of the vulnerable individuals and seeks to protect their interests.

Parental Involvement in Schools The relationships between parents or guardians, teachers, and members of school communities. Parental involvement has four goals: (1) offering parents opportunities to meaningfully influence educational programs and environments, (2) providing continuity between the home and the educational context, (3) creating a forum for parent education, and (4) empowering parents to set goals for their children and families. Parental involvement supports parents in their child-rearing roles and teachers in their educational roles and builds a feeling of community. Levels of involvement range from *minimum* (playing a supportive role for existing school programs, e.g., homework supervision or fund-raising), to *associate* (being vital in implementing existing programs, e.g., as classroom volunteers, library personnel, or PTA members), to *decision making* (sharing responsibility with school personnel for decisions regarding the future of the school and the quality of education, e.g., in governing boards or curriculum committees). Parent involvement is essential for reform and a factor in student success, improved attitudes, and higher graduation rates. For more information, see Olsen and Fuller (2007). **See also** School Reform

Parent Effectiveness Training (PET) A method of intervening in child behavior problems put forth by Thomas Gordon, who was influenced by person-centered therapy. PET eschews the use of punishment in favor of teaching children self-reliance. This is accomplished by the parent and child engaging in collaborative, noncoercive problem solving to arrive at mutually beneficial solutions. For more information, see Gordon (2000).

Parity Principle An approach to organizing a system in which there are parties with competing economic interests. Each party is given equal weight in the decision-making process. The classic example would be a union and the owners of the business with whom it negotiates a labor contract. Consequently, the entities created by collective agreement are usually administered by joint bodies composed of equal numbers of representatives from both sides.

Parliament The form of legislature existing in the United Kingdom. It is also common in countries based on the Westminster political system. In England, the role of the parliament is to examine and challenge the work of the executive branch, debate and pass all laws, and enable the government to raise taxes. There are two houses: the House of Commons and the House of Lords; the laws passed by one house, besides finance-related ones, which are within the purview of the House of Commons only, need to be approved by the other house. The House of Commons, composed of publically elected officials, holds the power to make legislation. The political party that wins the majority of seats in the House of Commons forms the government, or executive

P

branch. The party's leader becomes prime minister and appoints appropriate cabinet positions. The House of Lords is in the majority composed of appointments by the Queen, on the advice of the prime minister and the lord chancellor, and the bishops and archbishops of the Church of England. The House of Lords also passes legislation. England's highest court, the court of last appeals, is located in the House of Lords, until 2009, when a new 12-member supreme court will be created according to the Constitutional Reform Act of 2005. This court is scheduled to begin operation in October 2009. *See also* Legislature

Parole   Conditional release of a prisoner from prison to the community, under the supervision of a parole officer. The parolee may remain in the community if he or she respects the conditions for parole, which are imposed by the court. Parole conditions vary according to the individual, offense, and state. Conditions may include restrictions regarding living conditions or location, travel, activities, associations with certain individuals, employment, and so on. Parolees are required to report to their parole officers on a regular basis and may also be required to attend various programs or other forms of therapy, including substance use treatment programs, psychiatric treatment, anger management groups, and so on. If parolees do not fulfill the conditions for conditional release imposed by the court, parole may be revoked and the parolee may be sent back to prison. Parole is a type of community correction and is similar to probation with regard to the conditions imposed on the offender. *See also* Community-Based Corrections; Probation

Partial Reinforcement Effect   An effect wherein a behavior that is reinforced intermittently is more resistant to becoming extinct than a behavior that is continuously reinforced. In partial reinforcement schedules, only some responses are reinforced during learning, not each and every response. Thus, a behavior that is observed under this treatment shows increased resistance to extinction as well as increased performance. The predictability of behavior under reinforcement schedules was advanced by B. F. Skinner, using operant conditioning. The reliability of the schedules led to the development of applied behavior analysis as a means of controlling behavior. An example of a partial reinforcement schedule is the variable ratio schedule. Under this, reinforcement is delivered after a random number of responses that is based on a predetermined average. For more information, see Chance (2003) and Skinner (1938). *See also* Reinforcement

Participant Observation *(education)*   A set of ethnographic research methods in which the researcher gathers data by participating directly in a group's activities within their natural context. The goal of such research is to capture insights from the perspective of group members about their knowledge, attitudes, and patterns of behavior. *See also* Ethnography (education); Qualitative Research

Participant Observation *(sociology)*   A research strategy whereby an observer studies an individual or group of individuals to become familiar with their customs and practices. The observer is involved with the observed individual(s) in their natural habitat. Participant observation entails direct participation by the observer in the lives of the observed individual(s). One of the main benefits of participant observation relates to the fact that the observer has direct access to the research information. The main caveat associated with participant observation is the bias created by the knowledge of being observed. Social desirability may alter the routine behaviors and attitudes of the individual(s) being observed. *See also* Ethnography (sociology); Qualitative Research

Participant-Observer   A person observing while participating in a qualitative research study. A participant-observer will live with or become a part of the social group or phenomenon he or she is studying to gain a full understanding of what is being studied. It is important that the participant-observer maintain a balance between the two terms *participant* and *observer* to maintain his or her observer status. This will allow the researcher to analyze what is being studied while minimizing bias. Critics note the large potential for bias, not only in observations but also in the way terms are defined and concepts are described. Proponents argue that there is no more bias in this method then there is in a qualitative research survey. For public administrators, participant observation can provide a wealth of information about public policies. The use of participant-observer studies can help public administrators understand how policy decisions directly affect a group in society. *See also* Public Policy

Participatory Evaluation   Evaluation that is not controlled by external entities but rather is a form of self-assessment in which the participants of a program and other primary stakeholders are involved with the collection and interpretation of data to be used for improvement purposes. The goal of involving the primary stakeholders in the evaluation process is to identify the most relevant questions, to empower individuals to become involved and emerge as leaders, and to encourage involvement in improvement. Challenges of participatory evaluation include the time and cost associated with all stages of the process, limited training on how to conduct the evaluation, and the potential for conflicts. Often, an external evaluator will help facilitate the process in the role of a guide or a coach. *See also* Evaluation, Logic of

Participatory Management   An organizational leadership approach to management that gives more opportunity to workers or employees to influence decisions about their work and working conditions. When participatory management is first implemented, this type of organizational leadership may require systemic change in an organization. Projected results include increased morale and productivity.

Passive Listening The act of hearing without making comments or showing reactions while another person speaks. The listener's lack of comment or reaction may be a conscious or unconscious choice.

Passive listening is the opposite of active listening, in that the one who is hearing is not interested in comprehending the underlying messages beneath the content of the words voiced, is not evaluating the speaker fairly, and is not reconsidering previously held attitudes. Passive listening also is the opposite of empathetic listening in that the active hearer is not responding to the sentiments or underlying messages voiced by the speaker and is not expressing a perception of what the speaker is saying. A passive listener makes no attempt to ask questions in order to demonstrate involvement or to reinforce the speaker's perspective.

Studies in the fields of education, medicine, psychiatry, and psychology, for instance, show passive listening to be the least effective listening approach for bringing about positive results for students, patients, or mental health consumers. For instance, a 1969 study showed that blind students in various grade levels learned much better under active than passive learning conditions.

The results of an assessment of medical residents in psychiatry published in 2006 showed that they tend to listen to patients in a passive manner, without comment or empathetic response. The researchers recommend that residents take a more proactive approach to listening to their patients and suggest that psychiatric training prepare the doctors for active, empathetic listening. For more information, see Nolan and Morris (1969) and Rimondini et al. (2006). **See also** Active Listening (communication); Critical Listening; Empathetic Listening; Evaluative Listening

Pastoral Counseling A subfield of the counseling profession, in which clergy of various types provide mental health services by combining religiously based teachings and ministering with counseling/psychotherapy techniques derived from the secular-scientific community. Pastoral counseling is limited by its frequent lack of recognition by state licensure boards and insurance companies. **See also** Counseling

Patent A legal document in which the government decrees exclusive rights to an inventor to produce, use, and sell a given product for a determined period of time. The purpose of the patent is to protect inventors in highly competitive markets and to ensure that they are given the opportunity to reap the benefits of their invention(s). The patent disallows other parties from producing, using, or selling the inventor's product.

Paternalism A method of social control where an individual's actions are constrained "for their own good" by the state. Legal paternalism refers to laws created by the state to protect citizens from their own behavior; laws considered paternalistic include motorcycle helmet regulations, seat-belt laws, and the criminalization of suicide. Critics of legal paternalism find it demeaning; the end result might be a citizenry who have lost their powers of rational judgment. The British philosopher John Stuart Mill (1806–1873), an ardent defender of individual liberties, proposed the "harm principle," meaning that the state is justified in limiting individual freedom when harm will be caused to others but not when protecting individuals against themselves (unless one's faculties are limited). Proponents argue that the absence of paternalism in the legal system would lead to grave moral consequences that allow for individual vices or crimes against the self. Paternalistic laws can also serve to uphold the moral fabric of a given society (e.g., laws to regulate prostitution or homosexuality). A recent controversy involving legal paternalism revolves around the banning of trans fats. Medical studies have found that regular ingestion of trans fats is harmful to one's health; it can lead to high cholesterol and clogged arteries and aggravate diabetes. The benefit of trans fat is that it increases a food product's shelf life and enhances its taste. Despite protests from civil libertarians and the restaurant industry, New York City, in 2006, became the first major American municipality to ban the serving of trans fats in restaurants. For more information, see Dworkin (1972). **See also** Liberty

Path Analysis The combination of regression analysis with a graphic causal model. Like all forms of regression analysis, path analysis predicts or explains a dependent (or outcome) variable using information about one or more independent (or predictor) variables. The graphic model allows researchers to study both the direct and the indirect effects of the independent variables on the dependent variable. Figure 1 is a simple path diagram measuring the effects on adult income (dependent variable) of education and parents' income (independent variables).

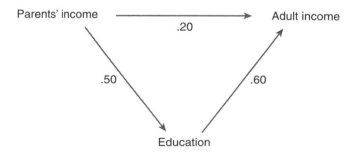

Figure 1 *Path Diagram*

The diagram shows that parents' income influences adult income directly, and indirectly through education. Is the direct effect stronger or the indirect effect? This can be determined by the numbers on the arrows; these are path coefficients, which are standardized regression coefficients. The direct effect is .20. The indirect effect is calculated by multiplying the path coefficients: $.50 \times .60 = .30$, which is larger than the direct effect. ***See also*** Regression Analysis; Structural Equation Modeling

Pathology   The science concerned with the origin of diseases, as well as the diagnosis and treatment of these diseases. In human pathology, this is achieved through examination of the human anatomy. There are two main areas of pathology: (1) anatomical pathology and (2) clinical pathology. Clinical pathology aims to investigate diseases based on bodily fluids (i.e., blood, urine, saliva). Anatomical pathology studies diseases based on tissues and organs. The science of pathology extends to nonhumans, such as animals (referred to as veterinary pathology) and plants (i.e., phytopathology). It can also be extended to psychological explanations of behavior (i.e., psychopathology).

Pathos   In rhetorical persuasion, there are three primary techniques. They are pathos, ethos, and logos. Pathos appeals to the audience's emotions. Such emotional appeal can be conveyed by the way a story is told or by the passion used in the delivery of a speech. The Greek philosopher Aristotle (384–322 BCE), in his *Ars Rhetorica,* laid the groundwork for all subsequent studies of the art of persuasion, of which pathos is the emotional component. For more information, see Aristotle (1959). ***See also*** Ethos; Logos

Patriarchy *(political science)*   A political or social system where men dominate in politics and family life. Patriarchy is a universal phenomenon and can be found in virtually every society in varying degrees. Reasons for the prevalence of patriarchy can be traced back to the beginnings of human life; these revolve around the biological differences between the sexes, such as women's ability to give birth and the accompanying responsibility of caring for the young. A second reason is men's superior physical strength, which allows them to take part in warfare, where great status was traditionally attained. In the United States, patriarchy is evidenced by the small number of female politicians, including the fact that no woman has ever been elected president. Inequality is also expressed in the extremely low number of female CEOs and the "pay gap," with women earning on average 70% of a man's salary for the same job. ***See also*** Matriarchy

Patriarchy *(sociology)*   A social structure in which the male figure is predominant in society, namely, in institutions such as the family, as well as in economic, political, religious, and other social institutions. In the household, the male is considered to be the representative of the family and takes primary responsibility for the welfare of his family. In a patriarchal society, males are granted authority over females and children, and the social structure is governed by males. In contrast to patriarchy, a matriarchal society refers to a social structure characterized by the predominance of female figures. ***See also*** Matriarchy

Patrol   The act of observing or monitoring a given area to ensure safety, security, or order. Patrol is generally carried out by skilled and trained individuals (police officers, security staff, etc.) and in a wide range of contexts. For instance, police officers perform daily patrol duties by supervising and monitoring activities and behaviors in public spaces. Police patrol became common in the 1970s during the reform/professional era of policing. Patrol aims to deter potential criminals from committing acts in a particular place. The effectiveness of patrol as a deterrent strategy has been questioned in studies such as the Kansas City Patrol Experiment. ***See also*** Kansas City Patrol Experiment

Pattern Matching   A method of theory conceptualization, data collection, and data interpretation commonly used when the number of cases is small, as in comparative case study research, or when subjects are not assigned randomly to control and experimental groups, as in quasi experiments. There are two basic types of pattern-matching analyses, focusing on (1) patterns in groups of *dependent* variables or (2) patterns in groups of *independent* variables. In the first type, the researcher might predict that a treatment or a program intervention would lead to a cluster of related outcomes. In the second type, a researcher predicts that instances of a particular outcome will be associated with a patterned group of independent variables. In the first case, the cause is known, and a pattern of outcomes is sought. In the second, the outcome is known, and a pattern of potential causes is investigated.

Pattern *matching* is also a field of computer science in which software is used to search for and identify specific sequences of symbols in long texts. Pattern *recognition* consists of searching for less strictly specified configurations of symbols. Pattern recognition is also a part of cognitive psychology; the emphasis is on identifying shapes, faces, texts, music, and so on. For more information, see Shadish, Cook, and Campbell (2002). ***See also*** Data, Extant/Existing; Variable (education)

Pauses   *See* Paralanguage

Peace Officer   An officer of the law who is responsible for enforcing and maintaining public order and peace. Examples of peace officers include police officers, customs officers, and probation and parole officers.

Pedagogy   Various methods, principles, strategies, techniques, theories, and philosophies employed by teachers during instructional activities. The term is often used to refer to the teaching of both children and adults, although some prefer to use the term *andragogy* when referring specifically to the teaching of adults. ***See also*** Liberation Pedagogy

Pedophilia/Pedophile A paraphilia (sexual disorder) that is characterized by a sexual preference for pre-pubescent children; a person who has this disorder. The American Psychiatric Association's *Diagnostic and Statistical Manual of Mental Disorders* (fourth edition; *DSM-IV-TR*) lists the following diagnostic criteria for pedophilia (sect. 302.2):

> A. Over a period of at least 6 months, [the person has experienced] recurrent, intense sexually arousing fantasies, sexual urges, or behaviors involving sexual activity with a prepubescent child or children (generally age 13 years or younger).

> B. The person has acted on these sexual urges, or the sexual urges or fantasies cause marked distress or interpersonal difficulty.

> C. The person is at least age 16 years and at least 5 years older than the child or children in Criterion A.

See also Sex Offense/Crime; Sexual Offender

Peel, Sir Robert The prime minister of the United Kingdom between 1834–1835 and 1841–1846. In 1829, when he was Home Secretary of England, he founded the first police force in Great Britain and created the Metropolitan Police. Sir Robert Peel advocated for many principles that form the basis of modern community policing practices. Peel believed that the police's main mandate was to prevent crime and disorder and that this should be achieved with minimal disturbances and intrusion in the lives of community members. Peel's policing model also emphasized the importance of partnership and collaboration between the police and community members. ***See also*** Law Enforcement

Penal Codes/Laws The part of a state's legal code that defines crimes and their punishment. Every state has its own penal code, in which it specifies the elements of each criminal offense and the range of punishments that might be imposed for the commission of the offense. ***See also*** Criminal Law (political science, sociology); Felon/Felony; Misdemeanor; Punishment (sociology); Statute/Statutory Law

Penology The science of punishment and its effects. Penology is sometimes described as a subarea within criminology. Although scholars of penology often study penitentiaries and prisons, the science of punishment encompasses the theories of punishment and social control through the management strategies of correctional administrators. Some penologists study penitentiary science (or the practice of institutional

punishment), while others study the evolution of penal law. Many of the most famous penologists of the past were penal reformers and correctional administrators (e.g., John Howard and Zebulon Brockway). Those who identify themselves as penologists today are quite often sociologists or criminologists whose area of expertise is in the area of punishment. ***See also*** Criminology; Deterrence (political science, sociology); Incapacitate; Penal Codes/Laws; Rehabilitation; Retribution

Percentile The percentage of cases that fall below a specific value in a distribution. For example, the 65th percentile is the value in a distribution below which 65% of the cases fall. The median of a distribution is equal to the 50th percentile. ***See also*** Descriptive Statistics (education, sociology)

Perception *(communication)* The intuitive process by which humans interpret the sounds, smells, and sights of the world around them. On a higher plane, perception refers to how humans intuit the verbal and non-verbal interactions between themselves and other individuals.

Perception is a broad term open to interpretation by scientists and social scientists, and perceptional concepts are studied in a variety of disciplines, including anthropology, biology, communications, education, health care, management, political science, psychology, and sociology. Perception is often linked to biases and prejudices concerning the political and religious views, the economic and cultural identities, and the physical appearances of other people. People react to each other depending on how they perceive their worth and their likeliness to be compatriots or adversaries.

Humans give names and symbols to the objects, events, and processes they observe in the world, as noted by the communications theorist James W. Carey; he added that language itself can distort perceptions of reality. For more information, see Carey (1992) and Neuliep, Hintz, and McCroskey (2005). ***See also*** Body Language; Cognition; Ethnocentrism (communication); Nonverbal Communication

Perception *(psychology)* The process of acquiring, selecting, interpreting, and organizing sensory information in the mind. Human beings perceive their environment and interpret information taken in through the senses. Human attention is selective in that we selectively attend to certain information while relegating other information to the background. There are a number of theories on how we perceive information and interpret and process it. The most well-known is the work of Gestalt psychologists, who believe that the whole is greater than the sum of its parts. For example, when you see a single dot, you perceive it as such, but when you see five dots grouped together, you see a line of dots and do not perceive them individually. They outlined several principles that influence the way we organize basic sensory input into whole patterns, such as

P

figure and ground theory, grouping, perceptual constancies, and illusions. For more information, see Gibson (1987). *See also* Perceptual Set

Perceptual Set   The tendency to see in a particular way that is based on one's experiences, emotions, expectations, and assumptions about the world. It is the readiness to detect a particular stimulus in a given context. For example, a new mother is perceptually set to hear the cries of her child. Oftentimes, a perceptual set will lead one to transform an ambiguous stimulus into one that the person was not expecting. People can develop very different views of the same situation and create different sets. A person's context and perceptual set can influence his or her attitude toward groups of people. For more information, see Bruner (1957). *See also* Perception (communication, sociology)

Peremptory Challenge   A right granted to the defense and prosecution teams during the *voir dire* to disallow the selection of particular potential jurors on the basis of personal biases that these individuals may have toward the case. Peremptory challenge seeks to create an objective and impartial jury and serves the purpose of ensuring a just and unbiased trial. Because both defense and prosecution teams provide input in the selection of jurors, preemptory challenge also results in a reduced likelihood that either side would view the verdict as biased or unjust. Counsel has a limited number of peremptory challenges and does not have to state the reason for dismissal of the potential juror. The reasons for dismissal cannot be based on gender or race. *See also* Jury

Perfect Competition   An idealized market structure with the following assumptions: (a) buyers and sellers have perfect knowledge of what is going on in the market place, (b) there are many buyers and sellers, (c) there is unrestricted entry into and out of the market, (d) the good in question is homogeneous (of the same quality), and (e) the seller of the product has limited or no control over the price (price taker) in the marketplace because of competition. The perfect competitor, therefore, faces an infinitely elastic demand curve, which is equal to his or her marginal revenue and average revenue.

The idealism of perfect competition serves the useful theoretical purpose of explaining why competition in the marketplace leads to an efficient outcome in the long run when all inputs are variable. Profit maximization, which is attractive in the short run because of the lack of restrictions to entry and the potential to earn economic profit, will allow other firms to enter the market. As firms enter the market, the available profit will be competed away, and some firms will exit the market. In the long run, the price that will prevail in the market will be equivalent to the least per unit cost (productive efficiency) and the cost of the scarce resources used to produce a good in alternative markets (allocative efficiency). For more information, see McConnell and Brue (2008), Salvatore (2002), and Schiller (2006). *See also* Elasticity; Equilibrium; Market Forces

Performance Appraisal *(education)*   The process of evaluating the quantity and quality of employees' work efforts. Performance appraisals are usually part of a broader performance management system that clarifies performance expectations, provides positive and corrective feedback regarding performance, and rewards employees for successful performance. Performance management systems encourage individuals to fulfill their responsibilities in order to ensure that the organization achieves its objectives. Performance appraisals serve three purposes: (1) to motivate employee productivity, (2) to identify training and development needs, and (3) to provide a basis for human resource (HR) decisions, such as pay, promotion, and termination.

Although no federal law requires employers to use formal performance appraisal systems, courts have consistently ruled that when performance appraisal results are used to make employment decisions, performance appraisals qualify as *tests* according to the *Uniform Guidelines on Employee Selection Procedures*. Thus, the contents of the performance appraisal must match the contents of the job, and performance appraisals must accurately measure job performance if the results are used in making HR decisions.

Since the content of performance appraisals should be reflected in the content of the jobs, the first step in the appraisal process is conducting job analyses to identify the tasks, duties, and responsibilities associated with each job. After the job duties and responsibilities are clarified, the performance standards for each are set. Performance standards may be based on nonjudgmental objective measurements, such as the number of units produced or tasks completed or the quality of production; or performance may be measured using subjective estimates of performance. Performance standards included in the appraisal should cover all important job dimensions. If important job dimensions are omitted, the appraisal is deficient. If the appraisal includes performance standards that are irrelevant to job performance, the appraisal is contaminated.

Several appraisal sources are available. Most frequently, a supervisor is the only appraiser of employees' performance. Some organizations allow subordinates to appraise their managers' performance, peers to assess coworker performance, and customers to assess the performance of employees with whom they interact, and some require self-assessments. A 360-degree appraisal collects perceptions of employee performance from several sources to provide a full-circle view of performance. Most experts agree that 360-degree appraisals should only be used for developmental purposes and not for HR decisions such as pay or promotions.

Performance is usually assessed either by comparing one employee's performance with another's or by comparing each employee's performance with performance standards. Appraisal methods comparing employees' performance include simple ranking, alternative ranking, paired comparisons, and forced distribution. Methods comparing an employee's performance against performance standards include graphic rating scales, behavior observation scales, mixed-standard scales, behaviorally anchored rating scales, and management by objectives (MBO).

The accuracy of performance appraisals depends on appraisers' abilities to avoid common rater biases or errors that tend to distort appraisal results. Common rater errors are leniency, severity, and central tendency (rating all employees at the high end of the rating scale, at the low end of the scale, and near the center of the scale on all dimensions, respectively). Other common rater errors include the halo and horn effects (rating an employee high or low on all job dimensions despite different levels of performance on each dimension).

An effective appraisal allows the rater to distinguish the strengths and weaknesses of each employee and allows raters to distinguish high performers from low performers. *See also* Evaluation (education)

Performance Appraisal *(public administration)* An evaluation of how well an employee has performed his or her job duties within an organization. It is usually based on the measurement of an individual's achievement of specific goals within a specified time period. A performance appraisal may be used to (a) identify an individual's training needs, (b) provide documentation for funding or grant requirements, (c) facilitate personnel changes (e.g., promotions, demotions, or changes in salaries), (d) improve the operation of an organization, and (e) provide feedback to the employee about his or her ability to perform specific job duties. Performance appraisals are normally conducted at regular intervals. *See also* Evaluation; Organization (public administration)

Performance Assessment An assessment that requires students to demonstrate and apply skill or ability to complete a hands-on task. For example, the performance task may require students to produce a product, a written response, or a spoken answer or complete a simulation. The student may be assessed on the completed product or on the processes used during the task. Performance assessments are also sometimes called authentic assessment, as the tasks that are used tend to model realistic situations. One example would be tests of driving ability used for issuing a driver's license. To standardize the scoring of a performance task as much as possible, a scoring rubric is used. *See also* Rubrics

Performance Auditing The execution of an appraisal to determine whether a program, function, operation, or management system or the procedures of a governmental or nonprofit entity are effective, efficient, and fulfilling their objectives. While entities, specifically governmental at the federal and state levels, are sometimes required to retain external audit bodies, usually the examination may be conducted by internal auditors. The process is intended to be objective and systematic and is usually executed using structured and documented methodologies. A performance audit usually has two parts: (1) an economy and efficiency review, which determines whether resources were used

efficiently, and (2) a program review, which evaluates whether resources were used for the purpose intended by the grantor of the resources.

The typical performance audit, like all audits, has three phases: (1) planning, (2) fieldwork, and (3) reporting. Prior to commencing the performance audit, its scope and plan must be defined. After determining specific objectives, a preliminary survey is conducted to obtain the information needed to write an audit program and estimate a budget.

Performance-Based Evaluation An evaluation that assesses programs or individuals on the basis of what they can do. The standard of achievement is the demonstrated ability to perform some act or accomplish a goal. For example, a piano student would be assessed by his or her ability to play a piece, not by his or her knowledge of music theory evaluated with a multiple-choice examination. *See also* Evaluation (education)

Performance Test A type of test intended to measure a person's ability to demonstrate the application of knowledge or skills on a given task. Performance tests tend to be constructed-response tests, in which a student both gives the response to a question and demonstrates the process by which the answer is obtained. *See also* Performance Assessment

Period An interval of time in which events of particular significance have occurred and that highlight a significant turning point. A period is shorter than an era but longer than an epoch. *See also* Epoch

Peripheral Nervous System (PNS) A part of the nervous system that facilitates communication between the central nervous system (CNS) and other parts of the body. The PNS consists of two types of cells—(1) those that carry information to the CNS (sensory nervous cells) and (2) those that carry information from the CNS (motor nervous cells). Sensory cells send information to the CNS from the organs or external stimuli. Motor cells carry information from the brain to the organs, muscles, and glands. For more information, see Robertson, Low, and Polinsky (1996). *See also* Central Nervous System (CNS)

Perjury A deliberate attempt to misinform and mislead. In legal cases, individuals who address the court are asked to take an oath before their testimony, promising to provide the truth and accurate facts. Perjury occurs in cases where the testimony fails to provide the truth to the best of the knowledge of the individual being questioned. Perjury is a criminal offense. *See also* Trial

Perpetrator An individual who has committed an offense. While this term generally refers to engagement in criminal offenses, it can also allude to other forms of offending. *See also* Offender/Offense

Personality An individual's unique and relatively stable pattern of behavior, thoughts, and emotions. The study of personality has been undertaken throughout the history of psychology, yet the debate still remains as to whether individual personalities are stable enough over time to warrant their study. Some state that people show too much variability across situations and that no stable predictions about behavior can be made from personality. Others argue that there is ample evidence to show that people behave in a consistent manner across situations, and even if contrasting patterns are displayed at times, these are functionally equivalent for that person. That is, the behaviors have the same meaning for the individual. Thus, behavior in any given situation is a complex interaction of both personality features and the situational factors of the world around us. This is known as the interactionist perspective and is currently accepted by most psychologists. There are numerous theories of personality, with contrasting views of the origins and nature of human uniqueness. None of these theories are accepted as a whole by psychologists, but each offers new insights and a unique view of the study of personality. For more information, see Nelson and Miller (1995). **See also** Personality Disorders (psychology)

Personality Disorders (education)   A family of 10 disorders specified in the *Diagnostic and Statistical Manual of Mental Disorders* (fourth edition; *DSM-IV*), which are divided into three groups (1) odd or eccentric; (2) dramatic, emotional, erratic, or manipulative; and (3) anxious, obsessive, or fearful. Personality disorders are listed on Axis II in the *DSM* system, whereas most other disorders are on Axis I. This distinction reflects the fact that personality disorders are chronic and enduring and are essentially maladaptive problems present within the individual's overall lifestyle and personality organization. Research suggests that personality disorders are highly resistant to both psychotherapy and medication, though recent research has yielded evidence-based psychotherapies for some of these disorders. *See also* Diagnostic and Statistical Manual (DSM) (education)

Personality Disorders (psychology)   A set of maladaptive and stable characteristics that are characterized by ongoing and rigid patterns of thought. These behavioral patterns are often inflexible, causing personal and social difficulties, as well as impairment in normal functioning. These behavioral deviations are manifested in cognition, affect, interpersonal functioning, or impulse control. Personalities are generally described as dramatic, antisocial, or obsessive. Individuals suffering from these disorders do not view their behavior as strange but as normal and beneficial—especially to them. Personality disorders have been grouped into three major clusters by psychologists. Cluster A includes those disorders that are marked by odd, eccentric behavior, including paranoid, schizoid, and schizotypal personality disorders. Cluster B consists of those disorders that are marked by dramatic, emotional behavior and include histrionic, narcissistic, antisocial, and borderline personality disorders. Cluster C disorders are characterized by anxious and fearful behaviors that include obsessive-compulsive, avoidant, and dependent personality disorders. There is no cure for personality disorders, and they are for the most part untreatable. Therapy and medication can help control them to a certain extent if the individual makes the conscious decision to take control of his or her own life. This is necessary to break the enduring pattern of a personality disorder. Some risks that have been found to act as precursors to the development of personality disorders are childhood abuse and neglect. Additionally, most personality disorders begin as problems in personal development that become prominent during adolescence. For example, a strong genetic link has been found with antisocial and borderline personality disorders. For more information, see Marshall and Serin (1997). **See also** *Diagnostic and Statistical Manual* (DSM) (psychology)

Personality Test   Tests that theoretically measure abstract personality traits, which vary in their presence in human beings and predispose individuals to certain patterns of thinking, feeling, and behaving. Prominent nonclinical uses include personnel screening/selection and career guidance. Typical clinical uses involve making determinations about the presence of maladaptive patterns of behavior or personality traits. **See also** Personality

Person-Centered Therapy (PCT)   An approach to counseling and psychotherapy developed by the humanist psychologist Carl Rogers in the 1940s. The defining purpose of PCT, also known as client-centered therapy, was to have a more personal relationship with patients and help them reach a state of realization so that they can help themselves. PCT is based on the theory that all patients, no matter what their difficulty, can improve without being taught anything specific by the therapist given a supportive environment that helps them achieve personal growth. PCT uses a nondirective approach, whereby patients are encouraged to express their feelings while the therapist listens and reflects on those revelations without analyzing what the feelings mean or offering suggested remedies. This is done with the goal of helping patients explore and understand their feelings for themselves. Patients are thus able to decide what kind of changes they would like to make, thereby achieving personal growth. Some of the core concepts of this therapy include (a) congruence—the therapist should openly express feelings and emotions that are flowing in the moment, (b) unconditional positive regard—the therapist should experience a positive attitude toward the client, (c) empathic understanding—the need to employ reflection and clarification in order to develop a deep understanding of the client, and (d) the actualizing tendency—it is the role of the therapist to provide conditions for personal development and growth. Though this type of therapeutic approach is generally not considered to be effective for severe psychopathologies, such as schizophrenia, components of this therapeutic style have had a great influence on many psychotherapeutic interactions. For more information, see Rogers (1980). *See also* Humanistic Theory

Personnel Evaluation   An assessment of personnel for purposes such as selection, performance appraisal, promotion, demotion, and merit increases. As a practice, personnel evaluation dates back at least to the civil servant examinations of the Chinese and Egyptian dynasties, more than 4,000 years ago. In the past 100 years, the principles and procedures of personnel evaluation have predominately come from the applied domains of work, and industrial and organizational psychology. *See also* Performance Appraisal (education)

Persuasion   The exercise of influence. Persuasion can be accomplished by various means, including argument, entreaty, and expostulation. Interpretations of the word are broad, ranging from coercion to behavior modification. *Persuade,* the predicate form of the word, is often used interchangeably with the word *convince,* but their Latin origins show them to differ, in that *convince* comes from a word that means to conquer, while *persuade* comes from a word that means to advise, to make appealing, or to sweeten.

Persuasion as rhetoric has been discussed among scholars as far back as the ancient Greeks. In contemporary times, persuasion has become a subject of communications science and is studied for its application to political processes, public relations and corporations, advertising and consumerism, interpersonal relationships, and societal change.

Persuasion theories include language expectancy, regarding the effects of linguistic variations on message perception, and inoculation theory, regarding message resistance. For more information, see Dillard and Pfau (2002) and Oxford University Press (2002). *See also* Language; Media; Perception (communication)

Phenomenological Perspective   The philosophical precursor to humanistic psychology, it is the study of consciousness from a subjective, first-person perspective, in contrast to an objectivist, third-person perspective. Skeptical of traditional scientific methods, the phenomenological approach emphasizes qualitative research methods based on self-reporting. Phenomenology is influential in qualitative research paradigms as well as humanistic approaches to psychotherapy. *See also* Person-Centered Therapy (PCT)

Phenomenology   The study of the structure and meaning of the lived experiences of a phenomenon for a group of individuals. The purpose is to reveal the hidden meanings, or essences, of a phenomenon by comparing individual experiences and describing the commonalities. This qualitative research method also seeks to discover how participants make meaning of their experiences. Examples of phenomena studied by a phenomenological researcher include hazing, the

freshman experience, test anxiety, and the experience of the death of a loved one.

In phenomenology, the researcher investigates the essence of an experience or phenomenon by examining the descriptions of the experiences given by participants. The end result of the investigation is to determine and describe what the experience means to the participants and to provide a complete description of it. The description involves not only what was experienced but also how it was experienced.

Phenomenological research is built on a strong philosophical foundation. Two popular types of phenomenology are (1) hermeneutic phenomenology (Van Manen, 1990) and (2) transcendental phenomenology (Moustakas, 1994). Hermeneutical phenomenology is concerned with interpreting the texts of life (hermeneutics) as they relate to lived experience (phenomenology). This type of phenomenology requires the researcher not only to describe but also to interpret the descriptions of study participants. Bracketing, the setting aside of one's own experiences and biases, is controversial and is not necessary in hermeneutical phenomenology. Transcendental phenomenology, also known as empirical, existential, or psychological phenomenology, focuses on the descriptions and experiences of the research study participants. In this type of phenomenology, bracketing is considered desirable so that researchers may more fully concentrate on the essence of participants' experiences without their own experiences and biases influencing the research. Researchers try to transcend their own biases and experiences in order to perceive anew the experiences of their participants. However, because bracketing is difficult to achieve, it may be considered a weakness of transcendental phenomenology.

Phenomenology may be the research method of choice when the essence of a person's experience must be explored, described, and potentially interpreted. Typically, phenomenology involves a small number of participants, but researchers will study the data generated by these participants (generally interviews) in great detail to arrive at the very heart of an experience. For more information, see van Manen (1990) and Moustakas (1994). *See also* Existentialism; Qualitative Research

Phenotype   An organism's observable properties, such as its morphology, development, of behavior. It is the result of what happens when various genes interact with one another and the environment. It is distinguished from a genotype, which consists of the underlying DNA sequence, which may or may not be observable. Some genes do not allow for variations of expression in the phenotype, such as blood type. For example, if your blood genotype is BO, your blood type will be B regardless of other environmental factors. For more information, see Churchill (1974). *See also* Genotype

Pheromones   Chemicals secreted by animals that transmit signals, usually to animals of the same species.

There are alarm pheromones, food trail pheromones, sex pheromones, and many others that affect behavior or physiology. Ants, bees, and other insects secrete chemicals that attract mates and "release" other behaviors. Some studies have suggested the possibility of the occurrence of pheromones in humans. For example, people might be using odor cues associated with the immune system to select mates who are not closely related to themselves. For more information, see Wyatt (2003).

Phobia   An intense, irrational, and persistent fear of a specific object, activity, person, or situation. The main symptoms are an excessive and unreasonable desire to avoid the feared subject. The most common phobias are fear of heights, airplanes, closed spaces, snakes, and spiders. Phobias are the most common form of anxiety disorders and are found in between 8% and 18% of Americans. Phobias are generally caused by a combination of external events and internal predispositions. For more information, see Bourne (2005). *See also* Anxiety Disorders

Phonics   An approach for beginning literacy instruction in which learners are explicitly taught basic letter, sound relationships and the rule for sounding out words. This method emphasizes decoding skills, as opposed to meaning and learners' experiences with language and the world, which is the focus of the whole language approach. *See also* Literacy/Illiteracy

Photography   The recording of light reflected off materials on media that can store this information and make it available later for reproducing a likeness of the material. The light is usually captured by a camera with a lens that focuses the light information on the recoding medium. Analog or film photography records on light-sensitive emulsion coated onto plastic rolls that are processed with chemicals and used to make photographic prints. Analog photography was first developed in the early part of the 19th century. Digital photography uses light information transmitted to an electronic sensor that translates and stores the data in digital formats. Digital data can be transformed into physical prints or transmitted electronically. Digital photography was developed at the end of the 20th century and is steadily replacing film photography for general consumer use. For more information, see Kelby (2006). *See also* Electronic Media; Film

Phrenology *(psychology)*   Was founded by Franz Joseph Gall, a Viennese physician, around 1800 and gained popularity in the 19th century. Phrenology is the pseudoscientific theory that psychological characteristics are revealed by bumps on the skull. Gall believed that speech, math ability, aggression, and other traits are localized to certain regions of the brain. Phrenologists believed that the mind has a set of different mental faculties, with each particular faculty represented in a different portion of the brain. Gall stated that all moral and intellectual faculties are innate, their manifestation depends on organization, and the form of the head represents the form of the brain and reflects the relative development of the brain organs. Phrenology laid the foundation for modern neuroscience. For more information, see Zola-Morgan (1995). *See also* Brain

Phrenology *(sociology)*   An early attempt to measure criminality, prior to the development of positivism and the scientific method. Developed by the German physician Franz Gall (1758–1828), phrenology was a process by which bumps on the skull were measured to determine brain development. Phrenology was based on the idea that each area of the brain had a specific function. It was believed that through systematic observation and experimentation, specific aspects of character, including criminality, could be associated with precise sections of the brain. The areas were said to be proportional to a person's personality and character tendencies; particular areas of the brain that were larger were believed to indicate a greater tendency to exhibit a given behavior or characteristic. Johann Spurzheim (1776–1832) spread these ideas in England and the United States. *See also* Positivism (sociology)

Physical Context   The space around something that is to be discussed in communication and that influences how we see that space. For example, a phrase; a word; or a work of dance, art, or drama can explain to us the meaning of the aspects of the environment that we are viewing or reading about at that moment. In the Middle Ages, a religious painting, for example, was created to be placed in a church or chapel and viewed more as a devotional object than for the its intrinsic merits. Today, such an object is perceived very differently in a museum, and in fact, it serves a different function. In addition, a more structured physical context, such as a superior's office in an organization, can connote a different style of communication than a casual conversation in a hallway.

Physical Geography   *See* Geography

Picket-Fence Federalism   Our country's history shows several stages of governance, with shifting roles and responsibilities between the federal and state governments. Prior to the 20th century, for example, state and federal relationships and responsibilities were in many respects mutually exclusive. Later, the Great Depression and the subsequent New Deal policies fostered more cooperation between federal and state governments as they worked to stimulate the economy, increase jobs, and provide and implement social policies. The 1960s saw a substantial increase in federal programs that were designed to address urban problems and to meet the needs of the disadvantaged (e.g., Medicare and Medicaid programs). The War on Poverty, during the Johnson administration, substantially increased funding to the local levels of government. Rather than providing funds to states, grant programs provided funding to local school districts, governments, and nonprofits. The application process required a clear strategy, a budget plan, inclusion of the public, and management strategies. Local governments and organizations worked diligently to apply for federal grants while determining how to raise matching funds and meet performance and reporting requirements. As the result of these grant programs, intergovernmental relations became more competitive in nature. The image of the picket fence is used to visually show how all levels of government had a stake and interest in addressing public policies and programs. Issues such as welfare, elementary and secondary education, and public housing are the vertical slats of the fence, while the federal, state, and local governments are the horizontal slats that provide reinforcement and support. ***See also*** Cooperative Federalism; Dual Federalism

Pictograph *(media studies)* Stylized pictures of objects that form an essential part of public communications—for example, the sign of a jagged arrow as a danger sign for live voltage. Emoticons, such as smiley faces, indicate the popular use of iconographic script in electronic text messages. Because they transcend individual languages (speakers of different languages will equally understand the message), pictographs (or pictograms) are not strictly a writing system, although it was from pictographs that written language largely developed. The critical change occurred when a script moved from denoting things—pictographic script—to denoting sounds (syllables and letters)—phonetic script. This change occurred gradually as pictures became conventionalized and simplified to such a degree that the original referent could no longer be recognized from the conventionalized markers. Those markers came to denote first syllables, then consonants, and then vowels and consonants combined to give us our modern alphabet, a relatively economic system of script. ***See also*** Oral Tradition; Papyrus; Parchment; Printing

Pictograph *(sociology)* A method of expression and communication that uses symbols and drawings to convey ideas. The pictograph refers to the symbol(s) used to express these ideas. Ancient hieroglyphs used pictures as a method of communication and are a well-known example of pictographs.

Pigeon Hole A political tactic that causes proposed bills to be stalled, or killed, by committee members. Committee members achieve this result through placing the bill at the bottom of their committee's agenda or simply refusing to vote or debate on it. Pigeonholing is one of the many forms of power that committee members wield. A bill becomes pigeonholed after it is drafted and introduced to the appropriate House and sent to a committee for review by the Speaker of the House. The term is also used in British politics and has the same meaning in reference to Committees of Parliament. ***See also*** Bill

Pirate An individual who, without consent from the original owner/inventor/author, makes unauthorized use of material that does not belong to him or her. Examples of piracy include plagiarism, violating copyright laws, or using unlicensed software.

Placebo Effect A form of treatment that is psychological in nature and routinely used by the medical field. A placebo is any type of medical intervention (including inactive drugs, counseling, or surgery) designed to improve one's condition merely through the power of suggestion. This is also known as a subject expectancy effect and occurs when a patient's symptoms are altered in some manner by an otherwise inert treatment due to the individual believing that it will work. This effect occurs when a patient takes an inert substance in combination with a suggestion that the pill will aid in healing and the patient's condition will improve. This effect has been shown to be robust through experimental research, whereby those who are assigned to receive placebo therapy are often better off than those who are not. For more information, see Harrington (1997). ***See also*** Hawthorne Effect (psychology)

Plagiarism The act of intentionally or unintentionally using another's words or ideas without proper attribution. Plagiarism commonly takes two forms. The first, often referred to as direct plagiarism, is the use of verbatim, or nearly verbatim, passages of another's written or spoken words without citing the original source or identifying the verbatim sections by the use of quotation marks or other means (e.g., block quotation). The second, often referred to as indirect plagiarism, is the paraphrasing of another's written or spoken words without identifying the source of the paraphrased material. Mosaic plagiarism is a type of indirect plagiarism where another's work is paraphrased and interspersed with new material in such a manner that it is impossible to determine which ideas are original and which are paraphrased. A third, less common, form of plagiarism is self-plagiarism or duplicate publication. This involves publishing the same material, or essentially the same material, in multiple outlets without citing the previous publications.

Plain Language Language that is more readily comprehensible to the public replacing the language of law and government. For some decades there have been attempts to demystify the specialized vocabulary of bureaucracy, and on June 1, 1998, President Bill Clinton signed a presidential memo requiring that the federal government's writing be in plain language. The memo came in the wake of a judgment that the difficulty of the documentation of the U.S. Immigration and Naturalization Service had violated the civil right to due process of certain aliens. Plain language avoids excessive use of acronyms and abbreviations, Latin phrases, and long noun clusters; it emphasizes directness, clarity, conciseness, and the use of everyday rather than arcane or highly specialized vocabulary (unless needed for technical precision). Practical examples include the use of (a) an informal style, using the second-person pronoun to address the reader directly; (b) the active rather than the passive voice; (c) the grammatical subject at the beginning of the sentence; (d) shorter sentences; (e) shorter paragraphs, addressing one topic only and using a topic sentence; (d) *must* or *will* instead of *shall;* (e) format features, such as boldface, italics, bullets, and so on, to break up information and guide the reader; and (f) ordinary words such as *so* instead of *accordingly* or *such that.* This last example illustrates one of the costs of plain language—the shrinkage of vocabulary to a limited range of qualifiers so overworked that the meaning can only be determined from the context. In preferring everyday words to special-use vocabulary, plain language writers continually balance loss of precision with comprehensibility. *See also* Communication; Communication Theory; Rhetoric

Plain View   A legal doctrine that authorizes police officers to seize unlawful material from a suspect without a warrant, granted that the object(s) is discernible to the officer without an unauthorized search. To ensure that the seizure is legal and conforms to the suspect's rights, the officer needs to have reasonable suspicion that the item is contraband or is possible evidence in relation to a crime. *See also* Search and Seizure

Planning-Programming-Budgeting System   An integrated decision-making approach to budgeting that entails the systematic analysis of government goals to inform decision making in meeting those goals. Alternative methods for obtaining those goals are also generated. Although the planning-programming-budgeting system (PPBS) was developed in the 1960s, one of the earliest influences on a program-budgeting initiative was by the Taft Commission on Economy and Efficiency in 1912. In the 1920s, large organizations, such as General Motors and Ford, tried program budgeting. RAND Corporation economists in the 1960s developed the widely used model that was then adopted by the Department of Defense through Secretary of Defense Robert McNamara. In 1965, President Lyndon B. Johnson directed the heads of federal executive departments to establish the PPBS.

The three-pronged approach of PPBS requires certain activities at each stage. Planning involves identifying the need, setting goals, determining objectives, and developing alternatives to the goals and objectives. Programming is the process of examining sacrifices, analyzing alternative methods, and making comparisons among the alternative methods regarding which is best. Budgeting comprises the legal and financial means for allocating resources. This part should not rely on short-term but rather on ongoing commitment that includes preparation, presentation, adoption, execution, and appraisal.

Following the interest generated at the federal level, in the 1970s, states began adopting PPBS and extended it to local school districts. However, PPBS failed to attain its intended goals. In the school systems, this failure was due in part to several misconceptions, including the beliefs that PPBS is primarily concerned with budgeting and can be implemented within a brief period, existing school functions can easily be converted to PPBS, and it is not necessary to attend to all elements of PPBS.

Though the label *PPBS* is not often heard anymore, its basic elements still exist in school budgeting processes. The major contribution of PPBS lies in the planning process—that is, the process of making program policy decisions that lead to a specific budget and specific multiyear plans. *See also* Budgeting

Plate Tectonics   A geological theory formulated in the 1960s, which posits that the earth's crust is composed of large irregularly shaped plates that move slowly past one another to produce changes in the earth's surface. The plates, which are approximately 100 kilometers in thickness, move only between about 1 to 12 centimeters per year. The plates are divided into smaller and larger plates, with approximately 14 main plates currently known. Most notably, plate tectonics is responsible for the formation and separation of large land masses, in particular the continents of the earth. Some of the main plates can be found in North America, South America, and the Pacific.

The theory of plate tectonics also explains the production of other major land formations, including mountains and volcanoes. In addition, plate tectonics, composed of three types of plate boundaries, accounts for volcanic activity, earthquakes, and oceanic activity. Tectonic activity at transform, convergent, and divergent plate boundaries explains how plate movements produce different land formations by sliding past, apart from, and toward each other, respectively.

The theory of plate tectonics, although relatively recent, is actually a combination of two accepted geological theories: (1) seafloor spreading and (2) continental drift. The theory of plate tectonics subsumes these two existing theories to more fully account for the major changes in the earth's surface. The theory of plate tectonics is widely accepted and stands in the forefront of modern geological theory.

Platform   The official stand of a political party and/or political candidate on issues of interest to voters; individual issues are known as "planks." In the United States, each party develops a platform in each election; candidates of the party usually endorse their party's platform, but some prefer to deviate from it. Platforms are not binding, and scholars estimate that elected officials follow their platform in about 50% of the cases. The first party platform in the United States dates back to the Virginia and Kentucky Resolutions of 1798–1799, written by Republican state legislators in opposition to the Federalist Alien and Sedition Acts.

Play Therapy The use of play and familiar toys or games with children and adolescents (and sometimes adults) to help find the causes of disturbed behaviors, to desensitize them to uncomfortable situations, and to help develop coping skills or work through developmental, emotional, or psychological difficulties. Play therapists are trained and often licensed. The activities or toy/games are chosen intentionally for therapeutic outcomes. "Free play" is often used to help diagnose difficulties or to assist children in expressing feelings that they are not able to verbalize. Structured play and group play are used when the therapist deems them beneficial. *See also* Child Abuse and Neglect; Early-Intervention Programs

Plea A response to an accusation. In court cases (civil or criminal), defendants may opt to enter one of three pleas in response to the charged offense: (1) guilty, (2) not guilty, or (3) *nolo contendere* (the defendant's decision not to plead either guilty or not guilty). There is also a fourth plea of insanity in some jurisdictions. When the defendant chooses to enter a guilty plea, the right to a trial and deliberation, which could possibly lead to a reduced sentence, is waived. The plea is generally announced at arraignment, which occurs when formal charges for any given offense are brought against the defendant in court. *See also* Guilty (sociology); *Nolo Contendere*; Not Guilty

Pleasure Principle A part of the theory of personality formulated by Sigmund Freud in the 19th century. According to psychoanalysis, it is the id's boundless drive for immediate gratification that motivates it to seek immediate and total gratification of all desires. When a person is deprived of things such as food, air, or sex, a state of tension builds up until this need is satisfied. The id is the pleasure-seeking part that attempts to reduce this tension. The pleasure principle guides one to seek pleasure and avoid pain. However, as one grows and matures, one begins to realize the necessity sometimes to endure pain and to defer gratification because of the obstacles one encounters in real life. For more information, see Freud (1940). *See also* Id

Plebiscite A poll that takes place when a government sends a single-issue question to the entire electorate for a vote. Plebiscites in the United States appear at the federal, local, and state levels, usually involving constitutional amendments, a proposed law, or the recall of an official or standing law. The term is named after the Plebian Council of Ancient Rome (494 BCE). *See also* Referendum

Pluralism *(education)* A belief in the reality and value of diversity. In metaphysics, this could refer to the idea that there are two or more kinds of ultimate reality, such as the physical and the spiritual. In social life, pluralism refers to a state of society in which members of diverse groups (ethnic, religious, racial, etc.) maintain some of their autonomy and traditions while still being part of a larger social whole. In political life, pluralism refers to the competitive power sharing characteristic of democracies. Cultural pluralists believe that distinct cultures can coexist in the same society and that assimilation is neither necessary nor desirable. Parallel beliefs exist in the field of research methodology.

In research methodology, pluralism is the belief that different methods may each contribute, in their own way, to broaden knowledge and deepen understanding. Pluralists reject methodological monism, or the belief that there is one best method for all research problems.

The kind of methodological pluralism that has recently attracted the most attention focuses on reconciling quantitative and qualitative methods of measurement and methods of analysis. If they cannot be reconciled, they can at least be mixed or juxtaposed in a study of the same phenomena. This methodology is usually called mixed-methods research. Mixed-methods research focuses on approaches that cross the quantitative-qualitative boundary. Answers to surveys coded numerically and answers to interview questions coded verbally are a frequent example. *Multimethod* research includes mixed-methods approaches and also covers other forms of methodological pluralism. For example, using verbal documents and qualitatively coded observations to better understand an institution is purely a qualitative multimethod research. Combining numerical data from field observations and numerical data from laboratory experiments is an example of quantitative multimethod research. Multitrait-multimethod research (MTMM) is another variant; it is used principally to assess discriminant and convergent validity. Two or more constructs are measured in two or more ways, and the results are displayed in an MTMM correlation matrix.

Whatever the specific combinations, the general attitude of mind behind all these varieties of mixed-methods and multimethod research is methodological pluralism. Methodological pluralism enhances the researcher's range of choices for investigating problems and increases opportunities for cross-validation. Methodological pluralism also often involves social pluralism, because bringing together the diverse knowledge and skills needed for multiple approaches to a research question frequently requires the teamwork of several researchers with different backgrounds. *See also* Cross-Validation; Mixed-Methods Research

Pluralism *(media studies)* Modern media providers must consider how to adapt their communications for reception by a pluralistic society—one that is highly diverse in its politics, ethnicities, religious faiths, gender identifications, and other defining characteristics. Observers who are wary of a hegemonic media marketplace—one in which the values of a privileged class are continually asserted and reinforced—have argued passionately for the adoption of a more pluralistic model of media communications—one that

P

promotes and affirms a diversity of backgrounds, identities, and experiences.

Advocates of diversity in media complain that when media images and viewpoints are dominated by a prevailing race, class, or gender, the public discourse is narrowed and degraded, as viewers unconsciously adopt and accept the simplified, unchallenging worldview of the status quo. It is feared that media purveyors, in search of higher ratings and dependable audiences, will favor predictable publications and programs that confirm audiences in their preexisting assumptions and biases rather than stimulating them toward broader tolerance and a deeper understanding of different people.

Controversy persists as to the best way to structure and maintain a pluralistic media environment. It seems evident that something is required other than, for instance, merely representing more ethnically diverse people on television. For one thing, a diverse collection of faces does not necessarily translate to diversity of content and message. Moreover, it is generally recognized that media that appear superficially diverse may still not engage in complex treatment of issues. Depicting more minority members on television, for instance, will do little to change popular attitudes if the characters portrayed are stereotypic and unimaginatively conceived. Media purveyors must also deal with the fact that no character or group of characters can accurately reveal life in all its complexity. For more information, see Croteau and Hoynes (2005). *See also* Pluralism (education, political science, public administration)

Pluralism *(political science)* A theoretical model in which various interest groups compete for influence in politics. Proponents of pluralism stress that this competition prevents any one group from exerting its dominance. Detractors note that the inequities of resources between interest groups places society's elites at a distinct advantage. The political theorist Robert J. Waste, in *Community Power: Directions for Future Research* (1986), identified four patterns of pluralism:

1. *Classical pluralism:* This ideal model of governance only works in a society with a small population. Policy making occurs in a public arena and is open to all individuals, who hold a diverse set of interests, to participate through debate and discussion. The citizens vote on negotiated legislation and agree to obey its terms.

2. *Hyperpluralism:* This is a system in which the state exerts less influence than political-interest groups, usually short-term in nature. Hyperpluralism is usually limited to large municipal settings and controversial political times. Many interest groups exist within this system and express themselves through protest politics.

3. *Stratified pluralism:* This is a system in which the policy arena is limited to those who are active, resourceful, and organized. This system excludes a large segment of the population who are inactive or apathetic.

4. *Privatized pluralism:* In this model, private-interest (business, commercial) and public-interest groups are in competition to influence policy decisions that will protect their interests. The level of resources of the interest group is essential in determining its prominence in decision outcomes. For more information, see Waste (1986). *See also* Interest Group (political science); Pluralism (education, media studies, public administration)

Pluralism *(public administration)* The belief that a mixture of different religions and ethnic groups within a single society is a positive thing. While the United States has long embraced the concept of political pluralism (hence the "melting pot"), Europe has been traditionally more resistant. Pluralism can also refer to the embrace of different ideas; by recognizing competing philosophies and perspectives, a society may better realize a larger common good. This is seen as essential to any open political system, which does not hold a single monopoly over the truth but rather seeks negotiation between a multiplicity of discrete interests and ideas. Although the abstract idea of pluralism is generally embraced, many social critics have questioned its larger consequences. For example, to what extent should societies be willing to accommodate minority cultural values that are viewed as harmful or repressive to the general population? *See also* Pluralism (education, media studies, political science)

Plurality A voting system in which the winner is one who has gained the most votes but not necessarily the majority of votes. This system is used when there is more than one candidate running for political office. There are four types of plurality majority voting systems that are commonly used: (1) single-member district voting, (2) at-large voting, (3) two-round runoff voting, and (4) instant runoff voting. Single-member district voting is the most commonly used system in Great Britain and the United States. The winner is the candidate who receives the plurality. At-large, voting is used mainly in municipal elections. The candidates' names appear on the ballot in one large district (e.g., a municipality), and voters have the same number of votes as seats to be filled; for example, 3 candidates should be chosen—from a choice of 10—to fill three city council seats. The winner receives the plurality. Two-round runoff voting is a majority voting system in which if no majority is achieved, a second election occurs between the top two candidates. This system is used frequently by the French. The fourth system, popular in Australia, instant runoff voting, requires voters to rank order candidates. If no majority is achieved, the candidate with the least votes is removed from the ballot. The votes of that candidate are automatically transferred to the voters' second choices. This process continues until a majority winner has been determined. For more information, see Douglas (2000).

Pocket Veto A presidential political tactic aimed to avoid a bill becoming law. A pocket veto is achieved if the president does not sign a bill in the 10 days required by Article 1, Section 7 of the Constitution and Congress has adjourned before the 10 days have passed. If Congress is in session during the 10 days, then the bill would become law. *See also* Bill; Veto

Podcasting   An audio- or video-content delivery service where digital media files are downloaded to portable players using Web technology. The term, first used in 2004, combines the Apple Computer iPod player with the concept of broadcasting. Computer users can subscribe to and automatically update a variety of podcasts—ranging from music to talk radio to TV episodes to public lectures—via Web-based media players (e.g., iTunes, MPlayer), many free of cost. Numerous radio shows make their programs available as podcasts, and increasingly, programs are created as original podcasts, existing only in that form. Originally of use for entertainment purposes, educators quickly adopted the technology to better reach a physically remote group or to engage a digitally attuned generation.

Police Misconduct   Offensive or inappropriate behavior on the part of police officers in the discharge of their official duties as law enforcement officials. Police misconduct may include the use of excessive force, arrests under false pretenses, mistreatment of individuals on the basis of sociodemographic characteristics, and other similar acts. Police misconduct is defined as an abuse of power, generally toward a more vulnerable target. Corruption is also considered to be a form of police misconduct. In recent years, there have been an increasing number of reported cases involving police brutality, some of which have resulted in the death of the victims. Various federal laws have been enforced by the U.S. Department of Justice to address the issue of police misconduct. *See also* Corruption (sociology)

Police Personality   The amalgamation of personality traits that are generally characteristic of police officers. Some of these characteristics include machismo, bravery, authoritarianism, cynicism, suspicion, and aggression. Over the past decades, the changing cultural values and the role of the media have altered the definitions and perceptions of police personalities. The concept of police personality is relevant in the recruitment process to ensure that candidates possess particular traits that are deemed to be crucial in the making of a proficient police officer. Various psychological assessment instruments are used in the screening process, such as the Minnesota Multiphasic Personality Inventory (MMPI) and the California Personality Inventory (CPI). The concept of police personality is not limited to the psychological traits observed at recruitment and is perceived to be a dynamic set of characteristics. As such, the police personality may be altered as the police officer's career progresses. These psychological traits may be developed with changing work circumstances and experiences. *See also* Police Subculture

Police Power   The authority of any given government to enact legislation for the purpose of protecting communities and promoting the welfare and safety of its citizens. While police power may refer to the establishment and development of police forces, it also entails the implementation of laws in various other areas, such as schooling, zoning, and sanitation. In the United States, laws are enacted on the basis of police power at the state level only. At the federal level, the enactment of laws occurs on the basis of powers granted through the Constitution. State governments pass on a substantial proportion of their police power to the various cities, counties, boroughs, and so on that make up the state.

Police Subculture   In the general sense, a subculture refers to a group of individuals characterized by a distinct set of values, beliefs, and behaviors. The police subculture refers to the beliefs, norms, attitudes, and values that characterize members of the police force, which may be distinct from the beliefs expressed by other individuals or social groups. The concept of the police subculture supposes that police officers adhere to beliefs and behaviors that may be distinct from those of ordinary citizens. Some of the values often associated with the police culture include bravery, solidarity, masculinity, loyalty, and discretion. As with processes of social learning in other forms of subcultures, these beliefs, norms, attitudes, and values may be transmitted from one generation of police officers to another. *See also* Police Personality

Policy *(education)*   A stated plan of action used to guide decision making. Policies are found in government, businesses, and organizations. A policy conveys the intentions of the entity to guide actions toward a particular goal. Policies may describe the procedures with which to conduct political, management, financial, or administrative processes.

Policy *(public administration)*   The term refers to what public officials within government choose to do, or not do, about public problems. Public problems are generally what the public considers to be unacceptable conditions that demand some form of intervention. Such problems may concern workplace safety, the quality of education, the environment, the economy, or human rights. The term *policy* generally refers to a strategic course of action that an individual or group takes to consistently address specific issues. Policies can be thought of as a set of prescriptions through which societies self-regulate and attempt to influence human behavior in an appropriate direction. Policies can have many different purposes. They may be designed to regulate behavior, to inform or educate the public, to ration, or to determine the appropriate level of involvement of government agencies via contracting or privatization. These aims and intentions are demonstrated through a variety of legal expressions, such as laws, executive orders, regulations,

P

and judicial rulings. These policy tools and legal expressions can define the intent of a policy at any given time. Public and private organizations are likely to operationalize policies as they manage policy inputs (the resources and administrative processes set up to achieve policy goals), policy outputs (the result of agency actions, such as the number of individuals served), and policy outcomes (the positive effects or benefits of policy actions for the public or in solving public problems). Policy tools and the mechanisms that initiate policies are instituted at the federal, state, and local levels. In some instances, policies may be implemented exclusively by a particular level of government. Medicare, for example, is implemented by the federal government. Medicaid is generally implemented by the states. Other policies may be implemented through coordination between the federal, state, and local levels of government. Education policy, while predominantly a local issue, is one such example of how the three levels of government relate with each other to provide access to quality education for all citizens. Governance, funding, and managing day-to-day operations of schools are generally the concern of local officials and administrators. States provide oversight of school district conditions and performance while providing school report cards to the public. Federal mandates require standardized testing in particular subject areas and grades, while providing technical assistance and funding to states to improve performance. More recent trends and government reforms also emphasize that policies can and should be implemented by nongovernmental organizations (whether faith-based or nonprofit organizations). The role of government, therefore, is to provide oversight in order to ensure that policies are implemented to its satisfaction and ultimately to the satisfaction of the public. For more information, see Kraft and Furlong (2007) and Simon (2007). *See also* Policy Analysis; Public Policy

Policy Analysis   A process that is a critical part of the policy-making process as it plays a significant role in problem definition, policy implementation, and evaluation of agency efforts to meet policy goals and objectives. It is most often associated with systematic assessment of policy alternatives to inform the public, stimulate debate, and lead to a desired course of action. Overall, policy analysis involves data collection and interpretation to clarify the causes and effects of public problems, as well as the consequences of employing various policy alternatives.

The policy analysis process involves several steps: (a) problem definition, (b) designing policy alternatives, (c) developing evaluative criteria, (d) assessing alternatives, and (e) drawing conclusions (Kraft & Furlong, 2007). Defining problems prompts policy analysts to ask questions such as the following: Who are being affected by the problem? What are the major causes? How might policy actions make an impact? Cell phone use while driving has emerged as a policy problem, as analysts work to determine its relationship

to auto accidents. While formulating policy alternatives, questions as to which policy options might be considered for addressing a problem are likely to arise. Examining the use of cell phones while driving, policy analysts and various decision makers are likely to consider a range of actions that could potentially reduce its occurrence. The aim is to determine which course of action will most likely change behaviors—in this case, regulating or discouraging driving while talking on a cell phone. The next step is to develop the criteria that are most suitable for the problem and the policy alternatives. In this stage, analysts and policy decision makers consider what the costs of a policy action are, which action is likely to be more effective, and whether the alternatives are politically and socially feasible. What criteria, for example, are most important for regulating the use of cell phones while driving? What options would be most effective for regulating this behavior? Will the public find these restrictions acceptable? After determining which activities or behaviors are likely to be addressed by the policy, analysts and decision makers will assess the various alternatives. In this case, they will examine the practices of other jurisdictions in addressing the problem of cell phone use while driving. Alternatives such as requiring hands-free technologies and imposing fines, among others, are likely to be discussed and vetted. Ultimately, a conclusion must be drawn as to which is the best course of action. In some instances, there may be very little consensus on what should be done, while in other instances, the analysis reveals a clear path of action. For more information, see Kraft and Furlong (2007). *See also* Evaluation (public administration); Policy (public administration); Policy Implementation

Policy Entrepreneur   Someone who establishes a novel project, organization, or political party. There are different types of entrepreneurs. Market entrepreneurs, for example, conceptualize innovative products or solutions in the hope of reaping significant profits for their ideas. The political entrepreneur bears both similarities and differences to his or her market colleague; in contrast to monetary gain, this type of entrepreneur instead seeks administrative change. Both also share some similarities and differences with social entrepreneurs, or persons who use innovative strategies to beneficially ameliorate a collective difficulty or hardship. Although social and political entrepreneurs each seek to promote structural change, they ultimately focus on distinctively different spheres of society. Of course, one should be cautioned against forming overly stringent categories, as the social, political, and economic realms are often deeply intertwined. For more information, see Bornstein (2007).

Policy Implementation   Many assume that the policy process ends when a law is passed. In practice, policy implementation marks the beginning of government activity that will affect the daily lives of citizens. Policy implementation involves assigning institutional resources within the bureaucracy to enact the policy program. Much of the work of implementation is in the hands of public managers and personnel who work in federal, state, and local agencies. Three activities—organization, interpretation, and application—are considered critical factors for successful implementation. Organization requires the establishment of resources, offices, and methods necessary to set the implementation wheels in motion. Interpretation involves the process of translating legislation into policy actions. In many instances, public managers are charged with translating vague legislative language and requirements into concrete programs with clear objectives, strategies for action, and criteria for objectively measuring the program's performance and results. Application requires a clear set of policies and processes that provide the directives the personnel need to coordinate their activities and services.

Bureaucracy, pressure groups, and the judicial system, all have varying degrees of influence in the implementation process. The bureaucracy provides the process and structure through which legislative intent becomes tangible program objectives and activities. Much of the emphasis is on rulemaking (also referred to as administrative law). Administrative rules guide the day-to-day implementation of the statute. These are often formulated by bureaucrats and are available for public review in the Federal Register or state administrative code manuals. Oversight is provided by the executive and legislative branches of government, with enforcement carried out by the courts. Public hearings permit pressure groups to provide important input for interpreting statutory intent and bureaucratic decision making. In many instances, organized groups will engage in information campaigns to inform the public and build awareness on key policy issues. Lobbying may be used to inform elected officials of the costs and benefits of fully funding the implementation of a statute. Pressure groups can also influence policy implementation through expert testimony or by building relationships via iron triangles or subgovernments. The court system plays a significant role in policy implementation when individuals or groups suggest that their constitutional rights are violated as a result of either a statute or any administrative rules that are established for implementation. Those seeking legal recourse have the burden of showing legal standing (sufficient evidence that they are harmed by the law or government action that is called into question). Failure to demonstrate legal standing will result in the court dismissing the case without further consideration of the claim of unconstitutionality. For more information, see Jones (1984) and Simon (2007). *See also* Issue Networks

Political Behavior Theorists are traditionally most interested in the formation of an individual's political ideology and the forces that influence voter behavior. This branch of political science, which studies what influences individual or institutional political behavior, is interdisciplinary, borrowing heavily from the fields of economics, psychology, and sociology.

Political Culture The unique pattern of beliefs about power and legitimacy that permeate a nation or a nation's subculture. Political culture is most concerned with long-standing, deeply rooted values rather than contemporary ones. One of the most influential works on political culture was by the American political scientists Gabriel Almond and Sidney Verba, who in their work *The Civic Culture: Political Attitudes and Democracy in Five Nations* (1963) noted three patterns of political culture: (1) participant, where citizens are aware of the central government and are active participants; (2) subject, where citizens are aware of the central government but have low participation rates or room for dissent; and (3) parochial, where citizens are unaware of the central government and are uninterested in politics. The authors concluded that democracy thrives in a participant culture, but still, some degree of subject and parochial culture should coexist. For more information, see Almond and Verba (1963). *See also* Political Participation

Political Economy Approach A phrase that refers to the study of the relationships between the buying, selling, and production within a society with respect to law, culture, and government. This approach originated with the moral philosophers of the late 18th century, most notably Adam Smith. As the field began to develop, it shifted toward mathematical analysis of consumption and production rather than the relationships of the entire social, political, and economic structure. As such, *political economy* was largely replaced by the term *economics*.

Today, *political economy approach* usually refers to a suite of distinct, but related, approaches to studying the political and economic behaviors of individuals and groups. This generally involves combining the tools of economics with those of other social sciences. Most frequently, *political economy* refers to an interdisciplinary approach that integrates economics, law, and political science to explain the influences of and relationships between economic systems (capitalist, socialist, mixed), the political culture and environment, and institutions. Many view this as an "applied" approach to topics in economics that are related to public policy. Examples include rent seeking, government fiscal policy, and market protection.

Some historians apply political economy analysis to assess how individuals or groups have managed their economic interests and used politics and institutions to achieve the desired outcomes. Political scientists frequently associate political economy with analysis grounded in rational choice (especially game theory). Commonly, this involves analyzing data derived from voter behavior.

On the cutting edge of this approach is the field of international political economy (IPE). IPE employs many

P

of the same analytical tools and assumptions of political economy; however, the focus of IPE is much broader. IPE examines international trade and finance, as well as local social, political, and economic development and growth.

There is a balkanized approach to the social sciences in the United States. As such, each field has its canon and has largely evolved in a disaggregated manner; arguably, this leads to practitioners in their respective fields knowing more and more about less and less. In the United States, there are but a handful of universities that offer political economy programs at the undergraduate or the graduate levels—Princeton University and Fordham University being the notable exceptions. Such programs are much more common in European universities. *See also* Economics; Economic System; Social Capital

Politically Incorrect   A term that describes any form of speech that would cause offense to an identity group. The term is a play on the antonym of the pejorative term *politically correct*. *Politically correct* was first used by the Supreme Court in *Chisholm v. Georgia* (1793); it was used in a literal sense regarding the correctness of a citizen's right to sue a state government. The concept of political correctness faded from usage until the 1930s, when the term was used sarcastically to refer to American communists. Thirty years later, moderate radicals called their more extreme counterparts "politically correct." In the 1980s, conservatives described the behavior of liberals, especially those associated with academia, who attacked others' viewpoints as politically correct. The term's usage has continued in modern American parlance, and it has even become the title of a popular book and television series. For more information, see *Chisholm v. Georgia* (1793).

Political Machine   The name given to politicians who engage in rampant patronage, usually associated with bribery and corruption (also known as political bosses). This practice was common in the northeastern cities of the United States from the early 20th century until the 1940s. Industrialization coupled with large-scale immigration created a fertile ground for political machines. The demand for jobs for the new immigrants and the advent of civil service positions allowed politicians to offer jobs in exchange for votes. Since the early 1950s, reforms and the increased intervention of state and federal governments in local politics have largely curbed the practices of political machines. *See also* Spoils System (political science)

Political Media   A term that to some degree encompasses all media. If one accepts the premise that all expression is in some sense political, then all media are to some degree political media. The media are involved in the political life of the modern world not only insofar as they report factually on political events but also as they represent politics in fictionalized portrayals, as in movies such as *Dave* and *Primary Colors*.

In our time, media interests also use extensive lobbying efforts and contribute heavily to political campaigns to achieve their legislative and regulatory goals. In 1999, for example, major Internet companies including AOL, eBay, and Yahoo! formed a lobbying consortium, known as NetCoalition.com, to block efforts to tax Internet commerce. Similarly, the Recording Industry Association of America has lobbied for limitations on the right to file for bankruptcy, to prevent performers from declaring bankruptcy and thus voiding long-term contracts they signed before becoming famous.

The power of the media to influence politics, of course, extends well beyond lobbying efforts, since the media exercise extensive control over information about public figures. Former Federal Communications Commission (FCC) Chair Reed Hundt has stated, "TV and newspapers are the gatekeepers of public perception and can make a politician popular or unpopular. . . . Politicians know that in their bones; the only ones who don't are the ones who don't get elected." According to David Croteau and William Hoynes, the media mogul Rupert Murdoch has frequently used his television and newspaper concerns to cast unfavorable attention on public officials who have resisted his political objectives. With the growth of media empires, there has arisen an omnipresent opportunity for the abuse of media power to influence the political process.

Another type of political influence occurs when corporate media ally themselves with the government to insert propagandistic messages into media content. An example occurred in 2000, when the White House Office of National Drug Control Policy reviewed scripts and advance footage of a number of popular television programs and awarded indirect financial incentives to networks based on the amount of antidrug material in the episodes' plots and dialogue. Media messages are subject to government influence in other ways as well. For instance, the Department of Defense, which routinely supplies information, access, and equipment to make military-themed movies seem more authentic, tends to provide this assistance only after government representatives review the film project and determine that the movie will portray the military in a sufficiently favorable light. For more information, see Croteau and Hoynes (2001). *See also* Media; Propaganda (media studies); Public Interest (media studies)

Political Participation   Activities of a state's citizenry aimed at influencing politics. Forms of political participation include voting, protesting, membership in political organizations, running for political office, or working on a political campaign. The freedom of all citizens to be politically active is an essential hallmark of a democracy. This concept traces back to the Ancient Greek philosophers, such as Aristotle, who wrote in the *Politics* (350 BCE) about the dual nature of *eleutheria* (liberty): the freedom to politically participate, "being ruled and ruling in turn," and the freedom to "live as you like." In contrast, political participation is outlawed under an authoritative regime, in which voting is restricted and strict adherence to government views is required.

In the United States, the majority of Americans participate in voting, but in no other form of politics. Voting participation has been in gradual decline in the United States since reaching a record high of 63% in the 1960 presidential elections; in 2004, 56% of Americans voted. Political theorists have attributed this phenomenon to a feeling of alienation among voters, a general mistrust of the government, the ambiguous nature of political parties, and the decline in the efficacy of elections (believing that one's vote makes a difference). According to the latest U.S. Census Bureau statistics, those most likely to vote in the United States are non-Hispanic whites, the older generation, more educated persons, people with higher annual salaries, and the employed. Those least likely to vote are Latinos, the younger generation, less educated persons, people with a low annual income, and the unemployed. For more information, see Conway (2000). *See also* Democracy (political science)

Political Philosophy   A discipline that is concerned with the ethical and moral standards of states, societies, and individuals. Scholarly debate in this discipline evaluates the facts about social organization in a society, particularly government. There are thus two distinctive aspects of political philosophy: (1) the ethically normative aspect and (2) the more descriptive-explanatory aspect. Within its normative concerns, we find themes such as justice, community, and political responsibility. Some of the questions scholars confront are the following: What features does a good government have? Should citizens have the right to oust their government? If so, which methods should be used? What should be the relationship between the individual and society? When should the government intervene in the lives of its citizens?

Among the founding fathers of Western political philosophy were Plato and Aristotle. During medieval times, St. Thomas Aquinas was an extremely influential philosopher, whereas during the European Renaissance and the Age of Enlightenment, Rousseau's *The Social Contract* and the works of Locke and Hobbes were quite prominent.

Contemporary political philosophers include feminists, certain minorities in the developing world (called subaltern), and scholars from the developed world, among others, who have made a compelling case for reassessment of the traditional paradigm set up by the founders of the discipline. Among these are the neo-conservatives, who follow the philosophy of Leo Strauss.

Feminist political philosophy is a field of inquiry that emphasizes the systematic study of historical conditions and social practices that produce and legitimate gender inequality. Feminist political theorists have together forced classical political theory to encompass what was once considered apolitical—the family, child-rearing practices, gender, the body, sexuality, and human

relationships. Simone de Beauvoir (France) and Iris Young (United States) are examples of contemporary feminist philosophers. For more information, see Berlin (1958), Boucher and Kelly (2003), Constant (1988), and Hirschmann and Di Stefano (1996). *See also* Politics (political science); Social Contract

Political Science   A discipline that can be traced back to the Ancient Greeks. Considered by many to be the first theorists in the discipline, thinkers like Plato and Aristotle wrestled with questions related to good government and the political system. As the discipline has broadened, it now largely coincides with political sociology in research themes, theory, and methodology. In the United States in the 1930s and 1940s, it was shaped by concerns about the systematic study of power, as it sought to differentiate itself from other disciplines such as economics and philosophy. Political science studies the distribution of power in different polities; the sources of power; how, when, and by whom it is exercised; as well as who gains and who loses in power struggles. These struggles may range from local-interest groups competing for positions of power in county government to a military dispute between two super-powers. From these observations, political scientists draw general propositions, hypotheses, and, ultimately, theories about power and politics.

The study of power takes various forms, from the investigation of individual political attitudes and behavior to the examination of state activities at the national and international levels. The study of power and how it is shared (or not) is applied to governmental institutions, across the world economy, and in terms of international relations rather than merely within particular nation-states.

By the mid-20th century, political science was beginning to fragment into different subfields, such as political philosophy, methodology, American politics, international relations, and political economy. Furthermore, differentiation occurred through the field of comparative politics and the study of the Cold War. The result was the emergence of subfields such as political party systems, comparative legislative behavior, federalism, polling, and elections. By the 1980s, there was a further change in what was being analyzed and for what purpose, with the "Bring back the state" focus on the impact that state authority can have on historical processes of political development.

The failure of political science to predict the sudden end of the Cold War and the demise of the Soviet empire raised troublesome questions about the quality of international relations theories and the accuracy of what had been presumed to have been solid knowledge about world politics. This failure also points to the contradiction in the use of the term *science* when dealing with humans. In other words, predicting human actions is a very inexact art rather than a science. Currently, the discipline has been consumed with interest in the political consequences of economic globalization and

P

the information and communications revolutions. For more information, see Almond (1990), Chilcote (2000), Krieger (2001), and Lipset (1981). ***See also*** Political Philosophy; Politics (political science); Social Science

Political Socialization   Socialization is the process of acquiring a sense of cultural norms. Human infants are not born with culture; they are transformed by significant agents of socialization (e.g., parents, teachers, peers) into social beings. Through socialization, we learn the language of our culture, the norms of our culture, and the roles we are to play in life.

Political socialization can best be defined as the long-term process by which political culture is transmitted in a society. It is how individuals learn political ideas and orientations and internalize particular political values and beliefs. Like the general sense of socialization, it is a lifelong process.

Our first political ideas are shaped within the family. Family tradition is particularly a factor in party identification, as indicated by the phrases "lifelong Republican" or "lifelong Democrat." Schools are also an important agent of political socialization. Children are introduced to elections and voting when they choose their class officers. The more sophisticated elections in high school and college teach the rudiments of campaigning. Political facts are learned through courses in social studies and history.

Peer influence plays a somewhat smaller role in a young person's political socialization. Although peer influence certainly affects teenagers' lifestyles, it is less evident in developing their political values. Exceptions are issues that directly affect students, such as the Vietnam War during the 1960s.

Much of our political information comes from the mass media: newspapers, magazines, radio, television, and, increasingly, online social networks. These are the dominant information sources. Television not only helps shape public opinion by providing news and analysis, but its entertainment programming also addresses important contemporary issues in the political arena, such as drug use, abortion, and crime.

Critics of political socialization have noted that political socialization research is merely descriptive and therefore not really a good empirical tool. Unlike some factors that remain constant (e.g., ethnicity), political attitudes can change over time and therefore cannot predict actual behavior (e.g., voting). For more information, see McLean and McMillan (2003). ***See also*** Political Culture; Socialization (sociology)

Political Sociology   A specialization of sociology that analyzes the social dynamics of power and authority relations within the state. Political sociology is particularly interested in the struggle to attain or influence state power. According to Irving Louis Horowitz, in *Foundations of Political Sociology* (1997), the central difference between political science and political sociology is in its emphasis; in the former, it is the state,

and in the latter, it is society. One of the most influential works of political sociology is Max Weber's *The Three Types of Legitimate Rule* (1958), which delineates three forms of legitimization of state power: (1) traditional—society accepts the power structure through convention, for example, monarchy; (2) rational-legal—society accepts the law on which the power is based, for example, a constitution; and (3) charismatic—society accepts the power based on the exceptional characteristics of or its belief in a mission adopted by the power holder, for example, Napoleon Bonaparte. For more information, see Horowitz (1997) and Weber (1958). ***See also*** Political Science; Sociology

Politician   An individual who holds elective office at the local, state, or federal level. In the United States, politicians are elected, but other nations may have self-appointed or hereditary political leaders, as in a dictatorship or monarchy, respectively. It is common for politicians to come from the field of law and/or other elective offices. There are usually certain minimum qualifications for politicians to possess in order to run for office. For example, the U.S. Constitution's Article 2, Section 1 requires that the president be at least 35 years of age, a natural-born citizen of the United States, and a resident for the past 14 years. The term *politician* is also used metaphorically for someone who is adept at managing people or affairs for his or her own ends. ***See also*** Election; Politics (political science)

Politics *(political science)*   The exercise or the study of power in a state or social organization. The term is derived from Aristotle (384–322 BCE), who wrote of the *polis* to refer to a state and system of order. Politics can mean a variety of things in multiple contexts, including strategizing, current affairs, the inner workings of a government, and conflict escalation or resolution. Political science is the study of politics and political systems from a sociological and/or philosophical standpoint. Much discussion of politics revolves around power and its social legitimization. One of the most cited works on political power is *The Three Types of Legitimate Rule*, by Max Weber (1958), which distinguishes three kinds of legitimization of state power: (1) traditional, where the power structure is authorized by convention—for example, in a monarchy; (2) rational-legal, where the power is sanctioned by law—for example, through a constitution; and (3) charismatic, where the power is accepted because of the exceptional characteristics of or people's belief in a mission adopted by the power holder—for example, Napoleon Bonaparte or Benito Mussolini. For more information, see Weber (1958). ***See also*** Politician

Politics *(sociology)*   In a general sense, the term refers to the study of relationships between individuals or groups and entities in a position of authority. More specifically, politics is a discipline that is preoccupied with the study of government. Politics is concerned with relationships between citizens of a society and the representatives of those citizens, as well as the policies implemented by members of government to preserve or further develop the best interests of the citizens. The study of politics also examines the various decision-making processes that occur at the governmental level. ***See also*** Politician

Poll   A public opinion survey, often concerning a political issue. Nonprofit, educational, media, and political organizations usually run polls, and the results can affect politicians' choices in regard to policy measures. An "exit poll" is conducted after a vote on an issue or a candidate, when voters are asked the nature of their vote. ***See also*** Public Opinion Poll

Polyandry   The practice of one woman having more than one husband simultaneously. Polyandry is one of the many forms of polygamy, which is defined as the practice of having multiple spouses at the same time. Although not very common in contemporary society, polyandry is still practiced in some parts of the world. ***See also*** Polygamy

Polychronic Behavior   A term that refers to the variety of activities, roles, and tasks that organizational members are expected to handle simultaneously, or at least concurrently. As competitive pressures mount, and as time itself is seen, increasingly, as a resource to be measured and monitored, firms are attempting to do more with less and to do it as quickly as possible. With the advent of increasingly efficient and portable technology, such as computers and cell phones, it is more and more common for individuals to engage in multiple tasks within the same time period. These trends promote polychronic behavior in most organizations.

Monochronic individuals attend to things serially or one at a time, and polychronic individuals attend to several things at a time. In workplace vernacular, workers are expected to "multiplex." Some studies have shown that when an organization's members are charged with accomplishing highly creative and intellectual tasks, polychronicity may actually promote greater creativity. Other research indicates, however, that for some members of an organization, polychronicity may serve to undermine the member's performance on particular tasks.

While polychronic behavior may mean doing two or more tasks simultaneously—for example, speaking on the phone while also typing at the computer—it also refers to being involved in several tasks or projects in a set time period. Thus, an organization's members may switch freely between projects, depending on situational and environmental demands. This parallel or distributed approach to work design contradicts the traditional monochronic approach to work organization. ***See also*** Monochronic Behavior

Polygamy   The practice of having more than one spouse simultaneously. The various forms of polygamy include polygyny (which involves one man with numerous wives), polyandry (one woman with numerous husbands), and group marriages (which involves more than one wife and more than one husband). Polygamy is still an acceptable practice in some societies. ***See also*** Polyandry

Polygenic   A trait or characteristic that is determined by the joint effect of two or more genes on the organism. While each gene may exert a negligible effect on the given trait, the joint effect of the genes may have a more substantial impact. When a trait is determined by one single gene, it is referred to as *monogenic*. ***See also*** Genes; Genetics

Polygraph *(psychology)*   An electronic instrument that records multiple channels of arousal and has been used mainly in the detection of deception. It measures and records physiological responses such as blood pressure, pulse, and respiration while the subject is asked a series of questions. It is based on the assumption that false responses will produce changes in the sympathetic nervous system that will be detectable, given that they will vary from baseline levels of physiological arousal. For more information, see Gale (1998). ***See also*** Lie Detector

Polygraph *(sociology)*   A device used to determine whether an individual is being truthful. Commonly referred to as a lie detector test, the instrument records the individual's physiological responses when asked specific questions; these physiological responses include measures of breathing, blood pressure, and pulse. Before being asked the questions of interest, a pretest is carried out to measure the change in physiological responses. Based on that level of change, it is possible to determine whether an individual is being truthful. Polygraphs can be used by the police when investigating suspects in a criminal case, though this material is generally inadmissible in court. ***See also*** Lie Detector

Polymorphism   In a broader sense, the term refers to the coexistence of different forms or shapes in the same population or the capacity to for a single property to have different states. For instance, in the field of biology, polymorphism occurs when the qualities of an organism exist in different forms in the population of a particular species.

Polytheism   The practice of worshiping and believing in the existence of more than one deity. Polytheists believe in the existence of various gods that are each characterized by distinct features. The term *pantheon* refers to the entire group of gods that characterizes a given polytheistic religion; this term is also used to designate the temples built in honor of these different deities. Ancient Greece was an example of a polytheistic society that believed in the existence of numerous different deities. Hinduism is an example

P

of a contemporary polytheistic religion. **See also** Monotheism

Pons   A brain-stem region that regulates brain activity during sleep and dreaming. It also plays a role in arousal, assists in controlling autonomic functions, and relays sensory information between the cerebrum and the cerebellum. It also contains important centers for regulating breathing. *Pons* is derived from the Latin word for "bridge." It is found directly above the medulla. It contains important neuronal pathways arising from the cerebrum and spinal cord, as well as the cerebellum. For more information, see Gazzangia (2004). **See also** Cerebellum

Ponzo Illusion   An optical illusion that is based on the suggestion that the human mind judges an object's size based on its background. This was first demonstrated by the Italian psychologist Mario Ponzo in 1913 by drawing two straight lines across a pair of converging lines. The horizontal line on top tends to look longer than the one below it. This tendency is known as the Ponzo illusion. The upper line looks longer because we interpret the converging sides according to the linear perspective. The two lines cast the same-size retinal image, so the one that seems more distant is perceived to be larger. The more depth perception cues there are in the background, the stronger the illusion. For more information, see Deregowski (1989).

Popular Culture   The culture "of the people." Culture has a broad semantic range broadened further by some attributives (high culture, popular culture, subculture, etc.). In this usage, one speaks of cultures in the plural to denote specific, local ways of life and the customs of a particular group rather than some universal notion of evolving civilization. The word *popular,* in use from the 15th century, ranges from the neutral sense of "belonging to the people" to the negative meaning of low, vulgar, and common on one end and the more positive sense of having general appeal, being widespread, and being well liked on the other. This latter, positive sense developed in the 18th century. The term *popular culture* has, however, never shed the taint of the vulgar. The abbreviation of the term in the mid-20th century to "pop," as in pop music or pop art, conveys the sense of trivial, superficial, and undiscriminating, despite the important innovations pop culture is capable of making. The objects of representation in pop art— mass produced, disposable, cheap, and endlessly replicated (e.g., Andy Warhol's Campbell's soup cans)— seriously critique the possibility of authenticity and originality in a consumer-driven society.

The gradual acquisition of the more positive meaning of *popular* and the emergence of popular culture must be understood in light of the changing structure of society and the economy. Capitalism, urbanization, and industrialization increasingly legitimated bourgeois tastes as the middle classes expanded and became wealthier. The surge of mass production in the mid-20th

century has arguably submerged the traditional markers of difference and the distinction between high and low culture into a global culture, differentiated primarily by income and consumer taste. The rise of the digital media and consumer Web sites enabled by the Internet has globalized access and further leveled the restrictions imposed by locality, class, race, ethnicity, and gender. Popular culture and culture have, thus, in many ways come to mean the same thing. **See also** Culture (communication, media studies); Mass Culture

Popular Justice   An informal system of social control, in contrast to the formal criminal justice system. It refers to a locally controlled system of social control, run by the community to uphold community norms.

Popular Prints   A term used to refer mainly to the relatively cheap mass-produced prints made on paper in the West during the 17th and 18th centuries. These prints were "popular" as distinct from the more expensive and higher-quality prints made for the "polite," elite society. Western printing technology at that time used either wooden blocks or copper plates. Printing using copper plates produced images with far greater detail than printing with wood blocks, but the copper eroded quickly, increasing costs. Popular prints were generally made from carved wooden blocks, which were far more resilient and lasted considerably longer than copper plates, allowing many more prints to be made. The prints were sold by traveling sales people and pinned, usually unframed, onto interior walls for decoration or carried around as talismans by their purchasers. Some included text or were made to accompany ballads or other musical lyrics. The subject matter varied widely and included illustrations of religious scenes and political satire. Relatively few of these prints from western Europe survive today. Many that do survive were collected by religious or secular authorities, suspicious of their popularity, wide distribution, and unauthorized content. In Russia, both copper plates and woodblocks were used to produce popular satiric illustrations of life under Peter the Great.

In cities, more expensive, finer prints were made using engraving or etching techniques and were frequently hand colored. Typical subject matter included royalty, famous places, and politically important figures.

By the mid-19th century, technology (lithography, etc.) had developed sufficiently for illustrated periodicals to appear, including the English *Punch* and the *Illustrated London News*. Sensational broadsheets or catchpenny prints were being produced in major cities, typically featuring executions or murders. In France, modern technology was being used to mass produce nostalgic images resembling the popular prints from previous centuries. In North America, prints were made celebrating heroic or sentimental scenes of Civil War life. For more information, see Platzker and Wyckoff (2000) and "Popular Prints" (2008). **See also** Mass Media; Print Media

Popular Sovereignty A government run by the people. The concept has its origin in the work of the English social contract theorists Thomas Hobbes (1588–1679) and John Locke (1632–1704) and the French philosopher Jean Jacques Rousseau (1712–1778), who believed that the state is subservient to the will of its citizens. In early American history, the term was used during the American Revolution to express the need for sovereignty from the king of England and in designing a democracy under the U.S. Constitution. The term took on a different meaning prior to the Civil War and was used to describe the right of new territories to decide, instead of Congress, whether or not to allow slaves, prior to approaching the Union for statehood. Proponents of the plan, especially from the North, referred to it as "squatter sovereignty." *See also* Sovereignty

Populism An international political movement that advocates the rights of the "common man" and social equality. In the United States, the Populist Party, also known as the People's Party, was founded in 1891; that same year, William Peffer of Kentucky became the first Populist in the U.S. Senate. In 1892, the Populists supported their own third-party presidential candidate, James P. Weaver, who won over a million votes in the general election. In 1896, two factions formed within the party: (1) the Fusion Populists, who sought to join with the powerful Democrat party, and (2) the Mid-Roader Populists, who advocated remaining independent and adopting an ideology midway between the ideologies of the two leading parties. In the presidential election of 1896, the Fusions voted to endorse the Democrats' candidate, William Jennings Bryan, and the Mid-Roaders supported the Populist vice presidential candidate, Tom Watson. Issues supported by the Populists included federal intervention to help ease the Depression, the eradication of poverty among farmers, and a crackdown on big-business abuses. Bryan lost the campaign to Republican William McKinley, and the party dissipated by 1908. Many Populist issues were revived by Progressive Theodore Roosevelt in his "Bull Moose" presidential campaign of 1912, which the former president entered after losing the Republican nomination. Although he lost the election to the Democrat nominee Woodrow Wilson, Roosevelt was the only third-party candidate in the nation's history to win more votes than one of the two major parties. For more information, see Clanton (1991). *See also* Democracy (political science)

Pornography Any material (audio/video, magazines, pictures, letters, etc.) intended for sexual stimulation. Some moral and religious groups have argued that pornography is immoral due to the sexually explicit messages it sends out. According to these groups, such messages conflict with the fundamental religious and family-oriented values put forth by conventional social institutions. These groups also argue that pornography promotes deviant sexual behavior as well as sexual promiscuity. Some feminist groups have expressed their disapproval of pornography, mainly because such material objectifies, exploits, and oppresses women. Groups that are opposed to pornography support the use of formal measures and sanctions to prevent individuals from viewing or being involved in the production of pornographic material. On the opposite end of the spectrum, liberal groups advocate against censorship, arguing that it constitutes a violation of individuals' right to freedom. To prevent individuals from expressing their preferences and beliefs is deemed a violation of the freedom of speech and expression. Censorship of pornography is also perceived by some as a violation of the right to privacy; sexual preferences are a private matter, and it is argued that individuals should have the right to express these preferences in private without external interference. Liberal groups further argue that viewing pornographic material does not cause any harm to anyone, and therefore, there is no basis for censorship. Child pornography is prohibited, but the regulations around this are still developing. For instance, the use of "virtual" child pornography is legally acceptable, since it uses computer images and not the images of real children. *See also* Censorship (media studies)

Portfolio Assessment A method of assessing learning based on a collection of student-generated materials that reflect what students are capable of doing on an ongoing basis. Various materials and samples of students' work are placed together in individual portfolios (either a physical container or electronic) and evaluated on a regular basis by the teacher and the student to identify strengths and the areas that need strengthening. By reflecting on the portfolio contents, goals are set by the teacher and the student for future learning. Portfolio assessment reflects the idea that informative assessment begins with the learner and that assessment should be based on multiple examples of a student's work rather than only on a classroom examination.

Positive Feedback The act of a sender receiving a response (that contains information) from a receiver. This information is characterized as being helpful to the sender and often provides evaluation in response to information that was transmitted by the sender. Positive feedback can be in the form of encouraging advice to aid in the sender's reformulation of the information to that receiver or others. It can also be an affirmation about the sender and/or the information, which can then influence the sender's personal attitude. Positive feedback is offered in interpersonal interactions in formal and informal settings and can help in the formation and continuation of healthy relationships. Positive feedback is part of the feedback loop in an exchange of communication, wherein there can be negative feedback as well. *See also* Negative Feedback

Positive Psychology This is a recent movement in psychology that builds on the work of the humanistic psychologists and counseling psychologists of the 20th century. Positive psychology focuses on strengths, virtues, and healthy/resilient individuals, as opposed to maladaptive behavior and psychopathology. This movement originated in the work of Martin Seligman, who argued in the 1990s for a strain of psychology that is decidedly humanistic in its focus on the positive dimensions of human behavior and also decidedly empirical and scientific in its attempts to investigate these positive dimensions. The latter feature distinguishes modern positive psychology from humanistic psychology's reliance on qualitative research methods and is in keeping with modern psychology's emphasis on positivistic and empirical research methods. Positive psychology is also influenced by the specialty of counseling psychology, which has traditionally focused on "normal," nonclinical populations and used a wellness model of mental illness in its approach to clinical intervention. Both of these emphases are similar to the approach taken by the proponents of the more recent positive psychology.

The typical foci of positive psychologist theorists and researchers are (a) happiness, (b) recreation, (c) relationships, (d) productivity, (e) self-efficacy, (f) occupational success, (g) personal meaning, (h) spirituality, (i) virtues, (j) moral behavior, and (k) culture. Positive psychology's research findings are also increasingly emphasized in the field of medical/health psychology. While it is sometimes criticized for adopting an overly optimistic approach to psychology, positive psychology proponents argue that it is important to understand the positive dimensions of life in their own right and that such understanding also yields important insights into how to better address human psychological and behavioral problems. For more information, see Seligman (1990, 1993). *See also* Counseling Psychology; Humanistic Counseling; Self-Efficacy (psychology)

Positive Regard   A broad term put forth by Carl Rogers that conveys human experiences such as love, affection, acceptance, nurturance, and so on. Rogers argued that individuals must experience this from others to have positive regard for themselves. Therefore, to be effective, according to Rogers, the therapist must hold the client in unconditional positive regard. *See also* Client-Centered Therapy

Positivism   *(education)*   A general philosophical movement that upheld empiricism, the logical analysis of thought and language, and verificationism. Positivism reached its apex with the Vienna Circle of Logical Positivism in the early 20th century.

The term *positivism* and many of its basic ideas originated with Auguste Comte (1798–1857). Comte advocated a strict empiricism, which rejected the possibility of knowledge of unobservable physical objects. Connected with this, he rejected metaphysical speculation as failing to keep imagination limited by observation. In addition to Comte, the Vienna Circle

itself was influenced by the logical methods of Gottlob Frege and Ludwig Wittgenstein, the mathematical developments of David Hilbert and Henri Poincaré, and the physical theories of Ernst Mach and Albert Einstein.

A central tenet of the Vienna Circle was the verifiability criterion of meaning. This criterion required that contingent, synthetic statements be empirically verifiable in some sense to be significant. The justification for this criterion came about through a linkage of verifiability with meaning, such that the meaning of a synthetic sentence was identified with its method of verification. Statements expressing necessary truths were treated by the Circle as analytic and thereby as reducible to tautologies through logical analysis. A related doctrine of the Circle was a form of reductionism, according to which statements about the physical world could be reduced, through logical analysis, to "protocol statements" expressing immediate, noninferentially justified experience. Through a combination of the verifiability criterion with the methods of logical analysis, the Circle thought it possible to demonstrate the meaninglessness of most traditional metaphysical statements.

Despite its influence, the positivism of the Vienna Circle was ultimately subjected to heavy criticism and has few contemporary defenders. One important line of criticism from the philosopher W. V. Quine rejected the positivists' distinction between analytic and synthetic statements as untenable, in part because Quine believed that it failed to acknowledge the theoryladenness, and hence the relativity, of analytic statements. Another line of criticism attacked the verifiability criterion as imposing overly restrictive constraints on meaningfulness. For instance, universal statements such as "For every action, there is an equal and opposite reaction" seem impossible to conclusively verify by any finite set of observations, yet such statements are clearly meaningful nonetheless. For more information, see Quine (1951/1953). *See also* Empiricism; Idealism; Metaphysics; Reductionism

Positivism   *(sociology)*   A major theoretical movement of the 20th century. The Positivist School rejected the notion of free will put forth by the Classical School, which stipulated that crime is a result of a conscious and free choice made by individuals. While the Classical School emphasized reforms in the law to tackle the issue of crime, positivist criminology aimed to explain criminal behavior through scientific experimentation and research. Cesare Lombroso is considered to be the father of positivism. With his theory of born criminals, Lombroso argued that individuals who engage in the most serious forms of offending tend to have primitive instincts and are derived from a lower life form ("atavistic throwback"). These individuals have very distinct physical characteristics (head size, asymmetry of the face, body type, etc.). In short, crime is inevitable for such individuals, as their actions are determined by their physical and psychological deficiencies. Other well-known positivists include Enrico Ferri, Raffaele Garofalo, and William Sheldon. Contemporary positivist criminology remains concerned with the etiology of crime. For more information, see Lombroso (1876). **See also** Classical Criminology; Lombroso, Cesare

Positron Emission Tomography (PET) Scan A revolutionary nuclear-medicine medical brain-imaging technique that can be used to map brain activity over time. It is based on the assumption that areas of high radioactivity are associated with brain activity. The level of activity in a given region of a brain can be measured by the amount of glucose it burns. A small amount of radioactive glucose is injected into the brain, and the scanner measures the amount of it that is consumed by different regions. Images of this are then reconstructed by computer analyses that produce a colored picture. Using the PET scan, psychologists have found that it may be possible to distinguish between different psychological disorders by measuring brain activity. Researchers have also found that different areas are activated when one thinks about the self. For more information, see *Kandel, Schwartz, and Jessell (1999)*. **See also** Computerized Tomography (CT) Scan

Posse Comitatus Act An act passed in 1878 in the United States that prohibited members of the federal military and related services (e.g., the army, the air force, the navy, etc.) from exercising the same powers as appointed officers of the peace. The Posse Comitatus Act prevented the federal government from using military personnel and resources for law enforcement purposes.

Possibilism The belief that culture is shaped by the actions of human beings rather than by nature. A discipline of cultural geography, and standing in direct opposition to geographic determinism, possibilism acknowledges the environmental influence over culture; however, possibilists believe that the environmental influence is a small one and the role of human interaction with the environment is the primary force in shaping culture. Environmental determinism, developed in the beginning of the 20th century, was replaced by possibilism and other forms of cultural geography later in the 20th century, as the idea that the physical environment shaped culture fell out of favor. **See also** Environmental Determinism

Postmodernism A somewhat amorphous concept that at its core involves calling into question modernist or positivist assumptions about the nature of reality. According to the postmodern standpoint, "reality" does not exist as a fixed, objective construct that can be studied; rather, reality is created through the interaction of human knowledge and learning with the world, at all levels from the individual, through the cultural, to the multicultural. In postmodernist thought, no sharp distinction is made between a "fact" and an "opinion": Individuals' beliefs about the world not only invariably color their interpretation of facts but actually *affect*

reality. Thus, in a sense, according to its own terms, postmodernism is inherently undefinable, since "knowledge" in the postmodernist construction is inherently fluid.

The foundational thinkers of postmodernism include Michel Foucault, Jacques Derrida, and Jean-François Lyotard. Foucault's work, in particular, has strong relevance to education, as he specifically addressed not only the construction of knowledge, a common theme in postmodernist works, but also, in *Discipline and Punish,* the nature and history of the school in society. In Foucault's conception, the school—the educational institution—underwent a transition over the course of the past three centuries, from a means to the end of education to an end in itself. The "time of training" became separated both from the rest of an individual's life span and from the rest of society, both physically and socially. Instead of undergoing apprenticeships and other forms of training that involved practical application and that were integrated into the social fabric, students began to be educated in schools, which separated them from the general public and educated them in a set of skills that were divorced from their ultimate practical application.

Another implication of postmodernism in the educational context is the concept of multiculuralism. Specifically, efforts made to move away from the assumption that the values of one cultural group (usually Western) are "true" and instead to accept and integrate perspectives from all cultures into the educational paradigm have their roots in the postmodernist perspective.

In research, the postmodernist paradigm is allied with qualitative research, with its focus on the subjective and intersubjective nature of knowledge and the blurring of the line between researcher and subject, where the researcher is understood to have personal biases that may affect the outcome of the research, and the goal is to present the research participants' viewpoints within a context. Adherents of both qualitative research and the postmodernist thought take issue with what they see as the underlying principles of quantitative methodology, namely, the idea than anything can be fully known and that a researcher's biases play no role in the outcome of the research. For more information, see Foucault (1977). **See also** Poststructuralism; Qualitative Research

Postpositivism A broad cluster of beliefs about research methods in the social and behavioral sciences. Postpositivism is most clearly defined by what it rejects or modifies—positivism. Positivism is an epistemological belief. Epistemology is the study of knowledge: what it is and how we obtain it. The most influential positivists were members of the Vienna Circle in the 1920s. They believed that knowledge can only be obtained scientifically. Furthermore, if something cannot be studied scientifically, then trying to study it in other ways is meaningless. The positivist definition of "scientific" was narrow and mandated the empirical verification of theories. Logical positivism added to this the contention that it is also possible to obtain positive knowledge through rigorous deduction based on the model of mathematics.

Postpositivism is sometimes used to mean any epistemological position that was opposed to positivism, after its heyday in the mid-20th century. More frequently, postpositivism describes those who have adjusted positivism in light of its many criticisms but have tried to salvage its core belief that positive knowledge can be gained through scientific means. Note that postpositivists do not say that knowledge can *only* be obtained through scientific means. One of the biggest differences between positivists and postpositivists is that the latter hardly ever call the work of people with whom they disagree "meaningless" and "nonsense." The use of those terms was among the defining characteristics of the original positivists, who wanted to root out "false" knowledge claims as much as come to positive conclusions. Some of the bitterness of the opponents of positivists stems from this name-calling. ***See also*** Epistemology; Positivism (education)

Postsecondary Education   The next level of education beyond secondary education (high school). Postsecondary education, also called higher education, encompasses institutions of higher learning, such as universities, community colleges, professional schools, as well as technical institutes. Typically, a degree or certificate is issued following completion of the course of study.

Postsecondary Governance   The internal structure, organization, and management of autonomous educational organizations, including the way they are operated. Governing structures vary widely throughout the world, but in the United States, in particular, governing structures typically include a governing board (board of regents, board of directors, etc.), the college/university president, a team of administrators (vice presidents and division directors), deans, department chairs, and some form of representation from student organizations, such as a student government president.

Poststructuralism   The name attributed to a large, diverse body of French theory that followed structuralism from the 1960s until the end of the 20th century, influenced by the events of World War II, the Algerian War, and May 1968. Poststructural scholars, including Jean Baudrillard, Hélène Cixous, Gilles Deleuze, Jacques Derrida, Michel Foucault, Félix Guattari, Luce Irigaray, Julia Kristeva, Jacques Lacan, and Jean-François Lyotard, throw into radical doubt humanist notions of language, discourse, power, knowledge, and the subject. Poststructuralism does not reject the aforementioned concepts; instead, it analyzes the historical contingency of the concepts and what they make possible and impossible, using methodologies such as Deleuzoguattarian schizoanalysis and rhizoanalysis; Derridean affirmative deconstruction; Foucauldian archaeologies, genealogies, and discourse analysis; Lacanian psychoanalysis; and Lyotardian paralogic legitmation.

Poststructuralism "troubles" the idea that language is neutral, by positing instead that it is a productive and culturally situated practice where meaning is constantly destabilized. Language produces discourse and makes possible certain structures, statements, ways of knowing, actions, and subject positions and has material effects that are always tangled in power relations. The poststructural subject is produced within the structures made possible by language, discourse, and power relations, and in turn, it is an active agent in the production of language, discourse, and power relations that subvert or uphold structures. Poststructural theories ask us to take seriously our responsibility for the use of language, the discourses we deploy, and our activities within structures of power, truth, and knowledge. For more information, see Spivak (1993) and St. Pierre (2000). ***See also*** Postmodernism

Posttraumatic Stress Disorder (PTSD)   An anxiety disorder that can develop after one is exposed to a horrifying event or ordeal in which physical harm occurred or was threatened. Traumas can be caused by a range of experiences, such as life-threatening accidents, fires, natural disasters, combat, and so on. It is indentified by symptoms such as recurring anxiety, sleeplessness, nightmares, vivid flashbacks, intrusive thoughts, attentional problems, and social withdrawal. In a study conducted by Ironson et al. (1997) on Miami residents caught in a major hurricane, results revealed that one third exhibited symptoms of PTSD and that the more injury, property damage, and loss they suffered, the more severe their symptoms were. Many forms of psychotherapy have been advocated for trauma-related problems such as PTSD. Basic counseling for PTSD includes education about the condition and provision of safety and support. For more information, see Cahill and Foa (2004) and Ironson et al. (1997). ***See also*** Anxiety Disorders

Poverty   A state of destitution in which individuals cannot conveniently afford the basic necessities of life—food, clothing, and shelter. As a standardized method of measuring poverty across the globe, the World Bank introduced the $1 and $2 per day thresholds in the 1980s to distinguish extreme from severe poverty in absolute terms. Those living on less than $1 per day are classified as living in extreme poverty. Some critics of this absolute measure contend that the benchmarks are exceedingly low.

In the United States, the poverty threshold is relative. As of 2009, an individual with an annual income of $10,830 does not have enough to cover basic needs, and a family of three with an annual income of $18,310 is considered poor.

There are several reasons why some people might be poor. These include lack of opportunity, inadequate education, unemployment, and adverse distributive policies. For more information, see Perkins, Radlet, and Lindauer (2006) and Warburton (2005). *See also* Developing Countries; Gross Domestic Product; Income; Welfare

Power *(communication)* The ability to act effectively and/or to exert control or influence. In positive terms, power can be seen as capable leadership, in pejorative terms, as manipulation or tyranny.

Power has been conceptualized by theorists in many disciplines. The sociologist Amitai Etzioni named three typologies of organizational power: (1) coercive, (2) normative, and (3) remunerative/utilitarian. Coercive power entails force or threat, normative power relies on compliance with organizational expectations and practices, and remunerative power uses rewards. The sociologist Steven Lukes categorized views of political power as being one-, two-, or three-dimensional. While each view shows elements of conflict and subject interest, the one-dimensional view is most concerned with who emerges as the winner of a struggle; the two-dimensional, with who decides which issues get chosen for decisive action; and the three-dimensional, with who controls political agendas.

In terms of media practice, power can be considered an influence in advertising, advocacy, and agenda setting. For more information, see Etzioni (1961), Lukes (1974), and Sisaye (2005). *See also* Coercion (sociology); Politics (sociology)

Power *(education)* One's influence over others. It is the ability to get things done. French and Raven (1959) described five types, or bases, of power: (1) reward power, (2) coercive power, (3) legitimate power, (4) referent power, and (5) expert power.

A person with the ability to reward others is said to have reward power. Thus, a university department chairperson might have reward power in the eyes of a faculty member because of his or her ability to assign teaching loads. The strength of one's reward power increases based on the perceived ability to provide continuous and greater rewards. So a department chairperson's reward power increases in the eyes of a faculty member as he or she is able to provide letters of recommendations for awards, recommendations for tenure and promotion, and the like.

Coercive power stems from the ability of one person to punish another or force that person to act against his or her will. The sponsor of an honor society might be seen to have coercive power by its members based on the minimum grade point average (GPA) they must maintain to remain active members. For example, if a member's GPA slipped below the minimum required for membership in the honor society, the sponsor would have the authority to dismiss the student from it.

Legitimate power is based on the belief that one person has the genuine right to influence others. Others feel an obligation to accept this influence, as it seems to spring from an authentic source. An example of legitimate power would be that of a professor in a college classroom. Students perceive the professor's power as legitimate since he or she has the academic credentials to qualify for such a teaching position.

Referent power is derived from a person's feeling of kinship, affiliation, or liking for another person or group. Sororities and fraternities on college campuses have referent power over their members and pledges. The greater the feelings of kinship or affiliation, the greater the referent power.

Expert power is attributed to an individual when others perceive him or her as having a particular type of knowledge or skill. Career services centers at universities are perceived as having expert power in the area of job placement. Expert power is limited, however, to the particular area of knowledge or skill. Career services centers would not, for example, be recognized by college students as places to seek other types of services, such as counseling or health services. For more information, see French and Raven (1959). *See also* Coercion (sociology)

Power Distance The extent to which members of institutions and organizations expect and accept that authority is distributed unequally and located in individuals and places at some remove from them. Power distance also describes the extent to which employees accept that superiors have more power, income, and/or influence than they actually have and that the decisions and opinions of their superiors are, by and large, the right ones.

The power distance in modest-sized organizations is small, where subordinates work closely with their superiors, the salary range is narrow between the top and bottom levels, and subordinates are consulted for organizational decisions. In larger organizations, members may feel that the power distance is much greater, where contact with superiors is limited, the salary range between the top and bottom levels is wide, and there is little or no member input into organizational decision making. Organizations with a large power distance are much more centrally organized, with clear chains of command. *See also* Organizational Culture (communication)

Power Test A timed knowledge test. Time limits are generally for administrative purposes and are not intended to affect performance. However, in some cases, time limits may indeed influence the rate or accuracy of responses, often evidenced by random guessing at the end of a test. *See also* Achievement Tests

Pragmatic Party The name of the fictional political party created in 2006 by the *Dilbert* cartoon series creator, Scott Adams. The party became an Internet blog sensation among its fans. Adams (2007) described the Pragmatic Party as follows:

> In my fantasy I form what I call the Pragmatic Party. All of my policies would be based on what is most practical . . . You need one Big Idea when you

run for President. I would explain that our current system of government was conceived prior to the Internet, electronic mass media, and sophisticated polling methods. 200 years ago the only practical form of government involved voting for a small group of individuals that would pretend to represent you. Now we have better tools and we should use them . . . The Pragmatic Party platform would always mirror the majority opinion of the country. When the majority opinion changed, so too would my platform. (p. 126)

Dilbert is the name of a popular American cartoon series, first appearing in 1989, which satirizes life in corporate America. For more information, see Adams (2007).

Pragmatics   The use of socially acceptable language patterns to clearly communicate. Pragmatics takes into consideration the actual semantics and linguistic aspects of communication. Furthermore, pragmatics takes into account cultural differences in the use of language devices and patterns. This may include euphemisms, metaphors, or devices; it also includes colloquialisms, dialectic differences, or variations of meaning within a context. Finally, pragmatics addresses *mores,* or the rules of conversation, which define what is socially appropriate or inappropriate. **See also** Diversity; Linguistics; Social Norm; Sociolinguistics

Pragmatism   a family of philosophies first formulated in the United States in the late 19th and early 20th centuries, most prominently by Charles Sanders Peirce (1839–1914), William James (1842–1910), and John Dewey (1859–1952). Pragmatism was formulated in reaction to the metaphysical excesses of 19th-century Continental philosophy (especially that of George Wilhelm Fredrick Hegel), the early modern philosophical debate between the rationalists (especially Descartes) and the empiricists (John Locke, George Berkeley, and David Hume), and the "spectator view" of philosophy (where the philosopher examines the "external world" and philosophizes about its nature), which dates back to Socrates and Plato. The goal was to bring philosophy back to the world of experiences, actions, and consequences and to avoid traditional dualisms that had been long debated in philosophy (sometimes since ancient times), such as appearance versus reality, freewill versus determinism, facts versus values, subjectivism versus objectivism, realism versus antirealism, and rationalism versus empiricism. The goal in pragmatism was to focus knowledge more on practical outcomes than on abstract philosophical debates that often led to either skepticism or dogmatism. The goal was to find workable "solutions" to problems in the world. The *pragmatic maxim* states that the meaning, or instrumental or provisional truth, of a concept, expression, or practice is determined by the experiences or consequences following the firm belief in or use of the concept or practice. Following are some of the principles of pragmatism: (a) search for a middle ground on dualisms and other polarized philosophical disputes; (b) reject dichotomous (either/or) thinking and related attempts to force all considerations of knowledge into deductive logical systems; (c) view knowledge as originating in the interaction of person/organism and environment; (d) view knowledge as individually/ socially constructed and simultaneously resulting from empirical discovery; (e) view theories instrumentally (i.e., not as true or false but as more or less instrumentally useful for predicting, explaining, and influencing); (f) take the ontological position of pluralism (i.e., that multiple perspectives and theories about complex phenomena can be "true"); (g) take the epistemological position that there are multiple routes to knowledge and that researchers make "warranted assertions" rather than claims of unvarying, eternal truths; (h) view inquiry as ongoing and operating within each individual as well as in science as we search for solutions to the problems we face; (i) incorporate values directly into inquiry and endorse equality, freedom, and democracy; (j) thoroughly accept the doctrine of fallibilism of research and knowledge; and (k) ultimately view Truth as what is obtained only at the end of history. Pragmatism takes other philosophies seriously (e.g., Anglo-American and Continental philosophy) but tries to identify what is true or useful in each and bring the best parts together for common causes and to solve social problems. **See also** Epistemology; Liberalism (education, political science); Pluralism (education, political science); Progressivism (education, public administration); Utilitarianism (education, political science)

Pre-Assessment of Learning   A strategy used by teachers to explore students' knowledge, skills, and attitudes about an instructional unit or topic. It takes place before the beginning of formal instruction to make decisions on learners' strengths and needs. Pre-assessment helps teachers determine what and how they should teach. **See also** Assessment

Precedent *(political science)*   The past cases that relate to the case being decided under a common-law system. This principle is known as *stare decisis,* Latin for "stand by what is decided." It is unusual and highly discouraged for a judge to depart from precedent, but if he or she does do so, the judge is required to detail the reasons for his or her departure in a written decision. If there are no available cases on the legal matter at issue in the court's jurisdiction, similar cases or ones from nearby jurisdictions are presented in its place. Precedent serves as an essential guide for law under a common-law system, since the written laws are usually vague and ambiguous; the details of the law's spirit thus need to be defined by the courts. **See also** Common Law (political science); *Stare Decisis*

Precedent *(sociology)*   A legal principle or rule established in an earlier case. To the extent possible, courts adhere to the principle of *stare decisis*, Latin for "stand by what is decided." When presented with a case with facts similar to already decided cases, courts rely on the precedents set in those earlier cases in rendering the current decision. ***See also*** Case Law; *Stare Decisis*

Predictive Validity The extent to which a test score predicts the future score on another criterion measure. For example, if the purpose of an admission test is to predict future college success, the correlation of the test score and the college grade average may be examined. ***See also*** Validity

Preemption The interests of the federal government are so great that federal law or regulation overrides any state law, although state governments might otherwise have jurisdiction over a particular issue. A definition of preemption begins with the constitutional fact of federalism, that both the federal government and the state governments are separate sovereigns. The first pillar of the preemption doctrine is the supremacy clause, Article 6 of the U.S. Constitution:

> This Constitution, and the Laws of the United States which shall be made in Pursuance thereof; and all Treaties made, or which shall be made, under the Authority of the United States, *shall be the supreme Law of the Land;* and the Judges in every State shall be bound thereby, any Thing in the Constitution or Laws of any State to the Contrary notwithstanding. A second pillar, which is also a limitation, is the commerce clause, Article 1, Section 8 of the Constitution: "The Congress shall have Power to regulate Commerce with foreign Nations, and among the several States, and with the Indian Tribes."

As originally conceptualized and explained by James Madison in 1788, the powers delegated by the proposed Constitution to the federal government, are few and defined. Those which are to remain in the state governments are numerous and indefinite. The former will be exercised principally on external objects, as war, peace, negotiation, and foreign commerce; with which last the power of taxation will, for the most part, be connected. The powers reserved to the several states will extend to all the objects which, in the ordinary course of affairs, concern the lives, liberties, and properties of the people, and the internal order, improvement, and prosperity of the state. The power of the states is called "the police power," or the authority to undertake action, such as issuing

> regulations designed to promote the public convenience or the general prosperity as well as those to promote public safety, health, and morals, and is not confined to the suppression of what is offensive, disorderly, or unsanitary, but extends to what is for the greatest welfare of the state.

(*Federalist* No. 45, "Alleged Danger From the Powers of the Union to the State Governments Considered")

Over time, however, the role of the federal government has grown, primarily by means of the commerce clause. Consequently, the federal government may act, by law and regulations—with federal agency regulations having the force of law (i.e., having supremacy over state law)—in a matter that may traditionally be one in which state governments have acted, such as labor relations. It is presumed, however, that where Congress legislates in a field traditionally occupied by the states, courts should start with the assumption that the historic police powers of the states are not to be superseded by the federal act unless that was the clear and manifest purpose of Congress. The Supreme Court of the United States has recognized two types of preemptive language: (1) express preemption, or specific prescriptive or nonprescriptive displacement of state laws, in which federal law is intended to displace state law, and (2) implied preemption. It has also identified two types of implied preemption: (1) field preemption, where the federal government "occupies the field" and leaves no room for state regulation, and (2) conflict preemption, where state law is in direct conflict with federal law.

President Clinton issued Executive Order No. 13,132, "Federalism," on August 4, 1999, revoking earlier orders, among other things, to establish guidelines for preemption. Section 4, Special Requirements for Preemption, mandates that the agencies, in taking action that preempt state law, shall act in strict accordance with governing law. They

> [(a)] shall construe, in regulations and otherwise, a Federal statute to preempt State law only where the statute contains an express preemption provision or there is some other clear evidence that the Congress intended preemption of State law, or where the exercise of State authority conflicts with the exercise of Federal authority under the Federal statute; (b) Where a Federal statute does not preempt State law . . . agencies shall construe any authorization in the statute for the issuance of regulations as authorizing preemption of State law by rulemaking only when the exercise of State authority directly conflicts with the exercise of Federal authority under the Federal statute or there is clear evidence to conclude that the Congress intended the agency to have the authority to preempt State law; (c) Any regulatory preemption of State law shall be restricted to the minimum level necessary to achieve the objectives of the statute pursuant to which the regulations are promulgated; (d) When an agency foresees the possibility of a conflict between State law and Federally protected interests within its area of regulatory responsibility, the agency shall consult,

to the extent practicable, with appropriate State and local officials in an effort to avoid such a conflict; and (e) When an agency proposes to act through adjudication or rulemaking to preempt State law, the agency shall provide all affected State and local officials notice and an opportunity for appropriate participation in the proceedings.

For more information, see Executive Order No. 13,132 (1999), Madison, Hamilton, & Jay (1788/1987), Senate Document No. 108–17 (2004), Senate Document No. 108–19 (2004), Senate Document No. 110–6 (2007), and *The Constitution of the United States of America, Analysis and Interpretation: Annotations of cases decided by the Supreme Court of the United States* (2002). *See also* Commerce Clause; Federalism; Federalist Papers; Supremacy Doctrine

Prehistoric   From a period of time before the existence of written or recorded history. Information from prehistoric times has generally been obtained through archaeological, anthropological, and other artifacts.

Prejudice *(media studies)*   The act of making a judgment about something without or before having relevant facts about it. Prejudice involves making and defending categories and using those categories to make decisions and carry out actions; prejudice does not usually change when new information or experience is available. Prejudice today often refers to racial prejudgments and attributing to an individual the preconceived negative qualities of the ethnic, gender, or racial group to which that person belongs. Prejudice, which involves usually negative and often unfounded stereotypes and generalizations, is hard to change because it is often supported beyond the individual: by the family or the community. Prejudices are learned as a member of a group because groups use various forms of prejudice to define who is part of the group and who is not.

In his classic study of prejudice, the psychologist Gordon Allport defined five aspects of prejudice that when applied to a society told how prejudiced that society was. On Allport's Scale of Prejudice, Scale 1 was Antilocution, saying negative things or making jokes about a group. At Scale 2, Avoidance is common, and the majority group isolates or avoids the minority. At Scale 3, called Discrimination, prejudice is acted out through denying the target group equal opportunities. At Scale 4, Physical Attacks by the prejudiced group on the minority group are carried out with the intent to cause physical harm. At Scale 5, Extermination, the total elimination of the minority group is the goal. For more information, see Allport (1954/1979). *See also* Ethnocentrism (communication); Stereotyping

Prejudice *(psychology)*   Negative feelings toward others based solely on their membership in a certain group. People often dislike others because they are different. Farley classified prejudice into three categories—cognitive

prejudice, affective prejudice, and conative prejudice. Cognitive prejudice refers to what people believe is true. Affective prejudice refers to what people like and dislike. Conative prejudice refers to how people are inclined to behave. These three types of prejudice are correlated, but all need not be present in a particular individual. For more information, see Farley (2005) and Miles, Mark, and Hazel (2002). *See also* Discrimination (sociology)

Prejudice and Discrimination   A rigid, overly simplified, and unfair generalization about a person or a social group. It can be positive or negative and is based on false or incomplete information. It typically is based on stereotypes, such that all members of the group are assumed to have a specific set of traits or characteristics. Prejudice leads to discrimination, an action or omission expressing disdain and/or prejudice and directed toward one or more persons due to their demographic affiliation(s). Acts of discrimination can be blatant or subtle. *See also* Stereotype (psychology)

Preliminary Hearing   An evidentiary hearing that takes place early in the criminal process to determine if there is probable cause to establish (1) that the alleged crime took place in the jurisdiction of the court and (2) that the person charged with the crime could have committed the crime. If probable cause is established, a formal charging document known as "information" is issued. Some jurisdictions use grand jury proceedings instead of preliminary hearings. At the end of the preliminary hearing, the judge schedules a date for the arraignment. *See also* Arraignment; Grand Jury; Indictment; Information; Probable Cause

Preoperational Stage   The second in four stages of cognitive development proposed by Jean Piaget (1896–1980). At some point during the child's second year, developments in memory lead to permanence with respect to people no longer in view; that is, the child understands that others are still there even if they are out of the child's visual field. Children also become more verbal and abstract in their thinking during this period, starting to use words and images to symbolize objects. In this stage, reasoning is typically intuitive and prelogical, and as such, children at this stage of development often have difficulty performing mental operations. This stage of development is further characterized by two features—egocentrism and conservation. For more information, see Piaget (1954). *See also* Cognitive Development

Preponderance of the Evidence   The increased power of evidence presented by one party in a civil case, which will result in a favorable verdict. A judge or jury will make a decision about the outcome of the case based on an assessment of the party that has presented the most convincing evidence. *See also* Civil Law (sociology); Verdict

Presentence Investigation Report   A report typically written by the Department of Probation and used by a judge in sentencing. A presentence investigation report is a concise but detailed offense summary that describes the nature and circumstances of the offense, the background and current status of the offender, and the impact of the offense on the victim and the community, and it often includes a sentence recommendation. Presentence investigation reports are seen as essential to the sentencing process because few cases ever go to trial and the vast majority of all convictions are secured through guilty pleas or plea bargains. **See also** Probation; Sentencing

President   A common title for the head of state in most republics, whether popularly elected or chosen by the legislature or a special electoral college. The title is also often adopted by dictators.

An English word, the term was originally used to refer to the presiding officer of a committee or governing body in Great Britain. Later, this usage was applied to state-level political leaders. As other countries followed the American and French revolutions and deposed their monarchies, the title "President" was commonly adopted as for the new heads of state. The first European president was the President of France, a post created in 1848. The first president of an internationally recognized African state was the President of Liberia, also in 1848. Today, many African nations and also South and Central American nations use the term.

The presidency of the United States is limited to acting as commander-in-chief of the U.S. Army and Navy and of the state militias, but "when called into the actual Service of the United States," the actual power of the U.S. President is much greater than this list would suggest. As commander-in-chief of a superpower in a world with nuclear weapons, the President has almost unlimited power. The restrictions on making treaties can be, and frequently are, evaded by calling them "executive agreements." Congress has tried to have a say in the "imperial presidency" but with no real success in foreign policy, primarily because this branch of government has given the President the powers in the first place, usually in an emergency. This happened at the beginning of the escalation of the Vietnam War, when Congress granted such authority to President Lyndon B. Johnson, after the "Gulf of Tonkin" incident.

In domestic policy, the power of the U.S. President is much weaker. He may run executive departments however he pleases, but even this is subject to having his administrators ratified by the Senate, which in recent years has been a substantial obstacle. Domestic policy making is best regarded as a game in which the President, the two houses of Congress (separately), and the federal courts have a set of interlocking veto powers. For any policy to be implemented, a number of the players with vetoes must agree (the number varying with the policy area). Presidents may be directly elected, indirectly elected, or appointed. The United States has a complicated process that involves the use of an electoral college. For more information, see Hart (1987) and Schlesinger (1973). **See also** Congress; Electoral College

Pretrial Detention/Release   Detention in a jail facility while awaiting trial. Those arrested and charged with a felony criminal offense face one of two pretrial dispositions: (1) they are released (on their own recognizance, conditionally, or on bail/bond) or (2) remanded to custody. The pretrial disposition decision usually occurs during the preliminary hearing and generally within 48 hours of arrest. When it comes to pretrial detention decisions, there is a presumption in favor of release. The type and seriousness of the offense and the defendant's employment status, prior record, and ties with the community are considered relevant in the pretrial release determination. For those detained pretrial, the time served while awaiting trial is typically deducted from the eventual sentence if found guilty. **See also** Jail; Preliminary Hearing

Prevalence   The total number of individuals who have the characteristic of interest in proportion to the population size at any given point in time. The prevalence of a given incident, social phenomenon, or disease is computed by dividing the total number of individuals presenting a given trait or the symptoms of a particular disease at a specific point in time by the total number of individuals in the population of interest. In contrast to prevalence, incidence assesses the number of cases (not individuals) of the characteristic or trait of interest over a one-year period, in proportion to the population size. **See also** Incidence

Price   The value at which goods, services, or assets can be bought and sold or exchanged. Price is said to be determined freely when the market forces of supply and demand are left to operate on their own without any external intervention. In such a situation, price is deemed to be an efficient allocator of resources and commodities. The price at which the expectations of buyers and sellers are realized, as a result of the meeting of minds, is known as the equilibrium price. Economic shocks, commodity availability, and inflexible prices have made it impossible to rely entirely on the free movement of prices. Consequently, policymakers intervene in markets to set prices. Examples of such intervention are minimum wage, usury laws, and federal funds rate. **See also** Commodity; Fiscal Policy; Laissez-Faire (economics); Market Forces; Stabilization

Primacy Effect   An effect that occurs when people are more influenced by information they receive early in an interaction than by information that appears later on. At the same time, when a person is engaged and alert, the influence of this effect is diminished. This effect occurs for two reasons. First, we become somewhat attentive to later information only when we have already formed an impression. The second reason is what is known as the change-of-meaning hypothesis. This states that once people form an impression, they later interpret inconsistent information in light of that impression. Depending on first impressions, the same information can be interpreted in multiple ways. The primacy effect is reduced when items are presented quickly and is enhanced when they are presented slowly. For more information, see Healy, Havas, and Parker (2000). *See also* Serial-Position Curve

Primary Election   An election where voters choose which candidate should run as a political party's candidate in a subsequent election. Primaries can be "open" or "closed." Open means that registered party members of the opposing party and/or independents may vote, although no voter can vote in both elections. Closed primaries are those restricted to voters who hold party membership. In the United States, primaries are held for election of the presidential nominee of each party. Some states choose to hold caucuses, meetings of party members where a vote is taken, instead of primaries, which involve individuals voting at a polling station. Primaries result in electoral votes that represent the votes of delegates who are sent to each party's respective convention, although a minority percentage of delegates at the Democratic Convention, sometimes called "superdelegates," are not bound to vote according to the primary results. *See also* Closed Primary; Election; Open Party Caucuses

Prime Meridian   The 0-degree longitude line that determines the time of the day. There are intervals on the prime meridian about 15 degrees long that stand for one hour in terms of measurement of the sun's revolution. The prime meridian passes through England, France, Togo, and down to Antarctica. It is opposite to the International Date Line and is also used for giving suitable directions. The Moon and Mars also have prime meridians. *See also* International Date Line

Priming   The tendency for a recently presented concept to prime responses to a subsequent target question. It is considered to be one of the manifestations of implicit memory. A property of priming is that the remembered item is remembered best in the form in which it was originally encountered. If a priming list is given in an auditory mode, then an auditory cue produces better performance than a visual cue. Subliminal presentation of information can also lead to priming. For more information, see Marcel (1983). *See also* Implicit Memory

Primitive   That which is less advanced, underdeveloped, or in early stages of development. Although the term *primitive* can be used in a variety of contexts, it is often used to describe the early stages of human evolution.

Printing   The process of setting written material or illustrations onto a surface such as paper by means of a press. The contrast between scribal and printing cultures was not as abrupt as is often considered to be. The designers of the early presses (Gutenberg, Manutius, Caxton, et al.) were motivated more to rival the professional scribe than to develop a system of mass production and distribution; it is only in hindsight that media theorists have ascribed to printing these dramatic consequences. The first books were meant to create a high-quality product that looked as good as the scribe's individual work but more quickly and more cheaply. Vellum was regularly used in the early printed books, for example, in the deluxe copies of the Gutenberg Bible. They were printed with spaces left for the illuminator to work on by hand, and the first type re-created the effect of calligraphy, with ligatures and ornate capitals that looked as if done by quill. Manuscript culture itself was much speedier than is suggested by the image of a solitary scribe laboring over one tome. Monastic scriptoria had developed a system of speeding up the production of copying by breaking the book up into its component-sewn gatherings and setting many scribes to work on just one gathering—an early model of assembly line production. The university towns later perfected this model by developing what is known as the *pecia* system of copying. Each *pecia* was one gathering of the book used as an exemplar and kept at the stationer's. By renting out the exemplar to multiple students, each borrowing and copying a different pecia from each other, the book could be reduplicated rapidly. A simplified script, abbreviations, thinner and cheaper parchment, and abandonment of ornamentation, all contributed to the rapidity of copying. The rising demand for texts among the laity (romances, devotional treatises, prayer books) maintained the need for such stationers even where no university was in residence. Movable type was a critical innovation in European presses, which till then used woodblock stamping (movable type was already known in Asia). Paper, another Asian development, was manufactured in Europe from as early as the 12th and 13th centuries, and the use in printing of paper rather than of parchment encouraged the final separation of print from manuscript culture. Books such as the Gutenberg Bible are large and heavy, and it was only with cheaper, smaller-format books, printed in the vernacular rather than in the scholarly languages of Latin and Greek, that the impact of printing began to be felt throughout literate society. Without the standardization and wide dissemination of ideas made possible by printing, it is questionable whether the Protestant Reformation and the Scientific Revolution could have had the impact they had in Europe. *See also* Culture (communication); Parchment; Printing Press; Print Media

Printing Press   The presses of Johannes Gutenberg and the early printers combined movable metal type with oil-based ink (more durable than water-based inks) and the hand press. A reusable mould enabled mass production of individual metal types for setting series of pages at a time. The earliest typography mimicked the scribal hand, then through the 16th and 17th centuries aimed to perfect the calligraphic art of well-proportioned letters plotted onto mathematical grids. But people were increasingly reading books to gain information, and in the mid-18th century, a family of French printers developed a typeface that embodied the Enlightenment spirit of rationality and elegant plainness—Didot. Technological advancement affected methods not only of printing but also of compositing. From the time of Gutenberg, the compositor used to have to assemble the type by hand, letter by letter, and then return each individual piece after the print run. In the late 19th century, the development of Linotype and Monotype mechanized typesetting by means of a keyboard.

Letterpress (or relief or typographic printing) refers to the process of pressing paper onto inked type. There are various kinds of letterpress methods. The flatbed press uses a flat surface for the plates of composed type against which paper is pressed, using either another flat surface (platen) or a cylinder rolling across it. The first cylinder flatbed press was in use by the early 19th century to print newspapers. In contrast to the jawlike motion of the platen press, the rotary press comprises two cylinders revolving in opposite directions: The plate cylinder carries the curved, inked print plates; the impression cylinder presses onto the plate cylinder the paper, which is fed continuously from a roll. Sophisticated variations of this basic model enable printing on both sides of paper in multiple types and colors, cutting, and folding, all at high speed. Its usefulness for newspaper production is evident. Lithography, developed in the late 18th century, contrasts with the letterpress by fixing the image to the paper chemically rather than by embossing or depressing it. The most widely used kind of commercial printing today for high-volume output is offset printing, a variation of the lithographic process, in which the blank areas of the page are protected by water and the image-bearing areas of the page are coated with oil-based ink. Because ink and water do not mix, the image is clean, sharp, and of high quality. Xerography (from the Greek *xeros,* dry), developed in the 20th century, is the method used in photocopying machines and laser printers. The image to be copied is illuminated, projected, and reproduced using developing powder (toner). ***See also*** Culture (communication, education); Newspaper; Parchment; Printing; Print Media

Print Media Printing on paper originated in China around the 8th century CE, with the use of wooden blocks carved to reproduce text or images. The Chinese also used baked clay movable type. Block printing spread to Europe in the 14th century. The first European printing press using movable metal type was probably developed around 1450 by Johannes Gutenberg in Mainz. By 1500, there were 250 printing presses in Europe. Early type attempted to mirror the appearance of handwriting. Early printers produced bibles, romances, lives of the saints, travel guides, sermons, ballads,

handbills, Latin and Greek classics in their original languages and the vernacular, and many other works to be read by an increasingly literate public. Formats included single sheets of paper called broadsheets or broadsides, chapbooks or booklets made of single large sheets folded in four, and multiple-page bound volumes.

Printing presses increased the speed and accuracy with which written works could be copied, thus increasing the ability of information to travel through and between communities. Printed works were used in the dissemination of new ideas, thoughts, and ideologies, from Luther and Calvin to Marx, as well as news of business matters; politics; scientific, geographic, and medical discoveries; and other events. Printed media, especially newspapers and other periodicals, constituted the sole mass media until the development and widespread adoption of radio broadcasting in the early 20th century, followed by television in the late 1940s and 1950s and the Internet in the 1990s.

Many works that were developed using print format are adding, or moving entirely to, an electronic format for Web delivery, including newspapers, popular magazines, academic journals, technical books, and even literary books. The print-on-paper format, however, remains the most suitable for long-term storage, without the data loss or retrieval problems of the electronic format. For more information, see Crowley and Heyer (2007), Febvre and Martin (1997), and Stephens (2007). ***See also*** Media, New; Newspaper; Publishing Industry; Tabloid Newspapers/Coverage; Typography; Visual Images

Prison/Prisoner Institutions designed for the confinement of convicted felons who have been sentenced to more than one year of incarceration. Prisons are distinct from jails in that prisons typically confine only sentenced offenders serving more than one year, while jails hold pretrial detainees as well as misdemeanants serving shorter sentences. Moreover, jails are typically administered by local law enforcement agencies, while prisons are administered by state departments of correction. Although there is evidence of confinement facilities of various types throughout history, the prison as we know it today is a relatively young institution. The birth of the modern prison is generally credited to the penal reformers of the late 1700s and the development of the penitentiaries in the United States in the early 1800s. Two competing models of a penitentiary system emerged in New York and Pennsylvania, and penal reformers of the time had high hopes for the potential of these new institutions. Within less than 50 years, it was clear that the penitentiaries had not achieved their lofty aims, and they were gradually replaced by reformatories, which were, in turn, gradually replaced by prisons. Today, prisons are generally places designed solely for punishment. Rehabilitation and reform are no longer the central aims of the institution. There are more prisons and prisoners today than at any previous time in history, and research suggests that, at

P

least in the United States, convicted offenders are more likely to be sent to prison and more likely to serve lengthy terms of imprisonment when they arrive. ***See also*** Imprisonment; Incapacitate; Incarcerate; Jail; Penology; Punishment (sociology); Retribution

Privacy, Right to A basic right that protects individuals from an invasion of their private and personal lives. Individuals have the freedom to choose to keep information about themselves and those surrounding them private. Article 12 of the Universal Declaration of Human Rights stipulates,

> No one shall be subjected to arbitrary interference with his privacy, family, home or correspondence, nor to attacks upon his honour and reputation. Everyone has the right to the protection of the law against such interference or attacks. (www.un.org/Overview/rights.html)

In 1974, the U.S. Congress adopted the Privacy Act, which prevented agencies (with some exceptions) from disclosing private information about individuals included in their official records.

Private Law The area of law that pertains only to private individuals, associations, and corporations. This differs from public law, which encompasses law relating to the government and the government's relations with private citizens, individuals, and associations.

Private law includes civil law (relating to contracts, torts, property, family), labor law, and commercial or business law. The distinction between public and private law dates back to the Middle Ages; it was codified into the Corpus Juris Civilis (534 AD), the compilation of Roman Law issued under the order of Justinian I of the Byzantine Empire.

Private law can also refer to legislation that benefits an individual or locality. Individuals usually apply for relief under private law if legal and administrative means prove unsatisfactory. Issues dealt with under private law include immigration (granting of citizenship or residency), taxation claims, veterans' claims, military decoration claims, and general claims against the government. At the federal level, private-law bills generally begin with the phrase "For the relief of." ***See also*** Civil Law (political science)

Private Market In public administration, economics, and political science, this term is essentially synonymous with the term *free,* or private, *market,* in which goods and services are both owned and exchanged without excessive government regulation or restriction. The antonym for this market is a command economy, in which government controls the means of production as well as all decisions in relation to production, distribution, and pricing. The private market operates on the simplest basis through supply and demand. Goods are allocated on the basis of who

can pay, not what the state commands. The pure free-market theorists even oppose taxation. Markets emerge as a result of certain economic decisions made by the producers of goods and services. Adam Smith and his intellectual descendants declare that such an economy results in spontaneous order, where the "invisible hand [which] promotes an end . . . by pursuing his own interest . . . promotes that [end] of the society more effectually" (Smith, *The Wealth of Nations,* 1776). Such a market is closely associated with the laissez-faire philosophy. In such capitalistic economies, the private market or sector takes on the responsibility for generating new wealth, businesses, technological developments, and higher standards of living. Influential economic theorists such as Ludwig von Mises and Frederic von Hayek believe that free markets are natural to a free society. In practice, however, the free or private market is an ideal or normative value. In reality, markets cannot operate in a society without some regulation against fraud and deceit. The government must provide a legal and political environment in which businesses can function freely. When government steps back, as it had done in the United States in the late 20th century, the market is open to manipulation and criminal activity. The 2008 economic collapse illustrates well the results of the irresponsible economic deregulation that began during the Jimmy Carter administration (1977–1981), picked up steam under Ronald Reagan (1981–1989), was abetted by the policies of both George H. W. Bush (1989–1993) and Bill Clinton (1993–2001), and finally reached its nadir, ending in almost total financial collapse, with the reckless economic policies of George W. Bush (2001–2009). For example, the financial crimes of free-market buccaneers in the early 21st century, with their sophisticated but mainly fraudulent financial instruments and outright large-scale con games and theft, brought the American financial and economic system to near meltdown and financially ruined millions of pensioners, businesses, charitable organizations, and institutional endowments.

Private-market value is another use of the term. This usage refers to the value of the parts as opposed to the whole of any economic entity. For instance, when a company is being taken over, analysts look at the value of its component parts to determine its real value. For more information, see Hayek (1944), Mises (1922/1951), Petsoulas (2001), and Smith (1776/2007). ***See also*** Capitalism (economics); Demand; Laissez-Faire (economics); Market; Supply

Private Sector The area of commerce that is not run, or is run in part, by the government. This sector differs from the public sector, which provides goods and/or services by, or on behalf of, the government. Common segments of the public sector include the police and the prison system, the military, transportation infrastructure, education, and health care for the poor. The number of public versus private sector institutions in a nation depends on its economic system; capitalism would have the least and socialism and communism the most. When government services or institutions are transferred to private ownership, it is called privatization. This global trend began during the 1980s, triggered by the growth in private industry and encouraging economic theory. Proponents of privatization believe that it increases efficiency due to free-market competition forces. Antagonists counter that there is less accountability and a potential for substandard performance due to the profit-making incentive. Examples of privatization include outsourcing, private financing of government ventures, and the transfer of publically owned business to private concerns.

The success of privatization is, however, dependent on necessary preconditions. These preconditions may require a period of transition and assurances that the new products are equally better or reliable. There is also the problem of market failure, which might have forced government officials to manage the organizations to begin with. There is no guarantee that a reversion to an unfettered market or the private sector will provide the necessary safeguards that prompted the government to assume ownership in the first place.

There is usually apprehension about turning over vital services, such as water supply and electricity, to the private sector because of adverse social and political consequences. Goods and services with inelastic demand provide exceptionally good opportunities for increased revenue by charging higher prices.

Market failure has been of concern in market economies for a long time. For example, in the 1930s, the Great Depression not only brought into existence extensive regulation of markets (a variance of privatization), it also created a safety net to protect people from adversities in old age—social security and unemployment insurance. Privatizing social security raises concerns. Similarly, the creation of the Federal Mortgage Association (Fannie Mae) was a response to the inability of the markets to create mortgage at reasonable terms for low- and middle-income individuals and families. Ultimately this created an arena for speculation so that many people lost their investments.

Although privatization may reduce costs and increase profits, it is worth noting that it provides opportunities for rent-seeking activities, corruption, nepotism, and unemployment (undesirable outcomes). The market failures of 2008–2009, the result of disastrous economic policies from the deregulations of the Carter administration to the George W. Bush administration's economic catastrophes, have brought the question of more extensive regulation back into the spotlight. *See also* Corruption (economics); Elasticity; Market Failure; Privatization (political science); Public Goods (economics); Public Sector

Privatization *(political science)* The transfer of services or institutions from state to private ownership. Ernst Ulrich Weizacker and his colleagues, in *Limits to Privatization* (2005, p. 6), identified four broad categories of privatization: (1) putting state monopolies in competition with private, or other state, operators; (2) outsourcing, whereby governments pay private actors to perform previously state-provided activities and services; (3) private financing, in exchange for delegated management, often turning the institution back over to the government after a period of profitable use; and (4) transfer of publicly owned assets into private hands. Privatization efforts under debate in the United States include the sale of Amtrak, a universal school voucher system, and the privatization of prisons, or at least certain prison services, such as health. For more information, see Weizacker, Young, and Finger (2005). *See also* Private Sector; Public Sector

Privatization *(public administration)* The government practice of engaging a third party to deliver a service but retain its role in policy. For example, government may contract with a private firm to take care of computer programming or with a nonprofit to deliver a service to welfare recipients. In each of these scenarios, government provides the parameters for the party providing or delivering the service and the funding. A majority of privatization has occurred in human services, as a result of the Personal Responsibility and Work Opportunity Reconciliation Act of 1996.

Contracting is the most common mechanism used for privatizing public services. A government that contracts regards the resources required to manage the contract as part of the cost of contracting. Moreover, it trains the contract managers to develop contract requirements as well as performance measures to be used for the contracts. Most often, young employees are hired with the expectation that they bring with them technical and managerial expertise that the government lacks. *See also* Private Sector; Public Sector

Privatization of Schools The controversial shifting of services in school districts from the control of public sector employees to that of private companies. This shift has been particularly evident in urban schools in areas with lower socioeconomic status. *See also* No Child Left Behind (NCLB); Public Versus Private Schools

Privileged Conversations (Reporters' Protection of News Sources) Reporters rely on sources to provide them with information for a story. These sources may speak "on the record" and be identified by name. Unnamed sources also provide valuable information and may be identified as an unnamed "government spokesperson" or "industry analyst" or some such similar term. Background or "deep background" information may be provided by people speaking "off the record," who are not identified even by occupation. The identity of unnamed sources is generally known only to the reporter and perhaps revealed to the editor. Many stories, particularly about sensitive and/or controversial issues, could not have been developed without the information supplied by anonymous and/or confidential sources. Legally, conversations between reporters and anonymous or confidential sources are considered somewhat privileged, similar to conversations between lawyer and client or doctor and patient, but with much less protection.

One of the most famous confidential sources was "Deep Throat," a high-ranking member of the FBI who provided information to the *Washington Post* journalists Bob Woodward and Carl Bernstein about the Watergate affair. Deep Throat confirmed their investigative research into the criminal activities of the Committee to Re-Elect the President. Publication of the stories led, eventually, to the resignation of President Nixon. After 30 years, the anonymity of Deep Throat was broken by his lawyer, who revealed Deep Throat to be Mark Felt.

Reporters who refused to reveal the identity of their sources to courts have on occasion been jailed and their employers fined. In *Branzburg v. Hayes* (1972), the Supreme Court found that reporters can be ordered to testify in front of a grand jury. One of the judges, while agreeing with the ruling, stated that when deciding privilege, a balance should be struck between freedom of the press and the government interest.

Shield laws have been passed by most state legislatures to give some protection to reporters. The House of Representatives Judiciary Committee passed on March 25, 2009, a federal shield law, the Free Flow of Information Act (HR 985), which is yet to come to a full vote in the House. Shield laws generally attempt to balance the freedom of the press with security and law enforcement needs. For more information, see *Branzburg v. Hayes* (1972) and Pearlstine (2007). ***See also*** Reporter; Shield Laws

Proactive Interference   The situation in which prior information inhibits our ability to recall something new. Underwood, in 1957, demonstrated that information learned before encoding a target item can worsen recall of that target item. Proactive interference can be demonstrated using the Brown-Peterson paradigm. A single Brown-Peterson trial consists of a study list, a retention interval, and then a recall period. Studies show that performance is usually close to perfect on the first trial and declines on subsequent trials that use study lists drawn from the same category. For more information, see Brown (1958) and Underwood (1957). ***See also*** Retroactive Interference

Probability Value (*p* Value)   The probability of the observed value of a sample statistic, or a more extreme value, if the null hypothesis were true. It is a conditional probability because it tells the researcher the probability of the observed result *if the null hypothesis were true*. The probability value does not tell the researcher the probability that the null hypothesis is true; it does not tell the researcher the probability that the alternative hypothesis is true; and it does not tell the researcher the probability that the null hypothesis is false. When the probability value is small, the researcher rejects the null hypothesis and tentatively

accepts the alternative hypothesis. ***See also*** Hypothesis Testing; Inferential Statistics

Probable Cause   A necessary condition in cases where law enforcement officials choose to deprive individuals of their liberty. Probable cause is present when there is reasonable ground to believe that an individual is or has engaged in an offense or will do so in the future. According to the Fourth Amendment in the U.S. Constitution, probable cause must be stronger than mere suspicion but does not necessarily imply the presence of strong evidence that will lead to a conviction. Probable cause is relevant to contacts with the police and with the court. For instance, a police officer may search or arrest an individual if he or she has probable cause to believe that the individual has engaged in illegal behavior. Furthermore, the court also has to establish that probable cause was present to prosecute the defendant. ***See also*** Reasonable Suspicion; Search and Seizure

Probation   A sentence to be served in the community under the supervision of a probation officer. Probation is the centerpiece of community corrections and accounts for the largest number of offenders under correctional supervision. The Department of Probation, which is typically housed within the court, has the dual role of investigation and supervision. The investigative role involves the preparation of presentence investigation reports for the court, while the supervisory role involves the active monitoring of offenders sentenced to probation. Offenders sentenced to probation serve their sentences in the community and are required to abide by a variety of conditions. Standard, treatment, punitive, and special conditions allow the probation sentence to be tailored to the needs of the offender. ***See also*** Community Corrections; Parole; Presentence Investigation Report

Problem-Oriented Policing (POP)   A form of policing aiming to identify particular crime problems in the community and to develop the most effective strategies that can be implemented to tackle these problems. Developed by Professor Herman Goldstein from the University of Wisconsin-Madison, problem-oriented policing emphasizes crime prevention principles, analysis and research, thorough evaluations of the effectiveness of the implemented strategies, and the importance of partnerships with the community and other public and private organizations and agencies. When problems are identified, the police work closely with members of the community and other agencies to find the most effective solution to address the situation. When the solution is implemented, an evaluation process occurs to assess whether the strategy was constructive in addressing the problem. ***See also*** Community Policing (COP)

Problem Solving *(communication)*   A systematic process undertaken by an individual or a group of individuals to identify and evaluate situations that are difficult, disagreeable, or harmful and to decide on methods to resolve such situations.

Scholars credited with early research and writings on the topic of problem solving include John Dewey in the 1910s and the team of James McBurney and Kenneth Hance in the 1930s. In the early 1980s, a group of Pennsylvania State University researchers studied nine problem-solving groups to determine whether the order of steps they followed made a difference in their rate of success. Reporting for the group, Randy Hirokawa noted that uniformity in the steps followed was not essential. However, those groups that approached problems in an analytical and evaluative manner before attempting to solve them had the highest rates of success; those that looked for solutions without taking the steps of identification and evaluation were less successful.

Writing from a business communications standpoint in 1997, Jay Knippen and Thad Green noted that a group problem-solving approach involving both management and workforce representatives both increased motivation and benefited the organization. They outlined the following seven steps: (1) establishing goals, (2) identifying problems and identifying constraints, (3) identifying alternatives, (4) evaluating the alternatives, (5) selecting the best solution, and (6) creating an implementation. For the final step, implementation, they suggested the following six-question approach: (1) What needs to be done? (2) How it should be done? (3) Who should do what? (4) When does it need to be done? (5) Where it should be done? (6) What is the budget? For more information, see Dewey (1910), Hirokawa (1983), Knippen and Green (1997), and McBurney and Hance (1939). *See also* Consensus (communication); Evaluation (public administration)

Problem Solving *(education)*   The process of applying knowledge and skills to create new solutions to problems. Although problem solving is developmental in nature, there is substantial evidence that problem-solving skills can be taught. Developmentally speaking, maturational and experiential processes combine to increase problem-solving capacity and success. The development of increasingly sophisticated strategy use, mental representation (e.g., language, maps), and cognitive self-regulation, for example, permits 14-year-olds to have far more problem-solving tools to draw on for successful problem solving than 6-year-olds.

Teaching problem solving is clearly a major educational goal. Bransford and Stein, in their 1984 book, *The IDEAL Problem Solver*, promote teaching of the process of general problem solving, using IDEAL (identify, define, explore, act, look) as a means to improve problem solving. Other teachable strategies include employing algorithms and heuristics. Algorithms entail using detailed, specific procedures for attaining a goal, such as solving a math problem. Heuristic strategies include dividing a problem into a series of smaller subgoals and devising a means of solving each (means-end analysis),

thereby making the problem more manageable. For more information, see Bransford and Stein (1984). *See also* Algorithm; Developmental Psychology

Procedural Law/Rights   The rules that govern the proceedings of a case in a court of law and determine whether a given case needs to go to trial. These guidelines include various procedural rights for the defendants, such as the right to remain silent, the right to be represented by counsel, and the right to be present and offer evidence at any given proceeding. *See also* Criminal Law (political science, sociology); Penal Codes/Laws; Substantive Law

Procedural Memory   A type of long-term memory that consists of our stored knowledge of well-learned habits and skills. These include activities such as driving, riding a bicycle, typing, and swimming. Procedural memory is oftentimes hard to verbalize, and it can be done without consciously thinking about it. It reflects a number of stimulus-response actions that are learned over a period of time. This type of memory is highly durable. For example, one remembers how to ride a bike even if one has not been on a bike for a number of years. Procedural learning seems to be associated with the cerebellum and the basal ganglia, as damage to those areas can affect it. For more information, see Fitts (1964). *See also* Implicit Memory; Memory (psychology)

Process Consultation   A philosophy, attitude, and methodology for nondirective helping and change within groups and organizations. A collaborative, empowering client-consultant relationship is established to codiagnose situations and codevelop appropriate remedies. The emphasis of process consultation is on *process* (how things are done between people in systems) rather than content. Process consultation involves activities designed to increase a system's awareness and understanding of its functioning, "ownership" of its processes, and a capacity for learning, to improve how its members work together. Schein (1999) stated that a central fundamental assumption of process consultation is that a consultant can only help a human system to help itself. The main function of the consultant is to build a readiness for change and pass on the skills of constructive intervention so that a client system may improve on its own. For more information, see Schein (1999). *See also* Organizational Change (education, public administration)

Process Evaluation   Researchers evaluating programs gather information about program *outcomes* by answering questions such as "Did the program achieve its goals?" and "Was the effect of the program substantial?" This kind of evaluation (sometimes called summative evaluation) is clearly important. Equally important is the evaluation of the *processes* the program followed in trying to achieve its goals. A process evaluation is also called an implementation evaluation and sometimes a formative evaluation. Outcomes evaluations tell you *what* was accomplished; process evaluations tell you *how* it was accomplished. Knowing the "bottom line" is necessary but not sufficient. To use what was learned from one program to plan or to improve other programs, you need to know about both outcomes and processes. Process evaluations are widely used in most organizations that conduct evaluations, public and private.

Evaluation researchers typically use a wide range of methods, and this is especially true of process evaluations, which usually collect both qualitative and quantitative data. Data from observations, documents, and interviews are often central to a process evaluation. A process evaluation usually takes an in-depth, case study approach. Documents such as meeting minutes and reports are important for establishing context and time lines. Interviews are frequently the key method for understanding program delivery. Interviews are conducted both with program officials and with the individuals and groups served by the program.

Process evaluation focuses on the early stages of development and actual implementation of the program, including any changes in goals and methods, such as adjustments to the context in which the program worked. Although summative assessment of the impact of the program is not the point of a process evaluation, judgments of quality are frequent, especially as they pertain to the administration, coordination, and delivery of services. Process evaluations often address the program's work in evaluating itself: What is the program's process for collecting, recording, and interpreting evaluative data about its activities? What is being learned, and to what use is it put?

Typical questions addressed by process evaluations are as follows:

- Is the program being implemented as planned?
- Who actually participated?
- Is the program reaching the kinds of people it was meant to reach? Are the participants willing? How long did they participate? How many dropped out?
- How does the program fit into its environment?
- What problems were encountered? Did they lead to alterations in program delivery or objectives?

Understanding exactly how a program operates is essential for three purposes: (1) improving the program as it is implemented, (2) drawing lessons for other programs, and (3) interpreting the results of outcome evaluations. For example, a program might work well because it devised a new method of delivery in response to a problem. A process evaluation should discover this; an outcome evaluation would probably miss it. *See also* Case Study Research (education); Program Development

Productivity   The amount of output of any aspect of production, such as labor, equipment, capital, per unit of input. Output can be measured in various ways: output per acre for land, yearly percentage for capital, output per hour for labor, and so on. A high national productivity typically indicates efficient production of goods and services and a competitive economy; however, growth in productivity can occur during periods of recession and increased unemployment as businesses cut jobs and seek to become more efficient. Many factors such as product, process, capacity, external influences, quality, and labor force affect productivity.

Productivity differs from measures of allocative efficiency, which take into account both the value of what is produced and the cost of inputs used, and although closely related, it is distinct from and not dependent on measures of profitability, which address the difference between the revenues obtained from output and the expense associated with consumption of inputs.

Generally speaking, productivity is used as a measure of how effectively an organization converts its particular resources into products or services. This measure is used to compare the effectiveness of an organization, country, department within an organization, or individual with the effectiveness of each of these or other entities of a similar nature over time for the same operation.

Productivity measurement has also become important for the formulation of monetary and fiscal policy. Productivity trends are used to predict potential economic growth. For example, if labor income grows faster than labor productivity, the expected result is inflation. Thus, productivity measurement is used in the difficult feat of balancing unemployment and inflation. Long-term productivity growth is commonly viewed as the determinant for sustainable economic growth.

Productivity studies are significant in understanding how productivity and economic growth can be increased. By analyzing productivity developments in different firms and industries and across regions and countries, productivity bottlenecks and opportunities for improvement can be determined. *See also* Economic Growth; Productivity Model

Productivity Model   To aid in determining productivity, it is necessary to use a model with which it is possible to calculate the results of the real process, income distribution process, and production process. Such a model is called the productivity model. The starting point is a profitability calculation, using surplus value as a criterion of profitability. The surplus value calculation is the only valid measure for understanding the connection between profitability and productivity or understanding the connection between the real process and production process. A valid measurement of total productivity necessitates considering all production inputs, and the surplus value calculation is the only calculation to conform to the requirement. *See also* Productivity

Professional Staff Development   A term that refers to activities that enhance one's professional career growth. In the field of education, these activities are designed to have a positive impact on classroom instruction and increase the educator's knowledge and skills. These may include experiences such as attending seminars and/or workshops, taking courses, or participating in in-service education. Membership in professional organizations and subscriptions to professional journals are examples of additional ways in which one might further one's professional growth. A certain amount of professional development may be required for educators to maintain licenses or certification.

Profiling The process of analyzing a crime scene and using information from that crime scene to determine the identity of the perpetrator, a process that can be helpful in narrowing down the number of suspects, among other things (also called criminal or psychological profiling). A profile may provide information that could include aspects of the perpetrator's personality, sex, age, and physical features, such as height and weight. With the help of this information, possible suspects may be identified, depending on whether they fit the profile. Profiles are based on the manner in which the crime was committed—the method of operation (or modus operandi [MO]). This includes the identity of the victim, commonalities among victims, the weapons used, the degree of aggression, whether there was sexual molestation, and so on. The FBI has identified four stages in the profiling process: (1) antecedent—the trigger that led to the commission of the act, (2) method and manner—the method of operation, (3) body disposal—whether the act took place at one or multiple scenes, and (4) postoffense behavior—whether the murderer is trying to become involved in the investigation through the police or the media. The FBI's crime scene analysis consists of six steps: (1) profiling inputs, (2) decision-process models, (3) crime assessment, (4) criminal profile, (5) the investigation, and (6) the apprehension. Criminal profiling draws on established theories of personality, such as those developed by Freud, Maslow, and the like, to develop offender profiles. Additionally, John Douglas of the FBI has spent years interviewing convicted perpetrators and learning about their motives and desires. For more information, see Turvey (1999). *See also* Forensic Psychology

Profit Generally calculated as the difference between total revenue and total cost. Total revenue is the product of price and quantity, the total amount of goods sold. It does not take into consideration the costs associated with producing and marketing the goods. Total cost reflects the variable and fixed costs incurred in the producing and marketing of a good. Profit may be measured from an economic or accounting perspective. Economic profit is calculated as the difference between total revenue and the combination of total cost and opportunity cost. The opportunity cost is a sacrificed alternative to facilitate the production of a good. This

may be in the form of foregone rent or interest on money. Accounting profit does not consider opportunity cost. For more information, see Boyes and Melvin (2002), McConnell and Brue (2008), and Warburton (2006). *See also* Fixed Cost; Price

Program Development The creation, the process, and the strategies that contribute to the generation and outcomes of a program. Program outcomes vary and can include foci that range from physical and cognitive outcomes to those that are social and/or emotional. Process strategies are comprehensive in that they represent a roadmap for attainment of the particular desired outcome(s).

Program Manager A person who oversees and manages an ongoing program, as opposed to a project manager, who manages a specific project, usually for a specified period of time. In a larger program, a program manager will oversee project managers and be responsible for planning, assessment, budgeting, and allocation of resources. *See also* Program Development

Progressivism *(education)* The educational application of pragmatism, organizing schooling around the needs, interests, and real experiences of students. The educational theory most closely associated with John Dewey, progressivism rejects the teacher-centered classroom, in which students are passive recipients of knowledge, and instead emphasizes student-active, real-life problem solving; individual development; and the continuity of experience. For more information, see Dewey (1916). *See also* Pragmatism

Progressivism *(public administration)* The term refers to a broad school of social and political philosophy that supports social justice and the advancement of workers' rights. The term was first used in reference to a widely based reform movement in the United States in the late 19th and early 20th centuries. Following the Civil War, this period was marked by widespread industrialization, the rapid expansion of cities, the completion of a national rail system, and the multiplication of the factory system.

Rampant growth of cities and industry created problems. Markedly, a large portion of the nation's wealth came under the control of a small number of people. Simultaneously, an increasing number of people fell into poverty, and workers faced gruelingly long hours of work, hazardous conditions, and poor pay. Progressive reformers strove to resolve to bridge the gap between the social classes and to protect the working class. Political corruption, business monopolies, and corporate power were believed by reformers to threaten democracy and were at the forefront of their concerns. Moreover, progressive reformers were advocates of workers' rights and social justice, as well as proponents of government-funded environmentalism, such as the creation of wildlife refuges and national parks.

Many of the principles that were laid out by the early progressives continue to serve as the foundation of modern progressive politics. Although the specific criteria for what constitutes progressivism and its related doctrines vary worldwide, there are multiple common tenets. Democracy, efficiency, social justice, regulation of large corporations and monopolies, and environmentalism are all often the underlying political, social, and economic concerns associated with progressivism.

Progressive political parties were created on three different occasions in the United States during the first half of the 20th century. The first, the Progressive Party, founded in 1912 by Theodore Roosevelt, has been acclaimed as the most successful third party in modern American history. Neither of the two subsequent parties, the Progressive Party created in 1924 or the Progressive Party created in 1948, was considered as successful as the first. Although progressivism, which is today often used in place of the term *liberal*, is not as popular in other parts of the world, such as Asia and Europe, as it is in North America, there are political parties and organizations that support many of the principles of progressivism.

Conservatism, which supports social stability and established traditions, and libertarianism, which advocates a hands-off approach to government, are regarded as views in opposition to progressivism. *See also* Conservatism; Liberalism (political science); Social Justice

Prohibition   In the American context, the term refers to a period during which the consumption, sale, and production of alcohol were prohibited. The Prohibition period occurred between 1920 and 1933, and the legislation was amended by President Franklin Roosevelt in 1933. The Prohibition is said to have contributed to the development of the underground market, as well as racketeering activities and organized crime groups, and is said to have had a substantial effect on the alcohol industry in the United States. Such legislation still exists in certain parts of the world, where the sale, consumption, and production, of alcohol remain strictly illegal.

Projection *(communication)*   The promotion or presentation of a person, an organization, or other entity in a constructed image, often for purposes of gaining favor with the public or attracting public favor away from an opponent. Advertising and public relations campaigns, for instance, project images of athletes or entire sports team as being "valiant warriors" or "America's team." Political candidates are projected as being "tough on crime" or dedicated to bettering the lives of "the working poor."

Projection can also refer to an individual's adaptation of another persona, frequently for entertainment purposes. The comedian Stephen Colbert, for example, projects the character of a politically conservative late-night talk show host. *See also* Public Relations

Projection *(psychology)*   A psychological defense mechanism proposed by the father of psychoanalysis,

Sigmund Freud. Projection occurs when people attribute their own unacceptable impulses onto others. For example, people who may be hostile toward certain ethnic groups may project their own hostile views onto "them," believing the ethnic group to be hostile. Projection reduces anxiety by allowing the expression of unwanted desires that may be subconscious in nature without letting the ego understand them. For more information, see Fonagy and Target (2003). *See also* Defense Mechanisms (psychology)

Projection and Projective Tests   Projection is a defense mechanism in which one ascribes the undesirable cognitions or emotions experienced by oneself to another person. For example, an unfaithful husband may constantly badger his wife with accusations related to her fidelity. Projective tests are open-ended assessment techniques in which a subject is presented with neutral or ambiguous stimuli and asked to respond. The subject's reply is analyzed as a projection. Projective measures include having the subject draw (traditionally a person or object), complete unfinished sentences, describe what is seen in an ink blot, or tell a comprehensive story while viewing a picture. *See also* Defense Mechanisms (education)

Projective Tests   A technique devised by psychoanalysts to delve into the unconscious without the use of psychotherapy. A projective test asks subjects to respond to an ambiguous stimulus, for example, an incomplete sentence, an inkblot, or a fuzzy picture. The underlying assumption of projective testing is that if a stimulus has no inherent meaning and can take on a multitude of interpretations, then whatever interpretation the subject puts on the stimulus is a projection of his or her own needs, wants, hopes, fears, and conflicts. Advocates claim that this ambiguity of the stimulus allows the subject to vent his or her inner thoughts. The most commonly known projective test is the Rorschach Inkblot Test, in which the subject is shown a series of irregular but symmetrical inkblots and asked to explain what they are. Projective tests have lost popularity among those who consider them to be unreliable. Additionally, the idea of repression that underlies these tests has been labeled as false by many psychologists with cognitive-behavioral orientations. Others have criticized the nature of the tests themselves, in that they depend heavily on the judgment of the examiner. At the same time, these are viewed as a nonthreatening manner in which to make the subject comfortable and then to introduce testing to the subject. For more information, see Hiller, Rosenthal, Bronstein, Berry, and Brunell-Neuleib (1999). *See also* Rorschach

Proof   Evidence that establishes that a given statement or allegation is true. Proof refers to the process that involves testing a given statement, as well as investigating alternative statements and explanations and demonstrating their inappropriateness. *See also* Research Methodology

Propaganda (*media studies*)   An attempt to deceive or coerce the recipients of a message by means of outright deception, selective information, or appeals to fears and emotions. Political propaganda is the use of these techniques to promote a political or power agenda or to cover up mistakes and illegal dealings. The widespread use of propaganda in political situations dominates the definition of propaganda as one of misinforming an audience or indoctrination. Information that is not structured to be propaganda is thought to be fair-minded and impartial, not favoring a particular point of view.

Propaganda shares with advertising, education, religious proselytizing, public relations, and governmental campaigns an effort to influence feelings, thoughts, and behavior through media messages. That the persuasion of an audience through media images and messages is thought to be commonplace can be seen in the concept of "spin," the idea that the manipulation of information to favor either an overt or a covert agenda is an expected part of contemporary communications. Through pundits, expert commentators, slanted statistics and research, and attractive visuals, messages from corporations, governments, or interest groups are presented to audiences, who are not given information for making their own judgments but are persuaded to accept the offered message as true and accurate.

From 1937 to 1942, The Institute of Propaganda Analysis tried to educate Americans in the identification of propaganda and how to fight it with critical thinking. The proposed seven basic techniques that could be recognized were as follows: (1) Name-Calling, (2) Glittering Generality, (3) Transfer, (4) Testimonial, (5) Plain Folks, (6) Card Stacking, and (7) Band Wagon. The use of these techniques for making persuasive messages can be seen in all types of communication. For more information, see Propaganda Critic: www.propagandacritic.com/articles/intro.why.html and Tye (2002). ***See also*** Advertising (media studies); Media; Media as a Cause of Crime; Stereotyping

Propaganda (*political science*)   A press campaign, usually sponsored by a military or government agency, to invoke emotional responses from its audience in order to influence and persuade mass numbers. It is a pejorative term and is often associated with negativity, deceit, and distortion. The word *propaganda* was originally a neutral term, derived from the Latin, meaning "to propagate" or "to sow." Current usage extends back to 1622, when Pope Gregory XV instituted the Office of the Propagation of the Faith (*Congretio de propaganda fide*) to supervise missionaries sent to the New World to stop the spread of Protestantism. It was not until World War I that the term began to be used in the English language. During the war, both the Allied and the Axis powers used mass media for their own objectives. Mediums for influence included news reports, books, leaflets, movie and television shows, and posters. The war campaign of one's enemies tended to be labeled propaganda, while one's own nation's campaign was considered to be the truth. ***See also*** Objectiveness in Media Coverage; Political Media; Public Interest (political science)

Propaganda Model   A controversial framework developed by Chomsky and Herman in their book *Manufacturing Consent* (1988), explaining why some stories and not others are reported by the media. The model describes how three elite institutions—mainstream media, government, and corporations—interact under a capitalist, market-driven system to the detriment of diverse press coverage.

According to Chomsky and Herman, information must successfully evade capture by any of the five "filters" if it is to appear as news. These filters are (1) ownership, (2) advertising, (3) sourcing, (4) flak, and (5) anticommunist ideology.

Dominant mainstream media are businesses, and as such, they seek to maximize their profits. To do so, they rely on advertising, from other businesses. Journalists rely heavily on inexpensive official sources for their information, including government spokespersons and public relations specialists. "Flak" may come in the form of libel suits or threats to withdraw advertising. Before and during the Cold War, anticommunist ideology biased or discouraged coverage of certain types of foreign news stories.

The model is used to explain why certain news stories appear and others do not. The stories that do not appear disappear into the filters, resulting in an effective, though unlegislated, censorship. Thus, workers striking against a communist government may be considered worthy victims suitable for news coverage; but strikers in a capitalist country may not. Or atrocities by the communist side in a civil war may be reported to a greater extent than those committed by the U.S.-supported side. Chomsky cites Federalist John Jay's words, "Those who own the country ought to govern it," and his propaganda model illustrates how in a market-driven democracy this might come about.

Criticisms of the model are many. Critics protest the implication that mainstream media frame news and debate only in the interests of the powerful and the wealthy, that the model is a conspiracy theory, and that it has no regard for journalistic professionalism and objectivity. For more information, see Herman (1996), Herman and Chomsky (1988), and Klaehn (2003). ***See also*** Objectiveness in Media Coverage

Property Rights   The rights to own and use property, emanating from natural and enacted laws. A property is a possession or entitlement that usually has exchangeable value. Public property, such as a park or a major bridge, is owned by the public, whereas private property denies the public a right to ownership or unfettered access.

Property may be physical, for example, land, a house, and an automobile, or intellectual, for example copyrights and patents granted to individuals and groups for their artistic creativity and innovations.

P

According to the Coase theorem, when private property rights (group rights that implicitly include individual rights) are well-defined and bargaining costs are low, economic outcomes are more efficient when settlements are negotiated rather than regulated. Of course, rights are never absolute. Enjoyment of ownership of them is contingent on reasonable use and benefit rather than abuse. However, regulation may not necessarily produce the best outcome and may even violate property rights.

Recent controversy over the enjoyment of the property right in international trade is closely related to its conflict with human rights and national self-determination. This controversy was heightened by the World Trade Organization's inclusion of Trade-Related Aspects of Intellectual Property Rights (TRIPs) in the international trade agreement. Developing countries argue for the right to produce life-saving drugs by compulsory licensing as a result of the acquired immune deficiency syndrome (AIDS) epidemic, but pharmaceutical companies and their host countries prefer to uphold patent rights as an intellectual right and a natural right. *See also* World Trade Organization (WTO)

Proportional Representation   An election system, practiced in many European democracies, in which representatives are elected in proportion to the votes received. This system contrasts with the majority and plurality—winner take all—voting systems common in Great Britain and her former colonies. The goal of proportional representation is to better represent minority groups, especially racial and ethnic minorities, and avoid "wasted" votes. There are many types of proportional representation systems, including party list, mixed-member, and preference voting. The party-list system is the most common; candidates receive the percentage representation in legislature that matches their proportion of the vote. A closed-list system is where a political party decides beforehand the order of candidates on the ballot. In an open-list system, voters decide the order in which candidates are chosen. The second system, the mixed-member system, is a true hybrid of proportional and winner-take-all; half of the representatives are selected through the winner-take-all process and half through proportional representation. In contrast, preference voting requires voters to rank order the candidates. Once a candidate is elected or comes in last place, his or her name is removed from the ballot, and the votes of that candidate are automatically transferred to the voters' second choices. This process continues until the winners have been determined. Disadvantages of proportional representation include legislative gridlock, too much power allotted to small parties, and less resistance to extremism. For more information, see Douglas (2000). *See also* Plurality

Proportional Tax   A tax that is applied to all or any type of income at the same rate and that does not change or fluctuate regardless of socioeconomic status.

These schemes typically exclude households whose incomes fall below a determined level (by statute). Such taxation is regressive, is usually unfair to the poor, and is not used in income tax systems in advanced societies, such as the United States and Canada. Individual state sales taxes, however, are usually regressive.

Prosecution   A criminal proceeding to determine a defendant's innocence or guilt. The term is also used to identify the government as the appellant party in a case. Crimes can only be prosecuted at the county, state, and federal levels by salaried government lawyers (prosecutors). A victim cannot hire a private attorney to represent him or her in a criminal trial. Private attorneys can be hired to sue a defendant after the criminal trial, in a civil court for tort claims. Prosecutors can only handle criminal cases; civil cases are therefore outside their jurisdiction. The chief prosecutor of a county, the state district attorney, and the attorney general can be either elected or appointed. *See also* Criminal Law (political science)

Prosecutor   A legal representative who is responsible for prosecuting cases on behalf of a government or the people. Also called a district attorney in most jurisdictions, the prosecutor's role is to present a case that will demonstrate that a given defendant is guilty of the charges brought against him or her. Prosecutors have legal training and act as representatives of the government at the local, state, and federal levels. At the local level, the prosecutor generally represents the county or city, while he or she represents the state and federal governments at the latter two levels. *See also* Prosecution

Prosocial Model   Media theorists have long postulated that depictions of antisocial behavior in mass media have tended to influence viewers to themselves incline toward antisocial activity. Whereas most studies in this area have focused on imitations of antisocial behavior, a substantial number of studies have also examined the power of the media to promote prosocial behavior. Prosocial models of media-influenced behavior contend that mass media can induce viewers to behave in more socially beneficial ways by portraying and praising kind and honorable behaviors.

In the early 1970s, around the same time that the Surgeon General's Scientific Advisory Committee on Television and Social Behavior was asserting that there may be a causal relation between violent visual images and aggressive behavior among people who had seen them, studies were also demonstrating that children also imitated observed behaviors such as altruism, postponement of gratification, and setting high standards of performance. In 1986, Susan Hearold argued that the data regarding the prosocial effects of media messages held up better under rigorous experimental conditions than did the evidence of antisocial effects. She further noted that prosocial effects were stronger for both boys and girls and that the potential for prosocial influence overrides the small but persistent negative effects of antisocial programs.

Most efforts to promote prosocial behavior through the media have been directed at younger (and, therefore, presumably more impressionable) audiences. Programmers interested in modeling prosocial behavior have struggled with a basic dilemma: how to convey their prosocial message in ways interesting and engaging enough to hold the attention of young audiences. V. O. Lovelace and A. C. Huston have identified three strategies for modeling prosocial behavior for children through the media. The first is to present characters who exhibit only prosocial behavior. Although the messages conveyed by such a character are unambiguous, this approach has the disadvantage of presenting flat, dramatically vapid characters. The second technique is to incorporate story lines in which characters resolve conflict by making prosocial choices. Positive consequences are attributed to prosocial behavior and negative consequences to antisocial behavior. The perceived disadvantage here is the concern that viewers will imitate the antisocial behaviors along with or in place of the prosocial. This second model is frequently employed in programs such as *Sesame Street*. The third strategy is to present both prosocial and antisocial behaviors without presenting a resolution within the program. Rather, the viewer is asked to offer his or her own solution to the presented conflict. This third approach is considered most effective in classroom or therapeutic settings, where an adult can supervise postviewing discussion or activity. For more information, see Hearold (1986), Hoffman (1970), Lovelace and Huston (1983), and Staub (1971). *See also* Mass Media

Prosopagnosia A rare disorder that impairs one's ability to recognize familiar faces, such as one's family members, friends, celebrities, and even one's own face. This often results from damage to the temporal lobes in the brain. Even though prosopagnosiacs cannot overtly recognize faces, research has shown that they exhibit greater electrical activity in the brain and increased autonomic arousal when presented with familiar as compared with unfamiliar faces. Thus, they exhibit some recognition but do not realize this. For more information, see Bruce and Young (2000). *See also* Memory

Prostitution The act of engaging in sexual behavior (not limited to intercourse) in exchange for money. Some view prostitution as degrading and exploitative work and have advocated for the abolition of prostitution. For instance, various organizations, such as WHISPER (Women Hurt in Systems of Prostitution Engaged in Revolt, which was founded by a former prostitute in New York), have expressed the need to eradicate the sex industry, including prostitution services, strip clubs, pornography, and similar services. Conversely, in recent years, there has been much debate surrounding the legalization or decriminalization of prostitution. Some have highlighted the numerous benefits associated with the legalization of prostitution, namely, exerting better control over the health and safety of individuals involved in this type of activity, enabling law enforcement to cope with more pressing crime issues, and preventing individuals from getting involved at a young age. *See also* Sex Offense/Crime

Protoculture The transmission of different behaviors between different generations of nonhuman primates. These behaviors tend to be quite basic and are acquired through a group learning process.

Provisionalism Open-mindedness and a willingness to display attitudes of flexibility and reasonableness. People who follow a code of provisionalism are compromisers and facilitators, who will consider the value of what others may deem important. They are willing to put aside previously held ideas for the purposes of discussion and experimentation.

The use of the term as a positive attribute is credited to Jack R. Gibbs, a university professor considered to be a pioneer in humanistic psychology. Writing in 1961, Gibbs pointed out that people can reduce the incidence of less productive, defensive encounters by communicating that they are willing to consider new concepts, attitudes, and behaviors. People who practice provisionalism, he maintained, are likely to help solve problems and avoid alienating people or making them feel defensive. Persons seeking information do not "resent help or company along the way," he wrote. For more information, see Gibbs (1961). *See also* Active Listening; Compromising; Problem Solving (communication)

Provocation The act of inciting or instigating some action or behavior from another person. Provocation is the attempt to stimulate a reaction from another, through words, behavior, or any other form of communication.

Proxemics The spatial separation between people as they interact. The anthropologist Edward T. Hall (1966) coined the term in his book *The Hidden Dimension*. The effects of proxemics, according to Hall, can be summarized by his rule: Intimate distance is for embracing, touching, and whispering; such close contact can often be used for intimidation. President Lyndon Johnson was noted for maintaining a close contact when trying to persuade people to accept his point of view. For more information, see Hall (1966). *See also* Kinesics; Social Distance

Proximity The nearness in place, time, order, occurrence, or relation. It is also a Gestalt principle of organization holding that (other things being equal) objects or events that are near to one another (in space or time) are perceived as belonging together as a unit.

Prozac An antidepressant that is part of the class of selective serotonin reuptake inhibitors (SSRIs). Also called fluoxetine, it acts by blocking the absorption and removal of serotonin from neural synapses without affecting other neurotransmitters. It is used for the treatment of clinical depression, obsessive-compulsive disorder, bulimia, and panic disorder. It has generally been proven to be effective in clinical trials, and its side effects tend to be minimal. Though its widespread popularity has not been without controversy, this drug is generally seen to be efficacious in treating particular forms of mental distress. For more information, see *Wong, Bymaster, and Engleman (1995)*. *See also* Depression (psychology)

Psychoactive Drug   A chemical that acts on the central nervous system and influences perceptions, moods, thoughts, or behaviors. Psychoactive drugs act as aphrodisiacs and may be used recreationally to alter consciousness, for spiritual purposes, or therapeutically as medication. They bring about subjective changes in consciousness that may make the user more alert or act as a mood upper (e.g., euphoria). Because of these reasons, these drugs are often misused or abused despite their negative consequences. Psychoactive drugs can become physically or psychologically addictive. Physical dependence leads to a need to continue drug use in order to satisfy intense cravings. Psychological dependence is when continued drug use is needed to maintain a sense of well-being. Exposure to such substances can cause changes in the structure and functioning of neurons, as the nervous system tries to reestablish homeostasis, which is unbalanced due to the ingestion of the drug. Additionally, continued use can produce tolerance, whereby larger doses are needed to produce the desired effect. There are four major classes of psychoactive drugs—sedatives, stimulants, hallucinogens, and opiates. Drug abuse is a major problem, especially among youth. The drugs most commonly abused include alcohol, barbiturates, cocaine, LSD, and marijuana. Drug rehabilitation involves a combination of psychotherapy and use of other psychoactive substances to break the cycle of dependency. For more information, see Siegel (2005). *See also* Drug

Psychoanalysis *(education)*   The term Sigmund Freud coined to describe his theory of psychological development and psychotherapy. Psychoanalysis views unconscious conflicts, particularly those linked to the sexual drive, as central to understanding psychopathology. Therapy is lengthy and involves the analyst eliciting and interpreting the client's free associations, dreams, and transference reactions to bring the unconscious conflicts into consciousness. *See also* Personality

Psychoanalysis *(psychology)*   A theory of personality pioneered by the eminent psychologist Sigmund Freud (1856–1939). Freud defined psychology as the study of conscious experience driven by largely unconscious forces. He believed that traumas in early childhood can have lasting effects on the individual, influencing later thought and behavioral patterns. Moreover, Freud theorized that we are driven by unconscious forces and

that these unconscious forces can be brought out through processes such as free association. He introduced this theory in 1900 in his book *The Interpretation of Dreams*. Freud explained the idea of the unconscious by comparing the human mind to an iceberg. The conscious part of the mind, or what the person is aware of, was thought to be the tip of the iceberg, while the much larger region below the surface is the vast region of the unconscious that contains feelings and thoughts hidden from awareness. Freud divided the human personality into three interacting parts, the id, ego, and superego. The id, believed to be the most primitive part, operates according to the pleasure principle, whereby it motivates the individual to seek immediate gratification of all desires. Alternatively, the superego was thought to motivate one to act in a highly moralistic manner. The ego, in turn, mediates the conflict between the immediate wants of the id and the strict morals of the superego, helping to achieve realistic forms of gratification and operating according to the reality principle. Based on his treatment of patients, Freud concluded that personality is shaped in the first few years of life and that the resolution of what is known as "psychosexual" conflicts is the reason for this development. These psychosexual stages are each marked by erogenous zones on the body that are most sensitive to erotic stimulation. The four stages are (1) the oral stage, (2) the anal stage, (3) the phallic stage, and (4) the genital stage. According to Freud, one needs to pass successfully through each one of these stages in order to develop a healthy personality and enjoy mature adult relationships. Although Freud's theories are met with skepticism by some, his ideas gave rise to a number of other psychoanalytic theories and personality tests. For more information, see Freud (1940). *See also* Defense Mechanisms (psychology); Personality

Psychographics   The examination of segments of the human population that are identified by consumer interests, values, personality, lifestyles, and opinions for the purposes of market research and advertising. Information about these subgroups is commonly concerned with consumer reasoning for purchasing products, the frequency of product usage, and consumer lifestyle (e.g., 20-something couples, families with young children, or retirees). These factors are considered as contributing to consumers' current and future purchasing decisions. Psychographic information can be collected through qualitative methods, such as focus groups, interviews, or questionnaires. Market researchers use these data to construct psychographic profiles, which are implemented to characterize and determine existing as well as prospective consumers. Marketing strategies are developed from psychographic profiles to target markets audiences for maximum product consumption. Strategies include advertising campaigns, the selection of appropriate media outlets for advertising and marketing, and appealing product characteristics (e.g., the color and shape of a perfume bottle). *See also* Demographics (economics, media studies)

Psychological Dependence The condition of drug users who need continued use to maintain a state of well-being. It is a dependency of the mind and can lead to a number of withdrawal symptoms associated with psychoactive drug use, including cravings, irritability, insomnia, depression, and anorexia. This results in psychological dysfunction, which replaces normal functioning. Psychological dependence is not limited to substance use, but it can include activities and various behavioral patterns such as gambling, Internet addiction, sexual addiction, and so on. For more information, see Hubbard, Marsden, Rachel, Harwood, Cavanaugh, and Ginzburg, (1989). **See also** Psychoactive Drug

Psychological Disorder A condition in which a person's thoughts, feelings, or behavior are thought to be in some way dysfunctional. Though the recognition and understanding of various disorders has changed over time, the most commonly used guideline for the classification of mental disorders is the American Psychological Association's (APA) *Diagnostic and Statistical Manual of Mental Disorders* (fourth edition; *DSM-IV*). This manual provides a comprehensive listing of psychological disorders, grouping them into 17 broad categories. According to the APA, a pattern of behavior is considered a psychological disorder if it satisfies three criteria: (1) the person experiences significant pain or distress, demonstrates an inability to work, is at an increased risk of death, and/or experiences loss of freedom; (2) the sources of the problem are internal to the person, whether biological factors, mental processes, or learned habits, and lead to abnormal responses to life events; (3) the problem being experienced is not merely a reaction to societal problems such as poverty, prejudice, or government policy. There are different models of abnormality that have been identified in the literature. These include the following: (1) the medical model—advocates that disorders, thoughts, and behaviors are caused by physical disease; (2) the psychological perspective—advocates that psychological disorders are caused by a person's past and present life experiences; (3) the sociocultural perspective—stresses that the social and cultural environment we live in can determine the type of psychological disorders we are susceptible to; (4) the synthetic model—combines all the above and advocates that no one model can explain the underlying causes of a disorder in its entirety. Many mental health professionals seek to diagnose individuals by ascertaining their particular mental disorder. Some professionals, however, may avoid diagnosis in favor of other assessment methods, such as formulation of a client's difficulties and circumstances. Treatment for psychological disorders varies depending on the particular disorder. It can range from case management, day treatment, inpatient treatment, to involuntary commitment of individuals who may be a danger or risk to others or themselves. According to the World Health Organization, approximately 450 million people worldwide suffer from mental disorders, and 1 of 4 people will suffer from some form of mental illness at some point in their life. For more information, see Kessler, McGonagle, Zhao, and Nelson (1995). **See also** Psychotherapy

Psychology The scientific study of behavior and the mind. Psychology is a science in that psychologists employ systematic, objective methods of observation to study any activity that can be observed, recorded, and measured. Additionally, psychologists study the mind (this includes both conscious and unconscious mental states) through inferences made from observable behavior. Psychology includes many subfields, including human development, health, industry, law, and so on. Psychology as a science began in 1879, when Wilhelm Wundt, also known as the father of psychology, established the first laboratory dedicated to psychological research at Leipzig University in Germany. Following this, William James published *The Principles of Psychology,* which laid the foundation for much of the study of psychology that followed. For more information, see Brain (2002) and James (1890). **See also** Developmental Psychology; Health Psychology

Psychology of Communication Communication is a manner in which we transmit and receive information. While we are not always doing it in a conscious manner, sometimes we are not even aware that we communicate a message to the external world. The communication process occurs between a sender and a receiver. It is a process that is shared by everybody and occurs on a constant basis; we communicate messages and concepts constantly, and this process operates in many directions and dimensions. The effectiveness of the communication process is heavily dependent on the level of understanding between the sender and the receiver. There are three most frequently recognized modes of communications: (1) the interpersonal communication, (2) intrapersonal communication, and (3) person-group communication. Person-to-person communication occurs between at least two individuals, and the level of its effectiveness is highly dependent on interpersonal communication skills. Intrapersonal communication occurs within the person, when we "talk to ourselves or with ourselves." This type of phenomenon occurs primarily when we attempt to solve problems. Person-to-group communication is staged when a person addresses a group of other individuals, such as in public engagement speaking, while giving a court testimony, or while preaching in a house of prayer.

Psychology is an academic and applied discipline involving the scientific study of mental process and behavior, including the phenomena of perception, cognition, and interpersonal relations.

The psychology of communication, or the mental dimensions of the sender-receiver interaction, constitutes the various elements of the communication process, which are highly interdependent with the individuals' frame of mind and their metal capacities. The psychology of communication explores the perception and cognition in interpersonal relations based on the

P

quality of the communication process. As the process of communication begins with a source or an idea that the sender wants to transmit to the receivers, the message needs to be encoded into a symbol in order to be transmitted to the receivers, who on their end need to decode the message into a meaning. The way the receiver decodes the message is directly related to the receiver's perception and cognitive abilities. The feedback to the sender will also depend on the interpersonal relationships the receiver has with the sender. A distortion of the communication process can occur at any stage, depending on the interaction between the sender and the receiver. There are three interpersonal modes of communication, verbal, nonverbal, and symbolic, and the decoding of all the modes depends heavily on the context of the overall situation, which sometimes overrides or interferes with a person's cognitive and perceptional processes. For more information, see Hunter, Mayhall, and Barker (2000) and Weaver (1972). *See also* Communication; Effectiveness (communication); Interpersonal Communication; Message; Psychology

Psychomotor Skills   The ability to physically manipulate objects in the environment using perceptual information. For example, the ability to write with a pencil or to stack blocks would require psychomotor skills. Several taxonomies exist that classify how learners progressively acquire and ultimately master these skills. *See also* Taxonomies

Psychopathy   The psychological construct that describes immoral and antisocial behavior. The modern conception of psychopathy was put forth by Hervey Cleckley in his work *The Mask of Sanity* (1941). According to his criteria, a psychopath is an intelligent person who is devoid of emotions, has no sense of shame, is charming and manipulative, and displays irresponsible behavior. Psychopathic personality disorders have been the most studied of any personality disorder. Psychopathy has been operationalized by Robert Hare in his Psychopathy Checklist-Revised (PCL-R). This assesses both the affective and the interpersonal components as well as antisocial deficits in the patient. At the same time, findings from psychopathy research have not been shown to aid in diagnosis or treatment of this disorder. Two types of psychopathy have been defined in the literature—primary psychopathy and secondary psychopathy. Primary psychopathy is seen as the main disorder patients are diagnosed with, whereas secondary psychopathy is seen as arising from another psychiatric diagnosis or the social circumstances of the patient. Some use the term *primary psychopathy* to differentiate between psychopathy that is biological in origin and *secondary psychopathy,* which results from a combination of genetic and environmental influences. Psychopathy is normally only diagnosed in adults and not in children or adolescents; some jurisdictions forbid this diagnosis in children. In cases in which psychopathic tendencies appear in children, it is diagnosed as conduct disorder. It is estimated that approximately 1% of the general population are psychopaths. For more information, see Cleckley (1941), Cooke, Forth, and Hare (1998), and Hare (2003). *See also* Oppositional Defiant Disorder (ODD)

Psychopharmacology   The study of the effects of drugs on psychological processes—moods, sensations, thinking, and behavior. A vast array of drugs are being used in this process with varying psychoactive properties, and they are used most commonly to treat mental disorders. Most of these work by acting on neurotransmitters—biochemicals that relay information between neurons. Psychoactive drugs originate from natural sources such as plants or through artificial synthesis in the laboratory. These drugs are different from sedative drugs, which were formerly in use and led to impaired motor and perceptual abilities and clouded consciousness. Antipsychotic drugs, on the other hand, can alleviate symptoms of anxiety and reduce delusions and hallucinations without the earlier side effects. This has led to the overprescription of drugs to reduce agitation and anxiety. For more information, see Gitlin (1996). *See also* Antipsychotic Drugs

Psychosexual   Stages   The various stages of development that children pass through in their first few years of life. This theory of development, proposed by Freud, states that each stage is defined by a different erogenous zone—a part of the body that is most sensitive to erotic simulation. Freud proposed four stages. (1) First is the oral stage, which occurs in the first year of life and is characterized by the mouth being the pleasure center. Feeding and weaning are the main sources of conflict at this stage. (2) Next is the anal stage, which was thought to occur during ages 3 and 4, when control over feces is a primary source of conflict and pleasure. Conflict is said to occur, for example, between the child who wants release and the parent who tries to discipline. (3) The third stage, which occurs between ages 4 and 6, is known as the phallic stage. Here, pleasure is felt in the genital area; during this stage, the child is said to be fascinated with his or her own body and is often seen playing with his or her sex organs in public, which may produce conflict with parents. (4) The fourth stage is referred to as the latency period, and it occurs between ages 7 and 12. During this stage, sexual impulses lie dormant, and children concentrate on same-sex friends. (5) The final stage is the genital stage. Following puberty, adolescents start to feel adult-like sexual urges. It is in this stage that the ego comes into play, as it mediates between biological drives and social prohibition. For more information, see Sim (1974). *See also* Psychoanalysis

Psychosurgery   A kind of medical treatment whereby portions of the brain are removed to treat psychological disorders. Historically, this started with prefrontal lobotomies, a surgical procedure where the nerves that connect the frontal lobe to the rest of the brain were cut to treat patients who were agitated, manic, or violent. The first systematic attempt at psychosurgery was conducted by Egas Moniz, who performed a prefrontal lobotomy in 1935. Currently, this procedure is considered medically inappropriate as there are a number of less invasive procedures available, such as psychiatric medication and electroconvulsive therapy. Additionally, specific regions of the brain can be destroyed through ultrasonic irradiation. For example, certain nerve fibers can be deactivated for people afflicted with uncontrollable seizures. It is used sparingly with some success on those for whom the other procedures prove to be unsuccessful. For more information, see Rogers (1992). *See also* Electroconvulsive Therapy (ECT)

Psychotherapy A term used for all types of treatment in which a trained psychologist uses psychological techniques to help persons in need of assistance. Psychotherapists employ a range of techniques that may assist in, for example, the development of social or interpersonal skills, relationship building, heightening of cognitive awareness, and behavior change, with the goal of improving the mental health of the client. The first specific school of psychotherapy can be traced back to Sigmund Freud in the early 1900s. Freud focused on problems that had no organic basis, theorizing that problems had psychological causes originating in childhood experiences. He developed techniques such as dream interpretation, free association, and transference. There are now a number of schools of thought regarding psychotherapy, including, cognitive behavioral, psychodynamic, existential, humanistic, and multisystemic approaches. Psychotherapy is usually a structured encounter between the therapist and the client, and in addition to the more typical face-to-face oral exchange, it may also involve drama, artwork, and writing exercises. Psychotherapy can be provided either individually or in a group setting and, typically, lasts anywhere from a few weeks to a year or more, though shorter and more goal-directed forms of therapy are becoming increasingly common. For more information, see Roth and Fonagy (2004). *See also* Clinical Psychology

Public Administration Definitions of this term vary widely due, in part, to the differing roles and perspectives of public administrators. However, definitions of public administration often include the following common elements: (a) the formulation and implementation of public policies, (b) a wide range of problems concerning human behavior and cooperative human effort, (c) the production of public goods and services, and (d) a foundation rooted in law. Public administration includes the practice of government, but *public administration* also refers to an academic field of study and can be compared with business administration. An MPA degree is similar to an MBA, except that the MPA degree entails ethics and sociological aspects usually not found in MBA curricula. Public administration developed as an academic study in the late 19th and early 20th centuries as a result of industrialization and urbanization in the United States.

Lorenz von Stein is considered the founder of the science of public administration. In the late 19th century, he promoted public administration as a science rather than a form of law. Von Stein recognized that public administration is a discipline comprising sociology, political science, administrative law, and public finance. In the United States, public administration as a science began to take shape in an article written in 1887 by Woodrow Wilson, who was a political scientist and the future U.S. President. In his article, Wilson favored (a) separation between politics and public administration, (b) consideration of government from a commercial perspective, and effective management through training civil servants and assessing their performance quality.

Public administration focused on the development and implementation of rational methods of managing production, especially large-scale production in the urbanized areas of the post–Industrial Revolution era. Beginning with Frederick Taylor's scientific management principles in the early 20th century, the focus was on maximizing the efficiency of work processes. Scientific management principles, coupled with the results of the Hawthorne experiments, promoted the view that organizations are highly rational. There was little or no accounting for the social or psychological side of human activity.

Whereas the 1920s stressed productivity, the 1930s stressed the management of large-scale organizations. This was exemplified by the acronym POSDCORB (planning, organizing, staffing, directing, coordinating, reporting, and budgeting), to explain the common functions that managers perform. In the 1940s, the focus began to shift to the positivistic approach of managerial decision making. It was not until the 1970s and 1980s that public organizations considered those whom an organization was designed to serve—the public. The shift resulted from perceptions that government was inept and unresponsive. The new public management, with its principles borrowed from economics and the private sector, emphasized empowering frontline managers, who worked directly with the public—its customers, and decentralizing government. The new prescription was to meet the needs of those being served rather than focus on internal production and control.

The 1970s and 1980s also shifted public administration from vertical organizational hierarchies to horizontal forms of control. This has become even more important since public administrations have steadily been dealing more directly with administrations representing the public sector, particularly with contracting goods and services.

Although management in public administrations has not changed greatly in the past 100 years, its greatest utility may be in running large and complex organizations. For more information, see Gillespie (1991), Rabin, Hildreth, and Miller (1998), and Taylor (1911/1967). *See also* Policy Analysis; Public Management; Public Policy.

Public Administration Theory Both an inter-disciplinary and an applied field. As such, no single theory can completely account for its complexities. Instead, public administration theory comprises elements of several fields, which in conjunction can inform a fuller understanding of public administration. The fields from which public administration theory borrows include organizational theory, social psychology, political theory, political science, and history. Public administrators have developed theories of public administration in the areas of political control of the bureaucracy, bureaucracy and democracy, and public management. Examples of other theories are post-modern theory, decision theory, rational choice theory, and theories of governance.

Bureaucracy and control of the bureaucracy are central to the politics-administration dichotomy, which dates back to the founding documents in American history. The belief that there should be a division between legislative, or political, powers and executive, or administrative, powers continues till today. Theories in this area have thus emphasized a council-manager model of government, where there is a fairly clear distinction between the popularly elected city council, with its responsibility to set law and policy, and the professional city manger the council employs, who is tasked with leading the bureaucracy and carrying out policy. Empirical studies, however, have found that this distinction is not so clear, especially in light of the fact that the most important aspect of public administration is its political nature. Rather, different jurisdictions show different levels of control over the mission, policy, administration, and management of the government process.

Theories of bureaucratic politics emerged to address the conflict emanating from the hierarchical and authoritarian nature of the bureaucracy, and the egalitarian and often inefficient values of democracy were raised in the 1950s. Theories in this area have focused on finding a way to legitimate the power of the bureaucracy in the context of democratic values. A central hypothesis of these theories states that a bureaucracy that reflects the diversity of the community it serves is more likely to respond to the interests of all groups in the making of policy decisions.

Public management theories start from the premise of scientific management that managers are responsible for defining and solving problems. In the 1960s and 1970s, public management was influenced by theories of democratic administration, such as flat hierarchies, worker self-management, project management, and the elimination of competition. In the 1980s, public manage-ment focused on describing management behavior in the ongoing routine of work. To do so, it commonly linked management and organization. Management was described as the formal and informal processes of guiding human interaction toward public organization objectives, whereas organization was the design and evolution of structural arrangements for the conduct of public administrators.

Postmodern theories use stories and narratives that detail how public administrators interpret laws and rules as well as their daily application to clients. Making sense of the bureaucracy is the core of empirical findings.

Decision theory is based on the notion of bounded rationality, whereby the practitioner must choose the most appropriate means for reaching desired ends. Decision theory models deal with limitations on rationality, such as goal ambiguity, resource limitations, incomplete information, and satisficing. In studies measuring decision theory, the decision is the unit of analysis.

Rational choice theory applies decision theory and economics to mathematical models to test the relation-ships between the preferences of citizens, politicians, and public servants and alternative courses of action. Rational choice theories explain why bureaucracies and bureaucrats do what they do, as well as how public goods are produced and consumed.

Several attempts to postulate a theory of governance have been made, but with differing results. Governance theories may include (a) an attempt to unify a broad area of government activity; (b) a new public management movement to define the normative area of government; (c) a body of theory on the blurring of jurisdictional borders, lateral relations, and the decline of sovereignty; and (d) the identification of systematic patterns of how administrators perform their jobs. For more information, see Frederickson and Smith (2003). *See also* Bureaucracy (public administration); Organizational Theory; Public Administration; Public Management

Publication A non-oral media text that offers information to readers through the written word and images. The information in these media messages is determined by its cultural and institutional context (like editorial staffs and the bodies of corporate ownership). Media outlets present publications for audience consumption. Advertisements are frequently featured in publications. Examples of publications include books, magazines, journals, or newspapers (in print or online). Many publications focus on specific subjects (e.g., journals featuring sociological research) and hobbies (e.g., travel). Publications target specific markets, particularly by gender (*Ladies' Home Journal)*, age (*AARP Magazine*), and ethnicity (*Ebony Magazine)*. In today's media landscape, many publications have moved from solely print environments to online as well; often, the information available in online formats is different from the offline version due to the incorporation of news updates or additional features to drive readers to the publication Web site. Some publications exist only in the online space. *See also* Industry (media studies); Media Outlet

Public Campaign An organized effort to influence the election of candidates for office, and the results of referenda (also called political campaigns).

Political campaigns in the United States are subject to federal and state laws that attempt to ensure fair elections. Laws govern campaign financing, advertising, corruption (including bribery and coercive voting), and speech. While open debate is encouraged, false claims and misrepresentations in the media are forbidden. Campaign violations may be prosecuted in the courts, and/or a legislative body may refuse to seat the winning candidate.

Political campaigns use mass media to communicate, adapting to each format in turn as they developed, from mass meetings in the 19th century to mass-circulation newspapers, radio, television, and the most recent arrival, the Internet.

New media have been used in political campaigns since the late 1990s. Candidates have Web sites describing their positions, biographies, and voting records. Fund-raising organizations enable donations to be made online. E-mail and text messaging are being used to reach potential voters. The Kerry versus Bush presidential election in 2004 was the first presidential campaign to make use of blogs. Interactive Internet media enable voters to quickly and easily express their opinions to campaign staff. Moveon.org is one of the best-known grassroots-organizing campaign sites, which was started by two Silicon Valley engineers during the Clinton-Lewinsky scandal of 1998. For more information, see Bartels and Vavreck (2000), Kobrak (2002), and Roberts and Hammond (2004). *See also* Media Campaigns

Public-Choice Economics

A branch of economics that is concerned with the scientific applications of economic modeling to political decision making. Nobel Laureate James Buchanan (1986) is credited with the discovery of the public-choice theory and its focus on the behaviors of stakeholders in the political process, such as party leaders, voters, lobbyists, politicians, administrators, and bureaucrats.

In this approach, a "choice" is the particular act of selecting among different options; whereas "public" refers to people; that said, people (collectively) do not make choices. Individuals make choices, and their choices may be characterized as either "private" or "public." An individual makes private decisions as he or she goes about his or her daily life; however, the individual makes "public choices" when he or she selects an option among the alternatives that affect that individual and others. These public choices are the primary unit of analysis in public-choice economics.

Traditionally, economic analysis of decision making was primarily concerned with the private choices made through market exchanges; moreover, traditional political science was typically focused on aggregate choices and behavior. Therefore, public choice is designed to interlink these social sciences by assessing political institutions within the economic theory and modeling of behaviors.

Frequently, public-choice practitioners emphasize comparative analysis of institutions, especially the relationships between political and economic entities. Whereas many social scientists assume that government policies can and should substitute for imperfections in market-led decision making, public-choice practitioners do not. The latter take a pragmatic approach and view both market- and government-driven processes as having imperfections, and therefore, the one may be an alternative but not a perfect replacement for the other. *See also* Economics

Public Communication *(communication)*

The process of encoding and emitting information and data to the general public. This process is evident in many industries and fields, including politics, business, health, and entertainment. Communication involves gathering information (or data), specifying the messages that need to be sent, transferring the messages through different channels, and sending this information to the target audience. Subsequent to gathering the information, the individual or organization collecting the information should know who the target audience is. The messages that are to be relayed can be phrased so that the target audience will understand the message. The channels involved with sending the messages should also be accessible to the target audience. Such channels include newspapers, magazines, the Internet, radio, and television. Ultimately, the messages should be received and understood by the target audience.

Public communication is a vital aspect of many industries. Without developing and using effective means of delivering messages to the public, the sender (the organization) and the receiver (the public) can be negatively affected by the lack of efficacy. For example, a political campaign involves many strategies to persuade the voting community to vote for a particular party. A political campaign would involve compiling the messages and ideas that are to be communicated, creating strategies to expose these messages based on the characteristics of the target audience, finding the appropriate channels to deliver the messages, and evaluating the success of the communication plans. If a party wanted to tell the audience that they are interested in tuition cutbacks for colleges, they could send this message to young adults between 18 and 25 years of age by using flyers and advertisements at campuses, on Web sites on the Internet, and in television commercials. In the business industry, public communication is crucial for advertisement and publicity purposes. This can also be applied to the entertainment industry, such as finding creative ways to advertise movies on the Internet. In the health field, campaigns need to be devised to deliver messages about important health problems and related issues.

Such communication is so important that it has become an industry in itself. Public relations and communications are fields related to public communication. In the entertainment industry, for example, public relations consultants and representatives play a significant role in handling the careers of celebrities. The messages they deliver can have an impact on the public images of the celebrities. For more information, see

P

Graber (2003). ***See also*** Mass Communication; Mass Media; Public Campaign; Public Relations; Target Audience

Public Communication *(media studies)* Communication with the public in general, not for a limited, specific audience. Public communication, in contrast to private, interpersonal communication, is usually carried out on behalf of an agency or organization. It includes political communication systems between and among people, mass media, and political institutions.

In the journalistic model of public relations, information is provided to the press and to the public as a one-way flow. In the context of public relations, public communication departs from the traditional journalistic model by approaching communication between an organization and the public as an interactive two-way flow, fostering relationship development. Negative associations with the term *public relations* include paternalism, deception, and manipulation; the term *public communication* has not earned such lack of respect.

Communication tools can involve more than press releases to the mass media. Scientists have long been concerned about popular antipathy toward science and public ignorance about scientific issues. Ways have been sought to surmount the perceived communication barrier between scientists and the general public. Scientific information generally flows to the public by way of gatekeepers: science journalists, who may not be educated in science but do have the skills to write for the public that few working scientists possess. Non-intermediated public communication by scientists is possible and might involve science fairs, public lectures, and open days at research centers.

The American Public Communications Council is a Washington-based lobbying group, formed in 1988 to represent the interests of independent payphone service providers. For more information, see Blumler and Gurevitch (1995), Bucchi and Trench (2008), Hackett and Carroll (2006), and Willems (2003). ***See also*** Mass Communication; Mass Media; Media Campaigns; Multistep Flow of Communication; Public Campaign; Public Information Officers; Public Relations

Public Defender A defense attorney provided for the offender and paid for by the state. Although the Sixth Amendment to the U.S. Constitution provides that all criminal defendants have the right to assistance of counsel, historically, very few defendants enjoyed that right because most could not afford attorneys. In *Gideon v. Wainwright* (1963), the U.S. Supreme Court ruled that attorneys would be provided for indigent defendants in both federal and state felony prosecutions. All states now have some mechanism for the provision of public defenders for indigent defendants. While many states have public defender offices, others pay defense attorneys on a contractual basis. For more information, see *Gideon v. Wainwright* (1963). ***See also*** Defense; Indigent; Legal Aid

Public Distance The lecturing distance (public speaking distance). E. T. Hall, an anthropologist, described the public distance as 13–26 feet. For example, this would be the distance that a manager typically uses to lecture his or her workers or when speaking to a group that the manager wants to keep in his or her view. Hall is of the view that maintaining a certain distance from others has the character of a nonverbal message. Its precondition is that the other person has the same need for space. If this is not the case, misunderstandings are likely to occur. The need for public space varies from culture to culture. For example, Hall points out that Germans tend to maintain relatively large public distances (large private spheres). ***See also*** Public Speaking

Public Education A tuition-free education with the theoretical promise of equal educational opportunities regardless of race, religion, or ability. There is supposed to be a commitment to high standards and high expectations for all students, but this standard has fallen through the years.

Public education is, in theory, providing equal educational opportunities for all school-age children. However, the community in which the school resides determines how much and/or how well a child is taught. In other words, higher taxes equate better school districts, which then enable the student to acquire a better and more profitable education. As a result, economically disadvantaged neighborhoods provide a less than adequate education.

The idea of free public education had its roots in the early republic era. Thomas Jefferson believed that it was to society's benefit to educate all its citizens for them to be able to provide leadership and support for the community. As a result, common schools were started around the same time. These schools were supported by taxes allocated for the town districts and taught reading, writing, arithmetic, and history. Thereafter came universal schooling, whose mission was educating all citizens for the common good. Public education was mandatory until the Progressive Era.

Public education is a system of governance that ensures public accountability. It benefits society by teaching democratic principles and common values. Public education is a means by which society shapes its future. Through public education, future generations learn societal norms and are ideally moulded into good, productive citizens. ***See also*** Accountability (education); Equity (political science)

Public Goods *(economics)* For goods such as recreational parks, the airwaves, and national defense, the principle of mutual exclusivity does not hold, where mutual exclusivity is the theory that precludes the common use of privately owned property. By definition therefore, the consumption of public goods by an individual does not preclude others from deriving utility or benefit from the consumption of such goods.

The freedom to use public goods has the potential of generating social problems in the form of common tragedies (abuse) and free-rider problems (enjoying the benefits of a good or service at the expense of others). For example, without private ownership rights or culpability for the use of public resources, potential abuse of such resources because of self-interest is real, even when the abuse is not collectively beneficial. Similarly, some will like to be protected from foreign invasion by a standing militia but will evade the payment of required taxes to provide for the national defense.

Once public goods are produced, the incentive to pay for them diminishes because those who are less inclined to pay for them are not precluded from enjoying the benefits of such goods. The costs and benefits associated with the production of public goods make it very unlikely for individuals to produce and own them. ***See also*** Market Failure

Public Goods *(public administration)*   Something that cannot be expended, depleted, or competed for by a member of society and that a member of society cannot be excluded from using. This is a theoretical economic concept, as in reality there is no such thing as a totally nonexcludable good; however, some argue that there are products or services that approximate the notion of public goods and, thus, find this analysis to be analytically pertinent.

Suppose an individual consumes a cookie; consequently, there would be no cookie for others to consume. Thus, it is possible to exclude others, thereby making the cookie a private good. Conversely, in many areas, drinking water or breathing air does not reduce the amount that is available for others to consume; moreover, it poses a significant challenge to restrict or exclude an individual's consumption of water and air.

Examples of public goods include lighthouses, national defense, and law enforcement; moreover, it is possible for technological advancements to yield public goods. An example would be streetlights. Conversely, technology may take a public good and make it private. An example would be the encryption of television signals, which can only be decoded by subscribers with the appropriate receiver.

Some argue that a public good is the consequence of a market failure, where inefficiencies are created in spite of market-like conditions and behaviors being present. When private entities do not derive benefits from their labors, their incentive for production may be insufficient for them to produce voluntarily. When this occurs, consumers, whose contribution to production is negligible, nonetheless accrue benefits. This is frequently referred to as the "free-rider problem." For example, visitors to Times Square can enjoy the security afforded by the police and the clean streets provided by the local administration yet contribute nothing by way of taxes to the costs of security and maintenance. ***See also*** Market Failure

Public Information Officers   Persons employed by government agencies, including the health and police departments, to provide information to the public regarding the agencies' policies and activities. Public information officers (PIOs) may have education and training in public relations or journalism or may be appointed to the position from within the ranks of the organization. They provide a single point of contact between the public, including journalists, and the agency personnel. A PIO is the spokesperson for the agency, usually the person who responds to journalists' questions and information requests, and passes on press releases from the agency. Agency policy may forbid other employees from communicating directly with the press. PIOs differ from public relations people in that they do not generally engage in marketing and advertising and they work for nonprofit organizations. They require familiarity with the culture, the normal procedures and policies, and the specialist knowledge of that organization. A PIO for a health department would be expected to have knowledge of diseases and the workings of the agency and would be called on to describe and explain the agency's responses to a public health emergency—for example, an outbreak of meningitis among schoolchildren—in such a way as to provide credible information without triggering a panic. For more information, see Federal Emergency Management Agency (2009), Lee (2008), and National Information Officers Association: www.nioa.org/. ***See also*** Public Communication (communication, media studies); Public Relations

Public Interest *(media studies)*   What benefits the public as a whole. This is a vague, immeasurable, and variously defined concept with a long history, often used interchangeably with the term *public good*.

In the utilitarian tradition of Jeremy Bentham and John Stuart Mill, public interest is "the greatest good for the greatest number." The media critic Walter Lippmann (1955) defined it as "what men would choose if they saw clearly, thought rationally, acted disinterestedly and benevolently."

The provision of public goods is said to be in the public interest. Public goods are available to everyone in a community regardless of whether or not they want to make use of them. Public health programs, public schools, pollution control programs, and parks are all considered public goods. Such public goods are generally financed by taxation. Community members cannot normally opt out of paying for public goods that they do not approve of; for example, people cannot legally refuse to pay that part of the tax that would go toward providing a service that they do not wish to have, such as education or defense.

In many countries, including the United States, governments distributed licenses to broadcast with the requirement that radio and television stations serve the public interest. What exactly this means has been the subject of much controversial debate between those who advocate a free market and those who prefer a trusteeship mode.

In English law, there is a principle of public-interest immunity. Government officials do not have to deliver documents in response to freedom-of-information requests if they can claim that doing so would be detrimental to the public interest. For more information, see Lippmann (1955) and McCauley, Peterson, Artz, and Halleck (2003). ***See also*** Public Service Broadcasting

Public Interest (*political science*)   A term applied to legislation or policy in which society at large shares an interest beyond mere curiosity and/or that affects the general well-being. The courts have often used the public-interest standard as an essential variable to be weighed in balancing tests. For example, in *Department of Justice v. Reporters Committee for Freedom of the Press* (1989), the Supreme Court ruled that nondisclosure of information under the Freedom of Information Act is permissible only if the personal privacy interest due to nondisclosure outweighs the public interest in obtaining the information. A public interest in this case was defined as "shed[ding] light on an agency's performance of its statutory duties" (pp. 1481–1483). Public interest is also a category of law that serves the public in some capacity. Most public-interest lawyers work for nonprofit and legal service organizations, prosecutor offices, government law offices, and public service law firms. For more information, see *Department of Justice v. Reporters Committee for Freedom of the Press (1989)*. ***See also*** Freedom of Information Act

Publicity (Prejudicial Publicity in the Media) Prejudicial publicity refers to media coverage of criminal trials that may be detrimental to the defendant. Two constitutionally protected rights converge and conflict: The Sixth Amendment of the U.S. Constitution grants defendants the right to a fair trial, while the First Amendment guarantees a free press and, thus, the right of the press to report trials. A small minority of criminal trials attract media attention. Even fewer get considerable and continuing media coverage (e.g., the O. J. Simpson case), and these may be reported as much as entertainment as news.

There is debate as to how damaging pretrial publicity is to a defendant and how potential damage (assuming it exists) can be mitigated. Much of the research in this area has been done with mock jurors in laboratory settings and so may not be applicable to real-life settings. Studies of real-life trials have shown that media coverage is overwhelmingly antidefendant—though whether and how this might affect the eventual trial outcome is hotly debated.

Mitigating actions available to judges and lawyers in individual trials include *voir dire* jury selection, during which potential jurors who admit to being biased can be dismissed; moving the trial to a different jurisdiction than where the crime occurred or selecting a jury from a distant location; banning cameras from the courtroom; lengthening the trial duration; sequestering the jury away from media reports; instructing the jury to ignore media reports; and, in extreme cases, ordering a new trial. For more information, see Brischke and Loges (2004). ***See also*** Crime News; *Voir Dire*

Public Law   Law that pertains to the following areas: (a) the relationship between private citizens and the state; (b) the organization, obligations, immunities, and powers of the state; and (c) the relationship between the state and foreign powers. Public law stands in contrast to private law, which only concerns relations between private individuals or corporations. Public law can be found in constitutional, administrative, criminal, and international law. The distinction between public and private law dates back to the Middle Ages; it was codified into the *Corpus Juris Civilis* (534 AD), the compilation of Roman Law issued under the order of the Roman (Byzantine) emperor Justinian I. Public law also refers to an act enacted by the state that applies to the general public. At the federal level, public law is enacted by Congress and signed into law by the president. A public law is indicated by the letters PL preceding the law's numerical citation. ***See also*** Private Law

Public Management   A generic term used to describe the issues relating to public service and administration. Similar to private organizations, public organizations must have decision makers, managers, and workers to run them. More important, there must be some sort of measurement to gauge their effectiveness and compliance with legislative mandates and controls.

Unlike the private sector, profit is not the prime motive for public organizations to exist. Serving a public purpose may often be a profitless endeavor. This forces managers to make decisions with a *different set of principles* in mind than their private sector counterparts. Selection of workers is a prime way to see this difference. Private companies may look for the best possible worker for the lowest cost. Public organizations must comply with various hiring regulations consistent with different federal, state, and local laws. Civil service exams and a fair method of employment selection are almost always mandated for government managers to use before making employment decisions. In the private sector, much more leeway is allowed in hiring decisions, and much fewer regulations are to be considered.

Additionally, public managers must also operate within the political sphere and under the public eye. When a worker at a plumbing-supply company makes an error, it is hardly ever reported in the local news unless extreme circumstances surround the event; however, if a police officer errs, there is a very good possibility that the department as a whole will be under scrutiny by the public at large, the media, and elected officials at various levels and branches of government.

It is now conventional wisdom that government should be more "businesslike." Some view this as propaganda stemming from people in favor of limited government. Others view this concept as a noble endeavor—something that could help government become more professional and more responsive to the general public. ***See also*** Public Administration

Public Opinion (*media studies*)　A product of people conversing among themselves about issues of common interest, it is much more than the sum of private opinions held by individuals. Interpersonal communication, individual opinions, mass communication, and public opinion are interactive.

In 1898, the French social psychologist Gabriel Tarde developed a model linking the press, conversations, opinion formation, and the resulting social and political action. The press set the agenda, dictating the topics of conversations held by the people, where opinions were developed during interpersonal debates, leading directly to some action being taken.

Hans Speier, in 1950, described public opinion as communication with two important components. First, people talked with each other, then the results of their deliberations were communicated upward to those in power. He saw that freedom of expression and freedom to influence others are essential for the existence of public opinion. Both Speier and Tarde emphasize the importance of conversations in forming public opinion.

Elisabeth Noelle-Neumann's "spiral of silence" theory illustrates the difference between those opinions that are held privately and those that are made public. She observed that an individual's perceptions of what others believe and feel influences whether or not that individual shares his or her true opinions. Individuals who believe that the majority opinion differs from their own view will remain silent in a political conversation, thus removing themselves from the conversations described by Speier and Tarde, in which public opinion is formed.

Opinion polls are often assumed to reflect public opinion but actually record an aggregate of private opinions. Public opinion is formed by individuals interacting with others, developing their opinions through back-and-forth conversations. Elites look to the media to convey public opinion but may be misled when the media rely on opinion polls and surveys. For more information, see Glasser and Salmon (1995), Noelle-Neumann (1984), Speier (1950), and Tarde (1898/1969). ***See also*** Agenda Setting (media studies)

Public Opinion (*political science*)　The aggregate attitudes and beliefs of a population. In democracies, public opinion holds great value for lawmakers in discerning what policy agendas are popular with the public and in understanding voting behavior. Government agencies and private organizations regularly run surveys to measure current trends in public thought. The origins of the concept of public opinion date back to philosophical arguments regarding its value among the ancient Greeks. Does the public know best how to govern a democracy, or should issues of governance be left to the most intelligent and talented people in society? The philosopher Aristotle (384–322 BCE) believed the former and Plato (427–347 BCE), the latter. Nearly a century later, the English philosophers Thomas Hobbes (1588–1679) and John Locke (1632–1704) also reflected on its value. Hobbes believed that involvement of the public was essential in forming the government but not in actual governance. In contrast, Locke, like Aristotle, valued the active participation of a diverse citizenry in politics. ***See also*** Agenda Setting (political science)

Public Opinion Poll　A survey of a population group or sample that measures public opinion on contemporary issues. The first known published public opinion poll in the United States dates back to 1824, when *The Harrisburg Pennsylvanian* reported that Andrew Jackson was the most likely winner in the bid for presidency against John Quincy Adams. Perhaps the most influential public opinion poll in modern American politics is the Gallup Poll, sponsored by the Gallup Organization. The organization, originally the American Institute for Public Opinion, was founded by the advertising executive George Gallup in 1935. Gallup began his career running studies for Hollywood studios on the box office potential. He later concentrated on politics and election forecasting. ***See also*** Public Opinion (political science)

Public Order Offense　An act that has been criminalized because it is seen as being disruptive to the orderly functioning (or moral standards) of a community. Public order offenses are typically the nuisance offenses, such as disorderly conduct and public drunkenness. Some also characterize consensual crimes (prostitution), victimless crimes (drug use), and vice crimes (gambling) as public order offenses. ***See also*** Misdemeanor

Public Policy　What government does and why it performs certain actions to address a public issue. Public policy is authoritative statements or laws made by governmental actors. Although formally the executive branch and political appointees play a significant role in policy formulation, it is the career civil servants who play a key role in bringing social problems to light. Policy making initiates with problem identification. Different groups, including interest groups and individuals, identify societal problems. For the problem to receive attention, it must be placed on the agenda, so that policymakers can begin to address what should be done about the problem and initiate policy formulation. Once the policy has been formulated and approved, it must be authorized to acquire a budget. After appropriations have been acquired, it is the task of administrative agencies and other actors, such as nonprofits, to implement the policy and perform program evaluation. Evaluation is a core component of

P

public policy and serves to determine if the goals of the policy were met. The findings are key in deciding if programs should be continued, tweaked, or terminated. Administrative agencies are key players not only in the implementation of public policy but also in its formulation. Agencies are close to the action and therefore have insight into what the problems are. Quite often, administrative agencies recommend legislative amendments to existing law. For more information, see Grover (2008).

Public Programs   Programs that are, by definition, publicly funded. Their benefits may be to reduce harms, educate, evaluate, and so on, in order to benefit the public. For example, public health programs are intended to protect and enhance the health of the public. In the United States, governments plan, administer, and coordinate public health programs and services, which include environmental health programs, mental health programs, cancer control, communicable disease control, child health services, health statistics maintenance, and immunization services.

In the United States, most health care programs are overseen by the cabinet-level Department of Health and Human Services (DHHS). DHHS's operations are divided between the Public Health Operating Divisions and Human Services Operating Divisions, which include Medicare, Medicaid, and the Administration for Children and Families. Major divisions of the DHHS include the National Institutes of Health, the Food and Drug Administration, the Centers for Disease Control, the Substance Abuse and Mental Health Services Administration, the Health Resources and Services Administration, the Agency for Toxic Substances and Disease Registry, the Indian Health Service, and the Agency for Healthcare Research and Quality.

Health care programs must be evaluated to determine whether they are effectively benefiting the public. Five aspects that should be evaluated are the program's (1) relevance to the needs of the population, (2) progress in terms of implementation, (3) efficiency in terms of outcomes achieved relative to the resources expended, (4) effectiveness or extent to which objectives are met, and (5) impact based on long-term outcomes. Evaluations can take the form of case studies, randomized experiments, and other statistical analyses. For more information, see Drummond, O'Brien, Stoddart, and Torrance (1997). **See also** Health Care System

Public Relations   A management tool that involves the use of psychological and sociological knowledge and skills to create and present a positive image of an organization (or individual) and its activities to the public. Public relations has become so widespread that few organizations of any size operate without public relations specialists. The number of public relations specialists is currently greater than the number of journalists employed in the United States.

Edward L. Bernays was one of the most influential and successful practitioners of public relations in the United States for much of the 20th century. A nephew of Sigmund Freud, he pioneered psychological techniques of mass persuasion. An elitist with little respect for ordinary people, Bernays advocated disseminating information indirectly and inconspicuously by way of propaganda and news reports rather than through direct publicity from his clients.

Public relations is not confined to commercial, for-profit businesses. Charities, nongovernmental organizations, and cultural and education institutions, all rely on public relations tools. Government agencies can use public relations to increase public support, increase awareness and use of its products and services, and educate the public and encourage compliance with regulations. For example, a city sanitation department might use public relations techniques to increase popular support for recycling. For more information, see Cutlip (1994), Ewen (1996), Heath (2005), Lee (2008), Stauber and Rampton (1995), and Watson and Noble (2007). **See also** News Management; Public Communication (communication, media studies); Public Information Officers

Public Sector   The term refers to the government, including departments, agencies, commissions, and government corporations, and the nonprofit sector, including both member-serving organizations and public-serving organizations. The public sector differs from the private sector in four respects: (1) structures, (2) incentives, (3) settings, and (4) purposes. Unlike in the private sector, the lines of authority are often blurred because one entity does not have complete authority with respect to a government policy or program. Another fundamental difference between the public and private sectors is in the matter of incentives. Incentives are often connected to resources. In the public sector, resources often do not come from the client, and therefore, clients are seen as a strain on resources; whereas in the private sector, employees have the incentive to retain customers. In addition, the two sectors differ in terms of setting; the public sector puts a high value on transparency and has higher turn-over rates than the private sector. Finally, unlike the private sector, whose purpose is profit, the public sector serves the common good. For more information, see Grover (2008). **See also** Government Nonprofit Organization; Private Sector

Public Service Broadcasting   A range of radio and television broadcasting services that exist to a greater or lesser extent independent of control by advertisers and states. Commercial broadcasters rely on income from advertisers and compete with other broadcasters for audiences and advertising. In contrast, public service broadcasting in most countries, though not the United States, is funded by license fees paid by the public who own radios or televisions and/or by government grants.

The British Broadcasting Corporation (BBC) is widely recognized to be one of the most successful public broadcasting services. In Britain, public service broadcasting started in 1923 with the founding of the BBC, intended to be a public service run in the national interest. Broadcasting was permitted only under license by the Post Office, and the BBC maintained a monopoly for many decades. Broadcasting was seen as too important a public utility to be commercialized. It was believed that market forces would dictate that commercialized competing broadcasters provide only programs catering to the lowest forms of mass appetite. From the start, the BBC aimed to provide not just entertainment but also access to the best of human knowledge while maintaining high standards and a high moral tone. The BBC aspired to inform and educate and provide a forum for open public discussion. By providing common access to public events and ceremonies, a shared public life could be created. BBC-owned transmitters currently provide services to 91% of the British population.

In most countries other than the United States, public rather than commercial broadcasting dominates and is seen as essential to maintaining and promoting the national culture. Some countries require that a certain minimum portion of broadcasting content be produced within the country and in the national language.

In the United States, public broadcasting is much more eclectic. Individual stations may be part of a network or independent. Many colleges have their own broadcasting services. NPR (National Public Radio) and PBS (Public Broadcasting Service) are networks of local stations, rather than single entities, and occupy niche positions, dwarfed by the commercial broadcasting stations. Financing is provided by appealing for funds directly to audiences, who are encouraged to pay to become members of their local stations. Additional financing is provided by corporate sponsorship, foundations, and grants. NPR develops some of its own programming and buys in the rest. Public broadcasters in the United States and elsewhere see themselves as providing programming of a higher intellectual and moral quality than commercial broadcasters would provide. For more information, see Avery (1993) and Schnell (1996). *See also* Network; Satellite Systems

Public Speaking   The act of talking to an audience to inform, persuade, and/or entertain. Academics, candidates for political office, clerics, corporate executives, heads of state, and social activists, among others, speak in public. Students are introduced to the conventions of public speaking as early as in the primary grades.

Public speaking is both an art and a science, involving development of presentation skills. Robert D. Freeburn, director of the Voice and Speech Centre in the United Kingdom, concedes that public speaking can be a frightening experience, and he notes that American research shows that audiences begin making conclusions about public speakers during the first 90 seconds of their presentations. He suggests that the initial tasks of an effective public speaker are to become aware of the audience to be addressed and to prepare appropriate material. A public speaker should develop an expressive vocal range and gestures that underscore the points made. Good posture and eye contact are essential. For more information, see Freeburn (1994). *See also* Body Language; Effectiveness (communication); Persuasion

Public Versus Private Schools   The distinction between public schools, funded by tax revenues, and private schools, funded through other measures, primarily through tuition payments made by students' families. Public schools are led primarily by local administrators in the public sector, admit all children who live in the district, and are obligated to follow local, state, and federal laws regarding education, which may affect funding and the curriculum. Private schools can be selective in admitting students and have fewer obligations to follow local, state, or federal laws, allowing for more freedom in curriculum selection. *See also* Financing of Schools

Publishing Industry   The industry that produces books, magazines, and newspapers and generates revenues from the sales of its products and from advertising. In 2007, the global publishing market had an estimated value of $444.1 billion, with the U.S. publishing market alone valued at $157.9 billion. Globally, advertising was the greatest source of revenue, accounting for a third of the market value. Newspapers and magazines together earned 39.2% of global revenue, with book sales making up 28.1%. Since 2003, the global market has grown at about 2.4% annually. The industry is dominated by large international firms, notably Bertelsmann AG, Time Warner Inc., and Reed Elsevier NV. Both Time Warner and Bertelsmann have diversified operations, which include nonpublishing business areas such as entertainment, communication, and services. Reed Elsevier concentrates on publishing of science, technical, education, legal, and medical books, periodicals, and databases in print and electronic formats.

The most common format for books, newspapers, and magazines is print, but publishers are delivering more of their products on the World Wide Web—most notably, national newspapers and magazines supported by online commercial advertising. Newspapers have lost a significant source of revenue with the movement of consumer adverts (small ads) away from local papers to Web services such as Craigslist. Sales of printed books are moving from physical bookstores, with their limited stock of titles, to Internet stores, such as Amazon. Sales of books in electronic form lag behind sales of printed books but are expected to increase. For more information, see Gomez (2008), Greco (2000), *Publishing Industry Profile: Global* (2007), *Publishing Industry Profile: United States* (2007), and *U.S. Industry Quarterly Review: Information Services* (2006). *See also* Newspaper; Print Media

Punishment *(psychology)*   Any stimulus that decreases the likelihood of a prior response. Skinner, a leading behaviorist, identified two types of punishment as part of his theory of operant conditioning. A positive punisher weakens a response through the presentation of an averse stimulus, for example, scolding a child. A negative punisher weakens behavior by removing a stimulus that is ordinarily characterized as positive, for example, taking a toy away from a child. For more information, see Ferster and Skinner (1957). ***See also*** Behaviorism (psychology)

Punishment *(sociology)*   A sanction imposed on a person or persons as a result of their wrongdoing. In criminal law, punishment is imposed following conviction for a criminal offense. The range of punishments that can be imposed for any given offense is specified in the penal code. Punishment can range from financial penalties (e.g., fines and restitution), to restrictions on freedom (through surveillance, house arrest, etc.), to the deprivation of liberty (through incarceration or imprisonment), to the forfeiture of life (through a death sentence). Deterrence, retribution, incapacitation, and rehabilitation are the four widely accepted purposes of punishment. ***See also*** Community-Based Corrections; Deterrence (sociology); Penal Codes/Laws; Penology; Rehabilitation; Retribution

Punitive Damages   Financial penalties imposed on defendants and awarded to plaintiffs in civil cases. Punitive damages are financial payments in excess of what would be required to compensate the plaintiff for actual losses and are intended to make the sanctions more punishing. ***See also*** Civil Law (political science); Civil Liability

P

Q

Qualitative Criminology An area of study that aims to document detailed information about human and social behaviors in issues that are of relevance to the disciplines of criminology and criminal justice. Some of the methods used to collect qualitative data include in-depth interviews, direct observation, and participation in the environment of interest. One of the major benefits of qualitative research is that it enables the collection of in-depth information about the topic at hand and provides a better tool for understanding the processes underlying the phenomenon at hand. One of the main pitfalls of qualitative research relates to the limited ability to generalize findings to a larger reference population. ***See also*** Quantitative Research; Research Methodology

Qualitative Data Analysis Qualitative data analysis (QDA) includes the strategies for summarizing and determining the meaning of qualitative research data included in this analysis. During QDA, the researcher explores the data and searches for patterns, themes, relationships, and significant statements. The researcher prepares the qualitative data, such as interviews and field notes, for analysis by transcribing verbal or written data into text data. Visual data also are important in qualitative research. Researchers are increasingly importing qualitative data into software designed specifically for QDA.

To obtain a general sense of the material, a researcher usually reads through the data several times; during this time, the researcher might jot down notes. The researcher must continually decide whether more data are needed because analysis in qualitative research often takes the form of interim analysis, which means that data collection and analysis are conducted cyclically during the research study.

Central to QDA are the activities of segmenting and coding. The researcher locates meaningful segments of data (e.g., text) and assigns a code (e.g., a symbol, category, concept, or short phrase) to label each segment. The researcher should choose codes to represent text segments that clearly describe people, places, events, activities, concepts, and processes in order to help the audience understand the study's central phenomenon. Types of codes include inductive codes (generated by the researcher during examination of the data), a priori codes (developed before examining the data), co-occurring codes (overlapping codes), and face sheet codes (codes applying to a complete document or case).

Sometimes enumeration of codes is conducted, in which the frequency of occurrence of codes is counted.

During QDA, many types of "relationships" might be found in the data. One's codes/categories might naturally fall into a hierarchy of concepts, which would form a hierarchical relationship. Typologies can be constructed from codes. Codes/categories can be depicted in diagrams and matrices to help the analyst and reader "see" relationships in the data. Spradley (1979) suggests searching for the following types of semantic relationships: strict inclusion, spatial, cause-effect, rationale, location for action, function, means-end, sequence, and attribution.

The content of qualitative data (e.g., codes, categories, descriptive phrases) often is collapsed into a few (five or six) themes. A relatively ordinary theme would be one that the researcher might expect to find throughout the course of his or her study (e.g., "bullying in school"). An unexpected theme would be one that comes as a surprise during the study (e.g., "tolerance of bullying in school"). Social science themes are those that reflect some social construct (e.g., "cliques in school"). Hard-to-classify themes contain ideas that overlap with several themes or don't easily fit into one theme (e.g., "discipline problems with girls"). Major and minor subthemes are those representing major ideas and minor ideas, respectively, in the researcher's database. Most qualitative researchers rely on the logic of induction and therefore emphasize that the themes should emerge out of the data rather than being forced onto the data. A researcher can be assured of a good qualitative analysis when multiple perspectives are represented, good quotable material is identified, all the research questions have been covered, and responses from several people to each question can be tied together to represent the different perspectives. For more information, see Spradley (1979). ***See also*** Data, Extant/Existing; Field Notes; Interview (education, sociology); Qualitative Research; Qualitative Research Validity Types

Qualitative Research A methodological paradigm that relies primarily on the collection of qualitative data (e.g., nonnumeric data such as words, pictures, images, categories). According to qualitative research, reality is subjective, personal, and socially constructed. The purposes of qualitative research are to explore, discover, construct, and describe phenomena experienced by people in specific contexts. The qualitative researcher usually does not make generalizations beyond the people in the research study. Qualitative researchers collect data through in-depth interviews, participant observations, field notes, and open-ended questionnaires. Rather than using standardized instruments of data collection, the research is said to be the "instrument of data collection." It is important in qualitative research to understand the emic, or insider's perspective, as well as the etic, or the "objective" outsider's perspective. Data are collected and analyzed for patterns, themes, and holistic features. The qualitative research report usually takes a narrative form, and it includes rich descriptions of the people and the context. Popular qualitative research methods are phenomenology, ethnography, case study, grounded theory, and historical research. In *phenomenology*, the researcher attempts to understand how one or more individuals experience a particular phenomenon (e.g., the experience of the death of a loved one). The focus is on the meaning, structure, and essences of a lived experience. In *ethnography*, the researcher studies the culture of a group of people, including their shared values, beliefs, norms, rituals, language, and material productions. The focus is on the cultural characteristics of the people or of a cultural scene. In *qualitative case study* research, the researcher provides a detailed account of one or more cases or bounded systems. A case might be examined for its intrinsic characteristics or studied instrumentally (to understand something broader than the particular case); multiple cases also can be studied in comparative case studies. In *grounded theory*, the researcher inductively generates a theory to explain a particular phenomenon. The focus is on constructing an explanation of how and why something operates. In *historical* research, the researcher writes about other people in other times; oral history is especially important for documenting how different times, places, and events were according to the people who experienced them. A strength of qualitative research is its ability to provide an in-depth understanding of humans and their circumstances. A potential weakness is the inability to generalize findings to other populations. ***See also*** Data, Extant/Existing; Field Notes; Interview (education, sociology); Objectivity/Objectivism; Participant Observation (education, sociology); Qualitative Data Analysis; Qualitative Research Validity Types; Subjectivity/Subjectivism

Qualitative Research Validity Types   The production of defensible research is important in all types of research, including qualitative research. A common label for "validity" in qualitative research is "trustworthiness." Although there are many published sets of qualitative research validity types, I focus here on the one constructed by Joseph Maxwell, which includes five validity types. First, *descriptive validity* refers to the factual accuracy of the account that is reported by the researcher. It answers the question "Did the researcher get the "facts" right?" The idea is to describe accurately the events, objects, behaviors, people, settings, times, and places that come up during data collection. Second,

interpretative validity refers to the degree to which the qualitative researcher accurately portrays the inner worlds or inner meanings given by the participants to what is studied. This is perhaps the most central concern in qualitative research. This type of validity is similar to Max Weber's concept of *verstehen*, or empathetic understanding of others' viewpoints, intentions, beliefs, and experiences; it also is similar to what ethnographers call the *emic perspective*. Third, *theoretical validity* refers to the degree to which the theoretical explanation developed in the study fits the data. A theory explains to a reader "how" and "why" a phenomenon studied operates. The concepts in a theory will be slightly more abstract than those documented for descriptive validity. Fourth, *internal validity* refers to the degree to which "cause-and-effect" claims are warranted. Qualitative researchers sometimes prefer to label this type of validity "credibility." Some qualitative researchers have little or no interest in causal relationships, and when they do, their interest is focused only on local causes and effects (i.e., what occurred for particular people in a particular setting). Fifth, *external validity* refers to the degree to which the research findings can be generalized to other people, settings, and times. Qualitative researchers sometimes label this type of validity "transferability." Because of its primary interest in local people and local contexts, qualitative research usually is not interested in external validity. Rather than making generalizations from their research studies, qualitative researchers recommend that the reader of a study decide how similar his or her situation is to the one reported and then make generalizations based on similarity of contexts and people. Robert Stake calls this (where the user rather than the researcher makes generalizations) *naturalistic generalization*. There are many strategies for achieving the above types of validity or trustworthiness, including triangulation, extended fieldwork, member checking, reflexivity, peer review, external auditing, and negative-case sampling. ***See also*** Emic and Etic Perspectives; Triangulation

Quality Circle *(education)*   A participative management concept that originated in Japan. A quality circle is composed of 8 to 10 volunteers linked by a common interest who meet regularly to identify, investigate, and solve problems in their organization. The circle has an elected leader and typically includes a facilitator. ***See also*** Quality in Education; Team Building

Quality Circle *(public administration)*   A participative management technique that seeks to involve employees in problem solving and decision making through the use of small (8–10 member) suggestion groups that brainstorm an issue. Apparently first proposed by statistician and management consultant W. Edwards Deming (1900–1993) for the reconstruction of post–World War II Japanese industry, it became remarkably successful there and was taken up by American companies in the 1970s. The technique is based on the assumption that the line workers know more about the problems of quality control and should be given responsibility for solving them early in the production process. In theory, such quality circles that are truly voluntary, give the workers responsibility for problem solving, and will result in greater productivity and job satisfaction. In some companies, however, management set the agenda and used them to undermine labor organizations. *See also* Brainstorming

Quality in Education   A concept derived from the total quality management (TQM) philosophy. The TQM philosophy was created and made popular, initially in the manufacturing industry, by consultants such as W. Edwards Deming, Joseph Juran, and Philip Crosby. TQM began gaining popularity in education during the late 1980s and 1990s, particularly in higher education. When applied to education, TQM stresses a customer-based approach whereby educational institutions provide customers (students, parents, employers, the community, etc.) with a service (education, educated individuals, etc.) that meets their needs. Quality is defined in terms of the customer's needs and desires. The customer, not the institution, decides what constitutes quality. TQM emphasizes strategy, leadership, teamwork, detailed analysis, and self-assessment. Continuous improvement of the service is called for when employing this model.

Quantitative Criminology/Study/Statistics   An area of study that focuses on the investigation and testing of hypotheses, theories, and paradigms in relation to topics that is relevant to the fields of criminology and criminal justice. Quantitative research relies on data that consist of numbers, statistics, and mathematical models. Quantitative research is based on principles of the scientific approach, which includes the collection, analysis, and interpretation of empirical data. Quantitative studies are concerned with external validity, which refers to the ability to generalize findings from a sample to the larger population of reference. *See also* Qualitative Research; Research Methodology; Sampling; Statistics (psychology, sociology); Validity

Quantitative Research   One of the three major research paradigms, which includes qualitative research, mixed-methods research, and quantitative research. Quantitative research relies primarily on the collection of quantitative data and has its own, unique set of assumptions and normative practices. Quantitative research usually assumes that human behavior exhibits some lawfulness and predictability that can be documented through empirical research. Goals include to describe, to predict, and to explain human phenomena. Quantitative researchers often try to study behavior under controlled conditions via experiments, in order to isolate the causal effects of independent variables. Popular methods of quantitative research are experimental research, survey research, and structured observational research. Quantitative data are collected based on precise measurement of variables using structured, standardized, and validated data collection instruments and procedures. Data are analyzed using descriptive and inferential statistics. The desired product is research findings that generalize broadly. Quantitative researchers attempt to minimize their biases during the research process by relying on standardized testing and measurement, continual testing of measurement procedures for reliability and validity, random selection of research participants, random assignment of research participants to comparison groups, measures of interrater reliability when multiple observers are used, and inferential statistics for estimating the values of population parameters and for testing statistical hypotheses. Although some writers continue to refer to quantitative research as "positivism," virtually all quantitative researchers and the associated philosophy of science have moved past traditional positivism (born in the 19th century in the work of Auguste Comte) and past logical positivism, popular in the first half of the 20th century (found in the writings of A. J. Ayer, Rudolf Carnap, Otto Neurath, Hans Reichenbach, and Moritz Schlick). Popular philosophies of science currently associated with quantitative research are postpositivism, naturalism, physicalism, and scientific realism. *See also* Descriptive Statistics (education, sociology); Experimental Research; Inferential Statistics; Longitudinal Versus Cross-Sectional Data; Measurement; Nonexperimental Research in Quantitative Research; Quasi-Experimental Research; Sampling in Quantitative Research; Validity in Quantitative Research; Variable (education, sociology)

Quantity Theory of Money   According to this theory, changes in the money supply will lead to proportionate changes in the price level or inflation. The quantity theory of money is represented by the equation $MV = PQ$, where M is the total money supply circulating in the economy during a specific period of time; V is the velocity, or the number of times or transactions per period or year in which the money is spent on final goods within the defined period; P is the average price level during the defined period; and Q is the physical quantity of all final goods produced in the defined period. The left-hand side of the equation, MV, is the total monetary expenditures on the final goods produced within the period, and this is related to the money supply spent on all the physical goods produced (Q) times the average sale price (P) of the final goods. This equation is an identity, and the right-hand side equals the left-hand side. It shows that the amount of money spent on all final goods produced is equal to all the money received by those selling these goods. The quantity theory equation assumes that velocity and quantity are fixed and held constant and only the money supply and the price level change. Velocity and quantity are fixed by the behavior of consumers and firms and by the choices they make. Velocity and quantity are therefore fixed in relation to the money supply. Since velocity and quantity are fixed, an increase in the money supply will lead to a proportionate increase in the price level or inflation. The theory suggests that the application of the quantity theory equation can be effective in controlling inflation. The quantity theory was first postulated in the 17th century and later formalized into an equation by Irvin Fisher (1867–1947). The quantity theory was later challenged by Keynesian economists, led by John Maynard Keynes. The quantity theory of money was supported by monetarist economists, led by Milton Friedman. Keynes suggested that an increase in the money supply will lead to greater economic activity and increased demand, which will lead to an increase in real income. Milton Friedman showed that velocity, which is relatively stable and predictable in the short run, can be held constant in response to variation in the money supply. Policies based on the quantity theory of money were adopted during the 1980s, which was a period of rising inflation caused by rising oil prices. Application of the quantity theory of money is simple: Control of the money supply will lead to control of inflation. On the other hand, followers of Keynesian economics believe that this does not stimulate demand and therefore increased spending by government on public works and projects will stimulate demand and will lead to an increase in real income. For more information, see Carbaugh (2007) and McEachern (2006). **See also** Inflation; Keynesian; Monetary Policy; Money Supply; Price

Quasi-Experimental Research   A term attributed to Campbell (1957) and Campbell and Stanley (1963), with a more extensive description by Cook and Campbell (1979) and Shadish, Cook, and Campbell (2002), referring to the use of designs where random assignment of participants to comparison groups is not used to structure the comparison groups. Sometimes random assignment is not possible because participants are already in intact groups or they may have a common characteristic that is not under the control of the researcher (e.g., gender, political preference, marital status). There is a controlled or explicit independent variable or treatment manipulation, as is the case in experimental research. There are recognized examples of these designs, each having a variety of design arrangements. Nonequivalent group designs compare results on a dependent variable between two or more groups where participants are not randomly assigned to the experimental conditions. This may involve only a posttest, but more often this involves both a pretest and a posttest on the dependent variable, giving at least a minimum of statistical comparison. The interrupted time series design involves one or more groups, where multiple measures of the dependent variable are taken over time, the treatment is introduced, and it is then followed by more multiple measures of the dependent variable over time. The regression-discontinuity design is based on comparisons of the linear regression *Y*-intercepts of a situation where the treatment is absent with a situation where the treatment is present. Because of the lack of random assignment of participants to comparison groups, quasi-experimental research is prone to selection threats to internal validity. Strategies have been proposed by these and other authors to minimize the threats to validity when using these designs. For more information, see Campbell (1957), Campbell and Stanley (1963), Cook and Campbell (1979), and Shadish, Cook, and Campbell (2002). **See also** Experimental Research; Nonexperimental Research in Quantitative Research

Question   In the United States, a political question occurs when a court, particularly the Supreme Court, decides that an issue before the court should be left to "politics," the legislative or executive branches, to resolve. Notable cases in which the Supreme Court decided that the issues were a political question include *Nixon v. United States* (1993), regarding a disputed Senate Rule concerning congressional impeachment. According to Jesse H. Choper, in *The Political Question Doctrine and the Supreme Court of the United States* (2007), legal scholars are in agreement that the use of the Political Question Doctrine is in serious decline in the American judicial system. For more information, see Choper (2007) and *Nixon v. United States* (1993). **See also** Executive Branch; Legislative Branch; Politics (political science)

Questionnaire   A list of questions or items used to gather data from a sample, usually in order to perform statistical analyses. Questionnaires may be online or in printed form. The format of questions and items may vary and may be either closed- or open-ended. **See also** Rating Scale; Survey Research

Quorum   The minimum number of people necessary for a legislative body to pass a bill. In the United States, Article 1, Section 5 of the Constitution states that a quorum of both houses of Congress exists when there is a majority present; the Senate *Rules of Order* further stipulate that the majority be composed of those "duly chosen and sworn." A practice known as "quorum-busting" occurs when members of a legislative body are purposefully absent to avoid a vote on and subsequent passage of a bill. Although this strategy has been used successfully to prevent the passage of legislation in state legislatures, the Senate was granted the authority in 1877 to arrest members for quorum busting. The Senate has occasionally made such arrests; the first act of physical compulsion to vote was evidenced in 1988, when the Capitol Police brought Senator Robert Packwood (OR-Rep) into Chambers at 1:17 a.m. for a campaign finance reform bill vote. **See also** Bill; Legislature

R

Race Discrimination   Negative actions, behaviors, or prejudice toward others based on race, color, ethnic origin, or nationality. Race discrimination originates from the belief that one race of people is superior to another race of people. Race discrimination is prohibited in education under Title 6 of the Civil Rights Act of 1964. Because they receive federal funds, most public schools, universities, and colleges are covered under Title 6. As such, they must ensure that services such as admissions, recruitment, financial aid, discipline, athletics, recreation, housing, grading, and classroom assignments are free of race discrimination.

Racism *(education)*   A belief that one is superior in socioeconomic, political, and intellectual standing with respect to a person of a different race or ethnic group. Racism can be expressed in an overt, covert, or unconscious manner. Racism denies individuals or groups opportunities to be recognized, respected, and accepted in society. It is founded on the belief that race is the primary determinant of both internal (social) and external (physical) traits and of the capacities of thought and reason. Racism is a learned behavior and thought process, which is generally passed down from generation to generation. It is not a natural phenomenon.

Racism *(psychology)*   The thought that particular human traits and abilities are a function of race and that a specific race is superior to others. Individuals described as racist are those who engage in discrimination or prejudice because of another's race. Although race has been commonly accepted as based on skin color or nation of origin, racial classifications are no longer so straightforward. In fact, there is no consensus on the definition of race, and modern social scientists tend to consider it a social or psychological construct rather than an objective, biological one. Though racial classifications are considered more complicated today than they once were, levels of racism have remained constant throughout the years worldwide. Historical events such as the Holocaust in Germany and slavery in the United States exemplify the most deleterious effects of racism. Hate groups, such as the Ku Klux Klan, and terrorist organizations, such as Al Qaeda, continue to perpetuate racist hate and violence in the world today. Nations such as the United States continue to enact local hate crime legislation and actively participate in global efforts to combat racist acts. For more information, see Smedley and Smedley (2005).

Radical   A political view associated with desiring to change "radically," or drastically, official institutions and alter the existing power relations in society. The term is derived from the Latin *radix,* or root. The term originated in late-18th-century England; one of the earliest known usages was by the radical Whig Parliamentarian Charles James Fox. Daniel Pope, in *American Radicalism* (2001) notes that radicalism is a chronologically contingent term: What is radical this generation may be status quo the next. In terms of political ideology, common terminology associates radicalism with the "left" (liberal) and reactionary views with the "right" (conservative) ends of the political spectrum. *Reactionary* is a pejorative term usually associated with ultraconservative political views. The term originated with the French Revolution (1789–1799) to describe those who opposed the revolt. For more information, see Pope (2001).

Radical Criminology   A school of criminological thought encompassing a range of theories about the origins of crime, characterizations of criminality, and the role of law in society. Radical criminologists focus on the relationships between crime, economic and political structures, and power distribution. A core tenet of radical criminology is that crime is a manifestation of a society's social structures. These theories posit that crime stems from capitalist principles such as greed, individualism, and alienation; law is constructed and enforced to maintain the status quo; and that which is identified as criminal is socially constructed.

The ideas and principles associated with radical criminology originate from the ideological and theoretical doctrines of Karl Marx and Frederrich Engels. Radical criminology was first introduced in the work of Willem Bonger, who, in the early 1900s, linked crime rates and capitalist development. Modern radical criminology materialized in the 1960s and 1970s as part of those decades' waves of radicalism. Modern radical criminologists—including conflict criminologists, labeling theorists, and critical criminologists—challenge the precepts of positivist and classical criminology. For more information, see Bonger (1905/1916). ***See also*** Conflict Criminology; Labeling Theory; Marxism (political science, sociology)

Radio   The transmission and reception of communication signals that consist of electromagnetic waves that travel through the air. Radio waves may travel either in a straight line or by reflection off the ionosphere or a communications satellite. Radio waves may be classified according to their physical length or by the number of cycles that they complete in a given time period. For radio transmission, audio data are imparted to a carrier wave by varying its amplitude, frequency, or duration by a process called modulation. AM (amplitude modulation) radio involves "side-band" frequencies at the upper and lower ends of a carrier wave, which register variations in the strength of the wave. FM (frequency modulation) radio involves the variation of the number of cycles through which the wave passes over time.

Radio first became possible after the British physicist Michael Faraday demonstrated that electrical currents can producer magnetic fields. A long-distance radio system was first perfected by the Italian inventor Guglielmo Marconi in 1901. The first commercial radio station, KDKA in Pittsburgh, first went on the air with returns from the 1920 presidential election. A communications boom ensued, and an additional 563 radio stations were licensed in the next two years. In 1926, the National Broadcast Corporation (NBC) established the first radio network. In 1927, Congress enacted the Radio Act, which both inhibited the threat of monopoly and established the agency now known as the Federal Communications Commission.

The artistic potential of radio remained unexplored until the 1930s, when radio flourished as a dramatic medium. The first means of simultaneous, nationwide entertainment, American radio gave the public memorable, long-running programs such as *One Man's Family, Fibber McGee and Molly,* and *The Shadow.* Also of enduring note was Orson Welles's *Mercury Theater,* now best remembered for its 1938 "War of the Worlds" broadcast, whose realistic rendering of a Martian attack nearly touched off a national panic. Radio broadcasts of sporting events, quiz shows, and big band music became commonplace, as did performances by stars such as Jack Benny, Bing Crosby, and George Burns and Gracie Allen. Radio also became a potent political tool, as reflected by the *Fireside Chats* of President Franklin Roosevelt.

Whereas the rise of television in the late 1940s and 1950s ended the reign of radio as a purveyor of dramatic programs, radio remained a significant medium in the fields of music, sports, and political opinion and was instrumental in the popularization of rock music. With the recent advent of satellite radio, a technology that enables the broadcast of digital signals from communications satellites and permits broadcast over a much larger geographic area than conventional radio signals, radio is currently enjoying a popular renaissance.

Random Assignment   A term used in the context of experimental research whereby participants are indiscriminately assigned to either an experimental or a control group. For an experimental design to employ true random assignment, each participant must have an equal chance of being selected for either group. The

purpose of randomly assigning participants to groups is to control for variables that may have a confounding effect on the dependent variable(s). Random number tables, or assigning every *n*th participant to one group or another, are common methods used to randomly assign participants. For more information, see Sidani (2006).

Random Assignment Versus Random Selection
Random assignment is a technique used after participants have been chosen for participation in a research study. This technique ensures that each participant has an equal chance of inclusion in the various conditions of an experiment. Random assignment is essential in the determination of a study's *internal* validity. Random selection, however, in which each member of a given population has an equal chance of being selected for participation in a research study (also referred to as *random sampling*), is important in the determination of a study's *external* validity. **See also** Sampling in Quantitative Research

Random Sample   A group of research participants selected randomly from a particular target population. A true random sample is one for which each member of the population of interest has an equal chance of being chosen. Random sampling is an essential initial step when conducting research as it is thought to generate a group of participants who are representative of the population as a whole. Most research samples represent *convenience* (i.e., not random) samples and leave themselves open to the potentially negative effects of sampling bias. One way to randomly sample from a population is to select every *n*th individual in a telephone directory to participate in a research study. For more information, see Kane (2002).

Rape, Forcible   A sexual act realized through force or intimidation. Rape is a sexual assault wherein someone has been made to submit to sexual acts against his or her will and without giving consent. It is one of the eight *index offenses* listed in the Uniform Crime Reports (UCRs). Historically, rape exclusively described sexual intercourse imposed on a woman by a man. The women's movement of the 1970s brought attention to the issue of rape and helped broaden its definition. The term has evolved and is now used to refer to a range of sexual acts. The specific genders of those involved are irrelevant to the legal use of the term. *Date rape* is a term that emerged toward the end of the 20th century and describes forced sexual acts that occur in the context of a dating relationship. The term *rape* is sometimes used to convey acute violation with or without a sexual component. **See also** Rape, Statutory; Sex Offense/Crime; Uniform Crime Report (UCR) (Part I/Part II Offenses)

Rape, Statutory   Sexual relations between a party the age of consent or older and a party under the age of consent, which is illegal. Sexual activity between such parties is against the law as it can never be consensual since one of the parties has been legally deemed incapable of agreeing to sexual activity. The act or acts are thereby taken as forced on the individual who is too young to understand or accede to such behavior. The person of consenting age can be charged with the crime of statutory rape even if no force was used to compel the underage party to participate. The age of consent varies by jurisdiction and ranges from 16 to 18 years in the United States. The sexual activity to which the term refers also varies and is defined by jurisdiction. ***See also*** Rape, Forcible

Rap Sheet   A slang term for someone's recorded criminal history. The document is a written accounting of an individual's arrests and convictions. *Rap sheet* is a term associated with police officers, though it has long since permeated popular culture and can be found in most dictionaries.

Rasch Measurement Theory   A theory that provides the basis for the one-parameter model of *item response* theories. George Rasch, a Danish mathematician, developed the model, and many social scientists have expanded its use. The primary purpose of the model is to develop a unidimensional, interval-level measurement system for a construct that can be construed in terms of *ability* (where someone falls on a trait, which is a function of the number of items correct or scored consistent with that trait) and *item* (how difficult it was to get the item correct or how much of the trait you need to agree with an item) parameters. These ability and item parameters can be estimated from the same set of data and are invariant, assuming that the items are independent of one another. The *item characteristic curves* generated in Rasch models are assumed to only reflect item difficulty. Other elements, such as how the item discriminates at different levels of ability or guessing parameters, are not included in the Rasch model. Because of its simplicity, it is very commonly used in the development of standardized tests.

Ratification   The term used when an official party approves a treaty or formal document. In the United States, Article 7 of the U.S. Constitution stated that ratification of the Constitution required approval by 9 of the 13 established states. Article 5 stipulates that amendments to the Constitution can be ratified when a bill has been approved by a two-thirds majority of both Houses and then continues to the states for three quarters of the states' approval. An amendment can also be ratified by the states calling for a Constitutional Convention to propose an amendment and then sending it for the three-quarters approval, but this method has never been attempted.

Rating Scale   The set of fixed-response choices that an individual selects from when rating the material provided in an item stem. Unlike a multiple-choice-test item, an item using a rating scale does not have a correct response. When determining what rating scale should be used with an item stem, the number and type of response choices must be determined. Perhaps the most popular are 5-point and 4-point rating scales, where each of the points is anchored with a number and/or a descriptive label. For example, here is a popular 5-point agreement scale with its anchors: (1) *strongly disagree,* (2) *disagree,* (3) *neutral,* (4) *agree,* and (5) *strongly agree.* Items that use this 5-point rating scale sometimes are called "Likert-type items" because Rensis Likert used this in the late 1920s, when he invented the technique of *summated rating scales* (i.e., using multiple items to measure a single construct and summing the item values into a single number).

Some researchers prefer to use an even number of items rather than an odd number of items, omitting the neutral category. This practice forces the respondent to choose a side for the statement, and research suggests that it can work well. Selection between a 4-point or 5-point rating scale is based on researcher preference, the needs of the research project, and the determination of what will work best with the particular research participants. The use of more than 4 or 5 points also is common; research suggests that one should use between 4 and 11 points on a rating scale. If you think that you want to use a "10-point" rating scale, it is recommended that 11 points be used (0–10) because if only 10 points are used (1–10), some respondents will incorrectly assume that 5 is the center point. Five is the center point on a 0-to-10 scale (but not on a 1-to-10 scale).

Researchers construct rating scales for many dimensions in addition to agreement. One might, for example, measure the following: approval (*strongly disapprove, disapprove, approve, strongly approve*), comparison (*much worse, worse, about the same, better, much better*), effectiveness (*not at all effective, not very effective, somewhat effective, very effective*), evaluation (*poor, fair, good, excellent*), and satisfaction (*very dissatisfied, somewhat dissatisfied, somewhat satisfied, very satisfied*). The key when constructing anchors for a rating scale is to make sure the "distance" between adjacent categories is the same. For example, the distance between *strongly agree* and *agree* is similar to the distance between *strongly disagree* and *disagree.*

Rational Choice   A theoretical perspective used to explain and account for how humans come to make the decisions that they do. Rational choice theories are wide-ranging, but each is built on the premise that people, using free will, choose their courses of action based on whether positive or negative outcomes will result from their choices. The idea of the rational man emerged with the rise of Enlightenment ideology during the 1700s. Rational choice asserts that individuals are compelled by self-interest and apply their rationale accordingly. Therefore, human decision making stems from a rationally conducted cost-benefit calculus. Humans aim to maximize gains while trying to limit or avoid pain and make decisions to realize such outcomes.

The idea of rational choice is applied in a multitude of disciplines, including economics, political science, and sociology. Theorists and practitioners in the field of criminal justice often use rational choice to explain criminal behavior and enact policies based on this theory to try to deter future offending. *See also* Deterrence (sociology)

Rational Emotive Behavior Therapy (REBT) *(education)*

In the mid-1950s, Dr. Albert Ellis developed REBT, which is classified as a *cognitive behavioral therapy*. Ellis theorized that emotions and behaviors result from thoughts and if a person modified his or her thoughts, then feelings and behaviors would be different. In Ellis's ABC model, there is an activating event and inferences are made (A), and then filtered through a person's beliefs and evaluated (B), which leads to an emotional and behavioral response (C). According to REBT, long-lasting change occurs when a person's core beliefs are modified because A triggers B, which causes C. For more information, see Ellis and Springer (2007). *See also* Cognition; Cognitive Behavioral Therapy (CBT); Cognitive Therapy (education, psychology)

Rational Emotive Behavior Therapy (REBT) *(psychology)*

A type of *cognitive behavioral therapy* (CBT) that was developed by Albert Ellis in the 1950s. Ellis's model assumes that individuals endorse unrealistic expectations for themselves and their environment, thereby interfering with their life goals. REBT focuses on identifying and addressing maladaptive cognitions that are believed to result in self-defeating behaviors and/or distressing feelings. It uses the "ABC" structure underlying the cognitive model, wherein relationships between (A) activating events, (B) beliefs about them, and (C) the emotional or behavioral consequences of the beliefs are explored. In addition to subscribing to the ABC framework, the REBT model endorses three main insights:

1. Although external circumstances have recognized psychological effects, psychological troubles are predominantly viewed as a matter of choice, the result of the unconscious or conscious selection of rational or irrational beliefs when a negative event occurs.

2. Past and present life experiences affect individuals, but it is their responses to such situations that cause disturbances.

3. Restructuring one's cognitions is possible but requires perseverance and hard work. Individuals undergoing REBT are encouraged to recognize the rationality of their thoughts and, when deemed irrational, substitute them with more adaptive ones.

Therapeutic techniques used in REBT are similar to those used in other cognitive therapies, such as homework assignments and role playing. Also, the therapist plays an active role, often seeking to dispute the client's irrational beliefs and taking a more aggressive approach than in most therapeutic models. REBT has been found to be efficacious for the treatment of anxiety and mood disorders (e.g., depression), but it seems to be less effective in the treatment of psychotic disorders since it requires the active participation of clients. For more information, see Ellis and Springer (2007) and Lega and Ellis (2001).

Rational Expectations

What economic agents use, in the absence of perfect foresight, to anticipate economic policies and minimize their effects. By incorporating past and present information, economic agents can aggregate information to such an extent that, on average, they are not consistently wrong. If economic agents can aggregate information and form rational expectations, forecasting errors will be the result of exogenous (stochastic) shocks or changes and not systematic miscalculation.

The theory has aroused controversy in economic literature. The theory's central thrust can be related to the ineffectiveness of stabilization policies when economic agents have rational expectations. For example, a 3% expansionary policy, which might cause a 3% increase in inflation, might prompt rational agents to demand higher wages of about 3% to offset the cost of inflation. This reaction increases inflation without any noticeable effect on output or employment. If expectations are rational, the theory maintains that further increases in inflation will be attributable to unanticipated shocks.

Rational expectations are based on the idea that the results of the past cannot continue to hold or predict future outcomes when economic conditions change (Lucas critique). By this proposition, rational expectation can be distinguished from *adaptive expectation*, which is based on forecasting the future based on past or inadequate information.

Rational expectation has also formed a foundation for other economic theories, such as the *random walk* or *efficient markets hypothesis*, the *permanent income* and life-cycle theories of consumption, and the theory of *tax smoothing*.

The efficient markets hypothesis was applied to asset pricing, which incorporates the notion that a sequence of observations on a variable follows a random walk if the current value gives the best possible prediction of future values. Stock prices for example, follow a random walk after adjustments have been made for discounting, dividends, and all available information.

The permanent income hypothesis by Milton Friedman postulates that consumption depends on present and future income (permanent income)—that is, the level of income that can be sustained with expectations of future income. Tax smoothing alludes to the ability of government to make future tax policies when people are already making plans in response to future tax policies. In all these situations, if economic agents can make prescient adjustments, policy results become questionable. For more information, see Friedman (1957), Muth (1961), and Rudebusch (2005).

Rationalism An epistemological belief that knowledge arises from and is verified by reasoning. Some rationalists contend that *only* deductions from innate concepts constitute true knowledge. Rationalist models for knowledge include mathematics and logic. Rationalism is often contrasted with *empiricism,* which holds that the source of knowledge is induction from observations of the external world. ***See also*** Deduction Versus Induction; Empiricism; Epistemology

Rationalization A defense mechanism whereby individuals attempt to justify their behavior by creating false, though plausible, explanations of behavior to themselves and others. For example, after getting caught cutting class by the principal, a student might justify his or her actions by pointing out that other students have engaged in the same behavior. It is one of the ego defense mechanisms identified by Sigmund Freud, falling within his conceptualization of personality structure (which comprises the id, ego, and superego). Ego defense mechanisms are thought to serve as an intermediary when internal conflicts arise between one's immediate gratification-seeking id and one's morally principled superego. Rationalization, along with other defense mechanisms, is thought to represent an unconscious response suppressing undesirable feelings from reaching conscious levels of awareness. For more information, see Tsang (2002). ***See also*** Defense Mechanisms (psychology)

Reactionary A pejorative term usually associated with ultraconservative political views. The term originated with the French Revolution (1789–1799), from the French *réactionnaire,* or reaction, to describe those who opposed the revolt. During the 18th century, reactionaries countered the French Revolution and fought for the return of a monarchical society. In the 19th century, reactionaries worked to restore the monarchy and the Church's power in state politics. In the 20th century, the opponents of socialism, communism, or other revolutionary forces, particularly in a European context, have been labeled reactionaries, whether rightly or not. Most recently, *reactionary* has been applied to proponents of radical, fundamental Islam.

Reaction Formation A defense mechanism whereby an individual's unacceptable feelings are altered unconsciously into the opposite sentiments. An example would be a man with homosexual desires joining an antigay protest or group. For more information, see Juni (1981). ***See also*** Defense Mechanisms (psychology); Rationalization

Reagan Doctrine The foreign policy of President Ronald Reagan from 1981 to 1988. The doctrine defined the strict anticommunist stance of the Reagan administration. It supported aid against communist regimes (or those remotely perceived as such) in Third World countries. The doctrine was declared in President Reagan's State of the Union address in 1985, when he called on the citizens of the United States to defy the Soviet Union's influence in Africa, Asia, and Latin America.

The doctrine enforced the United States' alleged responsibility to support right-wing insurgencies, such as in Nicaragua during its long and bloody war, which came to be known as the Contra War (1970–1987). And yet, despite the billionaire levels of military support, the United States failed to create a sound military force in Nicaragua. For some observers, such as Noam Chomsky, a critical voice against U.S. intervention, the Reagan doctrine against Nicaragua could be considered as state terrorism.

By the mid-1980s, it has been estimated that the United States had spent more than 1 billion dollars in military aid and more than 4 billion dollars in economic aid for the specific purpose of halting the spread of Soviet and communist influence in the Third World. In addition, the expansion of U.S. conventional forces to enhance U.S. regional intervention capabilities was undertaken

Economic pressure on the Soviet economy was also used in the war against left-wing partisans. To this end, the United States' European allies were encouraged (not always with success) to withdraw from existing commitments and abolish the favorable credit arrangements previously carried out with the Soviet Union. Arguably, the Soviet Union's collapse was due in part to its effort to keep up with American military spending while not having the gross national product to support such defense expenditures. For more information, see Chomsky and Achcar (2006), Lagon (1994), and *Reagan Doctrine* (1985).

Reaganomics The supply-side economic policies heralded by former President Ronald Reagan during his campaign for the presidency in 1980, which he later put into action during his administration. During his campaign run, President Reagan blamed the looming recession and high inflation and unemployment rates on the liberal, Keynesian economic policies of his predecessors. President Reagan denounced unnecessary government spending and involvement in the private sector. His administration advocated a decrease in government regulation, cuts in social welfare expenditures, individual and corporate tax cuts, massive increases in defense spending, and a balanced budget.

The Reagan administration set forth large-scale individual and corporate tax cuts in the President's Economic Recovery Tax Act of 1981. The act aimed to produce a "trickle down" effect in the form of increased capitalist investments, savings, and productivity. Congress also passed the Budget Reconciliation Act of 1981, which included a $39 billion cut in domestic spending. Five years later, Reagan supported the Tax Reform Act of 1986. This act eliminated the concept of

R

progressive taxation; two rates were established: for families making less than $29,750 or individuals making less than $17,850, and everyone else.

Against the backdrop of the Cold War, Reagan dramatically increased defense spending. In 1983, his administration proposed increasing the military budget by an estimated $33.8 billion. Among Reagan's most well-known defense projects was the Strategic Defense Initiative (SDI), popularly known as "Star Wars." The SDI aimed to guard against potential Soviet nuclear attack through the interception of in-flight ballistic missiles.

Realism   The view that phenomena in some domain(s) exist independently of our experience, knowledge, or perception of them. One might be an *ontological realist,* an *ethical realist,* a *scientific realist,* or some other type. In most cases, one can be a realist about one domain without necessarily being a realist about another.

Ontological (metaphysical) realism is the view that objects exist independently of our experience or perception of them and independently of the concepts or language through which they are understood and described. The scope of ontological realism can vary greatly. One might be a realist only about physical, spatio-temporal objects. Or realism might extend to include abstract objects, such as numbers, sets, or laws. One might also be a realist about the entities postulated by metaphysical theories, such as universals, relations, or bare particulars. A common objection to ontological realism is that objects are unintelligible apart from our experience or concepts of them.

Ethical (moral) realism is the view that there are moral facts or properties and that these facts or properties exist independently of human experience, cognition, or judgment. Ethical realism is typically accompanied by the views that real moral facts and properties are what are described, truly or falsely, by moral judgments and that, as such, moral facts and properties are knowable in principle. Together, these views entail that there can be objectively true moral judgments. One common objection to ethical realism is that moral facts or properties have no apparent place in a causal, naturalistic explanation of the world.

Scientific realism is the view that at least some of the entities, laws, or properties posited by fully developed scientific theories exist independently of those theories as real features of the natural world. Scientific realism often includes the view that true statements of scientific theory correspond with facts in the natural world, although scientific realists will often hedge this claim by allowing that any contemporary scientific theory is likely to be "immature" or incomplete. An important objection to scientific realism is the *underdetermination thesis.* This thesis holds that for any set of observations, there exist rival theories that are incompatible with each other yet compatible with those observations. If true, this thesis might force the rejection of the idea that there is a single scientific theory that corresponds with the world. ***See also*** Idealism; Metaphysics

Realist Evaluation   Seeks to investigate how, why, and for whom particular programs work. *Realist evaluation* is synonymous with *realistic evaluation.* It is rooted in scientific realism, which is said to be one of the dominant axes in modern European thinking. Realist evaluation is concerned with the nature and operation of causal forces. The essential ingredients for investigating these causal forces are *C-M-O* configurations, where *C* represents context, *M* represents mechanisms, and *O* represents outcomes. From *C-M-O* configurations, the way in which causation in the social world should be constructed is represented by the basic realist formula of $C + M = O$.

Reality Principle   A Freudian term referring to the operating mechanism of the ego, the aspect of personality responsible for organizing the manner in which an individual acquires what he or she wants from the real world. The reality principle is distinct from the *pleasure principle,* the underlying operational system of the id, which seeks immediate gratification in response to instinctual desires. For example, an individual who is sweating from the heat in a workplace without air conditioners may respond on the basis of the ego or the id. If operating solely on a pleasure-principled id, he or she might disrobe in front of coworkers; however, if the reality-principled and more intellectually based ego is involved, that person may exercise a more controlled cognitive response, such as buying a desk fan or taking a break outdoors. For more information, see Bornstein (2003). ***See also*** Ego (education, psychology)

Reality Programming   A type of media program (usually television but also radio or Internet) that presents ordinary people instead of actors in situations that appear real and unscripted. *Reality programming* is a general term that can include game shows; talk shows, featuring real people talking about their problems; hidden-camera shows, such as *Candid Camera;* and competitions such as *Dancing With the Stars* and *Project Runway.* *The People's Court* (started in 1981) and *Judge Judy* are examples of reality court shows in which people agree to air their problems on television, in front of a judge who renders a binding agreement. Makeover shows are designed to follow contestants as their lives, houses, or bodies are transformed. Makeover shows include *Extreme Makeover* and *The Biggest Loser* for physical transformations and *Extreme Makeover: Home Edition* for housing design. What all these programs have in common is the idea that the participants or contestants do not know the outcome of their participation in the show and that the audience is watching real events taking place.

Some reality shows, such as *Survivor* (started in 2000 in the United States) and *The Real World* (started in 1992), have preplanned activities and structured environments but claim to let the participants, through their decisions and actions, determine the outcome of events. Some programs invite audience participation: *American Idol* (started in 2002 in the United States) determines its winner by a vote by millions of viewers each week. Reality programming has proven very popular, with shows such as *American Idol* and *Survivor* always among the most watched. For more information, see *American Idol:* www.americanidol.com and *Survivor:* www.cbs.com/primetime/survivor16. ***See also*** Infotainment

Real Options Theory   The application of *option pricing theory* that is used to evaluate *call and put options* in order to evaluate investments in real assets, such as acquisition of plant, equipment, and other fixed assets. Whereas call and put options pricing deals with pricing financial assets, real options theory deals with strategic decision making in investment in real assets—plant, equipment, land, and buildings—by applying call and put options pricing models to *capital budgeting techniques.* Capital budgeting is the application of financial techniques to evaluate investments in projects and products that increase the value of the firm. These techniques will lead to an accept or reject decision of whether to undertake the project

A call or put option is the right and not the obligation to buy or sell a financial asset such as a stock. Similarly, a *real option* is the right but not the obligation to invest in real or physical assets. Financial options are generally traded on organized markets such as the Chicago Mercantile Exchange. However, real options cannot be traded on organized markets because the owner of a real option cannot sell its rights in the investment in a plant or equipment in an organized market.

Real options theory research is growing and has attracted much attention. Investing in real assets has options, similar to exercising a call or put option, to invest or not in real assets or projects. These investment options are sometimes difficult to evaluate using traditional capital budgeting techniques because many investment opportunities and projects contain embedded options that make the discount rates or risk-adjusted discount rates difficult to estimate. This problem can be dealt with by applying options pricing theory to assess whether to reject or accept an investment opportunity. Applying the real options model to the evaluation of an investment avoids the need to estimate the risk-adjusted discount rate.

Real options theory can also be used to value a business. Valuing a business the traditional way, such as using the price/earnings multiplier or calculating the present value of the future cash flows using the risk-adjusted cost of capital, does not give a good valuation for new businesses because new businesses tend to have negative earnings during the first few years. There are also many other applications of real options theory. It can be used to evaluate whether to sell or close down a project, whether to make further investments, whether to reduce the scale of a project's operation, or whether to defer a project and extend the life of an asset. For more information, see Hull (2006).

Reasonable Suspicion   A legal concept that structures and directs police procedure regarding the stopping and frisking of citizens. The standard of reasonable suspicion arose from the 1968 U.S. Supreme Court case *Terry v. Ohio.* In their landmark decision, the Court ruled that if the facts and circumstances of the situation, in their totality, would lead a reasonable person to likely suspect that a crime has been, is being, or will be committed, then indeed the police have "reasonable suspicion" and may stop someone and frisk him or her for weapons. This is considered an objective standard. Reasonable suspicion is not as high a standard as that needed for *probable cause* and thus allows for less police ingress. For more information, see *Terry v. Ohio* (1968). ***See also*** Probable Cause

Rebuttal   The act of a sender receiving an oppositional response from a receiver in an exchange of communication. This message is characterized as being a purposeful comeback that negates the stated argument of another party. It can involve information that directly contradicts that of the sender or the presentation of additional information to build an argument as evidence of the sender's inaccuracy. A rebuttal can occur in both formal and informal settings. Moreover, it can lead to a situation of argumentativeness. A rebuttal is considered to be part of an aggressive mode of verbal communication but can also involve nonverbal behavior. ***See also*** Debate

Recession   A state of the economy that occurs when there is a slowdown or downturn of economic activity for two consecutive quarters or more. The slowdown is a manifestation of increased unemployment above its natural (long-run) rate and plummeting real output (GDP).

Economists generally disagree on the reasons for a recession because it may be caused by a reduction in aggregate demand (consumption), a reduction in aggregate supply (production), or exogenous shocks. In trying to explain a recession, the two major schools of thought can broadly be classified in terms of demand and supply. Others believe that the economy can correct itself through built-in stabilizers such as unemployment compensation and tax receipts.

The fundamental challenge confronting policymakers when an economy is in a recessionary state is to design effective policies that will get the economy out of a recession and onto a path of recovery. Proponents of the *demand-side* theory believe in expansionary policies that will stimulate consumption, because it is believed that the effects of such a policy will have an immediate effect on the prospects of recovery if the policies are well targeted at those who will spend to get the economy out of a recession.

Supply siders believe that incentives should be created to stimulate production so that the unemployed could become employed, earn income, and increase spending. Supply siders also believe that the stimulation of production is good for long-term investment.

R

Remedial policies to get out of a recession fall into two broad categories: *expansionary fiscal* (tax cuts and/or increased government spending) and *expansionary monetary* (reduction in the interest rate and/or an increase in the money supply).

Critics of policy intervention argue that policies are futile because of lags (delay in getting the desired results). Lags have the potential to drive the economy off its natural course. Fiscal policy has a long *inside lag* because it takes a longer time for fiscal policy to be agreed on; monetary policy has a long *outside lag* because it takes a longer time for monetary policy to take effect. For more information, see Case and Fair (2003), Mankiw (2006), and McConnell and Brue (2008). ***See also*** Business Cycle (economics, public administration); Fiscal Policy; Monetary Policy; Stabilization

Recessive   The quality of being less dominant. *Recessive* is a term common to the discourse of genetics and refers to genes that require the presence of an identical match to manifest the characteristic or trait associated with that gene.

Recidivism   Recurrent criminal behavior on the part of those previously convicted of criminal activity. A *recidivist,* also known as a *repeat offender,* is someone who breaks the law after having been punished, treated, or educated as the result of a prior determination of criminal activity. A common and popular measure of penal and correctional effectiveness is the rate of recidivism. This is a complicated measure as it can require calculating the return to or continuation of offending or calculating only the rate at which people return to the criminal justice system postsanction.

Reciprocal Altruism   The notion that if you acted kindly toward an individual in the past, he or she will be inclined to act altruistically toward you in the future. The idea of reciprocal altruism is not based on an altruist's motivation, however. That is, it is not necessary for the altruist to anticipate anything in return for his or her kind acts; it is solely a recognition that altruistic individuals do typically benefit from reciprocal acts of benevolence over time. The concept of altruism more generally continues to generate debate among social scientists, particularly in light of the reciprocal effects of altruistic acts. While motivation is not a necessary component of the definition of reciprocal altruism, strategic individuals are often attracted to its beneficial effects and act kindly solely for the purpose of future rewards. For more information, see Nielsen (1994). ***See also*** Altruism (psychology)

Reciprocal Teaching   A collaborative instructional method for improving reading comprehension in which a teacher and a group of students dialogue about a segment of text. It includes teaching the following comprehension strategies: summarizing, questioning, clarifying, and predicting. First, a teacher models reading comprehension strategies and guides students in learning to use the strategies. Gradually, the teacher shifts responsibility to the students, who can actively use the strategies, assume the role of "teacher," and lead the discussion.

Reciprocity *(education)*   The principle, in counseling, that the contributions of each dyadic partner should be relatively equal. Reciprocity is applied to social interactions in exchange theory, is taught in social skills training, and is assessed in research by instruments such as the Social Reciprocity Scale. ***See also*** Social Exchange Theory; Social Skills Training

Reciprocity *(sociology)*   An exchange, between two or more parties, rooted in mutuality. Reciprocity is a cooperative trade of services, favors, goods, or aid. The terms of a reciprocal relationship rely on the principles of give-and-take: Each participant in the deal provides something, and each receives something. The gains and concessions should be comparable in value.

Recordings   Sound recording devices have been available to us for little over a century. For most of history, neither music nor speech, or any other sounds, could be captured and replayed. Sound recording devices were developed during the late 19th century, with the first commercial playback devices sold in 1889 in Germany and 1893 in the United States. Thomas Edison, in the United States, and Charles Cros, in France, were pioneers of sound reproduction in the late 19th century. In 1877, Edison was the first to record and play back speech using a "phonograph." He spoke into a horn fitted with a stylus at the narrow end that cut into soft wax on a cylinder, the depth of each cut reflecting the sound vibration. The earliest recordings used cylinders. Flat discs, introduced by Emile Berliner, gradually replaced the cylinders and had the advantage of being easier to mass reproduce. These cylinders and discs could play back sounds lasting up to four minutes.

Despite Edison's vision of phonographs as being useful chiefly for business purposes, by the early 20th century the entertainment possibilities were being explored by a rapidly expanding gramophone and phonograph industry. Short musical pieces were popular. Experiments with combining sound and moving images led eventually to movies with synchronized sounds, with the 1927 *Jazz Singer* being the first feature-length, commercially released "talkie."

In 1925, these purely acoustical/mechanical techniques of recording sound were supplanted by electrical recordings, which improved the recording fidelity (quality) dramatically. The recording time on discs remained short, about 4 minutes, until the long-playing record arrived in 1948 with space for 20 to 30 minutes.

By the mid-20th century, most commercial recordings were being made on magnetic tape rather than on a disc. Tape was cheaper, and it enabled editing. Multiple polyvinyl chloride (PVC) discs would then be made from the master tape for sale to consumers. Portable cassette tape players appeared in stores in the mid-1960s, allowing the general public not just to listen to prerecordings but to make their own recordings too. Compact discs arrived in the early 1980s. By the early 21st century, sound files were easily retrievable from the Internet, disrupting the traditional sales patterns of the music recording industry. For more information, see Morton (2006) and National Park Service (n.d.). *See also* Audio Tapes; Cablecasting; Cinema; Compact Discs; Telegraph; Television and Social Behavior; Video/Music Videos

Redirect   The trial process in which an attorney questions a witness after he or she has been cross-examined. The attorney who first questioned the witness conducts the redirect examination, which offers the opportunity to address any damaging testimony the opposing side introduced during the cross-examination.

Redistributive Policy   The practice of taxing high-income members of society to provide funds or services to lower income, disadvantaged, displaced, or otherwise less fortunate members of society. Governmental efforts at redistribution can be traced at least as far back as Chancellor Otto von Bismarck of Prussia in the late 1880s. Von Bismarck initiated a public pension program. In the United States, a major thrust in the direction of a greater government role in redistributive policy was undertaken in the mid-1930s with programs initiated as part of President Franklin D. Roosevelt's New Deal, such as the Social Security program (which included a public pension plan and a public assistance component to direct funds to those in greatest need) and unemployment insurance. Over the decades, the proportion of state and federal budgets devoted to redistributive programs has substantially increased. This increase has corresponded to a substantial growth in the number of civil servants administering these programs.

Reductionism   The attempt to analyze or explain the entities, properties, or concepts in one domain in terms of those of another. Reductions can take a variety of forms. A *conceptual reduction* might attempt to analyze the concepts of one area, such as the nonobservational vocabulary of a physical theory, in terms of those of another, such as the observational vocabulary. An *ontological reduction* might attempt to account for the entities of one scientific domain, such as biology, in terms solely of the entities of another, such as physics. An *epistemological reduction* might analyze the knowledge claims of one domain, such as mathematics, in terms of those of another, such as logic. *See also* Positivism (education, sociology)

Reenactments in News   Reenactments on television of real-life events have been used for decades to dramatize and publicize true-crime stories. "Crime-stoppers"-type programs typically show unsolved crimes, with appeals to the audience to call in with information that might help the police. Program producers work closely with the local police to gain access to information about the crimes, decide together what crimes to feature, what details to show, and what to keep from the public. Actors reenact the crime before the camera, using locations and props as similar as possible to the originals. Actors are chosen to resemble the victim, the witnesses, and the description(s) of the perpetrator(s).

The first series broadcasting reenactments of real-life crimes started in 1967 in West Germany. This program, *Aktenzeichen XY . . . ungelöst* (*File XY . . . Unsolved*) included political crimes, such as those thought to involve the Baader-Meinhof gang. A copycat British program *Crimewatch UK* took off in 1984 but with the intention of concentrating on ordinary offenses against people and property and staying away from politically motivated actions. *America's Most Wanted* followed in 1988.

These programs attract large audiences. Surveys have shown that information gathered from audiences has helped solve crimes and led to arrests. Some critics of the programs blame them for increasing fear of crime. Other critics view with suspicion the necessary media-police partnerships involved in making the programs, claim that the programs are incompatible with media objectivity, and denounce the unquestioning support shown for law enforcement authorities. Concerns that defendants' rights to a fair trial are jeopardized because of adverse pretrial publicity have also been raised. For more information, see Fishman and Cavender (1998), Leishman and Mason (2003), and Miller (2001). *See also* Crime News; Infotainment; Objectiveness in Media Coverage; Publicity; Videotaping in the Criminal Justice System

Referendum   The process in the United States whereby existing legislation—usually controversial in nature—goes before a local or state electorate for an approval vote. Referendums do not occur at the federal level, but many state legislatures provide for them. South Dakota, in 1898, was the first state to amend its constitution to include the referendum option. *See also* Direct Democracy

Reflation   An expansionary policy to increase aggregate demand and employment. According to Keynes, an increase in spending creates a multiplier effect, which increases output and further spending when an economy is operating at less than full capacity.

Expansionary monetary policy which is aimed at stimulating an economy can also be considered reflationary. In response to the virtual recession of January 2008 in the United States, the Federal Reserve lowered the federal funds rate to stave off a virtual recession that was partly the result of a mortgage crisis and its cascading effect. The Congress and the President also put forward a stimulus package to avert a recession. Policy intervention calls into question the self-correcting ability of the market, but it also shows that fiscal policy may not have its intended effect because of an inside lag. It takes Congress a while to respond, by which time the response may not have the intended effect. ***See also*** Business Cycle (economics); Fiscal Policy; Keynesian; Laissez-Faire (economics); Monetary Policy; Stabilization

Reflexivity   A methodological tool that involves a rigorous "troubling" of the production of knowledge throughout all the stages of qualitative inquiry. It includes self-reflection and understanding of one's role in the construction of meaning. As a compositional strategy, reflexivity aims to produce a more open-ended and multivoiced research account that moves between interpretation and description. For more information, see Denzin (1997) and Pillow (2003). ***See also*** Subjectivity/Subjectivism

Reform   The process or effort to change something for the better. The concept of reform can be applied to individual action, social-change movements, or organizations. It is the drive toward improving something using relatively noncontroversial and nonaggressive means. Reform is often contrasted with revolutionary or radical change.

Refutation   The act of proving false or wrong, or disproving, as in an argument. In a refutation, the goal is to deny the truth or accuracy of a verbal statement or a written document. The term *refutation* comes from the Latin *refutare,* meaning to check, suppress, or refute.

Region   An area of the world, either land or water, that shares characteristics distinguishing it from other parts of the earth. While a region provides boundaries, there are different theories about the defining traits of a region. Regions are constructs and therefore can be classified by natural characteristics or social characteristics, such as economy and culture. A natural region is one that is distinguished by similar natural physical features, such as mountainous terrain or heavy forestry. Other regions are delineated by socially constructed norms. Some of these regions are functional, otherwise known as *nodal regions,* as they are tied together by a common purpose, such as transportation or communication. Other regions are separated by social constructs, including culture, profession, economics, religion, and so forth. Many regions are uniform, meaning that they share the same features, whether the features are physical or cultural.

Regionalism   A political sentiment that favors the autonomy or political preferences of a particular geographical area (region) within a state. The boundaries of a region may be natural, political, economic, or racial/ethnic in nature. Regionalism can have the potential to lead to revolution and secession. After the fall of the Soviet Union in 1991, regionalism in the republics led to the outbreak of civil wars. For example, in Tadzhikistan, fighting broke out among Communist supporters—the "Rouge Khmers"—in the North and their mostly Sunnite Muslim opponents in the South. Russian Army

intervention, on behalf of the North, saved the fledgling country.

In the United States, prior to the end of the 19th century, regionalism was often referred to as *sectionalism.* Sectionalism divided the pre–Civil War United States into the North, the South, and the West. Slavery was one of the most defining distinctions between the North and the South, and a rivalry existed for control of the frontier West. Historians credit the Civil War (1861–1865) with solidifying the United States' North-South division. In Sid Noel's *From Power Sharing to Democracy* (2005), modern American regionalism is described as follows:

> The Northeast represents the old industries and the financial centres with a traditional working class. The midwest is more agrarian, small-town America. The South is the pocket with cheap labour, anti-unionism, and traditional conservatism. The West Coast is the mecca for the high-technology industries, where new ideas flourish. (p. 232)

American regionalism dictates political party affiliation to a large degree; for example, the South was strongly Democratic until the 1950s and the Democrat National Party's endorsement of the civil rights movement. Since the 1960s, the South has gradually become a Republican political stronghold. For more information, see Noel (2005) and Powell (2007).

Regional Policy   A nationally or internationally oriented policy to foster national or intraregional development or regional international trade. In the context of national development, it could be seen as a subsidy to enhance regional development, for which retaliatory action (countervailing or actionable duty under the World Trade Organization rules) should not be taken. The subsidy is generally reflective of the need to expand, an activity to which insufficient resources have been allocated (market failure).

Nations of a geographic region can also come together to have a common trading or regional trading policy with the rest of the world. This is usually the case with *customs unions, common markets,* and *economic unions.* Unlike a *free-trade area,* members of customs unions, common markets, and economic unions adopt a common regional trading policy against outsiders or nonmembers. The European Union exemplifies the advanced form of regional economic integration (common monetary policy) with a common regional economic policy. For more information, see Carbaugh (2007), Perkins, Radlet and Lindauer (2006), Pugel (2007), and Salvatore (2006). ***See also*** Economic Growth; Externality; Market Failure; World Trade Organization (WTO)

Registration   The term usually refers, in the United States, to draft registration, or the Selective Service. All male citizens and male aliens living in the United States between the ages of 18 and 25 must register with the armed services. If a draft is declared, men are chosen by random lottery and year of birth. The term also can refer to registering to vote in local, state, and national elections. *See also* Suffrage

Regression   A statistical means to summarize, evaluate, and determine various types of relationships between variables. *Logistical regression* is a statistical model used to predict the probability of a particular outcome using categorical or numerical data. *Linear regression* is a statistical method used to construct and identify the most meaningful line between independent and dependent variables. *See also* Statistics (psychology, sociology)

Regression Analysis   If there is a correlation between two metric (interval or ratio) variables, this relationship can be used for the prediction of values of one variable (the *criterion variable*) from values of the other variable (the *predictor variable*). *Simple linear regression* is the prediction of one criterion variable from a single predictor variable. An example would be the prediction of grade point average (GPA) at the end of the freshman year of college from a score on the SAT (formerly called the Scholastic Aptitude Test).

If more than one predictor variable is used, this is referred to as *multiple regression.* An example would be the use of the variables of SAT score, rank in high school class, average grade on selected high school courses, and high school quality score to predict GPA at the end of the freshman year. In multiple regression, each *partial regression coefficient* (one for each predictor variable), expresses the relationship between that predictor variable and the criterion variable, controlling for the other predictor variables in the regression equation.

Determination of the best prediction equation is usually based on the criterion of *least squares,* which involves minimizing the squared deviations of the observed and predicted values of the criterion variable. Once the best regression equation has been determined, it can be used to predict a value on the criterion variable, and *confidence intervals* can be placed around the predicted criterion score based on an estimate of the standard error of the regression. Most of the time, regression analysis is based on the linear relationships between variables, but *curvilinear regression* also is possible.

Regulation *(economics)*   The oversight and control of economic activities by government or its agents to ensure safety and health, efficiency, transparency, and equity. The desire to maximize profit without adequate consideration of social responsibility has prompted governments to regulate the activities of businesses.

Today, regulation can be found in almost all facets of business undertakings because of the potential of external effects and inequity. Regulations cover industrial activity and pollution, worker safety and compensation, consumer protection laws (including the rights to know and product safety), the requirement to disclose material information in securities markets and in banking and investment, and business organization (to ensure competition).

Combination laws or antitrust laws regulate business collusion and illegal pricing activities. Such regulation goes back to the 19th century during the era of big business, when trusts mushroomed to take advantage of monopolies and unfair prices. The U.S. Justice Department oversees mergers by evaluating law and industry concentration.

In the United States, Congress may enact regulatory laws or delegate the promulgation of rules and enforcement to specialized agencies such as the Securities and Exchange Commission, the Federal Reserve, NASDAQ (National Association of Securities Dealers Automated Quotation [system]), and NASA (National Aeronautics and Space Administration).

In the 1930s and 1980s, there was a strong desire to regulate markets after the Great Depression and the mortgage crises, respectively. In a similar vein, the stock and housing irregularities of major energy and investment companies in the first decade of the 21st century brought into focus the need for stringent regulation or enforcement. Regulation may not always provide the best results for market operations; as a result of which deregulation may be effected to remove bad or ineffective laws. The late 1970s and early 1980s saw a wave of deregulation in the United States to remove or amend old banking and investment laws. *See also* Deregulation; Externality; Market; Market Failure; Perfect Competition

Regulation *(public administration)*   A broad term that encompasses both rules and regulations, which are related terms but not synonymous.

There are three types of agency regulations:

1. Every agency head has the authority to issue "housekeeping" regulations, which are inherent with the position and may also be authorized by law—for example, in the case of the federal government, to issue regulations to govern the internal affairs of the agency. Regulations in this category may include subjects such as conflicts of interest, employee travel, and delegations to organizational components, including the custody, use, and preservation of its records, papers, and property. This does not authorize rulemaking that creates substantive legal rights.

2. Agencies also have inherent authority to issue procedural rules to govern their internal processes, as well as "interpretive" rules that express the agency's policy positions or views in a way that does not bind outside parties or the agency itself.

3. Last, there are "legislative" or "statutory" regulations. Regulations in this category, which can only be issued pursuant to a specific statutory grant of authority, create rights and obligations and address other substantive matters in ways that have the force and effect of law. In effect, these regulations constitute the exercise of authority delegated to the agency by law to further "legislate" by fleshing out the underlying statute that the agency is charged with implementing. The scope and

specificity of such a congressional delegation of legislative authority to an agency will often determine how much deference the courts will accord to the agency's regulations and to the agency's interpretation of the laws it implements. It is not unusual for Congress to grant agencies statutory authority to issue such regulations. When Congress enacts a new program statute, it typically does not prescribe every detail of the statute's implementation but leaves it to the administering agency to "fill in the gaps" by regulation.

As used in administrative procedures, the third example is the type of regulation that is the object of rulemaking. The term *rule,* in pertinent part, does not include any rule relating to agency management or personnel or any rule of agency organization, procedure, or practice that does not substantially affect the rights or obligations of nonagency parties.

By issuing regulations, an agency may voluntarily (and perhaps even inadvertently) limit its own discretion. Generally, "an agency must comply with its own regulations, even if the action is discretionary by statute." Generally, "legislative or statutory regulations that are otherwise valid (i.e., they are within the bounds of the agency's statutory authority) have the force and effect of law," which means "that the regulations are binding on all concerned, the issuing agency included, and that the agency cannot waive their application on an *ad hoc* or situational basis." The Supreme Court provided detailed instruction as to when an agency regulation is entitled to the force and effect of law. The regulation "must have certain substantive characteristics and be the product of certain procedural requisites." Specifically, the Court listed three tests that must be met: (1) the regulation must be a substantive or legislative regulation affecting individual rights or obligations—regulations that are interpretative only generally will not qualify; (2) the regulation must be issued pursuant to, and subject to any limitations of, a statutory grant of authority; and (3) the regulation must be issued in compliance with any procedural requirements imposed by Congress. This generally means the Administrative Procedures Act (APA), unless the regulation falls within one of the exemptions previously discussed.

A regulation that meets these three tests will be given the force and effect of law. A regulation with the force and effect of law is "binding on courts in a manner akin to statutes"; it has the same legal effect "as if [it] had been enacted by Congress directly"; it "is as binding on a court as if it were part of the statute"; it is "as binding on the courts as any statute enacted by Congress." A regulation with the force and effect of law is controlling, subject to the "arbitrary and capricious" standard of the APA. A regulation will generally be found arbitrary and capricious

if the agency has relied on factors which Congress has not intended it to consider, entirely failed to consider an important aspect of the problem, offered an explanation for its decision that runs counter to the evidence before the agency, or is so implausible that it could not be ascribed to a difference in view or the product of agency expertise.

For more information, see Comptroller General, Federal Appropriations Law (2008b, 2008c).

Regulatory Agency   An independent agency that is authorized by a government to create and enforce rules and regulations in the public interest. In the United States, regulations created by regulatory agencies are subject to review by both the President and Congress. According to the U.S. Office of Management and Budget's *Draft Report to Congress on the Costs and Benefits of Federal Regulations* (2000), there are three types of regulatory agencies in the United States: social, economic, and process. Social regulatory agencies serve to protect the public from products that harm their health, safety, and environment. These agencies also seek to increase consumer awareness. Economic regulatory agencies encourage economic health, including the stimulation of competition between market forces. Process regulatory agencies involve the collection of funds and their allocation to proper recipients and the provision and purchase of goods and services by the government and the public, respectively.

The first regulatory agency in the United States was the Interstate Commerce Commission (ICC) established in 1887. During the early 20th century, regulatory agencies continued to be created by Congress, mainly aimed at regulating financial and commercial concerns. There was a surge in economic regulatory agency formation during the New Deal era. Another marked increase in agency formation occurred in the 1960s and 1970s, reflecting a rise in consumer protectionism. Energy protection agencies were also developed during the 1970s in response to the oil crisis. The 1980s witnessed a push for deregulation of the business sector, resulting in the elimination of some regulations and regulatory agencies. This was followed by the enactment of reregulation policies in the early 1990s, only to be reversed again later that decade. An increase in environmental protection regulations occurred as we entered the 21st century. For more information, see Croley (2007) and U.S. Office of Management and Budget (2000).

Regulatory Policy   Policy is the process of making political, management, administrative, and financial decisions so as to meet specific goals. Although policy incorporates law, it is different in that policy guides actions likely to meet goals, whereas law either compels or prohibits behavior. Regulatory policy is the process of controlling individuals, institutions, businesses, and agencies to standardize acceptable practices and sanction those who are in violation of the law.

Regulatory policies originated in the 19th century as a response to the laissez-faire, monopolistic practices in the United States. The first federal regulatory agency, the Interstate Commerce Commission, was created in 1887 by the Interstate Commerce Act to address abuse and discrimination by the railroads.

The goal of regulatory policies is to protect the public's fundamental rights to life, liberty, and the pursuit of happiness. Regulatory policy is also intended to protect the public from harm. In other words, an organization may not, for example, allow dangerous working conditions for employees, sell unsafe drugs, pollute the air or water, or market tainted meat.

Rehabilitation The process and the goal of rehabilitating a criminal offender to become a law-abiding, productive citizen, one of the goals of the criminal justice system. Rehabilitation is a correctional perspective that emphasizes diagnosis, treatment, education, programming, and therapies rather than retribution and harsh punishment. Rehabilitationists believe that punishment should be used to transform people for the better, not harm them. The justification for this approach is utilitarian. A reformed person is believed to be a valuable and desirable outcome not only for the offender but also for society, as recidivism will be less likely and the community safer. Rehabilitation is a forward-looking, consequentialist philosophy in that it focuses on the future and the consequences of punishment. ***See also*** Deterrence (sociology); Retribution

Rehabilitation Counseling Counseling that focuses on helping individuals with disabilities regain adaptive functioning in their lives and achieve optimal health and independent living to the greatest extent possible. For individuals with disabilities, rehabilitation counselors facilitate emotional adjustment to loss and grief and assist with vocational counseling, if needed. ***See also*** Counseling

Reinforcement A term introduced by B. F. Skinner in the context of his theory of behaviorism and, specifically, operant conditioning. According to Skinner, a *reinforcer* is an event that follows a response and subsequently affects the likelihood of the response's reoccurrence. The two main types of reinforcement are referred to as positive and negative. *Positive reinforcement* consists of adding a stimulus after a behavior and is intended to increase the probability of continual engagement in the behavior, such as giving a rat a pellet after pressing a bar. *Negative reinforcement* consists of removing an aversive stimulus and is also intended to increase the probability of continual engagement in behaviors such as removing a shock after a rat presses a bar. For more information, see Cameron and Pierce (1994). ***See also*** Behaviorism (education, psychology); Operant Conditioning; Skinner Box

Reinforcement Versus Punishment Reinforcement is a key umbrella concept of behaviorism. Basically, it claims that behavior, as a response to the environmental events surrounding it, is more likely to reoccur if it has been rewarded (or reinforced) and that behavior is less likely to reoccur if its consequence has been aversive. Reinforcement, therefore, is a consequence of a response that increases the probability of the behavior's recurrence. It can be positive or negative, depending on its effect on behavior.

For an effective behavioral consequence, reinforcement presented or removed must have the following two important characteristics: (1) it must increase the rate of responding in a given environmental condition and (2) it must be immediately contingent on the execution of an appropriate response, hence the term *contingent stimulus*. As mentioned above, there are two types of contingent stimuli: *satisfying* and *aversive*. Contingent on the organism's response to environmental conditions, satisfying and aversive stimuli can be presented or removed for strengthening or weakening behavior. Both satisfying and aversive stimuli can be presented contingent on the response. Similarly, both satisfying and aversive stimuli can be removed. Thus, four types of reinforcement exist:

1. *Positive reinforcement:* the presentation, or adding, of a satisfying stimulus contingent on a response that results in the strengthening of that response and an increase in the frequency of its reoccurrence. An example is allowing a child more time for watching TV contingent on his behavior of going to bed on time. However, this is a good example only if the frequency of the child's going to bed on time increases.

2. *Punishment:* the presentation of an aversive stimulus contingent on a response that results in the weakening of that response and a decrease in the frequency of its reoccurrence. An example is when parents take away time for watching TV from a child when the child finds all kinds of excuses for not going to bed on time.

3. *Reinforcement removal:* the removal of a satisfying stimulus contingent on a response that results in the weakening of that response and a decrease in the frequency of its reoccurrence. An example is when a teacher takes fewer breaks when the students who are supposed to work productively in groups have goofed around.

4. *Negative reinforcement:* the removal of an aversive stimulus contingent on a response that results in the strengthening of that response and an increase in the frequency of its reoccurrence. An example is the removal of weekly quizzes by the teacher because his or her students have been doing their homework well.

Reinforcer A stimulus with the function of strengthening behavior. Reinforcers can be classified as *primary reinforcers,* which are biologically determined (e.g., food and sleep), and *secondary reinforcers,* whose function is associated with a primary or another secondary reinforcer (e.g., money and praise).

Reinforcers can also be classified according to the motivating values of reinforcement: *intrinsic* and *extrinsic*. Intrinsic reinforcers strengthen behavior resulting from an organism's natural needs. All primary reinforcers are intrinsic reinforcers. Depending on additional characteristics of an intrinsic reinforcer displayed, there are intrinsic (e.g., video games for learning) or extrinsic secondary reinforcers, whose function has been instructed (e.g., grades).

Reiterative Model   Forms of media that can be reproduced intact and without distortion. A book, for instance, by virtue of its static physicality and the process by which it is received, is accessible without restriction repeatedly and unmediated by the context in which it is consumed. Nonreiterative media, in contrast, are exemplified by electronic media, such as television and radio. Such media, consumed socially or collectively, are affected by the manner and context in which they are received. Repeated viewings will necessarily be distorted because the circumstances will be different each time, thereby potentially diminishing the quality of the message therein.

Relapse Prevention   The therapeutic steps taken to prevent an individual from returning to a particular substance, typically in the context of treatment for substance use disorders and coexisting mental disorders. A relapse is considered to have occurred at any point in which the individual has breached his or her sobriety to any extent. Relapse can be the result of a combination of any number of factors, such as returning to the same physical and social environment where the substance was used (including spending time with the same individuals) and failing to follow a treatment plan or stopping therapy.

There are various warning signs or "red flags" that may precede a relapse, such as the occurrence of major life events (positive or negative) and emotional states such as boredom. Contemporary relapse prevention techniques integrate principles from various theoretical models, including motivational interviewing, cognitive behavioral therapy, and distress tolerance. These models aim to familiarize recovering addicts with their personal triggers and warning signs, employ various recovery techniques, and develop a plan of action to reduce the desire to return to the substance of choice.

Commitment to therapy is a necessary first step for addicts engaging in relapse prevention, and support networks play a central role in the therapeutic process. Well-known "12-step" groups, such as Alcoholics Anonymous (AA) and Narcotics Anonymous (NA), provide structured networks for recovering addicts. In addition to various other techniques, these groups embrace a religious or spiritual path to full recovery and relapse prevention. Certain programs, such as Self-Management and Recovery Training (SMART) Recovery, employ similar techniques to AA and NA without the religious or spiritual focus. For more information, see Lawrence (2007). ***See also*** Substance Abuse

Relativism *(education)*   Broadly speaking, the idea of relativism is based on relations. Thus, *epistemological relativism* is the idea that the ways in which a certain group of people acquires knowledge are different from, and neither superior nor inferior to, the ways used by another group of people; *ethical relativism,* on the other hand, is the idea that a society's notions of right and wrong are unique to its social and historical conditions; and *ontological relativism* is the idea that notions of what constitutes reality and truth are also different from one perspective to another. Because relativism is often perceived as connoting radicalism, few philosophers and social scientists label themselves as relativists. However, traces of relativist thought are at the core of influential currents of modern thought such as interpretivism, phenomenology, pragmatism, constructivism, postmodernism, and pluralism.

Ethical relativism is arguably the most commonly known form of relativism. Its more frequent manifestation is in the sociopolitical realm in relation to the adoption of pluralist values. Ethical relativists argue that as societies become more multicultural, *universal* laws, norms, and notions of justice cannot be created or enforced. Instead of advocating for absolute normative systems, ethical relativists argue for the usefulness of understanding context and treating each ethical dilemma on a case-by-case basis.

Ontological relativism is built around the idea that reality is nuanced, indeterminate, multifaceted, constantly in flux, and inevitably dependent on historical, cultural, political, and economic contexts. Truth, reality, and being are therefore not essences but rather the products of experience, social position, perspective, interpretation, contingency, need, will, joint actions, and interest. Ontological relativist pursuits generally focus on deconstructing social realties—or rather, shedding light on how realities are constructed. Because relativists believe that things could be otherwise, their endeavors are often comparative across temporal periods or geographical spaces. However, ontological relativism does not engage in comparison to prove or establish what is best but simply to describe and interpret how unique social processes have produced unique outcomes.

Finally, *epistemological relativists*—similar to ontological relativists—argue that knowledge and systems of knowing depend on the same contingencies that shape being and realities (context, position, etc.). While epistemological relativism is potentially quite liberating and democratic—in that it debunks colonialism and paternalism at their very core—in its most radical fashion, it may result in solipsism (the idea that one's reality is irreducible to any other's and unknowable by anyone else), excessive doubt, intellectual paralysis, and the philosophical equivalent of schizophrenia. Apart from its radical excesses, relativism—of the ontological, epistemological, and ethical varieties—has played a key role in debunking the hegemony of universalist, modernist, and essentialist thinking. ***See also*** Epistemology; Ethics (public administration, sociology); Ontology

Relativism *(sociology)* The perspective that there is no universal or intrinsic means by which to judge the value or worthlessness of something. Varying concepts, practices, cultures, morals, behaviors, philosophies, and viewpoints are simply different from one another. None is, by its nature, of more or less value than any other.

Released on Recognizance (ROR) A legal term that describes a formal binding obligation or condition to which a person accused of a crime has obligated himself or herself. The accused is bound by the declaration he or she has made to the court. The pledge can take a variety of forms, including refraining from certain activities, the commitment to pay a fee, or the promise to return to court.

ROR stands for *release on own recognizance.* This is a legal phrase that refers to the unconditional pretrial release of an individual who has been charged with a crime. The accused is released with the expectation that he or she will appear in court at the time of the trial. ROR is a judicial determination. The decision is reached after assessing an individual's likelihood of returning to court. The criteria examined before determination include the nature of the crime being charged and the scale of evidence, as well as the employment status, ties to the community, and any other variables that relate to the character of the accused. ***See also*** Bail; Pretrial Detention/Release

Reliabilility The psychometric properties of measures are presented in terms of their *reliability* and *validity.* Reliability relates to the ability of a measure to produce consistent test scores. There are four general types of reliability: *interrater, test-retest, alternate forms,* and *internal consistency.* Interrater reliability refers to consistency across raters or evaluators; test-retest reliability refers to the consistency of scores on a test administered twice to the same individual; alternate forms reliability relates to the stability of scores on two parallel forms (e.g., A and B) of a test; and measures of internal consistency are investigated to determine levels of consistency among items in the same test. For more information, see DeVon, Block, and Moyle-Wright (2007).

Religion in Public Education (e.g., Creationism, Prayer, Religious Instruction) Religious issues in public schools are primarily legal and can be categorized into the categories of individual rights and limitations on government involvement. Legal issues were summarized in the 1998 *Joint Statement of Public Law,* in which 35 religious and civil rights groups agreed on interpretations of the law that have been the basis of iterations sent to public schools by the federal government. This document outlines both the individual religious rights protected by law and the limitations put on representatives of the "state." In public schools, students retain individual religious rights, while school employees, representing the government, are restricted when functioning as "official" representatives (teacher, administrator, or staff). Student religious rights applicable in schools include the right to religious speech; freedom of religious choice, expression, and practice (prayer, religious garb, distribution of religious literature to willing student recipients, display of religious symbols); freedom of assembly (for prayer or religious discussion); and limited free speech. School personnel have the right to religious free speech, to read religious texts, and to pray alone or with other school personnel during allocated personal time and not in the presence of students.

A neutral coverage of religion in various parts of the curriculum is legal, but teaching "about" religion is seldom done in public schools today. Some scholars argue for a broad inclusion of the study of religion in public school curricula (Nord & Haynes, 1998). Religion is an important part of culture and has played a significant role in history, politics, morality, war, the arts, and literature. The absence of the study of religion in public schools is not a neutral treatment of religion in public schools.

Student religious rights are restricted when they interfere with schooling (e.g., interrupting a lesson or assessment). Free speech regarding religion and religious practice (prayer) are restricted. Dress codes may restrict religious garb or display of symbols (jewelry, religious sayings on T-shirts).

Various groups work to change or maintain legalities regarding religion in public schools. These include People for the American Way, Family Research Council, Concerned Women for America, the American Civil Liberties Union (ACLU), The Heritage Foundation, and The Pew Forum. The ACLU is best known for supporting religious freedoms that keep government neutral regarding religion. People for the American Way and the Family Research Council are best known for supporting religious freedoms that allow government and individuals to promote the Christian religion. Law regarding religion in public schools has changed and will change according to the varying legal viewpoints of justices in the federal court system. Perhaps the most controversial facet of religious study in schools is the teaching of creationism or intelligent design on an equal basis to the more accepted scientific theory of evolution. This conflict continues in the state and federal courts. For more information, see Hudson (n.d.), Nord and Haynes (1998), and Riley (1998).

REM Sleep The terms *rapid eye movement* (REM) and *nonrapid eye movement* (NREM) were first coined by William Dement in the 1950s; he went on to become a leader in the field of sleep research. REM sleep occurs in the fifth stage of sleep and is associated with dreaming. It is a deep stage of sleep wherein the muscles remain in an extremely relaxed state nearing paralysis, making it difficult to awaken. Electroencephalograph (EEG) patterns indicate an "awake brain" during REM sleep, characterized by physiological changes such as increased breathing and heart rate. NREM sleep consists of sleep Stages 1 to 4 and is characterized by decreased brain activity, including minimal dreaming.

R

The stages of sleep are cyclical in that individuals pass through four or five cycles on average per night. The duration of NREM sleep is 90 to 120 minutes, with each stage lasting between 5 and 15 minutes, and Stages 2 and 3 being repeated before REM sleep occurs. Therefore, a normal sleep cycle has the following pattern: Stages 1, 2, 3, 4, 3, 2, REM. REM sleep occurs about 90 minutes after initial sleep onset. For more information, see Kavanau (2002).

Reparations   Payment or other compensation for having caused loss or injury. A common type of reparation in politics is for war damages caused by a defeated nation. Under the Treaty of Versailles (1919), Germany, after its defeat in World War I, had to pay $31.4 billion to the Allied powers. The troubled German economy made it difficult for the nation to ever fully pay back the owed monies. After World War II, Germany—once again—and Japan owed reparations to the Allied nations. The U.S. Marshall Plan (1948), which pumped $13 billion of economic and technical assistance into European reconstruction, helped the nations pay back the owed money. More recently, Nazi survivors are receiving reparations from public and private entities in Switzerland and Germany for losses suffered during the Holocaust.

Replication *(psychology)*   The process by which researchers duplicate the methods of previous empirical studies with the intention of eliciting results to be compared with or contrasted to the original findings. It is an essential component of the scientific method, as results from replication studies may either buttress or contradict previous research findings. As such, it is standard practice to provide a detailed account of the methods in a particular study in research reports for the benefit of those who wish to replicate the research. For more information, see Brennan (2001).

Replication *(sociology)*   The expectation that research done under the same conditions as a previous study, if the initial effort was valid, ought to yield similar findings. Replication is a concept associated with the scientific method and empirical research. It is a means to assess the strength of research conclusions and can reveal design flaws.

Reporter   An individual who researches, manages, and offers information to an audience through a media text. A reporter can adhere to the traditional notions of journalism or provide infotainment. Information can be obtained from interviewing people, observation of an event, speaking with an unnamed but credible source, and the study of public records. *See also* Gatekeepers

Representation *(media studies)*   The appointment of someone to act on behalf of another, in a legal and governmental sense. This idea of "standing in for another," which lies at the heart of representation, extends more philosophically to the arts, where for Plato and Aristotle it concerned the status of imitation (*mimesis*). For Aristotle, humans naturally represent or imitate things, because it is how they learn. Whatever the artistic medium, art does not passively reflect reality but actively shapes it. Modern aesthetics sometimes narrowly distinguishes between representative art (e.g., portrait painting) and nonrepresentational art (e.g., abstract painting), but representation is broader than mere description. Arguably, an original experience or reality is not accessible through anything other than its representations. For example, in dream analysis, the original dream is unrecoverable—all that remains are verbal representations of it. In this sense, all reality is uninterpretable unless mediated through our various representations of it. *See also* Construction of Reality; Discourse; Realism

Representation *(political science)*   One entity seeking to act on behalf of another. There are two types of representation in a democracy: (1) *representative democracy*, where legislators are elected by constituents who hold a duty to act in the best interest of their constituency, and (2) *direct democracy*, where legislators act in direct accordance to the wishes of their constituents. The United States practices representative democracy at the federal level, evidenced in the election of the president and members of both houses of Congress. On the other hand, at the state and local levels, measures such as the *initiative, referendum,* and *recall* are examples of direct democracy.

Representative Democracy   The most common form of democracy, in which representatives are elected by the people to make political decisions on their behalf. This system differs from a *direct democracy,* in which all citizens participate in political decision making. A direct democracy theoretically can only work where there are a small number of citizens, because people need to physically gather in one place and vote. Representatives are elected in a democracy in usually one of two ways: the *plurality-majority* method or the *proportional-representation* method.

The plurality-majority method is a "winner takes all" voting system in which the winner is the one who has gained the most votes. This system is common in Great Britain and her former colonies, including the United States. The majority system is usually employed when there are only two candidates running in an election; the winner requiring a majority of the vote. The plurality system is used when there is more than one candidate running for political office; the winner has received the most votes but not necessarily a majority. There are four types of plurality-majority voting systems that are commonly used: (1) single-member district voting, (2) at-large voting, (3) two-round runoff voting, and (4) instant runoff voting.

Proportional representation is an election system, practiced in many European democracies, in which representatives are elected in proportion to the votes received. This system is in contrast to the majority and plurality—winner takes all—voting systems. A goal of proportional representation is to better represent minority groups, especially racial and ethnic minorities, and avoid "wasted" votes. Some disadvantages of proportional representation include legislative gridlock, too much power allotted to small parties, and less resistance to extremism. For more information, see Douglas (2000).

Repressed Memory Memories that have been blocked out of consciousness because they are emotionally painful, according to Freudian psychoanalytic theory. When such memories are later recalled, either spontaneously or through psychotherapy, they are referred to as *recovered memories*. In the Freudian context, *repression* is considered to be a phenomenon in direct contrast to *suppression,* whereby undesirable thoughts or memories are intentionally pushed out of conscious awareness. Like his other theories, Sigmund Freud developed the theory of repression from clinical case studies rather than from true experimental investigation. Much of the recent research on repression revolves around the area of recovered traumatic memories via naturalistic studies. For instance, researchers may follow a cohort of abused children over the course of many years (i.e., longitudinal design) comparing their reported memories with the original incident(s) of abuse.

In recent years, the issue of recovered memories surrounding abuse has been met with tremendous controversy. During the 1980s and 1990s, a series of sexual abuse cases involving day care centers, as well as more recent events in the Catholic Church, wherein many adults came forward to report incidents of abuse that occurred during their youth, attracted attention throughout the country. While the veracity of child witness statements is hotly contested throughout the professional literature and the courts, the validity of recovered memories by adults who were victims of child abuse is even more contentious. These debates tend to focus on recovered memories, but before a memory can be recovered, it must have been previously repressed. Longitudinal research in the area of child abuse has provided preliminary evidence for the construct validity of repression, but what has become perhaps a more salient concern in this area of study is the accuracy of recovered memories. For more information, see Flathman (1999). *See also* Child Abuse and Neglect; Memory (education, psychology); Repression (education, psychology)

Repression *(education)* The means by which people divert information from the consciousness to avoid aversive thoughts and negative affect. It is often regarded as an unconscious process. For more information, see Freud (1915/1957). *See also* Defense Mechanisms (education, psychology)

Repression *(psychology)* A defense mechanism characterized by the unconscious omission of distressing memories, thoughts, or feelings from consciousness. In a highly controversial, though common, example of the purported process of repression, an adult may not have any recollection of being sexually abused as a child. Repression is thought to manifest via anxious or neurotic symptoms, which arise when memories of traumatic experiences threaten to enter one's consciousness.

Sigmund Freud placed this conflict intermediary mechanism within his conceptualization of personality structure (id, ego, and superego). For more information, see Derakshan and Eysenck (1997). *See also* Defense Mechanisms (psychology); Repressed Memory

Reproduction The biological process of creating progeny. To reproduce is to generate an offspring. Reproduction is a basic trait of all living organisms. Asexual reproduction generally involves a single "parent" and is often associated with plants, though not exclusively. Sexual reproduction typically involves a cellular exchange and a fertilization process.

Republic A nonmonarchical form of government in which some type of representative democracy exists. The term is derived from the Latin *res publica,* or commonwealth. Two major forms of republics exist: the *presidential* and the *parliamentary.* In the presidential form, citizens commonly elect both legislators and the president. Under the parliamentary system, citizens commonly elect their legislators, but the legislators elect the prime minister. In both types of republics, the legislative and executive branches check and balance each other's powers. Some republics have both a prime minister and a president; in this case, the two officials serve different state functions. The first known republic was formed in Athens, Greece, and lasted from 1068 BCE to 500 BCE.

The Republic (360 BCE) is also the title of the classical Greek philosopher Plato's influential work of political philosophy, in which the virtues of justice are questioned using the metaphor of both a city's governance and a human's conscience. For more information, see Plato (360 BCE/2007).

R

Republicanism A political philosophy that favors the governance of a nation through an emphasis on *liberty,* the *rule of law, popular sovereignty,* and *civic virtue.* Nations ruled through this ideology are called republics or commonwealths.

Republicanism envisions liberty as the absence of domination by either private individuals or the institutions of the state. Promotion of liberty is the ideal goal of republicanism.

The rule of law means that governance is by laws and not the arbitrary whims of individuals. Republicanism does not, therefore, favor nations ruled by monarchies, oligarchies, or dictators. The law, which is the coercive tool of the state, necessarily involves interference and, at least potentially, has the capacity to infringe on people's liberty. But the law is an exercise of domination only if the interference is intentionally or negligently harmful.

Republicanism prefers rule by popular sovereignty. This means that public institutions ought to be headed by leaders who are elected officials. In a republic, the collectivity of citizens places its trust in state leaders to ensure the dispensation of nonarbitrary rule. The leaders are, therefore, expected to rule through constitutional authority, or rule of law, rather than personal inclinations.

The trade-off of the protection of liberty through the rule of law and elected leaders is that citizens must also act virtuously. This means that they should exhibit actions that are necessary for the cultivation of the good of a community. Modern ideals of virtuous behavior are to refrain from breaking the law. When citizens act virtuously, then they will be protected from the interference of the law. *See also* Republic; Rule of Law

Research   The product and the action of methodological inquiry. Scientific research consists of investigations rooted in theory, logic, and empiricism. Research methods are wide-ranging and include traditional, feminist, anti-oppressive, and indigenous methodologies. Scholarly and scientific research is careful, structured inquiry that adheres to the constraints, requisites, and terms that discipline and researchers have developed and come to collectively accept. The design of an individual research project depends on the nature and context of that specific study. *Quantitative research* involves numerical measures and findings and allows for comprehensive statistical analysis. *Qualitative research* incorporates surveys, interviews, and direct observations so as to reveal nonnumerical data. *See also* Empiricism

Research Methodology   The study of research methods, including *research design*, as well as methods for *sampling, data coding, measurement*, and *analysis*. Methodology usually involves comparing different methods in terms of how effective they are for studying particular questions. Major types of designs include experiments, interviews, surveys, observational research, and archival research. Two main categories of sampling are *probability* and *nonprobability* sampling. In the first, researchers know the probability that cases will be chosen from the population; in the second, they do not. Names, ranks, and numbers are the three kinds of coding most often used in the social and behavioral sciences. Names are qualitative, numbers are quantitative, and ranks fall in between. Data such as names, ranks, or numbers (categorical, ordinal, or continuous) also shape choices about methods of analysis. Research methodology also includes considerations of the philosophies of science. *See also* Measurement; Sampling

Reserved Powers   Powers that are reserved for one section of the government to the exclusion of another. In the United States, reserved powers refer to those powers granted to the state governments and are mentioned in the Tenth Amendment of the U.S.

Constitution. Under the Tenth Amendment, "The powers not delegated to the United States by the Constitution, nor prohibited by it to the States, are reserved to the States respectively, or to the people." An example of a reserved power would be a state's marriage and divorce laws.

Reserved powers differ from *enumerated* and *concurrent* powers. Enumerated powers are those expressly given to the federal government in the Constitution, for example, the power to declare war. Concurrent powers are those shared between the federal and state governments, for example, taxation. The U.S. Supreme Court's decision in *McCulloch v. Maryland* (1819) broadly interpreted the powers of the federal government under the Constitution, countering the intended scope of the Tenth Amendment. For more information, see *McCulloch v. Maryland* (1819).

Resistance   A term used to describe (mainly) unconscious defensive acts to impede the progress of psychotherapy. Therapy clients may evidence resistance via overt actions during the therapy session, such as suddenly changing topics or losing their train of thought when difficult topics are touched on, or in more subtle ways, such as coming late to therapy sessions or missing them entirely. While resistance is ostensibly problematic, it is often considered to be positive by many who believe that it can be a sign that the therapist is approaching a core dilemma within the client. For more information, see Bystritsky (2006).

Resistance to Change   Individuals and systems generally seek stability and attempt to avoid the disequilibrium of imposed change. Resistance can be active or passive, overt or covert. Fear of the unknown, loss of status, and disruption of routine are some reasons for resistance. For more information, see Senge et al. (1999). *See also* Change Management

Response Set   A biased set of responses on self-report measures. Examples include *acquiescence,* the tendency for respondents to agree with items; *social desirability,* the tendency to portray the self in a favorable manner; and *deviance,* the tendency to respond in an atypical manner. Response sets can also emerge in observational rating scales and include errors of *leniency, central tendency,* and *halo effect.* Response sets can be avoided through the careful development of scales and training of raters. For example, acquiescence on a rating scale can be reduced by using *counterbalancing. See also* Likert Scale (education, psychology); Rating Scale

Response Time   The span of time it takes police officers to arrive at the scene of a crime after they have been called. Response time is used to measure how quickly or slowly a police force is, on average, responding to citizens' needs. This measure is regularly used to demonstrate the efficacy or failings of a police force. Rapid response time is often equated with aggressive policing, and it is assumed that a fast response will help solve or prevent crime. However, studies do not necessarily support that association.

Restitution   The act of compensating an injured party for any loss, harm, or damages they may have incurred. Some criminal sanctions require offenders to make some kind of restitution to the victim(s) of their crime. Restitution includes any gesture, monetary payment, or act that will help restore something or someone to their state prior to the criminal incident.

Restorative Justice   A nonpunitive justice paradigm often posited as an alternative to *retributive justice.* There is no definitive definition of restorative justice as it is a set of principles rather than a particular practice or program. Core values include victims' rights, informal social controls, reconciliation, mediation, restitution, community participation, and reintegration. According to restorative justice philosophy, three parties ought to be included in the response and resolution of criminal events: the victim, the offender, and the community. A variety of practices are associated with restorative justice, including victim-offender mediation, healing circles, family group conferencing, reparation boards, and victim-offender reconciliation programs. Restorative justice practices can be found throughout the world. *See also* Retributive Justice

Restraining Order   A judicial injunction that prohibits or mandates specific behavior. A restraining order can be issued without a formal hearing. The behavioral restrictions and directions found in a restraining order may vary. A well-known type of restraining order is one that requires a person to keep a certain distance from another individual.

Retribution   A principle stating that those who commit wrong acts must be punished. It is one of four sentencing philosophies in the criminal justice system. Retributivists assert that wrongful behavior warrants *just deserts*—that is, justly deserved punishment. Retribution is sometimes equated with vengeance or retaliation and is linked to the concept of *lex talionis*. The precept of an eye for an eye and a tooth for a tooth, seen as early as 1750 BCE in the Code of Hammurabi, is the first documented call for retribution. Retribution mandates that only those held responsible for their actions can, and must, be punished. Retribution is commonly cited as a fundamental reason for punishing criminal offenders, and it is often contrasted with rehabilitation. *See also* Deterrence (sociology); Incapacitate; Just Deserts; Rehabilitation; Retributive Justice

Retributive Justice   A justice model built on the principle of retribution. Retributive justice mandates punishment for those who commit wrongful acts. In a retributive justice system, punishment is a fair and deserved response to bad behavior. This philosophy of justice dates as far back as the Code of Hammurabi,

1750 BCE. Typically, retributivists call for *proportional punishment,* which means that the pain of the justly deserved sanction should be related to the nature of the bad act and that those who committed similar acts should receive similar punishments.

Retributive justice is a backward-looking philosophy that focuses on the wrongful act already committed. This is in contrast to the *restorative justice* model, which is forward looking and focuses on the restoration of the victim and the community. Evidence of retributive justice can be found in religious texts and penal doctrines from around the world. *See also* Just Deserts; Punishment (psychology, sociology); Restorative Justice; Retribution

Retroactive Interference   In the context of memory research, interference theory proposes that individuals forget information as a result of competition from other information. According to interference theory, there are two main types of interference: *retroactive* and *proactive.* Retroactive interference occurs when the introduction of novel information impairs one's ability to retain previously learned information. For example, if a student studied for a biology exam followed by mathematics, any interference generated from studying for the mathematics exam would be considered to be retroactive. Proactive interference occurs when previously learned information interferes with the ability to retain new information. Using the same example as above, any interference generated from studying biology would be considered to be proactive. Empirical research has shown that greater levels of interference are associated with greater levels of forgetting. For more information, see Bouton (1993). *See also* Memory (education, psychology)

Retrograde Amnesia   Amnesia simply refers to memory loss; however, amnesia experienced after a trauma is either classified as *retrograde* or *anterograde.* Retrograde amnesia consists of memory loss for events that preceded the traumatic event. For example, an individual involved in a severe car crash may not be able to recall events that occurred prior to the accident. Anterograde amnesia consists of memory loss for events that occur after the trauma, such as remembering new people or where one placed one's keys. The amount of memory loss varies dramatically across cases, ranging from minutes to years of previous memories being erased. It is not uncommon for both types of amnesia to co-occur. Injury to the hippocampal region of the brain has been implicated in amnesia, albeit indirectly, as harm to the hippocampus is thought to interfere with the hypothetical process of consolidation, which consists of the gradual transfer of information into an individual's long-term memory. For more information, see Squire, Clark, and Knowlton (2001). *See also* Amnesia; Anterograde Amnesia; Memory (education, psychology)

Revocation   The legal and procedural process by which *probation* or *parole* may be withdrawn. Both

R

probation and parole are conditional release from incarceration. If individuals violate the terms of their release, their freedom may be revoked. Probation and parole officers have considerable discretion when it comes to revocation. In 1972, the Supreme Court ruled in *Morrissey v. Brewer* that parole revocation requires due process. Parolees are entitled to an administrative hearing when faced with revocation. For more information, see *Morrissey v. Brewer* (1972). **See also** Parole; Probation

Revolution   A complete economic, political, cultural, or ideological transformation of a nation by its own citizens. A revolution differs from a coup because more than the leadership changes; instead, the underlying form of the government is transformed. Revolutions come in many forms and types: Chalmers Johnson (1964, pp. 27–28) in *Revolution and the Social System* found that the form depended on the following variables: (1) targets of the revolution, (2) identity of the revolutionaries, (3) revolutionary goals, and (4) whether revolution was planned or spontaneous.

The only political revolution that America experienced was the War of Independence, or the American Revolution (1775–1783), against the British for sovereignty. Some call the period of the 1960s and 1970s in the United States the "sexual revolution," because of the sociological transformation from a mainly conservative, puritanical culture to one that embraced sexual freedom and permissiveness. The origins of the sexual revolution have been traced to the publication of the *Kinsey Report* (1948) which detailed Americans' sexual habits. For more information, see Johnson (1964) and Kinsey, Pomeroy, and Mart (1948/1998).

Revolving Door   The practice, in some government regulatory agencies, whereby the appointed regulators are drawn from the segments of the private sector that they are assigned to regulate. Such individuals often move back and forth between these regulatory agencies and the affected industries. Critics suggest that such regulators may be doing the bidding of those whom they are meant to be regulating, rather than restraining the antisocial behaviors that may be found in regulated industries. Some jurisdictions have attempted to address this problem by setting minimal time intervals between assignments in the regulatory agencies and the taking of jobs in the regulated industries.

Alternatively, this is a pattern in which there is a frequent turnover of personnel in a company or organization.

Rhetoric   A body of specific techniques of persuasion, available to the good cause and the bad cause alike, and a philosophical position on truth, ethical responsibility, and human motivation. From its inception, rhetoric has borne this dual aspect. Its formal origins lie in public oratory, in the assemblies and courts of the Athenian *demos*. The sophists were the first to formalize the procedures of public oratory into strategies that could be

taught as an art, and they became disreputable for making the worse argument appear the better—hence our word *sophistry*. Plato argued that rhetoric, having no proper subject matter, was a bogus art. Defining it as the use of the available means of persuasion, Aristotle rehabilitated rhetoric to become a valid means of disclosing truth, if less precise than dialectic.

Classical rhetoric was divided into three essential parts: *invention* (discovering the argument), *arrangement* (marshalling the argument), and *style* (expressing the argument elegantly and appropriately). (*Memorization* and *delivery* were further parts.) From classical to early modern times, rhetoric was one of the seven liberal arts. The relationship between rhetoric and dialectic (i.e., logic) has often been illustrated with the image of rhetoric as the open palm, available to all, and dialectic as the closed fist, available only to the learned. Rhetoric also has a close relationship with poetics. The tropes and devices we associate with literature (metaphor, simile, etc.) all derive from rhetorical treatises on style. Rhetoric has gained a new lease of life in the study of the mechanics and strategies of prose composition and its strategies of argumentation.

In its more theoretical aspect, rhetoric studies the nature of persuasion itself as a communicative act, its relationship to the exercise of power, and the discursive codes that make utterances meaningful and persuasive (or not). This makes rhetoric a critical element in the study of communications, political spin, and media representation. **See also** Dialectic; Discourse; Rhetorical Communication

Rhetorical Communication   The best available means of persuasion. Rhetoric aims to alter the beliefs, attitudes, values, or actions of its target audience. Rhetorical communication is symbolic in nature. Some scholars argue that all communication is rhetorical. Others say that only symbolic communication aimed at persuasion is rhetorical; communication aimed at providing information or entertainment may not be aimed at persuasion and thus would not be rhetorical.

The Ancient Greeks and Romans divided rhetoric into three elements: *ethos, pathos,* and *logos*. *Ethos* meant both ethical proof in speech and credibility, *pathos* meant emotional proof, and *logos*—which literally meant the "word"—stood for the logic, reason, and substance of the message. In addition, they divided rhetoric into five canons: (1) invention (coming up with the ideas and support in the speech), (2) disposition (the organization of the speech), (3) style (use of language), (4) delivery (the physical presentation of the message), and (5) memory (mastery and command over the material of the speech). Traditional rhetorical messages rely heavily on the effectiveness of language. Nontraditional rhetoric, such as films or videos, may rely on visual imagery or sound to make a point without the use of words.

Today, rhetorical communication comes through a variety of methods. Speech, writing, photographs and other forms of art, cartoons, videos, films, theatrical performances, and songs, each may contain rhetorical communication. It comes through various channels: interpersonal, small group, public forums, mass media, and the Web. There is dispute over whether acts of violence, such as terrorist bombings, are rhetorical acts. Those who say that these are rhetorical acts point to their symbolic nature and their persuasive purpose; those who disagree point to the fact that these acts are actual rather than symbolic or point to a difference in kind, separating actual violence intended to intimidate from other symbolic acts.

The rhetor chooses a channel for the message: pamphlets, Web blogs, speeches in public forums, speeches on radio or television, political cartoons, plays, films, nonfiction books or essays, and fiction books and essays are examples of the different media used for persuasive messages. The medium chosen may determine aspects of the message's form, its content, the audience it will reach, and the audience response.

In any case, rhetorical communication comes in a variety of contexts. Rhetorical communication occurs in both a broad context and a specific situation. Context and situation both generate the communication and determines its effectiveness. Rhetoric is intended for specific audiences. Audience characteristics also determine how successful the rhetorical communication can be. However, some argue that rhetoric should be judged by the verdict of a universal audience, an idealized concept of intelligent and ethical people, rather than by the more ephemeral reactions of the immediate specific audiences.

Rhetoric of Apology   A formal acknowledgment of wrongdoing. The rhetoric of apology also can be employed with the underlying intent to win favor with an audience or to diminish the perception of fault.

The earliest known form of the rhetoric of apology is the apologia of Ancient Greece; classical figures such as Socrates composed and delivered apologiae in the courts in self-defense. Elements of self-defense and self-promotion in the rhetoric of apology can be found in former President Richard Nixon's resignation speech in 1974.

Apologies in the rhetorical manner have been issued by representatives of nations, sometimes decades or centuries after the fact—among them, that made by Pope John Paul II for centuries of Christian persecution of the Jews. In 2000, Assistant Secretary of the Interior Kevin Gover, a member of the Pawnee nation, issued a rhetoric of apology for 175 years of mistreatment of Native Americans by the federal Bureau of Indian Affairs. For more information, see Buck (2006) and Wilson (1976). ***See also*** Forensic; Persuasion

Right   A legal or moral principle of what is fair or just. A right can also refer to one's legal or moral entitlement or obligation, usually based in law or religion. In the United States, the rights of citizens are delineated in the Bill of Rights, the first 10 amendments to the U.S. Constitution. The amendments place limits on the powers of the federal government and protect an individual's private liberties. The Bill of Rights was included in the Constitution because its framers feared that a Constitution without one could lead to tyranny. At the First Congress of the United States, September 25, 1789, Congress proposed 12 amendments. Ten of the 12 amendments were approved; the first two, which dealt with congressional representation and compensation, were struck down.

Rightist   Those who are on the right side of the political spectrum, which ranges from the right (conservative) to the left (liberal). The terms *right* and *left* date back to the French Revolution (1789–1799) and the seating arrangements of aristocrats and radicals at the first meeting of the Estate General in 1789. The aristocrats sat to the right and the radicals to the left of the president's chair. *Reactionary* is a term associated with rightists; it also originated with the French Revolution, describing those who opposed the revolt against the monarchy. During the 19th century, the term *rightist* came to describe those who wanted the monarchy and the Church to play a more central role in European governance. In the 20th century, the term has been associated with opponents of socialism, communism, or other revolutionary views. In 21st-century American politics, rightists advocate religious values, military spending, and laissez-faire economics.

Riot   A collective, unstructured, violent event. A riot involves a group of people who come together and engage in violent activity that lasts for a stretch of time, threatens order, and causes injury or harm. Riots are serious events of group unrest that disturb the stability of the status quo. Some riots are rooted in social complaint or are driven by the desire for social change, while others have no explicit or unifying motivation. Examples of riots include the 1863 New York City draft riots, the unrest that broke out in many of America's cities after the 1968 assassination of Dr. Martin Luther King Jr., the 1971 Attica prison uprising, and the 1992 Los Angeles riots that exploded after the Rodney King verdict.

Risk   The chance that the expected outcome of an event may not occur. For example, if you expect your company to meet its year-end revenues objectives, there is a chance or risk that this may not happen. Business is often a risky undertaking, and some companies are more risky than others. Businesses are subject to many different kinds of risks—economic, technological, political, and financial. The risk to companies comes from many sources, including but not limited to the economy, government policies, competition, and regulation. The risk to a company is generally borne by the owners and shareholders. Management attempts to reduce these risks or control them by using risk management techniques such as diversification. For taking on risks, investors expect to be compensated and demand a higher return on risky ventures. For more information, see Hall and Lieberman (2005) and Ehrhardt and Brigham (2003).

Risk Management (*economics*) A long-term management strategy for dealing with unforeseen or uncontrollable contingencies that may cause harm. To manage risk effectively, an assessment must be made of potential risk. Risk assessment is, therefore, an integral component of risk management, although it is normally problematic to evaluate and quantify speculative risk.

Individuals, households, and businesses face risk in economic transactions and unpredictable earthly occurrences. Risks are associated with changing asset values or losses, raising capital, natural disasters, health, theft, and accidents. Economic agents with foresight must then anticipate uncontrollable adverse occurrences and adopt long-term safeguards to minimize the cost of their adversities.

Profit-maximizing companies incur risks in the process of raising capital to finance their growth. As such, risk management is inherently part of corporate finance. The cost of risk is factored into earnings. At the corporate level, risks are normally associated with employee and consumer injury, accidents, insurance costs, and losses from bad investments or loans. To hedge against bad loans, depository institutions use credit analysis (character, capacity, adequacy of capital, collateral, and current economic conditions) to manage accounts-receivable risk.

Individuals incur risks by investing in assets with volatile prices, by possessing goods that are susceptible to fire and natural disasters, and by becoming sick or infirm. Hedging and insurance policies provide mechanisms to manage the risks confronting individuals so that they can offset the full cost of adversities.

Full-time, professional managers can be contracted to manage the risks that emanate from losses, claims, insurance, and safety programs. Professionals who manage risk play a key role in identifying, minimizing, and financing potential risks. Management of institutional risk may be undertaken by a risk management committee.

Risk Management (*public administration*) The concept of identifying, analyzing, and taking steps to either mitigate or hedge the uncertainty involved in investment decisions. It is a relatively recent evolution of the term *insurance management*. Risk management is a concept employed by most companies to reduce or eliminate exposures to loss as they relate to a broad scope of activities and responsibilities that range from basic risks, such as fire and employee injuries, to financial risks, such as interest rates and derivatives. The concept refers to multiple threats caused by the environment, humans, organizations, technology, and politics.

Risk management is ideally conducted using a prioritization process, and typically five or six sequential steps are followed, depending on the nature of the organization and the magnitude of the decision at hand.

Risk management strategies are usually determined attuned with the primary objectives of an organization. According to C. Arthur Williams Jr. and Richard M. Heins in their book *Risk Management and Insurance,* the risk management process typically incorporates six steps: (1) determining the objectives of the organization, (2) identifying exposures to loss, (3) measuring those same exposures, (4) selecting alternatives, (5) implementing a solution, and (6) monitoring the results. These six steps, in some variation, are typical of the risk management process.

Risk management techniques, theory, and policies have most recently been applied in the criminal justice system, especially in determining "dangerousness" for sentencing violent and repeat offenders to prison. For more information, see Williams and Heins (1989).

Risky Shift If a group shows a lack of caution when making a decision, it is termed "risky shift" behavior. Several explanations have been offered to explain the phenomenon:

1. Group members rationalize that they have no personal responsibility for the results.

2. When contributions to the decision are anonymous or otherwise shielded from view, individuals feel that they will avoid criticism.

3. Those who endorse risk taking in the first place may be more powerful or persuasive than other participants and are thus able to gain the support of more cautious members.

Rites of Passage Transitional ceremonies or customs. A rite of passage is a ritual or practice that marks a person's move from one stage in their life to another. One's social standing may change after a rite of passage. Rites of passage are generally prescribed by culture and tradition. ***See also*** Ritual (sociology)

Ritual (*communications*) A category of repetitive and customary behaviors and activities performed communally, usually with the intention of bringing about some desired outcome. Rituals may be secular or religious and may mark the passage of time or a significant event such as a birth or a death; they may commemorate a past event or attempt to influence a future one. A ritual is sometimes thought to be a reenactment of myth connecting the present with the past. Many rituals are assumed to have the three-part structure originally associated with rites of passage (the transformation in a social position or condition). First, there is a separation from everyday life; then the ritual participants enter the in-between or liminal stage, during which the elements that can make the culture fall apart are made evident or acted out. The ritual ends with some form of reintegration or reincorporation that either moves the participants on to a new social order or solidifies the one already in existence. For more

R

information, see Bell (1997). ***See also*** Culture (communication, media studies, sociology); Myth

Ritual (*sociology*)   An action or body of practices regularly performed. Rituals tend to be prescribed by tradition, religion, or culture. A ritual can be a method for performing an act or the act itself. Ritual is generally understood as a repetitive or recurrent practice and is often associated with ceremony.

Rival Hypotheses   Conflicting explanations of the same phenomenon. Researchers often design their projects to decide between rival hypotheses. For example, one hypothesis to explain the relation between income and the death rate is that people with higher incomes have better access to medical care; another is that people with lower incomes live and work in less healthy environments.

Role   A set of rights and obligations of people in a social context. Roles are expected behaviors set by society. They relay social status. Norms define how a person acts in a given situation.

Role theory studies how one develops or adopts a certain role, whether through the environment, social position, others' expectations (labeling theory), the influence of society (structuralist), individual responses to behavior (symbolic interactionist), or roles in the organization. Role conflict arises when a person is forced to take on two different and incompatible roles at the same time.

Role Ambiguity   A role is said to be ambiguous when the expectations surrounding a single role are unclear, inherently contradictory, or highly varied and complex. An example is the dilemma frequently faced by human resource specialists: On the one hand, they are management's agents imposing discipline on employees; on the other hand, they advise employees about their rights and benefits. In complex organizations, especially when change is ongoing, role ambiguity can arise frequently, and managers should look for and clarify ambiguous roles where possible. Highly complex roles, such as those in executive ranks, may have inherent ambiguities whose resolution is neither practical nor desirable. Such roles are best filled by individuals with a high tolerance for ambiguity and pragmatic decision making.

Role Conflict (*education*)   Roles are "scripted" expectations for behavior from persons who occupy a given status. Role *conflict* can occur when social roles seem to require incompatible behaviors. For example, mothers are expected to act one way, police officers another. If you have done something illegal and your mother is a police officer, she is likely to experience role conflict when deciding what to do about your crime.

Role *strain* is tension among the roles linked to a particular social position. A teacher may feel strain between the roles of friendly advisor and objective judge of academic performance. Role *overload* is often associated with jobs that require employees to fulfill more functions than they can handle. ***See also*** Cognitive Dissonance (psychology)

Role Conflict (*public administration*)   A conflict that occurs when a contradiction arises between two or more roles, which are sets of expectations attached to a particular status in a social system. How a priest or boss or police officer is supposed to act is clear to most of us, and so is how we should act, generally, with respect to them. Everyone plays several roles in their daily lives, and different roles may present incompatible demands. A "boss" just up from the ranks is still a "friend" to his or her former workmates and current "subordinates." When the new "boss" has occasion to discipline an employee toward whom he or she would be indulgent as a "friend," a conflict between roles arises whose resolution is accompanied by considerable stress for all involved.

Role Playing   A therapeutic technique used in counseling that enables the client to rehearse a desired behavior by creating and performing a role. The simulation of the experience should closely mimic an experience similar to what is likely to occur in the client's life. Constructive feedback from the counselor can encourage the client to recognize both strengths and challenges in practicing the new skill. It is sometimes paired with imagery, wherein first a client imagines using a new adaptive coping strategy in a problem situation and then follows it with the imagery of acting out the new approach. ***See also*** Counseling

Romanticism   A cultural and artistic movement in Europe and America between 1770 and 1860. It is generally seen as a reaction against Enlightenment values and industrialism. It is characterized by a privileging of individualism, passion, imagination, social transformation, and nature. While Romanticism is typically associated with literature (Wordsworth and Keats in England, Goethe and Höelderlin in Germany, and Emerson and Whitman in America), music (Beethoven and Chopin) and painting (Turner and Goya) were also significantly influenced.

Rooting Reflex   In the first weeks and months after birth, infants engage in involuntary, instinctual reactions called reflexes. One such reflex is referred to as the rooting reflex, whereby a newborn turns its mouth toward a finger or nipple that makes contact with its cheek. The rooting reflex is an important innate reaction for babies as it helps ensure breastfeeding. Two additional involuntary reflexes infants are equipped with are the grasping and sucking reflexes. For more information, see Byrd, Nelson, and Manthey (2006).

Rorschach   The Rorschach Inkblot Test is an instrument used in the context of personality assessment. The test was published in a monograph (*Psychodiagnostik*) by Hermann Rorschach, a Swiss psychiatrist, who died at the young age of 38, well before the instrument gained worldwide attention. The Rorschach consists of 10 cards, each containing an inkblot; some are solely in black and white, while others include color. Respondents are asked to indicate what they believe the inkblot might be, followed by an explanation of their answer.

Various methods have been developed for scoring the Rorschach, but the most widely accepted and well researched is the Exner Comprehensive System developed by John E. Exner, Jr. The scoring criteria of the Comprehensive System and other scoring methods require evaluators to evaluate responses based on details such as the location of the card the respondent is attending to, various features such as color and shape, the content of responses, and the typicality of the responses.

The Rorschach is commonly described as a *projective* personality measure (as opposed to *objective*). Projective measures are foundationally grounded in the idea that individuals will project personality traits and life experiences onto ambiguous stimuli such as inkblots. There is a burgeoning area of commentary by scholars in the area of personality assessment, however, who are lobbying for the removal of the classificatory term *projective* to describe the Rorschach as they believe that it carries with it a negative connotation and perpetuates a sentiment that self-report measures are entirely "objective." The Rorschach also continues to attract controversy in the psychological literature, mainly with respect to its psychometric properties—namely, its reliability and validity. For more information, see Exner (2003) and Rorschach (1948). ***See also*** Projection and Projective Tests; Projective Tests

Routine Activities Theory

A criminological theory developed by Lawrence Cohen and Marcus Felson in 1979. In their theoretical analysis, Felson and Cohen contend that crime is the result of the simultaneous convergence of three conditions: (1) a motivated offender, (2) a suitable target (object, place, or person), and (3) the absence of a suitable guardian (camera, police, neighbor, etc.) Routine activities theory maintains that each of these elements must be present for crime to take place. This is a theory rooted in environmental criminology and focused on the opportunities for the occurrence of crime. To reduce the opportunities for crime, situational crime prevention models can be implemented. For more information, see Cohen and Felson (1979). ***See also*** Rational Choice; Situational Crime Prevention

Rubrics

Tools used to score constructed response assessments, such as essays and performance assessments. Rubrics can come in various forms, such as checklists, rating scales, or scoring grids or matrices. The purpose of the scoring rubric is to allow the most systematic and objective grading possible. By asking multiple raters to rate a set of constructed response assessments, reliability can be estimated by the level of concordance.

A *holistic* rubric is used to rate a task as a whole, in which the rater assigns a score based on an overall impression of the performance. Also called global, scoring, or rating rubrics, holistic rubrics allow for faster scoring by the rater. One disadvantage of the holistic rubric is the limited feedback that is available for the student. The *annotated holistic* rubric is a variation of the holistic rubric and allows the rater to add comments on strengths and weaknesses of the student, thus increasing the amount of feedback available. Another disadvantage of the holistic rubric is the increased possibility of rater bias. Errors in spelling or grammar and messy handwriting may influence a rater to give reduced scores.

An *analytic* rubric allows the rater to assign scores for different components or characteristics of the task. Generally, these scores are then summed to assign an overall score to the student. Also called point or trait rubrics, these types of rubrics take more time for the rater to complete. However, they also provide more feedback to the student regarding his or her performance. To create an analytic rubric, the developer must identify the major elements that constitute the given task. The identification of these key elements is another potential drawback of analytic rubrics, as this may be difficult for some beginning teachers. The major elements should coincide with the intended learning outcomes for a given task. For example, the developer may list the following as the major elements of an oral presentation assignment: organization, style, use of communication aids, and depth of content. Standards of performance for each element are then categorized. For example, each element could be rated using a defined set of criteria for what type of response constitutes excellent, average, or poor performance.

Rubrics may be used for either *summative* or *formative* purposes. Large-scale tests that include open-ended responses use rubrics in a summative format to provide a final score to each test taker. In classrooms, rubrics may be used in a formative manner, with the rubric possibly shared with students both before and after task completion. ***See also*** Objective (definition and types of); Performance Assessment

Rulemaking

The process for adopting, amending, or repealing a rule. Under the Federal Administrative Procedures Act (APA), *rule* means

> the whole or a part of an agency statement of general or particular applicability and future effect designed to implement, interpret, or prescribe law or policy or describing the organization, procedure, or practice requirements of an agency and includes the approval or prescription for the future of rates, wages, corporate or financial structures or reorganizations thereof, prices, facilities, appliances, services or allowances therefore or of valuations, costs, or accounting, or practices bearing on any of the foregoing.

Under the Model State APA, *rule* means the whole or a part of an agency statement of general applicability and future effect that implements, interprets, or prescribes law or policy or the organization, procedure, or practice requirements of an agency. The term does not include (a) statements concerning only the internal management of an agency and not affecting private rights or procedures available to the public; (b) agency declaratory orders issued under the APA; (c) a decision or order in a disputed case; (d) an intergovernmental or interagency memorandum, directive, or communication that does not affect the rights of, or procedures and practices available to, the public; (e) an opinion of the attorney general; (f) an executive order of the governor; (g) a statement that establishes criteria or guidelines to be used by the staff of an agency in performing audits, investigations, or inspections, in settling commercial disputes, in negotiating commercial arrangements, or in the defense, prosecution, or settlement of cases, if disclosure of the criteria or guidelines would enable law violators to avoid detection, facilitate disregard of requirements imposed by law, or give a clearly improper advantage to persons who are in an adverse position to the state; and (h) guidance documents.

Originally, the APA prescribed two types of rulemaking, which have come to be known as "formal" and "informal." Since 1990, a third type, negotiated rulemaking, a form of informal rulemaking has been enacted. The same categories are available in state governments.

Formal rulemaking under the APA involves a trial-type hearing (witnesses, depositions, transcript, etc.). This more rigorous, and today relatively uncommon, procedure is required only where the governing statute requires that the proceeding be "on the record."

Most agency regulations are the product of informal rulemaking—the notice and comment procedures. The first step in this process is the publication of a proposed regulation in the *Federal Register*. The *Federal Register* is a daily publication printed and distributed by the Government Printing Office. Publication of a document in the *Federal Register* constitutes legal notice of its contents. This is called a Notice of Proposed Rulemaking (NPRM)—that is, a document that describes and explains the regulations that the federal government proposes to adopt at some future date, and invites interested parties to submit comments related to them. These comments can then be used in developing a final regulation.

The agency then allows a period of time during which interested parties may participate in the process, usually by submitting written comments, although oral presentations are sometimes permitted. Next, the agency considers and evaluates the comments submitted and determines the content of the final regulation, which is also published in the *Federal Register,* generally at least 30 days prior to its effective date.

The agency is also required to publish a "concise general statement" of the basis and purpose of the regulation. This is commonly known as the preamble, the substance of which appears in the *Federal Register* under the heading "Supplementary Information." The preamble normally accompanies publication of the final regulation, although this is not required as long as it is sufficiently close in time to make clear that it is, in fact, contemporaneous and not a *"post hoc* rationalization." Apart from questions of judicial review, the preamble serves another highly important function: It provides, as its title in the *Federal Register* indicates, useful supplementary information. Viewed from this perspective, the preamble serves much the same purpose with respect to a regulation as legislative history does with respect to a statute.

Codifications of agency regulations are issued in bound and permanent form in the Code of Federal Regulations (CFR). The CFR is supplemented or republished at least once a year. Unfortunately, with rare exceptions, the preamble does not accompany the regulations in the CFR but is found only in the original *Federal Register* issuance. The CFR does, however, give the appropriate *Federal Register* citation.

The third form of rulemaking, negotiated rulemaking, allows an agency to consult with interested parties in the development of regulations. Under this legislation, a proposed regulation is drafted by a committee composed of representatives of the agency and other interested parties if the agency determines, among other things, that there are a limited number of identifiable interests that will be significantly affected by the regulation and that there is a reasonable likelihood that a committee can reach a consensus without unreasonably delaying the rulemaking process. Once the proposed regulation is developed in this manner, it remains subject to the APA's notice and comment requirements. The negotiated rulemaking procedure is optional; an agency's decision to use or not use it is not subject to judicial review. For more information, see National Conference of Commissioners on Uniform State Laws (2007b), 5 U.S.C. § 551(4), Model SAPA. loc. cit (27), Comptroller General, Federal Appropriations Law (2008a), and Department of Health and Human Services (n.d.).

Rule of Law   The democratic principle that no one is above the law. The rule of law concept traces back to Ancient Greece and the writings of Aristotle (384–322 BCE) and Plato (427–347 BCE). Athens in the 5th century BCE was one of the earliest examples of a rule-of-law society. All men over the age of 30, regardless of social class or wealth, were entitled to serve as jurists, legislators, and magistrates. Aristotle and Plato were wary of the Athen system because they feared rule by the majority. In the United States, the rule of law is based on the U.S. Constitution, which applies to each citizen, including the president, on an equal basis. The principle exists that a democratic society requires the respect of a set of well-defined and just laws created by a representative legislature, approved by the chief executive, and enforced by the independent judiciary branch.

Rules   Norms that can be formal or informal but are widely accepted by society. They are standards that we are expected to follow. They encompass a reason or reasons to act, feel, or believe a set of ideas that are accepted as qualifications or definitions. Rules regulate behavior and act as social controls. They are historically and culturally conditioned and frequently change.

S

Sacred Something regarded with reverence, often of a religious nature. Émile Durkheim (1858–1917) proposed that religion had social functions and was not limited to an individual experience. Basic to religion, he argued, was the *distinction between the sacred and the profane*. He viewed the sacred as the interests of the group, particularly unity, which were communicated through group symbols. The profane referred to more basic individual concerns. For more information, see Durkheim (2001).

Salience The notion that the media are capable of shaping audience opinion based on the importance assigned to a public issue or figure through their messages. This is similar to the idea of agenda setting. Salience is of particular consideration in the research of political communication. ***See also*** Gatekeepers; Industry (media studies)

Sample A population group used in a study. All scientifically sound surveys, including political surveys, are required to have randomly selected participants. Samples should also be controlled, meaning that the independent variable is what is measured and not some third variable. Otherwise, the sample would be considered biased.

Sampling A statistical procedure where some individual units are chosen for study from a population (the total number of units) to make inferences about the entire population. A sample is chosen because it is usually not possible to include or study every member of the population (the universe). A sample is drawn from a population based on several factors, including the size of the sample needed and access to the population. There are a number of sampling methods, including random sampling, where each member of the population has an equal and known chance of being included in the sample. It is vital that the sample be representative of the population if inferences are to be made about the larger group. ***See also*** Sample

Sampling Bias This bias occurs when some members of the population are more likely to be included in a sample than others. Given that a perfectly random sample is often impractical, most samples contain some bias. Sampling bias becomes problematic when the statistics are said to accurately reflect the larger population, as the results of the study may be skewed to reflect the biased sample. ***See also*** Sampling; Sampling Error

Sampling Distribution The resulting distribution of a sampled statistic (proportion, mean, variance, or their respective differences, etc.) from random samples of a given size (n). The sampling distribution has all the characteristics of any distribution, including measures of centrality, variability, and shape. The central limit theorem provides the basis for expecting a sampling distribution of a sampled statistic to become more like a normal distribution with reduced sampling error as sample size increases. The mean of the sampling distribution is expected to be the mean of the population from which the samples are randomly drawn. ***See also*** Central Limit Theorem; Sampling Error

Sampling Error The error that occurs from observing or studying a sample rather than all members of the population. The inferences made about the population based on the chosen sample contain inaccuracies, so the sample does not accurately reflect the population. Sampling error generally decreases as the size of the sample increases. Using a random sampling method can also minimize sampling error. ***See also*** Sampling; Sampling Bias

Sampling in Mixed-Methods Research Sampling in this type of research requires knowledge of sampling in qualitative and quantitative research because qualitative and quantitative sampling methods and strategies are systematically combined in mixed research. Typically, the mixed-methods researcher selects the qualitative sample using one of the qualitative-sampling techniques and the quantitative sample using one of the quantitative-sampling techniques. We focus here on classifying mixed-methods sampling using a typology of sampling designs developed by Anthony Onwuegbuzie and Kathleen Collins.

According to the Onwuegbuzie and Collins (2007) scheme, sampling in mixed research is classified into "mixed sampling designs." The sampling designs are classified on the basis of two major criteria: time orientation and sample relationship. *Time orientation* is determined by answering this question: "Do the qualitative and quantitative phases in the mixed research study occur concurrently or sequentially?" If the data are collected for the qualitative and quantitative phases of the study at approximately the same time, then this is known as a *concurrent* time orientation. In this situation, both sets of data are interpreted during data analysis and during the data interpretation stage. If the data are obtained in stages and the data from the first stage are used to shape selection of data in the second stage then this is known as a *sequential* time orientation. The second major criterion used in determining one's mixed sampling design is *sample relationship,* which is determined by answering this question: "Is the relationship between the quantitative and qualitative samples identical, parallel, nested, or multilevel?" In an *identical* sample relation, the same people participate in the quantitative and qualitative phases of the study. In a *parallel* sample relation, separate quantitative and qualitative samples are drawn from the same population for the study. In a *nested* sample relation, the participants selected for one phase are a subset of the participants selected for the other phase.

In a *multilevel* sample relation, the quantitative and qualitative samples are selected from different levels of a population.

The mixed sampling design matrix is constructed by combining the two major criteria just provided—time orientation (which has two types) and sample relationship (which has four types)—to form the eight *mixed sampling designs:* (1) identical concurrent sampling design, (2) identical sequential sampling design, (3) parallel concurrent sampling design, (4) parallel sequential sampling design, (5) nested concurrent sampling design, (6) nested sequential sampling design, (7) multilevel concurrent sampling design, and (8) multilevel sequential sampling design. Once the mixed sampling method has been determined, the researcher determines the qualitative and quantitative sampling methods and sample sizes. Then, the samples are located, and data are collected and analyzed using mixed-methods data analysis. For more information, see Onwuegbuzie and Collins (2007). *See also* Sampling in Qualitative Research, Methods of; Sampling in Quantitative Research

Sampling in Qualitative Research, Methods of

Sampling in this type of research is usually purposive (i.e., individuals or groups are selected that will provide the information needed to address the research questions). The goal is always to select information-rich cases when possible. Here, we list and briefly define the major types of sampling used in qualitative research, as identified by Anthony Onwuegbuzie and Nancy Leech (2007). First, in *maximum variation sampling,* the researcher purposively selects a wide range of cases. Second, in *homogeneous sample selection,* the researcher selects a small and homogeneous case or set of cases for intensive study. Third, in *extreme case sampling,* the researcher selects cases that represent the extremes on some dimension. Fourth, in *typical-case sampling,* the researcher selects typical or average cases. Fifth, in *critical-case sampling,* the researcher selects cases that are known to be important. Sixth, in *negative-case sampling,* the researcher purposively selects cases that disconfirm

the tentative generalizations being formed, so that the researcher can ensure that he or she is not just selectively finding cases to support his or her personal theory. Seventh, in *opportunistic sampling,* the researcher selects potentially useful cases as the opportunity arises during fieldwork. Eighth, in *mixed purposeful sampling,* the researcher mixes and matches the sampling strategies just listed into more complex sampling designs tailored to the needs of the particular research study. Ninth, in *theory-based sampling,* the researcher selects settings, individuals, and/or groups because their inclusion helps the researcher to develop a theory. Tenth, in *confirming/disconfirming sampling,* after data collection has commenced, the researcher purposively selects additional cases to verify or confirm the initial findings. Eleventh, in *snowball sampling* (also called *network sampling* or *chain sampling*), the participants already selected for the study are asked to recruit individuals with the same characteristic(s) of interest to join the study. Twelfth, in *intensity sampling,* the researcher selects settings, individuals, and/or groups because their experiences relative to the phenomena of interest are viewed as intense but not extreme. Thirteenth, in *politically important case sampling,* the researcher selects settings, individuals, and/or groups to be included or excluded based on their political connections to the phenomenon of interest. Fourteenth, in *convenience sampling,* the researcher selects settings, individuals, and/or groups that are conveniently available and willing to participate in the research. Fifteenth, in *criterion sampling,* the researcher selects settings, individuals, and/or groups because they represent one or more criteria. Sixteenth, in *quota sampling,* the researcher identifies desired characteristics and quotas of sample members to be included in the study. Seventeenth, in *random purposeful sampling,* the researcher selects random cases from the sampling frame and randomly chooses a desired number of individuals to participate in the study. Eighteenth, in *stratified purposeful sampling,* the sampling frame is divided into strata to obtain relatively homogeneous subgroups, and a purposeful sample is selected from each stratum. Nineteenth, in *multistage purposeful sampling,* the researcher selects settings, individuals, and/or groups representing a sample in two or more stages, with all stages reflecting purposive sampling of participants. Finally, in *multistage purposeful random sampling,* the researcher selects settings, individuals, and/or groups representing a sample in two or more stages, wherein the first stage involves random selection and the following stages involve purposive selection of participants. For more information, see Onwuegbuzie and Leech (2007). *See also* Sampling in Mixed-Methods Research; Sampling in Quantitative Research

Sampling in Quantitative Research

Sampling is the process of selecting cases to study. The sample is a subgroup of a population or universe. A study of an entire population is a census. Samples are studied to learn about the population. *Inference* is the process of drawing conclusions about a population based on information from a sample. For example, if 62% of the members of the sample favor gun control, 62% is an estimate of the percentage of the population that favors gun control. The quality of a sample (and inference) depends on the sampling method and sample size; probability samples of sufficient size produce *representative samples* (i.e., samples that provide good estimates of population parameters).

The two basic sampling methods are *probability* and *nonprobability*. With probability samples, the researcher knows the probability that cases will be chosen; this knowledge allows statistical inference about the population. In nonprobability sampling, the probability is unknown, and statistical inferences are of doubtful value. Among types of probability sampling, *simple random* sampling is a common benchmark; the cases are selected using a random process, such as a lottery or a random number generator. In *stratified random* sampling, the researcher first orders the sampling frame by groups (strata) in the population, such as men and women, and then draws a random sample from each of these. In proportionate stratified sampling, the sample sizes within the strata are made to be proportional to their population sizes. In *cluster* sampling, subgroups (clusters) of the population, such as counties, are chosen randomly. In one-stage cluster sampling, all individuals in the randomly selected clusters are included; in two-stage cluster sampling, individuals are sampled randomly from the clusters. In *equal-probability sampling methods* (EPSEM), each member of the population has an equal chance of being included in the sample. EPSEMs include simple random sampling, proportionate stratified sampling, cluster sampling when clusters are of equal size, and systematic sampling. EPSEMs produce representative samples.

Nonprobability sampling is common because probability samples are often difficult to obtain. The major disadvantage of nonprobability samples is that researchers cannot legitimately use probability statistics to make inferences about the population. *Convenience* sampling is the most widespread of the nonprobability samples. A *quota* sample is a stratified nonprobability sample. Researchers have quotas of respondents (e.g., a specific number of men and women), who are then selected nonrandomly. *Judgment* or *purposive* sampling is used to improve the representativeness of a nonrandom sample or when a particular hard-to-find type of person is needed. For example, when conducting learning experiments, it would be hard to randomly sample from millions of school students. Representativeness could be improved by recruiting students from categories of schools the researcher judged likely to be important, such as urban, suburban, and rural. This would be better than using convenience samples from three schools closest to the researcher's home. *See also* Probability Value (*p* Value); Survey Research

Sanction *(political science)* A punishment or the permission to act, depending on its context. In politics, the term typically refers to political and economic sanctions. These sanctions refer to punitive action taken by a nation against another, most often in the form of a boycott of political or economic relations. The United Nations (UN) under Article VII of its Charter (1945) allows the Security Council to enforce sanctions with the aim of restoration of international peace and security. Sanctions are applied when diplomatic efforts have failed. In addition to economic and trade sanctions, UN-sponsored sanctions can also entail arms embargoes, travel bans, and financial and diplomatic restrictions.

Sanction *(sociology)* A form of punishment. In civil law, this is usually a monetary fine against a party in a legal action for violating the rules of procedure or otherwise exploiting the judicial process. A judge who sanctions a party during a legal procedure has imposed a penalty. In the criminal justice system, a sanction is a punishment imposed by the judge and can include anything from fines to incapacitation within the community to incarceration. *See also* Community-Based Corrections; Incapacitate; Shock Probation/Shock Incarceration

Satellite Systems Communication satellites enable the transfer of media services over long distances more economically than by cable. Signals can be transmitted by satellites to receiving stations for local distribution by cable. Ted Turner's Atlanta-based WTBS became the first U.S. station to use satellite transmission to cable receivers in the 1970s. Turner developed CNN in the 1980s, broadcasting 24-hour news coverage directly to subscribers and selling news to local stations in direct competition with the three main networks. Following its spectacular coverage of the 1991 Gulf War, CNN became a prominent worldwide news provider.

Satellites orbit the earth and transfer data from and to earth stations. Manufacturing and launching satellites is hugely expensive and risky. Satellite launching is a predominantly state-run operation, though at least one commercial satellite-launching service exists.

DBS (Direct Broadcast Satellite) is direct broadcasting via satellites to viewers using receiving dishes. This service has been available in the United States since the 1970s but has had a much lower take-up rate by consumers than cable. *See also* Direct Broadcast Satellite Systems (DBS); Public Service Broadcasting

Satisficing *(education)* A decision-making strategy that seeks a choice that is good enough but not perfectly optimal, specifically when wanting to achieve a particular goal under constraints or limitations. Coined by Herbert Simon in 1955, *satisficing* is a combination of the words *satisfy* and *suffice*. *See also* Decision-Making Theory

Satisficing *(public administration)* The economic or "optimized" solution to a problem is one where the

S

agent, given his constraints, maximizes the utility of the outcome; however, the optimal choice is not always clearly understood by decision-making agents. Thus, satisficing refers to the tendency to accept the first choice that is perceived as "good enough."

The Nobel Laureate Herbert Simon, who argued that decision-making agents tend to have neither the cognitive resources nor the information needed to evaluate all possible outcomes and maximize their utility, coined the word *satisfice*. To illustrate his idea, Simon used the example of a mouse in a maze searching for a piece of Gouda; however, finding none, the mouse would eventually be "satisfied" with whatever kind of cheese it may come upon, such as cheddar.

Satisficing also occurs in groups where consensus-seeking activities can result in solutions where everyone agrees to a decision that may not be optimal. For more information, see Simon (1955) and Janis and Mann (1977). **See also** Decision-Making Theory

Savings   The part of a person's income that is not spent at the end of any given accounting period. Individuals, households, businesses, and government dis-save when current expenditures exceed current saving.

For a closed economy, expenditures by firms and individuals are in equilibrium when saving is equal to investment. If saving is greater than investment, then expenditure from the sources of income (wages, rent, salaries, and dividends) will not be sufficiently spent on output, thereby causing income to fall until saving and investment are realigned. Several factors contribute to the level of aggregate saving, namely, income, the expectation of price changes, the business cycle, and age.

Higher levels of income tend to generate more saving, but if economic actors expect the general price level to rise tomorrow, they will try to preempt the effects of inflation by spending more today. In times of economic hardship and unemployment, people tend to save less, but they tend to save more as they get older. For more information, see Mankiw (2006) and Melicher and Norton (2005). **See also** Business Cycle (economics, public relations); Closed Economy; Income

Scaffolding   An instructional method whereby a teacher models the concept or skill to be learned, leads students through guided practice activities, and then offers various levels of teacher support while students practice the concept or skill independently. The purpose is to create a learning environment where students build confidence while mastering new skills or concepts.

Scared Straight   A documentary was released in 1978 that depicted a group of juvenile delinquents being brought in front of a group of life-sentenced adult inmates at Rahway State Prison (now East Jersey State Prison), who yelled, screamed, and otherwise terrorized the youths so as to demonstrate that prison was not a place they would want to be. The goal was to demonstrate that prison life was not glamorous or exciting.

While most of the youth in the original group were scared into following a law-abiding lifestyle, later research found that scared-straight programs actually lead to increased offending. **See also** Boot Camp

Scatterplot (*education*)   A two-dimensional graphic of paired scores on two continuous variables, one plotted horizontally (X) and one plotted vertically (Y), providing a visual display of a possible relationship and a visual basis for describing any relationship as linear (straight line) or curvilinear (nonstraight line). **See also** Correlation (education)

Scatterplot (*psychology*)   A representation of paired x and y data points to depict the relationship between two variables. A scatterplot gives a researcher an overview of the direction and nature of the relationship between two observed variables. If the points of the scatterplot depict the same upward linear trend, it means that if one variable increases, the other increases as well. It can be assumed that the correlation between these variables is positive. If the points in the scatterplot depict the same downward linear trend, it means that if one variable increases, the other decreases. It can be assumed that the correlation between these variables is negative. If the scatterplot depicts scattered points with no linear trend, it can be assumed that there is no relationship between the variables. **See also** Correlation (psychology)

Schedules of Reinforcement   The delivery of reinforcement according to different specifications, specifying the contingencies of reinforcement. Delivery of reinforcers based on the passage of time is an interval schedule. Delivery of reinforcers based on the number of responses emitted by an organism is a ratio schedule. Furthermore, reinforcement can occur consistently (i.e., a fixed schedule) or intermittently (i.e., a variable schedule). As such, there are four possible schedules: fixed ratio (e.g., pay on a piecework basis), variable ratio (e.g., payoffs from slot machines), fixed interval (e.g., weekly quizzes), and variable interval (e.g., spot-checking quizzes). **See also** Reinforcer

Schemas (*education*)   Hypothesized knowledge structures that are organized and reflect one's prior knowledge. The other common plural form is schemata. Schemas function to control the encoding, storage, and retrieval of information. They serve as frameworks for comprehending new data, guiding actions, and bridging gaps in information obtained from the environment.

Schemas (*psychology*)   Knowledge structures of an event or concept, based on previous perceptions of that event or concept. Schemas have direct effects on memory performance. While schema-consistent information is encoded and remembered more easily, it is also the case that people tend to remember schema-inconsistent information more easily. If information violates an existing schema, more processing time is necessary to process that information, which in turn leads to deeper processing and easier retrieval of that information. Schemas can even lead people to recall information that was not initially presented. A study by Brewer and Treyens (1982) tested people's memories for the content of a professor's office. Nine out of 30 participants in the study recalled that books were present in the office, although there were none, as books tend to be part of a professor's office schema. Although schemas are often used in the context of the representation of information, people also have self-schemas. Self-schemas are knowledge structures one believes to be true about one's self. As this large body of knowledge is stored in an organized way, similar to general information, it is therefore referred to as self-schemas. While self-schemas can refer to specific aspects of one's personality, the integration of all self-schemas to represent all aspects of oneself is referred to as the self-concept. In other words, people's self-concepts are composed of their self-schemas. For more information, see Brewer and Treyens (1981). **See also** Self-Discrepancy Theory

Schizophrenia   A type of psychological disorder characterized by hallucinations, delusions (or other psychotic symptoms), and the loss of adaptive behavior in society. It has been estimated that schizophrenia may affect approximately 1% of the population. A person suffering from schizophrenia often displays irrational thought processes and a detachment from reality, often marked by the presence of delusional thinking. Delusions can be defined as irrational beliefs not based in reality, which are believed despite all evidence to the contrary. For example, a person with schizophrenia may, through a delusion of grandeur, believe that he or she is a famous prince or princess (regardless of evidence that this is not the case). Hallucinations, in contrast, refer to the experience of sensory stimuli in the absence of any real stimulus input. For example, persons suffering from hallucinations may hear the voice of the devil, taste poison in their food, or feel spiders crawling on their skin. Other symptoms of schizophrenia include the display of odd or unusual behavior, lack of personal hygiene, flat or restricted affect, and lack of interest in ordinary life activities. Schizophrenia has been classified into the following subtypes. Paranoid schizophrenia can be characterized as dominated by irrational thoughts of persecution, while catatonic schizophrenia can be characterized by motor disturbances, such as muscular strictness or random motor movements. Disorganized schizophrenia can be characterized by the loss of adaptive behaviors, displayed via symptoms such as social withdrawal or incoherence. A person who cannot be classified in any of the above categories is classified as the undifferentiated type. As this classification system has received criticism, a new system now classifies negative and positive symptoms of schizophrenia. Negative symptoms include apathy, social and emotional withdrawal, as well as speech problems, while positive symptoms include hallucinations, delusions, and other unusual but apparent symptoms. **See also** Delusions; Hallucinations

School Administration   The educational leaders and decision makers who manage the day-to-day activities of the school. School administrators are usually assistant principals and principals. The ability to make effective decisions is critical to the success of school administrators. They are responsible for hiring, firing, training, providing mentoring, and supervising the teachers and support staff of the school. Administrators oversee the budget for a school. They also establish and negotiate relationships with students, parents, employers, and the community. Administrators set the policies and procedures to achieve the established educational standards and goals of a school.

School Audit   An audit typically undertaken to determine why a school is performing poorly and what can be done to improve its performance. Audits are usually conducted by teams and can take from weeks to months to complete. The process of an audit should be constructive rather than punitive.

School Choice and Vouchers   A concept first recommended in the 1950s by the economist Milton Friedman. Based on the principles of a free-market economy, parents as consumers would have the right to choose their children's schools, thereby compelling schools to compete for students and consequently forcing schools to improve. According to the policy, parents are given vouchers (which are similar to an admission ticket). It is claimed by proponents that parents are free to shop for the best school for their children and give the voucher to the school they select. The school would receive a fixed sum for each voucher, thus providing the school's source of operating income. **See also** School Reform

School Culture/Climate   Patterns of activity and the structures governing interaction that are fashioned by the assumptions, beliefs, values, norms, symbols, and tangible artifacts of a system. These patterns and structures give significance and meaning to the members of an organization/school, shaping behavior and structuring members' perceptions. The culture tends to be shared by all or most members; it is something that the more experienced individuals pass on to newer members. Members sense the particular culture of an organization/school, but it generally exists as tacit knowledge and is difficult to express explicitly.

Climate has been used to describe the atmosphere within an organization/school. It consists of the recurring patterns of behavior, attitudes, and feelings that characterize everyday life in the system, reflecting the individual's subjective experience. Although culture and climate are related, climate is easier to assess and change. But the concept of culture is particularly important when attempting to manage systemwide change. For more information, see Morgan (1997). ***See also*** Organizational Change (education)

School Effectiveness and Improvement   Effective schools and the characteristics they commonly share positively affect student learning outcomes. Effective schools get results. Research into what makes a school "effective" is often used by school boards to guide the improvement plans of school systems. Some of the characteristics of effective schools are strong schoolwide leadership (administration and teachers); a mission and environment focused on learning for all students; high expectations of student success and mastery of content that is standards-based; ongoing and authentic assessments of student progress and teacher performance; productive, collaborative partnerships with parents and community sources; and ongoing professional development opportunities for teachers. When successfully implemented in the school environment, these multidimensional indicators directly correlate to increased student learning for all students. It is important to note that the possession of these traits does not ensure that a school will be effective, but it does increase the likelihood of success. ***See also*** School Evaluation; School Reform

School Evaluation   Assessment of the overall effectiveness of a school serving K–12 students. School evaluation addresses multiple educational expectations, including those of the state, the federal government, students, parents, teachers, administrators, and the community. School evaluations comprehensively address instruction and curriculum (e.g., curriculum standards, student academic and social outcomes), school services (e.g., transportation, food service), school administration (e.g., facilities, finance, information systems), human resources (e.g., teacher qualifications, development, and evaluation), as well as parent and community involvement. An example of school evaluation is reflected in the criteria and assessments of regional accrediting agencies providing school-level accreditation. ***See also*** School Effectiveness and Improvement

School Governance   The means by which schools are officially structured and managed. It is a complex model, which includes input from federal, state, and local education agencies, all of which are tasked with different decision-making functions. Federal mandates dictate to state authorities, which impose those demands on local agencies. ***See also*** School Administration

School Psychology   A specialty field of professional psychology. Training involves significant work in psychological consultation, neuropsychoeducational assessment, evidence-based interventions, program development and evaluation, and research methods/data analysis. Many practitioners work in educational environments, mental health centers, and social service/correctional facilities. Independent professional practice occurs at the doctoral level, but individuals with

an educational specialist degree are eligible to practice in school environments. For more information, see Fagan and Wise (2007). ***See also*** Psychology

School Reform   The constant movement to improve schooling and student achievement outcomes. Though dating back to the Committee of Ten (1892), more recently, *A Nation at Risk* (1983) is generally credited with bolstering the back-to-basics and school accountability movements. The most recent national example is the No Child Left Behind Act (2000). For more information, see National Commission on Excellence in Education (1983). ***See also*** Accountability (education)

School Violence   Verbal and physical aggression, uncivil behavior, bullying, and criminal acts in schools, which impede learning and take away from a positive school climate. School violence includes not only extreme physical acts such as rape, robbery, and homicide but also verbal acts such as making threats, quarreling with peers, and gossiping. The more subtle verbal acts, present in elementary schools and increasing most rapidly in middle and high schools, are of special concern because they can lead to the escalation of more serious forms of deviant behavior and crime. Victims of school violence suffer socially, psychologically, and academically, as they are more likely to be ostracized, suffer from lowered self-esteem and heightened anxiety, and become more likely to drop out. School-based prevention and intervention strategies hold promise for reducing such behavior. For more information, see Jimmerson and Furlong (2006). ***See also*** Aggression

Scientific Management *(education)*   An approach to managing personnel and resources that is characterized by a fixed division of labor, a clear hierarchy of authority, promotion based on seniority and/or merit, absence of interpersonal relationships, and control by rules. Relationships between managers and workers are governed by a strictly top-down hierarchical structure. ***See also*** Division of Labor; Efficiency; Management; Organizational Theory

Scientific Management *(public administration)*   A workflow management theory developed by the classical thinker Frederick Winslow Taylor (1865–1915). Taylor, generally considered the "father of scientific management," pioneered time and motion studies to determine the "one best way" to achieve the fastest, most efficient, and least fatiguing production methods. Workers are conceptualized as interchangeable parts of a large, impersonal production machine. Scientific management received its greatest public sector attention when Frederick Taylor in 1912 presented its core principles to the U.S. House of Representatives. He focused on the duties of management, which include (a) relying on more systematic methods of measuring and managing work elements rather than on rule-of-thumb methods; (b) determining strategies to select, develop, and place workers in their roles in order to achieve optimal production; (c) determining ways to achieve cooperation among workers to fully implement scientific management principles and procedures; and (d) developing logical divisions of worker and manager roles and responsibilities. Classical organization theory evolved from these elements. For more information, see Berkley and Rouse (2004), and Kettl and Fesler (2005). *See also* Division of Labor; Efficiency; Management; Organizational Theory

Scientific Socialism   Karl Marx and Friedrich Engels coined this term. They used the concept to illustrate the doctrines that they developed in their critique of bourgeois society in order to distinguish these doctrines from other socialist doctrines, which they considered "utopian socialism."

The modern socialist movement dates from the publication of Marx and Engels's *Communist Manifesto* in 1848. This short publication was an important document in the history of socialism because it outlined the theoretical basis for modern socialism.

In their work, Marx and Engels explained how societies are able to advance progressively from less advanced states (e.g., feudalism) to more sophisticated ones (e.g., capitalism). In their discussion of the relationship between state and classes, Marx and Engels identified further dimensions of their "stages" view of history, which were to become the cornerstones of "scientific" socialism.

Engels regarded their work as "scientific" in that they exposed the secret of capitalism through the discovery of "surplus value" (the value that capitalists appropriate from workers' labor) and explained how capitalism would eventually be overthrown and replaced by socialism. They thought that the concept made Marxist doctrines more attractive than rival socialist doctrines by suggesting that equality and the end of exploitation were not only desirable but also inevitable.

The reason why this socialism is called "scientific socialism" (as opposed to utopian socialism) is because, as in science, observation is essential to this theory. Thus, scientific socialism presented itself as both a well-grounded method as well as a content or body of scientific conclusions, later on becoming both a theory and a practice. That this reasoning was false became evident later, as did most uses of the word *science* when applied to human actions.

For more information, see Engels, Moore, and Marx (1970), Lichtheim (1962), and Marx and Engels (1848/1969). *See also* Capitalism (political science); Marxism (political science); Socialism (political science)

Scientific Theory   A logical model or explanation for a social phenomenon. Theory can be based on experimental results or observations where a pattern emerges (inductive reasoning) or can be proposed and then tested with experiments or observations (deductive reasoning). A scientific theory is a systematic and formal expression of all previous data; it should be predictive and testable or verifiable. Based on theories, hypotheses or predictions about the social phenomena can then be developed. No such theory based on the contingency of human actions can be truly predictive. Examples of social science theories include social control theory, strain theory, and social learning theory.

Search and Seizure   A legal power given to law enforcement officers to examine and confiscate evidence believed to be related to a crime, regulated by the Fourth Amendment of the U.S. Constitution. The power is limited based on the extent of the suspect's reasonable expectation of privacy in a given situation. To search a home, law enforcement officers must demonstrate probable cause that a crime has been committed, to obtain a search warrant from a judge. Alternately, the police are not required to obtain a warrant if the property owner consents to the search. In contrast, law enforcement need only demonstrate reasonable suspicion to search a person on a street. There is no standard of proof required to search garbage at the curb as trash, as there is no reasonable expectation of privacy. Evidence in an officer's plain view can also be seized without a warrant. When an illegal search and seizure is performed, the "exclusionary rule" states that the evidence may not be used against the suspect at trial. *See also* Exclusionary Rule (political science, sociology); Fruit of the Poisonous Tree; Warrant

Secondary Data   *(education)*   Preexisting data originally collected by individuals other than the current research investigator. Often, these data are examined in a manner different from their original purpose. Secondary data may be obtained from censuses, national databases, or large surveys. *See also* Data, Extant/Existing

Secondary Data   *(sociology)*   Statistical data or other information that is processed and analyzed by people other than the researcher who originally collected those data. Primary data, in contrast, are processed and analyzed by the researcher who originally collected them. In the social sciences, secondary data are commonly analyzed from large surveys, such as the General Social Survey (GSS), the U.S. Census, and Uniform Crime Report (UCR). Secondary data are generally stored in computer databases accessible to the public or with permission to researchers or institutions. *See also* Quantitative Research

Second-Best Theory   The acceptance of beneficial suboptimal result when the optimal result cannot be obtained for a general equilibrium. It is a theory that has wide appeal in market analysis and international trade. Market-clearing conditions, which are considered to be equilibriums or optimal solutions, are usually understood to be the best conditions for efficiency (given the resource constraints). Yet there are situations when distortions and market imperfections can prevent the realization of market-clearing results or the efficient use

S

of available resources. In such situations, pricing decisions or resource allocation cannot practically reflect the standard market prescriptions. Alternatives to the primary outcomes (second best) become as attractive as, if not better than, the primary unrealized market solution.

Richard Lipsey and Kelvin Lancaster are credited with proposing the second-best theory. They argue that when one optimal equilibrium condition is not attainable, all other preconditions for equilibrium will change, so that when there is market failure in one market, the rules for price determination in other markets are affected and aggregate welfare is not optimized. The failure of simultaneous equilibriums can generate a second-best situation when there is policy intervention (new constraints) to minimize market failure or the factors that inhibit the realization of the first best.

Lipsey and Lancaster separated the Paretian optimum (theoretical) from policy constraints (taxes and subsidies) and note that optimization can be obtained by combining the constraints to achieve the second best.

Covetous market-based solutions can be considered first best, but second-best, welfare-enhancing results can arise as a result of taxes, subsidies, and regulation of markets, or the regulation of international trade through tariffs and nontariff barriers, as long as policy intervention outweighs the cost of inaction and intervention.

The new trade theory is largely an application of the theory of the second best. Additionally, customs union (integration) has been used to make the case for the second best. For example, Jacob Viner showed that the removal of tariff from imports may in actual fact result in a reduction in the efficiency of world production. Meade also showed that a customs union has parallel effects on the utility of world consumption.

The concept poses a problem for rankings. Can there be a third best, and so on? To avoid ranking ambiguities, all other suboptimal results can be classified as second best, except when there is a clear basis for structural ranking. For more information, see Lipsey and Lancaster (1956), Meade (1955), and Viner (1950). **See also** Market Failure; Trade Theory, New

Securitization   The transformation of illiquid assets into securities through financial intermediation (usually a depository institution or investment banker). These securities are otherwise known as *asset-backed securities,* for example, mortgage-backed securities (MBS) or mortgage pass through. In this form of finance, debt instruments are usually aggregated into a pool (risk consolidation) that backs the issue of new securities to investors.

Securitization through financial intermediation enables financial intermediaries to raise capital to lend to their customers while minimizing risk of default as a result of inadequate collateral. Principal and interest payments are channeled to the holders of the securities.

Securitization enhances liquidity by converting long-term illiquid investments into liquid securities. These securities normally have an active secondary market and could be used to back other securities. They are usually denominated in $1,000 within the United States, with a maturity of five years.

There are inherent risks associated with the possession of MBS. Interest rate changes have an impact on the value of the securities. The value of the securities moves in a direction opposite to interest rate. As interest rate rises, the value of the securities (usually bonds) falls, and as interest rate falls, the value of the securities rises.

Mortgages can also be prepaid without penalty, meaning that outstanding loans can be paid before their maturity. Investors will therefore have no reliable idea of future interest payments, which exposes them to a timing risk. There is also the probability of payment default by homeowners.

Some intermediaries, such as Ginnie Mae, Fannie Mae, and Freddie Mac, offer guarantees against default risk. Private sector MBS may structure default risk without primary responsibility. It becomes incumbent on investors to insure their risks if they are risk-averse.

Risks may be distributed by ranking the bankruptcy priority of securities based on superiority (subordination). For example, first default losses may be allocated to the most junior class of bond, and progressively in that order. Risks may be minimized in securitization by using an overcollateralization buffer (the difference between the principal balance on outstanding loans in the pool and the principal balance on outstanding securities). Alternatively, excess spread differential can be used—the difference between loan payments (excluding service fees) and weighted-average payments going to securities holders. For more information, see Kidwell, Blackwell, Whidbee, and Peterson (2008) and Rosen (2007). **See also** Insurance; Risk Management (economics)

Sedatives   Drugs inducing calmness and sleepiness by inhibiting the activation of the central nervous system. Also referred to as *downers* or tranquilizers, sedatives are frequently used to relieve states of anxiety and tension. The opposite of stimulants, sedatives can be classified as barbiturates and nonbarbiturates. Similar to the effects of alcohol, barbiturates can make individuals feel intoxicated and cause slurred speech. Barbiturates can cause decreased heart beat and blood pressure in a person, and when taken in excess, they lead to accidental death. **See also** Stimulants

Segmentary Lineage   A group of descendants that form a lineage of varying sizes. Lineages can be composed of the descendants of one person and expand to include dozens of generations consisting of thousands of people. These larger units are divided into smaller sections through a process of segmentation or branching.

Segmentary Societies   Societies characterized by small farming families, where there is little differentiation of social status and the lifestyle is communal—also known as a tribal society. No one individual or group is dominant within the tribe. The groups are generally autonomous, and social control and cohesion is achieved by a balancing of group power.

Segregation The environmental and organizational separation of racial or ethnic groups. After the Civil War, former slaves were granted their freedom, but laws and policies of segregation continued for approximately 100 years. The Jim Crow laws enforced policies of segregation such as the disenfranchisement of blacks. Segregation was made official policy in 1896 in the Supreme Court case of *Plessy v. Ferguson,* which established a policy of separate but equal facilities for different races. For more information, see *Plessy v. Ferguson* (1896). ***See also*** Civil Liberties; Civil Rights

Seismic The term (derived from the Greek word *seismos,* for earthquake) refers to the waves that result from cataclysmic events such as explosions, earthquakes, or similar undulations that travel through the ocean or the earth as a result of some force that generates violent movement (e.g., tectonic plate stresses). In geographical terminology, there are body waves (in the interior of the earth) and surface waves (as in ocean waves). The word is frequently used to describe "earthshaking" social and political events, such as revolutions, that render society apart.

Selective Exposure A process that occurs when people seek out information that supports their preexisting viewpoints or decisions. It is one of several related concepts of media effects theories that first emerged in the 1950s, suggesting that mass media have only a limited effect on individuals and that people engage in selective exposure based on certain variables, such as family background, social class, and education. In 1960, Klapper, after reviewing the research to date on mass media, suggested that people use these self-protective devices when dealing with mass media and that the media have less power to change people's perceptions than to reinforce them. Prior to this time, theorists suggested that the media had much more influence over individuals and that people received and reacted to messages in a uniform way. For more information, see Klapper (1960). ***See also*** Media Effects; Selective Interpretation; Selective Perception

Selective Interpretation One of several selective processes, suggesting that when individuals are exposed to a message that is not in agreement with their beliefs, they will selectively interpret some or all of the message to support their viewpoint. A well-known study of this early limited-effects theory was performed by Kendall and Wolf. When a group of subjects were exposed to a series of cartoons that satirized a bigot, nearly two thirds of them or those who were prejudiced missed the point entirely and thought that the purpose of the cartoons was to reinforce prejudice. For more information, see Kendall and Wolf (1949). ***See also*** Media Effects; Selective Exposure; Selective Perception

Selective Perception A selective process in which individuals will accept only that information that is perceived to be in accordance with their existing beliefs. Alternatively, they will scrutinize any information that is not in accordance with their beliefs, often rejecting it by finding fault with the methodology and results. Earlier studies in communications research suggested that people received messages and were affected by messages in the same way. Later selective processes research, however, suggested instead that people's perceptions and interpretations of messages were affected by their education, class, and family background. For more information, see Klapper (1960). ***See also*** Media Effects; Selective Exposure; Selective Interpretation

Self-Actualization *(education)* The neurologist Kurt Goldstein first defined self-actualization as the primary motive of organisms to realize their unique innate potential. Abraham Maslow later described self-actualization as the pinnacle of psychological development, placed at the top of his hierarchy of needs. Maslow described self-actualized people as self-accepting, problem solvers, spontaneous, and reality oriented. ***See also*** Humanistic Counseling; Humanistic Theory

Self-Actualization *(psychology)* The highest tier of Maslow's pyramid of needs, defined as a person's desire to fulfill his or her potential. For example, if a person has great artistic talent but is forced to study accounting, the person will be frustrated as a result. Maslow proposed that a person who does not get the chance to fulfill his or her potential will be frustrated because the person's drive to achieve is inhibited.

Self-actualization plays an important role in a healthy personality. Maslow classified a self-actualizing individual as a person who has a healthy personality defined by continuous personal growth. Studying well-respected and acclaimed historical figures as well as the healthiest 1% of students, Maslow identified several characteristics of self-actualizing individuals. For example, self-actualizers tend to be in touch with reality and are comfortable and relaxed dealing with it. Self-actualizers also tend to be open to new experiences and are spontaneous and uncomplicated individuals. While they enjoy few, but close friendships, they are able to distance themselves and be independent of culture as well as environment. Self-actualizers are autonomous, independent, do not require other people for approval, and have a need for privacy. Furthermore, self-actualizers derive deep satisfaction from their work, while also having more "peak experiences," also referred to as "emotional highs," than other people. Self-actualizers tend to have a philosophical and nonhostile humor, while having clear ethical definitions of good and evil. Finally, self-actualizers demonstrate a balance between polar aspects of personality; for example, they can be both rational as well as intuitive. ***See also*** Self-Efficacy (psychology)

Self-Concept One's conception and perception of one's self that is based on cognitive processing of data or information about the self. These perceptions are neutral

S

and only become value laden (labeled as positive or negative) when based on social comparison or integrated with other self-constructs such as self-worth. ***See also*** Self-Efficacy (education, psychology); Self-Esteem

Self-Defense   A justification defense for committing a criminal act where it is argued that another reasonable person would have acted in the same way. The defendant must have acted with the realistic belief that he or she was in imminent danger of harm or death and had no other viable way to escape the situation.

Self-Disclosure   The act of disclosing an aspect of a therapist's personal background or perceptions to a client. The ethical consensus among practitioners is that self-disclosure carries more risks than benefits and only should be undertaken when a clear benefit to the client is present. Research has shown mixed results when applying self-disclosure in therapy.

Self-Discrepancy Theory   This theory proposes that incongruence between aspects of the self leads to either dejection-related or agitation-related emotions (Higgins, 1987). Incongruence between a person's actual self and ideal self is indicated by a lack of positive outcomes and will result in dejection-related emotions, such as disappointment and sorrow. Incongruence between a person's actual self and ought self is indicated by the presence of negative outcomes and will result in agitation-related emotions, such as threat and anxiety. Although it is similar to the concept of cognitive dissonance, self-discrepancy theory is novel because it is the first theory attempting to predict which type of emotions would result from discrepancies within the self. For more information, see Higgins (1987). ***See also*** Cognitive Dissonance (psychology)

Self-Efficacy (*education*)   Bandura defined this term as one's self-perceived ability at a task. Two aspects make self-efficacy a unique concept. First, it is personal. While influenced by opinions or comparison with others, this is an individual perception. Second, self-efficacy is task specific, so a person could consider himself or herself a mediocre skier but an excellent organizer.

According to Bandura (1977), self-efficacy is influenced by four main factors:

1. *Enactive attainment or mastery practice:* The more we practice, the more skillful we become. Greater skill increases involvement in that activity, and there is an upward spiral in mastery, choice, and self-efficacy.

2. *Modeling and vicarious learning:* As we see others engage in an activity, we compare ourselves with them. If we see ourselves as similar, we are more likely to attempt the activity (If he can do it, I can). Similarly, we watch others execute various subskills and try to mimic their behavior.

Conversely, we may watch others attempt maneuvers and fail; after watching them, we avoid similar actions, trying variations to prevent failure.

3. *Social persuasion:* When others either encourage or discourage a person's behaviors or choices, it may affect choice or level of involvement. The more power a person has in our life, the greater may be the effect of their opinions.

4. *Physiological arousal:* There are signals from our body as we engage in activities. Some are obvious, such as sweating, increased heartbeat, or pain. Others are more subtle but equally as effective in influencing our behaviors and decisions—such as production of endorphins or adrenalin.

Self-efficacy can be distinguished from self-esteem, self-concept, and self-worth semantically. Self-esteem encompasses feelings about oneself, such as pride or shame. Self-concept is based on cognitively processing data or information about oneself. Self-worth is related to how valuable a person feels. For example, a person may feel a sense of value within the family unit, either because the family expresses deep caring and commitment or because the family is made better because of skills or actions contributed by the individual (or both). Of these four constructs, *self-efficacy* is the most task specific, and therefore the least resistant to outside forces. The other three are more global and more vulnerable to a single experience. However, it is clear that the four self-constructs are interwoven, and each is affected by changes in the other three. For more information, see Bandura (1977). ***See also*** Self-Concept; Self-Esteem; Social Learning Theory (education)

Self-Efficacy (*psychology*)   The central construct of Bandura's (2001) social-cognitive theory. Self-efficacy refers to a person's belief whether he or she is capable of achieving a certain outcome. When self-efficacy is high, a person believes that he or she has the capacity to respond adeptly to a situation. When self-efficacy is low, a person believes that he or she lacks the capacity to adequately respond to a situation. The perception of self-efficacy is subjective and situation dependent; that is, a person may have high self-efficacy in one situation and low self-efficacy in another. For more information, see Bandura (2001). ***See also*** Modeling

Self-Esteem   Beliefs and feelings about self. In 1890, James defined self-esteem mathematically as successes divided by failures. Self-esteem is currently defined as one's satisfaction or happiness with self, regard for self, or belief in one's importance. For more information, see James (1890). ***See also*** Self-Concept; Self-Efficacy (psychology)

Self-Fulfilling Prophecy   The notion that one's beliefs or attitudes about oneself or others become reality. Used across many contexts, the self-fulfilling prophecy has been used to explain many phenomena. For example, stereotypes might be explained by the self-fulfilling prophecy when a person holds certain beliefs about a group and then treats persons belonging to the group accordingly, which, in turn, reinforces the initial stereotype. Similarly, a person's self-concept is supported when a person behaves in a way that is in accordance with how the person has conceptualized his or her own self. *See also* Self-Discrepancy Theory

Self-Incrimination Confessing or giving information that implicates oneself in an offense. The Fifth Amendment of the U.S. Constitution grants protection from incriminating oneself. Law enforcement officers are not permitted to use physical or psychological coercion during an interrogation. Prior to questioning a person in custody, the police must read the Miranda warning. For more information, see *Miranda v. Arizona* (1966). *See also* Miranda Rights

Self-Organization When social animals create their own ordered social structure or system. The system evolves without being guided by outside sources, and its power is generally decentralized. Examples include the Underground Railroad network, which aided fugitive slaves, and Critical Mass, the bicycle group that rides through cities around the world reminding people that cities are not bicycle friendly.

Self-Perception The theory that humans learn about themselves by inference, taking note of their attitudes, behaviors, emotions, and various internal states as they would observe those of other people. The theory was first advanced in the 1960s by the social psychologist Daryl J. Bern (also known by the surname Bem) as what he defined as "an alternative interpretation of cognitive dissonance phenomena."

The individual who observes himself or herself, Bem wrote in 1970, uses a self-selection rule: "What must my attitude be if I am willing to behave in this fashion in this situation?"

Though Bern viewed self-perception as key to an individual's self-knowledge, he and researchers who continue to study his paradigm caution that self-perceptions are not always rooted in reality but in the unconscious mind. Timothy Wilson and Elizabeth Dunn, for instance, suggest that to truly benefit from self-observation, people need to increase their cognizance of their personalities and nonconscious motives. For more information, see Bem (1967), Bern (1972), and Wilson and Dunn (2004). *See also* Cognitive Dissonance (communication); Perception (communication, psychology)

Self-Regulation The term refers to personal goal-directed behavior while learning or performing a task. This includes several other cognitive activities. Self-monitoring includes decisions about planning and organizing one's work, taking breaks, and knowing when

and where to seek help. Self-evaluation is determining one's progress toward goal achievement and appraisal of the quality of work completed thus far. This reflection or analysis influences problem solving, pacing, and changes in planning. Although self-regulation is an internal process, external cues may be influential, including comparing self with others, learning vicariously, and seeking and receiving help. *See also* Self-Concept; Self-Efficacy (education); Self-Esteem

Self-Report A research technique based on a person's own account of his or her behavior. The self-report technique often involves the participant completing a questionnaire. Several limitations of the self-report technique can be identified. For example, a person may bias his or her answers by trying to appear more socially fitting, which is called the social desirability bias. Other limitations include the misunderstanding of questions and the language used to phrase certain questions, which may bias responses. *See also* Survey (psychology)

Self-Report Studies A research methodology used by social scientists to learn about the behaviors and activities of an individual. The approach is commonly used when asking about involvement in crime or deviance. The survey or questionnaire is generally confidential and anonymous, to increase the likelihood that the respondent will answer honestly. *See also* Qualitative Research; Quantitative Research; Research Methodology

Semantic Network A knowledge representation modeling human cognition. In a semantic network, units of information are represented by nodes and are interconnected via links. Semantic networks operate on the assumption that concepts that have similar meaning are closely linked together. For example, "nurse" and "hospital" would be closely linked as they tend to be strongly associated. Due to spreading activation in the network, when the word *nurse* is activated, the word *hospital* would be more easily remembered than a less closely linked word, such as *moon*. For more information, see Collins and Loftus (1975). *See also* Cognition

Semantics The study or science of meaning as it relates to language. It is primarily the study of relationships between signs and symbols and what they represent. It is also the meaning or the interpretation of a word, sentence, or other language form. It is the study of abstract meaning. It is the study of linguistic development by classifying and examining changes in meaning and form.

A synonym for *semantics* is *significs*. Significs is the branch of semiotics dealing with the relations between signs and what they denote.

In linguistics, semantics had its beginnings in France and Germany in the 1820s, when the meanings of words were recognized as significant features in the growth of language. Among the foremost linguistic semanticists of the 20th century are Gustaf Stern, Jose Trier, B. L. Whorf,

S

Uriel Weinreich, Stephen Ullmann, Thomas Sebeok, Noam Chomsky, Jerrold Katz, and Charles Osgood.

Transformational grammar has emerged as a branch of semantics. This theory, developed largely by George Lakoff and James McCawley, is termed *generative semantics*. Transformational grammar has reemphasized the role of meaning in linguistic analysis.

According to Stephen G. Pulman, a perennial problem in semantics is the delineation of its subject matter. The term *meaning* can be used in a variety of ways, and only some of them correspond to the usual understanding of the scope of linguistic or computational semantics. A standard assumption in computationally oriented semantics is that knowledge of the meaning of a sentence can be equated with knowledge of its truth conditions: that is, knowledge of what the world would be like if the sentence was true.

Pulman believes that the most pressing needs of semantic theory are to find ways to achieve a wider and more robust coverage of real data. Recent work in semantics has shifted emphasis away from the purely sentence-based approach. For more information, see Pulman, Richie, Russell, and Black (1991). *See also* Language; Meaning

Semantic Selection   An indefinitely large set of alternative phrases that individuals may choose to use in their communication patterns. Semantic selection also refers to a broad range of grammatical alternatives, while allowing different metaphors for different nouns, verbs, and adjectives. It is based on a more in-depth knowledge of the domain or the language, is rather specific to the group of people who are familiar with this domain, and is not necessarily intended for general inference. This may present a problem with translation when the individual who speaks the given language is not familiar with the semantic selection alternatives and the translated phrases do not convey the same message as intended by the original sender. It can also produce various distortions when translated verbatim: The original message is encoded into meanings that differ from the domain of the language it was sent in. The knowledge contained in the domain of a given language and its grammar and syntax was assumed to be encapsulated and not changeable over time; however, in languages that are more dynamic and evolving, the domain knowledge changes all the time, which makes it even more of a challenge in a translation setting. The evolution of the semantic selection requires constant modifications in the application domain to allow for the most updated translation options. The modification itself is a complex process, as it requires detail orientation toward the variety of sources and the consequences of the changes. Some linguists refer to the semantic selection as a "meaning" that serves to define the relationship of signs to other signs in the message matrix or in the connection with the concept of "structure" of a language code, which represents a linguistic unit. Other linguists view the meaning of semantic selection in terms of the total linguistic context within which a given sign appears. For more information, see Haase and Stojanovic (2005) and Computer Laboratory (2009). *See also* Semantics

Semiotics *(education)*   The study of signs. In a broad sense, signs are anything that can stand for something else, such as words, images, sounds, objects, discourses, and text. Therefore, more precisely, semiotics studies the meanings of signs and how meanings are constructed through sign systems and their use. Semiotics allows us to understand that reality is not objective but rather constructed through meanings that are generated through codes, discourses, practices, and contexts. Semiotics owes its early development to the Swiss linguist Ferdinand de Saussure (1857–1913) and the American pragmatist philosopher Charles Sanders Peirce (1839–1914).

Saussure built his semiotic theory around the grammatical and syntactical properties of language. Shifting from the traditional sociolinguistic attention to how meaning varied over time, he focused on the differences among signs at a fixed point in time. His focus on differences yielded the observation that difference itself is the source of meaning. Saussure is also credited with establishing the basic distinction between a symbol that carries meaning (signifier) and a referent (signified). For him, a sign was the unity of signified and signifier. Followers of Saussurean approaches to semiotics were known as *structuralists*. Those who have drawn inspiration from Saussure yet transcended the key limitations of structuralism (e.g., Derrida, Barthes, Eco) are known as poststructuralists.

In contrast to Saussure, Peirce viewed meaning as emergent in the responses people direct toward signs. Peirce's model of signs is a triadic one, including the sign vehicle, the object to which the sign vehicle refers, and its interpretant—which roughly refers to the sense that is made of the relationship between sign vehicle and object. Peirce's theories also incorporated three types of signs: symbols (e.g., words), index (e.g., smoke as an indication of fire), and icon (e.g., photographs or reality-resembling sculptures). Followers of Peirce's semiotics are now numerous among proponents of pragmatism in philosophy, symbolic interactionism in social psychology, and social semiotics in cultural studies. For more information, see Chandler (2007). *See also* Pragmatics; Semantics; Text

Semiotics *(media studies)*   The system of implicitly and explicitly agreed-on signs within a community by which meaning is made. *Semiotics* is derived from the Greek *semeioun*, meaning "to interpret as a sign." It came to acquire its current meaning in the late 19th and 20th centuries with the work of the American logician, philosopher, and mathematician Charles Sanders Peirce and the Swiss linguist Ferdinand de Saussure. The sign proper is conventional, not natural; that is, its meaning is determined by a society's implicit or explicit agreement to assign a certain hermeneutic value to a thing. Colors, gestures, objects, and all phenomena thus behave like languages, shifting their meaning across time and place and according to context. Semiotics collapses the division between the study of language proper and that of any system of constructing and assigning meaning. One of Saussure's initial steps was to divorce the word as a linguistic sign from its referent: Thus, language denotes not objects in the real world but concepts, thereby becoming a self-referential system of signs that shift in relation to each other as new words are coined and as old words acquire new nuances and meanings. Saussure also emphasized that meaning is measured by the extent to which signs differ from one another. Thus, the meaning of *man* is measured by the extent to which it differs from *woman, lord, boy, animal,* and so on. Meaning is thus relational rather than intrinsic. Elements can relate to each other through contrast (a paradigmatic relation, as in *a* or *b*) or through association (a syntagmatic relation, as in *a* and *b*). This means that one cannot study individual signs in isolation from each other but as part of a system of meaning. In current contexts, semiotics applies the above principles to the study of all unspoken conventions in social life, such as body language, fashion, advertising, visual media, animal behavior, and so on. ***See also*** Discourse; Structuralism (education, media studies)

Senate   At the federal level, the upper house of Congress. As outlined in Article 1 of the U.S. Constitution, Congress is made up of two Houses, the Senate and the House of Representatives. The Senate provides equal representation (two Senators) for each state, while the House provides representation proportional to a state's population. Senators are elected to six-year terms and the House representatives to two-year terms. The Senate holds the exclusive powers of making treaties and approval of nominations to the president's cabinet, appointment of federal judges, and ambassadorships. In addition, only the Senate can try a public official for a crime against the United States. A bill can be introduced in either House, except for bills raising revenue, which can only be introduced in the House of Representatives. The name *senate* is derived from the Roman Senate (Latin *senex,* meaning old man), or board of wise old men. ***See also*** Congress; House of Representatives

Sensorimotor Stage   Piaget's first stage of child development, occurring from birth to 2 years of age. During the sensorimotor stage, children explore and learn about the world via their congenital senses rather than mental operations. This stage is responsible for the development of spatial abilities in the child. The milestone of the sensorimotor stage is the development of symbolic thought, which is exemplified in the concept of object permanence. For more information, see Piaget (1954). ***See also*** Object Permanence

Sensory Adaptation   The fading sensitivity to an ongoing sensory stimulus. The term applies to all the senses. An individual will experience a change in sensation over time, due to a steady decline in response to the sensory stimulation. For example, if one were to listen to prolonged noise, that noise would be experienced as less loud over time. Sensory adaptation is based on sensory neurons responding less over time. ***See also*** Just Noticeable Difference; Perception (psychology)

Sentencing   The phase of the criminal trial in which a judge gives the guilty defendant a sanction. Types of sentences include incarceration, monetary fines, and probation or other community supervision. When multiple crimes have been committed, the sentences can be served together, concurrently, where the period of incarceration equals the length of the longest sentence or the sentences can be served consecutively, where the length of time served is the total of all sentences. There are several sentencing models, including indeterminate sentencing, where a minimum and a maximum length of incarceration are stated and after serving the minimum sentence the person may be released on parole or other type of supervision based, in part, on institutional behavior. Determinate sentences provide a fixed length of incarceration. Mandatory sentences, such as three-strike laws, allow the judge no discretion regarding the length of the sentence—once convicted of a given offense, the sentence has been legislatively set. There are a number of goals of sentencing today, including general and specific deterrence, incapacitation, retribution, rehabilitation, and restitution. ***See also*** Determinate Sentence; Indeterminate Sentence; Mandatory Sentence; Punishment (sociology); Retribution

Separation Anxiety   A part of a child's development whereby the child develops a stronger preference for the primary caregiver and becomes emotionally distressed when separated from that caregiver. While children of the age of 2 to 3 months do not seem to express a preference for any caregiver, when reaching 6 to 8 months, a child will develop a distinct preference for the primary caregiver, which is often the mother. In conjunction with this preference for the primary caregiver, the child also develops a stronger attachment to that person and thus becomes emotionally distressed when that person leaves the child. Separation anxiety increases until it peaks at approximately 14 to 18 months, after which it tends to decline. For more information, see American Psychiatric Association, *Diagnostic and Statistical Manual of Mental Disorders* (fourth edition, text revision, 2000). ***See also*** Insecure Attachment

Separation of Powers   A democratic principle that limits the powers of any one branch of government. In the United States, it is also known as a system of "checks and balances" and was deliberately written into the U.S. Constitution. The framers developed the U.S. system in

S

an effort to avoid the tyrannical leadership emblematic of Great Britain at that time. Powers are separated among the three branches of the federal government (executive, legislature, and judiciary), and between the federal and state governments. There is a list of enumerated concurrent powers, those shared with the states, and exclusive powers, those exercised only by the federal government or the states, in the Constitution. Concurrent powers are held in common between the federal and state governments but otherwise operate in a mutually exclusive manner. If a conflict arises regarding a concurrent power, according to the supremacy clause, Article 6 of the U.S. Constitution, the federal interest will prevail. ***See also*** Executive Branch; Judicial; Legislative Branch

Separatism   A political movement that favors the autonomy and sovereignty of a nation that is presently a part of a larger sovereign state. Separatist movements are often based on ethnic, cultural, religious, or economic lines. Separatist movements can have the potential to lead to revolution and secession. For example, separatism was the leading cause of the American Civil War (1861–1865). The North and South had a major economic difference over the dependence on the institution of slavery for the health of the regional economy (Southern cotton plantations). Following the election in 1860 of the Republican candidate Abraham Lincoln (who did not win one Southern electoral vote), South Carolina, followed by Mississippi, Florida, Alabama, Georgia, Louisiana, and Texas, seceded from the Union. In recent world history, separatism occurred after the fall of the Soviet Union in 1991. For example, in Tadzhikistan, fighting broke out among Communist supporters—the "Rouge Khmers"—in the North and their mostly Sunnite Muslim opponents in the South. Russian Army intervention, on behalf of the North, saved the fledgling country. Into the 21st century, separatist movements continue in many nations, including Puerto Rico, the Basque movement in Spain and France, Ireland, and Canada (Western separatism in Alberta and French in Québec).

The opposite of separatism is nationalism, a political ideology that encourages the uniting of nations into a common statehood. Similarly, annexation, the opposite of secession, takes place when a geographical area is declared part of a state's sovereign territory. For more information, see Spencer (1998). ***See also*** Nationalism; Sovereignty

Sequester   During a trial, members of the trial jury are not allowed to go home at the end of the day but have to stay in a hotel so as to enable the court to limit the jurors' access to other people and media. The goal is to minimize possible bias in the outcome of the case. The court pays the costs of the hotel and all meals. ***See also*** Trial

Serial Murder/Serial Killer   Several murders committed over a period of time of weeks, months, or years by a single individual or team of people. Most serial killers have diagnosable psychological disorders, particularly an antisocial personality disorder (more commonly called *psychopathy*). Many serial killers exhibit "the terrible triad" of childhood: bedwetting, cruelty to animals, and fire setting. Serial killing is often sexually motivated. The offender fantasizes about the murder prior to killing, and victims often represent someone who earlier in the killer's life caused him or her pain. Organized serial killers, generally socially proficient, usually plan the murders, move their victims (either alive or dead), and take a memento or trophy from the victim to remember the event. In comparison, disorganized serial killers are generally not socially competent and may demonstrate noticeable mental illness. ***See also*** Psychopathy

Serial Position Curve   A U-shaped curve depicting memory for list items. Generally, items presented at the beginning and end of the list are remembered better than items in the middle. Increased recall of early items is referred to as the primacy effect. As there is greater opportunity to rehearse early items, there is greater likelihood that early items will be committed to memory and thus remembered better. Increased recall of late items is referred to as the recency effect. As recently presented items are still present in auditory short-term memory, recall of such items is improved. ***See also*** Short-Term Memory (STM)

Service Learning   A teaching and learning strategy allowing students to work cooperatively to improve their communities by addressing real-world issues and social problems. Students actively participate in community projects to meet instructional objectives and state content standards and to develop a sense of civic responsibility.

Set Induction   Also known as *anticipatory set,* it is an educational term used to describe the introduction in a lesson plan. The purpose is to garner students' interest in the learning activities, to focus their attention on the objectives of the lesson, and to motivate them to want to learn. ***See also*** Lesson Planning

Severance   A process in civil and criminal law when a judge separates a case into two or more separate trials or when a decision is made to hear multiple defendants' cases separately. ***See also*** Joinder

Sex Discrimination   Discrimination against an individual based on his or her gender. Sex discrimination, which includes sexual harassment, is prohibited in educational programs and activities receiving federal funds under Title IX of the Education Amendments of 1972. Title IX applies to most public schools, colleges, and universities. Sexual harassment includes behaviors ranging from requests for sexual favors to conditions that create a hostile environment for individuals of either gender, including same-sex harassment. Other types of discrimination that are prohibited under Title IX include discrimination based on pregnancy and failure to provide equal opportunity in athletics. For more information, see ED.gov. (2008). **See also** Sexual Harassment

Sexism The attitudes and beliefs of individuals as they relate to a person's gender. These beliefs and attitudes influence behaviors toward others and, in the educational setting, result in practices that are not gender fair. Examples of such practices include traditional role models in teaching, including women as elementary teachers and men as math and social science teachers; few women occupying leadership positions in education; certain courses being thought of as gender specific, such as home economics for females only and shop and agriculture classes for males only; students not encouraged to explore career and vocational paths viewed as nontraditional for their gender; and textbooks that do not depict an equal number of stories with male and female characters. Sexism generally means that an individual is being judged or treated as inferior due to gender. Usually, the individual's worth and value are viewed as less because of their gender.

Sex Offense/Crime A sexual act that is criminal because of physical coercion or a lack of consent to participate in the act. Common sex crimes include rape, sexual assault, child sexual abuse, marital rape, exhibitionism and voyeurism, sexual harassment, prostitution, and sex with animals. Ownership or viewing of child pornography is also a sex crime. Megan's law requires sex offenders to register with the local law enforcement when they are released from prison and move into an area. Parents of children in local schools and neighbors are then notified of the offender's presence. Many jurisdictions have adopted laws that prohibit sex offenders from living within a certain distance of where children congregate, such as schools or playgrounds. Most recently, penalties for sex offenders have been increased, with some states requiring confinement (civil commitment) in a psychiatric institution after serving a prison sentence. **See also** Sexual Offender

Sexual Harassment Sexually offensive demands, suggestions, or actions in a working environment that are unwelcome and often repeated by someone in a superior position to a subordinate. Title VII of the Civil Rights Act of 1964 recognizes two types of sexual harassment. Quid pro quo sexual harassment occurs when a subordinate receives favorable treatment in exchange for sexual favors. Hostile environment sexual harassment occurs when factors in the work environment severely and pervasively interfere with an employee's performance. **See also** Civil Rights Act of 1964

Sexual Offender A person who commits a crime of a sexual nature against another person. For example, forcible rape, statutory rape, and child sexual assault are types of sexual offending. Four different categories of sexual offenders have been classified by the MTC: R3 (Knight & Prentky, 1987). The pervasively angry rapist, also referred to as the anger retaliation type, can be characterized by aggression and violence. The attack lacks sexual arousal, and the victim is often mutilated as genital parts are cut, torn, or bitten. The motivation for the attack is primarily anger. Nonsadistic rapists, on the other hand, assault a person because of sexual arousal or motivation. While aggression may be part of the assault, the main attack is motivated to demonstrate the sexual prowess of the offender. Nonsadistic rapists are frequently described as shy and lonesome people who may not be socially adept. The sexually motivated rapist displays both sexual and aggressive motivations in his attacks. The offender believes that the victim enjoys being assaulted and that resistance to the assault is a game. This category of offender often displays antisocial behavior from an early age. The fourth category of offender is the impulse-opportunistic rapist, who assaults a person because the situation presents itself. That is, the assault may be committed within the context of another offense, such as a burglary. For more information, see Knight and Prentky (1987). **See also** Offender/Offense

Sexual Response Cycle The four stages of human sexual response. Based on observations and interviews with people, Masters and Johnson (1966) identified the following four stages. The first stage is the excitement phase, during which physical arousal increases quickly. This arousal is indicated by increased muscle tension, breathing, and heart rate, as well as increase in blood pressure. Due to vasocongestion, the enlargement of blood vessels, the penis erects, and the clitoris becomes harder and swells, while the vagina becomes lubricated. During the second stage, the plateau phase, physiological arousal still increases but at a notably reduced rate. For example, in women, the vaginal entry becomes tighter. The majority of men may secrete a small drop of fluid at the top of the penis. This drop may hold a small amount of sperm but is not the same as ejaculate. Depending on the length of foreplay, the sexual arousal may vary and fluctuate in men and women. The third stage is the orgasm stage, during which arousal is at its highest point. Orgasm results in muscular contractions and spasms in the pelvic region and in a male, ejaculation of semen. Though women may be less likely than men to experience orgasm during intercourse, they are more likely to be multiorgasmic—that is, capable of having more than one orgasm. The final stage of the sexual response cycle is the resolution phase, during which levels of arousal return back to normal. After climax, men often experience a refractory period—that is, a time during which the male does not respond to stimulation. For more information, see Masters and Johnson (1966). **See also** Observation (sociology)

Sexual Stratification Based on a person's gender, males and females are directed into hierarchical rankings

S

in society. Rewards such as power and wealth as well as inequalities are based on gender. Gender determines one's status and role; gender roles depend on cultural norms and can vary between societies.

Shared Powers   Powers shared in a separation-of-powers government. In the United States, the three branches of government at the federal level (executive, legislative, judicial) share the power to make laws and govern the nation, but each "check and balance" the other. Shared powers can also refer to "concurrent powers." Concurrent powers are held in common between the federal and state governments but otherwise operate in a mutually exclusive manner. If a conflict arises regarding a concurrent power, according to the supremacy clause, Article 6 of the U.S. Constitution, the federal interest will prevail. Examples of concurrent powers include the powers to collect taxes, borrow money, build public works, charter banks, establish courts, assist agriculture and industry, and protect public health. ***See also*** Concurrent Powers; Separation of Powers

Sheriff   A county's top law enforcement officer. There are about 3,000 county sheriffs' offices in the United States. The responsibilities of a sheriff's department vary according to the size and population density of the county. Duties generally include patrol, response to residents' calls, and criminal investigation. Sheriffs' offices may also serve summons, provide court security, and operate the county jail.

Shield   A substantial mass of metamorphic rock located at the center of a continent. One of the most significant shields is the Canadian Shield, which can be found over a large region in central Canada. As shields are found at the most interior layers of continents, they are sometimes referred to as continental shields.

Shield Laws   Legislation intended to protect journalists or other media professionals from being forced to appear as witnesses in court actions, to divulge confidential information, or to identify sources with whom they have interacted under an expectation of confidentiality. Shield laws establish a form of evidentiary privilege, providing that a reporter cannot be compelled by a subpoena or other court order to testify about a news story or the sources on which it was based.

In 1972, in the case of *Branzburg v. Hayes,* the U.S. Supreme Court held that the press has no constitutional right to withhold confidential information in a court proceeding. However, the case also provides that when seeking to compel the disclosure of such information, the government must "convincingly show a substantial relation between the information sought and a subject of overriding and compelling state interest." In the United States, no federal shield law exists, and state protections vary from one jurisdiction to the next. When this opinion was written, shield laws existed in 32 states and the District of Columbia. Three others offered qualified protection to journalists, while 15 states offered no shield law protection. Some existing shield laws apply only to civil, and not criminal, actions. Others recognize the journalist's right not to reveal confidential sources but do not protect the withholding of other information. In some states, the shield law has been codified; in others, it exists solely by state court precedent.

The propriety of shield laws remains a matter of legal and political controversy. Proponents insist that news gatherers should be allowed to do their jobs without the threat of government interference. Detractors argue that free speech protections should apply equally to all and that the government should not create special privileges for a protected class. In recent years, federal shield bills have been introduced in Congress without success. For more information, see *Branzburg v. Hayes* (1972). ***See also*** Journalism

Shock Probation/Shock Incarceration   A type of split sentence where offenders spend a brief amount of time in prison before being released on probation. The purpose is to demonstrate the seriousness and difficult conditions of prison so as to promote successful probation on release. One type of shock incarceration is "boot camp," where young or first-time offenders are briefly (from three to six months) placed in a facility where they are made to participate in intense physical activity and mandatory education and/or treatment programs. The military-like training is designed to build self-confidence, improve decision-making skills, instill anger management, and instill socialization skills. The point is to "shock" offenders so that they do not want to return and prefer to remain uninvolved with crime on release. ***See also*** Community-Based Corrections

Short-Term Memory (STM)   A temporary memory store in which information is held for a brief time. Information in short-term memory is rapidly lost if information is not transferred into long-term memory via, for example, rehearsal. The capacity of short-term memory has been identified as "seven, plus or minus two," which is also referred to as "The Magical Number Seven" (Miller, 1956). Recent research has indicated that information can be transferred into long-term memory via processes other than rehearsal and that semantic encoding may also take place. These findings indicate that short-term memory is more than a mere storage space and may actively be involved in information processing. Thus, the concept of short-term memory has been replaced with the theory of working memory (Baddeley, 2001). For more information, see Baddeley (2001) and Miller (1956). ***See also*** Long-Term Memory (LTM)

Signal Detection Theory   A psychophysical measure to investigate decision making based on sensory input. Signal detection theory is based on two measures: the individual's sensory sensitivity, also referred to as *d*, and the individual's criterion for acting on the sensory information provided, β. To measure these, an individual's responses under two different conditions are required. For example, in a visual experiment, the person may be asked to respond whether he or she has observed weak light (referred to as the signal) or no light (referred to as noise). As either a signal or noise was presented and the person responds that there either has or has not been a light, there can be four different types of responses. The correct responses can either be a hit, in which there was a signal and the individual indicated such, or a correct rejection, if there was no stimulus present. With regard to incorrect responses, there can either be a false alarm, when a person responds that there has been a stimulus when there has not been one. Alternatively, there can be a miss, when the stimulus was present but the person indicated that there was none.

There are two main advantages to signal detection theory. First, it provides a precise tool to convey what is encompassed by a stimulus, for example, by containing the spatial distribution of the stimulus, as well as how the stimulus changes over time. The second advantage of signal detection theory is its acknowledgment that perceptual measurements can also be influenced by nonsensory influences. Importantly, signal detection theory can provide measures for both sensory and nonsensory factors. Signal detection theory has been applied to other nonsensory decision-making contexts, such as memory, anxiety, and eyewitness identification. ***See also*** Just Noticeable Difference; Perception (psychology)

Simulations   Educational technology programs that model real-life problem-solving situations, particularly those dangerous or inaccessible to students. Immersed in such virtual environments, students learn skills for collaboration as well as solving complex problems. While sometimes interchangeably used, simulations and microworlds are different in two major ways. Simulations present ill-structured problems in extensive environments of data and resources, whereas microworlds embody the simplest models of domains such as mathematics or science and focus on their central principles. In addition, microworlds adapt to students' current cognitive states and offer a point of entry appropriate for students, whereas simulations usually do not.

Single-Case Research   Research that investigates the effect of an experimental treatment on one or a few research participants (Johnson & Christensen, 2008). It is frequently used in clinical settings where the goal is to evaluate a treatment for a particular individual rather than to determine the average effect for a population. There are several popular designs in single-case research. First is the *A-B-A-B design,* in which the letter A stands for baseline or nontreatment period, and B stands for treatment period. Multiple measurements of the outcome variable are taken within each period. Efficacy of the treatment is indicated by a high-low-high-low pattern (or a low-high-low-high pattern) of behavior (i.e., the behavior changes each time the treatment is administered, and it reverts to baseline when the treatment is

removed). If the behavior is not one that should revert, this design should not be used. Instead, the second design, the *multiple-baseline design,* should be used with three or four participants. For example, in Phase 1, baseline behavior is measured for three participants, and then the onset of treatment is staggered across the participants (i.e., in Phase 2 the treatment begins for Person 1, in Phase 3 the treatment begins for Person 2, and in Phase 4 the treatment begins for Person 3). Treatment efficacy is established when a change in behavior occurs only when the treatment is successively administered. Reversal is not needed because the treatment continues once started. Third is the *changing-criterion design.* Here, baseline performance is established, and a treatment condition is administered following the initial successful performance. Then, in successive stages, the participant's behavior is gradually altered by progressively increasing the criterion for success until the desired performance level is attained. For more information, see Johnson and Christensen (2008). ***See also*** Experimental Research Designs

Single-Party System   One in which one party only is allowed to hold legislative positions. The Communist Party in Cuba and China would be examples. Single-party systems are often associated with dictatorships, while two-party and multiparty systems are more often associated with democracies. The two-party approach is practiced in the United States and Great Britain and occurs when two political parties compete for influence and power in government. A multiparty system exists when a government's legislature consists of three or more political parties. Shifting coalitions and alliances are commonly formed in an effort to have political objectives met. ***See also*** Dictatorship; Two-Party System

Site *(geography)*   A specific physical location, encompassing both the location itself and the immediate surroundings. Usually referring to a particular place, a site can be used to classify an event or a structure, at either single or multiple locations.

Site *(sociology)*   A place or location of an event, structure, or object. A site can be the location of a future structure (construction site) as well as a virtual location (Web site). An archaeological site is a place where evidence of past activity, such as life or civilization, is collected.

Situated Cognition   The theory that meaningful learning takes place in complex, authentic situations, not in isolation. The interaction of learners with these situations influences their ability to develop a meaningful understanding of new concepts and skills and to transfer new skills to other relevant situations. Providing students with opportunities to allow the context of a situation to guide their learning more closely simulates how people learn in real-world situations. For more information, see Brown, Collins, and Duguid (1989).

S

Situational Crime Prevention   Based on the theory that crime is a rational decision, the approach considers the site where the crime is occurring and institutes strategies to reduce the opportunities for crime to occur there. Making the target less attractive is one approach to preventing crime, as is enlisting a capable guardian to watch over the target. A site can also be designed so as to reduce the probability of crime. Target-hardening techniques, such as building fences and installing lights, will increase the effort required to commit the crime. The rewards of criminal activity can also be reduced, for example, by attaching dye packs that explode when tampered with, making the item virtually unusable or sellable. The likelihood of identifying the perpetrator can be increased with tools such as caller identification systems, by publishing the names of prostitutes' customers in the newspaper, and so on. *See also* Operant Conditioning

Skinner Box   An experimental setting in which operant conditioning in animals is investigated. A Skinner Box, named after B. F. Skinner, usually comprises a small, enclosed space in which an animal can make responses while the consequences are controlled by the experimenter. For example, in experiments using rats, the typical setup of a Skinner Box would include a lever that the rat can push and from which it may receive food as a consequence. *See also* Experiment; Operant Conditioning

Slander   A type of defamation of an entity or a false spoken statement purposefully stated or implied to be fact that harms the reputation of a person, business, group, product, or government. Slander differs from libel, which is defamation in print or communicated through another type of media. *See also* Libel

Slang   Words or expressions not accepted as formal language but used often in everyday communication. Slang is more likely to be spoken than written and can reflect regional origins. Some people consider those who use slang to be undereducated or jargon-vulgar; certain slang words and expressions are thought to be offensive. *See also* Jargon

Sleep Apnea   A sleep disorder that is characterized by a person experiencing difficulties in sleeping due to interruptions in breathing. Following interruptions in breathing, a person gasps for air and, as a result, frequently awakens. In a person suffering from sleep apnea, the interruptions in breathing last more than 10 seconds and may occur several hundred times during one night. Sleep apnea is frequently accompanied by noisy snoring and occurs in 2% of females and 4% of males. *See also* REM Sleep

Sleeper Effect   When a message that initially carries little impact on an individual becomes stronger over time. This is opposite to the findings of most communications research, which suggest that the potency of a message decreases over time. It was first identified in 1949 by Carl Hovland, Lumsdaine, and Sheffield, when they looked at the effects of World War II propaganda films on army recruits. The sleeper effect occurs when there is a dissociation-discounting cue—for example, the message is presented by a nonreliable source, and so at first, the message is discounted. Over time, however, the message gains in potency as the message is dissociated from its source and the memory of the message does not decay as quickly as the memory of the source. For more information, see Hovland, Lumsdaine, and Sheffield (1949). *See also* Dissociation

Small Group   The study of communication within a group consisting of a limited number of participants is usually grounded in systems theory. A small group comprises less than 15 people, and usually, they go through a progression that leads from social awkwardness through rule establishment, conflict, and, finally, consensus. Several different theories of small-group development have been propounded in the past 40 years or so. To take but one example, B. A. Fisher's small-group development theory (1970) outlines four stages of development: orientation, conflict, emergence, and reinforcement. (1) When group members get to know each other, they experience primary tension, which results from the awkward feeling people have before they understand the common rules and expectations that give them a sense of being comfortable. (2) The members then experience conflict centered on a task, conflict that engenders debate, disagreement, and then consensus. (3) It is in the later stages that a social structure of the group emerges, with a means of communication. (4) Finally, in the reinforcement stage, group members bolster their final decision by using supportive verbal and nonverbal communication.

Other influential theories (among hundreds) are those of Stewart Tubbs, Kurt Lewin, Marshall Scott Poole, and Bruce Tuckman. For more information, see Fisher (1970). *See also* Group; Systems Theory

Small-Group Communication   The set of communicative and productive transactions among members of a group. While it is difficult to establish definitively what constitutes a "small" group, common factors are likely to be the extent to which members perceive themselves as constituting a small group, the extent to which members feel that they can predict communication patterns and behaviors in fellow members, the extent to which members feel that they can easily keep track of the activities of fellow group members, and the relatively easy availability of information common to each group member.

Small-group communication involves the ways in which members understand the group task or project, the ways in which members speak with one another, and the ways in which members characterize the processes and outcomes of their activities. One or more members may emerge as spokespeople, while others may take on more passive roles. If one member perceives that there is a majority viewpoint, he or she may be influenced to express a similar point of view, especially if his or her thoughts might be perceived as deviating markedly from the norm. On the other hand, the social makeup of the group may be such that all members feel equally comfortable, equally able to express themselves; in such cases, small-group communication will reflect greater input from the members of the group in general. *See also* Small Group

Smuggling The secret movement of items where prohibited, such as into a prison, across a nation's border, or onto an airplane (also known as trafficking). Motivations for smuggling include participating in illegal trade, such as with drugs or humans, theft of the item, and bringing banned items (contraband) into a prison, airplane, or other building.

Soap Opera Format A narrative entertainment media broadcast that is serialized and distributed in linked installments as opposed to distinct episodes. Serialized dramas were originally broadcast on radio in the United States in the 1930s and moved to television in the 1950s. The term *soap* refers to its sponsorship by manufacturers of household cleaning product. Since programs targeted housewives, other large corporate sponsors quickly realized the advertising potential of the format.

Soap operas in the United States are generally aired during the daytime and include a fictional cast of characters engaged in continuing, multiple and simultaneous plots. Narratives are set in everyday life and often incorporate contemporary social and cultural issues as plot bases. Some long-running examples include "As the World Turns," "One Life to Live," and "All My Children." In the United Kingdom, soap operas appear during evening prime time, with "Coronation Street" and "EastEnders" as popular examples. *See also* Entertainment Media; Narrative

Social Anomie A state of uncertainty and alienation in a society resulting from the absence of values and standards of behavior. Deriving from the Greek *anomos* (*a*, "lacking in" + *nomos*, "law"), *anomie* (or anomy) in its current use comes from the sociologist Émile Durkheim, who in *Suicide* (1897) describes an anomic society as lacking the norms, consensus, and goals exhibited by integrated societies. It results in feelings of alienation from the community and from oneself and feelings of helplessness. Any sudden change in social circumstances (good or bad) brings on a crisis and the disruption of prior value systems and shared expectations. Poverty at least protects individuals by forcing them to partially align their aspirations with their reduced resources. Affluence, however, lifts all the restraints on desires and goals inculcated by social means and conditioning. With infinite goals, no progress ever seems to be made, and disenchantment is inevitable. Anomic suicide removes the study of the phenomenon from the domain of individual moral weakness or illness and into structural terms as an indication of societal dysfunction or abnormality. In his analysis of society as the external regulative force that defines the individual's moral horizon of proper aspiration and desire, Durkheim adopts a Hobbesian view of human nature, which claims that because there is no "natural" term for human aspiration, it must be socially constructed and regulated. For Durkheim, earlier societies enjoyed solidarity through shared religion, the need for cooperation owing to the relative low density of the population, and fear of reprisal from repressive laws, but in the wake of secularism, economic materialism, and industrialization, anomie pervades modern society. Unfair division of labor alienates individuals even further, rendering any sense of the common good a meaningless abstraction. Edvard Munch's painting *The Scream* (1893), contemporaneous with Durkheim's work, visualizes the wordless horror, distorted vision, and alienation of modern existence. Samuel Beckett's play *En Attendant Godot (Waiting for Godot,* 1948–1949) sums up the dislocation between individuals, between humans and their environment, and between actions and meaningful goals.

The American sociologist Robert King Merton builds on the ideas of Durkheim to measure the reactions (from conformist to deviant) to anomic conditions brought about by the unbridgeable gap between desired goals (whether individual or common) and the means for achieving them. Faced with such discrepancy, individuals respond variously: by conforming to legitimate available means to attain goals; by retreating from both means and goals; by rebellion against the means, the goals, or both; by resorting to crime or other illegitimate means to achieve goals; by ritual conformity to acceptable means and simultaneous forfeiture of one's goals. The last two responses express anomie most purely in that in both cases the discrepancy between means and ends is at its bleakest. For more information, see Beckett (1954/1994) and Durkheim (1897/1997). *See also* Anomie

Social Capital (1) Aggregate productive assets, which contribute to output in the form of profit and human capital (education), and (2) beliefs and networks involving customs, relationships, and institutions that facilitate social interaction and collective action. The second connotation has more currency and extensive usage.

Social capital is critical for economic growth and sustainable development. It affects the ability of society to work as a unit in order to achieve common goals and clear policies. It is an integral precondition for inclusion, successful development projects, and nation building.

In its earliest form, it defines the virtues of sympathy, fellowship, and social interaction, which are necessary to build coherent and stable communities. These virtues can be strengthened through institutionalized relationships and acquaintances. In the 21st century, Putnam distinguishes physical capital from social capital in terms of social networks and the norms of reciprocity and trust that arise from them.

The World Bank breaks the term into five component parts: (1) groups and networks, (2) trust and solidarity, (3) collective action and cooperation, (4) social cohesion and inclusion, and (5) information and communication.

Groups and networks enable individuals to come together in order to promote personal relationships, which improve welfare. Trust and solidarity foster better collective action to resolve communal challenges. Social cohesion and inclusion minimize the risk of conflicts by promoting equitable access to benefits, and information and communication provide access to constructive information to negate negative ones.

Social capital is a significant concept for enhancing the effectiveness of World Bank community-based operations. To give the concept of social capital practical meaning, in order to translate the theory of social capital into a more practical construct, the World Bank developed the Social Capital Implementation Framework (SCIF), to determine how social capital can be incorporated into the multilateral operations. For more information, see Bourdieu (1983), Coleman (1988, 1990), Hanifan (1916), Putnam (1993), Smith (2007), Woolcock (2001), and World Bank (2008). ***See also*** Networking

Social Change A broad term referring to variations over time in a society's culture, the structure and function of social institutions, the structure and function of social roles, and the environmental stability of populations and communities. The change can occur at the macrolevel, such as with globalization or population growth; the middle level, such as with urbanization or changes in crime rates; or the microlevel, such as with changing norms of conduct. The change can be driven by forces within or beyond the society and be intentional or unintentional. Modernization and war are two powerful sources of social change. Explanations for social change include the evolutionary, cyclical, conflict, and functionalist models.

Social Class A hierarchical division of groups or individuals dependent primarily on various economic and social conditions. The factors that determine class vary between societies. For Karl Marx, there were two social classes, the owners of the means of production (the bourgeoisie) and the workers (proletariat). Within societies, types of social classes can also vary. For example, one's social class can be viewed in terms of occupation, education, wealth, age, gender, race, or health. Differential lifestyles, marked by factors such as dress, language, and tastes, characterize various social classes. The United States has traditionally been divided into the lower, middle, and upper classes. Today, class distinctions include the working class and the upper- and lower-middle classes. As the gap between the rich and the poor grows in the United States, the middle class is argued to be disappearing. ***See also*** Marxism (sociology)

Social Clock The expectations of society for individuals to complete or achieve certain milestones by a certain age. These expected milestones can include marriage, having children, and so on. There are cultural differences with regard to the social clock. For example, while it is anticipated in some cultures that people marry in their teenage years, other cultures may emphasize marriage in later years. One implication of the social clock is that people who have not completed certain milestones may feel inadequate. The social norms underlying the social clock are adaptable to change. For example, in many Westernized countries, the age at which women first give birth has increased in recent years. Consequently, the social clock that determines at which age women are expected to give birth has been adjusted. ***See also*** Stereotype (psychology)

Social Constructivism An epistemology/theory that emphasizes the idea that society and knowledge are produced by humans. Thus, knowledge is "constructed" at a given time by people through collective or individual action. The social constructionist assumes that people create their society and seek to examine how this construction is accomplished. ***See also*** Hermeneutics (education); Qualitative Research

Social Contract An agreement, arranged in a prepolitical state, by which people are said to abandon their natural state in order to form a society in which they agree to give up some rights and submit to political authority. In return, they will receive the safety of an organized state. The prepolitical state, also known as the *state of nature* or *natural state,* is the starting point for the social contract. It is the human condition as it exists in the absence of any social order. In the state of nature, an individual's action is bound only by his conscience. This arrangement is deemed legitimate to the extent that there is agreement among the people who are subjected to it. An important component of the social contract is the general will, which is a collective agreement of the common good. Included in the idea of the general will is the notion of reciprocated duties, whereby the sovereign is committed to the good of the individuals who constitute it and each individual is committed to the good of the whole.

The exact origin of the idea of a social contract is unknown, although some believe that it may have been a covenant from God. Two early social contract theorists were Socrates and Plato. However, social contract theory was first clearly articulated by Thomas Hobbes, John Locke, and Jean-Jacques Rousseau in the 17th and 18th centuries. Each philosopher, however, had different conceptions about the appearance of the prepolitical state and the effects of the political state on man's nature.

The 20th-century philosopher, John Rawls, brought social contract theory back into the philosophical discourse with his "original position" as a metaphor for the state of nature. According to Rawls, from the original position, individuals operating under a "veil of ignorance" would collectively agree on certain principles of justice. ***See also*** Civil Rights; Natural Rights

Social Control Theory   Attributed to Tavis Hirschi (1969), this theory states that criminality results when the bonds that tie a person to society weaken. The theory assumes that all people have the potential to engage in criminality, but most do not out of fear of damaging their relationships with others, such as family, friends, neighbors, figures of authority such as teachers, and employers. The relationship, or social bond, comprises four elements: attachment, commitment, involvement, and belief. Attachment to others is measured by a person's sensitivity to and interest in others. Commitment refers to the time and energy spent engaged in conventional activities such as getting an education and working at a job. Involvement in prosocial activities, such as attending school and spending time with the family or religious groups, does not leave time to engage in criminality. Belief in conventional ideals or moral values, such as honesty, responsibility, and fairness, will also bond a person to society. For more information, see Hirschi (1969). ***See also*** Criminology

Social Disorganization   A theory that states that conditions commonly found in urban environments enable criminality. A disorganized neighborhood is characterized by a breakdown of institutions of informal social control, including families, schools, and employment. Disorganized neighborhoods have high rates of unemployment, low rates of high school graduation, a concentration of poverty and single-parent households, high levels of population turnover, and poor-quality housing. These neighborhoods cannot provide sufficient social services, such as access to adequate education and health care, and job opportunities. People living in these areas may experience hopelessness and conflict, which can result in criminality. Disorganized neighborhoods are often in mixed-use areas, where businesses and residential housing exist together, contributing to a high level of anonymity and mobility, and thus a lack of cohesiveness among residents. As a result, collective problems cannot be efficiently solved. Socially disorganized neighborhoods become places where criminal activity is likely to occur. As a result, private and public investment in these areas is compromised, and the neighborhoods come to be characterized as high-crime areas. ***See also*** Criminology

Social Distance   The distance between different groups in society. Location distance and social distance are two very distinct concepts. Social distance plays out strongly especially in large cities, such as New York, especially Manhattan. There one has people living in similar locations or neighborhoods, but their social distance is great because of social class, wealth, race, ethnicity, and other social characteristics. Each social entity can have a different mental outlook or perception

of life, and communication between the two is very low context. William Julius Wilson (1987) argued that social isolation, or limited social contacts of inner-city communities with mainstream society, led to a variety of social problems, including welfare, dependency, dropout rates, crime, and other social pathologies. This concept of social distance and isolation applies to cities around the world. The Bogardus Social Distance Scale (a Gutman Scale) is a psychological testing scale developed by Emory S. Bogardus to empirically measure people's willingness to participate in social contacts of varying degrees of closeness with members of diverse social groups, such as other racial and ethnic groups, sex offenders, and gays and lesbians. For more information, see Wilson (1987). ***See also*** Social Ecology

Social Ecology   A neighborhood or area's environmental conditions that can contribute to people's experiences, including criminality and victimization. Cities, which have urban social ecologies, have higher rates of theft and violence than do suburban and rural communities. The social ecology of an area is characterized by several concepts, including the level of social disorganization, degree of community fear or siege mentality, level of poverty, and social isolationism. Collective efficacy, or communal trust and a willingness to maintain social control, is also a factor in a neighborhood's social ecology. For example, watching over other people's children is an indicator of social cohesion. The physical environment also comprises a neighborhood's social ecology. For example, well-lit streets versus vacant lots and abandoned buildings contribute to levels of crime in an area. ***See also*** Social Disorganization; Social Distance

Social Exchange Theory   A perspective in sociology and social psychology that explains human interaction as based on negotiated exchanges among individuals and groups. People use cost-benefit reasoning to decide how to act. Actions are based on expectations of rewards, such as approval or respect. The theory models social interaction as economic market interaction. ***See also*** Rational Choice

Socialism *(economics)*   A system of production and allocation of resources in which the means of production are considered to be collectively owned and equity or fairness in distribution of income is given a lot of consideration by policymakers. The common denominator of socialist regimes is that the state has a considerable responsibility to plan macroeconomic policies and intervene in market operations. State planning includes price determination, monitoring of output levels, and resource allocation.

The primary objective of state regulation is to determine the availability of goods, the prices at which they should be sold, and employment and rewards for the use of factor inputs.

There are theoretical advantages that have made socialism attractive for some governments. Socialism tends to minimize the problem or magnitude of market failure associated with free-market operations, and the distributive role of government tends to provide for those who will otherwise be priced out of markets.

The substitution of market outcomes with government wisdom may not necessarily provide optimal results. Excess demand creates shortages at suboptimal market prices, which generates rationing policies and stringent enforcement laws. Firms that do not maximize private profits are less motivated to innovate, and innovation as an integral part of growth may be compromised.

In the process of implementing socialism, it is not uncommon for individual rights to be violated or for resources to be inefficiently allocated because of the government's inability to make timely corrections to errors in decisions. Some governments in under-developed countries have ostensibly used the theory of socialism to prolong their stay in power and show zero tolerance for opposition to questionable economic policies; this is particularly true of some of the formerly nascent African economies in the postindependence era of the 1960s.

In the post–World War II period, the former Soviet Union and several eastern European countries adopted the socialist system. Changes in the world economy, which became much more apparent since the 1980s, have made the pristine form of socialism less viable today. The desire for political and economic freedom as well as the advent of globalization provoked insurrections and revolutions in countries such as Poland, Germany, and the Soviet Union, leading to political and economic reforms and the breaking up of the former Soviet Union. China has opened up its economy to become a member of the World Trade Organization. Socialism, like capitalism, is an economic theory that shows that no system can be comprehensive enough to disregard the mixture of market outcomes and policy intervention. Consequently, economic systems all over the world can best be characterized as "mixed," with varying degrees of intervention in the market. Prosocialist regimes tend to show more vigorous intervention relative to market-based capitalist regimes. The theory of social market is also an indicator of a market-policy compromise. ***See also*** Capitalism (economics, political science); Closed Economy; Free Trade; Laissez-Faire (economics); Market; Mixed Economy; Social Market; World Trade Organization (WTO)

Socialism *(political science)*   A political and economic theory that advances a system of collective or governmental ownership and management of the means of production and distribution of goods. In its modern conception, socialism originated as a remedy for the economic and moral defects of capitalism. Socialism is contrasted with capitalism in its main characteristics: the sanctity of private property, competition, and profit making. In place of these values, socialism stresses cooperation and the equitable distribution of wealth. Socialism also represents economic theories that argue

that resources should be owned by the state and that the state should assume responsibility for all economic planning and direction.

Socialists, those who advocate socialism, seek a democratically controlled economy run for the benefit of all. They argue that the competition of capitalists should be replaced by cooperation and that the business cycle of economic growth and decline be replaced by planned stability. They believe that property should be shared in common and private ownership of industry and land abolished.

Although indications of socialism may be traced back centuries to the early Christians, the roots of modern socialism lie in the western European countries of France, Germany, and England during the Industrial Revolution. Socialist thinking arose in the late 18th and early 19th centuries as a reaction to the economic and social changes that resulted in the rapid acquisition of wealth by factory owners and the increasing impoverishment of workers. The early socialist thinkers included Henri de Saint-Simon, François Marie Charles Fourier, François Noël Babeuf, and Robert Owen. These visionaries criticized the excesses of poverty and inequality created by the Industrial Revolution and hoped to bring about a society that included an equitable distribution of wealth and communities where private property was abolished.

In the 1840s, communism came to denote both advanced and militant leftist forms of socialism. In 1848, Karl Marx and Friedrich Engels wrote the *Communist Manifesto,* which described their doctrines. In this work, Marx and Engels further attacked the current socialist thinkers as utopian dreamers who disregarded the necessity of the revolutionary struggle to implement their principles. They argued that the current socialist thinkers had visions of a perfect egalitarian and communalist society without distinguishing between the bourgeoisie and the proletarian classes or recognizing the need for class struggle. These utopian socialists, as they were called, considered only a peaceful society and ignored the need for revolutionary action to impose change. Marx and Engels instead advocated a socialism that recognized the historical inevitability of conflict between capitalists and labor. Marx and Engels's revolution called for a forceful seizure of a previously developed capitalist system and redistribution of previously created wealth. They called this form of socialism *scientific socialism.* For more information, see Engels (1989), Marx and Engels (1848/1969), and Sassoon (1996). ***See also*** Communism (economics, political science); Democracy (political science); Democratic Socialism (economics); Marxism (political science)

Socialization *(media studies)*   The process whereby a culture reproduces itself by inducting individuals into its habits, roles, and belief systems. For the individual, it means adjustment to social expectations, thereby gaining approval and advancement. Socialization is not a process exclusive to humans and occurs within other species and between species (as in house-training a pet). The rules of behavior inculcated by socialization cannot be reduced to formulae one can learn in abstraction but are embedded in and acquired through relationships, observation of normative role models, efforts to secure approval, and "leisure" activities such as eating, dressing, storytelling, playing, and competitive games (sports). Socialization also shapes personality, morals, self-image, gendered behavior, and sexual orientation as children learn to relate to other significant individuals and to the general group. Family, school, and peer groups are major agents of socialization at this early stage. Socialization does not simply end with the onset of adulthood but continues as a learning process throughout life, though less dramatically than in childhood. Resocialization refers to transitions in adulthood in which the individual voluntarily or involuntarily enters a radically new environment (foreign country, career change, prison) and has to unlearn previously learned behaviors. In adulthood, peer groups, working colleagues, and the mass media are powerful agents of socialization. From the mid-20th century onward, the mass media have increasingly exercised a formative role on the individual both as child and as adult. As a concept, socialization can appear overly monolithic and controlling of the individual, who seems passive to the shaping forces from without. To balance this picture, it is important to note both the local level at which socialization occurs—for example, the family home and the differing socializing processes based on class, race, and ethnicity—and the influence of the individual over self and the group through interaction with it. *See also* Social Learning Theory (education, sociology); Social Pressure; Social Skills Training

Socialization *(sociology)*   A broad term that describes how a person learns to conform to a society's norms, values, and social roles. Learning these cultural aspects is necessary for successful participation in a given society. Agents of socialization include parents, teachers, and others in authority. Agencies of socialization include the family, religion, and the mass media. While the majority of socialization occurs during the younger years of a person's life, adults may experience resocialization as the result of overcoming an addiction or entering prison or the military. Some nonhuman animals also undergo a process of socialization, for example, domestication of dogs or cats. Dogs can also be socialized as working canines. When these animals remain unsocialized due to lack of human contact, they are regarded as feral or wild. *See also* Social Learning Theory (sociology)

Social Justice   The idea that all humans should be treated equitably regardless of their individual circumstances. Such circumstances include a person's ethnicity, race, gender, religion, and socioeconomic status. Laws that support and enforce this equitable treatment of all people are considered social justice laws.

Social justice laws strive to benefit individuals and groups, or societies, alike. The government of a society should be responsible for ensuring social justice, thus ensuring a higher quality of life for its citizens. While social justice encompasses economic justice (equitable distribution of wealth), it is often incorrectly equated with it.

Social Learning Theory *(education)*   Explained in full by Bandura (1977), this perspective proposes two ideas. First, much of our learning involves others. We can watch and learn (vicarious learning), we can be guided or instructed by others while we are learning (guided participation), and we can be influenced by others to learn or while learning (social persuasion). The second aspect of social learning theory is its emphasis on the continuous and reciprocal relationship between cognitive and behavioral learning within a social environment. Within the social context, several learning theories may be applied. Information process theory focuses on the mechanics of learning through attention (through the sensory register), the analysis and labeling of new information (working memory), and the cataloging and storage of that information (long-term memory). On the other hand, cognitive emphasis may be derived from the stage theory of Piaget, where social cues are perceived differently at different stages because of variations in developmental cognitive capacity or ability.

Alternatively, learning may be examined through the social-cognitive theory of Vygotsky (1978), through the mechanisms of *actual development* (what a person can already do), *potential development* (what capability of learning or doing the person has), and *proximal development* (what the person could learn to do with instruction or intervention by a tutor or mentor). Vygotsky proposed that the social context of learning provides scaffolding (cognitive support, such as demonstrating a process or reviewing steps) or cognitive apprenticeship (thinking through, problem solving, planning ahead, or supervised self-monitoring).

Although all social learning theory involves behavioral and cognitive interaction with others, behavioral theory may also be applied because it involves a system of reinforcement, whereby correct or expected behaviors are positively reinforced and undesirable or incorrect responses are punished or ignored.

Bandura posited that the most common and powerful aspect of environment is the social aspect, or the presence, contributions, and influence of the persons in that environment. As demonstrated, any cognitive application can be made within this social context of learning. For more information, see Bandura (1977), Piaget (1972), and Vygotsky (1978). *See also* Behaviorism (education, psychology); Cognitive Learning Theory; Social Constructivism

Social Learning Theory *(sociology)*   A criminological theory that states that behaviors and values are learned from observing others, whether prosocial or antisocial.

Theorists of this orientation assume that people are not born violent or criminal but learn violence and criminality from others. This not only follows from the theory of differential association but also includes a component that explains how behavior is modeled after others and includes positive and negative reinforcements. The modeling of behavior begins with interactions with family. When parents react to their children with violence, the children are more likely to interact with others using violent techniques. Experiences within a person's physical environment can also teach violence. Children who grow up in neighborhoods where they regularly view violence may come to perceive violence as acceptable or adopt the approach as a norm. Media sources also regularly show violence, and in many forums the violence is rewarded or glorified, thus reinforcing the acceptability of such behavior. ***See also*** Criminology; Differential Association

Social Loafing   A reduction in effort by an individual when asked to perform a task in a group setting rather than individually. The effect of social loafing was observed by Latané, Williams, and Harkins (1979), who found that individuals who were blindfolded and wore headphones worked harder at their task than when they believed that they were working as part of a group. Social loafing can be explained by the principle of diffusion of responsibility. That is, the greater the group size, the less responsibility there is for each individual. As an individual's responsibility decreases, he or she may contribute less to a project, as his or her efforts are less identifiable. Social loafing serves as a theory to explain loss of productivity in a group. For more information, see Latané, Williams, and Harkins (1979). ***See also*** Group Dynamics; Groups

Social Market   A theory that is designed to deal with market failure and traditional normative values. It became especially prominent in West Germany after the Nazi experience of extensive regulation of markets and dictatorship. The West Germans wanted an economy with less intensive regulation that would be responsive to the needs of its citizenry and not just the wealthy.

The concept is premised on the idea that competition can price the less fortunate out of the market and that the unchecked market is capable of evolving into monopolistic and oligopolistic structures. As such, economic policy since the 1950s has been directed at money and banking, monopolies and cartels, the labor market, and exchange rate policy.

The term *social* was preferred over *socialist* to differentiate the intensity of government intervention in the market. Social market could then be seen as a variant of the capitalist conception of markets and the response to market failure—the desire to bring free order to the market (*Ordo-Liberalismus*)—rather than total control of economic exchange. Yet it formed the basis of extensive socialist networks in Germany that are closely reflective of the social, political, and economic normative traditions. German unification and stabilization issues have made it much more difficult for the government to play a limited role in the market.

Tribe (1990) points out that the term gained definition only after economic recovery was under way in the Federal Republic and has consequently thereafter been associated with the more positive aspects of German economic development. As such, the concept has been identified with whatever is thought to be essential to the success of the postwar German economy. The theory best encapsulates the traditional idea that the state has some role to play in the economy but that some amount of precautionary intervention is desirable. For more information, see Tribe (1990). ***See also*** Business Cycle (economics); Market; Market Failure; Stabilization

Social Mobility   Movement by a group or an individual from one social level, or strata, in the hierarchy to another. Some societies known as *closed stratification societies* have strict boundaries between strata, while others known as *open stratification societies* allow for more movement between strata. A person whose parents did not go to college, rented an apartment, and worked at low-wage jobs may go on to college, own a home, and work at a high-paying white-collar job. This would be upward mobility. Conversely, those with advanced education and training may not be able to find employment in their field at a given time and may become unable to afford the kind of housing, education, or medical care they were accustomed to. There is a strong link between a person's level of education and social class. Critics argue, though, that access to education correlates to level of social class. Thus, a person in a lower social class will have reduced access to education and a reduced chance of social mobility, reproducing the same patterns of education and social class for a child as for his or her parents. ***See also*** Social Class; Social Stratification

Social Norm   An informal rule regarding social behavior. Social norms change over time and between cultures. In the United States, for example, cigarette smoking was once a generally accepted behavior. Most recently, knowledge about the health risks of smoking has led to a shift in its acceptability. Smoking has been banned in a number of places, including movie theaters, airplanes, and even prisons. Another example concerns gender roles and employment. Traditionally, in the United States, males were expected to earn more and provide for the family, while females cared for the children. Today, it is not uncommon for females to earn more than their male partners and for the male to stay home to care for the children.

Social Phobia   A high level of anxiety and self-consciousness experienced by a person during everyday interactions with other individuals. Also referred to as social anxiety disorder, social phobia may be limited to specific situations, such as public speaking, or may relate to all settings involving social interactions. Individuals suffering from social phobia are under the impression that they are being watched and evaluated by other people, and this may result in physical symptoms such as blushing, perspiring, feeling nauseous, and difficulties with speech. *See also* Anxiety Disorders; Phobia

Social Pressure A social demand or force that can compel a person to behave in a certain way or to adopt certain characteristics. Sources of the pressure include family members and peers, and media images. For example, people may feel social pressure to be married or have children by a certain age. Adolescent girls and boys may feel social pressure to match a given body type, even if unrealistic. Social pressure can then lead to stress or strain, such as when teenage girls become anorexic or teenage boys take steroids to alter their bodies.

Social-Psychological Context The environment of people grouped around a situation and the ways in which they view and interpret it. The social context influences how this situation or an individual is viewed. For example, a group of individuals watching a movie in a movie theater with their friends might interpret the movie or certain situations depicted in the movie in a way that is different from watching the same movie in a college or high school environment. While the first situation might be more pleasurable, the second might have a negative connotation if the course they are taking is a required course for the major and the groups of students in the class experienced some negative interactions among themselves during the semester. Depending on where the group is exposed to the given stimulus, their experience might be diametrically different.

Psychological context depends on who you are and what you bring to the interaction. Your needs, desires, values, and personality, all form the psychological context.

Humans communicate with each other across time, space, and contexts. Those contexts are often thought of as the particular combinations of people constituting a communication situation. Contexts of communication are best thought of as a way to focus on certain communication processes and effects. Communication context boundaries are changeable and tend to fluctuate. The interplay between the social and psychological contexts will produce a form of communication or interaction that will be devoid of objectivity and heavily grounded in the contextual variables of a given situation and the personal background of the individual or groups that define the situation. In organizational settings, the organization is a system taking in equivocal information from its environment, trying to make sense of that information, and using what was learned in the future. As such, organizations evolve as they make sense out of themselves and their environment, which is heavily influenced by the social and psychological contexts. For more information, see Stanford University (2009) and Weick (1996). *See also* Human Communication

Social Psychology A specialty of psychology that is concerned with the way an individual's perceptions and behaviors are influenced by his or her social environment. Social psychology encompasses a wide range of research areas, for example, people's self, attitudes and attitude changes, attributions, and attraction. Furthermore, social psychologists study how people behave in groups, for example, interpersonal perceptions, group behaviors and processes, and conformity and obedience. Finally, another area of interest for social psychologists is people's perception of others, including schemas, biases, stereotypes, and attitudes toward others.

With regard to person perception, there are several influential factors. For example, physically attractive people have been found to be associated with positive and desirable characteristics, potentially due to an overrepresentation of physically attractive people in the media. Furthermore, existing cognitive schemas influence the way people perceive and integrate new information. Another aspect potentially influencing person perception are stereotypes, which are beliefs held about a certain group.

Attributions are assumptions that a person makes about the causes of events and others' or one's own behavior. Attributions may be affected by biases. For example, according to the fundamental attribution error, people often assume internal attributes, such as traits and abilities, to explain other people's behaviors, rather than situational factors. According to the self-serving bias, people often attribute their own success to internal attributes, while mishaps are attributed to situational factors.

With regard to conformity and obedience, research has indicated that groups, and group behavior, influence a person's behavior. For example, people often try to conform; that is, a person adjusts his or her behavior in accordance with experienced social pressure. Interestingly, there is a relationship between level of conformity and group size. Conformity rapidly increases up to a group size of 4, after which it levels off. A concept similar to conformity is obedience, which is when a person complies with the demands of a person of perceived authority. Irrespective of their specialty, social psychologists employ rigorous scientific research methods, often based on quantitative and laboratory research. *See also* Attribution Theory; Conformity; Fundamental Attribution Error; In-Group Favoritism; Out-Group Homogeneity Bias; Qualitative Research; Quantitative Research; Research Methodology

Social Science Knowledge about the human world that has been obtained through empirical or scientific methods, including the objective, systematic collection of both qualitative and quantitative data. The social sciences collect data through methods including case studies, interviews, participant observations, and interviews. Social science is contrasted with natural or hard science, which focuses on the natural world, including biology and chemistry, and the humanities,

S

which focus on the arts. Examples of social science disciplines include anthropology, economics, geography, history, political science, psychology, and sociology. Social science can also be interdisciplinary, as with criminology/criminal justice, which can be studied from a number of social scientific perspectives. All predictive measures of the social sciences deal with human contingencies and thus cannot claim the hypothesis-testing validations or falsifications of the hard sciences; they therefore fall short in comparison with the hard sciences. The social sciences are also increasingly being studied in combination with the natural sciences in disciplines such as neuropsychology and sociobiology.

Social Skills Training Techniques aimed at improving the social capabilities of a person. As many psychological problems stem from interpersonal problems, this type of behavior therapy focuses on improving social skills via learning. The underlying assumption is that not all people are born with adept social skills and may not know how to cope interpersonally or express emotions adequately and appropriately. For example, a person may have difficulties in expressing affection or, alternatively, may have difficulty in expressing criticism constructively. Social skills training is based on the following three components: (1) modeling, (2) behavioral rehearsal, and (3) shaping. During modeling, the person is encouraged to observe other people who act in socially appropriate manners, with the goal of this observational process being the development of new socially appropriate behaviors, such as the use of eye contact. During behavioral rehearsal, the person is asked to practice these newly acquired behaviors, while a therapist typically guides rehearsal through constructive feedback. Behavioral rehearsal culminates in the person trying out the newly learned behaviors in the "real world." The final step of social skills training is shaping, during which the person is directed to attempt handling increasingly delicate and difficult social situations. Social skills training has been shown to be especially effective with social anxiety disorder, schizophrenia, and autistic spectrum disorders. ***See also*** Systematic Desensitization

Social Stratification The process by which the members of a society are hierarchically ordered into various strata or levels. Social stratification can be based on a number of characteristics, including age, ethnicity, gender, power, and wealth. Social stratification both differs and is reinforced by a society's culture. For example, the respect and deference shown to older people in some Asian societies can be contrasted with the emphasis on youth in the United States.

Social Studies A curricular discipline that examines all aspects of human cultures and civilizations, past and present. Contained within social studies are history, geography, economics, political science, anthropology, psychology, and sociology. Elementary and middle school social studies courses are generally taught holistically, while high schools typically separate the content areas into distinct courses.

Social Welfare Organized educational, cultural, medical, and financial assistance to those in need. Measures of assistance include care of destitute adults; treatment of the mentally ill; rehabilitation of criminals; care and relief of the sick, the handicapped, the young, and needy families; and educational activity for children. Access to such programs is considered a basic or inalienable right of those in need. Nations that provide social welfare programs are known as welfare states.

In the 16th century, the English poor laws made local authorities responsible for the collection of voluntary contributions to employ paupers on the one hand and provide direct relief to needy citizens on the other. The poor laws demonstrated a progression from private charity to a welfare state whereby the care and supervision of the poor were embodied in law. The laws further helped the destitute by guaranteeing a minimum level of subsistence. Relatives were simultaneously expected to assume responsibility for their poorer kin.

In 1883, the first modern social welfare system was implemented by the German government. This system supplied assistance to a wider range of groups than just the poor. Assistance included health insurance for workers, accident insurance, and retirement pensions. By the 1930s, most industrialized nations had some type of social welfare program.

In America, the colonists brought the English poor laws with them. In the earliest colonial times, there was recognition of an obligation to aid the needy, through almshouses and workhouses, when other efforts were deemed insufficient. Unlike the German system, the American social welfare programs that evolved were implemented in response to specific problems rather than resulting from a national agenda. Perhaps the most comprehensive and far-reaching social welfare program was that proposed by President Franklin D. Roosevelt. In 1933, the New Deal was implemented to provide relief to the unemployed and lift the United States out of the Great Depression. Most social welfare programs since the Depression have built on or subtracted from Roosevelt's programs. For more information, see Trattner (1979) and Gormley. ***See also*** Welfare

Social Worker The International Federation of Social Work defines social work as "promoting social change, problem solving in human relationships and the empowerment and liberation of people to enhance well-being. Utilizing theories of human behavior and social systems, social work intervenes at the points where people interact with their environments. Principles of human rights and social justice are fundamental to social work." A social worker is trained to help people acquire services fundamental to human need; to provide individuals, families, and groups with counseling and psychotherapy; to help communities develop, improve, and deliver social services; and to participate in the development of social policy. For more information, see Hare (2004) and International Federation of Social Workers (2000).

Society   A group of people or other nonhuman animals organized to cooperatively achieve common basic goals, including reproduction, sustenance, shelter, and defense. A society can also be a voluntarily organized group with political, cultural, or religious goals. Societies can be divided based on their levels of communication, economic development, and technology. Based on this hierarchy, there are hunters and gatherers, agricultural societies, industrial societies, and, today, digital and virtual societies. All societies are composed of social networks, have criteria for inclusion, and their own organization. Social networks are the relationships between individual members and groups within a given society. Criteria for inclusion may include possessing a specific skill or knowledge or having a certain personal attribute. Many modern human societies are organized primarily by their mode of production, but they can also be organized by factors such as political power or geography. ***See also*** Sociology

Sociolinguistics   The study of language development, use, and change and the social and cultural factors that affect language. The basic concept of sociolinguistics is that language is used for more than just direct communication and the form of language used is affected by the relationship between the people in the language exchange as well as factors such as age, gender, class, and ethnic heritage. Sociolinguistics draws on ideas from psychology, linguistics, anthropology, sociology, and communications as it studies the human use of language and the ways languages vary under different social conditions.

The development of ideas about the interactions between language and culture in the United States is attributed to the linguist William Labov, whose work on American dialects and class differences in language use and structure forms the basis of the discipline. Labov's study of African American Vernacular English, or Black English, as a legitimate dialect rather than a flawed use of Standard English was as important for the sociolinguistic techniques it demonstrated as for the social and political implications of his conclusions. Sociolinguistics also looks at how people talk to each other, how language is used to convey information about the self and others, how language is used to make things happen, and how dialects are chosen and used in different social situations. For more information, see Labov (1987). ***See also*** Language; Language Development; Linguistic Differences; Linguistics

Sociology   The scientific study of society and the various groups that constitute a given society. Sociology at the microlevel focuses on individuals and patterns of their behavior. At the middle level, sociology is concerned with phenomena that occur within and between organizations and communities. At the macrolevel, sociologists study changes in entire societies, such as those that result from war. The founding of sociology is based in the Enlightenment of the 1600s, when philosophers were developing the concepts of human reason. After the revolutions in France, England, and the early American colonies during the 1700s, tradition was challenged and increasingly replaced with science. The French philosopher Auguste Comte (1798–1857) is credited with coining the term *sociology*. The field was further developed in the 1800s by Karl Marx (1818–1883), Émile Durkheim (1858–1917), and Max Weber (1864–1920). The discipline was first taught by an independent academic department at the University of Chicago in 1892. ***See also*** Research

Sociology of Knowledge   The study of how knowledge is constructed and organized by humans. Knowledge includes what we know, believe, and value, including our cultural values and our perceptions of social reality.

Social reality is an abstract, changeable human construction. Social control mechanisms operate to stabilize our social reality. A significant part of our constructed social reality is made up of cultural values.

Social reality is constructed in three phases, according to Berger and Luckmann's (1966) treatise on everyday knowledge: externalization, objectivation, and internalization. In the externalization phase, culture provides meaning and is used to build the world. Objective culture includes physical items, while significative culture includes abstract elements such as language and values. Culture is objectified through institutionalization, historicity, legitimation, and language. Internalization occurs as a child is socialized into his or her world and as a human of any age is socialized into a particular subculture.

Mass media, including television, radio, newspaper, and magazines, portray and interpret the world around us and play a significant role in the creation of our social reality. If women were to be portrayed in the media solely as young, beautiful, and unintelligent, how would that affect our perceptions, expectations, and experiences of, and as, real women in our world as we live in it?

Social learning theory describes how people learn from observing others. It is not necessary to test and experience something to learn about it; we can learn by watching others and drawing conclusions from their experience. This occurs in both children and adults. Albert Bandura demonstrated in the 1970s that children were more likely to act aggressively toward dolls if they observed adults being aggressive with children. Many researchers have tried to prove or disprove a causative connection between viewing violence on television and/or video/Internet games and real-life aggressive behavior. Broadcast media have been used as educational tools—for example, in attempts to improve knowledge of farming techniques or health issues

S

through soap operas. For more information, see Allan (2006), Berger and Luckmann (1966), Burke (2000), Grindstaff and Turow (2006), and McCullagh (2002). ***See also*** Behavioral Effects; Causal Models of Aggression; Cultural Values; Selective Perception

Sociopath   An individual diagnosed with antisocial personality disorder (APD). Such individuals are characterized by their callous, unemotional, and exploitive interpersonal demeanor. They frequently violate the rights of others and feel little or no remorse. Some theorists differentiate between a sociopath and a psychopath, though both types are captured by the APD diagnostic criteria. ***See also*** Antisocial Personality Disorder

Sociotechnical Systems Theory   An approach to understanding a social system that emphasizes the complex, highly contextualized, and ubiquitous nature of the relationship between people and technology. This theory suggests that a complete understanding of any social system cannot be achieved without first studying the types of technologies employed by the people in the system. In addition, a complete understanding of any technology cannot be achieved without first studying the human factors that influenced the design, development, and utilization of the technology. Society and technology, therefore, should not be viewed as separate and discrete systems but as parts of a highly interrelated sociotechnical system. This theory is often applied in the field of organizational development to examine the effects of these sociotechnical interactions on the life of the organization. ***See also*** Society; Technology (education)

Sodomy   A term used to describe what is considered an unnatural sexual act, most often today meaning anal or oral intercourse. Biblical in its origin, the term has also been used to refer to other unholy acts that occurred in Sodom, including rape and torture of animals. In 2003, the U.S. Supreme Court ruled in *Lawrence v. Texas* that laws prohibiting same-sex sodomy were unconstitutional violations of privacy. For more information, see *Lawrence v. Texas* (2003).

Solicitor   A type of lawyer in commonwealth countries such as England, Ireland, Hong Kong, Australia, New Zealand, and Canada. There has traditionally been a difference between a solicitor, who represents and legally advises defendants, and a barrister, who is admitted to plead a case before a higher court. The solicitor can advise a barrister, but is not allowed to try a case before a higher court, and is usually called an "office lawyer." In England, this changed with the Courts and Legal Service Act of 1990, which allowed solicitors to appear, in some instances, in higher courts. The solicitor is also used as a judge to make a legal decision in certain jurisdictions.

Soma   The bulbous-shaped part of the neuron that encompasses the cell nucleus, as well as the chemical environment common in most cells. As neurons range in specialization, the soma (or cell body) can range in size from approximately 5 micrometers to more than 1 millimeter in invertebrates. Attached to the soma is the axon, which is responsible for transmission of information from the soma to the synapses at the axon terminal, to be received by other neurons, muscles, or glands. ***See also*** Axon; Neurons

Somatic Nervous System   Part of the peripheral nervous system and responsible for directing voluntary actions. While the central nervous system comprises the brain and the spine, the somatic nervous system is composed of the remaining nerves that establish the connection to the voluntary skeletal muscles and the sensory receptors. The somatic nervous system contains two different types of nerve fibers. Afferent nerve fibers are axons that transport incoming information from the outside to the central nervous system, while efferent nerve fibers are axons that transport outgoing information from the central nervous system to the outside. ***See also*** Autonomic Nervous System; Central Nervous System (CNS); Peripheral Nervous System (PNS); Sympathetic Nervous System

Somatoform Disorder   A physical illness that cannot be fully explained by organic causes and can be attributed *mostly* to psychological causes. In contrast, psychosomatic illnesses can be explained *in part* by psychological reasons, while malingering is the deliberate faking of an ailment for personal advantage.

There are three types of somatoform disorders. First, somatization disorder is marked by an individual who has a history of various illnesses that seem to be caused by psychological factors. The distinguishing characteristic of somatization disorder is that there is a wide array of physical ailments, ranging from cardiovascular and gastrointestinal to neurological ailments. A person with somatization disorder is often described as "clinging to ill health," as there is a succession of ailments, often involving the consultation of many physicians. Somatization disorder mostly affects women and tends to co-occur with depression and anxiety disorders.

Second, conversion disorder includes the loss of function, often in an individual organ. For example, symptoms include the partial or full loss of vision, hearing, or limb functioning, or paralysis. Conversion disorder is often discovered when the reported symptoms are inconsistent with the medical facts of the illness.

The third type of somatoform disorder is hypochondriasis. A person with hypochondriacal tendencies can be described as a person who continuously and excessively monitors his or her health and overinterprets potential physical symptoms, worrying that there could be an illness. When informed by a physician that there is no real ailment, the person may, for example, disregard the doctor's diagnosis, deem him or her incompetent, and seek the opinion of some other physician. Hypochondriasis is often accompanied by psychological disorders, such as depression and anxiety disorders. **See also** Hypochondriasis

Sovereignty The supreme authority of a nation. A sovereignty refers to the governing power of an independent nation, along with the accompanying power to dictate its political will. In contrast is a semi-sovereign state, which holds some degree of autonomy but a dominant country possesses ultimate control of it. The legal term *sovereign immunity,* also called *crown immunity,* refers to the doctrine that does not allow a citizen to bring suit against the government. In the United States, sovereign immunity exists but is waived under some limited circumstances. The Federal Tort Claims Act (1946) outlined conditions for tort suits against the federal government.

Speaker of the House The leader of the House of Representatives, elected by other members of the House. The Speaker usually shares the same party as the majority in the House. Under the Presidential Succession Act (1947), the Speaker is second in the line of succession after the vice president. The Speaker's responsibilities include calling the House to order, administering the oath of office to House members, presiding over House debates or delegating the power, setting the legislative agenda, and leading the appointment process for choosing committee chairs. In January 2007, Nancy Pelosi became the first female and first Italian American to hold the position of Speaker of the House. **See also** House of Representatives

Special Education With the implementation of PL 94–142 and its successor, the Individuals with Disabilities Act (IDEA), the United States passed federal legislation requiring the education of all students, regardless of their life situations or challenges. The legislation applies to K–12 schoolchildren, children from birth to age 3, and some adults. Special education involves modifying instruction and the environment for children with special needs. These needs include learning disabilities and cognitive-processing disorders; sensory and physical challenges; conditions such as attention deficit disorder, cerebral palsy, and autism; mental or developmental disabilities; speech and communication difficulties; and behavioral challenges and disorders. Services are provided in schools, homes, medical facilities, or group homes. **See also** Individualized Educational Plan (IEP); Individualized Family Service Plan (IFSP); Individuals with Disabilities Education Act (IDEA)

Speech The term has a variety of meanings in the social sciences. One refers to speech code theory, which attempts to explain a wide range of communicative conduct in a specific speech community. For example, in a speech code, one looks for particular symbols and meanings in the way a person speaks in a distinct culture; the words used help explain the characteristics of cultural conduct.

In a more general sense, speech refers to public speaking, or, more technically, elocutionism, or how one speaks in front of an audience. This meaning includes the art of persuasion, rhetoric, and the social psychology of interpersonal relationships. Late in the 20th century, the methodology derived from sociology, conversation analysis, found its way into the scholarly repertory. For more information, see Carbaugh (2005). **See also** Communication; Communication Theory

Speedy Trial A civil right guaranteed by the Sixth Amendment of the U.S. Constitution. However, due to an overburdened judicial system, with too many cases, too few judges, and legal procedures such as continuances, plea bargains, and other court delays, a speedy trial is a constitutional right generally not upheld. A speedy trial is designed to improve the credibility and availability of witnesses, avoid extended pretrial detention if the defendant is denied or unable to give bail, and decrease the opportunity for pretrial media attention, which could bias potential jurors. **See also** Trial

Spirituality This term is frequently defined in relation to the term *religion.* Typical distinctions between spirituality and religion are that the former is more private, idiosyncratic, fluid, and linked to personal meaning. In contrast, religion is more social, institutional, codified, and static. Spirituality also does not necessarily connote a belief in a supernatural or transcendent being.

Split Brain A brain in which there is no connection between the left and right hemispheres. Split-brain surgery involves the cutting of the connective tissue between the hemispheres. It is used as an attempt to alleviate the severity of epileptic seizures when all other treatments have failed. Research involving split-brain patients, that is, patients whose hemispheres have been surgically separated, provides information about what type of information is processed and stored in the left and right hemispheres. For example, research on split-brain individuals has indicated that incoming information into the brain is processed contralaterally— that is, in the opposite half of the brain where it normally is sent—and cannot be transferred or identified. Furthermore, research has indicated that the left side of the brain is predominant in processing language and higher-order processes, such as problem solving, reasoning, and organization. The right hemisphere has been identified as being predominant in processing visual-spatial tasks, such as color discrimination and face recognition. **See also** Brain

Split-Half Reliability A statistical method for testing the reliability of a psychometric measure. In split-half reliability, all test items of a measure are randomly divided into two sets, which are then administered to participants. For each participant, the scores for each half are then calculated and correlated with each other. The split-half reliability estimate is based on the correlation between these two total scores. Some limitations of split-half reliability are related to the division of items, that is, how to determine the best criterion by which the items should be split. For example, a simple top-half, bottom-half split is often not sufficient, due to practice effects, tiredness, and monotony. Other methods of testing reliability include the test-retest method and Cronbach's alpha. ***See also*** Reliability

Split Sentence A sentence whereby offenders are released to the community after being introduced to the pains of imprisonment for a brief period of time. The approach is based on the idea that offenders will be shocked by the conditions of prison and desist in committing crimes. Most commonly, the brief period of incarceration is paired with a sentence of probation. ***See also*** Community-Based Corrections; Shock Probation/ Shock Incarceration

Spoils System (*political science*) The practice of awarding political positions to loyal party members. The spoils system in the United States dates back to Thomas Jefferson, a Democrat-Republican, who aimed to keep rival Federalists out of federal positions. The expression comes from a speech by New York Senator William Learned Marcy in the U.S. Senate in January 1832: "To the victor, belong the spoils of the enemy." The comment was made after a speech by Kentucky Senator Henry Clay criticizing President Andrew Jackson for filling government posts with Democratic Party loyalists. Public attention to this matter peaked during the Ulysses S. Grant presidency, a Republican elected in 1868 for two full terms, whose administration was marked by corruption. The Civil Service Commission was created in 1871 to introduce reforms for filling civil service positions. ***See also*** Merit System

Spoils System (*public administration*) A system wherein the winner of an election awards administrative positions to his or her key allies. The term was derived from the famous speech delivered by New York Senator William Learned Marcy in 1832: "To the victor belong the spoils of the enemy." It was first used to characterize President Andrew Jackson's government appointments. On coming into power, a newly elected president has nearly carte blanche authority to choose his or her cabinet and closest officers (although admittedly not to the extent in previous centuries). Although it has been argued that these appointments are based on merit alone, party and personal loyalties undoubtedly play a central role in this selection process. Not surprisingly, the modern spoils system has both advocates and opponents. While the former argue that such a system allows smooth transitions in power, critics believe that such appointments are easily and frequently corruptible. This may be especially true in more transitional societies, where tribal and ethnic links often dominate the political power structure in place. For more information, see Hoogenboom (1961). ***See also*** Merit System

Spoils System (*sociology*) In American politics, this refers to the practice of the leaders of a political party appointing their supporters in jobs as a reward for their work, rather than awarding jobs based on merit. The practice dates back to the early 1800s and was prominent in the political era of policing. The Pendleton Act of 1883 created a Civil Service Commission to evaluate job candidates based on ability rather than party affiliation. President Theodore Roosevelt became known for reinforcing the civil service method at the federal level. The spoils system remained in effect longer at the local level, most famously with the Tammany Hall ring in New York City during the 1930s. ***See also*** Eras of Policing

Spontaneous Declaration An excited utterance or confession made without time for fabrication. An exception to the hearsay rule, a spontaneous declaration is admissible as evidence if the person who made the declaration is able to testify as a witness in the case. It was in *R. v. Smith* (1992) that the U.S. Supreme Court ruled that hearsay statements can be admitted if found to be sufficiently reliable. For more information, see *R. v. Smith* (1992).

Stability A broad term that generally means *balanced* or indicates a state of equilibrium. Countries may achieve economic stability, where inflation does not occur. Societies may reach population stability, where the number of births equals the number of deaths. Environmental or ecological stability can occur in nature. Political stability indicates that a society's government is not at risk of being overrun or ousted. Psychologically, stability can refer to a person's balanced emotional state, self-concept, or any number of other psychological concepts.

Stabilization A policy designed to check excessive short-term fluctuations of prices and output in a national economy due to shocks (unexpected or external changes). Shocks may be attributed to changes in aggregate demand and aggregate supply. For example, a sudden increase in aggregate demand, which causes the economy to increase production beyond the natural rate, will eventually put an upward pressure on the price level. An adverse supply shock attributable to the sudden rise in input cost, for example, oil prices or union activity, will reduce output and put an upward pressure on price.

An ideal approach to dealing with shocks is to find ways to expand consumption or employment during a recessionary period and contract consumption or excessive spending during inflationary periods. Countries with excessive balance-of-payments problems may also implement stabilization programs with the help of the International Monetary Fund (IMF) to curb inflation and reduce unemployment. A substantial number of countries in Latin America, Africa, and Asia have undertaken stabilization programs with the IMF in the 1980s and 1990s, with mixed results. For more information, see Lowenfeld (2003), Mankiw (2006),

Stiglitz (2003), and Warburton (2005). *See also* Business Cycle (economics); Fiscal Policy; International Monetary Fund (IMF); Monetary Policy

Staff Development   A program that prepares staff to assume future responsibilities by enhancing or creating competencies. Staff development readies the employee for promotion or a new position; in contrast, staff training seeks to enable the employee to perform his or her current job. Staff development can give employees opportunities to retrain and keep current skills. Through cross-training, where employees learn each other's jobs, development programs can ensure consistent productivity. Development programs can train current employees to ready them for future management vacancies and encourage employees to plan a career and gain the skills needed to progress. Staff development takes into consideration individual potential and talent and the staffing needs of the organization (Buford & Lindner, 2002). For more information, see Buford and Lindner (2002). *See also* Human Resource Management; Job Enrichment; Professional Staff Development; Training

Stage Theory   A theory of growth and development characterized by discrete stages (levels). Stage theory is associated with the idea that physical and psychological development occurs in stages over sequential periods of time. The essential concept is that each stage of development is characterized by specific and identifiable behaviors. Stage theory also holds that each stage of development is requisite to the next.

Stalking   The purposeful, malicious, and repeated following and harassing of another person. The visual or physical proximity to the victim is unwanted, as is any communication the stalker has with the victim. Stalkers may also verbally or in written form threaten their victims, causing them to fear imminent danger. Approximately half of all states have enacted statutes that make stalking a crime. Originally designed to protect women from past boyfriends or husbands, celebrities have also made use of the law against fans who are strangers following and harassing them.

Standard Deviation   In statistics, the square root of the variance, or spread, of a variable's values around the mean, or average of values. The variance is the average of the squared differences between the mean and the data points. A measure of statistical dispersion, a small standard deviation indicates that many of the data points are close to the mean, while a large standard deviation indicates that many of the data points are spread far from the mean. *See also* Statistics (sociology)

Standardization   A set of procedures for achieving uniformity in test administration and scoring. For test results to be comparable, it has to be ensured that testing conditions are as similar as possible. To achieve uniformity of procedure when administering a test,

detailed descriptions of how a test should be administered need to be given. Standardization of a psychometric instrument encompasses guidelines for the correct administration of materials, time limits for participants when completing tasks, oral instructions given by the test administrator, directions on how to handle questions, and so on. For example, when giving instructions, the rate of speech of the test administrator needs to be considered, as well as the tone of voice, inflection, and facial expressions, among others.

Another important aspect of standardization is to norm a test. That is, psychometric tests have no preestablished standards for evaluation. Norms need to be established in order to determine how a person performed in comparison with other people. To standardize a test, it needs to be administered to a large group of people, that is, a sample representative of the general public. This sample is referred to as the standardization sample. Norms are able to provide the mean of a measure, as well as indicate varying degrees of high performance or low performance. While standardization of an aptitude test provides an indication of a person's performance on a specific task, standardization of a personality test provides information regarding where a person falls on a personality scale or measure in relation to other people. *See also* Intelligence Quotient (IQ); Standard Score

Standards   Requirements that need to be met in order to achieve a prescribed level of excellence. Initially, standards-based education evolved in the early 1990s over concerns that American elementary and secondary students were not receiving an education that would prepare them to compete in a global economy, along with the realization that there were profound academic achievement gaps between minority and nonminority students. With the passage of the federal No Child Left Behind legislation in 2001, schools were challenged to state clearly measurable academic goals and to implement educational strategies to ensure that all students reached those goals. Schools responded by aligning curriculum, assessments, and professional development with their educational standards.

States were free to choose the educational strategies they deemed the most appropriate to help the students in their schools achieve standards, which also varied across states. The result was difficulty in comparing student achievement across states. This led to discussion of implementing of a common set of standards in all the states. Currently, there is disagreement over whether there should be national educational standards or different standards for each state. Critics of standards-based education argue that all students are not capable of attaining the same academic goals and should not be held to the same standards. Others claim that test scores have become the predominant method of standards assessment, forcing teachers and students to spend much of their class time on the content covered on tests, to the exclusion of everything else. *See also* No Child

Left Behind (NCLB); Standards-Based Curriculum and Instruction

Standards-Based Curriculum and Instruction Curriculum and instruction that are characterized and defined by a standards-based protocol. Standards-based curriculum and instruction are governed by the standards-based protocol or rules set forth by state and accreditation agencies. This protocol is used by institutions as a means for steering curriculum and instruction processes. Additionally, this protocol is also used by institutions as a means for justifying curriculum and instruction decisions. *See also* Standards

Standard Score An individual's score derived from the distance of the person's score to the mean, based on the standard deviation of the distribution. Standard scores are established via either linear or nonlinear transformations of the individual's raw scores. Scores that are linearly derived are frequently referred to as standard scores, or z scores. Scores need to be nonlinearly derived when a distribution curve is not shaped normally, and they may be skewed. *See also* Normal Curve (education); Stanine (psychology)

Standpoint Epistemology The idea that knowledge always exists from and within a particular perspective or standpoint. Because standpoint epistemology established its roots in feminist theory, the most common standpoint for knowledge is gender. Feminist standpoint theorists devoted much of their attention to female labor and asserted that all women are exploited. However, many feminists challenged this, arguing that different women have different experiences and perspectives. Patricia Hill Collins, for example, asserted that we should not group Caucasian women's experiences together with African American women's because of their different social positions. Today, standpoint epistemology recognizes that because there are a variety of situated experiences based on individuals' historical, ethnic, and social location in society, there are a variety of ways of knowing. For more information, see Harding (1991) and Collins (1990). *See also* Epistemology; Feminism

Standpoint Theory The notion that the social group to which a person belongs will directly influence the way in which that individual perceives and interprets daily experience. The theory, introduced by Hegel (1807), also entails the idea that the widest possible variety in standpoints—those places (real, social, conceptual) from which people perceive the world—will offer, in sum, a more comprehensive objectivity. Standpoint theory is frequently associated with one or more feminist approaches to knowledge, sometimes referred to as "situated knowledge," whereby the individual's thought processes and imagination are actually shaped by his or her social position. Put another way, the theory argues that knowledge and communication of that knowledge

will reflect one's social class. Standpoints, like points of view, are never complete and are necessarily skewed; one is never wholly embedded in a single such standpoint, and one can have multiple standpoints from which to view the world and express one's knowledge of it. *See also* Postmodernism

Stanford-Binet Intelligence Test A type of intelligence test, introducing the concept of a child's mental age. Responding to the request of an education commission in France, Binet and Simon developed the first test of general mental aptitude in 1905, the Binet-Simon Scale. The test quickly became successful and was widely used across Europe and America. In the United States, Terman and colleagues from Stanford University expanded the original scale and created the Stanford-Binet Intelligence Scale (Terman, 1916). Despite remaining close to the original scale, this test incorporated the concept of the intelligence quotient. The Stanford-Binet became one of the most widely administered psychological tests and is still administered today. One of the criticisms of the Stanford-Binet Intelligence Scale is its strong emphasis on verbal ability. For more information, see Terman (1916). *See also* Intelligence Quotient (IQ).

Stanine *(education)* Also called "standard nine" scores, they are a type of a normalized standard score. The normal distribution is divided into nine segments, with 1 representing the low end and 9 representing the high end. With the exception of scores 1 and 9, each segment represents one half of a standard deviation. For example, the middle 20% of the data are designated with a stanine score of 5. Publishers of nationally published instruments often use stanines to simplify scoring into single-numbered digits. The disadvantage of stanines is that the segments are not equal and are sample specific. *See also* Criterion- and Norm-Referenced Measurement

Stanine *(psychology)* Scores calibrated to a 9-point, normalized, standard scale, with a fixed mean of 5 and standard deviations of 2. Each stanine is based on the following percentage of scores in ascending order: 4% equals first stanine, 7% equals second stanine, 12% equals third stanine, 17% equals fourth stanine, 20% equals fifth stanine, 17% equals sixth stanine, 12% equals seventh stanine, 7% equals eighth stanine, and 4% equals ninth stanine. The lowest three stanines can be considered as below average, the middle three as average, and the highest three as above average. Although they represent an intuitive scale, stanines are less useful than percentiles. *See also* Normal Curve (psychology); Percentile; Standard Score

Stare Decisis A common-law principle by which past case law, or precedent, guides the decisions in later cases. It is unusual and highly discouraged for a judge to depart from precedent, but if he or she does do so, the judge is required to detail the reasons for his or her departure in a written decision.

State *(political science)* A geographical area that possesses some degree of political sovereignty. Although the terms are often used interchangeably, a difference exists between a state and a nation. A state is a political entity, while a nation is a culturally homogeneous group of individuals. There are nation-states, multinational states, and subnational states. When the geographic boundaries of a nation and a state are one and the same, it is called a nation-state—for example, Japan. A multinational state consists of many nations composing a single state—for example, the United Kingdom. The United States is often considered a nation-state because the states share a common American culture. *See also* Sovereignty

State *(psychology)* The condition a person happens to be in. States are applied across many different contexts, such as mental states, psychological states, or states of consciousness. Anxiety, for example, can be characterized as a physiological state, in conjunction with psychological interpretations. Psychological states, such as depression, may be related to other behaviors, such as gambling addiction. Furthermore, states have even been identified to have an effect on memory. For example, state-dependent learning experiments have demonstrated that the more encoding and retrieval conditions can be matched, the better the retrieval. *See also* Cannon-Bard Theory; James-Lange Theory

State Supreme Court The court of last resort in a state's judicial system, sometimes referred to as the court of appeals, supreme judicial court, or supreme court of appeals. After a verdict is rendered in a state's superior (sometimes circuit, district, or supreme) court, or highest court with general jurisdiction, the decision can be appealed to the state supreme court. Some states have intermediate courts of appeals that hear cases after the state's superior court but before the state supreme court.

Statistical Control When experimental controls are not possible, researchers resort to statistical methods to eliminate or "subtract" the effects variables. Experimenters control for these variables by assigning research participants to experimental groups, which receive treatments, and control groups, which do not. Having control groups allows researchers to isolate the effects of the treatment. For instance, to investigate the effects of income on adults' political beliefs, researchers cannot assign participants to different income levels to see what happens to their beliefs. Rather, researchers compare people with different incomes to see if their beliefs vary with their incomes, investigating whether there is a correlation between income and beliefs. If there is, it could be due to income, but it could also be explained by other variables. To eliminate those rival explanatory variables—such as age and education—the

researcher controls for them statistically. This statistical control is done by assigning average values to the control variables. This amounts to virtual assignment to a control group. *See also* Control Group

Statistical Power In hypothesis testing, researchers use statistical methods to determine whether the null hypothesis should be rejected. If the null hypothesis is false and the statistical analysis results lead the researcher to reject the null, then the researcher has made a correct decision. The probability of correctly rejecting a false null hypothesis is referred to as the *statistical power*. The researcher often sets a desired statistical power as one of the ingredients in the determination of the sample size needed in a research study. The following are ways to increase statistical power: (a) increase the sample size; (b) increase the alpha level (i.e., the level of significance), say from .05 to .10; (c) reduce experimental and measurement error in the estimate of variance; (d) increase the effect size (e.g., by increasing the strength of the treatment); and (e) conduct a justified directional hypothesis test if there are one or two groups. *See also* Hypothesis Testing

Statistical Versus Practical Significance In hypothesis testing, there are two types of outcomes. One is the determination of statistical significance, which is present when one rejects the null hypothesis. When one rejects the null hypothesis, however, one only knows that there is likely a nonzero relationship between the variables in the population. Practical significance is based on the potential usefulness of the research finding. Researchers use measures of effect size or strength of association to aid in determining practical significance. Effect sizes are measures of observed difference in units of standard deviation, such as Cohen's *d*, Glass's Δ, and Hedges's *g*. Strength-of-association measures estimate the proportion of variation in the dependent variable attributed to the independent variable. Examples are eta-squared, omega-squared, the intraclass correlation, and Cramer's *V*. *See also* Hypothesis Testing; Null Hypothesis (education, psychology)

Statistics *(psychology)* A way of describing, analyzing, and interpreting data based on mathematical science. Generally, statistics can be dichotomized into descriptive and inferential statistics. Descriptive statistics are used to summarize and describe data—for example, the range, median, mean, standard deviation—and can be depicted numerically or graphically. Similarly, correlations are used to describe the relationships between two variables. Inferential statistics are used to draw inferences about a data set and can be used to test hypotheses. ANOVA (analysis of variance), regressions, and data mining are inferential statistics techniques. The critical distinction between descriptive and inferential statistics is that causal relationships cannot be inferred on the basis of descriptive statistics and correlations alone. *See also* Correlation (psychology);

Descriptive Statistics (education, sociology); Inferential Statistics

Statistics *(sociology)*   The science of math that involves the analysis, explanation, and presentation of data, usually collected in one of the many academic disciplines, including both the social and natural sciences, and the humanities. When statistics are used to summarize a data set, they are referred to as descriptive statistics. Types of descriptive statistics include the mean (or average), median, and mode of a data set. When statistics from a sample are used to make assumptions about a larger population, they are referred to as inferential statistics. Examples of inferential statistics include correlation, regression, and time-series methods. ***See also*** Descriptive Statistics (sociology); Inferential Statistics

Status Conferral   Media attention confers status on people, things, and policies. By focusing on an individual or item, the media legitimize the status of that individual or item, enhancing prestige and authority. Lazarsfeld and Merton described status conferral as being one of the social functions of the media. They pointed out that it was not only favorable media attention that conferred status, such as a newspaper editorial endorsing a particular political candidate, but any media attention enhanced status.

People can become famous for being famous—celebrity status can be gained by sheer media coverage. In a circular belief, people believe that someone must be important because the media focuses attention on him or her. Celebrities appearing in advertisements confer status on a product.

How people are portrayed by the media affects their perceived status. More status is given to people who show anger rather than sadness; for example, President Bill Clinton supposedly gained status by displaying anger in front of the cameras while being questioned about his involvement with a White House intern. For more information, see Lazarsfeld and Merton (1948/2000).

Status Offense   An action prohibited for only certain groups of people, generally minors. The behavior would not be illegal if engaged in by an adult. The age of minor status differs from state to state. Examples of status offenses include running away, truancy, and underage drinking and smoking.

Status Recognition   Acknowledgment of the rank and social standing of an individual or a group of individuals within a community, workplace, or other organizational setting.

Status recognition is hierarchical and inequitable and depends on the human tendency to elevate some people to higher or lower planes of status based on a variety of social capital factors, including age, authority, class, employment, ownership, and power.

In Maoist China, for example, industrial workers were accorded high status recognition. In ancient societies, those who managed to live to an old age were accorded great respect and deference; the burgeoning population of senior citizens in contemporary times has lowered their status.

Writing the results of their five-culture study of the pursuit of status, Bernardo Huberman, Christoph Loch, and Ayse Onculer noted that among individuals who view status as having great value beyond material gain, recognition is a highly sought reward. For more information, see Ben-Israel and Ben-Israel (2002), Bian, Breiger, Davis, and Galaskiewicz (2005), and Huberman, Loch, and Onculer (2004). ***See also*** Equality (political science, public administration); Power; Rank

Statute/Statutory Law   Law put into effect by the state or federal government (in contrast to common law, case law, and administrative law). A statute begins as a bill proposed or sponsored by a member of the legislature, and if approved by both houses of the legislature, it is signed into law at the executive level. Statutes apply to specific situations, such as prohibiting a certain act, or can create a new governmental power. Statutes are often created in response to a new criminal phenomenon or to explain existing law. For example, statutes have been recently passed regarding identity theft and a number of computer crimes. ***See also*** Administrative Law; Bill; Case Law; Common Law (sociology)

Stereotype *(communication)*   A generalized, exaggerated, and simplistic label with a fixed meaning that is applied to an individual or a group. A stereotype does not take into account the unique characteristics of an individual or group. A stereotype is generally communicated through words (written and oral) but can also be conveyed in images. Stereotypes highlight people who are (or are not) representative of the dominant cultural ideologies. They are viewed as being an offensive means of description that formulates and perpetuates negative perceptions and opinions about individuals or groups. Stereotypes can be communicated culturally, institutionally, and through interaction (interpersonal, intergroup, intragroup, etc.). ***See also*** Prejudice (media studies, psychology)

Stereotype *(psychology)*   A belief that individuals who belong to a certain group have certain characteristics because they belong to that group. For example, gender stereotypes tend to associate certain characteristics with a person depending on whether the person is male or female. Women are assumed to be emotional and illogical, while men are assumed to be unemotional and logical. Ethnic stereotypes assume that people have certain characteristics because they are of a certain ethnicity. For example, Germans are assumed to be organized, the Scottish to be frugal, and the Irish to drink a lot. Occupational stereotypes assume that people have certain characteristics because they belong to certain occupational groups. For example, accountants are perceived as dull, IT people are seen as nerdy, and artists are seen as erratic. Stereotypes are based on schemas that have been formed about certain categories. While stereotypes overgeneralize the degree to which the characteristics of a group apply to all members of that group, stereotypes are a part of normal cognitive processing. As the brain attempts to process information as efficiently as possible, stereotyping saves cognitive energy by not having to classify each person individually. As a consequence, however, stereotypes can lead to inaccurate perceptions of individuals. *See also* Stereotype Threat

Stereotype Threat   The concept that if a person associates with a certain group, the person may be at risk of confirming negative stereotypes held about that group. If the negative stereotype about that group is in relation to academic performance, this may in turn affect the person's academic achievements. Stereotype threats have been demonstrated across a wide range of groups. For example, stereotype threats have been demonstrated in the context of race (Steele & Aronson, 1995). When the same difficult items of the Graduate Record Examination were given to African Americans and Caucasians, one third of participants were told that the test measured verbal ability and the other participants were told the test measured psychological factors in problem solving. While Caucasian students performed very similarly under both instructions, African Americans performed worse when being told that the test was measuring verbal ability. The same phenomenon has been observed in the context of gender. Stereotypically, it is perceived that men perform better at math tasks than do women. When this stereotype threat was activated, women had more negative thoughts about the task and performed worse than when the stereotype threat was not activated. An explanation for why stereotype threats may lead to decreased performance is that stereotype threats may trigger physiological responses—for example, increased blood pressure. For more information, see Steele and Aronson (1995). *See also* Stereotype (communication, psychology)

Stereotyping   The practice of assigning generalized, predetermined, and sometimes derogatory characteristics to an entire group of people, categorizing them without an analysis of their qualities or any experience with them. The term has taken on an almost entirely negative connotation, referring to unfounded generalizations based on race, gender, religion, ethnicity, or sexual orientation. The objection to stereotypes is based on the belief that the stereotyped generalizations are not accurate representations of the individual members of a group.

The popularization of the term to refer to a common way of dealing with complexity in the modern world is attributed to the journalist Walter Lippmann. Lippmann described modern life as covering the globe but our perceptions of it as limited by what we actually experience as well as what our culture has taught us to see. When our habitual ways of seeing and interpreting lead us to apply preexisting frames to new experiences and people without adjusting or changing them, the result can be a stereotype.

Categorizing people, activities, ideas, places, and things is a human necessity, and it is how humans organize and make sense of the world. Without categorization, it is impossible to define values, make judgments, and plan actions, so in a sense, stereotyping is a refusal to continue adjusting and reevaluating the categories we work with. Stereoptying also refers to a printing process in which setup type is impressed on a plate, made durable with metal, and impressions are pulled from the plate. The term originated in 1794 and was first used by Firmin Didot of Paris. For more information, see Ewen and Ewen (2006) and Lippmann (1922). *See also* Categorization; Postmodernism; Poststructuralism; Representation (media studies)

Stimulants   Drugs inducing excitement and awareness by increasing the activation of the nervous system. Also referred to as "uppers" or amphetamines, stimulants are used to alleviate fatigue and increase alertness. The opposite of sedatives, stimulants range from legal, mild stimulants, such as caffeine and nicotine, as found in soft drinks and tobacco, to stronger, illegal stimulants, such as cocaine, crack, and ice. Stimulants result in increased blood pressure and heart rate and reduced anxiety and appetite. The side effects of stimulants include increased aggressiveness and panic. *See also* Sedatives

Stimulation Hypothesis   This hypothesis holds that a subject who is exposed to a particular kind of message will accept and internalize the values expressed in that message and will become more likely to imitate the behavior that that message either expresses or seems to encourage. For instance, the hypothesis argues that a child who observes violent images on television is more likely to think, speak, and act violently and that a person exposed to pornography will be more inclined to approach sexuality in a socially unacceptable fashion. The stimulation hypothesis has been postulated in more than one form. One of these, the imitation hypothesis, argues that violent or sexual images educate viewers in forms of unacceptable behavior and incite them to engage in identical or closely comparable behaviors in real life. Another variant of the stimulation hypothesis, the disinhibition hypothesis, claims that these images lower people's social inhibitions, making them more generally inclined toward antisocial behavior. It can also be argued that violent or sexual images have the cumulative effect of producing more cultural acceptance of unacceptable behavior, creating a social environment in which aggressive or prurient impulses are less discouraged.

The stimulation hypothesis thoroughly contradicts the catharsis hypothesis, which contends that when the media present graphically violent or sexual images, it produces a release of tension in the viewer. The catharsis hypothesis maintains that viewers are satisfied with the vicarious experience of seeing forbidden behavior acted out for them and are thereafter less inclined to engage in the behavior directly. In hundreds of studies of the effects of television violence, only a handful have tended to confirm the catharsis hypothesis, whereas a great preponderance of data and clinical opinion support the stimulation hypothesis, that is, either the imitation hypothesis or the disinhibition hypothesis. For more information, see Severin (1988). ***See also*** Communication Theory; Message

Stimulus Generalization   The generalization of the conditioned response to stimuli that are similar to the initial stimulus causing the response. For example, Pavlov's infamous dog may have started to salivate on hearing a sound similar to the original sound that was used to elicit the conditioned response. Other examples include "Little Albert," who was conditioned to fear rats. A few days later, the child not only feared rats but also a rabbit, a dog, and even a Santa Claus mask. As not many stimuli in real life are exactly the same, stimulus generalization serves an adaptive purpose. As a general rule, the closer the stimulus is to the initial stimulus causing the response, the greater the likelihood of stimulus generalization. ***See also*** Classical Conditioning

Sting   A type of white-collar crime in which people use their position to trick others out of money. One example of a sting is a fake charity. Stings may also be a police tactic involving an undercover operation planned to counter a specific crime, such as catching people who sell illegal drugs.

Stockholm Syndrome   A psychological response that may occur when a seized hostage demonstrates loyalty to the hostage taker. The syndrome is named for the robbery of Kreditbanken in Norrmalmstrog, Stockholm, Sweden, in 1973, when the bank robbers held the bank employees captive for five days. The victims became emotionally attached to their captors and defended them publicly after being released. The term was first used by the criminologist and psychiatrist Nils Bererot. The term is also used to describe loyalty to an abuser, as in battered woman syndrome or other forms of abuse. The phenomenon is also referred to as *trauma bonding*. ***See also*** Hostage

Stop and Frisk   A type of warrantless search conducted in a public place when a law enforcement officer does not have probable cause to arrest a person but is suspicious enough, based on the person's behavior, to stop and search the person. Frisking is patting down the clothing of a person for the purpose of searching for a concealed weapon. Frisking falls under the Fourth Amendment protection against unlawful search and seizure. A law enforcement officer must have an articulable reason for conducting the stop and frisk, which is a lesser standard than probable cause. The standard was established in *Terry v. Ohio* (1968). For

more information, see *Terry v. Ohio* (1968). ***See also*** Reasonable Suspicion

Strategic Planning   Planning that can potentially help the members of an organization align key objectives with the capabilities to achieve them. It involves developing a plan of action that is the product of assessing key resources, internal organizational processes, and the external environment. Strategic planning may be used to set a long-term course or direction for an organization. It can help managers and staff identify what goals are most important and achievable for the organization. Public managers may also design strategic-planning activities to involve personnel at different levels of the organizational infrastructure, with the aim of developing a comprehensive plan and stimulating interest across agency departments and divisions. Denhardt and Denhardt (2006) identify key steps in the strategic-planning process: (a) stating or clarifying the organizational mission, (b) conducting an environmental analysis, (c) identifying strengths and weaknesses, (d) expressing the values of leaders, and (e) developing alternative strategies to achieve the desired results. For more information, see Denhardt and Denhardt (2006).

Strategy   A plan of action to aid in the communication and execution of a result. The desired goal of a strategy might be problem solving in an exchange of communication, optimizing effective and positive communication between parties, or development of a communication plan for a group of colleagues and their clients to discuss and accomplish a project. A strategy can be implemented in formal or informal contexts. It can be conceived by an individual or by two or more parties. Effective communication tactics can be learned through communication models and training programs, wherein the focus is on developing understandable and coherent messages between the sender and his or her audience. A strategy might include the use of rhetoric, attention to feedback mechanisms, or modification of oral style. ***See also*** Dissolution

Stratification (*education*)   The system of inequality in a society. Inequality comes in many forms. It may be political (power), social (prestige), and/or economic (money). These inequalities may be studied as they relate to groups and categories defined by gender, race/ethnicity, religion, or sexual preference. Important issues in stratification research concern the causes and outcomes of these inequalities, their degree of severity, and strategies to reduce inequality.

While anthropologists disagree about whether social stratification exists in all societies, it definitely persists in all large societies. But the amounts and types of inequality vary from one society to another. The gap between the rich and the poor or the powerful and the weak differs significantly among societies. One statistical index of the degree of inequality is the Gini coefficient. Gender and religious inequalities also vary sharply. The degree of social *mobility* (movement up or down) ranges from societies in which individuals are born into a caste to societies in which they have some opportunity to change their standing. ***See also*** Social Stratification

Stratification *(sociology)* The dividing of people in society into hierarchical levels or strata. Stratification can be based on factors including age, authority, ethnicity, gender, poverty, power, and wealth. Most commonly, stratification is based on a person's role in the society's mode of production. For example, in a capitalist society, a person who is a worker is in a lower stratum than an owner. ***See also*** Social Stratification

Stratified Random Sampling Sampling method that requires knowledge of the distribution of the target variable(s) in the population so as to choose a sample that is representative of that population. Examples of variables include gender and race or a factor of importance to the study, such as offense type or place of residence. The population is divided into strata based on the variable(s) of interest, and a random sample is chosen from each strata. ***See also*** Stratified Sampling

Stratified Sample Requires knowledge of the distribution of the target variable(s) in the population for division into strata based on the variable(s). Examples of variables include gender and race,or a factor of importance to the study such as offense type or place of residence. A sample is then drawn from each strata.

Stratified Sampling A random-sampling method that results in the sample having the same proportions on selected characteristics as found in the population. First, strata are identified; these *can be* crossed in a contingency table to determine the combinations. Second, the proportion in the sample in each stratum is selected to be the same as in the population, using random selection from the strata; this increases the likelihood that the sample will be representative of the population. For example, if 0.15 of the population are male and married, that will be *the pr*oportion of married males in the randomly selected sample from the population. ***See also*** Sampling in Mixed-Methods Research

Stratified Society A society that is characterized by a hierarchy of people based on status. Stratification can be based on factors including age, authority, ethnicity, gender, poverty, power, and wealth. Most commonly, stratification is based on a person's role in the society's mode of production.

Street Crime Generally, violent and/or property crime, such as theft or robbery. Street crime is punished more harshly than white-collar crime (i.e., suite crime), which is generally committed by people of affluence. Street crime is more likely to be committed by people of lower socioeconomic status.

Stress Any event perceived as a threat to a person's well-being and perceived as beyond the person's coping abilities. There are four major types of stress: frustration, conflict, change, and pressure. Frustration happens when reaching a goal seems temporarily impeded. For example, situations such as traffic jams or slow, crowded public transport can cause frustration. Although upsetting at the time, frustration is often not long lasting. Conflict takes place when an individual is uncertain as to how to respond to two conflicting goals. There are three types of conflict. An approach-approach conflict arises when an individual has to choose between two desired goals, while an avoidance-avoidance conflict is a choice between two undesirable goals. Finally, if a person has to decide whether to choose a goal that is both desirable and undesirable, it is referred to as an approach-avoidance conflict. The third type of stress, change, takes place when a change in life circumstances requires a person to readjust. For example, some of the most stressful life events requiring readjustment are the passing of a spouse, divorce, imprisonment, loss of a job, retirement, and so on. Finally, when a person is expected to perform certain behaviors, it is referred to as pressure. Pressure can be self-imposed or imposed by family or work settings. ***See also*** Conflict (sociology)

Stroop Test A cognitive test investigating automatic information processing. In the original Stroop test, named after its discoverer, Stroop, participants were asked to name the color of a written word where the word itself is a color word. For example, the word *green* would appear in red, and the participant would be expected to respond "Red," that is, naming the color of the written word. However, as reading is an automatic skill, many participants have difficulties naming the color of the word, as they cannot avoid also reading the word. As a result, the response time of participants was slowed down, or participants even responded incorrectly by naming the color word (*green*) instead of the color of the word (red).

The Stroop task supports Posner and Snyder's (1975) assertions of automatic processing. First, automatic processing can occur unintentionally. Second, automatic processing can occur without reaching conscious levels of awareness. Finally, automatic processing generally does not interfere with other cognitive activities. More recent versions of the test include the emotional Stroop test, in which the presented words are either negative-emotion-evoking words, such as hate, war, and so on, or neutral words. Similarly, participants are asked to name the color of the word. Results indicated that participants were slower in naming the color of negative-emotion words than neutral words. For more information, see Posner and Snyder (1975). ***See also*** Automaticity

Structural Equation Modeling A technique that combines path analysis, which is used to study the causal relations among variables, with factor analysis, which is used to improve the measurement of variables. Stuctural equation modeling (SEM) requires complicated calculations that are extremely impractical to do without using computer software. Among the more popular programs are LISREL, EQS, Amos, and Mplus.

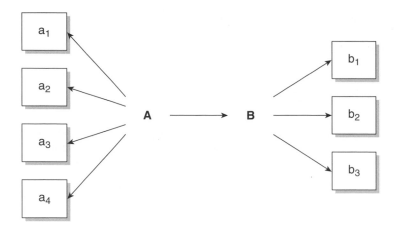

Figure 1   *Example of Structural Equation Modeling*

It is easiest to discuss SEM with a graphic example, as shown in Figure 1. Graphic representations are all but universal in SEM. The example is much simpler than a full SEM model, but it illustrates the main points. A researcher has a theory: *A* causes *B*. This is represented by an arrow from *A* to *B,* which leads to an important point: To use SEM, a researcher has to have a theory of the relationship between variables. Another researcher might believe that *B* causes *A*. SEM requires researchers to commit to a theory before they can begin the analysis. *A* and *B* could be any two variables. Say they are Attitude and Belief. These are good examples of variables studied using SEM: variables that are hard to measure because they are hard to observe directly. Such variables are usually called *latent variables.*

When measuring latent variables, using more than one instrument or indicator is a good practice; it enhances the quality of measurement of latent variables. Multiple measurements are seldom necessary with variables such as age or height; they are easily measured by an external observer. But attitudes and beliefs are internal and not as easily defined, observed, and measured. In the example graphic, *A* is measured in four ways, using four different indicators: a_1, a_2, a_3, and a_4. *B* is measured by three indicators: b_1, b_2, and b_3.

An SEM always has two components: a causal model and a measurement model. The causal model is $A \rightarrow B$, or Attitude causes Belief. The measurement model is represented by the arrows from *A* to a_1, a_2, a_3, and a_4 and the arrows from *B* to b_1, b_2, and b_3. These arrows describe how *A* and *B* are composite measures. In a full diagram, each of the arrows has a number attached to it. The arrow from *A* to *B* indicates the strength of the relation between the two; it is a type of regression coefficient. The arrows from *A* and *B* to their indicators show how well each of the indicators measures its latent variable. These arrows are labeled with correlations (factor loadings) of the indicator with its latent variable. Researchers in the social and behavioral sciences are often interested in latent variables and are usually interested in causation. SEM is popular because it combines these two interests. For more

information, see Kline (2005). ***See also*** Causation; Correlation (education, psychology); Factor Analysis (education, psychology); Path Analysis; Regression Analysis

Structuralism *(education)*   A theory based on the assumption that social or cultural practices are the result of the underlying structures that govern human behavior and interaction. Each society or culture operates on the basis of these structures. Differences among societies or cultures are explained through differences in these relationships. Structuralism posits that human actions are purposeful and methodical and are functional representations of the structures. It is argued that only a thorough investigation of the structures can result in an adequate understanding of the society or culture. ***See also*** Semiotics (education)

Structuralism *(media studies)*   A mode of inquiry emerging from application of the work of Ferdinand de Saussure to domains of meaning other than linguistic, notably the work of the anthropologist Claude Lévi-Strauss (*Anthropologie structurale* [*Structural Anthropology,* 1963] and *La Pensée sauvage* [*The Savage Mind,* 1968]). Lévi-Strauss's analysis of, for example, kinship relations or of food in terms of binary opposites such as "raw" and "cooked" laid bare all areas of social life to structural analysis. The contemporaneous works of Roland Barthes, Louis Althusser, and Jacques Lacan also apply structuralist principles to literature, political science, and psychology, respectively. Structuralist analysis was a radically leveling move, for objects of "high" culture yielded no more insights than those of popular or "low" culture; the very mystique of high culture could only exert itself on the strength of *not* being lowbrow. High culture needs low culture for its definition because its meaning is not intrinsic to itself but depends on a system of internal differences and codes (binary oppositions such as high/low, raw/cooked, etc.) that only emerge when phenomena are analyzed as part of a system rather than discretely (in Saussure's terms, when attention is paid to the implied system [*langue*] rather than to individual utterances [*parole*]). This prioritizing of system over individual instance gives structuralism its formalist and antihumanist bent, in that individual agency counts for little in the overall weight of social totalities. The tacit grammars of cultural systems influence meaning and behavior far more than any conscious intention or individual "free" will does. Structuralism works to disclose the deep structures of meaning that underlie the epiphenomenal appearances that can easily be mistaken for empirical reality. Precisely because meaning is deep and implied, no utterance can ever be taken at face value. We access the hidden meaning of things only by exposing the coded logic of appearance. This unmasking movement of structuralism showed many affinities with Marxism and Freudianism in their depiction of social and psychic reality as internally at variance with itself and as operating by indirection.

The challenge to classic structuralism that we call poststructuralism lies in the seeming orderliness of the systems and codes invoked to generate meaning. In an influential essay, "Structure, Sign, and Play in the Discourse of the Human Sciences," Jacques Derrida pointed out the covert dependence of all systemic structures on an invisible center that organizes meaning while itself remaining beyond analysis and that stays outside the play of meaning within shifting structures. Once these grounding assumptions of Western metaphysics are put into the play of meaning, the stability of all structures such as binary opposites is undercut. For more information, see Derrida (1980) and Lévi-Strauss (1963, 1968). ***See also*** Deconstruct; Empiricist Tradition; Semiotics (media studies)

Structuralism (*sociology*)   A broad term referring to the system of organizations in a society. The system creates a social structure. Parts of this structure are differentially available to members of a society, creating limited opportunities based on factors such as gender, power, and wealth. For example, access to the educational structural system is based on personal factors such as gender and socioeconomic status. ***See also*** Structuralism (media studies)

Student Diversity   The cultural differences among students based on race, ethnicity, gender, sexual orientation, socioeconomic status, religion, language, and ability/disability. It is a demographic reality of American public schooling. Moreover, demographic forecasting predicts that by 2030 half of all school children will be children of color. Student diversity, which can be related to learning-style differences and differences in academic outcomes, requires that teachers become more knowledgeable about diversity. ***See also*** Equal Educational Opportunity; Minority Group

Student/Learner-Centered and Constructivist Instruction/Learning   Constructivism is an educational philosophy that emphasizes learner agency in constructing knowledge while interacting with informational, material, and social resources in the learning environment.

There are two broad strands of constructivism on the two sides of a knowledge continuum: cognitive constructivism (Piaget, 1968) and sociocultural constructivism (Vygotsky, 1978). The former places more emphasis on knowledge as individually formed and possessed, whereas the latter views individual cognition as being inherently situated in sociocultural contexts.

Learner-centered instruction and learning lie at the core of constructivist instruction and learning. Guiding instruction and learning are the American Psychological Association's Learner-Centered Psychological Principles. These principles identify the specific contributions of both individual and social influences in four areas of psychological research: (1) cognitive and metacognitive factors, (2) motivational and affective factors, (3) developmental and social factors, and (4) individual differences. In the dialectic relationship between learning and development, learners bring in knowledge, skills, and attitudes to the educational setting; engage in knowledge sharing, building, and transforming; and develop accountable positioning as individuals. During the process, learners are provided support by peers and more capable adults for solving complex problems and making sense of experience.

With the learner participating in active knowledge construction, constructivist instructional principles emphasize the process more than the products of learning:

1. Embed learning in complex, realistic, and relevant environments.

2. Provide for social negotiation as an integral part of learning.

3. Support multiple perspectives and the use of multiple modes of representation.

4. Encourage ownership in learning.

5. Nurture self-awareness of the knowledge construction process.

Under these principles, collaborative learning and inquiry-based learning of various forms are two major methods of constructivist instruction and learning.

Piaget contributed the important concept of schema accommodation to constructivist teaching and learning. In encountering new experiences, the learner's existing schemas must be adjusted and modified to accommodate the events and account for the experiences.

Vygotsky's most influential concepts are the zone of proximal development (ZPD) and scaffolding. The ZPD is defined as the gap between the actual developmental level as determined by independent problem solving and the potential developmental level as determined through problem solving under adult guidance or in collaboration with more capable peers. Closely linked to the ZPD, scaffolding refers to the dynamic interactional process whereby the teacher or more capable peers operate as a supportive tool for learners for constructing knowledge. For more information, see Bonk and Cunningham (1998), Piaget (1968), and Vygotsky (1978). *See also* Learner-Centered Instruction

Student Outcomes   Information that is collected to depict students' development and learning as a result of specific educational interventions. Student outcomes can provide an overview of how students are learning, the areas for targeted improvements, and the specific strengths of a school or classroom. Student outcomes may be measured on an institutional or classroom level and may reflect cognitive, social, or affective domains. Analysis of student outcomes helps administrators, educators, and researchers evaluate the effectiveness of educational interventions ranging from schoolwide programs to classroom instruction.

Institutional-level student outcomes include indicators such as overall attendance, graduation, and retention rates. These data indicate how well the institution, as a whole, has met students' needs and prepared them for successful completion of a program (high school diploma, college degree, etc.). Classroom-level student outcomes include grades and performance on end-of-unit and achievement tests. These data allow students to demonstrate mastery of required skills and content while providing insight into the effectiveness of the teacher's instructional methods. *See also* Learning Outcomes

Student Rights   Students have the right to freedom of expression so long as their behavior, either in school or outside, does not substantially interfere with classwork, invade the rights of others, or violate school board standards of appropriateness. They are entitled to a free press so long as the articles that are published in the school paper support school goals. Though students have the right to freedom from unwarranted search and seizure, they may be searched if the school board deems it necessary. In this case, the search must be reasonable and connected to the violation under investigation. Students may also associate freely. *See also* Constitution (political science)

Students at Risk   Students are considered to be at risk of failing or dropping out of school due to continuous insufficient academic accomplishment. The following characteristics are generally associated with this designation: male, minority, low self-esteem, and low socioeconomic family status. At-risk students may also exhibit attention deficit disorders, view school as a negative environment, and be disruptive in the school setting. At-risk students may also have limited English proficiency, be struggling readers, and have a high absentee rate. These students sometimes come from undereducated families that do not value the benefits of education. At-risk students sometimes engage in unhealthy behaviors such as early sexual relations, drug and alcohol abuse, and poor nutritional habits. To decrease the risk of student failure, the educational community must attempt to identify at-risk students early in their schooling, provide developmentally responsive instruction, and regularly reevaluate the students for academic progress. At-risk students should not be given a watered-down curriculum; rather, they should be provided with a rich curriculum that is meaningful and relevant to the learner and have effective teachers who are knowledgeable and experienced in working with a diverse group of students; their learning should include higher-order thinking skills, and various forms of authentic assessment should be available for them to demonstrate their knowledge. The National Institute on the Education of At-Risk Students (At-Risk Institute) is one of five Institutes created by the Educational Research, Development, Dissemination and Improvement Act of 1994. These Institutes are located within the Office of Educational Research and Improvement at the U.S. Department of Education.

Students with Disabilities Act   The act, which is associated with Section 504 of the Rehabilitation Act of 1973 and the 1990 American Disabilities Act (ADA), states that schools must make reasonable accommodations and adaptations for students with disabilities, including individuals with physical, mental, or learning disabilities. School districts are required to offer the same opportunities for success and provide accessible school programs and accessible school facilities for disabled students. All public schools and those private schools that receive any federal funding are required to comply with the act. *See also* Individuals with Disabilities Education Act (IDEA)

Subculture   A group of people who not only have many of the traditions, rituals, values, and norms (i.e., culture) of the larger group but also have unique values and norms that differentiate them from this larger group. Ethnic groups, each with their own histories, have their own subcultures. Other subcultures can be based on factors ranging from sexuality to career type and from musical interest to favorite TV show. There are a number of subcultures that are considered deviant, including gangs, drug users, and people with numerous tattoos. Criminal subcultures may include people involved in white-collar crime, organized crime, or street crime. There are several aspects of youth culture, including the music, clothes, and language they favor. Cultural values can be dispersed through interaction with the group and observation of the group (such as with copycat school shooters) and be transmitted by the media and the Internet. *See also* Criminology; Culture (sociology)

Subjective Responsibility   The principle that an individual can only be found guilty of wrongfulness if he or she possessed the relevant *mens rea* (or criminal intent). The necessity of a "guilty mind," or the notion that an individual should only be punished for what he or she is responsible, undoubtedly embodies a cornerstone of contemporary American criminal justice. Although a number of crimes only require *actus rea* (or the guilty act), the vast majority of offenses demand some element of subjective responsibility. Determining *mens rea* generally requires three specific components: (1) culpability, (2) blameworthiness, and (3) evidence of fault. The parameters for determining subjective responsibility can be somewhat difficult to determine; this may be especially problematic in cases of insanity or justification. While the notion of legal insanity has gone through a number of historical permutations, that of justification is generally restricted to cases of self-defense (although the limits and extents of self-defense may be deeply contested). For more information, see Schulhofer (2001). ***See also*** Civil Liability; Objective Responsibility

Subjectivity The act of shaping ourselves as individuals and the subsequent ability to interact in the world. Subjectivity is determined by the processing of individuals, which is shaped by personal experience. Moreover, it can be reflected in one's decisions to adhere to social rules. Key elements that form one's subjectivity include gender, race, and class. Subjectivity is often discussed in relation to agency, the exertion of will to shape one's own world. Individuals' subjectivity, then, is crucial to the presentation and development of their mode of communication, as well as the potential for argumentativeness, articulation, attitude, avoidance, defensiveness, and oral style. ***See also*** Argumentativeness; Articulation; Attitude; Avoidance; Defensiveness; Oral Style

Subjectivity/Subjectivism A concept that is commonly discussed in social science research together with objectivity. Subjectivity is the idea that experiences are characterized by individual perception, standpoint, and social position. Objectivity, instead, is based on the notion that truth can be discovered once individuals move beyond their personal views and perceptions and aim for absolute and universal explanations. Modernist and positivist philosophers and scholars believe that an objective truth can be discovered through a systematic method of gathering and measuring empirical data and by allowing scientific inquiry to move beyond the idiosyncrasies of context. This view has been challenged by philosophers and scholars who assert that the notion of an objective reality is illusory because all knowledge is based on experience and embodied perception and is inseparable from context.

The latter view has its detractors as well. In fact, a radical view of subjectivity and subjectivism is offered by some postmodernist scholars, who argue that language predates experience and thus determines how we know, what we know, and who we are. Their subjectivism is radical because it rejects the need to gather empirical data based on either experience or objective reality. Such radical subjectivism advances the idea that all we can aim for, at best, is an appreciation of our condition as structured by the language-like form of consciousness and/or by the historical discursive traces that make up our knowledge, our ways of knowing, and our very idea of being. ***See also*** Objectivity/Objectivism

Subjects The individuals who are ruled over in a nation. The term is usually associated with monarchies. Citizens, in contrast, are associated with democracies. The Eleventh Amendment of the U.S. Constitution implies the citizen-subject distinction: "The Judicial power of the United States shall not be construed to extend to any suit . . . by Citizens or Subjects of any Foreign State."

Sublimation A coping mechanism whereby a person transfers psychic energy into a positive channel. Often referred to as a defense mechanism, sublimation can be considered the most constructive defense mechanism of all, as a person's sublimation may result in socially acceptable outlets such as art. An example of sublimation would be a person who feels sad or isolated, which results in the person singing rhythm and blues music. ***See also*** Defense Mechanisms (psychology); Projection (psychology); Rationalization; Reaction Formation; Repression (psychology)

Subliminal Message A message that is perceived below conscious levels of awareness. In 1957, James Vicary claimed that subliminally flashing brand names during a movie led to increased consumption of those products. He later admitted that these results were fabricated. Overall, research regarding the effects of subliminal messages is conflicting. While some research has indicated that there may be some priming effects, little research has shown any lasting effects on long-term memory. ***See also*** Priming

Subpoena A command to appear at a given time and place to provide testimony. A subpoena is also used to bring evidence such as documents, weapons, or photographs to court. Subpoenas are generally issued by judges and delivered by the lawyer whose client is in need of the testimony/evidence.

Subsidiarity A principle pronounced by Pope Pius XI in 1931 and written as a response to the Great Depression in the United States. This principle, found in the papal bulletin *Quadragesimo Anno*, states that a higher entity in the social order may not do for the lower order what the lower order is capable of doing for itself. Subsidiarity is a feature of federalism. In the United States, subsidiarity can be found in the Tenth Amendment of the Bill of Rights. It was asserted as countering the trend toward excessive centralization of government as well as communism and socialism.

The purpose of subsidiarity is to limit the role of the government in order to protect the place of private individuals and institutions while simultaneously justifying some role for the government. Only when a particular task cannot be undertaken by individuals will the task be handed to the level of government.

Although not originally intended as part of the European Economic Community in the 1950s, the European Union adopted subsidiarity in its 1992 Maastricht Treaty as one of its central principles. To the European Union, subsidiarity means that powers should only be shifted to the level of the European Union when member states themselves cannot achieve the same results. **See also** Bill of Rights (political science); Communism (political science); Federalism; Socialism (political science)

Substance Abuse   The excessive or improper use of mind- or mood-altering substances, especially alcohol and other drugs. Abuse results in negative consequences such as employment or relationship difficulties and loss of pleasure in previously enjoyable activities, and people with an abuse problem continue to use the substance despite self-awareness of the problem. In some cases, substance abuse leads to physical dependence. Substance abuse affects individuals, families, communities, and society. Oftentimes, there is a lack of understanding of the nature of substance abuse. Stigmatizing persons with abuse problems can result in refusal to self-identify one's problem and refusal to seek help.

Two popular explanatory models of substance abuse are the moral model and the disease model. The moral model views an addict as having character defects that lead to his or her substance use, and willpower is said to be enough to enable a person to stop using the substance. The disease model views an addict as suffering from a physical disease. More specific theories of substance abuse include (a) biopsychosocial theory, according to which addiction is related to dysfunctions of biology, psychology, and/or social interactions; (b) genetic theory, according to which substance abuse is genetically passed down from generation to generation; and (c) biological theory, according to which there are biological markers that cause some people to be susceptible to substance abuse. Psychological or adaptation theory focuses on psychological factors resulting in abusive beliefs and behavior.

Substantive Due Process   A guarantee under the due process clauses of the Fifth and Fourteenth amendments that appropriate justifications will be used whenever the government is taking away a person's life, liberty, or property, regardless of the procedures used. Substantive due process rights are not explicitly defined in the U.S. Constitution. Rather, these rights are "unenumerated." The concept of substantive due process developed around the time of the Civil War in the United States.

Prior to 1856, legal theorists focused on the procedural features of due process: whether the government was following fair procedures when depriving a person of life, liberty, or property. Substantive due

process was later introduced in 1856 in *Dred Scott v. Sandford.* In this case, the Supreme Court found that without due process, the Missouri Compromise of 1820 deprived slave owners of the liberty to own slaves, which violated the Fifth Amendment. After the *Dred Scott* case, the substantive due process doctrine lay dormant until 1905.

Starting with *Lochner v. New York* (1905), the Supreme Court used substantive due process in the early 20th century to protect economic liberties from government interference. In *Lochner,* the Court struck down a New York law that limited the number of hours a baker could work. The Court considered this law an interference with the liberty to contract between employer and employee. The Court thus ruled that the law violated the Fourteenth Amendment, which was ratified in 1868. Although the Supreme Court repudiated substantive due process in 1937, it still has been a factor in subsequent court rulings, especially those concerning privacy rights.

Among the many rights that the Supreme Court found in the latter part of the 20th century that were protected under substantive due process were the right to use birth control (*Griswold v. Connecticut,* 1965), the right to abortion in the first trimester (*Roe v. Wade,* 1973), and the right of competent adults to refuse medical treatment (*Cruzan v. Director Missouri Department of Health,* 1990).

In 1986, in *Bowers v. Hardwick,* the Court specified the contexts in which courts can protect substantive due process. Such rights should be protected only if they are enumerated in text—intended by the framers to be protected—and when a tradition of protecting such rights has been shown. For more information, see *Bowers v. Hardwick* (1986), Chemerinsky (1998–1999), *Cruzan v. Director Missouri Department of Health* (1990), *Dred Scott v. Sandford* (1856), *Griswold v. Connecticut* (1965), *Lochner v. New York* (1905), and *Roe v. Wade* (1973). **See also** Bill of Rights (political science); Due Process/Due Process Model

Substantive Law   Statutory or written law that defines crimes, punishments, civil rights, and responsibilities. Substantive law stands in contrast to procedural law, which defines the rules of the court and the rights of defendants within the criminal justice system. **See also** Procedural Law/Rights

Succession   The established order of leadership replacement among political leaders or monarchs. In the United States, the Presidential Succession Act (1947) delineates that in the case of the removal, death, or resignation of the President, he or she would be succeeded in the following order: the Vice President, the Speaker of the House, the President Pro Tempore, and then cabinet members in the order in which their departments were created.

The act was signed by President Harry Truman and replaced the 1886 version of the law, in which Congress had removed the President Pro Tempore and the Speaker of the House from the original act of 1792s line of succession.

Suffrage   The right to vote in a political election, as established by the government. Suffrage, if it exists at all, varies greatly between nations. Voting requirements traditionally depend on the following variables: gender, religion, wealth, education, race/ethnicity, age, residency, birth country, and criminal record. The U.S. Constitution contains many amendments reflecting the nation's suffrage history. The amendments allow nonwhite males (Fifteenth Amendment, 1870); women (Nineteenth Amendment, 1920); residents of Washington, D.C. (Twenty-Third Amendment, 1961); the poor—after abolishing the poll tax (Twenty-Fourth Amendment, 1962; extended to state elections in the Supreme Court decision of 1966, *Harper v. Virginia Board of Elections*); and 18- to 21-year-olds (Twenty-Sixth Amendment, 1971) to vote. Apart from the rights guaranteed by the Constitution, the states decide who can vote in their state. For example, the laws regarding the voting status of criminal felons and noncitizens are determined on a state-by-state basis.

Suite Crime   Also called white-collar crime, the term was originally coined by Edwin Sutherland to denote a crime committed by a person of high social status during the course of his or her employment. It refers to a type of corporate crime, such as fraud, insider trading, embezzlement, and computer crime. White-collar crime stands in contrast to street crime in that it is usually, but not necessarily, nonviolent. Suite crimes may also include offenses such as selling dangerous products to consumers and dumping toxic chemicals into the environment. *See also* White-Collar Crime

Summative Evaluation   Accountability-oriented evaluation that seeks to determine the merit, worth, and/or significance of an evaluand in order to inform decision making about the evaluand. This type of evaluation aids decision making about whether to continue or terminate a program or hire or fire a staff member. *See also* Evaluation (education); Evaluation, Logic of; Formative Evaluation

Sunshine Law   Transparency or openness in government, as when the windows are open and the sun shines in. The technical term is *freedom of information* laws. In the United States, the first sunshine law, the Freedom of Information Act, was signed into legislation by President Lyndon B. Johnson in 1966. This act applied only to the federal government. However, all 50 states have their own versions that apply to state governments. These laws keep open records on everything a government does, from minutes at meetings to budgetary records. Citizens have a right to request their government for information. There are certain records that are kept secret, such as items related to national security. When a state or federal government refuses to fill a request for information, the burden is on it, and not the requestor, to prove why it is necessary that the information be kept secret. These laws hold governments accountable for their actions while restoring the public's trust. *See also* Citizen Participation

Superego   One of the three core parts of Sigmund Freud's theory of the psyche in conjunction with the ego and the id. Originally derived from the German word *Überich*, the superego functions as a person's conscience and regulates the urges of the id. The superego develops from successfully mastering the Oedipus complex. The stronger the Oedipus complex was and the quicker it was repressed, the more the superego will reign as a conscience over the ego. As successfully resolving the Oedipus complex leads to identification with the father, the superego preserves the character of the father. For more information, see Freud (1923/2000). *See also* Ego (psychology); Id; Psychoanalysis (psychology)

Superpower   A country having the capacity to maintain dominating power and influence anywhere in the world so that it may attain the status of a global hegemon (Miller, 2005). Although the term *superpower* was around since the early 1920s, its common usage came from the post–World War II application to the United States, the British Empire, and the Soviet Union. Four major components of a superpower are military strength, economic wealth, political power, and cultural power. Other contributors to superpower status are large population size and control over a large geographical area. Britain was the sole superpower from the 19th century until World War II.

The British Empire, however, ceased to exist with the independence of its colonies. The concept of superpower thus came to mean the adversarial relationship between the United States and the Soviet Union during the Cold War. The superpower status of these two countries was defined by their possessions of nuclear weaponry, which made them more powerful than any other nation.

Thus, the age of superpowers has been considered by many to be the period from 1945, with the appearance of nuclear weapons and American and Soviet disagreement over the future of postwar Germany, to 1991, with the disappearance of the Soviet Union, which left the United States as the sole world superpower. This was the era of bipolarism, when international affairs was dominated by two very powerful states.

Today, there is speculation about who will become the next superpower in the 21st century. Some believe that China and India will be the next superpowers. Many others believe, however, that the world is multipolar since complex economic interdependencies dominate international relationships. In the end, some aver that no nation has maintained supremacy for more than several generations and that U.S. supremacy has already reached its zenith. For more information, see Miller (2005). *See also* Cold War

S

Supervision In the traditional sense, the function of directing, coordinating, and controlling the work of others. Supervision may also include training, instructing, motivating, evaluating, and rewarding employees. The purpose of supervision is to obtain maximum performance from employees. According to Douglas McGregor, the methods of supervision should be adjusted to the needs of employees. Employees who are motivated by lower-level needs require extrinsic rewards and more direction, while employees who identify with the goals and values of the organization will find their work more meaningful and will require less supervision. As workers are given more autonomy and responsibility, the function of supervision shifts to providing technical support, obtaining resources for the group, and serving as a liaison with other groups within the organization. When work groups become more self-directed, the supervisory functions may be shared among members of the work group, eliminating the need for a supervisor. For more information, see McGregor (1967).

Supply The various amounts of a good or service that producers or owners of the means of production are willing and able to make available for sale at alternative prices for a given period of time.

The law of supply holds that if the factors affecting supply, apart from the price of the good or service in question, don't change (ceteris paribus), as the price of that good or service increases, the producers or owners of the means of production will be induced to supply more.

Figure 1 *Law of Supply*

Figure 1 depicts the law of supply, which indicates that the quantity of a good or service supplied will increase as the price increases when other factors or variables remain unchanged. This positive correlation is contingent on other factors, which are generally considered to be the factors affecting supply. Some of these factors are resources (input cost), improvements in technology or innovation, taxes and subsidies, prices of other goods that may encourage a shift in

production when the cost of readjustment is minimal, producer expectation of prices, and the number of producers or owners supplying a good or service.

These factors are alternatively referred to as shifters because they determine whether supply will change at each of the original prices in the market. In other words, they cause a change in supply as distinct from a change in the quantity supplied. A change in the quantity supplied is the result of price changes associated with the price of a good directly under consideration in the market. Change in supply occurs when exogenous shocks to those variables (third variables), originally assumed to be constant, affect the original supply.

Taxes are intended to raise revenue, but they also discourage the production of certain goods—for example, alcohol and tobacco. Taxes increase the cost of production and therefore the supply. It becomes relatively expensive for consumers to consume goods that are increasingly taxed and for producers to recover their cost of production; consequently, supply falls. Subsidies produce the opposite effect. The total supply of output in a national economy is referred to as aggregate supply. For more information, see Boyes and Melvin (2002), Case and Fair (2003), McConnell and Brue (2008), Perkins, Radlet, and Lindauer (2006), Salvatore (2002), and Schiller (2008). ***See also*** Demand; Elasticity; Market

Supply-Side Policies A theory of economic stabilization that maintains that changes in aggregate supply rather than in aggregate demand are the major determinants of inflation, unemployment, and economic growth. Therefore, supply-siders argue that government policies that are intended to achieve stable prices and increased output must be targeted toward economic variables that can increase output and employment, such as the expansionary fiscal policy of tax reduction.

Supply-side economics presents tax reduction as an incentive to improve the work ethic and encourage saving and investment. The basic point of reference for tax evaluation is the marginal tax rate (the rate that is paid on the last unit of taxable income). Since the incentive to work, according to supply-siders, is highly contingent on disposable income (income after taxes), high marginal tax rates discourage worker productivity and put a tremendous burden on employers to invest, innovate, or employ more workers. Additionally, higher marginal tax rates are generally perceived by this school of thought to lead to tax avoidance and evasion—the obvious implication being a reduction in the tax revenue base as marginal tax rates reach prohibitive levels.

The tax Laffer curve (after the work of Arthur Laffer, but the concept antedates him by centuries; see Figure 1) is one of the widely used illustrations of the arguments of supply-siders, although there are substantial reservations about its accuracy.

Tax Receipts

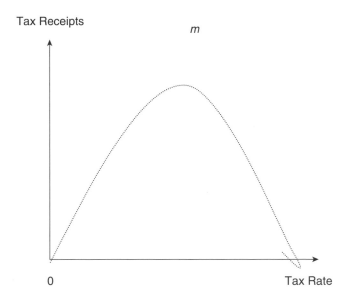

Figure 1 *Laffer Curve*

According to the Laffer parabola, tax receipts increase with the tax rate up to a certain critical point (*m*), after which there is an inverse relationship between tax rates and tax receipts. Beyond point *m,* as tax rate increases, tax receipts fall. The Laffer proposition, which was developed in the 1980s, seemed to explain economic performance reasonably well during the Kennedy and Reagan tax cuts of the 1960s and 1980s, but critics of the Laffer curve are apprehensive about the sensitivity of incentives to changes in the tax rate, particularly if tax incentives are poorly targeted.

Inasmuch as tax cuts can be beneficial to economic performance, Keynesians recommend tax cuts that will stimulate aggregate demand rather than aggregate supply, but the effects of tax cuts may well be indistinguishable if and when they are beneficial to both aggregate demand and supply—increasing workers' incentive to be productive on the one hand and increasing household disposable income on the other.

However, the empirical evidence of the Laffer argument is ambivalent. Workers tend to react to tax incentives differently—some preferring to work harder, while others increase their leisure time. Other concerns about the accuracy of the Laffer argument involve the appropriate timing of tax reductions (since policies might be susceptible to time lags, which can neutralize the intended outcomes of policy decisions) and the local maximum or optimum of tax receipts on the Laffer curve. For more information, see Mankiw (2006) and McConnell and Brue (2008). ***See also*** Aggregate Demand Curve; Aggregate Supply Curve; Business Cycle (economics, public administration); Gross Domestic Product; Recession

Supremacy Doctrine A clause found in Article 6 Section 2 of the U.S. Constitution, which states that federal law is superior to and overrides state law when the two conflict. "This Constitution, and the Laws of the United States which shall be made in Pursuance thereof; and all Treaties made, or which shall be made, under the Authority of the United States, shall be the supreme Law of the Land; and the Judges in every State shall be bound thereby."

The supremacy clause recognizes three sources of law as supreme: the Constitution, federal laws made in pursuance of the Constitution, and treaties of the United States. The two goals of the clause are to secure the supremacy of federal law and to prevent Congress from exceeding the scope of its powers, many of which are enumerated in the necessary and proper clause of Article 1 of the Constitution. Otherwise, states retain their remaining powers as stated in Article 10 of the Constitution.

Under the guiding principle of federalism, the founders of the Constitution recognized the overlapping sovereignty of state and federal powers to establish governing laws. This concurrent authority would inevitably give rise to conflicts between these laws. The founders chose to treat such conflicts as judicial rather than political questions. Since state courts are courts of general jurisdiction, the supremacy clause enlisted state courts to determine the bounds of federal power in the course of upholding the supreme law of the land. The supremacy clause authorized courts to determine whether a federal statute was made in pursuance of the Constitution. If so, the statute constitutes the supreme law of the land and displaces contrary state law. If not, then the statute binds neither the state nor the federal courts.

In a landmark decision on the supremacy clause, in *McCulloch v. Maryland* (1819), Chief Justice John Marshall delivered the opinion of the Supreme Court invalidating a Maryland law that taxed all banks in the state. According to the Court, Congress had the implied power to incorporate a bank within the limits of the necessary and proper clause. Since this incorporation statute was made in pursuance of the Constitution, the Supreme Court ruled that it was indeed valid. For more information, see Clark (2003) and *McCulloch v. Maryland* (1819). ***See also*** Congress; Constitution (political science); Federalism; Grants of Power

Supreme Court (U.S.) The highest appellate court in the United States and the court of last resort for all cases tried at the state and federal levels. It comprises the Chief Justice of the United States and eight associate justices, who are each nominated by the President and confirmed by the Senate. Justices serve on the court for life and step down when they retire, resign, or are impeached. Unlike other courts, the Supreme Court chooses the cases it will hear by granting a writ of certiorari, or a request for review, filed by the lower court. If the Court denies the writ, the decision of the lower court stands; if a writ is granted, by being approved by at least four of the nine justices, the Court agrees to hear the case and begins with a review of

S

written arguments, known as legal briefs. The Court has original jurisdiction in only certain cases, such as when one state sues another. The Court hears approximately 100 cases each year, although more than 7,000 petitions are presented per term. The Court chooses cases involving what are considered important legal issues, such as cases that pose a challenge to constitutional rights. ***See also*** Appellate Court (sociology); Chief Justice

Surveillance *(media studies)*   Monitoring—overt and covert—of crowds, private individuals, objects, and public and private places and activities. The word means "watching over" (French *sur + veiller*), implying that the supervision comes from the top down, whether the authority in question is state, institutional, corporate, or parental. Michel Foucault's *Surveiller et Punir* (*Discipline and Punish*) traces the emergence of surveillance as the characteristic mark of modern societies. Carceral models such as the panopticon, designed by Jeremy Bentham in 1791, only demonstrate in extreme form what occurs daily in civil society. Surveillance relies not only on technology in the obvious sense of hardware (24-hour cameras, satellites, listening devices, etc.) but also on techniques of power that exert mental rather than bodily control (e.g., spying, informing). The media's control of the flow of information enables them both to participate in state surveillance and to protect public interest by acting as a watchdog for abuses by the authorities. ***See also*** Censorship (communication, media studies); Technology (education, media studies)

Surveillance *(sociology)*   A broad term referring, in part, to monitoring of human behavior. Usually referring to visual observation, it can also include telephone tapping, secret listening devices, global positioning system (GPS) tracking, and electronic tagging of objects. Closed-circuit televisions (CCTV) are increasingly being placed in public places, including city streets. With augmented surveillance systems comes the threat of loss of privacy. ***See also*** Censorship (political science)

Survey *(psychology)*   A type of research involving the use of questionnaires or interviews to investigate human behavior or perceptions. Advantages of the survey method include ease of administration to large samples, particularly online surveys, and the anonymous nature of surveys may allow for insights into sensitive issues. Disadvantages of the survey method include issues with participants' honesty, as participants may bias answers to appear socially desirable. Participants may have memory issues and respond in accordance to "wishful thinking rather than realistically. ***See also*** Case Study Research (psychology); Experiment; Experimental Research; Naturalistic Observation

Survey *(sociology)*   A broad term referring to a collection of questions (a questionnaire) designed to gather qualitative or quantitative social science data. Examples of surveys include the census, opinion polls,

marketing research, and psychological instruments designed to identify mood or personality. Respondents may be asked the extent to which they agree or disagree with statements (Likert scale questions), to choose an answer to a question from a list provided by the researcher (closed-ended questions), or to provide their own answer to a question (open-ended questions). Surveys are administered by researchers in person, over the phone, through the mail, and, more commonly today, over the Internet. ***See also*** Questionnaire

Survey Research   Social science research in which the primary form of data collection is questionnaires or interviews. The focus of survey research is to gather information from a sample in order to make generalizations about the characteristics, opinions, or experiences of a larger population. Advantages of survey research include ease of collecting information from a large sample of respondents (e.g., through the Internet and telephone surveys), the flexibility of types of information collected, and the ability to standardize administration. Among the disadvantages are accuracy being dependent on respondents' memory, motivation, and willingness to be open and honest, and issues relating to nonresponse, which can result in biased or nonrepresentative samples. ***See also*** Open-Ended Versus Closed-Ended Questions; Sampling in Quantitative Research

Survival Analysis   An estimate of the probability of a dichotomous event occuring (such as death or success). Observation time is calendar fixed, and participants enter the set of data at different times and exit at different times and for reasons of the criterion event occurring (e.g., death or success) or other (censored) reasons. ***See also*** Statistics (sociology)

Suspended Sentence   A judge can determine a defendant's sentence and then defer that punishment on the condition that the defendant follows the rules of probation while living in the community. Suspended sentences are commonly used in cases involving first-time offenders who have committed a minor crime. Should the defendant violate the rules of probation, the original punishment will then be administered (e.g., the jail sentence).

Swing Voters   Those who may vote for either party in a political election, oftentimes switching their party vote depending on the candidate in question. In the United States, these voters usually consider themselves independents, conservative democrats, or liberal republicans. Swing voters play a large role in the outcome of elections; politicians campaign heavily to win their support.

Syllogism   A logical argument in which the conclusion follows from two prior premises. A categorical syllogism consists of a major premise, a minor premise, and a conclusion that follows—for example,

All cats are clever. (major premise)
Lily is a cat. (minor premise)
Therefore, Lily is clever. (conclusion)

Other types of syllogisms include disjunctive syllogisms and hypothetical syllogisms. ***See also*** Paradigm (education)

Symbolic Interactionism A school of thought in the social and behavioral sciences that emphasizes the socially constructed nature of meaning and human actions. This means that what people do and how they interact with each other, with objects, and with the environment are based on how they interpret the meaningfulness of these things. Those meanings are not inherent in the objects, but they are developed as a result of the social interactions between actors in a situation; and the ways in which everyone acts toward the object result in the understanding of it and its meanings. Meaning isn't recognized in an object but rather is developed through the use of that object. In this approach, every human act deals with the creation of meanings that are the result of social relations. Meanings are generated and regenerated as actions, actors, and situations change. This is different from most sociological or psychological research, which treats meaning as either fixed or peripheral to the research interest. Research on symbolic interaction is qualitative and consists of directly observing behavior and defining the situation in which that behavior is conducted. The originator of the term *symbolic interactionism,* Herbert Blumer, called these studies "naturalistic" and "down-to-earth" rather than abstract and removed from everyday life. All symbolic interactionist research is interested in human conduct in groups rather than in individual behavior. For more information, see Blumer (1969). ***See also*** Cultural Context; Meaning; Metacommunication; Symbols/Symbolic Reality

Symbols/Symbolic Reality Entities (objects, words, images, sounds) that stand in for or represent something other than, or more than, themselves. The thing indicated or referenced may be either abstract or concrete. Symbols act as bridges between two different entities: the real and the imaginary, the material and the immaterial, the visible and the invisible, the small and the large, and the local and the distant. Symbols are the basis of all communication: Languages use symbols to associate a word or a sound with ideas or things. The study of symbol systems is called *semiotics*. ***See also*** Construction of Reality; Semiotics (media studies)

Sympathetic Nervous System Part of the autonomic nervous system and responsible for directing the involuntary, visceral actions of muscles, blood vessels, and glands. Generally, the autonomic nervous system regulates the physiological arousal that accompanies experienced emotions. For example, the sympathetic nervous system mobilizes bodily resources to take action. If a person feels threatened, consequently, heart rate, blood pressure, breathing, and perspiration may increase. This is referred to as the fight-or-flight response, as the body can respond to the threat by either "fighting" or "fleeing" the perceived threat. As the body cannot remain in this mobilized and alert state, the parasympathetic nervous system is responsible for counteracting and normalizing the physiological arousal state. The sympathetic nervous system also lessens blood flow if there is an injury to the body. ***See also*** Autonomic Nervous System; Cannon-Bard Theory; Central Nervous System (CNS); Peripheral Nervous System (PNS); Somatic Nervous System

Synapse The part of the neuron through which the transmission of chemical messages takes place. Neural impulses, once they have reached the axon's terminal buttons, are transmitted via the release of neurotransmitters. These neurotransmitters may then bind with specific receptor sites. The synapse comprises this junction, through which neuronal transmission is passed. ***See also*** Axon; Neurons; Soma

Synchronous and Asynchronous Communication Two modes of computer-mediated communication (CMC). Synchronous communication is online communication enabled in real time via technologies such as instant messaging. Asynchronous communication is communication between a sender and a receiver who are not logged on at the same time (e.g., e-mail, online discussion forums).

Syndicated Programs/Syndicates Programs that are sold to multiple independent television stations. These programs can be first run as original programs that are not affiliated to any particular network or as reruns of former network programs. Either method can be quite lucrative, but in the case of a rerun, because the production costs have already been paid during its original network run, the sales can represent almost pure profit. Television syndication deals are handled on a cash or barter basis; that is, the program is either sold to the highest bidders in the various markets, or it is offered in exchange for a portion of the advertising revenue. ***See also*** Network

Synoptic Change The systematic approach to formulating, implementing, and monitoring strategy. It is a general approach to strategic management since this mode of thinking involves long-range planning and/or strategic planning. Synoptic change follows a well-defined and developed procedure for carrying out strategic functions. It involves changes that include a wide range of problem-solving approaches that are rational, sequential, and comprehensive.

The leader of the organization, often the CEO, uses explicit goals as screening devices and scans the environment for threats and opportunities. When discovered, plans are devised for evaluating alternative methods of exploiting opportunities or countering

S

threats. All consequences of the alternatives are identified, and the alternative that maximizes the return for the organization is chosen and implemented.

Synoptic change follows rational, comprehensive, and formal procedures that move an organization toward maximization of its goals, which are typically defined in economic or financial terms.

Synoptic change is contrasted with incrementalism, which argues that organizational complexity, personal values, group processes, and relative power substantially alter the rationality arrived at by synoptic change. Decisions are driven by the multiple constituencies that are represented in the strategy process, which replaces maximization of goals with satisficing as the various interests place constraints on the decision process. For more information, see Rabin, Miller, and Hildreth (2000). *See also* Strategic Planning

System   A broad term referring to a set of interdependent units that are integrated into a network. There are both naturally occurring and socially constructed systems. Natural systems include a geographical area's ecosystem where one part of nature is dependent on the existence of another. Social systems include the criminal justice system, comprising the police, courts, and corrections. In the United States, a system of social services can include income assistance, food assistance, job training, and medical care. Social systems are often criticized for being composed of units that do not effectively communicate or share information with each other and for "breaking down" when one part of the network becomes disconnected from the others. *See also* Network

Systematic Desensitization   A behavioral therapy intended to reduce or eliminate the consequences of phobias. Systematic desensitization follows a three-step therapy. During the first step, the therapist helps the client identify an anxiety hierarchy. To establish the anxiety hierarchy, the person has to list the anxiety-causing stimuli, as related to the specific phobia, in ascending order. The second step involves teaching the person relaxation techniques. While the type of relaxation technique may differ across therapists, what is important is that the person is able to engage in relaxation as directed by the therapist. During the third step, the person will address each item of the anxiety hierarchy while engaging in relaxation techniques. That is, the person imagines the anxiety-causing situation and tries to relax simultaneously. If the imagined situation remains anxiety causing, the imagining is stopped and the person solely focuses on relaxation. Starting with the least anxiety-causing item on the list, the person will progressively work through the list.

Systematic desensitization is based on the assumption that anxieties are acquired via classical conditioning. The purpose of the therapy is to weaken or eliminate the association between the conditioned stimulus and the conditioned response. Systematic desensitization can be used for many phobias—for example, snake phobias or fear of heights. Systematic desensitization has been shown to be effective in the treatment of phobias. *See also* Behavior Therapy (education, psychology); Classical Conditioning; Phobia

Systematic Risk   The risk remaining after diversifying a portfolio of stocks. This risk is referred to as market risk. Total risk is the overall variability of the returns of a financial asset. Total risk of a financial asset such as a stock is made up of two types of risks—systematic and unsystematic risk. Unsystematic or diversifiable risks can be diversified away by having a large, well-diversified portfolio of stocks. Systematic risk is the risk that remains, and it must be borne by investors for being in the stock market. This risk arises from external forces such as the economy and government policies. Systematic risk can be quantified by using a statistical technique to develop a risk-measuring barometer called *beta*. The beta of a stock measures the sensitivity of the stock to the market. Investors are compensated for taking on systematic risk but not unsystematic risk, which can be diversified away. For more information, see Ehrhardt and Brigham (2003). *See also* Risk

Systems Theory   The transdisciplinary study of the abstract organization of phenomena, independent of their substance or existence. Systems theory investigates both the principles common to all complex entities and the systems that can be used to describe them. In other words, it is the basic structure wherein one analyzes any group of objects that work together toward a result. This could be an organization of organisms or just one organism.

Systems can be either controlled (cybernetic) or uncontrolled. In controlled systems, information is sensed, and changes are made in response to that information. Kuhn refers to this as the detector, selector, and effector functions of the system. The detector deals with information about the intercommunication between systems. The selector is the rule that makes decisions, and the effector is the means by which transactions are made between systems.

Systems theory first appeared in biology in the 1920s because there was a need to explain the connection of organisms in ecosystems. This refers to the science of systems that resulted from Bertalanffy's general system theory (GST). Margaret Mead and Gregory Bateson (1979) developed interdisciplinary perspectives in systems theory (Bale, 1995).

The biologist Ludwig von Bertalanffy designed systems theory in the 1940s, and Ross Ashby added further elements to the theory. Ashby's emphasis was that real systems are open to and interact with their environments and that they can acquire qualitatively new properties through emergence, resulting in continual evolution (Ashby, 1956; Bertalanffy, 1950). Systems theory focuses on the parts and the way they connect to the whole. This organization that connects all to the whole determines a system that is independent of the concrete substance of the elements. Therefore, the concepts and principles of organization found in biology, physics, and so on, provide a different basis for their unification. Systems concepts include system-environment boundary, input, output, process, state, hierarchy, and goal directedness. For more information, see Ashby (1956), Bale (1995), Bateson (1979), and Bertalanffy (1950).

Systems Theory in Counseling   An application of general systems theory that proposes that persons should be examined and counseled within their social context. Systems theory in counseling proposes that personal conflict arises between or among persons. Therefore, the effective way to treat an individual is to view his or her problems as based on interrelationships with others. With couples, within families, or in groups, the therapist and the client collaborate to find patterns of behavior and communication between the client and significant others and to assess the patterns of words, thoughts, and actions that the client has (or could have) in relation to others. The system, rather than just the individual, usually requires work to restore healthy functioning. ***See also*** Family Therapy; Marriage Counseling

S

T

Tabloid Newspapers/Coverage Smaller in format than broadsheet newspapers, their coverage is typically more sensational, designed to have greater mass appeal than the more serious and intellectual broadsheets. News stories and editorials tend to be short, and their language is simple. Much of the content is given over to sports. During the 1920s and 1930s in the United States, tabloids were abundant, amply illustrated with photographs, reporting "gossip, sin, and scandal," but circulation dropped during the Depression. In the United States, tabloids currently tend to be local in terms of interests and sales, while English tabloids are national. English tabloids are renowned for their eye-catching and unsubtle sensational headlines, with "Gotcha" infamously announcing the sinking of an Argentine warship by the British navy, and for their images of scantily clad "Page 3 girls." ***See also*** News Coverage; Print Media

Taboo A category of objects, people, behaviors, or places that are considered by a culture to be dangerous, offensive, or disruptive to the social order. In anthropology, taboos are defined by a particular culture, but in psychoanalysis, a taboo is a condition of the unconscious, pointing to behaviors that all humans must repress. For more information, see Douglas (1966). ***See also*** Cultural Context; Culture (communication)

Target Audience A group of potential audience members or consumers who share demographic characteristics such as age, gender, race that a media outlet wishes to reach. Ultimately, the group—viewers or readers—is sought after by advertisers to whom an ad campaign or program content is specifically designed.

Tariff A tax that is placed on goods being imported into the country; the goods cannot enter the country unless the tax is paid. There are different types of tariffs, including the protective tariff that imposes high tariffs in an effort to artificially inflate the cost of imported goods in the domestic economy.

TASER A weapon used by police officers and civilians that employs nonlethal electroshock technology to stun and subdue a targeted subject from a distance. Originally a firearm, the TASER was later adapted without gunpowder and now has a single shot of two small electrodes. ***See also*** Firearm

Task Analysis An instructional design component in which content is defined and analyzed to address an instructional problem or need. In conducting analysis, content is articulated and then analyzed and sequenced appropriately. The content provides the basis for identifying instructional objectives and designing instruction.

Task analysis has the critical involvement of a subject matter expert (SME), who provides the instructional designer accurate and detailed information about the content. The instructional designer documents and identifies steps from the learner's perspective.

Generally, three task analysis methods can be used: (1) topic analysis, (2) procedural analysis, and (3) critical incident analysis. The first two analyses apply to concrete content and highly structured tasks that can be easily analyzed (e.g., how to upload photos on the computer). The third analysis is employed to analyze tasks that involve complex skills varying from instance to instance (e.g., how to be a group facilitator).

A topic analysis is used to identify cognitive knowledge such as facts, concepts, principles, and rules. An instructional designer working with the SME starts with the revelation of content structures and then identifies supporting details for each structure.

Procedural analysis is used to identify individual steps and their sequence. The designer uses a format (e.g., outline, table, flowchart) to document expert performance in the target environment and then logically organizes the steps and associated knowledge.

Critical incident analysis is used to identify interpersonal skills and attitudes. Interviews are conducted with several individuals, and different approaches for the same task and commonalities are identified.

These task analysis methods can be combined one way or another, depending on learner and contextual needs, levels of detail needed for instruction, and time and resources for instructional development. For more information, see Jonassen (1999). ***See also*** Instructional Objectives; Instructional Strategies

Task-Oriented Culture A concept that emphasizes the final outcome or the product above other, even human, considerations. Initiating structures is the main focus of task orientation, when goal attainment becomes the primary consideration that overrides relationship orientation and in a way sacrifices the individual for the benefit of the desired outcome.

Culture, among other variables, is composed of mores, rules, values, ethical considerations, principles, and attitudes toward certain concepts and behaviors. Culture depends on the way people think, act, and feel, and it is either explicit or implicit. Explicit culture addresses certain behavioral patterns, and implicit culture is more of an inferential concept that is more difficult to be defined in objective terms. When a task-oriented culture emphasizes the importance of work as its major value, it is easily observable when its members devote a disproportionate amount of time to the work environment, a concept that by itself is not challenged by any of its members. However, it would be hard to explain, in objective terms, why members of the task-oriented culture emphasize the importance of work-related time over time spent with one's family. Although no person adheres to all the values emphasized in a given culture, and the socialization process is very rarely completed, the overall impression is that nobody should challenge the value of the accepted task in favor of relationship orientation.

All cultures distinguish between the way things are supposed to be and the way they actually are. The task-oriented culture, for example, the Japanese culture, emphasizes a variety of "double codes," which manifest the Japanese norm of discouraging forthright communication. The distinction between the formal truth, or what is referred to as "tatemae," which is also referred to as a façade or a pretense, and real feelings, or what is called "honne" and refers to the truth one knows or senses, is especially legitimized among many government officials and provides for one mechanism of control and management of the task orientation.

While task-oriented cultures can elevate themselves in their product development and success on a global level, the preferred focus on task over relationship can lead to instances of individual and organizational corruption and, eventually, to the diffusions of these values and attitudes. The task orientation leaves little, if any, room for challenging unethical and immoral behaviors, not only legitimizing the final outcome but, at the same time, devaluating and degrading otherwise universally accepted "rights" and "wrongs," making it harder for the members of such a culture to integrate and adapt to other cultures and, therefore, making them even more insular. For more information, see Haberfeld (2005) and Johnson (2003). **See also** High-Context Culture; Low-Context Culture

Tax   A fee imposed on individuals, corporations, or trusts by a government entity. The purpose of a tax is to collect funds to pay for public needs and services. In the United States, taxes are collected at the local, federal, and state levels, and each respective level has established agencies to deal with tax enforcement and collection. Failure to pay taxes can result in fines and/or prison time. British taxes levied on American colonists were a leading trigger of the Revolutionary War; "No taxation without representation" became a war cry. These taxes

included the Sugar Act (1764), which placed a fee on foreign refined sugar, and the Stamp Act (1765), which required a British stamp or seal, for a fee, to be placed on public and legal documents. **See also** Taxation

Taxation   A fiscal policy through which governments raise revenue and influence production and consumption by levying taxes. Taxes are direct or indirect compulsory payments imposed by governments for a social purpose.

Direct taxes are imposed on payers directly, such as individual and corporate income taxes, while indirect taxes are imposed on the privileges or rights exercised by payers to consume or acquire certain goods—for example, import taxes (tariffs) and sales tax.

Taxes may also be regressive, proportional, or progressive. A tax is regressive when income tax payers in low-income brackets pay disproportionately higher rates than those in high-income brackets. In a proportional system, rates are evenly spread out irrespective of the level of income. A progressive system mandates those who are making more income to pay proportionally higher taxes.

Income tax rates are graduated, and the marginal tax rate is the rate paid on the last dollar of taxable income. The tax liability is the amount of taxes owed on income. The payment of taxes has raised concerns about legitimacy and methods, for which tax evasion has been a reaction. However, governments have severe laws against evasion, and fines or imprisonment can be the result of tax evasion or avoidance.

Taxation can be an effective tool to stabilize an economy when it is used wisely. A tax cut that is well targeted increases disposable income, and if an economy is in a recession, it can stimulate consumption and production to raise the level of national output or income. Conversely, to forestall overheating, policymakers can increase taxes, although it may seem to be a less attractive policy.

Taxation may also be used to discourage the production and consumption of certain goods. Taxes on nonessential goods such as tobacco and alcohol (excise taxes) raise the cost of production and consumption. Revenue from taxes is used to provide social amenities, create infrastructure, maintain law enforcement, and pay civil servants. **See also** Consumption; Income Tax; Stabilization; Tax Competition

Tax Competition   A competitive fiscal policy that encourages capital inflows and discourages capital outflows by reducing the amount of taxes on a taxable resource. Tax competition is particularly useful for long-term capital investment or movement. High levels of taxation contribute to tax evasion and the exodus of taxable resource to areas of lighter tax burden.

During the interwar years, some nations adopted a policy of competitive devaluation to promote exports and trade surpluses. Contemporary regulation of international trade and capital flows inveighs against unfair protective policies. Reduction in trade restrictions and economic integration (globalization) are inducing governments to be more responsive to the freer flow of economic resources and goods in order to capture the advantages of trade and factor movements.

Since taxes are a lucrative source of government revenue, their reduction poses potential problems for the provision of essential services. Incentives such as tax exemptions, holidays, and havens, which may be compensated for by subsidies, create an unfair competitive advantage for which a much more equitable or defensive system of policy harmonization may be required. Tax competition therefore creates a problem of tax reform that is sensitive to both competition and economic growth. ***See also*** Free Trade; Globalization (economics, political science); International Economics; Taxation; World Trade Organization (WTO)

Taxonomies The classification of different educational skills or abilities. Taxonomies are often used to define educational objectives and to classify instructional and assessment tasks. Taxonomies generally fall into one of three domains: cognitive, affective, and psychomotor. In 1956, Benjamin Bloom developed a taxonomy for the cognitive domain, which focuses on skills relating to memory, thinking, and reasoning. The cognitive taxonomy comprises six levels of complexity: knowledge, comprehension, application, analysis, synthesis, and evaluation. The least complex cognitive skill is knowledge, which focuses on the recall of facts or concepts. Knowledge-level skills may include defining, describing, and matching. Comprehension refers to a level of understanding in which the individual can interpret, translate, or describe. Examples of behaviors that demonstrate comprehension are giving examples, paraphrasing, or summarizing. Application refers to the ability of an individual to use acquired knowledge in a new situation and may include demonstrating, computing, solving, and manipulating. Analysis involves breaking down information into parts and may include classification, outlining, making inferences, and analyzing relationships. Synthesis is the ability to take parts of elements into a new whole or into a new pattern. Synthesis may include categorizing, designing, composing, and compiling. The most sophisticated cognitive level is evaluation, which is defined as making judgments or evaluations about information based on a specific set of criteria, either defined internally or externally. Evaluation may ask the student to appraise, justify, support, or criticize. The original Bloom's taxonomy was revised in 2001 by Anderson, Krathwohl, and several other contributors, who changed the levels from noun to verb format and reversed the order of synthesis and evaluation as being the most cognitively complex. Other cognitive taxonomies also exist, although Bloom's original and revised taxonomies remain the most commonly cited.

Taxonomies in the affective domain classify emotional reactions and feelings. Bloom's subcategories for the affective domain are receiving, responding, valuing, organization, and characterization. Receiving refers to being aware or conscious of something. Responding refers to reaction to a stimulus. Valuing refers to the attachment of a value to a phenomenon, object, or experience. Organization refers to putting together different values or ideas into one's own set of complex values. Characterization refers to the influence of the internal set of values on an individual's behaviors and life.

Skills in the psychomotor domain refer to abilities to physically manipulate objects and tools. While Bloom did not develop subcategories for the psychomotor domain, other researchers, including Harrow (1972), have continued this work. Harrow's classification levels include Reflex Movements, Basic-Fundamental Movements, Perceptual Abilities, Physical Abilities, Skilled Movements, and Non-Discursive Communication. For more information, see Anderson et al. (2001), Bloom, Engelhard, Furst, Hill, and Krathwohl (1956), and Harrow (1972). ***See also*** Objectives

Teacher Evaluation The process of collecting data for purposes of judging teacher quality and performance. Multiple sources of data, such as peer judgments, student and parent reports, and observations are used in the evaluations, which may be used for formative and summative purposes. ***See also*** Formative Evaluation; Summative Evaluation

Teacher Licensing Each state, in accordance with federal mandates for "highly qualified teachers," allows individuals to teach in state public and private schools. General requirements for licensure include a course load in educational history, theory, and pedagogy at an accredited college or university and successful completion of a supervised teaching assignment. ***See also*** National Board Certification; No Child Left Behind (NCLB)

Teacher Motivation Theory The arousal, direction, and persistence of voluntary teacher behavior. Although there is no single, widely accepted, overarching definition of work motivation, a number of theoretical approaches attempt to describe and explain it, including those that classify motivation as internal or external and theories that are need based, cognitive, and noncognitive. In general, theorists agree that teacher work motivation determines (a) whether teachers will put effort into an activity, (b) how long they will apply effort to an activity over competing activities, and (c) how intensely they continue.

With respect to description, motivation is often classified as either intrinsic or extrinsic. Thus, teachers can be motivated to engage in an activity because they find it stimulating, challenging, and satisfying (intrinsic) or because they might be rewarded with greater compensation and recognition (extrinsic).

The first major category of motivation theory is based on the notion of needs. When teachers, for example, feel a need for job security in light of declining student

T

enrollments, a tension develops that stimulates the search for a productive means to reduce the tension (e.g., extensive job search) and satisfy the need (e.g., a new job offer). Maslow's hierarchy of needs and Herzberg's two-factor theory represent this perspective. Herzberg proposes that individuals have two sets of basic needs, one focusing on survival (hygiene) and the other focusing on personal growth (motivator). Thus, teachers would be motivated by making sure that hygiene factors are present in the workplace to prevent dissatisfaction (e.g., good working conditions) and subsequently adding motivator factors to create job satisfaction (e.g., achievement). Job enrichment would be an example of this kind of activity.

Cognitive motivation theory, the second major category, suggests that conscious thoughts, beliefs, and judgments control motivation. Thus, it is how and what teachers think, believe, and judge that influence the extent of their motivation. Vroom's expectancy theory, Locke's goal-setting theory, Adams's equity theory, and Bandura's social-cognitive learning theory are the most widely recognized cognitive theories. While substantial scholarly support exists for each, goal-setting theory has enjoyed increased attention in recent years. Goals influence teachers' intention and commitment, which direct their behavior until they attain or change their goals. Goals that teachers see as specific, challenging, and reasonable have been more strongly linked to optimal performance than ambiguous and easy goals.

Noncognitive motivation or reinforcement theory (B. F. Skinner) attempts to explain behavior by directly observing the behavior and carefully considering its antecedents and outcomes. Teacher motivation to perform a behavior increases if followed by a positive consequence, such as increased compensation, but it decreases if followed by an aversive consequence, such as the removal of parking privileges. Internal needs, thoughts, or beliefs are irrelevant to explanations of behavior according to this theory. **See also** Motivation Theory

Teachers' Rights   At school, teachers serve students *in loco parentis*—"in place of parents." In the public sector, they act as agents of the state and are responsible for educating students and for keeping them safe in an orderly, well-maintained, and efficiently managed learning environment. Teachers may use reasonable force to safeguard both themselves and the student population. They have the right to due process under the law. Teachers have the right to academic freedom, allowing them to present educational material in a way that is uniquely their own as long as it fits within the parameters allowed by the school board. Freedom of speech for teachers can be censored by the school board if it is determined to be objectionable by their standards.

Team Building   In education, this term refers to scholarship and practices related to the creation and development of effective teams, often in work-related contexts. Team-building scholars seek to better understand small-group dynamics in terms of successful collaboration and the efficient fulfillment of objectives. In addition, scholars investigate methods for group assessment that involve both the group members themselves and external parties. Team-building scholars and practitioners engage team activities throughout the team life cycle, from recruitment and formation through completion and reorganization. Team building is often investigated in management studies and implemented within a broader organizational development context.

Team-building practitioners often focus on a core set of team-building principles and their related practices. Such principles can include the following:

Establishing and clarifying objectives: Properly framed, a shared understanding of group objectives can support increased communication between individual group members as well as overall productivity. Such objectives often relate to the completion of specific projects, interactions within the group, interactions between the group and their organization, and performance metrics.

Creating a shared purpose: In addition to specific objectives, many teams perform more effectively when they have a shared sense of how they contribute to the greater good of their organization or community.

Developing individual roles and responsibilities: Teams function optimally when individual members have a clear sense of their own role within the team and their particular responsibilities. Roles and responsibilities can shift over time as the group matures in its approach to reaching objectives.

Fostering a sense of ownership: Individual team members, and the group as a whole, are more effective when they have a sense of ownership with regard to their own process for achieving their objectives. Such ownership can increase motivation and reduce the possibility of satisficing in terms of accountability and productivity.

Establishing trust: A trusted relationship involves a negotiated reliance on the other. Trust among team members can have a powerful effect on team collaboration, supporting increased communication, a shared sense of responsibility, and innovative thinking. Social factors such as competition among team members can sometimes diminish self-disclosure and lead to a breakdown of trust.

Identifying and alleviating inhibitors to team effectiveness: In addition to supporting optimal functioning, team-building practitioners seek to uncover and mitigate those factors that inhibit team effectiveness. Such inhibitors can include poorly defined or inequitable roles and relationships, obstructive communication patterns, and organizational factors such as lack of resources.

Building self-assessment and feedback skills: Teams often have an increased sense of ownership, self-direction, and motivation when they themselves are involved in their own assessment.

See also Satisficing (education); Small-Group Communication

Team Policing A police strategy introduced in the 1970s in reaction to the perceived isolation of the police from the community due in part to changes in patrol techniques (e.g., increased use of police cars). Teams of police officers familiar with the neighborhood, including its community members and problems, would patrol a geographic area under the direction of a sergeant or lieutenant. Teams were meant to interrupt potential corruption and increase collaboration with local leaders and residents. Team policing never became a widespread solution because of law enforcement resistance, inadequate training, and studies showing short-term ineffectiveness. *See also* Patrol

Team Teaching A strategy that involves two or more teachers who work collaboratively in planning lessons, implementing instruction, and assessing student learning. Teachers may teach together in the same class at the same time or teach separately, yet they typically teach the same group of students.

Technical Subsystem The knowledge required to perform the various tasks used directly and indirectly in the transformation of inputs, such as tools, machines, procedures, methods, and technical knowledge, into outputs, such as manufacturing, accounting, marketing, and research. The type of technical subsystems contained in an organization is a function of the tasks required to perform the transformation processes.

The technical subsystem is mainly concerned with the technical resources needed to produce the product or service. Employees provide the expertise. Those working in the technical subsystem may shape organizational behavior by providing the specialized knowledge that informs policy decisions. It has long been recognized that the technical subsystem must further integrate with the social subsystem in the context of the total organization. This relationship is pivotal, since the kind of technology an organization chooses will determine whether it maximizes efficiency within the organization. For example, automating certain procedures may remove discretion from the hands of employees, which might decrease performance when considering the organizational humanism perspective that states that employees possessing autonomy and greater decision-making authority will be happier and reach self-actualization. While the technical subsystem is largely influenced by objective constraints and the social subsystem by subjective factors, both must reconcile psychological work requirements with the need to control potential problems in the transformation process. Both the technical and the social aspects of organizations are vital to performance, and their overall fit to an organization is critical. *See also* Organizational Change (public administration)

Technological Determinism The media theorist Marshall McLuhan in the 1960s coined the slogan "The medium is the message," which means that if it is the case that we initially shape the tools we use, it is equally true that the tools shape our way of perceiving, knowing, and ultimately all social interaction. In the instance of printing, mass production puts a book in everyone's hands, thereby encouraging private reading, raising literacy levels, and participating in the emergence of individualism and democracy.

McLuhan's slogan illustrates the principle of technological determinism, which asserts not only the formative effects that technology exerts over modes of perception and social interaction but also (and more contentiously) that technology has its own autonomy and follows the unfolding evolution of its own material logic rather than being summoned into existence by its creators. That is, technological innovation is more a matter of discovery than invention. In its extreme form, technological determinism posits technology as the primary formative cause of societal change and represents humans essentially as tool-making animals, as *homo faber.* Insofar as tools mediate between humans and nature, the media are the form par excellence of technological causation, for they *are* the message rather than being the mere communicator of the message. It is easy to be reductive about technological determinism, to assert, for example, that the invention of the stirrup caused chivalry, or the spinning jenny the Industrial Revolution.

Technological determinism contrasts with technological constructivism, which emphasizes the ideological directedness of new forms of production. The sociologist Émile Durkheim was one of the first thinkers to resist the domination of the technological in invoking the category of the "social" as something that stands independent of material causation. Whichever the side of the discussion taken, it is important to avoid speaking of technology in abstract terms divorced from the material conditions of its operation and sphere of influence. *See also* Culture (communication, media studies, sociology); Technology (media studies)

Technology *(education)* A broad term used to describe the application of knowledge to attain desired goals. It is usually manifested through the purposive use of tools, instruments, techniques, processes, methods, or systems in the attainment of the goal or end state. In education, the term *technology* is often used to describe the use of tools to augment or deliver all or part of an instructional module, such as calculators, audiovisual devices, computers, and the Internet. *See also* Educational Technology; Technology Integration

T

Technology *(media studies)*   No domain of social life is untouched by technology. The use of a stone lying ready at hand to crack a nut constitutes an instance of technology in its broad sense of instrumentality. The popular sense of the term refers, however, to the fashioning of a natural resource into hardware to enhance productivity and control one's environment. Deriving from the Greek word *techne,* "skill or art," technology implies a domain of resources that require skill to use (as in "technician" or "technical"). Technology has traditionally been thought to be an exclusively human phenomenon: Hence, humans create tools with their hands to perform activities for which animals use their claws and teeth. But from two sides, the exclusive hold of the human on technology has weakened: On one side, the line of distinction between human and animal inventiveness has blurred; on the other, the line between human and machine has become equally unsure, with fictional cyborgs or real-life robotic prostheses and implants.

Marx points to the domination of human relations by technology under capitalism. Under capitalism (the factory being an archetypal model for capitalist production), producers are separated from ownership of the means of production and from the commodities they produce, which belong to their employers. This estrangement of workers from the labor of their own hands results in alienation from self and from society—for Marx, the capitalist condition. The accelerated technology seen in the Industrial Revolution thus creates an alienated society. Marx was not against technology per se. Resistance to industrialization took many forms, not necessarily Marxist, as in Luddism, a movement in 19th-century England involving sabotage of the machines that threatened jobs.

The development of digital technology has had dramatic effects in social interaction and in the concept of technology itself. Where the Industrial Age produced physical objects, the primary product of the Digital Age is information—its collection, storage, manipulation, and transmission. The philosopher Jürgen Habermas observes how technical (or instrumental) rationality dehumanizes by using reason as a means to achieve goals rather than to select and justify goals. In doing so, he both reaffirms the connection between technology and instrumentality and questions the neutrality of technicality as an empty intermediary between humans and the world on which they act. The media theorist Neil Postman speaks of how such paradigms of thought lead to what he calls "technopoly," which valorizes "efficiency" as an end in itself where technical calculation takes priority over human judgment. Such critics call profoundly into question the assumption popular in the positive sciences that technological innovation represents social progress. *See also* Critical Theory; Marxism (sociology); Technological Determinism

Technology Integration   The process of using different technological tools to increase the quality of teaching and learning in instructional contexts. As technology evolves, it affects every dimension of society; the processes and the tools of education have also been affected by technological innovations. Technological advances have produced a variety of new media for producing effective learning environments. With regard to instructional methods and processes, technological integration increases the effectiveness of education in terms of time, budgeting, fostering learning, creating real-world contexts in classrooms, promoting multiple learning strategies concurrently, allowing students to learn individually and inductively, creating new assessment opportunities, and so on. The learning process will continue to advance along with advances in technology. *See also* Technology (education)

Telegenic Subjects   A person or a topic that is particularly suited to the medium of television and attracts and interests an audience.

The presidential candidate John Kennedy was considered to be more telegenic than his opponent Richard Nixon, appearing more charming, youthful, energetic, and handsome in televised debates in 1960. It is claimed that his election victory was due at least in part to his greater telegenic appeal.

Subjects who are considered telegenic get more television time and attract more advertising revenue, hence the proliferation of reality shows rather than, say, poetry recitals. Some media analysts are concerned that the emphasis on telegenic subject matter elbows out coverage of important issues. The nuances of complex issues may be communicated better by other media. People relying mainly on television for news may be making decisions based on incomplete information and may make less wise choices than they might if they were better informed. This is problematic as an informed citizenry is desirable for the effective working of a democracy.

Television was the dominant mass medium for the second part of the 20th century, reaching more people in the United States than radio or newspapers. Most people had access to a few local broadcast stations, which would produce some local material and acquire other shows produced for national broadcast, which would command huge audiences. Television audiences are now fragmenting among the increasing number of television stations enabled by cable, satellite, and digital technology. Niche markets for television channels are growing. In this environment, the subjective notion of what is telegenic is far more open to diverse interpretation than when television was dominated by a handful of broadcasting stations in the second half of the 20th century. For more information, see Postman (1985). *See also* Television and Social Behavior

Telegraph   The first technology to enable communication of information without physical movement (called the "Victorian Internet" of the telegraph). Optical telegraphs were in use from the end of the 18th century, consisting of people using lights, flags, or other devices to send semaphore signals from one tower or "beacon hill" to another a few miles away. The electrical telegraph was developed and became operational by the mid-19th century and was first used alongside railways to control switching and signaling.

An experimental line connected Baltimore and Washington in 1846, using technology developed by Samuel Morse. By 1850, there was 12,000 miles of telegraph in the United States. The first line to cross the continent was complete in 1861, making the Pony Express redundant. Messages that had taken 10 days to cross from Missouri to Sacramento were transferred by telegraph in seconds. Networks of telegraph lines connected telegraph offices in towns across the country. Messages would be exchanged between offices by means of the Morse code.

Telegrams were used to exchange commodity prices, reducing the price differences between markets. Personal information exchanges followed but, being expensive, tended to be short and were used for urgent news only.

The growing 19th-century newspaper industry eagerly adopted the telegraph, in a battle to be the first to get and report news from distant places. The Associated Press was founded in 1848, when six daily New York papers agreed to cooperate in using the telegraph to relay news stories. By the end of the 19th century, the organization was supplying news stories to newspapers across the United States. For more information, see Crowley and Heyer (2007) and Lebow (1995). **See also** Wire Services/News Groups

Telegraphic Speech   The laconic and efficient utterances that characterize speech during the two-word stage of language acquisition in child development, which generally occurs between 18 and 36 months of age. However, individuals who have suffered a stroke or other brain insult may use telegraphic speech. Telegraphic speech, first studied by Roger Brown in the 1970s, is brief, to the point, and leaves out nonessential words. For example, a child who wants to say "Mommy is sleeping" might say "Mommy sleep"; someone who wishes to say "The dog is running" might say "Dog running."

Television and Social Behavior   Television program content, viewer characteristics, and viewing context can have a measurable impact on viewer behavior. Considerable attention has especially been paid to the effects of violent and antisocial content, and research has centered on the potential negative effects on children. Out of concern about the effect of mass media portrayal of violence and its potential inducement of aggressive behavior in children, in 1972 the U.S. Surgeon General's Committee on Television and Social Behavior released a multivolume report on research on the impact of television on children. Because many studies showed a positive correlation, research on television effects continues to be a focus of social scientists and public concern.

The social behavior of adults is not immune to television effects. Dramas, comedies, and advertisement can both reflect and affect our social values. Negative behavior may be influenced by racial stereotypes portrayed on television shows or unbalanced news coverage. Television programs and advertisements influence consumer spending habits. People adjust their social schedule to accommodate their TV viewing schedule (though technological advances such as on-demand viewing has reduced this need), which may result in decreased social interaction. People also use television as background noise, to fill time, to reduce social unease, to stimulate conversation, and, often incidentally, for social learning.

Television viewing can have an impact on mass social action—telethons and public broadcasting auctions are proven methods of fund-raising. News coverage of events can affect how people feel about and act on issues. The Vietnam War, for instance, was dubbed the "living-room war," because the mass viewership of information about the war was believed to have had a significant impact on rallying viewers to demonstrate or vote in certain ways. News coverage of even fictional hypothetical events—natural disaster, financial climate, terrorism—can induce panic and in turn quell anxiety by providing crucial information.

While much of the research on television effects has been concerned with negative effects, many have also studied the prosocial attributes of the medium. Some advocates believe that watching television together strengthens the family unit. Others highlight the benefits of programming that portrays positive life situations intended to enhance the social and moral development of children and adolescents. Children can be exposed to and learn, for example, the values of altruism, self-control, and positive interactions. For more information, see Comstock (1972), Huston (1992), Mares and Woodard (2005), Newcomb (2007), and Sage (1997). **See also** Behavioral Effects; Copycat Effect/Crime; Crime Programming on Television; Media Effects; Prosocial Model; Stimulation Hypothesis

Temporal Context/Temporal Conception   These terms refer to temporarily related events in natural-language text. A temporal context scopes changing worldviews and serves as a tool for disambiguating time-dependent events or intervals. For example, the question, "Who was the President of the United States when Hurricane Katarina descended on New Orleans?" needs temporal event detection and context-based reasoning. There are several, standard, approaches to represent time or events in time. The most common approaches include absolute dating scheme, relative event ordering, and duration-based approaches. One of the main problems with temporal context is the lack of absolute timestamp for many events. Temporal conception addresses time as a medium of communication. It attempts to define the way people understand time and make use of it. The perception of physical time as a factor in an individual's subjective environment is itself a culturally changeable variable. No two people view the passage of time in the same way, although groups of people working in the same environments may view the passage of time in similar ways. For more information, see Moldovan, Clark, and Harabagiu (2009).

Tenure   After a probationary period (2–6 years) of satisfactory teaching service in a school district, an educator is guaranteed permanent employment. It is difficult for tenured educators to be released from teaching service, except in extreme circumstances such as illegal activity, without going through a prescribed professional improvement plan. *See also* Teacher Evaluation

Term Limits   The statutory limits on the number of terms a politician can serve in office. Term limits exist in Latin American countries as well as in Russia. In the United States, a form of term limit existed since the late 17th century. It was called rotation, and it mandated politicians to leave office for a period of time, although they were not barred from returning. The idea was to allow candidates to share in the fruits of power.

Gubernatorial term limits have existed in the United States since 1787. Today, about 40% of the states impose term limits on their respective governors. Executive term limits for the U.S. president have existed since 1951, with the ratification of the Twenty-Second Amendment of the U.S. Constitution. This amendment limits a president's service to 2 four-year terms. Congressional term limits, however, have a much more recent history in both state and federal governments.

Congressional term limits became an important issue during the late 1980s and early 1990s, when grassroots efforts were made to limit the terms of elected officials. However, in *Term Limits, Inc. v. Thornton* (1995), the Supreme Court ruled that states cannot impose term limits on federal representatives or senators. The only way to limit congressional terms would be to amend the Constitution. Subsequent to this decision, Congress failed to gain the two-thirds votes needed to pass such a constitutional amendment. And in March 1998, the Court let stand term limits for state lawmakers when it denied certiorari in an appeal to overturn term limits in California. Today, 16 states impose term limits for state legislators. Several states bar politicians for life from returning to the same office once the term has ended. For more information, see *Term Limits, Inc. v. Thornton* (1995). *See also* Congress; Legislative Branch; Writ of Certiorari

Territory *(geography)*   A geographical area that can be determinate or indeterminate but is usually under the jurisdiction of a state or national government. The term gives rise to political and social connotations expressed in variations, such as *territorial* or *territoriality*—the defense of a certain geographical entity. The term is also embedded in the *territorial imperative* theory of aggression, in which animals, humans, and nations seek to expand their physical space at the expense of others.

Such actions on the part of governments frequently lead to wars and other conflicts.

On a much more limited, political basis, the term refers to a nonsovereign nation that is controlled by the government of the nation in which the territory is located. Territories located in the United States are subject to the rule of the U.S. federal government. Puerto Rico, Guam, and the Virgin Islands are some of the more well-known territories in the United States. Although subject to the authority of the federal government, some of the territories, such as Guam, have established civilian self-governance.

Territory *(sociology)*   A defined geographical region (land or water) with varying levels of autonomy, over which another government exercises sovereignty. In some cases, territorial status may be in preparation for statehood. The Virgin Islands, Guam, and American Samoa are current territories of the United States.

Terrorism *(political science)*   The systematic use of terror or violence to achieve political goals. This definition of terrorism is not wholly adequate; more than 100 definitions of this term exist because there are many types of terrorism that differ in time, motivation, and manifestations, and there is no agreed-on definition. Nevertheless, elements of terrorism that are generally agreed on are its use or threatened use of violence to achieve some political aim, the acquisition and use of power, and the planned, calculated, and systematic characteristics of the act itself. Although terrorists themselves may embrace a specific ideology that justifies their acts, terrorism itself is not an ideology but rather one of the oldest forms of violence.

The pioneers of suicide terrorism were the Assassins, who operated between the 8th and 14th centuries in the area that now comprises Iran and Iraq. Since the Assassins used daggers to kill targets, who were usually well guarded, their chance of escape was generally nonexistent.

Terroristic acts have appeared in the *Old Testament* of the Bible and in Greek and Roman history. But the term *terrorism* was not popularized until the French Revolution in 1789. Terrorism was used as an instrument of governance to intimidate dissidents and those sympathetic to the previous regime. Thus, the resulting newly created political system, *la régime de la terreur,* connoted terrorism in a positive light.

After 1960, there was a rise in international terrorist attacks. The idea of modern terrorism arguably came into the public consciousness on July 22, 1968, when armed Palestinian men from the Palestinian Liberation Organization (PLO) hijacked an Israeli El Al commercial flight for the purpose of taking hostages in exchange for the release of Palestinian terrorists being held in Israel.

The perpetrators of terrorism may be either individual groups or whole governments. Some historical and current terrorist groups include left- and right-wing political groups, white supremacists, religious cults, antiabortionists, ecoterrorists, bioterrorists, cyberterrorists, and narcoterrorists. State-sponsored terrorism is supported by governments to eliminate their opponents. Examples of state-sponsored terrorism are found in many Asian, African, Middle-Eastern, and South American governments, as well as the tyrannical regimes of Adolf Hitler, Josef Stalin, and Benito Mussolini.

A new type of religious suicide/homicide terrorism emerged on September 11, 2001, which involved the deadliest terror attack on the United States, and pushed Islamic terrorism to the top of the American political agenda. In addition to an economic crisis in the airline industry and heightened security precautions, the United States changed its response to terrorism from that of the police model of arrest and prosecution to a preemptive-war model, which included the American attack on the Taliban regime in Afghanistan, followed by the 2003 invasion of Iraq. For more information, see Hoffman (1998) and Lacquer (2001). *See also* Ideology (political science, sociology); Tyranny

Terrorism *(sociology)*   The systematic use of violence designed to create a climate of fear among opponents, to coerce political change, to destabilize a government or society, or to publicize a cause. Attacks are intended to target or disregard the safety of civilians. Throughout history, a variety of organizations (e.g., political groups, religious groups, governments, extremists) have used terrorist techniques (e.g., bombing, hijacking, assassination) to fulfill ideological objectives. The concept was first introduced in reference to the French Revolution's Reign of Terror, though terrorism became more common after World War II. The United Nations and the governments of most countries define acts of terrorism as criminal acts. The deadliest terrorist attack in world history was perpetrated by members of the Islamist al-Qaeda network on September 11, 2001, in the United States, killing more than 3,000 people. An individual who carries out terrorist acts of violence is called a terrorist. *See also* Ideology (sociology)

Test Anxiety   Intense feelings of stress related to the testing situation. Moderate amounts of stress can be *facilitative,* leading students to study, take notes, read and research, attend class lectures or activities, and concentrate during the testing procedure. Facilitative anxiety is commonly linked to *state anxiety,* or specific event-related stress. With *state* test anxiety, the tension vanishes when the test-related activities end. After studying, a person with state anxiety can usually do other things, with no adverse effects. During class, moderate state anxiety leads a student to focus rather than to be off-task. During the test, moderate state anxiety directs the student's attention to reading carefully, proofreading, and other positive testing strategies. After the test, the anxiety disappears because the "state," or impetus for stress, has been removed.

Debilitating stress related to test taking, on the other hand, focuses on the negative aspects of testing. Fear of failure can block concentration during class activities, studying, and testing. This severe performance anxiety causes a person to focus on the results and the possible negative repercussions rather than on the content and preparation. Debilitative test anxiety is sometimes associated with more general *trait anxiety* or a constant fear or anxiety in life. This sort of test anxiety is sometimes found in perfectionists and others who need a strong sense of control in their world.

There are well-researched interventions for those with individuals experiencing test anxiety. Teachers give students helpful strategies for studying and test taking. Students learn relaxation techniques to help them concentrate. Students may be referred for group or individual therapeutic intervention to relieve and manage test anxiety. *See also* Anxiety Disorders

Testimony   An oral or written statement or declaration of fact given under oath by a witness in response to questions posed by an attorney at a trial in court or a deposition outside court. False testimony may result in a perjury charge. *See also* Witness

Test-Retest Reliability   A method used to assess the consistency of a measure from one point in time to another. Test-retest reliability is estimated by administering the same test to the same sample of people on two different occasions and correlating the scores obtained on each administration. This method assumes that the true ability of the test-taking sample does not change between administrations. The effects of practice or test familiarity can artificially deflate an estimate of test-retest reliability. *See also* Reliability; Spilt-Half Reliability

Texas Rangers   A group of mounted lawmen, formed in 1823, who patrolled ("ranged") the American frontier and provided law enforcement throughout Texas. In 1935, the State Highway Patrol absorbed the Rangers, and they became an investigative division of the Texas Department of Public Safety.

Text   In its proper usage, the term refers to any written document (script, novel, memo, etc.), but it has also a wider application and broadly refers to any meaningful cultural form, such as film or billboard ads. Texts communicate messages, with arguments often angled to support the central point. Texts have audiences, notional or real, and they have contexts, which give meaning to their message. Without that context of assumptions and implied codes, the meaning is not clear. The literary critic Terry Eagleton provides examples to show that the seemingly clearest "texts" are really quite ambiguous: "Dogs must be carried on the escalators" (Can one not get on without one?) or "Refuse to be put in this basket." This interpretative openness of texts that appear to be semantically "closed" shifts the emphasis away from the author to the reader, from words to how words are read. The title of an essay by Roland Barthes (1988) "From

Work to Text" encapsulates the epistemological shift away from the work as the effect of authorial intention to the text as a linguistic event. Text thus changes from being a message from an author to a reader to a depersonalized element within a discursive web of relations. Other French writers like Jacques Derrida and Julie Kristeva emphasize the ways in which every text holds other texts within it, thereby making every text intertextual. Emerging out of digital technology, hypertext partially realizes the philosophical vision of intertextuality in its networking of texts into a potentially endless "docuverse," a term coined by the information technologist Ted Nelson. For more information, see Barthes (1988). ***See also*** Discourse; Intertextuality

Thalamus   A dual-lobed structure of subcortical gray matter that is situated below the corpus callosum in the central part of the brain and controls the flow of all information to the cerebral cortex. The thalamus is composed of numerous nuclei that receive messages from all sensory organs via diverse brain regions and relay this information to various regions of the cortex. The thalamus can be considered the way station of the brain because axons from every sensory system (except olfaction) synapse at the thalamus before their information reaches the cerebral cortex. ***See also*** Brain

Theater   A word that combines the two ideas of spectacle and space, derived from the Greek *theatron* ("seeing place"). The etymology illustrates the influence Ancient Greece has exercised over Western theater. The earliest dramas probably comprised religious festivals in which the masses freely participated. Only with the emergence of the chorus out of the masses was the critical step taken toward the theatrical performance, with its division between actor and spectator. Theatrical space says much about the power relationship between the actor and the spectator. As theater became increasingly formalized and actors gained dominance over the chorus, purpose-built structures staged the plays. Stone amphitheaters, seating thousands, attest to the involvement of entire communities in these religious festivals. Despite Aristotle's deemphasizing of spectacle in tragic drama, the masks, dance, and elaborate scenery were central. Nonetheless, spectacle had its limits. Deeds deemed too sensational to see (e.g., Oedipus's self-blinding) were related rather than performed. The Christian Church regarded theater with suspicion, although the Middle Ages cultivated reenactments of biblical events (mystery plays), often performed in pageant wagons in the open street. Although there were some medieval fixed theaters, purpose-built playhouses did not gain prominence until the 16th century. The power of the playhouses is indicated by their closure during the era of Puritan censorship in England (1653–1659). During the 16th and 17th centuries, the proscenium became popular, in which the stage is framed with an arch marking the boundary between illusion and reality. The proscenium arch enabled the

development in the 19th century of the box set, in which the stage represents three walls of a room, with the audience forming a silently spectating fourth wall. This type of theatrical structure invites naturalism, with actors behaving as if the audience were absent. Reaction against naturalist theater took many forms but is most associated with the epic theater of Bertolt Brecht, whose alienation effects (*Verfremsdungeffekt*) were designed to dispel the hypnotic illusionism of Western theater, which stopped audiences from thinking critically. Although Western theater developed independently of Asian theater, Brecht's theater makes an interesting comparison with it, most notably in the distance actors maintain between themselves and their roles, where no effort is made to "get in character" as one does in the method acting of Stanislavsky. Contemporary theater is often freely experimental, with the lines between actor and audience, stage and auditorium, play and reality continually challenged. Movies are also performed in theaters, purpose-built structures for big-screen viewing. However, movie theaters rarely challenge the relationship between the passive audience and the onscreen action. Theater remains essentially a space of live performance. ***See also*** Drama; Film

Theft   The crime of intentionally taking the personal property or services of another person without freely given consent and with the intent to deprive the owner of it permanently. Theft is distinguished in statutory law from robbery, burglary, and embezzlement by the means and methods used.

Thematic Apperception Test (TAT)   A projective personality measure in which the subject is presented with a series of pictures of people engaged in some activity, either alone or with up to two others. Subjects are asked to generate stories about the pictures, which are vague enough to elicit a number of different responses yet intended to lead test takers to similar associations. Presumably the test takers will project themselves onto the story, revealing unconscious psychological processes. For more information, see Teglasi (2001). ***See also*** Rorschach

Thematic News Format   A format that both news media and news reporting can be described as having.

In terms of news media, thematic television and radio stations are those that carry only a specific type of program, such as sports, cartoons, or cooking programs. Thematic news channels provide continual news coverage—for example, CNN, Fox News Channel, Al-Jazeera. Rather than broadcasting a range of programming, such channels engage in "narrowcasting"—concentrating on a narrow range of program content.

News reporting can also be described as having a thematic format. This refers to news stories being presented in "frames" to define the context for the audience. Framing can be categorized as either episodic or thematic. Episodic framing focuses on a particular case or event, while a thematic frame adds a broader context and presents the story within a broader political or sociological framework. *See also* Agenda Setting (media studies); News/News Production

Theocracy   A form of government that claims to be directed by God or gods and divinely blessed. The term *theocracy* was coined from the Greek term *theokratia* in the 1st century by Flavius Josephus, a Jewish historian whose intent was to educate the Gentiles on the political system of the Jewish state. This system was in contrast to the monarchies, oligarchies, and republics existing in non-Jewish states.

Theocracy literally means "rule of God" or "rule by God." A theocracy is a state ruled by religious law. The leadership in a theocracy often comprises members of the clergy. Several forms of theocratic rule exist. The purest theocratic form is the hierocracy, in which the political sphere is dominated or replaced by religious institutions. In a hierocracy, society is ruled by a clergy or by priests who are believed to have a direct personal connection to God. It is sometimes called *priestly rule*. Few hierocracies have existed throughout history. Some hierocracies existed during the early years of Islam under Mohammed and the first caliphs, in Tibet from the 13th through the mid-20th centuries, among the early Mormons under Joseph Smith and Brigham Young in the 19th century, in Iran during the 1980s, in the Vatican under papal rule, and during the Taliban dominance of Afghanistan from 1996 through 2001.

Most theocracies, however, recognize that an ultimate authority may be vested in divine law but government is mediated through secularized political institutions. For example, the Egyptian kings were expected to rule according to the principles of justice, while the Roman emperors, who followed Eastern Orthodox Christianity, believed in ruling according to the revelation of truth. And for the Christian Calvinists of the 16th and 17th centuries, the clergy only had an advisory role in checking civil government.

In Western countries, the Age of Enlightenment in the 18th century marked the end of most theocracies. The end came as a result of the heavy beating that Europe endured from the religious wars in the 16th and 17th centuries. As a result, knowledge became dominated by rational inquiry as a defense against the superstitions and intolerances of religion. Today, secularization has further rendered a sharp dichotomy between the tenets of the church and the rules of the state in many Christian-dominated governments.

Even in the Islamic world, a Gallup poll taken in 2008 indicated that Muslims prefer a government that incorporates the Shari'a, or laws from the Koran, as a source of law. However, the government they prefer is a democratic one that resembles, rather than wholly adopts, the Westernized model. Interestingly, in 2006, another Gallup poll found that a majority of Americans wanted the Bible as either a source or the only source of legislation in the United States. For more information,

see Gallup (2008). *See also* Democracy (political science); Government

Theory *(communications)*   The set of assumptions and rules that guide systematic research and define the boundaries of the discipline. It is a set of statements about how the world of communication and its messages is thought to work. A theoretical stance affects what is studied as well as how it is studied. Communication, however, does not have one cohesive stance on its subject. Its theories range from cultural studies approaches using mass media theories about power and ideology to psychological approaches that look for actions by humans during communication that reduce anxiety and uncertainty or introduce control and deception. Other theoretical stances assume the activity or passivity of the recipient of messages, focus on decision making, study the structure and meaning of interpersonal relationships, or look at the institutions that produce and disseminate mass communications. Generally, communication theories focus on one of four areas: (1) interpersonal relations and face-to-face communications, (2) group communications and the workings of communities, (3) mass media and mass communication and the implications of the global media, and (4) cultural approaches that can include any type of communication interaction but always involve direct observation and field research. Theories in communication studies are not necessarily tested using the scientific method and objective criteria, as required in the natural sciences. Instead, data are interpreted, and the meaning or significance of a communication becomes the goal. For more information, see Griffin (2006). *See also* Discourse; Discourse Analysis; Mass Communication; Theory (psychology, sociology)

Theory *(psychology)*   An integrated set of propositions and concepts that is developed to account for a set of related observations and is used to generate testable hypotheses or predictions about future observations. Theories are not merely guesses or hunches. Rather, psychological theories are explanations of behavior that are developed after extensive carefully conducted research and observations across diverse settings and populations. *See also* Hypothesis (psychology); Theory (communications)

Theory *(sociology)*   An organized and consistent system of general propositions used to explain and predict a specific set of social phenomena. According to the scientific method, theories are generalizations that evolve from social research. Theories are always changeable according to new data and, therefore, must remain predictive of future phenomena and be logical and testable. Theories are distinguished from hypotheses, which are generally specific experimental applications of a theory. Feminist theories in sociology, for example, emphasize the role of gender inequality and male dominance in society. *See also* Hypothesis (sociology); Theory (communications)

Theory-Driven Evaluation An evaluation that seeks first to identify a program theory, whether derived from social science theory, stakeholder theory, or a combination of the two, which is usually represented in the form of a logic model. Second, theory-driven evaluations attempt to identify the mechanisms by which programs operate and produce their results, including the factors that mediate and moderate these results. Like realist evaluation, they are often designed to investigate how, why, and for whom a particular program works. *See also* Realist Evaluation

Therapy An intervention to help people cope, manage difficulties, adapt to life circumstances, or deal with crisis, disturbances, or disorders. The term is used interchangeably with psychotherapy (traditionally more intensive and long-term) or counseling (traditionally short-term and less intense). Treatments address a medical or physical condition or crisis, interpersonal relationships, cognitive challenges or disabilities, or emotional, psychological, or mental distress. Methods of intervention may include talk and communication, behavior changes, or the creative arts. The therapist is a trained and licensed professional with extensive supervised experience in working with clients. *See also* Cognitive Behavioral Therapy (CBT); Counseling; Gestalt Therapy; Marriage Counseling; Psychoanalysis (psychology).

Third Party An additional party that runs in a political election in which two parties is the norm. Third-party candidates can have the "spoiler effect" on a leading candidate, taking away a portion of his or her votes. In the United States, third-party candidates in past federal and state elections have included members of (a) the Green Party, (b) the Constitution Party, (c) the Libertarian Party, and (d) the Independent/Reform Party. Third-party candidates who have served as spoilers in U.S. presidential elections include Theodore Roosevelt (1912), George Wallace (1968), Ross Perot (1992), and Ralph Nader (2000).

Three-Strikes Laws A type of mandatory sentencing that targets habitual offenders for long-term incapacitation through imposing lengthy sentences of imprisonment. Borrowing their slogan from the well-known baseball saying "Three strikes, and you're out," these laws require that offenders who have two prior convictions for violent felony offenses be sentenced to 25 years to life on the third violent felony conviction. Although Washington passed the first three-strikes law in 1993, California's three-strikes law, which was passed in the aftermath of the abduction and murder of Polly Klaas, is the most well-known. Between 1994 and 1996, almost half of the states passed a three-strikes law. Although three-strikes laws are relatively new, habitual-offending statutes are not. Prior criminal record has always been taken into account during sentencing *See also* Habitual Offender; Mandatory Sentence

Threshold The minimum amount of a stimulus needed for it to be detected. For example, researchers may record varying levels of a sound to detect the conditions under which that sound can be detected. Sensory thresholds differ among individuals and can also differ within the same person depending on his or her physiological state. The smallest magnitude of a stimulus that can be detected is called the *absolute threshold,* and the smallest magnitude of difference in a stimulus is known as the *difference threshold.*

Title I A law designed to promote the education of students from disadvantaged backgrounds by requiring equal provision of services to students across the academic spectrum. (Its full name is Title I of the Elementary and Secondary Education Act of 1965.) Such services include school facilities, educational testing, well-trained teachers, and curricular materials. Title I also addresses the need for accountability on the part of educators and administrators through a variety of methods ranging from statewide assessment to local-level discretionary powers, mandates federal education funding specifically to promote these goals, and establishes the scope of federal responsibilities as related to their achievement.

Token Economy *(education)* A token symbolizes or stands for something else, such as tickets or points that are traded in for commodities or privileges. In a token economy, tokens are used as reinforcers or rewards to produce behavior change. An implementation plan specifies target behaviors, describes how tokens are to be awarded, and explains how tokens may be redeemed. To increase positive behaviors or decrease negative behaviors, tokens are awarded based on compliance. The system works best when (a) one behavior at a time is targeted, (b) the reinforcement is immediate, and (c) the rewards for accumulated tokens are desired or meaningful. *See also* Behaviorism (education); Contingency Contracting

Token Economy *(psychology)* A behavior modification procedure, based on operant conditioning principles, in which patients are given a conditioned reinforcer, such as tokens, for targeted behavior. Tokens can be exchanged for primary reinforcers such as snacks or social privileges. Token economies were once used on a widespread basis in institutions for mentally retarded or mentally ill individuals. When conducted fairly and consistently, patients tend to respond well. However, inconsistent implementation in large institutions, as well as ethical concerns over the undue influence on patients, have caused token economies to fall out of use. *See also* Behavior Modification; Operant Conditioning

Tolerance The term refers to curbing actions against something or someone disliked. The opposites of tolerance are persecution and discrimination, which involve acting against something or someone. Types of tolerance can be defined by their objects: political (public sphere), moral (private sphere), and social (characteristics of persons or groups). Tolerance is fundamental to democratic society: Governments must tolerate opposition; proponents of opposing views must allow others to express themselves and to vote. Tolerance is always limited; the sociopolitical definition of the limits of tolerance is crime, which is prohibited and punished, not tolerated. The tolerance levels of individuals and societies tend to be strongly correlated with their education levels. *See also* Discrimination (public administration)

Topography A major discipline of geography, the term refers to the study of the earth's physical features. More specifically, topography focuses on the features found on the earth's surface. Commonly studied features in this discipline include mountains, valleys, and rivers. However, topography is not limited to the study of naturally occurring features. The discipline also includes the study of man-made features, such as bridges and roadways. Topographers are concerned with the precise description of surface features, which includes the size, shape, and position of the feature under examination. The geographical information collected and analyzed by topographers is interpreted and presented in the form of topographic maps and charts. Topography is pertinent to the preservation and maintenance of the earth's natural resources and is also necessary for construction-site planning.

Tort A civil wrong or wrongful act, other than a breach of contract, either intentional (e.g., libel, wrongful death) or accidental (negligence), that causes harm to a person or property. Damages (symbolic or compensatory) are usually awarded. Torts may also be charged as crimes.

Totalitarian A type of government rule that is driven by an ideology that seeks control over all aspects of public activity. Totalitarian regimes reject liberal values. Instead, they exercise total control over the lives of subjects, including private morality, culture, religion, sports, science, politics, and economics. Totalitarian regimes are run by single-mass parties, whereby citizen participation in politics, such as voting, is compulsory. There is some disagreement about the relationship between totalitarian and authoritarian regimes. Some argue that totalitarian regimes are more repressive than authoritarian ones, whereas others believe that the two systems differ completely.

Totalitarianism A term that reflects the ideology of totalitarian regimes, may have been coined by Giovanni Gentile, a philosopher of fascism in Italy in the early 20th century. The term was later used in a speech by Benito Mussolini in 1925, in which he described his own regime as totalitarian. Modern totalitarian regimes made their appearance around the time of World War I, since the war required all state institutions to subordinate their interests to winning the war. The three prototype totalitarian regimes in the early 20th century were those of Mussolini's National Fascist Party, Stalin's Communist regime, and Hitler's National Socialist German Workers' Party. Although totalitarian regimes share some similarities, their ideological goals may differ. Communist regimes seek the establishment of classless societies, while the German socialists sought the establishment of a superior race of people.

There are six elements that totalitarian regimes share. First is the need for the center of power to possess the absolute truth with no tolerance for deviation. Second, an ideology is required to articulate the truth. Third, tactics including secrecy, terror, and systematic lying are used. Totalitarian leaders maintain power through propaganda and the use of terror through the secret police and military. Fourth, members of the party are used to interpret the regime's ideology for others. Fifth, implementers of the regime are used to run the state machinery. Sixth, there is a mass acceptance of the regime. For more information, see Schapiro (1972) and Soper (1985). *See also* Authoritarian; Cold War; Fascism; Ideology (political science); Liberalism (political science)

Totality of the Circumstances The requirement to consider all facts and the context rather than a single factor to evaluate concepts such as reasonable suspicion, probable cause, detention, and conditions of detention. Because there is often no single factor that defines probable cause for an arrest, for instance, officers must look at all factors known to them to determine if probable cause exists. *See also* Probable Cause; Reasonable Suspicion

Tracking The process of grouping students by ability, usually based on level of achievement, teacher recommendation, and parent wishes. Traditionally used in high schools to focus students on higher education or work after graduation, the most common tracks are (a) honors/advanced placement (AP), (b) college preparatory, (c) vocational/technical, (d) remedial, and (e) special education. *See also* Ability Grouping; Advanced Placement (AP); High School; Special Education; Vocational Education

Trade Area A concept with domestic and international dimensions. From a domestic perspective, a trade area incorporates the geographic proximity (trade zone) of customers and sellers. It is the geographic region from which a town gets most of its customers. From an international perspective, a trade area is normally associated with the economic integration of contiguous countries, known as a free-trade area.

Most retail businesses have a relatively fixed area where customers come from to do business. Businesses in a trade area attract customers from the neighborhood or workers who are employed in the vicinity. Changes in the residential size of the neighborhood or in job

T

availability affect the viability of the selling zone. The trade area for most small businesses is estimated to be about 3 to 5 miles.

A trade area can be defined by traffic flow, zip codes, retail gravity (estimates of the distance customers will travel to buy goods and services after comparing prices, quality, and other relevant factors), and commuting data (to define the boundaries of a trade area). The total market consists of populations in the host community and the population of the surrounding or adjoining towns in the trade area.

Identifying a trade area is important for businesses to understand how they can expand their markets, and it helps city and state policymakers engage in market analysis of the local area by using vital data on the number of customers, projected sales, and demand pull factors.

A free-trade area is a form of economic integration in which members remove trade barriers among themselves but retain the right to impose legal trade restrictions on nonmembers. The North American Free Trade Agreement (NAFTA), the Southern Common Market, and the Economic Community of West African States (ECOWAS) are examples of a free-trade area.

A free-trade area is one of four types of trading blocs. The others are customs union; common market; and economic union. For more information, see Carbaugh (2007), Myles (2003), Pugel (2007), and Salvatore (2006). **See also** Free Trade; Market; World Trade Organization (WTO)

Trade Theory, New

Trade Theory, New   A theory that argues that it is possible for protectionism to be sometimes better than free trade. This theory became more prominent in the 1980s as a result of the U.S. trade deficit with Japan. The idea of protection versus free trade is not a novel one, but the basis for trade theories has evolved over time. In fact, free trade has never been an absolute theory of trade. No nation can allow all sorts and conditions of goods to flow through its borders without some form of control. The question is, "To what extent should trade be permissible?"

In the 18th and 19th centuries, the mercantilists were concerned about the acquisition of wealth and unfettered trade. The argument then was that nations that wanted to be rich in order to raise large armies and fight expansionary wars must restrict imports as much as possible while exporting a lot to acquire bullion (precious metals).

The physiocrats David Hume and Adam Smith questioned the wisdom of trade restriction, and the concept of laissez-faire has played a much more dominant role in international trade and markets since the 19th century. The Great Depression of the 1930s drew attention to the need for regulated markets and trade.

The strength of the free trade argument has always been the notion of efficiency and improved consumer welfare. The new trade theory suggests that protection can equally improve consumer well-being in a large and diversified economy. The theory postulates that even though trade can contribute to growth, improvement in income does not necessarily translate into equitable income distribution between employers and employees.

The new trade theory extends the neoclassical tradition of economic analysis by reintroducing the concept of market imperfection, strategic trade theory, new growth theory, and political economy arguments into the explanation of international trade and the benefits of protection.

The pertinence of the new trade theory also finds favor in the developing countries, where economies of scale and imperfect competition are noticeable. These countries also allude to practical reasons to protect infant industries until they have the stature to compete in global markets. It is a theory that is sensitive to generic application because trade intervention is promoted to be selective and targeted with full realization of sector weaknesses and market imperfections.

New liberals are apprehensive of a government's wisdom to selectively target vital sectors of the economy in order to manage international trade. They find justification in the failures of sweeping and sudden reforms or intervention, which have proved to be calamitous in highly regulated economies. **See also** Absolute Advantage; Comparative Advantage; Fair Trade; Free Trade; Mercantilism

Tradition   A general term used to describe the beliefs, legends, rituals, or customs handed down from one generation to the next, especially orally or by example. Traditions may be societal, cultural, or religious and function as a way to transfer knowledge. While traditions are often assumed to be ancient, many traditions, in order to survive, adapt to contemporaneous economic, social, political, and cultural environments. Some scholars argue that tradition may be invented to maintain hegemony or power.

Traffic Law   The legal rules of the road, governing traffic movement and safety. Traffic rules apply to vehicles and drivers (e.g., registration, safety equipment) and to pedestrians (e.g., crossing rules). Traffic police may issue tickets for moving (e.g., speeding) and nonmoving (e.g., parking) violations.

Training   A planned effort to facilitate learning of the knowledge, skills, competencies, and attitudes needed for performing a specific task or job and furthering individual and organizational goals. Although training is typically associated with employees' acquisition of knowledge and learning in a cognitive sense, it also applies to the physical skill training of athletes, surgeons, fire fighters, physical therapists, and soldiers, to name a few, where certain physical skills are required to perform tasks optimally. Training increasingly is viewed as a vital part of a worker's lifelong need for continually updating skills to adapt best to rapidly changing workplace demands. For more information, see

Werner and DeSimone (2006). *See also* Organization Development (OD) (public administration)

Trait   A stable personality characteristic that is displayed consistently by an individual over time and across situations. The trait approach to understanding personality is a perspective that views an individual's personality as a combination of relatively enduring thoughts, attitudes, emotions, and behavioral tendencies that characterize an individual and allow for the prediction of the individual's future behaviors.

Trajectory   The path or course of an object through space. In the social sciences, the concept of a trajectory is used to describe the path of an individual or a group over a period of time, focusing on their stability and change. Specifically, in criminology, the life course theory of criminal behavior studies the trajectory of criminal behavior over the individual life course to determine the cause of decreases (desistance) or continued involvement (recidivism) in criminal behavior. *See also* Criminology

Transactional   Social exchanges between individuals. The most ideal transactional communications are give-and-take interactions in which an individual is confident about self-expression although open to the opinions and personal history of the other. The literature on transactional communication spans many fields, including psychology, management, and education.

The term *transactional* came into the vernacular during the second half of the 20th century with the psychiatrist Eric Berne's conception of how parental behaviors shape individual maturation and his development of a form of group therapy called transactional analysis. Those undergoing therapy are encouraged to focus on the adult, parent, and child components within themselves in order to attain awareness, spontaneity, intimacy, and, ultimately, personal autonomy. Berne's disciple Thomas Harris credits Berne with creating a "unified system of individual and social psychiatry" and eschewing psychiatric jargon while training mental health workers in "a public language" to enable change, self-control, self-direction, and freedom of choice. For more information, see Berne (1964) and Harris (1969). *See also* Interpersonal Communication; Persuasion

Transference   The unconscious redirection of feelings from one person to another. Such redirection of feelings can occur when a person projects the perceptions and expectations of one person (often a parental or other authority figure) onto his or her therapist and then interacts with the therapist as though the therapist is the person whose perceptions and expectations have been projected. Transference was first described by Sigmund Freud, who believed that early-childhood experiences with parents were crucial contributing factors to the development of personality and psychopathology. Freud considered transference

an important mechanism through which the psychoanalyst could understand the patient's feelings; however, it can also be problematic and can influence negatively the course of therapy. *See also* Psychoanalysis (psychology)

Transfer of Knowledge/Learning   The process of being able to take knowledge or learning (skills) from one context and applying it to another with similar characteristics. For organizational learning, this process relates to the practical problem of shifting knowledge/learning from one part of the organization to the entire organization. However, knowledge/learning transfer is complex because learning is often situated in particular situations or tied to specific contexts, knowledge resides in the execution of certain practices, and tacit knowledge is known but difficult to articulate. Transfer failures may represent a metacognitive problem, since individuals do not fully understand the utility of the knowledge or strategies they are learning. Practices that support the transfer of knowledge/learning include the development of communities of practice, mentoring, and guided practice. Transfer of knowledge/learning can also refer to transmission from research to practice, from the classroom to the workplace, or from academia to the community. For more information, see Perkins and Salomon (1994). *See also* Metacognition

Transformation   A change in the form, nature, or character of an individual or thing. In sociology, "social transformations" reflect changes in a culture and the associated collective identity, such as those that arise as the result of industrialization, forced migration, tourism, or democratization. Study of such social transformations analyzes the ways they affect individuals, groups, and cultures economically, socially, and politically. Much of the recent research on social transformation has focused on the impact of modernization and globalization on homogenization and diversity. *See also* Globalization (sociology)

Transformational Leadership   The concept of transformational leadership, as envisioned by Burns (1978), originally referred to moral political leaders who engaged with their followers in such a way that each was raised to a higher level of morality and motivation. The concept has since been applied in areas such as business, psychology, and education. For more information, see Burns (1978).

Transition   A change from one state or place to another. In sociology, the study of societal transition examines the effects of governmental, political, economic, or social transitions on the members of a group, culture, or society.

Transit Police   A specialized police unit charged with the prevention and investigation of crimes committed against a transit system, by or against passengers, or on system property. Transit police may be part of a police department or privately employed by the transit system.

Transparency   An indicator, closely related to accountability and openness, of how much information media organizations make available to their public about reporting and editorial decisions. Efforts to increase transparency in newsrooms include developing conflict-of-interest policies; revealing sources and source materials, including interview transcripts; opening editorial meetings to the public; and appointing public editors. **See also** Objectiveness in Media Coverage; Privileged Conversations

Treason   In U.S. law, this term refers to the crime of betraying one's country by levying war against it to overthrow the government or by giving assistance to its enemies in wartime. The Constitution requires the testimony of at least two witnesses to the same overt act (e.g., giving government secrets to other countries, espionage) or a confession in open court for conviction. According to congressional legislation, a traitor may be punished with death or imprisonment. Aaron Burr was tried for and acquitted of treason in 1807; there have been very few other treason prosecutions.

Treaty   A signed agreement between countries. A treaty can be between two or more countries, called a bilateral or multilateral treaty, respectively. Treaties commonly involve areas such as war reparations, arms agreements, trade relations, and financial concerns. In an effort to prevent secret treaties, the United Nations, under Article 102 of the Charter of the United Nations (1945), declared that "every treaty and international agreement entered into by a member state of the UN shall be registered with and published by the Secretariat." The U.S. Constitution, Article 2, Section 2, states that the president can sign treaties only on approval of two thirds of the Senate.

Trial   A court proceeding that takes place when a person accused of a crime pleads "not guilty." Witnesses are required to testify in court to give evidence of the defendant's guilt or innocence. Attorneys for the plaintiff and defendant are entitled to make opening statements, limited to an outline of what they plan to prove, and evidence is then presented by witnesses. Both sides may close with final arguments to summarize and comment on the evidence and legal questions. The judge or jury then retires to reach a verdict about the guilt or innocence of the defendant. **See also** Not Guilty; Verdict

Triangulation   The idea that using different theories, methods, data, and investigators will uncover different aspects of a problem. Triangulation is often viewed as a source of validity and as strengthening a study. The idea is to look at the problem from a different perspective, with different tools, with different sources of data, or with different researchers in order to compare with the original interpretation. The results either strengthen the original interpretation or lead the researcher in a different direction. **See also** Qualitative Research; Validity/Validation

Tribunal   A permanent institution (e.g., court, judicial body, board) composed of independent judges that carries out judicial or quasi-judicial functions, such as the adjudication of disputes. The International Criminal Court is a tribunal charged with trying genocide, crimes against humanity, and war crimes.

Tropics   The region of the earth found between the Tropic of Cancer and the Tropic of Capricorn. This region is marked by the absence of cold weather. Also known as the torrid zone, the tropics cover an area spanning from about 23 degrees north to 23 degrees south of the equator. There is very little change in the weather patterns in the tropics due to the region's close proximity to the equator. The tropics receive direct sun for a significant portion of the year, so the weather is usually hot and humid; although there is some variation in climatic conditions, the climate is considerably stable year-round, allowing ecosystems to develop and to flourish under these stable conditions.

Troposphere   One of the five atmospheric layers; the zone of the earth in which weather occurs. The troposphere, the lowest of all layers found in the atmosphere, spans from the earth's surface to the stratosphere. The layer dividing the two layers is known as the tropopause. The troposphere is characterized by temperatures that decrease with escalating altitude, whereas the stratosphere is characterized by temperatures that increase with altitude. The troposphere, which spans approximately 15 kilometers above the earth's surface, is the most compact of all the atmospheric layers and is home to most of the atmosphere's water vapor. In addition, the troposphere is the layer in which most of the earth's clouds are located.

Truant   A student who is absent from compulsory schooling or classes intentionally and without authorization. In some schools, repeated instances of truancy may result in punishment of the students (e.g., ineligibility for graduation or class credit) or parents (e.g., fines, mandated counseling). Truancy is a status offense.

True Bill   A grand jury's formal, written finding of probable cause of a crime to send a defendant to court for trial (also known as an indictment). A grand jury returns a "no true bill" if it finds no probable cause for indictment. **See also** Grand Jury

Truman Doctrine   The declaration of policy, pronounced by President Harry S. Truman, that wherever aggression threatened the peace of free nations, the security of the United States would become involved. Specifically, military and economic assistance would be provided for countries threatened by communist domination. This declaration effectively ended American isolationism.

In February 1947, the British Embassy in Washington, D.C., informed the United States that Britain could no longer continue aid to Greece and Turkey and that its aid would end by April 1, 1947. Britain expressed the hope that the United States could continue these aid efforts. Greece's economy and security had been deteriorating since World War II, and it was in the middle of a civil war. Turkey needed help in modernizing its society, especially its military. Truman was convinced that the communist influence, under Joseph Stalin, was intended to extend throughout Europe.

The Truman Doctrine originated in March 1947, from Truman's address to Congress. In this speech, he declared that the foreign policy of the United States should be to support any country whose independence was threatened by communism. Truman thus asked Congress to immediately provide $400 million in support to Greece and Turkey, which he feared would be targeted by Soviet communist domination.

Congress approved this change in foreign policy. In May 1947, Truman signed a bill, known as Public Law 75, that authorized U.S. aid to Greece and Turkey. Later the same year, Truman followed up with the Marshall Plan, which allowed U.S. economic aid to countries in Europe and Asia that were threatened by communist domination.

The Truman Doctrine was later used to justify U.S. action in both Korea and Vietnam. The policies of the Truman Doctrine continued the American idea of containment, which began with the initial American aid to Greece and Turkey. For more information, see Satterthwaite (1972). ***See also*** Containment; Isolationism

Trustee   A legal term for an individual who holds title to the property of another. The trustee possesses a fiduciary relationship to the beneficiaries and must abide by the rules of the trust. The property held in trust is usually an estate, interest, or power. Joint trusteeship is when more than one individual is appointed trustee.

Truth   A property of beliefs or statements, according to most contemporary theories. Thus, what is taken to require an explanation is simply stating in the predicate of a sentence that the statement or belief "is true." Theories of truth variously characterize truth in terms of the *correspondence* of a statement with a fact (correspondence theories), the *coherence* of a statement with a set of statements (coherence theories), or the ends of inquiry or the benefits true beliefs confer (pragmatic theories). These theories posit that truth is real and has substantive properties. An alternative, "deflationary" conception of truth claims that truth is not a genuine property and requires no special theoretical explanation. In short, "truth" is nothing more than an economy of expression in which the predicate of the sentence is repeated or is redundant to express agreement. For more information, see Horwich (1990).

Truth-in-Sentencing Laws   Laws that require that certain offenders serve most of their court-imposed sentences before becoming eligible for early release. Truth-in-sentencing (TIS) laws were passed in most states in the late 1990s to address the growing public discontent with the length of time offenders were serving. Traditionally, offenders served between one third and one half of their sentences prior to becoming eligible for parole release. TIS laws require that violent offenders serve at least 85% of their sentence before becoming eligible for parole. The federal government encouraged the passage of TIS laws by offering funds to subsidize prison construction costs to states enacting a TIS requirement. ***See also*** Parole

t* Score**   A test score that has been converted to an equivalent standard score in a normal distribution with a mean of 50 and a standard deviation of 10. To calculate a *t* score, convert the raw score to a *z* score (subtract the mean from the raw score, and divide that number by the standard deviation), then multiply by 10 and add 50. ***See also Statistics (psychology); *t* Test

t* Test**   An inferential test that allows a researcher to determine how likely it is that the difference between two group means occurred as a result of chance rather than as a result of the effect of the independent variable. The *t* value is calculated by dividing the difference between the means by the pooled sample standard deviation. If the resultant value of *t* is sufficiently large to exceed the threshold chosen for statistical significance, then the null hypothesis (that there are no differences between the group means) is rejected in favor of the alternative hypothesis (that there are true differences between the two group means). ***See also Statistics (psychology, sociology)

Tundra   The coldest of the earth's biomes. (The term derives its meaning from the term *barren land*.) Biomes are ecosystems in which organisms live in accordance with particular climatic conditions. The tundra is one of the six major biomes of the earth, with the other five being desert, forest, grasslands, marine, and rainforest. The tundra is characterized by very cold temperatures, a lack of precipitation, and very little biological diversity. While the tundra has a summer season, it is shorter in length, and temperatures do not rise above 50 degrees Fahrenheit. Tundras are generally treeless regions, as the cold temperatures keep the soil frozen and therefore growth is hindered. There are two types of tundras: arctic and alpine. Arctic tundras can be found in the Northern Hemisphere while alpine tundras are found in various mountainous regions of the earth. The depletion of natural resources in the arctic tundras, as well as the melting of the ice and release of gases there, has geopolitical and environmental implications. ***See also*** Ecosystem

T

Twin Studies (*psychology*)   The scientific study that attempts to determine the relative contributions of genes and the environment to behavior and/or personality characteristics. Because twins usually share the same environment and are treated similarly by parents, investigators can compare the similarities seen in identical twins, who share both genes and the environment, with those in nonidentical twins, who share the same environment but have different genetic makeups. If identical twins are more alike in some characteristics than are nonidentical twins, such characteristics may have a strong genetic component. In studies of intelligence, it has generally been found that identical twins are more similar to each other than they are to other siblings. Likewise, fraternal twins are less similar to each other than are identical twins. Twin studies also include adoption studies of identical twins reared apart, which allow the role of heredity to be highlighted. The most famous of such studies was the Minnesota Study of Twins Reared Apart, published in 1990. The Minnesota study reported that heredity was found to account for 70% of the variance in intelligence scores; however, these findings are limited to the extent that the researchers could not control for differences across adopted families. Most researchers consider the variance from inheritance to be closer to 50%. For more information, see Bouchard, Lykken, McGue, Segal, and Tellegan (1990). ***See also*** Genetics

Twin Studies (*sociology*)   The scientific study of identical (monozygotic) and nonidentical (dizygotic) twins to illuminate the roles of genetics and environment in human development. Originating in the 1870s, twin-study research has shown varying effects of heredity and environment on traits from height to intelligence. ***See also*** Genetics

Twitter   A Web-based social networking service cofounded by the software engineers Jack Dorsey and Biz Stone in 2006. The tool asks users the driving question "What are you doing?" and broadcasts the response (a "tweet") to other Twitter users who are registered and subscribed to their fellow users' updates ("followers"). The short text message updates are limited to fewer than 140 characters and can reach many users at one time. The impetus for the creation of the service was to provide an easy method to keep in touch with friends and family and simultaneously to quell the information overload perceived in the digital age of the early 21st century. Fans find it to be an effective communication and marketing tool, while critics contend that it is a trivia-gratifying fad. ***See also*** Blog/Blogging; Networking

Two-Factor Theory of Emotion   This theory was proposed in the 1960s by Stanley Schachter and Jerome Singer and states that people's experience of emotion depends on two factors: physiological arousal and the cognitive interpretation of that arousal. The theory dictates that when people perceive physiological symptoms of arousal, they look to the environment for an explanation of this arousal and label their emotional experience accordingly. Therefore, the same pattern of physiological arousal can give rise to different emotions. Schachter and Singer conducted an experiment in which participants were given a shot of adrenalin (epinephrine) and while some were told what side effects to expect (e.g., increases in blood pressure, heart rate, and respiration), others were not. The participants were then placed in either an experimental situation aimed at producing feelings of euphoria or one aimed at producing anger. Those who were told what side effects to expect reported less euphoria or anger, thus providing support for the theory that both physiological arousal as well as our labeling of that arousal are important to our understanding of emotion. For more information, see Schachter and Singer (1962).

Two-Party System   A system where there are two dominant nationwide political parties competing in elections. The United States and Great Britain are examples of two-party systems. A single-party system is one in which one party only is allowed to hold legislative positions; the Communist Party in Cuba and China would be examples. Single-party systems are often associated with dictatorships, while two-party and multiparty systems are more often associated with democracies. A multiparty system exists when a government's legislature consists of three or more political parties. Shifting coalitions and alliances are commonly formed in an effort to have political objectives met. ***See also*** Democracy (political science); Single-Party System

Two-Step Flow of Communication   A theory conceived by researchers studying voters during a 1940 election. The mass media of that time consisted of radio, newspapers, and cinema, all of which were assumed to have a great effect on people's opinions. Despite this, the researchers showed that personal influence was still an important factor in decision making. People's decisions were affected by conversations they had with friends, family members, and other contacts. Some people, labeled "opinion leaders" by the researchers, had greater influence on decision making within their social network. In addition, these opinion leaders were found to have greater exposure to media than other people and selectively passed on this media-derived information to their social network. Thus, the two-step model refers to media information flowing first to opinion leaders, then being passed on to a greater number of people.

Other researchers confirmed the existence of opinion leaders. Considerable research has been done in efforts to identify these leaders and their characteristics. They are of interest not just to advertisers and politicians but to communicators and educators in other fields, such as public health. For more information, see Infante, Rancer, and Womack (1997) and Lazarsfeld, Berelson, and Gaudet (1944). ***See also*** Multistep Flow of Communication

Type A class, group, or category of people or things based on shared characteristics. In sociology, Max Weber theorized "ideal types," which categorize human behavior by the creation of a single construct that deliberately oversimplifies and exaggerates for the purpose of explanation and analysis.

Type A Personality A personality type first described by two cardiologists, Friedman and Rosenman, in the 1950s. It can be understood as a set of behavioral characteristics that include intense ambition, competition, drive, preoccupation with responsibility, a sense of time urgency or impatience, and occasional hostility and cynicism.

Type A persons tend to be overachievers who multitask and prefer to work under the pressure of deadlines. For more information, see Friedman and Rosenman (1959). *See also* Type B Personality

Type B Personality A personality type, in contrast to the Type A personality, that is defined by a set of behavioral characteristics that include patience, calm, and a relaxed and easygoing attitude toward life. *See also* Type A Personality

Type I and II Errors The two erroneous outcomes that the statistical process of hypothesis testing can produce (the decision to reject or failure to reject the null hypothesis). As shown in the table below, Type I error refers to rejecting the null hypothesis when it is true. The probability of a Type I error is represented by α (alpha) and is usually set at .05 by practicing researchers. A Type II error refers to the failure to reject the null hypothesis when it is false. The probability of a Type II error is symbolized by β (beta). Type I errors are known as "false positives" and Type II errors are known as "false negatives."

		Null True	Null False
Decision made	Reject Null	Type I error	Correct
	Accept Null	Correct	Type II error

Typography The art and design affecting the appearance of type on the printed page, notably the font chosen, its size, and the spacing of text. Spacing between text is particularly important in poetry, advertisements, and art books. Traditionally practiced by a typesetter working with metal type, most publishers now compose, type, and lay out pages using computers. *See also* Text

Typology A system by which people or objects are distinguished and organized into groups, usually called types. The members of a group may be identified by shared attributes that are supposed to be mutually exclusive and collectively exhaustive. The classification of types facilitates the demonstration and analysis of data. However, the selection of combinations of variables as inclusion criteria for a typology is argued to be subjective and, therefore, potentially invalid or inexact. In early anthropology, typologies were used to divide people of different cultures into "races," a model that has since been discredited. *See also* Classification (sociology)

Tyranny A pejorative term referring to a single ruler who rules in self-interest against the will of his subjects. The word originated as a nonpejorative Greek word for "illegitimate ruler," meaning one who assumes rule without the support of a constitution, religion, or monarch. Tyrannies existed in large numbers in Ancient Greece; among the most notable is Peisistratus (607–528 BCE), who assumed rule of Athens following a coup. He was popular among the poorer classes and instituted cultural reform of the city. He is credited with paving the way for the later prominence of Athens. Another usage of the term is the expression "tyranny by the majority." Alexis de Tocqueville (1805–1859), a French political theorist, coined the expression in *Democracy in America* (1835). After observing democracy in France and the United States, he believed that a majority of voters imposing their will was a constant danger in a democracy. Tyrannies are often associated with despots, rulers with unlimited authority. *See also* Authoritarian; Democracy (political science); Despotism; Dictatorship; Totalitarian

T

U

Underground A clandestine organization or activity that involves illicit doings. In politics, an underground organization refers to a nationalist group that seeks to overthrow a government in power, through violent or nonviolent means. Drug markets are an example of an underground network of illicit activity.

Unicameral Legislature A unitary governmental system where power is concentrated in one central authority, such as a house or a chamber. It may or may not be nonpartisan. Although the most common legislative model is the bicameral parliament, congress, or assembly, unicameral models exist in many nations, such as Denmark, Finland, Israel, New Zealand, South Korea, Singapore, Sweden, Wales, Scotland, Northern Ireland, several African countries, as well as communist states. Countries with unicameral legislatures are often small and homogeneous, where members see no need for a second chamber.

Most American colonies were unicameral before 1776, except for Delaware and Pennsylvania, which were bicameral. After independence, however, only three states—Pennsylvania, Georgia, and Vermont—maintained a one-house system. All the others adopted a bicameral system similar to the newly formed Congress. Today, Nebraska is the only single-house state in the United States. It has been unicameral since 1937.

Advocates for unicameralism—the practice of having only one legislature—state several reasons for supporting a unicameral legislature. One reason is that bicameralism is no longer necessary for representative purposes. In American history, the two houses represented different socioeconomic groups and, later, political communities. Today, the same populations are represented in both houses in the state and federal legislatures. Also, unicameral legislatures are less costly to operate, more accountable to the electorate, more cooperative internally, and more deliberative in decision making. Finally, there is precedent of unicameral legislatures in U.S. history, as well as a record of unicameralism in other democracies around the world. ***See also*** Bicameral Legislature; Legislative Branch

Uniform Crime Report (UCR) (Part I/Part II Offenses) An annual crime report issued by the Federal Bureau of Investigation (FBI). The Uniform Crime Reporting Program is a national data-collection effort established in the late 1920s to improve the reliability of crime statistics. The FBI was charged with administering the Uniform Crime Reporting Program in 1930. UCR data are collected from local law enforcement agencies across the United States and include only crimes that are reported to the police. Although participation is voluntary, more than 90% of the United States is covered by the UCR program. The UCR reports offenses in two parts. Part I comprises the eight index offenses (four violent and four property), and Part II comprises all other offenses. Each year, the FBI issues selected findings from the UCRs in a report published under the title *Crime in the United States* (*CIUS*). The *CIUS* report includes sections on known offenses, clearances, persons arrested, and law enforcement employees. Weaknesses of the UCR include use of the "hierarchy rule," which means that only the most serious offense is counted; differences in the definition of offenses in various jurisdictions; and underreporting of offenses. ***See also*** Clearance Rate; Index Crimes/Offenses

Uniform Region *See* Region

United Nations An organization of voluntary signatory members of the United Nations (UN) Charter. The United Nations was founded in 1945 as a product of the vision of President Franklin D. Roosevelt and the Allied nations of World War II, who saw a need for a global police force to create order in the post–World War II era. The UN Charter, which was ratified by the original Allied nations, China, the Soviet Union, the United States, Britain, and later France, was aimed at maintaining international peace and security and providing solutions for global economic and humanitarian problems. The UN Security Council now has 15 permanent members, including the original 5. There are 10 nonpermanent members, who are elected for two-year terms by the General Assembly, and a total of more than 190 member countries. The UN's headquarters is in New York City, with additional offices in Geneva, Switzerland, and Vienna, Austria. Since the beginning of the 1990s, the UN has taken a more peacekeeping role, including supervising elections and providing police forces.

There are six organs of the United Nations. The first, the Security Council, is the most important and is responsible for maintaining global peace and security. The 5 permanent member states and 10 temporary seats comprise the Security Council. The second, the Secretariat, is headed by the Secretary General, who traditionally is elected to a five-year renewable term. The current Secretary General is Ban Ki-Moon of South Korea. The third, the General Assembly, is the deliberative body that makes resolutions and mediates disputes, although it does not create statutes or make binding decisions. Resolutions are passed by two thirds of the present majority. The General Assembly also elects the temporary member states. The fourth, the Economic and Social Council, coordinates intergovernmental agencies. The fifth, the International Court of Justice, is located in The Hague, Netherlands, and hears cases related to war crimes and ethnic cleansing. The sixth, the Trusteeship Council, was suspended in 1994. There are at least 14 specialized agencies, such as the International Labor Organization, the United Nations Children's Fund (UNICEF), the World Health Organization (WHO), the International Monetary Fund (IMF), the World Bank, and the Atomic Energy Commission.

The UN's effectiveness has encountered several obstacles throughout its history. Some of the obstacles are conflicts resulting from the Cold War, funding, the expansion of membership to Third World nations, corruption, allegations of sexual abuse by peacekeeping forces, and inaction with tragic results.

The coexistence of East-West ideologies has presented formidable challenges to the UN. Peacekeeping activities suffered during the Cold War when both the United States and the Soviet Union traded vetoes with each other over actions each disapproved. Both countries, in their continuing arguments over conflicts such as the Middle East, the wars in Africa, and the Korean Conflict, have used the UN as a forum for influencing other nations. In the late 1950s, the East-West rivalry prevented new membership for those antagonistic to each other's views. As a result of their conflict, both the United States and the Soviet Union have either outright refused or reduced payment for UN actions. The U.S. arrears had reached $1.3 billion at one time, although it has reduced since 2000.

The invitation of Third World nations to membership in the 1960s resulted in a power base loss to the United States. The resulting voting blocs, such as Arab nations, Latin American nations, and Asian and African nations, have taken a militant posture against the colonialism that the United States was seen to support.

Corruption has taken several forms. One of the most recent and widespread involved the Oil-for-Food Program in 1996. This program allowed Iraq to sell its oil on the world market and provide humanitarian aid for its people with the proceeds from those sales. The program was stopped in 2003 amid allegations that Saddam Hussein was receiving kickbacks, the director of the program was receiving bribes, and the son of Kofi Annan, the Secretary General of the UN, was procuring illegal contracts on behalf of a Swiss firm.

Peacekeeping forces have also been accused of child rape and soliciting prostitution in places such as Sri Lanka, Bosnia, Sudan, the Democratic Republic of Congo,

Haiti, and Liberia. Finally, the UN's failure to intervene in large-scale humanitarian crises contributed to the 1994 Rwandan genocide, the 1995 Srebrenica massacre, genocide in the ongoing Darfur civil war, and several other global tragedies.

The UN is probably most useful as a forum in which to discuss, rather than solve, international matters and disputes between countries. For more information, see Fasulo (2005). *See also* Communism; Westernization

Universal Design   An instructional design method that incorporates modes of instruction, application, and assessment of new concepts that take into account the learning styles, needs, and abilities of all learners. Traditional methods of instructional design approach planning with a "one-size-fits-all" mentality and assume that teachers will modify the design to fit diverse learners. Universal design assumes that all learners have unique needs and abilities and seeks to develop instruction that is flexible enough to meet these individual needs. This is accomplished by providing learners with multiple options for acquiring and demonstrating mastery of new concepts. For example, students might choose to either listen to a presentation or read a nonfiction source to gather data on a particular topic. They would then choose from a variety of options that would allow them to apply the new concept, synthesize it with prior knowledge, and produce a new product demonstrating mastery. For more information, see CAST (2008). *See also* Instructional Strategies

Universal of Communication   Communication is a manner in which we transmit and receive information, not always in a conscious manner; in fact, sometimes we are not even aware that we communicate a message to the external world. The communication process occurs between a sender and a receiver. It is a process that is shared by everybody and occurs on a constant basis. We communicate messages and concepts constantly, and this is a process that operates in many directions and dimensions. The effectiveness of the communication process depends heavily on the level of understanding between the sender and the receiver. There are three most frequently recognized modes of communication: (1) interpersonal communication, (2) intrapersonal communication, and (3) person-group communication. Person-to-person communication occurs between at least two individuals, and the level of its effectiveness depends highly on interpersonal communication skills. Intrapersonal communication occurs within the person, when we "talk to ourselves or with ourselves"; this type of phenomenon occurs primarily when we attempt to solve problems. Person-to-group communication is staged when a person addresses a group of individuals, such as in public speaking, while giving a testimony in court, or preaching in a house of prayer.

Universal is a concept referring to a set of values or norms or knowledge that occurs between entities and individuals. While effective communication depends on knowledge of the language, the grammar, and syntax structures, the most significant focus of universal of communication is knowledge about a problem to be solved.

For example, if one needs to communicate with a member of a specific profession about solving a problem related to that profession, the universal of knowledge of both the sender and the receiver should contain some level of knowledge related to the specific profession, to minimize and eliminate possible distortions. *Ontology,* a term that refers to the nature or relational common sense of being of some field of interest, is a framework of reference for the universal of communication, primarily used in the field of computer communication but also relevant to the other forms of communication. A shared ontology is necessary for communication between the sender and the receiver. Although the concept of universal of communication is predicated on the shared ontology, it is possible that the sender, the receiver, or both of them are experiencing a false sense of confidence with regard to the shared ontology and the final outcome is distorted based on their cognitive and perceptional skills and abilities. For example, one might be familiar with the vocabulary specific to a given profession, but the person's cultural background influences the way one may interpret a given concept. For more information, see Hunter, Mayhall, and Barker (2000) and Weaver (1972). *See also* Communication; Interpersonal Communication; Intrapersonal Communication; Message; Norm (communication); Ontology; Value

Universal Suffrage In its strictest sense, the term means that every human being in a country has the right to vote in that country. In reality, universal suffrage rarely exists in a nation due to restrictions on who is deemed eligible for voting. The French political scientist Frederic Bastiat in *The Law* (1850) explained the logic of voting restrictions based on one's capacity, because in a democracy the elector or voter does not vote just for himself or herself but for everybody. Suffrage restrictions traditionally depend on the following variables: gender, religion, wealth, education, race/ethnicity, age, residency, birth country, and criminal record. In the United States, apart from the rights guaranteed by the Constitution, state governments can decide who can vote in their state. For example, the laws regarding the voting status of criminal felons, noncitizens, and new state residents are determined on a state-by-state basis. The Supreme Court ultimately determines the constitutionality of state voting laws. For more information, see Bastiat (1850/2004).

University An institution of higher education with the authority to grant academic degrees in various disciplines or fields of study. A university usually consists of undergraduate and graduate divisions. Undergraduate studies lead to bachelor's degrees, while graduate studies lead to advanced degrees, such as master's or doctoral degrees.

Unlawful Entry Entry into an area, territory, or property that belongs to someone else, without the party's consent. Unlawful entry can be achieved through fraud or force. Burglary is a form of unlawful entry.

Unobtrusive Measures A term, attributed to Webb, Campbell, Schwartz, and Sechrest (1966), describing a set of data collection methods that do not directly require a participant to provide the information. Unobtrusive measures are considered to be nonreactive. Methods of data collection using flooring wear, wear and tear of physical objects, gravestones, garbage, secretive observation, and so on are cited as examples. For more information, see Webb, Campbell, Schwartz, and Sechrest (1966).

Upward Communication The flow of information from subordinates through a hierarchy of supervisors to the top executives in a workplace. Upward communication is a business management practice proposed in the latter half of the 20th century as an answer to the limitations posed by the earlier accepted practice of downward communication, in which all information considered pertinent within an organization comes from the top levels of management.

In theory, a management call for upward communication is supposed to foster cooperation at all levels of an organization. Management researchers, however, have found that expectations of upward communication can bring about resistance from the workforce and uncertainty about roles and courses of action in middle-level managers. Workers may want to keep, even "hoard," what they know about their jobs and about the equipment and techniques they use to do their jobs. They may see their job security and their vocational goals compromised if they are too forthcoming with the information requested. Often, they believe that they know more about their jobs than the managers who oversee how they do them. They also resent the lack of downward communication from management levels in response to the information they have sent upward and about the workplace in general.

Researchers have found that expectations of upward communication cause middle managers to feel caught between upper level management and the workforce they supervise. Researchers also have found that upward communication is most effective in organizations in which communication is open and transmitted from all directions. For more information, see Barrett (2002), Eisenberg and Witten (1987), and Goris (2007). *See also* Downward Communication; Horizontal Communication; Lateral Communication

U

Urbanization A process characterized by the growth and expansion of large cities. Urbanization involves the migration of large proportions of the population from rural to urban areas. The Industrial Revolution, which resulted in numerous technological innovations, led to increased urbanization. Various social issues accompanied the urbanization process, such as housing conditions, sanitation, welfare, and so on. ***See also*** Industrialism

U.S. Constitution and Education   The two are bounded by the educational system being a part of the government and the U.S. Constitution being the basic law of the land. However, education is not referenced in the U.S. Constitution; thus, the Tenth Amendment, known for its *reserved powers clause,* makes education a function of the state. The most recurrent educational law cases that come before the courts for interpretation focus on the protection of individual rights and are most commonly related to the First, Fourth, Eighth, and Fourteenth amendments. School cases based on the First Amendment generally involve the two religion clauses, the establishment of religion and the free exercise of religion. The right to freedom of speech, both pure and symbolic, has received increased court attention. Fourth Amendment cases filed in court generally focus on students' right to be protected from unlawful search and seizures. Eighth Amendment cases often address corporal punishment, which might be viewed as cruel and unusual. School cases based on the Fourteenth Amendment generally involve the due process clause and the equal protection clause. There are various federal statutes that affect educational systems, and many are tied to the acceptance of federal funds. ***See also*** Bill of Rights (political science); Law (political science); Reserved Powers

Utilitarianism (*economics*)   A theory that postulates that the criterion for evaluating ethical conduct in society and politics should be based on the greatest amount of satisfaction or utility that is derived from a conduct or policy. Alternatively, actions must be judged by their consequences. The theory is usually expressed as the greatest good of the greatest number, and its earliest form was propounded by Jeremy Bentham, James Mill, and John Stuart Mill.

There has been a tendency to separate act utilitarianism from rule utilitarianism, in an effort to determine whether the application of the theory should be based on acts or rules. Act utilitarianism is defined by the maximization of individual satisfaction, whereas rule utilitarianism is based on an aggregation of utilities permitted by law or regulation.

Rule utilitarianism maximizes the greatest good, in a situation where individual utilities cannot be obtained because of the disastrous social effect of maximizing all individual utilities. Rule utilitarianism avoids reliance on any source of authority for value judgment, except rules and regulations. To some, act and rule utilitarianism are not mutually exclusive because rules emanate from actions over time.

The early form of utilitarianism was concerned about the theories of self-interest and binding moral rules that drew inspiration from religion and precepts of natural law. An action was considered righteous only if it contributed to aggregate happiness.

The prototype definition of utilitarianism is fraught with controversy. Actions may be judged right or wrong because of intentions and not necessarily as a result of outcomes. Additionally, as Henry Sidgwick (1874) points out, aggregate utility does not necessarily translate into an equal distribution of happiness. His brand of utilitarianism distinguishes hedonism from self-evident principles of desire. The theory of distributive happiness has formed the basis of welfare economics, a situation in which few are rich and many are poor as a result of adverse income distribution—a perversion of the theory of aggregate happiness based on policy implementation and result. For more information, see Sidgwick (1874). ***See also*** Bentham, Jeremy; Utility

Utilitarianism (*education*)   A philosophy, first developed by Jeremy Bentham and later refined by John Stuart Mill, that states that happiness—defined as the development of one's natural abilities, and specifically higher mental faculties, which are seen as being unique to humankind—is the guiding moral principle or value. The role of society in utilitarianism is to provide its members with the opportunity for happiness through the development of those higher mental faculties. ***See also*** Bentham, Jeremy; Utility

Utilitarianism (*political science*)   A theory of morality that asserts that an action is right if it conforms to the principle of utility. Utilitarianism arose in the late 18th and early 19th centuries as a doctrine of social reform. Utilitarianism is a consequentialist belief that right or wrong can only be assessed by the goodness of consequences. Goodness is determined by an act that produces the greatest overall happiness.

Utilitarianism was first advanced by Jeremy Bentham in 1789 with his publication *An Introduction to the Principles of Morals and Legislation.* Bentham advocated the principle of utility, which stated that the moral value of an action is determined by how it promotes the greatest happiness for the greatest number. The principle of utility was the standard by which Benthamite utilitarians judged laws and social institutions. Social policies should be evaluated only in light of their effect on the general well-being of the populace. Bentham believed that only the consequence of an action mattered. The consequence was the achievement of pleasure and the avoidance of pain. The intention of the actor did not matter.

John Stuart Mill was another influential utilitarian; he published *Utilitarianism* as three magazine articles in 1861. Mill rejected Bentham's theory that the quantity of pleasure is the only measure of an act's value. According to Mill, pleasures qualitatively, as well as quantitatively, can differ from each other. Thus, the pleasures of intellect, feeling, and imagination are intrinsically better than the pleasures of mere bodily sensations. Also, unlike Bentham who believed in the totality of happiness, Mill argued that pain would be warranted if it resulted directly in the greater good of all.

Since its first articulation, several schools of utilitarian thought have emerged. They include two-level utilitarianism, negative utilitarianism, total utilitarianism, and speciesism. For more information, see Bentham (1789/2005) and Mill (1871). ***See also*** Bentham, Jeremy; Utility

Utilitarianism *(public administration)* A school of philosophy that contends that moral principles should be solely based on providing the greatest good for the greatest number of people. This idea is in strict contrast to deontology, which advocates that certain principles should not be violated regardless of their contribution to the greater good. The philosophers Jeremy Bentham and John Stuart Mill are usually credited with founding utilitarian thought, predicating their argument around the notion that people desire pleasure above all else. In such a scenario, it follows that people will seek to maximize their utility (or their amount of general pleasure) and minimize their pain. Furthermore, since pleasure offers the only gauge for human conduct, ethical behavior must be exclusively predicated on maximizing this value. Utilitarianism is thus ultimately a form of consequentialism, viewing actions as justified based solely on their outcome.

Thanks to its prominence in contemporary philosophical thought, utilitarianism has engendered a great deal of opponents. Many critics contend that utilitarianism strips people of their very humanity, casting individuals as simply "utility-generating maximizers." According to such theories, people are not merely guided by simple pleasure and pain but often have a host of different emotional motivations (or the very idea of self-sacrifice would be logically incoherent). Perhaps the utilitarians' greatest weakness lies in the fact that different actions make different people happy, and any notion of some abstract overall utility is therefore fundamentally incoherent. Indeed, although the early utilitarians (such as Bentham) believed that happiness could be quantitatively measured, the variables and means by which to do so have never been adequately agreed on. The consequences of strict utilitarianism in public administration or government can be frightening depending on the idea of who decides or persuades the population on what is the greater good. For more information, see Honderich (2005). ***See also*** Morality; Utilitarianism (economics)

Utility Satisfaction derived from the consumption of a good or service that is measured in *utils*. It is not very easy to quantify satisfaction, but economists use cardinal measure rather than ordinal measure to make comparative analysis. Ordinal measure does not provide useful information for comparative analysis because it is based on ranking, which does not indicate absolute measurable differences.

Cardinal measure indicates concrete numerical preferences. A consumer is in equilibrium when he or she allocates income to such an extent that the last monetary unit spent on each good or service produces the same amount of additional (marginal) utility.

Utility is a useful theory to explain consumer behavior in the market place. Consumers will usually demand more of a good when the price of a good falls because of real income and substitution effects (ceteris paribus). They may also be induced to buy more or less of a good because of the relationship between marginal utility and price. The price of a good must fall for consumers to be induced to buy more of a good since utility is subject to diminishing returns. For more information, see Case and Fair (2003), McConnell and Brue (2008), and Salvatore (2002). ***See also*** Budget; Consumption; Demand; Income; Price; Wealth Effect

Utilization-Focused Evaluation (Program Evaluation) Premises that evaluations should be judged by their utility and actual use; therefore, evaluators should design the evaluation process and select methods with a *focus* on intended use by primary intended users. The evaluation facilitator develops a working relationship with the intended users to help them focus and design the evaluation and follow through to use the findings. For more information, see Patton (2008). ***See also*** Evaluation (education)

U

V

Vagrancy The state of being without any means of financial support or domicile. Vagrancy is considered to be an offense and includes behaviors such as loitering, prostitution, drunkenness, and panhandling.

Validity Evidence that a test is measuring an intended construct, through investigation of theorized relationships between test scores and other measures. Convergent evidence is supported by positive relationships between the test scores and another instrument intended to measure a similar construct. Discriminant evidence is supported by a negative or zero relationship between the test scores and another instrument intended to measure a different construct. Both types of evidence are generally supported by correlational data. As an example, scores on a test intended to measure understanding of algebra concepts may be theorized to relate positively with a test of geometry understanding and to relate negatively with a test of reading ability. A positive correlation between the algebra and geometry test scores would be an example of convergent evidence. A negative correlation between the algebra and reading test scores would be an example of discriminant evidence. *See also* Validity/Validation

Validity/Validation The degree to which one measures what one sets out to measure in a given sample or, alternatively, the accuracy of the interpretations and decisions that are made based on test or measurement instrument scores. Several kinds of validity-related evidence can be used to support validity claims, including *criterion-*, *construct-*, and *content-related* evidence.

Criterion-related validity examines the degree to which a measure predicts a known construct or criterion of interest. For example, a standardized achievement test given to schoolchildren would have criterion-related validity if it adequately predicted academic performance, such as grades in school. Criterion validity includes two subtypes, predictive and concurrent validity. *Predictive validity* refers to the degree to which scores on one measure predict scores on a future criterion measure. When examining predictive validity, time must elapse between administration of the predictive and criterion measures. *Concurrent validity* refers to the degree to which a measure correlates with a measure of a related construct administered at the same point in time. For example, concurrent validity could be examined by looking at the correlation between standardized achievement test scores and current school GPA (grade point average).

Construct validity is the overarching type of measurement validity; it is the extent to which a higher-order construct is represented by a particular measure. Evidence of construct validity is gained by examining the relationships between a measure of the construct of interest and other measures designed to measure similar and different constructs. Specifically, convergent evidence and discriminant evidence are used to establish construct validity. *Convergent evidence* is obtained by investigating the relationship between the measure of interest and separate measures of the same construct. *Discriminant evidence* is obtained by investigating the relationship between the measure of interest and measures of theoretically different constructs. Construct validity exists when both convergent evidence and divergent evidence have been established.

Content-related validity evaluates the degree to which a measure examines a construct in its entirety. Content validity looks at all aspects of the research idea being studied. For example, a measure of child aggression would have content validity if it measured all components of aggression, such as both physical and verbal aggression. *See also* Construct Validity; Content Validity; Criterion Validity; Predictive Validity; Research Methodology

Validity in Quantitative Research Each of the major methodological paradigms (i.e., qualitative, quantitative, and mixed-methods research) has its set of criteria or standards for establishing the validity of the findings. Here, we list the major types used in quantitative research. We rely on the framework provided by the prominent quantitative research methodologists Thomas Cook and the late Donald Campbell. According to their framework, as outlined by Shadish, Cook, and Campbell (2002), quantitative research validity is divided into four major types: statistical conclusion validity, construct validity, internal validity, and external validity. *Statistical conclusion validity* refers to the degree to which the research study allows one to infer accurately that the independent and dependent variables are related and to infer accurately the size and direction of the relationship. *Construct validity* refers to the degree to which the constructs in a research study are accurately and appropriately represented. *Internal validity* refers to the degree to which the data in a research study allow one to make a warranted claim about cause and effect. Finally, *external validity* refers to the degree to which the data in a research study allow one to make warranted generalizations to other persons, settings, times, outcomes, and treatment variations. For more information, see Shadish, Cook, and Campbell (2002). *See also* External Validity; Internal Validity; Mixed-Methods Research Validity Types; Qualitative Research Validity Types

Valley   Generally described as a depression in the earth's surface resulting from erosion. More specifically, a valley is characterized as a low region of land usually encircled by either mountains or hills. In addition to its position between higher landforms, a valley typically has a stream or river along its base.

Value   The perceived worth of something in a media or communications outlet. In many cases this is difficult to define in objective terms because clearly, many channels of communication are ruled by the subjective theory of value and certainly by cultural relativism. How does one discern what is good? Perhaps we cherish popular culture and therefore say that it is valuable, but that certainly does not make it sui generis a matter of fact. Telling the truth in all matters is an absolute value, but the practice is not generally observed. For the meaning of *values* in communications, one must look to ethical theories. *See also* Ethics (communication)

Vandalism   A criminal offense that involves the deliberate destruction of private or public property without the owner's consent. There are varying degrees of vandalism, ranging from graffiti to complete destruction of personal or public property and rioting.

Variability   The degree of homogeneity or heterogeneity of data; the spread of scores from a reference point. When we have interval or ratio data, the measure of variability is usually the variance or standard deviation. Variance is the measure of variability around the mean. Because it is in the form of units of the squared variable (for example, (age in years)^2, (IQ)^2, X^2_{ACT}), we find its square root and get the standard deviation, which is in the same metric units as the original variable. When we have ordinal data, we use the interquartile range as our measure of variability. It is the difference between the 75th and 25th percentile points. The range, which is the difference between the high and low scores, is used as a rough measure of variability. It does not provide a very stable or useful measure of variability. When we have nominal data, about the only measure of variability we have is the number of different categories. *See also* Percentile

Variable (*education*)   A characteristic of data collected from physical entities, persons, or groups that reflects the attribute of interest that can take on different values. Variables can take on the form of categories (nominal), ranked observations (ordinal), or equal and additive interval observations (interval or ratio). There are recognized types of variables. An independent variable is used to label a treatment, differentiated groups, or causal influence. A dependent variable is the outcome, result, or effect. For example, drug dosage could be the independent variable and glucose level the dependent variable. An extraneous variable, sometimes called a confounder, is a variable present in an experimental or quasi-experimental situation that could have an effect on the dependent variable separately or in collaboration with the independent variable. A mediating variable is one that provides a facilitative linkage or conduit between the independent and dependent variables. A moderator variable is one that suppresses or stimulates the effect of the independent variable on the dependent variable. Terms sometimes used for variable labels in correlation and regression are *predictor variable* and *criterion variable*. The predictor variable is a variable used as a predictor for the criterion variable. When using the SAT (formerly called the Scholastic Aptitude Test) score to predict grade point average (GPA) at the end of the freshman year of college, the predictor variable is the SAT score and the criterion variable is GPA. *See also* Dependent Variable; Independent Variable

Variable (*sociology*)   A measure that is susceptible to change. Dependent and independent variables are among the most basic concepts in statistics. The independent variable refers to the variable that is manipulated by the researcher. The dependent variable refers to the variable for which changes in outcomes are measured, in relation to one or more independent variables. The independent variable is generally regarded as the predictor variable, and the dependent variable is often referred to as the outcome variable. *See also* Dependent Variable; Independent Variable

Variant   That which differs, changes, or is altered. A variant is an entity that is changing or distinct from a given norm.

Verbal Communication   The use of language and its symbols and sounds to convey messages. Communication that is verbal may also be accompanied by other forms of communication, including body language, images, sounds, and elements of voice and tone as well as nonverbal forms such as gesture, appearance, style, movement, and stress. Verbal communication is studied by a formal linguistic analysis of spoken words or by considering the interactions of people during a speech act. A study of the interpretation and meaning of verbal communications and its speech codes may also be conducted. It is also possible to look at the use of verbal communication in a social situation and analyze the effects of gender, class, ethnicity, education, and origin on the forms of verbalization. Verbal communication is problematic if accurate and effective transfer of information and messages is the goal because of the variability and fluidity of actual human speech. In addition, the interpretation of verbal communication is complicated by the assumptions and goals of both the speaker and the listener. Rules for verbally communicating effectively are taught in etiquette and public speaking, both of which attempt to control individual expressions in favor of culturally acceptable forms of verbal expression. Verbal communication is an exclusively human activity, although some higher primates have been trained to use some elements of sign language to communicate. *See also* Language; Meaning; Metacommunication; Speech

Verdict   The culmination of a decision-making process that follows a presentation of evidence regarding any given issue. In the context of the criminal justice system, a verdict refers to the judgment delivered by a judge or jury after having been presented the facts about a case. The verdict determines the guilt or innocence of the defendant. Once the verdict has been delivered, the judge decides on the appropriate sentence for the given offense. *See also* Judge; Jury

Veto   The power to block legislation. In the United States, the president can veto any bill presented to him by not signing it. He is required to return the bill to Congress with the proposed changes. Congress has the power to override the president's veto by a two-thirds majority of both Houses and have the bill become law. *See also* Bill; Law (political science)

Vice   An act, behavior, attitude, or habit that is considered immoral or corrupt and has a pejorative connotation. Examples of habits that may be regarded as vices are alcoholism and drug abuse. Vices are also associated with acts deemed as sexually immoral, such as prostitution.

Victim   A person who experiences a loss, a hardship, or an injury for any reason. A victim of a crime, or a person who experiences victimization, is a person who directly or indirectly experiences harm as a result of the criminal actions of another. Direct victims are primary victims, who experience the victimization firsthand. Secondary victims are those who know, are related to, or otherwise care for the primary victim (e.g., a spouse, parent, or friend). *See also* Victimology

Victimless Crime   Crime in which there is no identifiable victim, because there is either no obvious harm to another or because both parties have consented to engage in the conduct that is considered criminal. Vice behaviors such as gambling, drug use, and prostitution are often described as victimless crimes.

Victimology   The social-scientific study of victims and the social, psychological, physical, and financial harms that they suffer as a result of victimization. Those who study victimology are interested not just in the victim and the victim-offender relationship but also in the ways in which victims are treated by the criminal justice system, the media, and the public more generally. Victimologists study why some people are targeted for victimization while others are not and why some are more prepared to take risks associated with an enhanced probability for victimization. Victimology is a social science, and although some victimologists study non-criminal victimization, victimology is usually considered

a subfield of criminology. As social scientists, victimologists are researchers as opposed to advocates or practitioners. *See also* Victim

Victim Precipitation   A person who throws the first punch in a fight but then ends up more seriously injured is often said to have precipitated the victimization. Victim precipitation occurs when the victim of an offense has substantially contributed to his or her own victimization. *See also* Victim

Video/Music Videos   Primarily a visual art form, with a soundtrack but usually no dialogue. The shortness of the piece and lack of dialogue make plot and character development difficult. Videos convey emotion rather than narrative. Music videos are short films made to accompany a song. They are commercial entities, intended to advertise and market the song, and exist as a genre somewhere in between advertisements and movies.

Music videos may be divided into the performative and the conceptual. Performance videos typically show the musicians playing, usually before an audience or in a recording studio and shots of the band traveling or setting up. In contrast, Michael Jackson's 14-minute-long "Thriller" (1983) is a concept video with a strong narrative, using classic horror themes and culminating in a group of zombies dancing. At the other extreme, the "Bastards of Young" video by the avant-garde group The Replacements shows almost nothing but a record player and speakers.

During most of the 20th century, most recorded music was listened to without accompanying visuals. Music videos re-associated performers with their music. But music videos were not the first media attempts at combining music and visual images. Short musical films were produced in the mid-20th century showing Billie Holliday, Bing Crosby, and others performing, as well as animated features with symphonic soundtracks. Visual jukeboxes appeared briefly during World War II. Television in the 1950s used music pieces as fillers in between programs. In the 1960s, the Beatles, Pink Floyd, the Doors, and the Who all made promotional films. And in the mid-1970s, Queen came out with "Bohemian Rhapsody."

The 1980s, when cheap and easy video-editing technology became available, were the heyday of music videos. In 1981, MTV (music television) was launched as a niche cable channel showing promotional music videos, and until the early 1990s, the channel showed almost nothing else, 24 hours a day. MTV and similar stations provided a showcase for music videos, and the genre blossomed. The most successful music stars of the 1980s all made videos—for example, Michael Jackson, U2, Madonna, Bruce Springsteen. By the mid-1980s, almost all singles were released with an accompanying video.

Music videos have received much criticism for objectifying young women. The majority of music videos portray adolescent boys' fantasies of sexually available scantily clothed young women. Typical videos show many seminaked women dancing around male performers in adoring obsequiousness. A very few focus

V

on male rather than female bodies as objects of lust—for example, Salt-N-Pepa in "Shoop" and "Whatta Man."

By the late 1990s, MTV and similar channels were moving away from 24-hour music videos, showing instead reality and celebrity-focused shows. Music videos are now widely available on the Internet. For more information, see Austerlitz (2007) and Vernallis (2004). *See also* Recordings; Visual Images

Videotaping in the Criminal Justice System
Surveillance cameras have proliferated in public and private settings. Cameras mounted on buildings and light poles survey city streets, while interior cameras record inside malls, corner stores, subway stations, libraries, and public areas of apartment buildings. Video images can help resolve discussions about past events. Saved video images can be searched by a human—a slow, expensive procedure. Face recognition software can also be used. The cost-effectiveness of video surveillance as a crime-fighting tool is subject to debate. While research does not appear to show conclusively that cameras act as a crime deterrent, they are effective in recording incidents and reducing court time by encouraging guilty pleas. Civil liberties groups are concerned about the collection, archiving, and eventual use of video footage of people engaged in lawful activities, including political protests. Privacy is a concern; video clips from surveillance cameras of people engaged in intimate activities have been posted on the Internet.

Police patrol cars started carrying video recording devices from the late 1990s. Cameras, typically attached to the car dashboard, are set to record automatically when the car emergency lights are turned on or triggered manually. The first recorders used were analog, but digital devices are now more common. Video may be downloaded at the end of each shift to a data transfer system housed at a garage or a parking lot. Some cars are equipped with the ability to relay video in real time to receiving stations. Recordings are retained for varying amounts of time, depending on departmental policies. Video footage is used to corroborate or contradict statements of events by police officers and members of the public. The Los Angeles Police Department started equipping patrol cars with cameras on the advice of the post–Rodney King riots' Christopher Commission. Sound recorders are not made, as these would breach eavesdropping laws. Video clips can be seen on the Web sites of some police departments (e.g., the Ohio State Highway Patrol Video Gallery at www.statepatrol.ohio.gov/video.htm) and are shown on television during "real-life" cop shows. Traffic stops are frequent subjects.

Videotaped testimony is used in courts to enable child witnesses and victims to give evidence without entering the courtroom. This is of particular use in protecting children who are being asked to talk about sexual and physical abuse. Testimony may be prerecorded or may be by way of a live closed-circuit television feed. The constitutionality of such testimony was tested in a 1990 Supreme Court case, *Maryland v. Craig*. In this case, it was successfully argued that a 6-year-old child would be traumatized were he or she required to testify against the alleged abuser in the courtroom.

Videotaping and broadcasting of courtroom trials on television has been quite controversial. Concerns have centered on how recording the trial in this way affects the trial itself and thus the outcome of the trial; especially its effect on the witnesses and the jurors. For more information, see Bennett (2003), Foster (2004), Gill and Spriggs (2005), Lyon (2006), *Maryland v. Craig* (1990), and Norris and Wilson (2006). *See also* Privacy, Right to; Surveillance (media studies); Testimony

Vigilante   A person or group that pursues extralegal justice. Vigilantes and vigilante groups circumvent the criminal justice system using informal and often forceful means of pursuing justice of their own design. Vigilantes often resort to retaliation when they believe that the justice system has failed or will fail them.

Virtual Reality   A computer-based technology that provides experiences designed to simulate reality and the physical world. The participants in the virtual world are supposed to be immersed in the environment rather than just observing it. This can be accomplished through 3D graphics on a standard computer or television screen or through special viewing devices and body (mostly hand) controls. Software and hardware to produce virtual worlds, which were once proprietary and expensive, are now widely available on the consumer market. Virtual reality (VR) experiences can be individual or communal and are now common in amusement parks, game arcades, home gaming platforms, personal computers, motion pictures, museums, and schools. Applications for VR also include simulating medical procedures for training doctors, flight simulation for pilots, virtual tours of archaeological sites, and virtual visits to real estate properties for sale. For more information, see Moore (1998). *See also* Realism; Visual Reality

Visual Cliff   In developmental research, the visual cliff has been used to investigate the depth-perception abilities of infants. The visual cliff consists is a glass-topped table intended to create the impression of an abrupt drop-off. In their seminal work conducted in 1960, Eleanor Gibson and Richard Walk found that while depth perception seems to come about shortly after birth, fear and avoidance of the perceived threat increases with age. Most infants who had begun to crawl would not continue toward the ostensibly unsupported service even when their mothers called upon them from the other side.

Vision in Leadership   The practice of engaging others in shared goals for a purposeful future. A visionary leader exemplifies a strong, positive style of leadership based on values, background knowledge, and past experiences that establishes the tone of an organization and facilitates a culture of productivity.

Visual Images   Images predate words. Humans used images as a means of communication long before the

V

origin of writing. The first writing systems took the form of visual images—hieroglyphs.

Images were in use long before photography was invented. Coins bearing rulers' heads reminded the populace of whose authority they were under. Manuscripts were illustrated with creatures and biblical scenes. Printing presses published monotone woodcuts and engravings of animals and foreign lands and peoples, sometimes drawn from life, sometimes from travelers' tales. Religions have had different reactions to imagery. Christian churches in Europe relied on stained glass windows, carvings, statuary, and paintings in churches and engravings in books to convey and glorify biblical narratives to the illiterate and semiliterate. Islam forbade the making of images of people or of God.

In the 19th century, illustrated newspapers and magazines had a wide circulation, printing drawings and engravings and, later, photographs. In the 20th century, along with movies, photo-magazines for fans and general-interest/current-affairs magazines, notably *Life*, appeared.

Photographs have been praised for representing and communicating images of reality across time and space. Photographs and motion pictures taken at Nazi concentration camps at the end of the World War II in Europe convinced the public of the horrors that had occurred in a way that words had failed to do during the war. Death and photography have had a long history—an early use of daguerreotypes and photographs was to preserve the faces of family members, before or after death.

Photographs have been derided for obscuring reality. Widespread knowledge of how subject matter can be staged, and the resulting image manipulated, has given rise to general skepticism about the old claim that the camera cannot lie. The passionate debates that arise about the veracity of an image are evidence of the power of some images. Debate still surrounds the famous photograph of the flag raising over Iwo Jima, more than half a century after the events depicted. Images can be manipulated to show impossible situations—changing sizes, shapes, or locations and removing and/or adding people as their political fortunes change. More subtle editing involves improving the appearance of politicians and celebrities or, for some publications, emphasizing flaws.

Images have been used to convince, inspire, motivate, and sell by governments, propagandists, and advertisers. Images convey information and provoke emotion. Images may be chosen for what they signify—for example, an advertisement for perfume may signify the possibility of romance.

Under certain conditions, images may be chosen that do not convey new information. Some images used to accompany news reports have been criticized for their inability to convey complexity. A picture of a starving child conveys an image of famine without communicating the complex social, economic, and political factors leading to the disaster. The CNN effect was said by some to have driven U.S. foreign policy during the 1990s; that is, the issues portrayed by CNN images were those that the U.S. public demanded that their politicians address. The use of stock photographs by newspapers and television news programs bought from image banks such as Corbis has also been criticized for removing context from the stories being reported. But stock images are cheaper and easier to obtain than original, more relevant images from photojournalists. For more information, see Berger (1972), Crowley and Heyer (2007), Goldberg (1993), Newhall (1988), and Stephens (1998). ***See also*** Graphic; Popular Prints; Video/Music Videos

Visual Reality   Still and moving image cameras can be used to present a version of reality that seems incontrovertible because it is based in visual imagery that is captured by mechanical means. The visual basis of reality has been supported by definitions of reality that rely on being able to confirm the real through the senses, with vision being considered the most reliable. Documentary photography and movies are said to provide evidence of actual events or objects without the interpretational layers found in fictional material. But the ability of any sort of image-making to present an unvarnished, uninterpreted reality has been called into question by challenges to the film documentary form (by filmmakers like Michael Moore and YouTube, a video-sharing Web site); by the development of television programs presenting fake or spoofed news (Jon Stewart's "The Daily Show"), and by digital video and photography and imaging software that make manipulating images possible. For more information, see Tagg (1988). ***See also*** Construction of Reality; Virtual Reality

Vocalics   Also referred to as paralanguage, the term encompasses verbal cues, such as volume, rate, pitch, pausing, and silence, to convey meaning and emotion. Body language is also included in this form of communication. It is linked to other forms of nonverbal communication, such as facial expressions. ***See also*** Chronemics; Haptics; Kinesics

Vocational Education   Also called career and technical education, it is meant to provide individuals with the skills and knowledge to prepare them for trades or jobs in industry. While vocational education is often taught in high schools, it is also typically offered through community colleges or at an institute of technology.

Voice and Diction   The sound made through the mouth when talking or singing and how we express this utterance. There are two types of diction: (1) denotation, which is the literal meaning of a word, and (2) connotation, which refers to the feelings associated with a word. Diction also has an impact on the word choice of the speaker and syntax. Diction comprises utterance, inflection, verb, noun, connective, syllable, phoneme, and conjunction. Proper use of the voice and diction is crucial for effective communication. In another sense, the term refers to a value judgment, as when describing a singer or speaker as having a "good voice." ***See also*** Connotation; Denotation

Voice Identification   A technological method used to confirm identity through voiceprints and voice

V

recognition software. Similar to fingerprinting or iris recognition procedures, the use of voice identification devices is based on the premise that vocal characteristics are unique to each individual. Voice identification technology is often used for security purposes, and it is currently used by banks and credit card companies to reduce the risk of identity fraud.

Voir Dire   A French expression. The original meaning of the expression made reference to an oath to tell the truth. In the contemporary context, *voir dire* refers to the process by which individuals are examined and questioned by the judge and legal teams for selection as members of a jury. During the *voir dire* process, attorneys may dismiss potential jurors "for cause" or through a limited number of peremptory challenges (with no explanation for the dismissal, though the dismissal cannot be based on race, gender, or other discriminatory criteria). ***See also*** Jury; Peremptory Challenge

Vollmer, August   A police chief from California who played a key role in the development of the fields of law enforcement and criminal justice in the early 20th century. He founded the Berkeley Police School in 1908 and was responsible for various innovative developments in the area of policing. His numerous contributions to law enforcement include setting up the first scientific crime lab, developing a fingerprinting program, and emphasizing the importance of crime prevention efforts. Vollmer was one of the 11 members appointed to the Wickersham Commission. ***See also*** Wickersham Commission

Voyeur/Voyeurism   People who achieve sexual gratification from the sexual experiences of other people, or the action of doing so. Voyeurism refers to a behavior that involves sexual arousal resulting from the observation of other individuals, without their consent, while they carry out intimate behaviors. Voyeurs tend to observe other individuals as they remove their clothing or engage in sexual behavior. In Western societies, voyeurism is often perceived as a disorder or a perversion and, in many cases, a criminal offense.

V

W

Wages The pecuniary rewards for the use of units of labor. Wage rates may be determined by acquired skills, physical well-being, government, the market, employers, or trade unions. Wages can be inflexible because of nonmarket forces, and some economists believe that unemployment can be explained in part by wage rigidity (inflexibility—that is, the failure to achieve equilibrium in the labor market). Rigidity is caused by minimum-wage laws, unions and collective bargaining, and efficiency wage.

Governments may stipulate the minimum wage that should be paid and, by so doing, can create a permanent surplus. Unions influence the wage rate that should be paid by management through collective bargaining, and the efficiency wage keeps the wage rate above the market clearing value to induce productivity and reduce a firm's labor cost per unit of output. The efficiency wage also ensures retention of high-quality workers who are motivated to be productive rather than complacent. For more information, see Mankiw (2006) and McConnell and Brue (2008). *See also* Labor; Labor Theory of Value; Market

Wanton An adjective describing an act that can be obscene and offensive, or even cruel. A wanton act is unprovoked and illustrates a lack of restraint and consideration for the consequences of one's actions. A wanton act is often perceived as undisciplined or immoral.

War Crimes Crimes committed by soldiers, political leaders, or civilians during times of war that are punishable under international law. Although acts that would be criminal during times of peace are sometimes permissible in times of war (such as the killing of enemy soldiers), there are rules of war that are specified in the Geneva Conventions. Mistreatment of civilians or of prisoners of war and rape of civilians, soldiers, or prisoners in the context of war would each be considered war crimes under international law. The International Criminal Court at the Hague has been established to prosecute war crimes and crimes against humanity. *See also* International Law

Warden In a broader sense, a public official who is responsible for leading any given department or area (e.g., fire warden, prison warden). However, a warden is most often used to denote the head of a prison, who is responsible for overseeing operations within the prison. *See also* Prison/Prisoner

Warrant A decree that provides authorization to engage in a given act. Common examples of warrants are the search warrant, which provides legal grounds for police officers to search the premises of a suspected offender, or the arrest warrant, which enables a law enforcement official to arrest a particular individual. The warrant allows law enforcement authorities to search a premises and seize any illegal property found or arrest a suspect. Items found as a result of a search warrant may be used as evidence in court proceedings. The warrant is usually issued by a judge or other authorized officer, ensuring that the search or arrest conforms to legal regulations. *See also* Search and Seizure

Warren Commission A report produced in 1963 to investigate the facts relating to the assassination of President John F. Kennedy. The commission was named after the chief justice of the United States, Earl Warren, who was the chairman of the commission. The report provided various details about the assassination of President Kennedy and concluded that Lee Harvey Oswald alone was responsible for the act. The Warren Commission has been challenged numerous times since it was drafted, but no substantial proof has been brought forward to date to refute its claims.

Wealth Effect Otherwise known as the real-balance effect. When prices change, individuals become richer or poorer depending on the direction of price movements. The value of their assets (money, bonds, and other financial assets) increases or decreases as a result of changes in the purchasing power of their assets—that is, what their assets can buy in real or actual units.

When the price level falls, the assets of individuals and businesses increase, because they can purchase more (wealth effect appreciates). On the contrary, when the price level increases, the purchasing power of financial assets falls, thereby resulting in a depreciation of the value of wealth. The wealth effect has an impact on spending and investment. A declining wealth effect causes a reduction in spending and conversion of assets into cash, whereas an increase in the wealth effect leads to an increase in spending and conversion of cash into assets with higher returns (interest rate). For more information, see Boyes and Melvin (2002), McConnell and Brue (2008), and Schiller (2006). *See also* Aggregate Demand Curve; Liquidity

Weapon   An instrument used with the intent to harm, kill, or destroy. Weapons are often used in the context of a confrontation, for defensive or offensive purposes. Firearms, knives, and missiles are a few examples of different types of weapons.

Weathering   The geographical process by which rock and minerals are broken down. Weathering occurs when rocks and minerals are exposed to atmospheric agents such as wind and water; however, this is not the same as erosion, which occurs when land is transported or worn away by wind or water, usually after weathering. There are two types of weathering: chemical and mechanical. Chemical weathering occurs when the chemical composition of rock/mineral is transformed by the chemical elements of an atmospheric agent. Mechanical weathering, on the other hand, is the physical process by which rocks/minerals are broken down into smaller pieces. Mechanical weathering changes the physical nature of the rock/mineral but does not affect the chemical composition.

Wechsler Adult Intelligence Scales (WAIS)   One of the most widely used and researched intelligence tests. The WAIS was created by David Wechsler in 1955. It was adapted from an early measure developed by Wechsler in 1939, the Wechsler-Bellevue Intelligence Scale. The WAIS has since undergone a number of revisions and is currently in its third edition (WAIS-III, 1997), with plans for a fourth edition under way. The WAIS-III is composed of 14 subtests that produce raw scores, which are later converted into scaled scores based on comparison with an age-based normative sample. Subtests are divided into two main areas of cognitive functioning: verbal and performance. An overall full-scale intelligence quotient (IQ) score as well as both performance and verbal IQ scores are calculated. In addition, there are four main indexes for which scores are produced: Verbal Comprehension, Perceptual Organization, Working Memory, and Processing Speed. A full-scale IQ score may fall within one of seven main classifications: Very Superior (130+), Superior (120–129), High Average (110–119), Average (90–109), Low Average (80–89), Borderline (70–79), and Intellectually Deficient (69 or below). There is a significant body of literature supporting the use of the WAIS-III across various contexts. It is most commonly used in psychoeducational and neuropsychological evaluations, though it can be used for a variety of clinical purposes, including the diagnosis of mental retardation. According to the American Association on Intellectual and Developmental Disabilities (AAIDD), formerly the American Association on Mental Retardation (AAMR), mental retardation is a disability defined by significant limitations in both intellectual functioning and adaptive functioning. The AAIDD states that mental retardation is thought to be present in individuals who receive an IQ score of 70 or below. For more information, see Tulsky, Saklofskie, and Zhu (2003). ***See also*** Intelligence Quotient (IQ)

Weed and Seed Program   A program developed by the U.S. Department of Justice to help communities tackle various challenges such as crime, gang activity, and substance use, as well as neighborhood preservation and restoration. Components of weed and seed programs may vary from one area to another, but these programs all seek one common objective: to improve the quality of life in high-crime, disadvantaged neighborhoods.

Weightless Economy   A technologically innovative economy that is driven by human capital (knowledge product), information and communication technology, and biotechnology. In short, it is a capital-driven economy that has more to do with human capital relative to physical capital. An important aspect of the weightless economy is economic integration and diffusion of knowledge within the parameters of the acknowledgment and management of property rights.

Yet it is an economy that has inherent conflict, largely as a result of the perception of a conflict between intellectual property and human or sovereign right in the biotechnology sector, for example. The assertion of property rights and rewards may or may not result in inequity, for which proactive policy directives are important in the weightless economy.

The weightless economy is a growth-oriented economy in which consumers can now benefit from proximity and competition. It achieves greatest contemporary resonance in the arenas of telecommunications, intellectual property, product differentiation, and electronic libraries and databases (including entertainment and communication).

A distinguishing feature of the weightless economy is the prominence of the service sector, which has become increasingly as important as other sectors such as manufacturing, which once dominated the contribution to national wealth and international exchange. Additionally, the use of the common features of the contemporary weightless economy tends to be durable and nondiminutive. For more information, see Quah (1999). ***See also*** Economy, New; Globalization (economics); Innovation (economics); Liberalization

Welfare   Generally, the well-being of an individual or group. In an economic sense, the term describes governmental benefits or assistance given to impoverished people to enable them to maintain the minimum standard of living. First enacted in Germany in the 1880s, and adopted by most Western countries by the early 1900s, welfare laws and programs can be general or specific.

Welfare is often distributed through programs such as pensions, disability, national health insurance, and unemployment insurance. Individuals or families may apply for welfare due to disability, unemployment, lack of education or job training, or substance abuse. Qualifications vary depending on location and government. While welfare is typically dispensed by monetary means, it can come in other forms such as, for example, tax credits for working mothers.

Welfare can also be paid to companies or entities. This type of welfare, coined "corporate welfare" in 1956 by Ralph Nadar, refers to capital granted to companies in an industry that is perceived by government to need financial assistance in order to survive or expand. Corporate welfare is often paid in the form of favorable tax policy.

The provision of providing welfare benefits to poor people in the United States has been controversial throughout history. Until the Great Depression of the 1930s, assistance provided by state and local governments was minimal, with church and volunteer agencies providing the bulk of aid to the impoverished. Currently, almost all developed nations provide some type of economic or social benefits for the disadvantaged members of society. Nations where welfare programs are particularly prominent are typically known as welfare states.

Welfare programs vary greatly, depending on the nature of the recipient and the government's desired outcome. For example, welfare is given to nondisabled recipients to prevent them from becoming completely destitute, and they must periodically prove that they are actively seeking employment. Conversely, justification to provide assistance to disabled persons is more philosophical.

Welfare Economics A methodological approach to assess resource allocations and establish criteria for government intervention as it relates to the well-being of a community. Established as a well-defined branch of economics during the 20th century and often considered a normative branch, it uses microeconomic techniques and income distribution to simultaneously determine prosperity within an economy.

Welfare economics assesses social welfare, which refers to the overall well-being of a society. Such well-being or welfare is measured in terms of the individual economic activity of the people who make up the society. Moreover, welfare economics largely considers two concepts: income distribution and economic efficiency. Income distribution (in a country or the world) refers to how income is distributed between distinct groups of individuals. Economic efficiency refers to the unit of goods produced at the lowest possible cost. Economic efficiency can be viewed as dealing with the "size of the pie," while income distribution deals with the "division of the pie."

Welfare economics typically takes into consideration individual preferences and specifies a welfare improvement in Pareto efficiency terms. The term *Pareto efficiency* is named after the Italian economist Vilfredo Pareto and is often used in evaluating economic systems. If an economic system is Pareto efficient, it is implied that a certain allocation of income or resources may result in the improvement of individuals' well-being, with no individual being made worse off at their expense.

Welfare economics is often studied through either a neoclassical approach, developed by the economists Francis Ysidro Edgeworth, Alfred Marshall, and Arthur Cecil Pigou and the philosopher Henry Sidgwick, or the new welfare economics approach, created by the economists Vilfred Pareto, Nicholas Kaldor, and John Hicks. Neoclassical economics is largely considered mainstream at the microeconomic level and focuses on the determination of prices, outputs, and income distributions in markets through supply and demand. In the new welfare economics approach, efficiency and income distribution are treated separately. Furthermore, neoclassical economics measures utility as cardinal, or measurable by observation, while new welfare economics measures utility as ordinal, rejecting an objective measure and, instead, ranking commodity bundles.

There are two fundamental theorems of welfare economics. The first welfare theorem states that a Walrasian equilibrium is a Pareto-efficient distribution of resources. Such a theorem is true in a large and important class of general equilibrium models (usually static ones). The standard case is that if every resource has a positive quantity of every good, and every resource has a utility function that is convex, continuous, and strictly increasing, then the first welfare theorem holds.

The second welfare theorem is that a Pareto-efficient allocation can be achieved by a Walrasian equilibrium if every agent has a positive quantity of every good and preferences are convex, continuous, and strictly increasing.

Despite the apparent symmetry of the two theorems, the first theorem is much more general than the second, requiring far fewer assumptions.

Welfare can be measured either in terms of "utils" or dollars or measured ordinally in terms of Pareto efficiency. The cardinal method of measurement in utils is rarely used in theory today due to the aggregation problems that make the meaning of the method doubtful, except on widely challenged underlying assumptions. ***See also*** Neoclassical Economics; Social Welfare; Utility

Wellness A state of optimal health, often including physical, mental, and emotional aspects. Wellness is not simply the absence of disease. It also includes the presence of lifestyle choices that lead to increased well-being, including a healthy diet, moderate exercise, and participation in positive social relationships. ***See also*** Positive Psychology

Wernicke's Area An area in the brain named after the Polish-German neurologist Carl Wernicke. He discovered that damage to the left temporal lobe of the brain posterior to the primary auditory complex causes what is now referred to as Wernicke's aphasia—a condition in which individuals hear spoken language but cannot understand it. Wernicke's aphasia is also associated with difficulties related to the production of speech, such that individuals are able to produce grammatically correct sentences, though they lack in meaningful content. Wernicke's aphasia is typically presented in the literature, in contrast to Broca's aphasia, a condition whereby individuals have difficulty

W

producing grammatically correct speech. For more information, see Alexander (2000). **See also** Aphasia

Westernization   The influencing of the customs and practices of westernized societies on non-Western civilizations. Westernization includes the process of assimilating dominated societies into Western cultures. Westernization emerged in the mid-19th century with the colonization of India, when the British embraced a vision of world domination. At this time, other western European nations, as well as Russia and later the United States, were also seeking dominion over foreign nations. The British, however, took the lead and formed the model for other powerful nations to follow. This process was intended to promote freedom, justice, and peace, on the one hand, and demonstrate the raw power necessary to reshape the world in one's own image, on the other.

Scholars have questioned how the West came to dominate the rest of the world. One theory offered focused on the West's development of an agrarian lifestyle in place of a hunting or pastoral existence. Geographically, Europe was well-placed in terms of fertile land and temperate climates for domesticating crops and animals. Europe could therefore adopt new crops, livestock, and technology and provide itself with adequate nourishment. Furthermore, due to their ability to domesticate crops and animals, Europeans were in a position to get a head start over other societies in the development of writing, government, technology, weapons of war, and immunity to deadly germs. As a result, Europe was in a position to outbreed, conquer, and destroy societies resisting or unable to adopt such innovations.

By the beginning of the 20th century, the world was thus subjected to the political domination and way of life of western Europe and North America. About 85% of the world's land surface, including South America, Africa, Asia, and the Islamic world of the Ottoman Empire, had been absorbed into Western colonial empires.

A major effect of European domination was the integration of Western colonized nations into a world capitalist system, with the colonized nations acting primarily as sources of raw materials for Western industrial production. This turned colonized populations from agriculturalists into wage laborers. In addition, Christian missionaries, through education, converted or tried to convert colonized populations and instill Western values such as monogamy and the nuclear family. Colonization lasted until about the 1960s, when many of the colonial powers, weakened by World Wars I and II, gave independence to their overseas land holdings.

Today, Westernization still exists through globalization, which entails the loosening of trade barriers, through capitalistic ventures, and the promotion of democratization, both of which are values established by the Western world. Today, as a result of colonization, Westernized countries include Australia and New Zealand, Canada and Greenland, Israel, South Africa, and Central Europe. For more information, see Diamond (1999) and Von Laue (1987). **See also** Globalization (political science); Imperialism

Whistle-Blowing   The act of reporting to internal or external parties the wrongdoing found within an organization. Internal parties are stakeholders who work within the organization. External parties are persons or groups working outside the organization, such as the media, regulators, law enforcement personnel, or legislators. The term *whistle-blowing* derived from the practice of English bobbies, who would blow their whistles to alert citizens and other law enforcement officers of the presence of danger. A person who reports wrongdoing is known as a whistle-blower.

Although legislation protecting whistle-blowers dates to about a century ago, only recently have whistle-blowers received protection from retaliation by employers, due, in part, to decisions by corporations that ended in tragic consequences. In an unprecedented act, in 2002, *Time* magazine named three whistle-blowers as Persons of the Year. They were Cynthia Cooper of WorldCom, Sherron Watkins of Enron, and Colleen Rowley of the Federal Bureau of Investigation.

The first whistle-blowing legislation in the United States was introduced in 1863 by President Abraham Lincoln. The False Claims Act was created to combat fraud resulting from the sale of fake gunpowder, faulty rifles, rancid food, and ill horses and mules to the Union army during the Civil War. The act allowed private citizens to sue individuals and groups defrauding the government.

In 1986, Congress amended the False Claims Act by adding antiretaliation protections, as well as a provision for a whistle-blower to share in 30% of the proceeds of a successful lawsuit. The act further protects whistle-blowers from wrongful dismissal and allows for reinstatement, double back pay, interest on back pay, compensation for discriminatory treatment, and payment of reasonable legal fees.

Several other pieces of legislation have been passed to protect whistle-blowers from retaliatory acts of employers, such as termination, suspension, demotion, wage garnishment, and general mistreatment. In 1989, the Whistleblower Protection Act was passed and then amended in 1994. This legislation protects federal employees who disclose waste and fraud. The proposed Whistleblower Protection Enhancement Act of 2007, although not passed by the U.S. Congress, was designed to protect individuals who go public with corporate or governmental wrongdoing. Whistle-blower provisions are also found in other federal legislation as well as in state laws.

While legislation protected federal employees and contractors, there were few protections for whistle-blowers in private industry. That changed with the Sarbanes-Oxley Act of 2002 (SOX). This law was created in response to a rash of high-profile corporate scandals, such as Enron, WorldCom, and Tyco. Three major provisions of the act were passed. First, employees of publicly traded companies who report fraud to federal regulatory agencies, law enforcement, members or committees of Congress, or persons with supervisory authority over the employees are protected against retaliation. Next, the act compels auditors to develop reporting mechanisms for information provided by employees confidentially and anonymously. Third, the act extends beyond public corporations by protecting any person who reports violations of federal law to law enforcement.

White-Collar Crime Nonviolent criminal offenses that involve deception or concealment of information. White-collar crime is generally associated with members of the higher social classes. The concept of white-collar crime was first developed by the American sociologist Edwin H. Sutherland. Some examples of white-collar offenses include embezzlement, tax evasion, environmental crimes, and fraud. *See also* Suite Crime

Wickersham Commission A commission of 11 members, headed by George W. Wickersham, who were asked to investigate the causes of crime and to make recommendations for public policy and crime prevention strategies. The Wickersham Commission, or the National Committee on Law Observation and Enforcement, was established in 1929 in the United States. The commission paid particular attention to violations of the prohibition laws, which were quite common in the United States, and recommended a stricter enforcement of these laws. *See also* Prohibition

Wilson, O. W. A protégé of August Vollmer. While studying for a degree in criminology at the University of California, Wilson worked with the Berkeley Police Department. After graduation, he served as police chief in Fullerton (California) and later went on to serve in the same position in Kansas. One of his key contributions was the reorganization of the Wichita Police Department and the implementation of innovative law enforcement strategies, such as mobile crime labs. Wilson was well-known for his work ethics and his strong stand against police corruption. He also acknowledged the limits of the police's ability to prevent crime, mainly because he believed that poverty and other social factors were root causes of the crime problem and that the police had little influence over these issues. He also served in various European countries during World War II and was mainly responsible for public safety issues. Like Vollmer, he was involved in both law enforcement and academia. *See also* Vollmer, August

Wire Services/News Groups News agencies developed in the 19th century for the purpose of collecting news, particularly foreign news, and selling it to newspapers unwilling or unable to finance their own reporters. Although these agencies emerged before the widespread use of telegraphy, they flourished as telegraphy systems spread. News stories were sent by agency reporters down the wire, first to the agency for consolidation and rewriting and then out to newspapers who subscribed to the service. The agencies made sure that the stories were neutral in tone, without political bias. This was necessary as the papers that would publish the stories were widely varied in their editorial views, and removing potentially objectionable bias was essential if the agency wanted to keep and serve all its customers. Agency news thus earned a reputation for objectivity. Newspapers might rewrite the stories before publication but more usually printed the stories or selected parts verbatim.

In New York, in the 1820s, five newspapers agreed to work together to collect news from arriving ships. As telegraphy spread across the United States, more cooperative regional news-gathering groups developed, with some competing and others merging. Toward the end of the 19th century, the dominant agencies in the United States were the Western Associated Press and the New York Associated Press.

In Europe, the British Post Office acted as an agency, when early in the 19th century, it started selling news stories from foreign papers. In Paris, Agence Havas was founded in 1832, and Reuters was founded in London in 1851. From 1870 until the 1930s, foreign news gathering was centralized and dominated by noncompetitive agreements between the strongest Western agencies—Havas, Reuters, Wolff (in Germany), and The Associated Press. Thus, news from Africa might travel to Europe before arriving in Asia.

News agencies now include nonprofit, for-profit, and government-controlled (e.g., China's Xinhau) organizations. Western news agencies still dominate the international flow of news. Reuters is currently the largest worldwide agency. The Associated Press is a not-for-profit cooperative owned by 1,500 U.S. newspaper members, with more than 4,000 employees in 240 worldwide bureaus. The dominance of Western news agencies as the primary source of non-Western news for North American and European audiences may be somewhat challenged by local news organizations posting their stories on the Web and by the emergence of non-Western news networks broadcasting in English, such as Al-Jazeera. For more information, see Blondheim (1994) and Stephens (2007). *See also* Objectiveness in Media Coverage; Telegraph

Witness An individual who was present but was not involved in the perpetration of an act or event. In the context of the criminal justice system, witnesses are called on to help build a case in order to establish the guilt or innocence of the defendant. An individual who has witnessed a crime may be subpoenaed (summoned to court to testify). Credible witness testimony is often considered to be one of the stronger forms of evidence. *See also* Evidence

Work Design The identification of tasks or processes to be completed in order to fulfill the organization's objectives, the assignment of tasks and subtasks to individuals, and the coordination of individuals performing the tasks. Simplification, which is assigning one subtask to an individual, leads to greater efficiencies and economic advantages; however, simplification increases interdependence among workers and increases the need for coordination among workers. Simplification reduces the meaningfulness of a job and is more likely to result in lower levels of job satisfaction and motivation. Rotating individuals among tasks (job rotation), assigning several tasks to an individual (job enlargement), or allowing individuals more responsibility and control (job enrichment) may increase interest and job satisfaction. For more information, see Galbraith (1977). *See also* Job Enrichment; Job Satisfaction

Work–Family Balance   The juggling act people do between careers, family, and other personal or professional obligations to maintain their roles and responsibilities. Struggling with competing priorities is required to maintain balance. Work–family balance is a multifaceted matter concerning finances, personal goals, and time management.

Workforce   The pool of people engaged in or eligible for employment. The concept can be applied to different units, including a group of people (e.g., women), a single organization (e.g., the Acme Corporation), an industry (e.g., textiles), and a geographic region (e.g., city, county, state, nation).

Since workforce participation is a key component in long-term economic health and growth, workforce planning is a central element. Workforce planning allows units to anticipate changes in the workforce rather than react to them. These changes can include demographic, social, economic, and political factors that might increase or decrease the pool of available workers.

Working Memory   The mechanism by which individuals can temporarily store and manipulate information. It has been conceptualized as a temporary storage and workspace in the brain and is thought to be a key component in the ability to perform arithmetic and read. Working memory has also been implicated in affecting cognitive flexibility and planning abilities. The term *working memory* is very familiar to those conducting intelligence assessments with the Wechsler scales, as it is one of the four main indexes used in the measurement of IQ scores. For more information, see Jonides, Reuter-Lorenz, and Smith (1996). *See also* Memory (education, psychology)

Work Release   A program implemented to enable incarcerated individuals to take temporary leave from prison for the purpose of employment or training in the community while serving their sentence. Work release programs are restricted to individuals who meet certain criteria, including sentence length and type of conviction. The purpose of the work release programs is to facilitate the inmates' transition back into the community on release from prison. *See also* Furlough

World Trade Organization (WTO)   The organization that replaced the General Agreement on Tariffs and Trade (GATT) on January 1, 1995, the day on which the Uruguay Round came into effect. GATT was created in 1947, after World War II, to deal with problems associated with trade restrictions and poor economic performance, but it expired in 1994. The primary motives behind the creation of GATT, the promotion of less restricted trade and equity in trading relations, are inherent in the World Trade Organization (WTO), but unlike GATT, the WTO is structured to minimize procedural and enforcement problems associated with trade disputes.

Apart from procedural issues, changing social and economic conditions necessitated the resolution of urgent trade disagreements. Acquired immune deficiency syndrome (AIDS) and the desperate need for pharmaceutical drugs made the protection of intellectual property rights a critical issue to fight the creation of counterfeit drugs.

Nations that were severely affected by the AIDS epidemic argued for the right to issue patents to produce antiretroviral drugs, much to the chagrin of pharmaceutical companies and their host nations. Intellectual property rights took a broader dimension to include books, films, music, computer programs, and non-antiretroviral drugs under the WTO.

The service sectors, including banking, shipping, and insurance, also became subject to international regulation under the WTO. Other salient trade issues include dumping, agriculture, the environment, and tariff reductions. The issue of nontariff barriers—that is, restrictions other than tariffs—continues to be a major problem for the organization.

Members of the WTO have essential obligations that are set forth in Articles I through III and VI of the GATT. The major principles of the WTO are (a) liberalization of trade; (b) the nondiscrimination (most favored nation) rule; and (c) no unfair promotion of exports—for example, undue subsidy. For more information, see Carbaugh (2007), Folsom, Gordon, and Spanogle (2004), Friedman (2006), and Pugel (2007). *See also* Fair Trade; Free Trade; Globalization; Liberalization; Trade Theory, New

Worldview   An individual's or a society's philosophy or conception about the world. Worldviews are subjective outlooks influenced by personal experience, cultural norms, religious beliefs, social philosophies, and political ideologies, and they reflect apprehension as much as comprehension.

The term is a translation of the German *Weltanschauung*, with *welt* meaning "world" and *anschauung* meaning "outlook" or "view." According to the writer James Sire, the German term is believed to have been first articulated by the 18th-century German philosopher Immanuel Kant and first elaborated on by the 19th-century German romanticist and empiricist Wilhelm Dilthey.

Sire, who had written a few books on the subject of worldview in the latter half of the 20th century, reexplores the idea in his 2004 book, *Naming the Elephant: Worldview as a Concept*. He posits that worldview is not a mere set of basic concepts "but a fundamental orientation of the heart" and a commitment to understanding "the really real." He states that people's behaviors are reflected in their worldviews and their ability to grasp the worldviews of others.

Worldview does affect behavior, and a survey of history will produce countless examples of how worldview has influenced the course of events through the centuries. Worldview motivates the imperialist and the revolutionary and propels conquerors to send armies into the homelands of others. Worldview allowed Southern planters to believe that owning slaves was acceptable and tells the descendants of slaves that their claiming of reparation is justified. Worldview inspired those who plotted and carried out the September 11, 2001, terror attacks in America, and led the U.S. Congress to pass the 2001 Patriot Act and vote to fund wars in Afghanistan and Iraq.

The concept of worldview has been applied to many fields of study, including religion, history, philosophy, feminism, the natural sciences, management science, and computer science, and it invites debate on subjects as varied as Darwin and the evolutionary process, the truths or fallacies to be found in the world's major religions, and the wisdom of government practices.

Worldviews are not necessarily static. Boise (Idaho) State University faculty member Mohan Limaye writes that a survey he gave his international business students—85% of whom are white and Christian—showed significant perceptual changes in their worldviews after they were exposed to information about various cultures and religions throughout the world and to historical and current facts about America. The survey exercise also taught them that successful business communication depends on a variety of information sources in addition to those perceived to be standard business. For more information, see Limaye (2000), Sire (2004), Smedley (2007), and Tate (2007). ***See also*** Cognitive Dissonance; Cultural Relativism; Frame of Reference; Hegemony; Metaphysics

Writing Across the Curriculum A practice designed to improve the writing skills of students by providing them opportunities to write in all content areas. Writing across the curriculum develops stronger communication skills while allowing students to synthesize content information from multiple disciplines. For example, students may write a daily learning log to describe how they solve mathematical problems.

Writ of Certiorari A court order issued by the U.S. Supreme Court that directs a lower court to produce records for a case that it will hear on appeal. Originally, the Supreme Court was mandated to hear all cases on appeal, but this resulted in an overburdened docket. In the Judiciary Act of 1891, Congress authorized the Supreme Court the use of the writ of *certiorari*, which in Latin means "to be informed," to give the Court discretion to decide which cases it will hear. This eased the docket burden for a time. The Judiciary Act of 1925 provided even greater Supreme Court discretion, and in 1988, Congress increased the Court's discretionary role even further.

A petition for a writ of certiorari is a document that a losing party in a lower court files with the Supreme Court asking it to review the lower court's decision. Today, the Court receives around 8,000 petitions per term, which lasts between October and June. About 80 petitions get granted. The Court hears cases that raise a significant question of law, that result from a lower court's conflicting interpretation of the law, and that will promote a nationally uniform understanding of a legal point. Although it is a tradition rather than a written rule, the justices will grant certiorari based on the Rule of Four, which means that four of the nine justices favor granting the petition. If a petition is granted, then the case is scheduled for the filing of briefs and oral arguments.

When denying a writ of certiorari petition, the Court does not usually provide its reasons. Some reasons, however, may be untimeliness, a lower court's misapplication of the law, or the lack of finality from which the order was appealed. ***See also*** Supreme Court, U.S.

W

X

XYY Chromosomes   While most males generally have one X and one Y chromosome, some males have an extra Y chromosome. This disorder is referred to as the XYY syndrome, and criminological theorists have referred to such men as "supermales." While it has been suggested that the XYY syndrome may be associated with mental health issues and increased criminal behavior, the evidence regarding this issue has been found to be inconclusive.

X

Z

Zero-Tolerance Policing A law enforcement strategy aiming to severely punish offenders engaging in a specific type of offense for the first time, with no tolerance for the targeted behavior. Such policies can also be aimed at specific individuals. Various zero-tolerance policies have emerged in recent years. For instance, some jurisdictions have implemented zero-tolerance policies regarding the possession of weapons in schools. Zero-tolerance policies are also widely used for driving under the influence. In general, zero-tolerance policies are perceived as "tough-on-crime" policing strategies.

Zone of Proximal Development The range of tasks that a child cannot currently perform unassisted but can perform with some guidance from more competent individuals. The zone of proximal development is the "zone" in which effective learning can occur. The zone is dynamic and changes as learning occurs, and it varies according to person and task. It is the area that teachers and aids should focus on to promote learning and development. The concept originated in the early 20th century with the Russian psychologist Lev Vygotsky.

z **Scores** Standard scores with a mean (M) of 0 and standard deviation (SD) of 1, based on the conversion of raw scores (X) into units of standard deviation below or above the mean:

$$z = (X - M)/SD,$$

with a typical range of $\pm 3z$ from the mean.

Z

BIBLIOGRAPHY

13 Op.A.G. 516, August 31, 1871.

5 CFR 210.102(b)(1).

5 U.S.C. § 551(4).

Adams, J. S. (1963). Toward an understanding of inequity. *Journal of Abnormal Psychology, 67*(5), 422–436.

Adams, S. (2007). *Stick to drawing comics, monkey brain! Cartoonist ignores helpful advice.* New York: Portfolio.

Adams, T. (2007). Producers, directors, and horizontal communication in television news production. *Journal of Broadcasting & Electronic Media, 51*(2), 337–354. Retrieved August 5, 2008, from http://web.ebscohost.com/ehost/pdf?vid=3&hid=5&sid=b862c22a-ff7f-41fc-b2f1-cfe76059fce1%40SRCSM1

Adler, J. R. (Ed.). (2004). *Forensic psychology: Concepts, debates and practice.* Cullompton, UK: Willan.

Administrative Procedures Act, 5 U.S.C. § 551 *et seq.* (1946).

Adorno, T. W., Frenkel-Brunswik, E., Levinson, D. J., & Sanford, R. N. (1993). *The authoritarian personality* (Studies in Prejudice Series). New York: W. W. Norton. (Original work published 1950)

Adorno, T. W., & Horkheimer, M. (1972). The culture industry: Enlightenment as mass deception. In M. Horkheimer & T. Adorno (Eds.), *Dialectic of enlightenment* (pp. 120–167). New York: Herder & Herder.

Akera, A. (2001). Voluntarism and the fruits of collaboration: The IBM user group, Share. *Technology and Culture, 42*(4), 710–736.

Alali, A. O., & Eke, K. K. (Eds.). *Media coverage of terrorism: Methods of diffusion.* Newbury Park, CA: Sage.

Alexander, M. P. (2000). Aphasia I: Clinical and anatomic issues. In M. J. Farah & T. E. Feinberg (Eds.), *Patient-based approaches to cognitive neuroscience* (pp. 165–181). Cambridge: MIT Press.

Alexander, S. L. (2004). *Media and American courts: A reference handbook.* Santa Barbara, CA: ABC-CLIO.

Allan, K. (2006). *Contemporary social and sociological theory: Visualizing social worlds.* Thousand Oaks, CA: Pine Forge Press.

Allen, G. (2000). *Intertextuality.* New York: Routledge.

Allen, M. (2007). Effective opportunity and democratic deliberation. *Politics, 27*(2), 83–90.

Allport, G. (1979). *The nature of prejudice.* Reading, MA: Addison-Wesley. (Original work published 1954)

Almond, A. G. (1990). *A discipline divided.* Newbury Park, CA: Sage.

Almond, G., & Verba, S. (1963). *The civic culture: Political attitudes and democracy in five nations.* Beverly Hills, CA: Sage.

Al-Orabi, M. (2002, October 31). *Diplomacy: An ever developing set of concepts* (Concepts of Diplomacy Seminar Series). Berlin, Germany: Humboldt-University.

Altemeyer, B. (1996). *The authoritarian specter.* Cambridge, MA: Harvard University Press.

Alterman, E. (2008, March 31). Out of print: The death and life of the American newspaper. *New Yorker,* 48–59.

Althusser, L., & Balibar, E. (1968). *Lire le Capital.* Paris: François Maspero.

Ambady, N., & Rosenthal, R. (1992). Thin slices of expressive behavior as predictors of interpersonal consequences: A meta-analysis. *Psychological Bulletin, 111,* 256–274.

American Academy of Pediatrics. (2000, July 26). *Joint statement on the impact of entertainment violence on children* (Congressional Public Health Summit). Retrieved August 1, 2008, from http://www.aap.org/advocacy/releases/jstmtevc.htm

American Idol: www.americanidol.com

American Psychiatric Association. (2000). *Diagnostic and statistical manual of mental disorders* (4th ed., text revision). Washington, DC: Author.

Amin, S. (2008). "Market economy" or oligopoly finance capitalism? *Monthly Review: An Independent Socialist Magazine, 59*(11), 51–61.

Anderson, C. (2006). *The long tail: Why the future of business is selling less of more.* New York: Hyperion.

Anderson, J. (2000). *Learning and memory.* (2nd ed.) New York: Wiley.

Anderson, J., & Anderson, B. (1993). The myth of persistence of vision revisited. *Journal of film and video, 45*(1), 3–12.

Anderson, J. E. (1997). *Public policymaking* (3rd ed.). Boston: Houghton-Mifflin.

Anderson, L. W., Krathwohl, D. R., Airasian, P. W., Cruikshank, K. A., Mayer, R. E., Pintrich, P. R., et al. (2001). *A taxonomy for learning, teaching, and assessing. A revision of Bloom's taxonomy of educational objectives.* New York: Longman.

Anderson, P. (1985). Nonverbal immediacy in interpersonal communication. In A. Siegman & S. Feldstein (Eds.), *Multichannel Integrations of Nonverbal Behavior* (pp. 1–33). Hillsdale, NJ: Erlbaum.

Anderson, T., & Leal, D. (2001). *Free market environmentalism.* New York: Macmillan.

Aristotle. (1959). *Ars rhetorica.* New York: Oxford University Press. (Original written 4th century BCE)

Aristotle. (1996). *Poetics* (M. Heath, Trans.). London: Penguin Classics. (Original written c. 335 BCE)

Arizona Revised Statutes, ARS 36–301. Definitions.

Articles of Confederation. (2001). In J. J. Patrick, R. M. Pious, & D. A. Ritchie (Eds.), *The Oxford guide to the United States government.* New York: Oxford University Press. (*Oxford reference online,* City University of New York, John Jay College of Criminal Justice. Retrieved February 10, 2008, from http://www.oxfordreference.com/views/ENTRY.html?subview=Main&entry=t89.e39

Asch, S. E. (1946). Forming impressions of personality. *Journal of Abnormal and Social Psychology, 41,* 258–290.

Asch, S. E. (1955). Opinions and social pressure. *Scientific American, 193,* 31–35.

Asch, S. E. (1956). Studies of Independence and Conformity: I. A Minority of One against a Unanimous Majority," *Psychological Monographs 70*(9), 1–70.

Asch, S. E. (1987). *Social psychology* (Oxford Science Publications). Oxford, UK: Oxford University Press. (Original work published 1952)

Ashby, R. (1956). *Introduction to cybernetics*. London: Chapman & Hall.

Ashcroft v. The Free Speech Coalition, 535 U.S. 234 (2002).

Auerbach, C., & Silverstein, L. B. (2003). *Qualitative data: An introduction to coding and analysis*. New York: New York University Press.

Austerlitz, S. (2007). *Money for nothing: A history of the music video from the Beatles to the White Stripes*. New York: Continuum.

Auzenne, V. R. (1994). *The visualization quest: A history of computer animation*. Rutherford, NJ: Fairleigh Dickinson University Press.

Avery, R. (Ed.). (1993). *Public service broadcasting in a multichannel environment: The history and survival of an ideal*. New York: Longman.

Bacevich, A. (2008, October). The Petraeus Doctrine. *The Atlantic*, 17–20.

Back, H. (2008). Intraparty politics and coalition formation: Evidence from Swedish local government. *Party Politics, 14*(1), 71–89.

Baddeley, A. D. (1999). *Essentials of human memory*. Hove, UK: Psychology Press.

Baddeley, A. D. (2001). Is working memory still working? *American Psychologist, 56*(11), 851–864.

Baillargeon, R., & DeVos. J. (1991). Object permanence in young infants: Further evidence. *Child Development, 62*(6), 1227–1246.

Bale, L. S. (1995). Gregory Bateson: Cybernetics and the social and behavioral sciences. *Cybernetics and Human Knowing: A Journal of the Second Order, 3*(1), 27–45.

Ball-Rokeach, S. J., & DeFleur, M. L. (1976). A dependency model of mass-media effects. *Communications Research, 3*, 3–21.

Bandura, A. (1977). *Social learning theory*. New York: General Learning Press.

Bandura. A. (1997). *Self-efficacy: The exercise of control*. New York: Freeman.

Bandura, A. (2001). Social cognitive theory: An agentic perspective. *Annual Review of Psychology, 52*(1), 1–26.

Barlow, A. (2007). *The rise of the blogosphere*. Westport, CT: Praeger.

Barlow, D. H. (2002). *Anxiety and its disorders: The nature and treatment of anxiety and panic* (2nd ed.). New York: Guilford Press.

Barnlund, D. C. (1968). *Interpersonal communication: Survey and studies*. New York: Houghton Mifflin.

Baron-Cohen, S., & Klin, A. (2006). What's so special about Asperger syndrome? [Editorial]. *Brain and Cognition, 61*, 1–4.

Barrett, D. (2002). Change communications: Using strategic employee communication to facilitate major change. *Corporate Communications: An International Journal, 7*(4), 219–231.

Barrett, R. A. (1984). *Culture and conduct: An excursion in anthropology*. Belmont, CA: Wadsworth.

Barry, B. J., & Crant, M. (2000). Dyadic communication relationships in organizations: An attributional/expectancy approach. *Organizational Science, 11*(6), 648–664.

Bartels, L., & Vavreck, L. (2000). *Campaign reform: Insights and evidence*. Ann Arbor: University of Michigan Press.

Barthes, R. (1967). *Elements of semiology*. New York: Hill & Wang.

Barthes, R. (1977). *Image, music, text* (S. Heath, Trans.). New York: Hill & Wang.

Barthes, R. (1988). From work to text. In *Image, music, text* (S. Heath, Trans., pp. 155–164). New York: Macmillan.

Bastiat, F. (2004). *The law*. Whitefish, MT: Kessinger. (Original work published 1850)

Bates, S. (2001). The reporter's privilege, then and now. *Society, 35*, 41–54.

Bateson, G. (1972). *Steps to an ecology of mind*. New York: Ballantine.

Bateson, G. (1979). *Mind and nature: A necessary unity*. New York: Ballantine.

Batson, C. D. (1998). Altruism and prosocial behavior. In D. T. Gilbert, S. T. Fiske, & G. Lindzey (Eds.), *Handbook of social psychology* (Vol. 2, 4th ed., pp. 282–316). Boston: McGraw-Hill.

Baughman, J. (1992). *The republic of mass culture: Journalism, filmmaking, and broadcasting in America since 1941*. Baltimore: Johns Hopkins University Press.

Baum, W. M. (1994). *Understanding behaviorism: Science, behavior and culture*. New York: Harper.

Baum, W. M. (2005). *Understanding behaviorism: Behavior, culture and evolution*. Malden, MA: Blackwell.

Baxter, L. A., Wilmot, W. W., Simmons, C. A., & Swartz, A. (1993). Ways of doing conflict: A folk taxonomy of conflict events in personal relationships. In P. J. Kalbfleish (Ed.), *Interpersonal communication: Evolving personal relationships* (pp. 89–108). Hillsdale, NJ: Lawrence Erlbaum.

Beattie, G. (2003). *Visible thought: The new psychology of body language*. London: Routledge. Retrieved May 19, 2008, from http://books.google.com/books?

Beccaria, C. (1983). *An essay on crimes and punishment* (A. Caso, Ed.). Boston: International Pocket Library. (Original work published 1764)

Beck, A. T., & Emery, G. (with Greenberg, R. L.). (1985). *Anxiety disorders and phobias: A cognitive perspective*. New York: Basic Books,

Becker, H. S. (1994). "Foi por acaso": Conceptualizing coincidence. *Sociological Quarterly, 35*, 183–194.

Becker, L. B., & Whitney, D. C. (1980). Effects of media dependencies: Audience assessment of government. *Communications Research, 7*, 95–120.

Beckett, S. (1994). *Waiting for Godot: A tragicomedy in two acts*. New York: Grove Press. (Original work published 1954)

Beels, C. (2002). Notes for a cultural history of family therapy. *Family Process, 41*, 67–82.

Beer, S. H. (1993). *To make a nation: The rediscovery of American federalism*. Cambridge, MA: Belknap Press.

Bell, C. (1844). *Anatomy and philosophy of expression as connected with the fine arts*. London: Murray.

Bell, C. (1997). *Ritual: Perspectives and dimensions*. New York: Oxford University Press.

Belfer Center Newsletter. (n.d.). In America's National Interest: Preventing Terrorism. Retrieved August 24, 2008, from http://belfercenter.ksg.harvard.edu/publication/3859/in_americas_national_interest.html

Bellah, R. N. (Ed.). (1973). *Émile Durkheim: On morality and society. Selected writings*. Chicago: University of Chicago Press.

Belz, H. (2005). Cooperative federalism. In K. L. Hall (Ed.), *The Oxford companion to the Supreme Court of the United States*. Oxford, UK: Oxford University Press. (*Oxford reference online*, City University of New York, John Jay College of Criminal Justice. Retrieved February 10, 2008, from http://www.oxfordreference.com/views/ENTRY.html?subview=Main&entry=t184.e0274

Bem, D. (1967). Self-perception: An alternative interpretation of cognitive dissonance phenomena. *Psychological Review, 74*(3), 183–200. Retrieved March 11, 2009, from http://dbem.ws/SP%20Theory%20Cognitive%20Dissonance.pdf

Ben-Israel, G., & Ben-Israel, R. (2002). Senior citizens: Social dignity, status and the right to representative freedom of organization. *International Labour Review, 141*(3), 253–273. Retrieved from the ProQuest Social Science Journals database

Bennett, K. (2003). Legal and social issues surrounding closed-circuit television testimony of child victims and witnesses. *Journal of Aggression Maltreatment & Trauma, 8*(3), 233–271.

Benson, J. T. (1977). Organizations: A dialectical view. *Administrative Science Quarterly, 22*(1), 1–21.

Bentham, J. (2005). *An introduction to the principles of morals and legislation.* Whitefish, MT: Kessinger. (Original work published 1789).

Berelson, B. R., Lazarsfeld, & McPhee. (1954). *Voting: A study of opinion formation in a presidential campaign,* Chicago: University of Chicago Press.

Berger, C. R. (1997). *Planning strategic interaction: Attaining goals through communicative action.* Mahwah, NJ: Lawrence Erlbaum.

Berger, J. (1972). *Ways of seeing.* London: British Broadcasting Company/Penguin Books.

Berger, J. (2002). Reemergence of the feminine: A model for global leadership. *Perspectives in Business,* 31–36.

Berger, P. L., & Luckmann, T. (1966). *The social construction of reality: A treatise in the sociology of knowledge.* New York: Doubleday.

Berkley, G., & Rouse, J. (2004). *The craft of public administration.* New York: McGraw-Hill.

Berkowitz, L. (1993). *Aggression: Its causes, consequences, and control.* New York: McGraw-Hill.

Berlin, I. (1958). Two concepts of liberty. In *Four essays on liberty* (pp. 118–172). Oxford, UK: Oxford University Press.

Berlin, I. (1959). *Karl Marx: His life and environment.* New York: Oxford University Press.

Berman, S. (2001–2002). Opening the closed mind: Making assumptions, jumping to conclusions. *ETC: A Review of General Semantics, 58*(4), 429–439. Retrieved May 29, 2008, from web.ebscohost.com.ezproxy.pratt.edu:2048/ehost/results?vid=5&hid=104&sid=66d24114–4b72–4bac-9568–844ae810b9d6%40sessionmgr102

Bern, D. (1972). Self-perception theory. In L. Berkowitz (Ed.), *Advances in experimental social psychology* (Vol. 6, pp. 1–62). New York: Academic Press.

Berne, E. (1964). *Games people play: The psychology of human relationships.* New York: Grove Press.

Bernstein, B. R., & Agel, J. (1995). *Amending America: If we love the Constitution so much, why do we keep trying to change it?* Lawrence: University Press of Kansas.

Berry, J. M. (2005). Nonprofits and civic engagement. *Public Administration Review, 65*(5), 568–578.

Berry, J. W., Poortinga, Y. H., & Pandey, J. (1997). *Handbook of cross-cultural psychology.* Boston: Allyn & Bacon.

Bertalanffy, L. V. (1950). An outline of general systems theory. *British Journal for the Philosophy and Science, 1*(2).

Bertalanffy, L. von. (1976). *General systems theory: Foundations, development, applications* (Rev. ed.). New York: Braziller.

Berthoud, H. R., & Neuhuber, W. L. (2000). Functional and chemical anatomy of the afferent vagal system. *Autonomic Neuroscience: Basic & Clinical, 85,* 1–17.

Bettelheim, B., & Janowitz, M. (1964). *Social change and prejudice, including dynamics of prejudice.* New York: Free Press of Glencoe.

Bhagwati, J. (2004). *In defense of globalization.* New York: Oxford University Press.

Bian, Y., Breiger, R., Davis, D., & Galaskiewicz, J. (2005). Occupation, class, and social networks in urban China. *Social Forces, 83*(4), 1443–1468. Retrieved from the ProQuest Social Science Journals database

Bineham, J. L. (1988). A historical account of the hypodermic model in mass communication. *Communication Monographs, 55*(3), 230–247.

Blanshard, B. (1966). Reflections on economic determinism. *Journal of Philosophy, 63*(7), 169–178.

Blaug, M. (1992). *The methodology of economics: Or, how economists explain.* Cambridge, UK: Cambridge University Press.

Bleicher, J. (1980). *Contemporary hermeneutics: Hermeneutics as method, philosophy and critique.* London: Routledge.

Bliese, P. (2003). Modeling longitudinal and multilevel data [Book review]. *Organizational Research Methods, 6*(1), 132–134.

Bliese, P., Chan, D., & Ployhart, R. (2007). Multilevel methods: Future directions in measurement, longitudinal analyses, and nonnormal outcomes. *Organizational Research Methods, 10*(4), 551–563.

Blondheim, M. (1994). *News over the wire: The telegraph and the flow of public information in America, 1844–1897.* Cambridge, MA: Harvard University Press.

Bloom, B. S. (Ed.). (1956). *Taxonomy of educational objectives: The classification of educational goals* (pp. 201–207). Chicago: Susan Fauer.

Bloom, B. S. (1965). *Taxonomy of educational objectives. Handbook II: The affective domain.* New York: David McKay.

Bloom, B. S., Engelhard, M. D., Furst, E. J., Hill, W. H., & Krathwohl, D. R. (1956). *Taxonomy of educational objectives: The classification of educational goals. Handbook I: Cognitive domain.* White Plains, NY: Longman.

Bluck, S. (2003). Autobiographical memory: Exploring its functions in everyday life. *Memory, 11,* 113–124.

Blumer, H. (1969). *Symbolic interactionism: Perspective and method.* Englewood Cliffs, NJ: Prentice Hall.

Blumler, J. G., & Gurevitch, J. (1995). *The crisis of public communication.* New York: Routledge.

Boaz, D. (1998). *The libertarian reader: Classic and contemporary writings from Lao Tzu to Milton Friedman.* New York: Free Press.

Bogaards, M. (2004). Counting parties and identifying dominant party systems in Africa. *European Journal of Political Research, 43*(2), 173–197.

Bohm, D. (1996). *On dialogue* (L. Nichols, Ed.). London: Routledge.

Bolgar, H. (1964). Karl Buhler: 1879–1963. *American Journal of Psychology, 77*(4), 674–678.

Bolman, L. G., & Deal, T. E. (1997). *Reframing organizations: Artistry, choice, and leadership* (2nd ed.). San Francisco: Jossey-Bass.

Bonger, W. (1916). *Criminality and economic conditions* (H. P. Horton, Trans.). Boston: Little, Brown. (Original work published 1905)

Bonk, C. J., & Cunningham, D. J. (1998). Searching for learner-centered, constructivist, and sociocultural components of collaborative educational learning tools. In C. J. Bonk & K. S. King (Eds.), *Electronic collaborators* (pp. 25–50). Mahwah, NJ: Lawrence Erlbaum.

Boorstin, D. (1961). *The image: A guide to pseudo-events in America.* New York: Atheneum.

Boorstin, D. (1987). *The image: A guide to pseudo-events in America* (25th anniversary ed., p. 13). New York: Vintage.

Bornstein, D. (2007). *How to change the world: Social entrepreneurs and the power of new ideas.* New York: Oxford University Press.

Bornstein, R. F. (2003). Psychodynamic models of personality. In T. Millon & M. J. Lerner (Eds.), *Handbook of psychology: Personality and social psychology* (pp. 117–134). Hoboken, NJ: Wiley.

Bouchard, T. J., Jr., Lykken, D. T., McGue, M., Segal, N., & Tellegen, A. (1990). Sources of human psychological differences: The Minnesota Study of Twins Reared Apart. *Science, 250,* 223–228.

Boucher, D., & Kelly, P. (Eds.). (2003). *Political thinkers: From Socrates to the present.* New York: Oxford University Press.

Bourdieu, P. (1983). Forms of capital. In J. C. Richards (Ed.), *Handbook of theory and research for the sociology of education* (pp. 241–258). Westport, CT: Greenwood Press.

Bourne, E. J. (2005). *The anxiety & phobia workbook* (4th ed.). Oakland, CA: New Harbinger.

Bouton, M. E. (1993). Context, time, and memory retrieval in the interference paradigms of Pavlovian learning. *Psychological Bulletin, 114*(1), 80–99.

Bouton, M. E., Mineka, S., & Barlow, D. H. (2001). A modern learning theory perspective on the etiology of panic disorder. *Psychological Review, 108,* 4–32.

Bove, P. A. (1990). Discourse. In F. Lentricchia & T. McLaughlin (Eds.), *Critical terms for literary study* (pp. 50–65). Chicago: University of Chicago Press.

Bowers v. Hardwick, 478 U.S. 186 (1986).

Bowlby, J. (2005). *The making and breaking of affectional bonds.* New York: Routledge.

Boyd v. United States, 116 U.S. 616 (1886).

Boyes, W., & Melvin, M. (2002). *Economics.* Boston: Houghton Mifflin.

Brain, C. (2002). *Advanced psychology: Applications, issues and perspectives.* Cheltenham, UK: Nelson Thornes.

Brannon, L., Tagley, M., & Eagly, A. (2007). The moderating role of attitude strength in selective exposure to information. *Journal of Experimental Social Psychology, 43*(4), 611–617.

Bransford, J. D., & Stein, B. S. (1984). *The IDEAL problem solver: A guide for improving thinking, learning, and creativity.* New York: W. H. Freeman.

Branzburg v. Hayes, 408 U.S. 665 (1972).

Brehm, J., & Gates, S. (1993). Donut shops and speed traps: Evaluating models of supervision on police behavior. *American Journal of Political Science, 37,* 555–581.

Brennan, R. L. (2001). An essay on the history and future of reliability from the perspective of replications. *Journal of Educational Measurement, 38*(4), 295–317.

Brent, J. (1997). *Applied cost-benefit analysis.* Cheltenham, UK: Edward Elgar.

Breslin, R. W. (1981). *Cross-cultural encounters: Face-to-face interaction.* New York: Pergamon Press.

Brewer, W. F., & Treyens, J. C. (1981). Role of schemata in memory for places. *Cognitive Psychology, 13*(2), 207–230.

Bridges, W. (1991). *Managing transitions.* New York: Addison-Wesley.

Brischke, J., & Loges, W. (2004). *Free press vs. fair trials: Examining publicity's role in trial outcomes.* Matwah, NJ: Lawrence Erlbaum.

Broadbent, D. (1958). *Perception and communication.* London: Pergamon Press.

Bronfenbrenner, U., & Morris, P. A. (1998). The ecology of developmental processes. In R. M. Lerner (Ed.), *Theoretical models of human development* (5th ed., Vol. 1, pp. 993–1028). New York: Wiley.

Brown, J. (1958). Some tests of the decay theory of immediate memory. *Quarterly Journal of Experimental Psychology, 10,* 12–21.

Brown, J. S., Collins, A., & Duguid, P. (1989). Situated cognition and the culture of learning. *Educational Researcher, 18*(1), 32–42.

Brown v. Board of Education of Topeka, 347 U.S. 483 (1954).

Bruce, V., & Young, A. (2000). *In the eye of the beholder: The science of face perception.* Oxford, UK: Oxford University Press.

Brunell, T. (2004, September). *The effects of primary type on competitiveness in U.S. congressional elections.* Paper presented at the meeting of the American Political Science Association, Chicago, IL. Retrieved March 21, 2008, from http://www.allacademic.com/meta/p60258_index.html

Bruner, J. S. (1957). On perceptual readiness. *Psychological Review, 64,* 123–152.

Bruner, J. S. (1961). The act of discovery. *Harvard Educational Review, 31*(1), 21–32.

Bruskin & Associates. (1973, July). *What are Americans afraid of?* (The Bruskin Report, No. 53). Edison, NJ: Author.

Bryant, A. J. (Ed.). (2007). *The children's television community.* Mahwah, NJ: Lawrence Erlbaum.

Bryk, A. S., & Raudenbush, S. W. (1992). *Hierarchical linear models: Applications and data analysis methods.* Newbury Park, CA: Sage.

Bucchi, M., & Trench, B. (2008). *Handbook of public communication of science and technology.* New York: Routledge.

Buck, C. (2006). "Never again": Kevin Gover's apology for the Bureau of Indian Affairs. *Wicazo Sa Review, 21*(1), 97–126. Retrieved May 31, 2008, from http://muse.jhu.edu.ezproxy .pratt.edu:2048/journals/wicazo_sa_review/v021/21.1buck .html

Buergenthal, T., Shelton, D., & Stewart, P. D. (2002). *International human rights in a nutshell* (Nutshell Series). St. Paul, MN: West Group.

Buford, J. A., Jr., & Lindner, J. R. (2002). *Human resource management in local government: Concepts and applications for HRM students and practitioners.* Cincinnati. OH: South-Western.

Bulik, C. M., Sullivan, P. F., Wade, T. D., & Kendler, K. S. (2000). Twin studies of eating disorders: A review. *International Journal of Eating Disorders, 27,* 1–20.

Bunyan, J. (1678). *The pilgrim's progress.* New York: Oxford University Press.

Burgee, J. (1980). Nonverbal communication research in the 1970s: An overview. In D. Nimmo, (Ed.), *Communication Yearbook,* Volume 4. New Brunswick, NJ: Transaction Books.

Burgess, G. (1992). The divine right of kings reconsidered. *The English Historical Review, 107*(425), 837–861.

Burgess, G. (1996). *Absolute monarchy and the Stuart Constitution.* New Haven: Yale University Press.

Burke, M., & Miranti, J. (1992). *Ethical and spiritual values in counseling.* Alexandria, VA: American Association for Counseling and Development.

Burke, P. (2000). *A social history of knowledge: From Gutenberg to Diderot.* Cambridge, UK: Polity.

Burleson, B. R., & Planalp, S. (2000). Producing emotion(al) messages. *Communications Theory, 10,* 221–250.

Burns, J. M. (1978). *Government by the people: National, state, and local edition.* Englewood Cliffs, NJ: Prentice Hall.

Burns, T., & Stalker, G. M. (1961). *Management of innovation.* London: Tavistock.

Burnstein, E., Crandell, C., & Kitayama, S. (1994). Some Neo-Darwinian decision rules for altruism: Weighing cues for inclusive fitness as a function of the biological importance of the decision. *Journal of Personality and Social Psychology, 67,* 773–789.

Burr, V. (2003). *Social constructionism* (2nd ed.). London: Routledge.

Burton, M., & Lombra, R. (2003). *The financial system & the economy.* Mason, OH: Thomson South-Western.

Bush v. Gore, 531 U.S. 98 (2000).

Butcher, J. N. (Ed.). (2006). *MMPI-2: A practitioner's guide.* Washington, DC: American Psychological Association.

Butler, J. (1992). Contingent foundations: Feminism and the question of "postmodernism." In J. Butler & J. W. Scott

(Eds.), *Feminists theorize the political* (pp. 3–21). New York: Routledge.

Byrd, M. R., Nelson, E. M., & Manthey, L. M. (2006). Oral-digital habits of childhood: Thumb sucking. In J. E. Fisher & W. T. O'Donohue (Eds,), *Practitioner's guide to evidence-based psychotherapy* (pp. 718–725). New York: Springer Science/Business Media.

Bystritsky, A. (2006). Treatment-resistant anxiety disorders. *Molecular Psychiatry, 11*(9), 805–814.

Cahill, S. P., & Foa, E. B. (2004). A glass half empty or half full? Where we are and directions for future research in the treatment of PTSD. In S. Taylor (Ed.), *Advances in the treatment of posttraumatic stress disorder: Cognitive-behavioral perspectives* (pp. 267–313). New York: Springer.

Cameron, J., & Pierce, W. D. (1994). Reinforcement, reward, and intrinsic motivation: A meta-analysis. *Review of Educational Research, 64*(3), 363–423.

Campbell, D., & Fiske, D. (1959). Convergent and discriminant validation by the multitrait-multimethod matrix. *Psychological Bulletin, 56,* 81–105.

Campbell, D. T. (1957). Factors relevant to the validity of experiments in social settings. *Psychological Bulletin, 54,* 546–553.

Campbell, D. T., & Stanley, J. C. (1963). Experimental and quasi-experimental designs for research on teaching. In N. L. Gage (Ed.), *Handbook of research on teaching* (pp. 171–246). Chicago: Rand McNally.

Campbell, R., Martin, C. R., & Fabos, B. (2007). *Media & culture: An introduction to mass communication* (5th ed.). Boston: Bedford/St. Martin's.

Carbaugh, D. (2005). *Cultures in conversation.* Mahwah, NJ: Ablex.

Carbaugh, R. J. (2007). *International economics* (11th ed.). Mason, OH: Thomson South-Western.

Carey, J. W. (1992). *Communication as culture: Essays on media and society* (p. 25). London: Routledge.

Carlson, N. (2007). *Foundations of physiological psychology* (7th ed.). Essex, UK: Pearson.

Carney, D., Hall, J. & LeBeau, L. (2005, Summer). Beliefs about the nonverbal expression of social power. *Journal of Nonverbal Behavior, 29*(2), 105–123. Retrieved May 23, 2008, from http://vnweb.hwwilsonweb.com.ezproxy.pratt.edu:2048/hww/results/external_link_maincontentframe.jhtml?_DARGS=/hww/results/results_common.jhtml.16

Carty, R. K., & Stewart, D. (1996). Party and party systems. In C. Dunn (Ed.), *Provinces: Canadian provincial politics* (pp. 63–94). Peterborough, Ontario, Canada: Broadview Press.

Case, K. E., & Fair, R. C. (2003). *Principles of economics.* Upper Saddle River, NJ: Prentice Hall.

CAST. (2008). *Universal design for learning guidelines* (Version 1.0). Wakefield, MA: Author.

Cater, D. (1964). *Power in Washington: A critical look at today's struggle to govern in the nation's capital.* New York: Random House.

Cattell, R. B. (1971). *Abilities: Their structure, growth, and action.* New York: Houghton Mifflin.

Cattell, R. B. (1987). *Intelligence: Its structure, growth, and action.* New York: Elsevier.

Chance, P. (2003). *Learning and behavior* (5th ed.). Toronto, Ontario, Canada: Thomson-Wadsworth.

Chance, P. L., & Chance, E. W. (2002). *Introduction to educational leadership and organizational behavior.* Larchmont, NY: Eye on Education, Inc.

Chandler, D. (2001). *Semiotics for beginners.* Retrieved March 3, 2009, from http://www.aber.ac.uk/media/Documents/S4B/sem08c.html

Chandler, D. (2007). *Semiotics: The basics.* London: Routledge.

Chemerinsky, E. (1998–1999). Substantive due process. *Touro Law Review, 15,* 1501–1534.

Chevron U.S.A., Inc. v. Natural Resources Defense Council, Inc., 467 U.S. 837 (1984).

Chilcote, R. (2000). *Theories of comparative political economy.* Boulder, CO: Westview Press.

Childs, P., & Williams, R. J. P. (1997). Said: Knowledge and power. In P. Childs & R. J. P. Williams (Eds.), *An introduction to post-colonial theory* (pp. 97–121). London: Prentice Hall.

Chisholm v. Georgia, 2 U.S. 419 (*1793*).

Chomsky, N., & Achcar, G. (2006). *Perilous power: The Middle East and U.S. foreign policy: Dialogues on terror, democracy, war and justice.* Boulder, CO: Paradigm.

Choper, J. H. (2007). Introduction. In N. Mourtada-Sabbah & B. E. Cain (Eds.), *The political question doctrine and the Supreme Court of the United States* (pp. 1–22). Lanham, MD: Lexington Books.

Christensen, L., & Karp, S. (2003). *Rethinking school reform: Views from the classroom* (pp. 275–286). Milwaukee, WI: Rethinking Schools.

Churchill, F. B. (1974). William Johannsen and the genotype concept. *Journal of the History of Biology, 7,* 5–30.

Civil law. (2006). In E. A. Martin & J. Law (Eds.), *Oxford dictionary of law.* Oxford, UK: Oxford University Press. (*Oxford reference online,* City University of New York, John Jay College of Criminal Justice. Retrieved February 10, 2008, from http://www.oxfordreference.com/views/ENTRY.html?subview=Main&entry=t49.e621

Claessens, S., Cassimon, D., & Campenhout, B. V. (2007, December). *Empirical evidence on the new international aid architecture* (International Monetary Fund WP/07/277). Retrieved March 2, 2008, from http://www.imf.org/external/pubs/ft/wp/2007/wp07277.pdf

Clanton, G. (1991). *Populism: The human preference in America 1890–1900.* New York: Twayne.

Clapham, A. (2001). Human rights. In Joel Krieger (Ed.), *The Oxford companion to the politics of the world.* Oxford, UK: Oxford University Press. (*Oxford reference online,* City University of New York, John Jay College of Criminal Justice. Retrieved 10 February, 2008, from http://www.oxfordreference.com/views/ENTRY.html?subview=Main&entry=t121.e0330

Clark, B. (2003). The supremacy clause as a constraint on federal power. *George Washington Law Review, 71*(1), 91–130.

Cleckley, H. (1941). *The mask of sanity.* St. Louis, MO: Mosby.

Cohen, J. (1988). *Statistical power analysis for the behavioral sciences* (2nd ed.). Hillsdale, NJ: Lawrence Erlbaum.

Cohen, L. E., & Felson, M. (1979). Social change and crime rate trends: A routine activity approach. *American Sociological Review, 44,* 588–605.

Cohen, S. (1988–1989). The significance of "In the Name of Civil Liberties." *Law and Philosophy, 7*(3), 375–394.

Cohen, S. (2002). *Folk devils and moral panics: The creation of mods and rockers.* London: MacGibbon & Kee. (Original work published 1972)

Cohn, M., & Dow, D. (1998). *Cameras in the courtroom: Television and the pursuit of justice.* Jefferson, NC: McFarland.

Coleman, J. C. (1988). Social capital in the creation of human capital. *American Journal of Sociology, 94,* S95–S120.

Coleman, J. C. (1990). *Foundations of social theory.* Cambridge, MA: Belknap Press.

Coleman, L. (2004). *The copycat effect: How the media and popular culture trigger the mayhem in tomorrow's headlines.* New York: Pocket Books.

Collins, A. M., & Loftus, E. F. (1975). A spreading activation theory of semantic processing. *Psychological Review, 82,* 407–428.

Collins, P. H. (1990). *Black feminist thought: Knowledge, consciousness, and the politics of empowerment.* New York: Routledge, Chapman & Hall.

Communism. (2005). In J. Scott & G. Marshall (Eds.), *A dictionary of sociology.* Oxford, UK: Oxford University Press. (*Oxford reference online,* City University of New York, John Jay College of Criminal Justice. Retrieved February 10, 2008, from http://www.oxfordreference.com/views/ ENTRY.html?subview=Main&entry=t88.e334

Compaine, B. (2002). Global media. *Foreign Policy, 133,* 20–28.

Comparative and International Education Society: http://www .cies.us

Comptroller General, Federal Appropriations Law, 5 U.S.C. § 301, Departmental regulations, I GAO-04-261SP 3-2, *et seq.* (2008b).

Comptroller General, Federal Appropriations Law, 5 U.S.C. § 804(3), I GAO-04-261SP 3-2, *et seq.* (2008c).

Comptroller General, Federal Appropriations Law, I GAO-04-261SP 3-2, *et seq.* (2008a).

Computer Laboratory. (2009). *Lexical and semantic selection.* Cambridge, UK: University of Cambridge. Retrieved March 23, 2009, from http://www.cl.cam.ac.uk/~aac10/talks-etc/scl .ppt#349,8,Semantic selection

Comstock, G. (1972). *Television and social behavior.* Rockville, MD: U.S. Department of Health, Education and Welfare, National Institute of Mental Health.

Confederation. (2006). In E. A. Martin & J. Law (Eds.), *Oxford dictionary of law.* Oxford, UK: Oxford University Press. (*Oxford reference online,* City University of New York, John Jay College of Criminal Justice. Retrieved February 10, 2008, from http://www.oxfordreference.com/views/ENTRY.html? subview=Main&entry=t49.e789

Congressional Research Service, The Library of Congress. (2005, July). *The Individuals with Disabilities Education Act (IDEA): Proposed Regulations for P.L. 108-446.* Retrieved March 30, 2008, from http://digital.library.unt.edu/govdocs/crs//data/ 2005/upl-meta-crs-6940/RL32998_2005Jul18.pdf

Constant, B. (1988). The liberty of the ancients compared with that of the moderns. In B. Fontana (Ed.), *Political writings* (pp. 310–311). Cambridge, UK: Cambridge University Press.

Constitution of the United States of America. Article 1, Section 8. Retrieved March 24, 2008, from http:// www.law.cornell.edu/constitution/constitution.overview .html

Constitution of the United States of America, analysis and interpretation: Annotations of cases decided by the Supreme Court of the United States (2002, June 28). Washington, DC: Government Printing Office. (See also the *2004 Supplement: Cases Decided to June 29, 2004, 108th Congress 2d Session* and *2006 Supplement: Cases Decided to June 29, 2006, 110th Congress 1st Session*)

Containment, strategy of. (2001). In *The Oxford essential dictionary of the U.S. military.* New York: Berkley Books. (*Oxford reference online,* City University of New York, John Jay College of Criminal Justice. Retrieved February 10, 2008, from http://www.oxfordreference.com/views/ENTRY.html? subview=Main&entry=t63.e10019

Conway, J. C., & Rubin, A. M. (1991). Psychological predictors of television viewing motivation. *Communications Research, 18,* 443.

Conway, M. A. (1990). *Autobiographical memory: An introduction.* Philadephia: Open University Press.

Conway, M. A. (1995). *Flashbulb memories.* Brighton, Sussex, UK: Erlbaum.

Conway, M. M. (2000). *Political participation in the United States.* Washington, DC: CQ Press.

Cook, N. M. (1989). The applicability of verbal mnemonics for different populations: A review. *Applied Cognitive Psychology, 31,* 3–22.

Cook, T. D., & Campbell, D. T. (1979). *Quasi-experimentation: Design and analysis issues for field settings.* Chicago: Rand McNally.

Cooke, D. J., Forth, A. E., & Hare, R. D. (Eds.). (1998). *Psychopathy: Theory, research, and implications for society.* Dordrecht, The Netherlands: Kluwer.

Cooper, D. E. (1999). *Existentialism: A reconstruction.* Oxford, UK: Blackwell.

Corkin, S. (2002). What's new with the amnesic patient H.M.? *Nature Reviews Neuroscience, 3,* 153–160.

Cornell University School of Law. (2009). *Employment discrimination: An overview.* Retrieved March 3, 2009, from http://www.law.cornell.edu/wex/index.php/Employment_ discrimination

Corrigan, T., & White, P. (2004). *The film experience: An introduction.* Boston: Bedford/St. Martin's.

Cotton, J. (1985). Cognitive dissonance in selective exposure. In D. Zillmann & J. Bryant (Eds.), *Selective exposure to communication* (pp. 11–33). Hillsdale, NJ: Lawrence Erlbaum.

Cousins, M. (2004). *The story of film.* New York: Thunder's Mouth Press.

Cozby, P. C. (2004). *Methods in behavioral research* (8th ed.). Boston: McGraw Hill.

Craig, F., & Lockhart, R. (1972). Levels of processing: A framework for memory research. *Journal of Verbal Thinking and Verbal Behavior, 11,* 671–684.

Craig, F. I. M., & Lockhart, R. S. (1972). Levels of processing: A framework for memory research. *Journal of Verbal Learning and Verbal Behaviour, 11,* 671–684.

Creswell, J. (Ed.). (2002). Ethnographic designs. In *Educational research: Planning, conducting, and evaluating qualitative research* (pp. 481–519). Upper Saddle River, NJ: Merrill Prentice Hall.

Critcher, C. (2003). *Moral panics and the media.* Philadelphia: Open University Press.

Croley, S. P. (2007). *Regulation and public interests: The possibility of good regulatory government.* Princeton, NJ: Princeton University Press.

Croteau, D. R., & Hoynes, W. (2001). *The business of media: Corporate media and the public interest.* Thousand Oaks, CA: Pine Forge Press.

Croteau, D. R., & Hoynes, W. (2005). *The business of media: Corporate media and the public interest* (2nd ed.). Thousand Oaks, CA: Pine Forge Press.

Crotty, M. (1998). *The foundations of social research: Meaning and perspective in the research process.* London: Sage.

Crowley, D., & Heyer, P. (Eds.). (2007). *Communication in history: Technology, culture, society* (5th ed.). New York: Pearson Education.

Crowley, T. (1997). *An introduction to historical linguistics.* Melbourne, Victoria, Australia: Oxford University Press.

Cruzan v. Director Missouri Department of Health, 497 U.S. 261 (1990).

Cubitt, S. (2004). *The cinema effect.* Cambridge: MIT Press.

Cumberbatch, G., & Howitt, D. (1989). *A measure of uncertainty: The effects of the mass media.* London: J. Libbey.

Cummings, T. G., & Worley, C. G. (2005). *Organization development and change* (8th ed.). Mason, OH: Thomson South-Western.

Curran, J., & Gurevitch, M. (2005). *Mass media and society* (4th ed.). London: Hodder Arnold.

Current issues in comparative education (n.d.). Retrieved April 24, 2009, from http://www.tc.columbia.edu/CICE

Cutlip, S. (1994). *The unseen power: Public relations, a history.* Hillsdale, NJ: Lawrence Erlbaum.

Dahl, R. (2000). *On democracy.* New Haven, CT: Yale University Press.

Dahl, R. (2003). Madisonian democracy. In R. Dahl, I. Shapiro, & J. Cheibub (Eds.), *The democracy sourcebook* (pp. 207–216). Cambridge: MIT Press.

Dahl, S. (2004). *Intercultural research: The current state of knowledge* (Discussion Paper). London: Middlesex University Business School.

Dallek, M., & Boyer, P. S. (2001). Affirmative action. In P. S. Boyer (Ed.), *The Oxford companion to United States history.* London: Oxford University Press. (*Oxford reference online,* City University of New York, John Jay College of Criminal Justice. Retrieved February 10, 2008, from http://www.oxford reference.com/views/ENTRY.html?subview=Main&entry=t11 9.e0020

Daniels, J. P., & Vanhoose, D. D. (2005). *International monetary and financial economics.* Mason, OH: Thomson South-Western.

Dann, P. (2006). The political institutions. In A. Von Bogdandy & J. Bast (Eds.), *Principles of European constitutional law* (pp. 229–280). Oxford, UK: Hart.

Daruna, J. H., Dalton, R., & Forman, M. A. (2000). Attention deficit hyperactivity disorder. In R. E. Behrman, R. M. Kliegman, & H. B. Jenson (Eds.), *Nelson textbook of pediatrics* (16th ed., pp. 100–103). Philadelphia: W. B. Saunders.

Darwin, C. (1965). *The expression of the emotions in man and animals.* Chicago: Univerity of Chicago Press. (Original work published 1872)

Daubert v. Merrell Dow Pharmaceutical, 509 U.S. 579 (1993).

David-Fox, M. (1999). What is cultural revolution? *Russian Review, 58*(2), 181–201.

Davidson, R. H., & Oleszek, W. J. (2006). *Congress and its members* (10th ed.). Washington, DC: CQ Press.

Davidson-Shivers, G. V., & Rasmussen, K. L. (2006). *Web-based learning: Design, implementation, and evaluation.* Upper Saddle River, NJ: Prentice Hall.

Dawes, R. M., Faust, D., & Meehl, P. E. (1989). Clinical versus actuarial judgment. *Science, 243,* 1668–1674.

Deal, T. E., & Kennedy, A. A. (1982). *Corporate cultures: The rites and rituals of corporate life.* Harmondsworth, UK: Penguin Books.

DeFleur, M. L. (1970). *Theories of mass communication.* New York: David McKay Company.

Delisle, J. (1996). Multiple intelligences: Convenient, simple, wrong. *Gifted Child Today, 19*(6), 12–13.

Denhardt, R. B., & Denhardt, J. V. (2006). *Public administration: An action orientation* (5th ed.). New York: Pearson Longman.

Denzin, N. K. (1997). *Interpretive ethnography: Ethnographic practices for the 21st century.* Thousand Oaks, CA: Sage.

Department of Defense dictionary of military and associated terms (JP 1–02).

Department of Health and Human Services, Centers for Medicare & Medicaid Services. (n.d.). *Glossary.* Retrieved April 20, 2009, from http://www.cms.hhs.gov/apps/glossary

Department of Justice v. Reporters Committee for Freedom of the Press, 489 U.S. 749 (1989).

Dequech, D. (2001). Bounded rationality, institutions, and uncertainty. *Journal of Economic Issues, 35*(4), 911–924.

Derakshan, N., & Eysenck, M. W. (1997). Repression and repressors: Theoretical and experimental approaches. *European Psychologist, 2*(3), 235–246.

Deregowski, J. B. (1989). Real space and represented space: Cross-cultural perspectives. *Brain and Behavioral Sciences, 12,* 51–119.

Derrida, J. (1980). Structure, sign, and play in the discourse of the human sciences. In *Writing and difference* (A. Bass, Trans., pp. 278–294). Chicago: University of Chicago Press.

DeVon, H. A., Block, M. E., & Moyle-Wright, P. A. (2007). A psychometric toolbox for testing validity and reliability. *Journal of Nursing Scholarship, 39*(2), 155–164.

Dewey, J. (1910). *How we think.* Boston: D. C. Heath.

Dewey, J. (1916). *Democracy and education: An introduction to the philosophy of education.* New York: Macmillan.

Dewey, J. (1997). *Democracy and education.* New York: Free Press. (Original work published 1916)

Diamond, J. (1999). *Guns, germs, and steel: The fates of human societies.* New York: W. W. Norton.

Dick, W., Carey, L., & Carey, L. (2005). *The systematic design of instruction* (6th ed.). Boston: Allyn & Bacon.

Dillard, J. P., & Pfau, M. (2002). *The persuasion handbook: Developments in theory and practice.* Thousand Oaks, CA: Sage.

Douglas, A. J. (2000). *Behind the ballot box: A citizen's guide to voting systems.* Westport, CT: Greenwood Press.

Douglas, M. (1966). *Purity and danger: An analysis of concepts of pollution and taboo.* London: Routledge & Kegan Paul.

Dovidio, J. F., & Penner, L. A. (2001). Helping and altruism. In M. Brewer & M. Hewstone (Eds.), *Blackwell international handbook of social psychology: Interpersonal processes* (pp. 162–195). Cambridge, MA: Blackwell.

Dred Scott v. Sandford, 60 U.S. 393 (1856).

Drucker, P. (1954). *The practice of management.* New York: Harper & Row.

Drummond, L. (1981). The serpent's children: Semiotics of cultural genesis in Arawak and Trobriand myth. *American Ethnologist, 8*(3), 633–660.

Drummond, M. F., O'Brien, B., Stoddart, G. L., & Torrance, G. W. (1997). *Methods for the economic evaluation of health care programmes* (2nd ed.). Oxford, UK: Oxford University Press.

DuBois, E. C. (2001). *Equal rights amendment: The Oxford companion to United States history* (P. S. Boyer, Ed.). Oxford, UK: Oxford University Press. (*Oxford reference online,* City University of New York, John Jay College of Criminal Justice. Retrieved February 10, 2008, from http://www.oxfordreference.com/views/ENTRY.html?subview=Main&entry=t119.e0485

Duchenne, G. G. (1990). *The mechanism of human facial expression.* Cambridge, UK: Cambridge University Press. (Original work published 1867)

Dunkley, G. (2004). *Free trade.* New York: Zed Books.

Durkheim, É. (1977). *The division of labor in society.* New York: Free Press. (Original work published 1893)

Durkheim, É. (1997). *Suicide* (G. Simpson, Ed., J. A. Spaulding, Trans.). New York: Free Press. (Original work published 1897)

Durkheim, É. (2001). *Elementary forms of religious life* (C. Cosman, Trans.). New York: Oxford University Press.

Dusky v. United States 362 U.S. 402 (1960).

Dworkin, G. (1972). Paternalism. *The Monist, 56,* 63–84.

Dyson, P. (1999). *Dictionary of networking.* Hoboken, NJ: Wiley.

Eagleton, T. (1991). *Ideology: An introduction.* London: Verso.

ED.gov. (2008). *Civil rights: Sex discrimination.* Washington, DC: U.S. Department of Education. Retrieved October 1, 2008, from http://www.ed.gov/policy/rights/guid/ocr/sex.html www.ed.gov/policy/rights/guid/ocr/sex.html

Edmonds, R. (1979). Effective schools for the urban poor. *Educational Leadership, 37*(1), 15–24.

Efron, B., & Morris, C. (1977). Stein's paradox in statistics. *Scientific American, 236,* 119–127.

Ehrhardt, M. C., & Brigham, E. F. (2003). *Corporate finance: A focused approach.* Mason, OH: Thomson South-Western.

Eisenberg, E., & Witten, M. (1987, July). Reconsidering openness in organizational communication. *Academy of Management Review, 12*(3), 418–426.

Eisenberg, N. (1989). The development of prosocial and aggressive behavior. In M. H. Bornstein & M. E. Lamb (Eds.), *Social, emotional and personality development* (pp. 461–486). Hillsdale, NJ: Lawrence Erlbaum.

Elazar, D. J. (1991). *Federal systems of the world: A handbook of federal, confederal and autonomy arrangements.* Essex, UK: Longman.

Elkins, S. & E. McKitrick, E. (1993). *The age of Federalism, 1788–1800.* New York: Oxford University Press.

Ellis, A., & Dryden, W. (1997). *The practice of rational emotive behavior therapy* (2nd ed.). New York: Springer.

Ellis, A., & Springer, W. (2007). *The practice of rational emotive theory* (2nd ed.). New York: Springer.

Elster, J., & Slagstad, R. (1993). *Constitutionalism and democracy.* Cambridge, UK: Cambridge University Press.

Emery, D. R., Finnerty, J. D., & Stowe, J. D. (2004). *Corporate financial management.* Upper Saddle River, NJ: Pearson/Prentice Hall.

Endersby, J. W., & Krieckhaus, J. T. (2008). Turnout around the globe: The influence of electoral institutions on national voter participation, 1972–2000. *Electoral Studies, 27,* 601–610.

Engels, F. (1989). *Socialism: Utopian and scientific.* New York: International Publishers.

Engels, F., Moore, A., & Marx, K. (1970). *Socialism: Utopian and scientific.* Moscow: Progress.

Enzensberger, H. M. (2000). Constituents of a theory of the media. In P. Marris & S. Thornham (Eds.), *Media studies: A reader* (2nd ed., pp. 68–91). New York: New York University Press.

Epstein, R. (2003). *The pocket guide to critical thinking* (2nd ed.). Toronto, Ontario, Canada: Wadsworth.

ERIC: http://www.eric.ed.gov

Ericson, R. V., Baranek, P., & Chan, J. B. L. (1987). *Visualizing deviance: A study of the news organization.* Toronto, Ontario, Canada: University of Toronto Press.

Erikson, R. S., & Wright, G. C. (2001). Voters, candidates, and issues in congressional elections. In L. C. Dodd & B. I. Oppenheimer (Eds.), *Congress reconsidered* (pp. 67–92). Washington, DC: CQ Press.

Etzioni, A. (1961). *A comparative analysis of complex organizations: On power, involvement, and their correlates.* New York: Free Press.

Evans, G., & Newnham, J. (1992). *The dictionary of world politics: A reference guide to concepts, ideas and institutions.* New York: Simon & Schuster.

Ewen, E., & Ewen, S. (2006). *Typecasting: On the arts and sciences of human inequality.* New York: Seven Stories Press.

Ewen, S. (1996). *PR! A social history of spin.* New York: Basic Books.

Exec. Order No. 13,132, Federalism (Aug. 4, 1999), 64 Fed. Reg. 43,255 (Aug. 10, 1999).

Exner, J. E., Jr. (2003). *The Rorschach: A comprehensive system* (4th ed.). Hoboken, NJ: Wiley.

Eysenck, H. J., & Nias, D. K. B. (1978). *Sex, violence, and the media.* London: Temple Smith.

Fagan, T. K., & Wise, P. S. (2007). *School psychology: Past, present, and future* (3rd ed.). New York: National Association of School Psychologists.

Fama, E. F., Fisher, L., Jensen, M. C., & Roll, R. (1969). The adjustment of stock prices to new information. *International Economic Review, 10*(1), 1–21.

Farley, J. (2005). *Majority-minority relations* (5th ed.). Upper Saddle River, NJ: Prentice Hall.

Fast, J. (1971). *Body language.* New York: Penguin Books.

Fasulo, L. (2005). *An insider's guide to the UN.* New Haven, CT: Yale University Press.

Faust, J., Olson, R., & Rodriguez, H. (1991). Same-day surgery preparation: Reduction of pediatric patient arousal and distress through participant modeling. *Journal of Consulting and Clinical Psychology, 59,* 475–478.

Febvre, L., & Martin, H. J. (1997). *The coming of the book* (D. Gerard, Trans.). New York: Verso.

Federal Emergency Management Agency. (2009). *National Incident Management System (NIMS) basic guidance for public information officers (PIOs)* (FEMA 517). Washington, DC: Author. Retrieved March 7, 2009, from http://www.fema.gov/library/viewRecord.do?id=3095

Federal Judicial Center. (2001). *Effective use of courtroom technology: A judge's guide to pretrial and trial.* South Bend, IN: National Institute for Trial Advocacy.

Fenwick, C. G. (1938). Canada and the Monroe Doctrine. *American Journal of International Law, 32*(4), 782–785.

Ferster, C. B., & Skinner, B. F. (1957). *Schedules of reinforcement.* New York: Appleton-Century-Crofts.

Feshbach, S. (1961). The stimulating versus cathartic effects of a vicarious aggressive activity. *Journal of Abnormal and Social Psychology, 63,* 381–385.

Festinger, L. (1950). Informal social communication. *Psychological Review, 57,* 271–282.

Festinger, L. A. (1956). *When prophecy fails: A social and psychological study of a modern group that predicted the destruction of the world.* New York: Harper-Torchbooks.

Festinger, L. A. (1957). *A theory of cognitive dissonance.* Evanston, IL: Row, Peterson.

Fetterman, D. (1997). *Ethnography: Step by step.* Thousand Oaks, CA: Sage.

Field, B. C., & Field, M. K. (2006). *Environmental economics.* New York: McGraw-Hill.

Finer, H. (1972). Administrative responsibility in democratic government. In F. E. Rourke (Ed.), *Bureaucratic power in national politics* (3rd ed., pp. 326–337). Boston: Little Brown. (Original work published 1941)

Firth, J. R. (1957). *Papers in linguistics.* London: Oxford.

Fischhoff, B., & Beyth, R. (1975). I knew it would happen: Remembered probabilities of once-future things. *Organizational Behavior and Human Performance, 13,* 1–16.

Fisher, B. A. (1970). Decision emergence: Phrases in group decision making. *Speech Monographs, 47,* 53–66.

Fishman, M., & Cavender, G. (Eds.). (1998). *Entertaining crime: Television reality programs.* New York: Aldine de Gruyter.

Fitts, P. M. (1964). Perceptual motor skill learning. In A. W. Melton (Ed.), *Categories of human learning* (pp. 243–285). New York: Academic Press.

Flanagin, A. J., & Metzger, M. J. (2007). The role of site features, user attributes, and information verification behaviors on the perceived credibility of Web-based information. *New Media & Society, 9*(2), 319–342.

Flathman, M. (1999). Trauma and delayed memory: A review of the "repressed memories" literature. *Journal of Child Sexual Abuse, 8*(2), 1–23.

Fletcher v. Peck, 10 U.S. 87 (1810).

Flor, H., Birbaumer, N., Hermann, C., Ziegler, S., & Patrick, C. (2002). Aversive Pavlovian conditioning in psychopaths: Peripheral and central correlates. *Psychophysiology, 39,* 505–518.

Flynn John J. v. Cmsnr IRS, No. 00-1457a (D.C. Cir., 2001).

Foley, J. P. (Ed.). (1900). *The Jeffersonian cyclopedia: A comprehensive collection of the views of Thomas Jefferson.* New York: Funk & Wagnalls.

Folsom, R. H., Gordon, M. W., & Spanogle, J. A. (2004). *International trade and economic relations.* St. Paul, MN: Thomson-West.

Fonagy, P., & Target, M. (2003). *Psychoanalytic theories: Perspectives from developmental psychopathology.* London: Whurr.

Foot, D., & Stoffman, D. (1999). *Boom, bust and echo 2000: Profiting from the demographic shift in the new millennium.* Toronto, Ontario, Canada: MacFarlane Walter & Ross.

Fordham, B. (2004). A very sharp sword: The influence of military capabilities on American decisions to use force. *Journal of Conflict Resolution, 48*(5), 632–656.

Fortier, M. (1998). Equity and ideas: Coke, Ellesmere, and James I. *Renaissance Quarterly, 51*(4), 1255–1281.

Foster, J. B. (2006). *Naked imperialism: America's pursuit of global hegemony.* New York: Monthly Review Press.

Foster, R. (2004). *Police technology.* Upper Saddle River, NJ: Pearson/Prentice Hall.

Foucault, M. (1977). *Discipline and punish: The birth of the prison.* New York: Vintage Books.

Foucault, M. (1978). Method. In M. Foucault (Ed.), R. Hurley (Trans.), *The history of sexuality: Volume 1. An introduction* (pp. 92–102). New York: Vintage Books.

Fournier, D. M. (Ed.). (1995). *Reasoning in evaluation: Inferential links and leaps* (New Directions for Program Evaluation, No. 68). San Francisco: Jossey-Bass.

Fowler, F. (2004). *Education policy studies for educational leaders* (2nd ed.). Boston: Pearson.

Fowles, J. (1999). *The case for television violence.* Thousand Oaks, CA: Sage.

Frederickson, H. G., & Smith, K. B. (2003). *Public administration theory primer.* Boulder, CO: Westview Press.

Fredrich, C. J., & Brzezinski, Z. K. (1965). *Totalitarian dictatorship and autocracy* (2nd ed.). Cambridge, MA: Harvard University Press.

Freeburn, R. (1994). Speaking in public, part 1: Stand, speak, point and make them listen. *Executive Journal, 7*(4), 31–32.

French, J., & Raven, B. (1959). The bases of social power. In D. Cartwright (Ed.), *Studies in social power* (pp. 150–167). Ann Arbor, MI: Institute for Social Research.

Freud, A. (1937). *The ego and the mechanisms of defense.* London: Hogarth Press.

Freud, S. (1923). *The ego and the id.* New York: W. W. Norton.

Freud, S. (1940). *An outline of psychoanalysis* (The Standard Edition of the Complete Psychological Works of Sigmund Freud, Vol. 23). London: Hogarth.

Freud, S. (1957). Repression. In *The complete psychological works of Sigmund Freud* (J. Strachey, Trans.). London: Hogarth. (Original work published 1915)

Freud, S. (1966). *Introductory lectures on psycho-analysis.* New York: W. W. Norton.

Freud, S. (2000a). *The ego and the id and other works* (The Standard Edition of the Complete Psychological Works of Sigmund Freud, J. Strachey, Ed., Vol. 19 [1923–1925], pp. 1–66). New York: W. W. Norton. (Original work published 1923)

Freud, S. (2000b). *The interpretation of dreams* (The Standard Edition of the Complete Works of Sigmund Freud, Vols. 4 and 5, J. Strachey, Ed.). London: Hogarth.

Friedman, M. (1957). *A theory of the consumption function.* Princeton, NJ: Princeton University Press.

Friedman, M., & Rosenman, R. H. (1959). Association of specific overt behavior pattern with blood and cardiovascular findings: Blood cholesterol level, blood clotting time, incidence of arcus senilis, and clinical coronary artery disease. *Journal of the American Medical Association, 169*(12), 1286–1296.

Friedman, T. L. (2006). *The world is flat.* Union Square West, NY: Farrar, Strauss & Giroux.

Friedrich, C. J. (1978). Public policy and the nature of administrative responsibility. In F. E. Rourke (Ed.), *Bureaucratic power in national politics* (3rd ed., pp. 316–326). Boston: Little Brown. (Original work published 1941)

Frisch, M., & Ashbrook, J. M. (1992). *The Hamilton-Madison-Jefferson triangle.* Ashland, OH: Ashbrook Press.

Frye v. US, 293 F. 1013 (D.C. Cir. 1923).

Fuchs, C., & Collier, J. (2007). A dynamic systems view of economic and political theory. *Theoria: A Journal of Social & Political Theory, 113,* 23–52.

Fuguitt, D., & Wilcox, S. (1999). *Cost benefit analysis for public sector decision makers.* Westport, CT: Quorum Books.

Fullinwider, R. K. (1980). *The reverse discrimination controversy.* Totowa, NJ: Rowman & Littlefield.

Furman v. Georgia, 408 U.S. 238 (1972).

Furr, R. M., & Funder, D. C. (2007). Behavioral observation. In R. Robins, C. Fraley, & R. Krueger (Eds.), *Handbook of research methods in personality psychology.* New York: Guilford Press.

Fusfeld, D. (1999). *The age of the economist.* New York: Addison-Wesley Longman.

Gagné, R. M. (1977). *The conditions of learning* (3rd ed.). New York: Holt, Rinehart & Winston.

Galbraith, J. R. (1977). *Organization design.* Reading, MA: Addison-Wesley.

Gale, A. (Ed.). (1998). *The polygraph test: Lies, truth, and science.* London: Sage.

Gallois, C. (2003). Reconciliation through communication in intercultural encounters: Potential or peril? (Abstract). *Journal of Communication, 53*(1), 5–15.

Gallup. (2008). Do Muslims want democracy and theocracy? In *Who speaks for Islam?* Retrieved July 17, 2008, from http://www.gallup.com/poll/104731/Muslims-Want-Democracy-Theocracy.aspx

Gardner, H. (1983). *Frames of mind: The theory of multiple intelligences.* New York: Basic Books.

Gardner, H. (1999). *Intelligence reframed: Multiple intelligences for the 21st century.* New York: Basic Books.

Gazzangia, M. S. (2004). *The cognitive neurosciences III* (3rd ed.). Cambridge: MIT Press.

Geertz, C. (1966a). Religion as a cultural system. In M. P. Banton (ed.), *Anthropological approaches to the study of religion* (pp. 1–46). New York: Frederick A. Praeger Press.

Geertz, C. (1966b). *The interpretation of cultures.* New York: Basic Books.

Gelfand, S. A. (2004). *Hearing: An introduction to psychological and physiological acoustics* (4th ed.). New York: Informa Healthcare.

Gelman, A. (2006). Multilevel (hierarchical) modeling: What it can and cannot do. *Technometrics, 48*(3), 432–435.

Gelman, A., & Hill, J. (2006). *Data analysis using regression and multilevel/hierarchical models.* New York: Cambridge University Press.

George, F. K. (1947). The sources of Soviet conduct. *Foreign Affairs, 25,* 566–582.

Gerbner, G., & Gross, L. (1976). Living with television: The violence profile. *Journal of Communication, 26,* 172–194.

Gerbner, G., Gross, L., Morgan, M., & Signorelli, N. (1980). The mainstreaming of America: Violence profile no. 11. *Journal of Communication, 30,* 10–29.

Gerbner, G., Mowlana, H., & Nordenstreng, K. (Eds.). (1993). *The global media debate: Its rise, fall, and renewal* (The Communication and Information Science Series). Norwood, NJ: Ablex.

Giannelli, P. (1983). Chain of custody and the handling of real evidence. *American Criminal Law Review, 20*(4), 527.

Gibb, J. (1961). Defensive communication [Electronic version]. *Journal of Communication, 11*(3), 141–148. Retrieved March 6, 2009, from http://www.healthy.net/scr/Article.asp?Id=2533&xcntr=5

Gibson, E. J., & Pick, A. D. (2000). *An ecological approach to perceptual learning and development.* New York: Oxford University Press.

Gibson, J. J. (1979). *The ecological approach to visual perception.* Boston: Houghton Mifflin.

Gibson, J. J. (1987). *The ecological approach to visual perception* (New ed.). Hillsdale, NJ: Lawrence Erlbaum.

Gibson, J. J., & Gibson, E. (1955). Perceptual learning: Differentiation or enrichment? *Psychological Review, 62,* 32–41.

Gideon v. Wainwright, 372 U.S. 335 (1961).

Gigerenzer, G., Todd, P. M., & the ABC Research Group (Eds.). (1999). *Simple heuristics that make us smart.* London: Oxford University Press.

Giles, H., Fortman, J., Dailey, R., Barker, V. Hajek, C., Chernikoff, M., et al. (2005). Communication accommodation: Law enforcement and the public. In R. M. Dailey & B. A. Le Poire (Eds.), *Applied research in interpersonal communication: Family communication, health communication and communicating across social boundaries* (pp. 241–269). New York: Peter Lang.

Gill, M., & Spriggs, A. (2005). *Assessing the impact of CCTV.* London: Home Office Research, Development and Statistics Directorate. Retrieved March 21, 2009, from http://www.homeoffice.gov.uk/rds/pdfs05/hors292.pdf

Gillespie, R. (1991). *Manufacturing knowledge: A history of the Hawthorne Experiments.* Cambridge, UK: Cambridge University Press.

Gilligan, C. (1977). In a different voice: Women's conception of the self and morality. *Harvard Education Review, 47,* 481–517.

Ginott, H. G. (1995). *Teacher and child: A book for parents and teachers.* New York: Collier.

Ginsberg, A. (1995). *Howl* (B. Miller, Ed.). New York: Harper Perennial. (Original work published 1956)

Gitlin, M. J. (1996). *The psychotherapist's guide to psychopharmacology* (2nd. ed.). Englewood Cliffs, NJ: Prentice Hall.

Gitman, L. J., Smart, S. B., & Megginson, S. L. (2007). *Corporate finance.* Mason, OH: Thomson South-Western.

Glass v. Ickes, 117 F.2d 273 (D.C. Cir. 1940).

Glasser, T., & Salmon, C. (Eds.). (1995). *Public opinion and the communication of consent.* New York: Guilford Press.

Glasser, W. (1984). *Take effective control of your life.* New York: Harper & Row.

Gleaves, D. H., May, M. C., & Cardena, E. (2001). An examination of the diagnostic validity of dissociative identity disorder. *Clinical Psychology Review, 21,* 577–608.

Goldberg, V. (1993). *The power of photography: How photographs changed our lives.* New York: Abbeville.

Goleman, D. (1995). *Emotional intelligence: Why it can matter more than IQ.* New York: Bantam Books.

Golish, T. (1999). Students' use of compliance-gaining strategies with graduate teaching assistants: Examining the other end of the power spectrum. *Communication Quarterly, 47*(1), 12–32. Retrieved May 24, 2008, from http://web.ebscohost.com.proxy.libraries.rutgers.edu/ehost/pdf?vid=3&hid=109&sid=f417548c-41f0–4e1c-863b-5535c6f941f2%40sessionmgr102

Gomez, J. (2008). *Print is dead: Books in our digital age.* New York: Macmillan.

Goode, E., & Ben-Yehuda, N. (1994). *Moral panics: The social construction of deviance.* Cambridge, MA: Blackwell.

Gordon, M. (1964). *Assimilation in American life: The roles of race, religion and national origins.* Oxford, UK: Oxford University Press.

Gordon, T. (2000). *Parent effectiveness training: The proven program for raising responsible children.* New York: Three Rivers Press.

Goris, J. (2007). Effects of satisfaction with communication on the relationship between individual-job congruence and job performance/satisfaction. *Journal of Management Development, 26*(8), 735–752. Retrieved June 12, 2008, from http://web.ebscohost.com.proxy.libraries.rutgers.edu/ehost/results?vid=9&hid=108&sid=e4030d5c-1943–41c2-a9a2–0cd8fd7b2544%40sessionmgr103

Goris, J., Vaught, B., & Pettit, J. (2000). Effects of communication direction on job performance and satisfaction: A moderated regression analysis. *Journal of Business Communication, 37*(4), 348–368.

Gorman, J. M. (2003). Treating generalized anxiety disorder. *Journal of Clinical Psychiatry, 64,* 24–29.

Gorman, L., & McLean, D. (2003). *Media and society in the twentieth century: A historical introduction.* Malden, MA: Blackwell.

Gortner, H. F., Mahler, J., & Nicholson, J. B. (1989). *Organization theory: A public perspective.* Belmont, CA: Wadsworth.

Goss, B. (1982). *Processing communication: Information processing in intrapersonal communication.* Florence, KY: Wadsworth.

Gould, S. J. (1979). *Ever since Darwin.* New York: W.W. Norton.

Graber, D. A. (1980). *Crime news and the public.* New York: Praeger.

Graber, D. A. (2003). *The power of communication: Managing information in public organizations.* Washington, DC: CQ Press.

Graham, P. (Ed.). (1995). *Mary Parker Follett: Prophet of management.* Boston: Harvard Business School Press.

Grant, R. W., & Keohane, R. O. (2005). Accountability and abuse of power in world politics. *American Political Science Review, 99*(1), 29–43.

Grant, W. (2003). Confederation. In I. McLean & A. McMillan (Eds.), *The concise Oxford dictionary of politics.* Oxford, UK: Oxford University Press. (*Oxford reference online,* City University of New York, John Jay College of Criminal Justice. Retrieved February 10, 2008, from http://www.oxfordreference.com/views/ENTRY.html?subview=Main&entry=t86.e262

Greco, A. N. (Ed.). (2000). *The media and entertainment industries.* Needham Heights, MA: Allyn & Bacon.

Greeno, J. G., & Simon, H. A. (1988). Problem solving and reasoning. In R. C. Atkinson, R. J. Herrnstein, G. Lindzey, & R. D. Luce (Eds.), *Stevens' handbook of experimental psychology: Vol. 2. Learning and cognition* (2nd ed., pp. 589–672). Oxford, UK: Wiley.

Greenspan, A. (2007). *The age of turbulence.* New York: Penguin Press.

Greenwald, A. G., McGhee, D. E., & Schwartz, J. L. K. (1998). Measuring individual differences in implicit cognition: The Implicit Association Test. *Journal of Personality and Social Psychology, 74,* 1464–1480.

Gregg v. Georgia, 428 U.S. 153 (1976).

Gregory, I. (2003). *Ethics in research.* New York: Continuum International.

Grice, H. P. (1989). *Studies in the way of words.* Cambridge, MA: Harvard University Press.

Griffin, E. (2006). *A first look at communication theory* (6th ed.). New York: McGraw-Hill.

Grindstaff, L., & Turow, J. (2006). Video cultures: Television sociology in the "New TV" age. *Annual Review of Sociology, 32,* 103–125.

Griswold v. Connecticut, 381 U.S. 479 (1965).

Grover, S. (2008). *Managing the public sector* (8th ed.). Belmont, CA: Thompson/Wadsworth.

Gruber, H. E., & Vonèche, J. J. (Eds.). (1977). *The essential Piaget* (H. E. Gruber & J. J. Vonèche, Eds.). New York: Basic Books.

Gruber, J. (1987). *Controlling bureaucracies: Dilemmas in democratic governance.* Berkeley: University of California Press.

Grunig, J. (1992). *Excellence in public relations and communication management* (p. 71). Hillsdale, NJ: Lawrence Erlbaum.

Gujarati, D. N. (2006). *Essentials of econometrics.* New York: McGraw-Hill.

Gumbrecht, H. U., & Pfeiffer, K. L. (Eds.). (1994). *Materialities of communication* (Writing Science). Stanford, CA: Stanford University Press.

Gunderson, J. G. (2001). *Borderline personality disorder: A clinical guide.* Washington, DC: American Psychiatric Press.

Gustafson, K. L., & Branch, R. M. (2002). What is instructional technology? In R. A. Reiser & J. A. Dempsey (Eds.), *Trends and issues in instructional design and technology* (pp. 16–25). Upper Saddle River, NJ: Prentice Hall.

Gutek, G. (2006). *American education in a global society: International and comparative perspectives* (2nd ed.). Long Grove, IL: Waveland Press.

Gylfason, T. (1999). *Principles of economic growth.* New York: Oxford University Press.

Haase, P., & Stojanovic, L. (2005). *Lecture notes in computer science.* Berlin, Germany: Springer.

Haberfeld, M. R. (2005). *Police leadership.* Upper Saddle River, NJ: Prentice Hall.

Habermas, J. (1989). *The structural transformation of the public sphere: An inquiry into a category of bourgeois society.* Cambridge: MIT Press. (Original work published 1962)

Hackett, R., & Carroll, W. (2006). *Remaking media: The struggle to democratize public communication.* New York: Routledge.

Hackman, J. R. (1977). Work design. In J. R. Hackman & J. L. Suttle (Eds.). *Improving life at work: Behavioral science approaches to organizational change* (pp. 128–129). Santa Monica, CA: Goodyear.

Hackman, J. R., & Oldham, G. R. (1976). Motivation through the design of work: Test of a theory. *Organizational Behavior and Human Performance, 16,* 250–279.

Hafner, K., & Lyon, M. (1998). *Where wizards stay up late: The origins of the Internet.* New York: Simon & Schuster.

Hall, E., & Hall, M. (1990). *Understanding cultural differences* (pp. 6–7, 13–16). Yarmouth, ME: Intercultural Press.

Hall, E. T. (1966). *The hidden dimension.* Garden City, NY: Doubleday

Hall, E. T. (1976). *Beyond culture.* New York: Doubleday.

Hall, R. E., & Lieberman, M. (2005). *Macro economics: Principles and applications.* Mason, OH: Thomson South-Western.

Hamilton, A. (1788, March 21). The same subject continued, and re-eligibility of the executive considered from the New York packet. In *The Federalist papers* (No. 72). Retrieved March 5, 2009, from http://avalon.law.yale.edu/18th_century/fed72.asp

Hanifan, L. J. (1916). The rural school community center. *Annals of the American Academy of Political and Social Science, 67,* 130–138.

Harbutt, F. (2001). Containment. In P. S. Boyer (Ed.), *The Oxford companion to United States history.* Oxford, UK: Oxford University Press. (*Oxford reference online,* City University of New York, John Jay College of Criminal Justice. Retrieved February 10, 2008, from http://www.oxfordreference.com/views/ENTRY.html?subview=Main&entry=t119.e0354

Hartz, L. (1955). *The liberal tradition of America.* New York: Harcourt.

Hartz, L. (1964). *The founding of new societies: Studies in the history of the U.S., Latin America, South Africa, Canada, and Australia.* New York: Harcourt.

Harding, S. (1991). *Whose science? Whose knowledge?: Thinking from women's lives.* Ithaca, NY: Cornell University Press.

Hare, I. (2004). Defining social work for the 21st century. *International Social Work, 47*(3), 407–424.

Hare, R. (2003). *Psychopathy checklist-revised* (2nd ed.). Toronto, Ontario, Canada: Multi-Health Systems.

Harrington, A. (Ed.). (1997). *The placebo effect: An interdisciplinary exploration.* Cambridge, MA: Harvard University Press.

Harris, S. (2006). *Best practices of award-winning secondary school principals.* Thousand Oaks, CA: Corwin Press.

Harris, T. (1969). *I'm OK, you're OK: A practical guide to transactional analysis.* New York: Harper & Row.

Harrow, A. J. (1972). *A taxonomy of the psychomotor domain: A guide for developing behavioral objectives.* White Plains, NY: Longman.

Hart, J. (1987). *The presidential branch.* New York: Pergamon Press.

Hart, V., & Stimson, S. (1993). *Writing a national identity: Political, economic and cultural perspectives on the written constitution.* Manchester, UK: Manchester University Press.

Hayek, F. von. (1944). *The road to serfdom.* London: Routledge.

Healy, A. F., Havas, D. A., & Parker, J. T. (2000). Comparing serial position effects in semantic and episodic memory using reconstruction of order tasks. *Journal of Memory and Language, 42,* 147–167.

Hearold, S. (1986). A synthesis of 1,043 effects of television on social behavior. In G. Comstock (Ed.), *Public communication and behavior* (Vol. 1, pp. 66–135). New York: Academic Press.

Heath, R. L. (Ed.). (2005). *Encyclopedia of public relations.* Thousand Oaks, CA: Sage.

Heclo, H. (1978). Issue networks and the executive establishment. In A. King (Ed.), *The new American political system.* Washington, DC: American Enterprise Institute.

Heller, M. (2006). New ICTs and the problem of "publicness." *European Journal of Communication, 21,* 311–329.

Herbert, S. A. (1959). Theories of decision making in economics and behavioral science. *American Economic Review, 49,* 253–283.

Herman, E., & Chomsky, N. (1988). *Manufacturing consent: The political economy of the mass media.* New York: Pantheon.

Herman, E. S. (1996). The propaganda model revisited. *Monthly Review, 48*(3), 115–128.

Herman, E. S., & McChesney, R. W. (1997). *The global media: The new missionaries of corporate capitalism.* London: Cassell.

Herzberg, F. I., Mausner, B., & Snyderman, B. (1959). *The motivation to work* (2nd ed.). New York: Wiley.

Herzog, D. B., Dorer, D. J., Keel, P. K., Selwyn, S. E., Ekeblad, E. R., Flores, A. T., et al. (1999). Recovery and relapse in anorexia and bulimia nervosa: A 7.5-year follow-up study. *Journal of the American Academy of Child and Adolescent Psychiatry, 38,* 829–837.

Heyne, P. T., Boettke, P. J., & Prychitko, D. L. (2002). *The economic way of thinking* (10th ed). Upper Saddle River, NJ: Prentice Hall.

Higgins, E. T. (1987). Self-discrepancy: A theory relating self and affect. *Psychological Review, 94*(3), 319–340.

Hilgert, R. (1964). Modern organization theory and business management thought. *American Behavioral Scientist, 8*(25), 25–29.

Hiller, J. B., Rosenthal, R., Bronstein, R. F., Berry, D. T. R., & Brunell-Neuleib, S. (1999). A comparative meta-analysis of Rorschach and MMPI validity. *Psychological Assessment, 11,* 278–296.

Hilmes, M. (2007). *Only connect: A cultural history of broadcasting in the United States.* Belmont, CA: Wadsworth.

Hirokawa, R. (1983). Group communication and problem-solving effectiveness: An investigation of group phases [Electronic version]. *Human Communication Research, 9*(4), 291–305. Retrieved April 6, 2009, from http://pao.chadwyck.com.proxy.libraries.rutgers.edu/articles/displayItem.do?

Hirschi, T. (1969). *Causes of delinquency.* Berkeley: University of California Press.

Hirschman, A. O. (1970). *Exit, voice and loyalty: Responses to decline in firms, organizations, and states.* Cambridge, MA: Harvard University Press.

Hirschmann, N., & Di Stefano, C. (1996). (Eds.). *Revisioning the political: Feminist reconstructions of traditional concepts in Western political theory.* Boulder, CO: Westview Press.

Hobson, J. A., & McCarley, R. W. (1977). The brain as a dream state generator: An activation synthesis hypothesis of the dream process. *American Journal of Psychiatry, 132,* 1335–1348.

Hoem, J. (July 2006). Openness in communication [Electronic version]. *First Monday, 11*(7). Retrieved November 3, 2008, from http://firstmonday.org/issues/issue11_7/hoem/index.html

Hoffman, B. (1998). *Inside terrorism.* New York: Columbia University Press.

Hoffman, M. L. (1970). *Moral development: Carmichael's manual of child psychology* (Vol. 2, 3rd ed.). New York: Wiley.

Hofstede, G. (1980). *Culture's consequences: International differences in work-related values.* Beverly Hills, CA: Sage.

Hofstede, G. (Ed.). (1998). *Masculinity and femininity: The taboo dimension of national cultures.* Thousand Oaks, CA: Sage.

Holbert, R. L., & Stephenson, M. T. (2003). The importance of indirect effects in media effects research: Testing for mediation in structural equation modeling. *Journal of Broadcasting and Electronic Media, 47,* 556–572.

Holland, J. L. (1997). *Making vocational choices: A theory of vocational personalities and work environments.* Tampa, FL: Psychological Assessment Resource.

Holman, P., Devane, T., & Cady, S. (2007). *The change handbook* (2nd ed. rev.). San Francisco: Berrett-Koehler.

Honderich, T. (Ed.). (2005). *The Oxford guide: Philosophy.* Oxford, UK: Oxford University Press.

Hoogenboom, A. A.. (1961). *Outlawing the spoils: A history of the civil service reform movement, 1865–1883.* Urbana: University of Illinois Press.

Horkheimer, M. (1972). Traditional and critical theory. In *Critical theory: Selected essays* (M. J. O'Connell et al., Trans.; pp. 188–243). New York: Seabury Press. (Original work published 1937)

Horowitz, I. L. (1997). *Foundations of political sociology.* Edison, NJ: Transaction Publishers.

Horsky, S. (2006). The changing architecture of advertising agencies. *Marketing Science, 25,* 367–383.

Horwich, P. (1990). *Truth.* Oxford, UK: Basil Blackwell.

Houghtalen, R. P., & Privitera, M. R. (2007). Major mood disorders. In O. J. Z. Sahler & J. E. Carr (Eds.), *The behavioral sciences and health care* (2nd ed., pp. 333–343). Ashland, OH: Hogrefe & Huber.

Houghton, G. (Ed.). (2005). *Connectionist models in cognitive psychology.* New York: Psychology Press.

Hovland, C. I., Lumsdaine, A. A., & Sheffield, F. D. (1949). *Experiments on mass communication.* Princeton, NJ: Princeton University Press.

Howard, P. N. (2006). *New media campaigns and the managed citizen.* New York: Cambridge University Press.

Howell, D. C. (2007). *Statistical methods for psychology* (6th ed.). Pacific Grove, CA: Duxbury.

Hox, J. (1994, January 1). *Applied multilevel analysis.* Retrieved March 30, 2009, from http://www.geocites.com/joophox/publist/pubenjh.htm

Huang, N., & Kleiner, B. (2005). New developments concerning corporate communications. *Management Research News, 28*(10), 57–64. Retrieved June 12, 2008, from http://proquest.umi.com/pqdweb?

Hubbard, R. L., Marsden, M. E., Rachel, J. V., Harwood, H. J., Cavanaugh, E. R., & Ginzburg, H. M. (1989). *Drug abuse treatment: A national study of effectiveness.* Chapel Hill: University of North Carolina Press.

Huber, P. (1998, April). *Commentary: Saving the environment from the environmentalists* (Vol. 105, No. 4). Retrieved April 20, 2008, from http://www.manhattan-institute.org/html/_commentary-saving_the_environ.htm

Huberman, B., Loch, C., & Onculer, A. (2004). Status as a valued resource. *Social Psychology Quarterly, 67*(1), 103–114. Retrieved from the ProQuest Social Science Journals database

Hudson, D. (n.d.). *Evolution and creation.* Retrieved May 6, 2009, from http://www.firstamendmentcenter.org/rel_liberty/publicschools/topic.aspx?topic=evolution_creation

Huesmann, L. R. (2007). The impact of electronic media violence: Scientific theory and research. *Journal of Adolescent Health, 41*(6, Suppl.), S6–S13.

Hull, C. L. (1951). *A behavior system.* New Haven, CT: Yale University Press.

Hull, J. C. (2006). *Options, futures and other derivatives.* Upper Saddle River, NJ: Prentice Hall.

Human Genome Project Web site: http://www.ornl.gov/sci/techresources/Human_Genome/home.shtml

Humphrey's Executor v. United States, 295 U.S. 602 (1934).

Hunsaker, R. (1991, November 3). *Critical listening: A neglected skill.* Paper presented at the 77th annual meeting of the Speech Communication Association, Atlanta, GA. (Abstract retrieved May 28, 2008, from http://eric.ed.gov/ERICWebPortal/Home.portal?)

Hunter, D. R., Mayhall, P. D., & Barker, T. (2000). *Police community relations and the administration of justice* (5th ed.). Upper Saddle River, NJ: Prentice Hall.

Huntington, S. P. (1997). The erosion of American national interest. *Foreign Affairs, 76*(5): 28–49.

Huston, A. C. (1992). *Big world, small screen: The role of television in American society (child, youth, and family services).* Lincoln: University of Nebraska Press.

Hyman, A. (2005). The little word due. *Akron Law Review, 38,* 1–52.

Ibrahim, J. K., & Glants, S. A. (2007). The rise and fall of tobacco control media campaigns: 1967–2006. *American Journal of Public Health, 97*(8), 1383–1396.

Illeris, K. (2002). *Three dimensions of learning*. Roskilde, Denmark: Roskilde University Press.

Illinois General Assembly. (n.d.). *Illinois legislative glossary*. Retrieved February 19, 2009, from http://www.ilga.gov/legislation/Glossary.asp

Individuals with Disabilities Education Act (IDEA): Proposed regulations for P.L. 108–446. Retrieved April 21, 2009, from http://www.nectact.org/idea.asp

Infante, D. A., Rancer, A. S., & Womack, D. F. (1997). *Building communication theory* (3rd ed.). Prospect Heights, IL: Waveland Press.

Ingraham v. Wright, 430 U.S. 651 (1977).

Institute for Working Futures. (2005). *Interpersonal people skills*. Retrieved September 25, 2008, from http://marcbowles.com/courses/frontline/theme_intros/theme_b_intro.htm

International Federation of Social Workers. (2000). *Definition of social work*. Retrieved March 10, 2008, http://www.ifsw.org/p38000208.html

International trade (Leontief paradox). (2009). *Encyclopedia Britannica online*. Retrieved May 11, 2009, from http://search.eb.com/EB/article.61690

Ironson, G., Wynings, C., Schneiderman, N., Baum, A., Rodriguez, M., Greenwood, D., et al. (1997). Posttraumatic stress symptoms, intrusive thoughts, loss, and immune function after Hurricane Andrew. *Psychosomatic Medicine, 59*(2), 128–141.

Irwin, H. J., & Watt, C. A. (2007). *An introduction to parapsychology*. Jefferson, NC: McFarland.

Jacobs, H. H. (1997). *Mapping the big picture: Integrating curriculum and assessment K–12*. Alexandria, VA: Association for Supervision and Curriculum Development.

Jahnke, J. C., & Nowaczyk, R. H. (1998). *Cognition*. Upper Saddle River, NJ: Prentice Hall.

Jalongo, M. R. (2008). *Learning to listen, listening to learn: Building essential skills in young children*. Washington, DC: National Association for the Education of Young Children. (Abstract retrieved May 28, 2008, from http://eric.ed.gov/ERICWebPortal/Home.portal?)

James, W. (1884). What is an emotion? *Mind, 9,* 188–205.

James, W. (1890). *The principles of psychology*. New York: Henry Holt.

James, W. (2008). *Talks to teachers on psychology: And to students on some of life's ideals*. Sioux Falls, SD: NuVision. (Original work published 1899)

Janis, I. L., & Mann, L. (1977). *Decision making: A psychological analysis of conflict, choice, and commitment*. New York: Free Press.

Jarvis, P. (1987). *Adult learning in the social context*. London: Croom Helm.

Jensen, M. (1940). *The Articles of Confederation: An interpretation of the social-constitutional history of the American revolution, 1774–1781*. Madison: University of Wisconsin Press.

Jimmerson, S. R., & Furlong, M. (2006). *Handbook of school violence and school safety: From research to practice*. Mahwah, NJ: Lawrence Erlbaum.

Johnson, C. (1964). *Revolution and the social system*. Stanford, CA: Hoover Institution on War, Revolution, and Peace.

Johnson, D. T. (2003). Police integrity in Japan. In C. B. Klockars, S. K. Ivkovich, & M. R. Haberfeld (Eds.), *Contours of police integrity* (pp. 130–160). Thousand Oaks, CA: Sage.

Johnson, P. (1973). The unnecessary crime of conspiracy. *California Law Review, 61,* 11–88.

Johnson, R. B. (2001). Toward a new classification of non-experimental quantitative research. *Educational Researcher, 30*(2), 3–13.

Johnson, R. B., & Christensen, L. B. (2008). *Educational research: Quantitative, qualitative, and mixed approaches*. Los Angeles: Sage.

Johnson, S. (1755). *A dictionary of the English language: In which the words are deduced from their originals, and illustrated in their different significations by examples from the best writers: to which are prefixed, a history of the language, and an English grammer* (2 vols.). London: W. Strahan for J. and P. Knapton.

Johnston, J. (2007). *Media relations: Issues and strategies*. Crows Nest, New South Wales, Australia: Allen & Unwin.

Jonassen, D. H. (1999). Task analysis methods for instructional design. Mahwah, NJ: Lawrence Erlbaum.

Jones, C. (2003). International law. In I. McLean & A. McMillan (Eds.), *The concise Oxford dictionary of politics*. Oxford, UK: Oxford University Press. (*Oxford reference online*, City University of New York, John Jay College of Criminal Justice. Retrieved, February 10, 2008, from http://www.oxfordreference.com/views/ENTRY.html?subview=Main&entry=t86.e657

Jones, C. O. (1984). *Introduction to the study of public policy* (3rd ed.). Monterey, CA: Brooks/Cole.

Jones, E. E. & Harris, V. A. (1967). The attribution of attitudes. *Journal of Experimental Social Psychology, 3,* 1–24.

Jones, E. E., Wood, G. C., & Quattrone, G. A. (1981). Perceived variability of personal characteristics in in-groups and out-groups: The role of knowledge and evaluation. *Personality and Social Psychology Bulletin, 7*(3), 523–528.

Jones, F. H. (2000). *Tools for teaching*. Santa Cruz, CA: Fredric H. Jones.

Jones, S. R. G. (1992). Was there a Hawthorne effect? *American Journal of Sociology, 98*(3), 451–468.

Jonides, J., Reuter-Lorenz, P. A., & Smith, E. E. (1996). Verbal and spatial working memory in humans. In D. L. Medin (Ed.), *The psychology of learning and motivation: Advances in research and theory* (Vol. 35, pp. 43–88). San Diego, CA: Academic Press.

Josephson, J. R., & Josephson, S. G. (Eds.). (1996). *Abductive inference: Computation, philosophy, technology*. New York: Cambridge University Press.

Jung, C. (1981). *The archetypes of the collective unconscious* (Collected Works of C. G. Jung, G. Adler & R. F. C. Hull, Trans., Vol. 9, 2nd ed., Pt. 1). Princeton, NJ: Princeton University Press. (Original work published 1934)

Juni, S. (1981). Theoretical foundations of reaction formation as a defense mechanism. *Genetic Psychology Monographs, 104*(1), 107–135.

Kahneman, D., & Miller, D. T. (1986). Norm theory: Comparing reality to its alternatives. *Psychological Review, 93,* 136–153.

Kahneman, D., & Tversky, A. (2000). *Choices, values, and frames*. Cambridge, UK: Cambridge University Press.

Kahneman, D., Tversky, A., & Slovic, P. (Eds.). (1982). *Judgment under uncertainty: Heuristics and biases*. Cambridge, UK: Cambridge University Press.

Kaminski, J. P. (2001). Articles of Confederation. In P. S. Boyer (Ed.), *The Oxford companion to United States history*. New York: Oxford University Press. (*Oxford reference online*, City University of New York, John Jay College of Criminal Justice. Retrieved February 10, 2008, from http://www.oxfordreference.com/views/ENTRY.html?subview=Main&entry=t119.e0113

Kandel, E. R., Schwartz, J. H., & Jessell, T. M. (Eds.). (1999). *Principles of neural science* (3rd ed.). New York: Elsevier.

Kandel, E. R., Schwartz, J. H., & Jessell, T. M. (Eds.). (2000). *Principles of neural science* (4th ed.). New York: McGraw-Hill.

Kane, M. (2002). Inferences about variance components and reliability-generalizability coefficients in the absence of random sampling. *Journal of Educational Measurement, 39*(2), 165–181.

Kaplan, H. R., & Tausky, C. (1977). Humanism in organizations: A critical approach. *Public Administration Review, 37*(2), 171–180.

Karoly, P. (1993). Mechanisms of self-regulation: A systems view. *Annual Review of Psychology, 44,* 23–52.

Katz, E., & Lazarsfeld, P. F. (1955). *Personal influence: The part played by people in the flow of mass communications.* Glencoe, IL: Free Press.

Kaufman, H. Emerging Conflicts in the doctrines of public administration. *American Political Science Review, 50*(4), 1057–1073.

Kavanau, J. L. (2002). REM and NREM sleep as natural accompaniments of the evolution of warm-bloodedness. *Neuroscience & Biobehavioral Reviews, 26*(8), 889–906.

Kavoori, A. P., & Fraley, T. (Eds.). (2006). *Media, terrorism, and theory: A reader.* New York: Rowman & Littlefield.

Keeves J. P. (1997). *Educational research, methodology, and measurement: An international handbook* (2nd ed.). Oxford, UK: Pergamon.

Keim v. United States, 177 U.S. 290 (1900).

Keim, loc. cit.

Kelby, S. (2006). *The digital photography book.* Berkeley, CA: Peachpit Press.

Kellehear, A. (1993). *The unobtrusive researcher: A guide to methods.* St. Leonards, New South Wales, Australia: Allen & Unwin.

Keller, J. M. (1987). Development and use of the ARCS model of instructional design. *Journal of Instructional Development, 10*(3), 2–10.

Kelley, H. H. (1973). The process of causal attribution. *American Psychologist, 28,* 107–128.

Kelling, G., & Wilson, J. (1982). Broken windows. *The Atlantic, March.* Retrieved April 30, 2009, from http://www.theatlantic.com/doc/198203/broken-windows

Kelly, D. (1998). *A life of one's own: Individual rights and the welfare state.* Washington, DC: Cato Institute.

Kendall, P., & Wolf, K. (1949). The analysis of deviant cases in communication research. In P. F. Lazarsfeld & F. Stanton (Eds.), *Communications research, 1948–1949* (pp. 153–154). New York: Harper.

Kendall, P. C., & Clarkin, J. F. (1992). Introduction to special section: Comorbidity and treatment implications. *Journal of Consulting and Clinical Psychology, 60,* 833–834.

Kennedy, R. (2002). The ideology of American isolationism: 1931–1939. *Cercles, 5,* 57–76.

Kent, S. L. (2001). *The ultimate history of video games.* Roseville, CA: Prima.

Kessler, R. C., McGonagle, K. A., Zhao, S., & Nelson, C. B. (1995). Lifetime and 12-month prevalence of *DSM-III-R* psychiatric disorders in the United States. *Archives of General Psychiatry, 51,* 8–19.

Kettl, D. F., & Fesler, J. (2005). *The politics of the administrative process.* Washington, DC: CQ Press.

Keynes, J. M. (1936). *The general theory of employment, interest and money.* Cambridge, UK: Cambridge University Press.

Kidwell, D. S., Blackwell, D. W., Whidbee, D. A., & Peterson, R. L. (2008). *Financial institutions, markets, and money.* Hoboken, NJ: Wiley.

Kierstyn, v. Racine Unified School District, 228 Wis.2d 81, 596 N.W.2d 417 (S. Ct. Wis. 1999), citing to Lister, 72 Wis.2d at 301.

Kilmann, R. H., & Thomas, K. W. (1977). Developing a forced-choice measure of conflict-handling behavior: The mode instrument. *Educational and Psychological Measurement, 37*(2), 309–325.

Kingdon, J. (1995). *Agendas, alternatives and public policies* (2nd ed.). New York: HarperCollins.

Kinsey, A. C., Pomeroy, W. B., & Mart, C. E. (1998). *Sexual behavior in the human male.* Bloomington: Indiana University Press. (Original work published 1948)

Kirk, R. (1967). *Edmund Burke: A genius reconsidered.* Wilmington, DE: Intercollegiate Studies Institute.

Kirschenbaum, H., & Henderson, V. L. (Eds.). (1989). *The Carl Rogers reader.* Boston: Houghton Mifflin.

Klaehn, J. (2003). Behind the invisible curtain of scholarly criticism: Revisiting the propaganda model. *Journalism Studies, 4*(3), 359–369.

Klapper, J. T. (1960). *The effects of mass communication.* Glencoe, IL: Free Press.

Kleiven, J. (1973). Verbal communications and the intensity of delivery. *Scandinavian Journal of Psychology, 14*(1), 111–113.

Kline, R. B. (2005). *Principles and practice of structural equation modeling* (2nd ed.). New York: Guilford Press.

Kmiec, K. (2004). Comment: The origin and current meanings of judicial activism. *California Law Review, 92*(5), 1441–1478.

Knight, R. A., & Prentky, R. A. (1987). The developmental antecedents and adult adaptations or rapist subtypes. *Criminal Justice and Behavior, 14*(4), 403–426.

Knippen, J., & Green, T. (1997). Problem solving. *Journal of Workplace Learning, 9*(3), 98–99.

Knowles, M. S. (1980). *The modern practice of adult education: From pedagogy to andragogy* (2nd ed.). New York: Cambridge Books.

Kobayashi, T., Ikeda, K., & Miyata, K. (2006). Social capital online: Collective use of the Internet and reciprocity as lubricants of democracy. *Information, Communication & Society, 9*(5), 582–611.

Kobrak, P. (2002). *Cozy politics: Political parties, campaign finance, and compromised government.* Boulder, CO: Lynne Rienner.

Koger, G. (2006). Cloture reform and party government in the Senate, 1918–1925. *Journal of Politics, 68*(3), 708–719.

Kohlberg, L. (1973). The claim to moral adequacy of a highest stage of moral judgment. *Journal of Philosophy, 70,* 630–646.

Kohlberg, L. (1984). *Essays on moral development: The psychology of moral development* (Vol. 2). San Francisco: Harper & Row.

Kornhauser, W. (1959). *The politics of mass society.* Glencoe, IL: Free Press.

Kouvelaskis, S. (2005). The Marxian critique of citizenship: For a rereading of the Jewish question. *The South Atlantic Quarterly, 104*(4), 707–721.

Kovach, B., & Rosenstiel, T. (2001). *The elements of journalism: What newspeople should know and the public should expect.* New York: Crown.

Kraft, M. E., & Furlong, S. R. (2007). *Public policy: Politics, analysis, and alternatives* (2nd ed.). Washington, DC: CQ Press.

Kramnic, I. (Ed.). (1999). *The portable Edmund Burke.* London: Penguin Books.

Krebs, D. L., & Denton, K. (1997). Social illusions and self-deception: The evolution of biases in person perception. In J. A. Simpson & D. T. Kenrick (Eds.), *Evolutionary social psychology* (pp. 21–47). Hillsdale, NJ: Lawrence Erlbaum.

Krieger, J. (Ed.). (2001). *Oxford companion to world politics.* New York: Oxford University Press. (*Oxford reference online,* City

University of New York, John Jay College of Criminal Justice. Retrieved February 10, 2008, from http://www.oxfordreference.com/views/ENTRY.html?subview=Main&entry=t121.e0603

Kroker, A., & Kroker, M. (Eds.). (1997). *Digital delirium*. New York: St. Martin's Press.

Kruglanski, A. (2004). *The psychology of closed mindedness*. New York: Psychology Press.

Krugman, P. R., & Obstfeld, M. (2006). *International economics: Theory and policy*. Boston: Addison-Wesley.

Kubow, P., & Fossum, P. (2003). *Comparative education: Exploring issues in international context*. Columbus, OH: Merrill/Prentice Hall.

Kuhn, T. (1962). *The structure of scientific revolutions*. Chicago: University of Chicago Press.

Kura, N. O. (2001). *Congress of the United States: Power, structure, and proceedings*. Hauppauge, NY: Nova.

Kyvig, E. D. (1998). *Explicit and authentic acts: Amending the U.S. Constitution, 1776–1995*. Lawrence: University Press of Kansas.

Labov, W. (1987). *Some observations on the foundation of linguistics*. Retrieved August 2, 2008, from http://www.ling.upenn.edu/~wlabov/Papers/Foundations.html

Lacquer, W. (2001). *A history of terrorism*. Edison, NJ: Transaction.

Lagon, P. M. (1994). *The Reagan doctrine. Sources of American conduct in the cold war's last chapter*. Westport, CT: Greenwood Press.

Landow, G. P. (1992). *Hypertext: The convergence of contemporary critical theory and technology*. Baltimore: Johns Hopkins University Press.

Lang, G. E., & Lang, K. (1983). *The battle for public opinion: The President, the press, and the polls during Watergate*. New York: Columbia University Press.

Langer, E. J. (1975). The illusion of control. *Journal of Personality and Social Psychology, 32*, 311–328.

Langer, L., & Wilhelm, T. (2005). The ideology of state supreme court chief justices. *Judicature, 89*(2), 78–87.

Langer, S. (1957). *Philosophy in a new key: A study in the symbolism of reason, rite, and art*. Cambridge, MA: Harvard University Press.

Lapin, D. (2004). It's communication, stupid! *Public Management, 86*(1), 32–33.

Larson, C., & Ovando, C. (2000). *The color of bureaucracy: The politics of equity in multicultural school communities*. Belmont, CA: Wadsworth.

Lasswell, H. D. (1927). *Propaganda technique in the World War*. New York: Knopf.

Latane, B., & Nilda, S. (1981). Ten years of research on group size and helping. *Psychological Bulletin, 89*, 308–324.

Latané, B., Williams, K., & Harkins, S. (1979). Many hands make light the work: The causes and consequences of social loafing. *Journal of Personality and Social Psychology, 37*(6), 822–832.

Lau v. Nichols, 414 U.S. 563 (1974).

Lawrence v. Texas, 539 U.S. 558 (2003).

Lawrence, A. J. (2007). Therapeutics for alcoholism: What's the future? *Drug and Alcohol Review, 26*, 3–8.

Lazarsfeld, P. F., & Katz, E. (1948). *The people's choice*. New York: Columbia University Press.

Lazarsfeld, P. F., Berelson, B., & Gaudet, H. (1944). *The people's choice: How the voter makes up his mind in a presidential campaign*. New York: Duell, Sloan & Pearce.

Lazarsfeld, P. F., & Merton, R. K. (2000). Mass communication, popular taste and organized social action. In P. Marris & S. Thornham (Eds.), *Media studies: A reader* (2nd ed., pp. 18–30). New York: New York University Press. (Original work published 1948)

Lazzarini, R. (2003). *Myelin biology and disorders*. New York: Elsevier Academic Press.

Lebow, I. (1995). *Information highways and byways: From the telegraph to the 21st century*. New York: Institute of Electrical and Electronics Engineers.

Ledingham, J. (2003). Explicating relationship management as a general theory of public relations. *Journal of Public Relations Research, 15*, 181–198.

LeDoux, J. (2007). The amygdala. *Current Biology, 17*, 868–874.

Lee, M. (Ed.). (2008). *Government public relations: A reader*. Boca Raton, FL: CRC Press.

Lee, R. D., Johnson, R. W., & Joyce, P. G. (2008). *Public budgeting systems*. Boston: Jones & Barlett.

Lega, L. I., & Ellis, A. (2001). Rational emotive behavior therapy (REBT) in the new millennium: A cross-cultural approach. *Journal of Rational-Emotive & Cognitive Behavior Therapy, 19*(4), 201–222.

Lehman, A., Myers, C. P., & Corty, E. (2000). Assessment and classification of patients with psychiatric and substance abuse syndromes. *Psychiatric Services, 51*(9), 1119–1125.

Leishman, F., & Mason, P. (2003). *Policing and the media; Facts, fictions and factions*. Uffculme, Devon, UK: Willan.

Lerner, R. M., & Steinberg, L. (Eds.). (2004). *Handbook of adolescent psychology*. New York: Wiley.

LeRoy, K., & Saunders, C. (2006). Australia: Dualist in form, cooperative in practice. In R. Blindenbacher & A. Ostien (Eds.), *Dialogues on legislative, executive, and judicial governance in federal countries* (A Global Dialogue on Federalism Booklet Series, Vol. 3, pp. 6–9). Montreal, Quebec, Canada: McGill-Queen's University Press.

Levin-Rozalis, M. (2000). Abduction: A logical criterion for programme and project evaluation. *Evaluation, 6*(4), 415–432.

Levin-Rozalis, M. (2004). Revisited: A tracer study ten years later. Detective process. *Journal of Early Childhood Research, 2*(3), 271–296.

Lévi-Strauss, C. (1963). *Structural anthropology* (C. Jacobson & B. Schoepf, Trans.). New York: Doubleday Anchor Books.

Lévi-Strauss, C. (1968). *The savage mind (Nature of human society)*. Chicago: University of Chicago Press.

Lezak, M. D., Howieson, D. B., Loring, D. W., Hannay, H. J., & Fischer, J. S. (2004). *Neuropsychological assessment* (4th ed.). New York: Oxford University Press.

Li, P. P. (2007). Guanxi as the Chinese norm for personalized social capital: Toward an integrated duality framework of informal exchange. In H. W. Yeung (Ed.), *Handbook for research in Asian business* (pp. 250–265). Cheltenham, UK: Edward Elgar.

Lichtheim, G. (1962). *Marxism*. New York: Praeger.

Lieberman, J. A., Stroup, S., McEvoy, J., Swartz, M., Rosenheck, R., Perkins, D., et al. (2005). Effectiveness of antipsychotic drugs in patients with chronic schizophrenia. *New England Journal of Medicine, 353*, 1209–1223.

Lievrouw, L., & Livingstone, S. (Eds.). (2002). *Handbook of new media: Social shaping and social consequences*. London: Sage.

Lijphart, A. (1968). Typologies of democratic systems. *Comparative Political Studies, 1*(1), 3–44.

Likert, R. (1967). *The human organization: Its management and value*. New York: McGraw-Hill.

Limaye, M. (2000). Perception is the thing: Presenting variant worldviews in the international business communication classroom. *Business Communication Quarterly, 63*(3), 24–38. Retrieved May 31, 2008, from http://web.ebscohost.com.proxy.libraries.rutgers.edu/ehost/pdf?vid=3&hid=8&sid=ca988b5d-dfca-4ed1-b030-8fe0dba3a8f1%40SRCSM1

Lindberg, T. (2004). Neoconservatism's liberal legacy: Striking a balance between freedom and equality. *Policy Review, 127*.

Retrieved May 5, 2008, from http://www.hoover.org/publications/policyreview/3436416.html

Lindlof, T., & Taylor, B. (2002). Qualitative analysis and interpretation. In *Qualitative communication research methods* (chap. 7, Coding and Categorization, pp. 214–215). Thousand Oaks, CA: Sage.

Linkins, R. L. (2007). Satisfy the demands of justice: Embrace electronic recording of custodial investigative interviews through legislation, agency policy, or court mandate. *American Criminal Law Review, 44*(1), 141–173.

Lippman, M. R. (2006). *Contemporary criminal law: Concepts, cases, and controversies.* Thousand Oaks, CA: Sage.

Lippmann, W. (1922). *Public opinion.* New York: Free Press Paperbacks.

Lippmann, W. (1947). *The cold war.* London: H. Hamilton.

Lippmann, W. (1955). *Essays in the public philosophy.* Boston: Little, Brown.

Lipset, S. M. (1981). *Political man: The social bases of politics.* Baltimore: Johns Hopkins University Press.

Lipsey, R. G., & Lancaster, K. (1956). The general theory of second best. *Review of Economic Studies, 24*(1), 11–32.

Livert, D., Rindskopf, D., Saxe, L., & Stirratt, M. (2001). Using multilevel modeling in the evaluation of community-based treatment programs. *Multivariate Behavioral Research, 36*(2), 155–184.

Lochner v. New York, 198 U.S. 45 (1905).

Locke, J. (1988). *Two treatises of government.* P. Laslett (Ed.). Cambridge, UK: Cambridge University Press.

Loeske, D. (2003). *Thinking about social problems: An introduction to constructionist perspectives.* Piscataway, NJ: Aldine Transaction.

Lombroso, C. (1876). *L'uomo delinquente* [Criminal man]. Milan, Italy: Hoepli.

Lovelace, V. O., & Huston, A. C. (1983). Can television teach prosocial behavior? *Prevention in Human Services, 2,* 93–106.

Lowenfeld, A. (2003). *International economic law.* New York: Oxford University Press.

Lucas, S. E. (2007). *The art of public speaking* (9th ed.). New York: McGraw-Hill.

Ludy, B. (2005). A history of clinical psychology as a profession in America (and a glimpse at its future). *Annual Review of Clinical Psychology, 1,* 1–30.

Luft, J. (1984). *Group process: An introduction to group dynamics* (3rd ed.). Mountain View, CA: Mayfield.

Lukes, S. (1974). *Power: A radical view.* London: Macmillan.

Lukes, S. (1990). Socialism and capitalism, left and right. *Social Research, 57*(3), 571–577.

Lum, C. M. K. (2006). *Perspectives on culture, technology and communication: The media ecology.* Cresskill, NJ: Hampton Press.

Lyon, D. (Ed.). (2006). *Theorizing surveillance: The panopticon and beyond.* Portland, OR: Willan.

MacFarquhar, R., & Schoenhals, M. (2008). *Mao's last revolution.* Cambridge, MA: Belknap Press.

Machin, D., & Niblock, S. (2006). *News production: theory and practice.* New York: Routledge.

Madison, J., Hamilton, J., & Jay, J. (1987). *The Federalist papers.* London: Penguin Classics. (Original work published 1788)

Madsen, E. A., Tunney, R., Fieldman, G., Plotkin, H. C., Dunbar, R. I. M., Richardson, J. M., et al. (2007). Kinship and altruism: A cross-cultural experimental study. *British Journal of Psychology, 98,* 339–359.

Makielski, S. J., Jr. (1967). The preconditions to effective public administration. *American Society for Public Administration, 27,* 148–153.

Malinowski, B. (1947). The problem of meaning in primitive languages. In R. Ogden and I. A. Richards (Eds.), *The meaning of meaning* (pp. 296–336). London: Harcourt Brace.

Malone, J. C. (1990). *Theories of learning: A historical approach.* Belmont, CA: Wadsworth.

Malone, Rev. P. (2007). Cracking the code. *U.S. Catholic, 72*(10), 24–29.

Malthus, M. (1798). *An essay on the principle of population.* Retrieved April 25, 2009, from http://www.esp.org/books/malthus/population/malthus.pdf

Manipulation. (2008). In *Oxford English dictionary.* Retrieved October 24, 2008, from http://mccclib.mccc.edu:2074/cgi/entry/00301234?

Mankiw, N. G. (2006). *Macroeconomics.* New York: Worth.

Mankiw, N. G. (2007). *Principles of microeconomics.* Cincinnati, OH: Thomson South-Western.

Mansbridge, J. J. (2001). *Equal rights amendment: The Oxford companion to the politics of the world* (2nd ed.). Oxford, UK: Oxford University Press. (*Oxford reference online,* City University of New York, John Jay College of Criminal Justice. Retrieved February 10, 2008, from http://www.oxfordreference.com/views/ENTRY.html?subview=Main&entry=t121.e0227

Mapp v. Ohio, 367 U.S. 643 (1961).

Marbury v. Madison, 5 U.S. 137 (1803).

Marcel, A. J. (1983). Conscious and unconscious perception: Experiments on visual masking and word recognition. *Cognitive Psychology, 15,* 197–237.

Marcus, P. (2002). Conspiracy. In K. L. Hall (Ed.), *The Oxford companion to American law.* Oxford, UK: Oxford University Press. (*Oxford reference online,* City University of New York, John Jay College of Criminal Justice. Retrieved February 10, 2008, from http://www.oxfordreference.com/views/ENTRY.html?subview=Main&entry=t122.e0172

Mares, M. L., & Woodard, E. (2005). Positive effects of television on children's social interactions: A meta-analysis. *Media Psychology, 7,* 301–322.

Markman, E. (1989). *Categorization and naming in children: Problems of induction.* Cambridge: MIT Press. Retrieved May 22, 2008, from http://books.google.com/books?hl=en&lr=&id=gtF-Iasx9BcC&oi=fnd&pg=PP11&dq=Markman&ots=iZfHKCT_Fu&sig=lpB17sCTMCIcS68wBpR_Sd1FzTc

Markovic, M. (1982). *Democratic socialism: Theory and practice.* New York: St. Martin's Press.

Markowitz, H. M. (1952). Portfolio selection. *Journal of Finance, 7*(1), 77–91.

Marrow, A. F. (1969). *The practical theorist: The life and work of Kurt Lewin.* New York: Basic Books.

Marshall, W., & Serin, R. (1997). Personality disorders. In S. M. Turner & R. Hersen (Eds.), *Adult psychopathology and diagnosis* (pp. 508–541). New York: Wiley.

Martin, D. W. (2004). *Doing psychology experiments* (6th ed.). Belmont, CA: Thompson/Wadsworth.

Marx, K. (1992). *Capital: A critique of political economy* (Vol. 1, B. Fowkes, Trans.). London: Penguin Group.

Marx, K., & Engels, F. (1969). *The communist manifesto* (Marx-Engels Selected Works, Vol. 1, pp. 98–137). Moscow: Progress. (Original work published 1848)

Maryland v. Craig, 497 U.S. 836 (1990).

Maslow, A. H. (1943). A theory of human motivation. *Psychological Review, 50*(4), 370–396.

Massachusetts v. Environmental Protection Agency, 549 U.S. 497 (2007).

Masters, W. H., & Johnson, V. E. (1966). *Human sexual response.* Oxford, UK: Little, Brown.

Mathison, S. (Ed.). (2005). *Encyclopedia of evaluation.* Thousand Oaks, CA: Sage.

Mattelart, A. (2000). *Networking the world: 1794–2000.* Minneapolis, MN: University of Minneapolis Press.

Mayer, J. D., & Salovey, P. (1993). The intelligence of emotional intelligence. *Intelligence, 17*(4), 433–442.

McAlinden, A. M. (2005). The use of shame with sexual offenders. *British Journal of Criminology, 45,* 373–394.

McBurney, D. H., & White, T. L. (2007). *Research methods* (7th ed.). Belmont, CA: Thomson Wadsworth.

McBurney, J., & Hance, K. (1939). *The principles and methods of discussion.* New York: Harper & Brothers.

McCauley, M., Peterson, E., Artz, B., & Halleck, D. (Eds.). (2003). *Public broadcasting and the public interest.* Armonk, NY: M. E. Sharpe.

McChesney, R. W. (2004). *The problem of the media: U.S. communication politics in the twenty-first century.* New York: Monthly Review Press.

McClelland, D. C. (1973). Testing for competence rather than for intelligence. *American Psychologist, 28,* 1–14.

McClelland, D. C. (1985). *Human motivation.* Glenview, IL: Scott-Foresman.

McClusky, H. Y. (1963). The course of the adult life span. In W. C. Hallenbeck (Ed.), *Psychology of adults* (pp. 10–19). Washington, DC: Adult Education Association.

McComas, M. (1992). Amending the Constitution. *Constitution, 4*(2) 26–31.

McCombs, M. E., & Shaw, D. L. (1972). The agenda-setting function of mass media. *Public Opinion Quarterly, 36,* 176–184.

McConnell, C. R., & Brue, S. L. (2008). *Economics* (17th ed.). New York: McGraw-Hill.

McCornack, S. (2007). *Reflect and relate: An introduction to interpersonal communication,* New York: Bedford/St. Martin's.

McCornack, S., Levine, T., Morrison, K., & Lapinski, M. (1996). Speaking of information manipulation: A critical rejoinder. *Communications Monographs, 63*(1), 83–92.

McCornack, S. A. (1992). Information manipulation theory. *Communication Monographs, 59,* 1–16.

McCornack, S. A., & Levine, T. R. (1990). When lies are uncovered: Emotional and relational outcomes of discovered deception. *Communication Monographs, 57,* 119–138.

McCrae, R.R., Costa, P.T. (2004). A contemplated revision of the NEO Five-Factor Inventory. *Personality and Individual Differences, 36,* 587–596.

McCullagh, C. (2002). *Media power: A sociological introduction.* New York: Palgrave.

McCulloch v. Maryland, 17 U.S. 316 (1819).

McEachern, W. A. (2006). *Economics: A contemporary introduction.* Mason, OH: Thomson South-Western.

McFarlane, J., Welch, J., & Rodgers, J. (2006). Severity of Alzheimer's disease and effect on premorbid measures of intelligence. *British Journal of Clinical Psychology, 45,* 453–463.

McGrain v. Daughtery, 273 U.S. 135 (1927).

McGregor, D. (1960). *The human side of enterprise.* New York: McGraw-Hill.

McGregor, D. (1967). *The professional manager.* New York: McGraw-Hill.

McGregor, D. (2006). *The human side of enterprise* (Annotated ed.). New York: McGraw-Hill.

McKinney, R. J. (2006). *A research guide to the Federal Register and the Code of Federal Regulations.* Retrieved April 30, 2009, from http://www.llsdc.org/fed-reg-cfr

McLean, I., & McMillan, A. (Eds.). (2003). *The concise Oxford dictionary of politics.* New York: Oxford University Press. (*Oxford Reference Online,* City University of New York, John Jay College of Criminal Justice. Retrieved December 8, 2007, from http://www.oxfordreference.com/views/ENTRY.html?subview=Main&entry=t86.e1039

McLuhan, M. (1964). *Understanding media: The extensions of man.* New York: McGraw-Hill.

McLuhan, M., & Powers, B. R. (1989). *The global village: Transformations in world life and media in the 21st century.* New York: Oxford University Press.

McManus, J. (1994). *Market-driven journalism: Let the citizen beware?* Thousand Oaks, CA: Sage.

McNair, B. (1996). *Mediated sex: Pornography and postmodern culture.* London: Arnold.

McQuail, D. (1992). *Media performance: Mass communication and the public interest.* London: Sage.

Meade, J. E. (1955). *The theory of customs unions.* Amsterdam, The Netherlands: North-Holland.

Mealey, L. (1995). The sociobiology of sociopathy: An integrated evolutionary model. *Behavioral and Brain Sciences, 18,* 523–599.

Melicher, W. R., & Norton, E. A. (2005). *Finance.* Hoboken, NJ: Wiley.

Merriam, S. B., Caffarella, R. S., & Baumgartner, L. M. (2007). *Learning in adulthood: A comprehensive guide* (3rd ed.). San Francisco: Jossey-Bass.

Merryman, J. (1969). *The civil law tradition: An introduction to the legal systems of western Europe and Latin America.* Stanford, CA: Stanford University Press.

Merton, R. K., Fisk, M., & Curtis, A. (1946). *Mass persuasion: The social psychology of a war bond drive.* New York: Harper.

Mervin, D. (2003). Affirmative action. In I. McLean & A. McMillan (Eds.), *The concise Oxford dictionary of politics.* London: Oxford University Press. (*Oxford reference online,* City University of New York, John Jay College of Criminal Justice, Retrieved February 10, 2008, from http://www.oxfordreference.com/views/ENTRY.html?subview=Main&entry=t86.e12

Mervin, D. (2003). Bill of rights. In I. McLean & A. McMillan (Eds.), *The Concise Oxford dictionary of politics.* New York: Oxford University Press. (*Oxford Reference Online,* City University of New York, John Jay College of Criminal Justice. Retrieved February 20, 2008, from http://www.oxfordreference.com/views/ENTRY.html?subview=Main&entry=t86.e121

Mezirow, J. (2000). Learning to think like an adult: Core concepts of transformation theory. In J. Mezirow & Associates (Eds.), *Learning as transformation: Critical perspectives on a theory in progress* (pp. 3–33). San Francisco: Jossey-Bass.

Michell, J. (1990). *An introduction to the logic of psychological measurement.* Hillsdale, NJ: Lawrence Erlbaum.

Michels, R. (1999). *Political parties: A sociological study of the oligarchical tendencies of modern* democracy (E. Paul & C. Paul, Trans.). Piscataway, NJ: Transaction Publishers. (Original work published 1911)

Miles, H., Mark, R., & Hazel, W. (2002). Intergroup bias. *Annual Review Psychology, 53,* 575–604.

Mill, J. S. (1871). *Utilitarianism* (4th ed.). London: Longmans, Green, Reader, & Dyer.

Mill, J. S. (1989). *On liberty* (J. S. Mill: "On Liberty" and Other Writings, S. Collini, Ed., pp. 1–116). Cambridge, UK: Cambridge University Press. (Original work published 1859)

Mill, J. S. (2004). *Principles of political economy.* Amherst, NY: Prometheus Books. (Original work published 1848)

Miller, G. A. (1956). The magical number seven, plus or minus two: Some limits on our capacity to process information. *Psychological Review, 63*(2), 81–97.

Miller, H. (2001). *"Crimewatch" solved: The inside story.* London: Boxtree.

Miller, K. I. (2006). *Organizational communication: Approaches and processes* (4th ed.). Belmont, CA: Wadsworth.

Miller, L. (2005). China an emerging superpower. *Stanford Journal of International Relations, 6*(1).

Miller, M. M., & Reese, S. D. (1982). Media dependency as interaction: Effects of exposure and reliance on political activity and efficacy. *Communications Research, 9*, 227–248.

Miller, R., Benjamin, D. K., & North, D. C. (2007). *Economics of public issues.* Boston: Addison-Wesley.

Mills, C. W. (1958). *Causes of World War III.* New York: Simon & Schuster.

Mills, C. W. (1963). *Power, politics, and people: The collected essays of C. Wright Mills.* New York: Oxford University Press.

Miltenberger, R. G. (2003). *Behavior modification: Principles and procedures* (3rd ed.). Pacific Grove, CA: Wadsworth.

Mio, J. S., Barker-Hackett, L., & Tumambing, J. (2005). *Multicultural psychology: Understanding our diverse communities.* New York: McGraw-Hill.

Miranda v. Arizona, 384 U.S. 436 (*1966*).

Mises, L. von. (1951). *Socialism: An economic and sociological analysis.* New Haven, CT: Yale University Press. (Original work published 1922)

Mishan, E. J., & Quah, E. (2007). *Cost benefit analysis.* New York: Routledge.

Model SAPA. loc. cit (27).

Moldovan, D., Clark, C., & Harabagiu, S. (2009). *Temporal context representation and reasoning.* Richardson, TX: Language Computer. Retrieved March 13, 2009, from http://dli.iiit.ac.in/ijcai/IJCAI-05/PDF/1538.pdf

Monell v. Department of Social Services, 436 U.S. 658 (1978).

Monroe v. Pape, 365 U.S. 167 (1961).

Montessori, M. (1912). *The Montessori method.* New York: F. A. Stokes.

Monti, P. M., Rohsenow, D. J., & Hutchison, K. E. (2000). Toward bridging the gap between biological, psychobiological, and psychosocial models of alcohol craving. *Addiction, 95*(Suppl. 2), S229–S236.

Moore, M. (1998). *Virtualities.* Bloomington: Indiana University Press.

Morgan, G. (1997). *Images of organization.* Thousand Oaks, CA: Sage.

Morikawa, K. (2003). An application of the Muller-Lyer illusion. *Perception, 32*, 121–123.

Morrissey v. Brewer, 408 U.S. 471 (1972).

Mortensen, C. D. (1994). *Problematic communication.* New York: Praeger.

Mortensen, C. D. (1997). *Miscommunication.* London: Sage.

Morton, D. L., Jr. (2006). *Sound recording: The life story of a technology.* Baltimore: Johns Hopkins University Press.

Moustakas, C. (1994). *Phenomenological research methods.* Thousand Oaks, CA: Sage.

Mueser, K., Drake, R., & Wallach, M. (1998). Dual diagnosis. A review of etiological theories. *Addictive Behaviors, 23*(6), 717–734.

Munn v. Illinois, 94 U.S. 113 (1877).

Muth, J. A. (1961). Rational expectations and the theory of price movements. *Econometrica, 29*(6), 315–335.

Myers, K. (1983). Understanding advertisers. In H. David & P. Walton (Eds.), *Language, image, media* (pp. 205–223). Oxford, UK: Basil Blackwell.

Myles, E. A. (2003). *Understanding your trade area: Implications for retail analysis.* Mississippi State: Mississippi State University Extension Service. Retrieved March 6, 2008, from http://msucares.com/pubs/publications/p2321.pdf

Nacos, B. L. (2002). *Mass-mediated terrorism: The central role of the media in terrorism and counterterrorism.* New York: Rowman & Littlefield.

Nathan, R. P. (2001). Federalism. In J. Krieger (Ed.), *The Oxford Companion to the Politics of the World* (2nd ed.). New York Oxford University Press. (*Oxford reference online,* City University of New York, John Jay College of Criminal Justice. Retrieved February 10, 2008, from http://www.oxfordreference.com/views/ENTRY.html?subview=Main&entry=t121.e0243Berthold

National Clearinghouse for English Language Acquisition and Language Instruction Educational Programs. (2008). *NCELA FAQs.* Retrieved February 26, 2009, from http://www.ncela.gwu.edu/expert/faq/03history.html

National Commission on Excellence in Education. (1983, April). *A nation at risk: The imperative for educational reform.* Retrieved April 13, 2009, from http://www.ed.gov/pubs/NatAtRisk/index.html

National Communication Association. (1999). *How Americans communicate.* Retrieved from http://www.natcom.org/research/Roper/how_americans_communicate.htm

National Conference of Commissioners on Uniform State Laws, (Draft) Revised Model State Administrative Procedure Act, Section 102, Definitions (19) (2007a, April).

National Conference of Commissioners on Uniform State Laws, (Draft) Revised Model State Administrative Procedure Act, Section 102, Definitions (28) (2007b, April).

National Information Officers Association: http://www.nioa.org

National Park Service. (n.d.). *Edison: Sounds.* Retrieved April 20, 2009, from http://www.nps.gov/archive/edis/edisonia/sounds.html

Neff, W. D., & Goldberg, J. M. (1960). Higher functions of the central nervous system. *Annual Review Psychology, 22*, 499–524.

Negroponte, N. (1995). *Being digital.* New York: Alfred A. Knopf.

Neher, A. (1991). Malsow's theory of motivation: A critique. *Journal of Humanistic Psychology, 31*, 89–112.

Neisser, U. (1967). *Cognitive psychology.* New York: Appleton-Century-Crofts.

Nelson, L. J., & Miller, D. T. (1995). The distinctiveness effect in social categorization: You are what makes you unusual. *Psychological Science, 6*, 246–249.

Nelson, T. (1965). The hypertext. In Proceedings of the World Documentation Federation Conference.

Neuliep, J., Hintz, S., & McCroskey, J. (2005). The influence of ethnocentrism in organizational contexts: Perceptions of interviewee and managerial attractiveness, credibility, and effectiveness. *Communication Quarterly, 53*(1), 41–56. Retrieved from the ProQuest Social Science Journals database, Document ID: 836500741

Nevins, A., & Commager, H. S. (1992). *A pocket history of the United States.* New York: Simon & Schuster.

Newcomb, H. (2007). *Television: The critical view.* New York: Oxford University Press.

Newhall, B. (1988). *The history of photography.* New York: Museum of Modern Art.

New York County Lawyers' Association. (n.d.). *Report on the electronic recording of police interrogations.* Retrieved 23 March, 2009, from http://www.nycla.org/publications/revisedvideotapereport.pdf

New York State Department of Civil Service. (2008). *Manual for administrative law judges and hearing officers.* New York: Author.

New York State Unified Court System. (n.d.). *Glossary.* Retrieved March 9, 2009, from http://www.nycourts.gov/kiosk/glossary.htm

New York Times v. Sullivan, 376 U.S. 254 (1964).

New York University. (2009). *Interclass debates.* Retrieved March 24, 2009, from http://www.nyu.edu/classes/op/writing/debate_content.htm

Nicholas, J., & Price, J. (1998). *Advanced studies in media.* Walton-on-Thames, UK: Nelson.

Nichols, R. (2006). The struggle to be human. *International Journal of Listening, 20,* 4–12. (Keynote address at the first annual convention of the International Listening Association, 1980)

Nickerson, R. S. (1998). Confirmation bias: An ubiquitous phenomenon in many guises. *Review of General Psychology, 2,* 175–220.

Nielsen, F. (1994). Sociobiology and sociology. *Annual Review of Sociology, 20,* 267–303.

Nietzsche, F. (1955). *Beyond good and evil.* Chicago: Henry Regnery. (Original work published 1886)

Nihei, Y., & Miura, T. (2002). Applied research as a basis for basic research. *Japanese Psychological Research, 44,* 121–123.

Nixon v. United States, 506 U.S. 224 (1993).

Noel, S. (Ed.). (2005). *From power sharing to democracy: Post-conflict institutions in ethnically divided societies* (Studies in Nationalism and Ethnic Conflict). Montreal, Québec, Canada: McGill-Queen's University Press.

Noelle-Neumann, E. (1984). *The spiral of silence: Public opinion—our social skin.* Chicago: University of Chicago Press. (Original work published in German in 1980)

Nolan, C., & Morris, J. (1969). Learning by blind students through active and passive listening. *Exceptional Children, 36*(3), 173–181. Retrieved May 23, 2008, from http://web.ebscohost.com/ehost/detail?

Nord, W., & Haynes, C. (1998). *Taking religion seriously across the curriculum.* Alexandria, VA: Association for Supervision and Curriculum Development.

Nordenstreng, K., & Griffin, M. S. (1999). *International media monitoring* (Hampton Press Communication Series). Cresskill, NJ: Hampton Press.

Norris, C., & Wilson, D. (Eds.). (2006). *Surveillance, crime and social control.* Burlington, VT: Ashgate.

Ohayon, M. M. (2000). Prevalence of hallucinations and their pathological associations in the general population. *Psychiatry Research, 97*(2/3), 153–164.

Olfson, M., Marcus, S. C., Druss, B., Elinson, L., Tanielian, T., & Pincus, H. A. (2002). National trends in the outpatient treatment of depression. *Journal of the American Medical Association, 287,* 203–209.

Olmstead, J. A. (2002). *Creating the functionally competent organization: An open systems approach.* Westport, CT: Quorum Books.

Olsen, G., & Fuller, M. L. (2007). *Home-school relations: Working successfully with parents and families* (3rd ed.). New York: Allyn & Bacon.

Ong, W. (1988). *Orality and literacy: The technologizing of the word.* New York: Routledge.

Onwuegbuzie, A. J., & Collins, K. M. T. (2007). A typology of mixed methods sampling designs in social science research. *The Qualitative Report, 12,* 281–316. Retrieved October 8, 2008, from http://www.nova.edu/ssss/QR/QR12-2/onwuegbuzie2.pdf

Onwuegbuzie, A. J., & Johnson, R. B. (2006). The validity issue in mixed research. *Research in the Schools, 13*(1), 48–63.

Onwuegbuzie, A. J., & Leech, N. L. (2007). Sampling designs in qualitative research: Making the sampling process more public. *The Qualitative Report, 12*(2), 238–254. Retrieved October 8, 2008, from http://www.nova.edu/ssss/QR/QR12-2/onwuegbuzie1.pdf

Oregon School Activities Association. (2009). *2008–09 speech handbook.* Retrieved March 24, 2009, from http://www.osaa.org/publications/handbook/0809SPEECHHandbook.pdf

Orwell, G. (1945, October 19). You and the atomic bomb. *The Tribune.*

Oxford reference online, City University of New York, John Jay College of Criminal Justice. Retrieved April 23, 2008, from http://www.oxfordreference.com/views/ENTRY.html?subview=Main&entry=t86.e671

Oxford University Press. (2002). *Oxford American college dictionary.* New York: Author.

Ozinga, J. R. (1991). *Communism: The story of the idea and its implementation* (2nd ed.). Englewood Cliffs, NJ: Prentice Hall

Pagani, M. (Ed.). (2005). *Encyclopedia of multimedia technology and networking.* Hershey, PA: Idea Group Reference.

Panama Refining Co. v. Ryan, 293 U.S. 388 (1935).

Parenti, M. (1993). *Inventing reality: The politics of news media* (2nd ed.). New York: St. Martin's Press.

Parenti, M. (1995). *Against empire.* San Francisco: City Lights.

Parsons, T. (1959). The role of general theory in sociological analysis: Some case material. *Alpha Kappa Deltan: A Sociological Journal, 29*(1), 12–38.

Patrick, J. J., Pious, R. M., & Ritchie, D. A. (2001). *The Oxford guide to the United States government.* New York: Oxford University Press. (*Oxford reference online,* City University of New York, John Jay College of Criminal Justice. Retrieved February 10, 2008, from http://www.oxfordreference.com/views/ENTRY.html?subview=Main&entry=t89.e65

Patton, M. Q. (2002). *Qualitative research and evaluation methods* (3rd ed.). Thousand Oaks, CA: Sage.

Patton, M. Q. (2008). *Utilization-focused evaluation.* Thousand Oaks, CA: Sage.

Paulos, J. A. (1995). *A mathematician reads the newspaper.* New York: Basic Books.

Pavlov, I. P. (1902). *The work of the digestive glands* (W. H. Thompson, Trans.). Philadelphia: Griffin.

Pavlov, I. P. (1960). *Conditional reflexes.* New York: Dover. (Original work published 1927 by Oxford University Press, http://psychclassics.yorku.ca/Pavlov)

Payne, W. L. (1985). A study of emotion: Developing emotional intelligence; self-integration; relating to fear, pain and desire (theory, structure of reality, problem-solving, contraction/expansion, tuning in/coming out/letting go) (Doctoral dissertation, Union for Experimenting Colleges and Universities, 1985). *Dissertation Abstracts International, 47*(01), 203A.

Pearlstine, N. (2007). *Off the record: The press, the government and the war over anonymous sources.* New York: Farrar, Straus & Giroux.

Pedraza, S. (1999). Immigration in America at the turn of this century. *Contemporary Sociology, 28*(4), 377–381.

Peirce, C. S. (1955a). Abduction and induction. In Justus Buchler (Ed.), *Philosophical writing of Peirce* (pp. 150–156). New York: Dover.

Peirce, C. S. (1955b). The criterion of validity in reasoning. In Justus Buchler (Ed.), *Philosophical writing of Peirce* (pp. 120–128). New York: Dover.

Perkins, D. H., Radelet, S., & Lindauer, D. L. (2006). *Economics of development*. New York: W. W. Norton.

Perkins, D. N., & Salomon, G. (1994). Transfer of learning. In T. Husen & T. N. Postelwhite (Eds.), *International handbook of educational research* (2nd ed., Vol. 11, pp. 6452–6457). Oxford, UK: Pergamon Press.

Perry v. Sindermann, 408 U.S. 593 (1972).

Perse, E. M. (2000). *Media effects and society*. Mahwah, NJ: Lawrence Erlbaum.

Peters, B. G. (2007). *American public policy: Promise and performance* (7th ed.). Washington, DC: CQ Press.

Petsoulas, C. (2001). *Hayek's liberalism and its origins: His idea of spontaneous order and the Scottish enlightenment*. London: Routledge.

Petty, R. E., & Cacioppo, J. T. (1996). *Attitudes and persuasion: Classic and contemporary approaches*. Boulder, CO: Westview Press.

Pfeffer, J. (1981). Understanding the role of power in decision making. In J. M. Shafritz & J. S. Ott (Eds.), *Classics in organization theory* (pp. 304–318). Belmont, CA: Wadsworth Group.

Piaget, J. (1928). *The child's conception of the world*. London: Routledge & Kegan Paul.

Piaget, J. (1936). *La naissance d'intelligence*. Neuchatel, Switzerland: Delachaux et Niestlé.

Piaget, J. (1954). *The construction of reality in the child*. New York: Basic Books.

Piaget, J. (1965). *The moral judgment of the child* (M. Gabain, Trans.). New York: Free Press. (Original work published 1932)

Piaget, J. (1968). *Six psychological studies* (A. Tenzer, Trans.). New York: Vintage Books.

Piaget, J. (1972). *The psychology of the child*. New York: Basic Books.

Piaget, J. (1983). Piaget's theory. In P. Mussen (ed.)., *Handbook of child psychology.* (4th ed.). Vol. 1. New York: Wiley.

Piaget, J. (1999). The stages of the intellectual development of the child. In A. Slater & D. Muir (Eds.), *The Blackwell reader in developmental psychology* (pp. 35–42). Oxford, UK: Blackwell. (Reprinted from *Bulletin of the Menninger Clinic, 26*, 120–128, 1962)

Picker, J. M. (2001). International law. In P. S. Boyer (Ed.), *The Oxford companion to United States history*. Oxford, UK: Oxford University Press. (*Oxford reference online*, City University of New York, John Jay College of Criminal Justice. Retrieved 10 February, 2008, from http://www.oxfordreference.com/views/ENTRY.html?subview=Main&entry=t119.e0784

Pierce, K. (2005, November). A criminal conspiracy primer: What you need to know about the "darling of the modern prosecutor's nursery." *Emergency Envelopes, 1*(1).

Pillow, W. (2003). Confession, catharsis, or cure? Rethinking the uses of reflexivity as methodological power in qualitative research. *International Journal of Qualitative Studies, 16*(2), 175–196.

Pinel, J. P. J. (2005). *Biopsychology* (6th ed.) Boston: Allyn & Bacon.

Plato. (2007). *The republic* (D. Lee, Trans.). London: Penguin Classics. (Original work published 360 BCE)

Platzker, D., & Wyckoff, E. (2000). *Hard pressed: 600 years of prints and process*. New York: Hudson Hills Press.

Plessy v. Ferguson, 163 U.S. 537 (*1896*).

Plomin, R., DeFries, J. C., McClearn, G. E., & McGuffin, P. (2001). *Behavioral Genetics* (4th ed.). New York: Worth.

Plucker, J. A., Callahan, C. M., & Tomchin, E. M. (1996). Wherefore art thou, multiple intelligences? Alternative assessments for identifying talent in ethnically diverse and low income students. *Gifted Child Quarterly, 40*, 81–92.

Pope, D. (Ed.). (2001). *American radicalism*. Malden, MA: Wiley-Blackwell.

Pope, K., & Vasquez, M. (2007). *Ethics in psychotherapy and counselling: A practical guide* (3rd ed.). Indianapolis, IN: Wiley.

Popham, W. J. (1993). *Educational evaluation*. Needham Heights, MA: Allyn & Bacon.

Popular prints. (2008). In *Grove art online*. New York: Oxford University Press. Retrieved April 9, 2008, from http://www.groveart.com

Posner, M. I., & Snyder, C. R. R. (1975). Attention and cognitive control. In R. L. Solso (Ed.), *Information processing and cognition: The Loyola Symposium* (pp. 58–85). Hillsdale, NJ: Lawrence Erlbaum.

Postman, N. (1979). *The information environment: Teaching as a conserving activity* (pp. 33–48). New York: Delacorte.

Postman, N. (1985). *Amusing ourselves to death: Public discourse in the age of show business*. New York: Viking.

Powell, D. R. (2007). *Critical regionalism: Connecting politics and culture in the American landscape*. Chapel Hill: University of North Carolina Press.

Powell v. Alabama, 287 U.S. 45 (1932).

Poythress, M. P., & Slobogin, C. (2007). *Psychological evaluations for the courts*. New York: Guilford Press.

Prince, S. (2004). *Movies and meaning: An introduction to film*. Boston: Pearson.

Propaganda Critic: www.propagandacritic.com/articles/intro.why.html

Publishing industry profile: Global. (2007, November). Retrieved April 19, 2008, from the Business Source Premier database.

Publishing industry profile: United States. (2007, November). Retrieved April 19, 2008, from the Business Source Premier database.

Pugel, A. T. (2007). *International economics*. New York: McGraw-Hill.

Pulman, S. G., Richie, G. D., Russell, G. J., & Black, A. W. (1991). *Computational morphology: Practical mechanisms for the English lexicon*. Cambridge: MIT Press.

Purdy, J. E., Markham, M. R., Schwartz, B. L., & Gordon, W. C. (2001). *Learning and memory* (2nd ed.). Belmont, CA: Wadsworth/Thomson Learning.

Putnam, R. D. (1993). *Making democracy work: Civic traditions in modern Italy*. Princeton, NJ: Princeton University Press.

Pyryt, M. C. (2000). Finding "g": Easy viewing through higher-order factor analysis. *Gifted Child Quarterly, 44*, 190–192.

Quah, D. T. (1999). The weightless economy in growth. *Business Economist, 30*(1), 40–53.

Quine, W. V. O. (1953). Two dogmas of empiricism. In *From a logical point of view*. Cambridge, MA: Harvard University Press. (Reprinted from *Philosophical Review, 60*, 20–43, 1951)

Quinn, M. P. (1997). *Utilization-focused evaluation: The new century text*. Thousand Oaks, CA: Sage.

R. v. Smith, 2 S.C.R. 915 (*1992*).

Rabin, J., Hildreth, W. B., & Miller, G. J. (1998). *Handbook of public administration*. New York: Marcel Dekker.

Rabin, J., Miller, G., & Hildreth, B. (2000). *Handbook of strategic management*. Boca Raton, FL: CRC Press.

Rabkin, J. A. (2001). Conservatism. In J. Krieger (Ed.), *The Oxford companion to the politics of the world* (2nd ed.). Oxford, UK: Oxford University Press. (*Oxford reference online*, City University of New York, John Jay College of Criminal Justice. Retrieved February 10, 2008, from http://www.oxfordreference.com/views/ENTRY.html?subview=Main&entry=t121.e0155

Rahim, M., Kaufman, S., & Psenicka, C. (2004, June 6–9). A model of the styles of handling conflict, marital satisfaction, and instability. Paper presented at the IACM

17th Annual Conference, Pittsburgh, PA. Retrieved April 24, 2009, from http://ssrn.com/abstract=602765

Rahim, M. A. (2002). Toward a theory of managing organizational conflict. *International Journal of Conflict Management, 13*(3), 206–235. Retrieved April 30, 2009, from http://papers.ssrn.com/sol3/papers.cfm?abstract_id=437684

Rakove, J. N. (1979). *The beginnings of national politics: An interpretive history of the Continental Congress.* New York: Alfred Knopf.

Ratner, S., & Abrams, J. (2001). *Accountability for human rights atrocities in international law: Beyond the Nuremberg legacy.* Oxford, UK: Oxford University Press.

Rauch, J. (2001). The new old economy: Oil, computers, and the reinvention of the earth. *The Atlantic Monthly, 287*(1), 35–49.

Reagan doctrine. (1985). Retrieved October 4, 2008, from http://www.state.gov/r/pa/ho/time/rd/17741.htm

Reigeluth, C. M. (Ed.). (1999). *Instructional-design theories and models: A new paradigm of instructional theory* (Vol. 2). Mahwah, NJ: Lawrence Erlbaum.

Reiter, C., Rifkin, H., Garssen, B., & Van Schawk, A. (1989). Comorbidity among the anxiety disorders. *Journal of Anxiety Disorders, 3*, 57–68.

Rescher, N. (1978). *Scientific progress: A philosophical essay on the economics of research in natural science.* Pittsburgh, PA: University of Pittsburgh Press.

Reuter, P. (1983). *Disorganized crime: The economics of the visible hand.* Cambridge: MIT Press.

Rhodes, R. (2000). *The media violence myth.* Retrieved August 1, 2008, from http://www.abffe.org/myth1.htm

Ricardo, D. (1996). *Principles of political economy and taxation.* Amherst, NY: Prometheus Books. (Original work published 1817)

Riccio, D. C., Millin, P. M., & Gisquet-Verrier, P. (2003). Forgetting back: Retrograde amnesia. *Current Directions in Psychological Science, 12*, 41–44.

Ricoeur, P. (1981). *Hermeneutics and the human sciences.* New York: Cambridge University Press.

Riley, R. (1998). *Religious expression in public schools* (U.S. Department of Education guidelines). Retrieved May 6, 2009, from http://www.ed.gov/Speeches/08-1995/religion.html

Rimondini, M., Del Piccolo, L., Goss, C., Mazzi, M., Paccaloni, M., & Zimmermann, C. (2006). *Communication* skills in psychiatry residents: How do they handle patient concerns? *Psychotherapy & Psychosomatics, 75*(3), 161–169. Retrieved May 23, 2008, from http://content.karger.com

Rindskopf, D. (2006). Heavy alcohol use in the fighting back survey sample: Separating individual and community level influences using multilevel latent class analysis. *Journal of Drug Issues, 36*(2), 441–462.

Ritchie, A. D. (1989). *The Constitution.* New York: Chelsea House.

Rittberger, B., & Bulpitt, P. (2003). Federalism. In I. McLean & A. McMillan (Eds.), *The concise Oxford dictionary of politics.* New York: Oxford University Press. (*Oxford reference online*, City University of New York. Retrieved February 10, 2008, from http://www.oxfordreference.com/views/ENTRY.html?subview=Main&entry=t86.e471

Roberts, R. N., & Hammond, S. J. (2004). *Encyclopedia of presidential campaigns, slogans, issues and platforms.* Westport, CT: Greenwood Press.

Robertson, D. (1985). *A dictionary of modern politics.* Philadelphia: Taylor & Francis.

Robertson, D., Low, P. A., & Polinsky, R. J. (1996). *Primer on the autonomic nervous system.* San Diego, CA: Academic Press.

Robinson, P. (2005). The CNN effect revisited, *Critical Studies in Media Communication, 22*(4), 344/349.

Roe v. Wade, 410 U.S. 113 (1973).

Rogers, C. (1959). A theory of therapy, personality and interpersonal relationships as developed in the client-centered framework. In S. Koch (Ed.), *Psychology: A study of a science* (3rd ed., pp. 184–256). New York: McGraw-Hill.

Rogers, C. (1980). *A way of being.* Boston: Houghton Mifflin.

Rogers, C., & Farson, R. (1987). Active listening. In R. Newman, M. Danzinger, & M. Cohen (Eds.), *Communicating in business today.* Lexington, MA: D. C. Heath.

Rogers, C., & Roethlisberger, F. (1991). Barriers and gateways to communication. *Harvard Business Review, 69*(6), 105–111. Retrieved May 11, 2008, from http://web.ebscohost.com/ehost/detail?vid=4&hid=9&sid=f6166ffe-2987–4f3f-985b-cb96838c0618%40sessionmgr3http://web.ebscohost.com/ehost/detail?vid=4&hid=9&sid=f6166ffe-2987-4f3f-985b-cb96838c0618@sessionmgr3 (Original work published 1951)

Rogers, C. R. (1965). *Client-centered therapy: Its current practice, implications, and theory* (with chapters contributed by Elaine Dorman, Thomas Gordon, and Nicholas Hobbes). Boston: Houghton Mifflin.

Rogers, E. R. (1962). *Diffusion of innovations.* New York: Free Press of Glencoe.

Rogers, J. E. (1992). *Psychosurgery: Damaging the brain to save the mind.* New York: HarperCollins.

Rolls, E. T. (1999). *The brain and emotion.* New York: Oxford University Press.

Romzek, B., & Dubnick, M. (1987). Accountability in the public sector: Lessons learned from the Challenger tragedy. *Public Administration Review, 47*(3), 227–238.

Rondinelli, D. A. (1980). Government decentralization in comparative perspective: Theory and practice in developing countries. *International Review of Administrative Sciences, 47*, 133–145.

Rorschach, H. (1948). *Psychodiagnostik.* Bern, Switzerland: Hans Huber.

Rose, C. (2005). *How to win campaigns: 100 steps to success.* Sterling, VA: Earthscan.

Rosen, R. J. (2007). The role of securitization in mortgage lending. *Chicago Fed Letter, November*, 244.

Rosenthal, S. B. (1993). Peirce's ultimate logical interpretant and dynamical object: A pragmatic perspective. *Transactions of the Charles S. Peirce Society, 29*, 195–210.

Rosenwald, L. (2000). The theory, practice and influence of Thoreau's civil disobedience. In W. Cain (Ed.), *A historical guide to Henry David Thoreau* (pp. 153–180). Cambridge, UK: Oxford University Press.

Rosenzweig, R. (1999). Crashing the system? Hypertext and scholarship on American culture. *American Quarterly, 51*(2), 237–246.

Ross, C. A. (1997). *Dissociative identity disorder: Diagnosis, clinical features, and treatment of multiple personality.* New York: Wiley.

Roszak, T. (1995). *The making of a counter culture: Reflections on the technocratic society and its youthful opposition.* Berkeley: University of California Press. (Original work published 1969)

Roth, A., & Fonagy, P. (2004). *What works for whom? A critical review of psychotherapy research* (2nd ed.). New York: Guilford Press.

Ruben, B., & Lievrouw, L. (Eds.). (1990). *Mediation, information, and communication.* New Brunswick, NJ: Transaction Publishers.

Rudebusch, G. D. (2005). Assessing the Lucas critique in monetary policy models. *Journal of Money, Credit and Banking, 37*(2), 245–272.

Ruggiero, V. (1989). *Critical thinking: Supplement to becoming a master student.* Rapid City, SD: College Survival.

Rumelhart, D. E., McClelland, J. L., & the PDP Research Group. (1986). *Parallel distributed processing: Explorations in the microstructure of cognition* (Vol. 1). Cambridge: MIT Press.

Ryan, M. L. (2004). *Narrative across media: The languages of storytelling* (Frontiers of Narrative). Lincoln: University of Nebraska Press.

S. Doc. No. 108-17, 2d Sess., 108th Cong. (2004). Washington, DC: Government Printing Office.

S. Doc. No. 108-19, 2d Sess., 108th Cong. (2004). Washington, DC: Government Printing Office.

S. Doc. No. 110-6, 1st Sess., 110th Cong. (2007). Washington, DC: Government Printing Office.

S. Rep. No. 752 at 26, 1st Sess., 79th Cong. (1945). Washington, DC: Government Printing Office.

Sachs, G. S., Koslow, C. L., & Ghaemi, S. N. (2000). The treatment of bipolar depression: Review article. *Bipolar Disorders, 2,* 256–260.

Sage. (1997). *National television violence study.* Thousand Oaks, CA: Author.

Said, E. W. (1978). *Orientalism.* New York: Random House.

Salovey, P., & Mayer, J. D. (1990). Emotional intelligence. *Imagination, Cognition, and Personality, 9,* 185–211.

Salvatore, D. (2002). *Microeconomics.* New York: Oxford University Press.

Salvatore, D. (2006). *International economics.* New York: Wiley.

Sam, D. L. (2006). Acculturation and health. In D. L. Sam & J. W. Berry (Eds.), *Cambridge handbook of acculturation psychology* (pp. 452–468). New York: Cambridge University Press.

Sam, D. L., & Berry, J. (Eds.). (2006). *Cambridge handbook of acculturation psychology.* New York: Cambridge University Press.

Sambhava, P. (Compiler). (1993). *The Tibetan book of the dead: The great book of natural liberation through understanding in the between* (R. Thurman, Trans.). New York: Bantam Books.

Sarafino, E. P., & Goehring, P. (2000). Age comparisons in acquiring biofeedback control and success in reducing headache pain. *Annals of Behavioral Medicine, 22,* 10–16.

Sartori, G. (1962). Constitutionalism: A preliminary discussion, *American Political Science Review, 56,* 853–864.

Sassoon, D. (1996). *One hundred years of socialism: The West European left in the twentieth century.* New York: New York University Press.

Satterthwaite, J. (1972). The Truman Doctrine: Turkey. *Annals of the American Academy of Political and Social Science, 401*(America and the Middle East), 74–84.

Sauer, C. (1925). The morphology of landscape. *University of California Publications in Geography, 2,* 19–54.

Schachter, S., & Singer, J. E. (1962). Cognitive, social, and physiological determinants of emotional state. *Psychological Review, 69*(5), 379–399.

Schacter, D. L. (1987). Implicit memory: History and current status. *Journal of Experimental Psychology: Learning, Memory, and Cognition, 13,* 501–518.

Schapiro, L. (1972). *Totalitarianism.* New York: Praeger.

Schein, E. (1999). *Process consultation revisited.* New York: Addison-Wesley.

Schein, E. H. (2004). *Organizational culture and leadership* (The Jossey-Bass Business & Management Series). San Francisco: Jossey-Bass.

Schenck v. United States, 249 U.S. 47 (1919)

Schiller, B. R. (2006). *The economy today.* New York: McGraw-Hill.

Schiller, H. I. (1969). *Mass communications and American empire.* New York: A. M. Kelley.

Schlesinger, A. M., Jr. (1947). The Supreme Court: 1947. *Fortune,* January, 202, 208.

Schlesinger, A. M., Jr. (1973). *The imperial presidency.* Boston: Houghton Mifflin.

Schmidt, W. S, Shelley, M. C., & Bardes, A. B. (2006). *American government and politics today.* Florence, KY: Wadsworth.

Schmitz, D. F. (2006). *The United States and right-wing dictatorships.* Cambridge, UK: Cambridge University Press.

Schneider, F., & Enste, D. (2002). *Hiding in the shadows: The growth of the underground economy* (Economic Issues, No. 30). Retrieved February 23, 2008, from http://www.imf.org

Schnell, P. (1996). Public service broadcasting: The history of a concept. In P. Marris & S. Thornham (Eds.), *Media studies: A reader* (2nd ed., pp. 120–134). New York: New York University Press. (Reprinted from *Understanding television,* pp. 11–29, by A. Goodwin & G. Whannel, Eds., 1989, London: Routledge)

Schoenwald, S. K., Ward, D. M., Henggeler, S. W., & Rowland, M. D. (2000). Multisystemic therapy versus hospitalization for crisis stabilization of youth: Placement outcomes four months postreferral. *Mental Health Services Research, 2,* 3–12.

Schonfeld, I., & Rindskopf, D. (2007). Hierarchical linear modeling in organizational research: Longitudinal data outside the context of growth modeling. *Organizational Research Methods, 10*(3), 417–429.

Schudson, M. (1978). *Discovering the news: A social history of American newpapers.* New York: Basic Books.

Schulhofer, K. (2001). *Criminal law and its processes: Cases and materials* (7th ed.). New York: Aspen.

Schultz, W. (1958). *FIRO: A three-dimensional theory of interpersonal behavior.* New York: Rinehart.

Schumpeter, J. (1939). *Business cycles: A theoretical, historical, and statistical analysis of the capitalist process.* New York. McGraw-Hill.

Schumpeter, J. A. (1950). *Capitalism, socialism and democracy.* New York: Harper & Brothers.

Scott, J. (Ed.). (2002). *Social networks: Critical concepts in sociology.* London: Routledge.

Scriven, M. (1991). *Evaluation thesaurus* (4th ed.). Newbury Park, CA: Sage.

Scruton, R. (1982). *A dictionary of political thought.* New York: Harper & Row.

Seligman, M. E. P. (1990). *Learned optimism.* New York: Knopf.

Seligman, M. E. P. (1993). *What you can change and what you can't: The complete guide to successful self-improvement.* New York: Knopf.

Senate Report No. 752 (1945).

Senge, P., Kleiner, A., Roberts, C., Ross, R., Roth, G., & Smith, B. (1999). *The dance of change: The challenges to sustaining momentum in learning organizations.* New York: Currency Press.

Serrano v. Priest, 5 Cal.3d 584 (1971).

Severin, W. J. (1988). *Communication theories: Origins, methods, uses* (2nd ed.). New York: Longman.

Severin, W. J., & Tankard, J. W., Jr. (1997). *Communication theories: Origins, methods, and uses in the mass media* (4th ed.). New York: Longman.

Shadish, W. R., Cook, T. D., & Campbell, D. (2002). *Experimental and quasi-experimental designs for generalized causal inference.* New York: Houghton Mifflin.

Shafritz, J., & Ott, J. (2001). *Classics of organization theory* (5th ed.). Belmont, CA: Wadsworth/Thompson Learning.

Shaughnessy, J., Zeichmeister, E. & Zeichmeister, E. (2000). *Research methods in psychology.* Boston: McGraw-Hill.

Sheehan, M. (1996). *The balance of power: History and theory.* New York: Routledge.

Shepard, S. B. (1997, November 17). The new economy: What it really means [Electronic version]. *Business Week*. Retrieved April 13, 2009, from http://www.businessweek.com/1997/46/b3553084.htm

Shermer, M. (1997). *Why smart people believe weird things*. New York: W. H. Freeman.

Shimojo, S., Kamitani, Y., & Nishida, S. (2001). Afterimage of perceptually filled-in surface. *Science, 293,* 1677–1680.

Shutze, R. (2009, May). *From dual to cooperative federalism: The changing structure of European law*. Oxford, UK: Oxford University Press.

Sidani, S. (2006). Random assignment: A systematic review. In R. R. Bootzin & M. E. Patrick (Eds.), *Strengthening research methodology: Psychological measurement and evaluation* (pp. 125–141). Washington, DC: Author.

Sidgwick, H. (1874). *The methods of ethics*. London: Macmillan.

Siegel, R. K. (2005). *Intoxication: The universal drive for mind-altering substances*. Rochester, VT: Park Street Press.

Silber, M. H. (2001). Sleep disorders, *Neurologic Clinics,* 19, 173–186.

Silverstone, R. (2005). The sociology of mediation and communication. In C. Calhoun, C. Rojek, & B. Turner (Eds.), *The Sage handbook of sociology* (pp. 188–207). London: Sage.

Sim, M. (1974). *Guide to psychiatry* (3rd ed.). London: Churchill Livingstone.

Simon, C. A. (2007). *Public policy: Preferences and outcomes*. New York: Pearson Longman.

Simon, H. (1947). *Administrative behavior: A study of decision-making processes in administrative organizations* (4th ed.). Glencoe, IL: Free Press.

Simon, H. (1991). *Models of my life*. New York: Basic Books.

Simon, H. A. (1955). A behavioral model of rational choice. *Quarterly Journal of Economics, 69,* 100–118.

Simon, H. A. (1979). Rational decision making in business organizations. *The American Economic Review,* 69(1), 493–513.

Sinclair, U. (1906). *The jungle*. New York: Simon & Schuster.

Sire, J. (2004). *Naming the elephant: Worldview as a concept*. Downers Grove, IL: InterVarsity Press.

Sisaye, S. (2005). Teams and management control systems: A synthesis of three organizational development approaches. *Leadership & Organization Development Journal, 26*(3), 172–185.

Skinner, B. F. (1938). *The behavior of organisms*. New York: Appleton-Century-Crofts.

Skolnick, J. (2005). Corruption and the blue code of silence. In R. Sarre, D. K. Das, & H. Albrecht (Eds.), *Policing corruption: International perspectives* (pp. 301–316). Lanham, MD: Lexington Books.

Slater, A., & Bremner, G. (Eds.). (2003). *Introduction to developmental psychology*. Malden, MA: Blackwell.

Slomanson, W. R. (2003). *Fundamental perspectives on international law*. London: West Group.

Sluga, H. D., & Stern, D. G. (Eds.). (1996). *The Cambridge companion to Wittgenstein*. Cambridge, UK: Press Syndicate of the University of Cambridge.

Smart, S. B., Megginson, W. L., & Gitman, L. J. (2007). *Corporate finance* (2nd ed.). Mason, OH: Thomson South-Western.

Smedley, A. (2007). *Race in North America: Origin and evolution of a worldview* (3rd ed.). Boulder, CO: Westview Press.

Smedley, A., & Smedley, B. D. (2005). Race as biology is fiction, racism as a social problem is real: Anthropological and historical perspectives on the social construction of race. *American Psychologist, 60*(1), 16–26.

Smelser, N. J. (1976). *Comparative methods in the social sciences*. Princeton, NJ: Prentice Hall.

Smith, A. (1977). *An inquiry into the nature and causes of the wealth of nations* (E. Cannan, Ed.). Chicago: University of Chicago Press. (Original work published 1776)

Smith, A. (1994). *The wealth of nations* (E. Cannan, Ed.). New York: Modern Library. (Original work published 1776)

Smith, A. (2000). *The theory of moral sentiments*. Amherst, NY: Prometheus Books. (Original work published 1759)

Smith, A. (2007). *The wealth of nations*. Hampshire, UK: Harriman House. (Original work published 1776)

Smith, G. (1986). *Morality, reason, and power: American diplomacy in the Carter years*. New York: Hill & Wag.

Smith, M. K. (2007, December). Social capital. In *The encyclopedia of informal education*. Retrieved February 18, 2008, from http://www.infed.org/biblio/social_capital.htm

Smith, W. S. (1998). Our dysfunctional Cuban embargo. *Orbis, 42*(4), 533–545.

Smythe, D. W. (1981). On the audience commodity and its work. In D. W. Smythe (Ed.), *Dependency road: Communications, capitalism, consciousness, and Canada* (pp. 22–51). Norwood, NJ: Ablex.

Smythe v. Ames, 169 U.S. 466 (1898).

Soley, L. (2004). *Censorship, Inc.: The corporate threat to free speech in the United States*. New York: Monthly Review Press.

Solomon, R. L. (1980). The opponent-process theory of acquired motivation: The costs of pleasure and the benefits of pain. *American Psychologist, 35*(8), 691—712.

Solow, R. (1956). A contribution to the theory of economic growth. *Quarterly Journal of Economics, 70*(1), 65–94.

Sombart, W. (1916). *Der Moderne Kapitalismus* [Modern capitalism] (3 vols. in 6). Munchen und Leipzig, Germany: Duncker & Humblot.

Soothill, K., Francis, B., & Ackerley, E. (2007). Kidnapping: A criminal profile of persons convicted, 1979–2001. *Behavioral Sciences and the Law, 25*(1), 69–84.

Soper, S. (1985). *Totalitarianism: A conceptual approach*. Lanham, MD: University Press of America.

Spalding, D. A. (1872). On instinct. *Nature, 6,* 485–486.

Sparks, R. (1992). *Television and the drama of crime: Moral tales and the place of crime in public life*. Philadelphia: Open University Press.

Speier, H. (1950). Historical development of public opinion. *American Journal of Sociology, 55,* 376–388.

Spencer, M. (1998). *Separatism: Democracy and disintegration*. Lanham, MD: Rowman & Littlefield.

Sperling, G. (1960). The information available in brief visual presentations. *Psychological Monographs: General and Applied, 74*(11, Whole No. 498), 1–29.

Spivak, G. (1993). *Outside in the teaching machine*. New York: Routledge.

Spradley, J. P. (1979). *The ethnographic interview*. Fort Worth, TX: Holt, Rinehart, & Winston.

Spreen, O., & Risser, A. H. (2003). *Assessment of aphasia*. New York: Oxford University Press.

Sproule, J. M. (1997). *Propaganda and democracy: The American experience of media and mass persuasion*. New York: Cambridge University Press.

Squire, L. R., Clark, R. E., & Knowlton, B. J. (2001). Retrograde amnesia. In Animal models of memory consolidation [Special issue]. *Hippocampus, 11*(1), 50–55.

Squire, L. R., Knowlton, B., & Musen, G. (1993). The structure and organization of memory. *Annual Review of Psychology, 44,* 453–495.

Squires, D. A., Huitt, W. G., & Segars, J. K. (1983). *Effective schools and classrooms: A research-based perspective*.

Alexandria, VA: Association for Supervision and Curriculum Development.

St. Pierre, E. A. (2000). Poststructural feminism in education: An overview. *International Journal of Qualitative Studies in Education, 13*(5), 477–515.

Stanford encyclopedia of philosophy. Heredity and heritability. Retrieved March 2, 2009, from http://plato.stanford.edu/entries/heredityhttp://plato.stanford.edu/entries/heredity/http://plato.stanford.edu/entries/heredity/

Stanford University. (2009). *Glossary.* Retrieved March 23, 2009, from http://www.stanford.edu/group/arts/nicaragua/student/mural/glossary.html

Stangor, C. (2007). *Research methods for the behavioral sciences* (3rd ed.). Boston, MA: Houghton Mifflin.

Staples, W. G. (1997). *The culture of surveillance: Discipline and social control in the United States.* New York: St. Martin's Press.

Starling, G. (2008). *Managing the public sector* (8th ed.). Belmont, CA: Thompson Wadsworth.

Starr, P. (1982). *The social transformation of American medicine.* New York: Basic Books.

State of Maine Supreme Judicial Court Administrative Order JB-05–2. Protocol for Issuance, Distribution, and Publication of Administrative Orders Effective: August 1, 2005.

Staub, E. (1971). A child in distress: The influence of nurturance and modeling on children's attempts to help. *Developmental Psychology, 5,* 124–132.

Stauber, J. C., & Rampton, S. (1995). *Toxic sludge is good for you: Lies, damn lies and the public relations industry.* Monroe, ME: Common Courage Press.

Steele, C. M., & Aronson, J. (1995). Stereotype threat and the intellectual test performance of African Americans. *Journal of Personality and Social Psychology, 69*(5), 797–811.

Steele, R., & Black, J. (1999). *Codes of ethics and beyond.* Retrieved March 12, 2008, from http://www.poynter.org/content/content_view.asp?id=5522

Steffens, L. (1957). *The shame of the cities.* New York: Dover. (Original work published 1904)

Steinmetz, S. (2008). *Semantic antics: How and why words change meaning.* New York: Random House.

Stephens, M. (1998). *The rise of the image, the fall of the word.* New York: Oxford University Press.

Stephens, M. (2007). *A history of news* (3rd ed.). New York: Oxford University Press.

Sternberg, R. J., & Soriano, L. J. (1984). Styles of conflict resolution. *Journal of Personality and Social Psychology, 41*(5) 15–26.

Stevens, L. (1973). *Individualism.* Oxford, UK: Basil Blackwell.

Stiglitz, J. E. (2003). *Globalization and its discontents.* New York: W. W. Norton.

Stossel, S. (1997). The man who counts the killings. *The Atlantic Monthly, 279*(5), 86–104.

Stratton, K. R., Howe, C. J., & Battaglia, F. C. (1996). *Fetal alcohol syndrome, diagnosis, epidemiology, prevention, and treatment.* Washington, DC: National Academy Press.

Stuart, G., Spruston, N., & Hausser, M. (2007). *Dendrites.* New York: Oxford University Press.

Suber, P. (2004). *Open access overview: Focusing on open access to peer-reviewed research articles and their preprints.* Retrieved May 1, 2008, from http://www.earlham.edu/~peters/fos/overview.htm

Sullivan, J., Albrecht, T., & Taylor, S. (1990). Process, organizational, relational, and personal determinants of managerial compliance-gaining communication strategies. *Journal of Business Communication, 27*(4), 331–355. Retrieved May 24, 2008, from http://web.ebscohost.com/ehost/results?

Sullivan, T. P. (2004). *Police experiences with recording custodial interrogations.* Chicago: Northwestern University School of Law, Center on Wrongful Convictions. Retrieved 23 March, 2009, from http://www.law.northwestern.edu/wrongfulconvictions/issues/causesandremedies/falseconfessions/SullivanReport.pdf

Surette, R. (1990). Estimating the magnitude and mechanisms of copycat crime. In R. Surette (Ed.), *The media and criminal justice policy: Recent research and social effects* (pp. 87–102). Springfield, IL: Charles C Thomas.

Surette, R. (1992). *Media, crime, and criminal justice: Images and realities.* (Contemporary Issues in Crime and Justice Series). Pacific Grove, CA: Brooks/Cole.

Survivor: www.cbs.com/primetime/survivor16

Sutherland, E. H. (1939). *Principles of criminology* (3rd ed.). Philadelphia: J. B. Lippincott.

Sutton, A. J., Abrams, K. R., Jones, D. R., Sheldon, T. A., & Song, F. (2000). *Methods for meta-analysis in medical research.* West Sussex, UK: Wiley.

Svanikier, J. (2007). Political elite circulation: Implications for leadership diversity and democratic regime stability in Ghana. *Comparative Sociology, 6,* 114–135.

Tagg, J. (1988). *The burden of representation: Essays on photographies and histories.* Amherst: University of Massachusetts Press.

Tarasoff v. Regents of the University of California, 551 P.2d 334 (1976).

Tarde, G. (1903). *The laws of imitation.* New York: Holt.

Tarde, G. (1912). *Penal philosophy.* Boston: Little Brown.

Tarde, G. (1962). *The laws of imitiation.* Gloucester, MA: Patterson Smith. (Original work published 1903)

Tarde, G. (1969). Opinion and conversation. In T. Clarke (Ed.), *Gabriel Tarde on communication and social influence* (pp. 297–318). Chicago: University of Chicago Press. (Original work published 1898)

Tate, A. (2007). The mind of the master class: History and faith in the Southern slaveholders' worldview [Review]. *Journal of Social History (1527–1897), 40*(3), 788–790. Retrieved May 31, 2008, from http://z3950.muse.jhu.edu.proxy.libraries.rutgers.edu/journals/journal_of_social_history/v040/40.3tate.pdf

Taylor, F. W. (1967). *The principles of scientific management.* New York: W. W. Norton. (Original work published 1911)

Taylor, S. E. (1990). Health psychology. *American Psychologist, 45*(1), 40–50.

Tebbel, J. W., & Zuckerman, M. (1991). *The magazine in America: 1741–1990.* New York: Oxford University Press.

Ted Nelson's Web site: http://hyperland.com/mlawLeast.html

Teglasi, H. (2001). *Essentials of TAT and other storytelling techniques assessment.* Hoboken, NJ: Wiley.

Terman, L. M. (1916). *The measurement of intelligence.* Boston: Houghton, Mifflin.

Term Limits, Inc. v. Thornton, 514 U.S. 779 (1995).

Terry v. Ohio, 392 U.S. 1 (1968).

Thomas, G. C., III. (1998). *Double jeopardy: The history, the law.* New York: New York University Press.

Thomas, H. (2007). *Watchdogs of democracy: The waning Washington press corps and how it has failed the public.* New York: Scribner.

Thomas, K., & Kilmann, R. (1983). The Thomas-Kilmann conflict mode instrument. In D. Cole (Ed.), *Conflict resolution technology* (pp. 57–64). Cleveland, OH: Organizational Development Institute.

Thompson, J. B. (1995). *The media and modernity: A social theory of the media.* Stanford, CA: Stanford University Press.

Thompson, K., Leintz, P., Nevers, B., & Witkowski, S. (2004). The integrative listening model: An approach to teaching and learning listening. *Journal of General Education,*

53(3–4), 225–246. Retrieved May 31, 2008, from http://wfsearch.webfeat.org/cgi-bin/WebFeat.dll?

Thorndike, E. L. (1898). Animal intelligence: An experimental study of the associative processes in animals. *Psychological Review Monograph Supplement, 2*(8), 1–109.

Thorndike, E. L. (1920). A constant error on psychological rating. *Journal of Applied Psychology, 4*, 25–29.

Thucydides. (431 BCE). *History of the Peloponnesian War* (Richard Crawly Trans.) (The Internet Classics Archive). Retrieved 5 March, 2009, from http://classics.mit.edu/Thucydides/pelopwar.html

Thurstone, L. L., & Thurstone, T. G. (1941). *Factorial studies of intelligence.* Chicago: University of Chicago Press.

Tichenor, P. J., Donohue, G., & Olien, O. (1970). Mass media flow and differential growth in knowledge identifiers. *Public Opinion Quarterly, 34*, 159–170.

Tjosvold, D., Johnson, W., Johnson, R., & Sun, H. (2003). Can interpersonal competition be constructive within organizations? *Journal of Psychology, 137*(1), 63–84. Retrieved from the ProQuest Social Science Journals database

Tobach, E. (2006). Identity of comparative psychology: Its status and advances in evolutionary theory and genetics. *International Journal of Comparative Psychology, 19*, 129–150.

Todaro, M. P., & Smith, S. C. (2006). *Economic development* (9th ed.). New York: Pearson.

Todaro, M. P., & Smith, S. C. (2008). *Economic development* (10th ed.). Upper Saddle River, NJ: Pearson.

Toulmin, S. (1958). *The uses of argument.* Cambridge, UK: Cambridge University Press.

Toulmin, S., Riecke, R., & Janik, A. (1979). *An introduction to reasoning.* New York. Macmillan.

Trattner, W. (1979). *From poor law to welfare state: A history of social welfare in America* (2nd ed.). New York: Free Press.

Treffert, D. A., & Wallace, G. A. (2003). Islands of genius. *Scientific American, 14*, 14–23.

Triandis, H. C. (1989). Self and social behavior in differing cultural contexts. *Psychological Review, 96*(3), 506–520.

Tribe, K. (1990). German neo-liberals and the social market economy. *Economic Journal, 100*(401), 630–632.

Tsang, J. (2002). Moral rationalization and the integration of situational factors and psychological processes in immoral behavior. *Review of General Psychology, 6*(1), 25–50.

Tsebelis, G., & Money, J. (1997). *Bicameralism.* Cambridge, UK: Cambridge University Press.

Tukey, J. W. (1977). *Exploratory data analysis.* Reading, MA: Addison-Wesley.

Tulsky, D. S., Saklofskie, D. H., & Zhu, J. (2003). Revising a standard: An evaluation of the origin and development of the WAIS-III. In D. S. Tulsky, D. H. Saklofske, G. J. Chelune, R. K. Heaton, & R. J. Ivnik (Eds.), *Clinical interpretation of the WAIS-III and WMS-III* (pp. 43–92). San Diego, CA: Academic Press.

Tulving, E., & Thomson, D. M. (1973). Encoding specificity and retrieval processes in episodic memory. *Psychological Review, 80*, 352–373.

Turow, J. (1997). *Breaking up America: Advertisers and the new media world.* Chicago: University of Chicago Press.

Turvey, B. (1999). *Criminal profiling: An introduction to behavioral evidence analysis.* San Diego, CA: Academic Press.

Tversky, A., & Kahneman, D. (1974). Judgement under uncertainty: Heuristics and biases. *Science, 185*, 1124–1130.

Tye, L. (2002). *The father of spin: Edward L. Bernays and the birth of public relations.* New York: Holt.

Tylor, E. B. (1974). *Primitive culture: Researches into the development of mythology, philosophy, religion, art, and custom.* Croydon, UK: Gordon Press. (Original work published 1871)

Ulam, A. B. (1973). *The rivals: America and Russia Since World War II.* New York: Viking Press.

Underwood, B. J. (1957). Interference and forgetting. *Psychological Review, 64*, 49–60.

United Kingdom House of Lords Decisions. (1843, May 26–June 19). *Daniel M'Naghten's case.* Retrieved March 22, 2009, from http://www.bailii.org/uk/cases/UKHL/1843/J16.html

United Nations. (2002). Freedom to believe: A defining freedom. *UN Chronicle, 43*(3), 14. Retrieved March 31, 2009, from http://www.un.org/Pubs/chronicle/2006/issue3/0306p14.htm

United Nations Educational, Scientific and Cultural Organization. (n.d.). *Cultural diversity.* Retrieved March 24, 2009, from http://portal.unesco.org/culture/en/ev.php-URL_ID=2450&URL_DO=DO_TOPIC&URL_SECTION=201.html

Ury, W. (1985). (M. Lynsky, ed.) *Beyond the hotline: How crisis control can prevent nuclear war.* Boston: Houghton Mifflin.

USLegal. (n.d.) *Adverse impact law and legal definition.* Retrieved February 25, 2009, from http://definitions.uslegal.com/a/adverse-impact

U.S. Department of Education: http://www.ed.gov

U.S. Department of Education, Office of Special Education and Rehabilitative Services. (2000, July). *A guide to the individualized education program.* Jessup, MD: U.S. Department of Education, Editorial Publications Center. Retrieved March 30, 2008, from http://www.ed.gov/parents/needs/speced/iepguide/index.html#team

U.S. Department of Justice. (1947). *Attorney General's manual on the Administrative Procedures Act.* Retrieved March 6, 2009, from http://www.law.fsu.edu/library/admin/1947cover.html

U.S. General Accounting Office, Office of the General Counsel. (2004). Agency regulations and administrative discretion. In *Principles of Federal Appropriations Law* (GAO-04-261SP) (3rd ed., Vol. 1, chap. 3, pp. 3-2, *et seq.*). Retrieved February 23, 2009, from http://www.gao.gov/atext/d04261sp.txt

U.S. House of Representatives. (2003). *How our laws are made.* Retrieved February 19, 2009, from http://thomas.loc.gov/home/lawsmade.bysec/publication.html

U.S. industry quarterly review: Information services. (2006, 2nd Quarter). Retrieved April 19, 2008, from the Business Source Premier database.

U.S. Office of Management and Budget. (2000). *Draft report to Congress on the costs and benefits of federal regulations.* Washington, DC: Author.

U.S. Office of Personnel Management. (n.d.). Glossary of terms used in processing personnel actions. In *The guide to processing personnel actions* (chap. 35). Washington, DC: Author.

U.S. Senate. (n.d.) *Senate glossary.* Retrieved February 19, 2009, from http://www.senate.gov/pagelayout/reference/b_three_sections_with_teasers/glossary.htm

U.S. Term Limits, Inc. v. Thornton, 514 U.S. 779 (1995).

U.S. v. Nixon, 418 *U.S.* 683 (1974).

U.S. v. Reynolds, 345 U.S. 10 (1953).

Vadi, M., Allik, J., & Realo, A. (2002). *Collectivism and its consequences for organizational culture.* Tartu, Estonia: University of Tartu.

van Manen, M. (1990). *Researching lived experience: Human science for an action sensitive pedagogy.* London, Ontario, Canada: University of Western Ontario.

van Manen, M. (1997). *Researching lived experience* (2nd ed.). London, Ontario, Canada: Althouse Press.

Vernallis, C. (2004). *Experiencing music video: Aesthetics and cultural context.* New York: Columbia University Press.

Viner, J. (1950). *Customs union issue*. New York: Carnegie Endowment for International Peace.

Vines, D., & Gilbert, C. (Eds.). (2004). *The IMF and its critic: Reform of global financial architecture*. Cambridge, UK: Cambridge University Press.

Vocate, D. R. (1994). *Intrapersonal communication: Different voices, different minds*. Mahwah, NJ: Lawrence Erlbaum.

von Dornum, D. (1997). The straight and the crooked: Legal accountability in ancient Greece. *Columbia Law Review, 97*(5), 1483–1518.

Von Laue, T. (1987). *The world revolution of Westernization: The twentieth century in global perspective*. New York: Oxford University Press.

Vroom, V. H. (1994). *Work and motivation*. San Francisco, CA: Jossey-Bass.

Vygotsky, L. S. (1978). *Mind in society: The development of higher psychological processes* (M. Cole, V. John-Steiner, S. Scribner, & E. Souberman, Eds.). Cambridge, MA: Harvard University Press.

Walsh, K. (2004). *Talking about politics: Informal groups and social identity in American life* (pp. 1–2). Chicago: University of Chicago Press.

Walton, D. N. (1999). *Appeal to popular opinion*. University Park: Pennsylvania State University Press.

Waluchow, W. J. (2007). Judicial review. *Philosophy Compass, 2*(2), 258–266. Retrieved April 21, 2008, from http://www.blackwellcompass.com

Wandycz, P. (2006). Nationalism and patriotism: The contribution of Andrzej Walicki. *Dialogue & Universalism, 16*(1/2), 105–114.

Warburton, C. E. S. (2005). *The evolution of crises and underdevelopment in Africa*. Lanham, MD: University Press of America.

Warburton, C. E. S. (2006). *Research and profit maximization in finance and economics*. Lanham, MD: University Press of America.

Ward, S. J. A. (2004). *The invention of journalism ethics: The path to objectivity and beyond*. Montreal, Quebec, Canada: McGill-Queen's University Press.

Washington's farewell address to the people of the United States (Senate Document No. 106–21). (2000). Washington, DC: Government Printing Office. (Published in *The Independent Chronicle*, September 26, 1796. Retrieved March 23, 2009, from http://www.access.gpo.gov/congress/senate/farewell/sd106-21.pdf

Waste, R. J. (1986). *Community power: Directions for future research*. Beverly Hills, CA: Sage.

Watson, A. (Trans., Ed.). (1998). *The digest of Justinian* (2 vols.). Philadelphia: University of Pennsylvania Press.

Watson, J. B. (1913). Psychology as the behaviorist views it. *Psychological Review, 20*, 158–177.

Watson, T., & Noble, P. (2007). *Evaluating public relations: A best practice guide to public relations planning, research and evaluation* (2nd ed.). London: Kogan Page.

Watson Wyatt Worldwide. (2009). *Executive summary, 2007/2008 communication ROI study; secrets of top performers: How companies with highly effective employee communication differentiate themselves*. Retrieved February 26, 2009, from http://www.watsonwyatt.com/research/resrender.asp?id=2007-US-0214&page=1

Weaver, C. H. (1972). *Human listening: Processes and behavior*. New York: Bobbs-Merrill.

Weaver, W., & Shannon, C. E. (1963). *The mathematical theory of communication*. Champaign: University of Illinois Press.

Webb, E. J., Campbell, D. T., Schwartz, R. D., & Sechrest, L. (1966). *Unobtrusive measures: Nonreactive research in the social science*. Beverly Hills, CA: Sage.

Weber, M. (1922). Characteristics of bureaucracy. In *Wirtschaft und Gesellschaft [Economy and Society]* (Pt. 3, chap. 6, pp. 650–678). Tübingen, Germany: J. C. B. Mohr. Retrieved March 9, 2009, from http://www.faculty.rsu.edu/~felwell/TheoryWeb/readings/WeberBurform.html

Weber, M. (1949). Objectivity in social science and social policy. In E. A. Shils & H. A. Finch (Eds. &Trans.), *The methodology of the social sciences* (50–112). New York: Free Press. (Original work published 1904)

Weber, M. (1958). The three types of legitimate rule (H. Gerth, Trans.). Berkeley Publications in Society and Institutions, *4*(1), 1–11.

Weber, M. (1991). *Essays in sociology* (H. H. Gerth & C. Wright Mills, Eds.). London: Routledge.

Wechsler, D. (1939). *The measurement of adult intelligence*. Baltimore: Williams & Wilkins.

Weeks v. U.S., 232 U.S. 383 (1914).

Weick, K. E. (1996). *Sensemaking in organizations*. Thousand Oaks, CA: Sage.

Weinberg, G. M. (1975). *An introduction to general systems thinking*. New York: Wiley.

Weinberg, L. (1991). The Monroe mystery solved: Beyond the unhappy history theory of civil rights litigation. *Brigham Young University Law Review, 1991*(2), 737–766.

Weiss, C. H. (1988). Evaluation for decisions: Is anybody there? Does anybody care? *Evaluation Practice, 9*, 5–19.

Weiss, T. G., Forsythe, D. P., & Coate, R. A. (2004). *The United Nations and changing world politics* (4th ed.). Boulder, CO: Westview Press.

Weizacker, E. W., Young, O. R., & Finger, M. (2005). *Limits to privatization: How to avoid too much of a good thing* (p. 6). London: Earthscan.

Werner, J. M., & DeSimone, R. L. (2006). *Human resource development* (4th ed.). Mason, OH: Thomson.

West, M., & Farr, J. (Eds.). (1991). *Innovation and creativity at work*. Chichester, UK: Wiley.

Westbrook, C., Roth, C. K., & Talbot, J. (2005). *MRI in practice* (3rd ed.). Cambridge, UK: Blackwell.

Westchester Institute for Human Services Research. (2002). Ability grouping. *The Balanced View: Research Based Information on Timely Topics, 6*(2). Retrieved March 4, 2008, from http://www.sharingsuccess.org/code/bv/ability grouping.pdf

Westfeldt, W., & Wicker, T. (1998). *Indictment: The news media and the criminal justice system*. Nashville, TN: First Amendment Center.

Whitefield, S. (2003). Communism. In I. McLean & A. McMillan (Eds.), *The concise Oxford dictionary of politics*. Oxford, UK: Oxford University Press. (*Oxford reference online*, City University of New York, John Jay College of Criminal Justice. Retrieved February 10, 2008, from http://www.oxfordreference.com/views/ENTRY.html?subview=Main&entry=t86.e245

White House. (2009). *Our government: The executive branch*. Retrieved April 13, 2009, from http://www.whitehouse.gov/our_government/executive_branch/

Wickens, C., Lee, J., Liu, Y., & Gordon-Becker, S. (2004). *An introduction to human factors engineering*. Harlow, UK: Pearson Prentice Hall.

Willems, J. (2003). Bringing down the barriers: Public communication should be part of common scientific practice. Nature, 422, 470.

Williams, C. A., Jr., & Heins, R. M. (1989). *Risk management and insurance*. New York: McGraw-Hill.

Williams, R. (1977). From medium to social practice. In *Marxism and Literature*. New York: Oxford University Press.

Wilmot, W. (1987). *Dyadic communication* (3rd ed.). New York: Random House.

Wilson, G. (1976). Strategy of explanation: Richard M. Nixon's August 8, 1974, resignation address. *Communication Quarterly, 24*(3), 14–20. Retrieved May 31, 2008, from http://gh9wn9pv9q.cs.serialssolutions.com.proxy.libraries.rutgers.edu/results?

Wilson, J. Q., & Kelling, G. L. (1982). Broken windows: The police and neighborhood safety. *The Atlantic Monthly, 249,* 29–38.

Wilson, K. G. (2000). *Deregulating telecommunications: U.S. and Canadian telecommunications, 1840–1997.* Lanham, MD: Rowman & Littlefield.

Wilson, P. H. (2000). *Absolutism in Central Europe.* New York: Routledge.

Wilson, S. (1995). *Mass media/mass culture: An introduction.* New York: McGraw-Hill.

Wilson, T., & Dunn, E. (2004). Self-knowledge: Its limits, value, and potential for improvement. *Annual Review of Psychology, 55,* 493–518. Retrieved November 15, 2008, from the ProQuest Psychology Journals database

Wilson, W. (1968, December 9). The study of administration. In A. S. Link (Ed.), *Proceedings of the American Philosophical Society* (Vol. 112, No. 6, pp. 431–433). Retrieved April 30, 2009, from http://www.jstor.org/stable/985941 (Original work published 1877)

Wilson, W. J. (1987). *The truly disadvantaged: The inner city, the underclass, and public policy.* Chicago: University of Chicago Press.

Winston, C. (1993). Economic deregulation: Days of reckoning for microeconomists. *Journal of Economic Literature, 31*(3), 1263–1289.

Wolff, R. P. (1998). *In defense of anarchism.* Berkeley: University of California Press.

Wolfgang, M. E., Figlio, R. M., & Sellin, T. (1972). *Delinquency in a birth cohort.* Chicago: University of Chicago Press.

Wong, D. T., Bymaster, F. P., & Engleman, E. A. (1995). Prozac (fluoxetine, Lilly 110140), the first selective serotonin uptake inhibitor and an antidepressant drug: Twenty years since its first publication. *Life Science, 57,* 411–441.

Woodward, J. (1965). *Industrial organization: Theory and practice.* London: Oxford University Press.

Woolcock, M. (2001). The place of social capital in understanding social and economic outcomes. *Isuma: Canadian Journal of Policy Research, 2*(1), 1–17.

World Bank. (1993). *The east Asian miracle.* New York: Oxford University Press.

World Bank. (2008). Social capital. In *PovertyNet.* Retrieved February 18, 2008, from http://www.worldbank.org/poverty/scapital/whatsc.htm

World Council of Comparative Education Societies: http://www.wcces.net

Wrench, J., & Butterfield, M. (2003). Increasing patient satisfaction and compliance: An examination of physician humor orientation, compliance-gaining strategies, and perceived credibility. *Communication Quarterly, 51*(4), 482–503. Retrieved May 24, 2008, from vnweb.hwwilsonweb.com.ezproxy.pratt.edu:2048/hww/results/getResults.jhtml?

Wright, C. R. (1960). Functional analysis and mass communication. *The Public Opinion Quarterly, 24,* 605–620.

Wright, J. R. (2002). *Interest groups and Congress: Lobbying, contributions, and influence.* New York: Longman Classics.

Wrightsman, L. S., & Fulero, S. M. (2005). *Forensic psychology.* Belmont, CA: Thomson Wadsworth.

Wundt, W. M. (1888). Selbstbeobachtung und innere Wahrnehmung. *Philosophische Studien, 4,* 292–309.

Wyatt, T. D. (2003). *Pheromones and animal behaviour: Communication by smell and taste.* Cambridge, UK: Cambridge University Press.

Yanovitzky, I., & Stryker, J. (2001). Mass media, social norms, and health promotion efforts: A longitudinal study of media effects on youth binge drinking. *Communication Research, 28,* 208–239.

Yates, J. (1993). *Control through communication: The rise of system in American management.* Baltimore: Johns Hopkins University Press.

Yu, C. H. (1994, April). *Abduction? Deduction? Induction? Is there a logic of exploratory data analysis?* Paper presented at the annual meeting of the American Educational Research Association, New Orleans, LA.

Zajonc, R. B., Murphy, S. T., & Inglehart, M. (1989). Feeling and facial efference: Implications for the vascular theory of emotion. *Psychological Review, 96*(3), 395–416.

Zambok, C. E., & Klein, G. (Eds.). (1997). *Naturalistic decision making.* Mahwah, NJ: Lawrence Erlbaum.

Zola-Morgan, S. (1995). Localization of brain function: The legacy of Franz Gall (1758–1828). *Annual Review of Neuroscience, 18,* 359–383.

Zubin, J., & Spring, B. (1977). Vulnerability. A new view of schizophrenia. *Journal of Abnormal Psychology, 86,* 103–126.

Zucker, R. (2001). *Democratic distributive justice.* Cambridge, UK: Cambridge University Press.

Zwart, T., & Verhey, L. F. M. (2003). *Agencies in European and comparative perspective.* Antwerp, Belgium: Intersentia.